THE IRWIN SERIES IN MARKETING

Consulting Editor
Gilbert A. Churchill, Jr.
University of Wisconsin, Madison

FOURTH EDITION

CONTEMPORARY

Courtland L. Bovée

William F. Arens

IRWIN

Homewood, IL 60430

Boston, MA 02116

Cover photo: David Bentley
Cover and part lettering: Jack Scott

Sponsoring editor: Steve Patterson
Developmental editor: Eleanore Snow
Project editor: Jean Roberts
Production manager: Irene H. Sotiroff
Designer: Michael Warrell
Art manager: Kim Meriwether
Artist: Rolin Graphics Inc.
Compositor: Better Graphics, Inc.
Typeface: 10/12 ITC Garamond Light
Printer: Von Hoffmann Press, Inc.

Library of Congress Cataloging-in-Publication Data

Bovée, Courtland L.
    Contemporary advertising/Courtland L. Bovée, William F. Arens.—
—4th ed.
        p.   cm. — (Irwin series in marketing)
    Includes index.
    ISBN 0-256-09196-X
    1. Advertising.   I. Arens, William F.   II. Title.   III. Series.
HF5821.B62   1992
    659.1—dc20   91-28798

Printed in the United States of America
1 2 3 4 5 6 7 8 9 0 VH 8 7 6 5 4 3 2 1 0

To John V. Thill
Friend and colleague
C.L.B.

To Stan
The man, the teacher, the friend
Les beaux souvenirs vivent pour toujours.
W.F.A.

PREFACE

The essence of advertising's global significance may have been captured by British novelist Norman Douglas when he remarked, "You can tell the ideals of a nation by its advertisements." Indeed, while the advertising business may have been viewed as a particularly American institution in the first half of the 20th century, that is certainly no longer the case. Today, everyone living and working in the modern world is influenced by advertising. Thus, the study of advertising has taken on new importance, not only for students of business or journalism—who may one day be practitioners—but also for students of sociology, psychology, political science, economics, history, language, art, or the sciences, all of whom will continue to be consumers of advertising.

There are six major reasons why students profit from studying advertising. It can help them to:

Understand the impact of advertising on the domestic economy and on the economies of foreign nations.

Comprehend advertising's role in fashioning society and, conversely, society's impact on advertising.

See how advertising fits within the broader disciplines of business and marketing.

Learn how advertising relates to journalism and the whole field of human communications.

Appreciate the artistic creativity and technical expertise required in advertising.

Discover what advertising people do and how they do it, and the career opportunities the field offers.

STUDENT-ORIENTED FEATURES FOR THE 21ST CENTURY

Our mission in the previous editions of *Contemporary Advertising* has been to present advertising as it is actually practiced—to put flesh on the bones of academic theory. As we approach the 21st century, our purpose remains the same. We believe advertising should be taught as it really is—as a business, as a marketing tool, as a creative process, and as a dynamic, hybrid discipline employing elements of the various arts and sciences. And we believe it should be taught in a manner and style relevant to today's student.

For these reasons, we have written and developed *Contemporary Advertising* around a number of exclusive student-oriented features.

Award-Winning Graphic Design

Contemporary Advertising has always been distinguished by its exceptional packaging and award-winning graphic design. That's important for a book which purports to teach about advertising design and art direction, and it contributes to learning by making the text material inviting and accessible to the widest range of students. In the Fourth Edition, the elegance of this design is further enhanced with beautiful part and chapter openers—and made even more reader-friendly with the introduction of chapter learning objectives and divisional and chapter overviews.

Chapter-Opening Vignettes

To capture and hold student interest, each chapter opens with a story—written in a warm, narrative style—about an actual situation illustrating a basic concept in the study of advertising. This opening example is then often used throughout the chapter to demonstrate how textbook concepts are applied in real-life situations. For example, the history of the world's most successful packaged good—Coca-Cola—is used throughout Chapter 1 to define the functions of advertising and to trace the development and growth of modern advertising; the recent historic emergence of J. C. Penney as the largest U.S. department store chain is used in Chapter 6 to illustrate the depth and complexity of marketing and advertising research processes; and the entire subject of media planning and selection in Chapter 12 is wrapped around the story of how Del Monte shifted from television to magazines for its packaged goods advertising.

Extensive Illustration Program

The best way to teach is by setting a good example. Each of the 19 chapters is beautifully illustrated in full color with current, award-winning advertisements and campaigns that demonstrate the best in the business from the last three years. In fact, *Contemporary Advertising* is still the most extensively illustrated textbook on the market, and all the major media are represented—print, electronic, outdoor—in a balanced manner. All the examples and illustrations used in this text are carefully selected both for their quality and for their relevance to students.

Furthermore, we have included many local as well as national ads, and business-to-business as well as consumer ads. In-depth captions tell the stories behind many of the ads and explain how the ads demonstrate the concepts discussed in the text.

The text is also heavily illustrated with diagrams, charts, graphs, and tables that encapsulate useful information about advertising concepts, the advertising industry, media, and production.

Full-Color Portfolios

In addition to the individual print ads and actual frames from TV commercials, the book contains several multipage portfolios of outstanding creative work. Some of these are the "Art Director's Portfolio," the "Copywriter's Portfolio," "Portfolio of Corporate Advertising," "Portfolio of Outstanding Magazine Advertising," and "Portfolio of International Advertising."

Creative Departments

The "Creative Department" is a special section that appears in two chapters of the book and describes how an interesting ad was created from beginning to end. A print ad for Lipton International Soup Classics is featured in the first Creative Department. And the second features the creation of the very popular current series of TV commercials for Taster's Choice coffee.

Advertising Laboratories

Active participation enhances learning, so "Advertising Laboratories" are incorporated into every chapter. These thought-provoking sidebars to the world of advertising introduce students to topics of current interest or controversy and then involve them in the subject by posing questions that stimulate critical thinking. Some of the many topics presented in Ad Labs include subliminal advertising, marketing warfare, bottom-up marketing, and the psychological impact of color.

Ethical Dilemmas in Advertising

Today's students will be 21st-century practitioners. As such, they will face new and challenging ethical issues, and they will need to exercise greater sensitivity than their 20th-century counterparts. Therefore, we have incorporated a series of nine current ethical dilemmas in advertising—interspersed throughout the book—to focus attention on some of the most critical social issues facing advertisers today. Some of these include advertising to children, the targeting of ethnic minorities, and negative political campaign advertising.

Practical Checklists

Advertising is a very broad subject encompassing many disciplines, and one of the dilemmas advertising students and practitioners face is handling and organizing large volumes of information and then creatively converting these data into effective advertising. Because of this, students truly appreciate the numerous handy checklists that appear regularly throughout the text. These are useful for stimulating memory, organizing thinking, and reinforcing important concepts. Some examples are the "Checklist of Product Marketing Facts for Copywriters"; "Checklist of What Works Best in TV"; "Checklist of Design Principles"; and "Checklist of Ways to Set Advertising Budgets," to mention just a few. Many students plan to become professionals in the field. As such, they will find that these checklists are an invaluable, practical resource for developing marketing and advertising plans, writing and designing effective ads and commercials, selecting and scheduling media, evaluating advertising work, and making advertising decisions. As a result, the checklists greatly enhance the long-term value to the book.

Local Advertising Coverage

Throughout the book, *Contemporary Advertising* addresses the needs of both small and large advertisers with its many examples, case histories, Ad Labs, checklists, and advertisements. Moreover, this is one of the few texts to devote adequate attention to the needs of the small retail advertiser, with a complete chapter on the subject of local advertising.

Additional Pedagogical Aids

Because of the inclusion of separate chapters on local advertising, international advertising, corporate, public relations, and noncommercial advertising, and marketing and advertising research, *Contemporary Advertising* will remain the most comprehensive and up-to-date text on the market.

Each chapter concludes with a summary followed by questions for review and discussion. Both of these pedagogical aids are designed to help students review chapter content and assimilate what they have learned. Throughout the text, key ideas and terms are highlighted with boldface type and are defined when introduced. The definitions of all these terms are collected at the end of the book in the most thorough and extensive glossary in the field.

CHANGES IN THIS EDITION

Our continuing goal has been to personally involve students as much as possible in the practical experiences of advertising while simultaneously giving them a solid understanding of advertising's role in both marketing management and the human communication process. In the pursuit of this objective, we have instituted a significant number of modifications and improvements in the Fourth Edition of *Contemporary Advertising*.

First, throughout the book, we have updated all statistics and tables and also augmented the documentation of academic and professional source material, thereby giving *Contemporary Advertising* the most current and extensive compendium of academic and trade references in the field. We have included the results of important recent research and introduced interesting new building-block models to facilitate student comprehension of the often complex processes involved in marketing, consumer behavior, and human communication.

Second, many new, real-world examples have been added. These were selected not only for their currency but also for their relevance to students. Likewise, most of the chapter-opening stories are new. Some of these advertising success stories include the introduction of Acura, the turnaround of Motel 6, the expansion of Gotcha surfwear, and the image-building of Timberland shoes. All the Ad Labs, checklists, and full-color portfolios have been updated, expanded, or replaced with more current examples.

In recent years, the technology of advertising has changed dramatically. For example, in just the last five years, the computer has revolutionized the way advertising is planned, designed, produced, and scheduled. The Fourth Edition of *Contemporary Advertising* deals with this revolution in detail in several chapters.

In light of the increasing globalization of business, we have placed greater emphasis on international advertising. The international chapter has been extensively revised and updated to reflect the increased importance of advertising as Central Europe moves toward a market economy and as Western Europe unites to create a new marketing environment in 1992. In addition, throughout the text, numerous international examples are used.

Finally, thanks in large part to the contributions of the professional community, a major new feature of the Fourth Edition is a total North American orientation. This is important for two reasons.

First, *Contemporary Advertising* is widely used in Canada. Moreover, many of the academic and trade references for the text emanated from Canadian journals and publications. Therefore, we have approached the subject of domestic advertising as it is practiced in both the United States and Canada. In so doing, we have also included a wide variety of high-quality Canadian ad examples throughout the book—in both English and French—with which Canadian students and professors will be familiar.

Second, it's important that U.S. students, who are often less knowledgeable about Canada than Canadian students are about the United States, develop familiarity with the importance of our closest neighbor. Canada is already the largest trading partner of the United States, and it is only going to become larger in light of the free trade agreement.

Finally, as mentioned earlier, the social aspects of advertising have become so important that we have introduced the series of nine Ethical Dilemmas in Advertising as a major new feature in the Fourth Edition.

Other highlights of this revision include:

Chapter 1: "The Dimensions of Advertising." This chapter has been renamed, restructured, extensively revised—and also shortened. The discussion on the evolution of advertising has been strengthened and, at the same time, focused on the historic technological changes that have dramatically affected the business. The functions and effects of advertising have been simplified and clarified, and the discussion of economics is now centered on the macroeconomic effects.

Chapter 2: "The Social, Ethical, and Regulatory Aspects of Advertising." The chapter now addresses ethics lapses and ethical dilemmas in advertising. The discussion of consumer groups has been strengthened. The chapter now offers a more balanced presentation of what's right and wrong about advertising. The section on government has been reworked to give students a more interesting and engaging presentation, and the chapter expands the coverage of the Federal Trade Commission.

Chapter 3: "The Advertising Business: Agencies and Clients." This chapter has been revised to make it more people-oriented—who advertising people are, what they do, and what they are responsible for. The discussion of agencies has been moved forward of the discussion of advertisers so that, when the advertiser's in-house agency is discussed, students will already know what an agency is. The section on client-agency relationships has been updated to include some of the latest account switches.

Chapter 4: "The Importance of Marketing and Consumer Behavior to Advertising." As the first chapter in Part II, Chapter 4 has been renamed and completely restructured in order to focus the concepts of marketing and consumer behavior on people and, at the same time, orient the discussion from the advertiser's point of view. In the discussion on marketing, new information is presented about needs and utility. Material on consumer behavior, previously in Chapter 5, has been moved up to this chapter, reorganized, and strengthened with new information, models, and terminology on both the human communication and the consumer behavior processes. The discussion is now also more operational so students can see how the concepts presented actually affect ad making.

Chapter 5: "Market Segmentation and the Marketing Mix: Matching Products to Markets." Like Chapter 4, this chapter has been renamed, expanded, and completely restructured to include all the marketing mix information previously covered in Chapter 4. The Clearwater Federal story has been strengthened to include a hypothetical demonstration of how new market research technology might have been used to locate and aggregate actual market segments leading to the selection of a profitable target market. The treatment of the 4 Ps is now more focused on the development of a total product concept aimed at matching the perceived needs, wants, or desires of the target market. This section is further enhanced with new material on products, services, and branding.

Chapter 6: "Marketing and Advertising Research: Inputs to the Planning Process." The J. C. Penney story has been updated to include its 1990 campaign: "Fashion Comes to Life." The basic steps in the research process have been clarified and made more action-oriented. The chapter presents new sources of research information, shows new examples of how research affects advertising creativity, and clarifies the concepts of *validity* and *reliability*.

Chapter 7: "Marketing and Advertising Planning." A new chapter-opening story—the successful introduction of the Acura automobile—serves as a foil for the principles and concepts discussed throughout this chapter and is highlighted with many illustrations and examples. New material on top-down and bottom-up marketing and advertising planning makes the chapter more practical from the small advertiser's point of view. Additional examples related to the allocation of advertising funds during recessionary economic cycles also make the chapter extremely timely.

Chapter 8: "Creative Copywriting." We have expanded the sections on how advertisers develop the copy platform and the "big idea" in advertising. Included is an example of an actual copy platform from Foote, Cone & Belding for Sunkist. To assist in understanding the objectives of good copy, a new model, the copywriter's pyramid, is introduced—similar to the well-known advertising pyramid from Chapter 5. Also introduced in this chapter is information on the most popular word processing programs used by copywriters. The chapter is accented with a completely new illustration program that students will find relevant and timely.

Chapter 9: "Creative Art Direction." This chapter has been heavily revised to focus on the role of art in various advertising forms—print, television, packaging, and even radio, and much of the descriptive material has been shortened and moved to Ad Labs. The aesthetic potential of advertising art is demonstrated through the chapter-opening story of Timberland's recent award-winning image campaign. The new technology of desktop publishing is introduced. Material on television creativity—previously in Chapter 11—has been moved to a new section in this chapter dealing with the role of art in radio and television commercials. Finally, we have created a completely new illustration program and Art Director's Portfolio of current, student-relevant ads to enliven the text matter.

Chapter 10: "Creative Production: Print Media." The role of the computer in print production keys the chapter-opening story of the creation of a beautiful, award-winning business-to-business ad for NYNEX. This leads to a new, in-depth discussion of the impact of desktop publishing on ad making. Reflecting this, the material on typesetting has been updated, and new student-relevant examples demonstrate the possibilities offered by typography. The chapter has been carefully edited to ensure that students gain the most practical information possible on how to produce quality print media materials, and the chapter even includes a new section on how to think like a printer to save money on print runs.

Chapter 11: "Creative Production: Electronic Media." The incredible turn-around of Motel 6, thanks to radio advertising, is the new chapter-opening story that highlights this chapter on electronic production. The radio production section has been expanded and made more operational with new information on the use of microphones and the coordination of studio, sound booth, and control room. The television section opens with an involving story about a new, state-of-the-art MTV campaign for Gotcha surfwear. Again, the impact of the computer is discussed as it relates to TV production; and the section on shooting commercials has been expanded to include material on lights, cameras, and action. A new Creative Department on the current, very popular campaign for Taster's Choice coffee serves as a climax to the chapter and the whole creative unit by showing how these commercials were developed and shot, from concept through production.

Chapter 12: "Media Planning and Selection." The chapter has been carefully revised to increase clarity, coherence, and balance. The more lively writing style now engages students more readily in chapter topics. The chapter expands the coverage of sources of media information. Examples have been added to enrich the material and engage student interest.

Chapter 13: "Print Media." The chapter has been expanded to include magazine readership sources. Careful revision has resulted in a more logical organization. The discussion of vertical publications has been expanded, and the distinction between classified ad space and display ad space has been clarified.

Chapter 14: "Electronic Media." The number of advertiser-oriented examples has been increased. The material on the use of and confidence in people meters has been fully updated. The chapter now includes a full discussion of how the networks are responding to the success of cable television.

Chapter 15: "Direct Mail and Outdoor Media." The chapter has been expanded to more fully cover direct mail and to more equally address the various functions of direct mail. The number of examples has been increased to better explicate the chapter material. The chapter expands discussions of research and direct mail, implications of the mailing list, and creative direct-mail techniques.

Chapter 16: "Sales Promotion and Supplementary Media." The chapter probes deeper into the partnership between sales promotion and advertising. The sections on specialty advertising and alternative media have been carefully revised and strengthened. The chapter has been expanded to include a discussion of how growth in the use of sales promotion has been at the expense of advertising. The discussion of display allowances has been expanded.

Chapter 17: "Local Advertising." The discussion of factors that influence local advertising budgets now includes details about *how* those factors influence budgets. The chapter expands on the importance of Yellow Pages to local advertisers. Cooperative advertising is now discussed in much greater detail and explained more thoroughly. The number of examples has been increased to more fully illustrate the chapter material.

Chapter 18: "Public Relations, Corporate Advertising, and Noncommercial Advertising." The discussions of publicity, political advertising, and advocacy advertising have been expanded to emphasize their importance. The topic of special events receives more attention, emphasizing its growing importance, especially in music and sports events. The relationship between publicity and public relations is more clearly discussed.

Chapter 19: "International Advertising." The chapter strengthens the focus on advertising while de-emphasizing the discussion of marketing. The discussion of media planning has been deepened and expanded. A "Portfolio of International Advertising" is now included to brighten the text, engage student interest, and deepen understanding.

SUPPLEMENTARY MATERIALS

While the text itself is a complete introduction to the field of advertising, it is accompanied by a number of valuable supplemental materials designed to assist the instructor.

Instructor's Manual

The instructor's manual offers a wealth of suggestions for classroom lectures and discussions. It includes answers to all discussion questions, course and subject outlines, and a comprehensive testing program to facilitate the administration of examinations.

Video Supplements

To illustrate how the principles discussed in the text have actually been applied in business, the book is supplemented by two special video programs. One of these was produced exclusively for *Contemporary Advertising* for instructor use in the classroom and includes a wide variety of local, national, and international commercials specifically referenced with voice-over introductions to specific chapters. This video is not only text-specific in subject matter, but it even includes some of the commercials discussed in the text—such as the Taster's Choice and Gotcha campaigns from Chapter 11.

The second video was produced by the Advertising Educational Foundation, to whom we express our deep gratitude and appreciation, and includes a behind-the-scenes look at the advertising process at work. Included on the video: the development of a TV commercial designed to introduce a new Johnson & Johnson product, Acuvue Disposable Contact Lenses; the production of a print ad for Jell-O gelatin; and a summer TV ad for Coca-Cola. These are all excellent adjuncts to the chapters on creativity and production.

Offered at no charge to adopters of *Contemporary Advertising*, these video supplements are designed to help the instructor teach real-world decision making and demonstrate some of the best current examples of television advertising from around the world.

Color Transparencies

Also available to instructors is a high-quality selection of overhead transparencies. These include over 100 additional ads besides those found in the text and a selection of many of the important models and graphs presented in the text—all produced in full color.

Testing Systems

An extensive bank of objective test questions carefully designed to provide a fair, structured program of evaluation is available in several formats:

Irwin Computerized Test Generator System—a convenient and flexible question retrieval device for mainframe systems, providing an extensive bank of questions to use as is or with additional questions of your own.

Irwin Computerized Testing Software—a microcomputer testing system that provides convenient and flexible retrieval from an extensive bank of questions to use as is or with additional questions of your own.

COMPUGRADE—a microcomputer gradebook that stores and prints all grades by name or ID number. Capable of weighting and averaging grades.

Teletest—a toll-free phone-in service to request customized exams prepared for classroom use.

USES FOR THIS TEXT

Contemporary Advertising was originally intended for the undergraduate student in business and journalism schools. Because of its practical, hands-on approach, depth of coverage, and marketing management emphasis, it is also widely used in independent schools, university extension courses, and courses on advertising management. The wealth of award-winning advertisements also makes it a resource guide to the best work in the field for students in art and graphic design courses as well as for professionals in the field.

Many of the stories, materials, and techniques included in this text come from our own personal experiences as a college professor and as a full-time marketing and advertising executive. Others come from the experiences of professional friends and colleagues. We hope that this book will be a valuable resource guide, not only in the study of advertising but later on in practice. In all cases, we hope that through reading this text, students will experience the feel and the humanness of the advertising world—whether they intend to become professionals in the business, to work with practitioners, or simply to become more sophisticated consumers.

ACKNOWLEDGMENTS

We are deeply indebted to many individuals in advertising and related fields for their personal encouragement and professional assistance. These include, but are certainly not limited to: Alistair Gillett and Steve Makransky at Young & Rubicam; Victoria Horstmann, Charles Meding, Ted Regan, and Fred Posner at N. W. Ayer; Jan Sneed at Warwick Baker & Fiore; David Kreinick at Creative Media, Inc.; Peter Farago at Farago Advertising; Ella Strubel, Wally Petersen, and Mark Hart at Leo Burnett; Dennis Chase and James Lawson at *Advertising Age*; Tom Exster at *American Demographics*; Joyce Harrington at the American Association of Advertising Agencies; Steve McCauley at R. C. Auletta and Company; Jigisha Patel, Chiat/Day/Mojo, Los Angeles; Adelaide Horton, Chiat/Day/Mojo, New York; Maryanne O'Brien, Patricia Davidson, Nadine Howe at Fallon McElligott; Cindi Rowe, BBDO/West; Ann Jenneman Smith at Procter & Gamble; Thomas Hripko at the Richards Group, Dallas; Larry Jones and Nicoletta Poloynis at Foote, Cone & Belding; Russ Hanlin and Ray Cole at Sunkist Growers, Inc.; Mike Salisbury at Salisbury Communications; Kim Randall at Ketchum Advertising; Robert Hines at the Hines Company; Gerry Rubin and Joan Egan at Rubin Postaer; Earl Cavanah at Scali, McCabe, Sloves; Joe Sedelmaier and Marsie Wallach at Sedelmaier Film Productions; and Raphaële at Raphaële Digital Transparencies.

For their warm, open, and gracious contributions, we extend our appreciation, *avec tous nos remerciements*, to all our Canadian friends, especially Elisabeth Cohen, Daniel Rabinowicz, and Paul Lavoie at Cossette Communication-Marketing; Yves Gougoux, Caroline Jarvis, and Sylvie Thauvette at BCP Stratégie Créativité; *et particulièrement*, Jean Pelletier and Normand Grenier at the Publicité-Club de Montréal. Also, great appreciation for timely assistance to Dieter Kaufmann (President of the Toronto Art Director's Club) at Anderson Advertising; Mary N. Neill at Chiat/Day/Mojo (Toronto); Allison Findley at Ogilvy & Mather, Toronto; and Emily Bain, Kathleen Vollebregt, and Colleen Evans at Young & Rubicam/Toronto.

Special thanks also to several good, longtime friends whose contributions, continuous support, and wise counsel we appreciate far more than they could ever know: Al Ries at Trout & Ries; Susan Irwin at McCann-Erickson; John O'Toole at the American Association of Advertising Agencies; Sid Stein at Rutgers University; Rance Crain at *Advertising Age*; Homer Torrey, formerly of J. C. Penney Co.; Randy Grimm at National Decision Systems; and, for patient and loyal support, business partner Stanley L. Urlaub.

In addition, we are appreciative of the support, encouragement, generous assistance, and friendship of Tom Michael, Roger Tilton, Alayne Harris, Kelly Seagraves, Mark McCormick, Mark Salik, Professor E. L. Deckinger, Mike Sims,

Suzie Toutant, Jim Moran, Littleton Waller, Rob Settle, Pam Alreck, Joe Hoyt, Bill Kimmelman, Jann Pasler, Atsuo Mihara, Mary Beth McCabe, Barnard and Sylvia Thompson, Don and Ann Ritchey, Carlos and Yolanda Cortez, Susan Harding, Jim and LeAnna Zevely, Fred and Brenda Bern, Mitch Moshtaghi, Bill and Olivia Werner, Alan and Rita Moller, and—for giving so much to so many for so long—Stanley D. Woodworth, gone from our midst but never forgotten.

We appreciate the patience and support of our far-flung families, all the Bovées and the Arenses, and especially Olivia, for her unwavering tolerance.

A special thank you to Terry Anderson, Kathleen J. Lenz, Mike Vassolo, Colleen Pang, Kate Bertrand, George Dovel, Marian Burk Wood, and Jackie Estrada for their specialized knowledge and expert assistance. Likewise, great appreciation to Jack Whidden for his experience and in-depth conceptual and editorial assistance and to Debbie Campbell, Rebecca Smith, and Bonnie Dowd for being there when we needed them most.

In the effort to make this the most timely and current book on the market, the huge Irwin A-team, which invariably found a way to do the impossible, was led by Steve Patterson, Eleanore Snow, Michael Warrell, Mike Hruby, Jean Roberts, Irene H. Sotiroff, John Black, Bill Setten, and Jerry Saykes, all of whom had to put up with us on an almost daily basis. We appreciate your tolerant indulgence of our individual and collective idiosyncrasies and foibles, and we thank you for a job incredibly well done.

We also wish to recognize and thank the American Academy of Advertising, an organization whose publications and meetings provide a valuable forum for the exchange of ideas and for professional growth.

We are deeply grateful to the many academic reviewers whose ideas and critical insights were invaluable in the preparation of this edition. They include Hugh G. Daubek, Purdue University, Calumet; Joby John, Bentley College; Susan A. Schneider, Endicott College; Ronald D. Taylor, Mississippi State University; Peter B. Turk, University of Akron; Sharon Brock, Ohio State University; J. Nicholas DeBonis, California State University, Fullerton; Karen Porter, University of Montana; Michael F. Weigold, University of Florida, Gainesville; D. Joel Whalen, DePaul University; and G. Gelderloos, Grand Rapids Junior College.

To all of you, thank you. You make it happen.

Courtland L. Bovée
William F. Arens

CONTENTS IN BRIEF

PART I

ADVERTISING PERSPECTIVES 2

1 The Dimensions of Advertising 4
2 The Social, Ethical, and Regulatory Aspects of Advertising 42
3 The Advertising Business: Agencies and Clients 78

PART II

DEVELOPING MARKETING AND ADVERTISING STRATEGIES 116

4 The Importance of Marketing and Consumer Behavior to Advertising 118
5 Market Segmentation and the Marketing Mix: Matching Products to Markets 154
6 Marketing and Advertising Research: Inputs to the Planning Process 198
7 Marketing and Advertising Planning 236

PART III

CREATING ADVERTISEMENTS AND COMMERCIALS 276

8 Creative Copywriting 278
9 Creative Art Direction 316
10 Creative Production: Print Media 350
11 Creative Production: Electronic Media 384

PART IV

ADVERTISING MEDIA 420

12 Media Planning and Selection 422
13 Print Media 456
14 Electronic Media 494
15 Direct Mail and Outdoor Media 534
16 Sales Promotion and Supplementary Media 574

PART V

SPECIAL TYPES OF ADVERTISING 600

17 Local Advertising 602
18 Public Relations, Corporate Advertising, and Noncommercial Advertising 638
19 International Advertising 670

Appendix A: Marketing Plan Outline 698
Appendix B: Advertising Plan Outline 704
Appendix C: Career Planning in Advertising 708
Endnotes E-1
Credits and Acknowledgments C-1
Glossary G
Name and Company Index I-1
Subject Index I-8

CONTENTS

PART

I

ADVERTISING PERSPECTIVES   2

CHAPTER 1

THE DIMENSIONS OF ADVERTISING   4

Advertising Defined   6
Classifications of Advertising   8
*By Target Audience   8   By Geographic Area   12   By Medium   14
By Purpose   14*

Advertising's Evolution   16
*The Impact of Printing   17   The Industrial Revolution and Early U.S.
Advertising   17   The Communications Revolution   18   The Dawning
of Responsibility   18   The Rise of Broadcast Advertising   21*

The Development of Modern Advertising   22
*The Positioning Era   22   The "Me" Decade   23   The Age of
Marketing Warfare   24   The Information Age   25*

Functions and Effects of Advertising   26
The Economic Impact of Advertising   32
*Effect on the Value of Products   33   Effect on Prices   34   Effect on
Competition   36   Effect on Consumer Demand   37   Effect on
Consumer Choice   37   Effect on the Business Cycle   37   Economic
Impact of Advertising in Perspective: The Abundance Principle   38*

Ad Lab 1-A: It Had to Be Good to Get Where It Is!   6
Ethical Dilemma in Advertising: Truth in Advertising—Is It Puffed Up or
Overblown?   20
Coca-Cola Illustrates the History of Modern Advertising   28

CHAPTER 2

THE SOCIAL, ETHICAL, AND REGULATORY ASPECTS OF ADVERTISING   42

The Social Impact of Advertising   44
Social Criticisms   44   Social Benefits   51

Advertising Ethics and Social Responsibility   52
    Advertising Ethics   53   Advertisers' Social Responsibility   54

Federal Regulation of Advertising   55
    *Federal Trade Commission   55   Food and Drug Administration   59
    Federal Communications Commission   61   Patent and Trademark
    Office   61   Library of Congress   63*

State and Local Regulation   63
    *Regulation by State Governments   64   Regulation by Local
    Governments   64*

Recent Court Rulings Affecting Advertisers   64
    *First Amendment Rights   65   Privacy Rights   66   Comparative
    Advertising   66*

Nongovernment Regulation   67
    *The Role of the Better Business Bureau (BBB)   67   National Advertis-
    ing Review Council   68   Regulation by the Media   70   Regulation
    by Consumer Groups   74   Self-Regulation by Advertisers   75
    Self-Regulation by Ad Agencies and Associations   76*

Ad Lab 2-A: Unfair and Deceptive Practices in Advertising   52
Ad Lab 2-B: Advertising to Children: What You Can and Cannot Do   69
Ad Lab 2-C: The Issue of Issue Ads   72

CHAPTER 3

THE ADVERTISING BUSINESS: AGENCIES AND CLIENTS   78

Who Makes Up the Advertising Business?   80
    The Organizations   80   The People   80

What Advertising People Do: Fundamental Tasks   82
    *Administration   82   Planning   82   Budgeting   82
    Coordination   82   Creating Ads   84*

The Advertising Agency   84
    *The Role of the Advertising Agency   84   Types of Agencies   86
    What Agency People Do   89   How Agencies Are Structured   94
    How Agencies Make Money   96   How Agencies Get Clients   98*

The Advertisers (Clients)   100
    Large Advertisers   100   Small Advertisers   106

The Client-Agency Relationship   107
    *Stages in the Client-Agency Relationship   107   Factors Affecting the
    Client-Agency Relationship   110*

Ad Lab 3-A: How Big Is the Agency Business?   85
Checklist for Agency Review   108
Ethical Dilemma in Advertising: The Conflict over Client-Agency
Conflicts   110
Checklist for Ways to Be a Better Client   112
Ad Lab 3-B: Megamergers Make Agency Supergroups   113

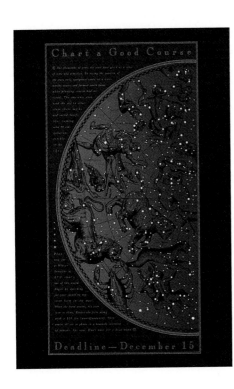

PART
II

DEVELOPING MARKETING AND ADVERTISING STRATEGIES   116

CHAPTER 4

THE IMPORTANCE OF MARKETING AND CONSUMER BEHAVIOR TO ADVERTISING   118

The Importance of Marketing to Advertising People   120

What Is Marketing?   121
*Needs and Utility   122   Perception, Exchanges, and
Satisfaction   123   The Evolution of Marketing Theory   125
The Marketing Exchange Cycle   125   The Key Participants in the
Marketing Process   125*

How Advertisers Reach the Market   128
*The Art and Science of Advertising   128   The Marketing
Communication Process   129*

The Importance of Knowing the Consumer   131
*Consumer Behavior from the Advertising Perspective   132   Personal
Processes in Consumer Behavior   133   Interpersonal Influences on
Consumer Behavior   143   Nonpersonal Influences on Consumer
Behavior   148   The Purchase Decision and Postpurchase
Evaluation   149*

Ad Lab 4-A: Understanding Needs and Utility   122

Ad Lab 4-B: Positioning Strategy—Or, How to Penetrate the Perceptual
Screens   138

Ad Lab 4-C: Subliminal Manipulation: Fact or Fantasy?   144

Ad Lab 4-D: Applying Consumer Behavior Principles to Ad Making   151

CHAPTER 5

MARKET SEGMENTATION AND THE MARKETING MIX: MATCHING PRODUCTS TO MARKETS   154

The Majority Fallacy   155

The Product Marketing Process   156

The Market Segmentation Process   156
*Identifying Consumer Market Segments   157   Identifying Business
Market Segments   165   Aggregating Market Segments   168*

The Target Marketing Process   170
*Target Market Selection   170   The Marketing Mix: Matching Products
to Markets   171*

Advertising and the Product Element   172
*Product Life Cycle   173   Product Classifications   176   Product
Positioning   178   Product Differentiation   179   Product
Branding   180   Product Packaging   183*

Advertising and the Price Element   186
 *Key Factors Influencing Price   186   The Impact of Pricing Strategies
 on Advertising   188*

Advertising and the Place Element   189
 *Direct Marketing   190   Indirect Marketing   191   Vertical Marketing
 Systems   193*

Advertising and the Promotion Element   194
 *Personal Selling   195   Advertising   195   Public Relations   196
 Sales Promotion   196   Collateral Materials   196*

The Marketing Mix in Perspective   196

Ethical Dilemma in Advertising: Warning: Market Segmentation May Be
Hazardous to Your Business   160
Ad Lab 5-A: Marketing Reebok: The Product Element and the Market   172
Ad Lab 5-B: Marketing Reebok: The Price Element and the Market   191
Ad Lab 5-C: Marketing Reebok: The Place Element and the Market   193
Ad Lab 5-D: Marketing Reebok: Deciding on the Promotion Element   195

CHAPTER 6

MARKETING AND ADVERTISING RESEARCH: INPUTS TO THE PLANNING
PROCESS   198

The Need for Research in Marketing and Advertising   200
 Marketing Research   201   Advertising Research   202

Basic Steps in the Research Process   202
 *Analyze the Situation and Define the Problem   202   Conduct
 Informal (Exploratory) Research   203   Use Internal Secondary
 Data   204   Collect External Secondary Data   204   Establish Research
 Objectives   208   Conduct Formal Research   209   Interpret and
 Report the Findings   219*

Applying Research to Marketing and Advertising Strategy   220
 *Developing Marketing Strategy   220   Developing Advertising
 Strategy   221   Creative Concept Testing   224   Testing and
 Evaluation of Advertising   226*

Ad Lab 6-A: Using Marketing Research for New-Product Development   205
Ad Lab 6-B: How Does Sampling Work?   216
Checklist for Developing an Effective Questionnaire   218
Checklist of Methods for Pretesting Advertisements   230
Checklist of Methods for Posttesting Advertisements   232

CHAPTER 7

MARKETING AND ADVERTISING PLANNING   236

The Marketing Plan   242
 *What Is a Marketing Plan?   242   Effect of the Marketing Plan on
 Advertising   242   Elements of the Marketing Plan   244*

The Advertising Plan   252
   *Review of the Marketing Plan 252   Setting Advertising
   Objectives 252   Advertising Strategy and the Creative Mix 258*

Reversing the Planning Process: Bottom-Up Marketing   262
   *The Tactic: A Singular, Competitive Mental Angle 263   The Secret
   to Successful Planning 266*

Allocating Funds for Advertising   266
   *An Investment in Future Sales 268   Methods of Allocating
   Funds 270   The Bottom Line 274*

Ad Lab 7-A: The Era of Marketing Warfare   238

Checklist for Situation Analysis   245

Ad Lab 7-B: MaxiMarketing—How Small Advertisers Build the Inverted
Pyramid   257

Checklist for Developing Advertising Objectives   258

Ad Lab 7-C: Creative Use of the Creative Mix   264

Ad Lab 7-D: How Economists View the Effect of Advertising on Sales   269

Checklist of Ways to Set Advertising Budgets   271

PART

III

CREATING ADVERTISEMENTS AND COMMERCIALS   276

CHAPTER 8

CREATIVE COPYWRITING   278

Copywriting and Advertising Strategy   280
   Elements of Message Strategy 281   Developing the Big Idea 284

The Copywriter's Pyramid: Setting Copy Objectives   287
   *Attention 288   Interest 290   Credibility 290   Desire 291
   Action 291*

Understanding the Copywriter's Terminology   291
   *Headlines 292   Subheads 297   Body Copy 298   Boxes and
   Panels 308   Slogans 308   Seals, Logotypes, and Signatures 308*

Common Pitfalls in Writing Copy   309
   *Obfuscation 309   Filibustering 310   Clichés, Triteness, and
   Superlatives 310   Abstractness and Vagueness 310
   "Me-Me-Me" 310   No, Not Negativity 311   Euphemisms 311
   Defamation 311*

The Writing Process: Tools of the Trade   313

Checklist of Product Marketing Facts for Copywriters   282

Ethical Dilemma in Advertising: When Advertisers Dare to Compare   288

Ad Lab 8-A: Applying the Copywriter's Pyramid to Print Advertising   293

Ad Lab 8-B: The Eye versus the Ear   299

Checklist for Writing Effective Copy   301
Copywriter's Portfolio   304
Ad Lab 8-C: Creating Names for Products   312

CHAPTER 9

CREATIVE ART DIRECTION   316

What Is Art?   318
The Role of Art in Creating Print Advertising   319
*Laying Out the Ad   319   The Use of Layouts   323   Steps in
Advertising Layout   325   Which Kind of Layout Design Works
Best?   327   The Advertising Visual   328*

The Role of Art in Package Design   336
*Packaging Forms and Materials   337   Packaging Specialists   338
When Should a Package Be Changed?   339*

The Role of Art in Radio and Television Advertising   339
*Developing the Concept for the Commercial   339   Types of Television
Commercials   346   The Role of Art Direction in Perspective   348*

Checklist of Artistic Principles   320
Ad Lab 9-A: The Role of the Advertising Artist   322
Ad Lab 9-B: Which Ad Would You Select?   324
Ad Lab 9-C: Techniques for Creating Advertising Visuals   331
Art Director's Portfolio   333
Ad Lab 9-D: The Psychological Impact of Color   336
Ethical Dilemma in Advertising: Imitation or Plagiarism—What's the
Difference?   344

CHAPTER 10

CREATIVE PRODUCTION: PRINT MEDIA   350

The Production Process   352
*Role of the Production Manager   353   Impact of Computers on Print
Production   354*

Planning Print Production   356
Typography   358
*Classes of Type   358   Type Groups   359   Type Families   360   Type
Structure and Measurement   361   Type Selection   362   Type
Specification and Copy Casting   364   Typesetting Methods   365*

The Printing Process   367
*Preparing Materials for the Press (Prepress)   367   Thinking like a
Printer   369   Methods of Printing   370   Printing in Color   374
Selecting Papers for Printing   375   Preparing Materials for Print
Media   381*

Ad Lab 10-A: Celestial Seasonings Uses Some Unforgettable
Characters   365
Creative Department: From Concept through Production of a Magazine
Advertisement   376

CHAPTER 11

CREATIVE PRODUCTION: ELECTRONIC MEDIA 384

Producing Radio Commercials 386
Writing Radio Copy 386 Types of Radio Commercials 387

The Radio Production Process 389
Preproduction 389 Production: Cutting the Spot 390
Postproduction: Finishing the Spot 394

Producing Television Commercials 394
Television Production Techniques 396 The Television Production
Process 400 The Film versus Tape Debate 412 Costs 413

Checklist for Creating Effective Radio Commercials 386
Ad Lab 11-A: Creative Ways to Sell on Radio 388
Checklist for Creating Effective TV Commercials 396
Ethical Dilemma in Advertising: In Political Advertising, the Nays Have
It 400
Creative Department: From Concept through Production of a Television
Commercial 414

PART

IV

ADVERTISING MEDIA 420

CHAPTER 12

MEDIA PLANNING AND SELECTION 422

Media Planning: An Overview 424
The Players 424 The Challenge 425

The Role of Media in the Marketing Framework 428
Marketing Objectives and Strategy 428 Advertising Objectives and
Strategy 428

Defining Media Objectives 430
Audience Objectives 430 Message-Distribution Objectives 432

Developing a Media Strategy 435
Geographic Scope 435 Nature of the Medium and the
Message 437 Message Size, Length, and Position
Considerations 439 Competitive Strategy and Budget
Considerations 439 Stating the Media Strategy 440

Media Selection and Scheduling 441
Considerations in Selecting Individual Media 441 The Media
Mix 447 Scheduling Criteria 448 The Use of Computers in Media
Selection and Scheduling 452

Ad Lab 12-A: Off-the-Wall Media that Pull Customers off the Fence 426
Ad Lab 12-B: Media Selection: As the Creative Person Sees It 438

CHAPTER 13

PRINT MEDIA 456

Using Newspapers in the Creative Mix 458
*Advantages of Newspapers 458 Some Drawbacks to
Newspapers 459 Who Uses Newspapers? 460 How Newspapers Are
Categorized 461 Types of Newspaper Advertising 466*

How to Buy Newspaper Space 469
*Understanding Readership and Circulation 469 Rate Cards 469
Co-Op Insertions 472 Insertion Orders and Tear Sheets 473*

Using Magazines in the Creative Mix 473
*Advantages of Magazines 473 Some Drawbacks to
Magazines 478 Special Possibilities with Magazines 480 How
Magazines Are Categorized 482*

How to Buy Magazine Space 485
Understanding Magazine Circulation 485 Rate Cards 489

Sources of Print Media Information 490

Portfolio of Award-Winning Magazine Advertisements 474
Checklist of What Works Best in Print 480
Ad Lab 13-A: Innovations in Magazine Advertising 481

CHAPTER 14

ELECTRONIC MEDIA 494

Overview of the Broadcast Television Medium 496
*Audience Trends 496 Growth of Television Advertising 497 Types
of Broadcast Advertising 498*

Using Broadcast Television in the Creative Mix 500
*Advantages of Broadcast Television 501 Drawbacks of Broadcast
Television 503*

Television Audience Measurement 506
*Rating Services: "The Book" 507 Television Markets 508
Dayparts 509 Audience Measures 510 Gross Rating Points 510*

Buying Television Time 511
*Requesting Avails 511 Selecting Programs for Buys 511
Negotiating Prices and Contracts 512*

Overview of the Cable Medium 512
Audience Trends 513 Ratings 514 Who Uses Cable? 514

Using Cable Television in the Creative Mix 515
*Advantages of Cable 515 Drawbacks of Cable 517 Buying Cable
Time 518 Other Forms of Television 518 Advertising on
Videocassette Rentals 519*

Overview of the Radio Medium 520
Who Uses Radio? 520 Radio Programming and Audiences 520

Using Radio in the Creative Mix   522
  Advantages of Radio   523   Drawbacks to Radio   526

Buying Radio Time   527
  *Types of Radio Advertising   527   Radio Terminology   528   Preparing
  a Radio Schedule   532*

Checklist of What Works Best in Television   503
Ethical Dilemma in Advertising: Children's Television Advertising: The
Medium and the Message   506
Ad Lab 14-A: Where Do Those Infamous TV Ratings Come From?   508
Checklist of What Works Best in Radio   526
Ad Lab 14-B: The Reports that Make or Break Radio Stations   529

CHAPTER **15**

DIRECT MAIL AND OUTDOOR MEDIA   534

Direct-Mail Advertising   536
  Direct Mail versus Direct Marketing   536   Growth of Direct Mail   539

Using Direct Mail in the Creative Mix   540
  *Types of Direct Mail   540   Buying Direct-Mail Advertising   542
  Advantages of Direct Mail   546   Drawbacks to Direct Mail   550*

Outdoor Advertising   553
  *Standardization of the Outdoor Advertising Business   553   Buying
  Outdoor Advertising   553   Advantages of Outdoor Advertising   556
  Drawbacks to Outdoor Advertising   561*

Transit Advertising   566
  *Types of Transit Advertising   566   Buying Transit Advertising   568
  Advantages of Transit Advertising   571   Drawbacks to Transit
  Advertising   572*

Ethical Dilemma in Advertising: The Direct-Mail Privacy Crisis   542
Ad Lab 15-A: College Grad Gets Job through Mail   547
Checklist of What Works Best in Direct Mail   551
Ad Lab 15-B: How to Use Color in Outdoor Advertising   556
Checklist of What Works Best in Outdoor   562
Portfolio of Outdoor Advertising: A 20th-Century Art Form   563

CHAPTER **16**

SALES PROMOTION AND SUPPLEMENTARY MEDIA   574

Role of Sales Promotion   576
  *Benefits of Sales Promotion   577   Drawbacks of Sales
  Promotion   577*

Sales Promotion Techniques   577
  Push Strategy Techniques   578   Pull Strategy Techniques   582

Supplementary Media 591
 *Specialty Advertising 591 Trade Shows and Exhibitions 593
 Directories and Yellow Pages 594 Emerging Media 595*

Ad Lab 16-A: The 10 Commandments of Creative Promotion 584
Ad Lab 16-B: Smell: Powerful Armament in the Retailer's Arsenal 589

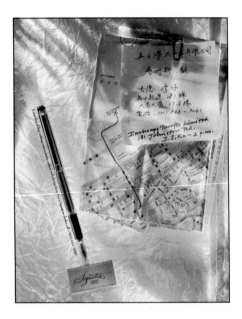

PART
V

SPECIAL TYPES OF ADVERTISING 600

CHAPTER 17

LOCAL ADVERTISING 602

Local Advertising: Where the Action Is 604
 Types of Local Advertising 605 Objectives of Local Advertising 607

Planning the Advertising Effort 608
 *Analyzing the Local Market and Competition 609 Conducting
 Adequate Research 609 Determining Objectives and Strategy 611
 Establishing the Budget 614 Planning Media Strategy 617*

Creating the Local Advertisement 627
 Creating the Message 628 Seeking Creative Assistance 631

Checklist of Local Advertising Objectives 608
Ad Lab 17-A: Mistakes Commonly Made by Local Advertisers 613
Checklist for Setting Local Advertising Budgets 618
Checklist for Creating Local Advertising 630
Ad Lab 17-B: The Co-Op Battleground 636

CHAPTER 18

PUBLIC RELATIONS, CORPORATE ADVERTISING, AND NONCOMMERCIAL
ADVERTISING 638

The Role of Public Relations 640
 *Advertising versus Public Relations 640 Advertising versus Public
 Relations Practitioners 641*

Public Relations Activities and Tools 641
 *Crisis Communications 642 Public Relations Activities 643 Public
 Relations Tools 648*

Corporate Advertising 652
 *Public Relations Advertising 652 Corporate/Institutional
 Advertising 652 Corporate Identity Advertising 661 Recruitment
 Advertising 662*

Noncommercial Advertising 662
  *Examples of Noncommercial Advertising 663 Types of
  Noncommercial Advertising 664 The Advertising Council 667*

Checklist for Writing News Releases 648
Portfolio of Corporate Advertising 654
Ethical Dilemma in Advertising: When Is Advertising Not Really
Advertising? 658
Ad Lab 18-A: David Ogilvy Talks about Corporate Advertising 660

CHAPTER 19

INTERNATIONAL ADVERTISING 670

Growth and Status of International Advertising 672
Managing International Advertising 674
  Worldwide Marketing Structures 675 Agency Selection 678

Creative Strategies in International Advertising 681
  *Market Considerations 681 Media Considerations 686 Message
  Considerations 689*

Ad Lab 19-A: Advertising in the Soviet Union 674
Portfolio of International Advertising 682
Checklist for International Media Planning 690

APPENDIX A: MARKETING PLAN OUTLINE 698

APPENDIX B: ADVERTISING PLAN OUTLINE 704

APPENDIX C: CAREER PLANNING IN ADVERTISING 708

ENDNOTES E-1

CREDITS AND ACKNOWLEDGMENTS C-1

GLOSSARY G

NAME AND COMPANY INDEX I-1

SUBJECT INDEX I-8

CONTEMPORARY

Advertising

PART

I

ADVERTISING PERSPECTIVES

There are many ways to look at advertising—as a business, as a creative process, as a social phenomenon, or even as a fundamental ingredient of a market economy and the free enterprise system. This first unit defines advertising and its functions, examines its economic effect, discusses the social and legal aspects of advertising, and looks at who the major participants are in the advertising business.

Chapter 1, "The Dimensions of Advertising," gives an overview of the profession. A working definition of advertising is presented, as are the various functions and classifications of advertising. The chapter discusses the modern history of advertising and its overall impact on the free enterprise system from both micro- and macroeconomic points of view.

Chapter 2, "The Social, Ethical, and Regulatory Aspects of Advertising," presents a healthy discussion of some of the common criticisms of advertising and debates the ethical and social responsibilities of companies that advertise. The role of government, industry, and consumer groups in regulating advertising is discussed, and important laws governing the practice of advertising are enumerated.

Chapter 3, "The Advertising Business: Agencies and Clients," depicts how people and groups organize themselves—as advertisers and agencies—to create and produce advertising. The chapter describes the role of advertising agencies and the way clients structure their advertising departments. Finally, the chapter elaborates upon the critical factors affecting the client-agency relationship.

Perception and Reality

THE DIMENSIONS
OF ADVERTISING

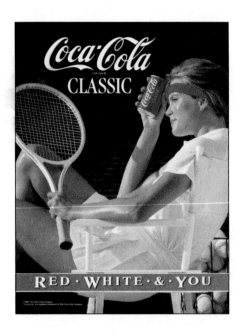

Objective: To define what advertising is and to introduce a functional overview of the profession. To grasp the depth and breadth of advertising, the advertising person must understand the broad elements of the field. In addition to basic advertising terminology, these include: the classifications of advertising; the evolution of advertising technology and strategic thinking; the functions and effects of advertising; and advertising's overall economic impact. These elements set the framework of understanding for the more detailed study of advertising to follow.

After studying this chapter, you will be able to:

☐ Define advertising and differentiate it from public relations.

☐ Understand and describe the different classifications of advertising.

☐ Discuss the key milestones in the evolution of modern advertising.

☐ Explain the significance of marketing warfare to product advertising.

☐ Express the impact of technology on advertising in the 1990s.

☐ Enumerate some of the most important functions of advertising.

☐ Debate the effect of advertising on the value and the price of products.

☐ Explore the impact of advertising on competition and on consumer choice.

He didn't realize it at the time, but John S. Pemberton, an inconspicuous pharmacist in Atlanta, Georgia, had just invented what would soon become the most successful consumer product in history. In fact, it would revolutionize the beverage industry and write a new chapter in the history of marketing and advertising.

As legend goes, Dr. Pemberton developed his concoction while working over a three-legged pot in his backyard in 1886. From the juices of certain plants and nuts, he produced a sweet-tasting brown syrup. When it was accidentally mixed with soda fountain water, the syrup created a remarkable, sparkling taste. On May 8, 1886, Pemberton's new elixir was placed on sale as a soda fountain drink for 5 cents a glass at Jacobs' Pharmacy in downtown Atlanta (see Exhibit 1-1). It was an immediate success. On May 29, a newspaper ad in the *Atlanta Journal* invited Atlantans to try "the new and popular soda fountain drink." The ad also proclaimed that Coca-Cola, as Pemberton called it, was "Delicious and Refreshing," a theme that continues today.

Through the years, the Coca-Cola Company has used a variety of advertising slogans and headlines, including:

The great national temperance beverage.

Thirst knows no season.

The pause that refreshes.

Enjoy Coca-Cola.

For a complete list of Coca-Cola's slogans, campaigns, and themes spanning more than 100 years, see Ad Lab 1-A. The list chronicles not only the history of the world's most successful product but also the history of modern advertising.

EXHIBIT 1-1

Coca-Cola was first served at Jacobs' Pharmacy in downtown Atlanta in 1886. The soda fountain drink, which cost 5 cents a glass at the time, was an immediate success.

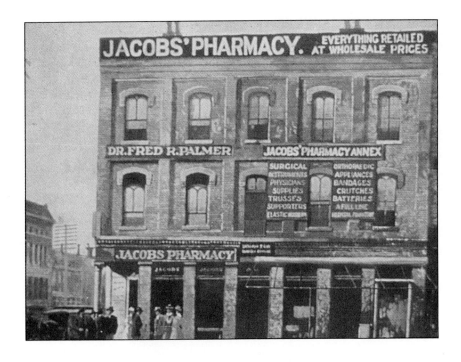

ADVERTISING DEFINED

What is advertising? According to McCann Erickson, Inc., the advertising agency that develops Coca-Cola's national campaigns, advertising is "truth well told." This philosophy has been echoed by Coke's management for many years:

> [Coke's advertising] should be a pleasurable experience, refreshing to watch and pleasant to listen to. It should reflect quality by being quality. And it should make you say, "I wish I'd been there. I wish I had been drinking Coke with these people."[1]

That's what advertising is to Coca-Cola. But can the same be said for other products and services in the marketplace today? How do we define the advertising we see for those commodities?

Albert Lasker, who has been called the father of modern advertising, said that advertising is "salesmanship in print." That may well be. But he gave us that definition long before the advent of radio and television and at a time

---

AD LAB 1-A

It Had to Be Good to Get Where It Is!

1886 Drink Coca-Cola.	1933 Bounce back to normal.
1904 Delicious and refreshing.	1933 Don't wear a tired, thirsty face.
1904 Coca-Cola . . . satisfies.	1935 Coca-Cola . . . the pause that brings friends together.
1905 Coca-Cola revives and sustains.	
1905 Wherever you go . . . you'll find Coca-Cola.	1937 America's favorite moment.
1906 The drink of quality.	1938 The best friend thirst ever had.
1906 The great national temperance beverage.	1938 Thirst asks nothing more.
1907 Coca-Cola is full of vim, vigor and go—is a snappy drink.	1939 Coca-Cola goes along.
	1939 Coca-Cola has the taste thirst goes for.
1908 Get the genuine.	1939 Whoever you are, whatever you do, wherever you
1909 Whenever you see an arrow, think of Coca-Cola.	may be, when you think of refreshment, think of
1911 Enjoy a glass of liquid laughter.	ice-cold Coca-Cola.
1917 Three million a day.	1940 Within easy reach of your thirst.
1920 Coca-Cola . . . good things from 9 climes poured into a single glass.	1940 America's year-round answer to thirst.
	1941 Work refreshed.
1922 Thirst knows no season.	1941 Coca-Cola belongs . . .
1923 Enjoy thirst.	1942 The only thing like Coca-Cola is Coca-Cola itself.
1925 It has the charm of purity.	1942 Coca-Cola has that extra something.
1925 With a drink so good . . . 'tis folly to be thirsty.	1942 The best is always the better buy.
1925 Six million a day.	1942 It's the real thing.
1926 Coca-Cola is the shortest distance between thirst and refreshment.	1943 Universal symbol of the American way of life . . . Coca-Cola.
1927 It had to be good to get where it is.	1943 With a taste all its own.
1927 Around the corner from anywhere.	1945 The happy symbol of a friendly way of life.
1927 At the little red sign.	1945 Why grow thirsty?
1928 Coca-Cola . . . a pure drink of natural flavors.	1946 The world's friendliest club . . . admission 5¢
1929 The best served drink in the world.	1946 Yes.
1929 The pause that refreshes.	1947 Coca-Cola . . . continuous quality.
1932 Ice-cold sunshine.	1947 Continuous quality is quality you trust.
1932 Thirst come, thirst served.	

when the nature and scope of advertising were considerably different than they are today.

Today, we all have strong concepts of what advertising is—and we also tend to have very strong opinions and prejudices about it. Advertising may be defined as a communication process, a marketing process, an economic and social process, a public relations process, or an information and persuasion process, depending on the point of view.

We shall discuss some of these views shortly, but first let's determine a working definition of advertising as it is presented in this book:

> **Advertising** is the nonpersonal communication of information, usually paid for and usually persuasive in nature, about products (goods and services) or ideas by identified sponsors through various media.

Let's take this definition apart and analyze its components. Advertising is directed to groups of people, rather than to individuals, and is therefore

1947	The quality of Coca-Cola is a friendly quality you can always trust.
1948	Where there's Coke there's hospitality.
1949	Coca-Cola . . . along the highway to anywhere.
1950	Thirst, too, seeks quality.
1951	For home and hospitality.
1951	You taste its quality.
1952	What you want is a Coke.
1952	Coke follows thirst everywhere.
1953	Drive safely . . . Drive refreshed.
1953	Midsummer magic.
1955	Bright and bracing as sunshine.
1956	Coca-Cola . . . makes good things taste better.
1956	The friendliest drink on earth.
1956	Gives a bright little lift.
1956	Coca-Cola puts you at your sparkling best.
1957	Sign of good taste.
1958	The cold, crisp taste of Coke.
1959	Cheerful life of Coke.
1959	Relax refreshed with ice-cold Coca-Cola.
1959	Be really refreshed.
1959	The cold, crisp taste that so deeply satisfies.
1961	Coca-Cola refreshes you best.
1963	The big bold taste that's always just right.
1963	Things go better with Coke.
1963	Go better refreshed.
1964	Coca-Cola gives that special zing . . . refreshes best.
1965	Enjoy Coca-Cola.
1965	For extra fun—take more than one! Take an extra carton of Coke!
1966	Coca-Cola has the taste you never get tired of.
1968	Tells your thirst to go fly a kite.
1968	Wave after wave—drink after drink.
1968	For twice the convenience, bring home two cartons of Coke.
1968	It's twice time.
1970	It's the real thing.
1971	I'd like to buy the world a Coke.
1972	Coke . . . goes with the good times.
1975	Look up America, see what we've got.
1976	Coke adds life . . .
1980	Have a Coke and a smile.
1982	Coke is it.
1985	We've got a taste for you (new Coke). America's real choice (Coca-Cola Classic).
1986	Catch the Wave (new Coke). Red, white and you (Coca-Cola Classic).
1988	Can't beat the feeling (Coca-Cola Classic).
1989	Can't beat the real thing (Coca-Cola Classic).
1991	Can't beat the real thing (Coca-Cola Classic).

Laboratory Applications

1. Which slogans are outdated? Why?

2. Which slogans persuade the reader to take action?

3. What slogans can you suggest to reflect Coca-Cola's positioning in the 1990s?

nonpersonal. The groups, for example, might be teenagers who enjoy rock music or older adults who attend cultural events. In either case, advertising to these groups is not personal or face-to-face communication.

Direct-mail advertising often attempts to personalize the message by inserting the receiver's name one or more times in the letter. But direct mail is still nonpersonal; a computer inserted the name. And the signature on the direct-mail advertisement is produced electronically.

Most advertising is *paid for* by sponsors. General Motors, Kmart, Coca-Cola, and the local supermarket pay money to the media to carry the advertisements we read, hear, and see. But some ads are not paid for by their sponsors. The American Red Cross, United Way, and the American Cancer Society are only three of hundreds of organizations whose messages are customarily presented by the media at no charge as a public service.

Most advertising is intended to be *persuasive*—to win converts to a good, service, or idea. A company usually sponsors advertising to convince people its product will benefit them. Some ads, though, such as legal announcements, are intended merely to inform, not to persuade.

In addition to promoting tangible **goods** such as suits, soap, and soft drinks, advertising also helps sell the intangible **services** of bankers, beauticians, and bike repair shops. And increasingly, advertising is used to sell a wide variety of **ideas**—economic, political, religious, and social. It's important to note here that, for the sake of simplicity, in this text the term **product** refers to both goods and services.

For a message to be considered an advertisement, the sponsor must be *identified.* This seems obvious: Naturally, the sponsor usually wants to be identified—or else why pay to advertise? But a distinguishing characteristic between advertising and *public relations* is that certain public relations activities like *publicity* are normally not openly sponsored. This subject will be explored further in Chapter 18.

Advertising reaches us through various channels of communication referred to as the **media.** In addition to the traditional mass media—radio, television, newspapers, magazines, and billboards—advertising also uses direct mail, shopping carts, blimps, and videocassettes.

With this working definition in mind, let's consider some varieties of advertising.

CLASSIFICATIONS OF ADVERTISING

The word *advertising* is often preceded by an adjective that indicates the kind of advertising being discussed. Advertising can be classified by four main criteria: target audience, geographic area, medium, and purpose. These classifications are summarized in Exhibit 1-2.

By Target Audience

Advertising is usually aimed at a particular segment of the population—the **target audience.** When you see an ad that doesn't appeal to you, it may be because the ad is not aimed at any of the groups of people you belong to. For example, a television commercial for denture cream would probably offer little relevance to a teenager. Similarly, young parents may have very little interest in an ad for a senior citizen condominium.

There are many kinds of target audiences. The two major classifications, though, are consumers and businesses.

EXHIBIT 1-2   The Classifications of Advertising

☐ **By target audience**
  Consumer advertising
  Business advertising
    Industrial
    Trade
    Professional
    Agricultural (farm)

☐ **By geographic area**
  International advertising
  National advertising
  Regional advertising
  Local (retail) advertising

☐ **By medium**
  Print advertising
    Newspaper
    Magazine
  Broadcast advertising
    Radio
    Television
  Out-of-home advertising
    Outdoor (billboard)
    Transit
  Direct-mail advertising

☐ **By purpose**
  Product advertising
  Nonproduct advertising
  Commercial advertising
  Noncommercial advertising
  Action advertising
  Awareness advertising

Consumer Advertising

Most of the ads in the mass media—television, radio, newspapers, and magazines—are **consumer advertisements.** They may be sponsored by the manufacturer of the product or the dealer who sells the product. They are typically directed at **consumers**—people who will buy the product for their own, or someone else's, personal use. For example, a magazine ad for Coca-Cola may be aimed at both the purchaser and the user, who may or may not be the same person. A TV commercial for dog food, however, is aimed at the purchaser, not the user, of the product. Both examples, though, would still be referred to as *consumer advertisements.*

Business Advertising

People who buy or specify goods and services for use in business make up the target audience for **business advertising.** The majority of consumer advertising appears in mass-consumer media. Business advertising, on the other hand, tends to be concentrated in specialized business publications or professional journals, in direct-mail pieces mailed to business establishments, or in trade shows held for specific areas of business. Until recently, business advertising was rarely seen in the mass media. In fact, business advertising is often said to be invisible because unless you are actively involved in some business you are not likely to see it.

Business advertising comes in four distinct types: *industrial, trade, professional,* and *agricultural.*

Industrial advertising is aimed at individuals in business who buy or influence the purchase of **industrial products.** Industrial products include goods and services used in the manufacture of other goods (plants, machinery, equipment) or that become a physical part of another product (raw materials, semimanufactured goods, components). Industrial products also include goods or services that are used to conduct business and that do not become part of another product. These might be capital goods (office machines, computers, desks, operating supplies) or business services the user engages. The ad for a capital goods item in Exhibit 1–3 uses the headline in a

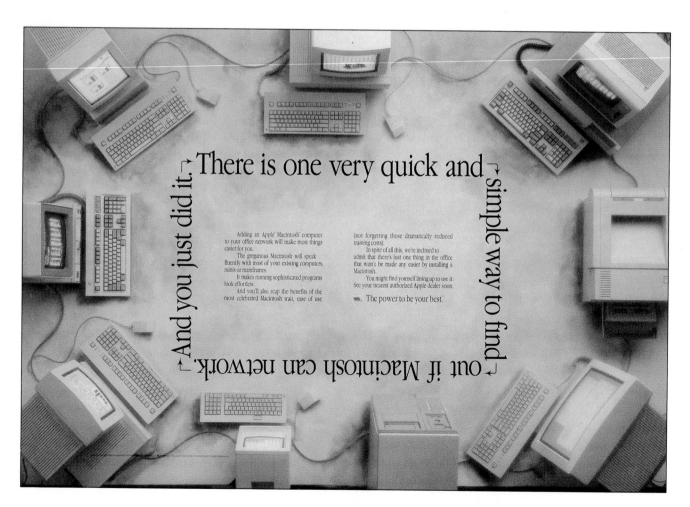

EXHIBIT 1–3

Apple of Canada uses industrial advertising to announce the networking capabilities of the Macintosh computer to business people who buy or influence the purchase of capital goods prod-ucts. Apple's agency, Baker Lovick/BBDO, used the headline creatively to lead the reader around the network of computers that operate differently.

very creative manner to lead business owners and purchasing agents into understanding the answer to two major questions in the computer world today—Does the Macintosh computer operate on existing computer networks and is it compatible with other types of computers?

Advertising for such products as computer mainframes and software systems in *Iron Age, Electronics, Business Week,* and the like would be referred to as *industrial advertising.* In recent years, some of these products have been advertised in mass-consumer media like radio and television, but the target audience is still businesspeople who purchase or use industrial goods.

Manufacturers use **trade advertising**—the advertising of goods and services to middlemen—to stimulate wholesalers and retailers to buy goods for resale to their customers. For example, an ad for Coca-Cola in a trade publication like *Progressive Grocer* might be aimed at getting food store

STERLING LITHO GLOSS PRINTS WITH A FLOURISH, RUNS WITH A FLAIR.

In the ancient art of calligraphy, masters of this Oriental discipline have passed their secrets down through a hundred generations.

In the modern art of lithography, there is another "secret" known to serious practitioners through the years: STERLING® Litho Gloss paper.

STERLING is treasured for its bright, white styling and sparkling gloss. Its smooth, uniform surface gives snap and depth to bolder colors, perfect fidelity to subtle colors and shapes.

And printers know that STERLING runs as beautifully as it prints, because we've built in all the qualities that make this a truly production-oriented sheet.

They also know that when deadlines are tight, fast PressDate® Service will get them through. On orders of 2,500 to 40,000 lbs. (60, 70, 80, or 100lb., 25x38—500 basis) finished to your specified size, we'll ship in five days or less. For full details, call your Westvaco representative.

And for next-day delivery of customized dummies and white and printed samples, call Westvaco Direct Response℠ at 1-800-235-3782.

This advertisement was lithographed 8-up on a 40x52 sheet of STERLING Litho Gloss, 80lb., 25x38—500 basis. Precision sheeted by Westvaco's AccuTrim™ machines. Westvaco Corporation, Fine Papers Division, 299 Park Avenue, New York, NY 10171.

Westvaco
It works.

© 1988 Westvaco Corporation

EXHIBIT 1-4

Three features of this ad work together in appealing to members of the printing trade. First, the ad was printed on Sterling Litho Gloss paper before being bound into a trade magazine. This enabled the ad to stand out from other pages, and it also demonstrated the advertiser's claim of high quality. Finally, the promise of prompt delivery of industrial-sized orders demonstrates the company's desire to obtain greater distribution of the product through high-volume/high-quality professional printers and the designers who specify papers.

managers to stock more Coke on their shelves. Some items advertised to the trade, such as office equipment, store fixtures, or specialized business services, might be bought for use in the middleman's own business. The major objective of trade advertising, though, is to obtain greater distribution of the product being sold, either by developing more sales outlets or by selling more products to existing outlets. For example, Exhibit 1-4 features the Westvaco paper company's ad lauding the benefits of its Sterling Litho Gloss paper—and its ability to ship large orders promptly—to get the attention of the printing trade, the retailers who actually recommend the use of such paper to end users who need printing.

Professional advertising is aimed at individuals normally licensed to practice and operate under a code of ethics or a set of professional standards—such as teachers, accountants, doctors, dentists, architects, engineers, and lawyers. Often the publications used for professional advertising are the official organs of professional societies, such as the *Archives of Ophthalmology,* published by the American Medical Association, or the *Music Educators Journal,* published by the Music Educators National Conference.

Professional advertising has three objectives: (1) to convince professional people to buy items, equipment, and supplies by brand name for use in their work; (2) to encourage professionals to recommend or prescribe a specific product or service to their clients or patients; and (3) to persuade the person to use the product personally.

Farming is still the largest industry in the United States and Canada. Farmers are consumers, of course, but they are businesspeople, too, and as such they make up the audience for **agricultural** (or **farm**) **advertising.** Agricultural advertising is aimed at establishing awareness of particular brands of agricultural goods; building dealer acceptance of advertised products; and creating preference for products by showing the farmer how the products will increase efficiency, reduce risks, and widen profit margins. Publications such as *California Farmer* and *American Vegetable Grower* serve these markets.

By Geographic Area

A neighborhood dress shop would most likely advertise in the local area near the store. On the other hand, many U.S. and Canadian products are advertised in foreign countries from Africa to Asia. The four classifications of advertising based on geography are international, national, regional, and local.

International advertising is advertising directed at foreign markets. Travel to Europe and you might see advertisements for Crest toothpaste in Norwegian. In Russia, you'll find the virtues of Pepsi-Cola and McDonald's extolled. Visit Brazil and see print and TV ads (in Portuguese) for products advertised daily in the United States and Canada, such as Levi's or Pierre Cardin products (see Exhibit 1-5). As a field of study, international advertising has grown so fast and become so important that we have devoted an entire chapter (Chapter 19) to the subject.

Advertising aimed at customers in several regions of the country is called **national advertising,** and its sponsors are called **national advertisers.** The majority of advertising we see on prime-time network television is national advertising.

Many products are sold in one area or region, but not the whole country, hence the need for **regional advertising.** Publications such as *The Wall*

Entre na dimensão Pierre Cardin.
Um universo de moda muito exclusivo.

PIERRE CARDIN

EXHIBIT 1-5

International advertising requires the correct use of concepts and language. In South America, advertisers generally use Spanish. But for the marketer wanting any share of the dynamic Brazilian market, Portuguese is obligatory.

This Pierre Cardin ad, created in Rio, uses an avant-garde, surrealistic theme that could be used successfully in many countries: "Enter the Pierre Cardin dimension. A most exclusive universe of fashion."

EXHIBIT 1-6

Witty headlines, combined with strong visuals, captured attention in this local outdoor and transit ad campaign for Chicago's Adler Planetarium. The modest three-month campaign was produced by the agency as a public service, saving the taxpayers money while increasing traffic and revenues for the city planetarium.

EXHIBIT 1-7
Corporate or institutional advertising promotes a company's mission or philosophy rather than a specific product. Goodwill is often the reward. This institutional ad reaches two audiences with its salute to the hardworking and proud people of Baltimore, citizens who are both employees as well as patients of Kaiser Permanente.

SFX: Piano music

VO: To friends . . . and families. To those full of history and hard work. To those who have just arrived and those who have been around a bit longer. A salute . . . to the proud people of Baltimore. From Kaiser Permanente. The people who are proud to be taking care of you.

Street Journal and *Time* sell space on either a national or a regional basis. Thus, an airline that operates in only, say, the West Coast area might purchase ad space in the regional edition of certain national publications.

Advertisers such as department stores, automobile dealers, and restaurants use **local advertising,** because the majority of their customers come from only one city or local trading area. Exhibit 1-6, for example, is an ad for the Adler Planetarium, which primarily serves the Chicago market area. Local advertising is often called **retail advertising** simply because most of it is paid for by retailers. However, not all retail advertising is local. Increasingly, major retail chains such as Sears and Kmart advertise beyond the local areas where their stores are located.

By Medium

Advertising can be classified on the basis of the *medium* used to transmit the message (e.g., radio advertising). An **advertising medium** is any *paid* means used to present an advertisement to its target audience. It does not, therefore, include "word-of-mouth" advertising. The principal **media** (plural of medium) used in advertising are newspapers, magazines, radio, television, direct mail, and out-of-home media such as outdoor signs, billboards, and transit ads (on buses or trucks).

By Purpose

Another way to classify advertising is on the basis of the sponsor's general objectives. Some advertising, for example, is designed to promote a particular good or service. Other ads promote ideas. Some advertising is meant to generate profits for the advertiser; some ads are sponsored by nonprofit groups. Some ads are meant to call the target audience to some action; others are only intended to create awareness or understanding of the advertiser's good or service.

Product versus Nonproduct Advertising

Product advertising is intended to promote goods and services. Nonproduct advertising is designed to sell ideas. When Citgo places an ad for its gasoline, it is a product ad. Ads for insurance or legal services are also product advertisements.

On the other hand, if Citgo tells about its ability to drill for oil without disturbing or polluting the environment, the ad is promoting the company's mission or philosophy rather than a particular product. This form of advertising is called **corporate, nonproduct,** or **institutional advertising.** Corporate advertising can have various objectives: to counter public criticism or to promote noncontroversial causes such as support for the arts or charities, for example. The corporate ad by Kaiser Permanente seen in Exhibit 1-7 helps to build goodwill for the company by saluting the people it serves, in this case the people of Baltimore. This type of advertising will be the focus of Chapter 18.

Commercial versus Noncommercial Advertising

Commercial (for profit) **advertising** promotes goods, services, or ideas for a business with the expectation of making a profit. **Noncommercial** (nonprofit) **advertising** is sponsored by or for a charitable institution, civic group, or religious or political organization. Many noncommercial advertisements seek money and are placed in the hope of raising funds. Others hope to change consumer behavior ("Buckle up for safety"). Chapter 18 also discusses noncommercial advertising.

Action Advertising versus Awareness Advertising

Rapp and Collins, advertising professionals and authors of *Maxi-Marketing,* have categorized ads on the basis of expected consumer response.[2] They point out that some ads are intended to bring about immediate action on the part of the reader, whereas some have a longer-term goal.

Mail-order advertisements, for example, are typical of **action advertising.** Some newspaper and magazine ads include cents-off coupons or a form for the reader to use to request catalogs or additional information. These ads seek an immediate, direct action from the reader. For example, the ad in Exhibit 1–8 for Pearle Vision Centers eye care products features coupons that imply what action the reader should take and strong visuals suggesting how stylish the customer will look with Pearle's products.

Advertising that attempts to build the image of a product or familiarity with the name and package is called **awareness advertising.** The objective may be to create interest in the product and to influence readers or viewers to select a specific brand the next time they are in the market for that product category. Most ads on TV and radio could be classified as awareness advertising. Some, however, are a mixture of action and awareness advertising. It is not uncommon to see a 60-second TV commercial that devotes the first 50 seconds to image building and the last 10 seconds to a local phone number for further information.

This action advertisement stimulates an immediate, direct response from readers by suggesting two incentives. Pearle's glasses will make you look good, and by cutting out the coupon, you can save money.

Experienced advertisers, though, exercise caution in the use of action devices. The more they are used, the more they tend to detract from the image-building qualities of an ad. And that can adversely affect the advertiser's longer term marketing objectives.

ADVERTISING'S EVOLUTION

As you can see, advertising today takes many forms. And as we can all attest from experience, advertising has considerable influence on contemporary society and commerce. But this was not always the case.

Thousands of years ago, ancient civilizations had only unsophisticated hand tools for producing goods, so the quantity and variety of available goods was negligible. People lived in small, isolated communities, and the distribution of goods was also limited. There was no need to stimulate mass purchases; there were no mass media and, therefore, there was little need for advertising.

Most historians believe advertising was introduced by Greek and Roman merchants who benefited from expanded contact with other societies, a higher level of production due to the use of more sophisticated tools, and enhanced communication. An increased demand for goods created a greater need to advertise their availability. Thus, signs carved in clay, wood, or stone were hung in front of shops so passersby could see what products the merchants offered. Most people could not read, so the signs often only symbolized the goods for sale, such as a jerkin for a tailor's shop (see Exhibit 1-9).

Throughout history, social and technological developments have similarly affected advertising and communication, sometimes profoundly. The popular phrase "The medium is the message," coined by Marshall McLuhan, points out the connection between technology and communication.[3] McLuhan's

EXHIBIT 1-9

Here is an example of one of the earliest forms of advertising. Until the advent of public schooling, most people could not read—so signs often featured only a symbol of the goods or services for sale, such as the jerkin on this tailor's sign in Williamsburg, Virginia.

legacy is the idea that technological advances have evoked social changes. As we examine the evolution of advertising, a number of proofs for McLuhan's theory can be seen.

The Impact of Printing

The introduction of the printing press in Germany in the 1450s was a major event in the history of civilization—and probably the most important development in the history of advertising. Johannes Gutenberg, the inventor of the printing press and its system of changeable letters, changed the way people lived and worked.

Before the printing press became a usable tool, most people could not read or write. Monks and scholars, scattered throughout Europe in monasteries and a few major cities, read and wrote in Latin. The average person had to memorize anything important, and most information was transmitted orally. To put it mildly, this system had its limitations. Because oral communication could not be substantiated, the vast majority of people lived a life without documentable facts. And because dialects varied from region to region, most news never traveled much more than 50 miles.[4]

The introduction of printing marked a dramatic turning point. Facts could now be established and substantiated in text. People no longer had to rely on their memories for data storage and began to rely on printed materials. Movable letters provided the flexibility to print in local dialects. The slow hand-transcription of Latin texts by the monks gave way to more rapid mass printing by a less select group. Entrepreneurs bought printing presses, mounted them in wagons, and traveled from town to town selling printing. Thus, as this new technology made possible the first formats of mass advertising—posters, handbills, and newspaper advertisements—printing facilitated the development of the first mass media.

By 1472, the first advertisement printed in English appeared: a handbill, tacked on church doors in London, announcing a prayer book for sale. The first newspaper ad appeared on the back of a London newspaper in 1650, offering a reward for the return of 12 stolen horses. Later, ads appeared for coffee, chocolate, tea, real estate, and medicines, as did "personal ads." Such advertising was directed to a limited number of people who were customers of coffeehouses where the newspapers were read.

In the American colonies, the *Boston Newsletter* began carrying newspaper ads in 1704. Later, Benjamin Franklin made ads more readable by using large headlines and by surrounding the ads with considerable white space. In fact, Franklin was the first American known to use illustrations in ads.

The Industrial Revolution and Early U.S. Advertising

The Industrial Revolution began in England in the mid-1700s and reached the United States by the early 1800s. Machinery began to replace animal power. Manufacturers now could mass-produce goods with uniform quality; and for the first time, it cost less to buy a product than to make it oneself.

In order to mass-produce, however, manufacturers needed mass consumption. They could no longer be content to sell only in their local area. Manufacturers soon realized the tremendous value of advertising as an aid in selling to the exciting frontier markets in the West as well as to the growing industrial markets in the East.

In July 1844, the first magazine ad appeared in the *Southern Messenger,* a publication edited for a short time by Edgar Allan Poe. Magazines were the initial medium used by manufacturers to reach the mass market and to stimulate mass consumption. Magazines made national advertising possible—and thereby the sale of products nationwide.

Historians consider Volney B. Palmer the earliest advertising agent in the United States. Setting up business in Philadelphia in 1841, Palmer contracted with newspapers for large volumes of advertising space at discount rates and then resold this space to advertisers at a higer rate. The advertisers usually prepared the ads themselves. In 1890, N. W. Ayer & Son, another Philadelphia advertising organization, offered its services to advertisers. This company was the first advertising agency to operate as agencies do today—planning, creating, and executing complete advertising campaigns for clients in return for a commission paid by the media or for fees received from advertisers. Today Ayer is considered the oldest advertising agency in the United States.

The Communications Revolution

Technological advances of the 19th century created the greatest changes in the advertising industry since the 1450s. Consider the introduction of photography in 1839, which changed the way newspapers and advertisements were illustrated. Before photography, products could be depicted only by handcrafted woodcuts or engraved metal drawings. Photography added credibility and a whole new world of creativity to advertising—it allowed products, people, and places to be shown as they really were, rather than as visualized by the artist.

The telegraph, introduced in 1844, enabled news to travel over great distances in little time, thereby diminishing regionalism. The invention of other important communications devices in the late 19th and early 20th centuries—including the telephone, typewriter, phonograph, and motion pictures—enabled people to communicate as never before.

Other developments during the 19th century directly affected the growth of advertising. The rapidly growing population provided an increasingly large market for manufacturers. At the same time, the number of people who could read increased substantially. The literacy rate was up to 90 percent by the late 1800s. This large reading public provided an audience that could understand printed advertising messages.

The development of a nationwide railroad transportation system quickly moved the United States into a period of spectacular growth. And in 1896, the federal government inaugurated rural free delivery (RFD). Direct-mail advertising and mail-order selling flourished with mass production. Manufacturers had an ever-increasing variety of products for their catalogs. And they had a means of delivering their advertising (via newspapers and magazines) and their goods to the public.

The Dawning of Responsibility

The United States entered the 20th century as a great industrial nation. A national marketing system had evolved, enhanced and propelled by advertising. But during the first two decades of the 1900s, advertising underwent an era of reexamination. Decades of unsubstantiated advertising claims for products like the health jolting chair in Exhibit 1-10 had caused widespread resentment and resulted in a consumer revolt. The focal point of the attack

EXHIBIT 1-10

In the 1880s, advertisements in
weekly newspapers for health
gimmicks and patent medicines
were typical. They exemplified
the attitude of manufacturers at
that time, known by the Latin
expression *caveat emptor* ("let
the buyer beware"). The result
was the first consumer movement
in this country leading to regulatory legislation.

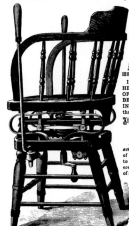

NEW IDEAS AND INVENTIONS

From a weekly New York newspaper of the 1880's.

The Health Jolting Chair
COPYRIGHT.

The most important Health Mechanism ever produced

A Practical Household Substitute for the Saddle-Horse

It affords a PERFECT means of giving EFFICIENT exercise to the ESSEN-TIALLY IMPORTANT NUTRITIVE ORGANS OF THE BODY in the most DIRECT, CONVENIENT, COMFORTABLE, and IN-EXPENSIVE manner.

Suitable for all ages and for most physical conditions.

INDISPENSABLE TO THE HEALTH AND HAPPINESS OF MILLIONS OF HUMAN BEINGS WHO MAY BE LIV-ING SEDENTARY LIVES through choice or necessity.

It preserves Health, cures Disease, and prolongs Life.

An *ingenious, rational, scientific, mechanical* means of overcoming those impediments to the taking of proper exercise, erected by the artificial methods of modern society.

For certain classes of invalids a veritable Treasure-Trove.

A CONSERVATOR of NERVOUS ENERGY.

No dwelling-house is com-pletely furnished without The Health Jolting Chair.

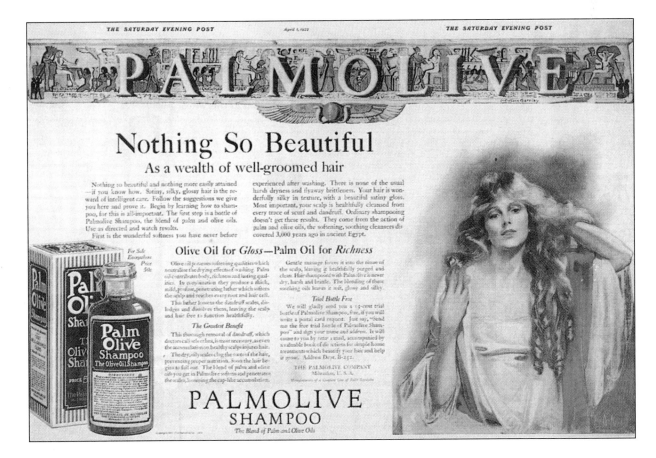

EXHIBIT 1-11

After World War I, the greater
emotional impact of color was
used more and more by advertisers—despite higher cost. Here
is an early example of such a full-
color ad, produced in 1922 for
Palmolive shampoo.

was the advertising for patent medicines and health devices. Regulation came from the government and from within the advertising industry itself.

In the 1920s, after World War I, the "era of salesmanship" arrived, and advertising truly became "salesmanship in print." Testimonial advertising by movie stars became popular. Full-color printing became the norm and was employed lavishly by magazine advertisers. The 1922 ad in Exhibit 1–11 is an early example of a color ad.

On October 29, 1929, the stock market crashed, the Great Depression began, and advertising expenditures were drastically reduced. However, perhaps out of desperation, false and misleading advertising continued to thrive. Several best-selling books exposed advertising as an unscrupulous exploiter of consumers, giving root to the consumer movement and resulting in further government regulation.

Because of the sales resistance of consumers and the budget-cutting attitude of management during the Depression, advertising turned to research to regain its credibility and effectiveness. Daniel Starch, A. C. Nielsen, and George Gallup founded research organizations to delve into the attitudes and preferences of consumers. By providing information to advertisers on public opinion, the performance of advertising messages, and the sales of

ETHICAL DILEMMA IN ADVERTISING
Truth in Advertising—Is It Puffed Up or Overblown?

Fluff and puff are the bricks and mortar of most consumer advertising, or so it seems. Perhaps that's because the main factor that differentiates one product from another is advertising. Traditionally, puffery has been immune from legal constraints because it's considered a statement of opinion rather than fact. That means people aren't expected to believe it when an advertiser says "Our service can't be beat!" But sometimes it's difficult to distinguish between puffery and truth. And although the FTC contends that reasonable people won't believe puffery, research has consistently shown that many do.

At one time or another, most companies venture into the gray area that exists between the unvarnished truth and outright deception. Food and toy advertisers often use special effects to exaggerate their products' qualities, for example. Since the government began regulating toy industry commercials, however, some of the worst examples of overblown puffery have occurred in the world of automotive advertising, where reality often takes a backseat to dramatization.

One of the industry's most memorable spokespersons is Joe Isuzu, a character famous for his inability to tell the truth. Jerry Della Femina cryptically states that his agency created Joe Isuzu to "get information to the consumer, which is usually fed in the worst way possible." Hal Riney, chairman of Riney & Partners, sees this "antitruth" ap-

proach as a possible solution to a problem that pervades the advertising industry at large. "We used up all our superlatives on lesser claims and made it difficult to come up with language that sounds believable when something really is different or special," he says.

Many people found the irreverent Isuzu commercials amusing; but nobody's laughing about the Volvo scandal. To make a point about Volvo's durability and safety in an accident, the company made a commercial that showed a lineup of cars being run over by a monster truck called Bear Foot. Only the Volvo survived the ordeal intact. However, an investigation by the Texas attorney general's office found that the demonstration was fraudulent. Volvo later admitted that its production company had artificially reinforced the Volvo's structure and then cut the support pillars on the competitors' cars.

Both Volvo and their ad agency maintained their innocence even though everything was done in clear view of hundreds of hired spectators. In the end, Volvo's reputation was crushed. The company was required to pay hundreds of thousands of dollars in investigative costs, and it also ran ads apologizing for the deception. The ad agency was forced to resign the account.

Some industry experts think the Volvo debacle will make advertisers more careful about crossing the line between puffery and dishonesty. Rick Kurnit, partner at a advertised products through food stores and drugstores, these firms gave birth to a whole new business activity—the marketing research industry.

The Rise of Broadcast Advertising

A powerful new advertising medium—radio—started on November 2, 1920, in Pittsburgh, Pennsylvania. It rapidly became the primary means of mass communication. World and national news could now arrive direct from the scene, and a whole new world of family entertainment—music, drama, sports—became possible. Suddenly, radio enabled national advertisers to reach the large, captive audiences tuned to popular programs. In fact, the first radio shows were produced by the advertisers that sponsored them.

The greatest expansion of any medium, though, occurred after the initial television program was broadcast in 1941. Following World War II, the use of television advertising grew rapidly. In 1955, color TV was born. Today, television has become the second largest advertising medium (after newspapers) in terms of total dollars spent by advertisers.

law firm that works with ad agencies says, "There is no doubt in my mind that post-Volvo, both the networks and the [Federal Trade Commission] will be focusing in on the demonstration issue." Sean Fitzpatrick, vice chairman of McCann-Erickson, adds, "If the cinematography is aiding you and convincing people that you can do things you can't do, then I'd say any reasonable person would say that's wrong. If nothing else, it's a matter of ethics."

But can the public really be blamed for doubting advertisers' claims? The FTC hasn't taken the lead in protecting consumers, and watchdog groups aren't powerful enough to be effective. Most people don't know that ad agencies must submit detailed affidavits verifying that no tricks have been used during the filming of demonstration commercials—and that some advertisers are more scrupulous about this than others. According to a Honda spokesman, the company has a policy to use a dramatization label "whenever we depict something in a commercial that could possibly be misconstrued." But as consumer cynicism grows, some industry experts fear that the actions of a few may have undermined the credibility of all advertisers. Donnie Deutsch, creative director at Deutsch, New York says, "The public thinks all advertising is [bull] anyway . . . [even though] . . . there are thousands of things that are done right and legitimately."

Given the fierce competition in the marketplace and the lack of legal restraints, the question is not *whether* but *how much* puffery is allowable. Prudent consumers must maintain a healthy skepticism about the advertising they see. They must also try to distinguish fact from fiction while keeping in mind the meaning of the ancient admonition *caveat emptor*: let the buyer beware.

Questions

1. Ron Jackson, CEO of Jackson/Riley & Co., a Cincinnati ad agency, claims that an integral part of selling is "emotion, romance, and the metaphor of ideas," that is, puffery. Do you think that advertisers should be allowed to puff up their product claims using these kinds of nonrational appeals? If advertisers were forced to tell only the literal truth, how would that affect creativity in advertising?

2. Do you think that *all* puffery should be outlawed? If so, how would similar products (toothpaste, detergents, cereals, for example) go about differentiating themselves from the competition? Would it be morally preferable for some companies to go out of business rather than increase their sales by puffing up the claims about their products?

THE DEVELOPMENT OF MODERN ADVERTISING

Since World War II, the growth of advertising and the money spent on it has been phenomenal. As the war economy changed to a peacetime economy, the manufacturers of war equipment reverted to mass producing and advertising consumer products, offering greater luxury, style, and convenience.

The postwar prosperity of the late 1940s and early 1950s were marked by a consumer society vigorously chasing itself up the social ladder by buying more products to keep up with the Joneses. Ads of the era stressed product features that implied social acceptance, style, luxury, and success. Rosser Reeves of the Ted Bates advertising agency introduced the idea that every advertisement must point out the product's **USP—unique selling proposition**—those features that differentiated it from competitive products. But soon there were so many imitation USPs that consumers couldn't take any more. Ford Motor Company regretfully discovered this when consumers failed to accept another medium-priced, chromium-plated, "keep-up-with-the-Joneses" car model—the Edsel—despite massive advertising expenditures (see Chapter 4).

The transition to the image era of the 1960s, then, was a natural evolution. During this period, the emphasis in advertising shifted from product features to product image, or personality. Cadillac became the image of luxury and the bourgeois symbol of success surpassed only by the aristocratic snootiness of Rolls-Royce. Even products like shirts were given an image (see Exhibit 1-12).

The Positioning Era

In the early 1970s, Jack Trout and Al Ries wrote that just as the "me-too" (imitative) products of the 1950s killed the product era, the me-too images of the 1960s killed the image era. The 1970s saw a new kind of advertising strategy, where the competitor's strengths became as important as the adver-

EXHIBIT 1-12

By the 1960s, the emphasis in advertising had shifted from listing product features in an ad to promoting the product's image. This shift stemmed from the success of people like David Ogilvy in creating highly successful image campaigns like the "man in the Hathaway shirt." It was David Ogilvy's first big hit in the advertising business and rapidly became a classic campaign of the era. The eye-patched actor in the series, George Wrangell, lent an air of aristocratic British class to the product. His attitude of discriminating taste added value to the perception of the product and tripled Hathaway's annual sales.

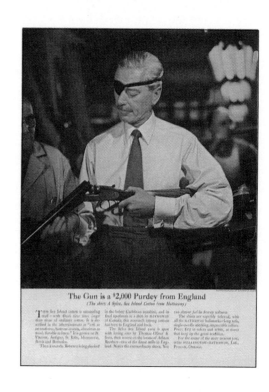

The Gun is a $2,000 Purdey from England
(The shirt: A Sykes, Sea Island Cotton from Hathaway)

tiser's. This was called the **positioning era,** and Trout and Ries were its greatest advocates. Acknowledging the importance of product features and image, they insisted that what was really important was how the product ranked against the competition in the consumer's mind.

The most famous ads of the positioning era were Volkswagen ("Think small"), Avis ("We're only No. 2"), and 7UP ("The uncola"). Exhibit 1-13 shows Volkswagen's now classic "Think Small" ad. Many other manufacturers tried it with great success. Trout and Ries also pointed to product disappointments of the period—like Life Savers gum and RCA computers—and suggested that poor positioning was the reason.[5]

The "Me" Decade

Trout and Ries did not address the consumer movement, which received its greatest impetus from the disillusioning setbacks of the Vietnam War, the Watergate scandals, and the sudden shortage of vital natural resources. These issues fostered cynicism and distrust of the establishment and everything traditional, and gave rise to a new twist in moral consciousness. On the one hand, individual irresponsibility and self-indulgence were defended in the name of personal self-fulfillment. On the other hand, the concept of corporate self-fulfillment was attacked in the name of social accountability. All this led to another evolution in the style and the subjects of advertising.

By the mid-1980s, Americans had already witnessed an avalanche of ads—especially in the toiletry and cosmetics industries—aimed at the "me" generation that played off the self-fulfillment climate ("L'Oreal. Because I'm worth

EXHIBIT 1-13

Jack Trout and Al Ries called this "probably the most famous ad of the 60s." In their view, it helped usher in the positioning era of the 70s. By opting for the "small" position in consumers' minds, Volkswagen assumed a leadership rank that took many years and millions of competitors' dollars to overcome.

Think small.

it."). At the same time, the nation's largest industrial concerns were spending millions of dollars on corporate advertising to extol their social consciousness and good citizenship for cleaning up after themselves and otherwise protecting the environment.

Likewise, following the energy shortages of the 1970s and 1980s, a new marketing tactic called **demarketing** appeared. Producers of energy and energy-consuming goods used marketing and advertising techniques to actually slow the demand for their products. Ads appeared asking people to refrain from operating clothes washers and dryers during peak periods of the day when electricity is in high demand by businesses. In time, demarketing became a strategic tool for certain noncommercial, issue advertisers such as the Minnesota Department of Health, whose antismoking commercial is shown in Exhibit 1-14. Some financial and health-care institutions also used demarketing to segment prospective customers. By actively discouraging patronage from some customers, for example, the banks could concentrate on those who appeared most profitable.[6]

The Age of Marketing Warfare

In the 1980s, Trout and Ries published a new book, *Marketing Warfare,* in which they portrayed marketing as a war that businesspeople must be prepared to wage. Many of their ideas came from a classic book on military strategy, *On War,* written in 1831 by Karl von Clausewitz, a Prussian general.

In *Marketing Warfare,* Trout and Ries outlined four strategic positions in the marketplace: *defensive, offensive, flanking,* and *guerrilla.* The **defensive strategy** belongs to the dominant company in a given market, which must defend itself against the onslaught of competitors aiming to knock it off the top of the mountain. The second- and third-place companies must use an **offensive strategy** to capture portions of number-one's market. The third strategy, adopted by the middle companies in the hierarchy, is a **flanking strategy,** in which these companies must point up the qualities that make them different from the top three. Finally, the remaining companies must adopt a **guerrilla strategy** to carve out small niches they can defend successfully in the larger marketplace.[7] (A more in-depth review of Trout and Ries's comparison of war and marketing strategies is presented in Chapter 7, Ad Lab 7-A.)

At the end of the 1980s, the economy began to slow, and too many companies began chasing too few consumer dollars. The intensity of the advertising that followed provided additional evidence that marketing warfare strategies were enduring. For example, Coke and Pepsi's long-running battle heated up, with a series of counterpoint ads featuring a procession of celebrities choosing one cola or the other.

As the decade of the 90s began, a new form of advertising appeared to be evolving. Based on comparative advertising, this new form was an intensified demarketing approach that sought to scare or shame buyers away from competitors' products. For example, AT&T commercials depicted a small-business owner complaining about his phone system (from a competing company) as he loses sales waiting for a service person to arrive. To increase the anxiety of this portrayal, the camera continually swept the scene as if held by an amateur. A similar camera technique was used in a Chrysler commercial showing the company's CEO Lee Iacocca haranguing colleages about

EXHIBIT 1-14

Demarketing—slowing the demand for certain products—became a strategic tool for some noncommercial, issue-oriented advertisers. In this ad, produced for the Minnesota Department of Health, animals are used to show the foolishness of smoking.

VO: If you think this looks ridiculous, remember smoking is just as unnatural for you as it is for them.

Americans' inferiority complex, which leads them to overvalue Japanese cars and undervalue American brands.[8]

At the same time, a five-year study by the Ayer advertising agency found that consumers and consumer product companies were moving in opposite directions. For the 90s, this meant diminished effectiveness of company brands. Ayer found that consumers would become increasingly diverse and fragmented, while companies would be under pressure to simplify and consolidate. Fred Posner, Ayer's executive VP and director of research, urged marketers to redefine and reembrace the concept of branding (discussed in Chapter 5) and to use advertising and all other marketing activities to build a deep and relevant relationship with the consumer into their brands' personalities.[9]

Echoing the need for more effective and relevant advertising in the 90s, Tom McElligott, the head of Chiat/Day/Mojo's advertising offices in New York, London, and Toronto, asserted, "There's a growing appreciation among consumers for advertising that is charming, intelligent, and smart."[10]

The Information Age

During the last decade, several significant new technologies have affected advertising considerably. One was the penetration of cable television and satellite receivers into a vast number of American homes. Many cable channels are devoted to single types of programming, such as straight news, home shopping, sports, or comedy. This has transformed television from the most widespread of mass media to a somewhat more specialized medium.[11] Now smaller companies and companies with products that appeal to a limited market can use television to reach audiences with particular interests.

Another change in the TV world has been the growing presence of videocassette recorders. For many consumers, watching movies on video at home has replaced going to the movie theater. Advertisers have watched this trend with interest. Some videos now begin with an ad, shot in a suitable cinematic style, that sells a product valued by that particular movie's audience. In one expensive example, a woman trekking to the kitchen for a Pepsi encounters a series of hazards similar to the adventures of Indiana Jones. Again, this technological trend has allowed special-interest advertising through what has traditionally been considered a mass medium.

Computer technology has had its own impact. Personal computers, modems, electronic mail, electronic bulletin boards, even facsimile machines give advertisers new media for reaching potential customers. But these options are largely replacements for print media, and their advertising tends to be more information-oriented than image-oriented. Expanded access to computer power has benefited advertisers in another way as well. Now even the smallest companies can maintain a database for direct mail. This, too, is an excellent medium for reaching people with particular interests, as Chapter 15 will explain.

Advertising has come a long way from the simple sign on the bootmaker's shop. Today it is a powerful device that announces the availability and location of products, expresses the quality and value of those products, and even imbues brands with personality while simultaneously defining the personality of the people who buy them. In turn, advertising itself is shaped by the technology used to convey its message to potential customers.

FUNCTIONS AND EFFECTS OF ADVERTISING

EXHIBIT 1-15

In 1886, John Pemberton, the creator of the famous Coca-Cola formula, went into business to market the new product. Ninety-nine years later, when a change in the historic original formula was announced, consumers revolted, and the world's favorite soft drink began to lose its market position. The following year, on its 100th birthday, the Coca-Cola Company truly celebrated—the return of Pemberton's original formula as "Coca-Cola Classic" had transported the company to new heights, well beyond its former top market position.

Advertising performs several functions for any business with something to sell, and its effects on that organization may be dramatic. Consider the beginnings of the Coca-Cola Company. Dr. Pemberton (pictured in Exhibit 1-15) and his partner, Frank M. Robinson, came up with a name for their new drink and decided to write the name in a unique way. Later, the name and script were trademarked with the U.S. Patent Office to ensure their sole usage by the Coca-Cola Company in its advertising and packaging. This demonstrates perhaps one of the most basic marketing functions of advertising—*to identify products and differentiate them from others.* The many functions and effects of advertising are listed in Exhibit 1-16.

No sooner had Pemberton and Robinson named the product than they ran an ad to tell people about it and where they could get it. Within a year, as more soda fountains began to sell the product, handpainted oilcloth signs with "Coca-Cola" began to appear, attached to store awnings. Then the word *drink* was added to inform passersby that the product was a soda fountain beverage. Here we see another basic function of advertising: *to communicate information about the product, its features, and its location of sale.*

In 1888, with Pemberton in ill health, Asa G. Candler bought the rights to Coca-Cola for $2,300. Candler was a promoter and a firm believer in advertising. He printed and distributed thousands of coupons offering a complimentary glass of Coca-Cola, shown in Exhibit 1-17. People who received free coupons tried the product and then tried it again. That's another reason for advertising: *to induce consumers to try new products and to suggest reuse.*

After more people tried the soft drink, liked it, and requested it, more pharmacies bought the product to sell to their customers. *Stimulating the distribution of a product* is yet another function of advertising.

Up to that time, Coca-Cola had been sold only at soda fountains. One of the many purposes of advertising, though, is *to increase product usage.* In 1899, the first Coca-Cola bottling plant opened in Chattanooga, Tennessee. The second opened the following year in Atlanta. Now people could buy bottles of Coke to take with them and enjoy at home.

As with anything popular, imitators immediately appeared, and the battle against these competitors has been continuous from the beginning. Another major purpose or function of advertising is *to build brand preference and loyalty.* Candler's use of an ongoing, consistent promotional campaign helped accomplish this.

EXHIBIT 1-16	Functions and Effects of Advertising as a Marketing Tool

☐ To identify products and differentiate them from others.

☐ To communicate information about the product, its features, and its location of sale.

☐ To induce consumers to try new products and to suggest reuse.

☐ To stimulate the distribution of a product.

☐ To build brand preference and loyalty.

☐ To lower the overall cost of sales.

Coupons encouraged people to try the new soft drink in its early years. This is an example of one used in the 1890s.

In 1916, the famous Coca-Cola bottle with its distinctive contour design was introduced. This helped identify Coke and differentiate it from competitors to such an extent that the bottle was registered as a trademark by the U.S. Patent Office. At the same time, the bottle enhanced the company's other promotional efforts and also assured the public of the standardized quality of Coke with every purchase. Exhibit 1-18 portrays the evolution of the famous Coke bottle.

For more than a hundred years, now, Coca-Cola has used the media to communicate advertising messages to mass audiences. The purpose is to satisfy the most important overall function of advertising: *to lower the cost of sales.* The cost of reaching a thousand people through advertising is usually far less than the cost of reaching just one prospect through personal selling.

For example, consider how much it would cost to have a sales rep make a *personal* sales call on every football fan who watches the Super Bowl on TV in order to sell each a bottle of Coke. It would be unbelievably expensive. The McGraw-Hill Laboratory reports that in 1985 the average face-to-face sales call cost a company well over \$220.[12] Today the cost would be even higher. If we multiply \$220 by the more than 100 million people who watch the Super Bowl, the cost is mind-boggling, over \$22 *billion*. However, for *only* \$750,000 the advertiser could buy a 30-second TV commercial during the Super Bowl and tell those same 100 million people about Coca-Cola. That's a lot less. In fact, through advertising, you could talk to a *thousand* of those prospects for only \$7.50—about 3 percent of what it costs to talk to *one* prospect through personal selling.

From this brief history of the Coca-Cola Company, we can see that advertising may perform a variety of functions for any business and that it may

Continued on page 32

The bottling of Coca-Cola overcame the limitations of fountain dispensing and led to worldwide distribution—the first in a series of now-classic marketing innovations. The bottle design of 1899 was changed in 1916 to the unique, contour design that became so recognizable that it was granted registration as a trademark 44 years later, an honor accorded only to a handful of other packages. The bottling concept led to the creation of the first six-bottle carton in the early 1920s. In 1929, Coke was first sold via ice-cooled machines located at work sites, and the distinctively shaped Coca-Cola fountain glass we know today appeared. And at the 1933 World's Fair, the first counter dispenser to mix syrup with carbonated water belonged to Coca-Cola.

COCA-COLA ILLUSTRATES THE HISTORY OF MODERN ADVERTISING

A. Coca-Cola was already in wide distribution "at all (soda) fountains" before the Ford name became a household word. In those days, only the wealthy could afford an automobile, and it was still considered quite avant-garde. Thus, it was an attractive and interesting association for Coke illustrated in this 1905 advertisement.

b. With the "charm of purity," a single Coke, one of 6 million per day, was served by a white-uniformed bellhop in this classic 1925 advertisement.

C. Coca-Cola discovered the benefits of merchandising very early. This 1934 tray with pictures of famous movie stars Maureen O'Sullivan and Johnny Weismuller (Tarzan) proved appealing to their fans.

D. While many ads of the 1930s showcased movie stars, later advertising, such as this 1943 ad, reflected life during wartime. Coke followed the troops, with a total of 64 bottling plants shipped abroad during the war and set up as close as possible to combat areas in North Africa, Europe, and the Pacific. An order from Coca-Cola's president gave the assurance that "every man in uniform gets a bottle of Coke for 5¢ wherever he is and whatever it costs the company."

E. As Coca-Cola spread around the world, ads and news coverage in major American magazines continued to echo the themes of refreshment and availability. The *Time* magazine cover that appeared in the 1950s describes Coke as the world's "friend."

G. Max Headroom, the first computerized celebrity presenter, was a popular symbol of New Coke for several years.

F. "I'd like to teach the world to sing in perfect harmony. I'd like to buy the world a Coke and keep it company." A product such as Coca-Cola rarely changes; society, though, is constantly changing. Consequently, the advertising must change to reflect current lifestyles. This commercial featuring children from around the world singing the Coke song atop a hill in 1969 (first three frames) was so popular when it first aired that 20 years later, Coke invited the same singers back—with *their* children—to perform a "hilltop reunion" (last frame).

H. Two weeks after Grandpa—played by Art Carney—buries a piece of Grandma's fruitcake and a magic pinecone in an empty Rockefeller Center planter, he

and his grandson return to find the planter now filled with one of the world's most beautiful Christmas visions: the glorious

Rockefeller Center Christmas tree. This spot, which first aired in 1989, has become a Coca-Cola holiday classic.

I. Entering the 90s, Coke told us, "You can't beat the feeling." This slogan was used in a variety of settings in both print and television advertising—the latter combined with a beautiful musical score that played off the historic jingle of "I'd like to teach the world to sing."

J. One of the sports stars Coca-Cola has used in recent years is basketball's Michael Jordan. His legendary jumping ability inspired this spot, titled "Moon Jordan," in which the goal of his rocket-like leap into outer space is to capture a stray bottle of Coca-Cola.

EXHIBIT 1-19

Advertising plays a vital role in communicating messages that create awareness for political, moral, and social issues like the one featured in this dramatic ad for the Save the Battlefield Coalition.

dramatically affect that organization. As we shall see in this and subsequent chapters, advertising communication also plays an interesting and important role in the overall economy and in society. The ad in Exhibit 1-19, for example, represents an effort to make a local population examine its priorities.

THE ECONOMIC IMPACT OF ADVERTISING

As the world's industrial output has grown, so has the use of advertising. In 1990, U.S. advertising alone represented a total expenditure of $124 billion and made up 2.37 percent of the gross national product.[13] In relation to the total U.S. economy, this may not seem like a lot, but, in fact, advertising is an industry that significantly affects the economy.

The economic effect of advertising can be likened to the opening "break" shot in pool or billiards, as shown in Exhibit 1-20. The moment a company begins to advertise, a chain reaction of economic events takes place. Usually the extent of the chain reaction is very difficult to measure; but as in billiards, its scope is certainly related to the force of the shot. And because it inevitably occurs at the same time as a host of other economic events, even the direction of the chain reaction is often in dispute.

For example, consider these questions about the effect of advertising: Does advertising affect the value of products? Does advertising raise or lower prices? Does advertising promote competition or discourage it? What is the effect of advertising on the total demand for a product category? Does advertising make more consumer choices available or less? How does advertising influence the business cycle? These are just some of the many frequently asked (and difficult to answer) questions related to the chain of economic events caused by the effective use of advertising.

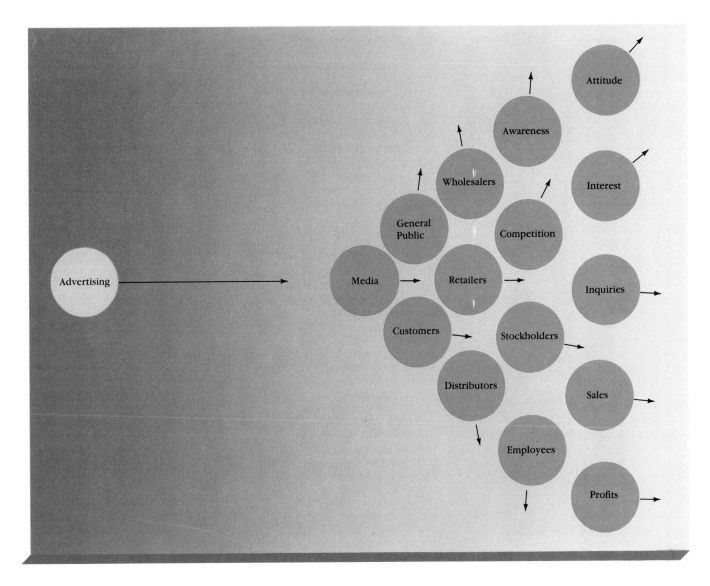

The billiard-ball principle describes the chain reaction of economic events that takes place the moment a company begins to advertise. As in billiards, the magnitude of these events depends, to a great extent, on the force of the initial advertising impact.

Effect on the Value of Products

Why do most people prefer Coca-Cola to some other cola? Why do more women prefer Estee Lauder to some other unadvertised, inexpensive perfume? Is it because the advertised products are better products? Not necessarily. But advertising can add *perceptual* value to a product in the consumer's mind.

In the mid-1960s, Dr. Ernest Dichter, a psychologist now known as the father of motivational research, supported the view that a product's *image*, which is produced partially by advertising and promotion, *is an inherent feature of the product itself.*[14] In subsequent decades, numerous studies concluded that even though an ad may say nothing verbally about the product's quality, the positive image conveyed by advertising may denote quality, make the product more desirable to the consumer, and thereby add value to the product.[15] This is why some people will pay more for Bufferin

Research has shown that the image of a product, which is produced partially by advertising and promotion, is an inherent feature of the product. Claims and promises become known over time, and that reassures consumers of the product's reliability. As a result, people are willing to pay more for Bufferin aspirin than for an unadvertised house brand about which they know little or nothing.

for an unadvertised house brand next to it on the store shelf (as shown in Exhibit 1-21)—even though most aspirin is the same.

Advertising also creates value by educating customers, for example, about new uses for products. Kleenex was originally advertised as a make-up remover; later it was promoted as a disposable handkerchief. Customers can also be educated by indicating *how* to use a product. As shown in Exhibit 1-22, computer software companies like Lotus Development Corporation often use their ads to demonstrate the look, feel, and application of their software programs in use. This technique is ideal for such difficult, complex products. Ads that educate have the net effect of increasing the product's value in the minds of customers.

One advantage of the free market system is that consumers can choose the values they want in the products they buy. If low price is important, for example, consumers can buy an inexpensive economy car. If image and luxury are more important, they can buy a fancy sedan or a racy sports car. Many of our wants are emotional, social, or psychological rather than functional. Advertising allows people in a free society the opportunity to satisfy those wants.

Effect on Prices

If advertising adds value to products, then it follows that advertising also adds costs. Right? And if companies stopped all that expensive advertising, then products would cost less. Right?

Wrong.

There is no question that in some cases advertised products cost more than unadvertised products. However, the opposite is true in many cases. In recent years, for example, the Federal Trade Commission and the Supreme Court have ruled that because advertising has the competitive effect of

For complex products like computer software, advertising can create value by demonstrating how to use the product. Moreover, to remain competitive, computer software companies like Lotus must regularly develop new features for their products. But if these updated products were not heavily advertised, the value of the product would not change in the perception of the customers.

keeping prices down, professional people such as attorneys, accountants, and physicians must be allowed to advertise.

Any broad, sweeping statements about the positive or negative effect of advertising on prices are likely to be too simplistic. Nevertheless, some important points can be made about the relationship between advertising and prices:

☐ As one of the many costs of doing business, advertising is indeed paid for by the consumer who buys the product. The amount spent on advertising, though, is usually very small compared with total sales.

☐ Advertising is just one element of the mass-distribution system that enables many manufacturers to engage in mass production. The long, uninterrupted runs used in mass production lower the unit cost of products. These savings can then be passed on to consumers in the form of lower prices. In this indirect way, advertising may be credited with lowering prices.

☐ In some industries subject to government price regulation (agriculture, utilities), advertising has historically had no effect on prices whatsoever. In the 1980s, though, the government began deregulating many of these industries in an effort to restore free market pressures on prices. In these cases, advertising does affect price—often downward, sometimes upward.

☐ In retailing, price is a prominent element in many ads, so advertising tends to hold prices down. In manufacturing, companies use advertising to stress the features that make their products better than those of competing firms; thus, advertising tends to hold prices up.

Effect on Competition

The complaint is often heard that small companies or newcomers to an industry can't possibly compete with the immense advertising budgets of big business. The belief seems to be that advertising restricts competition.

Some say that advertising campaigns by big companies with large advertising budgets have ruined small companies. It's possible that intense competition does tend to reduce the number of businesses in an industry. However, it also may be that the firms eliminated through competition were those that served the consumer least effectively.

In many cases, advertising by big companies only has a limited effect on small businesses because no advertiser is large enough to completely dominate the whole country. Local oil companies, for example, compete very successfully with national oil companies on the local level—a fact portrayed in the ad in Exhibit 1-23. And nonadvertised store brands of food compete with nationally advertised brands on the very same shelves.

In industries characterized by heavy advertising expenditures, though, it is certainly true that advertising may inhibit the entry of new competitors. In fact, in some markets, the original brands probably benefit greatly from this

EXHIBIT 1-23

Despite stereotypical opinions to the contrary, very few advertisers are actually large enough to dominate the mindset of the whole country. For example, many people believe that the big oil companies are an international cartel. Union Oil created this ad to dispel that myth following two major energy crises when the big oil companies were accused of "rigging" the emergencies to raise prices. The ad pointed out that there are many local oil companies out there competing for our gasoline dollars, and they're doing so quite successfully in many regions of the country. The result has been that Americans have historically enjoyed gasoline prices that are among the lowest in the world.

form of advertising barrier. But heavy spending on new plants and machinery is also a barrier—and usually a far more significant one than marketing costs.

Overly simplistic statements that attribute unreasonable power to advertising fail to acknowledge the importance of other, usually more significant influences on competition such as product quality, price, convenience, and customer satisfaction.

Effect on Consumer Demand

The question of advertising's effect on total consumer demand is extremely complex. Numerous studies show that promotional activity does have some effect on aggregate consumption, but there is no agreement as to the extent. The effects of many social and economic forces, including technological advances, education levels of the general populace, increases in population and in per capita income, and revolutionary changes in lifestyle are more significant.

For example, the demand for CD players, microwave dinners, and personal computers has expanded at a tremendous rate, thanks in part to advertising but especially to favorable market conditions. At the same time, advertising has done little to slow the decline in popularity of such items as men's and women's hats, fur coats, and manual typewriters.

We might conclude, therefore, that advertising can help to get new products off the ground by stimulating demand for the product class. But in declining markets, advertising can only hope to slow the rate of decline. We can also conclude that in growing markets, advertisers generally compete for shares of that growth. In static or declining markets, they compete for each other's shares.

Effect on Consumer Choice

For manufacturers, the best way to beat the competition is to make their product different. For example, look at the long list of automobile models, sizes, colors, and features available to attract the most discriminating buyers. And as Exhibit 1-24 shows, grocery shelves may carry 15 to 20 different brands of breakfast cereals—something for everybody.

The freedom to advertise gives manufacturers an incentive to create new brands and improve old ones. When one brand reaches a point of market dominance, smaller brands may disappear for a short time. But inevitably, the moment a better product comes along and is advertised skillfully, the tables suddenly turn and the dominant brand rapidly loses to the new, better product.

Effect on the Business Cycle

The relationship between advertising and the gross national product (GNP) has long been a subject of debate. In recent years, John Kenneth Galbraith, a perennial critic of advertising, has conceded that by helping to maintain the flow of consumer demand, advertising has helped sustain employment and income. He further maintains that, in spite of the decline in the value of the

EXHIBIT 1-24

EXHIBIT 1-24

The competition for consumer dollars is fierce in the $6 billion ready-to-eat cereal business. Here, cereal boxes set themselves apart by trying to attract attention. The result: packages that feature the same wordings, type styles, and visuals that appear regularly in print advertising. In essence, the package may be the brand's best advertisement.

dollar, the U.S. trade deficit has persisted because advertising and marketing activities have established certain foreign products in consumer preference and use.[16]

Historically, when business cycles dip, worried executives cut advertising expenditures. That may help immediate short-term profits, but studies prove that businesses that continue to invest in advertising during a recession fare considerably better after the recession.[17] However, no study has ever shown that if everybody just kept advertising, the recessionary cycle would be turned around.

We must conclude, therefore, that when business cycles are up, advertising contributes to the increase. When business cycles are down, advertising may act as a stabilizing force.

Economic Impact of Advertising in Perspective: The Abundance Principle

To individual businesses like Coca-Cola, the local car dealer, and the little convenience store on the corner, advertising pays more in results than it costs. If advertising did not pay, no one would use it; and the various news and entertainment media, which depend on advertising for financial support, would all go out of business.

For the consumer, advertising costs less than most people believe. The cost of a bottle of Coke includes about a penny for advertising. And the $15,000 price tag on a new car includes a manufacturer's advertising cost of less than $200.

To the economy as a whole, the importance of advertising may best be demonstrated by the **abundance principle.** This states that in an economy that produces more goods and services than can be consumed, advertising serves two important purposes: It keeps consumers informed of their selection alternatives, and it allows companies to compete more effectively for consumer dollars.

The U.S. and Canadian economies produce an enormous selection for consumers. More than 10,000 different items are on the average supermarket shelves. Each automobile manufacturer markets dozens of models. Clothing and shelter alternatives are seemingly endless. In short, both the U.S. and Canadian economies are characterized by many suppliers competing for the consumer dollar. This competition generally tends to produce more and better products at similar or lower prices.

As a competitive tool, advertising has stimulated this phenomenon. Moreover, because North American consumers have more income to spend after

EXHIBIT 1-25

No amount of advertising can achieve long-term acceptance for products that do not meet consumer approval. Despite spending millions of dollars to advertise Studebaker as the "postwar leader in motor car style," the company is no longer in business—as is the case with many other manufacturers whose names are not familiar to our generation.

Actual color photograph of 1947 Studebaker Champion Regal De Luxe 4-door sedan

This dream car is this year's style star...
the refreshingly different postwar Studebaker

Three generations of Thorntons help to safeguard Studebaker quality—Seated, in this final assembly picture, is 64-year-old Russell E. Thornton. Alongside are his son, Everett V., and Everett's son, Kenneth. Members of this family, like many of their neighbors, have been Studebaker craftsmen for years. Russell Thornton has five sons in all at Studebaker.

Most people say that even the windows of this postwar Studebaker help to give it a special distinction.

The low-swung, roomy body gleams with more glass than you ever saw in a car before.

The effect is fascinating. But the practical result is enormously increased driving vision—alongside, behind and ahead.

You find the same useful end served by everything else that contributes to this Studebaker's eye appeal.

The car's whole design has a marvelous effect on the way it performs, handles and rides.

This Studebaker is the first car, too, with self-adjusting brakes. Its dash dials are glareproofed by wartime aviation's "black light."

See for yourself how much safer and more enjoyable motoring can be, because of Studebaker's leadership in styling.

Drop in at a showroom for a look at Studebaker's new Champion, Commander and special long-wheelbase Land Cruiser.

STUDEBAKER
The postwar leader in motor car style

©The Studebaker Corp'n, South Bend 27, Indiana, U.S.A.

their physical needs are satisfied, advertising also stimulates the innovation and sale of new products.

However, no amount of advertising can achieve long-term acceptance for products that do not meet consumer approval. Less than a dozen of the 50 best-known automobile brands developed in this century are still with us despite major advertising expenditures. Exhibit 1-25 is an ad for one of those long-gone brands. Only 2 of the nation's 10 largest industrial firms in 1900 remain in the top 10 today despite massive advertising.

As advertising has stimulated a healthy economy, it has also stimulated a financially healthy consumer who is more informed, better educated, and more demanding. One of the loudest consumer demands has been for accountability by manufacturers in their advertising. This has led to an unprecedented level of social and legal regulation, the subject of our next chapter.

Summary

Advertising is defined as the nonpersonal communication of information usually paid for and usually persuasive in nature, about products, services, or ideas by identified sponsors through various media.

Advertising may be classified by target audience (consumer, industrial), by geography (local, international), by medium (radio, newspaper, television), or by its function or purpose (product advertising, noncommercial advertising, action advertising).

Advertising began in ancient times when most people could not read or write. As manufacturing and communication technologies developed, so did advertising. Printing was the first major technology to affect it, and cable television and computers are the most recent. Since World War II, advertisers have attempted to differentiate products through positioning strategies and other techniques.

As a marketing tool, advertising serves several functions:

☐ To identify and differentiate products.
☐ To communicate information about the product.
☐ To induce the trial of new products by new users and to suggest repurchasing by existing users.
☐ To stimulate a product's distribution.
☐ To increase product use.
☐ To build brand preference and loyalty.
☐ To lower the overall cost of sales.

Aside from marketing, advertising may also serve several other functions in the economy and in society.

The economic impact of advertising can be likened to the opening shot in billiards—a chain reaction that affects the company that advertises as well as its competitors, customers, and the business community.

On a broader scale, advertising is often considered the trigger on America's mass-distribution system that enables manufacturers to produce the products Americans want in high volume, at low prices, with standardized quality. Disagreement exists, however, about whether advertising adds value to products, makes products more or less expensive, encourages or discourages competition, affects total consumer demand, narrows or widens consumer choice, and affects national business cycles.

Although controversy surrounds most of these economic issues, few dispute the abundance principle, which states that, in an economy that produces more goods and services than can be consumed, advertising keeps consumers informed of their choices and helps companies compete more effectively.

Questions for Review and Discussion

1. How does advertising for the American Cancer Society compare with the standard definition of advertising?
2. Is an ad for an office computer industrial advertising, trade advertising, or professional advertising?
3. What is the difference between the media used for local advertising and for regional advertising?
4. How did the railroad affect the growth of advertising?
5. What examples can you think of (or conceive of) in which companies or organizations use a demarketing strategy?
6. What examples can you give to demonstrate the primary functions of advertising today?
7. As a consumer, are you more likely to save money by buying at a store that doesn't spend a lot of money on advertising? Explain.
8. In what ways can advertising increase a product's value?
9. How would you explain the overall effect of advertising on consumer choice?
10. How would the advertising for a new shopping center affect your local economy? Are retailers in your area advertising more or less because of current economic conditions?

THE SOCIAL, ETHICAL, AND REGULATORY ASPECTS OF ADVERTISING

Objective: To identify and explain the various social, ethical, and regulatory issues that advertisers must consider. Society, for example, tells advertisers what is offensive, excessive, and irresponsible. Government agencies, nongovernmental groups, and the courts help determine what is deceptive and unfair. To be socially responsible, ethical, and law abiding, as well as effective, an advertiser must have a clear understanding of all these issues.

After studying this chapter you will be able to:

☐ Identify the most common social criticisms of advertising.

☐ Describe the ways in which advertising benefits society.

☐ Differentiate between ethical dilemmas and ethical lapses within the advertising environment.

☐ Explain how various federal agencies regulate advertising to protect consumers and competing advertisers.

☐ Describe the role state and local governments play in regulating advertising.

☐ Discuss recent court rulings that affect advertisers.

☐ Analyze the primary means nongovernment organizations use to regulate advertising.

On a flight from New York to Chicago, John O'Toole, then chairman of Foote, Cone & Belding advertising agency, sat next to a woman who inquired what he did for a living. When he responded that he was in advertising, she stated somewhat scornfully, "I think advertising is destroying our language."

O'Toole debated whether to launch into his "case for national advertising as a preserver of clear, concise, colorful, and correct English." He refrained from that. Nor did this well-known poet tell his seatmate that advertising is "a portal for introducing new constructions and expressions into a constantly evolving language to enrich and renew it." He felt the flight would be far too short for such a long dissertation.

As he reported in a memo to his agency, O'Toole decided simply to cite an institution that, in his thinking, has done a far more thorough job than advertising in debasing our language.

Regular readers of these memos will assume that I took out after the federal government, or Harvard Business School, or that perennial favorite, the legal profession. Not so.

I didn't have to look beyond the vehicle we were in to find a first-class miscreant: the airline industry.

I showed her this paragraph I had just read in the in-flight magazine.

"TWA is required by the federal government to ensure compliance with the regulations concerning smoking on board its flights. For the comfort and safety of all, we earnestly solicit each passenger's cooperation in strictly observing these rules. Persistent disregard could result in the offending passenger's disembarkation."

What I think they're saying, amidst all the passive and conditional gobbledygook (I like that one, too), is this:

"The government makes us enforce the no-smoking rules. Please obey them or we'll have to throw you off the plane."

Now being thrown off a plane, presumably in flight, is a disquieting prospect. So perhaps they deliberately obscured the thought with gratuitous verbiage to soften its impact. Whatever the motive, comprehension is the victim.

Pompous as it sounds, *disembarkation* is a more accurate word to describe getting off an airplane than the one they normally use: *deplaning*. "We will be deplaning tonight," says the flight attendant, "through the forward exit." I have an image of passengers standing at the forward exit picking tiny planes off their persons and dropping them out into the darkness. We are not deplaning. Actually the plane is depeopling. But what's wrong with just "getting off"? Then there's the matter of redundancy in airline talk. "For your own personal safety and convenience," for example. Or, "Be sure your seat backs and tray tables are returned to their original upright positions."

Compare that kind of language, which is the airline itself speaking, to the precision of advertising speaking for the airline: "Fly the friendly skies." "You're going to like us." "Doing what we do best."

Anyone who concludes advertising is the offender deserves to be disembarked.[1]

John O'Toole, currently president of the American Association of Advertising Agencies, is one of the most articulate "defenders of the faith" in advertising. However, the advertising industry has had to deal with a growing number of equally articulate critics who condemn it for a wide variety of sins far worse than the simple misuse of the English language. These attacks have led to a stream of actions by consumer groups, business organizations, and governmental bodies to regulate what advertisers say and do in their advertising.

THE SOCIAL IMPACT OF ADVERTISING

This chapter first addresses the major social criticisms of advertising and the benefits of advertising. Then it examines advertising ethics and the social responsibility of advertisers. Finally, it discusses regulatory methods that the government, business organizations, the media, consumer groups, advertisers, and their agencies use to remedy advertising abuses that have led to many of the criticisms.

Social Criticisms

Advertising is the most visible activity of business. By inviting people to try their products, companies also invite public criticism and attack if their products don't live up to the promised benefits. Proponents of advertising say it is therefore safer to buy advertised than unadvertised products. Because makers of advertised items put their company name and reputation on the line, they try harder to fulfill their claims and promises—even when they promise customers they can look like a million bucks, as did the advertiser in Exhibit 2-1.

Advertising is widely criticized not only for the role it plays in selling products but also for its influence on our society. As a selling tool, advertising is attacked for its excesses. Some critics charge that, at its worst, advertising is downright untruthful, and, at best, it presents only positive information about

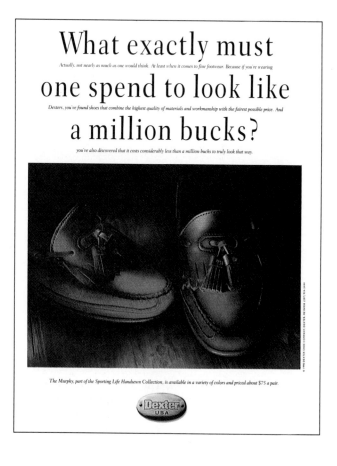

products. Others complain that advertising psychologically manipulates people to buy things they can't afford by promising greater sex appeal or improved social status. Still others attack advertising for being offensive, in bad taste, or simply too excessive.

Adequately detailing all the pros and cons of the charges against advertising would require volumes. It is important, however, to understand the essence of some of the more common criticisms and the impact they have on advertising.

Does Advertising Debase Our Language?

The very reasons John O'Toole likes advertising are the reasons defenders of traditional English usage don't like it. They feel advertising copy is too breezy, too informal, too casual, and therefore improper. Advertising, they believe, has destroyed the dignity of the language. Read the copy in Exhibit 2-2 and decide for yourself if it has any merit.

EXHIBIT 2-2

The misuse of the English language in the body copy of this ad might appall grammarians and might be used to bolster critics' assertions that advertising debases our language. Critics might also call the copywriter to task for stereotyping the audience (farmers). Nevertheless, this cleverly written ad won numerous awards from the advertising industry.

The fact is, to do its job, advertising must speak to people. It must be understandable and readable. Some critics don't acknowledge that ads are designed for specific audiences and therefore should reflect different language usage and patterns. Advertising research shows that people respond better to a down-to-earth, conversational tone than to a more dignified, formal tone. Good copywriters thus develop a style that is descriptive, colorful, and even picturesque as well as warm, human, and personal. Because of the need for brevity, they try to use simple words that are lively and full of personality. And they use punctuation to build a conversational tone rather than to construct purely grammatical sentences.

Not all copywriters are good copywriters, however, and literary license is a feeble excuse for what is sometimes just plain bad English.

Does Advertising Make Us Too Materialistic?

Some critics claim advertising adversely affects our value system by suggesting that the means to a happier life is in the acquisition of more material things instead of spiritual or intellectual enlightenment. Advertising, they say, encourages people to buy more automobiles, more clothing, and more appliances than they need—all with the promise of greater status, greater social acceptance, and greater sex appeal. For example, critics point out that millions of Americans own 20 or more pairs of shoes, several TV sets, and often more than one vehicle. But these critics fail to realize that they often tend to force their own values on others.

Frankly, we all have needs and desires beyond the basics of food, clothing, and shelter. One benefit of a free society is that we can choose the degree to which we wish to indulge our desires, needs, and fantasies. Some people prefer a simple life without an elegant house, fancy cars, and trips abroad. Others enjoy the material pleasures of a modern, technological society. There are advertising sponsors at both ends of that spectrum. Food companies offer natural products as well as convenience packaged goods. Shoe companies offer simple sandals as well as formal footwear.

Proponents of advertising also point out that material comfort or security is necessary before a person can devote time to higher cultural and spiritual values. Therefore, the stress on material things doesn't rule out spiritual and cultural values. In fact, it may create a greater opportunity for attaining such values, since the satisfaction of a person's higher desires is more likely when that person's lower, more basic desires have been met.[2] Proponents also point out that, through its support of the media, advertising has brought literature, opera, drama, and symphonies to millions who otherwise might never have experienced them.

Does Advertising Manipulate Us into Buying Things We Don't Need?

An oft-heard criticism is that advertising forces people to buy things they don't need by playing on their emotions. Some critics believe advertising's persuasive techniques are so powerful that consumers are helpless to defend themselves.

The fact, is, however, that no matter how much advertisers try to convince us that using their product will make us sexier or healthier or more successful, they can't *make* us buy a product we don't want. No matter how many ads we see for disposable diapers, we won't buy any if we prefer cloth diapers—or don't have a baby. Exhibit 2-3 illustrates that advertising power-

EXHIBIT 2-3

No cigarette ad has ever told the truth in a more compelling way than this antismoking ad, yet people continue to smoke. That's because ads simply can't force people to buy products—or ideas—that they don't really want.

EXHIBIT 2-3

No cigarette ad has ever told the truth in a more compelling way than this antismoking ad, yet people continue to smoke. That's because ads simply can't force people to buy products—or ideas—that they don't really want.

ful ideas doesn't guarantee a sale if people aren't interested. And even if an ad convinces us to buy a product once ("This frozen pizza looked really great on TV"), it can't get us to buy the product again if we don't like it ("Ugh! This tastes like cardboard!").

Those who accuse advertising of manipulating consumers—assuming that people can't resist advertising's hypnotic messages—have little respect for their decision-making abilities or common sense. Wilson Bryan Keys, who wrote several books on subliminal advertising, is convinced that sexual messages are intentionally embedded in many ads in order to seduce consumers at a subliminal level. However, proof of such embedding is nonexistent.[3] Besides, if it were that easy to seduce consumers into buying, why do so many more products fail than succeed in the marketplace? And why are some products highly successful with minimal or no advertising? As sociologist Michael Shudson points out in *Advertising, the Uneasy Persuasion,* the powers of advertising have been greatly exaggerated.[4] People simply don't pay that much attention to ads. And when they do pay attention, they may not recall what product went with which ad. In fact, most Americans are highly skeptical of advertising. In one study, only about 20 percent of consumers surveyed indicated that advertising directly played the major role in their choices.[5]

Another aspect of the manipulation argument is that advertising *creates* artificial needs, such as a need for underarm deodorants because of our anxiety about "offensive" body odors. Shudson suggests that any new consumer product that does not disappear quickly is probably related to deep social currents. In other words, just because deodorant *critics* don't see a "need" for such products doesn't mean that deodorant *users* don't perceive a need. Do you *need* a VCR, frozen orange juice, or ballpoint pens? You could live without them, but you'd probably buy them even if they weren't advertised. The role of advertising, then, is to help you decide *which* brand to purchase.

Robert Samuelson, writing in *Newsweek* magazine, makes the case for the "sovereignty of the consumer."[6] He argues that rather than corporate America controlling consumer buying habits through advertising, it's the other way around: Consumers control the marketplace by choices they make with their discretionary income. The microwave oven, for example, is one of today's best-selling consumer appliances not because it's been heavily advertised but because it meets a need of busy people.

In short, marketers have found that the only logical way to advertise and sell products is to satisfy genuine needs and wants rather than to "invent" needs to go with otherwise useless products.

Is Advertising Excessive?

One of the most common complaints about advertising is simply that there is too much of it. Experts say the average American is exposed to over 500 commercial messages a day. Consumer groups protest "billboard blight" along our highways. Local politicians criticize sign pollution in their communities. We are constantly bombarded at home with ads on radio and television, in newspapers, and through the mail. Advertisements also reach us in our cars and in elevators, parking lots, hotel lobbies, movie theaters, and subways.

With so many products competing for our attention (over 10,000 in the average supermarket), companies must often shout to be heard, and advertising is their megaphone. Our tolerance of advertising in the print media seems to be greater than in the broadcast media—probably because we can simply turn the pages and ignore it if we so desire. Broadcast media tend to be more intrusive and therefore receive greater criticism.

Advertising professionals themselves are concerned about the negative impact of ad proliferation. Most media impose voluntary restrictions on advertising volume. However, because mass distribution supports our free enterprise system, advertising volume is here to stay. And most Americans seem to accept this as the price we have to pay for free television, freedom of the press, and our high standard of living.

Is Advertising Offensive or in Bad Taste?

Many people find advertising offensive to their religious convictions, morality, or political perspectives. Others find advertising techniques that emphasize sex, violence, or body functions in bad taste.

Taste is highly subjective: What is good taste to some is bad taste to others. And tastes change. What is considered offensive today may not be offensive in the future. For example, people were outraged when the first advertisement for underarm deodorant was published in 1927 in the *Ladies Home Journal,* but today, no one questions such an ad. Some people find liquor and tobacco ads offensive, while others find them entertaining or informative.

Up until 1987, ads for birth control products were virtually absent from television, but fears about AIDS finally led cable and local TV stations to begin carrying carefully designed commercials for condoms. The ads had to meet certain restrictions specified by the stations, but the standards of taste for condom ads varied from station to station.[7] Some of the first ads to be accepted did not even mention the word *condom.* The AIDS scare has also led many print media, including *USA Today* and the *New York Times,* to reverse their policy against carrying condom advertising. However, the three major networks are still unwilling to accept condom ads—although numerous network affiliates have chosen to air them.

In the not-so-distant past, nude figures were rarely seen in print advertisements. Today, nudity is often featured in ads for grooming and personal hygiene products. Where nudity is relevant to the product being advertised, people are less likely to regard it as obscene or offensive.[8] Often the products themselves are not offensive, but the way they are advertised may be open to criticism. Advertising frequently emphasizes the sensational aspects of a product, particularly a book or motion picture. Shock value may be used to gain attention, especially by inexperienced copywriters. This sensationalism is often a reflection of the tastes and interests of the American people, however. If the ads don't attract the people they seek, the advertising campaign will falter and die. The audience, therefore, has the ultimate veto authority by ignoring offensive material.

It is unrealistic to assume that advertising, particularly mass advertising, will ever be free of this criticism. But reputable advertisers try to be aware of what the general public considers tasteful advertising.

Does Advertising Perpetuate Stereotypes?

Advertisers have become increasingly sensitive to stereotyping minorities and women in their ads. Blacks, Hispanics, Italians, Chinese, Native Americans, and other members of minority groups are now portrayed more favorably in ads, not only because of pressure from watchdog groups, but because it's just good business—these consumers represent sizable target markets for products. In fact, some advertisers have created campaigns designed to appeal to specific minority groups, such as the ad for a book in Exhibit 2-4. In addition,

EXHIBIT 2-4

As more major companies use niche marketing to tap into small, but profitable market segments, targeting ads toward specific racial and ethnic groups has become an increasingly important—and sometimes controversial—part of the advertising business.

new advertising agencies staffed or owned by minorities are successfully reaching minority markets.

The image of women in advertising has also changed significantly in the past few years. Feminists protested in the past that the great majority of ads portrayed women as homemakers and mothers constantly seeking advice and help from men or as sex objects whose role was to be dominated by men and to fulfill men's desires. Today, fewer and fewer ads show women in the traditional housewife/mother role. Rather, women are portrayed in expanded roles as corporate managers, doctors, lawyers, and even construction workers. In home settings, husbands are shown taking equal responsibility for such household tasks as cooking, cleaning, and taking care of the kids.

This changing portrayal of women in advertising has not come about simply because advertisers did not want to antagonize feminists. Rather, it has occurred in response to changes in the marketplace. More than 50 percent of all women work outside the home, more than 10 million of them in professional and managerial careers. That is a sizable market of upwardly mobile consumers that many advertisers are attempting to reach, as Northwestern Bell is doing in the ad shown in Exhibit 2-5. In fact, as one advertising analyst put it, "The income of baby-boomer women is not going to diminish. Advertisers would be foolish to treat this as a fad."[9]

Many consumers do not object to the use of sex per se. In fact, Gloria Steinem, after accepting a steamy ad for Calvin Klein's Obsession perfume to run in *Ms.* magazine, said, "Sexuality and nudity are a part of life, and if it's

EXHIBIT 2-5

An increasing number of ads, like this one for Northwestern Bell, are featuring busy career women as opposed to the traditional housewife/mother. This change may be as much in response to market forces (working women are constituting a larger and larger target market) as to feminist pressures.

(SFX: MUSIC UP, AMBIENT NOISE, SHUFFLING PAPERS, ETC.) WOMAN (TO HERSELF): Well . . . it's been a long and productive day. Oh listen, Jerry, thanks an awful lot for the suggestion. We'll get back to this again next week, OK?

FEMALE VO ON PHONE INTERCOM: Mrs. Harrison, there's a phone call for you. It's your daughter.

WOMAN: I'll take it in my office, Pat.

SINGER VO: Drift away, drift away . . . How the time disappears . . . Just the blink of an eye and the days turn into years . . .

SINGER VO: Drift away, drift away . . . How the time drifts away . . .

DAUGHTER VO ON PHONE: I need some advice again, Mom.

WOMAN (AD LIB UNDER): Don't pressure yourself so much, honey. You just have to try to relax and get through it.

appropriate it's fine."[10] The objections have to do with ads that demean women or that imply violence toward or exploitation of them.

The trend for the 1990s appears to be toward more romantic images and less explicit sex. An executive creative director of a New York-based ad agency said, "People are saying 'like please, enough already.'"[11]

Some advertisers are even dropping the sexy images altogether. Chrysler's Dodge division, for example, replaced young female models in slinky black outfits with young male models in pin-striped business suits for its 1991 auto shows around the country. Ford Motor Company went even further by using male and female actors who were demographically correct for each vehicle—like a balding, 15- to 20-pound overweight male actor for the typical pickup truck buyer.[12]

Is Advertising Deceptive?

Perhaps the greatest criticism of advertising is that it attempts to deceive the public. Deception in advertising has also received the greatest regulatory scrutiny, as we will discuss in the next section.

Critics define deceptiveness not only as false and misleading statements but also as any false impression conveyed, whether intentional or unintentional. Advertising deception can take a number of forms, and many of these are highly controversial with no hard-and-fast rules. Common practices considered deceptive include those listed in Ad Lab 2-A.

Consumers must have confidence in advertising if it is to be effective. Continued deception is self-defeating because, in time, it causes consumers to turn against a product. Even meaningless but legal *puffery*, such as claims of being the "best," "greatest," or "premier," is sometimes believed and therefore deceptive. Furthermore, there is little evidence that deceptive advertising actually helps sales anyway.

Advertising puts the advertiser on record for all who care to look. Because of greater scrutiny by consumers and the government, it is in the advertiser's own interest to avoid trouble by being honest.

Social Benefits

Advertising professionals acknowledge that over the years advertising has often been used irresponsibly. But they like to use the analogy of a high-powered automobile: If a drunk is at the wheel, there's going to be a lot of damage. The problem, though, is not the car but the drunk at the wheel.

Proponents of advertising say advertising benefits society in a number of ways. Economically, it encourages the development of new and better products; it gives consumers a wider variety of choices; it helps keep prices down; and it encourages competition. It also subsidizes the media, supports freedom of the press, and provides a means for the dissemination of public information about health and social issues as well as about products and services.

Advertising has been and still is sometimes misused. But advocates believe that the abuse heaped on it is no longer justified and is so excessive it makes all advertising appear bad. They point out that, of all the advertising reviewed by the Federal Trade Commission in a typical year, 97 percent is found to be satisfactory.[13]

Eric Clark analyzed the advertising industry in his book, *The Want Makers: Lifting the Lid off the World Advertising Industry; How They Make You Buy.*

AD LAB 2-A
Unfair and Deceptive Practices in Advertising

The courts have held that these acts constitute unfair or deceptive trade practices and are therefore illegal.

False Promises

Making an advertising promise that cannot be kept, such as "restores youth" or "prevents cancer."

Incomplete Description

Stating some, but not all, of the contents of a product, such as advertising a "solid oak" desk without mentioning that only the top is solid oak and that the rest is made of hardwoods with an oak veneer.

Misleading Comparisons

Making meaningless comparisons, such as "as good as a diamond," if the claim cannot be verified.

Bait-and-Switch Offers

Advertising an item at an unusually low price to bring people into the store and then "switching" them to a higher priced model than the one advertised by stating that the advertised product is "out of stock" or "poorly made."

Visual Distortions

Making a product look larger than it really is— for example, a TV commercial for a "giant steak" dinner special showing the steak on a miniature plate that makes it appear extra large. Or showing a "deluxe" model that is not the same as the one offered at a "sale" price.

False Testimonials

Implying that a product has the endorsement of a celebrity or an authority who is not a bona fide user of the product.

False Comparisons

Demonstrating one product as superior to another without giving the "inferior" item a chance or by comparing it with the least competitive product available, such as comparing the road performance of a steel-belted radial tire with that of an average "economy" tire.

Partial Disclosures

Stating what a product can do but not what it cannot do, such as claiming that an electrically powered automobile will go "60 miles per hour—without gasoline" and not mentioning that it needs an eight-hour battery recharge every 100 miles.

Small-Print Qualifications

Making a statement in large print ("Any new suit in stock— $50 off!") only to qualify or retract it in smaller type elsewhere in the ad ("With the purchase of a suit at the regular price").

Laboratory Application

What examples have you seen of deception?

He concluded that the worst of all worlds would probably be one without advertising. Clark said advertising "is needed to spread useful information. It has energy and extravagance. It can be fun—most of us have favorite ads that actually engender affection. But it is also a big, powerful, highly talented, and immensely wealthy industry."[14] It is up to both advertisers and consumers to ensure that advertising is used intelligently and responsibly.

ADVERTISING ETHICS AND SOCIAL RESPONSIBILITY

Numerous laws determine what advertisers can and can't do. There is a significant amount of leeway within the confines of those laws, however. That maneuvering room is where ethics and social responsibility come into play. It is possible for an advertiser to act unethically or socially irresponsibly without breaking any laws. Many attorneys, for example, believe that using client testimonials in ads is unethical, yet the practice is legal in several states. A tobacco company might be considered socially irresponsible for sponsoring a rock concert for college students, but would be acting within the law. In other words, ethical advertising means doing what the *advertiser* believes is morally right for a given situation. Social responsibility, on the other hand, means doing what *society* views as best for the welfare of people in general or for a specific group of people.

Advertising Ethics

Before the beginning of this century, there was little regard for advertising ethics. As consumers, the government, and special-interest groups became concerned with advertising practices, however, advertisers developed higher standards of ethical conduct. To better understand the ethical issues advertisers must wrestle with today, consider two categories of ethics topics: ethical dilemmas and ethical lapses.

Ethical Dilemmas

An **ethical dilemma** refers to a situation in which there are two conflicting, but valid, sides to an issue. So how would you, as an advertising person, go about resolving an ethical dilemma? The best approach is to answer three questions: (1) Which course of action will produce the most good for the greatest number of people? (2) Will either course of action violate someone else's rights? (3) Will either course of action result in unfair treatment of any affected party?[15]

Consider the issue of product placements in TV programs—such as the mention of Junior Mints in "thirtysomething," a shot of Quaker Oats Squares in "Roseanne," and IBM computers in "L.A. Law." Those products didn't appear just by chance, nor did the companies who make them pay to get them on the shows.[16] In fact, paid product placements on TV are illegal unless they are disclosed; but if they are disclosed, the networks generally won't approve them.[17] Behind the scenes, however, some advertisers provide free products in return for free exposure. Critics say the practice hurts traditional advertisers who pay $100,000 or more for a 30-second spot. It's an ethical dilemma for both advertisers and broadcasters.

Ethical Lapses

An **ethical lapse** refers to a situation in which an advertiser makes a clearly unethical and sometimes illegal decision. Volvo, for example, tarnished its impeccable reputation when it rigged a commercial to make it appear that its cars could withstand being run over by a heavy pickup truck, as shown in Exhibit 2-6. William Hoover, a senior vice president for Volvo, said the company "feels pretty dumb."[18] Unlike an ethical dilemma, where there is an unresolved interpretation of an ethical issue, an ethical lapse is a clear case of unethical behavior.

John P. Tully, an Illinois judge, is another example of an advertiser who suffered an ethical lapse. Judge Tully ran a controversial campaign for the state appellate judgeship. When the state's Judicial Inquiry Board investigated his campaign, it determined that Judge Tully's ads were inaccurate and misleading. Stephen Gillers, an ethics specialist at New York University

EXHIBIT 2-6

Volvo suffered an embarrassing ethical lapse in producing a rigged commercial, not to mention the fact that such blatant deception is illegal.

School of Law, said courts in Michigan and Ohio have ruled that campaign claims similar to Judge Tully's violate the canon of conduct that requires judges to "maintain the dignity appropriate to judicial office."[19]

Advertisers' Social Responsibility

Social responsibility is closely related to advertising ethics. Measures of social responsibility can change more rapidly than ethical positions, however. The AIDS scare, for example, caused many advertisers to voluntarily tone down the use of sex in advertisements. Concerned citizens, consumer advocates, and special-interest groups also put a great deal of pressure on advertisers when the public's welfare is at risk.

RJR Nabisco, for example, canceled plans for two new cigarette brands—Uptown, aimed at blacks, and Dakota, which targeted uneducated young women—in the heat of opposition from consumer-advocacy groups.[20] And Lorillard (the maker of Kent, Newport, and True cigarettes) was accused of being opportunistic when it announced plans to run yellow stripes on the corner of all its print and billboard ads in a show of support for U.S. troops in the Persian Gulf. A media specialist with the Advocacy Group pointed out that "If [Lorillard was] genuinely interested in preserving and protecting human lives, they would quit marketing their lethal products to people."[21] Environmental concerns are also putting pressure on advertisers to be more socially responsible. Many companies are now spreading the word through advertising about their socially responsible endeavors, as Amoco Chemical has done in its ad shown in Exhibit 2-7. Chevron also advertised its sense of social responsibility when it launched its "People Do" ads in the mid-1980s to explain how the company delayed a gas pipeline project in Wyoming to avoid upsetting the mating season of local grouse.[22] And Wal-Mart recently launched a "green" campaign to point out merchandise that is environmentally friendly.[23]

Most advertisers today strive to maintain high ethical standards and socially responsible advertising practices; but the sins of the past still haunt them. What was once an unchecked, free-swinging business activity is now a closely scrutinized and heavily regulated profession. Advertising's alleged past excesses and shortcomings (whether rightly or wrongly charged) have created layer upon layer of laws, regulations, and regulatory bodies. These are used by consumer groups, government, special-interest groups, and even other advertisers to review, check, control, and change advertising.

FEDERAL REGULATION OF ADVERTISING

The federal government imposes strict controls on advertisers through laws and their judicial interpretations. Various government agencies determine the scope of the laws and serve to enforce them. Major federal regulators of advertising include the Federal Trade Commission, the Food and Drug Administration, the Federal Communications Commission, the Patent and Trademark Office, the Library of Congress, and others outlined in Exhibit 2-8. The jurisdictions of these agencies often overlap, which can make the advertiser's efforts to comply with regulations even more difficult.

Federal Trade Commission

The **Federal Trade Commission (FTC)** is the major regulator of national advertising for products sold in interstate commerce. Initially, the FTC protected only competitors from false advertising. But in 1938, Congress passed the Wheeler-Lee Amendment, which gave the FTC power to protect both consumers and competitors from deceptive and unfair advertising. Unfortunately, the definition of *deceptive* and *unfair* is a matter of some controversy.

Defining Deception

Prior to 1983, the FTC interpreted *deceptive* as advertising that had "the tendency or capacity to mislead substantial numbers of consumers in a material way." Then in 1983, FTC chairman James C. Miller III drafted a new definition he believed would prevent the FTC from having to deal with so many trivial violations. Miller defined **deceptive advertising** as any ad in which "there is a misrepresentation, omission, or other practice that is likely to mislead the consumer acting reasonably in the circumstances, to the consumer's detriment."

Many people believe this revised definition puts a greater burden on the FTC to prove that deception has actually taken place. Furthermore, it indicates the FTC must show that consumer decisions were actually influenced in a material way. Finally, its reference to a "reasonable" consumer implies that an ad's effect on unthinking or ignorant consumers is not a main consideration.

Critics of the new definition worry that it will now be harder and more costly to win deceptive advertising cases.[24] They also fear that advertisers will feel freer to use deceptive practices because they perceive the FTC as more lax. However, the FTC remains a powerful regulator of advertising practices. For example, the commission recently cracked down on deceptive half-hour TV ads that viewers might mistake for regular programming.[25] It also looks at environmental claims (such as biodegradable, degradable, photodegradable, and recyclable). Because of confusing terminology, the National Association

---

EXHIBIT 2-8   Federal Regulators of Advertising

Federal Trade Commission
Regulates all commerce between the states. Formed in 1914, the FTC is the leading federal regulatory agency for advertising practices and is the subject of the greatest criticism by the advertising profession.

Federal Communications Commission
Formed by the Communications Act of 1934, has jurisdiction over the radio, television, telephone, and telegraph industries. It maintains indirect control over advertising through its authority to license or revoke the license of all broadcast stations.

Food and Drug Administration
Has authority over the advertising, labeling, packaging, and branding of all packaged goods and therapeutic devices. It requires full disclosure labels, regulates the use of descriptive words on packages, and has jurisdiction over the packaging of poisonous or otherwise hazardous products.

Patent and Trademark Office
Regulates registration of patents and trademarks. It enforces the Trade-Mark Act of 1947.

Library of Congress
Registers and protects all copyrighted material including advertisements, music, books, booklets, computer software, and other creative material.

Alcohol and Tobacco Tax Division
Has almost absolute authority over liquor advertising through its powers to suspend, revoke, or deny renewal of manufacturing and sales permits for distillers, vintners, and brewers found to be in violation of regulations.

Office of Consumer Affairs
Is the chief consumer protection department in the federal government. Established in 1971, the OCA coordinates, maintains, and publicizes information on all federal activities in the field of consumer protection. Publications produced and circulated by the OCA include consumer education guidelines, monthly newsletters, and a consumer services column that is released to some 4,500 weekly newspapers.

U.S. Postal Service
Has authority to halt mail delivery to any firm or person guilty of misusing the mails. The U.S. Postal Service maintains control over false and deceptive advertising, pornography, lottery offers, and guarantees that deceive or defraud.

Department of Agriculture
Closely monitors the distribution of misbranded or unregistered commercial poisons. The Department of Agriculture (USDA) works with the FTC to enforce regulations governing certain products. The USDA Grain

of Attorneys General requested that the FTC and EPA work jointly with the states to develop uniform national guidelines for environmental marketing claims.[26]

Defining Unfairness

Unfair advertising differs from deceptive advertising in that it may actually be nondeceptive but still be unfair to the consumer. According to FTC policy, unfairness exists when a consumer is "unjustifiably injured" or when there has been a "violation of public policy" (such as of other government statutes). Practices considered unfair are claims made without prior substantiation; claims that tend to exploit such vulnerable groups as children and the elderly; and instances in which the consumer cannot make a valid choice because the advertiser omits important information about the product or about competing products mentioned in the ad.[27]

In its 1984 case against International Harvester, for example, the FTC found that the company's failure to warn of a safety problem was not deceptive but did constitute an unfair practice.[28] Advertising organizations have argued that the word *unfair* is vague and "can mean whatever any given individual's value judgment may assign to it."[29] They have lobbied for Congress to eliminate the FTC's power to prosecute on unfairness grounds. Congress has not been receptive to this proposal, however.

Division has regulatory authority over false and deceptive advertising for seeds and grain products. The Grain Division is also empowered to initiate action against violators.

Civil Aeronautics Board
Regulates air traffic and advertising of all air carriers engaged in interstate commerce.

Securities and Exchange Commission
Was established in 1934 and has jurisdiction over all advertising of stocks, bonds, and other securities sold via interstate commerce. The SEC requires that public offerings of such issues contain full disclosure of all pertinent information on the company and the securities offered so that the prospective investor can make an informed buying decision. This disclosure must mention any negative elements that may affect the investment.

Department of Justice
Normally does not initiate legal action against persons or firms charged with violating the federal laws governing advertising. Instead, the Department of Justice enforces these laws and represents the federal government in the prosecution of cases referred to it by other federal agencies.

Consumer Product Safety Commission
Was established in 1972 to develop and enforce standards for potentially hazardous consumer products. It derives its power from four acts: the Flammable Fabrics Act of 1954, the Federal Hazardous Substances Act of 1960, the Children Protection Act of 1966, and the Standard for the Flammability of Children's Sleepwear of 1972. It has jurisdiction over the placement of warning statements in advertisements and other promotional materials for products covered under these acts. Its authority extends to household products, toys, and hazardous substances that cause accidental poisoning. The Consumer Product Safety Commission actively investigates product advertising and labeling violations brought to its attention by consumers and consumer protection groups. Continued violations by product makers are grounds for prosecution and punitive action by the Attorney General.

Investigating Suspected Violations

How does the FTC decide which advertisers to investigate? Complaints against advertisers usually come from consumers, competitors, and the FTC's own staff members who monitor ads in various media. The FTC has broad powers to go after suspected violators and to demand information from them.

Substantiation One thing the FTC looks at closely is whether an advertiser can substantiate product claims. For example, the FTC may ask to see supporting data if a suspected violator cites survey findings, scientific studies, and the like. Advertisers are expected to have supporting data in hand before running an ad, although the FTC does allow for postclaim evidence in some instances.[30] The FTC does not solicit substantiation from advertisers it is not investigating.

Endorsements The FTC also scrutinizes ads that contain questionable endorsements or testimonials. Like the advertisers who place the ads, endorsers must be able to substantiate their claims. Celebrity endorsers in particular face the possibility of being held personally liable for misrepresenting a product or service.[31] Many consumers don't believe celebrities because they think they'll say anything if they're paid enough. However, the FTC expects product endorsers to take reasonable steps to ensure the claims they make are true, as Johnny Cash had to do before agreeing to endorse the Technics electronic piano shown in Exhibit 2-9.

Affirmative Disclosures In addition to being able to substantiate positive claims about a product, advertisers must make affirmative disclosure of their product's limitations or deficiencies. Examples of affirmative disclosure include

EXHIBIT 2-9

Celebrity endorsements are popular because they lend interest and credibility to an advertiser's claims. This ad's seemingly contradictory visual and headline should make the reader curious enough to want to learn how an electric piano can sound like a guitar.

EPA mileage ratings for automobiles, pesticide warnings, and statements that soft drinks containing saccharin may be hazardous to one's health.

Remedies

When the FTC determines that an ad is deceptive or unfair, it has three courses of action: (1) request the advertiser to sign a consent decree, (2) issue a cease-and-desist order, and (3) require corrective advertising.

Consent Decree A *consent decree* is a document the advertiser signs agreeing to stop the objectionable advertising. Before signing the decree, the advertiser can negotiate and bargain with the FTC over specific directives that will govern subsequent advertising claims.

Cease-and-Desist Order If an advertiser does not sign a consent decree, the FTC may issue a cease-and-desist order prohibiting further use of the advertisement. Before the cease-and-desist order is final, a hearing is held before an administrative law judge. (Exhibit 2-10 presents a flowchart of the entire FTC complaint procedure.) Most advertisers sign the consent decree after the hearing and agree, without admitting guilt, to halt the advertising. Only a small percentage appeal cease-and-desist orders. Advertisers who violate either a consent decree or a cease-and-desist order are subject to a fine of up to $10,000 per showing of the ad.

Corrective Advertising The FTC may also require corrective advertising, which means a portion of the company's advertising for a period of time must be used to explain and correct the offending ads. The initial case establishing the FTC's authority in this area involved a Profile bread advertisement. The ad claimed that each slice contained fewer calories than slices of other brands. However, the ad did not mention that slices of Profile were thinner than those of other brands. The FTC ordered the company to allocate 25 percent of its advertising budget for one year to correct this misleading statement. Another classic case of corrective advertising was Listerine's $10.2 million worth of ads stating, "Listerine will not help prevent colds or sore throats or lessen their severity."

To help other advertisers avoid such expensive punishment, the FTC will review advertising before it runs and will give "advance clearance" in an advisory opinion. In addition, the FTC publishes *Industry Guides* and *Trade Regulation Rules,* which provide advertisers, agencies, and the media with ongoing information about FTC regulations.

Food and Drug Administration

A unit of the Department of Health and Human Services, the **Food and Drug Administration (FDA)** has authority over the labeling, packaging, and branding of packaged foods and therapeutic devices. The FDA requires manufacturers to disclose all the ingredients on product labels, in all product advertising featured in stores, and in all accompanying or separately distributed product literature. The label must accurately state the weight or volume of the contents. Labels on therapeutic devices must give clear instructions for use. The FDA is authorized to require warning and caution statements on packages of poisonous or otherwise hazardous products. It regulates "cents off" and other promotional statements on package labels.

FTC complaint procedure

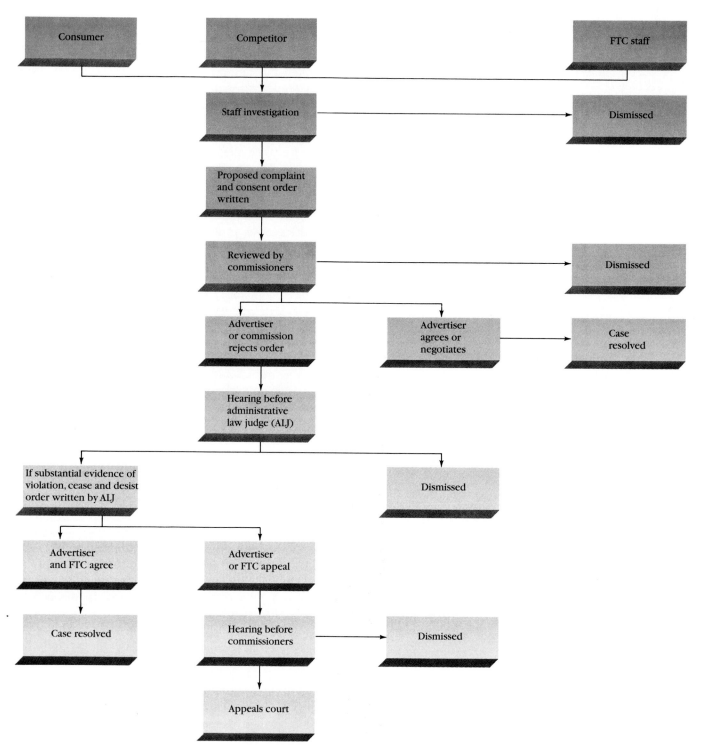

EXHIBIT 2-10

Flowchart of the FTC complaint
procedure.

If you love
your family;
give them a pat.

REAL BUTTER

EXHIBIT 2-11

The Food and Drug Administration scrutinizes food ads that make nutritional claims. If this ad had claimed that butter has fewer calories than margarine, the California Milk Advisory Board would have had to do some explaining to the FDA.

The FDA also has jurisdiction over the use of words such as *giant* or *family* when used to describe package sizes.

In response to the proliferation of consumer-oriented drug ads in the mid-1980s, the FDA ruled that any ad for a brand-name drug must include every piece of information that is in the package insert.[32] That meant advertisers would have to run lengthy commercials or use minuscule type in print ads. However, pharmaceutical companies found a way around the FDA ruling by not specifically mentioning the brand name. Upjohn, for example, developed a successful advertising campaign for its antibaldness drug by using only the Upjohn name in the ad, by talking about baldness in general, and by suggesting that the consumer see his doctor for further information.[33]

In 1987, the FDA lifted a long-standing ban on nutritional and health claims on food labels. Suddenly it was legal to use phrases like *high-fiber* or *low-cholesterol.* While the new policy boosted sales in many categories of packaged foods, it also led to exaggerated claims that outraged consumer groups and the FDA. As a result, President Bush signed into law the 1990 Nutritional Labeling and Education Act. Although the new law doesn't ban nutritional and health claims, it does require the FDA to come up with definitions for a wide range of terms, such as *light, low fat,* and *reduced calories.*[34]

Among advertisers affected by the FDA's tougher stand on food product claims is Perrier. When the FDA learned that the French company's mineral water doesn't exactly go untouched from Mother Nature to consumers' lips, regulators forced Perrier to drop the words "naturally sparkling" from its labels.[35] As a result of increased FDA scrutiny, many advertisers are now more cautious about their health and nutritional claims, such as the California Milk Advisory Board's claims about butter in Exhibit 2-11.

Federal Communications Commission

The seven-member **Federal Communications Commission (FCC)** was established as a result of the Communications Act of 1934. It has jurisdiction over the radio, television, telephone, and telegraph industries. Through its licensing authority, the FCC has indirect control over broadcast advertising. The FCC stringently controls the airing of obscenity and profanity, and it has restricted both advertising content and which products may be advertised on radio and television. For example, the FCC required stations to run commercials about the harmful effects of smoking even before Congress banned cigarette advertising on television and radio (per the Public Health Cigarette Smoking Act of 1970).

However, the FCC has since dropped many of its rules and regulations for both radio and TV stations, having decided that marketplace forces can do an adequate job of controlling broadcast media. For example, the FCC no longer limits the amount of time that can be devoted to commercials. And stations no longer have to maintain detailed program and commercial logs. However, stations still keep records of commercial broadcasts so advertisers can be assured of value received for the advertising time they purchased.

Patent and Trademark Office

A **trademark,** according to the Lanham Trade-Mark Act (1947), is "any word, name, symbol, or device or any combination thereof adopted and used by a manufacturer or merchant to identify his goods and distinguish them from

Term	Meaning	Examples

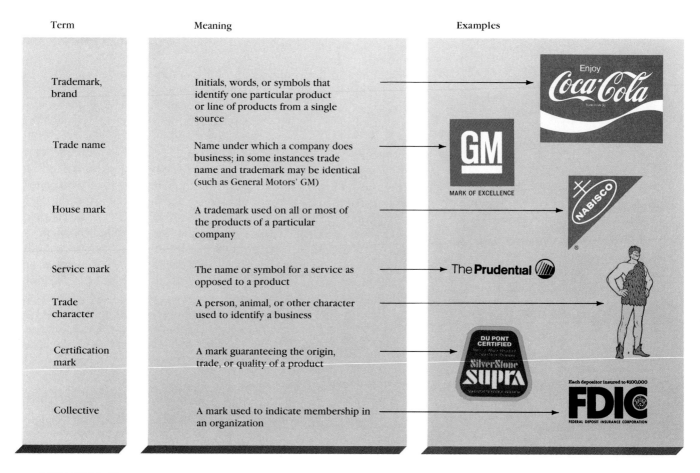

Trademark, brand	Initials, words, or symbols that identify one particular product or line of products from a single source	
Trade name	Name under which a company does business; in some instances trade name and trademark may be identical (such as General Motors' GM)	
House mark	A trademark used on all or most of the products of a particular company	
Service mark	The name or symbol for a service as opposed to a product	
Trade character	A person, animal, or other character used to identify a business	
Certification mark	A mark guaranteeing the origin, trade, or quality of a product	
Collective	A mark used to indicate membership in an organization	

EXHIBIT 2-12

Trademark terminology.

EXHIBIT 2-13

To keep the word from becoming generic, Xerox Corporation has conducted an active campaign to remind the public that the name Xerox is a registered trademark.

those manufactured or sold by others." See Exhibit 2-12 for examples of trademark terminology.

Ownership of a trademark may be designated in advertising or on a label, package, or letterhead by the word *Registered,* the symbol ®, or the symbol ™. If someone uses a trademark that is owned by another and refuses to discontinue such use, the trademark owner can ask the courts to order the violator to stop.

Ironically, advertising's very success can sometimes cause the demise of a trademark. This is precisely what happened to famous trademarks like thermos, escalator, and cellophane. The owners lost out when the courts declared the trademarks "generic," which means a term has come into common use and is now the dictionary name for the product. Other examples of lost trademarks include shredded wheat, yo-yo, cube steak, and trampoline.

Most trademark owners take particular care to prevent their trademark from becoming generic. They see to it that it is always distinguished from surrounding words and followed by the generic name of the product (Band-Aid brand adhesive bandages, Scotch brand tape, Kleenex tissues, Jell-O brand gelatin).[36] They never refer to the trademark in the plural. It is not three Xeroxes but three Xerox copies. Xerox even advertises the fact that its name is a registered trademark, as shown in Exhibit 2-13.

Library of Congress

The **Library of Congress** registers and protects all copyrighted material, including advertising. A **copyright** issued to an advertiser grants the exclusive right to print, publish, or reproduce the protected ad for a period of time equal to the life span of the copyright owner plus 50 additional years. An ad can be copyrighted only if it contains original copy or illustrations. Slogans, short phrases, and familiar symbols and designs cannot be copyrighted. Although a copyright prevents a whole advertisement from being legally used by another, it does not prevent others from using the general concept or idea of the ad or from paraphrasing the copy and expressing it in another way.

The use of any original creative written, musical, illustrative, or other material by an outside source in an ad without the express written consent of its creator is an infringement of copyright that may constitute grounds for legal action. For this reason, advertisers and agencies obtain permission before they use creative material from any outside source.

Copyright is indicated in an advertisement by the word *Copyright,* the abbreviation *Copr.,* or the copyright symbol © near the name of the advertiser. An ad that has foreign or international copyright protection usually contains the year of copyright as well. These copyright marks are also used to denote protection in other forms of print advertising, including booklets, sales brochures, and catalogs.

STATE AND LOCAL REGULATION

In addition to federal regulations, advertisers are subject to numerous state and local laws and enforcement agencies governing the areas in which the advertising occurs. During the federal deregulation trend of the 1980s, state and local governments took a more active role in enforcing their laws against false or deceptive advertising. As a result, advertisers are now more diligent in keeping an eye on varying state and local advertising regulations when designing ads that will appear in numerous states.

Regulation by State Governments

State legislation governing advertising is often based on the "truth-in-advertising" model statute developed in 1911 by *Printer's Ink,* which for many years was the major trade paper of the industry. The statute holds that any maker of an advertisement found to contain "untrue, deceptive, or misleading" material shall be guilty of a misdemeanor. Today 46 states—not including Arkansas, Delaware, Mississippi, and New Mexico—enforce laws patterned after this statute to control fraudulent and deceptive advertising.

All states also have what are referred to as "little FTC acts," or consumer protection acts, which govern unfair and deceptive business practices. Under such acts, states themselves can investigate and prosecute cases, and individual consumers can bring civil suits against businesses. To increase their clout, some states are teaming up on legal actions—most recently to challenge allegedly deceptive ad promotions in the airline, rental-car, and food-making industries. As William Howell, senior assistant attorney general in Florida points out, "Many of the food manufacturers could litigate some of the smaller states into the ground, but they might not be willing to fight it out against 10 states simultaneously."[37]

State actions can sometimes lead to changes in national campaigns. The Beef Industry Council, for example, changed its "Beef Gives Strength" campaign when the New York attorney general's office found the ads deceptive, since eating beef alone cannot increase strength and endurance.[38]

Advertisers also need to be aware of unique state regulations governing what can and cannot be advertised and what can be depicted in ads. Some states prohibit certain types of wine and liquor advertising, for example, and most states restrict the use of federal and state flags in advertising.

Regulation by Local Governments

Many cities and counties, usually through consumer protection agencies, enforce laws regulating local advertising practices. These agencies function chiefly to protect local consumers against unfair and misleading practices by area merchants.

The New York City Department of Consumer Affairs, for example, charged Sears, Roebuck with engaging in misleading advertising—such as advertising clothing discounts without explaining where prices started.[39] Instead of changing its ads and perhaps avoiding the bad publicity, Sears sued New York City, insisting that its ads comply with federal advertising laws and are protected by the First Amendment. According to Angelo J. Aponte, New York's consumer-affairs commissioner, his office has negotiated advertising changes with more than a hundred retailers since the laws in question took effect 20 years ago, and all except Sears have complied when contacted.[40]

RECENT COURT RULINGS AFFECTING ADVERTISERS

Both federal and state courts made a number of significant rulings in recent years pertaining to important advertising issues, including First Amendment rights, privacy rights, and comparative advertising.

First Amendment Rights

Historically, the Supreme Court has distinguished between "speech" and "commercial speech" (defined as speech that promotes a commercial transaction). However, in the last decade or so, it has made a series of decisions suggesting that truthful commercial speech is also entitled to full protection under the First Amendment.[41]

In 1977, for example, the Court declared state bar association bans on members' advertising to be in violation of the First Amendment. Now, a third of all lawyers in the nation advertise.[42] Exhibit 2-14 presents just one of the many ads lawyers have aired on TV. A few states even permit client testimonials in lawyer ads. Jim Schernecker, a Wisconsin personal injury and divorce lawyer, notes that his firm gained 200 new clients as a result of a $25,000 local TV ad campaign featuring client testimonials.[43] To help guard against deceptive and misleading legal ads, the American Bar Association has issued advertising guidelines for attorneys.

In 1982, the Supreme Court upheld an FTC order allowing physicians and dentists to advertise. Since then, advertising by medical and dental organizations has exploded. Exhibit 2-15 is just one example of the different types of services medical organizations now advertise.

In 1986, the Court made a ruling that many observers interpret as a setback to the First Amendment rights of commercial speech. The case involved a ban on gambling advertisements in Puerto Rico, where gambling itself is legal. Responding to a challenge of the law by one of the casino owners, the U.S. Supreme Court upheld the Puerto Rican legislature's power to ban the advertising, ruling that even truthful ads for goods and services may be restricted by the state to protect the "health, safety, and welfare" of its citizens. What has the advertising industry upset is the decision's implications for the

EXHIBIT 2-14

Before 1977, you couldn't have seen ads like this on TV because state bar associations banned advertising by lawyers. Now lawyers spend an estimated $60 million a year on TV ad time alone. Joel Hyatt, with 185 legal clinics in 22 states, spends about $5 million a year on TV advertising.

JOEL HYATT: His office was just across from the State House and he took all comers, big and small. His fees were so low, they alarmed his fellow lawyers. And on top of that, Abraham Lincoln *advertised.* For the same reason Hyatt Legal Services does today: To bring the law closer to people. Lincoln always told you his fee up front. And we do that today. Hyatt Legal Services. A good idea that just keeps getting better. I'm Joel Hyatt, and you have my word on it!

EXHIBIT 2-15

Medical and dental organizations, from individual practitioners to clinics and hospitals, have become major advertisers in print, broadcast, and outdoor media since restrictions on this type of advertising were lifted in 1982.

Starting March 2, We're Lowering The Cost Of Mammograms To $50. Just Think What You Could Save.

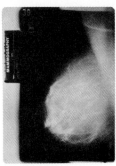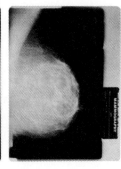

Considering 250 women in Rhode Island will die of breast cancer this year, a mammogram could save your life.

Which is why we urge you to take advantage of our special, low-cost mammography screenings available only during March and April.

A mammogram is a safe, low-dosage x-ray that can detect breast cancer three to five years before you can feel a lump.

To qualify, you must be over 40 years old with no symptoms of breast disease and must not have had a mammogram in at least two years.

All screenings will be done at the Ambulatory Patient Center at Rhode Island Hospital from 3:30 p.m. to 8:00 p.m. Special parking will be provided.

And if you can't afford the $50, don't worry. Nobody is going to be denied an important opportunity like this.

To register, call 277-4881 Monday through Friday, 9 a.m. to 4 p.m., starting February 17th.

And call soon. Because when it comes to detecting breast cancer, you can never be too early.

Rhode Island Hospital
Providence, Rhode Island

advertising of other products that a government might deem harmful, particularly tobacco and alcohol.

Privacy Rights

Another issue the courts have addressed in recent years is the violation of an individual's right to privacy. Most advertisers realize it is illegal to use a person's likeness in an ad without the individual's permission, but the courts recently have ruled that even using a "look-alike" can violate that person's rights.

The case that led to this decision involved an ad for Christian Dior. The ad depicted a fictional wedding attended by a number of well-known celebrities, including one who appeared to be Jacqueline Kennedy Onassis but was, in fact, a professional look-alike. Onassis sued and won on the grounds that the use of the look-alike without her permission constituted a violation of her right to privacy.[44] Other courts have ruled that privacy rights continue even after a person's death.

Comparative Advertising

Comparative advertising claims superiority to competitors in some aspect, as shown in Exhibit 2-16, for example. Such ads are legal so long as the comparison is truthful. In 1986, a federal appeals court in California upheld a $40 million damage award against now-bankrupt Jartran for ads that unfairly discredited U-Haul.[45] And in 1989, a Washington, D.C., court ordered Ralston Purina Company to pay $10.4 million in damages to Alpo Petfoods for misrepresenting its dog food.[46]

EXHIBIT 2-16

With encouragement by the FTC to "name names," comparative ads have flourished. Here Visa turns the tables on American Express with one of its ". . . and they don't take American Express" ads.

With the signing of the 1988 Trademark Law Revision Act, more businesses than ever are expected to sue over comparative advertising. The new law closes a loophole in the Lanham Act, which previously governed comparison ads but made no mention of misrepresenting another company's product. Under the new law, anyone who "misrepresents the nature, characteristics, qualities, or geographical origin of his or her or another person's goods, services, or commercial activities" is vulnerable to a civil action.[47]

In addition to being truthful, comparative ads must make the comparison in terms of some objectively measurable characteristic. Procter & Gamble and Chesebrough-Pond's, for example, sued each other for false advertising, but neither won its case. The court found much of their "scientific" testimony "incomprehensible," and concluded that both parties should probably remove ad claims that their hand lotion is the most effective available.[48]

NONGOVERNMENT REGULATION

Advertisers have achieved substantial voluntary self-regulation in recent years. This reflects their desire for acceptance and growth in a competitive marketplace where consumer confidence is essential. However, advertisers still are subject to considerable nongovernment regulation by business-monitoring organizations, the media, consumer groups, and advertising agencies and associations.

The Role of the Better Business Bureau (BBB)

The largest of the business-monitoring organizations is the **Better Business Bureau (BBB).** Established in 1916, the Better Business Bureau has national and local offices funded by dues from over 100,000 member companies. It operates primarily at the local level to protect consumers against fraudulent and deceptive advertising and sales practices. When local bureaus contact violators and ask them to revise their advertising, most comply.

The BBB's files on violators are open to the public. Records of violators who do not comply are sent to appropriate government agencies for further action. The BBB often works with local law enforcement agencies to prosecute advertisers guilty of fraud and misrepresentation. Each year, the BBB investigates thousands of advertisements for possible violations of truth and accuracy.

The Council of Better Business Bureaus, Inc., is the parent organization of the Better Business Bureau and part of the National Advertising Review Council. One of its functions is helping new industries develop standards for ethical and responsible advertising. It also provides ongoing information about advertising regulations and recent court and administrative rulings that affect advertising. In 1983, the **National Advertising Division (NAD)** of the Council of Better Business Bureaus published guidelines for advertising to children, a particularly sensitive area (see Ad Lab 2-B).

National Advertising Review Council

The **National Advertising Review Council (NARC)** was established in 1971 by the Council of Better Business Bureaus, Inc., in conjunction with the American Association of Advertising Agencies, the American Advertising Federation, and the Association of National Advertisers. Its primary purpose is to promote and enforce standards of truth, accuracy, taste, morality, and social responsibility in advertising.

NARC is regarded as the most comprehensive and effective regulatory mechanism in the advertising industry. Indeed, a U.S. district court judge noted in a 1985 case that the "speed, informality, and modest cost" as well as expertise of the self-regulatory organization give it special advantages over the court system in resolving advertising disputes.[49]

NARC Operating Arms

NARC has two operating arms: the National Advertising Division of the Council of Better Business Bureaus and the **National Advertising Review Board (NARB).**

The NAD is a monitoring and investigative body. It monitors advertising practices and reviews complaints about advertising from consumers and consumer groups, brand competitors, local Better Business Bureaus, NAD monitors, and others. The NARB serves as the appeals board for NAD decisions. The NARB consists of a chairperson and 50 volunteer members: 30 national advertisers, 10 agency representatives, and 10 laypeople from the public sector.

The NAD/NARB Review Process

Most complaints filed with the NAD concern advertising that is false or misleading or that departs from taste, morality, or social responsibility. As shown in Exhibit 2-17, the NAD even runs ads that include a complaint form. The NAD does not reveal the identity of the challenger except with permission.

AD LAB 2-B
Advertising to Children: What You Can and Cannot Do

Many people are concerned about the effects advertising has on children. Watchdog groups, for example, believe that some toy commercials create unreasonable expectations through animation and other special effects. They are also concerned about children being overexposed to sugary breakfast cereal and snack-food commericals. While kids don't buy the groceries, 78 percent of parents say that kids do influence their cereal purchases. It's difficult for parents to teach good eating habits if they're constantly being undermined by TV commercials. Sure, parents can simply turn off the TV, but kids should be able to watch their favorite programs without being taken advantage of.

To protect children from unfair advertising techniques, TV networks have established highly restrictive guidelines for children's advertising. Network censors closely scrutinize all ads submitted for Saturday morning programs in particular. However, many advertisers complain that network regulations are so precise that no room is left for creativity in ads. For instance, only 10 seconds of a toy ad may contain animation and other special effects, and the last 5 seconds must display all toys shown earlier in the ad and disclose whether they are sold separately and whether batteries are included.

The Council of Better Business Bureaus also polices advertising to children. Staff members regularly monitor commercials on network children's shows and check ads in children's comics and magazines against the following guidelines:

1. Advertisers should always take into account the target audience's level of knowledge, sophistication, and ma-

turity. Children have a limited capability for evaluating the credibility of what they see; therefore, advertisers have a special responsibility to protect children from their own susceptibilities.

2. Advertisers should not directly or indirectly stimulate unreasonable expectations of product quality or performance. Imaginative and make-believe play is an important part of a child's growing-up process; therefore, advertisers should exercise care not to exploit that imaginative quality of children.

3. Advertisers should communicate in a truthful and accurate manner with full recognition that the child may learn practices from advertising that can affect his or her health and well-being.

4. Advertisers are urged to capitalize on advertising's potential to positively influence social behavior. Wherever possible, advertising should reflect positive and beneficial social standards such as friendship, kindness, honesty, justice, generosity, and respect for others.

5. Advertisers should contribute to the parent-child relationship in a constructive manner. Although parents have the primary responsibility of providing guidance for their children, many other influences affect a child's personal and social development.

Laboratory Applications

1. Do you believe any of these guidelines are too restrictive?

2. Are there any additional guidelines you would suggest?

VO: Get ready for a toothpaste that tastes so great, kids will rush to brush. New Crest for Kids, with a flavor that is so different,

some kids call it berrylicious. No matter what they call it they'll rush to brush. And while they're enjoying the flavor they'll be

fighting cavities too. New Crest for Kids. It tastes so great they'll rush to brush.

EXHIBIT 2-17

The NAD actively encourages
consumers to register specific
complaints about misleading or
deceptive advertising. By voicing
their disapproval, people can
help the NAD protect both the
public and those advertisers who
do tell the truth.

EXHIBIT 2-17

The NAD actively encourages consumers to register specific complaints about misleading or deceptive advertising. By voicing their disapproval, people can help the NAD protect both the public and those advertisers who do tell the truth.

When the NAD finds a valid complaint, it contacts the advertiser, specifying any claims to be substantiated. If substantiation is inadequate, the NAD requests modification or discontinuance of the claims. No investigation is conducted if the advertiser withdraws the claims in question before receiving the NAD's first inquiry or if the claims are the subject of litigation by a government agency.

If the NAD and an advertiser reach an impasse in their discussions, either party has the right to review by a five-member NARB panel (consisting of three advertisers, one agency representative, and one layperson). The panel's decision is binding on the NAD. If an advertiser refuses to comply with the panel's decision, the NARB will refer the matter to an appropriate governmental authority and so indicate in its public record. Exhibit 2-18 presents a flowchart of the NAD/NARB review process.

In all its years of operation, no advertiser who participated in the complete process of an NAD investigation and NARB appeal has declined to abide by the panel's decision.[50] In fact, very few cases have made it to the NARB. Of 103 NAD investigations conducted in 1990, 19 ad claims were substantiated, 58 ads were modified or discontinued, and only 2 decisions were disputed and referred to the NARB for resolution.[51]

Both the NARB and the NAD issue monthly reports to help establish practicable standards for the advertising industry. The NARB also sponsors advisory panels to study such specialized topics as comparative advertising and women in advertising. To help advertisers avoid complaints, the NAD evaluates and renders decisions about proposed advertising campaigns prior to their completion and placement in the media.

Regulation by the Media

Almost all media maintain some form of advertising review and reserve the right to reject any material they regard as objectionable, even if it is not

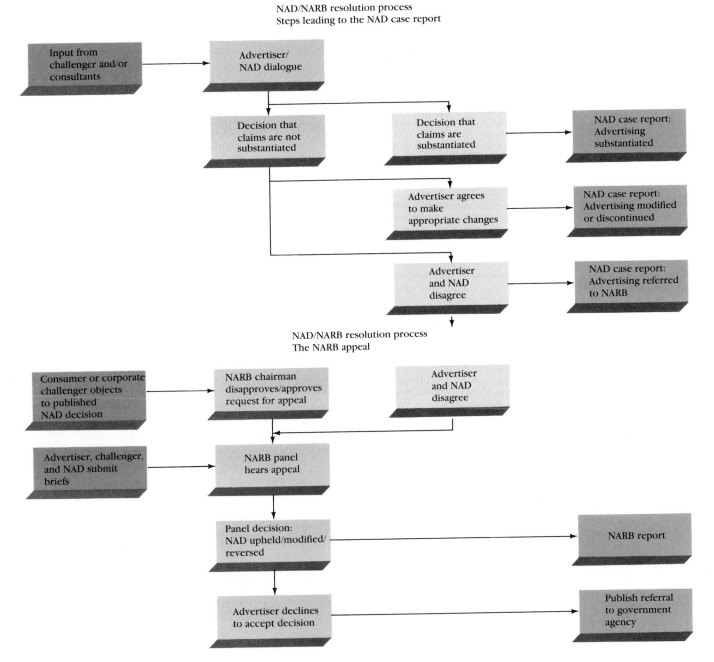

NAD/NARB resolution process
Steps leading to the NAD case report

NAD/NARB resolution process
The NARB appeal

EXHIBIT 2-18

Flowchart of the NAD/NARB review process.

deceptive. Many people view the media as a major source of regulation—in some cases as more effective than the FTC.

Television

Of all the media, the television networks conduct the strictest review of advertising. Advertisers are required to submit all commercials intended for a network or affiliated station to the broadcast standards department of the network. Estimates are that as many as half of all commercials (in storyboard form) are returned to the advertisers with suggestions for changes or greater substantiation of claims.[52] Some ads are totally rejected for violating network policies, as discussed in Ad Lab 2-C.

AD LAB 2-C
The Issue of Issue Ads

The TV commercial depicts a dilapidated courtroom 30 years from now. Testifying in front of a teenage prosecutor and a jury of other youngsters, an old man tries to explain why nothing was done decades before to protect them from the ravages of deficit spending: "It was all going to work out somehow, but no one was willing to make the sacrifices." When the young prosecutor says, "In 1986, the national debt had reached $2 trillion. Didn't that frighten you?" The old man shrugs helplessly. "Are you ever going to forgive us?"

This commercial, produced by W. R. Grace & Co., was rejected by all three networks. The networks claimed the ad violated their policies against carrying "issue" advertising that advocates a particular point of view. Part of their concern stemmed from the Fairness Doctrine, which requires giving equal time to opposing points of view. But the networks also have a policy of rejecting advocacy ads if they feel that such ads allow those with the most money to have their opinions heard. The Supreme Court ruled in 1973 that networks can reject paid editorial messages without violating the Communications Act or the First Amendment.

The Grace case has prompted some commentators to point out, however, that the networks may have gotten too paranoid in their attempts to determine what might or might not be "controversial." The Grace commercial was accepted and aired by cable networks and independent stations as well as by some network affiliates. At one point in the controversy over the network rejection of the ad, 122 independent TV stations banded together and aired the commercial as a public-service announcement, free of charge. CBS eventually accepted the ad after Grace made one minor change in it, and ABC subsequently said it would accept the ad if it were resubmitted. NBC, however, stood by its evaluation of the commercial as "controversial" and refused to air it.

Corporations that wish to place issue ads on network television argue that the airwaves belong to the public and that it is a violation of their First Amendment rights for the networks not to carry their ads.

The networks defend their position by citing the 1973 Supreme Court decision and by pointing out that they are fulfilling their obligations to free speech and public service through their news and public affairs programming.

Laboratory Applications

1. Do you think networks should alter their policy on corporate issue advertising? In what way?

2. The FCC has repealed the Fairness Doctrine, but Congress is currently considering legislation that would make the doctrine law. Are you in favor of such legislation? Why or why not?

OLD MAN: I've already told you, it was all going to work out somehow. There was even talk of an amendment. But no one was willing to make the sacrifices. I'm afraid you're much too young to understand.

BOY: Maybe so. But I'm afraid the numbers speak for themselves. By 1986, for example, the na-

tional debt had reached 2 trillion dollars. Didn't that frighten you?

ANNCR VO: No one really knows what another generation of unchecked federal deficits will bring.

OLD MAN: This frightens me.

BOY: No more questions.

OLD MAN: I have a question. Are you ever going to forgive us?

ANNCR VO: But we know this much. You can change the future. You have to. At W. R. Grace, we want all of us to stay one step ahead of a changing world.

The policies of the three major networks are all based on the original National Association of Broadcasters Television Code. (The code was suspended by the NAB in 1983 following court invalidation of part of it for violating the Sherman Antitrust Act.) However, the network policies vary enough from each other that preparing commercials acceptable to all can be a real headache. Cable networks and local stations tend to be much less stringent in their requirements, as demonstrated by their acceptance of condom ads.

One of the more recent issues to arise in TV advertising is the use of superimposed product disclaimers ("supers") that advertisers use to comply with network rules and regulations. Once limited primarily to aspirin commercials warning "use only as directed," supers are now used by a variety of advertisers including Chrysler, AT&T, and American Express. Some commercials were getting so cluttered with minuscule supers, however, that network executives started ordering revisions to ensure legibility.[53]

Radio

Review of radio advertising is handled primarily at the local level. There are 19 radio networks, but unlike TV networks, they supply only a small percentage of their affiliates' programming. Therefore, they have very little or no say in what their affiliates advertise. A radio station is also less likely to return an advertising script or tape for changes. At KLBJ in Austin, Texas, the station looks mainly at whether the advertising is illegal, unethical, or immoral.[54] One of the biggest concerns for radio stations is that the spot not detract from the rest of the programming or offend listeners. KLBJ, for example, will not air more than one spot per advertiser per hour to avoid irritating listeners. When radio stations do reject taped commercials from advertisers, it's usually because the sound is distorted or too loud, or the overall production quality is poor.

Every radio station typically has its own unwritten guidelines on what is allowable in commercials. Rarely is anything cast in stone, however. KDWB, a Minneapolis-St. Paul station with a contemporary hit format and a large teenage audience, turned down a psychic who wanted to buy advertising time, but allowed condom and other contraceptive ads after some serious internal debate over the issue.[55] KDWB also puts time restraints on certain ads aimed at young teenagers, such as commercials for rock concerts. KSDO in San Diego, a station with a business and information format, won't air commercials for X-rated movies, topless bars, or anything related to excessive drinking.[56]

Magazines

National magazines monitor all advertising, particularly those by new advertisers and for new products. Newer publications that are eager to sell space may not be so vigilant; but some established magazines, including *Time* and *Newsweek,* are highly scrupulous. Many magazines will not accept advertising for certain types of products. *The New Yorker,* for example, will not accept discount retail store advertising, ads for feminine hygiene products, or self-medication products. *Reader's Digest* will not accept tobacco advertising.

Some magazines test every product before accepting the advertising. *Good Housekeeping* is one example. If *Good Housekeeping* tests do not substantiate the advertiser's claims, the ad is rejected. Products that pass may feature the *Good Housekeeping* "Seal of Approval" on their labels and in advertising. *Parents Magazine* offers a similar product seal and warranty.

Newspapers

Newspapers also monitor and review advertising. Larger newspapers have clearance staffs that read every ad submitted. Most smaller newspapers rely on the advertising manager, sales personnel, or proofreaders to check ad copy.

The general advertising policies set forth in *Newspaper Rates and Data* (Standard Rate and Data Service) include such restrictions as "No objectionable medical, personal, matrimonial, clairvoyant, or palmistry advertising accepted; no stock promotion or financial advertising, other than those securities of known value, will be accepted." Another rule prohibits the publication of any ad that might easily be mistaken for regular reading material unless it features the word *advertisement* or *advt*.

In addition, most papers have their own codes of acceptability governing advertising. These codes can range from 1 page for small local papers to more than 50 pages for large dailies such as the *Los Angeles Times.* Some of these codes are quite specific in what they will and will not allow. The *Detroit Free Press,* for example, will not accept classified ads containing such words as *affair* or *swinger.* The *Kansas City Star and Times* requires advertisers who claim "the lowest price in town" to include in the ad a promise to meet or beat any lower price readers find elsewhere within 30 days.[57]

One problem advertisers face is the lack of uniformity to newspaper advertising codes. A survey conducted by the *Los Angeles Times* found, for example, that ads for handguns are totally prohibited by the *Boston Globe,* are accepted by the *Chicago Tribune* only if the guns are antique, and are permitted in the *Orlando Sentinel* so long as the guns are not automatic.[58] Newspapers do revise their policies from time to time, however. This occurred recently when many large papers reversed their policy on the acceptability of condom advertising.

Regulation by Consumer Groups

Of all the regulatory forces governing advertising, consumer protection organizations have achieved the greatest growth in recent years. Starting in the 1960s, the consumer movement became increasingly active in fighting fraudulent and deceptive advertising. Consumers demanded not only that products perform as advertised but also that more product information be provided so people can compare and make better buying decisions.

The impact of the consumer movement and its growing pressure for more stringent advertising regulation soon gave rise to a new word: **consumerism,** or social action designed to dramatize the rights of the buying public. Since then, one fact has become clear to both advertisers and agencies: The American consumer has the power to influence advertising practices.

The growing consumer movement has caused advertisers and agencies to pay more attention to product claims, especially those related to energy use (such as the estimated miles per gallon of a new auto) and the nutritional value of processed foods (such as sugar-coated breakfast cereals). Consumerism has fostered the growth of consumer advocate groups and regulatory agencies. It has also promoted more consumer research by advertisers, agencies, and the media in an effort to learn what consumers want—and how to provide it. Many advertisers agree that the creation of customer relations departments and investment in public goodwill ultimately will pay off in improved consumer relations and sales.

Consumer Information Networks

Several large organizations serve as mass-communication networks for the exchange of consumer information, enabling consumers to express their views on advertising and marketing infractions. These organizations include the Consumer Federation of America (CFA), the National Council of Senior Citizens, and the National Consumer League. They have the following functions: (1) to serve as a central clearinghouse for the exchange and dissemination of information among its members; (2) to aid in the development of state, regional, and local consumer organizations; and (3) to work with and provide services to national, regional, county, and municipal consumer groups.

Consumer interests also are served by several private, nonprofit testing organizations such as Consumers Union, Consumers' Research, and Underwriters Laboratories.

Consumer Advocates

Consumer advocate groups focus on issues that involve advertising and advertisers. These groups act on advertising complaints received from consumers as well as on those that grow out of their own research.

Their normal procedures are (1) to investigate the complaint; (2) if warranted, to contact the advertiser and ask that the objectionable advertisement or practice be halted; (3) if the advertiser does not comply, to release publicity or criticism about the offense to the media; (4) to submit complaints with substantiating evidence to appropriate government agencies for further action; and (5) in some instances, to file a lawsuit and seek to obtain from the courts a cease-and-desist order or a fine or other penalty against the violator.

Self-Regulation by Advertisers

Most large advertisers gather strong data to substantiate their claims. They maintain careful systems of advertising review to ensure that ads meet both their own standards and industry, media, and legal requirements. Most advertisers also reflect a sense of social responsibility in their advertising. Falstaff Brewing Company, for example, specifically avoids implying that beer will give people "a lift." It also rejects any appeals to adolescents and children and any references to sex.

In addition, many industries maintain advertising codes that reflect standards and practices that companies in the industry have agreed to follow. These codes also establish a basis for complaints. For example, a member may ask the executive board of the association to review existing competitive conditions in terms of the industry's advertising code.

However, industry advertising codes are only as effective as the enforcement powers of the individual trade associations. Since enforcement may conflict with antitrust laws that prohibit interference with open competition, trade associations usually exert peer pressure on member companies that violate their codes rather than resort to hearings or penalties.

Self-Regulation by Ad Agencies and Associations

Most advertising agencies monitor their own practices. In addition, professional advertising associations oversee the activities of member agencies to prevent problems that may trigger government intervention. Advertising publications actively report issues and actions before the courts in an effort to educate agencies and advertisers about possible legal infractions.

Advertising Agencies

Although the advertiser supplies information about a product or service to its agency, it is the agency's responsibility to research and verify all product claims and comparative product data before using them in advertising. The media may require such documentation before accepting the advertising, and substantiation also may be needed if government or consumer agencies challenge the claims.

Agencies can be held legally liable for fraudulent or misleading advertising claims. For this reason, most major advertising agencies have in-house legal counsel and regularly submit their advertisements for review. If any aspect of the advertising is challenged, the agency will ask its client to review the advertising and either confirm claims as truthful or replace unverified material.

Advertising Associations

Several advertising associations are actively engaged in monitoring industrywide advertising practices. The **American Association of Advertising Agencies (AAAA),** an association of advertising agencies throughout the United States, controls agency practices by denying membership to any agency judged unethical. The AAAA *Standards of Practice* and *Creative Code* set forth advertising principles for member agencies.

The **American Advertising Federation (AAF)** helped to establish the FTC, and its early "vigilance" committees were the forerunners of the Better Business Bureaus. The AAF "Advertising Principles of American Business," adopted in 1984, defines standards for truthful and responsible advertising. Since most local advertising clubs belong to the AAF, this organization has been instrumental in influencing agencies and advertisers to abide by these principles.

The **Association of National Advertisers (ANA)** comprises 400 major manufacturing and service companies that are clients of member agencies of the AAAA. These companies, pledged to uphold the ANA code of advertising ethics, work with the ANA through a joint Committee for Improvement of Advertising Content.

Summary

As advertising has proliferated in the media, the criticism of advertising has also intensified. Detractors say advertising debases our language, makes us too materialistic, and manipulates us into buying products we do not need. Furthermore, they say, advertising is not only excessive but also offensive or in bad taste and even deceptive.

Proponents of advertising admit that advertising has been and sometimes still is misused. However, they point out that the abuse heaped on advertising is often unjustified and excessive and that advertisers have been responsive to criticism by making efforts to avoid stereotypes, to control the proliferation of ads, and to make ads more informative and entertaining. Advertisers realize that the best way to sell their products is to appeal to genuine consumer needs and to be honest in their claims.

Advertising was once an unchecked, free-swinging business activity. However, growing pressure from consumers, special-interest groups, and increased government regulation has caused advertisers to develop higher standards of ethical conduct and social responsibility. One result of past abuses by advertisers is the current large body of laws and regulations governing advertising. Regulation comes in several forms: from federal, state, and local government agencies; nongovernment regulation by business-monitoring organizations, the media, and consumer groups; and self-regulation by advertisers and the advertising industry.

The FTC is the major federal regulator of advertising. Its recent definitions of what constitutes "deceptive" and "unfair" advertising have been controversial. In determining whether ads are deceptive or unfair, the FTC looks for substantiation of claims and scrutinizes endorsements and testimonials for signs of deception. If the FTC finds the advertiser at fault, it may issue a cease-and-desist order or require corrective advertising.

The FDA keeps an eye on advertising for food and drugs in addition to regulating product labels and packaging. The FCC has jurisdiction over the radio and television industries, but deregulation has severely limited the amount of control the FCC has over advertising in these media. The Patent and Trademark Office governs ownership of trademarks, trade names, house marks, and similar distinctive features of companies and brands. The Library of Congress registers and protects all copyrighted materials.

State and local governments also have enacted consumer protection laws that regulate aspects of advertising.

The federal and state courts have been involved in several advertising issues, including First Amendment protection of "commercial speech," the right of professionals such as lawyers and doctors to advertise, infringements of advertising on the right to privacy, and lawsuits over comparative advertising.

Nongovernmental sources of advertising regulation include the Council of Better Business Bureaus and the National Advertising Division. The NAD has been the most effective nongovernment regulatory body. It investigates complaints received from consumers, brand competitors, or local Better Business Bureaus and suggests corrective measures. Advertisers that refuse to comply are referred to the National Advertising Review Board (NARB), which may uphold, modify, or reverse the NAD's findings.

Other sources of nongovernment regulation include monitoring by the print media and broadcasting codes and policies. Consumer organizations and advocates also exert some control over advertising by investigating and filing complaints against advertisers and by providing information to consumers. Finally, sources of self-regulation include advertisers, industries that offer their own advertising standards and guidelines, and advertising agencies and organizations that make up the advertising industry.

Questions for Review and Discussion

1. Is advertising's responsibility to lead or to reflect society? Explain.

2. Do you believe advertising tends to create monopolies? How?

3. Why have feminists been so upset about certain advertising? Is their displeasure reasonable?

4. Explain the difference between an ethical dilemma and an ethical lapse. How does an advertiser's ethics differ from an advertiser's social responsibility?

5. What is the relationship between the FTC and the advertising industry? Do you feel the FTC has overstepped its authority? Explain. Can you cite recent examples of FTC action against advertisers?

6. If you were to help the FDA draft guidelines for health claims in food ads, what items would you include?

7. In what way does "commercial speech" differ from free speech? Should this distinction be maintained, or should advertising be given the same First Amendment protection as other types of speech?

8. What effect, if any, does physician advertising have on the practice of medicine?

9. It is estimated that 35 percent of current advertising is comparative. What is the value of comparative advertising? What are the drawbacks?

10. What is the importance of the NAD/NARB system to consumers and advertisers?

THE ADVERTISING BUSINESS: AGENCIES AND CLIENTS

Coffee with a twist.

Introducing Café Peach Crème, flavoured with a hint of real peach liqueur.
Pamper yourself with our newest cup of tenderness.

Objective: To depict how people and groups organize themselves to create and produce advertising. The advertising person may serve in any of a variety of roles and needs to understand the fundamental tasks of both the agency and the client, the role of the media and suppliers, how agencies acquire clients and make money, and the overall relationship between the agency and the client.

After studying this chapter you will be able to:

☐ Explain what organizations are the major participants in the advertising business and their relationship to one another.

☐ Define an advertising agency and give examples of the main types of agencies.

☐ Explain what the various people in an advertising agency do.

☐ Describe the way advertising agencies are typically structured.

☐ Illustrate how agencies get new clients and how they make money in the business.

☐ Suggest how different types of advertisers might structure their advertising departments.

☐ Debate the advantages and disadvantages of an in-house advertising agency.

☐ Discuss the factors that affect the client-agency relationship and suggest ways to improve that relationship.

rank Perdue was being interviewed for an article in *Esquire* magazine. "I could say I planned all this," he said, "but I was just back there with my father and a couple of other guys working my ass off every day. I wasn't even sure for a long time that I even liked the chicken business. But my advantage is that I grew up having to know my business in every detail. I dug cesspools, made coops, and cleaned them out. I know I'm not very smart, at least from the point of view of pure IQ, and that gave me one prime ingredient of success—fear. I mean a man should have enough fear so that he's always second-guessing himself."

He pulled a wrinkled clipping from his wallet. The words were Alexander Hamilton's: "Men give me credit for some genius. All the genius I have lies in this. When I have a subject in hand, I study it profoundly. Day and night it is before me. I explore it in all its bearings. My mind becomes pervaded with it. Then the effort I have made is what people are pleased to call the fruit of genius. It is the fruit of labor and thought."

Chickens are not a very glamorous business. And Frank Perdue didn't know anything about advertising. But when Madison Avenue learned that this chicken farmer from the Delmarva Peninsula (located between the Chesapeake Bay on the west and the Atlantic Ocean on the east) was ready to take a big plunge into advertising, everybody scrambled for the account. So many people were fawning all over Perdue that it made him uncomfortable. He pulled back for a while.

To make sure that nobody put him in that position again, Perdue immersed himself in advertising day and night. He devoured great volumes on the subject, and he can still drop quotes by people like David Ogilvy and Rosser Reeves the way other people cite the Bible or Shakespeare. He haunted an advertising institute, studying all the pamphlets and textbooks. He called up advertising journalists and radio and TV station managers in New York, systematically trying to pick brains. Hardly anyone knew him, but many helped simply because they were impressed by his industrious curiosity.

By the time he was ready to be courted again by Madison Avenue, Perdue was an expert. Altogether, he interviewed almost 50 agencies, and eventually narrowed his list to a championship flight of nine. Then he really went on the offensive—grilling, double-checking, interviewing. He called one very prominent agency and asked its representatives to have lunch with him in the Oak Room of the Plaza Hotel. The whole top executive force trooped over to the Plaza, licking their chops, convinced Perdue was going to tell them he had selected their agency for his chickens. Instead, as soon as they settled at the table, Perdue announced they hadn't even made his final list, but he would appreciate it if they would rank the nine agencies still in the running. Stunned and flabbergasted, the agency boys dived into another round of martinis and patiently did as he requested.

The losers were really the lucky ones. When Perdue called up Ed McCabe, the copy chief at Scali, McCabe, Sloves, for about the 800th time in a week, McCabe finally blew his cork. "You know, Frank," he said, "I'm not even sure that we want your account anymore, because you're such a pain in the ass." McCabe recalls, "You know all he said to that? He just said, 'Yeah, I know I'm a pain in the ass, and now that we've got that settled, here's what I want to ask you this time.'"

Sometime later, Perdue picked McCabe's agency. One of the first commercials they shot, in a campaign built around Perdue himself (another idea he never cottoned to), won an award for excellence. Ed McCabe won more honors than any other copywriter in the nation that year because of his work on the Perdue campaign. Frank Perdue, pictured in Exhibit 3-1,

IT TAKES A TOUGH MAN TO MAKE A TENDER CHICKEN.

When it comes to chicken, Frank Perdue is a tough bird. His standards are even higher than the Government's. In fact 30% of the chickens that U.S.D.A. inspectors call Grade A don't make the grade with him.

And even though it costs him an extra $3 million a year, he refuses to freeze or blast-chill his chickens the way so many others do. Perdue fresh, young chickens are packed in ice and shipped to arrive fresh, not freshly defrosted.

He won't allow his chickens to be fed a diet that costs chicken feed, either. Perdue chickens are raised on a more expensive, all-natural diet that consists mainly of corn, soybean meal, and marigold petals. Which explains why they always have that distinctive, healthy, golden-yellow glow. And why they're always so moist, tender, and delicious.

What Frank Perdue will do is give you your money back—no questions asked—if you're not completely satisfied.

Now you know why he's so tough.

PERDUE FRESH Young Chicken

EXHIBIT 3-1

Frank Perdue appeared in more than 100 commercials promoting the features that make his chickens better. Always the reluctant model, Perdue had to be persuaded to appear in ads by agency creatives who strongly believed that his image could sell poultry.

became the biggest chicken man in the nation's biggest city and a celebrity to boot.

The rest is history. Perdue's sales doubled every two years. Throughout the 1980s, as fast-food and convenience restaurants specializing in chicken proliferated, Perdue became one of the two major suppliers in the Northeast.[1] By 1990, Perdue Farms had 12,000 employees, was selling over 7 million broiler chickens and 2.8 million pounds of turkey per *week,* and realizing revenues of over $1.1 billion per year.[2] That makes Perdue Farms the fourth largest poultry producer in the nation and one of the top 50 private companies in the United States. But after appearing in over 100 commercials and spending untold millions of dollars to promote his birds, Frank Perdue may be as much in the advertising business as in the chicken business.

As Frank once said to a magazine interviewer: "I could write a book about advertising."[3]

WHO MAKES UP THE ADVERTISING BUSINESS?

Like Frank Perdue, many people who consider themselves a part of some other industry become involved with advertising as well. That's because virtually every successful organization does some sort of advertising. When you add advertising agencies and their personnel to the numbers, you find a large, complex, and pervasive industry.

The Organizations

The advertising business is composed of two main groups—advertisers and agencies. The **advertisers** (or *clients*) are the companies that, like Perdue Farms, advertise themselves and their products. Advertisers range in size from small independent stores to huge multinational firms and in type from small industrial concerns to large service organizations. Assisting them are the **advertising agencies** that plan, create, and prepare advertising campaigns and materials for the advertisers.

In addition to these two groups are the **media,** which sell time (in electronic media) and space (in print media) to carry the advertiser's message to the target audience. And finally, there is another group known as the **suppliers.** These include the photographers, illustrators, printers, typesetters, video production houses, and many others who assist both advertisers and agencies in the preparation of advertising materials.

This chapter examines the two main groups—advertisers and agencies: who they are, what they do, and how they work together to create effective advertising. Subsequent chapters deal with both the media and the suppliers of advertising to provide a picture of the full breadth and complexity of the advertising business and also the career opportunities in the field (the latter are covered in detail in Appendix C).

The People

Many of us think of advertising people as the copywriters and art directors who work for the advertising agencies. But in reality, the people who work for the clients are also very much involved in the advertising business. In fact, the majority of people in advertising are employed by the advertisers. Virtually every company has an advertising department of some size, even if it is just one person who shares the advertising responsibility with other job functions.

The importance of the company's advertising people varies, depending on several factors: the size of the company, the type of industry in which it operates, the size of the advertising program, the role of advertising in the company's marketing mix, and most of all, the involvement of the firm's top management in the advertising function.

Company presidents and other top executives, who are naturally quite interested in how their company or product is portrayed, are often directly involved in advertising decisions. Sales and marketing personnel frequently provide input to the creative process, assist in choosing the advertising agency, and help evaluate proposed advertising programs.

Large companies may have a separate advertising department employing from one to several hundred people and headed by an advertising manager who reports to a marketing director or marketing services manager, as shown in Exhibit 3-2. These departments often resemble advertising agencies in structure and function.

Creative people—artists, writers, and photographers—are employed by the advertising departments of large companies and by independent advertising agencies to produce the ads. Their work is coordinated by someone who takes responsibility for the entire campaign or product—perhaps a creative director or a product manager.

Product engineers and designers often make recommendations about product features or provide information about competitive products. Similarly, administrative people in accounting or purchasing frequently consider the impact of advertising programs on the company's financial status or help determine appropriate budgets for the next campaign.

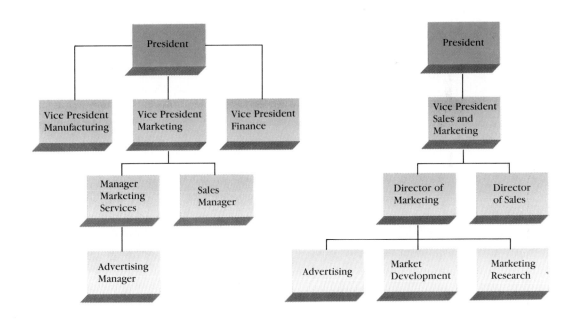

EXHIBIT 3-2

Many large companies have a separate advertising department. Their "clients" are the other departments within the company, and they offer writing, art, multimedia, and media placement services. Smaller ad departments generally send work to subcontractors, while large departments handle the majority of work on-site.

Even the clerical staff may get involved in the advertising process by virtue of their position within the organization and their knowledge of company activities. It is not uncommon, in fact, for secretaries in small firms to be promoted to the position of administrative assistant and eventually to manager of a department like advertising.

WHAT ADVERTISING PEOPLE DO: FUNDAMENTAL TASKS

The ways advertising departments and agencies function are as varied as the people who operate them. Regardless of how responsibilities are divided, however, all advertisers and agencies must do certain things. They all must understand and have some expertise in communications to perform the basic functions necessary to a successful advertising program. These functions include administering, planning, budgeting, coordinating, and creating.

Administration

Organizing and staffing the advertising department or agency and supervising and controlling its activities are normal administrative functions. An advertising manager (or committee) is also responsible for recommending specific advertising programs based on the client's marketing plans and budgets. It is imperative, therefore, that the advertising manager thoroughly understand the major factors influencing the client's marketing activities. Advertising managers should also establish an efficient procedure for handling inquiries, analyzing competitive advertising, and evaluating their own ads.

Planning

Occasionally it is necessary to draw up formal advertising proposals for management's approval, but meanwhile the planning process should be ongoing. Planning is a constant and never-ending process of defining and redefining goals and objectives, developing strategies, scheduling advertisements, and evaluating advertising results. The development of marketing and advertising plans is discussed in greater detail in Chapter 7.

Budgeting

The advertising budget is usually determined annually or semiannually. The advertising manager formulates the budget and presents it to top management, which always has the last word on how much will actually be allocated to advertising functions. The advertising manager then sees that the budget is followed and not squandered on items on the black list in Exhibit 3-3 before each of the advertising tasks has been performed.

Coordination

Business activities usually fall into three broad functional areas: production, finance, and marketing. Advertising, like sales, is a marketing activity. The

Chargeable	Debatable	Not chargeable
Space and time costs in regular media	Catalogs for consumers	Premium handling charges
Advertising consultants	Classified telephone directories	House-to-house sample distribution
Ad-pretesting services	Space in irregular publications	Packaging charges for premium promotions
Institutional advertising	Advertising aids for salespeople	Cost of merchandise for tie-in promotions
Industry directory listings	Financial advertising	Product tags
Readership or audience research	Dealer help literature	Showrooms
Media costs for consumer contests, premium and sampling promotions	Contributions to industry ad funds	Testing new labels and packages
Ad department travel and entertainment expenses	Direct mail to dealers and jobbers	Package design and artwork
Ad department salaries	Office supplies	Cost of non-self-liquidating premiums
Advertising association dues	Point-of-sale materials	Consumer education programs
Local cooperative advertising	Window display installation costs	Product publicity
Direct mail to consumers	Charges for services performed by other departments	Factory signs
Subscriptions to periodicals and services for ad department	Catalogs for dealers	House organs for salespeople
Storage of advertising materials	Test-marketing programs	Signs on company-owned vehicles
	Sample requests generated by advertising	Instruction enclosures
	Costs of exhibits except personnel	Press clipping services
	Ad department share of overhead	Market research (outside produced)
	House organs for customers and dealers	Samples of middlemen
	Cost of cash value or sampling coupons	Recruitment advertising
	Cost of contest entry blanks	Price sheets
	Cross-advertising enclosures	Public relations consultants
	Contest judging and handling fees	Coupon redemption costs
	Depreciation of ad department equipment	Corporate publicity
	Mobile exhibits	Market research (company produced)
	Employee fringe benefits	Exhibit personnel
	Catalogs for salespeople	Gifts of company products
	Packaging consultants	Cost of deal merchandise
	Consumer contest awards	Share of corporate salaries
		Cost of guarantee refunds
		Share of legal expenses
		Cost of detail or missionary people
		Sponsoring recreational activities
		Product research
		House organs for employees
		Entertaining customers and prospects
		Scholarships
		Plant tours
		Annual reports
		Outright charity donations

EXHIBIT 3-3

These three lists identify those budget items that should be charged to the advertising budget (white), items that are debatable (gray), and items that should not be charged to it (black).

advertising manager, therefore, must coordinate advertising activities with other marketing functions, as well as with production and finance activities. For example, sales and advertising people often determine which product and packaging features may improve customer satisfaction, and they must communicate that information to the production department. The accounting department may be consulted for records on overhead, ad production, and media costs, because controlling costs is a joint responsibility. Similarly, the agency's or client's legal department helps protect the company from trademark and copyright infringement and keep it from inadvertently violating truth-in-advertising laws.

Advertising departments and agencies are also the liaison between the firm and outside advertising services such as the media and suppliers. The department or agency has the responsibility of screening and analyzing the various services available, making recommendations to management, and (usually) deciding which outside services to use. The advertising manager then supervises and evaluates the work performed.

Creating Ads

The creative function is the most visible of advertising's fundamental tasks. It consists of three main elements, all overseen by the advertising manager: copywriting, art direction, and production. The end product is a combination of words and pictures that depicts goods or services to prospective customers. Without some creative output, the advertising agency or department would have little purpose.

We discuss the creative elements in detail in Chapters 8 through 11. But now we'll take a closer look at how advertising people are organized and the two major groups that employ them: the agencies and the clients.

THE ADVERTISING AGENCY

Why would a shrewd businessperson like Frank Perdue, who spends millions of dollars a year advertising his chickens, want to hire an advertising agency? Couldn't he save money by hiring his own people and creating his own advertising in-house? And how does Scali, McCabe, Sloves win such a multi-million-dollar advertising account? Must an agency's accounts all be that big for the agency to make money? And how do smaller agencies make money?

A discussion of the agency side of the advertising business can shed some light on these issues and give a clearer understanding of why so many advertisers use agencies.

The Role of the Advertising Agency

An **advertising agency** is an independent organization of creative people and businesspeople who specialize in developing and preparing advertising plans, advertisements, and other promotional tools. The agency also arranges or contracts for the purchase of advertising space and time in the various media. It does all this on behalf of different advertisers, or sellers—its **clients**—in an effort to find customers for their goods and services.[4]

This definition offers some good clues as to why so many advertisers hire advertising agencies. First, the definition points out that agencies are independent: They are not owned by the advertiser, the media, or the suppliers. This independence allows the agency to bring an outside, objective viewpoint to the advertiser's business. Good agencies possess the savvy, skill, and competence to serve the needs of a variety of clients because of their daily exposure to a broad spectrum of marketing situations and problems. The needs of some clients can be immense. Ad Lab 3-A provides an overview of the extent of the ad agency business in the United States.

The agency employs specialists in applying the complex art and science of advertising to business problems. They include administrators and other businesspeople, and writers, artists, market and media analysts, researchers, or other specialists. They have day-to-day contact with outside professional suppliers who illustrate advertisements, take photographs, set type, retouch art, shoot commercials, and record sound—all the steps required to produce quality work. They keep abreast of the latest advances in technology, the most recent changes in prices, and the most current production problems.

The agency provides yet another service to the client by arranging and contracting for the purchase of broadcast time and magazine or newspaper space. For one thing, it saves the client money. Most media allow the agency to keep 15 percent of the gross amount of money placed in their medium.

AD LAB 3-A
How Big Is the Agency Business?

Although New York, Los Angeles, and Chicago are the three leading advertising centers in North America (Toronto and Montreal being the major centers in Canada), advertising today is a worldwide business. In fact, in 1990, Tokyo (with $22.2 billion in billings) was barely behind New York (with $24.7 billion) as the world advertising capital. Today, any city in the United States or Canada with at least 100,000 people has advertising agencies. And many small cities and towns support one or more agencies. Of over 10,000 agencies in the United States, however, the top 500 represent about $54 billion in domestic billing—that is, the amount of client money the agency spends on media and equivalent activities. That's almost half of all U.S. advertising expenditures.

Interestingly, the top 10 U.S. agencies (which account for approximately one-tenth of 1 percent of all agencies) handle over 50 percent of the total volume of business done by the top 500 agencies—and that's just their U.S. billing. Many of them have overseas operations equal to or greater than their U.S. billings (see table).

An estimated 73,000 people are employed in the United States by the top 500 domestic advertising agencies today. Most agencies, however, have a low "body count" compared with that of other professions. When an agency staff is well balanced in skills and versatility, only five or six people can easily handle $1 million in annual billing. In agencies that bill $20 million or more per year, this ratio is usually even lower.

Basic information about advertising agencies in the United States can be found in the *Standard Directory of Advertising Agencies*. Known as the "Red Book" because of its cover color, this guide to the industry lists the names and addresses of most of the nation's agencies by state. It names the associations to which they belong, if any, and the media associations that recognize them for credit purposes. It also lists each agency's annual billings by media classification, the names and titles of its executives, and the names of its current accounts.

A related volume, the *Standard Directory of Advertisers*, lists the names of thousands of U.S. companies that advertise and the names and titles of their executives. Also cited are the names of their advertising agencies, their total annual advertising budget, and the principal media they use.

Laboratory Application

From your library, obtain a copy of the agency "Red Book." Are agencies in your town listed? If so, how many? If not, what is the town nearest you that has agency listings? How many?

Top 10 U.S.-Based Consolidated Agencies in Worldwide Gross Income (millions of dollars)

Rank (income)	Agency	Worldwide gross income 1990	Rank (billings)	Worldwide billings 1990
1	Young & Rubicam	$1,001.4	(1)	$7,519
2	Saatchi & Saatchi Advertising Worldwide	825.7	(2)	5,709
3	Ogilvy & Mather Worldwide	775.3	(3)	5,375
4	McCann-Erickson Worldwide	744.7	(5)	4,994
5	BBDO Worldwide	723.8	(4)	5,222
6	Backer Spielvogel Bates Worldwide	715.6	(6)	4,899
7	J. Walter Thompson Co.	690.7	(7)	4,852
8	Lintas: Worldwide	676.5	(9)	4,510
9	DDB Needham Worldwide	625.2	(8)	4,592
10	Grey Advertising	583.3	(11)	3,910

U.S.-based consolidated agencies are ranked by worldwide gross income and billings. D'Arcy Masius Benton & Bowles is ranked 10th by billings.

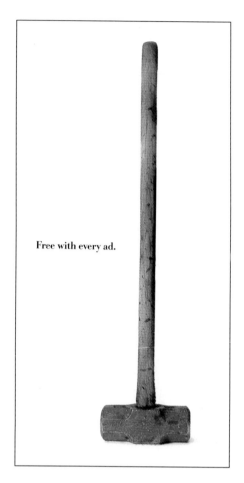

Free with every ad.

EXHIBIT 3-4

If a client wants the impact power of a sledgehammer, this ad suggests hiring Franklin Dallas Kundinger Advertising.

This **agency commission** reduces the amount of money the advertiser must pay the agency for its services. In return for this commission, the agency is expected to maintain an expertise in the various media available to the advertiser. This is no small task.

Finally, agencies work for a variety of different sellers (advertisers) to find customers for their goods and services. Agencies work for their *clients,* not for the media or the suppliers. Their moral, ethical, financial, and sometimes even legal obligation is to their clients—to find the best prices, give the best-quality work, and help the clients grow and prosper. Just as a well-run business seeks professional help from an attorney, accountant, banker, or management specialist, advertisers use agencies because they are usually equipped to create more effective advertising (as promised in the agency ad in Exhibit 3-4)—and select more effective media—than the advertisers can do themselves. Today, almost all sizable advertisers rely on an advertising agency for expert, objective counsel and unique creative skills.

Types of Agencies

Advertising agencies are normally classified by the range of services they offer (full-service or à la carte) and by the type of business they handle (consumer or industrial).

Full-Service Agencies

The modern **full-service advertising agency** serves its clients in all areas of communications and promotion. Its services are essentially grouped into advertising and nonadvertising categories. Advertising services include planning, creating, and producing advertisements and performing research and media selection services. Nonadvertising functions run the gamut from packaging to public relations to producing sales promotion materials, annual reports, trade-show exhibits, and sales training materials.[5]

Full-service agencies include the general consumer agency and the business or industrial agency.

General Consumer Agencies A **general agency** is willing to represent the widest variety of accounts. In practice, however, it concentrates on consumer accounts—companies that make goods purchased chiefly by consumers. Soaps, cereals, automobiles, pet foods, and toiletries are examples. Most of the advertising produced by the general agency is placed in consumer media—television, radio, billboards, newspapers, and magazines—that are commissionable to the agency. As a result, the general agency has traditionally obtained most of its income from media commissions.

General agencies include the international superagencies and the other large firms in New York, Chicago, Los Angeles, Minneapolis, Montreal, and Toronto we frequently hear about: names like Saatchi & Saatchi; Ogilvy & Mather; Foote, Cone & Belding; Ayer; Cossette Marketing-Communications; and Young & Rubicam, which advertises its Canadian offices in Exhibit 3-5. However, they also include the thousands of smaller **entrepreneurial agencies** that inhabit every major city in the United States and Canada: Rubin/Postaer, Los Angeles; Ruhr/Paragon, Minneapolis; Lyle Goodis and Associates, Toronto; BCP, Montreal; The Martin Agency, Richmond.

Profit margins in the entrepreneurial agencies are often slim, but their service is often more responsive to the smaller clients they serve, and their

RESIST THE USUAL.
YOUNG&RUBICAM

EXHIBIT 3-5

Young & Rubicam Canada, a general agency, couldn't resist the urge to run this ad to promote its un-"usual" creative nerve.

work is frequently startling in its creativity.[6] Moreover, some entrepreneurial agencies have carved a niche for themselves by serving the needs of particular market segments. These include, for example, the many agencies now proliferating that produce ethnic specialty ads like the one shown in Exhibit 3-6. The better known of these shops include: Bermudez Associates, Los Angeles; Castor Spanish International, New York; Burrell Advertising, Chicago; and Sosa & Associates, San Antonio, to name just a few.

Industrial Agencies An **industrial agency** represents clients that make goods to be sold to other businesses. Computer hardware and software, smelting furnaces, locomotives, and radium counters are examples of such goods. Business and industrial advertising is a very important aspect of the profession, requiring highly developed technical knowledge plus the ability to translate it into precise and persuasive communications.

Most **industrial** (also called **business-to-business**) **advertising** (such as the ad for *Crain's New York Business* in Exhibit 3-7) is placed in trade magazines and other business publications. These media are commissionable, but since their circulation is smaller, their rates are far lower than those of consumer media. The commissions are usually not large enough to cover the cost of the agency's services, so industrial agencies frequently charge the client an additional service fee. Though this can be expensive, especially for small advertisers, the failure to obtain an industrial agency's expertise may carry an even higher price tag in lost marketing opportunities.[7]

Business and industrial agencies may be large international firms like Maclaren/Lintas in Toronto, or like HCM/New York, which handles such major industrial corporations as Ashland Chemical, IBM, and United Technologies; or they may be smaller firms experienced in such specialized areas as recruitment advertising (help wanted), health and medicine, or electronics.

EXHIBIT 3-6

As awareness of the opportunities presented by ethnic markets has grown, so has the number of ad agencies specializing in ads aimed at those market segments. Ethnic specialty ads typically feature an individual from the particular ethnic group being targeted and usually appear in publications, or are broadcast on shows, whose audiences are primarily from that ethnic background.

EXHIBIT 3-7

This business-to-business ad created by Goldsmith/Jeffrey, New York, for *Crain's New York Business* magazine uses tongue-in-cheek humor to dramatize that 70 percent of its readers are corporate CEOs, chairmen, and presidents. The ad is aimed at people in the advertising trade to convince them to use the magazine as an advertising medium for their clients. Goldsmith/Jeffrey produces consumer as well as business-to-business advertising.

70% of our subscribers happen to be well-known CEOs, Chairmen, and Presidents. Out of respect for their anonymity, our lawyers have requested we not print their pictures but this innocuous stock photo instead.

CRAIN'S NEW YORK BUSINESS
To advertise, call (212) 210-0250.

A *la Carte Services*

In recent years, the trend toward specialization has produced a number of offshoots from the agency business. Among these are the small agency-type groups called *creative boutiques* and specialty businesses such as *media-buying services*.

Creative Boutiques Some talented specialists—like art directors, designers, and copywriters—set up their own creative services, or **creative boutiques.** Working for advertisers and occasionally subcontracting to advertising agencies, their mission is to develop exciting creative concepts and to produce fresh, distinctive advertising messages.

Because advertising effectiveness depends largely on originality in concept, design, and writing, advertisers tend to value this quality highly. However, the boutique's creative services usually do not include the marketing and sales direction that full-service agencies offer. This tends to limit the boutique to the role of a creative supplier.

For small advertisers, though, the creativity, responsiveness, and economy of the creative boutique are often worth these trade-offs. Moreover, good creative boutiques can be found in almost every metropolitan area.

Media-Buying Services As a counterpart to the creative boutiques, some experienced media specialists set up organizations that purchase and package radio and television time. The largest of these **media-buying services** is Western International Media in Los Angeles, which places over $720 million worth of media advertising annually for clients such as Walt Disney Co., Arco, USAir, and Times-Mirror Corp.[8] But there are many smaller ones such as Creative

Media, Inc., in New York, which places media for advertisers such as Citibank, AIWA, Great Cuts, and VISA.

Media-buying services owe their success in part to the fact that radio and TV time is "perishable"; that is, a 60-second radio spot at 8 P.M. cannot be sold after that hour has arrived. Thus, radio and television stations try to presell as much advertising time as possible and discount their rates to anyone who buys a large amount of time. The media-buying service negotiates a special discount rate with radio and TV stations and then sells this time to advertising agencies or advertisers.

As part of their service, media-buying firms provide their customers (both clients and agencies) with a detailed analysis of the media buy. Once the media package is sold, the buying service orders the spots on each station involved, verifies performance, sees to it that stations "make good" for any spots missed, and even pays the media bills.

Compensation methods used by media-buying services vary. Some receive a set fee. Others operate on an incentive basis, receiving a prescribed percentage of the money they save the client.

What Agency People Do

The American Association of Advertising Agencies (AAAA) is the national organization of the advertising agency business. It maintains very high membership standards and endeavors to be the most responsible speaker for the advertising industry. Its 750 agency members, representing the largest and oldest agencies in the business, place almost 80 percent of all national advertising handled by agencies in the United States—plus a large portion of the local and regional advertising.[9]

The AAAA *Service Standards* explains that an agency's purpose is to interpret to the public, or to desired segments of the public, information about a legally marketed product or service. How does it do this? First, the agency studies the client's product to determine its strengths and weaknesses. Next, it analyzes the present and potential market for the product. Then, using its knowledge of the channels of distribution, sales, and the available media, the agency formulates a plan for carrying the advertiser's message to consumers, wholesalers, dealers, or contractors.

Finally comes execution of the plan. That includes writing, designing, and producing ads and commercials, contracting for media space and time, verifying media insertions, and billing for services and media used.

The agency also cooperates with the client's marketing staff to enhance the effect of advertising through package design, sales research and training, and production of sales literature and displays.[10] This collateral material is often produced internally by the client's own staff, but the agency's creative expertise can prove invaluable.[11]

To understand these various functions more fully, let's look at all the agency people who were probably involved—directly or indirectly—in the creation, production, placement, or supervision of the ad in Exhibit 3-8 for Perdue Chickens. Scali, McCabe, Sloves, the agency Frank Perdue selected to handle his account, was not one of New York's largest agencies. In fact, at the time it was one of the smaller shops, but it had piled up an impressive record of award-winning advertising with several other accounts, such as Nikon and Dictaphone. As a full-service agency, Scali, McCabe, Sloves provides all the services suggested by the AAAA service standards.

EXHIBIT 3-8

Scali, McCabe, Sloves was a relatively small shop when Frank Perdue gave the agency his account, but it had won many awards, a factor that some advertisers find reassuring when choosing an agency.

Account Management

Scali, McCabe, Sloves's account management team is an essential part of the agency's organization. **Account executives (AEs)** are the liaison between the agency and the client. Responsible on the one hand for mustering all the agency's services for the benefit of the client and on the other hand for representing the agency's point of view to the client, the account executive is often caught in the middle. AEs, therefore, are virtually in business for themselves. It has been said that they must be tough, tactful, diplomatic, creative, communicative, persuasive, knowledgeable, sensitive, honest, and courageous—all at once. And they must be on time for meetings.[12]

Scali, McCabe, Sloves and other large agencies have many account executives who report to **management** (or **account**) **supervisors,** who in turn report to the agency's director of account services.

To survive, agencies must grow. The best creative people always want to work for the "hot shops," the ones attracting all the new business and receiving all the awards for outstanding advertising. Growth requires a steady flow of new projects, and this is usually the responsibility of account management people. Sometimes new assignments arise from new products developed by existing clients. In other cases, clients may seek out agencies whose work they are familiar with. Scali, McCabe, Sloves receives 15 to 20 calls per week, for example, because they are well known for the work they have done on Perdue Chickens, Maxell recording tape, Pella windows, and other major campaigns.

Most agencies keep a constant eye open for new business and assign certain account managers or agency principals—as in Exhibit 3-9—to targeting prospective clients and selling the agency's services.

EXHIBIT 3-9

Using one-line statements (clichés often heard in the ad business) that imply the failures of the competition, Gigante Vaz & Partners placed this ad in the trade publications to tout its strengths. The "competing" agency names are fictitious.

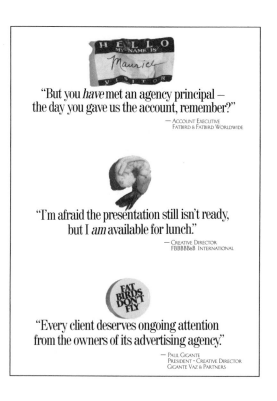

Research

Clients and agencies must give artists all the information they need to do a job—because advertising is based on information. An agency's staff of artists and copywriters can't be expected to create on intuition alone. Before any advertising is created, therefore, agencies must research the uses and advantages of the product, analyze the current and potential customers, and try to determine what will influence them to buy. Chapters 5 and 6 discuss some of the many types of research conducted by advertising agencies to discover this information.

Planning

The planning process actually begins before research and continues afterward. For the Perdue account, Sam Scali, Ed McCabe, and Alan Pesky, the director of account services, initiated this process with the client to determine Perdue's marketing and advertising objectives. They then met with the agency's market analysts, media planners, and other creative people to determine the appropriate advertising strategy. The results of research were considered, and the evaluation of the agency's planning team was then distilled into a detailed marketing and advertising plan. Once the client approves this plan, it becomes the blueprint for the agency's creative and media program. (This process is discussed in depth in Chapter 7.)

Creative Concepts

Most advertising relies heavily on **copy**—the words that make up the headline and message of the ad. People like Ed McCabe who create these words are called **copywriters.** Their work requires the skill to condense all that can be said about a product into a few points that are salient and pertinent to a given advertisement. Thus, what copywriters *don't* say is often just as important as what they *do* say. Copywriters usually work closely with the agency artists and production staff.

The agency art department is composed of art directors (like Sam Scali) and graphic designers whose primary job is to **lay out** advertising—that is, to illustrate in sketches how the various components of an ad fit together. When their assignment is to conceive a television commercial, the artists lay it out in a comic-strip series of sequential frames called a **storyboard.**

Most large agencies have their own art departments. The ad in Exhibit 3-10, for example, is seeking a new art director for a St. Louis advertising agency. Other shops prefer to purchase art services from independent studios or outside free-lance designers (discussed in Chapter 9).

Advertising Production: Print and Broadcast

Once the advertisement is designed and written and the client approves it, the ad goes into production. This is the responsibility of the agency's print production manager or broadcast producers and directors (discussed in Chapters 10 and 11).

For print advertising, the production department buys type, photographs, illustrations, and other components needed for the finished art. Production personnel then work with photoplatemakers, color separators, and other graphic arts suppliers to obtain the materials needed for the media.

If the ad is a broadcast commercial, the broadcast production personnel take the approved script or the storyboard and set about producing the finished product. Working with actors, camerapeople, and the production specialists (studios, directors, editors), they produce the commercial on tape (for radio) or on film or videotape (for television).

Media

When Frank Perdue started advertising his chickens, the agency recommended subway posters as an initial medium for three reasons: It required only a small budget, the art could be used again in butcher-shop windows, and the message would be read by the target market (working mothers and lower- to middle-income groups). Later, as the campaign developed and more money became available, more expensive media (newspapers and TV) were used.

The media director's job is to match the profile of the desired target market with the profiles of the audiences of a wide range of media. The media are then evaluated for efficiency and cost, and the media director recommends the best medium or media combination to use (covered in Chapter 12).

Unbiased and authenticated media information is one of the most valuable services an agency can offer the client.

Traffic

One of the greatest sins in the advertising agency business is to miss a deadline—and the whole business revolves around deadlines. If Scali, McCabe, Sloves misses the deadline for an ad in a monthly trade magazine read by Purdue's grocers, they will have to wait another whole month for that ad to appear. That would not please Frank Perdue—or any other client.

The job of the agency traffic department, therefore, is to make sure the work flow is smooth and efficient. It coordinates all phases of production and checks to see that everything is completed on time and that the media receive all ads and commercials before the deadline.

As the keystone position in the agency, the traffic department is often the first position for entry-level college graduates and is an excellent place to learn agency operations. (See Appendix C for information on careers in advertising.)

Additional Services

Many agencies provide a variety of additional services and employ specialists to perform these tasks. Scali, McCabe, Sloves, for instance, has a highly regarded sales promotion department used by most of the firm's clients to produce dealer ads, window posters, point-of-purchase displays, dealer contest materials, and sales material.

Other agencies maintain public relations and direct-marketing specialists, home economics experts, package designers, or economists, depending on the nature and needs of their clients.

Agency Administration

Like any business, an agency requires management. Prospective employees, for example, must be interviewed and then hired, trained, and periodically reviewed. In small agencies, this function may be handled by the firm's principals; but in large agencies, a well-staffed personnel department is a must. Large agencies may also have people occupied in data processing, purchasing, financial analysis, insurance, and even real estate and property maintenance functions.

It has been said that agencies are as much in the bookkeeping business as in the advertising business. Scali, McCabe, Sloves, for example, receives invoices every day from radio and TV stations, magazines, newspapers, billboard companies, transit companies, type houses, platemakers, free-lance artists and illustrators, talent agencies, photographers, television production companies, sound studios, music producers, printers, and so on. These bills are totaled by the accounting department on periodic invoices to the clients. When client payments are received and recorded, the accounting department then pays all the media and outside suppliers.

Dealing with variations in media commissions, agency markups, errors in invoices, cash discounts, and the complex flow of large amounts of cash for dozens of clients requires a highly competent accounting staff. At the same time, the staff must monitor the agency's income and expenses and keep management informed of the company's financial status.

In short, an advertising agency is a business, and to succeed, it must be run like one.

How Agencies Are Structured

An advertising agency organizes its functions, operations, and personnel according to its size, the types of accounts it serves, and whether it is local, regional, national, or international.

In small agencies (annual billings of less than $10 to $15 million), each person often wears many hats. A typical structure is illustrated in Exhibit 3-11. The owner or president usually supervises daily business operations and may be in charge of new business development as well. Account executives and account supervisors generally handle client contact. The account executive may also produce creative concepts for the clients and even write copy. Artwork may be produced by an inside art director or purchased from an independent studio or free-lance designer. Most small agencies have a production and traffic department or an employee who fulfills these functions. They also may have a media buyer, but in very small agencies the account executives also purchase media time and space for their accounts.

Medium and large agencies generally have a more formal organization and are usually structured in a departmental or group system.

In the **departmental system,** each of the agency's varied functions—account services, creative services, marketing services, and administration—is set up as a separate department, as shown in Exhibit 3-12. Each department is called on as needed to perform its specialty. The account executive handles the client contact, the **creative department** writes the ad and lays it out, marketing services selects media, and so forth.

But as agencies get larger they tend to use the **group system,** in which the agency is divided into a number of "little" agencies or groups, as shown in Exhibit 3-13. The group may serve only one large account or, in many cases, three or four smaller clients. Each group, headed by an account supervisor, comprises account executives, copywriters, art directors, a media director, and any other specialists required to serve the particular needs of that group's clients. A very large agency may have dozens or more groups. It may even have separate production and traffic units to serve each one.

In small agencies, the line between the head of the agency and the lowest-level personnel is fairly short and direct. In such cases, the agency head has more control over ad development and management.

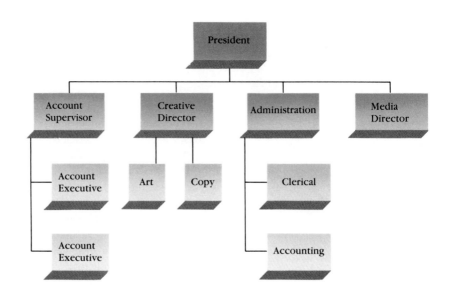

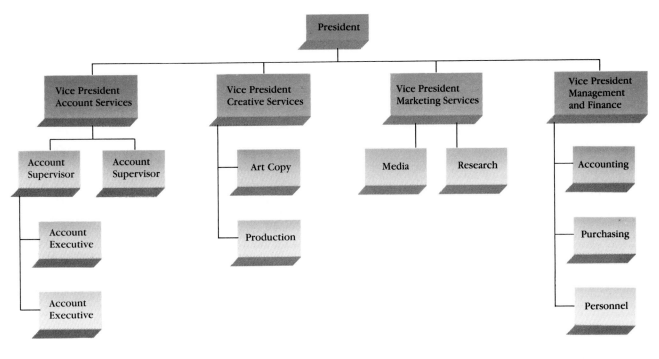

EXHIBIT 3-12

In the departmental system, each of the agency's varied functions—account services, creative services, marketing services, and administration—is relatively independent in operation and offers a specialized role. Often, departments can become autonomous to the point where flexibility is decreased.

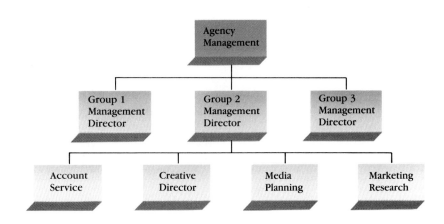

EXHIBIT 3-13

In the group system, a large agency is divided into a number of smaller "agencies" or groups. Each group is composed of all the personnel required to serve the needs of that group's clients. This system helps huge agencies remain flexible in times when rush work or unique solutions are needed.

Each of these systems has its advantages. The organization that best enables the agency to provide its services effectively, efficiently, and profitably is the one that should be implemented.

How Agencies Make Money

Like any other business, an advertising agency must make a fair profit on the services it renders. Lately, though, achieving this profit has become more and more difficult. The megamerger trend, the reduction of traditional media advertising budgets, shifts in promotional emphasis from media advertising to sales promotion vehicles, increased production costs, and the fragmentation of media vehicles have all cut into agency profits. Moreover, the amount of agency service needed differs from client to client, which forces agencies to develop various compensation methods in order to arrive at an equitable financial arrangement.[13] Basically, agencies make money from three sources: *media commissions, markups* on outside purchases, and *fees* or *retainers*. We discuss each of these briefly below.

Media Commissions

Agencies save the media considerable expense in sales and collections. So, historically, the major media have allowed recognized agencies to retain a 15 percent **media commission** on any space or time they purchase for their clients. (For outdoor advertising, the commission is usually 16⅔ percent.) The way this system works is simple. Assume you are an advertiser and plan to spend $1,000 on a magazine ad for your company. Your agency buys the space from the magazine, places the order, and delivers the ad to the magazine. When the ad appears, the magazine bills the agency $1,000. The agency then bills you $1,000. You pay the agency the total amount. The agency then keeps its 15 percent commission ($150) and sends $850 to the magazine. If you spent $1 million, the agency's commission would be $150,000, and it would remit $850,000 to the media. For large accounts (those billing more than $10 million annually), the agency has traditionally provided its creative services, media services, and accounting and account management services—plus a host of other *free* services such as public relations or sales promotion assistance—for this fee. Agencies are now beginning to insist that clients pay for free services.[14] For smaller accounts, the commission is usually not enough to cover the cost of even basic services, so the agency requires additional compensation.

Markups

To create a magazine ad, the agency normally buys type, photography, illustrations, and a variety of other services or materials from outside suppliers. These suppliers do not normally allow agency commissions, so the agency buys these services and adds a markup to the client's bill.

Traditionally, advertising agencies have added a 17.65 percent markup to outside purchases. The reason for this figure goes back to the tradition of the

15 percent commission. When you add 17.65 percent to an invoice, the amount added becomes 15 percent of the new total, as follows:

$$\$850 \ \times \ 17.65\% = \$150$$
$$\$850 \ + \ \$150 = \$1,000$$
$$\$1,000 \ \times \ 15\% = \$150$$

Thus, by adding a markup of 17.65 percent to, say, a photography bill of $850, the agency ends up with $150—or 15 percent of the total bill—the traditional agency commission.

Some media, especially local media, also do not allow agency commissions. Local newspapers, for example, may allow a commission on the higher rates they charge national advertisers but not on the lower rates charged to local advertisers. Therefore, advertising agencies using these media frequently use a markup formula of 17.65 percent to calculate a commission. In this case, when your firm places an ad costing $1,000, the agency bills you $1,176.50. The agency keeps the $176.50 markup and remits the $1,000 to the medium.

In recent years, many agencies have found that the 17.65 percent markup does not cover the cost of dealing with outside suppliers, especially on smaller accounts where the sums spent are minor. As a result, some agencies have increased their markups to as much as 20 to 25 percent. While this has helped, the squeeze on agency profits still tightens every year and has forced many agencies to move to a fee system in place of, or in addition to, commissions and markups.

Fees

Assume you are a very small advertising agency (fewer than 10 employees) with several local advertising clients. Perhaps your largest advertiser spends only $20,000 per month in commissionable media, yet you spend a lot of time servicing the account, providing in-depth media plans, staging in-store promotions, supervising press interviews, and developing posters and displays for windows and counters. It becomes obvious that the $3,000 per month you receive from the media commissions does not begin to cover the amount of work you, your secretary, art director, copywriter, and media person devote to this client. You need to charge your client an additional fee for your work to cover all of these costs. How do you determine a reasonable amount? Today, this question is being asked by large and small agencies alike as an increasing number of clients are seeking ways to compensate their agencies for solving client problems rather than for just placing media.[15]

Agencies that serve their clients on a fee basis usually use one of two pricing methods. The first is a **fee-commission** combination. With this method, the agency establishes a fixed monthly fee for all its services to the client. If, during a given month, the agency earns any media commissions for time or space purchased for the client, it retains these commissions in addition to the fee.

The second method is a **straight fee** or **retainer** and is similar to the retainers paid to attorneys or accountants for their legal and financial services. This is frequently used for services that produce no commission income, such as research for public relations, brochures, or annual reports.

Straight fee arrangements are also used for accounts in which media commissions are credited back to the client against the fee.

Recently, there has also been a new trend toward an **incentive system,** whereby the agency shares in the client's success when a campaign attains specific, agreed-upon goals. DDB Needham, for example, offers clients a "guaranteed results" program. If a campaign wins, the agency earns more; if it loses, the agency earns less. Kraft General Foods also rates the performance of its various agencies: A-graders get an extra 3 percent commission; C-graders are put on review.[16] This trend is typical of the predicted major issue of the 90s in agency-client relationships—accountability.

How Agencies Get Clients

To succeed, advertising agencies must have clients. But where do those clients come from? What can an agency do when it has a staff of artists, copywriters, account executives, media people, secretaries, and bookkeepers but not enough billing to pay the salaries?

An advertising agency, like any other business, has a product or a service to sell. Clients come to an advertising agency much the same way they come to an attorney, a doctor, a hairdresser, or a clothier: by referral, through advertising, because they were solicited, or because of reputation.

EXHIBIT 3-14

Although most major agencies get their new clients by referral, a few opt to advertise. In this example, Martin/Williams suggests that clients come to Minneapolis not for the weather but for the agency's outstanding creative work. Interestingly enough, Minneapolis has indeed become one of the major advertising centers in the United States.

Referrals

Most good advertising agencies get their clients by referral—from existing clients, from friends, or simply because of their reputations. The president of one company asks the president of another company who does those great ads, and the next week the agency gets a call. If an agency feels a prospective client may pose a conflict of interest with an existing client, it refers the new client to another agency.

In the case of local advertisers, media representatives frequently refer clients to an agency they have a working relationship with. It's important, therefore, for agencies to maintain good relationships with their existing clients, with the media, and with other agencies, and it is common practice to put the word out when they are looking for new business.

Solicitations for New Business

Lesser-known agencies cannot rely on referrals but must take a more aggressive approach, seeking new business through direct solicitation or any other means available. An agency may decide to openly solicit new business by advertising, writing solicitation letters, making "cold" calls on prospective clients, or following up leads from sources within the business. Few agencies simply advertise their services. The Martin/Williams agency ad in Exhibit 3-14 is an exception. One survey turned up some amusing answers as to why agencies don't advertise—considering the business they are in. Among the most common responses:

> "Advertising is not very effective."
> "We have never been able to agree on an advertising theme."
> "We have never budgeted for advertising."[17]

The important task of soliciting new business usually falls to one of the agency's principals, since the rest of the staff is normally assigned to the work of existing clients. Once a new business prospect has been found, however, staffers may be called in to help prepare the presentation.

Reputation and Community Relations

Agencies frequently find that their best source of business is simply their good reputation. Realizing that a good reputation takes a long time to develop, most agencies participate in activities that help raise their profile in the business community.

Many agencies submit their best ads to competitions to win awards and gain notoriety for their superior creativity. (Most of the ads in this text, for example, are award winners.) Some agencies work *pro bono* (for free) for charities or nonprofit organizations such as the Lung Association in Exhibit 3-15; others assist local politicians (although this may be controversial in some towns); and some are active in the arts, education, religion, or social circles. Some agencies give seminars; others write articles in magazines; and many others become active in advertising clubs or other professional organizations. All these activities help the agency become known and respected in the community.[18]

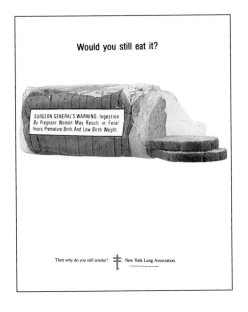

Would you still eat it?

SURGEON GENERAL'S WARNING: Ingestion By Pregnant Women May Result in Fetal Injury, Premature Birth, And Low Birth Weight.

Then why do you still smoke?   New York Lung Association.

EXHIBIT 3-15

This *pro bono* advertisement was created for a nonprofit organization, the New York Lung Association, and gives us a dramatic visual and a conceptual twist to drive home its point.

Presentations

Once an advertiser's management becomes interested in an agency, they may ask the agency to make a presentation. This may mean anything from a simple discussion of the agency's philosophy, experience, personnel, and track record to a full-blown audiovisual show complete with slides, films, sample commercials, or even proposed campaigns.

Some advertisers ask for or imply that they want the agency to make a **speculative presentation,** meaning they want to see what the agency would do for them before they hire them. But most agencies prefer to build their presentations around the work they have performed for other advertisers. This way, the agencies can demonstrate their versatility, philosophy, expertise, and depth of understanding of the marketplace and the client's business—without giving away their ideas.

The presentation process allows the agency and the advertiser to get to know each other before they commit to working together. Advertising is a very human business, and the advertiser-agency relationship is a peculiar kind of marriage. But as in any marriage, there must be mutual friendship, trust, and communication.

THE ADVERTISERS (CLIENTS)

Whether or not it uses an advertising agency, virtually every successful business uses advertising to help attract new customers and retain old ones. The size and function of a company's advertising department depends on a variety of factors, however—and so does the way the department is organized and managed.

Large Advertisers

No two firms, product lines, or markets are exactly alike. Therefore, the method of organization depends on the unique circumstances of each company. The two basic management structures that large companies use are *centralized* and *decentralized* organizations.

Centralized Organization

What do Wheaties, Betty Crocker, Red Lobster restaurants, and Garfield fruit snacks have in common? They are just a few of the many products owned and marketed by General Mills, Inc., of Minneapolis, Minnesota. One of the 20 largest national advertisers, General Mills operates a vast advertising and marketing services department with 350 employees and a $538 million annual advertising budget under its "Company of Champions" culture.[19]

General Mills' Marketing Services, located at corporate headquarters in Minneapolis, is really many departments within a department. As a **centralized advertising department,** it administers, plans, budgets, and coordinates the promotion of more than 50 brands. It also supervises 26 outside advertising agencies and operates its own in-house agency for new or smaller brands.

Organized around functional specialties (market research, media, graphics, copy), Marketing Services consults with General Mills' brand managers and consolidates many of their expenditures for maximum efficiency. The

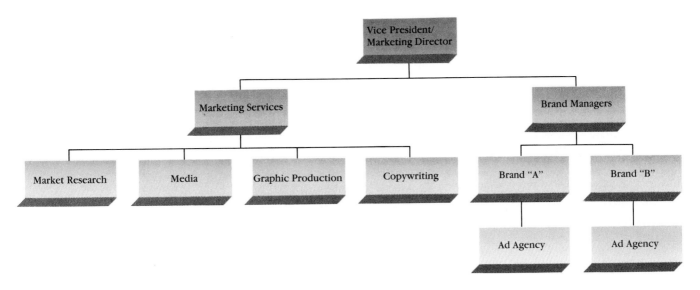

EXHIBIT 3-16

This is how General Mills operates its centralized advertising department. Typically, the advertising manager reports to a marketing vice president or marketing director. Other than this consistent feature, companies may organize their departments differently.

media department, for example, is involved daily in all media plans and dollar allocations with the various marketing divisions. The production and art services department handles the package design for all brands and the graphic requirements of the company's in-house agency. In addition, Betty Crocker Kitchens provides promotional services for the various marketing programs associated with Betty Crocker products.

The result is a highly effective series of mostly unrelated advertising programs for a wide variety of products and brands, all directed from one central spot. While this structure may sometimes make it more difficult for management to provide a general overview of marketing strategies and execution, it does give General Mills great efficiency in its advertising programs and affords the company appreciable savings.

The centralized advertising department is the most common type in large organizations for several reasons. For one thing, maintaining continuity in the company's various communications programs is more feasible than if the organization were decentralized—and the cost savings are substantial. Communication flows more easily in the organization. The need for several staffs of highly paid advertising specialists is eliminated. And lower-level personnel need not be exceptionally skilled or experienced in all areas because the firm's top management can assume some of the advertising decision making.

Exhibit 3-16 shows the centralized department at General Mills. Many companies organize their departments differently, however. Typically, the advertising manager reports to a marketing vice president, and the department is usually organized in one of five ways:

1. By product or brand.
2. By subfunction of advertising (such as sales promotion, print production, TV/radio buying, and outdoor advertising).
3. By end user (consumer products, industrial products).

4. By media (radio, television, newspapers, and so forth).

5. By geography (western advertising, eastern advertising).

The way these large centralized departments work depends primarily on management's philosophy, the firm's marketing needs, and the nature of the company's customers and products.

Decentralized Organization

As companies become larger, take on new brands or products, acquire subsidiaries, and establish divisions in several parts of the country (or several countries), a centralized advertising department often becomes highly impractical. A company may then begin to **decentralize** its advertising and establish departments assigned to the various divisions, subsidiaries, products, countries, regions, brands, or other categories that most suit its needs. The final authority for each division's advertising rests with the general manager of the particular division.

Procter & Gamble in Cincinnati, Ohio—commonly referred to as the nation's number-one marketing practitioner—is a 155-year-old, $24-billion company that manufactures and sells over 200 different consumer products internationally.[20] Many P&G brands are the leaders in their fields: Tide, Ivory soap, Pampers diapers, Duncan Hines cake mixes, Crisco shortening, Crest toothpaste (illustrated in Exhibit 3-17), and Charmin paper products, to mention just a few.

The nation's second-largest advertiser, with expenditures exceeding $1.7 billion annually, Procter & Gamble has eight consumer product divisions, five industrial product divisions, and four international divisions. Historically, each division has been set up almost like a separate company, with its own

research and development department, manufacturing plant, advertising department, sales force, and finance and accounting staff. Every brand within a division has a **brand manager,** two assistant brand managers, and one or two staff assistants. The whole purpose of this system is to ensure that each brand's manager contributes the single-minded drive and personal commitment necessary for success.[21]

The brand manager reports to an associate advertising manager who oversees three or four brand groups. The associate advertising manager reports to the division's advertising manager, who in turn is responsible to the division's general manager.[22] Each P&G brand manager has his or her own advertising agency that develops and creates the brand's media advertising. The division's advertising department helps coordinate sales promotion and merchandising programs across brands, and the corporate advertising department's media and research supervisors provide statistical information and guidance.

For new recruits fresh from college, P&G's brand manager development program has been legendary as the Marine Corps of marketing. Apprentice brand managers live with and learn the statistics of their brand's performance against competitors. They are assigned to work on store displays. They develop sales projections for their brand, help plan advertising budgets, and coordinate with other sections of the division's advertising department: media, copy, art and packaging, sampling and couponing, and legal. They learn how market research helps determine the package, scents, sizes, and colors people want; how product research improves the brand in response to competition; and how the division's sales force tries to muscle more shelf space for the brand in the supermarket.

This decentralized brand manager system, the most sacred of sacred cows at P&G for many years, has come under attack for a variety of ills. Primarily, it can no longer satisfy the needs of a rapidly changing marketplace, and it is too product-oriented rather than market-oriented.[23] As a result, in 1987, P&G reviewed the system and grafted onto it new executive titles such as "category" brand managers, "future" brand managers (for products planned for the future), and regional marketing managers. Competition between brand managers traditionally typified the old system, but the company has now developed teams that include manufacturing, sales, and research managers who all work together for the common good of the company.[24] While the system is still decentralized, many activities are becoming more centralized for economy, efficiency, and control. For example, the function of buying advertising space and time from the media—usually performed by agencies—is now sometimes performed by the company internally.[25]

For large, multidivision companies, decentralized advertising offers a number of advantages. For instance, it more easily conforms to the specific problems and needs of the division. Flexibility is increased, allowing quicker and easier adjustments in campaigns and media schedules. New approaches and creative ideas are introduced more easily. And the results of each division's advertising may be measured independently of the others. In effect, each division is its own marketing department, and the advertising manager reports to each division head as shown in the chart in Exhibit 3-18.

However, decentralized department heads sometimes tend to be more concerned with their own budgets, problems, and promotions than with determining what will benefit the firm as a whole. The potential power of repetitive corporate advertising is often diminished by the lack of uniformity in the advertising among divisions. Rivalry among brand managers may

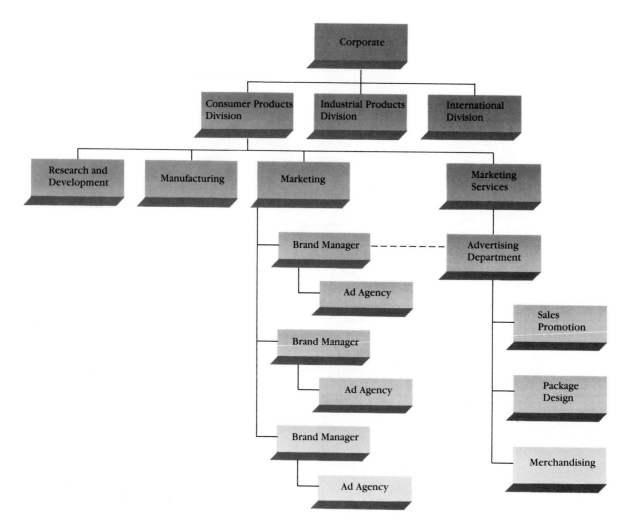

EXHIBIT 3-18

In a decentralized advertising department, each division is its own marketing department. This provides good flexibility for management and the creative staff.

become fierce and deteriorate into secrecy and jealousy. It is virtually impossible to standardize advertising styles, themes, or approaches. In fact, after one multidivision company decentralized, it had difficulty just getting the product brand managers to use the same logo in their various ads and brochures.

In summary, both centralized and decentralized advertising departments have their advantages. What works successfully in one market, though, may not work in the next. There are no constants in determining which form or organization is best. And no organizational structure is purely one form or the other. They are, in fact, all different and individually designed to fit the needs of the company.

The In-House Agency

Some companies have set up their own wholly owned **in-house agencies** (or *house agency*) in an effort to save money and centralize their advertising activities. Many large firms, including Bristol-Myers, Procter & Gamble, and General Foods, have turned to in-house media buying to monitor and control soaring media costs.[26]

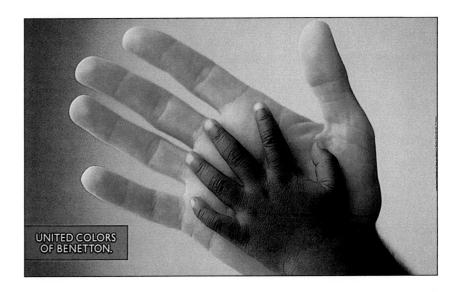

EXHIBIT 3-19

Many companies prefer to handle their own advertising and organize their own in-house agencies. This is especially true when people at the top are personally concerned about advertising quality—an important feature that helps sell certain products such as personal-care items and image products.

The full-service house agency is a total-capability advertising department, set up and staffed to do all the work of an independent full-service agency. All aspects of advertising creativity, production, and media placement are performed in-house. Being fully self-contained, it can develop and accomplish almost every type of advertising, publicity, and sales promotion the company requires.

Advertisers set up their own agencies for several reasons. Usually they hope to save money by cutting overhead expenses and keeping the 15 percent commission the agency typically gets for placing ads in the media. Moreover, with a house agency the company does not incur the standard markup on printing or art production, which ranges from 17.65 to 25 percent when such items are purchased through an outside agency.

Advertisers likewise feel they can receive more attention from their agency if the company is its only client. House agencies tend to have a greater depth of understanding of the company's products and markets, and they can usually respond better to pressure deadlines because they can focus their full resources on the project. Although outside agencies may be able to produce just as quickly, they often have to hire free-lance help, thereby incurring potentially large overtime charges.

Finally, many companies feel that management has better control of and involvement in the advertising when it is done in-house by company people—especially when the organization is a "single-business" company whose products and services are similar.[27] This top-level involvement has certainly been true in the case of Benetton's advertising pictured in Exhibit 3-19.

In spite of these advantages, many full-service house agencies do not succeed. In attempting to save as much of the independent agency's commission as possible, some companies sacrifice considerably more than they gain.

First, while the in-house agency offers greater flexibility, it is often at the expense of the creativity offered by outside agencies.[28] Large, independent agencies provide experience, versatility, and diverse talent. In-house agencies, on the other hand, typically find it quite difficult to attract and keep the best creative talent. In part, this may be because of the slower wage-raise policy in some corporations. But more important, creative people generally fear getting trapped in what they perceive to be a "stagnant" environment lacking the incentive, vitality, and stiff competition of the agency world.

Perhaps even worse than the loss of creativity is the loss of objectivity the independent agency normally brings to the client. Advertising suffers when it becomes company-oriented rather than consumer-oriented. By overly reflecting the internal politics, policies, and views of corporate management, it becomes stiff and self-serving. The result, all too often, is simply boring.

For years, advertisers and agencies have squabbled over the pros and cons of in-house advertising agencies. Independent agencies consider many house agencies to be nothing more than company ad departments, and they often resent the fact that the media allows these "intruders" to collect the commissions they feel should be reserved for "real" agencies. It's unlikely this argument will be settled in the near future.

Small Advertisers

A small retailer—say, a hardware, clothing, or electronics store—might have just one person in charge of advertising. That person, usually called the **advertising manager,** performs all the basic tasks discussed earlier—the administrative, planning, budgeting, and coordinating functions. In many cases, the advertising manager might also lay out the newspaper ads, write the advertising copy, and select the media to be used. However, unless the manager is also a commercial artist or graphic designer, it is unlikely that he or she physically creates the actual advertisements, setting type and doing the mechanical pasteup of materials (discussed in Chapter 10). On the other hand, a larger chain of stores might have a complete advertising department staffed and equipped to perform a range of activities internally. These may include *advertising production, media placement,* and *marketing support services.* We'll discuss each of these briefly.

Advertising Production

If a firm does not use an advertising agency, the advertising department may be responsible for creating and producing all advertising materials. This means writing the ads, designing the way they will look on the page or on TV, ordering type, arranging for photos or illustrations or broadcast talent, then assembling all the parts into a usable advertisement or commercial. The department would then need its own staff of artists, copywriters, and production specialists to produce this work, and the department's head would likely report to the company's sales or marketing manager, as diagrammed in Exhibit 3-20.

Media Placement

The people who work in company advertising departments often perform the media function, too. This means analyzing and evaluating available media vehicles according to coverage, cost, services to advertisers, and editorial content. The department would then develop media schedules in line with the budget, purchase media space and time, and verify performance.

EXHIBIT 3-20

A small advertiser with a high volume of advertising work—such as a regional department or grocery store chain—might set up an advertising department according to the structure outlined in this chart.

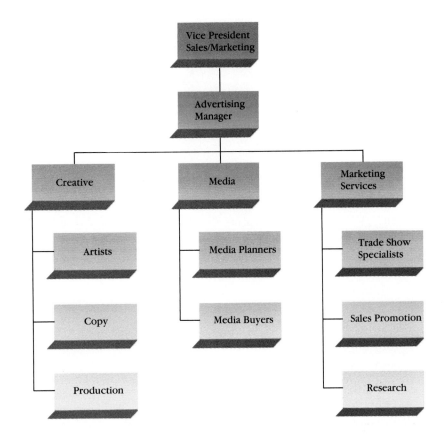

EXHIBIT 3-20

A small advertiser with a high volume of advertising work—such as a regional department or grocery store chain—might set up an advertising department according to the structure outlined in this chart.

Other Marketing Support Services

An advertising agency often is retained to prepare media advertising, while the company's advertising department performs other marketing support services such as producing sales materials and displays for distribution to managers, salespeople, dealers, and distributors.

Some advertisers produce their own product photography, technical films, trade-show exhibits, and direct-mail campaigns, and perform various other functions. The degree of responsibility depends on the company.

THE CLIENT-AGENCY RELATIONSHIP

Many factors determine the success of a company's advertising program. But numerous studies have turned up one consistent determinant—the nature of the relationship between the advertiser and its agency.[29] Indeed, it is clear that if an advertiser's relationship with its creative source is less than satisfactory, then that creativity will suffer. It is important to understand the various stages every agency-client partnership passes through and the factors that affect their relationship.

Stages in the Client-Agency Relationship

Just as people and products have life cycles, so do relationships. In the advertising business, the life cycle of the agency-client relationship includes

☑ Checklist for Agency Review

Rate each agency on a scale from 1 (strongly negative) to 10 (strongly positive).

General Information

☐ Agency size compatible with our needs.
☐ Strength of agency's management.
☐ Stability of agency's financial position.
☐ Compatibility with type of clients agency handles.
☐ Range of services agency is able to offer.
☐ Cost of agency services; billing policies.

Marketing Information

☐ Agency's ability to offer marketing counsel.
☐ Agency's understanding of the markets we serve.
☐ Agency's experience dealing in our market.
☐ Agency's success record; case histories.

Creative Abilities

☐ Well-thought-out creativity; relevance to strategy.
☐ Agency's art strength.
☐ Agency's copy strength.
☐ Overall creative quality.
☐ Effectiveness compared to work of competitors.

Production

☐ Faithfulness to creative concept and execution.
☐ Diligence to schedules and budgets.
☐ Agency's ability to control outside services.

Media

☐ Existence and soundness of media research.
☐ Effective and efficient media strategy.
☐ Ability to achieve objectives within budget.
☐ Strength at negotiating and executing schedules.
☐ Attitude toward periodic review of plan and budget.

Personality

☐ Agency's overall personality, philosophy, or position.
☐ Compatibility with client staff and management.
☐ Willingness to assign top people to account.

References

☐ Rating of agency's work by current clients.
☐ Rating of agency's work by past clients.
☐ Rating of agency's reputation by media.
☐ Rating of agency's strength by financial sources.
☐ Overall rating of agency's people or attitude by references.

Additional Considerations or Comments

_____
_____
_____
_____
_____
_____
_____
_____

---

four very definite stages: prerelationship, development, maintenance, and termination.[30] Each stage has unique characteristics that ultimately affect the longevity of the partnership. One cynic has rephrased this by saying that in the agency business, every day after you are hired you are one day closer to being fired. And as discussed earlier, the number of agency switches every year would seem to confirm this point of view.

The Prerelationship Stage

The **prerelationship stage** includes all time before an agency and client officially get together to do business. They may never have heard of one another, or may know each other only by reputation or through social contact—but whatever the case, it affects their perceptions of each other. During the prerelationship, those all-important first impressions are formed. Once the agency meets the prospective client, makes a good impression, and is invited to "pitch" the account, they have the opportunity to get to know each other a little and may begin working together. Through the presentation, the agency's effort will invariably be to maintain the best impression it possibly can—because the advertising agency is selling, and the client is buying. (The Checklist for Agency Review offers guidelines clients can use in choosing an agency.)

The Development Stage

Once the agency has been appointed, the **development stage** begins. In this so-called honeymoon period, both the agency and the client are at the peak of their optimism, and they are most anxious to quickly develop a mutually profitable mechanism for working together. Expectations are at their highest, and both sides are most forgiving. However, this is also when reality first sets in. During development, the rules of the relationship are established—either directly or nonverbally. The respective roles get set very quickly, the true personalities of all the players are discovered, the first work of the agency is created, and the agency's work product and work process are awaited with great expectation and then judged very thoroughly by the client. The agency also discovers how well the client pays its bills, how receptive the client is to new ideas, and how the client's various personalities are to work with. The first problems in the relationship occur during the development stage. If they are successfully handled, then the maintenance phase may begin soon afterward.

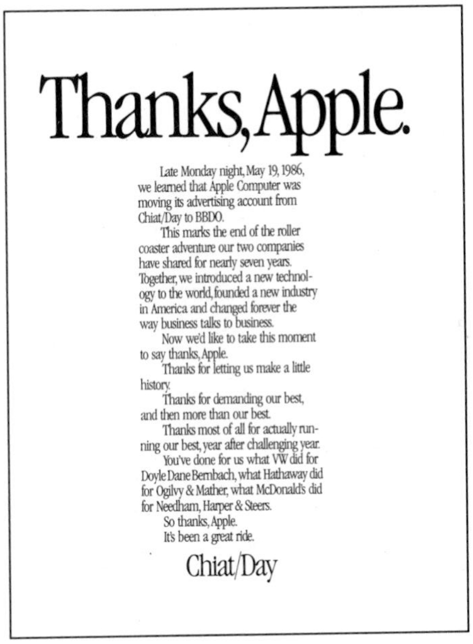

The Maintenance and Termination Stages

Maintenance is just that. It is the day-to-day working relationship that, when successful, may go on for many years. Sunkist, for example, has had the same advertising agency—Foote, Cone & Belding—for over 85 years. Unilever likewise has worked with J. Walter Thompson for a similar length of time, and AT&T has been with N. W. Ayer for 80 years. Unfortunately, though, the average client-agency relationship is much shorter—usually no more than seven or eight years.[31] During the maintenance stage, all the problems come up sooner or later, and each player's testiness is eventually observed. Whether it is a dispute over billing, a difference of opinion about strategy or execution, or a disagreement over responsibility for an expensive printing error, problems are normal occurrences. How they are resolved is the true test.

At some point, an irreconcilable difference may occur, and the relationship must be terminated. It may simply be that one party or the other decides it is time to move on. In 1991, for example, several long-standing client-agency relationships were terminated. After 25 years of work, Wells Rich Green lost the Benson & Hedges account. Similarly, Della Femina McNamee was replaced by Isuzu; and Ayer lost the J. C. Penney account (the story of how Ayer originally got the Penney account is discussed in Chapter 6).[32] The way the **termination** itself is handled will affect both sides for a long time and is an important factor in determining the possibility of the two ever getting back together. Several years ago, for example, Chiat/Day showed exceptional class when it placed the ad shown in Exhibit 3-21 after losing the Apple Computer account.

Thanks, Apple.

Late Monday night, May 19, 1986, we learned that Apple Computer was moving its advertising account from Chiat/Day to BBDO.

This marks the end of the roller coaster adventure our two companies have shared for nearly seven years. Together, we introduced a new technology to the world, founded a new industry in America and changed forever the way business talks to business.

Now we'd like to take this moment to say thanks, Apple.

Thanks for letting us make a little history.

Thanks for demanding our best, and then more than our best.

Thanks most of all for actually running our best, year after challenging year.

You've done for us what VW did for Doyle Dane Bernbach, what Hathaway did for Ogilvy & Mather, what McDonald's did for Needham, Harper & Steers.

So thanks, Apple.

It's been a great ride.

Chiat/Day

EXHIBIT 3-21

A client may decide, for one reason or another, to terminate its relationship with an agency. But the two may get back together again if the parting is handled well. When it lost the Apple Computer account several years ago, Chiat/Day gave the advertising profession a lesson in "class" with its public thank you letter to the client. The agency had produced an array of brilliant, highly creative ads that had been very instrumental in Apple's success.

Factors Affecting the Client-Agency Relationship

Naturally, many forces influence this marriage. They may best be grouped in four categories: chemistry, communication, conduct, and changes. We discuss each of these four Cs briefly below.

Chemistry

The most important critical factor is the personal *chemistry* between the client's employees and the agency's staff.[33] Good chemistry can create opportunities between the two and can overcome most problems. Poor chemistry creates problems where none exist and ruins a potentially good campaign. Agencies are usually very conscious of this and make efforts to "wine and dine" their clients in hopes of improving this chemistry. Some clients take advantage of these overtures, but the smart clients try to do their part to improve the chemistry with their agencies.

ETHICAL DILEMMA IN ADVERTISING
The Conflict over Client-Agency Conflicts

The biblical maxim that "No one can serve two masters" is a guiding principle of the advertising business, at least for clients. They become very concerned when their agencies do work for anyone that resembles the competition. John Powers, VP-director of marketing services at Eastman Kodak, sums up the prevailing attitude quite succinctly: "When we sign on with an agency, they say they want to be our full partners and increase our profits. How can they also increase my competition's profits and remain my partner?" With so much rivalry in the marketplace, it's no wonder some say that conflict with clients is the number-one problem facing the advertising business.

Part of the problem is the conflict over what constitutes a conflict. Everyone agrees that an agency shouldn't work on directly competing clients like Cheerios and Wheaties, for instance. But is it really a conflict if an agency handles Procter & Gamble's Sure deodorant and Colgate-Palmolive's Colgate toothpaste? The products certainly don't compete, but the companies do—in dozens of ways. Many advertisers believe that such indirect competition does represent a conflict, and the client's perception of the situation is the litmus test that determines if a conflict exists.

Clients worry that if their agency also serves the competition, confidential information might be revealed. Kent Mitchell, VP-marketing services at General Foods, says,

"Agencies working for you know your thinking, your tactical moves, and if you have worked together for a while, you've built up a certain amount of information about the industry you would like to protect." Besides confidentiality, clients also fear that an agency might not give equal time and talent to two competing accounts. These concerns often make client-agency relationships tense affairs rather than happy marriages.

The conflict problem is much more complex than it seems at first glance. Ronald Coleman, president of the Business/Professional Advertising Association echoes the belief that an "agency shouldn't get involved with any client that could be a competitor of an existing client." But that's easier said than done. Big, successful agencies attract big, successful clients, who in turn have so many different brands that conflict is virtually unavoidable.

Despite that fact, some clients have been unyielding in their attitudes. Procter & Gamble insists their agencies cannot do business with any company that competes with them in any product category. And McDonald's makes its agencies agree not to work for another fast-food account for a minimum of six months after resigning the McDonald's business. Important clients like these can make their demands stick. But is it really ethical to ask an agency to commit all its resources and loyalty to a single account, particularly when the client spreads its business among a number of agencies?

Communication

Poor *communication,* a problem often cited by both agencies and advertisers, can lead to misunderstandings of objectives, strategies, or tactics. It makes the work process inefficient and eventually hurts the end product. It should go without saying that constant and open communication is the key to the understanding and mutual respect essential to a good relationship.[34] Yet sometimes it seems this is most difficult to achieve due to poor systems or poor discipline or poor attitudes on both sides.

Conduct

Dissatisfaction with agency performance is perhaps the most commonly cited reason for agency switches.[35] *Conduct* includes what everyone in the relationship does—both the work process and the work product. Does the client give timely, accurate information to the agency? Does the agency understand

Keith Reinhard, chairman of DDB/Needham Worldwide, asks, "If you can't continue to grow at 15 percent with the present group of clients and you can't get new ones when they're all merging into each other's arena, what do you do?" For years, agencies have experimented with ways to minimize conflicts. Some build "Chinese walls" between agency teams handling competing accounts. Others create separate offices. Still others divide themselves into subsidiary businesses. But none of these solutions addresses the underlying problem, which is lack of trust.

Clients and agencies both agree that the best approach to handling potential conflicts is to be straightforward and honest, but that often puts agencies in an impossible bind. What happens if one client develops a new product that edges into the same category of another client? Would the agency be ethically required to resign one of the accounts? Should the agency go to either client and say, "I have a problem with something you don't know about and I can't tell you whom it involves or what it is"? In these cases, John Warwick, chairman of Warwick Baker & Fiore Advertising, offers some simple advice. "We live our lives by certain behavior codes, and business should really be guided by the same principles," he says.

Fortunately, indications are that some clients are learning to coexist in an atmosphere of mutual trust. Recently, Young & Rubicam wanted to pick up the Breyers' ice cream account from Kraft at a time when the agency also serviced General Foods' Jell-O Pudding Pops. Surprisingly, neither Kraft nor General Foods perceived any conflict in this situation. If more clients learn to have faith in their agencies, and if the agencies act ethically, perhaps the conflict over conflicts will be replaced by better client-agency relationships.

Questions

1. Imagine you're the advertising manager for a very successful brand of coffee and your ad agency of many years tells you it's thinking of accepting an assignment from a soft drink company. Would you view this as a potential conflict? If so, would you fire the agency or would you lay down new ground rules to ensure that no breach of ethics could occur?

2. Henry Kornhauser, CEO of Kornhauser & Calene, believes that conflicts shouldn't be as important as they are, because each brand has its own character. He claims that the key criteria should be: How good a job is the ad agency doing? How much advanced thinking and idea generation is the account getting? And how are the brand's sales doing? Do you agree with Kornhauser?

the client's problem and market and offer realistic alternatives to the client? Does the work measure up to the client's subjective idea of good advertising? Does the client appreciate good work when it's presented? Are bills paid promptly without nitpicking, or is billing always a problem? Does the client give the agency any creative freedom? Does the agency ever exercise leadership? And does the agency bring work in on time and on budget? (For more

Checklist for Ways to Be a Better Client

□ *Look for the big idea.* Concentrate first on positioning and brand personality. Too many products have neither. Do not allow a *single* advertisement—no matter how brilliant—to change your positioning or your brand personality.

□ *Learn the fine art of conducting a creative meeting.* Deal with the important issues first: strategy, consumer benefit, reason why.

□ *Cultivate honesty.* Tell your agency the truth. Make sure your advertising tells the truth and *implies* the truth as well.

□ *Be enthusiastic.* When you like the advertising, let the creative people know you like it. Applause is their staff of life.

□ *Be frank when you* don't like *the advertising.* Copywriters won't hate you for turning down an idea if you give them a *reason.*

□ *Be human.* Try to react like a person, not a corporation. Be human enough to laugh at a funny advertisement, even if it is off-strategy.

□ *Be willing to admit you aren't sure.* Don't let your agency press you by asking for the order *immediately* after a new copy presentation. You may need time to absorb what they've been thinking about for a long while.

□ *Insist on creative discipline.* Professionals don't bridle at discipline. A strategy helps creative people zero in on a target.

□ *Keep the creative people involved in your business.* Successful copywriters want to know the latest market shares just as much as you do. Tell them what's happening, good *and* bad.

□ *Don't insulate your top people from the creative people.* Agency creative people want to receive objectives directly from the top—not filtered through layers. Good work is done in an atmosphere of involvement, not insulation.

□ *Make the agency feel responsible.* Be a leader, not a nitpicker. *Tell them what you think is wrong, not how to fix it.*

□ *Don't be afraid to ask for great advertising.* Let your agency know you have confidence in them to deliver more than just "good solid advertising." Aiming for greatness involves trying new directions—and some risks.

□ *Set objectives.* If you expect action and results, you must know where you want to go. So set objectives for your advertising and your business.

□ *Switch people, not agencies.* If there are problems, ask for new people to work on your account. A different copywriter or account executive on your business may provide a fresh approach, without depriving the business of necessary continuity.

□ *Be sure the agency makes a profit on your account.* Clients who demand more service than the income can cover are shortsighted. In a good relationship, the agency grows as the client grows.

□ *Avoid insularity.* Don't isolate yourself with the same people. Force yourself to go beyond the comfortable world of your own lifestyle.

□ *Care about being a client.* Creative people do their best work on accounts they like, for clients they like to work with. *Good clients.* That doesn't mean *easy* clients. That's why good clients wind up with the best writers and the best account executives.

□ *Suggest work sessions.* Set up informal give-and-take discussions where copywriters can air rough ideas and you can talk about your objectives. These sessions are especially helpful just before the agency starts a complex assignment.

on how clients hold up their end of the relationship, see the Checklist for Ways to Be a Better Client.)

Changes

Changes occur in every relationship. Unfortunately, some of them may damage the agency-client partnership. The client's market position may

---

AD LAB 3-B
Megamergers Make Agency Supergroups

Historians will record the 1980s as the decade of merger-mania. America's largest corporations gobbled one another up to make the big still bigger and the small proportionately smaller still. The advertising agency business was not immune to this peculiar virus. And in fact, according to some sources, the agencies caught this disease from their corporate clients—as a result of either trying to emulate them or keep up in size.

Some of the agencies infected by this contagion included Bozell & Jacobs, Kenyon & Eckhardt, Doyle Dane Bernbach, BBDO, Needham Harper Worldwide, Young & Rubicam, Dancer Fitzgerald Sample, and many others. But the biggest empire builder of all was London-based Saatchi & Saatchi PLC, which rapidly became the world's largest agency by acquiring, in succession, Compton Advertising, Dancer Fitzgerald Sample, and the giant Ted Bates Worldwide. In addition, the Saatchi brothers, Charles and Maurice, also bought up a host of other firms in related communications fields, including the major research firms of Yankelovich, Skelly and White and Clancy Shulman.

Saatchi & Saatchi's rationale for the megamergers was globalization. Because more and more large companies sell their wares worldwide, the Saatchi brothers reasoned that the secret of success was to grow like fury and offer large clients a global service. In its thirst for such growth, the group often paid too much for the acquisitions, the most notable example being Ted Bates.

Saatchi & Saatchi Co. didn't stay at the top for long. In 1990, it was number two in worldwide gross income—a full billion dollars behind the London-based WPP Group, which includes the U.S. giants J. Walter Thompson Co. and Ogilvy & Mather Worldwide. Cash is also flowing out faster than it used to. Many of Saatchi & Saatchi's deals entailed deferred payments to the old owners. These payments zapped the group's cash flow—and will continue to do so for some time. Going global also led to mistakes, such as opening an office in Japan without local help. Some insiders say it has been losing $1 million a year.

The shuffling of agency decks in the 1980s resulted in the establishment of several advertising supergroups with gross billings in the billions of dollars. However, it also resulted in a period of unprecedented turmoil due to the inevitable conflicts of client loyalties, confusion of employees, and misunderstanding of management direction. With the Ted Bates merger, for example, Colgate-Palmolive withdrew its $100 million account from Bates since Saatchi handled Colgate's prime competitor, Procter & Gamble. Futher defections from the agency after the merger quickly climbed to a total of $300 million. This, no doubt, caused other potential mergerers to pause and consider the potential jeopardy.

Fortune magazine reported that with this consolidation of the industry, new consideration had to be given to how agencies operate, how to handle the issue of competing clients within one agency, and how to foster creativity in a large organizational structure. As Colgate's Chairman Reuben Mark said, "The most important thing when you work with an agency is to get truly great creative [work]. I fail to see how these mergers are going to improve the creative [product]."

This view was echoed by James Tappan at General Foods, who said they did not believe that agency megamergers represent the client's best interest.

At the time, agency spokespeople defended the merger trend. According to Robert Bloom of the Bloom Companies, the effect of a merger on an agency is based not on the size of the merged company but rather on the intimacy of the client relationship. That relationship, though, has sometimes been difficult to maintain in an institutional environment.

Laboratory Applications

1. Do you think the consternation of major advertisers over the agency mergers was warranted? Why or why not?

2. What effect do you think the megamerger trend had on small or medium-sized agencies? Why?

change as new competitors come on the scene and do a better job. Client policy may change, or new management personnel, who prefer their own team of players, may arrive. Agencies may lose some of their creative staff to other agencies. Or with the megamerger wave, client conflicts may arise when one agency buys another that handles competing accounts (see Ad Lab 3-B). The law pertaining to principal-agent relations holds that an advertising agency cannot represent a client's competition without the client's consent.[36] For example, a few years ago, when Saatchi & Saatchi bought the Ted Bates agency, it suddenly became the world's largest advertising agency—but it also immediately lost Bates's Colgate-Palmolive account because of the conflict with Saatchi & Saatchi's client Procter & Gamble. While changes cannot be avoided, the way they are handled determines the future of the relationship.[37]

Summary

The advertising business comprises two main groups: advertisers (clients) and agencies. In addition, there are the media and suppliers of advertising. The people in the advertising business may work for any of these organizations and may include creative people, product people, top executives, or even clerical personnel. In effect, the advertising a company uses affects virtually every person in the organization.

Fundamental to all advertisers and agencies are the tasks of administration, planning, budgeting, coordination with other departments or outside advertising services, and creative supervision.

Advertising agencies are independent organizations of creative people and businesspeople who specialize in the development and preparation of advertising plans, advertisements, and other promotional tools on behalf of clients.

Agencies may be classified by the range of services they offer and the types of business they handle. The two basic types of agencies are the full-service agencies and the agencies that offer à la carte services. The latter include creative boutiques and media-buying services. Further, agencies may specialize in either consumer or industrial accounts.

The people who work in agencies may be involved in research, planning, creative services, traffic, media, account management, new business, administration, or a host of other activities.

Agencies may also be organized into departments based on functional specialties or into groups that work as teams on various accounts.

Agencies may charge fees or retainers, receive commissions from the media, or mark up outside purchases made on behalf of their clients. Most agencies get their clients through referral, advertising, community relations, or personal solicitation.

The way a client's advertising department is organized depends on many variables. The two basic structures are the centralized and the decentralized department, and there are advantages and disadvantages to both. The centralized organization is the most typical and may be structured by product, by subfunction of advertising, by end user, or by geography. Decentralized departments are typical of large far-flung organizations that have numerous divisions, subsidiaries, products, countries, regions, or brands that need to be served.

Some advertising departments take responsibility for ad production, media placement, and other marketing support services. Some firms have even developed in-house advertising agencies in hopes of saving money by keeping the normal agency commissions for themselves. However, they have sometimes saved money but lost objectivity and creativity.

The client-agency relationship goes through a number of stages. Numerous factors affect the relationship, including chemistry, communication, conduct, and changes.

Questions for Review and Discussion

1. What roles do the major organizations involved in the advertising business perform?

2. If a client has an advertising agency, does it still need an advertising manager? Why?

3. In what ways can a full-service advertising agency help a manufacturer of industrial goods?

4. What do you think are the most important points for an advertiser to consider in selecting an agency?

5. Do you think an advertiser should change agencies on a regular basis? Why or why not?

6. What are the advantages and disadvantages of an in-house advertising agency?

7. How does an advertising agency make money, and what is the best way to compensate an advertising agency? Explain.

8. How does the client-agency relationship typically evolve, and what can clients and agencies do to protect the relationship?

9. Should advertising agencies advertise for clients? Why?

10. What methods can you think of that an advertiser or advertising agency might use to locate suppliers and evaluate their services?

PART

II

DEVELOPING MARKETING AND ADVERTISING STRATEGIES

The success of any business depends upon its ability to attract customers willing and able to make monetary exchanges for products and services. To do this, a business must find, understand, and communicate with potential customers where they live, work, and play. Part II examines the marketing process, the nature of consumers, the relationship between products and market groups, and the research and planning processes that make for marketing and advertising success.

Chapter 4 describes products and markets and how advertisers use the marketing process to create effective advertising. The consumer as a rejector or acceptor of products and how the complex, consumer decision-making process affects the design of advertising are discussed.

Chapter 5 discusses market segments, the aggregation of segments, and the influence of target marketing on a product concept. The elements of the marketing mix and their use as tools in understanding and improving a product concept are shown.

Chapter 6 points out the value of research in improving marketing and advertising effectiveness. It describes how to organize and gather data and properly evaluate and report results. The application of research to advertising and the objectives and techniques of concept testing, pretesting, and posttesting are discussed.

Chapter 7 details the creation of effective marketing and advertising plans, particularly analyzing, setting realistic and attainable objectives, and developing creative strategies to achieve those objectives. Top-down and bottom-up marketing, advertising strategies, and methods for allocating resources are discussed.

Friends, Foes, and War

Chart a Good Course

For thousands of years the stars have given us a sense of time and direction. By noting the position of the stars, early navigators could set a trustworthy course, and farmers could know when planting season had arrived. The ancients also used the sky to illustrate their myths and sacred beliefs, thus naming some 88 constellations visible in the sky.

Plan now for a Winter Semester at BYU that's out of this world. Begin by watching for your intent to register form in the mail. When the form arrives, it's your turn to shine. Return the form along with a $50 fee (nonrefundable). Then you're all set to phone in a heavenly selection of classes. Act now. Don't wait for a blue moon.

Deadline—December 15

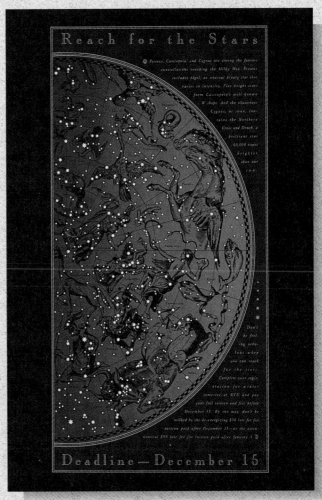

Reach for the Stars

Perseus, Cassiopeia, and Cygnus are among the famous constellations touching the Milky Way. Perseus includes Algol, an unusual binary star that varies in intensity. Five bright stars form Cassiopeia's well-known W shape. And the illustrious Cygnus, or swan, contains the Northern Cross and Deneb, a brilliant star 60,000 times brighter than our sun.

Don't be feeling nebulous when you can reach for the stars. Complete your registration for winter semester at BYU and pay your full tuition and fees before December 15. By the way, don't be milked by the de-energizing $50 late fee for tuition paid after December 15—or the astronomical $90 late fee for tuition paid after January 5.

Deadline—December 15

THE IMPORTANCE OF MARKETING AND CONSUMER BEHAVIOR TO ADVERTISING

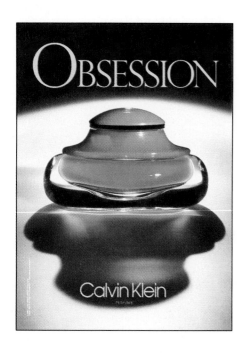

Objective: To highlight the importance of the marketing function in business and to define the important role advertising plays in presenting the company and its products to the market. Since markets are made up of people, the successful advertising person must understand the relationship between marketing and the way consumers behave. It is that relationship that ideally shapes advertising.

After studying this chapter, you will be able to:

☐ Define marketing and explain its importance to advertisers.

☐ Discuss the concept of product utility and the relationship of utility to consumer needs.

☐ Explain what is meant by the expression, "The perception is the reality."

☐ Describe who the key participants are in the marketing process.

☐ Outline the consumer perception process.

☐ Discuss the interpersonal influences on consumer behavior.

☐ Explain how advertisers try to deal with the problem of cognitive dissonance.

In the middle of this century, after nine years of work, the Ford Motor Company introduced what was not destined to be one of its better ideas—the Edsel. Named after one of Henry Ford's sons, the car was touted as the latest breakthrough in engineering design. The Edsel offered a host of features such as safety rim wheels and self-adjusting brakes. The automatic transmission was controlled by push buttons located in the middle of the steering wheel. Ford Motor Company spent over $250 million to design, engineer, and produce this marvel. Eventually, 110,000 Edsel cars were built and distributed to dealers across the country. The company then spent over $30 million advertising the Edsel in print and electronic media. The company spared no effort—and certainly no dollars—in marketing the Edsel.

Yet within two years Ford had discontinued the production of the Edsel, cutting losses at $350 million. What went wrong? Why did the Edsel fail so miserably?

Did the car sell poorly because potential buyers didn't know about it? Not really; the Edsel was extensively advertised. Individual ads followed proven standards of effective copywriting and layout. And in keeping with the Edsel's advanced design, the print ads even dared to be innovative for their time by integrating unusually small headlines into the overall ad design, as seen in Exhibit 4-1.

If the advertising was not to blame, what really was? Did the company rush into producing the Edsel without fully considering the consumer acceptance it might get? By that era's standards, Ford carefully analyzed the market at the

EXHIBIT 4-1

Ford Motor Company told us hopefully that the Edsel was here to stay. The automaker was wrong, however. With a loss of $350 million in 1959 dollars, the Edsel was perhaps the largest single product marketing disaster in U.S. history.

beginning of the process. Prior to the development and manufacturing of the Edsel, Ford's marketing research department surveyed potential customers for answers to these basic questions: Does the car-buying public want this car? Does it appeal to them? Do they need this car, or do other cars already fill the same need? At the price customers will be able or willing to pay for this car, can we cover all the costs of manufacturing, distribution, advertising, and sales? After covering all those costs, can we still make a worthwhile profit on this car?

In 1954, when Ford first asked these questions, the survey responses were weak affirmatives; when the survey was repeated in 1956, the results were even more negative. Unfortunately, top management ignored the survey results. They remained confident of their product's features and of their ability to pull the Edsel through its nationwide dealer network with $30 million in consumer advertising. The result was a costly failure.

The Edsel Syndrome

The Edsel story offers some good lessons. To succeed today, top management must listen and respond to the marketplace. They must respect the importance of marketing and know how to weigh the data uncovered by their marketing people. Companies that ignore this are risking experiencing their own Edsels.

For those in the field of advertising, the Edsel story demonstrates another important principle—advertising cannot save a product that hasn't been marketed correctly, even if the ad campaign itself is superior. Many years later, in an *Advertising Age* survey of advertising professionals across the country, Edsel was voted the biggest product failure in history. One advertising person commented, "I happen to think that was a pretty good ad campaign. Mismarketing, to be sure. But okay advertising."

Unfortunately, the business world is not always so kind. All too often, advertising is made the scapegoat for management's misfires.

THE IMPORTANCE OF MARKETING TO ADVERTISING PEOPLE

The advertising community constantly faces the challenge of how to present goods, services, and ideas effectively through the media to potential buyers. To do this successfully, advertisers must first understand the subtle relationship between the product and the marketplace. This relationship is the province of marketing. So, to begin, we must examine the role of marketing to fully understand its significance to advertising.

Every business organization performs a number of activities on a daily basis. Management typically classifies these diverse activities into three broad functional divisions:

☐ Production/manufacturing.
☐ Administration/finance.
☐ Marketing.

Students who major in business study a variety of subjects related to one or all of these general functions. For instance, courses in purchasing, quality control, and manufacturing relate to the production/manufacturing function. Courses in accounting, human resources, and management relate to the administration/finance area. And while some students may study advertising in schools of journalism or communications, advertising is typically a specialty area studied within the broader field of marketing, along with marketing research, product distribution, inventory control, and sales management, to mention a few.

The role of marketing may be one of the more misunderstood and overlooked elements of business. For example, businesspeople often emphasize that a business can't survive without proper financing. And many point out that without the production of goods or services, there is no reason to be in business. But to know what products or services to produce, businesspeople first must use marketing research to determine that a demand even exists for such products. And then, to obtain financing for the endeavor, the entrepreneur will have to create a plan for marketing the products that will be acceptable to financing sources. In short, as important as finance and production are, marketing is still the only business function whose primary role is to attract revenues into the company to recover the initial investment capital and to earn consistent profits.

Advertising people help the organization achieve its marketing goals. So do the people involved in marketing research, sales, product distribution, and inventory control. And the activities of these other marketing specialists have a relationship to, and an impact on, the advertising a company employs. Therefore, an effective advertising specialist must have a broad understanding of the marketing context advertising operates in.

Advertising professionals must also have a good understanding of how people act and think—and why people buy what they buy—for in the end, customers are nothing more than people. This area of study is the province of another specialty—consumer behavior—and an understanding of it helps advertisers perform their primary task of bringing products into the consciousness of consumers.

The purpose of this chapter—in fact of this whole unit—is to define and outline the whole subject of marketing in order to clarify advertising's proper role in the marketing function and to introduce the underlying market and human factors that ultimately shape advertising.

WHAT IS MARKETING?

Over the years, as the field of marketing has evolved, so has the definition of the term. Typically, these definitions depend on the perspective of the definer.[1] Because it's important to understand the concept of *marketing* as it relates to the people who work within the sphere of *advertising,* we shall define the term as follows:

> **Marketing** is the process of planning and executing the conception, pricing, promotion, and distribution of ideas, goods, and services to create exchanges that satisfy the perceived needs, wants, and objectives of individuals and organizations.[2]

The first important element of this definition is the statement that marketing is a process—a series of actions or methods that take place sequentially. In the case of marketing, the process includes conceiving products, pricing them strategically, promoting them through sales and advertising activities, and making them available to customers through a distribution network. The ultimate goal of the marketing process is to earn a profit by uniting a product or service with customers who need or want it. As we shall see in Chapter 7, the marketing plan and the advertising plan formalize this process in written form and guide it in a prescribed sequence.

Needs and Utility

A second important element in the definition of marketing is its focus on the special relationship between a customer's needs and the product's problem-solving potential. This is generally referred to as the product's **utility,** and it extends to the product's ability to provide both symbolic or psychological want satisfaction and functional satisfaction.[3] Ad Lab 4-A discusses the relationship between needs and utility.

In the initial stages of the process, marketers may use research to discover what needs and wants exist in the marketplace and to define the product's general characteristics in the light of economic, social, and political trends.

For example, an automobile manufacturer who notes that more couples are having children may decide to introduce a new station wagon model. Additional research may then answer the questions of which group of consumers are most concerned with multipassenger utility (e.g., baby boomers); how much these potential customers expect to spend on a car; and what other features are important to them (e.g., safety features). The ultimate goal is to use this marketing information to shape a new product or service during the conceptual stage or to reshape an existing product to more fully satisfy the customer's needs and wants. The ad in Exhibit 4-2 features language that indicates the advertiser believes completely in its research and the shaping of the product. For example, the ad's "voice" speaks as if it knows the reader very well—revealed by such phrases as "Curiosity runs in your family,"

AD LAB 4-A
Understanding Needs and Utility

No matter how well made a product is, superior quality by itself is not enough to sell anything. Marketing is needed to tout the advantages of a graphite tennis racket, the high performance of a new sports car, or even the prompt service at a bank.

Production and marketing, therefore, work in tandem to create goods and services that satisfy consumers' needs. The power to satisfy those needs is called *utility.* Four types of utility are important to consumers: utility of form, possession, time, and place.

Consumers obtain *form utility* from the product itself. However, mere production of a product like bicycles doesn't necessarily guarantee consumer satisfaction. Consumers must want one of those bicycles—or no need is satisfied, and no utility occurs. The production side of business, then, is guided by marketing decisions. What do consumers really want to purchase and why?

Even when form utility has been provided, marketers need to consider ways to give consumers possession of the product. Consumers must be able to obtain it and then have the right to use or consume it. Money is typically exchanged for *possession utility.* A sample bicycle on display, not for sale, may be just what a consumer wants. But if he or she cannot buy it, the bicycle has no possession utility.

Providing the consumer with the product when he or she wants it is known as *time utility.* Having an ample supply of bicycles, sports cars, or bank tellers at the time of consumer need is thus another marketing requirement.

Place utility—having the product available where the customer can get it—is also vital to business success. Bicycles and sports cars aren't usually sold if customers have to travel far out of their way to get them. Customers are even less likely to travel long distances for everyday needs. That's why banks have branches. That's why the 24-hour convenience markets, which sell gasoline and a few basic food items, have become so popular.

In summary, form, possession, time, and place utility are essential components of marketing success.

Laboratory Application

Choose a product and describe in detail how it provides you with form, possession, time, and place utility.

Ford Motor Company introduced the Explorer in response to market research showing that families wanted a four-wheel drive vehicle with ample interior space and a variety of optional amenities.

"You're always searching for the new and unexpected," and "Your Explorer is ready." The audacity to make such statements can only come from having studied the market thoroughly, from using that information to shape the product and the advertising, and from having complete confidence in that research.

Businesspeople have often given the marketing process short shrift or have misunderstood how to use it. Many products have been introduced without a clear idea of their utility to the customer. But as we have seen, the consequences of such a short-sighted policy can be severe. The Edsel fiasco is a case in point. At a Ford executive committee meeting in 1954, Robert S. McNamara asked, "What is this new car intended to offer the car-buying public?" Unfortunately, his question was never fully answered. Many marketing experts believe that by the time the Edsel was introduced, the American public already had a glut of chrome-filled, medium-priced cars to choose from. In another marketplace, the Edsel may have had utility; but by the time it was introduced, the American car-buying public had neither the need nor any desire for it.

Perception, Exchanges, and Satisfaction

The final part of the definition of marketing reads: ". . . to create exchanges that satisfy the perceived needs, wants, and objectives of individuals and organizations." Three related concepts are presented here: *perception, exchanges,* and *satisfaction..*

Perception

Consider first the concept of *perception* and how it relates to marketing and advertising. Classic studies have shown that people take action only when they have a goal. More important, however, they must perceive the goal and accept it as such before they will act.[4] Herein lie the roots of effective marketing—and, most especially, advertising. Advertisers must first help potential customers to perceive the existence of the product (awareness) and its value in supplying a want or need (utility). Once customers are aware of the product and its value and establish the goal of satisfying their want or need, they may be motivated to act. And the greater the customer's need, the greater the potential value or utility of the need-satisfying product.

Advertising plays a key role in creating awareness of a product and a sense of value in customers' minds. By using loud noises, sudden movements of light, and sensuous music, for example, a television commercial can capture a customer's attention and stimulate his or her emotions toward the goal of need or want fulfillment.[5]

Exchanges

Now consider the concept of **exchange,** in which one thing of value is traded for another thing of value. Any business transaction where one person sells something of value to another person is an exchange.

It is fairly common for people engaging in a business exchange to feel apprehensive about losing, to worry that the exchange may not be equal— even though the exchange may truly be equitable. The perception of unfairness is particularly likely if the consumer has little knowledge or experience of the product. Under such conditions, it is very important for the more knowledgeable party (in this case, the seller) to reassure the buyer that an equal exchange is possible. If the seller can provide the information and inspiration the buyer seeks, then the two may agree that a *perceived equal-value exchange* exists. Without this perception, the likelihood of an exchange is very remote.

One role of marketing is to discover whether potential customers are likely to perceive that an equal-value exchange is possible and which functional or symbolic needs, wants, and objectives relate to such perceptions. This information guides the company through another role of marketing— **product shaping**—designing and building products to solve the customer's problems. It also helps the company's promotional staff and advertising agency develop advertising appeals for the product.

In recent years, all U.S. carmakers have experienced turbulent times. It wasn't so very long ago that Chrysler Corporation went bankrupt and stayed in business only thanks to a government bailout. Chrysler President Lee Iacocca then turned the company around by giving car buyers two things: the basic utility they needed in a car and the perception they were getting an equal-value exchange for their money. Using advertising and public relations to inform potential customers that Chrysler products were "better engineered," Iacocca demonstrated that the product had been changed to have the proper utility. Then, by being the first to offer a whopping 6-year or 60,000-mile warranty, he gave consumers the perception their investment would be well protected. These two marketing moves had the desired effect. Consumers responded to Iacocca's appeal and within 36 months gave Chrysler the most profitable year in its history—allowing Chrysler to repay the government loan ahead of schedule.

Lee Iacocca represents another element in the exchange cycle. In this case, he was more than the man at the top of Chrysler; he was the man who created the programs that gave the product its exchange value. And he was willing to put his reputation on the line—a personal act—to assure people these

Using extensive advertising and public relations, Lee Iacocca made a personal commitment to quality as he informed potential customers that Chrysler products had utility and value.

programs had value. Appearing in a series of ads taped in his office and on the production floor (as seen in Exhibit 4-3), he spoke straightforwardly to the issues. Such a personal commitment to a product's quality is reassuring, and it encouraged people—on a person-to-person basis—to make the exchange.

Satisfaction

The concept of *satisfaction* is still an issue even after an exchange has occurred. Customers must be satisfied that their needs are met by their actual use of the product or they won't perceive that an equal-value exchange has taken place. If the product performs adequately or well, happy customers can lead to more sales. Advertising can reinforce this by giving customers the information they need to defend the product against skeptical peers, family members, and business associates, and to persuade other prospects to become customers. Of course, if use of the product does *not* reinforce the exchange, the negative effect can be even more far-reaching.

The Evolution of Marketing Theory

Over the years, the concept of *marketing* has been shaped by the relationship between the availability of goods and customers' ability or desire to own or use them.

Until a century ago, very few products were available compared to the number of consumers who wanted them, and business focused on making more products. Marketing simply transported and distributed these limited goods. Demand was high; there was no requirement to promote products as we do today. Marketers refer to this as the **production-oriented period.**

As mass production developed, however, more goods and services became available, and the focus of marketing changed to selling. Sales techniques were used to attract consumers to a particular company's goods and services and to distract them from competing products. This **sales-oriented period** was marked by extravagant advertising claims and a business attitude expressed by the Latin phrase *caveat emptor* ("let the buyer beware"). Occasionally the government stepped in as a referee, as Chapter 2 noted, to ensure that fair business practices prevailed.

In the last half of this century, as a deluge of products flooded the marketplace, business has found it more profitable to try to determine in advance what customers want and then to develop goods and services that will satisfy those desires. This is called the **marketing-oriented period.** Companies steered by the marketing concept are more concerned with shaping goods and services to meet the needs of customers than with trying to force consumers to buy whatever the company wants to produce. They are intensely interested in the consumer's point of view and allow that point of view to dictate many company activities.

As Chapter 18 explains, even many nonbusiness organizations not driven by a profit motive also operate under the marketing concept, seeking to develop services that satisfy their constituents' needs.

The Marketing Exchange Cycle

For firms operating under the marketing concept, the task of marketing is to manage the **marketing exchange cycle.** This responsibility is divided into three areas, as shown in Exhibit 4-4:

The marketing exchange cycle consists of several steps: (1) Consumers express their wants through research studies or their actions at the cash register. (2) Marketers must interpret this demand for management, which then funds and develops products to satisfy the needs. (3) Marketers then develop and implement a system to make the products available and execute the exchange. The consumers then decide to buy or reject the new or altered product—thus expressing their wants or needs again. Marketing, therefore, begins and ends with the consumer.

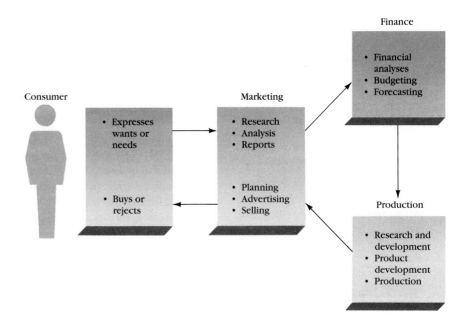

1. Discovering, locating, and measuring the needs, attitudes, and desires of prospective customers.
2. Interpreting this information for management so goods and services may be improved and new ones developed.
3. Devising and implementing a system to make the good or service available, to inform prospective customers about the product's need-satisfying capabilities, and to execute the exchange.

As you can see, the cycle begins and ends with the consumer.

Where does advertising fit into this responsibility? Advertising is primarily concerned with the third phase in the marketing exchange cycle: informing consumers about the product and persuading them to buy it. Sometimes advertising may even be directly involved in the exchange, as in the case of mail-order advertising. But in any case, advertising cannot be effective unless all the company's marketing activities are coordinated and performed well.

The Key Participants in the Marketing Process

Satisfactory exchanges depend on three types of participants: *customers, markets* (groups of customers), and *marketers*.

Customers

Customers are the people or organizations who consume goods and services. They include three general categories: *current customers, prospective customers,* and *centers of influence*.

Current customers have already purchased something from a business and may purchase on a regular basis. One measure of a business's success is the number of current customers it can boast and those customers' continuing goodwill. **Prospective customers** include people who are about to make an exchange or are considering it. Should the exchange be made, a prospective customer becomes a current customer. **Centers of influence** are customers, prospective customers, or opinion leaders whose actions are respected and may be emulated by others. A center of influence can often be the link to many prospective customers.

Markets

The second type of participant in the marketing process is the *market,* which is simply a group of current and prospective customers. A **market** comprises potential customers who share a common interest, need, or desire, who can use the offered good or service to some advantage, and who can afford or are willing to pay the purchase price. As we shall examine more fully in Chapter 5, a market rarely includes everybody. Companies advertise and sell to four broad classifications of markets:

1. **Consumer markets** include people who buy goods and services for their own personal use. Both Chrysler and Ford, for example, aim at the consumer market. But they also cater to different groups or segments within that market: single women, upscale young families, older retired people, outdoor sports enthusiasts, business executives, or people who live in a certain part of the country. Chapter 5 discusses some of the many ways to categorize consumer groups.

2. **Business markets** are composed of organizations that buy natural resources, component products, and services that they either resell or use in making another product. Two subtypes are reseller markets and industrial markets. **Reseller markets** buy products for the purpose of reselling them. Chrysler, for example, aims a portion of its marketing activities at a reseller market—its dealers. Likewise, a food manufacturer like Rosarito Mexican Foods first needs to convince food wholesalers and then retail grocers to carry its brands, or they will never be sold to consumers. Reseller markets, therefore, are extremely important to most companies—even though most consumers may be completely unaware of any marketing or advertising activities aimed at them.

   Industrial markets, which buy products needed for the production of other goods and services, are also beyond the general consumer's view. Plant equipment and machinery manufacturers aim at industrial markets, as do office suppliers, computer companies, and telephone companies who run ads such as that shown in Exhibit 4-5. Chapter 5 lists additional types of industrial markets, categorizing them by such factors as their industry segment or geographic location or size.

3. **Government markets** buy products for the successful coordination of municipal, state, federal, and other government activities. Consider all the vehicles used by the post office; the weapons bought by the police and the military; and the desks, computers, and even pencils used by tax collectors. Some firms have been immensely successful selling only to government markets.

4. **International markets** include any of the other three markets that are located in foreign countries. Every country has consumers, resellers, industries, and governments. Targeting those groups across national boundaries presents interesting problems, however, as Chapter 19 discusses.

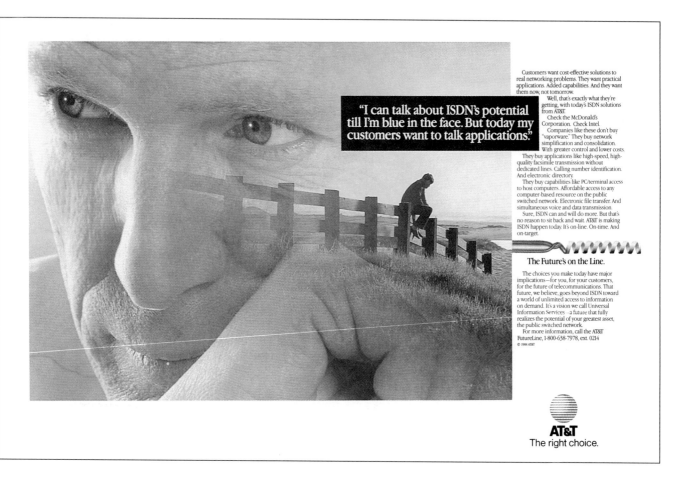

EXHIBIT 4-5

Customers in industrial markets buy products needed to produce other goods and services or to operate their businesses. This AT&T ad is a good example of advertising aimed at the industrial marketplace.

HOW ADVERTISERS REACH THE MARKET

Marketers

The third participant in the marketing process is the marketer. **Marketers** include every person or organization that has a good or service or idea to sell. Manufacturers market tangible consumer and business products. Farmers are marketers of wheat; doctors market medical services; banks, stockbrokers, and insurance companies are marketers of financial products and services; and political organizations are marketers of philosophies and candidates. And marketers, of course, are also the prime users of advertising.

Now that we understand what marketing is, how the marketing exchange cycle works, and who the key participants in the marketing process are, let's briefly consider how marketers and advertisers communicate with their markets. We look first at the nature of advertising as a science and an art and then at the basic process we humans use (whether through advertising or some other means) to communicate with one another.

The Art and Science of Advertising

Some people regard advertising as an art. Others consider it a science. Actually, it is a unique combination of the two. Talented, creative people with

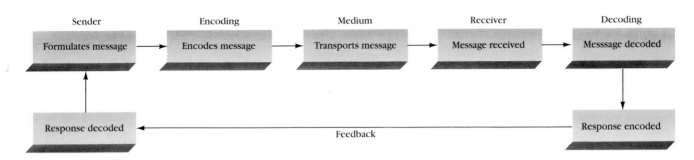

Sender	Encoding	Medium	Receiver	Decoding
Formulates message	Encodes message	Transports message	Message received	Messsage decoded

| Response decoded | Feedback | Response encoded |

EXHIBIT 4-6

This model of the human communication process shows what happens when people share ideas.

specialized knowledge in the **communicating arts** (writing and printing, drama and theatrical production, graphic design, photography, and so on) breathe life into the art of advertising. The appropriateness of advertising creativity (the art), though, depends on the facts about people and groups of people that marketers gain from studies of the marketplace. These are typically considered the province of the **behavioral** or **social sciences** (anthropology, sociology, psychology, etc.). How an advertiser blends scientific data with art determines the character of a campaign. The richer and more accurate the data and the more communicative the art, the more successful the campaign.

In this and the next two chapters, we will examine some of the scientific aspects of advertising. And in Chapters 8 through 11, we will see how scientifically obtained data support the creative processes.

The Marketing Communication Process

From the first cry at birth, our survival depends on our ability to inform or to persuade others to take some action. And as we develop, we learn to listen and to respond to others' messages. So, to understand how marketers communicate, let's look first at how humans communicate.

The model in Exhibit 4-6 summarizes the series of events that take place when people share ideas. The communication process begins when one person *formulates* and *encodes* an idea as a message and sends it via some *medium* to another person. The person receiving the message must *decode* it, formulate a new idea, and then encode and send a new message. A message that acknowledges or responds to the original message constitutes *feedback,* which also affects the encoding of a new message.[6]

We all communicate and usually don't think much about these complex processes. But the same basic sequence applies to marketing communications—so advertising people cannot afford to take the process for granted. Their jobs depend on getting the message into the market's collective awareness.

Encoding

In the **encoding** stage, advertisers translate an idea or message into words and illustrations—or symbols. In abbreviated messages such as advertising, words and symbols are especially important. For symbols to work, sender and receiver must agree on their meaning.[7] For example, many car ads use an animal (cougar, jaguar, eagle) to represent the product because they are accepted as symbols of power, strength, or speed. This can be an effective

EXHIBIT 4-7

The synergism of graphic design, visual, and text printed on this billboard makes a powerful statement for Wrangler jeans. The billboard medium itself, though, adds greater impact to the message because of its highly visible placement and intrusive nature on the highway.

technique when people view their car as a projection of their personal image rather than as a simple utilitarian device for getting around. Coming up with such symbols—encoding messages in terms that others will understand—is one of the challenges of advertising.

The Medium

Another essential communication concept in marketing is the **medium,** the means or instrument by which the message is carried to the receiver. When a salesperson speaks, vocal chords vibrate air—the medium—which, in turn, vibrates the prospect's eardrums, creating the perception of sound and voice. The message is in the words that are spoken. In print advertising, the publication is the medium, and as shown in Exhibit 4-7, the combination of words and graphics in the ad is the message.

As Marshall McLuhan observed nearly 30 years ago, though, the particular nature of any given medium affects the message dramatically, regardless of the message content.[8] The salesperson's voice—that is, the vibrating air coming from the larynx—gives color, character, and emphasis to the presentation. Similarly, a radio commercial is limited to sound; there are no colors, no graphics. But we still get a "picture" through radio, thanks to inflection, sound effects, and music. As McLuhan pointed out, since it focuses intensely on just one sense—hearing—radio can achieve great emotional "heat."

As a tool of marketing communications, each medium offers certain advantages and disadvantages in the transmission of advertising messages. So, as we shall see in Chapters 12 through 15, harnessing the particular atttributes of a medium and recognizing its limitations are critical to the success of any advertising program.

Decoding

The way the message is **decoded**—interpreted by the receiver—is another challenge for the advertising person. We've all had the unpleasant experience of being misunderstood. And that, of course, is the last thing a marketer wants. Unfortunately, message interpretation is only partially determined by the words and the medium used. The unique characteristics of the receivers are also very important—and the sender often knows little or nothing about them. Attitudes, perceptions, personality, self-concept, and culture are just some of the many influences that affect the way people receive and respond to messages and also how they behave as consumers in the marketplace.

Complicating this problem is the fact that the sender's advertising message must compete with hundreds of others every day. Thus, the sender doesn't know *how* the message is received, or even *if* it's received, until some acknowledgment takes place.

Feedback

That's why feedback is so important. **Feedback** verifies that the message was received. In advertising, feedback may come in a variety of forms: redeemed coupons, telephone inquiries, visits to a store, requests for more information, sales, or responses to a survey. Dramatically low responses to an advertisement indicate a break in the communication process. Questions arise: Is the product wrong for the market? Is the message unclear? Is the right medium being used? Without feedback, these questions cannot be answered.

To better understand and anticipate how people will decode and respond to marketing communications, advertising professionals constantly monitor human perceptions, attitudes, motivations, and actions. This leads us into the broad subject of consumer behavior.

THE IMPORTANCE OF KNOWING THE CONSUMER

Have you met Joe Shields? Chances are you have. But—since he's fictitious—you may know him by another name. He's 22 years old, a little taller than average, good-looking and clean shaven, and has curly, medium-length hair. Joe dresses casually but well, and he loves to have a good time. You have probably seen him cheering at football games or on the beach playing volleyball with the guys and chatting with female friends.

Joe's not only large physically, but he has a strong personality, too. He plans to be a lawyer one day, which is no surprise. He is already somewhat opinionated, and he certainly has a way with words. Joe's not afraid to say what he wants, and he usually gets it. His friends look for his approval and tend to follow his lead. Joe's parents are obviously pretty well-off. His dad develops real estate and seems to know everybody in town.

With or without his parents, Joe does well. Currently a business major, he enjoys college and is conscientious about his work. But that doesn't stop him from having a good time. He's not a loner, nor a homebody. He likes to go out and he likes to party. But he's not at all rowdy. In fact, at times, he can be rather serious and quiet.

Perhaps "casual" is the best way to describe Joe, because even his personal relationships seem to be light and easy rather than heavy and serious. Marriage and a family are a long way off, at least until after law school.

Do you recognize Joe? How well do you know him? Well enough to describe what kind of products he'd prefer? Do you think he eats out, or does he prefer cooking for himself? Does he ski? If so, what brands of gear does he buy? What radio stations does he listen to? What television programs? Does he read the newspaper? If you were trying to advertise a sports car to Joe, what type of appeal would you use? What media?

Advertising people constantly try to attract individuals and groups of individuals (markets) to their products. To succeed, they need to understand

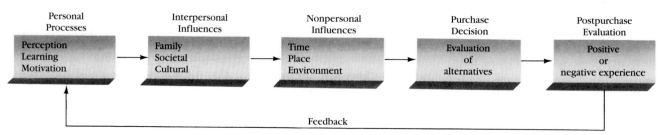

EXHIBIT 4-8

Shown here are the fundamental elements of the consumer decision-making process. A number of factors—personal, interpersonal, and nonpersonal—affect consumer response to an advertisement. The decision-making process then requires a purchase decision. If the consumer decides to buy the product, the final step is an evaluation of whether or not the purchase was a good one The result of this evaluation is fed back to the personal pro-cesses, where it affects future perceptions, learning, and motivation. For the complete model of this process, see Exhibit 4-22 at the end of this chapter.

what makes people like Joe Shields behave the way they do. The advertiser's goal is to get enough relevant market data to develop accurate profiles of potential buyers—to find the common ground (and symbols) for communication. This involves the study of **consumer behavior:** the activities, actions, and influencers of people who purchase and use goods and services to satisfy their personal or household needs and wants.[9] The behavior of **industrial buyers**—the people who purchase industrial goods and services for use in their business—is also very important. We examine in detail this aspect of buying behavior in Chapter 5, as part of the discussion on market segmentation.

Consumer Behavior from the Advertising Perspective

Social scientists have developed many sophisticated theories of consumer behavior. They have given the marketing community a wealth of data and a variety of theoretical models to explain the sequence of behaviors involved in making a purchase decision. For our purposes, we shall look at this information from the viewpoint of the advertiser.

The primary mission of advertising is to reach prospective customers like Joe Shields to influence their awareness, attitudes, and buying behavior. To do this, an advertiser must make the marketing communication process work at its highest level of efficiency.

The moment a medium delivers an ad message to Joe Shields, Joe's mental computer runs a rapid evaluation program called the **consumer decision-making process.** This involves a series of subprocesses that are affected by a variety of influences. The conceptual model in Exhibit 4-8 presents the fundamental building blocks in the consumer decision-making process.

First, three **personal processes** govern the way Joe discerns raw data (stimuli) and translates them into feelings, thoughts, beliefs, and actions. These include the perception, the learning, and the motivation processes.

Second, an advertiser needs to understand how Joe's mental processes and behavior are affected by two sets of influences. **Interpersonal influences** on consumer behavior include the consumer's *family, society,* and *culture.* **Nonpersonal influences**—factors often outside the consumer's control—include such things as time, place, and environment. All of these further affect the personal processes (perception, learning, motivation) mentioned above.

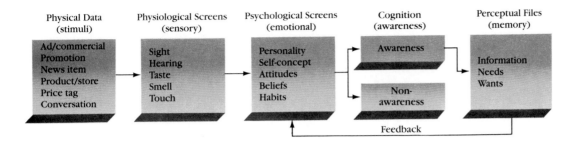

Physical Data (stimuli)	Physiological Screens (sensory)	Psychological Screens (emotional)	Cognition (awareness)	Perceptual Files (memory)
Ad/commercial Promotion News item Product/store Price tag Conversation	Sight Hearing Taste Smell Touch	Personality Self-concept Attitudes Beliefs Habits	Awareness / Non-awareness	Information Needs Wants

Feedback

EXHIBIT 4-9

The consumer perception process model shows that, when confronted with an advertisement or some other buying stimulus, the consumer processes data through sensory and emotional screens before deciding whether the data should be filed mentally as simple information or as a solution to needs or wants.

After dealing with all these processes and influences, Joe faces the pivotal decision, to buy or not to buy? But taking that final step typically requires yet another process, the **evaluation of selection alternatives**—where brands, sizes, styles, and colors are chosen. And even if the purchase is made, Joe's *postpurchase evaluation* will have a dramatic impact on all his subsequent purchases.

Like the marketing communication process, the decision-making process is circular in nature. The advertiser who understands this process can develop messages that are more capable of reaching and being understood by consumers.

Personal Processes in Consumer Behavior

The first task in advertising any new product is to create awareness (perception) that the product exists. The second is to provide enough information (learning) about the product for the prospective customer to make an informed decision. Finally, the advertiser wants to be persuasive enough to stimulate the customer's desire (motivation) to purchase and repurchase the product. Hence, the three personal processes of consumer behavior shown in Exhibit 4-8—perception, learning, and motivation—are extremely important to advertisers.

By studying and understanding these mental processes, advertisers can better evaluate how people perceive their messages. They can determine what people think or know about their products, whether they have a particular attitude about them, and how prospective customers might develop the habit of purchasing them.

The Consumer Perception Process

The perception problem is the first and greatest problem advertisers face. Some advertisers spend millions of dollars on national advertising, sales promotion, and point-of-purchase displays, only to discover later that consumers have little or no memory of their product or promotion. Similarly, the average adult is exposed to over 300 advertisements a day, but only a handful get noticed, and even fewer are remembered.[10] How can these things happen? The answer lies in the concept of *perception*. To understand these phenomena, let us look at what perception is and how the consumer perception process works.

Perception is our personalized way of sensing and comprehending the stimuli we are exposed to.[11] This definition suggests several key elements for understanding the consumer perception process, as shown in Exhibit 4-9.

Stimulus First is the concept of an outside **stimulus.** This is physical data that can be sensed by the person. When Joe Shields looks at a new automobile,

In this ad, the "hidden" image is the logo for Colombian coffee—Juan Valdez and his faithful companion. DDB Needham Worldwide chose to design the ad as a color-blindness test to cleverly get across the message that consumers should look for the logo as a sign of quality. Interestingly, for those who are truly red-green color blind, the ad will have difficulty penetrating the reader's physiological screen.

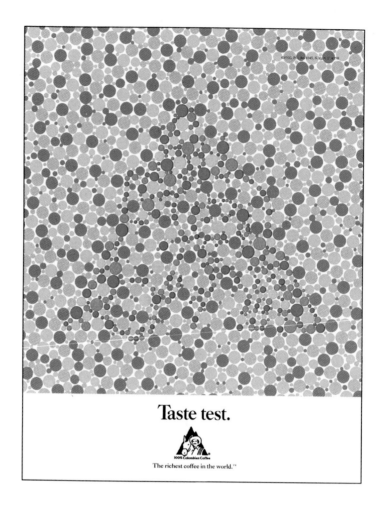

Taste test.

The richest coffee in the world.™

what is the stimulus? It's simply an organized collection of colored paint, tires, glass, and steel. That's the physical data, or stimulus. Likewise, when we look at a theater ad in the newspaper, what really hits us is the reflection of light off ink on paper, in the symbolic form of type, art, and photography. That's the stimulus, technically. But, for our purposes, we can assume that a stimulus is any ad, commercial, or promotion that confronts us.

Similarly, a stimulus could appear in the form of a window display at Macy's, the brightly colored labels on Dole fruit cocktail cans, or even a price tag on the skis at the Sport Chalet. These objects are all physical in nature. Like the ad shown in Exhibit 4-10, they stimulate our senses—with varying degrees of intensity—in ways that can be measured.

Perceptual Screens The second key element in the definition of perception is the personalized way of sensing the data—which brings us to the subject of *screens*. Before any data can be perceived, it must first penetrate a set of **perceptual screens,** the perceptual filters that messages must pass through.[12] The **physiological screens** comprise the five senses—sight, hearing, touch, taste, and smell. They detect the incoming data and measure the dimension and intensity of the physical stimulus. Obviously, a sight-impaired person would not be able to read an ad in *Sports Illustrated*. Likewise, if the type in a movie ad is too small for the average reader, it won't pass the threshold of sight, and perception will suffer. Similarly, if the music

EXHIBIT 4-11

Alpine cleverly uses a bent music staff to illustrate what a driver might perceive when the car hits a bump. This is an example of an attempt to pass through the consumer's psychological screen, which brings personal feelings and interests into the decision-making process.

EXHIBIT 4-12

When research showed that female consumers perceived Maidenform's line of bras as old-fashioned and conservative, the company responded with a bolder advertising approach and added more sex appeal to the product.

in a furniture store's TV commercial is too loud, the viewer may change channels or even turn the TV off. Here, the advertiser's message is effectively screened out, and perception will not occur.

We are limited not only by the physical capacity of our senses but also by our feelings and our interests. The consumer uses **psychological screens** to evaluate, filter, and personalize information according to subjective standards. More emotional in nature, these screens make evaluations based on criteria that include innate factors—such as the consumer's personality and instinctive human needs—and learned factors such as self-concept, interests, attitudes, beliefs, past experience, and lifestyle. These screens help consumers formulate summary notions and concepts from sometimes unwieldy or complex data that may otherwise be too difficult to articulate. For example, the perceptual screens help us accept or reject symbolic ideas such as the one suggested in Exhibit 4-11.

For example, one study asked female consumers how they perceived the Maidenform line of bras. Many respondents described it as old-fashioned and conservative, a brand worn by older women as opposed to young career women.[13] That was the respondents' reality. The product didn't fit their **self-concept**—the image we carry in our mind of the type of person we are and whom we desire to be. As a result, much of Maidenform's advertising didn't penetrate the consumers' screens. It went unnoticed, and sales suffered. Maidenform's response was to use a bolder advertising approach to appeal to modern young women, as shown in Exhibit 4-12.

As the Maidenform example shows, advertisers face a major problem in the way consumers use their perceptual screens. Consumers unconsciously screen out or modify many sensations that bombard them by rejecting those that conflict with their previous or current experiences, needs, desires, attitudes, and beliefs.[14] They simply focus attention on some things and ignore others. This is called **selective perception.** Hence, 4-Day Tire Stores may run many ads in the daily newspaper, but these ads won't get through the psychological screens of consumers who don't need tires. Later, they will be unable to remember seeing the ads.[15]

Cognition The third key element in our definition of perception is the concept of comprehension, or **cognition.** Once our senses detect the stimulus and allow it through the screens, we have an *awareness* of it. Since it relates to our previous experiences, we simultaneously *comprehend* and accept it. Now the act of perception has taken place.

This moment is an important experience for the consumer. The comprehension and acceptance of the stimulus make the perception come alive, placing it instantly in the consumer's reality zone.

Each of us has his or her own reality. For example, you may consider the tacos and burritos advertised by Del Taco to be "Mexican" food. That perception is your reality, even though someone from Mexico might tell you that, *in reality,* a fast-food taco bears little resemblance to an "authentic" Mexican taco. That person's reality, based on his or her perception, is considerably different. As seen in Exhibit 4-13, advertisers quite often use stereotypical themes to reach a more widely shared interpretation of reality.

Mental Files At the point of cognition, the consumer has to make a judgment—where to file the perception. The mind is like a memory bank, and the stored memories in our minds are called the **mental files.** When we perceive new

EXHIBIT 4-13

Many consumers perceive that fast-food tacos are authentic Mexican food, when in reality there may be little resemblance in taste or preparation. This ad for Dos Locos restaurant points up the difference.

information, it must be filed, or it will be instantly forgotten. We do this both consciously and, more often, subconsciously.

We have files for our needs and wants, attitudes, preferences, beliefs, and habits. We even have files full of random information gleaned from past learning. Some of our files are very specific: for industries, products, services, brand names.

In today's highly communicative society, our senses are bombarded by stimuli, and our mental files are crowded with information. To cope with the complexity of stimuli like advertising, we rank products and other data in our files by importance, by price, by quality, by features, or by a host of other descriptors. But unfortunately for many advertisers, consumers can rarely hold more than seven brand names in any one file—more often the number is one or two. The remainder either get discarded to some other file category or rejected altogether.[16] How many brands of coffee can you name?

Because of our limited memory, we resist opening new files, and we avoid accepting new information that is incongruent with what is already filed.[17] But once a new perception enters our files, the information from that perception alters the database upon which our psychological screen feeds. Thus, our mental files are major contributors to the screen-building process. For example, when a computer owner hears the word *mouse,* the mouse most relevant to his or her experiences, needs, and wants is most likely to come to mind first. This is portrayed in Exhibit 4-14.

Since screens are such a major challenge to advertisers, it's important to have some understanding of what is in the consumer's mental files and, if possible, to modify those files in favor of the advertiser's product. (See Ad Lab 4-B, "Positioning Strategy—Or, How to Penetrate the Perceptual Screens.") That brings us to the second process in consumer behavior—learning.

The Consumer Learning Process

Each new perception that we file in our minds is an additional step in learning. In fact, many psychologists consider learning to be the most fundamental

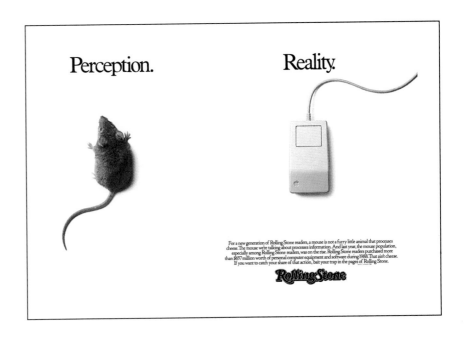

AD LAB 4-B
Positioning Strategy—Or, How to Penetrate the Perceptual Screens

Al Ries (chairman of the board) and Jack Trout (president) of Trout & Ries, Inc., are widely known for developing the "positioning" approach to advertising. Their book *Positioning: The Battle for Your Mind,* from which the following is adapted, has become an industry text. As a result, *positioning* has become the buzzword of advertising and marketing people not only in this country but around the world.

Positioning is a simple principle that can best be demonstrated by asking yourself some simple questions. Who was the first person to fly solo across the North Atlantic? Right, Charles Lindbergh. Who was the second person to fly solo across the North Atlantic? Not so easy to answer, is it? Similarly, the first company to occupy the position in a prospect's mind is going to be awfully hard to dislodge: IBM in computers, Hertz in rental cars, Coke in cola.

Like a memory bank, the mind has a slot or position for each bit of information it has chosen to retain. In its operation, the mind is a lot like a computer. But there is one important difference. A computer has to accept what is put into it, whereas the mind does not. In fact, quite the opposite. As a defense mechanism against the volume of today's communications, the mind screens and rejects much of the information offered it. In general, the mind accepts only new information that matches its prior knowledge or experience. It filters out everything else.

For example, when a viewer sees a television commercial that says, "NCR means computers," he doesn't accept it. IBM means computers; NCR means National Cash Register. The computer "position" in the minds of most people is filled by a company called IBM. For a competitive computer manufacturer to obtain a favorable position in the prospect's mind, it must relate its company to IBM's position.

To cope with advertising's complexity, people have learned to rank products and brands. Imagine a series of ladders in the mind. On each step is a brand name, and each different ladder represents a different product category. For advertisers to increase their brand preference, they must move up the ladder.

This is difficult, especially if the new category is not positioned against an old one. The mind has no room for the new and different unless it is related to the old. Therefore, if you have a truly new product, it's often better to tell the prospect what the product is not, rather than what it is.

The first automobile, for example, was called a "horseless" carriage, a name that positioned the concept against the existing mode of transportation. Words like *off-track betting, lead-free gasoline,* and *tubeless tires* are examples of how new concepts can best be positioned against the old ones.

Number-One Strategy

Successful marketing strategy usually consists of keeping your eyes open to possibilities and then striking before the product ladder is firmly fixed. The marketing leader is usually the one who moves the ladder into the mind with his or her brand nailed to the one and only rung.

Once there, what can a company do to keep its top-dog position? As long as a company owns the position, there's no point in running ads that scream "We're No. 1." It is much better to enhance the product category in prospects' minds. IBM ad campaigns typically ignore the competition and sell the value of computers—all computers, not just the company's types.

Number-Two Strategy

Most companies are in the number two, three, four, or even worse category. Nine times out of 10, these also-rans set out to attack the leader. The result is disaster.

In the communication jungle, the only hope is to be selective, to concentrate on narrow targets, and to practice segmentation. For example, Anheuser-Busch found an opening for a high-priced beer and filled it with Michelob. Advertisers must assess the competitors. They must locate weak points in their positions and then launch marketing attacks against them. Savin developed small, inexpensive copiers and took advantage of a weakness in the Xerox product line.

Simply stated, the first rule of positioning is this: You can't compete head-on with a company that has a strong, established position. You can go around, under, or over, but never head to head. The leader owns the high ground, the top position in the prospect's mind, the top rung of the product ladder.

Laboratory Applications

1. What type of car do you drive? What position does it occupy in the automobile market? Number one? Lower? What marketing strategy would be most appropriate for advertising that model?

2. Find a magazine ad that appeals to you. First identify the product category. Then identify the strategy used by the advertiser. Would you guess that the product is number one in its category? Or is it competing with number one? From what you know of the product and its position in the marketplace, is the strategy appropriate? Explain why or why not.

3. Can you think of any new concepts that were advertised by positioning them against old concepts? What slogans did they use?

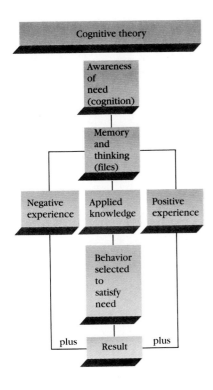

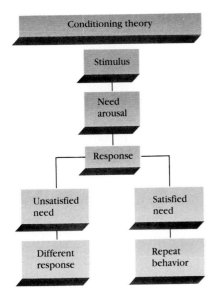

EXHIBIT 4-15

The two theories of learning are *cognitive theory*, which views learning as a mental process, and *conditioning theory*, which treats learning as a trial-and-error process.

process in human behavior; but from the advertiser's perspective, perception is most important because it precedes learning. In truth, perception and learning are a continuum, overlapping each other.

Like perception, learning works off the files and also contributes to them. Learning produces our habits and skills. It also contributes to the development of attitudes, beliefs, preferences, prejudices, emotions, and standards of conduct—all of which affect our perceptual screens and our eventual purchase decisions.

By definition, **learning** is a relatively permanent change in thought process or behavior that occurs as a result of reinforced experience. There are numerous theories of learning, but advertisers classify most into two broad categories: *cognitive theory* and *conditioning theory*. The applicability of each typically depends upon the level of consumer involvement (high or low) required to make a purchase. **Cognitive theory** views learning as a mental process of memory, thinking, and the rational application of knowledge to practical problems. This theory may be an accurate description of the way people evaluate a complex purchase such as insurance, stocks and bonds, or industrial goods and services. **Conditioning theory**—also called *stimulus-response theory*—treats learning as a trial-and-error process and is more applicable to the less complex, basic purchases consumers make every day. Some *stimulus* triggers the consumer's need or want, which in turn creates the drive to *respond*. If the response reduces the drive, then satisfaction occurs, and the response is rewarded or reinforced. This produces repeat behavior the next time the drive is aroused, demonstrating that learning has taken place.[18] Exhibit 4-15 shows simple diagrams of these two theories.

What if the purchase turns out to be unsatisfactory? Learning still takes place, but then something else happens. As John O'Toole says, "The mightiest weapon consumers have, and the one manufacturers fear most, is their refusal to repurchase. Advertising is powerful in that it can get them to buy a product once. But if it doesn't please them, the heaviest media budget in the world won't get them to buy again."[19]

When customers feel the product fails to meet standards or advertising promises—implied or stated—they tell others. This is especially true with single purchases such as concerts, theatrical performances, and impulse purchases. Many people tend to wait—to read newspaper reviews and to listen to their friends' opinions—before buying. Have you ever noticed how fast a bad movie dies at the box office? Bad word of mouth creates negative attitudes and beliefs and cancels the marketer's dream of creating new audiences, repeat business, or brand loyalty.

In contrast, good word of mouth works to create repeat purchases—leading to a purchasing habit. This is particularly important for businesses committed to long leases, large staffs, and many stores.

Superior product performance, good service, and reminder advertising all provide purchase reinforcement. If learning is reinforced enough and repeat behavior is produced, a purchasing habit may result.

Repetition is important to learning. Just as a student prepares for an exam by repeating key information to memorize it, an advertiser must repeat key information to prospective and current customers so they can better remember the product's name and its benefits. Repeat messages help break through a customer's perceptual screens by rekindling memories of key information from prior ads. In Exhibit 4-16, Quebec-based Cossette Communications-Marketing used pairs of billboards for its client Provigo stores, each featuring a strong visual element similar to the other, and positioned to be seen in succession. The repetition proved to be a highly successful awareness technique, producing $100 million in sales in just six months.[20]

Mario's stories.

Provigo's fish.

Marcel's jalopy.

Provigo's lemon.

EXHIBIT 4-16

This billboard ad for Provigo grocery store chain was part of a total campaign that not only created great awareness but also unusual reader interest and word of mouth. The double exposure of successive billboards reinforced the advertiser's message and stimulated consumer learning and memory.

Learning Produces Habits The natural extension of learning is **habit,** an acquired or developed behavior pattern that has become nearly or completely involuntary. The old cliché, "People are creatures of habit," is true.

Most consumer behavior is habitual for three interconnected reasons—it's safe, it's easy, and it's essential. First, regardless of how we learned to make our purchase decision (cognitive or conditioning process), we have discovered a reliable product or service. Because the purchase has been proved *safe,* we can now allow ourselves to repurchase it through habit.

Second, habit is *easy.* Having to consider an alternative to our usual choice forces us to think, evaluate, compare, and then decide. This is difficult, time-consuming, and risky.

Finally, because it's both safe and easy, we come to rely on it for our daily living. Considering the high volume of purchases made by the average consumer every day, habit is *essential.* Imagine trying to rethink every purchase decision you make. It would be virtually impossible—not to mention impractical.

A major objective of many advertisers is to produce the phenomenon known as *brand loyalty,* which comes directly from the habit of repurchasing. **Brand loyalty** is the consumer's conscious or unconscious decision—expressed through intention or behavior—to repurchase a brand continually.[21] This occurs because the consumer perceives that the brand offers the right product features, image, quality, or relationship at the right price.[22]

In the quest for brand loyalty, advertisers have three aims related to habits:

1. *Breaking habits:* to get consumers to *unlearn* an existing purchase habit—that is, to stop buying their habitual brand and try a new one. Advertisers frequently offer incentives to lure customers away from old brands or stores.

2. *Acquiring habits:* to help consumers learn to repurchase their brand or repatronize their establishment. For example, to get you started, record clubs offer free products the first month tied to a contract to purchase more later on.

3. *Reinforcing habits:* to remind current customers of the value of their original purchase and to encourage them to continue purchasing. Many magazines, for example, offer special rates for regular subscribers.

Developing loyalty is a long-term objective of all marketers. Ironically, though, achieving brand loyalty today is more difficult than ever before due to the increased sophistication of consumers and to the legions of habit-breaking activities of competitive advertisers.[23]

Learning Produces Attitudes Attitudes and habits are two sides of the same coin. Habit is the behavioral side; attitude is the mental side. An **attitude** is the acquired mental position we hold in regard to some idea or object. It is the positive or negative evaluations, feelings, or action tendencies that we have learned and cling to. To advertisers, gaining positive consumer attitudes is critical to success. Like habits, attitudes must be either capitalized upon or changed. The Pepsi challenge campaign, for instance—that held taste comparison tests all over the country—was aimed at changing Coca-Cola drinkers' attitudes.

Learning Defines Needs and Wants The learning process is both instantaneous and long term. The moment a perception is filed, some learning takes place. When we smell food cooking, we may become aware that we are hungry. As we collate the information in our mental files, comparing new perceptions with old, further learning takes place. The need may become a want. This then leads us into the next personal process—motivation.

The Consumer Motivation Process

Motivation refers to the underlying drives that contribute to the individual's purchasing actions. These drives stem from the conscious or unconscious *goal* of satisfying the needs and wants of the consumer. **Needs** are the basic, often instinctive, human forces that motivate a person to do something. **Wants** are "needs" that are learned during a person's lifetime.[24]

Motivations cannot be directly observed. When we see people eat, we assume they are hungry, but that assumption may not be correct. People eat for a variety of reasons besides hunger—because they want to be sociable, because it is time to eat, or because they are bored or nervous.

Often a combination of motives underlies the decision-making process. The reasons (motives) some people stop shopping at Lucky Supermarket and switch to Von's may be that the Von's market is closer to home and has a wider selection of fresh produce and (most likely) that they see other people like themselves shopping at Von's. Any one of these factors might be enough to make the shopper switch even if the prices on many items are lower at Lucky.

In an attempt to better understand what motivates people, Abraham Maslow developed the following classic model called the **hierarchy of needs:**

1. Physiological needs: oxygen, food, drink, sex, rest.
2. Safety needs: infantile dependency; avoidance of situations that are unfamiliar, threatening, or might lead to injury or illness; economic security.

3. Social needs: friendship, affection, a sense of belonging.

4. Esteem needs: self-respect, recognition, status, prestige, success.

5. Self-actualization: living up to one's potential (self-fulfillment).

Maslow maintained that the physiological and safety needs are dominant in human behavior and must be satisfied before the higher, socially acquired needs (or wants) become meaningful.[25]

The promise of satisfying a certain level of need establishes the basic promotional appeal for many advertisements. However, in such affluent societies as the United States, Canada, Western Europe, and Japan, most individuals pay little attention to physiological needs; they take satisfaction of these needs for granted. Thus, as shown in Exhibit 4-17, marketing and advertising campaigns for many products portray the fulfillment of social, esteem, and self-actualization needs, and many offer the rewards of better personal or love relationships.

People with needs and wants are frequently unaware of them. For example, before the desktop computer came along, most people were completely unaware of any need or want for it. However, the moment a consumer consciously recognizes a product-related want or need, an interesting process is set in motion. The consumer must first evaluate the need or want and then decide to either accept or reject it as worthy of action. Acceptance converts the satisfaction of the want or need into a *goal*, which, in turn, creates the dedication—or the motivation—to reach a particular end result. In contrast, rejection removes the necessity for action and thereby eliminates any motivation to buy.

The lesson here is that advertising cannot serve simply as an awareness builder. It must do more. Advertising must stimulate a decision about wants and needs. An ad that effectively portrays a chicly dressed model receiving enviable attention may stimulate the recognition on the part of some men and women of their need to be noticed and appreciated. If they accept this need, the readers of the ad will formulate a goal: to shop for clothes that attract the appropriate attention or recognition of others. If the name of the product or store is clearly presented in the ad, the advertiser may experience an increase in sales.

In some cases, advertisers have been accused of going too far in stimulating consumers' needs and wants. Some people have asserted that certain liquor ads, for example, hide distorted images of sexual references within the convoluted shadows and highlights of the featured glass, liquid, and ice cubes. The allegation is that such imagery offers the implied promise that liquor will help resolve the need for a more active sexual life. Are these claims true? Can decisions about needs and wants be encouraged by images and messages so well disguised that we're not even sure we've received them? For an answer, see Ad Lab 4-C, "Subliminal Manipulation: Fact or Fantasy?"

Advertisers must realize that people usually are motivated by the goal of satisfying some combination of two or more needs, and the needs may be both conscious and unconscious. *Motivation research* has offered some insights into the underlying reasons for unexpected consumer behavior. This subject is discussed more thoroughly in Chapter 6.

The lesson for advertisers is to carefully consider the goals that lead to consumer motivations before creating advertising messages. For example, in an ad for Denny's Restaurants, it might be a costly mistake to portray the goal as a romantic interlude if the real goal that motivates most Denny's customers is simply the satisfaction of their need for a nutritious, low-priced meal.

Interpersonal Influences on Consumer Behavior

For the advertising professional, it's not enough just to know the personal behavioral processes of perception, learning, and motivation. Important **interpersonal influences** affect—and sometimes even dominate—these processes, and they also serve as guidelines and measuring sticks for consumer behavior. These interpersonal influences can best be categorized as the *family,* the *society,* and the *cultural environment* of the consumer.

Family

Just think for a moment about where your attitudes and beliefs about ethical values, religion, work, gender roles, other ethnic groups, political philosophy, sexual behavior, right and wrong, and economics come from. They receive their initial direction in the family setting. From an early age, family communication affects our socialization as consumers—our attitudes toward many products and our purchasing habits.[26] This influence is usually strong and long-lasting. Learning as a child that the "right" headache relief is St. Joseph aspirin and the "right" name for appliances is General Electric goes a long way toward shaping the purchasing behavior of adults.

In recent years, however, research has indicated that family influence is diminished as working parents take a less active role in raising their children and as youngsters look outside the family for social values.[27] As this happens, the influence of society and culture intensify.

Society

The community we live in exerts a strong influence on all of us. When we affiliate with a particular societal division, or value the opinions of certain people, or identify with some special-interest group, it affects not only our views on life but also our perceptual screens and eventually the products we buy.

AD LAB 4-C
Subliminal Manipulation: Fact or Fantasy?

Is it possible to manipulate people with subliminal advertising? This intriguing controversy started back in the 1950s when Vance Packard's best-seller, *The Hidden Persuaders,* described an experiment that appeared to show that if a message was perceived, perhaps unconsciously, at levels below the "limen," or perceptual threshold, it could motivate consumers.

The experiment involved showing movies while at the same time projecting the words *Eat Popcorn* and *Drink Coca-Cola* on the screen for 1/3,000 of a second. Sales figures jumped 57 percent for popcorn and 18 percent for Coca-Cola during the six-week term of the experiment. As expected, this finding caused quite a furor. Some states passed laws to prevent the practice. However, this study has never been replicated successfully. One reason perhaps was that a number of factors may have affected the results of the experiment. For example, the movie being shown during the experiment period was *Picnic,* which included many scenes of people eating and drinking in hot summer weather.

If subliminal advertising could persuade people "against their will," profound ethical questions would be raised. But there is general agreement that it is not possible. First, the threshold (or level) at which people perceive visual and aural stimuli varies greatly. Obviously, people with good eyesight perceive visual stimuli more easily than people who wear glasses. Furthermore, researchers are able to measure *galvanic skin response (GSR)*—changes in the electrical activity of the skin—when certain stimuli are introduced. But no GSR can be detected during supposed subliminal perception states. The conclusion, therefore, is that no message has been perceived. And even if a message were perceived, it could be easily distorted: "Drink Coke" might make a viewer "go smoke" or "think jokes."

The subliminal perception controversy has been rekindled with the publication of books that accused advertising people of planting hidden sexual messages in print ads—particularly in the ice cubes portrayed in liquor advertising.

Subliminal Seduction (subtitled "Here Are the Secret Ways Ad Men Arouse Your Desires to Sell Their Products") and *Media Sexploitation* include numerous examples of what the author (Wilson Bryan Keys) believes are sexual symbols, four-letter words, and pornographic pictures buried in the otherwise bland content of various ads. He concludes that such "hidden persuaders" were carefully contrived by major advertisers and their agencies to seduce consumers at a subliminal level.

The fact is that virtually all photographs used in national advertising are retouched, either by hand or by electronic means, in order to correct imperfections or add visual effects to the picture (see Chapter 10). At this point in the production process, it is entirely possible for some mischievous creativity to take place. A photo retoucher could, for example, add some carefully disguised sexual element into an ad which, when reduced down to final size, would not be noticeable and would only be known to him or her. However, this would be considered highly unprofessional and unethical in the business, and if discovered, it would be cause for immediate termination of the offender. It would also seriously endanger the agency's relationship with its client.

As far as Mr. Keys's idea of the insidious cunning of marketing decision makers goes, it is interesting to note that in more than 600 pages on the subject, he mentions not a single individual who admits to, or even accuses others of, being involved in subliminal embedding.

Dr. Jack Haberstroh, professor in the School of Mass Communications at Virginia Commonwealth University, investigated Keys's charge that S-E-X is embedded on the face of Ritz crackers. His research even included a visit to a Ritz cracker factory. He concludes that the charges of S-E-X written on Ritz crackers in particular and of subliminal advertising in general are "preposterous, absurd, ludicrous, and laughable."

Laboratory Applications

1. Would words with sexual connotations hidden in an advertisement motivate you to purchase a product? Why or why not?

2. Do you feel that appeals to the consumer's prurient interests can help sell products? If so, what kinds of products?

Societal Divisions Traditionally, sociologists have divided societies into social classes: upper class, upper-middle class, lower-middle class, and so on. They believe that people in the same social class tend toward similar attitudes, status symbols, and spending patterns.

But today, this does not apply to most developed countries. North American society, especially, is extremely mobile—physically, socially, and economically. Americans, for example, believe strongly in "getting ahead,"

EXHIBIT 4-18	Contemporary Social Classes

Name	Description
Upper Crust	Metropolitan families, very high income and education, manager/professionals; very high installment activity
Mid-Life Success	Families, very high education, managers/professionals, technical/sales, high income; super-high installment activity
Movers and Shakers	Singles, couples, students, and recent graduates, high education and income, managers/professionals, technical/sales; average credit activity, medium-high installment activity
Successful Singles	Young, single renters, older housing, ethnic mix, high education, medium income, managers/professionals; very high bankcard accounts, very high installment activity, very low retail activity
Stars and Stripes	Young, large school-age families, medium income and education, military, precision/craft; average credit activity
Social Security	Mature/seniors, metro fringe, singles and couples, medium income and education, mixed jobs; very low credit activity
Middle of the Road	School-age families, mixed education, medium income, mixed jobs; very high revolving activity, very high bankcard accounts
Trying Metro Times	Young, seniors, ethnic mix, low income, older housing, low education, renters, mixed jobs; low credit activity, medium-high retail activity
Low-Income Blues	Blacks, singles and families, older housing, low income and education, services, laborers; low credit activity, medium-high retail activity
University USA	Students, singles, dorms/group quarters, very low income, medium-high education, technical/sales; low credit activity, high percent new accounts

The groups outlined in this exhibit are just 10 of 50 Microvision lifestyle segments defined by National Decision Systems, a division of Equifax.

"being better than your peers," "moving up," and "winning greater admiration and self-esteem." As the famous U.S. Army campaign illustrates, advertisers often capitalize on this broad-based desire to "be all that you can be."

Due to this mobility, to dramatic increases in immigration, and to the high divorce rate, social class boundaries have become quite muddled. Single parents, stockbrokers, immigrant shopkeepers, retired blue-collar workers, and bankers, for example, all see themselves as part of the great middle class.[28] So middle class just doesn't mean anything anymore. From the advertiser's point of view, social class no longer represents a functional or operational set of values.

To deal with these often bewildering changes, marketers have sought new ways to classify societal divisions and new strategies for appealing to them. Some of these are discussed in Chapter 5. Exhibit 4-18 outlines some of the more contemporary classifications marketers use to describe society today: for example, Stars and Stripes, Mid-Life Success, University USA, and Movers and Shakers.

Reference Groups Most of us are concerned with how we appear in the eyes of other people. We may even pattern our behavior after members of some groups we affiliate with. This is the significance of **reference groups**—people we try to emulate or whose approval concerns us. Reference groups can be personal (family, friends, co-workers) or impersonal (movie stars, professional athletes, business executives). A special reference group—our peers—exerts tremendous influence on what we believe and on the way we behave. To win acceptance by our peers (fellow students, co-workers, colleagues), we may purchase a certain style of clothing, choose a particular place to live, and acquire habits that will earn their approval. The ad in Exhibit 4-19 alludes to peer acceptance to help stimulate the desire for the advertiser's attractive set of kitchen knives and accompanying wooden stand.

Often an individual is influenced in opposite directions by two reference groups and must choose between them. For example, a college student may feel pressure from some friends to join a Greek house and at the same time be influenced by others to live independently with them off-campus.

Opinion Leaders An **opinion leader** is some person or organization whose beliefs or attitudes are respected by people who share an interest in some specific activity. All fields (sports, religion, economics, fashion, finance, politics) have opinion leaders. An opinion leader may be a knowledgeable friend or some expert we don't know personally. We reason, "If so-and-so believes Spalding is the right tennis racket, then it must be so. She knows more about the game than I do." Thus, the purchasing habits and testimonials of opinion leaders are important to advertisers.

EXHIBIT 4-19

Consumers often purchase products they feel their peers will approve of. This ad by Chicago Cutlery uses the appeal of social influence to promote its knives.

The advertiser must thoroughly understand its market when choosing an opinion leader as a spokesperson for the company or product. Even though some top executives may not personally relate to the spokesperson, the company must allow market tastes and interests to dictate their actions. If the company's advertising or spokesperson is out of tune with the market, the credibility of the opinion leader—and the company—will be undermined. The ad in Exhibit 4-20, for example, is an interesting case of a company seeking to relate to its target market through the use of a cutting-edge professional—Glen Plake, "extreme" skier extraordinaire.

Culture and Subculture

Culture imposes a tenacious influence on the consumer. Americans love to eat hot dogs, peanut butter, corn on the cob, and apple pie. Canada, Russia, Germany—every country has its own favorite specialties. It is nearly impossible for an advertiser to change these tastes.

The United States and Canada embrace many subcultures, some of them quite large. They may be based on race, national origin, religion, or geographic proximity. The advertiser must understand these subcultures, since differences among them may affect responses to both products and advertising messages.

The United States, in particular, is a great melting pot of minority subcultures. According to the U.S. Census Bureau, 31 million blacks, 21 million Hispanics, and 7 million Asians lived in the United States in 1990—plus an unknown number of undocumented foreign nationals. In 1990, these three minority groups alone accounted for over 21 percent of the American population; and by the year 2000, they may account for more than 25 percent.[29]

Subcultures tend to transfer their beliefs and values from generation to generation. Racial, religious, and ethnic backgrounds affect their preferences

EXHIBIT 4-20

Glen Plake, a well-known extreme skier, endorses Look ski bindings in this ad. By implication, if Plake likes Look bindings, they must be good—because he should know.

Companies are now recognizing that a special appeal to minorities makes good business sense. In this example, State Farm focuses on the Hispanic market by featuring insurance agent Ernie Lopez.

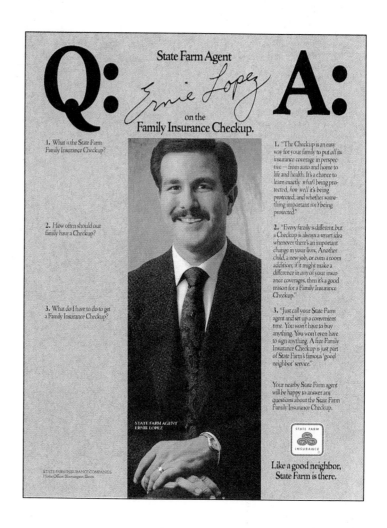

for styles of dress, food, beverages, transportation, personal-care products, and household furnishings, to name a few. In recent years, advertising agencies that specialize in growing minority markets have boomed as more and more advertisers recognize that an appeal tailored to minorities makes good business sense.[30] An extremely important element in a minority market ad is a visual featuring an individual from the targeted groups, like the State Farm ad in Exhibit 4-21 aimed at the Hispanic market.

Similarly, the social environment in other countries is also based on their particular language, culture, literacy rate, religion, and lifestyle. Their customs cannot be ignored by advertisers, particularly those that market products globally. International advertising is discussed in Chapter 19.

In summary, there are as many interpersonal influences on a consumer as personal processes. They all have an important effect on our mental files, screen building, and subsequent purchase decisions. An awareness of these interpersonal influences helps marketers create the strategy behind much advertising.

Nonpersonal Influences on Consumer Behavior

Numerous **nonpersonal influences** may also affect the consumer's final purchase decision. The most important nonpersonal influences are *time,* *place,* and *environment.* These influences are typically outside the consumer's control. But in certain cases, advertisers may affect them.

Time

The old saw, "timing is everything," certainly applies to marketing and advertising. A special three-day weekend sale may provide just the added incentive to break through the perceptual screen and bring a customer into the store. But running a commercial for that sale on Sunday evening would certainly be a foolish waste of advertising dollars.

Likewise, the consumer's particular need may be a function of time. Consumers certainly don't need snow tires in the summer (although some off-season promotions do work). On the other hand, if we unexpectedly get a flat on the highway, the time factor is suddenly the most important consideration in evaluating a purchase decision for new tires. As we shall see in our chapters on media, all marketing activities (including advertising) must be planned with the consumer's time clock in mind.

Place

Once Joe Shields decides to purchase a product, he may still hesitate if he doesn't know where the product is sold or if it is not available in a convenient or preferred location, Similarly, if consumers believe that a particular brand is a specialty good, but then it suddenly appears everywhere, their "specialness" perception of the product may be diminished. For these reasons, marketers carefully weigh consumer demand when deciding where to build stores or offer their products, and they devote much advertising time and space to communicating the convenience of location. *Place* is an important element of the marketing mix and will be discussed further in Chapter 5.

Environment

Many *environments*—ecological, political, technical, economic, household, and point-of-sale location, to mention a few—can affect the purchase decision. For example, advertisers can't expect to penetrate the perceptual screens of consumers who don't have the economic capacity to afford the purchase. And no matter how well you advertise them or how inexpensively you price them, NRA memberships aren't likely to be a hot item with members of the Audubon Society. On the other hand, an enticing display next to the cash register is known to improve the sale of low-cost impulse items. Thus, advertisers must consider the influence of the purchase environment on the consumer's decision processes.

The Purchase Decision and Postpurchase Evaluation

Now, let's examine the process involved in a typical purchase decision—the decision to buy a new blouse—made by a typical consumer like Joe Shields' younger sister, Christine. To help follow this process and see the interrelationship of the many behavioral factors we've discussed, study the complete model of the consumer decision-making process shown in Exhibit 4-22.

Christine still lives at home and is just about to enroll at the local community college. Although she has a part-time job, she is still supported by her parents and therefore has to act responsibly in their eyes particularly when it comes to spending money.

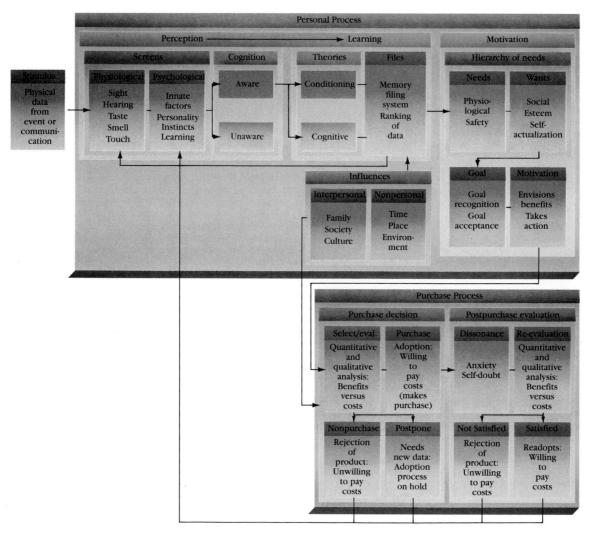

EXHIBIT 4-22

The complete model of the consumer decision-making process in its complexity.

One day Christine is thumbing through the most recent issue of *Elle*. Her eyes are attracted to a warmly colored ad portraying an elegantly dressed young woman enjoying a gourmet candlelight dinner with an attractive man. But the blouse is what catches Christine's attention. Its feminine tailoring, understated design, and rich silk fabric exude the essence of class—it's her kind of style. (See Ad Lab 4-D: "Applying Consumer Behavior Principles to Ad Making.") Christine's eyes drift across and down the page. The signature reads: "Escada at Saks Fifth Avenue."

She wants it!

The next day she's at Saks. The ad has done its work; the purchase decision process is well underway. At the point of making a purchase decision, consumers like Christine typically search, consider, and compare alternative brands.

Upon reaching the designer-wear department, Christine heads for the rack of designer blouses and begins her *search*. While looking for the advertised blouse, she encounters a variety of alternative styles and labels by names she knows and trusts: Donna Karan, Liz Claiborne, Yves St. Laurent, Chanel.

Consumers evaluate alternatives (called the **evoked set**).[31] To do this, they establish **evaluative criteria**, the standards they use to judge the

AD LAB 4-D
Applying Consumer Behavior Principles to Ad Making

When Jonathan's Uptown restaurant in Charlotte, North Carolina, chose Loeffler Ketchum Mountjoy to handle its advertising, the agency worried that they might have to try to deliver two messages, because Jonathan's featured two major benefits—fine dining and jazz music. They knew that consumers can become confused quite easily when advertisers try to communicate multiple messages simultaneously. The obvious consumer question becomes "Is it a restaurant? Or is it a jazz club?"

As with many ad campaigns, research played an important role for Jonathan's. After researching the advertising done by other restaurants in Charlotte, recounts Kathy Izard, art director, the agency realized that Jonathan's possessed something rare in restaurant advertsing—the potential to establish a unique position. Jonathan's was a place to spend an entire evening.

Moreover, with that position both of Jonathan's features could be presented as part of one "big idea." Now the

agency could move forward to focus on ways to penetrate consumers' perceptual screens and get the consumer learning process working. One of the ads they developed to accomplish the task is shown below.

Laboratory Applications

Study the visuals, the words, and the overall design of this ad for Jonathan's. How do these elements help the advertisement accomplish the following tasks:

1. Penetrate consumer perceptual screens.
2. Stimulate consumer learning.
3. Utilize the consumer's existing perceptual files.
4. Stimulate consumer wants and needs to affect motivation.

features and benefits of alternative products. Not all brands make it to the evoked set. In fact, based on the mental files of most consumers, usually no more than four or five brands are considered—which presents a real challenge to advertisers. If none of the alternatives meets the evaluative criteria, the consumer may reject the purchase or postpone the decision.

Christine finds the advertised dream blouse. It doesn't look exactly the same on the hanger as in the ad, however. And she's also found two others to her liking—all attractive, all expensive. As she carries the blouses to the fitting room, she considers their unique qualities of style and design: "This one may be a little too dressy." "This one I could wear to parties." "This one would be okay for school, but I'm not sure about evening."

Christine compares the blouses, considering style, material, possible uses, and price (they were all within 10 dollars of each other). She decides the advertised Escada really does make her look great. The purchase decision is completed when she signs on the dotted line, using her mother's charge card.

On the way home, Christine considers what she's just done. The **postpurchase evaluation** has just begun. She suddenly envisions her mother's reaction. It could be negative. Maybe she shouldn't have spent so much on just one blouse. She starts to worry—and to plan.

"It really is a lovely blouse, and it's very well made, and I'll get a lot of use out of it," she says to herself (to her mother). "And it's going to make me look totally . . ."

A key feature of the postpurchase evaluation is *cognitive dissonance.* The **theory of cognitive dissonance**—also called **postpurchase dissonance**[32]—states that people strive to justify their behavior by reducing the dissonance, or inconsistency, between their cognitions (their perceptions or beliefs) and reality. In fact, research has shown that, to combat dissonance, consumers like Christine are more likely to read advertisements about the brands they have already purchased than about new products or competing brands.[33]

When Christine gets home, she quickly hangs the new blouse away in the recesses of her closet. She goes downstairs, opens up to the ad in *Elle,* pores over it one more time, and then leaves it open to that page on the coffee table (for her mother to discover). She then goes upstairs and phones her friend Jennifer. She describes the purchase, emphasizing its value, the good use and enjoyment she will have wearing it, and how expensive it was.

During the postpurchase period, the consumer may enjoy the satisfaction of the purchase and thereby receive reinforcement for the decision. Or, the purchase may turn out to be unsatisfactory for any of a variety of reasons. In either case, feedback from the postpurchase evaluation will update the mental files in the consumer's mind, affecting perceptions and similar purchase decisions in the future.

Joe and Christine Shields may each typify a particular group of consumers. Marketers are interested in defining target markets and developing effective marketing strategies for groups of consumers who share similar characteristics, needs, motives, and buying habits. These are the subjects of market segmentation and the marketing mix, the focus of Chapter 5.

Summary

Marketing is the process companies use to make a profit by satisfying their customers' needs for products. A more complicated concept at the core of marketing is the perceived equal-value exchange, which implies three phases in the marketing-exchange cycle: finding out who customers are and what they want; interpreting this information for management in order to shape products; and devising strategies to inform customers about the product's utility and to make it available to them.

Advertising is concerned with the third step in the marketing process. It is one of several tools that marketers can use to inform, persuade, and remind groups of customers, or markets, about their goods and services. Its effectiveness depends on the communication skill of the advertising person. It is also effective only to the extent that other marketing activities, such as market research, are correctly implemented.

There are three categories of participants in the marketing process: customers, markets, and marketers. To reach customers and markets, advertisers use the marketing communication process, which is an extension of the human communication process.

Because their job is to match people and products, advertisers are keenly interested in consumer buying behavior. The objectives of consumer advertising are to motivate, modify, or reinforce consumer attitudes, perceptions, beliefs, and behavior. This requires the effective blending of the behavioral sciences (anthropology, sociology, psychology) with the communicating arts (writing, drama, graphics, photography). The behavioral characteristics of large groups of people give directional force to advertising aimed at those groups. Thus, advertising uses trends in mass-consumer behavior to create fashion or habit in specific consumer behavior.

To be successful, advertising people must understand the complexity of human behavior. Consumer behavior is governed by three personal processes: perception, learning, and motivation. These processes determine how consumers see the world around them, how they learn information and habits, and how they actualize their personal needs and motives. Two sets of influences also affect consumer behavior. Interpersonal influences include the consumer's family, society, and culture. Nonpersonal influences include time, place, and environment. These factors combine to determine how the consumer behaves. By evaluating the effect of these factors on groups of consumers, advertisers may determine how best to create their messages.

Questions for Review and Discussion

1. What is a process? Give an example of an advertising-related process.
2. What is utility, and how does it relate to advertising?
3. What is the significance of the perceived equal-value exchange?
4. What is a market, and what are the different types of markets?
5. How does an advertising person control or influence the communication process?
6. Which consumer behavior process presents the greatest problem to advertisers?
7. How does the learning process affect your behavior as a consumer?
8. What is the significance of Maslow's hierarchy of needs to advertisers?
9. How do environmental influences affect consumer behavior?
10. How does the theory of cognitive dissonance relate to advertising?

MARKET SEGMENTATION AND THE MARKETING MIX: MATCHING PRODUCTS TO MARKETS

Objective: To describe how marketers use behavioral characteristics to cluster prospective customers into market segments. Since no one product or service can possibly please everybody, the marketer needs to select from the identified segments those specific target markets that offer the greatest potential for sales. By so doing, the marketer gains the information and the direction necessary to fine-tune a suitable mix of various product-related elements (the 4Ps), including advertising, to match the needs, wants, or desires of the target market.

After studying this chapter, you will be able to:

☐ Understand the principle of the majority fallacy and its relationship to market segmentation and advertising.

☐ Discuss the steps in the marketing process and how they are linked.

☐ Grasp the role of market segmentation and identify the principal methods used to segment consumer and business markets.

☐ Explain the process of aggregating market segments and the importance of aggregation to the marketing process.

☐ Discuss the target marketing process and its relationship to the product concept.

☐ Describe the elements of the marketing mix and their importance to the product concept and to advertising.

☐ Explain the role and importance of branding.

Some years ago, at an advertising seminar for the Savings Institutions Marketing Society of America (SIMSA), delegates were shown a variety of advertisements from savings institutions around the country. The savings officers in the audience were to grade each ad on a scale of 1 to 10. One of the ads was an amusing example of tongue-in-cheek humor by Clearwater Federal Savings and Loan Association, which at that time was an established savings institution in Florida with over $450 million in assets.

A millionaire was pictured standing in the hallway of his mansion before a large, ornately framed painting. The headline on the ad read: "I keep the family jewels in the safe behind the portrait of my first wife. I keep my money at Clearwater Federal." This was followed by a column of light, humorous copy, which told how rich the man was, how security conscious he was, and how much he liked all the free services at Clearwater Federal that helped keep his money safe from his *second wife's* shopping sprees. The ad, shown in Exhibit 5-1, was signed: "Clearwater Federal. Where those who've made it keep it."

Most savings and loan executives who viewed the ad gave it a very low rating. They said they didn't like it because it would appeal only to a limited group (the very rich) and not to everybody.

THE MAJORITY FALLACY

Their reaction is a typical example of the **majority fallacy**—a common misconception that to be successful a product or service must appeal to everybody or at least to the majority of people.

EXHIBIT 5-1

Clearwater Federal spoke to a very interesting market segment in this tongue-in-cheek ad. Those who are wealthy can afford to laugh at themselves, and those desiring wealth can enjoy the joke, too. However, most bank executives viewing this ad failed to understand its sophisticated humor or marketing strategy. Their assumption, that the ad should appeal to everybody rather than just to a limited group, is an example of the *majority fallacy*.

Today, sophisticated marketing and advertising people know this is just not true. When several products or services compete for the same customers, each may attract only a small fraction of the total market. A new competing product will often achieve deeper penetration and a stronger, more entrenched marketing position if it aims at just one specific group of customers (like wealthy people) rather than at the entire population.

Clearwater Federal actually did a good job of selecting a very profitable market segment (that is, wealthy people or those who like the symbols of wealth) and then diligently catering to it. This group, though, represented just one narrow subset of the total financial institution market. Similarly, Reebok achieved its initial, dramatic success by creating a specialized shoe for just one segment of the fitness market rather than aiming at the whole world of footwear customers. The fact is with today's diverse consumer needs, wants, and perceptual files, it's totally unrealistic to think that one product or service—be it footwear or financial institutions—will appeal to or be purchased by "everybody."

THE PRODUCT MARKETING PROCESS

The **product marketing process** (the procedural side of the marketing exchange cycle discussed in Chapter 4) is the sequence of activities marketers perform to select markets and develop marketing mixes that eventually lead to exchanges. This process is shown in Exhibit 5-2. From the marketing person's point of view, the product marketing process begins with a new product idea or with an existing good or service.

But at this point, marketers and advertisers face a dilemma. On the one hand, they must find groups of people within a total population with similar needs and tastes that can be satisfied by the product. On the other hand, they must amass *enough* of these groups to make the product marketing process successful—and profitable. Realizing they can't appeal to everybody, marketers therefore turn to the techniques of market segmentation and target marketing—the subjects of this chapter—in their pursuit of the exchange.

THE MARKET SEGMENTATION PROCESS

Marketing and advertising people constantly scan the market to get the overall lay of the land—to see what needs and wants exist and how they might be better satisfied. One way they do this is through **market segmentation,** a two-step strategic process of (1) *identifying* groups of people (or

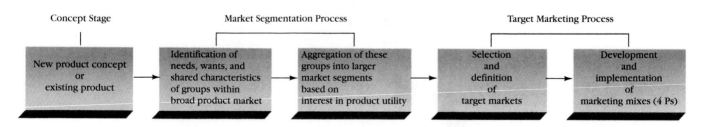

EXHIBIT 5-2

The product marketing process consists of three stages: the concept stage, the market segmentation stage, and the target marketing stage.

organizations) with certain shared characteristics within the broad product market; and then (2) *aggregating* (combining) these groups into larger market segments according to their mutual interest in the product's utility. The purpose is to give the company a selection of market segments large enough to target. Once a target is selected, the foundation is laid for developing a suitable mix of marketing activities—including advertising.

Because markets are heterogeneous and consist of many segments, a company may differentiate products and marketing strategy for every segment, or it may concentrate all its marketing activities on only one or a few segments. The Clearwater Federal ad, for example, suggests that the institution identified and targeted a single market segment from all possible others and then catered to it specifically with financial products and services and advertising. That may seem to be a simple task, but it's not. In fact, to do it well is a major accomplishment in marketing today. As we shall see, Clearwater's single segment was really a combination of several smaller groups that shared a common interest.

Identifying Consumer Market Segments

The concept of *shared characteristics* is critical to the market segmentation process. Marketing and advertising people have learned that, based on their needs, wants, and mental files, consumers leave many "footprints in the sand"—the variable characteristics of where they live and work, what they buy, and how they spend their leisure time, for example. By following these footprints, marketers can locate and define groups of consumers with similar needs and wants, create messages for them, and know how and where to send the messages.

As Exhibit 5-3 shows, marketers have lumped these variables into a variety of categories (geographic, demographic, behavioristic, and psychographic) as a basis for identifying behavioral groups and segmenting consumer markets.

Geographic Segmentation

One of the simplest methods of segmenting markets is by **geographic** location. People who live in one region of the country frequently have needs, wants, and purchasing habits that differ from those in other regions. People in the Sunbelt states, for example, purchase more suntan lotion than people in the North or Midwest. On the other hand, consumers in the North and in Canada purchase heavy winter clothing and special equipment for dealing with rain, snow, ice, sleet, and subzero temperatures.

When marketers analyze geographic data, they study sales by region, county size, city size, specific locations, and types of stores. Many products sell well in urban areas but poorly in suburban or rural areas. On the other hand, the market for a swimming pool contractor is very small in center-city areas but considerably larger in suburban areas.

Even in local markets, geographic segmentation is important. A retailer may attract people from only one part of town to his west-side store and therefore carry goods of special interest to people in that neighborhood. Or a local, liberal politician might send a mailer only to those precincts where the voters typically support liberal causes.

Demographic Segmentation

Demographics is the study of the numerical characteristics of the population. People can be grouped by sex, age, ethnicity, religion, education,

EXHIBIT 5-3   Methods Used to Segment Consumer Markets

Variables	Typical breakdowns
Geographic	
Region	Pacific; Mountain; West North Central; West South Central; East North Central; East South Central; South Atlantic; Middle Atlantic; New England
County size	A, B, C, D
Climate	Northern, southern
City or SMSA size	Under 5,000; 5,000-19,999; 20,000-49,999; 50,000-99,999; 100,000-249,999; 250,000-499,999; 500,000-999,999; 1,000,000-3,999,999; 4,000,000 or over
Density	Urban, suburban, rural
Demographic	
Age	Under 6, 6-11, 12-19, 20-34, 35-49, 50-64, 65+
Sex	Male, female
Family size	1-2, 3-4, 5+
Family life cycle	Young, single; young, married, no children; young, married, youngest child under six; young, married, youngest child six or over; young, unmarried, with children; older, married, with children; older, unmarried, with children; older, married, no children under 18; older, single; other
Income	Under $10,000; $10,000-20,000; $20,000-30,000; $30,000-40,000; $40,000-60,000; $60,000-100,000; $100,000 and over
Occupation	Professional and technical; managers, officials, and proprietors; clerical, sales; craftspeople, supervisors; operatives; farmers; retired; students; homemakers; unemployed
Education	Grade school or less; some high school; graduated high school; some college; graduated college
Religion	Catholic, Protestant, Jewish, other
Race	White, black, Asian
Nationality	American, British, French, German, Scandinavian, Italian, Latin American, Middle Eastern, Japanese
Behavioristic	
Purchase occasion	Regular occasion, special occasion
Benefits sought	Economy, convenience, prestige
User status	Nonuser, ex-user, potential user, first-time user, regular user
Usage rate	Light user, medium user, heavy user
Loyalty status	None, medium, strong, absolute
Readiness stage	Unaware, aware, informed, interested, desirous, intending to buy
Marketing-factor sensitivity	Quality, price, service, advertising, sales promotion
Psychographic	
Societal divisions	Upper crust, movers and shakers, successful singles, social security, middle of the road, metro ethnic mix
Lifestyle	Straights, swingers, long-hairs
Personality	Compulsive, gregarious, authoritarian, ambitious

occupation, income, and other quantifiable factors. For example, companies that sell products to middle-aged consumers may find it useful to know the size of that market segment along with where they live and how much they earn. Similarly, a company planning to distribute a new authentic Mexican food product might consider an area's Hispanic population as a good primary target market and want to measure that group's size as well as its distribution of income and age. In Canada, the large French-speaking community likewise presents unique marketing opportunities. How would you describe the probable demographic characteristics of the people in Clearwater Federal's target market?

EXHIBIT 5-4	Heavy Usage Patterns of Various Age Groups

Age	Name of age group	Merchandise purchased
0-5	Young children	Baby food, toys, nursery furniture, children's wear
6-19	Schoolchildren and teenagers	Clothing, sporting goods, records and tapes, school supplies, fast food, soft drinks, candy, cosmetics, movies
20-34	Young adults	Cars, furniture, housing, food and beer, clothing, diamonds, home entertainment equipment, recreational equipment, purchases for younger age segments
35-49	Younger middle-aged	Larger homes, better cars, second cars, new furniture, computers, recreational equipment, jewelry, clothing, food and wine
50-64	Older middle-aged	Recreational items, purchases for young marrieds and infants, travel
65 and over	Senior adults	Medical services, travel, pharmaceuticals, purchases for younger age groups

Exhibit 5-4 demonstrates how, as people grow older, their responsibilities and incomes change, as do their interests in various product categories. Marketers have tried to chart these life cycle changes and have drawn many conclusions about product appeals for each stage.[1]

The study of geographic and demographic data uncovers useful statistical information about markets, but it fails to provide much information about the psychological makeup of the people in those markets. Not all people of one sex, one age group, one income group, or one town have the same wants, attitudes, or beliefs. In fact, people in the same demographic or geographic segment may have widely differing product preferences.

Behavioristic Segmentation

Many marketers believe the best starting point for determining market segments is to cluster consumers into groups based on their attitude toward, use of, or response to actual products or product attributes. This is generally called **behavioristic segmentation.** Behavioral segments are determined by a number of variables, the most important of which may be categorized as *purchase occasion, benefits sought, user status,* or *usage rate.*

Purchase-Occasion Variables Buyers might be distinguished by *when* they buy or use a product or service—the **purchase occasion.** Air travelers, for example, might fly for business or for vacation. Thus, one airline ad might promote business travel while another promotes tourism. The purchase occasion might be affected by seasonality (water skis, snow skis, raincoats), by frequency of need (regular or occasional), or by some fad-and-fade cycle (candy, computer games). When the marketer can discover some commonality in the purchase occasion of certain groups or organizations, then there is a potential for creating a target segment. One consulting organization, Advertiming, was formed just to recommend the scheduling of media advertising based on a sophisticated system of correlating consumer purchase patterns with weather forecasts.[2]

Benefits-Sought Variables Determining the major benefits consumers seek in a product (high quality, low price, status, speed, sex appeal, good taste) enables marketers to design products and advertising around those particular benefits. Gillette aims at one narrow segment of the hair-care market with its For Oily Hair Only product by offering a major benefit. Other hair-care companies may market "only natural ingredients" or "buy shampoo—get conditioner free" offers. **Benefit segmentation,** as this is often called, presents such excellent opportunities to marketers that it is the prime objective behind many consumer attitude studies today and, as Exhibit 5-5 shows, is the basis for many successful advertising campaigns.

User-Status Variables Many markets can be segmented by the **user-status** of prospective customers (i.e., nonusers, new users, regular users, potential

ETHICAL DILEMMA IN ADVERTISING
Warning: Market Segmentation May Be Hazardous to Your Business

In early 1990, R. J. Reynolds Tobacco was poised to roll out a new product named Uptown. The idea of a light menthol cigarette in a sleek black and gold package held great promise—until Dr. Louis Sullivan spoke up. The Secretary of Health and Human Services openly accused Reynolds of "promoting a culture of cancer" among blacks. "This brand is cynically and deliberately targeted toward black Americans," Sullivan said. "I strongly urge you to cancel your plans to market a brand of cigarettes that is specifically targeted to black smokers," he added.

This unprecedented public attack by the nation's top health official caused such an uproar in the black community that Reynolds was forced to scrap its plans to test-market Uptown, at an estimated loss of $10 million. Reynolds cried foul. "This represents a loss of choice for black smokers and a further erosion of the free enterprise system," executive vice president Peter Hoult said.

The advertising community at large was also up in arms because Sullivan had called into question the ethics of market segmentation, one of the industry's tried and true techniques. Advertisers everywhere feared that the Uptown disaster would make it just that much more difficult to market their products to minorities, women, and children.

Market segmentation has long been accepted as a precise, effective way for advertisers to target potentially prof-

itable audiences for their products. And that's become increasingly important in the tobacco industry, where the percentage of Americans who smoke is steadily declining. As their customer base shrinks, cigarette makers have struggled to position brands toward specific market segments.

The rate of smoking among blacks is declining more slowly than among whites and is even increasing among young, poor, uneducated blacks, so they represent a tempting target. But marketing specialists and antismoking activists agree that Reynolds' big mistake was its blatant declaration that Uptown was specifically aimed at blacks. "We're an honest company; what do you say when the audience is going to be predominantly black?" a Reynolds spokesman said. Some industry experts were shocked that Reynolds caved in so quickly. "When big companies are challenged by consumer groups, they almost always stick to their guns," said Al Ries, chairman of Trout & Ries. "This shows the enormous power that consumer public opinion can have."

But the hue and cry that upset Reynolds' plan also harmed the black business community. For years, black consumers have demanded that industries advertise in black neighborhoods and media; but until recently, most cigarette companies took black smokers for granted. Now, by directly targeting this group, millions of ad dollars

EXHIBIT 5-5

Porsche uses benefit segmentation to target its prime consumers: people who understand the value of a dollar and the depreciation costs of most cars.

With a resale value of 99.43%, this is a true economy car.

You don't buy a new Porsche, you invest in one. That's because with a resale value of nearly 100%, you'll not only keep your money, you'll get to enjoy it.

PORSCHE

(Dealer Name)

1986 911 Carrera. Resale prices vary by model, region, condition of car, and mileage. Base on 5/89 NADA Official Used Car Guide, nine-edition national average. Based upon past performance. Past performance is no guarantee or representation of future performance. © 1989 Porsche Cars North America, Inc.

would have poured into the black community. Black-owned companies would be able to sell more billboard space and more ads in black magazines and newspapers. So why not take advantage of the bonanza? As *Philadelphia Magazine* publisher David Lipson points out, "It's a fact that blacks smoke a lot of cigarettes, and R. J. Reynolds wanted to design a product for the black market. What's wrong with that?"

What's wrong, indeed? Well, in addition to bringing more dollars into the black community, cigarette advertising would also bring more destruction. As Dr. Sullivan said, "Uptown's message is more disease, more suffering, and more death for a group already bearing more than its share of smoking-related illness and mortality." On the other hand, Walker Merryman, vice president of the Tobacco Institute, said that Sullivan "must believe that there are some adults in the population who can't be trusted to look at a cigarette promotion and make their own decision." And Sullivan isn't the only one with strong convictions. The Association of National Advertisers insists that restricting the industry's right to target specific markets is censorship and a violation of First Amendment rights.

Both sides in this dispute clearly believe that they're acting ethically. But troubling questions persist. True, cigarettes are legal products, but they're also deadly. And Dr. Sullivan's actions seem questionable considering that he's supposed to protect the health of all Americans, not just a select group. Ultimately, individual responsibility can't be ignored, because no amount of advertising can force a person to smoke cigarettes.

Market segmentation has always been a powerful advertising tool and freedom of expression a cherished American right. But rights must be balanced against duties and freedom against responsibility in order to achieve the greatest good for all the people.

Questions

1. Considering that all cigarette makers use market segmentation to focus their advertising, does it seem ethical to single out a specific brand for condemnation simply because of its audience?

2. Robert Schmidt, chairman of Levine, Huntley, Schmidt & Beaver, has publicly announced that "We will never create any cigarette advertisements. There has to be some social conscience to an ad agency." Do you agree? If you worked at the agency handling hundreds of millions of dollars in R. J. Reynolds billing, would you work on a cigarette account even if you believed that smoking is harmful? Would you be willing to sacrifice your job for your principles?

users, and ex-users). By targeting one or another of these groups, marketers might develop new products for nonusers or new uses for old products. This also closely parallels the habit-related goals of advertisers, discussed in Chapter 4.

Usage-Rate Variables Marketers realize that it is usually easier to get a heavy user to increase usage than to get a light user to do the same. Thus they measure **usage rates** to define consumers as light, medium, or heavy users of products. This is also called **volume segmentation.** In many product categories, 20 percent of the people consume 80 percent of the product. Marketers are usually interested in defining who comprises that 20 percent as closely as possible and aiming all their advertising at them. For example, as Exhibit 5-6 shows, 67 percent of the population never purchases dog food. On the other hand, 17 percent buys 87 percent of all the dog food sold. Logically, a company that markets dog food would rather attract one heavy purchaser to its brand than one light purchaser.

Marketers try to find common characteristics among heavy users of their products. This way, product differences may be more easily defined and advertising strategies more simply drawn. For example, the heavy users of bowling alleys have traditionally been working-class men between the ages of 25 and 50 who watch more than three and one-half hours of television a day and prefer to watch sports programs. We can readily see the implications a bowling equipment advertiser can draw from that in determining an advertising campaign.

EXHIBIT 5-6

Usage rates vary in many product categories. For example, of all households, only 4 percent doesn't buy ready-to-eat cereals (nonusers), about half (48 percent) buys 13 percent of the product (light users), and the other half (48 percent) buys 87 percent of the product (heavy users).

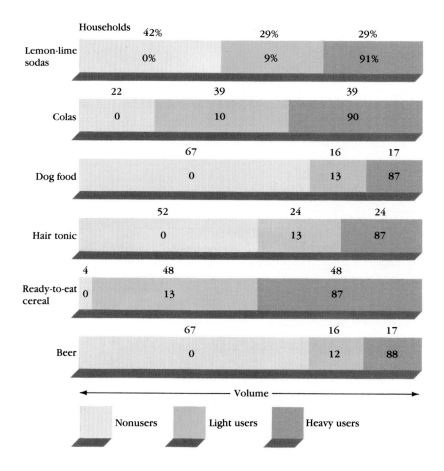

Marketers of one product sometimes find their customers are also heavy users of other products. If so, then they can define their target markets in terms of the usage rates of those other products. Recent research from SRI International's VALS 2 program (discussed in the next section) indicates that heavy users of home computers are also heavy users of foreign luxury cars, sports cars, backpacking equipment, binoculars, expensive bicycles, and literary magazines.[3]

Psychographic Segmentation

For many consumer product categories, customers are more likely to be swayed by the product's appeals to their emotions and cultural values than by how it performs functionally.[4] For this reason, advertisers have found *psychographic segmentation* an interesting method of defining consumer markets. **Psychographics** refers to the grouping of people into homogeneous segments on the basis of psychological makeup—namely, values, attitudes, personality, and lifestyle. Psychographics goes beyond standard demographics and behavioristics to indicate customers' dreams, hopes, and fears. It classifies people according to what they feel, what they believe, the way they live, and the products and services they use.[5]

Most of us desire to be seen as a particular type of person, so we use those brands that offer the user imagery we subscribe to. One study conducted by BBDO for General Electric, for example, found that consumers thought the GE brand attracted only conservative, older, business types. To change that image—and thereby appeal to a broader range of consumers—GE adopted its now famous "Brings Good Things to Life" campaign.[6]

By discovering as many descriptive qualities of their markets as possible, marketers hope to end up with rich target market profiles that enable them to focus all of their marketing and advertising activities efficiently. Exhibit 5-7 presents an example of how users of different toothpaste brands were segmented by benefits sought, demographics, behavioristics, and psychographics.

For years, marketers have attempted to categorize consumers by personality and lifestyle types in the hope of finding a common basis for making product appeals. Monitor, a service developed by Yankelovich, Skelly and White, was the first major syndicated study of changing U.S. values.[7]

EXHIBIT 5-7   Segmenting the U.S. Toothpaste Market

Benefit segments	Demographics	Behavioristics	Psychographics	Favored brands
Economy (low price)	Men	Heavy users	High autonomy, value-oriented	Brands on sale
Medicinal (decay prevention)	Large families	Heavy users	Hypochondriac, conservative	Crest
Cosmetic (bright teeth)	Teens, young adults	Smokers	High sociability, active	Macleans, Ultra Brite
Taste (good tasting)	Children	Spearmint lovers	High self-involvement, hedonistic.	Colgate, Aim

Another classification system, VALS (values and lifestyles), was originated by Arnold Mitchell at SRI International and was quickly adopted by marketers across the country. In 1989, VALS 2 was introduced, which updated the program and offered a new psychographic typology for segmenting U.S. consumers and predicting their purchase behavior.[8]

Values and Lifestyles (VALS) Using a two-dimensional structure based on self-orientation and resources, the **Values and Lifestyles (VALS)** system classifies eight types of consumers who exhibit distinctive behavior and decision-making patterns and who manifest particular product consumption tendencies. The groups are balanced in size—each falling between 8 and 17 percent of the population—so each truly represents a viable target market segment. In addition, neighboring groups within the defined network have similar characteristics, so segments can be aggregated.[9] For a graphic depiction of the VALS 2 network, see Exhibit 5-8.

Advertisers have found radio an excellent medium to reach some of the VALS lifestyle groups. The style of music a radio station plays satisfies the emotional and entertainment needs of certain groups of listeners. For example, conservative, blue-collar people with traditional values of home, family, and church often choose the "country music" station. This group also typically falls into the VALS 2 Believer and Maker segments (which comprise 29

EXHIBIT 5-8

The VALS 2 (Values and Lifestyles) classification system places consumers with abundant resources near the top of the chart and those with minimal resources near the bottom. Horizontally, the chart segments consumers by their basis for decision making: principles, status, or action. The boxes intersect to indicate that some of the categories may be considered together. For instance, a marketer may find it useful to categorize "Fulfilleds" and "Believers" together. However, it would be unproductive to try to link "Experiencers" with "Believers."

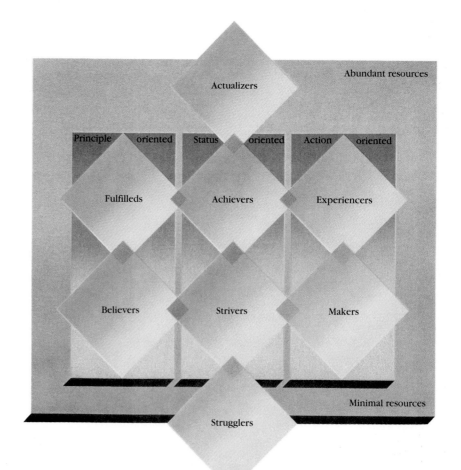

percent of the U.S. population). Most radio markets have no more than 12 unique radio formats, so SRI's eight values and lifestyles typologies can fit radio listenership reasonably well.[10]

Arbitron, the company that measures radio station audiences for advertisers, has found that radio station formats also divide the population neatly by age and sex. For example, higher-income men and women over the age of 45, who often fall into the VALS Actualizer, Fulfilled, and Achiever categories, typically listen to the news-and-talk radio station.

What other media do you think offer characteristics suitable for segmenting VALS groups? Magazines? Newspapers? Television? Why?

Numerous advertising agencies have jumped on the VALS bandwagon. Young & Rubicam, for example, has used VALS for a variety of its clients, including Mercury Capri, Dr Pepper, Kodak Instant Cameras, and Merrill Lynch. By using VALS to understand their customers, advertisers hope to better establish an emotional bond between the brand and the consumer.

For instance, Experiencers—who are typically young, vital, enthusiastic, and rebellious—make up much of the market for fast foods, music, movies, and video.[11] They are targeted with highly sensual and exciting ads by movie studios and recording companies.

Limitations of Psychographics Advocates of VALS and other psychographic methods claim their greatest value is in developing creative strategies for advertising messages that directly address the emotional factors that motivate consumers. However, the markets for many nationally advertised products comprise a cross section of the U.S. public far broader than one or two psychographic segments. In these cases, critics say psychographics may offer little real value at all in developing persuasive sales messages.[12]

VALS and similar methods of classification are often faulted for being oversimplifications of consumer personalities and purchase behavior.[13] While the VALS methodology defines personality on certain premises, there are also many other premises for defining personality.

Notwithstanding these challenges, when marketers understand the attitudes, lifestyles, and personalities of the people who buy their products or services, the implications are considerable. Companies can better select potential target markets and match the attributes and the image of their products with the types of consumers using the products. This aids in the definition of specific advertising objectives, development of media plans, and efficient budgeting of the marketers' dollars.[14] These potential benefits suggest that VALS and other psychographic segmentation systems will no doubt continue to flourish until something considerably better comes along.

Identifying Business Market Segments

Business (or industrial) markets include manufacturers, utilities, government agencies, contractors, wholesalers, retailers, banks, insurance companies, and institutions that buy goods and services to help them in their own business. These may be raw materials or parts that go into the product, or they might be desks, office equipment, vehicles, or a variety of business services used in conducting the business. The products sold to business markets are often intended for resale to the public, as in the case of retail goods.

In all these situations, identifying target markets of prospective business customers is just as complex as identifying consumer market segments. In most cases, many of the variables used to identify consumer markets can be used for business markets. For example, most organizations may be segmented by geographic location and by several behavioristic variables, such as benefits sought, user status, usage rate, and purchase occasion. But business markets also have several special characteristics. They normally use a systematic purchasing procedure; they may be classified by SIC code; they may be concentrated geographically; and they may have a relatively small number of buyers.[15] These characteristics have important implications for advertisers seeking special ways to segment industrial markets.

Business Purchasing Procedures

When businesspeople evaluate new products for purchase, they typically use a process that is far more complex and rigid than the consumer purchase process described in Chapter 4. Industrial marketers must design their advertising programs with this in mind.

Large firms invariably have a purchasing department that acts as a professional buyer. Its job is to evaluate the need for products, analyze proposed purchases, seek approvals from those who will use the product and authorizations from managers who will pay for the product, make requisitions, place purchase orders, and generally supervise all the product purchasing in the firm. The purchase decision, therefore, may take weeks, months, or even years before a sale is finally made. This is especially true with government agencies. Frequently, purchase decisions also depend on factors besides price or product quality—delivery time, terms of sale, service requirements, certainty of continuing supply, and others.[16]

When analyzing market segments, many industrial marketers consider the purchase decision process of various segments before determining the appropriate target market. Many new companies, for instance, target other small companies where the purchase decision can be made quickly and use commission-only representatives to call on larger firms that require more time to consummate the sale.

Standard Industrial Classification

The U.S. Department of Commerce classifies all businesses—and collects and publishes data on them—by **Standard Industrial Classification (SIC) codes.** These codes are based on broad industry categories that are subdivided into major divisions, subgroups, and then detailed classifications of firms in similar lines of business, as shown in Exhibit 5-9. The federal government reports the number of establishments, sales volumes, and number of employees, broken down by geographic areas, for each SIC code. Many companies can relate their sales to their industrial customers' lines of business. The SIC codes are a great help in segmenting those markets and performing research.

Market Concentration

The market for many industrial goods is heavily concentrated in the Midwest, the mid-Atlantic states, and California. For example, the stylized map in Exhibit 5-10 on p. 168 shows that, for manufactured goods, more than 50 percent of U.S. industry is located east of the Mississippi and north of the Mason-Dixon line. This greatly reduces the number of geographic targets for the industrial marketing efforts of many companies.

EXHIBIT 5-9

This is an example of how the SIC codes for selected businesses (product categories) in the apparel industry might be broken down. A business marketer wanting to sell goods or services to firms in the apparel industry might use the SIC codes in directories or on subscription databases to locate prospective companies.

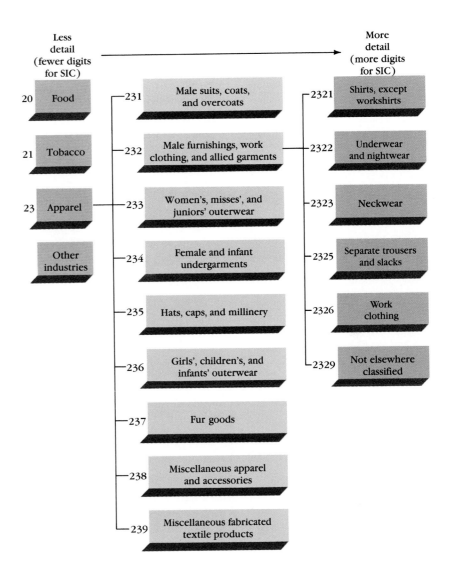

Moreover, industrial marketers deal with a very limited number of buyers. Less than 4 percent of all the companies in the United States account for nearly 60 percent of the production employees and over two-thirds of all the manufacturing dollars.[17] Thus, customer size is a critical basis for market segmentation. A firm may decide to concentrate its marketing efforts on a few large customers or to target its products to the more numerous smaller customers. Steelcase, for example, which manufactures office furniture, divides its marketing efforts between major accounts its sales force calls on directly and dealer accounts that resell its products to many small purchasers.

Business marketers can further segment their markets by end users. For example, since computers are now used in virtually every kind of business, a firm that develops a new computer software product may decide to design it specifically for use in one specialized industry, such as banking, or for general use in a variety of industries.

In general, the analysis of industrial markets and behavior is as great a challenge as the analysis of consumer buying behavior and market segments. Both are critical to the formulation of effective marketing and advertising plans.

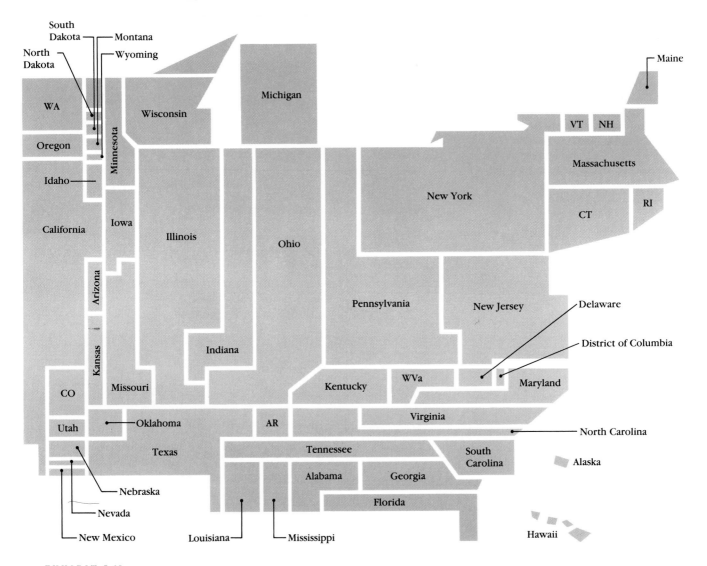

EXHIBIT 5-10

The states in this map are represented in proportion to the value of their manufactured products.

Aggregating Market Segments

Once marketers have grouped the broad product-based market by shared characteristics (geographic, demographic, behavioristic, or psychographic), they can proceed to the next step in the market segmentation process. This involves (1) selecting groups that have a mutual interest in the product's utility and (2) reorganizing and aggregating (combining) them into larger market segments based on the potential they offer for sales and profitability.

Let's take a closer look at how this process might work for Clearwater Federal from beginning to end. First, the founders of Clearwater Federal want to know—even before opening a new bank—the growth potential for banks and savings and loans in their local area. In other words, they need to discover the **primary demand trend** of the total market for financial institutions. To do this they use a variety of *marketing research* techniques (discussed in Chapter 6).

Assuming the primary demand trend is positive, Clearwater Federal now must identify the needs, wants, and shared characteristics of the various groups within the financial marketplace. To accomplish this, they may retain

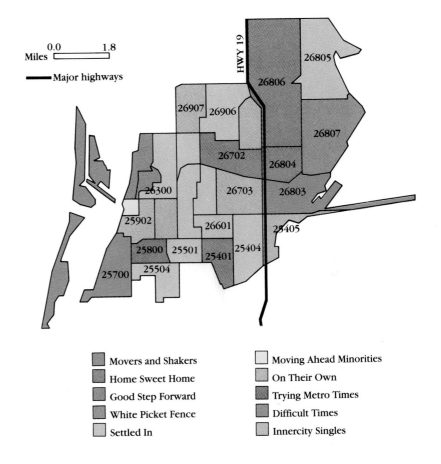

Clearwater Federal Savings & Loan
Clearwater, Florida
Dominant Microvision Segment by Census Tract

the services of a large database company like National Decision Systems to profile the local market area.

The data reveals a wide variety of prospective customers with financial needs in the Clearwater area. These include groups the average person would term doctors, lawyers, retail merchants, housewives, students, blue-collar workers, fixed-income retirees, teachers, and entrepreneurs. However, the database company measures and analyzes the groups by demographic and lifestyle characteristics and refers to them with the new terms mentioned in Exhibit 5-11: White Picket Fence, Movers and Shakers, On Their Own, Settled In, Good Step Forward, and Innercity Singles. Some of these people are well-to-do; most are not. But all have money to save, and many have the need to borrow (although, of course, not all can qualify).

Selecting Groups Interested in Product Utility

Clearwater Federal needs to select groups that would likely qualify for and be most interested in the basic utilities or benefits the institution plans to offer. These benefits include local financial services close to where the people live and work; federally insured savings accounts with slightly higher interest than banks; and specialized loans for real estate or home remodeling. The groups interested in these features make up the total possible local savings and loan market for Clearwater Federal.

Now, should Clearwater Federal try to appeal to all of these people? Or should it aim at some specialized segment? Part of the challenge of market segmentation is estimating the share of the total market a company might capture if it (1) aims at the whole market or (2) caters only to a specific market segment. As we discussed earlier, in highly competitive markets (like financial services), it is usually wise to avoid the majority fallacy.

Combining Groups to Build Target Market Segments

At this point, Clearwater Federal needs to find groups that are relatively homogeneous and at the same time offer good potential for profit. This is a creative process of looking at the market differently—sorting, rearranging, and combining the various utility-interested groups into possible target market segments.

Because Clearwater is basically a middle-class area, the market data turns up a large percentage of demographic and lifestyle segments that typically include older people on fixed incomes and young to middle-aged people on medium incomes: On Their Own (21 percent), Settled In (20 percent), and Good Step Forward (10 percent). Many of these people are renters rather than homeowners and thus not prime targets for real estate lending. But they might be interested in high-interest savings accounts.

On the other hand, a couple of small niche segments appear—young to middle-aged people with medium to high incomes: Movers and Shakers (2.4 percent) and Home Sweet Home (14.4 percent). By combining these with the young professionals in the Good Step Forward segment (10 percent), Clearwater Federal discovers it might create a new and interesting target market segment: young to middle-aged people on their way up the ladder of prosperity. These people might like the trappings of wealth, and Clearwater Federal could develop an image and promote services related to success, affluence, and prestige.

THE TARGET MARKETING PROCESS

Once the aggregating process is completed, a company can proceed to the **target marketing process.** As we shall see, the way this is accomplished will determine the content, look, and implementation of the company's advertising.

Target Market Selection

The first step in the target marketing process is to assess which of the newly created segments are large enough to offer the greatest potential for profits and which can be most successfully penetrated. The company designates one or more segments as a **target market**—that group of segments the company wishes to appeal to, design products for, and aim its marketing activities toward.[18] It may even choose to designate another set of segments as a secondary target market and aim some of its resources at it.

Let's look at Clearwater Federal's designated target market. It comprises individuals who are middle-aged or older and comfortably well-off; young to middle-aged with high income and aspiring to wealth; and young people of moderate income with a desire to affiliate with the upper classes. This represents over 25 percent of the total local financial market, a significant target that—if it can be won—possesses the potential for substantial profits.

Clearwater Federal offers what these prospects need and want: the safety and high interest of a federally insured savings account; a wide spectrum of relevant free services; loans for home purchases and remodeling; and an attractive location frequented by well-educated, affluent individuals.

If Clearwater Federal were to discover that the wealth-related segment is not large enough to be profitable, it would have to select a different target market. Its other marketing and advertising activities would have to change as well.

Now, for an exercise, look at Ad Lab 5-A (p. 172) and consider how Reebok selected its target market.

The Marketing Mix: Matching Products to Markets

Now that Clearwater Federal has a specific target market in sight, it must take steps to ensure it is truly ready to enter the marketplace.

Fortunately, once a company defines its target market, it knows exactly where to focus its attention and resources. Planning other marketing activities becomes greatly simplified because it knows which specific data to use. Now it can shape the product concept—even to the extent of designing special privileges for its target market (like free notary service)—and establish the proper pricing of services. It can determine the need and location of stores, dealers, or branches, and it has the basis for preparing the most convincing advertising messages. In other words, the whole mix of marketing activities can be aimed at making the product as attractive and accessible as possible. We will examine the marketing mix from the perspective of the advertiser. But first, let's examine what we mean by the *product concept*.

As we discussed in Chapter 4, a product offers utility. In fact, a product generally offers a number of utilities—perceived by the consumer as a *bundle of values*.

With this in mind, marketers and advertisers generally try to shape their basic, functional product into a total **product concept:** the consumer's perception of a product as a bundle of utilitarian and symbolic values that satisfy functional, social, psychological, economic, and other wants and needs.

Shaping a total product concept is no small task. It requires careful management of all the *marketing mix* elements, for they all contribute to the consumer's perception of the product. And if these elements are not managed properly, the product concept may lose its value in the mind of the consumer.

Companies engage in many activities to enhance the product concept: They might make the product bigger, add color, raise or lower the price, open more stores or branches, offer cents-off coupons, or advertise it differently. Marketers traditionally categorize and focus these activities under the broad headings of *product, price, place,* and *promotion* and give them the moniker of the **Four Ps (4 Ps).**[19] The 4 Ps are also called the elements of the **marketing mix,** and they represent the various determinants of a company's marketing strategy. By adding to, subtracting from, or modifying these four elements, each company strives to affect the product concept and improve sales.

AD LAB 5-A
Marketing Reebok: The Product Element and the Market

Today, Reebok is a well-known brand of athletic shoe featuring a number of product lines, but in 1980 it was virtually unknown. Named after the swift, graceful African antelope, Reebok International was the newest name for one of Britain's oldest shoe manufacturers, Joseph W. Foster & Sons Athletic Shoes. Foster's first introduced the spiked track shoe around the turn of the century, and members of the 1924 British track team, highlighted in the film *Chariots of Fire,* all wore Foster running shoes.

In 1979, Reebok was eager to enter the North American market, so they teamed up with Paul Fireman. Fireman's family had been in the camping and sporting goods business for some time, and he had been looking for a new and exciting product. Reebok looked like it.

As he sought to give Reebok a "foothold" in the marketplace of the early 80s, total U.S. industry sales were already reaching the $1 billion mark. The competition was formidable. He had to find a way to do war with the big boys—Nike, Converse, Adidas, and others. This was no small task. Converse, for example, was the strongest company targeting the basketball segment. Nike was strongest with runners, exactly the market that Reebok's manufacturer had traditionally served. Nike had a 35 percent share of the market, followed by Adidas and Converse with about 10 percent each.

How was Fireman's fledgling company going to compete against this kind of strength? He had to examine the marketplace, logically studying basic marketing fundamentals such as the product life cycle, positioning, and the consumer decision-making process as guidelines. He knew athletic shoes were now being scientifically designed for individual sports events. For example, a print ad from Nike pictured 10 athletic shoes used for 10 different sporting purposes: distance running, cross-country, sprinting, long jump, javelin throw, all-purpose running (two types), high jump, triple jump, shot put, and discus. At the same time, professional sports shoes were becoming popular with nonprofessionals—shoes for tennis, basketball, and jogging were already being sold in shoe stores, and markets such as aerobics, fitness, and walking were soon to follow.

Fireman realized he could be supplied with quality manufactured sports shoes and could offer some unique features: attractive styling with soft leather uppers in a wide range of colors, a tradition of Olympic running shoes and British quality, the trademarked Foster Heel Cradle, special cooling mesh toe, water-repellant and air-breathing Gore-Tex inner liner, and a dual-density midsole. Also, he had to look ahead, because the running shoe market was not a growing market like others. He also knew what he didn't have—a huge budget like his competitors, and a complete distribution system.

Because it was unrealistic to think that Reeboks would appeal to or be purchased by "everybody" (the majority fallacy), Fireman sagely recognized that the athletic footwear market actually contained a sufficient number of market segments to support Reebok's current product line—his first offering to the U.S. public—as well as a number of segments into which he could create and market new products.

By 1986, he had it all. Reebok had significantly penetrated the U.S. market and was the leader with 31.2 percent share of the athletic shoe market. Fireman had overcome

Advertising, as one of the activities within the promotion element, plays vastly different roles in the marketing of various items. These differences are the result of company decisions about the appropriate mix of other marketing activities used to achieve its objectives.

The remainder of this chapter focuses on the relationship of the 4 Ps to the advertising a company may use.

ADVERTISING AND THE PRODUCT ELEMENT

In developing a marketing mix, marketers generally start with the product element. The major activities typically associated with the **product element** include the way the product is designed and classified, positioned, branded, and packaged. Each of these affects the way the product is advertised.

Because life is not a spectator sport.

Nike that year, a lead Reebok maintained through the rest of the decade. By 1990, Reebok shared 59 percent of the marketplace along with Nike and a newcomer, L.A. Gear.

Today, Reebok continues to defend its market position. For example, in the fall of 1991, it introduced a line of sports casual shoes for men and women with a series of print ads. And for its Classic line, it launched a multi-million-dollar ad campaign.

Laboratory Applications

1. Examine Reebok's product features and the variety of market segments mentioned in the story above. Can you identify the market segment that was yet untapped in 1980 and would eventually propel Reebok to first place in athletic shoes? The woman in the Reebok ad is wearing the appropriate outfit—including the new line of shoes—for Reebok's new market segment.

2. From your reading of the text, discuss which market segments were available in 1980 to support Reebok's traditional product? Can you think of any market segment for athletic shoes that wasn't available in 1980? If so, would you advise Reebok to design and market a shoe for that segment (if so, prepare a list of reasons why)?

3. Discuss how you might use the Olympic tradition and Foster's trademarked Heel Cradle to develop a positioning statement for Reebok.

A major issue is how long the product has been in the marketplace in relation to market demand and competition, and this requires an understanding of the *product life cycle.*

Product Life Cycle

Marketers theorize that just as humans pass through stages in life from infancy to death, products (and especially product categories) also pass through a **product life cycle,**[20] illustrated in Exhibit 5-12. When an advertising person receives a new assignment, one of the first tasks is to identify which stage of the life cycle the product (or product category) is in. The product's position in the life cycle can have a great impact on the advertising used. The life cycle also gives numerous clues to other time-related questions of the marketing

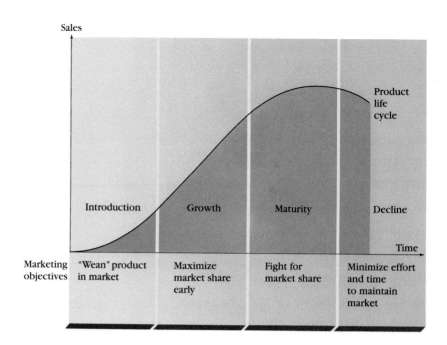

Sales

Introduction   Growth   Maturity   Decline

Product
life
cycle

Time

Marketing
objectives

"Wean" product
in market

Maximize
market share
early

Fight for
market share

Minimize effort
and time
to maintain
market

EXHIBIT 5-12

Every product has a life cycle, although the shape of the curve may change depending on the product category. Marketing objectives also change as the product proceeds from one stage of the cycle to the next. So do marketing strategies. In the introductory and growth stages, promotional activities are aimed at creating product awareness and inducing trial. In later stages, efforts may be aimed at suggesting competitive comparison or maintaining brand loyalty.

environment, such as industry growth potential, competitive pressure, and ease of entry. Marketing and advertising people have identified four major stages in the product life cycle: *introduction, growth, maturity,* and *decline.*

For example, when a major new product is introduced, nobody knows about it. In educating consumers about the new product, therefore, the company will also have to stimulate **primary demand**—that is, consumer demand for the whole product category. That's the objective of Intel's ad for its new 486 microprocessor in Exhibit 5-13.

When the videocassette recorder was first introduced, consumers had no previous perceptual files labeled *video;* they were labeled *television.* Thus, the advertisers' first aim was to create enough consumer demand to **pull** the product through the channels of distribution. Promotional activities had to educate the consuming public about the new product and its category, stressing information about what VCRs were, how they worked, and the rewards of owning one. A range of other promotional efforts to the retail trade—called **push** strategy—was also used to encourage distributors and dealers to stock, display, and advertise the new products.

During the **introductory**—or *pioneering*—**phase** of any new product category, companies must be prepared to incur considerable costs for product development and for initial advertising and promotion to educate customers, build widespread dealer distribution, and encourage demand. The company may not realize profits on the product until some point in the growth stage, and it must be well capitalized to be able to continue advertising and weather this initial period.

As sales volume begins to rise rapidly, the product enters the **growth stage.** This period is characterized by *market expansion,* as more and more customers, stimulated by mass advertising and word of mouth, make their first, second, and third purchases. At this point, potential competitors see the new product's success and recognize the growth opportunity. They enter the market by introducing new brands, and that creates even more purchase pressure on the marketplace. Sheer momentum now carries overall category

The 486™ PC. It may be a little more power than you're used to.

486™ Never before has this much power been plugged into a business PC.
Presenting the Intel 486 microprocessor—a veritable powerhouse that's been harnessed for business.

©1990 Intel Corporation

A 486 microprocessor-based PC has everything it takes to run today's high-powered applications. And run them the way you need to—simultaneously and at lightning speed.
Plus, it's compatible with the hard-

ware and business applications you already own, so you won't spend any extra time or money on training.
The 486 PC. Plug it in and start shocking the corporate world.
For additional information, call

1-800-548-4725 and ask for "The 486 Microprocessor Means Business" brochure.

intel
The Computer Inside.™
486 is a trademark of Intel Corporation.

EXHIBIT 5-13

Intel used this ad to educate business consumers about its new microprocessor, which packed more power than they were used to dealing with. Thus, it had to explain what needs the product would fill. Since the 486 would eventually be found in a variety of computers, Intel's interest is really in stimulating primary demand for the whole 486 product category rather than a particular brand of computer that uses the 486.

sales upward, boosting sales of the individual brands within the category. The ratio of advertising expenditures to total sales begins to decrease, and individual firms may realize their first substantial profits.

During the 1980s, for example, the demand for VCRs exploded, quadrupling sales year after year. By the end of the decade, over 66 percent of all U.S. homes (over 175 million people) had VCRs, and a variety of competitive brands—many with unknown names—had entered the scene to cash in on this growth.[21]

In the **maturity stage,** as the marketplace becomes saturated and the number of new customers dwindles, industry sales reach a plateau. As competition intensifies, profits also diminish. Promotional efforts are increased, but the emphasis is on **selective demand** to impress customers with the subtle advantage of one brand over another. At this stage, companies increase sales only at the expense of competitors. Therefore, the strategies of market segmentation and product positioning—as well as price promotion—become more important during this shakeout period as weak companies fall by

Crest shows three formulations of its product in this ad, all containing the Fluoristat cavity-fighting ingredient. While Crest has been a mature product for many years and has experienced tremendous competition from other brands, P&G has played an effective number-one positioning role, matching its competitors' moves with defensive moves of its own to constantly revitalize the product and extend the product life cycle.

the wayside and those left fight for even the smallest increases in market share.[22]

Late in the maturity stage, as products approach the end of their life cycle, companies frequently take a variety of actions to try to extend the product's life. They may try to add new users, increase the frequency of use by existing customers, develop new uses for the product, or change the size of packages, design new labels, or improve quality. By 1990, for example, VCRs were available in a wide variety of configurations and were sold at significantly lower prices than when first introduced. Ads stressed features and low prices, and the product had become a staple of the discount merchandisers.

Finally, products enter or approach the **decline stage** due to obsolescence or changing consumer tastes. Companies may then choose to cease all promotion and phase the products out quickly, as in the case of the Edsel automobile, or let them die slowly, like old brands of home movie film.

They may also attempt to revitalize the product in order to prolong the mature stage. As the ad in Exhibit 5-14 shows, Procter & Gamble created a new "great-tasting gel" formulation for its Crest toothpaste, developed "advanced formula Fluoristat" and new "plaque fighters," and built these features into Crest as improvements designed to extend the product's effective life.

Product Classifications

The way a company classifies its product is important in defining both the product concept and the marketing mix. As Exhibit 5-15 shows, there are

EXHIBIT 5-15   Product Classifications

By market

Consumer goods	Products and services we use in our daily lives (food, clothing, furniture, automobiles).
Industrial goods	Products used by companies for the purpose of producing other products (raw materials, agricultural commodities, machinery, tools, equipment).

By rate of consumption and tangibility

Durable goods	Tangible products that are long lasting and infrequently replaced (cars, trucks, refrigerators, furniture).
Nondurable goods	Tangible products that may be consumed in one or a few uses and usually need to be replaced at regular intervals (food, soap, gasoline, oil).
Services	Activities, benefits, or satisfactions offered for sale (travel, haircuts, legal and medical services, massages).

By purchasing habits

Convenience goods	Purchases made frequently with a minimum of effort (cigarettes, food, newspapers).
Shopping goods	Infrequently purchased items for which greater time is spent comparing price, quality, style, warranty (furniture, cars, clothing, tires).
Specialty goods	Products with such unique characteristics that consumers will make special efforts to purchase them even if they're more expensive (fancy photographic equipment, special women's fashions, stereo components).

By physical description

Package goods	Cereals, hair tonics, and so forth.
Hard goods	Furniture, appliances.
Soft goods	Clothing, bedding.
Services	Nontangible products.

many ways to classify products. They may be classified as consumer or industrial products. They may be grouped by markets—that is, by who buys them, or by the purchasing habits of the buyers. They may be classified according to some physical description. Or they may be classified by how fast they are used up or by how tangible they are.

When most people speak of a *product,* they usually mean a physical entity—a *good.* Does it take up space? Can it be touched? Yet people often pay for benefits that are not so physically real, such as insurance or an annuity. The fact is, a product may be either tangible or intangible—like services.

A **service** is a bundle of benefits that may or may not be physical, are temporary in nature, and come from the completion of a task.[23] The railroad is an example. Rail service is transitory—used and priced on a time and distance basis. It offers the functional benefits derived from the task of transporting people, livestock, and freight. But it can also offer psychological benefits as well, as shown in Exhibit 5-16 on p. 178. The railroad relies on the use of *specialized equipment*—vehicles able to pull huge loads over a unique track. This makes it an **equipment-based service.**

In contrast, let's look at a **people-based service**—a bank or savings and loan—that relies upon the talents and skills of individuals rather than on highly technical or specialized equipment. What would Clearwater Federal be without its manager, loan officers, and tellers? People make a financial institution run. Advertising itself is another example of a people-based service.

EXHIBIT 5-16

In addition to offering functional benefits, an equipment-based service like Amtrak also offers psychological benefits, such as providing travelers with a more intimate view of the land.

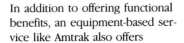

ANNCR: VO: It is grand and powerful, the land of the Empire Builder. The sky is bigger. Nature is stronger. The forces that shaped this earth still live. And where the Rockies are most forbidding, you will pass through and travel on to an ocean named for peace. Ride Amtrak's Empire Builder from Chicago to the Pacific Northwest . . . and feel your place in the universe. SONG: All aboard America, all aboard Amtrak. All aboard America, all aboard Amtrak.

Product Positioning

Once the advertising person understands the product's stage in the life cycle and how it's classified, the first strategic decision can be made—**positioning** the product. As we discussed in Ad Lab 4-B in Chapter 4, consumers rank products in their mental files. Part of the marketing effort, therefore, is to determine what desirable positions are open in the consumer's mind and to try to develop products that can occupy a number-one or number-two position.

Products may be positioned in many different ways. Generally, they are ranked by the way they are differentiated or by the particular market segment to which they appeal.[24] A product may even be positioned by the way it is classified (e.g., as a convenience good rather than a shopping good). As Exhibit 5-17 shows, Xerox—the one-time king of copiers—now positions itself as "The Document Company." This is a strategy to *reposition* itself, moving from the narrow, mature, glutted, copier market to the broader, growing, document-handling market. At one stroke, Xerox redefines the business it is in and creates a new number-one position for itself.

How was Clearwater Federal positioned? Like Xerox, the clue to how a company is trying to position itself is often found in the slogan underneath

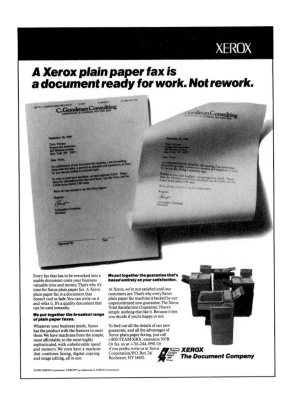

the logo (advertising people humorously call this the *slogo*). Clearwater
Federal used the tongue-in-cheek line: "Where those who've made it keep it."
This claim directly positioned Clearwater Federal as the place for the upscale
market—where successful people bank and save. While humorous, it also
differentiated Clearwater Federal by making all other financial institutions
appear lesser—through the implication that people who *haven't* made it
bank elsewhere. Thus, Clearwater Federal created the appearance of being in
a number-one position.

Product Differentiation

The concept of **product differentiation** is the competitive strategy of
creating a difference in a product that appeals to the preferences of a distinct
market segment. It has long been a basic method companies use to expand
markets. For example, the simple addition of pastel colors to a product line
can attract a new set of customers who were previously uninterested in the
product. But not all product differences need be so obvious. The differences
between products may be *perceptible, hidden, or induced.*

Perceptible Differences

Differences between products that are visibly apparent to the consumer are
called **perceptible differences.** For example, a red automobile is visibly
different from a black one and may appeal to more people without increasing
the manufacturing cost. Similarly, refrigerators are designed with right- and
left-hand doors, single doors, and double doors and in different colors.

Hidden Differences

Hidden differences are not so readily apparent. Trident's whole marketing strategy resulted from the *position* of its sugarless gum. The brand looks and tastes the same as other brands, but it is differentiated, albeit imperceptibly, by the use of artificial sweeteners. The same is true with many food products (caffeine-free colas) and automobiles (front-wheel drive). The differences may be imperceptible—or hidden—at first, but they do exist, and they may greatly affect the desirability of the product. However, these differences have no value to the product unless the consumer is aware of them—a problem answered by advertising.

Induced Differences

For many product classes, such as aspirin, salt, gasoline, packaged foods, liquor, and financial services, **induced differences** may be created by advertising or other promotional devices. One of the most successful product introductions in recent years was the Mitsubishi Eclipse sports car. The car was exactly the same as the Plymouth Laser (both were manufactured by Diamond Star Motors in Normal, Illinois—a joint venture between Chrysler and Mitsubishi). It was differentiated solely through unique branding, distribution, dealer service, and advertising. All these factors added **perceived value** to a product that was functionally no different than a competitor. Similarly, banks, brokerage houses, and insurance companies traditionally use advertising and promotion to differentiate themselves because the services and financial products they offer are virtually identical.[25] Research showed, for example, that Canada's leading supplier of natural gas, Linde, was seen by its customers as part of a faceless industry. So Linde pursued a massive, companywide effort (comprehensive employee training and intensive advertising) to make *customer service* a key factor in differentiating it from competitors.[26]

As Sunkist has so successfully demonstrated (see Exhibit 5-18), the ability to create the perception of differences in functionally similar products and services has made the strategy of product differentiation very popular and the effective use of branding, advertising, and packaging quite important.

Product Branding

The fundamental differentiating device for all products is the **brand**—the combination of name, words, symbols, or design that identifies the product and its source and differentiates it from competitive products. Without brands, consumers really wouldn't know one product from another, and advertising them would be a nearly impossible task.

Yet the decision regarding branding strategy is often difficult. A manufacturer may decide to establish an **individual brand** for each product it produces. Lever Brothers, for example, markets its various toothpastes under the individual brand names of Aim, Pepsodent, and Close-up. This way, the company can designate a distinct target market segment for each product and then develop a separate personality and image for each brand.[27] However, as any advertising professional knows, this is costly.

On the other hand, a company like Heinz may choose to use a **family brand** and market different products under the same umbrella name. When Heinz promotes its catsup products, it hopes its relish products are helped as

It's got sweet and juicy written all over it.

EXHIBIT 5-18

Good oranges are good oranges. But by putting the brand name on its best fruit and advertising consistently for 80 years, Sunkist has created the perception that its product is better than the non-branded orange. This is a juicy example of an induced difference.

well. This may be cost-effective, but if the products in the family do not share the same level of quality, the family brand image could be hurt by one bad tomato.

Since it is so expensive for manufacturers to market **national brands** (also called *manufacturer's brands*), some companies use a *private-labeling strategy*—they manufacture the product and sell it to **middlemen** (distributors or dealers) who place their own brand on the product for their particular outlets. These **private brands** are typically sold at lower prices in large retail chain stores and include familiar names like Kenmore, Craftsman, Cragmont, and Party Pride. In this case, the responsibility for creating brand image and familiarity rests on the particular distributor or retailer.

These decisions are difficult but critically important, because the brands a company owns may be its most important capital asset. Imagine for a moment the value of owning a brand name like Coca-Cola, or Nike, or Porsche, or Sunkist. In fact, this value is so great that some companies pay a substantial fee just for the right to use some other company's brand name. Thus, we have **licensed brands** like Sunkist vitamins, Coca-Cola clothing, Porsche sunglasses, and Mickey Mouse watches..

Role of Branding

As products have proliferated, the role of branding has taken on added significance. For the consumer, the brand offers instant recognition and identification of a sought-for product. But more important, the brand also represents the promise of a consistent, reliable standard of quality, taste, size, durability, or even emotional satisfaction. This adds value to the product for both the consumer and the manufacturer.

Brand differentiation must be built on the differences in images, meanings, and associations elicited by products and brands.[28] In fact, the No Excuses line of clothing was first conceptualized as a brand—because of the potential for humorous associations—before the marketer even had a product to sell.[29] Ideally, when consumers see a brand on the shelf, their mental files should instantly register comprehension of that particular brand's promise and inspire confidence in what to expect. But this, of course, depends on their level of familiarity with and acceptance of the brand.

Levels of Brand Acceptance

As McCarthy and Perreault point out, there are five levels of brand acceptance: (1) **brand nonrecognition**—when people are not aware of the brand; (2) **brand recognition**—when they are aware of it or recognize it in the store; (3) **brand rejection**—when they have tried it and will not do so again unless it changes its quality or image; (4) **brand preference**—when people usually choose the brand over competitors; and (5) **brand insistence**—when they will accept no substitutes.[30] Naturally, advertisers endeavor to achieve brand preference and insistence or, as we pointed out in Chapter 4, *brand loyalty*.

Over time, the goal of all brand advertising and promotion is to build greater *brand equity*. **Brand equity** is the totality of what consumers, distributors, dealers—and even competitors—feel and think about the brand over an extended period of time. It is, in short, the value of the brand's capital.

For the advertiser, the job of building brand equity requires time and money. Brand value and preference drive market share, but share points are usually won only by the advertisers who consistently win the ad spending war.[31]

But, as shown in Exhibit 5-19, most important is consistency in message and tone in all communications, from advertising to packaging, in order to maintain the personality and image of the brand.

EXHIBIT 5-19

Omni Hotels puts its logo on everything from matchbooks to grooming products to reinforce its image in the minds of guests.

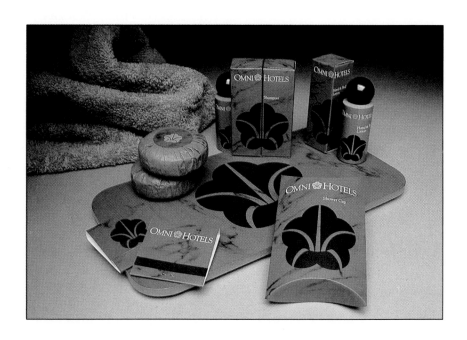

Product Packaging

The product's package is an integral component of the product element—but it is also a medium. In the average supermarket, more than 10,000 items compete for customer attention and dollars. Because of the emphasis on self-service, it is the package that often determines the outcome of this competition. The package quickly reveals the brand to current users and is designed to convince nonusers to try its contents for the first time.

Advertiser and agency creative departments are at the forefront of this battle, and their challenge is to make the package exciting, appealing, and at the same time functional. The five considerations in package design are *identification, containment and protection, convenience, consumer appeal,* and *economy.* If handled in a unique and creative manner, these functions may even become **copy points**—copywriting themes—in the product's advertising.

Identification

Packaging has become so important as an identification device that companies such as Heinz and Coca-Cola have adhered to the same basic bottle and label designs for years. Why? Because it is the unique combination of the trade name, trademark, or trade character—reinforced by the design of the package—that quickly identifies the product's brand and differentiates it from competitors. For example, the unique design and packaging of Speedo products in Exhibit 5-20 differentiate them from other water-sports accessories.

Shoppers seldom wear their reading glasses. So, just to penetrate their physiological screens, packages must offer high visibility and clear legibility. Product features must be easy to read, and color combinations should provide high contrast—all aimed at differentiating the product.[32]

This does not mean a package should be gaudy or garish. To penetrate the consumer's psychological screen, the package design must reflect the tone, the image, and the personality of the desired product concept. In fact, the

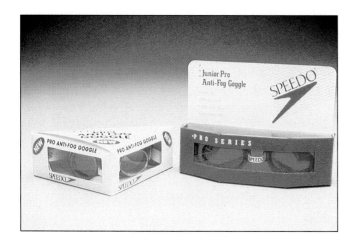

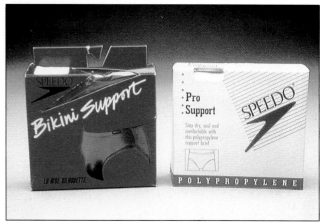

EXHIBIT 5-20   Speedo has a distinctive logo that it uses on all packaging. The combined use of logo design and consistent colors gives the entire Speedo line an overall integrity that complements each of its products.

package often reveals more about the product concept than the product itself; and, in many product categories, the quality of the package is perceived as an inherent factor in the quality of the product.

Containment and Protection

The basic purpose of any package is to hold and protect the product. While marketers must design an interesting package, they must also ensure that it will keep the product fresh and protect its contents from shipping damage, water vapor (for frozen foods), grease, infestation, and odors. Consumers don't expect contaminated food, leaky packages, cut fingers, or tampering by criminals; and packages must adhere to the protection requirements established by both the government and trade associations.

Convenience

Retailers want packages that are easy to stack and display, and they also look for a full range of sizes to fit their customers' needs. Consumers, likewise, want ease in storing and opening packages. So these are important design considerations.

Products for a dressing table, for example, should be packaged so they don't spill or tip over easily. Shampoo bottles should be easy to grip. But convenience cannot interfere with protection. Spouts make pouring much easier, for example, but they may also limit the package's physical strength.

Consumer Appeal

Consumer appeal in packaging is the result of many factors—size, color, material, and shape. A choice of sizes, for example, can satisfy different needs and budgets.

Color, too, is an important consideration, as shown in Exhibit 5-21. From many studies, researchers have learned that certain colors have special meanings to consumers. General Foods, for example, changed the Sanka package to orange when it learned that its yellow label suggested weakness.

A package's shape, as Exhibit 5-22 (p. 186) certainly demonstrates, may also offer an opportunity for consumer appeal based on whimsy, humor, romance, or some other form of creativity. Containers of Janitor in a Drum and heart-shaped packages of Valentine's Day candy instantly tell what the product is and what it is used for, and the packaging of several items together may offer convenience as well as a discount price.

Another opportunity for creativity and appeal is to design a package with a secondary use. For example, Kraft manufactures a cheese glass that, once emptied, can be used for serving fruit juice. Some tins and bottles even become collectibles. These packages are really premiums that give the buyer extra value for the dollars they spend.

Economy

The manufacturer's use of a particular package depends on its cost. The costs of the features we have discussed—protection, identification, convenience, and consumer appeal—all add to the basic cost of materials and printing.

Sometimes a small increase in production costs may be more than offset by increased customer appeal. These benefits may make a considerable difference to the consumer and affect both the product concept and the way

EXHIBIT 5-21

This packaging for computer software grabs the eye with color. The background for the Music Construction Set was originally gold, but it was changed to blue-green. Similarly, the red borders are eye-grabbers.

EXHIBIT 5-22

The Certifiably Nuts packaging features little straitjackets and a whimsical message on the bottom of the point-of-purchase display, revealed only when the product is removed.

the product is advertised. For example, the Kleenex package that dispenses one tissue at a time has been pictured in many ads. The same is true with the variety of medicines now offered in child-proof plastic bottles. And today, numerous promotional opportunities await manufacturers who can design packages that are not only cost-effective but environmentally friendly.[33]

ADVERTISING AND THE PRICE ELEMENT

It is very common for companies—especially small ones—to request input from their advertising people about pricing strategies, including the price charged, terms, and pricing offers.[34] Since the **price element** of the marketing mix has such a dramatic effect on the consumer's perception of the product concept, advertising managers must understand the factors that influence price, the strategic options available, and the consequent impact on the firm's advertising. This requires the ability to blend analysis with creativity.

Key Factors Influencing Price

Certain basic factors typically influence the way a company determines the price for its products. These include market demand, the cost of production and distribution, competition, and corporate objectives. Since price plays such an important role in advertising, we must consider these factors briefly.

Market Demand

Most people are familiar with the law of supply and demand. If the supply of a product stays the same and the desire (or demand) for it increases, the price tends to rise. If the demand decreases below the available supply, then the price tends to drop; and this can dramatically affect the message in advertising. These factors are diagrammed in Exhibit 5-23.

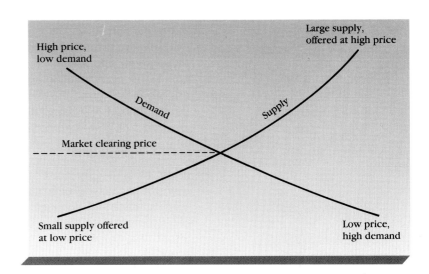

This graph plots demand versus price and supply versus price. The demand curve is a schedule of the amounts demanded at various prices. The supply curve is a schedule of the amounts offered for sale at various prices. The point where the two curves cross is called the *market clearing price*, where demand and supply are in balance. It is the price that theoretically clears the market of supply.

In the recession of 1990-91, many auto manufacturers were faced with a glut of unsold new cars and declining customer demand. Several companies decided to advertise substantial factory rebates—in effect, a price cut—to prospective car buyers to motivate them to buy. Dealers immediately sold more cars because of the lower price. In this case, no amount of image or awareness advertising would have had the same effect as simply cutting the price. But, of course, the use of advertising was essential to communicate the price cut.

Marketing theorists believe that for new durable-good products, advertising works with word-of-mouth communication to generate an awareness of product attributes. Once consumers perceive that the product's value warrants the purchase price, sales will occur. As product experience and information spread, the risks typically associated with new products diminish, which effectively increases the consumer's willingness to purchase at a higher price.[35] For advertisers, the implications of this theory are immense.

Production and Distribution Costs

The price of goods depends largely on the costs of production and distribution. As these costs increase, they must be passed on to the consumer, or the company will eventually be unable to meet its overhead and be forced to close its doors.

In such a case, advertising may be called upon to enhance the product image in order to justify the higher price. To the consumer, the issue is the "perceived equal exchange." The challenge for advertising, then, is to convince the consumer that the value of the exchange is indeed equal.

Interestingly, many premium-priced products are touted for the very fact that they do cost more. L'Oreal, for instance, successfully promoted the expensive luxury of its hair-care products with the line: "I deserve it."

Competition

Every company battles for sales in a competitive environment. And a product's relative price position versus competitors contributes to the consumer's perception of that product. Thus, as we mentioned earlier, the price element is an integral part of the product concept.

Marketers believe that in many product categories the perception of the price relative to the competition is more important than the absolute price of the item. For the advertiser, maintaining that perception during periods of intense price competition and fluctuation is very challenging, but critically important. And protecting the company's perceived price position should be the guidepost for any recommendations offered by advertising managers.[36]

Corporate Objectives

Prices are also influenced by the company's objectives. When introducing new products, companies often set a high price initially to recover development and start-up costs as quickly as possible. On the other hand, the objective may be to position the product as an inexpensive convenience item aimed at a broad target market. In this case, ads would likely stress the economy of the product.[37]

As products enter the maturity stage of their life cycle, corporate objectives tend to aim at increased market share, and advertising and promotion become more competitive and intensive. This tends to exert a downward pressure on prices.

Variable Influences

Prevailing economic conditions, consumer income and tastes, government regulations, marketing costs, and the supply of raw materials also influence the price of products and, thus, the advertising for them. Only after considering all these factors can marketing management determine the appropriate pricing strategy.

The Impact of Pricing Strategies on Advertising

A company has relatively few options for determining its price strategy. And these depend on the desired product concept. Say you are opening a retail store. Your plan is to sell audio equipment, CD players, car stereos, and peripheral products. One of your first decisions is how to price your merchandise. Consider the following alternatives.

Competitive Pricing Strategy

You could run ads declaring: "We won't be undersold!" Your ads could show or list a wide variety of products with a large, bold price next to each item. This would mean lower profit on each item and would require constant monitoring of competitive prices. It would also make you vulnerable to retaliatory actions by your competitors. Another approach to competitive pricing is to point out what a value your product is compared to high-priced brands.

Comparative Pricing

You could run ads for a new sound system showing the regular list price and your special low price. By always comparing your low price with "normal" lists prices, you inform customers that your store offers discount prices on these items.

Skimming Strategy

If yours is the only audio store in the area, you might need to start with relatively high prices to recover all the money you had to spend furnishing, decorating, stocking, and promoting the store. Your ads would probably feature convenience and service. Later, you might lower your prices if a competitive store opens up.

Penetration Pricing

You might open the store and offer lower prices than you intend to have later on. In this case, you hope to penetrate the market quickly by creating immediate traffic and sales. As your store develops regular customers, you gradually raise prices to a more profitable level. Your initial advertising might feature low prices, whereas your later ads would promote store services, quality products, wide selection, or convenience.

Promotional Pricing

To introduce a new line of equipment or to clear out old lines, you might use promotional pricing techniques. Two-for-one sales or end-of-month sales are typical retail efforts to maintain traffic, stimulate demand, or make room for new merchandise.

Loss-Leader Pricing

A special promotional strategy common to retail selling is the loss-leader strategy. You might select one sound system and advertise it at $100 below your cost. The purpose is to create store traffic and sell other regularly priced merchandise in addition to the loss leaders. This presents the problem, though, of bait-and-switch advertising, which is illegal and unethical. If you offer loss leaders, you must have them in stock and be prepared to sell them without trying to talk customers into buying higher-priced items instead.

Prestige Pricing

Rather than competing on the basis of price, you might prefer to offer the finest audio equipment available, the best service, free delivery, and friendly, knowledgeable clerks in plush surroundings. In this case, your ads might not mention prices at all. The ad in Exhibit 5-24 (p. 190), for example, is aimed at a select clientele who can afford to pay higher prices in exchange for convenience, service, and quality. To understand Reebok's pricing strategy, see Ad Lab 5-B, "Marketing Reebok: Price Element and the Market."

Which of these strategies would you select for your new audio store? Why? What are the advantages and disadvantages of each? How would they affect your advertising?

ADVERTISING AND THE PLACE ELEMENT

Every company must ask how and where their customers will buy their products. At the factory? From a door-to-door salesperson? In a store? Before the first advertisement can be created, this question of the **place element**— or distribution—must be answered. Companies may use two basic methods of distribution: direct or indirect.

Some ads, such as this one from Cornes Motors, are quite obviously designed to appeal to people who care about prestige.

The people who buy cars here at Cornes Motors are a demanding lot.

They feel, quite rightly, that they've earned the privilege of driving the best motorcars in the world.

covering more than 540 square feet, handcut from eleven complete hides.

The meticulousness.

The conscientiousness.

And, oh yes, the ashtrays.

Our customers are accustomed to having things done for them. But they're still amazed when their new car empties its own ashtrays.

But even so, after a simple test drive in a Bentley Turbo R, the most discriminating driver tends to walk away a bit awed.

Awed by the power churned out by the hand-assembled engine. Enough power to rival the quickest Porsche.

Awed by the magnificent interior, with walnut surfaces, polished like glass, at your fingertips always.

The Connolly leather everywhere,

They empty themselves, without even being asked, into a concealed bin.

If you'd like to know more about the Bentley Turbo R, or the other Bentley models, please visit us at 9010 Miramar Road.

You'll find that we'll go to extreme lengths to serve you. And, even more impressively, so will our cars.

CORNES MOTORS

Bentley   Ferrari   Rolls-Royce

Direct Marketing

Direct marketing is like moving the store to the customer's location. The mail-order house that communicates directly with consumers through mail-order ads and catalogs is one of the many types of companies engaged in direct marketing. It builds and maintains its own database of customers and uses a variety of media to communicate with those customers.

Today, the field of direct marketing is growing rapidly as companies discover the benefits of control, cost efficiency, and accountability. For example, many companies are using **telemarketing** programs to increase productivity through person-to-person telephone contact. Advertisers have known for some time that by using the telephone to follow up direct-mail advertising, results can be increased by 2.5 to 10 times over the response achieved by mail alone.[38]

AD LAB 5-B
Marketing Reebok: The Price Element and the Market

Once Reebok had selected its new target market and product concept in 1980, it decided on a premium pricing strategy that aimed at the higher end of the aerobics market. As you may recall from the Reebok story in Ad Lab 5-A, the total market revenues at that time were $1 billion. In 1990, reported total market revenues reached $5.55 billion. Along with this growth came increased costs. Reebok's ad budget, for example, was $60 million in 1989, but this accompanied a sales growth of 5.2 percent for the year. With continued growth, Reebok can be flexible in its pricing strategies for each line of shoe.

Laboratory Applications

1. Reviewing the Reebok story in Ad Lab 5-A, describe how the product's features justified the higher price to Reebok's target market—aerobics participants.

2. Visit two or three stores where Reeboks are sold. Can you determine the company's current pricing strategy or strategies?

Indirect Marketing

Manufacturers seldom have their own storefront. Most companies market their products through a distribution channel that includes a network of middlemen. A **middleman** is a business firm that operates between the producer and the consumer or industrial purchaser—someone who deals in trade rather than production.[39] The term includes both wholesalers and retailers, as well as manufacturers' representatives, brokers, jobbers, and distributors. A **distribution channel** comprises all the firms and individuals that take title, or assist in taking title, to the product as it moves from the producer to the consumer.

To help the massive flow of manufactured goods, various types of indirect distribution channels have developed to make products available to customers more economically than the manufacturers could accomplish through direct marketing. National appliance companies, for example, contract with exclusive regional distributors who buy the products from the factory and resell them to local dealers, who, in turn, resell them to consumers. Many industrial companies market their products through reps or distributors to original-equipment manufacturers (OEMs). These OEMs, in turn, may incorporate the product as a component in their own product, which is then sold to their customers.

The advertising a company uses depends on its method of distribution. Much of the advertising we see is not prepared or paid for by the manufacturer at all but rather by the distributor or the retailer as in Exhibit 5-25 (p. 192). In fact, over the years, members of the distribution channel have given enormous promotional support to the manufacturers they represent.

As part of their marketing strategy, manufacturers must determine the amount of market coverage necessary for their products. Procter & Gamble, for example, defines adequate coverage for Crest toothpaste as almost every supermarket, discount store, drugstore, and variety store. Other products might need only one dealer for every 50,000 people. Consumer goods manufacturers traditionally use three types of distribution strategies: *intensive, selective,* and *exclusive.*

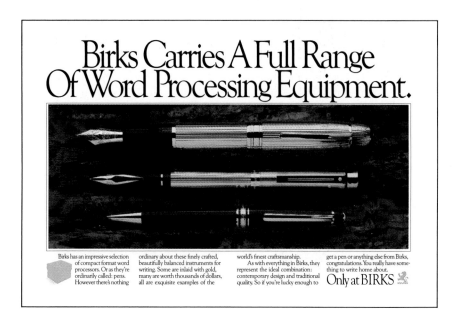

Intensive Distribution

Soft drinks, candy, Bic pens, Timex watches, and many other convenience goods are available to purchasers at every possible location because of **intensive distribution.** This enables the consumer to buy with a minimum of effort. The profit on each unit is usually very low, but the volume of sales is high. For this reason, the sales burden is usually carried by the manufacturer's national advertising program. Ads appear in trade magazines to **push** the product into the retail "pipeline" and in mass media to stimulate consumers to **pull** the products through the pipeline. As a manufacturer modifies its strategy to more push or more pull, special promotions may be directed at the trade or at consumers.

Selective Distribution

By limiting the number of outlets through **selective distribution,** manufacturers can cut their distribution and promotion costs. Many hardware tools, for example, are sold selectively through discount chains, home-improvement centers, and hardware stores. Manufacturers may use some national advertising, but the sales burden is normally carried by the retailer. In this case, the manufacturer may share part of the retailer's advertising costs through a **cooperative advertising** program, and the retailer agrees to display the manufacturer's products prominently.

Exclusive Distribution

Some manufacturers grant **exclusive distribution** rights to a wholesaler or retailer to sell in one geographic region. For example, a town of 50,000 to 100,000 people will have only one Chrysler dealer and may not even have a Mercedes dealer. This is also common in the high-fashion business and in the marketing of some major appliance and furniture lines. What is lost in market coverage is often gained in the ability to maintain a prestige image and premium prices. Exclusive distribution agreements also force manufacturers

AD LAB 5-C

Marketing Reebok: The Place Element and the Market

Reebok International sounds worldwide, but it is a U.S. company that distributes a British-made product named after an African antelope. It competes against German brands (Adidas and Puma) and other major U.S. brands (Nike and Converse). It also competes with brand names featuring geography: L.A. Gear, British Knights, and K-Swiss.

Many U.S. products sell to Europeans who are drawn to American street fashions. As of March 1991, Reebok and Nike showed an acceleration in European sales, while Adidas—still Europe's number one—slumped due to long-term problems stemming from unfocused advertising, high costs, and a glut of products.

Laboratory Applications

1. Should Reebok make a special marketing effort to capture more market share in Europe, especially since Adidas has lost some momentum? If so, cite your reasons.

2. If Reebok decided to push a new line of athletic shoes in Europe, should it choose a brand name that alludes to geography? If so, should the name be American, European, or African?

and retailers to cooperate closely in advertising and promotion programs. For example, a Reebok retailer may receive substantial advertising allowances from the manufacturer for advertising Reebok shoes in its local media. (See Ad Lab 5-C, "Marketing Reebok: The Place Element and the Market.")

Vertical Marketing Systems

To be efficient, members of the distribution channel need to cooperate closely with one another. This need has given rise in recent years to the development of the **vertical marketing system (VMS)**—a centrally programmed and managed distribution system that supplies or otherwise serves a group of stores or other businesses. The VMS is designed to profit from economies of scale and to maximize the marketing impact of all the stores in its chain. Sears Roebuck, which owns the manufacturers of many products sold in its stores, is one type of VMS called a **corporate marketing system.** Others include **administered systems,** like Magnavox, which, as the dominant channel member, gains strong retailer support because of the traditional strength of the brand's reputation; and **contractual systems,** like IGA Food Stores, which is a voluntary chain of independent members sponsored by a single wholesaler.[40]

Other types of contractual systems include retail cooperatives, which set up their own wholesaling operations to better compete with chains, and **franchises,** like Wendy's or PIP Printing (see Exhibit 5-26), in which dealers (or *franchisees*) pay a fee to operate under the guidelines and direction of the manufacturer (or *franchisor*). Franchises in areas such as fast food, automotive service, and other retail specialties have been so successful that now over 33 percent of all retail sales in the United States are made through franchise outlets.[41] As a result, similar vertical marketing systems are even developing in the new do-it-yourself health-care business—retail dentistry, urgent/primary-care centers, and freestanding day surgery clinics.[42]

IS THIS ALL YOU'RE WAITING FOR?

If all you're getting out of the corporate rat race are a few perks and the perfunctory gold watch, it's time to rethink your career strategy.

Owning a PIP Printing franchise can be the right move. At the right time. Here's an opportunity to call your own shots. To be with the leader in the business printing industry. An industry that's taken the fast track to an estimated $15 billion. And shows no signs of slowing down.

PIP Printing franchise owners benefit from over 20 years of proven experience. Experience that enables us to offer absolutely top-notch support in R&E. Training. Marketing. Advertising. And the most comprehensive operations support in the business printing industry.

If this sounds like what you've been waiting for, give us a call. There's never been a better time.

Prime locations and resales available.
Call **1-800-292-4747, extension 99**

PIP *PRINTING*

The Best Business Printer In The Business.™

Offering made by prospectus only. Cash requirements of $25,000 down, with $52,000 working capital plus living expenses. Financing available through PIP Printing. Based on data as of 12/15/90. © 1991 PIP Printing

The VMS offers both manufacturers and retailers numerous advantages: reduction of nonessential product offerings; streamlining of product and information flow; reduced duplication of efforts; standardization of record-keeping; centralized coordination of marketing efforts; and both substantial savings and continuity in advertising.[43] A common store name and similar product inventories mean that a single newspaper ad can promote all of a chain's retailers in a particular trading area.

Now that we've seen how advertising relates to the product, price, and place elements, let's take a brief look at the promotion element to see how advertising relates to it.

ADVERTISING AND THE PROMOTION ELEMENT

Once it has determined the first three elements of its marketing mix, the company is ready to plan its promotional activities. As a part of the promotion element, advertising is just one of the promotional tools companies have the option of using. (See Ad Lab 5-D, "Marketing Reebok: Deciding on the Promotion Element.")

AD LAB 5-D
Marketing Reebok: Deciding on the Promotion Element

In its initial 1980 promotional program, Reebok included sampling to aerobics instructors, direct selling to dealers by Reebok's sales staff, and advertising in trade and consumer magazines to promote its new line of aerobics shoes.

Over the years, Reebok has dramatically increased its ad budgets and has created a series of campaigns designed to catch the attention of various segments of the market. It increased its 1989 budget by 50 percent to $60 million. In early 1989, it ran its "Legends" campaign that targeted ethnic groups and teenagers and introduced Reebok's new Energy Return System shoes. Later in the year, it ran a performance-centered campaign titled "Physics of Physiques." And in 1990, its ads returned to the younger market by featuring Paula Abdul in its commercials, who introduced its "Club Reebok" footwear *and* apparel.

In addition, Reebok began using a "sales promotion agency," and thereby joined a recent and growing shift away from pure advertising agency creativity and ad placement services to a broader base of promotional services.

Laboratory Applications

1. If you were the brand manager for Reebok, how might you use the promotion mix? Would you use public relations? Sales promotion? Collateral materials? How?

2. Given the same situation, would you consider the services of a sales promotion agency rather than a public relations firm and/or advertising agency? Discuss your answers in detail.

The **promotion element** includes all the marketing-related communications between the seller and the buyer. Marketers have a variety of marketing communication tools. These tools can be grouped into *personal selling* and *nonpersonal selling* activities. **Personal selling** includes all person-to-person contact with customers. **Nonpersonal selling** activities—which use some medium as an intermediary for communication—include advertising, public relations, sales promotion, and collateral materials.

Personal Selling

Some consumer products are sold by clerks in retail stores, others by salespeople who call on customers directly. In business-to-business marketing, personal selling is often considered the most important activity of marketing. It establishes a face-to-face situation in which the marketer can learn firsthand about customer wants and needs; and customers, being offered that opportunity for satisfaction, find it more difficult to say no.

Advertising

Advertising has been called mass or nonpersonal selling. As we have discussed, advertising is used to inform, persuade, and remind customers about particular products and services. And in some cases—like mail order—advertising even closes the sale.

Some products lend themselves to advertising more than others. Typically, certain factors are particularly important for advertising success, such as:

☐ High primary demand trend for the product.

☐ Chance for significant product differentiation.

☐ High relative importance to the consumer of a product's hidden qualities (as opposed to external qualities).

☐ The opportunity to use strong emotional appeals.

☐ Substantial sums to support the advertising.

Where these conditions exist, as in the cosmetics industry, large advertising expenditures are favored, and the ratio of advertising to sales dollars is often quite high. For completely undifferentiated products, such as sugar, salt, and other raw materials or commodities, the importance of advertising is usually minimal, and price is usually the primary influence. An interesting exception to this is Sunkist, a farmers' cooperative that successfully brands an undifferentiated commodity (citrus fruit) and markets it internationally.

Public Relations

Whereas advertising is paid-for communication, **public relations** usually has no clear or overt sponsorship. Many firms use public relations activities such as publicity (news releases, media advisements, feature stories) and special events (open houses, factory tours, VIP parties, grand openings) as supplements to advertising to inform various audiences about the company and its products and to help build corporate credibility and image. Public relations, as we will discuss in Chapter 18, is an extremely powerful tool that should always be considered in the design of a company's promotional mix.

Sales Promotion

Sales promotion, the subject of Chapter 16, is a broad category covering nonmedia advertising activities such as free samples, displays, trading stamps, sweepstakes, cents-off coupons, and premiums. *Reader's Digest,* for example, is famous for its annual sweepstakes designed to increase circulation. Manufacturers print and distribute over 300 billion coupons per year. Of these, only 4 percent are ever redeemed. But this accounts for approximately $2.5 to 3 billion annually that manufacturers give their customers to try their products.[44] Similarly, financial institutions spend untold millions on premiums to attract new accounts.

Collateral Materials

As mentioned in Chapter 3, **collateral** refers to all the accessory advertising materials companies prepare to accompany an advertising or public relations campaign. These generally include booklets, catalogs, brochures, films, trade-show exhibits, sales kits, annual reports, and point-of-purchase displays.

THE MARKETING MIX IN PERSPECTIVE

With the target market designated and the various elements of the marketing mix determined, the company has not only a complete product concept but also a strategic basis for marketing to that target. Now it can formalize its strategies and tactics in a written marketing and advertising plan. As part of the planning process, though, companies typically use a variety of marketing and advertising research procedures. We discuss these in the next chapter before dealing with the formal planning process.

Summary

The majority fallacy is a common misconception that says a product or service must appeal to the majority of people to be successful. In fact, by aiming at specific target market segments, new products usually compete better and achieve deeper market penetration than if they try to aim at the whole market.

The product marketing process is the sequence of activities marketers perform to select markets and develop marketing mixes that eventually lead to exchanges.

Market segmentation is the process of identifying groups of people with certain shared characteristics within a broad product market and aggregating these groups into larger market segments according to their mutual interest in the product's utility. Marketers use a variety of methods to identify behavioral groups and segment markets. The most common bases for segmentation are geographic, demographic, behavioristic, and psychographic.

Business markets are often segmented in the same way as consumer markets: by geographic location and by several behavioristic variables. In addition, they may be grouped by business purchasing procedures, by SIC code, or by market concentration.

The next step in the segmentation process involves selecting those groups that have a mutual interest in the product and aggregating them into larger market segments by the potential they offer for sales and profit. From these segments, companies can then select a target market at which to aim all their marketing activities.

The target marketing process includes designating the specific segments to target and developing a mix of marketing activities aimed at refining the product concept, serving and appealing to the market, and effecting the marketing exchange. The product concept is the consumer's perception of the product as a bundle of utilitarian and symbolic need-satisfying values.

Every company can add, subtract, or modify four major elements in its marketing program to achieve a desired marketing mix. These elements are referred to as the 4 Ps: product, price, place, and promotion.

The *product* element includes the way the product is designed and classified, positioned, branded, and packaged. Just as humans pass through a life cycle, so do products—and product categories. The location of a product in its life cycle may determine how it is advertised.

To satisfy the variety of consumer tastes, marketers build differences into their products. Even the product's package is part of the product concept. The product concept may also be developed through unique positioning against competitive products in the consumer's mind.

Price refers to what and how a customer pays for a product, and companies can use many common pricing strategies. Some products compete on the basis of price, but many do not.

The term *place* refers to how and where the product is distributed, bought, and sold. Companies may use direct or indirect methods of distribution. Consumer goods manufacturers use several types of distribution strategies.

Promotion refers to the marketing-related communication between the seller and the buyer. Tools of the promotional element include personal selling, advertising, public relations, sales promotion, and collateral materials.

Advertising is considered nonpersonal selling and is most effective when there is a high demand for the product, a chance for significant product differentiation, an importance to the consumer of hidden product qualities, the opportunity to use strong emotional appeals, and substantial sums to support an advertising program.

Questions for Review and Discussion

1. How does the majority fallacy relate to the subject of market segmentation?
2. How could you use VALS to develop the marketing strategy for a product of your choice?
3. How does the segmentation of business markets differ from that of consumer markets?
4. What is the most important factor to consider when determining the elements of the marketing mix?
5. What is the difference between a product and a product concept?
6. What are some examples of product positioning not discussed in this chapter?
7. What effect does the product life cycle have on the advertising a company employs?
8. What factors influence the price of a product?
9. How do the basic methods of distribution affect advertising?
10. What product characteristics encourage heavy advertising? Little advertising? Why?

MARKETING AND ADVERTISING RESEARCH: INPUTS TO THE PLANNING PROCESS

Objective: To describe how marketers and advertisers use research as a tool to measure and evaluate specific information—both objective and subjective—about the marketplace and the marketing environment. The information gained from research is the glue that ties consumer behavior, market segmentation, and marketing and advertising planning together. Therefore, advertisers need to know the basic, overall research process, including the advantages and disadvantages of different methodologies and techniques. Finally, they need to understand how research findings are applied to marketing and advertising decision making.

After studying this chapter, you will be able to:

☐ Discuss how research helps advertisers segment markets and select target markets.

☐ Diagram and explain the fundamental steps in the research process for marketing and advertising.

☐ Delineate the differences between formal and informal research and primary and secondary data.

☐ Understand how to create a proper statement of research objectives.

☐ Explain the different methodologies used in quantitative and qualitative research.

☐ Define the concepts of validity and reliability in research and explain their importance.

☐ Recognize the issues and pitfalls in creating questions for research surveys.

☐ Debate the pros and cons of advertising testing.

☐ Relate how research helps companies use advertising to build a desirable product concept.

Now it was up to Agi—and to the several creative teams working under her. The agency that came up with the best campaign would win the account and the lucrative commissions that go along with placing millions of dollars worth of advertising.

In the advertising business, it was what they call a *plum account*—big and juicy—the kind every agency wants a crack at. In fact, just about every big agency in New York had competed for it, but now the choice had been narrowed down to four finalists. Ayer (formerly N.W. Ayer), the oldest agency in the United States, was one of them. To capture this $50 million plum, Agi (pronounced ah-szhee) Clark and her people had to gain the client's confidence in Ayer and demonstrate that the confidence would not be misplaced.

They were given an assignment, and it was not a simple one. To win they had to come up with a new image for J. C. Penney—one that would be both honest and credible, and would reposition the company and revolutionize the $200-billion-a-year department store industry. A transformation of this magnitude would require years to complete—probably more than a decade—and this promised a long-term, lucrative relationship to the winning agency. With this prospect, Ayer was willing to spend tens of thousands of dollars for the research and concept development that would make J. C. Penney (and the agency) successful.

The nation's third-largest retailer with more than 1,300 stores nationwide, J. C. Penney (shown in Exhibit 6-1) had been struggling with image problems. For decades, the retailer had been a mass merchandiser of a wide range of household commodities. But in recent years Penney's had changed. For

EXHIBIT 6-1

J. C. Penney saw its challenge as a positioning problem—to position itself as a "regional comparison retailer in competition with department and specialty stores similarly oriented." As the company had evolved from a mass merchandiser to a department store offering appealing selections and a variety of styles, colors, and brands of good-quality, fashionable merchandise, consumers were becoming confused. Penney's had to communicate its new image. One of the more visible changes was the modernized logo and storefront shown here.

one thing, it began to offer more fashionable apparel, which seemed to confuse customers. Was Penney's a nationwide discount retailer? A department store for fashionable apparel? Penney's customers said it wasn't the latter, but then they didn't know what is *was,* either. Agi Clark's assignment was to find a way to change that—to communicate that J. C. Penney was indeed changing, that now it really did offer quality, fashion, and style, but at the same time that the company had not forgotten its traditional promise of high value, fair prices, and honest dealing with customers.

Clark's colleagues at Ayer provided reams of research information about retail industry trends and Penney's position in the market. The agency's research and account teams analyzed sales data, tested consumer attitudes, and studied Penney's strengths and liabilities to find the most effective way to change Penney's image and boost its sales. They knew that to get customers to consider Penney's for their fashion purchases, they had to convince them that Penney's had changed. Somehow they had to connect Penney's to the modern, active lifestyle of upscale American consumers—tie it to the way they work, the way they relax, the way they play; make "human contact" (Ayer's slogan and advertising philosophy).

This wasn't the first time Clark had played the high-stakes game. As a senior vice president and executive creative director, she had already directed campaigns for several of Ayer's well-known clients like DeBeers ("A diamond is forever"), AT&T ("Reach out and touch someone"), and others. Her years on the DeBeers account had given Clark invaluable working experience with outstanding photographers, film directors, makeup artists, and hair stylists, but she had never really worked on an honest-to-goodness fashion account. She hoped that very fact, along with her knowledge of the American consumer, would enable her to bring a fresh approach to this campaign.

In countless meetings with her teams of art directors and copywriters, the concepts began to evolve. The teams came up with a design concept that was at once modern, fashionable, forward-looking, and simple—a whole new look and feel that could be used in magazine and newspaper ads and even on TV. OK. But what about the copy concept? What approach would be credible to the one-third of the women who make two-thirds of the fashion purchases?

The ideas and layouts piled up. They could tie Penney's to the new brand names it carried. They could tell customers that Penney's had "changed its looks but not its values." They could compare J. C. Penney with other well-known department stores. Clark consulted with Chuck Meding, Ayer's senior VP and the management supervisor who headed the Penney's account team. Finally, they settled on four basic concepts.

"All right," Agi said, "let's send these over to research for testing." But instinctively she felt she knew which concept would test best—the one that played off Penney's long history of responding to customers' needs. Tell them: "WE'VE CHANGED BECAUSE YOU'VE CHANGED."

THE NEED FOR RESEARCH IN MARKETING AND ADVERTISING

As we discussed in Chapter 5, advertising people are keenly interested in "what makes people tick." When companies like J. C. Penney plan to spend $30 or $40 or $50 million on advertising, they don't want to risk losing it on ads or commercials their target customers won't notice or respond to. They also don't want to waste time and money placing their messages on TV shows their customers don't watch or in magazines they don't read or on billboards if they don't drive cars.

Advertising is expensive. In 1990, the cost of a single 30-second commercial on prime-time network TV averaged $122,200. That equates to an average of $9.74 to reach 1,000 TV households—more than double the cost in 1980. Likewise, a single color-page ad in a national magazine averaged $18.44 to reach a thousand prospects.[1] That's too much money to risk if people won't see the ad, don't pay attention to it, don't like it, don't believe it, or forget it two minutes after it's gone. That's why advertising decision makers need research. Without it, they use intuition or guesswork. In our fast-changing, competitive economy, this invites failure.[2]

All the research and work paid off. Penney's liked Ayer's new concept. Armed with the concept and a $22 million fall budget plus its own marketing and merchandising know-how, J. C. Penney launched an assault on the department store industry in the mid-80s. Stated simply, their goal was to change the shopping habits of America.

Big bucks were at stake. U.S. consumers like clothes and fashionable merchandise. In fact, they spend more in department stores than many countries spend on food or national defense. And annually they consume more than $1,000 worth of department store merchandise for every man, woman, and child in the United States. An increase of just 1 percent in share of this total market means an added $2 billion in sales. A decrease of just 1 percent means a similar loss. These are high stakes; and the higher the stakes, the greater the advertiser's need for marketing and advertising information.

Marketing Research

Unfortunately, managers never have *all* the information they need to make the best decisions. That's where research comes in. The term **marketing research** refers to the systematic gathering, recording, and analysis of information to help managers make marketing decisions.[3] For firms that operate under the marketing concept (discussed in Chapter 4), marketing research plays a key role in identifying consumer needs and market segments, developing new products and marketing strategies, and assessing the effectiveness of marketing programs and promotional activities.

The importance of this information depends on the amount of risk involved in the decisions to be made. In Chapter 4, we mentioned the colossal failure of the Edsel automobile The mistake of ignoring research findings cost Ford Motor Company $350 million and earned them the dubious award from *Advertising Age* for the greatest marketing failure in history.

Major advertisers like J. C. Penney have no desire to take the record away from Ford. Thus, over the years as the stakes in business have gotten larger, so has the dependence on sophisticated information. Today, over $4.7 billion per year is spent on marketing, advertising, and public opinion research. The 25 largest research organizations—led by Dun & Bradstreet Corp.—account for close to 55 percent of this amount.[4]

Actually, marketing research is useful in all stages of the management process. For instance, marketing research is used just as much in fields like financial planning and economic forecasting as in traditional marketing areas like advertising.

Advertising Research

Many advertising decisions cannot be made from an agency's intuition or knowledge of the product. Without research data, Agi Clark would have had no assurance of consumers' attitudes toward J. C. Penney or the other department stores. Before she could develop a campaign, Clark needed to know how consumers perceived Penney's, its strong points or liabilities, how that compared with competitive stores, and what image would be most credible.

For that information, Clark needed advertising research. **Advertising research** is the systematic gathering and analysis of information specifically to facilitate the development or evaluation of advertising strategies, advertisements and commercials, and media campaigns. It is a subset of marketing research, as is **market research,** which is simply information gathering about the particular market or market segment.

Finally, to develop media strategies, select media vehicles, and evaluate their results, advertisers use a subset of advertising research called **media research.** This particular type of research is usually performed by subscribing to any of a variety of well-known **syndicated research services** (e.g., A. C. Nielsen, Arbitron, Simmons, and Standard Rate & Data Service) that continuously monitor and publish information on the reach and effectiveness of the media vehicles—radio, television, newspapers, and so on—available in every major geographic market in the United States and Canada.

In this chapter, we explore the basic procedures and techniques used in marketing and advertising research today. We will consider the importance of research to the development of marketing and advertising plans and strategies, and we'll look at the ways research can be used to test the effectiveness of ads and campaigns both before and after they have run.

BASIC STEPS IN THE RESEARCH PROCESS

The manager of marketing research and planning at J. C. Penney was Sid Stein. He had been with the company more than 15 years and had seen significant management changes take place. But now he would play a key role in one of the largest repositioning efforts in corporate history. Penney's board chairman, William Howell, had selected a committee of four to assess Penney's competitive environment and to determine a clear direction for the future of the company. Sid was to chair the committee; and over the next year, the research performed by his department would prove to be one of the most rewarding activities he had ever been involved in. It would make a significant contribution to the positioning strategy the committee was charged with developing.

Analyze the Situation and Define the Problem

As Exhibit 6-2 shows, the first step in the marketing research process is to evaluate the specific situation under consideration in order to identify and define the problem the company is experiencing. This may be a difficult and time-consuming task, but it's worthwhile if it results in a thorough definition of the problem. Good research on the wrong problem is a total waste of effort. Sid Stein was already well aware of the problem at J. C. Penney. His responsibility had been to conduct ongoing marketing research for the

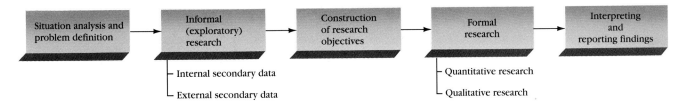

Situation analysis and problem definition → Informal (exploratory) research → Construction of research objectives → Formal research → Interpreting and reporting findings

— Internal secondary data
— External secondary data

— Quantitative research
— Qualitative research

EXHIBIT 6-2

The marketing research process begins with an evaluation of the company's situation and a specific definition of the problem. If this first step is not accomplished accurately, future money spent on formal research will likely be wasted.

company and to develop a **marketing information system**—a set of procedures and methods for generating an orderly flow of pertinent information for use in making marketing decisions.[5] The company was not running blind; Sid already had a good idea of the company's situation and why Penney's position in the market seemed to be slipping.

During the 1960s and early 70s, Penney's had a very broad merchandise mix. Customers could find everything they needed, from automotive products to home furnishings and appliances. At Penney's, you could get paint, hardware, lawn and garden supplies, home entertainment products, and apparel. The strategy had been one-stop shopping, "from a spool of thread to a refrigerator." As regional shopping centers emerged and flourished, Penney's set its course and in time occupied more space in these regional malls than any other retailer in the country. The company experienced tremendous growth, and its sales doubled or tripled in most categories. But Penney's research also showed that even though sales were increasing it was steadily losing its share of the total market, particularly in the highly profitable women's apparel department.

Penney's researchers believed the "contemporary" woman shopped at Penney's for commodity merchandise such as sheets, towels, underwear, and bathrobes but did not spend many of her fashion apparel dollars there. Yet, that contemporary group—about one-third of the population—accounts for two-thirds of women's apparel sales. Moreover, they discovered a perceptual gap between the way consumers viewed J. C. Penney and competing department stores with respect to fashionability and quality in women's apparel. It became apparent that in the process of trying to satisfy all consumers, Penney's may have inadvertently neglected certain groups, especially the higher-spending segments. Since 1975, Penney's had tried to respond to these consumer attitudes by adopting a segmentation strategy that led to the upgrading of the merchandise, but they had not done so fast enough. The competition had moved faster in upgrading their products and images, and the consumer perception gap had remained unchanged.

As a result, Stein was confronted with several problem *symptoms.* His first objective therefore was to discover the *causes* of these symptoms through informal research. Then the problem could be more accurately defined and analyzed before designing any formal research studies.

Conduct Informal (Exploratory) Research

The second step in the research process is simply to learn more about the market, the competition, and the business environment and to better define the problem through informal exploratory research. The researchers may discuss the problem with informed sources inside the firm; with wholesalers, distributors, or retailers outside the firm; with customers; or even with competitors. The point is not to waste time and money interviewing a large number of people at this point, but to find those few individuals who have the most information to offer

In all research, two types of data are used: *primary* and *secondary.* As we shall see later, **primary data** is information collected directly from the marketplace about the specific problem at hand. But this is expensive and time-consuming. During the exploratory research stage, therefore, it is usually less expensive to use **secondary data**—information that has been previously collected or published, usually for some other purpose by the firm or some other organization. This information is more readily available, either internally or externally, and can be gathered more quickly than primary data.

Use Internal Secondary Data

Company records are often a valuable source of secondary information. **Internal data** useful to a marketing or advertising manager include product shipment figures, billings to customers, warranty-card records, advertising expenditures, sales expenses, correspondence from customers, and records of meetings with sales staffs.

J. C. Penney's well-developed marketing information system provided an analysis of sales data, a review of past tracking studies, and an examination of previous marketing research data. This signaled the problem the company faced. In another situation, an advertiser might discover from an analysis of marketing expense data that sales to certain customers or territories are unprofitable in relation to the cost incurred producing the sales.

Collect External Secondary Data

Much information is available—usually at little or no cost—if the researcher just knows where to look for it. It might be government-issued materials, such as census data or publications from the U.S. Department of Commerce; published information from market research companies, trade associations, or various trade publications; or even computerized databases. Ad Lab 6-A, for example, presents a practical guide marketing and advertising people might use to find information pertaining to the vitamin market. Many of these same sources would be applicable to other markets as well.

Generally, collecting secondary data is less costly and time-consuming than collecting primary data. However, there are problems with secondary data. The information may be obsolete or not relevant to the problem at hand. The information may not be valid or reliable, depending on the way it was collected. And the very wealth of available information may be overpowering relative to the size of the problem being studied.

Some of the most frequently used sources of secondary data include:

☐ Library reference materials (*Business Periodicals Index* and *Canadian Periodical Index* for business magazines, *Reader's Guide to Periodical Literature* for consumer magazines, *Public Information Service Bulletin,* the *New York Times Index,* and the *World Almanac and Book of Facts*).

☐ Government publications (the *Statistical Abstract of the United States* or *Statistics Canada Catalogue*).

☐ Trade association publications (annual fact books containing government data and information gathered by various industry groups listed in the *Directory of National Trade Associations* and the *Directory of Associations in Canada*).

☐ Research organization publications (literature from university bureaus of business research, Nielsen retail store audits, MRCA consumer purchase diaries, Standard Rate & Data Service, *Canadian Advertising Rates & Data,* all available on a subscription basis). Exhibit 6-3 on p. 208 is an ad from one such organization—CACI Marketing Systems.

☐ Consumer/business publications (*Business Week, Forbes, Fortune, American Demographics, Canadian Consumer, Canadian Business, Advertising Age, Computer Marketing, Marketing* (Canada), and thousands more).

☐ Computer database services (DIALOG Information Service, IQuest from CompuServe, Dow Jones News Retrieval Service, and Corporate Canada Online, available by subscription to individuals and organizations that have access to a computer equipped with a modem).

When Sid Stein and his staff reviewed all the internal data and outside secondary research on Penney's situation, they found that Penney's was *not* losing sales so much to the specialty shops and mass merchandisers as to

AD LAB 6-A
Using Marketing Research for New-Product Development

You are the advertising manager for a major manufacturer of prescription drug products, and management is interested in marketing a line of products to the proprietary market. After a lengthy brainstorming session, you determine that your company has the research and development capability to produce a superior line of proprietary vitamin products that could be sold through your existing distribution channels.

The problem is to assess the opportunities available for entering the over-the-counter vitamin business and to evaluate the potential for obtaining market share and sufficient profit levels. Management is also interested in how quickly and thoroughly advertising can reach the appropriate market segments.

The first step in obtaining the required information on the vitamin market is to review some of the many general reference guides available today (see the chart on pages 206-7). As the chart shows, there are four general sources of data: the government (directories, reports, announcements, statistical data); trade and other types of organizations (directories, association bulletins and reports); consumer and business press (magazines, newsletters, and data guides specifically aimed at the trade); and formal publications (reports, professional journals, industrial indexes, and studies). You will find that many of the resources listed on the chart are useful for uncovering data about other products, too.

These sources often make for a good start, but because they contain mostly secondary data, you will probably need additional information of a more specific nature before completing your research. Fortunately, these publications often list the addresses and telephone numbers of qualified persons at the source who can give you additional information. In most cases, they will lead you to a number of less obvious data sources, which may turn up information of key significance to your overall findings. At this stage, you will also be able to reach the "industry experts" who may confirm (or disagree with) your assessment of the opportunities to participate in the vitamin market.

Having systematically gone through all these steps, your search is completed. With 50 pounds of data in hand, the real job begins—understanding what you've collected.

Laboratory Application

Find an ad for a product in a field that you are familiar with and go to the largest library in your area (preferably your university or main city library). Identify at least two sources from each of the four source categories described above that cite data relevant to the product shown in the ad. Use these data sources to answer the following questions:

1. How can the information you uncovered help improve the ad? Which of the four source categories proved most useful for improving the ad?

2. If you had to choose advertising and promotion media for your next campaign, which sources would be most suitable for selecting the best media to "spread the word"? Be specific.

continued on next page

AD LAB 6-A *(continued)*

A Guide to Obtaining Information on the Vitamin Market

Topics	Government	Trade and other organizations	Consumer/ business press	Publications
General reference guides	*U.S. Government Organizational Manual*	*Encyclopedia of Associations*	*Business Publications Rates & Data*	Business Periodicals Index
	Federal Statistical Directory	*Directory of Associations in Canada*	*Consumer Magazine & Agri-Media Rates & Data*	Funk & Scott Index of Corporations & Industries
	Government reports and announcements		*Canadian Advertising Rates & Data*	Index Medicus
	Statistics Canada		Media Measurement Service (Canada)	Thomas Register of American Corporations
				Pharmaceutical News Index
				Reader's Guide to Periodical Literature
Specific to the vitamin market Issues				
Nature of the product	National Technical Information Service (Department of Commerce)	Vitamin Information Bureau	*Consumer Reports*	*Journal of the AMA*
Vitamins and how they are used		American Dietetic Association	*Today's Health*	*New England Journal of Medicine*
New products and/or external issues influencing the market	National Center for Health Statistics (HHS)	National Science Foundation	*Drug Topics*	*FDA Reports* (newsletter)
			Prevention Magazine	
			American Druggist	
			Product Marketing	
Role of government				
Impact of existing and potential government rules and regulations	Food & Drug Administration (HHS)	The Proprietary Association	Articles appearing in business and drug trade magazines and medical journals	*Pharmaceutical News Index*
	Reports of congressional committees	Pharmaceutical Manufacturing Association		*FDA Reports*
		Consumer groups		
Consumer behavior				
Level of vitamin usage by consumers	National Technical Information Service (Department of Commerce)	Consumer groups	*Prevention Magazine*	*Findex Directory of Market Research Reports, Studies & Surveys*
Consumers' perceptions and attitudes concerning vitamins	National Center for Health Statistics (HHS)	Print Measurement Bureau (Canada)	Readership studies of general consumer and trade magazines	

Topics	Government	Trade and other organizations	Consumer/ business press	Publications
Competition Nature of the competition and extent of leverage in the market	Form 10-Ks (SEC)		Articles appearing in business and drug trade magazines	*Moody's Industrial Manual* Standard & Poor's corporation records *Value Line Investment Survey* *Dun & Bradstreet Reports* National Investment Library annual report Disclosure, Inc., annual report *Thomas Register of American Corporations* *Canadian Trade Index*
Market trends and developments Size of the market and growth rate Major vitamin categories and relative growth Traditional distribution channels and the major retail outlets Seasonal patterns or regional skews	Census of Manufacturers (Department of Commerce) Survey of Manufacturers (Department of Commerce) Current industrial reports (Department of Commerce) Statistics Canada	The Proprietary Association Pharmaceutical Manufacturers Association	*Product Marketing* *Drug Topics* *Supermarket Business* *Canadian Business* Articles appearing in business and drug trade magazines	*Standard & Poor's Industry Surveys* *Pharmaceutical News Index*
Advertising Kinds and levels of advertising support Creative strategies employed by advertisers			*Advertising Age* *Marketing Communications* *Marketing* (Canada) *Info Press Communications* (Canada)	Leading National Advertisers Publishers Information Bureau

other department stores. But Penney's long tradition of mass merchandising had created confusion in the minds of its own management and, most important, in the minds of its customers. Even Penney's management personnel at the store, district, regional, and corporate levels were not really clear about who the competition was. And consumers had difficulty describing just what kind of store J. C. Penney was.

This all meant one thing to Sid Stein and his committee: More than anything else, they had to chart an unequivocal course for the company and communicate it clearly. Everyone—their 170,000 employees, the thousands of suppliers and vendors, the financial community, and the public—had to understand just what J. C. Penney stood for. To set this course, though, they needed more questions answered. Stein decided to do some formal research specifically designed to identify who department store customers were and to clarify their perceptions of J. C. Penney and the competition. To do this, Stein first had to establish specific research objectives.

Establish Research Objectives

A concise statement of the research problem and objectives should be formulated at the beginning of any research project. In other words, a company must decide what it is after, and then these objectives must correlate with the company's marketing and advertising plans.[6] For example, one statement of Penney's problem and research objectives might have been written as follows:

Problem A, Market Share:

J. C. Penney's sales, while still increasing, seem to have lost their momentum and are not even producing the profit expected by our shareholders. In the last year, our share of the market has even slipped in several departments, from X percent in the home furnishings department to Y percent in the women's apparel department. Our studies indicate we are losing sales to other department stores in the same malls where our stores are located and that customers are confused about our position in the market.

Problem A, Research Objectives:

To answer the following questions: (1) Who are our customers? (2) Who are the customers of other department stores? (3) What do these customers like and dislike about us and about our competitors? (4) How are we currently perceived? and (5) What do we have to do to clarify and improve that perception?

This hypothetical statement of the problem is specific and measurable; the questions asked are relevant to the problem; and the pieces of information requested are directly related to one another.

The answers to these questions would provide the information base for Penney's evolving positioning strategy. That, in turn, would determine the kind of stores and merchandise the company would have and facilitate the development of practical marketing and advertising plans. In short, it would set the company's course for years to come.

Conduct Formal Research

When a company or organization wants to collect primary data directly from the *field* (marketplace) about a specific problem or issue, it uses **formal research.** The two types of formal research are *quantitative* and *qualitative.* There are several ways to perform each type, and there are important considerations with both..

Basic Methods of Quantitative Research

Advertising researchers use **quantitative research** to develop hard numbers so they can completely and accurately measure a particular market situation. The three basic research methods used to collect quantitative data are *observation, experiment,* and *survey.*

Observation   The **observation method** is used when researchers actually monitor the actions of the person being studied. It may take the form of a traffic count by outdoor billboard companies, a television audience count through instruments hooked to TV sets, or a study of consumer reactions to products displayed in the supermarket.

One development that has greatly assisted the observational method is the use of product labels with the **Universal Product Code (UPC).** As shown in Exhibit 6-4, this consists of a series of linear bars and a 10-digit number that identifies the product. With the aid of optical scanners, supermarkets can electronically observe which products are selling. The UPC label not only facilitates speed and accuracy at the check-out counter and timely inventory control but also permits the evaluation of alternative marketing plans, media vehicles, and promotional campaigns.[7]

At first, the scanner data were so detailed and voluminous they were too much for many advertisers to handle. Now, thanks to the desktop computer and new expert software systems like CoverStory from Information Re-

EXHIBIT 6-4

The Universal Product Code on product packages reduces human error at the check-out counter. It also allows for instant inventory control and, most important to advertisers, provides a convenient system for accumulating sales data and a wealth of very accessible market research information for marketing and advertising planning.

sources Inc. (IRI), marketing and advertising managers can click a mouse and let the computer sift through the data to find out how a product fared in different regions with different promotions and facing different competitors. Then the software automatically writes a report in plain English.[8]

The use of the UPC has "caused an explosion in learning how promotion affects purchasing," says IRI chairman Gian Fulgoni. In one case, scanner data indicated that a 40-cent coupon on a tube of toothpaste could create $147,000 in profits, but a 50-cent coupon on the same item would create a $348,000 loss.[9]

Advertisers used to assume that changes in market share and brand position usually appear slowly over time. But the ability to observe the actual incidence of sales has shown that the packaged-goods market is extremely complex and volatile. Moreover, the effects of advertising are invariably entangled and at cross-purposes with the effects of other advertising, both competitive and noncompetitive.[10] Thus, at the local level, weekly sales and share figures may fluctuate considerably, and gauging the short-term effectiveness of advertising may be uncertain at best.

Experiment The **experimental method** is designed to measure actual cause-and-effect relationships. An experiment is a scientific investigation in which a researcher alters the stimulus received by a test group or groups and compares the results with that of a control group that did not receive the altered stimulus. This type of research is used primarily for test-marketing new products in isolated geographic areas and in testing new advertising campaigns prior to national introduction. For example, a new campaign might be run in one geographic area but not in another. The sales results in the two areas are then compared to determine the effectiveness of the campaign. However, strict controls must be used so that the variable that causes the effect can be accurately determined. And because it is so difficult to control all the marketing variables, this method is very expensive and not easy to use.

Survey The **survey** is the most common way to gather primary research data. The researcher hopes to obtain information on attitudes, opinions, or motivations by asking questions of current or prospective customers. The political poll is a common survey we are all familiar with. The three common ways of conducting surveys are by telephone, by mail, and by personal interview. Each has distinct advantages and disadvantages, as shown in Exhibit 6-5.

Sid Stein's department ran a continuous stream of consumer surveys in locations around the country, asking shoppers to rate Penney's and competitive stores on issues of quality, integrity, fashionability, stylishness, newness/oldness, selection, store appeal, and so on.

In survey after survey, shoppers said they thought J. C. Penney stood for honesty, integrity, and value. That was the good news. But they also said Penney's stores were unexciting. And across the board, they perceived Penney's merchandise as lower quality and less stylish and contemporary than the merchandise carried by the other department stores. That was the bad news. Moreover, the interviews convinced Sid and his committee they *were* getting the same customers as the other department stores, but these customers were buying disproportionately less "fashionable" merchandise at Penney's. The problem, therefore, ran much deeper than women's, or even men's, apparel. It affected every department where product characteristics such as style, appearance, and timeliness were considered important by Penney's target customers.

EXHIBIT 6-5	Comparison of Data-Collection Methods		
	Personal	**Telephone**	**Mail**
Data-collection costs	High	Medium	Low
Data-collection time required	Medium	Low	High
Sample size for a given budget	Small	Medium	Large
Data quantity per respondent	High	Medium	Low
Reaches widely dispersed sample	No	Maybe	Yes
Reaches special locations	Yes	Maybe	No
Interaction with respondents	Yes	Yes	No
Degree of interviewer bias	High	Medium	None
Severity of nonresponse bias	Low	Low	High
Presentation of visual stimuli	Yes	No	Maybe
Field worker training required	Yes	Yes	No

Basic Methods of Qualitative Research

At this point in the research, J. C. Penney wanted to understand its sales problem more clearly, especially since the company was rated so highly for honesty, integrity, and value. Penney's researchers thus initiated a series of *focus-group sessions* to probe customers' perceptions of who Penney's most frequent shoppers were, who they weren't, and why. They also held interviews with more than 400 members of Penney's management at the store, district, regional, and corporate levels to determine their views and solicit their suggestions.

Qualitative research seeks in-depth, open-ended responses aimed at getting people to share their thoughts and feelings on a subject in order to gain impressions rather than definitions.[11] Advertisers use a variety of research methods to understand the "why" of consumer behavior.

No matter how skillfully posed, some questions are hard for the consumer to answer. It is especially difficult for consumers to give the real reasons for their product choices. If asked why they bought a particular car, for instance, they might reply that it handles well or is dependable, but not that driving it makes them feel like James Bond or an oil tycoon.[12] Thus, qualitative research is used more and more to give advertisers a general impression of the market, the consumer, or the product. Some advertisers refer to it as **motivation research.** The methods used in qualitative research are usually described as *projective* or *intensive* techniques.

Projective Techniques   To get an understanding of people's underlying or subconscious feelings, attitudes, opinions, needs, and motives, researchers use **projective techniques**—asking indirect questions or otherwise involving consumers in a situation where they can express feelings about the problem or product. Peter Hume, a researcher in Toronto, used projective techniques to discover that Campbell soups had an image of "cuddle-tum" food, as he calls it, in people's minds. This caused a revision in the company's advertising from a "gives-you-zip" appeal to a "hearth-and-home" approach, as shown in Exhibit 6-6.

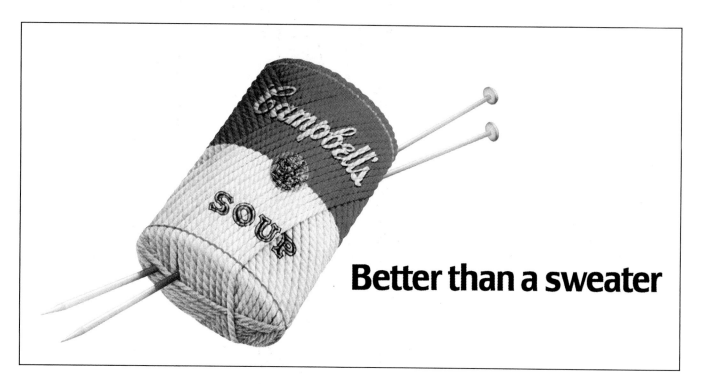

Better than a sweater

EXHIBIT 6-6

Peter Hume, a "brand character" researcher and principal of the Canadian account planning firm Abraxas, informed his client Campbell's Soup of Canada that its existing ads promoting "zip" didn't match the brand image in consumers' minds. They saw Campbell's as "cuddle-tum" food and still had memories of the Campbell's Kids, says Hume. The new billboard shown here featured a more "hearth-and-home" approach.

This technique has long been used by psychologists for clinical diagnosis and is now being adapted to marketing use. All such techniques require highly experienced researchers. For example, when Ayer vied for the J. C. Penney account, it conducted several studies using a projective technique in a series of shopping-center interviews. In one study, Ayer personnel showed pictures of different types of shoppers to people in the mall and asked them where they thought these shoppers probably bought their clothes.

Intensive Techniques Researchers use several **intensive techniques,** all of which require great care in administering the questions. One technique, the **in-depth interview,** uses carefully planned but loosely structured questions to enable the interviewer to probe respondents' deeper feelings. Although these interviews are very helpful at discovering individual motivations, they are also very expensive, extremely time-consuming, and limited because of the lack of skilled interviewers.

The **focus-group method** is one of the most useful intensive research techniques. Eight to 10 people, "typical" of the target market, are invited to a group session to discuss the product, the service, or the marketing situation for an hour or more. A trained moderator guides the often free-wheeling discussion, and the group interaction reveals the participants' true feelings or behavior toward the product. Focus-group meetings are usually recorded and may even be viewed or videotaped from behind a one-way mirror, as shown in Exhibit 6-7. Focus groups are not intended to represent a valid sample of

EXHIBIT 6-7

Focus-group sessions are usually held in comfortable settings where participants can feel relaxed about discussing their attitudes and beliefs. One of the interesting features of focus groups is that group interaction can hang up on seemingly small issues and overemphasize others. Because of this, some researchers refrain from using focus groups, while others feel that the distortion of a small issue is a symptom of a larger product problem.

the population. However participants' thinking can often be used prior to a formal survey to assist in questionnaire design.[13] Or as in the case of Penney's, focus groups following a survey can put flesh on the skeleton created by raw data.

Chevrolet held a series of focus-group studies and learned that consumers believed the company had let them down by not building cars for the needs of modern Americans. In 1986, as a result of those studies, Chevrolet launched its "Heartbeat of America" campaign to impart a distinctive corporate identity and to unify the image of its cars and trucks.[14]

Considerations in Conducting Formal Research

Quantitative (descriptive) research methods require formal design and rigorous standards for collecting and tabulating information. This is the only way to minimize inaccuracies and ensure *valid* and *reliable* data for future decision making.

Let's understand these two important terms. Assume a market contains 10,000 individuals, and you want to determine the market's attitude toward a proposed new toy. You walk into a restaurant and show a prototype of the toy to five people, and four say they like it. If you then extend that to your entire market, you might predict an 80 percent favorable attitude. Is that test *valid*? Hardly. For a test to be **valid,** the results of your test must reflect the true status of the market.[15] Five people would certainly not be enough to truly reflect the market.

Moreover, if you repeated your test with five more people in the restaurant, you might come up with an entirely different response. And if you repeated it again, you might come up with a third result. If that happened, it would show that your test also lacks *reliability.* For a test to be **reliable,** it must be repeatable, producing the same result each time it is administered. Exhibit 6-8 shows graphically what these two important terms mean.

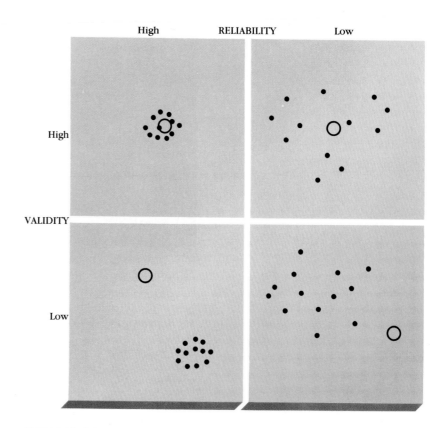

EXHIBIT 6-8

What do researchers mean by the terms *validity* and *reliability?* Using the analogy of a dartboard, the bull's-eye is the *actual* average of a value among a population of people (such as their average age). The marks of the darts thrown at the target are analogous to the averages that might be obtained by polling various *different* sets of people. The left column in the chart shows high reliability, or *repeatability,* because the results are all very similar—the ages of the group members are all fairly close. The right column shows low reliability, because the darts are randomly scattered on the target—meaning the group con-

sists of people of varying ages. In contrast, the top row shows the pattern for high validity. The marks are all centered on the bull's-eye—so they reflect the true status of the market. The bottom row shows the effect of systematic bias and, therefore, low validity. Thus, in the lower left quadrant, we see that a biased group—a senior citizens club—might all give similar answers (reliability), but their responses would not reflect the actual average of the total population. It requires experience to design effective sampling tests because a bias of the designer or a random error can lead to invalid or unreliable sampling results.

The validity and reliability of any research project, then, depends on several key elements. The most important of these are the sampling methods used, the way the survey questionnaire is designed, and the methods used for data tabulation and analysis. We discuss these briefly below.

Sampling Theories When J. C. Penney wants to know what consumers think about its products or its image, it cannot possibly ask everybody in the country. However, it is important that the results of the research accurately reflect the **universe** (the entire target population) of department store customers. Researchers therefore select a **sample** of the population they expect will give a representative minipicture of the population's true characteristics.[16] To accomplish this, they must make several basic decisions: Who is to be surveyed? How many people should be surveyed? How should the respondents be chosen?

A sample can be representative only if it reflects the pertinent characteristics of the universe the researcher wants to measure. For example, if we survey people who normally do not vote in an election, we will not get a result representative of the voters. The **sample unit,** or whom we survey, is therefore very important.

Theories of sampling are drawn from the mathematical theories of probability. To be considered adequate, a sample must be large enough to achieve satisfactory precision or stability. As shown in Ad Lab 6-B, the larger the sample size, the more reliable the results. However, adequate sample size has nothing to do with the size of the population. Good reliability can often be obtained with samples representing only a fraction of 1 percent of the population if the proper procedure is used. The two most commonly used sampling procedures are *random probability samples* and *nonprobability samples.*

Random probability samples give every unit in the universe an equal chance of being selected for the research. For example, if a researcher wishes to know a community's opinions on a particular issue, all members of the community constitute the universe. Selecting various members of the community at random produces an unbiased sample and the most accurate results, but it also presents certain difficulties. It requires that every unit be known, listed, and numbered so that each has an equal chance of being selected. This is often prohibitively expensive and sometimes impossible, especially in the case of customers for nationally distributed products. Every year J. C. Penney participates in a national probability study conducted by R. H. Bruskin Associates to identify the company's shopper base and to learn how it resembles the targeted competition—that is, department stores. These studies, when compared to earlier studies, provide an evaluation of how Penney's shopper base has changed over time.

Nonprobability samples do not give every unit in the universe an equal chance of being included. That means there is no guarantee the sample will be representative. Therefore, the researcher's level of confidence in the validity of the responses cannot be determined as it can when the statistical methods of probability sampling are used.[17] Nonetheless, researchers use nonprobability samples extensively because they are less expensive and less time-consuming and because random sampling is often not feasible. When only a general measure of the data is needed, nonprobability sampling can be extremely useful, and most marketing and advertising research studies use this method. For example, in the case of J. C. Penney, the nonprobability method of interviewing shoppers in malls was sufficient to determine the shopping preferences, image perceptions, and attitudes of its customers.

How Questionnaires Are Designed The construction of a good questionnaire requires considerable expertise. Much bias in research is blamed on poorly designed questionnaires. Typical problems include asking the wrong types of questions, asking too many questions, using the wrong form for a question (which makes it either too difficult to answer or too difficult to tabulate), and using the wrong choice of words. The sample questionnaire in Exhibit 6-9 (p. 217) shows some types of questions used in typical surveys.

AD LAB 6-B
How Does Sampling Work?

Information today exists on a scale that is either so large or so microscopic that it is overwhelming for most people to comprehend. To make sense of much of this data, therefore, statisticians have learned to use numbers to—in effect—paint pictures of the information.

By taking *samples* of the population, statisticians give marketing and advertising people the ability to analyze the behavior or attitudes of large masses of people. And as more advertisers seek to determine in advance the results of their advertising expenditures, the more valuable the statistician becomes.

Statistics are used to establish probabilities. The more information you have about a person, for example, the greater the probability you can predict his or her behavior. Sampling is a way to collect data—and the more samples of data taken, the clearer the probabilities can be pictured.

The way sampling works is easily demonstrated by the dots in the photos below. Four different dot patterns of varying courseness have been used to print the same picture onto the page. You can see that the clarity of the image is improved by using a greater number of dots that are finer in size. The clearest image contains several hundred thousand dots (representative of a total population) while the others have 2,000 dots, 1,000 dots, and 250 dots (representative of different samples of the population). The black dots in the pictures are distributed in proportion to their positions in the original black, white, and gray photo of the child (the dots remain evenly distributed throughout the image, with the bigger black dots creating the darkness of the hair while smaller black dots allow more of the whiteness of the paper to show in the child's light face).

These pictures are representative of a specific type of sampling research called *area probability sampling*—the type often used by national polling organizations and market research firms to predict election and other outcomes. When you think of each dot in the picture as representing a household within a neighborhood, you can see that the more households visited during the sampling period, the clearer your picture will be of the neighborhood—and the greater your chance of predicting the probable expression of attitudes and the behavior of each member of a household.

Interestingly, the 1,000-dot image is considered only twice as sharp as its neighbor with 250 dots—even though it has four times the number of dots. That is true with sampling, too. To double the accuracy, one must *quadruple* the sample size.

If you pull back from the pictures, you'll discover the 1,000- and 250-dot images improve in clarity. We may not see a lot of detail, but we can get a fairly reliable idea of what the child looks like. Similarly, a random sampling of only 1,200 homes, for example, can provide a reasonably accurate projection of how consumers will react to an ad, product, or service anywhere in the nation.

Laboratory Applications

1. Take the picture of the child in this ad lab and show it to 10 people and ask them if the child is a girl or a boy. Total the number of responses for "boy" and the number for "girl." Now, have a few classmates or friends each show the picture to 10 other people and total the responses. Are their totals consistent with yours? In other words, was the initial sampling of your 10 classmates enough to accurately predict the response of the wider population? If not, how large a sample do you think you would need to reliably predict the view of the wider population?

2. How do you think sampling might be used to determine the popularity of network TV shows? (Don't look at Chapter 14 for the answer.)

1. Do you intend to shop at any J. C. Penney store between now and Sunday?
   Yes 1   No 2   (If no, skip question 5)

2. Do you intend to go into J. C. Penney to buy something in particular or just to browse?
   Buy 1   Browse 2

3. Have you seen any of the items you intend to buy advertised by J. C. Penney?
   Yes 1 (continue)   No 2 (skip to question 5)

4. Where did you see these items advertised? Was it in a J. C. Penney advertising flyer included with
   your newspaper, a J. C. Penney flyer you received in the mail, on the pages of the newspaper itself,
   on TV, or somewhere else?

   Flyer in newspaper   _____
   Flyer in mail   _____
   Pages of newspaper   _____
   On TV   _____
   Somewhere else (specify)   _____
   Don't recall   _____

5. Now, I would like you to rate the J. C. Penney advertising insert on the attributes listed below. Please place an "X"
   in the box at the position that best reflects your opinion of how the insert rates on each attribute. Placing an "X"
   in the middle box usually means you are neutral. The closer you place the "X" to the left or right phrase or
   word, the more you believe it describes the J. C. Penney insert.

Looks expensive								Looks cheap
Cleverly done								Unskillful
Appealing								Unappealing
Shows clothing in an attractive manner								Does not show clothing in an attractive manner
	1	2	3	4	5	6	7	

6. Please indicate all of the different types of people listed below that you feel this J. C. Penney
   advertising insert is appealing to.

Young people	_____	Quality-conscious people	_____
Bargain hunters	_____	Low-income people	_____
Conservative dressers	_____	Budget watchers	_____
Fashion-conscious people	_____	Older people	_____
Rich people	_____	Middle-income people	_____
Professionals	_____	Blue-collar people	_____
High-income people	_____	Women	_____
Men	_____	Office workers	_____
Someone like me	_____	Smart dressers	_____
Career-oriented women	_____	Other (specify)	_____

EXHIBIT 6-9

J. C. Penney used a personal interview questionnaire similar to this to determine the feelings of shoppers toward the store, its merchandise, and its advertising.

Consider the simple question: "What kind of soap do you use?" The respondent doesn't know what the word *soap* means. Is it hand soap, shampoo, laundry detergent, dishwashing soap, cleansing cream, or dishwasher detergent? And take the word *kind*. Does that mean what brand, what size, or what use? Finally, what constitutes *use?* Does that mean what do you buy? You might buy one *kind* for yourself and another *kind* for your spouse. You probably use several different *kinds.* Answering the question accurately is

Checklist for Developing an Effective Questionnaire

☐ *List specific research objectives.* Be sure the reason for the study is clear. Avoid the expense of collecting irrelevant data.

☐ *Write short questionnaires.* Don't tax the patience of the respondent, lest careless or flip answers result.

☐ *State questions clearly* so there is no chance for misunderstanding. Avoid generalities and ambiguous terms.

☐ *Write a rough draft first.* After all the information points have been covered, then polish it.

☐ *Use a short opening statement.* Include your name, the name of your organization, and the broad purpose of the questionnaire.

☐ *Put the respondent at ease* by opening with one or two inoffensive, easily answered questions.

☐ *Ask general questions before the more detailed ones.* Structure them so they flow logically.

☐ *Avoid questions that suggest an answer or that could be considered "leading" questions.* They tend to bias the results.

☐ *Include a few questions that will serve to cross-check earlier answers.* This aids in ensuring validity.

☐ *Put the demographic questions (e.g., age, income, education) and any other personal questions at the end of the questionnaire.*

☐ *Pretest the questionnaire* with 20 to 30 persons to be sure that the questions are being interpreted as intended and that all the information sought is included.

impossible. Worse, if the question is answered, the researcher doesn't know what the answer signifies and will likely draw an incorrect conclusion. (See the Checklist for Developing an Effective Questionnaire.)

Effective survey questions have three important attributes: focus, brevity, and simplicity. They focus directly on the issue or topic of the survey. They are as brief as possible while still conveying the intended meaning. And they are expressed as simply and clearly as they can be.[18]

There are many ways to ask essentially the same question. Say you are conducting a survey on J. C. Penney's advertising. Exhibit 6-10 lists four common types of questions that might elicit responses about the quality of Penney's ads. There are also many ways to ask the questions within these four types. For example, additional choices might be added to the multiple-choice format. Neutral responses might be removed from the scale format so the respondent would have to answer on either the positive or the negative side. And there is obvious bias in the dichotomous question.

The important point is that questions should elicit a response that is both accurate and useful to the researcher's needs. For this reason, all questionnaires should be tested on a small subsample to detect any confusion, bias, or ambiguities.

Data Tabulation and Analysis The collected data must be validated, edited, coded, and tabulated. Answers must be checked to eliminate errors or inconsistencies. For instance, one person might give the answer "two years," while another says "24 months." These must be changed to the same units for correct tabulation. Some questionnaires may be rejected because the answers are obviously the result of misunderstanding. Finally, the data must be counted and summarized. For very small studies, tabulation may be manual. But most research projects today use computers to count the answers and produce cross-tabulations of the data.

EXHIBIT 6-10	Different Ways to Phrase Research Questions

Type	Questions
Open-ended	How would you describe J. C. Penney advertising?
Dichotomous	Do you think J. C. Penney advertising is too attractive? ____ Yes ____ No
Multiple choice	What description best fits your opinion of J. C. Penney advertising? ____ Modern ____ Well done ____ Believable ____ Unconvincing ____ Old-fashioned
Semantic differential (scale)	Please indicate on the scale how you rate the quality of J. C. Penney advertising. ___ ___ ___ ___ ___ 1 2 3 4 5 Poor Excellent

For example, many researchers want a cross-tabulation of product use by age group or other important demographic information. The researcher may apply some advanced statistical techniques to the raw data and pass them through the computer again to seek additional findings. At this point, the cost of the research study can go through the ceiling if an unskilled advertiser wants to see all the cross-tabulations possible. The researcher must use skill and imagination to select only cross-tabulations that will show significant relationships.

Interpret and Report the Findings

Marketing and advertising research is used to help solve management problems. If it doesn't do that, it's not worth the cost. Some research costs are shown in Exhibit 6-11. The researcher, therefore, must prepare a complete analysis of the information gathered. Tables and graphs may be used, but it is important that they be explained in words management can understand. Technical jargon (such as "multivariate analysis of variance model") should be avoided or at least confined to an appendix. The report should state the problem and research objective, a summary of the findings, and the researcher's conclusions drawn from an unbiased analysis of the data. The researcher's recommendations for management action should also be described, and the whole report should be offered with an oral presentation to allow for management feedback and to highlight important points. A description of the methodology, statistical analysis, and raw data the report is based on constitutes the report's appendix.

EXHIBIT 6-11	How Much Research Costs Using Professional Firms	
Type of research	**Features**	**Cost**
Telephone	500 20-minute interviews, with report	$15,000–$18,000
Mail	500 returns, with report—33 percent response rate	$8,000–$10,000
Intercept	500 interviews, four or five questions, with report	$15,000
Executive interviews (talking to business administrators)	20 interviews, with report	$2,500–$7,500
Focus group	One group, 8 to 10 people, with report and videotape	$2,500–$3,800

APPLYING RESEARCH TO MARKETING AND ADVERTISING STRATEGY

Thus far, we have seen how Sid Stein and his marketing research and planning department, in a step-by-step process, uncovered Penney's problem of declining market share, evaluated the company's competitive strengths and weaknesses, and measured consumer attitudes toward it. All this information was vital to the development of the company's positioning statement, marketing strategy, and subsequent advertising plans.

Developing Marketing Strategy

The pieces were all beginning to fit together, and the corporate direction for the next decade was set. The nation's third-largest retailer was going to change from a mass merchandiser to a "fashion-oriented national department store." The J. C. Penney Stores Positioning Statement had the complete involvement and commitment of Penney's top management.

To begin this evolution, the company announced two strategic moves for the 1980s. The first involved major changes in Penney's merchandise mix. In all stores, the automotive, paint and hardware, and lawn and garden departments would be discontinued. With the additional selling space made available, Penney's would make more dominant statements in its apparel lines by bringing in designer and upscale private brands—Hunt Club, Stafford, Worthington, Jacqueline Ferrar, and Original Arizona Jean Co., the label for which is shown in Exhibit 6-12. It would also bring in the national brands customers wanted, which would help improve the perception of quality and fashionability (Levi Strauss, Nike, Haggar, Van Heusen, Joneswear, Napier, and Vanity Fair).

Second, Penney's began a five-year, $1.5 billion modernization program to inject fashion and excitement into all its stores. Turning a battleship the size of J. C. Penney around could not be done overnight. It would take time and a

EXHIBIT 6-12

One of Penney's new higher taste-level private brands is the Original Arizona Jean Company. It follows the tradition of the large leather labels found on jeans, but its irregular, decorative edge make it unusual and lively.

lot of money. But by the end of the decade, virtually all of Penney's metropolitan stores would be modernized.

The program was finally underway. The target market had been selected and the marketing strategy determined. Now it was time to start letting the public know. That meant advertising—and more research.

Developing Advertising Strategy

It is difficult to say where marketing research ends and advertising research begins, and in fact there is often quite an overlap. There are typically four categories or types of advertising research:

1. Advertising strategy research (for defining the product concept, target market selection, message-element determination, or media selection).
2. Creative concept development research (to measure acceptability of different creative concepts).
3. Pretesting of ads and commercials.
4. Posttesting of ads, commercials, and campaigns (for evaluating a campaign after it has run).

The remainder of this chapter discusses these four types of advertising research. Exhibit 6-13 presents the timing, research problem, and techniques involved in the four categories.

At this point, it is important to understand how advertisers apply the marketing research procedures we have discussed to basic advertising strategy and concept development (Categories 1 and 2).

EXHIBIT 6-13   Categories of Research in Advertising Development

	Category 1: Strategy determination	Category 2: Concept development	Category 3: Pretesting	Category 4: Posttesting
Timing	Before creative work begins	Before agency production begins	Before finished artwork and photography	After the campaign has run
Research problem	Product concept definition	Concept testing	Print pretesting	Advertising effectiveness
	Target market selection	Name testing	Television storyboard pretesting	Consumer attitude change
	Message-element selection	Slogan testing	Radio commercial pretesting	Sales increases
Techniques	Consumer-attitude and usage studies	Free-association tests	Consumer jury Matched samples	Aided recall Unaided recall
		Qualitative interviews	Portfolio tests Storyboard test Mechanical devices	Sales tests Inquiry tests Attitude tests
		Statement-comparison tests	Psychological rating scales	

We have already seen how J. C. Penney used its initial marketing research results to discover which consumers currently shopped at Penney's, which did not, and how the general market perceived Penney's position in the marketplace. From the advertiser's point of view, this was the first element of Category 1 research. Let's review for a moment the results of this as it applied to product concept development..

Product Concept Definition

For decades, J. C. Penney had been positioned in the consumer's mind as a major mass merchandiser of basic apparel, housewares, hardware, and commodities like bedding and towels. The attributes applied to the firm in consumers' minds were honesty, integrity, and good value. But in recent years, Penney's had changed. It had introduced more fashion-oriented products and eliminated some departments such as automotive and hardware. But the consumer still did not associate the characteristics of fashion, style, and quality with the J. C. Penney name. From its quantitative and qualitative studies, Penney's knew its customers did not shop there for contemporary apparel, nor was Penney's really perceived as a department store. In fact, as Penney's changed, the consumer perception became unfocused until they weren't sure what the J. C. Penney product concept was anymore.

Now Penney's wanted to establish a new product concept by repositioning itself in the marketplace and changing the way consumers viewed it—usually no small task. As we discussed in Chapter 4, it is normally easier to position a product consistent with existing consumer attitudes and perceptions than to reposition it by emphasizing other uses or attributes.[19]

Trout and Ries, the authorities on positioning, would agree. However, they also believe it is virtually fruitless to try to dislodge a market leader unless the

EXHIBIT 6-14

The Hunt Club label captured the spirit of the consumer who related to the "polite" sports. To both create awareness and reinforce the image of its new Hunt Club label, Penney's installed new fixtures and displays in its men's casual-wear departments across the country.

leader is making serious positioning mistakes. For many years, J. C. Penney's main competition (as a mass merchandiser) had been Sears and Kmart, and Penney's was not winning. It was still the number-three retailer.

What Stein and the J. C. Penney management team banked on was that the very fuzziness in the consumer perception of Penney's business could work to its advantage, enabling it to change its basic product concept.

By repositioning itself as "a fashion-oriented national department store with traditional attention to quality and value," Penney's would remove itself from competing head-to-head with Sears. Then, instead of being in a number-three position, it could jump to number one—"the only truly national department store chain in the country."

To accomplish this task, though, Penney's knew it had to not only upgrade its stores and merchandise lines (such as adding the Hunt Club section shown in Exhibit 6-14) but also gradually change and clarify the consumer perception of its stores. Repositioning any brand or product is an expensive and time-consuming process. To reposition a national chain of retail stores is an even more difficult and risky task. And maintaining credibility with the consumer during the transition period is an absolute necessity. For this reason, Penney's was willing to commit a lot of years, fortitude, and millions of dollars to its new advertising campaign.

Target Market Selection

Penney's qualitative studies had showed that, contrary to popular belief, the "traditional J. C. Penney customer" was the *same* as the "traditional department store customer." These consumers were attracted to regional centers where they could compare merchandise before buying. They were looking for fashionable apparel and home furnishings, and they wanted the opportunity to compare the offerings of several stores. Penney's heavy users, or "frequent" shoppers, were in the mall, but they shopped less often at Penney's than at the other department stores.

Numerous quantitative studies showed that Penney's mix of male and female shoppers was about the same as that of the other department stores, with a slight edge in men but a slight disadvantage in the high-spending category of 18- to 34-year-old women.

Penney's identified specific market segments to target, which they named *Traditional Consumers* and *Updated Consumers*. These two groups represented both the largest share of the population (54 percent) and the largest share of fashion purchases (64 percent).

The Traditional Consumers were described as predominantly young married people (60 percent aged 18 to 44) with children and good incomes ($25,000 to $50,000) who wanted classic, long-lasting fashions. They defined value in terms of quality first, then fashion and price.

The Updated Consumers were more active and innovative. Over half were aged 18 to 44, incomes were high (30 percent over $50,000), 80 percent owned their own homes, half had attended college, and most were married, although only 50 percent had children. They valued fashion first, followed by quality and price.[20]

This was the opportunity Penney's wanted—to appeal to these key, contemporary, fashion-buying segments with the offerings these customers wanted.

Message-Element Determination

At this point, Ayer came into the picture. Penney's had a very important message to communicate to its customers; and after evaluating all the advertising agency presentations, Penney's selected Ayer to help develop the message. And that meant more research.

Studies aimed at the selection of advertising message elements focus on particular themes and claims that may be promising and are "concerned with the likes and dislikes of consumers in relation to the brands and products being considered."[21] In its qualitative attitude studies, and with the help of Agi Clark's creative group, Ayer discovered numerous themes that might be used: "Penney's looks different, but the value's the same"; "You're changing, so is Penney's"; and so on. The agency decided to immediately begin concept testing to discover which message-element options might prove most successful in the repositioning effort. This was the company's Category 2 research aimed at advertising-concept development.

Creative Concept Testing

Ayer prepared four tentative advertising concepts, each with an illustration and a headline stressing a different Penney's appeal, as shown in Exhibit 6-15. The agency then gathered numerous focus groups of volunteer consumers into their unique "developmental lab," which combines intensive qualitative interviews with certain quantitative techniques. While a discussion leader moderated the conversation, each group was shown the series of ads. The groups' reactions were measured, taped, and observed by Ayer staff behind a one-way mirror.

Fashions for people. Not mannequins.

JC Penney.
Fashion, American Style.

We've changed our looks.
Not our values.

JC Penney.

We've changed
because you've changed.

JC Penney.

No, not Saks.
JC Penney's.

We're the best dressed Penney ever.

EXHIBIT 6-15

The four layouts used in Penney's concept testing each stressed a different appeal. In a series of intensive interviews, the reactions of shoppers to the various themes were monitored and measured.

The focus groups were nearly unanimous in their choice: the message that announced Penney's change but related it to the change in the customers themselves. The reason for their choice was clear: J. C. Penney was indeed changing. It did have more fashions than ever before. Why? Because *they,* the customers, had changed, and they needed more fashion than ever before. The message was logical and straightforward. The focus groups found it to be a believable position and a great promise. And that convinced Ayer to make it the backbone of the new campaign.

Once the concept of how to announce the change was accepted, Ayer had to develop a campaign that would express the results and show the benefits of that change to the consumer. Agi Clark and her creative teams developed a series of ads for magazines and TV using the campaign idea: "YOU'RE LOOKING SMARTER THAN EVER." They believed that theme complimented the customer for looking and being smarter than ever and simultaneously made the promise that J. C. Penney would also be smarter than ever before.

Bringing the two ideas together, the introductory ads read: "THERE'S A CHANGE IN PENNEY'S BECAUSE THERE'S A CHANGE IN YOU. YOU'RE LOOKING SMARTER THAN EVER. J. C. PENNEY" (see Exhibit 6-16 on p. 226). Ayer liked it. Penney's liked it. But that wasn't enough. Now it was time to pretest to be sure this campaign would get the attention and recognition Penney's hoped for.

There's a change in Penney's because there's a change   in you.

Today, you're both as comfortable on Wall Street as Sesame Street, and you want clothes that can take you there in style. So we're taking a new look at how you want to look. One of the most exciting

changes at JCPenney is our exclusive Halston III™ Collection. Designed by Halston, it's a totally coordinated look for today's American woman.
Men can look to the Lee Wright® Collection for contemporary designs. Or to the Stafford® Collection for

more traditional styles. And for the career woman, we have the newest fall collections.
Today there's more style in everything you do, and more style than ever at JCPenney.

You're looking smarter than ever. JCPenney.

EXHIBIT 6-16

The first ad in Penney's new campaign showed off the company's solid commitment to sophisticated style and fashion flair. It also demonstrated Penney's responsiveness to its customers. The campaign had two objectives. The first was to announce the change in Penney's from the perspective of the customer; the second was to explain the benefits these changes would bring to the customer.

Testing and Evaluation of Advertising

In some instances, advertising is the largest single cost in a company's marketing budget. According to *Advertising Age,* the nation's 100 leading advertisers spend $35.6 billion a year on advertising.[22] No wonder its effectiveness is a major concern! Companies can't stop advertising, nor do they want to. But they *do* want to know what they are getting for their money—and if their advertising is working.

Testing is the primary tool advertisers have to ensure that their advertising dollars are being spent wisely. It may prevent costly errors in judging which advertising strategy and media will produce the greatest results. And it can give the advertiser some measure (besides sales results) of a campaign's effectiveness.

Objectives of Testing

Category 3 of advertising research—**pretesting**—is used to increase the likelihood of preparing the most effective advertising messages. Pretesting can help advertisers detect and eliminate communication gaps or flaws in message content that may ultimately result in consumer indifference or negative audience response (such as changing the channel).[23] **Posttesting,** the fourth category of advertising research, is designed to determine the effectiveness of an advertisement or campaign *after* it has run. The findings obtained from posttesting can provide the advertiser with useful guidelines for future advertising.

Several areas of advertising that may be evaluated in pretesting include markets, motives, messages, media, budgeting, and scheduling. As we will see in Chapter 7, several of these variables are basic elements of the *creative mix* (advertising strategy), and most are under the advertiser's control to add, subtract, or modify. Many of these same variables can be posttested. However, in posttesting, the objective is normally to evaluate rather than to diagnose. The intent is not to make changes but rather to understand what has already happened.

Markets Advertisers may pretest advertising strategy and commercials against various market segments or audience groups to measure their reactions. In this process, the advertiser may even decide to alter the strategy and target the campaign to a different market. In posttesting, advertisers are interested in determining the extent to which the campaign succeeded in reaching its target markets. Changes in awareness within the market segment or increases in market share, for instance, may indicate successful advertising exposure.

Motives The consumer's motives are outside of the advertiser's control, but the messages the advertiser uses to appeal to those motives are not. By pretesting advertisements, the advertiser can gauge various appeals that might influence a purchase decision based on the individual's needs and motives.

Messages Every advertising message has variables. Pretesting may be used to determine *what* a message says (from the customer's point of view) and to determine *how well* it says it. Variables tested might be the headline, the text, the illustration, and the typography—or possibly the message concept, the information presented, or the symbolism inherent in the ad, as the interviewer is asking for in Exhibit 6-17.

On the other hand, through posttesting, the advertiser can determine to what extent the advertising message was seen, remembered, and believed. Changes in consumer attitude or perception, for instance, indicate success in this area.[24] Similarly, success might be measured by the ability of consumers to accurately fill in the blanks in a campaign slogan or to identify the sponsor.

EXHIBIT 6-17

Survey workers may interview consumers about what brands of soap they use, if they recall a particular soap ad in the newspaper or on TV, and more. Because survey work is usually part-time and pays reasonably well, it is an ideal entrée to the field of research for marketing and advertising students.

Media Today the cost of media advertising is soaring while at the same time the size of media units is diminishing. As a result, advertisers are demanding ever-greater media accountability.[25] Pretesting can influence four types of media decisions: classes of media, media subclasses, specific media vehicles, and units of space and time.

Media classes refer to the broad media categories: print, electronic, outdoor, and direct mail. **Media subclasses** are radio or TV, news magazines or business publications, and so on. The specific **media vehicle** refers to the particular program or publication. For example, on radio, the media vehicle might be the all-rock radio station in Dallas or, on TV, the program "Cheers" on KNBC in Los Angeles. Exhibit 6-18 (p. 228) is an ad for a print media vehicle—*Parade* magazine. And **media units** mean half-page or full-page ads, 15- or 30-second spots, or 60-second commercials, and so forth.

After the campaign has run, posttesting can determine how effectively the media mix reached the target audience and communicated the desired message. Audience measurement is discussed fully in Chapters 12 through 14.

Budgeting How large should a company's total advertising budget be? How much of this should be allocated to various markets and media? To specific products? Spending too little on advertising can be as hazardous as spending too much; but how much is "too little"—and how much is "too much"?

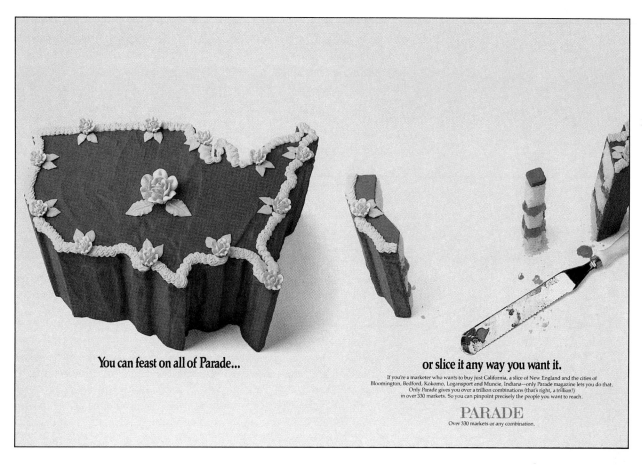

You can feast on all of Parade...   or slice it any way you want it.

If you're a marketer who wants to buy just California, a slice of New England and the cities of
Bloomington, Bedford, Kokomo, Logansport and Muncie, Indiana—only Parade magazine lets you do that.
Only Parade gives you over a trillion combinations (that's right, a trillion!)
in over 330 markets. So you can pinpoint precisely the people you want to reach.

PARADE
Over 330 markets or any combination.

EXHIBIT 6-18

This ad for *Parade* magazine is aimed at the advertising trade to tell them that they can have their cake and eat it, too. With this media vehicle they can pinpoint their geographic markets in a timely fashion like a local newspaper does, but get the quality of a magazine. *Parade* is a syndicated weekly magazine inserted inside the Sunday edition of daily newspapers.

Advertisers use various pretesting techniques to determine the optimum levels of expenditure before introducing national campaigns. (Chapter 7, "Marketing and Advertising Planning," provides further information on budgeting.)

Scheduling Advertisers can test consumer response to a product ad during different seasons of the year, or days of the week. They can test whether frequent advertising is more effective than occasional or one-time insertions, or whether year-round advertising of, say, a gift product is more effective than advertising that is concentrated during the Christmas gift-buying season.

Overall Results Finally, advertisers want to measure overall results to evaluate the extent to which advertising accomplished its objectives. That is the purpose of *posttesting,* and its results might be used to determine how to continue, what to change, and how much to spend in the future.

All these tests are designed with the hope of discovering to what extent advertising is the *stimulus* and which changes in consumer behavior are *responses.* Perhaps the greatest problem for the researcher, though, is to determine which and how many advertiser-controlled variables to measure and which consumer responses to survey.

Methods Used to Pretest Broadcast Ads

Although no infallible means of predicting advertising success or failure has been developed, certain popular pretesting methods can give the advertiser

EXHIBIT 6-19

TV commercials introduced Penney's Wyndham collection of coordinated separates for the working woman. In one 30-second spot, a fashion executive and her assistant were shown dashing to a presentation. The successful meeting ended with the supervisor giving credit to her hard-working assistant. All the commercials and print ads emphasized attractive people in real-life situations.

some useful insights if properly applied. (See the Checklist of Methods for Pretesting Advertisements.)

Several methods are used specifically to pretest radio and television commercials. The most common of these are central location tests, trailer tests, theater tests, and live telecasts, as described in the checklist. Advertisers also occasionally use sales experiments and physiological testing techniques.

In **central location tests,** videotapes of test commercials are shown to respondents on a one-to-one basis, usually in shopping center locations. Questions are asked before and after exposure to the commercials. J. C. Penney, for example, ran central location **clutter tests** of Ayer's television commercials in six dispersed markets before the campaign began. These tests had several objectives. By cluttering the Ayer commercials with other noncompetitive control commercials, Penney's could measure the effectiveness of the commercials in getting attention and increasing brand awareness; it could measure comprehension and resultant attitude shifts; and it could detect any weaknesses in the commercials.

As expected, the commercials created by Agi Clark's team, such as the one shown in Exhibit 6-19, fared well in pretesting. The campaign was launched and continued to run for five years with minor variations on the main theme.

Methods Used to Pretest Print Ads

In 1990, J. C. Penney decided to update its positioning statement and announce that its remarkable transformation had been accomplished. After considerable research, Ayer developed a new campaign theme, "Fashion comes to life," to reflect and reinforce all the positive changes taking place at Penney's and to tie these changes to their target customers' lifestyles.[26] Exhibit 6-20 is an ad from the new campaign.

Recent research has shown that *likability* is the single best determinant of whether a commercial—and the subsequent campaign—will be successful.[27]

EXHIBIT 6-20

"Fashion comes to life" is Penney's theme for the 90s. The campaign represents the culmination of over a decade of image development from a mass merchandise store to a fun shopping experience featuring style and quality.

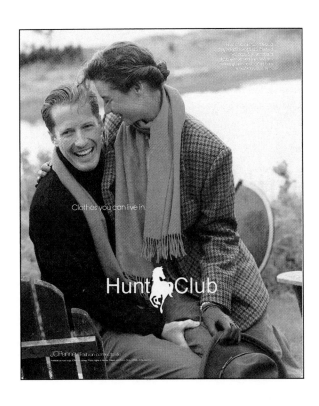

Checklist of Methods for Pretesting Advertisements

Print Advertising

☐ *Direct questioning.* Specific questions are asked about advertisements. Often used in testing alternative advertisements in the early stages of development.

☐ *Focus groups.* A free-wheeling discussion and interview is conducted with two or more people about a product, service, or marketing situation.

☐ *Order-of-merit tests.* Two or more advertisements are shown to respondents with instructions to arrange the advertisements in rank order.

☐ *Paired-comparison methods.* Each advertisement is compared by respondents with every other advertisement in a group.

☐ *Portfolio tests.* Test ads are interspersed among other ads and editorial matter in an album-type portfolio. Consumers in an experimental group are shown this portfolio. At the same time, consumers in a control group are shown the same portfolio but without the test ads. Afterward, members of both groups are questioned to determine their recall of the portfolio contents and the advertisements being tested.

☐ *Mock magazines.* An actual magazine is used instead of a portfolio. Test ads are "stripped into" the magazine, and it is left with respondents for a specified time. Respondents are then questioned about the test ads. Also used as a posttesting technique.

☐ *Perceptual meaning studies.* Ads are shown to respondents in timed exposures on a specially designed electronic tachistoscopic presentation instrument. Questions are given about recall of the product, brand, illustration, copy, and main idea of the ad.

☐ *Direct-mail tests.* Two or more alternative advertisements are mailed to different prospects on a mailing list. By keying each ad, the source of the orders can be traced. The ad that generates the largest volume of orders is presumed to be the most effective.

Broadcast Advertising

☐ *Central location projection tests.* Test commercials are run on a projector in a central location like a shopping center. Questions are asked before and after exposure to the commercials to determine brand awareness and to detect weaknesses in the commercials.

☐ *Trailer tests.* TV commercials are shown to people in trailers at shopping centers. Shoppers are then questioned about the commercials and are given packets of coupons that enable them to purchase products seen in the commercials at reduced prices. A matched sample of consumers who have not viewed the commercials are given identical packets of coupons. The impact of the commercials is measured in part by the difference in coupon redemption rates between the two groups.

☐ *Theater tests.* Electronic equipment enables respondents to indicate what they like and dislike as they view TV commercials in a theater setting.

☐ *Live telecast tests.* Test commercials are shown on closed-circuit or cable television. Respondents are interviewed by phone to test their reactions. Commercials may also be evaluated by sales audits at stores in the areas where the commercials were run.

☐ *Sales experiments.* Alternative commercials are run in two or more different market areas to determine which ads are the most effective.

Physiological Testing

☐ *Pupilometric devices.* Dilation of the pupil of the subject's eye is measured and presumed to indicate the subject's reaction to the illustration.

☐ *Eye-movement camera.* The route the subject's eye travels is superimposed over an advertisement to show the paths it takes and the areas that attracted and held attention. Used to obtain information on the placement of headlines, proper length of copy, and the most satisfactory ad layout.

☐ *Galvanometer.* A 25 milliampere current is passed through the subject, in at the palm and out at the elbow. When subject reacts to the advertisement, sweat gland activity increases, electrical resistance decreases, and the current passes through faster. These changes are recorded on a revolving drum apparatus. It is assumed that the more tension an ad creates, the more effective it is likely to be.

☐ *Voice-pitch analysis.* A tape recording is made of a consumer's explanation of his or her reaction to an ad. A computer is then used to measure the changes in voice pitch caused by emotional responses to the ad. This technique presumes a direct link between voice pitch and advertising effectiveness.

☐ *Brain-pattern analysis.* A brain scanner monitors the reaction of the brain while ads are presented. Proponents of this approach believe that brain waves indicate whether people respond favorably or unfavorably to commercials.

Therefore, before running the campaign on network TV and in national magazines, Penney's tested some more. On a national level, they conducted two qualitative studies and one very large quantitative study. They wanted to know if their target customer segments found the campaign likable. They also wanted to be sure the ads effectively built the perception of "affordable personal style"—Penney's desired product concept.

For example, to pretest Ayer's proposal for newspaper and magazine advertisements, Penney's interviewed women from both the Traditional Consumer segment and the Updated Consumer segment in central locations around the country. Respondents were asked direct questions like: What does the advertising say to you? Does the advertising tell you anything new or different about the company? If so, what? Does the advertising reflect activities you would like to participate in? Is the advertising believable? What effect, if any, does it have on your perception of the merchandise sold at Penney's? Do you find the ads likable?

As a method of pretesting, **direct questioning** is designed to elicit a full range of responses to the advertising. From customer responses, researchers can infer how well advertising messages convey key copy points. The researcher notes verbatim comments made by the respondents, which often reveal more subtle but meaningful reactions to the advertisement. Direct questioning is especially effective for testing alternative advertisements in the early stages of development. Respondents are virtual participants in the creative process at a time when their reactions and input can best be acted on.

In addition to direct questioning and focus groups, which we have already discussed, other techniques for pretesting print ads include order-of-merit tests, paired-comparison methods, portfolio tests, mock magazines, perceptual meaning studies, and direct-mail tests.

The Challenge of Pretesting

There is no one best way to pretest advertising variables. Different methods have been devised to test for different aspects of effectiveness. But each has its own peculiar set of advantages and disadvantages, and this constitutes a formidable challenge to the advertiser.

Pretesting is generally considered valuable in distinguishing very strong advertisements from very weak ones, but much controversy still surrounds the validity of any other research findings. Since the test itself occurs in an artificial setting, test respondents may cease being typical prospects and assume the role of expert or critic and give answers that may not reflect their real buying behavior. Consumers who do not have strong opinions about the test ad are likely to invent opinions on the spur of the moment to satisfy the interviewer. Some do not want to admit they could be influenced by the advertisement. Others may try to please the interviewer by voting for the ads they feel they *should* like rather than those they actually do like.

Likewise, researchers encounter problems when they ask people to compare a variety of ads and rank them for interest, personal pertinence, credibility, and comprehensibility. Respondents are likely to rate the one or two ads that make the best first impression as the highest in all categories. This is called the **halo effect.** Also, whereas questions about the respondent's ultimate buying behavior may be the most interesting, responses in this area may be the least valid. Behavior *intent,* in other words, may not become behavior *fact.*

Within the industry, some creative people typically mistrust commercial testing because they believe it stifles creativity. One of these is Marty Myers, the director of creative services for Miller Myers Bruce DellaCosta advertising agency in Toronto. He says that "test commercials, animatics, photomatics, and their ilk are an expensive charade, a multimillion-dollar industry built on fear—the fear of the linear, literal advertising person or advertiser who needs numbers to bolster his decision, so that if the project goes awry, he can't be blamed." Yet, notwithstanding this view, his agency has used research to great advantage for brands such as Dial soap.[28]

Despite the variety of challenges to pretesting, the issue comes down to dollars. Small advertisers rarely pretest; but then their risk is not as great, either. On the other hand, when advertisers risk millions of dollars on a new regional or national campaign, they *must* pretest to be sure the ad or commercial is interesting, believable, likable, and memorable to the consumer—and that it supports the brand image.

Posttesting Techniques

When Ayer launched its campaign for J. C. Penney, the client was anxious to know if customers saw and paid attention to it and what impression it made. So Ayer undertook a series of posttesting activities.

Posttesting is generally more costly and time-consuming than pretesting, but it permits ads to be tested under actual market conditions without the unnatural conditions of pretests. Advertisers can reap the benefits of both pretesting and posttesting by running ads in a few select markets before launching a major nationwide campaign.

A variety of quantitative and qualitative methods are used to determine what awareness or attitude changes the ads have achieved and what impact the advertising has had on sales. The most common posttesting techniques fall into five broad categories: aided recall, unaided recall, attitude tests, inquiry tests, and sales tests. Each of these has distinct advantages and limitations. (See the Checklist of Methods for Posttesting Advertisements.)

For example, **attitude tests** usually seek to measure the effectiveness of an advertising campaign in creating a favorable image for a company, its

---

Checklist of Methods for Posttesting Advertisements

☐ *Aided recall* (recognition-readership). To jog their memories, respondents are shown certain advertisements. Questions are then asked to determine whether the respondents' previous exposure to the ads was through reading, viewing, or listening.

☐ *Unaided recall.* Questions are asked of respondents without prompting to determine whether they saw or heard advertising messages.

☐ *Attitude tests.* Direct questions, semantic differential tests, or unstructured questions are given to measure changes in respondents' attitudes after an advertising campaign.

☐ *Inquiry tests.* Additional product information, product

samples, or premiums are offered to readers or viewers in an ad. Ads generating the most responses are presumed to be the most effective.

☐ *Sales tests.* Numerous types are used. Measures of past sales compare advertising efforts with sales. Controlled experiments may be used—for example, radio advertising in one market and newspaper advertising in another—followed by an audit of the results. Consumer purchase tests measure the retail sales that result from a given campaign. And store inventory audits measure advertising effectiveness by determining the inventory of retailers' stocks before and after an advertising campaign.

BRC

Please look over these pictures and words from a TV commercial and answer the questions on the right.

(Woman #1) My dog is so big ... we just built him a two-story dog house.

(Singing)
brand name dog food, *
If you've got a big dog.

(Boy) My dog is so big ... we see eye to eye on everything.

(Singing)
brand name dog food,
If you've got a big dog.

(Man) Introducing new brand name. The only dog food made for the special nutritional needs of big dogs. Growth food for large-breed puppies and adult food for large-breed adults.

(Woman with sheep dog) My dog is so big ... (rolls over and laughs)

(Singing)
brand name dog food,
If you've got a big dog.

Do you remember seeing this commercial on TV?

7-1 ☐ Yes   -2 ☐ No   -3 ☐ Not sure-I may have

How interested are you in what this commercial is trying to tell you or show you about the product? Would you say you were:

Very	Somewhat	Not
8-1 ☐ interested	-2 ☐ interested	-3 ☐ interested

Please check any of the following if you feel they describe this commercial.

9-1 ☐ Amusing	10-1 ☐ Interesting
-2 ☐ Appealing	-2 ☐ Irritating
-3 ☐ Clever	-3 ☐ Lively
-4 ☐ Convincing	-4 ☐ Original
-5 ☐ Dull	-5 ☐ Phony
-6 ☐ Easy to forget	-6 ☐ Pointless
-7 ☐ Effective	-7 ☐ Silly
-8 ☐ Gentle	-8 ☐ Uninteresting
-9 ☐ Imaginative	-9 ☐ Well done
-0 ☐ Informative	-0 ☐ Worth remembering

* We have blocked out the name. Do you remember which brand was being advertised?

Do you have:

11-1 ☐ Hero	12-1 ☐ A large dog
-2 ☐ Mighty Dog	-2 ☐ A small dog
-3 ☐ Mainstay	-3 ☐ No dogs
-4 ☐ Don't know	

13-

EXHIBIT 6-21

Bruzzone Research Company uses a direct-mail questionnaire to evaluate recall and attitude toward a dog food commercial. Questionnaires are sent across the country to 1,000 households chosen at random from either auto registrations or telephone listings. Other users of this service include General Motors, Gillette, Holiday Inns, and Polaroid.

brand, or its products. The standard presumption is that favorable changes in attitude predispose consumers to buy the company's product. On a regular basis, J. C. Penney uses lengthy questionnaires in shopping mall surveys— similar to the one in Exhibit 6-21 for the dog food product—to determine shifts in attitudes as a result of its TV commercials and newspaper inserts. The tests also seek to compare the ratings of the company and competitors with regard to products, services, and other attributes.

Likewise, Nissan interviews 1,000 consumers every month to track brand awareness, familiarity with particular vehicle models, recall of commercials, and shifts in attitude or image perception. If a commercial fails, it can be spotted and pulled in short order.[29]

The Challenge of Posttesting

Each posttesting method offers unique opportunities for advertisers to study the impact of their advertising campaigns. However, each also has definite limitations.

Recall tests measure specific behavior, not opinions or attitudes. They can also yield useful data on the relative effectiveness of different advertising components, such as size, color, or attention-getting themes, as illustrated by .

One of the leading firms in recall testing is Starch INRA Hooper. When it presents a readership report to its clients, the firm includes a copy of the magazine used in the test. In this Burger King advertisement from Ebony, for example, labels show readership of the ad as a whole and of component parts (headline, visuals, copy).

the Starch scores in Exhibit 6-22. Recall tests do not measure advertising effect, however; they merely measure what has been noticed, read, or watched. But readership or audience does not necessarily add up to product sales.

Attitude tests, on the other hand, are often a better measure of sales effectiveness than recall tests. An attitude change relates more closely to the purchase of the product, and a measured change in attitude gives management the confidence to make informed, intelligent decisions about advertising plans.[30] Unfortunately, though, many people find it difficult to determine their attitudes and to express them.

Inquiry tests—in which consumer responses to an ad for information or free samples are tabulated—enable the advertiser to test the attention-getting value of advertisements as well as their readability and understandability. They also permit fairly good control of the variables that motivate reader action, particularly if a split-run test is used (split runs are covered in Chapter 13). Unlike some methods, the inquiry test can be effective in testing small advertisements.

Unfortunately, inquiry tests are valid only when applied to ads that can logically use an offer to elicit inquiries. Such inquiries, though, may not even reflect a sincere interest in the product or its purchase. And since responses to a magazine offer may take months to receive, inquiry tests can be time-consuming.

Since the principal objective of most advertisers is increased sales, **sales tests** are logically popular. Unquestionably, sales tests can be a useful measure of advertising effectiveness when advertising is the dominant element, or the only variable, in the company's marketing plan.

However, it is often difficult to gauge to what extent advertising has been responsible for sales, since many other variables (competitors' activities, the season of the year, and even the weather) usually affect sales volume. Sales response to advertising is usually long range rather than immediate. Sales tests, and particularly field studies, are often costly and time-consuming. And, finally, most of them are useful only for testing complete campaigns, not individual ads or the components of an advertisement.

Summary

Marketing research is defined as the systematic gathering, recording, and analysis of data to help managers make decisions about the marketing of goods and services. Marketing research is useful in identifying consumer needs, developing new products and communication strategies, and assessing the effectiveness of marketing programs and promotional activities.

Conducting research involves several steps: first, to analyze the situation and define the problem; second, to conduct exploratory research by analyzing internal data and collecting secondary data; next, to set research objectives; then, to conduct formal research using either quantitative or qualitative methods; and finally, to interpret and report the findings.

Quantitative techniques include observation, experiment, and survey and are used to accurately measure a particular market situation. Marketers use qualitative research to get a general impression of the market. The methods used in qualitative research may be projective or intensive techniques.

The success of quantitative surveys depends on the sampling methods used and the design of the survey questionnaire. The two sampling procedures used are random probability and non-probability samples. Survey questions should have the attributes of focus, brevity, and simplicity.

Advertising research is used to develop strategies and test concepts. Research results help the advertiser define the product concept, select the target market, and develop the primary advertising message elements.

Advertisers use testing to ensure that their advertising dollars are spent wisely. Pretesting is used to detect and eliminate weaknesses in a campaign. Posttesting is used to evaluate the effectiveness of an advertisement or campaign after it has run. Testing helps evaluate several variables, including markets, motives, messages, media, budgets, and schedules.

Many techniques are used in pretesting, including central location tests, clutter tests, and direct questioning. Pretesting is subject to numerous problems including artificiality, consumer inaccuracy, and the halo effect of consumer responses.

The most commonly used posttesting techniques are aided recall, unaided recall, attitude tests, inquiry tests, and sales tests. Each has numerous opportunities and limitations.

Questions for Review and Discussion

1. How important is research to advertisers? Why?
2. What example can you think of that demonstrates the difference between marketing research and market research?
3. Which kind of research data is more expensive to collect, primary or secondary? Why?
4. Have you ever used observational research personally? How?
5. Do people use quantitative or qualitative research to evaluate movies? Explain.
6. Which of the major surveying methods is the most costly? Why?
7. What example can you give of research that offers validity but not reliability?
8. What specific example can you think of where research could help in the development of advertising strategy?
9. How would the halo effect bias an effort to pretest a soft drink ad?
10. How would you design a controlled experiment to test the advertising for a chain of men's stores?

MARKETING AND ADVERTISING PLANNING

If Cheops had only had MacProject II.
New people who manage can manage to do more. Upgrade hot line: 800-544-8554.

Objective: To describe the process of marketing and advertising planning and portray the important elements within each type of plan. For marketers and advertisers to achieve success, they need to understand the basic process of analyzing situations, setting realistic, attainable objectives, and developing strategies to achieve them. An incremental part of this process is the allocation of marketing and advertising resources, so advertisers must know the basic methods used by marketers to budget for marketing activities.

After studying this chapter, you will be able to:

☐ Explain the role and the elements of a marketing plan.

☐ Describe how a marketing plan and advertising plan are related.

☐ Discuss the difference between objectives and strategies in marketing and advertising plans.

☐ Give examples of market-need and sales-target objectives.

☐ Debate the suitability of top-down and bottom-up marketing and advertising planning.

☐ Enumerate the major ways advertising budgets are determined.

☐ Describe how the share-of-market/share-of-voice method can be used for new product introductions.

From its humble beginnings right after World War II as a small Japanese shop converting bicycles into motorbikes, Honda Motor Company grew to become the number-one motorcycle manufacturer in the world. This achievement was only the first in an impressive series of marketing successes.

Starting from scratch, Honda then clawed its way to the top ranks of the Japanese automobile industry, challenging mighty Toyota and Nissan every step of the way. The Honda Civic and its nonpolluting, gas-saving CVCC engine first came on the scene in 1975, at a time when oil crises, pollution, and economic stagnation were on everyone's mind. The Civic was an immediate success with Americans looking for good mileage, smooth performance, reliability, and a reasonable price. Then the Honda Accord was introduced to an avid market in 1976—somewhat fancier, slightly more expensive, but equally appropriate for the market.

With these cars, Honda proved that a Japanese automobile company could successfully sell cars in the United States, the world's biggest market. Then it proved that it could manufacture the same cars in a U.S. plant—and do so with such high quality that, by the late 1980s, an imported U.S.-built Honda would be viewed back in the homeland as a status symbol by the fastidious Japanese.

With a record like this, some companies might have been tempted to sit back and bask in the glory of victories already won. But not Honda. As discussed in Ad Lab 7-A, marketing is war and the marketplace is the battlefield. Honda was not about to be a passive participant on this battlefield. By the late 80s, U.S. car dealers were selling more Honda Accords than any other foreign-nameplate automobile—by far.[1] But the executives at American Honda were astute observers of their adopted turf. Looking toward the 90s, they saw changes developing in the U.S. car market.

A progressive automobile company like Honda didn't believe the future lay in making simple incremental improvements to a successful concept. Honda's research projected that total car sales would increase only 12 percent in the late 80s and early 90s. But for cars costing $18,000 or more, growth was projected at 28 percent. Thus, just as it had earlier moved from motorcycles into automobiles and from the domestic into the worldwide arena, Honda again upped the ante. It decided to move into the higher-priced market.

The idea was not without peril. Mercedes-Benz, BMW, Audi, Volvo, and others already had solid reputations and significant prestige in the market for luxury performance cars. And their customers were exceedingly loyal.

To get around that loyalty, Honda decided to target customers who had not yet formed a strong attachment to any particular brand—in other words, the segment of customers buying their first luxury performance automobile. The company could develop an intermediate product in the $18,000 to $25,000 price range. Upscale, young professionals would find the price attractive, and they would be impressed with the technological innovations Honda planned to incorporate.

In 1986, Honda introduced the Acura Legend, priced in the $20,000 range, and a lower-priced sports sedan—the Acura Integra—and again made marketing history. The new Acura (shown in Exhibit 7-1, p. 241) was more than a nameplate—it was a whole new automotive division, supported by a separate dealer and service network and its own brand advertising. The new division succeeded in cultivating an image of exclusivity while retaining a canny link to the dependable Honda name.

Meanwhile, the car-enthusiast media reported another development: Honda's successes on the Grand Prix racing circuit. As a result, car buffs

continued on page 240

AD LAB 7-A
The Era of Marketing Warfare

Chapter 4 introduced Jack Trout and Al Ries's idea of *positioning,* which is primarily an advertising concept.

In this chapter, we share Trout and Ries's advice on marketing, taken from their book *Marketing Warfare.* The basic idea is to approach the marketplace as though it were a battlefield. Much of the language of marketing has been borrowed from the military.

We launch a marketing campaign. Hopefully, a breakthrough campaign.

We divide people into divisions, companies, units. We report gains and losses. Sometimes, we issue uniforms.

From time to time, we go into the field to inspect those uniforms and review the progress of the troops. We have been known to pull rank.

In short, we have borrowed so many things from the military that we might as well adopt the strategic principles of warfare that have guided military thinking for centuries.

On War

Our "textbook" for marketing warfare is the classic book on military strategy, *On War,* written in 1831 by a Prussian general, Carl von Clausewitz. The book outlines the principles behind all successful wars. Two simple ideas dominated Clausewitz's thinking.

First is the principle of *force.* Says Clausewitz, "The greatest possible number of troops should be brought into action at the decisive point." Clausewitz studied all of the military battles of recorded history and found that in the vast majority of cases, the larger force prevailed. "God," said Napoleon, "is on the side of the big battalions."

The second principle is related to the first. It's *superiority of the defense.* Take Napoleon at Waterloo. Napoleon actually had a slight superiority in numbers, 74,000 men versus Wellington's 67,000. But Wellington had the advantage of being on the defense. And, of course, the defense prevailed. So this year we predict that Crest will be the best-selling toothpaste and McDonald's the largest fast-food company—regardless of what the competition does. A well-established defensive position is extremely strong and very difficult to overcome.

The Strategic Square

So how do the principles of warfare apply to marketing? It all comes down to what we call the "strategic square":

Out of every 100 companies

One should play defense	Two should play offense
Three should flank	And 94 should be guerrillas

Look at this strategic square from the point of view of the U.S. automotive industry.

General Motors	Ford Motors
Chrysler	American Motors

General Motors is the leader and gets more than half the business. Its primary concern ought to be defense.

Ford, on the other hand, is a strong number two. It's the only automobile company in a position to mount offensive attacks against GM.

Chrysler is a distant third and should avoid direct attacks. Rather, it should try flanking moves: smaller, bigger, cheaper, more expensive, and so on.

What can you say about American Motors? Head for the hills and become a guerrilla. The company should find a market segment small enough to defend. For AMC, the broad area of, say, "small cars" would be too much. But the Jeep business is distinctive and important enough to protect and make the most of. AMC's claim to that portion of the market should be further extended to include other four-wheel-drive vehicles. [Note: After Trout and Ries wrote this, AMC was sold to Chrysler, which has maintained the Jeep brand.]

Offensive Warfare

Let's look more closely at each of the four types of marketing warfare, starting with offensive warfare.

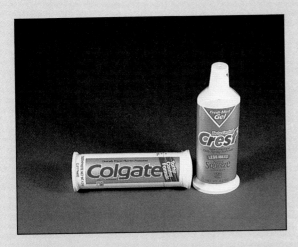

Colgate had a strong number-one position in toothpaste. But rival Procter & Gamble knew a thing or two about Carl von Clausewitz.

"Many assume that half efforts can be effective," said Clausewitz. "A small jump is easier than a large one, but no one wishing to cross a wide ditch would cross half of it first."

P&G launched Crest toothpaste not only with a massive $20 million advertising budget but also with the American Dental Association "seal of approval." Crest went over the top and is now the number-one selling toothpaste in the country.

Overtaking the leader is not that common. Most companies are happy if they can establish a profitable number-two position. How can anybody topple Listerine, the king

of halitosis hill? With its "medicine breath" attacks on Listerine, Scope aimed straight for Listerine's weakest position. The campaign improved Scope's position and secured its long-term position. But Listerine is still the leader, by a slim margin. A well-established defensive position is extremely strong and very difficult to overcome.

To sum up, here are the rules of the road in waging offensive marketing warfare:

1. The main consideration is the strength of the leader's position. No matter how strong a number-two or -three company is in a certain category or attribute, it cannot win if this also is where the leader is strong.

2. The attack should be launched on as narrow a front as possible. The "full line" of products is a luxury only for leaders. Offensive war should preferably be waged with single products.

3. The attack should be launched at the leader's weakest position.

Defensive Warfare

The "battle of migraine mountain" is an example of the advantages of quick response on the part of the leader. Datril, as you might remember, opened up a war on Tylenol with a price attack. Johnson & Johnson immediately cut Tylenol's price, even before Datril started its price advertising. Result: It repelled the Datril attacks and inflicted heavy losses on the Bristol-Myers entry.

Here are the principles of defensive marketing warfare:

1. Defensive marketing warfare is a game only market leaders should play.

2. The best defense is a good offense. A leader should introduce new products and services before the competition does.

3. Strong competitive moves should always be "blocked." In a word, rapidly copy the competitive move. Too many companies "pooh-pooh" the competitor until it's too late.

Flanking Warfare

The third type of marketing warfare is where the action is for most companies.

Here's Clausewitz's suggestion: "Where absolute superiority is not attainable, you must produce a relative one at

(continued)

AD LAB 7-A (continued)

the decisive point by making skillful use of what you have." In practice, this means attacking IBM where IBM is weak, not where it is strong—as Apple did successfully on the low end. Orville Redenbacher is successfully flanking the popcorn market leader with a high-priced brand. And who won the marketing battle between Cadillac and Lincoln Continental? Answer: Mercedes [and now the Japanese carmakers].

Here are the principles of flanking marketing warfare:

1. Good flanking moves must be made into uncontested areas. [Apple] introduced a small computer before IBM did.

2. Surprise ought to be an important element. Too much research will often snatch defeat from the jaws of victory by wasting time, the critical element in any successful flanking attack.

3. The pursuit is as critical as the attack itself. Too many companies quit after they're ahead.

Guerrilla Warfare

The fourth type of marketing warfare is guerrilla warfare. Most of America's companies should be waging guerrilla warfare.

The key attribute of successful guerrilla wars is flexibility. A guerrilla should not hesitate to abandon a given product or market if the tide of battle changes.

Here are the principles of guerrilla marketing warfare:

1. Find a market segment small enough to defend. It could be small geographically or in volume.

2. No matter how successful you become, never act like the leader.

3. Be prepared to "bug out" at a moment's notice. A company that runs away lives to fight another day.

Bottom Up

Trout and Ries's latest book is *Bottom-Up Marketing* (discussed later in this chapter). In it they continue the military analogy.

"Deep penetration on a narrow front is the key to winning a marketing war," they say. By this they mean that smaller companies should keep their product narrowly focused on a single concept. Too many companies "spread their forces over a wide front."

Trout and Ries use the Battle of France at the beginning of World War II as the key analogy. In 1940, the British Expeditionary Forces were in Holland and Belgium. The French Army was hiding behind the fortifications of the Maginot Line. So the Germans went down to the front and found a weak link between the British and French armies. There they concentrated all of their panzer (tank) divisions. Six weeks later, the Germans were at the English Channel. The Battle of France was over.

Concentrating forces as the Germans did is a powerful tactic. Many small, specialized companies have learned to use it against strong competitors—they find an unusual tactic, focus all their resources on it, and turn it into a successful strategy.

In fact, Trout and Ries report that today most large corporations face the problem of fending off focused attacks by smaller companies.

Laboratory Applications

1. Think of a successful product and explain its success in terms of marketing warfare.

2. Select a product and explain how marketing warfare strategy might be used to gain greater success.

became aware that the new Acura models were based on state-of-the-art engineering and design developed for racing. And they also quickly realized that Acura was prevailing over European technology on European turf. From 1987 on, Acura won car-magazine kudos for its technology, and consistently scored tops in customer satisfaction and dealer service—accomplishments duly noted in its advertising (see Exhibit 7-2). Most important for American Honda, Acura was outselling its more established European competitors.[2]

For our purposes, the Acura story demonstrates that marketing success usually depends less on advertising creativity and more on overall strategy.

EXHIBIT 7-1

Introducing a new automobile is an ambitious undertaking. Without careful planning based on research, the marketing and advertising campaign for Acura could not have succeeded. In one broad sweep, this ad attempts to reposition all the competitive makes as a confusing collection of product badges and labels—while positioning Acura as "an automotive statement" in precision-crafted performance. This approach says something interesting about the company's assessment of those people most likely to be interested in the Acura.

EXHIBIT 7-2

J. D. Power & Associates, an organization not dependent upon car manufacturers' dollars, consistently found that Acura buyers were highly satisfied with the automobile. From the beginning, Acura engineers looked for ways to build in driver-oriented features and comforts. They proved that customer-satisfaction awards are no fluke; they are the logical result of paying attention to the details of the product element of the marketing plan. Many car owners base their final buying decision on the J. D. Powers Customer Satisfaction Index.

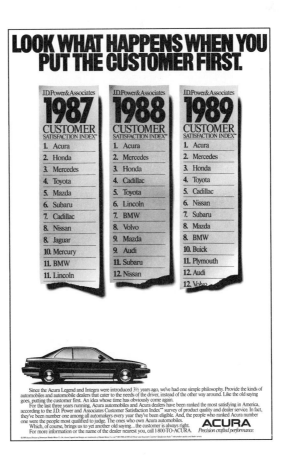

Good advertising strategy depends on careful marketing planning. This process of marketing and advertising planning is the means by which we can bring together the topics of the last three chapters: consumer behavior, market segmentation, the various elements of the marketing mix (including advertising), and marketing and advertising research.

THE MARKETING PLAN

What did Acura do to successfully appeal to its target market and achieve its goals in so short a time? It didn't start out with the track record of its European competitors in the luxury performance market; it had to develop a name for itself from scratch.

Did it succeed because of great advertising? Perhaps. But where did the ideas for the advertising come from? How did its agency decide what to write the ads about, where to run them, and what to say?

The answer lies in one word: *planning*.

Yet, as numerous marketing experts have pointed out over the years, more money is wasted—absolutely poured down the drain—on ineffectual advertising because of a woeful lack of adequate planning than for any other reason.

So what is a marketing plan? And what is an advertising plan? What is the difference, and what is their relationship? Let's deal with the first question first to better understand the overall success of Acura's introduction.

What Is a Marketing Plan?

The written marketing plan is like a nautical chart to the sailor. The planning process helps companies find the right course and then maintain its heading. Inasmuch as marketing is the *only* source of income for a company (except possibly for investments), the marketing plan may be the most important document a company can possess.

The **marketing plan** serves a number of very important functions. First, it assembles all the pertinent facts about the organization, the markets it serves, and its products, services, customers, competition, and so on in one spot. It also brings all these facts up-to-date. Second, it forces the functional managers within the company to work together—product development, production, selling, advertising, credit, transportation—to focus efficiently on the customer.[3] Third, it sets goals and objectives for specified periods of time and, finally, lays out the precise strategies and tactics that will be used to achieve them. Thus, as Exhibit 7-3 shows, it musters all the company's forces for the marketing battlefield.

Effect of the Marketing Plan on Advertising

If it truly does all these things, then the marketing plan should have a profound effect on the organization's advertising program. For one thing, the marketing plan enables analysis, criticism, and improvement of all company operations, including past marketing and advertising programs.

Second, it dictates the future role of advertising in the marketing mix. It determines which marketing activities will require advertising support and which advertising programs will need marketing support.

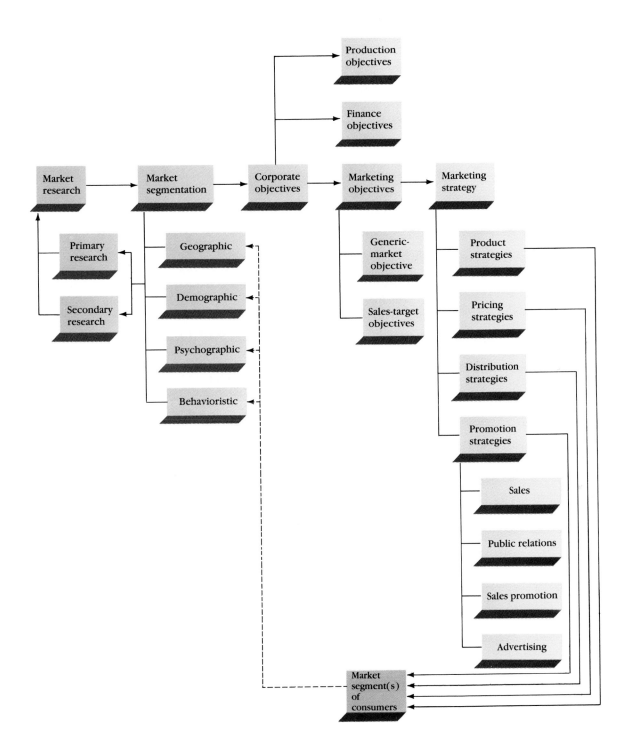

EXHIBIT 7-3

The marketing planning model above shows that planning is a continuous process that relies on blending the results of marketing research with company objectives in order to create sound strategies. These strategies are then applied to influence the market's buying patterns. Feedback from the market restarts the cycle.

Finally, it provides focus and guidance to advertising creativity. It reduces the temptation to go off on tangents; it enables better implementation, control, and continuity of advertising programs; and it ensures the most efficient allocation of advertising dollars.[4]

In short, successful organizations do not separate advertising plans from marketing. They view each as a vital building block for success.[5]

Elements of the Marketing Plan

The written marketing plan must reflect the goals of the company's top management and still be consistent with the capabilities of the company's various departments. Depending on its scope, the plan may be quite long and complex—as in the case of J. C. Penney or Acura—or, as in the case of a small firm or a single product line, it might be very brief, covering only, say, a six-month period. Regardless of length, the basic marketing plan should have four principal sections: *situation analysis, marketing objectives, marketing strategy,* and *action programs.*

In addition to these four sections, extended marketing plans for large companies also include a section on measurement, control, and review; a section on resource allocation; and an executive summary at the beginning to briefly state the contents of the whole plan. Subjects that relate purely to marketing are beyond the scope of this text. Those that relate to advertising, though, will be covered in this chapter. As a practical tool for both students and practitioners, we present a complete marketing plan outline in Appendix A at the end of this text.

Situation Analysis

The **situation analysis** section is an objective statement of where the organization is today and how it got there. Therefore, it is invariably the longest portion of the marketing plan, and preparing it may be a difficult and time-consuming task. This section should present all relevant facts about the company's history, growth, products and services, sales volume, share of market, competitive status, markets served, distribution system, past advertising programs, results of marketing research studies, company capabilities, strengths and weaknesses, and any other pertinent information.

The Checklist for Situation Analysis suggests some of the most important elements to consider. The situation analysis should also include information on key factors outside the company's immediate control—for example, the economic, political, social, technological, or commercial environments the company operates in. Only when all this information is assembled and the accuracy of the data is *agreed upon* by company executives can management hope to draw conclusions about planning for the future.[6]

What was Honda's situation when it began planning the introduction of the new Acura? The auto industry had already undergone a major change, from the age of big, style-oriented American cars to the age of small, technology-oriented foreign cars. However, the latter trend was beginning to show signs of maturity as greater numbers of competitors struggled to differentiate a plethora of similarly priced, similarly equipped compact and subcompact products. Meanwhile, economic conditions had improved, particularly in the price and availability of fuel. And demographic trends—such as more two-income families with more discretionary income—were contributing to the demand for higher-priced luxury cars. Over time, Honda had built a solid

Checklist for Situation Analysis

The Industry

- □ *Companies in industry:* dollar sales, strengths, and so forth.
- □ *Growth patterns within industry:* primary demand curve, per capita consumption, growth potential.
- □ *History of industry:* technological advances, trends, and so on.
- □ *Characteristics of industry:* distribution patterns, industry control, promotional activity, geographic characteristics, profit patterns, and so forth.

The Company

- □ *The company story:* history, size, growth, profitability, scope of business, competence in various areas, reputation, strengths, weaknesses, and so on.

The Product or Service

- □ *The product story:* development, quality, design, description, packaging, price structure, uses (primary, secondary, potential), reputation, strengths, and weaknesses.
- □ *Product sales features:* exclusive, nonexclusive differentiating qualities, product's competitive position in mind of consumer, and so forth.
- □ *Product research:* technological breakthroughs, improvements planned.

Sales History

- □ *Sales and sales costs:* by product, model, sales districts, and so on.
- □ *Profit history.*

Share of Market

- □ *Sales history industrywide:* share of market in dollars and units.
- □ *Market potential:* industry trends, company trend, demand trends.

The Market

- □ *Who and where is market,* how has market been segmented in the past, how can it be segmented in future, what are consumer needs, attitudes, and characteristics? How, why, when, and where do consumers buy?

- □ *Past advertising appeals* that have proved successful or unsuccessful in speaking to consumer needs.
- □ *Who are our customers,* past customers, future customers? What characteristics do they have in common? What do they like about our product? What don't they like?

Distribution

- □ *History and evaluation* of how and where product is distributed, current trend.
- □ *Company's relationship* with members of the distribution channel and their attitudes toward product/company.
- □ *Past policies* regarding trade advertising, deals, co-op advertising programs, and so on.
- □ *Status* of trade literature, dealer promotions, point-of-purchase, displays, and so on.

Pricing Policies

- □ *Price history:* trends, relationship to needs of buyers, competitive price situation.
- □ *Past price objectives:* management attitudes, buyer attitudes, channel attitudes.

Competition

- □ *Who is the competition?* Primary, secondary, share of market, products, services, goals, attitudes. What is competition's growth history and size?
- □ *Strengths of competition:* sales features, product quality, size. Weaknesses of competition.
- □ *Marketing activities of competition:* advertising, promotion, distribution, sales force. Estimated budget.

Promotion

- □ *Successes and failures* of past promotion policy, sales force, advertising, publicity.
- □ *Promotion expenditures:* history, budget emphasis, relation to competition, trend.
- □ *Advertising programs:* review of strategies, themes, campaigns.
- □ *Sales force:* size, scope, ability, cost/sale.

**PRACTICE NURSING
WHERE A NURSE'S
OPINION COUNTS.**

Nurses are a valuable part of the Army health care team. Just ask Captain Regina Tellitocci, R.N., Fitzsimons Army Medical Center in Denver.
    "Health care really is a team effort in the Army. Army nurses are involved with patient care eight hours a day, so our opinion counts.
    "The Army's rank structure helps a lot. We are comfortable enough that we feel free to discuss patient care or test results with the doctors.
    "When doctors and nurses work together, it always works to the patient's benefit. Things get diagnosed faster—and treated faster.
    "Army nurses are expected to give their opinions. As officers, we take on leadership roles quicker."
    You, too, can discover a world of opportunity in the Army Nurse Corps. If you have a BSN, and are registered to practice in the U.S., or if you're still a student, call 1-800-USA-ARMY, ext. 438, or write: Army Nurse Opportunities, P.O. Box 7713, Clifton, NJ 07015.

**ARMY NURSE CORPS.
BE ALL YOU CAN BE.**

EXHIBIT 7-4

The army offers job opportunities and excellent traning in a variety of fields for men and women. This ad for the Nurse Corps— aimed at teachers as well as students—promoted the fact that army nurses play a more important role on the health care team than civilian nurses. This fact reinforced the army's advertising theme: "Be all you can be."

reputation for innovation and user-friendly technology, quality, and service. Heading into the late 80s, the company thought it saw an opening it could exploit—a niche between the moderate-priced cars it had always built and the high-priced luxury market.

Marketing Objectives

Once the situation analysis data are assembled and agreed upon, the organization's management can determine specific marketing objectives to be attained within the time covered by the marketing plan. For example, in its efforts to recruit new soldiers every year, the U.S. Army sets specific numerical objectives for the regular army, the Army Reserve, and specific units within the army (such as the Nurse Corps advertised in Exhibit 7-4)—as well as quality objectives based on the mental aptitude and education of enlistees.

In contrast, for a manufacturer or distributor introducing a new product, marketing objectives might be expressed as follows:

1. Introduce the product to regional test markets and achieve a 10 percent share in those markets by the end of the first year.
2. Achieve national distribution to at least 40 states by the end of the second year.
3. Achieve a 10 percent share of the national market by the end of the third year.

Naturally, the marketing objectives must take into consideration the amount of money the organization has to invest in marketing and production, its knowledge of the marketplace, and its analysis of the competitive environment.

Marketing objectives should be logical deductions from the review of the company's current situation, management's prediction of future trends, and its understanding of the hierarchy of company objectives.[7] For example, **corporate objectives** are usually stated in terms of profit or return on investment. Or they may be stated in terms of net worth, earnings ratios, growth, or corporate reputation. **Marketing objectives,** on the other hand, derive from the corporate objectives but should relate to the needs of specific target markets and to specific sales objectives. These are referred to as general *market-need objectives* and specific *sales-target objectives.*[8]

The purpose of setting **market-need objectives** is to shift management's view of the organization from a producer of products or services to a satisfier of target market needs.[9] For example, rather than seeing itself as a piano company, Yamaha viewed itself as a provider of personal music entertainment. So, while overall demand for pianos was falling 10 percent each year, Yamaha developed a sophisticated technology that, in effect, reinvented the player piano, and sales skyrocketed.[10] The broader view of creating value for customers allows management to consider additional options.

Today, many consumer product companies are good examples of this view. A soap company may now recognize that its basic product is cleaning, not soap. Or, as Revlon founder Charles Revson once said, a cosmetic company's product is hope, not lipstick. And an insurance company sells financial security and opportunities, not just policies. What needs do you think Mirolin is offering to satisfy with its Mirocast Whirlpool tub in Exhibit 7-5?

EVER WONDER
WHY SOME PEOPLE
CALL THEIR
BATHROOM
A RESTROOM?

Perhaps it was first introduced as a polite alternative by the genteel society.

But today, in this increasingly stressful world, the whirlpool has given the name true meaning.

The pioneering designers of the Mirocast Whirlpool believed that every bathroom should be a restroom.

That everybody should benefit from the rapturous effects of massaging jets placed in strategic, anatomical locations. That everybody should experience the departure of stress and tension while lying in an ergonomically designed cradle.

What they designed is just such a whirlpool.

The Mirocast Whirlpool series is quite unlike any other whirlpool. It offers sizes, shapes and an assortment of contemporary colours to suit every taste. And each one features the jets, motor and hardware that has garnered much critical acclaim for comfort, safety and reliability.

The best way to see these whirlpools is to visit an authorized Mirocast dealer.

Or visit a friend, with a restroom.

©1989 Mirolin Industries Inc. Mirostone, Mirolin and Mirolin logo are registered trademarks of Mirolin Industries Inc. 200 Norseman Street, Toronto, Ontario.

Mirocast Whirlpools   ◈ Mirolin

EXHIBIT 7-5

Companies must keep the big picture in mind because they really produce more than goods. They fulfill people's dreams for a better life. This Canadian ad for Mirocast Whirlpools is offering far more than the cleaning benefit typically associated with bathtubs. It answers the market's higher-level needs for rest, relaxation, safety, reliability, and aesthetic appeal. This view is made possible when the advertiser includes *market-need objectives* in the development of its marketing and advertising plans.

Sales-target objectives, on the other hand, should be specific, quantitative, and realistic goals to be achieved within a specified time period. If Honda simply stated its marketing objective was to sell as many Acuras as possible, the objective would be nonspecific, unquantified, and unmeasurable. Instead, Honda defined its goal as selling 58,000 Acura Legends and Integras nationwide in 1986, 105,000 in 1987, and 180,000 in 1990. These objectives were specific to product and market, quantified to time and amount, and—judging by the results—fairly realistic. In 1986, 52,900 Acuras were sold; in 1987, 109,500; and in 1988, 128,200. In 1990, Americans bought 138,300 Acuras.

Objectives may be expressed in a number of ways. For instance, many marketing organizations set objectives by the following criteria:

☐ Total sales volume.

☐ Sales volume by product, market segment, customer type.

☐ Market share in total or by product line.

☐ Growth rate of sales volume in total or by product line.

☐ Gross profit in total or by product line.

Other criteria for marketing objectives might relate to additions or deletions to the product line, creation of new distribution channels, development of new pricing policies, or retraining of field sales staff. Some firms today even include objectives relating to social responsibility, such as the preservation of natural resources, participation in community projects, and support of educational programs or institutions.[11]

As we will see in our discussion of the advertising plan later in this chapter, specific marketing objectives also have an important impact on advertising objectives. Only by setting specific objectives can management measure the degree of marketing and advertising success it is achieving.

Marketing Strategy

The third major section of the marketing plan is the statement of how the company will accomplish its marketing objectives. The **strategy** is the total directional thrust of the company, the "how to" of the marketing plan. For example, if you must travel from Boston to San Francisco, your objective is to get to San Francisco. Your strategy, then, might be to take the train, to take the plane, or to go around Cape Horn on a square-rigged schooner.

In marketing terms, the objectives are what you want to accomplish, and the strategy determines the methods.

People often confuse the terms *objectives* and *strategy*. This is understandable, for, as Fred Posner, director of marketing research for Ayer, points out, one person's strategy may be another person's objective: "The meaning will often depend on where you sit—whether you look at the marketing battlefield from a tank turret, a field command tent, or a computer console."[12]

The chairman of the board may have the objective of increasing the stock dividend. His strategies for accomplishing this may include increasing sales. To the marketing director, the chairman's strategy (increased sales) becomes an objective. The marketing director may decide that to increase sales she will use advertising to persuade current users to use the product more often. That, then, becomes the advertising agency's objective. The agency then concludes that its strategy is to make the product most appealing to its light users by defining more use occasions where the product is appropriate.

To be effective, a marketing strategy must stand the test of time. It must be an ingenious design for achieving a desired goal, and it must be results oriented. The particular marketing strategy a company selects has a dramatic impact on its advertising. The marketing strategy affects the amount of advertising to be used, the creative thrust of advertisements, and the advertising media employed. In short, the marketing strategy determines the objectives for advertising and provides the key to the advertising strategy.

Selecting the Target Market   The strategy a company chooses depends not only on its marketing objectives but also on the particular market being approached. The first strategic step, therefore, is to select the *target market*. To some extent, this may already have been accomplished at the time corporate objectives were set. But, as we discussed in Chapters 5 and 6, by using the processes of market segmentation and research, management should define its target market very tightly within the scope of the broader market segment.

For instance, following the situation analysis, Honda executives decided to focus on the luxury performance market. But within that market were two segments: old-money people who had always driven a Mercedes-Benz or comparable luxury car, and new-money people who were moving up into the market. Honda executives decided to start by focusing on those who were just entering the market for luxury performance cars. But beyond that, what did Honda know about its target market?

Acura targets the luxury performance market. More specifically, however, the Acura marketing strategy focused on the active, younger, more iconoclastic segment of the market. The headline in this ad is a dead-on appeal to those people.

This is how the Acura sales brochure in Exhibit 7-6 characterized the upscale, young professionals the car was designed for:

> There are those few individuals for whom the word uncommon was invented. Who, because of their natural leadership ability, are never by themselves. Yet because of their unwillingness to accept the status quo, always stand apart from the crowd. This quest to go above and beyond carries over into every aspect of their lives. Including mode of transportation. . . .

Determining the Marketing Mix The second step in the development of the marketing strategy is to determine a cost-effective marketing mix for *each* target market the company pursues. As we discussed in Chapter 5, the mix will consist of a blend of the *4 Ps: product, price, place,* and *promotion.*

What was Acura's marketing mix? First, the company carefully developed and manufactured a solidly engineered, driver-oriented product that was supported by Honda's well-established commitment to service and customer satisfaction. Second, it set a pricing strategy that put the Acura at the low end of the luxury performance market—but allowed no factory rebates—to reinforce the image of quality.

Next, it created a completely new automotive division and nationwide distribution system for Acura—separate from the Honda network—and in numerous cases, brought in dealers who already had experience selling other makes of luxury cars. And finally, the Acura division initiated a promotional program that included extensive training programs for dealer sales and service staffs (personal selling), Grand Prix racing to establish a reputation for technological excellence among industry analysts and knowledgeable consumers (publicity), and a full program of television, magazine, and radio advertising to develop the distinct Acura personality (see Exhibit 7-7).

Companies have a wide variety of marketing strategy options. For example, a company might decide to increase distribution, initiate new uses for a product, increase or change a product line, develop entirely new markets, or

EXHIBIT 7-7

In its television ads, Acura followed through on the theme set in its print ads: This is an automobile for people with class who appreciate good engineering.

VO: The antilock brakes on the 1990 Acura Integra were inspired by those used to stop jet aircraft. And while you might expect to find such technology on a multi-million-dollar airplane, you might not expect to find it on an automobile that costs . . . considerably less.

go into discount pricing. Each of these tends to emphasize one or more of the marketing mix elements, and the selection depends greatly on the product's position in the market and its stage in the product life cycle.

Positioning Strategies David Ogilvy has said that the first decision in marketing and advertising is also the most important: *how to position your product.* To Ogilvy, *positioning* is defined as "what the product does and who it is for."[13] His agency (Ogilvy & Mather) developed the advertising for the Unilever product, Dove. As Ogilvy points out, they could have positioned Dove as a detergent bar for men with dirty hands. But when Lever Bros. (now Unilever) introduced Dove in 1957, it decided to position the new product as a complexion bar for women with dry skin, complete with a demonstration of the cleansing cream pouring into the bar. Dove maintained its position for 30 years, and the strategy never changed. Every commercial today still uses the same cleansing cream demonstration, and Dove is consistently the number-one brand in the $1.5 billion bar soap category.[14]

Companies usually have two choices in selecting a position. One is to pick a similar position next to a competitor and battle it out for the same customers ("Avis is only No. 2"). Another is to find a position not held by a competitor—a hole in the market—and quickly move to fill it, perhaps through product differentiation or market segmentation.

For example, a company might elect to position itself through *price/quality differentiation.* Like L'Oreal, it could offer a higher-quality product concept at a higher price, with the theme line: "I'm worth it" (see Exhibit 7-8). Or it could advertise the same quality at a lower price, like Suave, saying; "Why pay more for the same?"

What was Honda's strategy for positioning the Acura? Instead of trying to woo loyal customers from the well-entrenched nameplates, it decided to intercept new customers headed into the luxury performance market, as Exhibit 7-9 shows. At the time, this $18,000 to $25,000 range was a relatively empty niche, occupied only by Volvos, Audis, and the lowest-end Mercedes and BMWs. (The Toyoto Lexus and Nissan Infiniti have since followed Acura into the top end of this niche.) Furthermore, its racing program won so much attention among trend-setting car enthusiasts that Honda established an unassailable position as number one in engineering, thereby beating the Europeans at their own game.

The many variations of product differentiation strategies, price/quality strategies, positioning strategies, and segmentation strategies make finding the one best strategy exhaustive work. It is most important for marketing and advertising managers to overcome the normal barriers to strategic thinking and work together to generate a list of creative alternatives.[15] These must then be evaluated in terms of satisfying the needs of the marketplace, securing advantages over the competition, and creating company profits.

Tactics (Action Programs)

Once the overall marketing objectives and marketing strategy have been set, the company may determine what specific actions should be undertaken and by whom, and when to implement each element within the marketing mix. Some of these actions may be externally oriented, dealing with standard marketing communication and distribution issues. Others may be internally

With beautiful, sophisticated spokeswomen, L'Oreal aims to emphasize quality over price. The ad's tone signals that its hair-coloring products may cost more than the competition, but to paraphrase the theme line, the women who use it are "worth it."

CYBILL: Thank goodness you're all listening. I have an announcement that will knock your socks off. Preference by L'Oreal is new and better. I know you think it's

already practically perfect. Well me too! But nothing conditions better than new Preference. And it gives hair glorious shining color. So if you want to feel all

new and better, pull up your socks and say, "I'm worth it."

ANNOUNCER VO: New richer Preference by L'Oreal.

In this value-oriented ad, Acura solidly positioned itself as an alternative to the entrenched competition. By stating that luxury companies "manufacture" prices, the ad implies that high price is not a valid means of judging a car in Acura's category. This also reinforces the idea that Acura's relatively low price has more validity. This double message had great appeal for many first-time luxury-car buyers—because it was sensible.

oriented, dealing with the effective use of technology, capital, and human resources.[16]

A company's objectives indicate where it wants to go; the strategy indicates the general method and the intended route; and the **tactics** (or action programs) determine the shorter-term details of how to implement those methods and routes.[17]

In the case of a manufacturer of men's shirts, for example, a strategy might be to produce only the highest-quality designer products, charge a premium price, sell only through better department stores, and rely heavily on advertising to promote the line. The action programs might then be to develop a fashionable shirt that will give two years of normal wear, be available at Bullocks and Macy's, sell for $53.95, and be supported by a $1.5 million advertising budget divided equally between retailer co-op newspaper ads and national men's magazines.

It is in this world of action programs that advertising campaigns live. In the next section, therefore, we discuss the process used for planning advertising.

THE ADVERTISING PLAN

Advertising is a natural outgrowth of the marketing plan. In fact, a company's communications or **advertising plan** is prepared in much the same way as the marketing plan. The company follows the same process of performing analyses, setting objectives, and determining strategy. From the strategy, specific tactics or advertising programs are conceived and created. A complete advertising plan outline is presented in Appendix B at the end of this text.

Review of the Marketing Plan

The advertising manager's first task is to review the marketing plan. It is important to understand where the company is going, how it intends to get there, and the role advertising will play in the marketing mix. Therefore, the first section of the advertising plan is a premises or situation analysis section. This briefly restates the company's current situation, target markets, long- and short-term marketing objectives, and decisions regarding market positioning and the marketing mix.

Setting Advertising Objectives

Once the organization's marketing objectives and strategies have been set, the advertising manager can determine the specific tasks assigned to advertising. Unfortunately, some corporate executives have little idea of the specific tasks or objectives of their advertising programs. They describe the purpose of advertising with vague expressions such as "keeping our name out in front" or "giving ammunition to the sales force."

This ignorance may be largely the fault of advertising managers themselves, many of whom tend to state misty, generalized goals like "creating a favorable impression of the product in the marketplace in order to increase sales and maximize profits." Such wishy-washy gobbledygook serves the manager by protecting the program from ever being measured for effectiveness. However, it also reinforces the negative attitude shared by many executives about the large amount of money "wasted" on advertising. These executives think their money is wasted because they don't understand what the advertising is intended to do, how much it costs to do it, or how to measure the results.

Understanding What Advertising Can Do

Advertising objectives should be defined specifically, but doing so requires a clear understanding of what advertising can do. Most advertising programs, of course, hope to eventually cause some action on the part of the prospective customers. In fact, as we discussed in Chapter 1, **action advertising** attempts to induce the prospective customer to act immediately—by mailing a coupon or dialing a phone number to order the product from the advertiser. For example, the ad in Exhibit 7-10 is designed to stimulate interest *and inquiries* from pediatricians about how to get paid immediately for their services—by accepting the American Express card.

However, it is usually unfair to assign advertising the responsibility of achieving sales goals.[18] Sales goals are marketing objectives, not advertising objectives, and—typically—only a very small percentage of people exposed to particular ads are expected to act right away. Before customers can be persuaded to buy, a number of very important steps must be accomplished. Most advertising, therefore, seeks to inform, persuade, or remind its intended

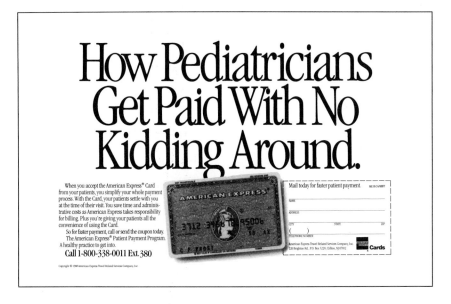

EXHIBIT 7-10

In this carefully designed *action ad* (also called a *direct-response ad*), American Express uses a direct visual line from headline to card to coupon to make its point fast. The headline is so commanding in size that readers tend to feel the company is politely yelling at them—compelling them to cut out the large coupon just to relieve the tension. The picture of the card is nearly as dominant as the headline because it *is* the product and because it completes the idea set up in the headline. The featured benefit of faster, no-hassle payments engenders a comforting feeling, while the toll-free number offers the ultimate in ordering convenience.

The advertising pyramid is a useful tool for setting advertising objectives because it represents the tasks advertising can perform and indicates how advertising may affect those who see and hear it. Compared to the large number of people made aware of the product by an ad (the base of the pyramid), the number who eventually act on its message is typically quite small (the top of the pyramid).

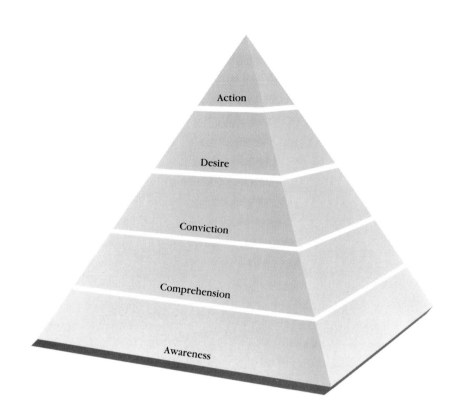

audience over an extended time about the company, good, service, or issue being advertised. This is the type of advertising generally used by retailers, manufacturers, banks, insurance companies, services, and associations.

The Advertising Pyramid: A Guide to Setting Objectives

A simple way to understand the tasks advertising can perform is to think of advertising as building the pyramid shown in Exhibit 7-11. Before a new product is introduced, prospective customers live in a desert of unawareness, totally oblivious to the product's existence. The first objective of any advertising, therefore, must be to lay the foundation of the pyramid by creating an **awareness block**—to acquaint some portion of those unaware people with the company, good, service, or brand.

The next task, or level of the pyramid, is to develop the **comprehension block**—to communicate enough information so that some percentage of that foundation group is not only aware of the product but also recognizes its purpose and perhaps some of its features.

Next, advertising needs to communicate enough information about the product and its features to persuade a certain number of people to believe in its value. This is called the **conviction block.** Of those who become convinced, some can be moved to the next block of people who actually **desire** the product. And finally, after all the preceding steps have been accomplished, a certain percentage of those who desire the product will reach the top of the pyramid, the **action block.** These people may request additional information, send in a coupon, go to a store to see the good, or even purchase it.

At this point, it's important to understand that our pyramid is not static. The advertiser actually works in three dimensions: time, dollars, and people. Advertising takes time to get up speed, especially for products that are not purchased regularly.[19] Over an extended time, as more and more dollars are spent on advertising, the number of people who become aware of the product increases. Likewise, as more people comprehend the product, believe in it, and desire it, more will take the final action of purchasing it.

Ideally, advertising objectives should be specified to time and degree in such a way that success can be measured by research studies and tests.[20] For example, in a classic treatise on this subject, Colley suggested a soap manufacturer might list the following advertising objective: "Among the 30 million housewives who own automatic washers, increase—from 10 percent to 40 percent in one year—the number who identify Brand X as a low-sudsing detergent and the number who think it gets clothes cleaner."

As we shall point out shortly, this theoretical approach has some problems. However, for our purposes in understanding the nature of advertising communication and the importance of trying to make advertising accountable, let's apply this principle to the development of objectives at each stage of the advertising pyramid for Acura.

Specific advertising objectives for the first-year introduction of the Acura might have read as follows:

1. Communicate within the first year the existence and availability of the Acura automobiles to 75 percent of the 700,000 people who annually buy luxury performance cars.
2. Inform 75 percent of this "aware" group that the Acura is a technologically superior car in the luxury performance class with many driver-oriented creature comforts; that it is a brand new nameplate backed up by Honda's reputation for service, quality, and value; and that it is sold only through dedicated Acura dealers.
3. Convince 75 percent of the "informed" group that the Acura is a very high-quality car, reliable, and exclusive.
4. Stimulate the desire within 75 percent of the "convinced" group to test-drive an Acura.
5. Motivate 50 percent of the "desire" group to actually go to their local Acura dealer to test-drive a Legend or Integra.

It's important to note here that these advertising objectives are specific as to time and degree and are quantified like marketing objectives. That means that, theoretically, at the end of the first year, a consumer attitude study could be performed to determine how many people are *aware* of the Acura, how many people *understand* the primary features of the car; and so on. If these results can be measured statistically, so can the effectiveness of the advertising program.

All things being equal, if Acura's hypothetical advertising objectives for the first year were all achieved, and if we assume that about half of those who test-drive a car buy one, Acura would gain approximately an 8 percent share of the targeted market by the end of year one. In fact, Acura did set a sales goal of 58,000 units for 1986, and it actually sold 52,900.

Acura's second-year objective was to sell 105,000 units, and it actually sold 109,500. To accomplish this goal, the company had to increase the percentages of people who were aware of the product, believed in it, and were willing to test-drive it. Much of this could be accomplished by advertising; but once the customer was in the store, it was the dealer's responsibility to close the sale through personal selling.

In some cases, the process can be accelerated by using sales promotion devices—such as heavy sampling of a product—to convert people from

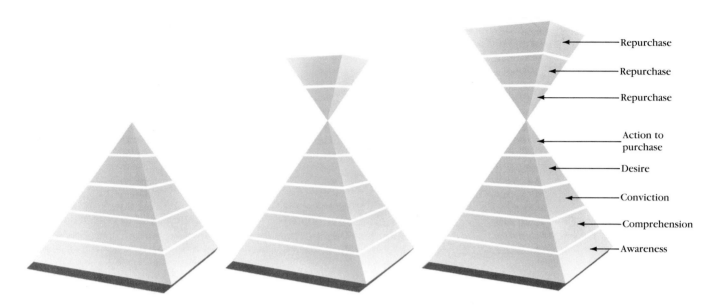

Repeat purchases are represented by the inverted pyramid. As more people purchase and repurchase the product, the inverted pyramid grows wider and taller to symbolize the ever-expanding numbers of loyal customers. Is it possible for the inverted pyramid to grow larger than the original advertising pyramid underneath it? How about for products that have limited advertising but very good word of mouth?

being totally unaware one day to being users of the product the next. This can be extremely expensive. Still, as we shall see in Chapter 16, many manufacturers use couponing and other sales promotion tools to speed up the results of their advertising.

Satisfied Customers Invert the Pyramid

Once a certain percentage of people have actually made the purchase decision, a new advertising objective may be introduced: to stimulate reuse of the product. As more and more people decide to purchase and repurchase, our pyramid model changes. A new inverted pyramid like the one in Exhibit 7-12 will be built on top of the old one to represent the growing number of people who have joined the action block and developed the repurchasing habit.

The inverted pyramid is actually built by customer satisfaction and good word of mouth. The greater the satisfaction and the more people told about the product, the faster the inverted pyramid will expand. At this point, **reinforcement advertising** is often used to remind people of their successful experience with the product and to suggest reuse. This can be optimized by small and large advertisers alike through a series of techniques referred to as *maximarketing*. (See Ad Lab 7-B, "MaxiMarketing—How Small Advertisers Build the Inverted Pyramid.")

The problem with these models and theories in real life is that they tend to oversimplify the complex phenomenon of consumer behavior: how communication takes place, how learning is achieved, how needs and desires are stimulated, and how consumer purchasing actually happens. They pay little or no attention to the dynamics of changing consumer tastes and preferences, to the nature of different classes of products with different life cycles, to the activities of competitors, or to the fact that people can come into and leave the market continuously at various levels of the pyramid due to any of innumerable internal and external stimuli besides advertising.

The hypothetical pyramid model, though, does give advertisers a simple way of looking at the long-term building and reinforcing effects of media advertising. It also helps them realize that, as they find consumers at various

AD LAB 7-B

MaxiMarketing—How Small Advertisers Build the Inverted Pyramid

Advertising to the masses is enormously expensive—prohibitively so for small firms. A national TV campaign generally costs millions of dollars, and even a local version may cost tens or hundreds of thousands. No wonder many small advertisers have stalled out instead of expanding.

One solution has been advanced by Stan Rapp and Tom Collins, who own one of the top direct-response advertising agencies in the country. They see a solution to the small advertiser's dilemma in some of the tools of their trade: computers, credit cards, and 800-number telephones. All are now within the reach of small companies. Rapp and Collins advocate using these tools to establish "lifetime" personal ties with clients, an approach they term *maximarketing* or *direct marketing* (not to be confused with one of its predecessors, direct-mail marketing). The result is a customized database of those who have bought before and who are likely to buy in the future. Directly marketing to the people who make up such a database maximizes the dollars spent. It also allows the small advertiser to simultaneously promote a product and capture a "share of mind," a loyalty that translates into future sales.

The three common denominators of any selling process are reaching the prospect, making the sale, and developing the relationship. In maximarketing, the company starts by finding the strongest prospects. First, it obtains an appropriate database. For many small advertisers, that may be a list of previous buyers or of service customers. Mailing lists (often already on computer disk) are also available at a reasonable cost from many other sources, ranging from the local chamber of commerce to one of the national database compilers. However, the advertiser who buys a list from elsewhere must often sift out the key prospects. With a list of solid prospects, the advertiser can then mail out carefully targeted information.

Responses to mailings are the measure of success for maximarketers. In traditional marketing, advertising success has been measured in terms of the cost per reader or viewer, the percentage of people who recall seeing the ad, and other similarly indirect measures. It is much more practical to judge an ad's effectiveness by the number of

sales it generates. Measuring response offers four major benefits: (1) It helps to correctly target advertising; (2) it helps in comparing the efficiency of media, offers, brand images, and product benefits; (3) it shows who is interested in the product; and (4) it provides information for refining the database of customers and prospects.

Rapp and Collins also recommend that advertising strive for "accountability." Response to advertising is one aspect of accountability. Another aspect is "activation." Getting a prospect to act right away—say, by mailing a coupon—is the goal. Ways to achieve this goal are to set specific deadlines and to offer quantitative, not subjective, incentives for responding. Making a sale, the second step in marketing, is not the immediate focus.

The third step in marketing, developing the relationship, is the ultimate goal of maximarketers. Commonly, large companies have spent most of their dollars on mass advertising and have devoted pennies to handling the responses to that advertising. The maximarketer takes exactly the opposite tack: Spend less on advertising, and spend what's left on turning responses from interested prospects into repeat business.

The way to develop "loyal friends" is to mail advertising to a carefully selected list and thereafter to rework the respondents. The list can be expanded by doing two jobs at once with any mailing—for example, putting information about a related product into the package or promoting related services. Done right, maximarketing forges a relationship with a customer that outlasts any single sale. And what's better for small advertisers, it doesn't sink the company.

Laboratory Application

Open any direct-mail package you have recently received. Analyze how well it reflects the maximarketing approach. Does it seem to have correctly targeted you as a strong prospect? How does it encourage you to take action? Is the main offer linked to a related product or service?

levels of the pyramid, the advertising communication needs, objectives, and strategies for achieving them all change. For new products, building awareness will probably be the primary objective. For well-known, established products, advertisers will want to focus on building appeal or enhancing consumer attitudes. For well-known and well-liked products facing stiff competitive activity, advertisers may want to build market share by promoting additional purchases with ads that stress action. (See the Checklist for Developing Advertising Objectives.)

Checklist for Developing Advertising Objectives

Does the advertising aim at closing an *immediate sale?* If so, the objectives might be to:

☐ Perform the complete selling function (take the product through all the necessary steps toward a sale).

☐ Close sales to prospects already partly sold through past advertising efforts ("Ask for the order" or "clincher" advertising).

☐ Announce a special reason for buying now (price, premium, and so forth).

☐ Remind people to buy.

☐ Tie in with some special buying event.

☐ Stimulate impulse sales.

Does the advertising aim at *near-term* sales by moving the prospect, step by step, closer to a sale (so that when confronted with a buying situation the customer will ask for, reach for, or accept the advertised brand)? If so, the objectives might be to:

☐ Create awareness of existence of product or brand.

☐ Create "brand image" or favorable emotional disposition toward the brand.

☐ Implant information or attitude regarding benefits and superior features of brand.

☐ Combat or offset competitive claims.

☐ Correct false impressions, misinformation, and other obstacles to sales.

☐ Build familiarity and easy recognition of package or trademark.

Does the advertising aim at building a "long-range consumer franchise"? If so, the objectives might be to:

☐ Build confidence in company and brand which is expected to pay off in years to come.

☐ Build customer demand, which places company in stronger position in relation to its distribution (not at the "mercy of the marketplace").

☐ Place advertiser in position to select preferred distributors and dealers.

☐ Secure universal distribution.

☐ Establish a "reputation platform" for launching new brands or product lines.

☐ Establish brand recognition and acceptance, which will enable the company to open up new markets (geographic, price, age, gender).

Specifically, how can advertising contribute toward increased sales? Among objectives would be to:

☐ Hold present customers against the inroads of competition.

☐ Convert competitive users to advertiser's brand.

☐ Cause people to specify advertiser's brand instead of asking for product by generic name.

☐ Convert nonusers of the product type to users of product and brand.

☐ Make steady customers out of occasional or sporadic customers.

☐ Advertise new uses of the product.

Advertising Strategy and the Creative Mix

Our discussion of marketing planning showed that the *marketing objective* is what the company wants to achieve, whereas the *marketing strategy* indicates how it is going to accomplish it. Similarly, the *advertising* (or *communications*) *objective* tells where the advertiser wants to be with respect to consumer awareness, attitude, and preference, whereas the *advertising* (or *creative*) *strategy* tells how to get there.

Marketing strategy refers to the way the marketing mix (product, price, place, and promotion) is blended. Promotional strategy (discussed in Chapter 5) refers to the way the **promotional mix** (personal selling, advertising, public relations, sales promotion, and collateral) is used. Similarly, **advertising strategy** is determined by the **creative mix,** which comprises the advertising elements the company controls to achieve its advertising objectives.

□ Persuade customers to buy larger sizes or multiple units.

□ Remind users to buy.

□ Encourage greater frequency or quantity of use.

Does the advertising aim at some specific step that leads to a sale? If so, objectives might be to:

□ Persuade prospect to write for descriptive literature, return a coupon, enter a contest.

□ Persuade prospect to visit a showroom, ask for a demonstration.

□ Induce prospect to sample the product (trial offer).

How important are "supplementary benefits" of end-user advertising? Among objectives would be to:

□ Aid salespeople in opening new accounts.

□ Aid salespeople in getting larger orders from wholesalers and retailers.

□ Aid salespeople in getting preferred display space.

□ Give salespeople an entrée.

□ Build morale of company sales force.

□ Impress the trade (causing recommendation to their customers and favorable treatment of salespeople).

Is it a task of advertising to impart information needed to consummate sales and build customer satisfaction? If so, objectives may be designed to use:

□ "Where to buy it" advertising.

□ "How to use it" advertising.

□ New models, features, package.

□ New prices.

□ Special terms, trade-in offers, and so forth.

□ New policies (such as guarantees).

To what extent does the advertising aim at building confidence and goodwill for the corporation among various groups? Targets may include:

□ Customers and potential customers.

□ The trade (distributors, dealers, retail people).

□ Employees and potential employees.

□ The financial community.

□ The public at large.

Specifically, what kind of images does the company wish to build?

□ Product quality, dependability.

□ Service.

□ Family resemblance of diversified products.

□ Corporate citizenship.

□ Growth, progressiveness, technical leadership.

The elements of the creative mix include:

□ The target audience.
□ The product concept.
□ The communications media.
□ The advertising message.

The Target Audience: Everyone Who Should Know

The **target audience** refers to the specific people the advertising is intended to address. That typically includes more segments than just the target market. In the marketing plan for Acura, the target market was described as upscale, young professionals interested in buying their first luxury performance automobile. In the advertising plan, however, the target audience included the

Lightly frosted, crunchy, delicious.
You don't have to be a kid to love the
taste of *Kellogg's Frosted Flakes*® cereal.
"They're Gr-r-reat!®"

EXHIBIT 7-13

The product concepts for
Kellogg's Frosted Flakes and General Mills' Total are reflected in
the packaging and advertising for
the two products. Typically, the
product name dominates the
package and is styled to have an
individual look. Many cereals feature a cartoon character like Tony
the Tiger that reinforces product
differentiation by creating personality for the product.

target market, but it also included well-educated, upper-income achievers
concerned with issues, trends, events, and personal growth. As opinion
leaders, they would be important in the decision-making process of potential
Acura buyers.

When determining the target audience, it is important to consider not just
who the end user is but also who makes the purchasing decision and who
influences the purchasing decision. Children, for example, may exert a strong
influence on where the family decides to eat. McDonald's thus includes
children as a target audience and concentrates much of its advertising spending on campaigns directed to them.

The Product Concept: Presenting the Product

From the advertiser's point of view, the particular "bundle of values" the
advertiser presents to the consumer is the **product concept.** For example,
both General Mills' Total cereal and Kellogg's Frosted Flakes are similarly
priced brands aimed at the U.S. ready-to-eat breakfast cereal market. However, the product concepts are completely different. Total is presented as a
nutritious cereal packed with vitamins ("100 percent of your daily requirement"), whereas the concept of Kellogg's Frosted Flakes (shown in Exhibit
7-13) is a good-tasting, sweet cereal that adults like as much as kids do.
Ideally, the advertiser's view of the product concept matches the one held by
the consumer—although this is certainly not always the case.

EXHIBIT 7-14

The FCB grid (developed by the Foote, Cone & Belding advertising agency) is used to classify products and brands so advertisers can more easily understand the nature of the purchase from the consumer's point of view. The grid has two dimensions. One moves from how demanding (high involvement) to how undemanding (low involvement) it is to make the purchase decision, while the other dimension looks at the emotional aspects, from "think" (least emotional) to "feel" (most emotional). The range of products shown on the chart typifies the degree and type of consumer effort needed to buy each product.

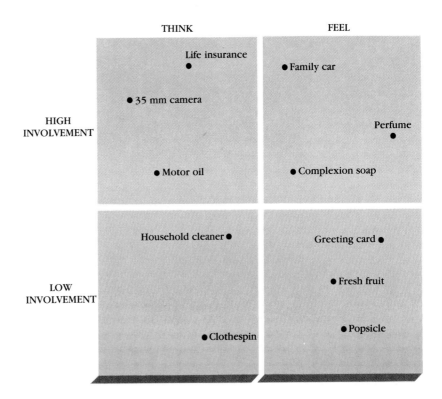

When writing the advertising plan, the advertising manager should develop a simple statement to describe the product concept—that is, how the advertising will present the product. To create this statement, the advertiser must first consider how the consumer perceives the product and weigh this against the company's marketing strategy for the product. How is the product positioned in the market? How is the product differentiated from the competition? Is price/quality differentiation used? What stage of the life cycle is the product in? How is the product classified, packaged, branded? All these considerations influence the product concept.

What was the product concept for the Acura? Functionally, the Acura boasted certain high-performance and driver comfort features, such as antilock brakes and easily reached radio switches. Conceptually, though, it was the upscale representative of Honda's tradition of excellence, offering European luxury styling and power at an affordable price.[21] It was both a luxury car and a performance car for those who, as one ad stated, "have arrived but weren't affected by the trip."

The product concept can be developed in many ways. To assist its people in this process, the Foote, Cone & Belding advertising agency developed the FCB grid shown in Exhibit 7-14. This depicts the *degree* and the *kind* of involvement the consumer brings to the purchase decision for different products. Some purchases, like automobiles, require a great deal of involvement. Others, like soap, require little. The *kind* of involvement may range from very rational (thinking) at one extreme to very emotional or symbolic (feeling) at the other. Testing consumer involvement is difficult, and both the degree and kind of involvement with different products may change. But by analyzing involvement, the advertiser may be able to hone the creative strategy and get to the idea stage more quickly.[22]

The Communications Media: The Message Delivery System

In the creative strategy, the **communications media** refer to the various methods or vehicles that will transmit the advertiser's message. These may include traditional media such as radio, television, newspapers, magazines, or billboards. Or, they may also include direct mail, publicity, and certain sales promotion techniques such as sample packs or coupons or events such as trade shows.

Introducing a new product concept is a daunting task and, when an image of quality is part of the message, an expensive one. Acura's advertising agency, Ketchum Advertising (which was different than Honda's agency), used television advertising to generate broad and immediate awareness of the new nameplate and followed up with radio advertising, on a more frequent schedule, to assist recall. Full-color, detailed magazine ads were also central to the plan. Research showed that Acura's target consumers often spend substantially more time reading than watching television, and for information they often relied on technical publications, such as auto-enthusiast magazines.

Media considerations will be discussed more fully in Chapter 12. It's important to understand here, though, that the media to be used are determined by considering audience or readership statistics, potential communications effectiveness, relevance to the rest of the creative mix, and cost at the time the advertising plan is developed.

The Advertising Message: What the Advertising Communicates

What the company plans to say in its advertisements and how it plans to say it—verbally and nonverbally—make up the **advertising message.** As we shall discuss in Chapter 8, the combination of copy, art, and production elements forms the message in an advertisement. There are an infinite number of ways to combine these elements, and the most creative of these define the state of the art of contemporary advertising (see Ad Lab 7-C, "Creative Use of the Creative Mix," on p. 264).

Acura wanted its message to center on technology, ergonomics (driver comfort), and prestige, with a certain rebellious twist to emphasize the difference between the Acura and old-line luxury performance cars. For example, the headline in one ad reads, "In a world of badges and labels, Acura presents an automotive statement that relies on neither." Ketchum's print ads for the Legend used two-page magazine spreads in luscious color dominated by a photograph of the car. The copy detailed the car's advanced features and consistently emphasized quality. The logo was accompanied by the tag line: "Precision crafted performance." In later ads, when Acura went through its first major design change, the pictures in the ads changed, but as Exhibit 7-15 shows, the tone of the ads remained the same.

REVERSING THE PLANNING PROCESS: BOTTOM-UP MARKETING

The marketing and advertising planning processes we've just examined—analyzing the situation, establishing objectives, setting strategy, and determining tactics—is a proven methodology for large companies. It is generally referred to as **top-down planning** and is ideal for complex, bureaucratic organizations—allowing management to participate at all levels, starting with the board of directors' objectives.

But how does a little company plan—particularly if it wants to become a big company?

This ad announces Acura's new design while emphasizing the car's quality engineering. The strong, simple visual allows the elegantly typeset headline to pique your interest when it says Acura's engineers forgot everything they'd heard about the Acura Legend.

Planning is frequently a dilemma for small firms. They know they should plan, but they're not sure how to do it or where to begin. Because everybody is both player and coach, the day-to-day details seem to come first. With everybody wearing a lot of hats, no one person is responsible for planning; and, besides, "We just can't afford to waste time planning."

However, there is a solution: **bottom-up marketing.**

As mentioned in Ad Lab 7-A on Marketing Warfare, Trout and Ries suggest the best way for a company to develop a competitive advantage is to focus on an ingenious tactic and develop it into a strategy. By reversing the normal process, advertisers sometimes make important discoveries.[23] For example, some researchers at Vicks developed an effective, new liquid cold remedy but then discovered that it put people to sleep when they used it. Rather than throwing out the research, Vicks positioned the formula as a nighttime cold remedy. The "first nighttime cold remedy" was an advertising tactic that worked because it was based on the principle of being first. NyQuil went on to become the most successful new product in Vicks' history and the number-one cold remedy.

The Tactic: A Singular, Competitive Mental Angle

By planning from the bottom up, managers can find things to exploit. The tactic is a competitive mental angle that is unique enough to produce results. But advertisers should find just one tactic—not two or three or four. Trout and Ries suggest that a tactic is like a nail, and the strategy is the hammer that drives it in. Once a tactic is discovered, the advertiser can build a strategy around it, focusing all the elements of the marketing mix on the tactic.

The combination of the tactic and the strategy is what creates a position in the consumer's mind. Thus, when Tom Monaghan thought of the tactic of delivering pizza to the home, it was the totality of the strategy focused on this singular idea that enabled him to make a fortune at Domino's (see Exhibit 7-16 on p. 266).

The company's advertising plan is an excellent place to discover a competitive tactic. But opportunities are hard to spot, because they often don't

AD LAB 7-C
Creative Use of the Creative Mix

AVO: Out of hairspray? Snyder's has 28 brands of hairspray.

Before.

After.

If you stop to consider what some metal products can be recycled to create, today's trash will be tomorrow's treasure. And when you stop to consider the possibilities of recycling, we hope you'll stop and consider us. We're Kasle Recycling. 2210 West Oliver Avenue in Indianapolis. (317) 637-3471. **Kasle Recycling**

Sail readers aren't all cut from the same cloth.

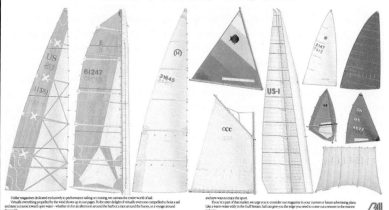

Unlike magazines dedicated exclusively to performance sailing or cruising, we canvass the entire world of sail. Virtually everything propelled by the wind shows up in our pages. To the utter delight of virtually everyone compelled to hoist a sail and steer a course toward open water – whether it's for an afternoon around the harbor, a race around the buoys, or a voyage around the world.

Whatever their motivation, 170,000 experts and novices alike read Sail each month. That's a larger paid circulation than any other sailing magazine. They pass on their copies to yield a total readership of over half a million, then go on to fuel the market for new products and new ways to enjoy the sport.

If you're a part of that market, we urge you to consider our magazine in your current or future advertising plans. Like a warm-water eddy in the Gulf Stream, Sail can give you the edge you need to come out a winner in the marine industry.

Call Dick Devlin at 617-241-9500. He'll explain why there's only one word you need to know for your advertising to succeed – Sail.

Laboratory Application

Describe which elements of the creative mix are being emphasized in each of these advertisements.

WE'RE DELIVERING OUR BEST TO YOU.

USE COUPONS ON BACK FOR GREAT DEALS
DELIVERED IN 30 MINUTES OR LESS.

IT'S TIME FOR DOMINO'S PIZZA.

Check your local White Pages for the Domino's Pizza nearest you.

EXHIBIT 7-16

Domino's tactic for rising above the many competing pizza restaurants was home delivery. This television ad shows some of the elements that helped support the tactic: clearly identified delivery vehicles and pizza boxes, and polite, customer-oriented delivery people.

ALLOCATING FUNDS FOR ADVERTISING

look like opportunities. They look like angles or gimmicks. When people saw the first Toys Я Us stores, did they say, "This is going to be the biggest toy store in America?" Or did they say, "Why is the R backwards?"

Small company managers with limited staffs are often besieged by the details of their businesses. This often denies them the luxury of looking at the forest because they are surrounded by too many trees. But they are actually in a very advantageous position because, surrounded with the details of the business, they are more likely to come in contact with a good tactic that can be developed into a powerful strategy.

The Secret to Successful Planning

Whether the advertiser is a large corporation or a small company, the key to successful planning is information. The corporation's information usually comes from stacks of data; the small company's information comes from the details of the day-to-day business or the successful implementation of a tactic. Information leads to direction. And once direction is established, planning becomes an easier and more rewarding process.

A singular direction allows the pieces of both the marketing plan and the advertising plan to fall into place. The advertising plan, for example, can lay out the general direction of the campaign for the allotted time period. Then, when it comes to creating the individual advertisements or commercials, a similar process can be repeated. The same questions may be asked: What is the overall strategy of the campaign? Who are we talking to? What is the specific objective of this ad? What is the best way to do it? What media should we use? What do we want to say? How do we want to say it? Answering those questions will be the objective of the next two parts of this text: "Advertising Creativity" and "Advertising Media." But first, we need to understand how companies allocate the money needed to implement their advertising strategies.

In 1990, after eight years of unprecedented growth, the United States and Canada experienced the first throes of a recession. Interest rates were high, real estate sales dropped, construction of new homes slowed down, defense spending was cut, and unemployment began to rise. To make matters worse, threats of war in the Mideast caused fear of higher fuel prices. Consumer confidence was sinking, and with it, retail sales.

As sales dropped and company owners fretted over the red ink on their bottom lines, many executives marched into their advertising departments and ordered the immediate curtailment of planned advertising programs. Many cut their advertising budgets to zero. But some time later, as the government announced the beginning of the turnaround, these same executives were behind their desks worrying that sales were still down. And their stockholders were wondering how their companies had just lost several percentage points in market share to the competition. (See the position of the American Association of Advertising Agencies on this subject in Exhibit 7-17.)

The fact is, money is the motor that drives every marketing and advertising plan. If you suddenly shut the motor off, it may coast for a while, but before long, it stops running. No advertising or marketing plan is complete, therefore, without a discussion of what the program will cost and how the money will be spent. And the advertising department has to convince management that the suggested level of expenditure makes good business sense—sometimes even in the face of an adverse economic climate.

IN A RECESSION, THE BEST DEFENSE IS A GOOD OFFENSE.

It's a recession. Your instincts demand that you cut the ad budget. But, as the McGraw-Hill Research[1] analysis of business-to-business advertising expenditures during the 1981-82 recession shows, it's those with the courage to maintain or increase advertising in a recession who reap a major sales advantage over their competitors who panic and fall back into a defensive posture. And this advantage continues to expand long after the recession is over.

Effects of Advertising in a Recession on Sales (Indices)

Companies that Maintained or Increased Advertising in Both 1981 and 1982

Companies that Eliminated or Decreased Advertising in Both 1981 and 1982

Year	Maintained/Increased	Eliminated/Decreased
1980	100	100
1981	137	96
1982	159	88
1983	195	89
1984	283	106
1985	375	119

McGraw-Hill Research, 1986.

Recessions last an average of 11 months, but any advertising decision made during one can have permanent repercussions. The McGraw-Hill study demonstrates that nervous advertisers lose ground to the brave and can't gain it back. In 1980, according to the chart seen here, sales indices were identical, but by 1985 the brave had racked up a 3.2 to 1 sales advantage. A similar study done by McGraw-Hill during the 1974-75 recession corroborates the 1980's research.

A recession is the single greatest period in which to make short- and long-term gains. And, surprisingly, increasing advertising modestly during one has much the same effect on your profits as cutting advertising does. According to The Center for Research & Development's October 1990 study of consumer advertising during a recession, advertisers who yield "to the natural inclination to cut spending in an effort to increase profits in a recession find that it doesn't work."[2] This study, relying on the PIMS[3] database, also uncovered that aggressive recessionary advertisers picked up 4.5 *times* as much market share gain as their overcautious competitors, leaving them in a far better position to exploit the inevitable recovery and expansion.

Chevrolet countered its competitors during the 1974-75 recession by aggressively beefing up its ad spending and attained a two percent market share increase. Today, two share points in the automotive industry are worth over $4 billion. Delta Airlines and Revlon also boosted ad spending in the 1974-75 recession and achieved similar results.

Continuous advertising sustains market leadership. And it's far easier to sustain momentum than it is to start it up again. Consider this list of market category leaders: Campbell's, Coca-Cola, Ivory, Kellogg, Kodak, Lipton and Wrigley. This is the leadership list for 1925. And 1990. These marketers have maintained a relentless commitment to their brands in both good times and bad. Kellogg had the guts to pump up its ad spending during the Great Depression and cemented a market leadership it has yet to relinquish.

These are the success stories. Space and diplomacy don't allow the mention of the names of those who lacked gusto and chose to cut their ad spending in recessionary times.

But if you would like to learn more about how advertising can help make the worst of times the best of times, please write to Department C, American Association of Advertising Agencies, 666 Third Avenue, New York, New York 10017, enclosing a check for five dollars. You will receive a booklet covering the pertinent research done on all the U.S. recessions since 1923. Please allow 4 to 6 weeks for delivery.

[1] McGraw-Hill Research, 1986. [2] The Center for Research and Development ©1990.
[3] Profit Impact of Market Strategies, The Strategic Planning Institute, Cambridge, MA.

AAAA

EXHIBIT 7-17

This ad by the American Association of Advertising Agencies makes a very persuasive case for continuing to advertise—even increasing advertising—during a recession.

An Investment in Future Sales

Accountants and Internal Revenue Service agents consider advertising a current business expense. Consequently, many executives treat advertising as a budget item to be trimmed or eliminated like other expense items when sales are either extremely high or extremely low. Although this is certainly understandable, it is also regrettable.

The cost of a new plant or distribution warehouse is considered an investment in the company's future ability to produce and distribute products. Similarly, advertising—as one element of the promotion mix—should be considered an investment in future sales. While advertising is often used to stimulate immediate sales, its greatest power is in its cumulative long-range effect.

Advertising builds a consumer preference and promotes goodwill. This, in turn, enhances the reputation and value of the company name. At first, advertising may move a person to buy a new kind of potato chip, but it also affects that person's next purchase of potato chips, and the one after that, and the one after that. This same advertising may also influence the consumer to try the firm's other snacks.

Thus, while advertising may be considered a current expense for accounting purposes, it can also be considered a long-term capital investment. For management to consider advertising as an investment, however, it must have some understanding of the relationship between advertising and sales and profits.

Relationship of Advertising to Sales and Profits

As we have discussed previously, many internal and external variables influence the effectiveness of a company's marketing and advertising efforts. Moreover, the research methodology that measures the relationships between advertising and sales, and between sales and profit, is far from perfect and can give only rough estimates. However, enough data are available to verify certain facts:

☐ In consumer goods marketing, increases in market share are more closely related to increases in the marketing budget than to price reduction strategies—and market share is a prime indicator of profitability.[24]

☐ Sales normally increase if there is additional advertising. At some point, however, the rate of return will decline. (See Ad Lab 7-D, "How Economists View the Effect of Advertising on Sales.")

☐ Sales response to advertising may build over time, but the durability of advertising is brief, so a consistent investment in advertising is important.[25]

☐ There are minimum levels below which advertising expenditures will have no effect on sales.

☐ There will be some sales even if there is no advertising.

☐ There are saturation limits imposed by culture and competition above which no amount of advertising can push sales.

To management, these facts, verified by numerous studies, might be interpreted into simple advice on how to allocate funds for advertising: Spend more until it stops working. But in reality, the issue is not that simple. It is actually full of complexities. For instance, advertising is not the only marketing activity that affects sales. Increased sales or market share may be due to perceived product quality and consumer word of mouth.[26] It might also be related to new-product introductions, the opening of more attractive

AD LAB 7-D

How Economists View the Effect of Advertising on Sales

Normally, the quantity sold will depend on the number of dollars the company spends advertising the product. And within reasonable limits (if its advertising program is not too repugnant), the more dollars spent on advertising, the more a company will sell—up to a point. Yet, even the most enthusiastic advertising agency will admit, reluctantly, that it is possible to spend too much on advertising.

To decide rationally how much to spend on this part of its marketing effort, management obviously should know just how quantity demanded is affected by advertising expenditure—how much more it will be able to sell per additional dollar of advertising and when additional advertising dollars cease being effective. It needs to have, not a fixed number representing potential demand, but a graph or a statistical equation describing the relationship between sales and advertising.

Notice that in our illustration most of the curve goes uphill as we move to the right (it has a positive slope). This means that additional advertising will continue to bring in business until (at a budget of x million dollars) people become so saturated by the message that it begins to repel them and turn them away from the product.

Even if the saturation level cannot be reached within the range of outlays the firm can afford, the curve is likely to level off, becoming flatter and flatter as the amount spent on advertising gets larger and larger and saturation is approached. The point at which the curve begins to flatten is the point at which returns from advertising begin to diminish. When the total advertising budget is small, even a

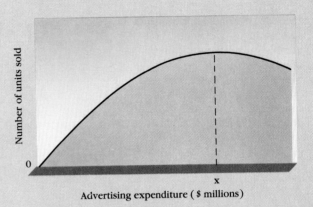

$1 addition to the campaign may bring in as much as $10 in new sales and so be very much worthwhile to the firm. But when the market approaches saturation, each additional dollar may contribute only 30 cents in new sales, and that is not sound business.

Laboratory Applications

1. Can you give an example of when the advertising expenditure curve would have a negative slope?

2. Economists suggest that the quantity sold depends on the number of dollars the company spends on advertising. Is that a safe assumption? Discuss.

outlets, better personal selling, or seasonal changes in the general business cycle.

Furthermore, most companies do not have a clear-cut way to determine the relationship between sales and profit. What if the company sells many products? Then we have the problem of determining which advertising is contributing to which product.

One thing remains clear. Since the response to advertising is spread out over an extended time, advertising should be viewed as a long-term investment in the company's future profits. Like all expenditures, advertising should be evaluated for wastefulness. But historically, companies that make advertising the scapegoat during periods of economic fluctuation invariably end up discovering they have lost substantial market share when the economy returns to stable growth.[27]

The Variable Environments of Business

Every business operates in several environments simultaneously, and the way the company relates to these environments may determine its success or failure. Before attempting to determine the advertising allocation, therefore,

EXHIBIT 7-18

This Canadian ad for the Bermuda Department of Tourism takes up-to-the-minute note of the economic environment in which its tourist industry operates. More favorable exchange rates will make Canadians more willing to travel to Bermuda. Therefore, just in case they aren't drawn by the island's many charms, they will have a rational reason to visit—they'll get more for their money than they did the year before.

the advertising manager must consider the status of the economic, political, social, and legal environments. The level of general economic activity, social customs and attitudes, and the tax structures all affect both total industry sales and corporate profits on sales. Economic conditions, for example, were certainly a consideration in the creation of the ad in Exhibit 7-18.

The manager must consider the institutional and competitive environments. What is the level of sales within the industry? The company can expect only a share of the total market demand. What activities of competitors might either help or hinder the company from making sales and achieving profits?

Finally, the manager should consider the internal environment. The activities of the company itself in relation to its competitors and its markets will have a bearing on the effectiveness of advertising expenditures.

A thorough reappraisal of these factors at the time the advertising allocation is determined may profoundly affect how much the company feels it can or should allocate and on what particular activities.

Methods of Allocating Funds

The typical attitude of business executives toward the advertising budget is relatively simple to understand. They will spend more money as long as they can be assured it will bring in a profit. If one more dollar in advertising will produce one more penny of profit, isn't it worth the expense? However, that point of equilibrium is hard to predict in advance when advertising budgets are being developed.

Over the years, a number of methods have been developed to help companies determine how much to spend on advertising. The most common of these are the percentage-of-sales, percentage-of-profit, unit-of-sale, competitive-parity, share-of-market, and task methods. (See the Checklist of Ways to Set Advertising Budgets.)

Some organizations rely solely on one technique, while others use several in combination. Recently, the tendency has been to shy away from the simpler methods of the past, such as percentage of sales, and to use more sophisticated methods. However, no technique for allocating advertising funds is adequate for all situations. The three methods discussed in this section are

Checklist of Ways to Set Advertising Budgets

☐ *Percentage of sales.* Advertising budget determined by allocating a percentage of last year's sales, anticipated sales for next year, or a combination of the two. The percentage is usually based on an industry average, on company experience, or else arbitrarily.

☐ *Percentage of profit.* Similar to percentage of sales except that percentage is applied to profit—either past years' or anticipated.

☐ *Unit of sale.* Also called the *case-rate method,* this is another variation of percentage of sales. Specific dollar amount is set for each box, case, barrel, or carton produced. Used primarily in assessing members of horizontal cooperatives or trade associations.

☐ *Competitive parity.* Allocates dollars according to the amounts spent by major competitors. Also called *self-defense method.*

☐ *Share of market/share of voice.* Allocates advertising dollars by maintaining a percentage share of total industry advertising comparable to or somewhat ahead of its percentage share of market. Often used for new-product introductions.

☐ *Objective/task method.* Also referred to as the *budget buildup method,* this method has three steps: defining objectives, determining strategy, and estimating the cost to execute that strategy.

☐ *Empirical research method.* By running a series of experimental tests in different markets with different budgets, companies determine which is the most efficient level of expenditure.

☐ *Quantitative mathematical models.* Computer-based programs developed by certain major advertisers and agencies that rely on input of sophisticated data, history, and assumptions.

☐ *All available funds method.* Go-for-broke technique generally used by small firms with limited capital who are trying to introduce new products or services.

---

primarily those used to arrive at national advertising budgets. Additional techniques used by retailers, who operate under a different set of variables, are discussed in Chapter 17, "Local Advertising."

Percentage-of-Sales Method

The **percentage-of-sales method** is one of the most popular techniques used to set the advertising appropriation. It may be based on a percentage of last year's sales, anticipated sales for next year, or a combination of the two. Businesspeople like this method because it is the simplest, it doesn't cost them anything, it is related to revenue, and it is considered safe. The problem is knowing what percentage to use. As Exhibit 7-19 (p. 272) shows, even among leaders within the same industry, percentages allocated to advertising vary widely.

Usually, the percentage is based on an industry average or on company experience. Unfortunately, it is too often determined arbitrarily. The problem of using an industry average is that it assumes that every company in the industry has similar objectives and faces the same marketing problems. When the percentage is based on company history, it assumes that the market is highly static, which is rarely the case.

However, this method does have some advantages. When applied against future sales, it often works well. It assumes that a certain number of dollars are needed to sell a certain number of units. If the advertiser knows what that percentage is, the correlation between advertising and sales should remain constant if the market is stable and competitors' advertising remains relatively unchanged. Furthermore, management tends to think in terms of percentages, whether income or outgo. They think of advertising in the same way, so

EXHIBIT 7-19   Advertising Expenditures by the Top 25 Leading Advertisers, 1990 ($ in millions)

Category	Rank	Company	U.S. advertising expenditures	U.S. sales	Advertising as percent of U.S. sales
Automotive	21	Chrysler Corp.	$ 528.4	$26,887	2.0
	16	Ford Motor Company	616.0	56,902	1.1
	4	General Motors Corp.	1,502.8	86,967	1.7
	17	Toyota Motor Corp.	580.7	N/A	N/A
Cameras and film	11	Eastman Kodak	664.8	10,118	6.6
Pharmaceuticals	25	American Home Products	415.4	4,608	9.0
	24	Bristol-Myers Squibb	428.7	7,017	6.1
	12	Johnson & Johnson	653.7	5,427	12.1
	15	Warner Lambert	630.8	2,445	25.8
Restaurants and food	8	McDonald's Corp.	764.1	3,871	19.7
	20	General Mills	539.0	6,377	8.5
	5	Grand Metropolitan PLC	882.6	8,025	11.0
	18	Kellogg Co.	577.7	3,044	19.0
	14	Nestlé SA	635.9	N/A	N/A
	13	RJR Nabisco	636.1	12,125	5.3
Retail	9	Kmart Corp.	693.2	32,070*	2.2
	3	Sears, Roebuck & Co.	1,507.1	55,972*	2.7
Soaps and cleaners	1	Procter & Gamble Co.	2,284.5	15,276	15.0
	19	Unilever N.V.	568.9	8,680	6.6
Soft drinks	6	PepsiCo Inc.	849.1	14,047	6.0
Publishing and entertainment	10	Time Warner	676.9	8,550	7.9
	23	Walt Disney	435.7	5,844*	7.5
Telephone	7	AT&T	796.5	37,285*	2.1
Tobacco	2	Philip Morris Cos.	2,210.2	36,014	6.1
Wine, beer, and liquor	22	Anheuser-Busch Cos.	459.2	11,612*	6.1

* Indicates worldwide sales

this method is simple. Also, because this method is common in the industry, it diminishes the likelihood of competitive warfare.

The greatest shortcoming of the percentage-of-sales method is that it violates a basic marketing principle. Marketing activities are supposed to stimulate demand and, thus, sales; marketing activities are not supposed to occur as a result of sales. And if advertising automatically increases when sales increase and declines when sales decline, it ignores all the other environments of business that might be suggesting a totally opposite move. It may also become simply a self-fulfilling prophecy.

Share-of-Market/Share-of-Voice Method

In markets with very similar products, a high correlation usually exists between a company's share of the market and its share of industry advertising. Knowing this, some firms set a goal for a certain portion of the market and then apply the same percentage of industry advertising dollars to their budget.

The **share-of-market/share-of-voice method,** which was developed by J. O. Peckham, executive vice president of the A. C. Nielsen Company, has the advantage of being a bold attempt to achieve a sales objective.[28] According to Peckham, a company's best chance of holding its share of the market is to keep a share of advertising (voice) somewhat ahead of its market share. For example, if you have a 30 percent share of the market, you should spend 35 percent of the industry's advertising dollars. Of course, one shortcoming is that there is no guarantee your competitors will not increase their advertising budgets.

The share of market/share-of-voice method is commonly used for new products.[29] According to Peckham's formula, when a new product brand is introduced, the advertising budget for the first two years should be about one and a half times the brand's targeted share of the market in two years. This means that if the company's two-year sales goal is 10 percent of the market, it should spend about 15 percent of the industry's advertising during the first two years.

The share-of-market method assumes that to gain share of market, you must spend more than your share of advertising dollars to first gain a share of the consumer's mind. This is a logical approach to budgeting strategy. However, one hazard of this method is the tendency to become complacent. Companies compete on more than one basis, and advertising is just one tool of the marketing mix. Therefore, simply maintaining a higher percentage of media exposure will usually not be enough to accomplish the desired results.[30] Despite the body of thought that sales promotion diminishes the consumer perception of a product's value, national packaged goods marketers still spend 69 percent of their marketing budgets on consumer and trade promotion rather than on consumer advertising.[31] Thus, companies must maintain an awareness of *all* the marketing activities of their competitors, not just advertising.

Objective/Task Method

The **objective/task method** is also known as the **budget buildup method.** In recent years, it has gained considerable popularity and is now used by the majority of major national advertisers in the United States and Canada.[32] It is one of the few logical means of determining advertising allocations. It defines the objectives and how advertising is to be used to accomplish them. It considers advertising a marketing tool to generate sales.[33]

The task method has three steps: defining the objectives, determining strategy, and estimating the cost. After specific, quantitative marketing objectives have been set, the advertiser develops programs to be used in attaining them. If the objective is to increase the number of coffee cases sold by 10 percent, the advertiser determines which advertising approach will work best, how often ads are to run, and which media to use. The proposed cost of this program is determined and becomes the basis for the advertising budget. It is necessary to consider this budget in light of the company's financial position, of course. If the cost is too high, the objectives may have to be scaled down. Likewise, after the campaign has run, if the results are better or worse than anticipated, the next budget may require appropriate revisions.

The task method forces companies to think in terms of goals and whether they are being accomplished. Its effectiveness is most apparent when the results of particular ads or campaigns can be readily measured. Due to its nature, the task is adaptable to changing conditions in the market and easily revised as dictated by results.

Although it is easy to look back and determine whether money was spent wisely, it is often very difficult to determine in advance the amount of money needed to reach a specific goal. This is the major drawback to the task method. Likewise, although techniques for measuring the effect of advertising are improving, they are still weak in many areas. As techniques become more exact, though, advertisers are using the task method more and more.

Additional Methods

There are several other methods for allocating funds that advertisers use to varying degrees. The **empirical research method** uses experimentation to determine the best level of advertising expenditure. By running a series of tests in different markets with different budgets, companies determine which is the most efficient level of expenditure.[34]

Since the introduction of computers, there has been a great deal of interest in the use of **quantitative mathematical models** for budgeting and allocating advertising dollars. Foote, Cone & Belding, for example, developed a response-curve database from tracking studies on more than 40 clients' products and services. This program analyzes media programs and estimates customer response.[35] Many other sophisticated techniques have also been developed to facilitate various activities such as marketing and advertising planning, budget allocation across multiple product offerings, new-product introductions, and media analysis.[36] However, for the most part, these models are not easily understood by line executives, and each typically relies on data that may be unavailable or on estimated relationships between uncertain variables.[37] Therefore, while they are now widely employed by major national advertisers, they typically require very sophisticated users and, for the most part, are still too expensive for the average business to obtain.

The Bottom Line

All these methods potentially assume one of two fallacies. The first fallacy is that advertising is a result of sales. Advertisers know this is not true, and yet the widespread use of the percentage-of-sales method indicates that many businesspeople think advertising should be a result of sales.

The second fallacy is that advertising creates sales. Only in rare circumstances (where direct-action advertising is used) can advertising be said to create sales. Advertising locates prospects and stimulates demand. It may even stimulate inquiries. Salespeople likewise may locate prospects and stimulate demand. They also close the sale. But, in reality, only customers create sales. It is the customer's choice to buy or not to buy the product, not the company's choice.

The job of advertising is to inform, persuade, and remind. In that way, advertising affects sales. However, advertising is just one part of the whole, and advertising managers must keep this in mind when preparing their plans and their budgets for management.

Summary

The marketing plan may be the most important document a company possesses. It assembles in one place all the pertinent facts about a company, the markets it serves, its products, and its competition and brings all these facts up-to-date. It sets specific goals and objectives to be attained and describes the precise strategies that will be used to achieve them. Thus, it musters all the company's forces for the marketing battlefield and in so doing dictates the role of advertising in the marketing mix and provides focus for advertising creativity.

The marketing plan should contain four principal sections: situation analysis, marketing objectives, marketing strategy, and action programs. A company's marketing objectives should be logical deductions from an analysis of its current situation, its prediction of future trends, and its understanding of corporate objectives. They should relate to the needs of specific target markets and specify sales objectives. The sales-target objectives should be specific, quantitative, and realistic.

The first step in developing a marketing strategy is to select the target market. The second step is to determine a cost-effective marketing mix for each target market the company pursues. The marketing mix is determined by how the company uses the 4 Ps of product, price, place, and promotion. Advertising is one of the promotional tools companies may use.

Advertising is a natural outgrowth of the marketing plan, and the advertising plan is prepared in much the same way as the marketing plan. It includes a section on analysis, advertising objectives, and strategy.

Advertising objectives may be expressed in terms of moving prospective customers up through the advertising pyramid (awareness, comprehension, conviction, desire, action). Or they may be expressed in terms of generating inquiries, coupon response, or attitude change.

The advertising (or creative) strategy is determined by the advertiser's use of the creative mix. The creative mix is composed of the (1) target audience, (2) product concept, (3) communications media, and (4) advertising message. The target audience includes the specific groups of people the advertising will address. It is usually larger than the target market. The product concept refers to the bundle of product-related values the advertiser presents to the customer. The communications media are the vehicles used to transmit the advertiser's message. The advertising message is what the company plans to say in its advertisements and how it plans to say it. One way for small companies to accomplish the marketing and advertising planning task is to work from the bottom up—taking an ingenious tactic and building a strategy around it.

Several methods are commonly used for allocating funds to advertising. Historically, the most popular method has been the percentage-of-sales approach. Other approaches include the share-of-market/share of voice method and the objective/task method. The latter involves defining the advertising objective, determining the strategy, and estimating the cost to conduct that strategy.

Questions for Review and Discussion

1. What is a marketing plan and why is it possibly the most important document in a company?

2. What examples can you give to show the difference between market-need objectives and sales-target objectives?

3. What basic elements should be included in any marketing plan?

4. What examples can you give to show how one person's strategy might become another person's objective?

5. What is the most important consideration in developing any marketing strategy?

6. What are the elements of an advertising plan and an advertising strategy?

7. How can bottom-up marketing be used by small companies that want to become big companies?

8. What is the best method of allocating funds for advertising a real estate development? Why?

9. What types of companies would tend to use the percentage-of-sales method? Why?

10. How could a packaged foods manufacturer use the share-of-market/share-of-voice method to determine its advertising budget?

CREATING ADVERTISEMENTS AND COMMERCIALS

Once advertising objectives and strategies have been determined, the advertiser can turn to developing message strategy and creating ads and commercials. Part III looks at ad creation from three sides: verbal (copywriting), nonverbal (art direction), and the actual production of ads (both print and electronic media).

Chapter 8 introduces the copywriter as a creator of advertising messages and explains how the copy platform is developed. The focus is on the big idea as the key to creativity and on methods for developing ideas. The copywriter's pyramid is given as a model of the objectives of good copy. Key copywriting terms are introduced, and the integral parts of an ad are explained.

Chapter 9 first defines *art* in advertising and then presents the role of art in print, radio, and TV advertising and package design. The terms and steps in the layout of print advertising are presented, with in-depth discussion of advertising visuals. Finally, the role of art in creating various types of radio and television commercials is discussed.

Chapter 10 depicts the complexity of print production and the dynamic impact of computerization. It focuses on typography as a key communication device in advertising. The chapter explores the printing process in detail and the advantages and limitations of various printing methods. Finally, it shows how a successful consumer goods ad was created from concept through production.

Chapter 11 presents an overview of radio and TV commercial production. Techniques used in radio advertising and the production process are shown. Likewise, the various types of TV commercials are presented, with an in-depth look at the production process. Finally, the chapter examines how one famous and popular TV commercial came to life from initial concept through final production.

Enlightened Inspiration

Bending Rules.
Schoolbook Hillbilly Schoolbook Hillbilly
hy–phen–a–tion hy-phen-a-tion
Art Dept., 322 Forest Ave., Suite No. 7, Bldg. 2, Palo Alto, CA 90431
Art Dept., 322 Forest Ave., Suite No. 7, Bldg. 2, Palo Alto, CA 90431
"Type is to read." "Type is to read."
"Design is an attitude." "Design is an attitude."
(x-height) (X-HEIGHT) (x-height) (X-HEIGHT)
378 CAMBRIDGE AVENUE P.O. BOX 3260 PALO ALTO, CA 94306 PHONE 408-932-1010
378 CAMBRIDGE AVENUE P.O. BOX 3260 PALO ALTO, CA 94306 PHONE 408-932-1010
First National, Inc. 8701 Embarcadero Road Menlo Park, CA 94203 714-258-7201
First National, Inc. 8701 Embarcadero Road Menlo Park, CA 94203 714-852-7201
MAY 1987
JUNE 1987
JULY 1987
AUGUST 1987
ALIGN-MENT OF TYPE SHOULD ALWAYS BE DONE OPTICALLY, RATHER THAN MECHANI-CALLY
ALIGN-MENT OF TYPE SHOULD ALWAYS BE DONE OPTICALLY, RATHER THAN MECHANI-CALLY
Herb Lubalin (1918-1981) —art director, graphic designer, and typographer— was presented a knotted T-square from his design staff in the early 60's with the inscription, "To Herb Lubalin for successfully ignoring this instrument for so many years." This poster is dedicated to him for bending and breaking typographic rules to make typography a better communication tool. Special thanks to Alan Peckolick of Alan Peckolick & Associates, New York, for the rights to use the image of the T-square.
This poster was produced using POSTSCRIPT. All typefaces shown are from the Adobe Type Library. For a complete listing of our current typefaces, please write to Adobe Systems Incorporated, 1870 Embarcadero Road, Palo Alto, CA 94303. (800) 29-ADOBE. In California (800) 85-ADOBE.
ADOBE SYSTEMS INCORPORATED

CREATIVE COPYWRITING

SEE THE ONLY ATHLETES WHO SCRATCH THEMSELVES MORE THAN BASEBALL PLAYERS.

Come to this year's Dog-Frisbee Championship and you'll see some great throwing, running, and catching. Not to mention some embarrasing sniffing, scratching, and licking.

THE ASHLEY WHIPPET DOG FRISBEE CHAMPIONSHIPS
For more information, call 1-800-423-3268, or write P.O. Box 16279, Encino, CA. 91416

Objective: To describe the role of the copywriter as a creator of advertising messages. Since the advertising message is a key element of advertising strategy, it is important to understand how research and advertising planning affect what the copywriter writes. Students need to understand the key terms used in creating both print and broadcast ads and what is required to create effective advertising copy. And finally, they should recognize the common problems and pitfalls in copywriting.

After studying this chapter, you will be able to:

☐ Explain how important copywriting is to advertising.

☐ Describe the role of the copywriter in relation to other team members involved in the creation of an advertisement.

☐ Discuss the five objectives of copy in an advertisement and point out the role of each objective in communicating the complete message.

☐ Identify the parts of an advertisement and describe how they relate to the objectives of advertising copywriting.

☐ Define the various types of headlines and the elements that make up body copy.

☐ Discuss and debate the common pitfalls in writing copy.

☐ Explain the process of copywriting from start to final copy.

History teaches us a lot—even about advertising. Here's a history lesson, compliments of Henry Ford.

Back in 1910, Ford had spent over five years and untold thousands of dollars to perfect his new Model T automobile. Now the first cars were ready, and it was time to advertise. But what sort of ad should he run? Ads at that time were mostly artwork or photos with few, if any, words. But Ford believed art alone couldn't sell his Model T. It had to be described—in detail.

A few weeks later, readers of the *Saturday Evening Post* were startled to see a black-and-white ad, two pages long, that contained no pictures. Instead, it was all words!

"When Ford speaks the world listens."

"Buy a Ford car because it is better—not because it is cheaper."

"The reason why can be given in a very few words . . ."

The "very few words" totaled about 1,200. They told how Henry Ford invented the Model T. They detailed the financial condition of the Ford Company. And they listed its 28 factories, assembly plants, and branches.

Ford did everything he could to make people want to read the ad—except show a picture. The language was simple and direct. The headlines and subheads were long, but provocative. The ad was laid out in an easy-to-follow editorial style with short paragraphs and many subheadings in bold type. There was even a panel on the right with a coupon at the bottom—to mail in for more information (see Exhibit 8-1).

The ad was a first. It contained more words—or **copy**—than any ad of the day. It also caused some industry leaders to rebuke Ford. "Pictures sell cars," one said flatly, "not words."

EXHIBIT 8-1

This 1910 advertisement, written by Henry Ford himself over the protests of all the "experts," contained 1,200 words—the longest copy of any advertisement of its time. It also sold more autos than any ad in previous history.

But Ford stood his ground and proved he was right. And what he proved still holds true today: Words do sell.

COPYWRITING AND ADVERTISING STRATEGY

Henry Ford's primary advertising objective was to inform prospective customers about the new Model T and convince them it was the best automobile buy on the market. In addition, he hoped to stimulate desire and action on the part of some readers to test-drive the new Ford car—or at least to mail in the coupon for a brochure and additional information. The ad's tremendous success was indicated by the number of requests Ford received for information on the car and by the substantial increase in sales. In fact, the ad was soon credited with stimulating more sales than any other auto ad in history. And it gave Henry Ford his "jump-start" toward what was to become, 10 years later, the largest and most profitable manufacturing company in the world. But what was the creative strategy that enabled Ford's ad to achieve that success?

A review of Chaper 7 reminds us that advertising or creative strategy consists of four elements:

1. The target audience.
2. The product concept.
3. The communications media.
4. The advertising message.

Who was Ford's target audience? In this case, it consisted of the millions of U.S wage earners who had never owned an automobile—people making their first purchase. These were people who wanted a reliable car but who couldn't afford to pay $1,900 for a Hudson automobile or some other make. The average salary in those days was around $20 per week.

What was the product concept? Even back then, the product concept was more than just the functional product—the Model T. The ad tells us the Ford Motor Company was already presenting a product concept that included economy, quality, reliability, and service in a brand-new, state-of-the-art transportation package.

The communications media included print media—newspapers and magazines—like the *Saturday Evening Post*. There wasn't any radio yet, much less TV; so these were the mass media of the day.

What was the advertising message—or message strategy? **Message strategy** is determined by what the company wants to communicate and how it wants to express the message. Ford wanted to convey the message that here, finally, was a car the average family could afford, that it was reliable, and that the Ford Motor Company would stand behind this car with quality service.

How to communicate that concept involved developing a *verbal* and *nonverbal* presentation of the message that would be simple, interesting, informative, entertaining, enjoyable, and helpful.

In Chapter 9, "Creative Art Direction," we will discuss the nonverbal, graphic side of message strategy. The subject of this chapter, **copywriting,** concerns the verbal element of message strategy. The combined product of the art director and the copywriter is the creative nucleus, which is then translated through the production process into the final advertisement or commercial.

Elements of Message Strategy

Before the copywriter starts to think about writing an ad, he or she must understand the marketing and advertising strategies completely. This includes the message strategy. If the advertising plan has not spelled it out in detail (which is often the case for smaller advertisers), the copywriter should immediately build a message strategy, in collaboration with the art director if possible (or creative director, if there is one) and get it approved before going any further. The fastest way to have an ad rejected is to write a brilliant, creative piece of work that has nothing to do with the strategy set for the campaign.

The message strategy includes three specific elements:

☐ Copy platform—what you're going to say and how you're going to say it.

☐ Art direction—what you're going to show and how you're going to show it.

☐ Production values—what you're going to create mechanically and how you're going to create it.

To develop these elements, the copywriter and the art director (often under the direction of a creative director) need first to review the marketing and advertising plan, analyze the facts, and study the market, the product, and the competition. (See the Checklist of Product Marketing Facts for Copywriters on p. 282.) All through this process, input—and often direction—from agency account executives and account managers and from client sales, marketing, product managers, or research people is very helpful.

Certain basic questions should be asked and answered: How is the market segmented? How will the product be positioned? Who are the best prospects for the product? Is the target audience different than the target market? What is the key consumer benefit? What is the product's (or company's) current image?

At this point, research data are important. Research identifies the best prospects; it identifies the best strategy; it can find the most important consumer appeals or product claims. *What* the advertising says is often more important than *how* it is said. But the reverse can also be true. So, as we discussed in Chapter 6, the message strategy should be tested.

Writing the Copy Platform

In developing the message strategy, the copywriter (or the creative director) needs to create the **copy platform,** a document that serves as the creative team's guide for writing and producing the ad.[1] The copy platform is a written strategy statement about the most important issues to be considered in the advertisement or the campaign—the *who, why, what,* and *how* of the advertising:

1. *Who is the most likely prospect for the product?* The copy platform must define the prospect tightly in terms of demographic, psychographic, and behavioristic qualities. If possible, it should describe the typical prospect's personality.

2. *Why?* Does the consumer have specific wants or needs that should be appealed to? In Chapter 5, we discussed some of the many types of **appeals,** or approaches, advertisers use to communicate need satisfaction.

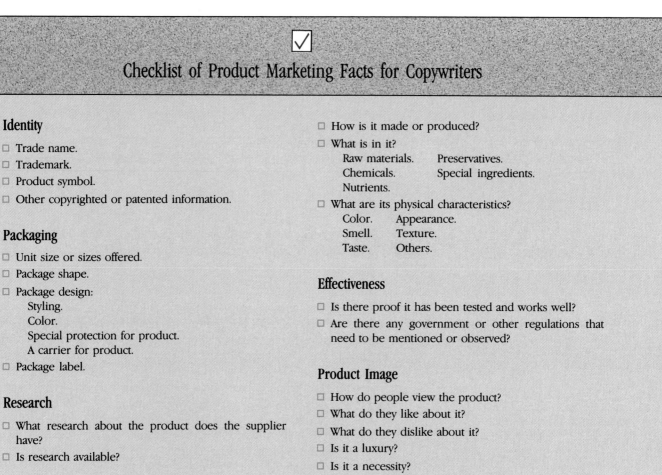

✓

Checklist of Product Marketing Facts for Copywriters

Identity

☐ Trade name.
☐ Trademark.
☐ Product symbol.
☐ Other copyrighted or patented information.

Packaging

☐ Unit size or sizes offered.
☐ Package shape.
☐ Package design:
   Styling.
   Color.
   Special protection for product.
   A carrier for product.
☐ Package label.

Research

☐ What research about the product does the supplier have?
☐ Is research available?

Performance

☐ What does it do?
☐ What might it be expected to do that it does *not*?
☐ How does it work?

☐ How is it made or produced?
☐ What is in it?
   Raw materials.   Preservatives.
   Chemicals.   Special ingredients.
   Nutrients.
☐ What are its physical characteristics?
   Color.   Appearance.
   Smell.   Texture.
   Taste.   Others.

Effectiveness

☐ Is there proof it has been tested and works well?
☐ Are there any government or other regulations that need to be mentioned or observed?

Product Image

☐ How do people view the product?
☐ What do they like about it?
☐ What do they dislike about it?
☐ Is it a luxury?
☐ Is it a necessity?
☐ Is it a habit?
☐ Is it self-indulgent?
☐ Do people have to have it but wish they didn't?

The two broadest categories are **rational appeals** and **emotional appeals.** The former is an appeal to the consumer's practical, functional need for the product or service. The latter relates to the consumer's psychological, social, or symbolic needs. Other types of appeals used by advertisers may fall into one of these two broad categories. These include positive and negative appeals, fear and sex appeals, humor appeals, and quantitative or qualitative appeals, among others. For a sampling of possible advertising appeals, see Exhibit 8-2. Depending on the overall message strategy, any or all of these appeals may be used to gain attention, create a personality for the product or service, and stimulate consumer interest, credibility, desire, and action.

3. *What product features satisfy the consumers' needs?* What kinds of support are there for the product claim? What is the product's position? What personality or image—of the product or the company—can be or has been created? And what perceived strengths or weaknesses need to be dealt with?[2]

Life Cycle

- ☐ What is its life or use span?

Competitive Information

- ☐ Who are the competitors?
- ☐ Does it have any advantages over them?
- ☐ Does it have any disadvantages?
- ☐ Are they all about the same?
- ☐ Do rival products present problems that this one solves?

Manufacturing

- ☐ How is it made?
- ☐ How long does it take?
- ☐ How many steps in the process?
- ☐ How about the people involved in making it?
- ☐ Are there any special machines used?
- ☐ Where is it made?

History

- ☐ When was it created or invented?
- ☐ Who introduced it?
- ☐ Has it had other names?
- ☐ Have there been product changes?
- ☐ Is there any "romance" to it?

Market Position

- ☐ What is its share of the total market?

Consumer Use

- ☐ How is the product used?
- ☐ Are there other possible uses?
- ☐ How frequently is it bought?
- ☐ What type of person uses the product?
- ☐ Why is the product bought?
  Personal use.
  Gift.
  Work.
- ☐ What type of person uses the product most (heavy user)?
- ☐ What amount of the product is bought by the heavy user?
- ☐ Where does the best customer live?
- ☐ What kind of person is a heavy user or buyer?

Distribution

- ☐ How widely is the product distributed?
- ☐ Are there exclusive sellers?
- ☐ Is there a ready supply or limited amount?
- ☐ Is it available for a short season?

EXHIBIT 8-2   Selected Advertising Appeals

Appetite	Sympathy for others	Novelty
Taste	Devotion to others	Safety
Health	Guilt	Courtesy
Fear	Pride of personal appearance	Rest or sleep
Humor	Home comfort	Economy in use
Security	Pride in appearance of property	Economy in purchase
Cleanliness	Pleasure of recreation	Efficiency in operation or use
Sex attraction	Entertainment	Dependability in use
Romance	Opportunity for more leisure time	Dependability in quality
Social achievement	Avoidance of a laborious task	Durability
Ambition	Enhancement of earnings	Variety of selection
Personal comfort	Style (beauty)	Simplicity
Protection of others	Pride of possession	Sport/play/physical activity
Social approval/approval of others	Curiosity	Cooperation

4. Finally, *how should this be communicated?* What style, approach, or tone will be used in the campaign? And generally, what will the copy say?

The answers to all these questions will help make up a copy platform similar to the one shown in Exhibit 8-3. Later, after the first ad is written, the copywriter should review the copy platform again to see whether the ad measures up. If it doesn't, the writer should reject it and start again.

Developing the Art Direction and Production Values

While the creative team is determining what it wants to say and how it wants to say it, it will also consider the other elements of the message strategy—the nonverbal aspects. We shall examine both art direction and production in the following chapters, but it is important to point out here that the process of developing the elements of message strategy is rarely accomplished step by step. Rather, because they are inevitably intertwined, all the elements normally evolve simultaneously. Most important though, the completed strategy statement is the prerequisite for developing the creative idea the ad or campaign will center on.

The message strategy must ensure that the advertising will be saying the right thing to the right person in the right context in the right tone and in the right manner—and that it will be designed to achieve the advertising objectives set by the advertiser and the agency's account management team. With that in place, we're ready for the next stage of development: getting the idea.[3]

Developing the Big Idea

For all creative people, the idea stage is always the toughest—but it's also the most rewarding. It is the long, tedious, difficult task of assembling all the pertinent information, analyzing the problem, and searching for some verbal or visual concept of how to communicate what needs to be said. It means establishing a mental idea or picture of the advertisement, commercial, or campaign before any copy is written or artwork begun.

The process may be called **visualization** or **conceptualization,** and it is the most important step in creating the advertisement. It is the creative point where the search for the **big idea**—that flash of insight—takes place. The big idea is a bold, creative initiative that "synthesizes the purposes of the strategy, joins the product benefit with consumer desire in a fresh, involving way, brings the subject to life, and makes the reader or the audience stop, look, and listen."[4]

What's the difference between *strategy* and an *idea?* An idea adds meaning, interest, memorability, and drama to what is stated in a strategy document. For example, the copy platform might have read:

Inform suburban families that the new Honda station wagon offers the same style and performance as the popular Honda Accord only with more space and greater power.

But the big idea, shown in Exhibit 8-4 (p. 286), was to show a beautiful, larger-than-life visual of the new vehicle under the simple headline:

More of a good thing.

While strategy requires deduction, an idea requires inspiration.[5]

Henry Ford notwithstanding, the big idea in advertising is rarely just a copywriting idea. It's almost invariably a combination of both art and copy—

COPY PLATFORM

Sunkist Foodservice Lemon Promotion Ad

Request

Sunkist has asked us to produce a 4/C, 1/2 page direct response coupon ad to sell their Sunkist Lemon Tap Promotion to Corporate Cafeterias.

Background

Corporate cafeterias are the number one growth segment in the foodservice industry. To attract this segment, Sunkist foodservice designed a turn-key promotion (a promotion that provides all the directions and materials to make the promotion a success). To sell the promotion initially, Sunkist sent out a direct mail piece which provided information on the promotion and included an order form postcard for requesting the kit. While 7% of the inventory was sold, sales didn't meet Sunkist's expectations. To boost sales, Sunkist has decided to advertise the promotion.

Description of Promotion

A free gift (a lemon tap and recipe booklet) is given to customers in exchange for ordering any food or drink garnished with a Sunkist lemon. Sunkist has assembled a complete promotional kit that helps to easily organize and implement the entire promotion, from start to finish.

Promotion's Value to the Cafeteria

Increases traffic and creates excitement for both cafeteria patrons and personnel.

Advertising Objectives

☐ To motivate the target to buy the promotion via the ad's coupon.
☐ Or, to at least call the Sunkist foodservice hotline and ask any questions.

Key Selling Point

☐ You get everything you need to make the promotion a success. And it's so easy to implement.

Input

1. The ad must provide enough information about the promotion to eliminate any doubts or questions that would prevent the target from clipping the coupon and sending in the $30.00 for it.
2. The coupon is a vital part of the ad. Please refer to the attached copy of the return postcard for the information that the coupon should contain.
3. An 800 number must appear in the ad. The copy should read something like "To order or answer any questions, please call the Sunkist Foodservice hotline at 1-800-221-7318."
4. Foodservice operators like to see what they're buying. Therefore, the visual (or a visual) should show the essential elements of the promotion. Also, all artwork that's used for the promotion is available for us to pick-up.

Media

☐ Publication: *Foodservice Director*
☐ Issue Dates: July 15th & August 15th

EXHIBIT 8-3

This sample copy platform identifies the elements of the message strategy, presents the overall thrust of the advertisement or campaign, and supplies any highly relevant specific information as a guide for the creative staff. From this, the "big idea"—generally in the form of a spirited headline and/or visual—will evolve. The creative director, who most likely was once a writer, is usually responsible for supervising the development of the copy platform.

EXHIBIT 8-4

Honda's big idea for its new station wagon was utter simplicity—typical of Honda advertising over the years. A large, dominant visual of the car and a catchy, word-play headline play off the positive consumer perception of the Honda Accord—the biggest-selling car in the United States. This ad builds immediate awareness and credibility for the new vehicle.

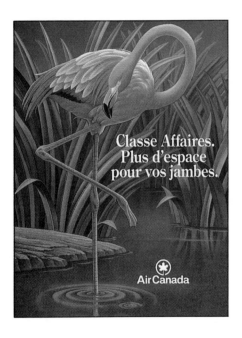

EXHIBIT 8-5

The large, stylized illustration of a flamingo with legs dominating the middle of the ad emphasizes the benefit of more leg room on Air Canada. Note how the pinks play off the greens in this beautifully illustrated poster ad—creating instant awareness and positive feelings.

as we shall discuss more thoroughly in Chapter 9. One strategy, for example, was to inform French-speaking business travelers in Quebec that Air Canada offered the benefit of greater leg room in its executive class. The agency, Cossette Communications, came up with a big idea: show a beautifully rendered, stylized, long-legged flamingo standing in a marsh with a simple yet humorous headline: "Classe affaires. Plus d'espace pour vos jambes." ("Executive class. More space for your legs.") As Exhibit 8-5 shows, the big idea in this case is neither the copy nor the art, but rather the synergistic effect of the two working together. This turned out to be just one of a series of outstanding creative ads that used the big idea of the stylized birds combined with a double entendre headline. Another was a pelican with an overinflated beak pouch. The headline: "Air Canada Cargo."

Big ideas are probably the most important element in advertising. But how do copywriters and art directors come up with big ideas? That question is often asked of the best minds in the business. Creativity, they say, is often the combination of two or more previous ideas, joined or altered to produce a new idea. In fact, the ability to share ideas is what makes teaming creative people so popular.

With some of their many suggestions for developing big ideas, a beginning copywriter could start a very practical tickler file. For example: cash in on your personal experience with the product; learn from the experience of others; talk with the manufacturer; talk with customers (and competitors' customers); study the product (look at it from a different angle); review previous advertising for the product; study competitors' ads (what are they *not* saying?); adapt an idea from an unrelated product category (copywriters and art directors all keep *swipe* files, but don't ever just copy somebody else's idea); examine customer testimonials; exaggerate and then solve the prospect's problem (what is the most important thing to him or her?); brainstorm some outrageous approaches (what flies and carries lots of cargo?); boldly sketch some buzzwords on sheets of paper and tape them to the walls; focus on a single concept and express it simply; write from the heart (get emotional); put your subconscious mind to work to find a relevant metaphor; tell the truth (the unmitigated, whole truth); and develop variations on a successful ad.[6]

For advertisers, recognizing a big idea and evaluating it are almost as difficult as coming up with one.[7] David Ogilvy recommends asking ourselves five questions to evaluate ideas:

1. Did it make me gasp when I first saw it?
2. Do I wish I had thought of it myself?
3. Is it unique?
4. Does it fit the strategy to perfection?
5. Could it be used for 30 years?[8]

As Ogilvy points out, you can count on your fingers the campaigns that have run five years or more. They are the superstars—the campaigns that keep on producing results and memorability through thick and thin: Dove soap (33 percent cleansing cream), Ivory soap (99 44/100 percent pure), Perdue Chickens ("It takes a tough man to make a tender chicken"), U.S. Army ("Be all you can be").

THE COPYWRITER'S PYRAMID: SETTING COPY OBJECTIVES

In Chapter 7, we presented the advertising pyramid as a simple hierarchical model for setting certain kinds of advertising objectives based on how people typically behave. Copywriters can use a similar, five-step structure—with only a slight variation in terminology—as a simple guide for setting copy objectives in writing an advertisement or commercial (see Exhibit 8-6).

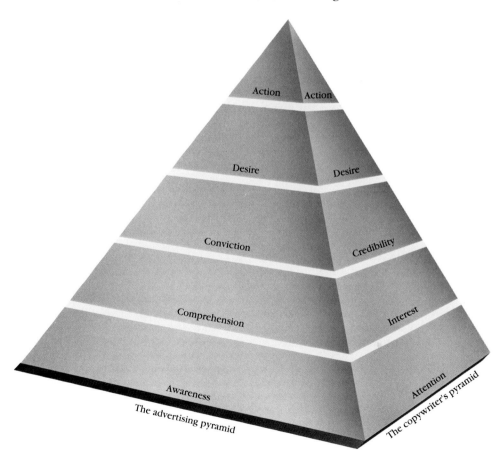

EXHIBIT 8-6

The copywriter's pyramid can help develop copy objectives for an ad or commercial.

The purpose of copywriting is usually to persuade or remind a group or groups of individuals to take some action to satisfy a need or want. But, first, people need to be made aware of the problem or (if the problem is obvious to them) of a solution. To create awareness, the copywriter first has to get people's attention. Next, the prospect's interest in the product has to be stimulated and credibility gained in the product claims. The copywriter then focuses on generating desire and finally on stimulating action. Since these five elements should be present in almost every ad or commercial, let's examine each briefly.

Attention

As we discussed in Chapter 4, an ad or commercial is a stimulus, and breaking through the physiological screens is the first task of the stimulus in creating perception. Attention, therefore, is the first objective of any ad and the fundamental building block in the copywriter's pyramid.

In print advertising, the headline is often the major attention-getting device. For example, the ad in Exhibit 8-7 for Luis Gomez, master dog trainer, is all headline. It uses large type and a didactic statement to catch the eye, and then a provocative question to engage the reader's mind. Many other devices can also be used to gain attention. In print media, these might include

ETHICAL DILEMMA IN ADVERTISING
When Advertisers Dare to Compare

It started in the 1950s when TV housewives began comparing their favorite laundry detergents to the mysterious Brand X. But it wasn't until 1971 that most advertisers dared to compare. That's the year the FTC actually encouraged comparative advertising in the belief that it would help consumers make better choices. By 1987, more than one in three ads identified the competition. Today, there's increased concern about the proliferation of comparative ads, because some advertisers use questionable techniques to outshine the competition, and that means consumers end up being misinformed rather than well-informed.

Academic studies have shown that comparative advertising is risky business at best. Direct comparisons do attract attention for low-share brands, but they often hurt established products by increasing awareness of competitors and fostering brand-name confusion. So there's never a guarantee that comparative advertising will meet its dual goals of consumer education and gaining awareness for the advertiser.

Observers believe the main problem with comparative advertising is that some companies draw erroneous conclusions from dubious data. A good example of how a true statement can create a false impression occurred when Sorrell Ridge took on Smucker's in a TV campaign. The

commercials claimed that Smucker's preserves are made mostly from corn syrup, refined sugar, and a little fruit while stressing that Sorrell's are all fruit and fruit juice. That's true, as far as it goes. But as Smucker's president, Richard Smucker, pointed out, Sorrell had made a fraudulent comparison. "We make an all-fruit product, but their comparisons are against our traditional fruit line."

As competition becomes more cutthroat, things are getting even rougher. As Bob Wolf, vice chairman of Chiat/Day Advertising, notes, "Comparative advertising has become really pointed and mean."

If some advertisers have cast ethical considerations aside, the Trademark Law Revision Act of 1988 now makes it easier for injured parties to sue. The new law prevents advertisers from misrepresenting "another person's goods, services, or commercial activities." Michael Epstein of Weil, Gotshal & Manges notes, "I don't think there's going to be a tenfold increase in suits, but companies will have to be more careful about their advertising."

Debatable comparative ads are particularly easy to create when the comparisons are subjective. Recently, Coca-Cola has taken issue with a number of Pepsi ads that claim Diet Pepsi is the "taste that beats Diet Coke" and "the undisputed champion" of taste. And even seemingly objective data can lead to allegations of unfairness. As one

The attention-getting, boldly visual headline is nearly the whole
ad in this case. On billboards and
in media that are dense with
distractions, getting attention is a
very big hurdle. Can you find the
two errors in punctuation in this
award-winning ad?

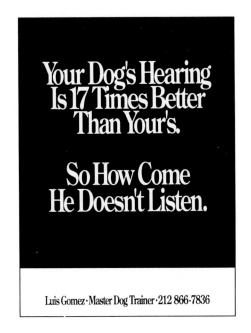

**Your Dog's Hearing
Is 17 Times Better
Than Your's.**

**So How Come
He Doesn't Listen.**

Luis Gomez · Master Dog Trainer · 212 866-7836

marketing executive said, "If you torture the numbers long
enough, they'll talk." Ford, for example, has been critical of
Chevrolet ads that talk about how many people have
switched to Chevy trucks. Ford contends that Chevy's research techniques don't meet professional standards; furthermore, the ads don't say how many people replaced
their Chevrolets with other brands.

Determining whether comparative claims are true can
be very difficult. Each company seems to have its own
research methodology, and all advertisers depend on the
television networks for clearance. One reason so many
dubious claims have been aired is that the networks simply
can't keep up with changing research standards. Moreover,
the networks don't act fast enough when a challenge is
filed. In many cases, disputed ads have been aired for
months while the networks have gone back to check the
data.

To remedy this situation, Coca-Cola has proposed that
an independent agency be created to help advertisers and
networks evaluate comparative claims. Network executives
maintain that such an agency would just add another level
of bureaucracy and make clearance even more time-consuming. Of course, it's the networks' business to clear—
and run—commercials as quickly as possible.

Industry experts believe that as competition increases,
so will comparative advertising. But if the ethical problems
aren't resolved soon, consumers might stop trying to separate the truth from the lies. John Ruhaak, vice president of
advertising for United Airlines, believes that the real bottom line is that advertisers' credibility with consumers is
being jeopardized. "If we try to juggle the facts in our
advertising rather than sell the value of our product, consumers won't believe our brands." If that's true, instead of
searching for craftier ways to make comparative claims,
advertisers should simply devise more ethical ways to
promote their products.

Questions

1. In the Sorrell Ridge-Smucker example given above,
   do you think Sorrell's behavior was unethical even
   though not necessarily illegal? Do you think that
   Sorrell should be compelled to either tell the whole
   truth or drop its comparative advertising claims
   altogether?

2. What guidelines would you use to determine whether
   comparative advertising is fair to both the competition
   mentioned in the ads and to consumers?

dynamic visuals, unusual layout, vibrant color, or dominant ad size; in electronic media, they include special sound effects, music, or visual techniques.

The copywriter has little or no control over some factors. The size of the ad—or length of the commercial—may influence how well or quickly it penetrates the screens, and this is often determined before a copywriter is assigned to write the ad. Similarly, a TV spot's position in a cluster of commercials between shows—or an ad's position in a publication—may determine who will see it. The copywriter must take all these factors into account before deciding on an attention-getting device.

The attention-getting device (e.g., headline, visual) should create drama, with power, impact, and intensity; but it must also be appropriate. It must relate to the product, to the tone of the ad, and to the needs or interests of the intended audience.[9] This is especially true in business-to-business advertising. For example, a manufacturer of laboratory ovens ran an ad with the headline: "The American work ethic is alive and well in Philadelphia." While that was probably good news to patriots and local politicians, not many patriots and politicians are known to be heavy users of laboratory ovens.[10]

Headlines that promise something but fail to deliver will not make a sale; in fact, the advertiser may alienate a potential customer. For example, ads that use racy headlines or nude figures unrelated to the product or sales ideas may attract attention but will often lose sales.

Interest

The second step in writing an advertisement is to create interest. This step relates to the customer's psychological screens. You've gotten your prospect's attention. She's looking at your advertisement. But if you can't keep her interest, you're going to lose her. So you have to talk to her, about her, and about her problems and needs. You may even want to use the word *you* frequently.

Interest is the bridge between attention and credibility. It is an important step. There are several effective ways to build and maintain interest. The copywriter might use cartoon characters or other interior visuals, subheads, storyline copy, or charts and tables. In radio, the copywriter might use an interesting, fast-paced dialogue between two believable characters. Television frequently uses quick cuts from one subject to another to maintain interest in the action—and the outcome—of the commercial. We discuss some of these techniques later in this chapter and in subsequent chapters on advertising production.

Credibility

The next step up the copywriter's pyramid is to establish credibility—often by playing off the consumer's own perceptual files. Research has shown that people read what interests them and ignore what doesn't.[11] At the same time, they are more sophisticated, skeptical, and cynical today than in years past. They may find the comparisons in some ads between Brand X and Brand Y not only irrelevant to their interests, but insulting to their intelligence. In such cases, the ad or commercial fails, and product sales often suffer.

Well-known presenters sometimes lend credibility to commercials. For example, comedian Bill Cosby has been hired to represent a variety of products, including Jell-O and Coke, because of his personable, believable, down-to-earth style. In print ads, advertisers often show independent test results to substantiate product claims. To work, these "proofs" must give honest support and not be the result of statistical manipulation. Advertisers and agencies must remember that there are a lot of consumers out there with extensive product knowledge—even in specialized areas.

Desire

Building the desire block in the copywriter's pyramid is not easy and is often an overlooked step. To heighten desire, advertisers must show the product— or the result of using the product—to great advantage and inform the reader or viewer of the important benefits of the product or service.

One way to nourish desire is to help prospects visualize themselves enjoying the product or service. This is easier to do in television than in print. In newspaper and magazine ads, copywriters may use words and phrases like:

Picture yourself . . .

Imagine . . .

Be the first . . .

The desire step is where the execution skill (in the art, copy, and production) of the advertiser's agency or creative team becomes paramount. Knowing the customer is most important in this step. Each new benefit should heighten desire because it is matched with a real or perceived need of the customer. Even if there is only one benefit, it must be presented in such a way that prospective customers believe it and immediately understand its application to their own needs and situations.

Action

The final step up the copywriter's pyramid is to the action block. Here the purpose is to motivate the reader to do something—to send in a coupon, call the number on the screen, or visit the store—or at least to agree with the advertiser. The action might be immediate or future. Action may be explicit: "Fill out and mail today"; or it may be implicit: "Fly the friendly skies." However it is done, there should be some request for action in the copy, as shown in Exhibit 8-8 (p. 292). The advertiser is asking for the order. But prospects are generally preoccupied; they need a course of action spelled out for them. That's what good copywriting does. (See Ad Lab 8-A, "Applying the Copywriter's Pyramid to Print Advertising," on p. 293.)

UNDERSTANDING THE COPYWRITER'S TERMINOLOGY

All advertisements comprise many elements or components that may be moved, enlarged, reduced, reversed, changed, or eliminated until a new look or approach is achieved. We need to understand these elements, their functions, and the terminology used in copywriting.

In print advertising, the key elements are the *headline,* the *visual, subheads, body copy, boxes and panels, slogans, seals, logotypes (logos),* and *signatures.*

Two devices in this United Way ad help impel the reader to action. First, the highly visible headline strikes an emotional appeal and simultaneously makes a pun about coupons with its use of the word *redeem*. Second, the highly visible coupon is a visual prompt to habitual coupon clippers.

In commercials for electronic media—radio and television—the copy is normally spoken dialogue and is referred to as the **audio** portion of the commercial. The audio may be delivered as a **voice-over** by an announcer who is heard but not seen. Or it may be **on-camera dialogue** by an announcer, a spokesperson, or actors playing out a scene. When copy is actually written on the screen, it may then be described by the same terms used in print advertising, which we shall discuss briefly here. (Copywriting for electronic media has some special aspects, which we discuss more specifically in Chapter 11.)

Headlines

Many advertisers consider the headline the most important element in a print advertisement. The term **headline** refers to the words in the leading position of the advertisement—the words that will be read first or that are positioned to draw the most attention. Therefore, headlines are usually set in larger type than other portions of the advertisement.

Role of Headlines

A headline has numerous functions. First of all, the headline must attract attention to the advertisement—fast. Surveys have shown that it should take only four seconds to capture the reader's attention.[12] Otherwise, the entire message may be lost. To promote its "eternity ring" to husbands, DeBeers used an effective headline:

You once said, "I do."
Now you can say, "I'm glad I did."

AD LAB 8-A
Applying the Copywriter's Pyramid to Print Advertising

Copywriters create awareness and stimulate action by applying the five objectives of advertising copy that are illustrated in the copywriter's pyramid in Exhibit 8-6. Notice how these objectives have been pursued in the ad shown here.

Attention: To grab the reader's eye, the left side of this ad uses a "larger-than-life" photo of the product and a how-to headline in interesting type—with lots of white space.

Interest: The second part of the heading ("to liters") completes the how-to statement in a clever and intriguing way. The reader will want to find out how a measurement of distance can be converted to a measurement of volume.

Credibility: The copy explains how the seemingly contradictory headline can be true. The free offer of the jug indicates to the reader that the manufacturer is interested in his or her business, as does

the offer of a chance to win a prize in the Great Outdoors Giveaway.

Desire: To make the offer even more appealing, the line "You could end up a very happy camper" provides a positive prospect for the readers—allowing them to envision themselves enjoying a weekend in the great outdoors.

Action: The copy explicitly urges that the reader spend $8.00 or more on Stanley tools and also enter the contest.

Laboratory Applications

1. Find an ad that exhibits the five elements of the copywriter's pyramid. (Beware: The desire step may be hard to find.)

2. Why do so many good ads lack one or more of the five elements listed here? How do they overcome the omission?

The Coleman Company, Inc.

BADGE OF THE PROFESSIONAL® The design of the POWERLOCK® Tape Rule case is a registered trademark of The Stanley Works. © 1989 Stanley Tools, Division of The Stanley Works.

HOW TO CONVERT FEET

TO LITERS.

It's a very simple equation. Just buy $8.00 or more of Stanley tools, and we'll give you a coupon good for a 2-liter jug from Coleman. Free.

You'll also get a chance to win the Ultimate Coleman Campsite in the Stanley Great Outdoors Giveaway. So enter today. You could end up a very happy camper.

STANLEY helps you do things right.

BARRY RACKS UP ZZZ's.

MAZDA'S TOO. Barry Wilson of Wilson's Auto Repair has been fixing cars for over twenty years. It's a good bet he can fix yours. At a fair price, too.
Overhauls, electrical, brakes & shocks, tune-ups, lube & oil changes, air conditioning, transmission, clutch, front wheel drive, 24-hour towing.
271-3579 313 Saturn S. of Kingsley Garland

Barry
WILSON'S
AUTO REPAIR

EXHIBIT 8-9

The headline in this ad flags Nissan owners, the target audience, as well as a secondary audience, Mazda owners. Other ads in the series selected Ford owners, Dodge owners ("Barry oversees Caravans"), and Honda owners.

This headline not only gets across a great idea fast, it also selects the reader—that is, it tells whether the ad's subject matter interests the reader. The idea is to engage and involve the reader, suggesting a reason to read the rest of the ad. In Exhibit 8-9, the headline of Barry Wilson's Auto Repair ad, "Barry Racks Up ZZZ's," immediately selects Nissan owners. A subhead further selects Mazda owners.

Audiences may be selected by demographic criteria (age, sex, income, marital status) or by psychographic criteria. However, psychographic qualification can backfire if caution is not exercised. A noted copywriter, Stan Freeberg, once developed a headline for an airline ad that used psychographic qualification. The headline read: "Hey, you with the sweaty palms!" The campaign was short-lived.

When applicable, the headline should lead the reader directly into the body copy. One good example is:

Headline: "What kind of man reads *Playboy?*"
Body copy: "He's a man who demands the best life has to offer."

Ideally, headlines should present the complete selling idea. A print ad can effectively reinforce a television campaign, but the headline should still tell the whole story.[13] Nike accomplishes this in its beautiful magazine and outdoor advertisements with nothing more than the visual of a runner or athlete, the logo, and the headline: "Just do it." Working off the visual, the headline creates the mood, suggests the image, and asks for the sale, all at once. Not only that, it is memorable. It can trigger a recognition response in the consumer's mind and reinforces current customers.

Research has shown that, on average, three to five times as many people read the headline as read the body copy. Therefore, if you haven't done some selling in the headline, you've wasted the greatest percent of your money.[14] David Ogilvy also suggests that advertisers should not be afraid of long headlines. His best headline, he says, contained 18 words: "At 60 miles an hour the loudest noise in the new Rolls-Royce comes from the electric clock."[15] (He must have read Henry Ford's ad!)

Headlines should offer customers a benefit—and the benefit should be readily apparent to the reader and easy to get.[16] For example, "Picture Perfect Typing. Smith Corona."

Finally, the headline should present product news of interest to the reader. Consumers look for new products, new uses of old products, or improvements on old products. Therefore, "magic" words that imply newness can increase readership and should be used whenever applicable.[17] Some examples include: *free, now, amazing, suddenly, announcing, introducing, it's here, improved, at last, revolutionary, just arrived,* and *important development.*

Types of Headlines

Copywriters and advertising academicians have been trying to classify types of headlines and body copy for years. There are probably as many different classifications and types as there are authors on the subject. One author, for example, has come up with 23 "basic" types of headlines for which he has developed names that range from "teaser" to "so what?"

The advertising practitioner would probably say "so what?" to the whole subject. However, the student of advertising and the businessperson with limited experience in the field may find a brief discussion of common types of headlines and copy styles helpful. This should facilitate understanding the role of copy and the skill required to write effective advertising.

The *San Francisco Examiner* used a benefit-oriented headline to promote its new ink. Notice how the typeface and graphic elements of the ad suit the image of a big-city daily newspaper. The visual provides a humorous contrast.

Generally, we can classify effective advertising headlines into five basic categories: *benefit, provocative, news/information, question,* and *command.*

Benefit headlines make a direct promise to the reader. Two good examples are "We'll give you a permanent without making waves in your budget" (Prime Cuts haircutting salon) and "New non-rub ink covers the news, not you," shown in Exhibit 8-10.

News/information headlines include many of the how-to headlines and headlines that seek to gain identification for their sponsors by announcing some news or providing some promise of information. Sea World began its television announcement of a new baby whale with a black and white headline on the screen: "It's a Girl." The L.A. City Fire Department provided "hot" news on billboards created *pro bono* by USC advertising professor Larry Londre. The ads showed a house totally consumed in flames; the timely headline read: "Burned on the 4th of July." This gave the reader considerable information in a very short sentence. A small subhead just above the Fire Department logo read: "There's nothing cool about fireworks." Here was important information, believable and memorable.

The agency for *Rolling Stone* magazine found that many upscale advertisers looked askance at the publication because they perceived its readers as young radicals—left-over hippies. Fallon McElligott developed a campaign using a series of two-page spreads with the simple news/information headline: "Perception . . . Reality." A photo on the left illustrates a preconceived notion of the *Rolling Stone* reader, while the right page shows another photograph that conveys the truth. For example, Perception—a flower-painted VW bus; Reality—a Ford Mustang (see Exhibit 8-11 on p. 296). Ad pages in *Rolling Stone* increased substantially the next year.[18]

Copywriters use **provocative headlines** to provoke the reader's curiosity. To learn more, the reader must read the body copy. Of course, the danger is that the reader won't read on, and the headline won't sell anything. To avoid this problem, provocative headlines are usually coupled with visuals that offer clarification or some *story appeal.*

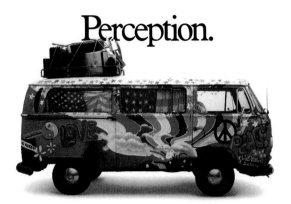

If you still think a Rolling Stone reader's idea of standard equipment is flowers on the door panels and incense in the ashtrays, consider this: Rolling Stone households own 5,199,000 automobiles. If you've got cars to sell, welcome to the fast lane. Source: Simmons 1984

The simple combination of words and pictures here makes a dramatic statement for *Rolling Stone* magazine. Its audience is not what many people think it is. The headline can be classified as news/information.

Look at the Prudential-Bache ad, for example, in Exhibit 8-12. The top third of the ad is all headline: "Once again, nobody else on Wall Street can give you a quote like this." To know the rest of the story, the reader has to read on. The accompanying visual is a photograph of a folded *Wall Street Journal*—May 1, 1990—with an article printed large enough to read and headlined: "Pru-Bache Ranked First for Fifth Consecutive Time." In this interesting case, the ad's provocative headline leads to the headline of the article, which in effect is a news/information subhead for the ad. The text of the article then becomes the body copy of the ad.

Question headlines can be dangerous. If you ask a question the reader can answer quickly, or (even worse) negatively, the rest of the advertisement may not get read. Imagine a headline that reads: "Do you like food?" The reader answers "of course" and turns the page.

A good question headline will pique the reader's curiosity and imagination.[19] The classic question headline of all time was Miss Clairol's: "Does she? Or doesn't she?" Used on TV and in print, this campaign put Clairol's hair-coloring product on top for many years. Likewise, an American Airlines advertisement asked: "If you don't show your kids where America began, who will?" The ad was designed to motivate educated parents to think about future travel plans. It accomplished its objective.

The provocative headline in this ad for Prudential-Bache Securities gets your attention and leads your eye to the visual. The viewer's interest is piqued with the realization that the visual *is* the text. Showing the actual article enhances credibility. The article presents a positive testimonial and valuable information from a reliable and unbiased source—features the ad could never achieve otherwise.

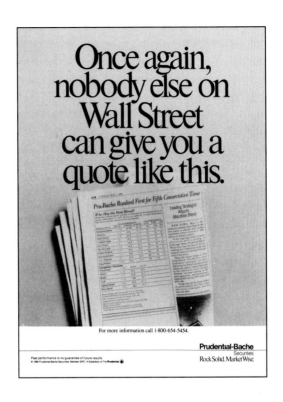

A **command headline** orders us to do something and therefore might seem negative. Yet we pay attention to such headlines. They motivate us through fear or emotion or because we understand the inherent correctness of the command. For example, "Drive safely. The life you save may be your own," is difficult to challenge. Other command headlines are more pleasant, such as "Listen to what you've been missing in cassette sound" (3M Company). And some may be couched in the form of a request: "Please don't squeeze the Charmin" (Charmin bathroom tissue). Perhaps the best command headline of all time was: "Promise her anything but give her Arpege."

We have touched on only a few types of headlines in this brief discussion. Trying to categorize all of them could take a lifetime and serves little purpose. Many headline types are easily combined, and some—like the one in Exhibit 8-13 (p. 298)—absolutely require clarifying visuals. Provocative headlines and question headlines usually require more support from definitive photos or illustrations. A good exercise for any copywriter is to create a checklist of basic headline categories and then to write several different types for each new project. That is one way to find the best solution to the problem at hand.

Subheads

Subheads are misnamed—they can appear above the headline as well as below. They may also appear in the body copy or the text of the advertisement. A subhead that appears above the headline is called a **kicker.**

Subheads are little headlines. While they usually appear in a smaller type size than the headline, they are almost invariably larger than the body copy or text type size. Subheads may appear in **boldface** (heavier) type or in a different ink color.

EXHIBIT 8-13

"Kiss it goodbye" informs the reader that the pictured symbol—a way of life for all IBM-compatible microcomputer users—is being replaced by new software. This headline and visual work together to instantly deliver the dramatic promise. The text goes on to promote "point and click" software.

The purpose of the subhead is to transmit key sales points—fast! Most individuals read only the headline and subheads. Subheads should be reserved for important facts that may not be so dramatic or memorable as the headline information. Some may even require more space than a headline because they communicate more information and require more words.

The subheads should reinforce the headline and advertisement theme. Fidelity Federal's "Is your bank taking you to the cleaners?" is a headline well reinforced by the subhead: "If your bank isn't paying you interest on your checking account, no matter what your balance is, they're cleaning up. Instead of you."

Body Copy

The advertiser tells the complete sales story in the **body copy,** or **text,** as it is sometimes called. Set in smaller type than headlines or subheads, the body copy is a logical continuation of the headline and subheads. It is also where the sale is closed.

The text should relate to the campaign appeal and to the reader's self-interest, and it must explain how the product or service being advertised satisfies the customer's need. The text may concentrate on one or several benefits as they relate specifically to the target audience. Copy should be written as if the writer were conversing with one person. In fact, copywriters often read their copy aloud just to hear how it sounds—even if it's intended for print media. The ear is a powerful copywriting tool. (See Ad Lab 8-B, "The Eye versus the Ear.") Here are some pointers that experts have arrived at after years of copy research:[20]

☐ Stress one major idea.

☐ Position the product clearly.

☐ Emphasize the consumer's ultimate benefit.

☐ Keep the brand name up front and reinforce it.

AD LAB 8-B
The Eye versus the Ear

Jack Trout and Al Ries, who pioneered the concepts of positioning, marketing warfare, and bottom-up marketing, here share their views on another controversial subject: the eye versus the ear.

It's a fact of life that we succeed or fail based on our preconceptions—preconceptions that we seldom think about, that we seldom debate. Today, there's an advertising preconception that is deeply rooted and fallacious.

Which Is More Powerful?

Which is more powerful, the eye or the ear? Has anybody ever asked you that question? Probably not, because the answer is obvious. Chances are that deep down inside you believe the eye is more powerful than the ear.

After all, 500 years before Christ, Confucius said, "A picture is worth a thousand words."

These seven words, not pictures mind you, have lived for 2,500 years. And the way things are going, these seven words will probably never die. What agency president, creative director, or art director hasn't quoted Confucius at least once in his or her career?

After analyzing hundreds of effective positioning campaigns, though, we ran into a surprising conclusion.

The programs were all verbal. There wasn't a single positioning concept that was exclusively visual. Could Confucius have been wrong?

In order to set the record straight, we went back to find out what Confucius actually said. We took the Chinese characters and had them translated.

Confucius said, "A picture is worth a thousand pieces of gold." Not words, but gold. Son of a gun! Here all these years we thought he was knocking words.

What Is a Picture Worth?

We all know television pictures are expensive. But what is a picture worth on television? That is, just the picture without the sound. Not much. As a matter of fact, without the words on the package or the graphics on the screen, pictures in a TV commercial have almost no communication value. But add sound, and the picture changes. If pictures alone make no sense, how about the sound alone? Strange as it may seem, the sound alone in a television commercial usually carries an easy-to-understand message.

Most classic print advertisements illustrate the same principle. The visual alone makes no sense. Naturally, a print ad with both pictures and words is more effective than either alone. But individually, which is more powerful—the verbal or the visual?

Sound Alone Is Powerful

Evidence from controlled laboratory studies shows that when you present a list of words to people either auditorily, say, on tape, or visually, say, on slides, people remember more words if they hear the words than if they see them.

A recent study from Northwestern University shows that if you try to convince people about a product and you do it with just a verbal message, people are much more convinced about your product. They like it better; they want to buy it more than if you accompany those verbal messages with pictures. The verbal message alone seems to create in people's minds more of a positive feeling for the product.

Two Kinds of Words

There are two kinds of words: printed and spoken. We often confuse the two, but there's a big difference.

The ear is faster than the eye. Repeated tests have shown that the mind is able to understand a spoken word in 140 milliseconds. A printed word, on the other hand, can be understood in 180 milliseconds.

To account for this 40-millisecond delay, psychologists speculate that the brain translates visual information into aural sounds that the mind can comprehend.

Not only do you hear faster than you see, your hearing lasts longer than your seeing. A visual image—picture or words—fades in one second unless your mind does something to file away the essence of the idea. Hearing, on the other hand, lasts four or five times as long.

That's why it's easy to lose your train of thought when you read printed words. Often you have to backtrack to pick up the sense of the message. Because sound lasts much longer in the mind, the spoken word is easier to follow.

Thus, listening to a message is much more effective than reading it. First, the mind holds the spoken words in storage much longer, enabling you to follow the train of thought with greater clarity. And second, the tone of the human voice gives the words emotional impact that no picture can achieve.

But other things happen in your mind when you listen to the spoken word.

Auding and Reading

In newborn children, the process of listening occurs first, and then the process of *auding,* which is listening to the spoken language and comprehending the language. Only later do people actually learn to read.

(continued)

AD LAB 8-B *(continued)*

Ordinarily, when children enter the school system, they learn to decode through the process of phonics training. So there is a very intimate relationship between written language and oral language, inasmuch as written language is ordinarily recoded into an internal form of the earlier-acquired oral language skill.

In other words, the mind apparently translates printed words into spoken equivalents before it can understand them. (Beginning readers often move their lips when reading.)

Now we know why a deaf person has so much trouble learning to read—there are no sounds to translate the words into—and why a blind person has no trouble learning to read braille.

We also know the reason for the 40-millisecond difference between the printed and the spoken word. Printed words make a mental detour through the aural portion of the brain.

The ear drives the eye. There is much evidence that the mind works by ear, that thinking is a process of manipulating sounds, not images—even when pictures or photographs are involved.

Implications for Advertising

The implications of these findings for the advertising industry are staggering, to say the least. In many ways, they call for a complete reorientation from a visual to a verbal point of view.

We're not saying that the visual doesn't play an important role. Of course it does. But the verbal should be the driver, and the pictures should reinforce the words. All too often the opposite is the case.

Laboratory Applications

1. What are some of the possible implications of these findings for the way advertising is created? For the ways copy is written? For the media used by advertisers?

2. Do you agree with Trout and Ries's findings? What do you think most consumers prefer for communication and entertainment, the eye or the ear? What do most advertisers prefer for communicating their messages?

☐ Keep copy lean and tight. Tell the whole story and no more. When finished, stop.

☐ Support audio with video.

In writing copy, we look for the techniques that provide the greatest sales appeal for the idea we are presenting. (See the Checklist for Writing Effective Copy.) Copy styles fall into many categories. Some common types of copy styles include *straight sell, institutional, narrative, dialogue/monologue, picture-caption,* and *device..*

In **straight-sell copy,** the text immediately explains or develops the headline and visual—or the pictures on the screen—in a straightforward attempt to sell the product. Since the product's sales points are ticked off in order of their importance, straight-sell copy is particularly advantageous for consumer products that may be difficult to use and in direct-mail advertising and industrial situations. Many camera ads, for example, use this straight, factual copy style to get the message across. The straight-sell approach emphasizes the reason the consumer should buy something.

Sometimes the advertiser uses **institutional copy** to sell an idea or the merits of the organization or service rather than sales features of a particular product. Often institutional copy is also narrative in style because it lends warmth to the organization. Banks, insurance companies, public utilities, and large manufacturing concerns are the most common users of institutional

Checklist for Writing Effective Copy

☐ *Make it easy on your reader.* Write short sentences. Use easy, familiar words.

☐ *Don't waste words.* Say what you have to say—nothing more, nothing less. Don't pad, but don't skimp.

☐ *Stick to the present tense, active voice*—it's crisper. Avoid the past tense and passive voice. Exceptions should be deliberate, for special effect.

☐ *Don't hesitate to use personal pronouns.* Remember, you're trying to talk to just *one* person, so talk as you would to a friend. Use "you" and "your."

☐ *Clichés are crutches.* Learn to get along without them. Bright, surprising words and phrases perk up readers, keep them reading.

☐ *Don't overpunctuate.* It kills copy flow. Excessive commas are the chief culprits. Don't give your readers any excuse to jump ship.

☐ *Use contractions whenever possible.* They're fast, personal, natural. People talk in contractions. (Listen to yourself.)

☐ *Don't brag or boast.* Write from the reader's point of view, not your own. Avoid "we," "us," "our."

☐ *Be single-minded.* Don't try to do too much. If you chase more than one rabbit at a time, you'll catch none.

☐ *Write with flair.* Drum up excitement. Make sure the enthusiasm you feel comes through in your copy.

☐ *Read your copy aloud*—to see how your copy sounds and to catch errors. The written word is considerably different from the spoken word.

---

copy—in both print and electronic media. However, beware of what David Ogilvy refers to as the "self-serving, flatulent pomposity" that characterizes the copy in many corporate ads.[21]

Advertisers use **narrative copy** to tell a story. It often sets up a problem and then creates a solution using the particular sales features of the product or service. It may then suggest that you use the same solution if you have that problem. An ad for Quebec Tourism shows a young couple seated at a sidewalk cafe, gazing into each other's eyes. Under the headline "Romanti-Que," the copy reads like an intimate entry in a diary: "Somewhere between the *salade d'endives* and the last spoonful of *mousse au chocolat,* we fell in love all over again."

By using **dialogue/monologue copy,** the advertiser can add the believability that narrative copy sometimes lacks. The characters portrayed in a commercial, such as those in Exhibit 8-14 (p. 302), or in a print ad do the selling in their own words, through a testimonial or quasi-testimonial technique, or through a comic-strip panel. However, beginning copywriters often have trouble writing this kind of copy unless they have some playwriting experience. Not everything people say is interesting. If it is not done well, dialogue copy can come off as dull or—even worse—hokey.

Sometimes in a print ad it is easier to tell the story through a series of illustrations and captions than through the use of a copy block alone. Then **picture-caption copy** is used. This is especially true when the product is shown in a number of different uses or when it is available in a variety of styles or designs.

A common technique is to use some form of **device copy.** Typical devices include wordplays, humor, poetry, rhymes, great exaggeration, gags, and other tricks or gimmicks. Don't downgrade device advertising. A device

SFX: (Phone ring/pick up.)

ESTELLE: Irving's Earthworms.

EDGAR: Estelle...Edgar. I need six gross for Betty's Bait Shack.

ESTELLE: You got it.

SFX: (Phone click/ring/pick up.)

ESTELLE: Irving's Earthworms.

EDGAR: Estelle...Edgar. I need four gross for Fred's Fish Farm.

ESTELLE: No sweat.

SFX: (Phone click/ring/pick up.)

ESTELLE: Irving's Earthworms.

EDGAR: Estelle...Edgar. I need eight gross for Tackle Town.

ESTELLE: Edgar...why don't you call these orders in all at once?

EDGAR: I'm afraid I'll get cut off.

ESTELLE: Are you calling on a GTE public phone?

EDGAR: Yeah.

ESTELLE: On a local call, you can talk as long as you want.

EDGAR: For 20 cents?!

ESTELLE: For 20 cents. You can even get free operator assistance, access to any long distance carrier, use a calling card and get refunds if you goof up.

EDGAR: All on a GTE phone?

ESTELLE: You got it.

EDGAR: Just think...I can travel all over, calling in orders from the really big bait shops.

ESTELLE: Edgar...

EDGAR: Carp 'N' Carry, Halibut Heaven...

ESTELLE: Edgar...

EDGAR: I could even call my mother... collect...

ANNCR: On the road and need to make a call? Look for a GTE public phone. We're keeping calling...simple.

EDGAR: There's only one problem in the meantime...

ESTELLE: What's that?

EDGAR: What am I gonna do with 600 dimes?

EXHIBIT 8-14

The dialogue copy for this GTE radio ad keeps us interested with a play on business names and word rhythms. Note that very few of the statements are complete sentences, which is the way most people talk in casual conversation. As an exercise, count the number of product features and benefits presented in the context of this humorous phone conversation.

carried out rationally is believable. And frankly, some of the best advertising uses unique devices, both in body copy and in headlines. An ad for the household lubricant WD-40 shows a close-up of the spray can aimed directly at the reader. The copy says: "Take a shot at tools with moving parts, lawnmowers, sticky locks, and squeaky hinges. Anything that moves. WD-40. America's troubleshooter."

Humor is a popular form of device copy, particularly in broadcast advertising, as the ad for U S West shows in Exhibit 8-15. In fact, many creative directors look for humor in copy to serve as entertainment value in advertising. One ad touched parental funny bones by featuring a cute little boy dipping into a bag of Kraft marshmallows, with the headline: "A marshmallow a day keeps your freckles on straight."

Humor can be effective when the advertiser needs high memorability in a short time, and it may be used to destroy an outmoded attitude or use pattern that affects a product. However, humor is also very subjective. It should always be used carefully and never in questionable taste. Some researchers believe humor can even be detrimental when used for financial services and insurance.[22]

The four basic elements used in the construction of body copy are the *lead-in paragraph, interior paragraphs, trial close,* and *close.*

Lead-In Paragraph

The **lead-in paragraph** is a bridge between the headline, the subheads, and the sales ideas presented in the text. It transfers reading interest to product interest.

> *Headline:* "It was easier to turn a Porsche into a luxury car than vice versa."
> *Lead-in paragraph:* "Ever since the first 356 rolled off the assembly line and into automotive history, enthusiasts have associated the name Porsche with one thing. Performance."

The lead-in paragraph may perform other functions as well. In short-copy ads (an increasing trend) and outdoor advertising, the lead-in paragraph may be the only paragraph. It may include the promise, the claim-support information, and the close. An ad for the Minneapolis Planetarium, for instance, shows a large cartoon of Buck Rogers under the headline: "The Buck Stops Here." The single paragraph of body copy reads "When you've had enough of science fiction, try some science fact at the Minneapolis Planetarium."

Interior Paragraphs

This is where the copywriter builds interest and desire and provides proof for claims and promises. A good ad or commercial not only has to be truthful but also believable to be effective. With increased consumer awareness and sophistication, claims must be made carefully. And proof should be offered. Proofs may fall into the following categories:

☐ *Research:* government or private studies.

☐ *Testing:* by case history, testing firm, consumers, or the advertiser.

☐ *Usage:* product market rank, case history, testimonial, endorsements.

☐ *Guarantee:* trial offers, demonstration offers, free samples, warranty information.

The keys to good copy are simplicity, order, credibility, and clarity. Or, as John O'Toole says, what's important is "that the prose be written clearly, informatively, interestingly, powerfully, persuasively, dramatically, memorably, and with effortless grace. That's all."[23] (To see some good examples of ads that do just that, study the Copywriter's Portfolio.)·

Trial Close

Interspersed in the interior paragraphs should be requests for the order. Good copy asks for the order more than once. In mail-order advertisements particularly, it is necessary to ask for the order several times. Consumers may decide to buy without reading the entire body copy. The **trial close** gives them the option to make the buying decisions early.

Close

An advertisement's **close** asks consumers to do something and tells them how to do it. This is the action block in the advertisement when the sale, in its broadest sense, is made. Of course, not all advertisements sell products or services. The advertiser may be looking for a change in attitude, an understanding of its point of view, a vote, or a new preference for its product or service.

The close can be direct or indirect, a subtle suggestion or a direct command. English Leather's close is certainly indirect: "My men wear English Leather or they wear nothing at all." This headline is repeated in the last sentence of the body copy, suggesting indirectly that if you want to please a woman, you will wear English Leather; or conversely, if you want to please a man, you will buy him English Leather. A direct close seeks immediate response in the form of either a purchase or a request for further details. The U.S. Coast Guard commercial in Exhibit 8-16, directed to boaters, gives a very

(continued on p. 308)

EXHIBIT 8-15

A humorous approach helps this radio spot for U S West make its point in a short time. The busy signal that underlies most of the monologue is a gimmick that grabs the listener's attention.

EXHIBIT 8-16

The action step in this TV commercial is not selling a product or service, but still relies heavily on stirring viewers to action. In this U.S. Coast Guard commercial, arresting visuals combine with a stern admonition to boaters to wear their life jackets.

ANNCR: There are life jackets to fit every boater and life jackets to fit every boating situation. And buckling up one of these makes sense for any boater. Because life jackets won't work unless you wear them, and you should Know Before You Go.

COPYWRITER'S PORTFOLIO

A. The diary technique of the copy in this tourism ad helps personalize it. The smattering of identifiable French terms makes Quebec seem exotic, but not too exotic.

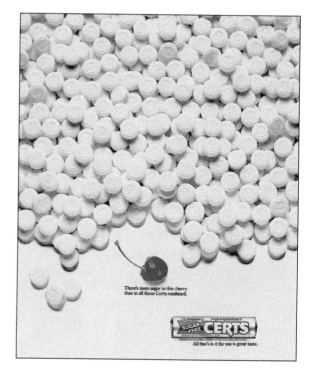

B. The limited copy in this Certs ad makes a telling point, in type so small the reader really has to become involved to get the message.

C. Steve Wozniak, the founder of Apple Computer and a U.C. Berkeley alumnus, suffered a bout of temporary amnesia after a plane crash. When he later donated to his alma mater, he funded a memory-research program at the university. But he also made the day for Chiat/Day Advertising copywriter Brian O'Neill who wrote this ad for the U.C. Berkeley Foundation, Cal's nonprofit, alumni fund-raising organization. The provocative, news/information headline—supported by the newspaper clipping—is a copywriter's dream come true.

AMNESIA VICTIM REMEMBERS CAL.

Apple founder donates money for research

A few years ago, Steve Wozniak was involved in an accident he would never forget.

A near-fatal plane crash left Wozniak an amnesiac.

If you recall, this is the same man who invented the personal computer—by cranking out page after page of computer code from memory.

And just like that, his entire database was erased.

The amnesia subsided five weeks later, but "Woz" still couldn't get over the memory of losing his memory.

Then he remembered Cal.

His generous donation is now helping to fund an ongoing memory research program.

Conducted by Cal's Psychology Department, this breakthrough work is using computers to develop a whole new approach to memory rehabilitation.

But remember:

Cal is not a "state-supported" university, so programs like this depend heavily on alumni contributions.

So for those of you who might've forgotten, our Donor Line number is (415) 642-1212.

Give us a call.

And Woz, if you're reading this, we'd just like to say thanks.

If it weren't for you and the rest of our esteemed alumni, Cal wouldn't be the great university that it is today.

And don't you forget it.

U.C. BERKELEY
It's not the same without you.
U.C. Berkeley Foundation, 2440 Bancroft Way, RM. 301, Berkeley, CA 94720.

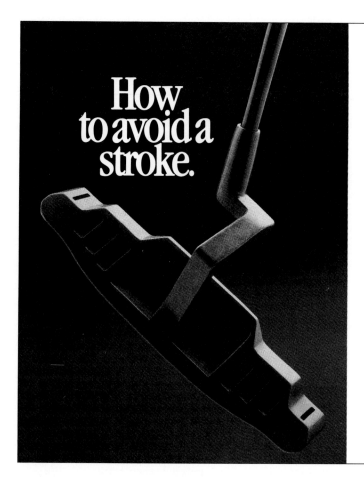

How to avoid a stroke.

The Spalding Centerline™ Putter. It's unique head design will help you put the ball in the hole.

You've heard your customers telling this story a million times. First, they hit the ball pure off the tee. Then they stuck their approach shot 15 feet from the pin. But from there, things became, shall we say, unpleasant.

What can you do to help? Introduce them to our new Centerline putters.

Just by looking at it, you can see the Centerline represents an entirely new concept in putting.

We've designed the Centerline Putter to offer superior alignment because it has an innovative hosel that promotes proper club head and hand positioning.

And because of the shape of the precision milled, elongated hitting surface, and positioning of the club head to shaft, the Centerline virtually makes a player align the putter head with the center of the hole.

And in case a player does make an off-center hit, we've incorporated heel/toe weighting to reduce club head twisting.

The Centerline has a stiff, black chrome shaft from True Temper® and the exclusive Spalding Ultra Feel grip by Eaton®.

It's available in extreme offset, medium offset, and zero offset for right handed players and medium offset for lefties.

To sum up, we think Centerline putters will help your customers get lower numbers on the course.

And help you get higher numbers at your cash register.

Centerline putters are available in extreme, medium, and zero offset for righties, and medium offset for lefties.

SPALDING
Professional Golf Clubs

C88

D. The "big idea" in this Spalding golf club ad is a play on words. It is reinforced by a strong visual.

Expect light, moderate and heavy winds through the weekend.

In fact, powerful performances are forecast from every section of The Minnesota Orchestra for the new season. We have the turbulence of Rachmaninoff. The gentle airs of Mozart and Debussy. The brisk pacing of Beethoven. And much more. All waiting for you weekends from September through May, when you subscribe.

Enjoying the season is a breeze with the many exciting series we offer. Tickets are available for Wednesday, Friday or Saturday evenings at Orchestra Hall. Or for Thursday or Saturday evenings at the Ordway Music Theatre in St. Paul. And there are plenty of good seats left for the weekend, including our popular Friday night series.

Choices range from five and six concert Mini Series to the 24 concert Imperial Series. With a subscription you can save up to 36% over single ticket prices. And what is more important, you get the richness of experience that comes with repeated attendance, as well as the one-of-a-kind moments that happen only in a live performance.

Best seats go fast, so call 371-5656. And subscribe while conditions are still favorable.

The Minnesota Orchestra 1989/90 Subscription Series.
Edo de Waart, Music Director

E. Not-for-profit organizations benefit just as much from good copywriting as commercial organizations do. This ad for the Minnesota Orchestra combines a clever metaphorical headline, an attractive visual, and informative copy to attract attention and interest.

compelling reason for wearing a life jacket. The ad closes with a simple, direct warning: "Know Before You Go."

The close should simplify the reader's response, making it as easy as possible for the reader to order the merchandise, send for information, or visit a showroom. The close tells the reader where to shop or what to send. A business reply card or a toll-free telephone number may be included. In fact, everything the reader needs to take action should be in the close or near it.

Boxes and Panels

Boxes and panels are generally used in ads that contain coupons, special offers, contest rules, and order blanks to set these features apart from the rest of the ad.

Specifically, a **box** is copy with a line drawn around it. A **panel** is an elongated box that usually runs the whole length or width of an ad. Sometimes it may be shaded or completely black, with text or copy shown in reverse (white lettering).

Boxes and panels are used to draw greater attention to a specific element or message in an advertisement.

Slogans

Many **slogans** (also called **theme lines** or **tag lines**) begin as successful headlines. Through continuous use, they become standard statements, not just in advertising but for salespeople and company employees, as in AT&T's "Reach out and touch someone." Slogans become a battle cry for the company. In fact, the word *slogan* comes from the Gaelic term for *battle cry*.

Slogans have two basic purposes: to provide continuity for a campaign and to reduce a key theme or idea to a brief, memorable positioning statement. DeBeers's ads, for example, still claim the famous promise in their slogan: "Diamonds are forever." On the other hand, First Interstate Bank's promise in Exhibit 8-17, "We go the extra mile for you," may be a good tag line but probably lacks the endurance to become a full-fledged slogan.

Slogans should be like old friends who stay the same year after year. You recognize them instantly, and you feel you understand them. Some slogans endure because they encapsulate a corporate philosophy, such as Hallmark's "When you care enough to send the very best." Another example of a corporate philosophy is Zenith's slogan, "At Zenith, the quality goes in before the name goes on."[24] Unfortunately, though, many slogans do not measure up to these lofty expectations. Rather, they fall into Ogilvy's category of "interchangeable fatuous bromides."[25]

Effective slogans are short, simple, memorable, easy to repeat, and most important, helpful in differentiating the product or the company from its competitors: "When it rains, it pours" (Morton Salt). Rhyme, rhythm, and reason—not to mention alliteration—are valuable copy aids in writing slogans.

Seals, Logotypes, and Signatures

The term **seal** is the subject of much confusion among advertising students. For some, it indicates the seals of approval offered by such organizations as the Good Housekeeping Institute, Underwriters Laboratories, and Parents

Institute. Seals are given only when a product meets standards established by these institutions. Since the organizations are all recognized authorities—and have great credibility—it is beneficial to include the seals in an advertisement. The seals provide an independent, valued endorsement for the advertised product.

For others, the term *seal* refers to the company seal or trademark. These are actually called **logotypes.** Logotypes (logos) and **signature cuts** (sig cuts) are special designs of the advertiser's company name or product name. They appear in all company ads and are like trademarks because they give the product individuality and provide quick recognition at the point of purchase.

COMMON PITFALLS IN WRITING COPY

Today's consumer is intelligent, educated, and discriminating. Copy style, therefore, should reflect consumer tastes and values. Generalizations are not convincing—the consumer is looking for specific information to form judgments and make purchase decisions. Being specific means leaving out the trite advertising clichés like *amazing, wonderful,* and *finest.*

Words cost money. A print ad may cost $50 a word or $5,000 a word, depending on the medium. At those prices, every word counts. Words that do not sell cost more money than words that do, so use words that sell. Avoid the following pitfalls that plague beginning copywriters and annoy customers.

Obfuscation

The fundamental requirements of any advertisement are that it be readable and understandable. Avoid $10 words (like *obfuscation*) that nobody understands. Write simply in the everyday, colloquial English people use in conversation. Use small words. You will get your point across better if you use words and phrases that are familiar to your reader. Use short sentences. The longer the sentence, the harder it is to understand. Compare these paragraphs:

> The Armco vacuum cleaner not only cleans your rugs and drapes, it's invaluable on hard surfaces such as vinyl floors, wood floors, even cement. You won't believe how incredibly smooth and quiet the machine is as it travels across your sparkling floors.

> The Armco vacuum cleaner cleans rugs . . . drapes. It cleans hard surfaces like woods and vinyl floors. Even cement! The Armco vacuum cleaner is smooth . . . quiet. Try it! Make your floors sparkle with new cleanliness.

Thousands of advertisements compete for your reader. The more understandable your advertisement, the more likely it will be read.

Filibustering

We have discussed the importance of brevity. Look at this headline for Nike: "Just do it." Now imagine if it weren't concise: "We know running and exercising is hard work and exhausting, but you really should do it, because it's good for you. And, by the way, when you're doing it, please wear our shoes."

Long-winded filibusters should be confined to the Senate. They are not allowed in advertising. Be complete, but be concise.

Clichés, Triteness, and Superlatives

Overused expressions do nothing for copy. Most superlatives (greatest, large economy) and clichés (tried and true, a penny saved is a penny earned) may once have been exciting statements, but time has worn their value into rags.

Certainly clichés can communicate, and not all stock expressions are clichés. But clichés erode consumer confidence. They contribute to an out-of-date image.

Abstractness and Vagueness

Abstract words, such as *fine, really,* and *OK,* do not provide specificity. Since they can't be measured, they are not easily understood or evaluated.

Superior copy is concrete and matched to the experience of the audience to which it appeals. Words should have tangible dollars-and-cents value. For example, in an ad for a new high-tech product, avoid vague, boastful generalities like: "Supporting the Nutech Spectra-flanstran are technological advances that give these instruments incredible capability." Be specific: "The Nutech Spectra-flanstran provides military specification tolerances to .005 inches."[26]

"Me-Me-Me"

The advertisement must appeal to the reader's self-interest, not the advertiser's. To get your message across and persuade the reader, use the "you

EXHIBIT 8-18

This notable television commercial for Alaska Airlines is one of a series depicting the common indignities of air travel. Alaska Airlines, in contrast, emphasizes "you," the flying public, in its services and in its ad copy.

ANNCR: Do the little things on your airline work as well as they should? Before you get on an Alaska Airlines plane, we make sure everything is ship-shape, inside and out.

attitude." Talk about the customer's needs, hopes, wishes, and preferences. In a commercial from Alaska Airlines' famous campaign, the voice-over announcer asks the audience how well things work on their airline (see Exhibit 8-18). Note the use of *you* and *your*. Talk about the customer, and you are talking about the most interesting person in the world. For example:

Me	You
We are pleased to announce our new flight schedule from Cincinnati to Philadelphia, which is any hour on the hour.	You can take a plane from Cincinnati to Philadelphia any hour on the hour.
We believe this vacuum cleaner is technically superior to any other on the market.	Your house will be more beautiful because you'll be using the most powerful, easy-to-use vacuum on the market.

No, Not Negativity

Think negatively, write negatively, and you may produce a negative response. Readers usually respond better to a positive viewpoint. Stress what things are or what they can be instead of what they are not. Remember, words often have connotations apart from their literal meanings. Also, be aware that different people react to the same word in different ways. Even *love,* that most beautiful word, may have a positive meaning for a romantic, single person and a negative implication for someone who has just been burned.

Euphemisms

To **euphemize** is to substitute an inoffensive, mild word for a word that is offensive, harsh, or blunt. A copywriter euphemizes to put a good face on something. Calling toilet paper "bathroom tissue" doesn't change its appearance or function, but it may soften the social acceptability for people. Other euphemisms are "previously owned cars" (for used cars), "package store" (for liquor store), "memorial gardens" (for cemeteries), "underarm wetness" (for sweaty armpits), "irregularity" (for constipation), and "midriff bulge" (for fat gut). But be careful in choosing euphemisms. They can be misleading, can weaken your message, and if considered fraudulent, can invite investigation by the Federal Trade Commission.

Euphemisms are frequently used in the process of naming products. Since copywriters often get involved in that endeavor, it is worthwhile to study some of the approaches used in developing brand names (see Ad Lab 8-C, "Creating Names for Products," on p. 312).

Defamation

Avoid portraying real people in a bad light. All advertising copy is governed by the laws of **defamation,** which prohibits making false statements or allegations about a person or holding a person up to contempt. Defamation in print advertising is called **libel.** In broadcast advertising or verbal statements, it is called **slander.** Defamation occurs when people's names are used

AD LAB 8-C
Creating Names for Products

Copywriters are often called on to develop names for companies or products. Here's how they do it:

Personal Names

One way to label a product is to name it after yourself: Gerber baby foods, Ford cars. Problems occur, however, because people have similar names. Names can be copied, and it is difficult to stop other people from using their own name on their products. Using fictitious names, like Bartles & Jaymes, may avoid this problem.

Geographic Names

If a geographic name is used in an arbitrary manner, like Newport cigarettes, it may function as a trademark. However, if it identifies a product's place of origin or suggests where the product may have come from (like Detroit Auto Works), it cannot be protected as a trademark.

Coined or Invented Names

The most distinctive names are often coined. Kodak was coined by George Eastman because he wanted a name beginning and ending with an infrequently used letter. Kleenex, Xerox, Betty Crocker, and Polaroid have an advantage because they are short, pronounceable, and arbitrary. It's unlikely others will use anything similar. In recent years, the computer has been used to generate unique coined names for both companies and products.

Initials or Numbers

Some common examples are IBM computers, RCA televisions, and A-1 steak sauce. In general, initials and numbers are not recommended as product names. How do you position your new RQS Company? What would the name Harris 5500 say about your product?

Company Name

The company name is sometimes also used as a brand name—Texaco, Gulf, Shell. More typically, though, companies choose to develop different names for their products so as to avoid confusion and create greater value for the brand itself.

Foreign Words

Perfume companies often use French words to project an image of romance (Vol de Nuit). Auto manufacturers use foreign words to add mystery and intrigue: Cordova, Biarritz. Restaurants use them to identify the kind of food they serve: Del Taco, L'Auberge, La Scala.

Licensed Names

Companies may license names for their marketability (Snoopy toothbrushes, Sunkist vitamins). The cost of using a licensed name is often steep, and the use of the name has tight restrictions.

Arbitrary Dictionary Words

The most successful products often have dictionary names: Tide detergent, Whirlpool appliances, Arrow shirts. Dictionary words that have nothing to do with the product description are more easily protected than words that have some relationship to the product. They may also give the product an image. Fragrance advertisers have used steamy advertising and shock-value names—Obsession, Poison, Decadence—to pique consumer interest.

Laboratory Applications

1. Look through publications for an example of each category of product name (other than the names mentioned here). Which category is easiest to find? Which is most difficult?

2. Product names that are closely related to the product description are less likely to be protected by trademark law. Why do you suppose that is?

3. If you were opening a clothing boutique or a restaurant, what would you call it? Explain why you would choose that name.

or references are made to them in a libelous or slanderous manner. The size of audience is not a defense; a libelous statement, for example, need only be read by more than one person to be defamation.

THE WRITING PROCESS: TOOLS OF THE TRADE

As the copywriter develops the text of ads and commercials, the actual task of forming the copy takes place. This requires tools of the writer's trade as well as a sequence of editing processes.

In times past, the copywriter's tools were very simple: pencils, pads, markers, typewriter, and red or blue editing pens. First drafts were often done in pen or pencil and then typed, edited, retyped, and reedited. This has all changed. Today, word processing on personal computers (or terminals connected to a central processor and central printer) has become a requirement for all agencies—large and small—and even for most free-lancers. For most writers, the tools now consist of a computer (IBM-compatibles and Macintosh are favorites), a dot matrix or laser printer, and word-processing software (Microsoft® Word, WordPerfect®, MacWrite™, and Write Now are a few favorites). The better programs offer a complete thesaurus, spell checker, and a variety of style sheet templates, which all contribute to unparalleled ease and efficiency in editing, formatting, and file storage.

As with any creative process, the copywriter's work is always subject to the approval process (see Exhibit 8-19). The larger the agency and the larger the client, the more formidable this seems to become. All copy must first be approved within the creative department by senior copywriters and creative

EXHIBIT 8-19

The copy approval process can be formidable as agencies and clients grow larger and larger.

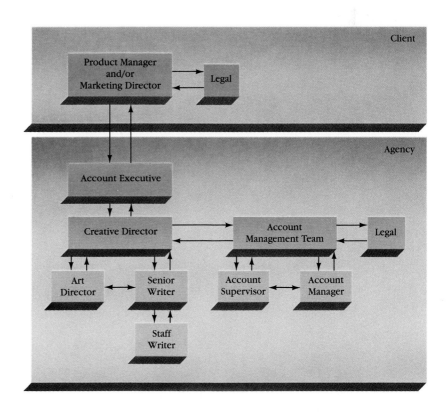

directors. Then the agency's account management team takes a few whacks at improving it. Next, client product managers and marketing staff approve or disapprove the copy. Finally, both the agency and the client legal departments scrutinize the copy for potential pitfalls that could pose a legal or unfair practices problem.

Throughout this process, the writer must be prepared to gracefully accept and/or rebut the inevitable critiques, additions, and deletions and be able to adopt any valid corrections. Redlining by editors is so commonplace that writers must develop thick skins and not be surprised by the edits that may be reedited from moment to moment. Under these circumstances, maintaining artistic purity is extremely difficult and requires patience, flexibility, maturity, and the skill to articulate an important point of view.

Since the whole study of advertising concerns the discipline of writing, no single chapter on the topic of copywriting can ever be complete. For that reason, we will continue to discuss certain copywriting issues in subsequent chapters on advertising production and media as they pertain to those subjects.

Summary

Copy is the verbal presentation, and art is the nonverbal, or visual, presentation of the message strategy. Before beginning to write, the copywriter (usually under the guidance of a creative director) must understand the intended marketing and advertising strategies. This typically requires a review of the marketing and advertising plans, an analysis of the facts, and an examination of the creative strategy. The copywriter should develop a brief written copy platform that tells what the copy will say and how it will support the message strategy.

Once the copy platform is established, the search for the big idea begins—the most important step in creating an advertisement. The big idea is the creative flash that adds meaning, interest, memorability, and drama to the strategy statement. It is the essence of the ad or commercial.

To create effective advertising, creative people use the copywriter's pyramid—similar to the advertising pyramid—as a model to gain attention, create interest, achieve credibility, heighten desire, and stimulate action.

The key copy elements in print advertising are headlines, subheads, body copy, boxes and panels, slogans, seals, logotypes, and signatures. In electronic media, copy is normally spoken dialog and is referred to as the audio portion of the commercial. The copy may be delivered as a voice-over by an unseen announcer or on camera by an announcer, spokesperson, or actor.

Many types of headlines and copy styles are used in print advertising. Good advertising headlines can generally be classified into five basic categories: benefit, provocative, news/information, question, and command. Copy styles also fall into several categories: straight sell, institutional, narrative, dialogue/monologue, picture caption, and device.

The pitfalls for unsuspecting copywriters are many and varied. The most common are obfuscation; filibustering; clichés, triteness, and superlatives; abstractness and vagueness; "me-me-me"; negative thinking; misleading euphemisms; and unintentional defamation.

Today, virtually all advertising copywriters use word processing as the primary tool of the trade, which makes computer literacy a must. Likewise, as advertising copy goes through the editing process, copywriters must be prepared for an inevitable—and sometimes long—succession of edits and reedits from agency and client managers and legal departments before the work is ever finally approved and run. As a result, copywriters are required to be more than just creative; they must be patient, flexible, and mature and be able to exercise great self-control.

Questions for Review and Discussion

1. Based on an advertisement you have selected in this chapter, what is the advertiser's message strategy?
2. Based on a television commercial of your choice, how well has the advertiser followed the steps up the copywriter's pyramid? Explain.
3. Select a magazine advertisement you like. What functions are provided by the various elements in the ad?
4. Choose an advertisement you don't like. How would you rewrite the headline using three different styles?
5. Find an advertisement with a tag line. What is its function, and what is your opinion of it?
6. Select an advertisement or commercial you like. What issues do you believe the advertiser considered in writing the copy platform? Discuss.
7. What are the basic functions of a headline?
8. What are some of the most effective methods for making copy interesting?
9. Find an advertisement you don't like. What is the message strategy? Which type of headline is used? What is the copy style? Do you think the copy and headline reflect the strategy? What don't you like about the ad? Why?
10. What is the difference between defamation, libel, and slander?

CREATIVE ART DIRECTION

Objective: To present the role of art in print, radio, and television advertising and in package design. Artists include a variety of specialists who follow specific procedures for conceptualizing, designing, and producing advertising materials. To be successful, advertising people must be conversant in the commercial art terms used to communicate in the business. They must also develop an aesthetic sensitivity to be able to recognize, evaluate, and recommend quality work.

After studying this chapter, you will be able to:

☐ Define *art* as the term is used in advertising.

☐ Describe the roles played by various types of artists in the advertising business.

☐ Explain how advertising layouts are used and the steps involved in creating layouts.

☐ Understand the purpose and use of different types of visuals in advertising.

☐ Evaluate the importance of art in package design.

☐ Explain how art directors affect radio commercials.

☐ Define the basic terms used in scriptwriting for television and radio.

☐ Discuss the advantages of the major types of television commercials.

For 17 years, the Timberland Company's award-winning ads had relied upon beautifully lit, studio-shot, product photography to sell its line of outdoorsman shoes, boots, jackets, and all-weather gear. One ad pictured a column of water rolling out of a spigot onto the golden-rough, natural leather toe of a Timberland boot. The headline read: "For long wear and rugged good looks, just add water." But now it was the 90s—and time for a change.

John Doyle, art director for Boston-based Mullen Advertising, was given the job of creating a new series of ads for the recently acquired Timberland account. Doyle chose to break with the studio look—strobe lights softened by scrims and reflectors—and take Timberland's products outdoors into nature's expansive settings and full spectrum of light. "We wanted people to be visually transported to a different place," says Doyle, "where they could feel the environment and the elements."

They came up with a big idea—Timber Land—as the focus for the campaign. Timber Land would be a utopian natural setting of extraordinary landscapes and crystalline waters where the mountains dramatically disappeared into the clouds. Great creativity, as well as photographic talent and skill, would be needed to express such a wondrous place.

Doyle had seen the work of New York photographer Eric Meola, considered a master at capturing the look and feel of monumental subject matter. He chose Meola for the job, noting that Meola's "shots are so intriguing a viewer is compelled to spend time with them—which is just what we needed for this campaign."

In advertising, it's a challenge for all creative people to come up with images and sounds that are powerful, compelling, and exceptional. As John Doyle and Eric Meola undertook the task of photographing Timber Land, they accepted another inevitable challenge of creativity—the need to come up with something new and fresh.

They spent 44 days shooting in Alaska, Arizona, and Scotland. In the process, they auditioned over 200 models (but found only two who looked sophisticated yet rugged); they spent days scouting the local populations for additional models; they struggled to survive blinding snow gusts; they rented six planes to stage shots at the 7,000-foot level of Mount McKinley; and they had to shoot a cliff-climbing model across a cavernous channel of sea water. After all this, Meola and Doyle captured just nine shots of Timber Land that they deemed usable. Fortunately, these were enough to start the campaign.

Now John Doyle had to turn his attention to further development of the ads. Although the big idea had been identified as Timber Land, the final look for the ads along with final copy had yet to be completed. As we pointed out in Chapter 8, the initial stages of creating an advertisement are always the toughest. John Doyle not only worked closely with Eric Meola, he also had to complete the design of the ads. As for the copy, brainstorming with the copywriter, Paul Silverman, had produced a lot of ideas; but only a few variations on the theme "Timber Land" could be considered real winners. It's at this point in the creative process that the art director and copywriter are often reminded of the phrase: "Creativity is 10 percent inspiration, 90 percent perspiration."

At last it all came together. Meola's stunning wide-angle shots across lakes, plains, and mountainous landscapes with a lone person in the foreground were capped by Silverman's headlines: "Timberland. Because the earth is two-thirds water"; and "Timberland. Where the elements of design are the elements themselves." In designing the ads (see Exhibit 9-1), Doyle used a

Timberland's new advertising campaign for its boots represents a departure from the studio photography and witty headlines typical of this product category. Here the reader is offered the adventure of traveling to a new and wondrous utopia—"Timber Land." The mood and tone of this pristine environment serve as a metaphor for the quality and image of the advertised product.

special typeface whose elegant character added the suggestion of quality to the spacious design.

This was it—the look and concept that expressed the mystique of Timberland. And the image that would carry Timberland successfully into the new decade.[1]

In the case of Timberland, as in most cases, the nonverbal aspect of an advertisement or commercial carries fully half the burden of communicating the message. The way an advertisement *looks* will often determine to a great extent the way it *feels*. That, in turn, will flavor the message and determine the degree to which the advertiser's words are understood and believed. In this chapter, therefore, we discuss advertising concepts from the standpoint of the visual details: the art in advertising—what it is, where it comes from, how it's done.

WHAT IS ART?

When the word *art* is mentioned, most people immediately think of visual art—a painting or photograph. In print advertising, this is called the **visual,** and it is usually the reproduction of a photograph, a computer-generated image, or a hand-rendered illustration. However, the visual isn't the only art in a print ad. In advertising, the term **art** can also refer to the whole presentation—visual, verbal, and aural—of the commercial or advertisement. For example, in most cases, the words in the copy have been artfully chosen to communicate not only the facts about the product, but the positive feelings you should expect to experience with its use. Then the text is carefully set in an appropriately designed typeface and precisely arranged by an artist to further improve its readability and to interact well with the visual. *Art* also refers to the style of photography or illustration, the way color is used, and the arrangement of elements in an ad so that they relate to one another in size and proportion.

In short, if *copy* is the spoken language of an ad, *art* is the body language. This is true for both print ads and the commercials we see and hear on electronic media. Art directors are as important as copywriters when it comes to writing and producing the commercials we see on TV. Why? Because they are concerned with what the commercial *looks like* and *feels like*. TV requires the artful use of both sight and sound to creatively attract and keep the viewer involved. In fact, many of the top agencies even have their art directors help write radio commercials. They believe effective radio advertising combines sounds and words to create visual *word pictures* in the mind of the listener. The art director can be very instrumental in orchestrating this visual (and visceral) impression of the radio commercial. The particular blend of such writing, visual designs, and sounds makes up any advertisement's particular expressive character. Thus, even though the quality of the art is in the eye of the beholder, *every* advertisement employs *art*.

As most writers, visual artists, musicians, filmmakers, and video directors know, the creative elements they share are identifiable, but difficult to define. For example, the principles of balance, proportion, and movement serve as guides for bringing images, type, sounds, colors, inspirations, and qualities of the medium together into a single communication. The creative person understands these principles and uses them to organize the nature of sounds, images, and words so that they have relevance to one another. (See the Checklist of Artistic Principles.)

Because the art forms used in advertising are so diverse, a great amount of effort is generally needed to creatively meld the visual, aural, and verbal elements into a complete and powerful statement. But this effort must be made if the ad is to make an impact powerful enough to break through the customer's physiological and psychological screens and reach the mental files.

The Role of Art in Creating Print Advertising

What set Timberland's advertising campaign apart was the *big idea*—the same thing that sets all good advertising apart. In this case, the big idea of photographically creating an ultrapristine, natural utopia as a setting for the company's products demanded a unique artistic vision. For the ads to be relevant to the audience, the objectives of the company, and the verbal presentation in the copy, the art concept *had* to be peerless and brilliantly executed.

Laying Out the Ad

One of the impressive features about the Timberland ads is the layout and design. Note how in Exhibit 9-2 the copy is dominated by the size and spaciousness of the photograph. In fact, the overall layout of the ad is governed by the concept of space. The sparse text—which gives the ad breathability—is set with the Timberland logo in a neat, easy-to-read, four-column format to fit comfortably into the two-page spread. Likewise, the effective balance of art and copy elements breaking into the margins on either side of the ad further enhances the feeling of spaciousness. Depth—a way of gaining space *into* the picture—is handled by placing the shoes upon the surface of the picture plane, while the photographic landscape disappears into the horizon deep behind the plane. The three-dimensional effect is accentuated by leaving the shadows under the shoes and the logo. This spacial quality gives the ad a total unity and balance in spite of the number

Checklist of Artistic Principles

Balance

The reference point that determines the balance of a layout is the optical center. The optical center is about one-eighth above the physical center, or five-eighths from the bottom of the page. Balance is the arrangement of the elements as they are positioned on the page—the left side of the optical center versus the right, and above the optical center versus below. There are two kinds of balance—formal and informal.

☐ Formal balance. Perfect symmetry is the key to formal balance: *Matched elements* on either side of a line dissecting the ad have equal optical weight. This is used to strike a dignified, stable, conservative image.

☐ Informal balance. By placing elements of *different* size, shape, intensity of color, or darkness at different distances from the optical center, a visually balanced presentation can be achieved. Just like a teeter-totter, an object of greater optical weight near the center can be balanced by an object of less weight placed farther from the center. Most advertisements use informal balance because it makes the ad more interesting, imaginative, and exciting.

Movement

The principle of design that causes the reader of an advertisement to read the material in the sequence desired is called *movement*. This can be achieved through a variety of techniques.

☐ The placement of people or animals in the advertisement can cause their eyes to direct our eyes to the next important element to be read.

☐ Mechanical devices such as pointing fingers, rectangles, lines, or arrows (or, in television, moving the actors or the camera or changing scenes) direct attention from element to element.

☐ Comic-strip sequence and pictures with captions force the reader to start at the beginning and follow the sequence in order to grasp the message.

☐ Use of white space and color emphasizes a body of type or an illustration. Eyes will go from a dark element to a light one, from color to noncolor.

☐ Design can take advantage of the natural tendency of readers to start at the top left corner of the page and proceed on a diagonal Z motion to the lower right corner.

☐ Using size itself attracts attention because readers are drawn to the biggest and most dominant element on the page and then to the smaller elements.

Proportion

☐ Elements in an advertisement should be accorded space based on their importance to the complete advertisement. For best appearance, elements are usually given varying amounts of space in some proportion to avoid the monotony of equal amounts of space for each element.

EXHIBIT 9–2

This ad, another of the award-winning series for Timberland, required uncommon vision and incredible attention to detail. Art director and designer John Doyle went to extraordinary lengths to find just the right creative collaborators, settings, and models—all to fashion a "body language" in this ad that would pierce the reader's physiological and psychological screens and beguile the prospect into venturing out to a spacious new environment.

Contrast

☐ An effective way of drawing attention to a particular element is to use contrast in color, size, or style. For example, a reverse ad (white letters on a dark background) or a black-and-white ad with a red border or an ad with an unusual type style creates contrast and draws attention.

Continuity

☐ Continuity refers to the relationship of one ad to the rest of the campaign. This is achieved by using the same design format, style, and tone for all advertisements, by using the same spokesperson in commercials, by incorporating an unusual and unique graphic element in all ads, or by the consistent use of other techniques such as a logo, a cartoon character, or a catchy slogan.

Unity

☐ Unity is the ad's bonding agent. It means that although the ad is made up of many different parts, these elements relate to one another in such a way that the ad gives a harmonious impression. Balance, movement, proportion, contrast, and color may all contribute to unity of design. In addition, many other techniques can be used.

☐ Type styles from the same family.

☐ Borders around ads to hold elements together.

☐ Overlapping one picture or element on another.

☐ Judicious use of white space.

☐ Graphic tools such as boxes, arrows, or tints.

Clarity and Simplicity

☐ Any elements that can be eliminated without damaging the effect the advertiser is trying to achieve should be cut. Too many different type styles, type that is too small, too many reverses, illustrations, or boxed items, and unnecessary copy make a layout complex and too busy. They make the advertisement hard to read and hurt the overall effect desired.

White Space (Isolation)

☐ White space is the part of the advertisement not occupied by other elements (even though the color of the background may be black or some color other than white). White space can be used to focus attention on an isolated element. Put a vast amount of white space around a block of copy and it almost appears as if it's in a spotlight. White space has a great deal to do with the image the artist desires to create.

and variety of elements in the ad. The Timberland campaign is a vivid demonstration of how layout and design create body language for the advertising.

For print media, the first work from the art department is usually in the form of a **layout,** which is simply a pencil design of the advertisement within the specified dimensions. The term is used when referring to newspaper, magazine, and outdoor and transit advertisements. For direct-mail and point-of-purchase materials, which often require a three-dimensional presentation of the message, the layout is referred to as a **dummy.** For television, the script of a commercial is first seen as a layout in the form of a **storyboard,** a series of pictures or frames that correspond to the script.

The initial layouts or storyboards may be done by any of a variety of artists who work under the art director. (See Ad Lab 9-A, "The Role of the Advertising Artist.") Working in collaboration with copywriters, the artists draw upon all their expertise in graphic design—including photography, typography, and illustration—to create an effective ad or commercial.

AD LAB 9-A
The Role of the Advertising Artist

Several different types of people are employed in advertising art. All of them may be called *artists,* or *commercial artists,* even though they perform entirely different tasks. What is often surprising to nonadvertising people is that some of these "artists" may not be able to draw particularly well. Instead, they have been trained for other artistic specialties.

Art Directors

Art directors are responsible for the visual presentation of the ad. They are normally involved, along with a copywriter, in developing the initial concept of the ad. They may do the initial sketches, or layouts, of what the ad might look like. From that point on, though, they may not touch the ad again themselves. Their primary responsibility is to supervise the ad's progress to completion.

The best art directors are good at presenting ideas in both words and pictures. They are usually graphic designers with broad experience and a good understanding of consumers. Moreover, they should be good managers of people. They may have a large or small staff under them, depending on the organization. Or they may work freelance (as an independent contractor), in which case they themselves probably do more of the work that would normally be handled by assistants in agency art departments.

Graphic Designers

The way advertising materials are initially designed establishes the artistic direction and eventually determines the result. Graphic designers are precision specialists who are preoccupied with the shape and form of things. Their effort in advertising is to arrange the various graphic elements (type, illustrations, photos, white space) in the most attractive and effective way possible. While they may work on ads, especially as free-lancers on special projects, they are more typically involved in the design and production of collateral materials, such as posters, brochures, and annual reports.

In an agency, the art director often acts as the designer. Sometimes, however, a separate designer is used to offer a unique touch to a particular ad.

Illustrators

The artists who paint or draw the pictures we see in ads are called *illustrators.* One of the greatest illustrators in the 20th century was Norman Rockwell, whose pictures brought life in middle America to the cover of the *Saturday Evening Post* every week.

Illustrators are specialists. They are so specialized, in fact, that many frequently concentrate on just one type of illustrating. Automotive, fashion, and furniture are typical examples. Furniture illustrators, for example, might draw a manufacturer's sofa in pencil or with watercolors, paying great attention to the upholstery or wood veneer and showing it all off in a beautiful living room setting.

Very few agencies or advertisers retain full-time illustrators, so most advertising illustrators free-lance. Typically, the agencies hire different illustrators for different jobs depending on the particular needs and the desired look and feel of the ad.

Production Artists

Production (or pasteup) artists are responsible for assembling the various elements of an ad and mechanically putting them together the way the art director or designer has indicated. Good production artists are fast, precise, and knowledgeable about the whole production process (described in Chapter 10). In addition, they have the tenacity to stand the tedious task of bending over a drawing board all day assembling little pieces of type, drawing perfectly straight, clean lines with a pen, or cutting delicate photographs with a sharp knife. To be a production artist today, computer literacy is a must, since the whole process of advertising art is rapidly being computerized.

Most designers and art directors start their careers as production artists and work their way up. It's very difficult work, but it is also important since this is where the ads actually come together in their finished form.

Laboratory Applications

1. Look at the Nissan ad in the Art Director's Portfolio on page 336 and explain which advertising artists were probably involved in its creation and what the responsibility of each artist was.

2. What advertising artists would be involved in creating an all-copy ad such as the famous Henry Ford ad shown in Exhibit 8-1 in Chapter 8?

EXHIBIT 9-3

A layout is used to present an idea to the client and to guide all those who will be involved in producing the ad: artists, photographers, copywriters, and so on. Frequently, slight changes in the concept will occur after presenting the layout, as in this ad for Chicago Cutlery.

The Use of Layouts

A layout is an orderly formation of all the parts of the advertisement. In print, the *layout* refers to the arrangement of the headline, subheads, visual(s), copy, picture captions, trademarks, slogans, and signature (or logotype). In television, *layout* refers to the placement of characters, props, scenery, and product elements; the location and angle of the camera; and the use of lighting.

The layout has two purposes. Mechanically, the layout works as a blueprint. The layout of the print ad in Exhibit 9-3, for example, shows where the parts of the ad are to be placed, it guides the copywriter in determining the amount of copy to write, it helps the illustrator or photographer determine the size and style of pictures to be used, and it helps the art director plan the size and style of type to be used. Finally, the layout is also helpful in determining costs.

The same is true in television advertising. However, the storyboard usually acts more as an approximation of how the commercial will look. We discuss this further later in this chapter and in Chapter 11, "Creative Production: Electronic Media."

The second purpose of the layout is psychological or symbolic. As the Timberland story suggests, the ad's layout and execution create the feeling of the product. The way the layout is designed can be crucial in determining the image a business or product presents. For example, many grocery and other retail stores lay their ads out in a cluttered, busy manner with rows and rows of items and bold, black prices. This is typical of bargain-basement advertising, and the purpose is to create the image of volumes of merchandise at low prices. On the other hand, stores that offer better-quality merchandise, service, and status at higher prices tend to use large, beautiful illustrations, often in color, small blocks of copy, and ample white space. Many of these ads don't even mention price.

Both types of layouts communicate store image and provide blueprint directions for the production artist. Therefore, when designing the initial layout, the art director must be very sensitive to the desired image of the product or business and use a format that projects that image. (See Ad Lab 9-B, "Which Ad Would You Select?") In the case of Timberland, image was a primary reason for the combination of a dominant, spacious photograph and sparse, elegant copy. The ad instantly presents a highly credible image.

AD LAB 9-B
Which Ad Would You Select?

Creating great advertising requires trust between the advertising manager and the creative team. Both must possess the courage to give the advertiser what is needed, rather than what he or she wants. The agency needs the courage to present it. The advertiser needs the vision to recognize its greatness and the courage to buy it. Mike Turner, the senior vice president of Ogilvy & Mather and managing director of OM's Houston office, offered this fictitious example of how a fearful agency account team systematically botched up a marvelous advertisement.

In this example, Ad 1 is the famous Hathaway shirt ad as it originally was conceived in the mid-1950s. The ad created an outstanding image for Hathaway and made the agency, Ogilvy & Mather, famous. However, an account team terrified of taking risks nearly destroyed it at its birth.

When the ad was presented to an account executive at the agency, he added the ugly panel at the left (Ad 2) and changed the strong, simple statement to a lackluster headline. Next, in came a woman (Ad 3) to add sex appeal. Then (Ad 4), off went the "risky" eyepatch. Why? Because people might associate it with unpleasant eye diseases.

As Turner says, "This account team was so busy trying to outguess what the client wanted that they never gave one moment's thought to what was needed, and in the process a great advertisement was destroyed."

Laboratory Applications

1. What would you have done if the agency had presented these four layouts? Would you have had the courage to buy the "risky" ad? Or would you have taken the "safe" route?

2. Identify a current ad that works despite an unconventional or risky approach.

1

2

3

4

Steps in Advertising Layout

Each step in the layout process serves a particular purpose; and for a specific ad, some or all may be performed. Layouts act as guides in the development of the ad or commercial by both those who are working on it and those who must approve it.

Thumbnail Sketches

Thumbnail sketches are extremely rough, rapidly produced drawings used to try out ideas. The best sketches can be chosen for further development. There are two forms of thumbnails. Some art directors prefer to sketch out their ideas on tracing paper or foolscap in miniature—approximately one-fourth to one-eighth the size of the finished ad, as shown in Exhibit 9-4A. Others like to work larger than life and use a full 8½" × 11" (or larger) sheet for each sketch, tearing pages off and starting again after each try.

Rough Layout

The next step in the layout process is the rough layout, which the artist draws to the size of the actual advertisement. As shown in Exhibit 9-4B, the headlines and subheads are lettered onto the layout, the intended illustrations and photographs are sketched in, and the body copy is simulated by using pencil lines.

If the advertisement is to be a television commercial, the proposed scenes in the commercial are drawn in **storyboard** form—in a series of boxes shaped like TV screens. The copy corresponding to each scene is indicated beneath each frame along with a description of sound effects and music.

Comprehensive Layout

The **comprehensive layout,** or comp, is a facsimile of the finished advertisement and is prepared so the advertiser can gauge the final effect of the ad. Copy is set in type and pasted into position, and the illustrations are very carefully drawn. If a photograph will be included, it is pasted into position as well.

In national consumer advertising, the cost of producing layouts is usually covered by the commission the agency receives on the client's media billings. Comps, though, are normally created for the client's benefit rather than for the agency's, so it's not uncommon to charge the client for this expense.

Mechanical

In print advertising, the type and the illustrations or photographs are pasted into the exact position where they will appear in the final ad. This **mechanical** (or **pasteup**) is then used as a direct basis for the next step in the reproduction process—creating color keys, prints, and film of the finished ad, shown in Exhibit 9-4C. The whole production process will be discussed further in Chapter 10.

The advent of desktop publishing and the standardization of electronic interchange between typesetting and prepress equipment has enabled the mechanical steps to be eliminated from many types of jobs. In fact, in many agencies today, the job of the production artist has changed from pasteup to computer operation. (See Chapter 10, "Creative Production: Print Media," for a more in-depth discussion.)

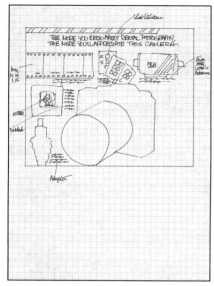
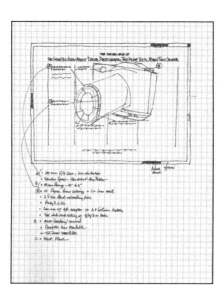
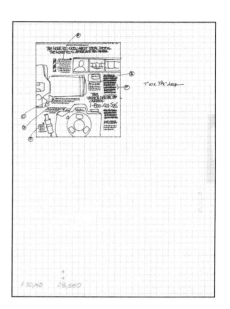

A.

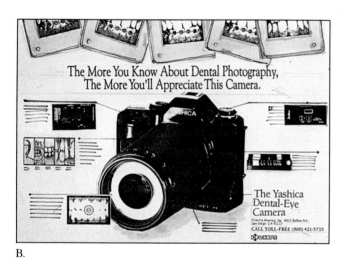

B.

C.

A. Thumbnails are small sketches used to try out various layout ideas. They provide a rapid, inexpensive way to discover the best method for visually matching the copy platform.
B. The rough layout is a larger sketch done to actual size.
C. The finished advertisement for Kyocera's Yashica Dental-Eye camera, as well as the layouts, was produced by Tom Michael and Bob Hines of Market Design in Solana Beach, California.

Dummy

A **dummy** is usually prepared for layouts of brochures and other multipage materials used in advertising. It is put together, page by page, to look exactly like the finished product. A dummy may go through the thumbnail, rough, comprehensive, and mechanical stages just as a regular print layout does.

Generally, an artist makes a dummy by hand, using color markers on tissue paper, mounting the layouts on sturdy paper, and then cutting and folding the dummy to size. Often the dummy is quite elaborate, with colored photos, press-on lettering, and photostats, and spray-coated to look glossy. Today, advertising art and computer suppliers offer complete systems that encompass the entire process of making ad comps as well as dummies. These include color-coded papers, markers, printing inks, and transparency films

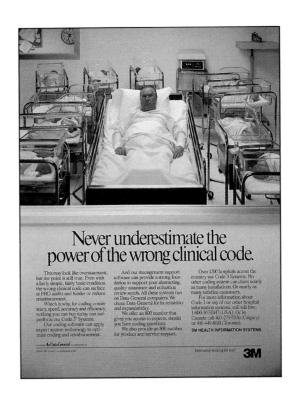

EXHIBIT 9-5

The headline helps stop readers in this business-to-business ad for 3M and combines with the visual to help get the message into the prospect's mental files for better recall later. The words are important, but the visual is what adds meaning and interest to the provocative/command headline. The standard layout of visual, headline, body copy, and logo promises superior ad readership.

(and their electronic equivalents) for making both comps and dummies that are easy for printers to match.

Which Kind of Layout Design Works Best?

Readership studies in recent years indicate that 85 percent of ads do not even get looked at.[2] Moreover, these studies also show—contrary to popular belief—virtually no relationship between the level of ad spending and the recall performance of an ad. What is important, though, is the quality of the advertising.[3] Thus, we are reminded once again of the importance of achieving attention and interest, which in print is greatly influenced by the way an ad is laid out.

Traditionally, the highest-scoring print ads have a standard, poster-style layout with a single, dominant visual that occupies between 60 and 70 percent of the ad's total area.[4] In fact, some research has shown that ads scoring in the top third for stopping power devote an average of 82 percent of their space to the visual.[5] Next in ranking are ads that have one large picture and two smaller ones. The visuals stop the reader and arouse attention, so their content must be interesting.

Headlines also stop the reader and may contribute more to long-term memory than the visual. Research shows that short headlines with one line are best but that a second line is acceptable. The total headline area should fill only 10 to 15 percent of the ad, so the type need not be particularly large. Headlines may appear above or below the visual, depending on the situation (see Exhibit 9-5). David Ogilvy believes that headlines below the illustration gain about 10 percent more readership.[6]

Research also shows that readership drops considerably if ads have more than 50 words. Therefore, if the purpose is to attract a large number of readers, copy blocks should be kept to less than 20 percent of the ad.

Conversely, however, with many products, the more you tell the more you sell.[7] So don't be afraid of long copy if it's *appropriate*. As Henry Ford discovered, long-copy ads can certainly be effective if they are laid out in a readable fashion.

Finally, most people who read ads are also interested in who placed the ad. Company signatures or logos need not be particularly large, however, or occupy more than 5 to 10 percent of the area. For best results, the signatures or logos should be placed in the lower right-hand corner or across the bottom of the ad.

The Advertising Visual

Most people unfamiliar with advertising think an artist is someone who paints or draws. As we discussed in Ad Lab 9-A, however, many advertising artists have relatively little talent for drawing or painting. Their talent may lie in the area of design or art direction or in the mechanical areas of pasteup, production, or computer operation.

The artists who paint, sketch, and draw in advertising are called **illustrators.** The artists who produce pictures with a camera are called **photographers.** Together they are responsible for all the *visuals,* or pictures, we see in advertising.

Purpose of the Visual

Most readers of advertisements (1) look at the picture, (2) read the headline, and (3) read the body copy, in that order.[8] If any one of these elements fails, the impact of the advertisement decreases. Since the visual carries such a great deal of responsibility for the success of an advertisement, it should always try to offer story appeal. Some advertisements have no visuals because someone made a conscious decision that a picture was not needed for effective communication to occur. If a visual is used, it should accomplish at least one, and preferably more, of the following tasks:

☐ Capture the attention of the reader.
☐ Identify the subject of the advertisement.
☐ Qualify readers by stopping those who are legitimate prospects and letting others skip over the ad if they are so inclined.
☐ Arouse the reader's interest in the headline.
☐ Create a favorable impression of the product or the advertiser.
☐ Clarify claims made by the copy.
☐ Help convince the reader of the truth of claims made in the copy.
☐ Emphasize unique features of the product.
☐ Provide continuity for all advertisements in the campaign through the use of a unified visual technique in each individual ad.[9]

Determining the Chief Focus for Visuals

In the Timberland campaign, the ads were dominated by large, single visuals that demonstrated the environment in which the product was used rather than the product itself. But more important, the visuals captured a mood and created a feeling—a context for the consumer's perception of the product.

Selecting the chief focus for advertising visuals is a major step in the creative process. It often determines how well the big idea is executed. Print advertising has many standard subjects for ad visuals, typically more product-related than the Timberland approach. The 10 most common subjects include:

1. *The package containing the product.* This is especially important for packaged goods because it helps the consumer identify the product on the grocery shelf.

2. *The product alone.* Most advertising people discourage this approach for nonpackaged goods because of the lower-than-average readership scores achieved by ads that show the product alone. However, the Godiva chocolate ad in Exhibit 9-6 is an excellent example of how this technique can be used to advantage.

3. *The product in use.* Automobile ads almost invariably show the car in use while talking about the ride, the luxury, the handling, or the economy. Cosmetic ads usually show the product in use with a close-up photograph of a beautiful woman wearing the mascara, the lipstick, or the eye shadow being advertised. The Timberland ads also show the products in use; they're just too small to see in the totality of the visual.

4. *How to use the product.* Recipe ads featuring a new way to use food products historically pull very high readership scores.

5. *Product features.* Computer software ads frequently show a photograph of the monitor screen so the prospect can see how the software features are displayed.

6. *Comparison of products.* The advertiser compares its mouthwash with another, or claims its electric razor gives a closer shave than competitors A, B, and C.

7. *User benefit.* When Sylvania introduced its new 10-bulb flash cartridge, it illustrated user benefit through a series of 10 photographs of the

EXHIBIT 9-6

The Godiva mystique was spawned by the campaign's elegant poster-style layouts and stunning photographic treatment of the sculpted sweets. A vast departure from typical candy advertising, the ad implies the premium price without ever mentioning it.

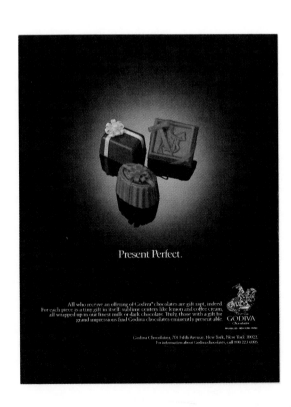

EXHIBIT 9-7

One way to depict a product is by featuring its negative appeal—that is, what happens if you don't have the product. The negative element in this ad helps us stretch our minds into the future and reminds us that our present beliefs could seriously affect our future happiness.

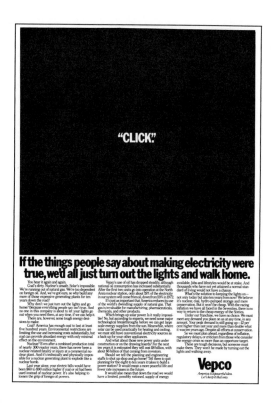

Mona Lisa. The headline keyed the humor: "Now you have two more chances to get it right." It is often difficult to illustrate user benefits, especially intangible benefits. However, marketers know that the best way to get a customer's attention is to show how to benefit from the product.

8. *Humor.* There is no doubt that much advertising is entertainment. Humor in the right situations can make a positive, lasting impression. It can also destroy credibility if used incorrectly, however. Caution is always recommended when dealing with serious subjects. When appropriate, though, humor is like Pernod: "It grows on you."

9. *Testimonial.* A common type of illustration is the photo of a celebrity or of an actual user touting the product. The "before and after" variation of the testimonial illustration has proven very effective for weight-loss products, skin-care lotions, and body-building courses.

10. *Negative appeal.* Sometimes, it is stronger to point out what happens if you don't use the product than if you do use it. Electricity, for example, is something we all take for granted, and illustrating it in use might be very difficult. Illustrating it *not* in use, however, is very simple—and can be compelling, as Exhibit 9-7 shows.

Choosing the Visual

One dynamic aspect of advertising is the infinite number of pictures that can be used to communicate the benefits of a product or service. The kind of picture used is often determined during the visualization process (see Ad Lab 9-C, "Techniques for Creating Advertising Visuals"). But frequently the desired visual is not determined until the art director or designer actually lays out the ad. Advertising managers and art directors often keep checklists handy (as well as an extensive file, or *morgue*, of noteworthy ads, photos, and illustrations) to serve as idea ticklers.

AD LAB 9-C
Techniques for Creating Advertising Visuals

Visuals in an ad help consumers envision a fact or concept—and they do so with immediacy. The type and size of the visual depends upon several factors: the role it should play in the ad, cost, technical limitations, the time required to produce it, effect desired, printing requirements, and the availability of the particular professional to produce what is needed in the medium desired.

The two basic types of visuals used in advertising are photographs and illustrations (drawn, painted, or computer generated).

Photography

A good photograph usually can make several important contributions to an advertisement.

Provides Realism Photography's ability to capture details brings the "real thing" into an ad. Good color photography can give viewers an exciting, realistic look at all kinds of products, from up-close views of high-tech products to wide landscape vistas.

Photographs—especially news-type photos—put you right on the spot. You're on the goal line when the touchdown is scored. Knowing the photographer had to be there, you personally become involved in the action.

Makes the "Cartoon Effect" Come Alive Photography lends an added dimension of realism to subjects that otherwise seem unusual or cartoonish. For instance, had the famous eye-patched Hathaway man been shown as a drawing, it would have lacked the dynamic realism and story appeal expressed by the photograph of the actual man.

Adds Mood, Beauty, and Sensitivity Photography can deliver a mood. It can carry a tremendous emotional wallop—like a documentary photograph of an abused child or, in contrast, a studio portrait of a child enhanced by techniques that emphasize warmth and sensitivity.

Photography may be used to create high sensuality or achieve a high artistic level.

Offers Speed, Flexibility, and Economy A drawing or painting usually takes considerably longer to complete than a photograph—in fact, many photographs can be taken and developed overnight. If custom photographs are budget breakers, stock photos of popular situations, people, and places are available at reasonable prices.

The process of using photography is relatively simple. The photographer shoots a wide variety of poses at various angles and with various light settings. Then, in the case of black-and-white and color print photography, the negatives are printed actual size on a contact sheet unretouched.

With a magnifying glass, the art director finds and proofs the most suitable photo. Most color photos are taken as transparencies (slides), and the art director uses a light table or slide viewer to make selections.

Photography offers flexibility since photographs can be cropped to any size or shape and retouched with a paintbrush or airbrush to improve the image.

Cautions, Though For photographs that are commissioned or bought by an advertiser or agency, any individuals who appear in the picture must sign a standard model release (available from many stationery stores), which grants permission to the advertiser for the photo's use. For children, the release must be signed by the parent or guardian.

In addition, copyright laws state that the image belongs to the artist (photographers and illustrators included); hence, a payment for each use of the photo is normal. The price a photographer charges usually depends on the intended use, frequency of use, and the size of the market.

Illustration

Hand-drawn or painted illustrations offer different benefits than photographs. Some things cannot be photographed: certain concepts and past and future events. Likewise, a line drawing may more clearly portray a product or instill the proper mood. Illustrations may also be used to exaggerate a subject—such as the flamingo in the Air Canada ad in Chapter 8.

Illustrators are limited only by their own skill. Unlike photographers who must capture a scene (either in nature or with expensive staging), the illustrator has the freedom to create the image desired, while adding personal style.

Illustrators use a number of techniques (or media) to produce illustrations, including (1) pencil, crayon, and charcoal; (2) ink and ink wash; (3) scratchboard; (4) airbrush; (5) oil, acrylic, tempera, and watercolor; and (6) the computer.

Line Drawings Line drawings use lines to depict an image. Ideal for sharp and clearly detailed subjects, line drawings are usually created in black-and-white, with no shades of gray. The mediums used include pencil, crayon, and charcoal, which are known for their dry, scratchy appearance; and ink, which can appear wet. Sometimes referred to as pen-and-ink drawings, line drawings are less costly to reproduce than drawings with tonal values. Technical drawings and cartoons are frequently done as line drawings. Line drawings are usually inexpensive and often the least time-consuming type of illustration.

(continued)

AD LAB 9-C *(continued)*

Wash Drawings When tones and grays are desired, a wash drawing might then be used. Essentially, it's an ink applied in various shades of one color using a brush filled with varying degrees of ink and water. There are two types of wash drawings: tight and loose. A tight drawing is detailed, realistic, and done with both a pen and a brush. A loose wash drawing is more impressionistic and done with a brush only; this technique is used by fashion and furniture illustrators in newspaper advertising.

Scratchboard Using special paper with a soft, chalky surface called *scratchboard,* the illustrator applies black ink to the area that will carry the illustration. Then, using a sharp object for scratching—ideally a stylus meant for scratchboard—the ink is removed, leaving a white line. It's as if the artist is adding light to the image with each scratch. This technique gives the impression of extremely fine workmanship and tends to require many hours of meticulous craftsmanship.

Other Illustrative Techniques Numerous other illustrative techniques can be employed. Airbrush is used for its ability to create fine shadings and edges rather than lines; and oil, tempera, and watercolor illustration are used for their wet appearance. Computer-generated drawings can be created to appear as other mediums: ink line drawings, graphic renderings (featuring flat fields of colors or patterns with lines and text on top), airbrush, and photographs (using digitized photography).

Laboratory Applications

1. Select five ads from the text and describe which visualization technique is used for each and how effective it is.
2. Select an ad from the text and propose a different visual or visualization technique from the one used. Describe the rationale for your choice.

Talon, Inc., has used a humorous approach for years to advertise its various zipper models to consumers and to the clothing trade. Other ads include a photograph of a football with a zipper on it and even one of a kangaroo with a zipper on the pouch.

What if you're advertising a zipper? How exciting is a picture of a zipper. Do you show it on a man's pants or a woman's dress? Do you picture it opened or closed? Or do you picture something else? (See Exhibit 9-8.)

Selecting the appropriate photograph or visual for an advertisement is a difficult creative task and is often what separates the great from the not so great. (See the Art Director's Portfolio for examples of dynamic, creative ads.)

Art directors deal with several basic issues in the selection of visuals:

☐ Is a visual needed for effective communication to occur?

☐ Should it be black-and-white or color, and is this a budgetary decision?

☐ What should the subject of the picture be, and is that subject relevant to the advertiser's creative strategy?

☐ Should an illustration or a photograph be used?

☐ What are the technical and budgetary requirements to achieve the desired visual solution?

These very basic questions are all too often overlooked. They should be asked and answered in the initial planning stages of the advertisement, and they should be asked again when the advertisement is being produced. This is where pretests, such as paired comparisons, come in (as we discussed in Chapter 6).

Just as an exercise, thumb through any chapter in this book and study any one of the advertisements shown. Ask yourself the questions listed above as they apply to the ad you chose. On any day, in any given agency, top art directors perform this exercise routinely.

ART DIRECTOR'S PORTFOLIO

A. The art director carefully placed the small headline in this ad for Garuda Airlines to allow the National Geographic-style photograph to accomplish its task of capturing attention and reader interest.

B. Lincoln is taking President's Day off, but TCF isn't. This illustration allows the art director to express the impossible, reinforce the big idea, and catch the eye and mind of the reader—all at once.

C. An imaginative blend of type, creative copywriting, and art combine to lure readers into this ad for The Nature Company, a retailer of all kinds of nature-related products.

D. Only an advertiser with a highly recognizable logo like McDonald's could get away with this billboard—run in French-speaking Quebec. It's the ultimate play on symbols. When you pronounce the J and the M together in French, it sounds the same as *j'aime*—meaning "I love." Thus, "I love McDonald's." The art director ingeniously used the mysterious smile of Mona Lisa to further reinforce the concept of love and reassure us that we've read this surprising ad correctly.

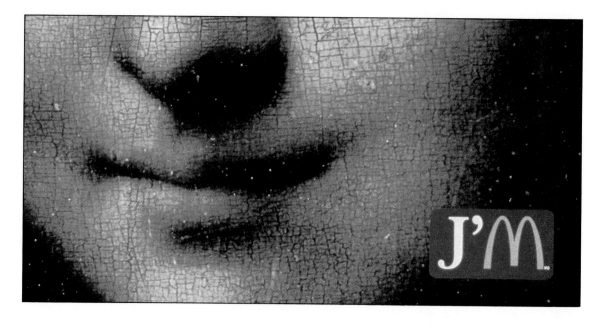

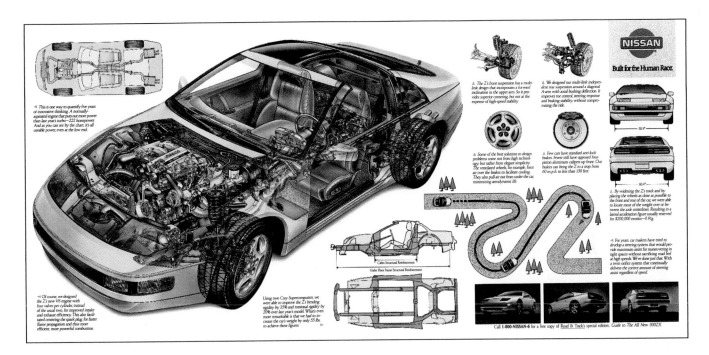

E. The automobile enthusiast is sure to be drawn into this information-filled array of copy, detailed illustrations, and photography. This spread is actually three pages of a fold-out brochure—thus, no headline.

AD LAB 9-D
The Psychological Impact of Color

Reaction to color, says Walter Margulies, is generally based on a person's national origin or culture. For example, "warm" colors are red, yellow, and orange; "these tend to stimulate, excite, and create an active response." Those from a warmer climate, apparently, are most responsive to those colors.

Violet and "leaf green" fall on the line between warm and cool. Each can be one or the other, depending on the shade used.

Here are some more Margulies observations:

Red Symbol of blood and fire. A runner-up to blue as people's "favorite color" but the most versatile, the hottest color with highest "action quotient." Appropriate for Campbell's soups, Stouffer's frozen foods, and meats. Conveys strong masculine appeal—shaving cream, sports equipment, automobiles.

Brown Another masculine color, associated with earth, woods, mellowness, age, warmth, comfort—the essential male; used to sell anything (even cosmetics)—Revlon's Braggi.

Yellow High impact to catch consumer's eye, particularly when used with black; psychologically right for corn, lemon, or suntan products.

Green The symbols of health and freshness; popular for tobacco products, especially mentholated; also soft drinks—7UP.

Blue Coldest color, with most appeal; effective for frozen foods (ice impression); if used with lighter tints becomes "sweet"—Wondra flour; Morton Salt.

Black Conveys sophistication, high-end merchandise, and is used to simulate expensive products; good as background and foil for other colors.

Orange Most "edible" color, especially in brown-tinged shades; evokes autumn and good things to eat.

Laboratory Applications

1. Based on Margulies's observations, explain the moods or feelings that are stimulated by specific color advertisements or packages illustrated in this text.
2. Name products for which a redesign using different color combinations might make the product or package more attractive.

THE ROLE OF ART IN PACKAGE DESIGN

No discussion of advertising art direction can be complete without giving some attention to the design of product packages. Perhaps the best way to emphasize the importance of package design is to point out the amount of money spent on it: over $70 billion in 1990, fully as much as is spent on media advertising in the United States.[10] In fact, many businesses spend more money on packaging than they do on advertising. A major reason for the heavy emphasis on packaging is the trend toward self-service, which requires that the package play a major role in both advertising and selling.

Packaging encompasses the physical appearance of the container and includes design, color, shape, labeling, and materials. In designing a package, consideration should be given to three factors: its stand-out appeal, how it communicates verbally and nonverbally, and the prestige or image desired.

Like advertising, packaging communicates both verbally and nonverbally. For example, one bread manufacturer decided that a green wrapping would connote freshness. The only problem was, the customers associated it with fresh mold! Perhaps the company simply chose the wrong shade of the color—an easy mistake to make with green. (See Ad Lab 9-D, "The Psychological Impact of Color.")

Even after consumers buy the product, they must continually be "sold" on it. Research has shown that the consumer has an active relationship with

EXHIBIT 9-9

Packages have as much effect on consumer buying decisions as ads do and are designed with just as much care. The idea for the Hombre six-pack and bottle labels evolved from a series of sketches the designer made on napkins while having lunch with the client. The image conveyed by the type style and the illustration is of prime importance for so-called nonrational products.

packaging and responds to a package intuitively. Therefore, package design can be as powerful a tool as advertising in building a product's brand image.[11]

Packaging establishes the personality, the image, and the prestige of the brand. Therefore, the design must give consideration to what the consumer thinks others would regard as prestigious. This is especially important with the so-called nonrational products—such as health and beauty aids, perfume, sports accessories, and confection gifts—for which fancy, whim, and mystique all operate in place of rational choice.[12]

As in Exhibit 9-9, the package must literally sell the product off the shelf. This can be done by using shape, color, size, interesting visuals, or even texture to deliver a marketing message, give product information, and indicate in-use application.[13] Additionally, the package should continue promoting the product in the home, creating brand image and loyalty. Therefore, packages should be designed to open and close easily and not be awkward to handle.[14]

Packaging Forms and Materials

Packages come as wrappers, cartons, boxes, crates, cans, bottles, jars, tubes, barrels, drums, and pallets. Packages are made of many substances—primarily paper, steel (or "tin" cans as in Exhibit 9-10 on p. 338), aluminum, plastic, wood, glass, burlap, and other fibers. Newer packaging materials include plastic-coated papers, ceramics, shrink and wax wraps, and even straw. Metal foils that protect the contents and add to the attractiveness of the package have become common. Plastic provides a lightweight, safe, unbreakable container. Important improvements in packaging include amber-green glass wine bottles that protect the contents from damage by light and heavy-

EXHIBIT 9-10

The "tin" cans are standard for canned fish, but the elegantly designed paper wrappers are not. They, and the gift boxes, signal that Gold Seal salmon is a premium product—a far cry from the main ingredient in Aunt Betty's salmon-noodle casserole.

duty, gray computer diskette jackets that reflect heat and protect the diskette from damage.[15] The relatively new plastic film pouch for food products has become a substitute for tin cans and makes packages even more flexible, light, and compact.

With the public's growing concern for the environment, recyclable tin-coated steel and aluminum packages have enjoyed a recent resurgence in popularity. Similarly, the popular aerosol spray can is rapidly becoming free of fluorocarbons in order to protect the ozone layer.[16]

Packaging Specialists

Management ultimately makes the final design decisions about packages and labels. However, because packaging is closely related to advertising, and because of the similar techniques used in advertising and packaging, the advertising department and the advertising agency usually play an important role in package development. Many advertising agencies design labels and packages and prepare the copy that goes on them. Often, their help is vital because they coordinate their work with the overall theme of the advertising campaign they have devised for the product. Also, packaging is now sometimes considered part of the advertising and sales budgets of manufacturers who previously viewed it as a facet of production.

However, packaging problems have become so complex in recent years that advertisers and their agencies increasingly use packaging specialists. These specialists usually fall into one of three groups:

1. Outside package-consulting firms, staffed by experienced designers and artists, that provide complete package design.
2. Design departments of larger corporations that have their own personnel to work on packaging and who probably played a role in designing the product as well.

3. Container manufacturers that sell metal, paper, plastic, or other packaging materials and often provide help with package design as a service to their present and potential customers.

When Should a Package Be Changed?

There are many reasons why even successful packaging gets changed. If a product is altered or improved, repackaging may be required. New packaging may be necessitated by substitutions in materials, such as aluminum or plastic. Competitive pressure or environmental concerns may also influence alterations in the existing package.

As the number of working women has increased and television has declined as an advertising medium, package design is being used more often as a way to communicate product value. This has resulted in more frequent package redesigns as companies strive to keep the brand image projected by the package current with constantly changing consumer perceptions.[17] Advertisers spend millions of dollars in researching a new image and then promoting it.

However, a decision to stay with the present packaging can be as crucial as a decision to change it, and marketers should always exercise caution when considering a change. Even when a decision to change has been made, designers often change the packaging very gradually so consumers will not be confused.

THE ROLE OF ART IN RADIO AND TELEVISION ADVERTISING

Upon receiving a flood of calls from amputees, executives at the Du Pont Corporation knew their new commercial was a success.

Created by BBDO Worldwide from an inspiration by a Du Pont department head, the ad featured Bill Demby, a Vietnam veteran who lost his legs in a rocket attack. In the TV spot, Demby is introduced to the viewer while on his way to a pick-up game of basketball in an urban neighborhood. On his arrival, he is acknowledged by the other players; but as he pulls off his sweatpants, attention focuses on his two artificial legs. As Demby freely dashes, jumps, scrambles, and shoots, the voice-over describes that he is wearing the "Seattle Foot," a prosthesis designed by the Prosthetics Research Study in Seattle, Washington. It features an inner keel made of Du Pont's Delrin acetal resin that mimics the unique springing action found in a natural leg. Suddenly, Demby falls. Play stops. He's offered a helping hand but jumps right up, and the rapid fire action begins again. As the spot ends, an out-of-breath player calls out: "Hey, Bill, you've been practicing!" (See Exhibit 9-11.)

Developing the Concept for the Commercial

Creating concepts for broadcast commercials is similar to the process used in creating print ads, and getting through the first phases can be the toughest. For BBDO, coming up with the big idea was not so much a challenge as coming up with the main "actor." They wanted the credibility that a real Vietnam veteran could offer. As it turned out, the creative team needed not only a Vietnam vet with his own Seattle Foot, but also someone who was telegenic, physically strong, and able to display athletic skills. "You'd be surprised how difficult a task that proved to be," says Cathy Mendel, BBDO account supervisor. "After exhausting all the traditional casting sources," she

In this ad, the story line is a framework within which to portray the value of the product and demonstrate its ruggedness. The story itself began without a specific person in mind, but as you can see from this storyboard, Bill Demby—a real-life beneficiary of the product—helped make the product's utility come alive.

(Music under)

ANNCR: When Bill Demby was in Vietnam, he dreamed of coming home and playing a little basketball.

MAN: Hey, Bill!

ANNCR: A dream that all but died when he lost both legs to a

Vietcong rocket. But then researchers discovered that a Du Pont plastic could help make truly lifelike artificial limbs.

(SFX: sounds of game in progress)

ANNCR: Now Bill's back, and some say he hasn't lost a step. At

Du Pont, we make things that make a difference.

MAN: Hey, Bill, you've been practicing!

ANNCR: Better things for better living.

recalls, "we finally looked at participants in the Disabled Games. That's where we found Bill Demby." The storyboard shown in Exhibit 9-12 was then personalized to fit Bill's story.

Where do the concepts and characters we see and hear every day on radio and TV come from? Simply put, they are usually born in the minds of the men and women who conceive the original commercial—the art director, the copywriter, and the creative director.

Initially, if the concept is to create a dramatic scene, the script may call for an actor to play the part of a fictitious character. Or the creative team may decide it wants to use a well-known celebrity to lend credibility to the product. In any case, as we saw with Bill Demby, casting these characters is a major area of deliberation at the time the commercial is written.

During the casting process, the most important consideration is relevance to the product. For example, it's usually considered unwise to use a comic to sell financial products—or mortuary services, for that matter. And in spite of

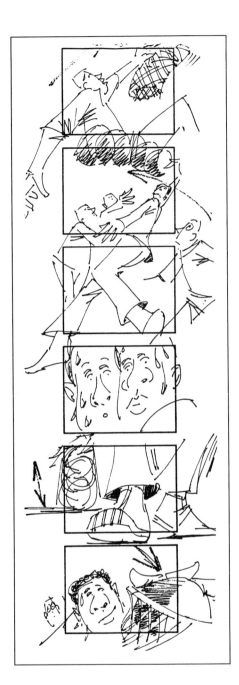

EXHIBIT 9-12

This ad revolves around a single character, Bill Demby, and how a Du Pont product contributes to "better living" for him. One of the "arts" of TV and radio ads is choosing a viable character who can make the product credible and appealing. Once Bill was chosen for the ad, this "impressionistic" storyboard was developed to depict his story and the action that would be incorporated into the ad.

Bill Cosby's success for advertisers such as Jell-O, Ford, McDonald's, and Coca-Cola, David Ogilvy doesn't even believe in using celebrities. Viewers, he says, tend to remember the celebrity more than the product.[18]

As the concept for the commercial evolves, the creative team defines the characters' personalities and usually writes a brief but detailed description of them. These descriptions serve as guides in casting sessions in selecting prospective actors who interview and audition for the roles. Sometimes, a Frank Bartles and Ed Jaymes (of Bartles & Jaymes fame) will be discovered—solid, believable characters who go beyond a simple role and actually create a personality or image for the product.

Basic Mechanics of Script Development

A television script is divided into two portions. The right side is labeled **audio** and lists the spoken copy, sound effects, and music. The left side is the **video**—for the camera action, scenes, and stage directions. Exhibit 9-13 (p. 342) shows a script for AT&T prepared by Ayer advertising in New York.

Once the basic script has been conceived, the writer and art director prepare a *storyboard*. The typical storyboard is a sheet preprinted with a series of 8 to 20 blank television screens (frames). The video scenes are sketched into the frames by the art director, and the audio (plus instructions for the video) is typed underneath. Due to space limitations, many abbreviations are used. See Exhibit 9-14 (p. 343) for some of the more common ones.

The visual value of television is such a powerful element that the art director's role (relative to the copywriter) is particularly important today—more than ever before.[19] The art director carefully designs a layout of each scene in much the same way as in a print ad—arranging actors, scenery, props, lighting, and camera angles—to maximize impact, beauty, and emotion. The storyboard helps both agency and client personnel visualize the complexities of the commercial, estimate the expense, discover any weaknesses in concept, present it to management for approval, and guide the actual shooting. At its best, though, the storyboard is still just an approximation of what the final commercial will look like. Actual production sometimes results in many changes in lighting, camera angle, focal point, and emphasis. The camera sees many things the artist didn't consider, and vice versa.

During the last decade, the cost of both television production and media has soared, greatly increasing the pressure on agencies to pretest their commercial concepts before final production. To supplement the storyboard or pretest the concept, therefore, a commercial may be taped in rough form using the writers and artists as actors.[20] Or an **animatic** may be shot—a film strip composed of the sketches in the storyboard accompanied by the audio portion of the commercial synchronized on tape.

However, even an animatic now costs $10,000 or more to produce. Here again, though, the computer is having a cost-saving impact. Peter Farago of Farago Advertising, for example, has developed a Macintosh-based random-access computerized editing system that enables the agency to create moving pictures on the screen (after scanning storyboard sketches into the computer), lay sound in behind them, then transfer the entire package onto videotape to send to the client.[21]

This system cuts the cost to produce testable material from about $11,000 down to around $1,100. "We're doing video comps, if you will, on a Macintosh," says Farago.[22] While this technology is still new, it is being adopted by more and more agencies as they look for ways to serve their clients' creative needs better for less money.

EXHIBIT 9-13

This script for the AT&T calling card is designed to reinforce the decision of those who never left AT&T for a competitor. The frustration of the man trying to make a long-distance call on a competitive carrier while double-parked comes through the script—even without seeing the commercial. And the spot acts as a warning for anyone considering the competition.

NW Ayer Incorporated
1345 Avenue Of The Americas, New York, N.Y. 10105

CLIENT AT&T	PROGRAM
PRODUCT Testimonial	FACILITIES
TITLE Meter Maid	DATE 3/27/90
NUMBER AXLL 9099 AS PRODUCED	LENGTH :30

VIDEO	AUDIO
OPEN ON MCU OF MAN GETTING OUT OF CAR THAT HE JUST DOUBLE PARKED ON A BUSY STREET.	MUSIC UNDER THROUGHOUT. MAN VO: This is gonna be a piece of cake right?
CUT TO MLS OF MAN RUNNING TO CURB.	Pull over, make a fast call.
CUT TO MCU OF MAN DIALING ON PAY PHONE.	But I'm using this other long distance company. Now, ...
CUT TO CU OF POLICE TRAFFIC VEHICLE.	First, they have me ...
CUT TO MCU OF MAN DIALING PHONE.	dialing all these numbers just to get them. Then I gotta dial the ...
CUT TO ECU OF TRAFFIC VEHICLE SIREN.	number I'm calling.
CUT TO CU OF MAN LOOKING FRUSTRATED.	MAN UNDER: You call this easy?
CUT TO ECU OF MAN ON PHONE.	MAN VO: Then I still have to dial all these other numbers.
CUT TO MS OF TRAFFIC VEHICLE. CUT TO CU OF METER MAID.	MAN UNDER: Come on, I'm double parked.
CUT TO CU SHOTS OF MAN ON PHONE.	MAN VO: So yeah, I make the call.
CUT TO SHOT OF METER MAID WRITING TICKET.	MAN UNDER: Thank you. MAN VO: To the tune of 35 bucks.
CUT TO MS OF MAN RUNNING OUT OF BOOTH.	CLIFF ROBERTSON VO: With the AT&T card, calling is easy.
CUT TO PC SCREEN WITH NAMES.	Another reason people are coming back to AT&T.
CUT TO AT&T LOGO. SUPER: The Right Choice. 1 800 225-7466	Aren't you glad you ...
CUT TO MLS OF MAN PICKING UP TICKET OFF CAR WINDOW.	never left.

F-440 Rev 10/81

The Art of Scripting

In Chapter 8, we presented fundamentals of writing advertising copy. Television commercials demand that additional attention be given to credibility, believability, and relevance. That goes well beyond the use of words and includes the work of the art director.

David Ogilvy points out that the millions of dollars spent on TV commercial research have resulted in the following principles:

☐ The opening should be a short, compelling attention getter—a visual surprise, compelling in action, drama, humor, or human interest.
☐ Demonstrations should be interesting and believable—authentic and true to life; they should never appear to be a camera trick.
☐ The commercial should be ethical, in good taste, and not offend local mores.
☐ Commercials should be entertaining (to hold the viewers' attention), but the entertainment should be a means to an end and not interfere with the message.

EXHIBIT 9-14   Cut, Zoom, and Wipe, Please! (Common abbreviations used in TV scripts)

CU:	Close-up. Very close shot of person or object.
ECU:	Extreme close-up. A more extreme version of the above. Sometimes designated as BCU (big close-up) or TCU (tight close-up).
MCU:	Medium close-up. Emphasizes the subject but includes other objects nearby.
MS:	Medium shot. Wide-angle shot of subject but not whole set.
FS:	Full shot. Entire set or object.
LS:	Long shot. Full view of scene to give effect of distance.
DOLLY:	Move camera toward or away from subject. Dolly in (DI), dolly out (DO), or dolly back (DB).
PAN:	Scan from one side to the other.
ZOOM:	Move rapidly in or out from the subject without blurring.
SUPER:	Superimpose one image on another—as showing lettering over a scene.
DISS:	Dissolve (also DSS). Fade out one scene while fading in another.
CUT:	Instant change of one picture to another.
WIPE:	Gradually erase picture from screen. (Many varied effects are possible.)
VO:	Voice-over. An off-screen voice, usually the announcer's.
SFX:	Sound effects.
DAU:	Down and under. Sound effects fade as voice comes on.
UAO:	Up and over. Voice fades as sound effects come on.

☐ The general structure of the commercial and the copy should be simple and easy to follow. The video should carry most of the weight, but the audio must support it.

☐ Characters become the living symbol of your product—they should be appealing, believable, and most of all, relevant.[23]

These are just a few of the principles research has shown to be true.

To illustrate these principles, look at the award-winning, 30-second commercial for Jarman's shoes illustrated in Exhibit 9-15. Created by the Bloom Agency in Dallas, this is a classic example of a well-written, well-designed, simple, interesting, credible, and entertaining commercial. It was also relatively inexpensive to produce.

First, look at the commercial as a whole. It has one dominant mood and gives a single, unified impression. There are a minimum number of people. The situation is high in human interest. The structure is *simple* and easy to follow. The presenter is *appealing,* authoritative, and credible, and the whole commercial is a *close-up* of him. The entertainment value is high but perfectly *relevant.* In fact, everything not relevant to the commercial's objective has been deleted. The *sales points* are demonstrated smoothly, and the *product name* is mentioned frequently. Finally, there is a strong *closing identification* illustrating the name and the product.

EXHIBIT 9-15

This commercial for Jarman shoes demonstrates the basic principles of creating an effective television ad.

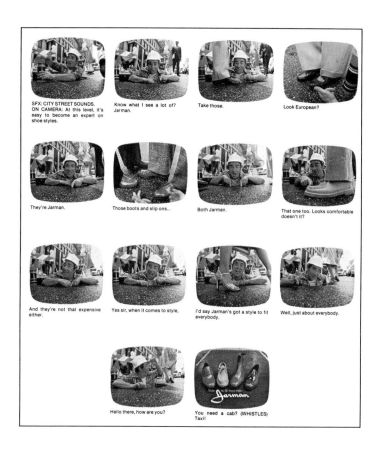

SFX: CITY STREET SOUNDS. ON CAMERA: At this level, it's easy to become an expert on shoe styles.

Know what I see a lot of? Jarman.

Take those.

Look European?

They're Jarman.

Those boots and slip ons...

Both Jarman.

That one too. Looks comfortable doesn't it?

And they're not that expensive either.

Yes sir, when it comes to style,

I'd say Jarman's got a style to fit everybody.

Well, just about everybody.

Hello there, how are you?

You need a cab? (WHISTLES) Taxi!

ETHICAL DILEMMA IN ADVERTISING
Imitation or Plagiarism—What's the Difference?

When two companies run ads that are strikingly similar, is it imitation, plagiarism, or coincidence? Well, it depends on your point of view. In the mid-1980s, Rubin Postaer & Associates created a commercial for American Honda that ended with the frame turned sideways while the car blasted off like a rocket. Five years later, Leo Burnett Advertising created a commercial featuring astronaut Scott Carpenter and his son in which they compared an Oldsmobile to a spaceship. At the end, the Olds turned sideways and blasted off—just like the Honda. Larry Postaer, creative director at the Honda agency claimed, "That was a direct steal from us." But Burnett executives denied pilfering the visual. Burnett's president, Rick Fizdale, said he wasn't even familiar with the Honda commercial.

That's been the historical pattern of the debate: angry accusations followed by denials, and then everything blows over till next time. Some advertisers try to ignore the problem by convincing themselves that being copied is actually good. Hugh Thrasher, executive VP of marketing for Motel 6, says of his often-imitated Tom Bodett commercials: "We think these [copycat] ads just remind people of the originality of our concept." Others like Nancy Shalek,

president of L.A.'s Shalek Agency, maintain, "If you haven't been ripped off, you're really in trouble."

It's doubtful that the debate about the difference between imitation and plagiarism will be resolved soon. Part of the problem is that creative advertising is essentially derivative, with popular movies, books, and music providing the basis for countless ads. As Millie Olson, executive creative director at Ketchum Advertising, San Francisco, points out, "We try to follow the trends and speak the language people are speaking."

The moment a genuine breakthrough occurs, everybody jumps on the bandwagon. Some of the best—and most imitated—recent campaigns include the shaky-camera spots for AT&T and the down-home Bartles & Jaymes commercials. Copying the style of these ads is easy, because plagiarism is almost impossible to prove. Today, the only rule seems to be: When you imitate, make enough changes to avoid being so obvious that you draw flak from the originator.

Surprisingly, clients haven't entered the debate over copycat advertising. Perhaps that's because they're more comfortable with well-worn ideas rather than with bold, original concepts. The prevailing attitude seems to be that

Looking at some of the mechanics, note that there seems to be only one scene throughout. There are, in fact, four different camera setups. But the *unity* is so strong the changes are hardly noticeable.

Examine the opening scene. Before one word is spoken, we know who the man is and what he's doing. He looks the part and acts the part. In 12 words, he has established the whole context of the commercial and is into the sell. By the second frame of the storyboard, he has already said the product name once and made a case for the popularity of the product. By the third frame, he's proving his first sales point and is into the second—style. Then he hits the name again. Two frames later, he hits it again, and then there is a third sales point—comfort. One more frame and he hits the fourth sales point—price. Then he hits the name again and the fifth point, which also selects the target market—for men only. Finally, the last shot shows the shoes, the name, and the strong tag line: "Style to fit your style."

In all, the commercial contains only 76 words, yet it says so much. That's what makes a commercial memorable.

As an exercise, take a few minutes to compare some of the other television spots with which you're familiar to that Jarman commercial. How many can you think of that are so concise? So simple? So appealing? So credible? These are the qualities that make commercials effective.

ads are just tools of the trade. If something's working for the competition, why not use it?

Perhaps the real crux of the problem is that imitation is an accepted part of the advertising business. Many of the industry's most talented art directors and writers collect competitive ads to use for inspiration. And because advertising is a highly collaborative process, it's often difficult to determine the extent of the creative contribution of each individual working on a campaign. With personal responsibility so unclear, it becomes easier to shirk professional ethics.

But every so often, someone creates an ad that goes so far beyond the "gray zone" that it helps clarify the boundaries of what's ethically permissible and what's not. One such campaign promoted Mint Condition, a new candy for smokers. The ad showed a cowboy on a horse coming toward the reader. In the foreground were two flip-top boxes of mints; the theme under them read: "Come to Mint Condition." Visually, it was a dead ringer for a classic Marlboro ad right down to the typeface used. Mint Condition's president, Joel Gayner, defended the ads saying they "make something even more original through changing it three degrees." Philip Morris's lawyers weren't amused by the parody and considered an infringement suit.

But even flagrant infringement cases are very hard to win, because ideas aren't protected by copyright laws, and creative advertising is an idea business. That's why some industry leaders have become passionate about the need for personal ethics. As Jim Golden, executive producer of DMH MacGuffin says, "All we have in this business are creativity and ideas. The moment someone infringes on that, they're reaching into the very core of the business and ripping it out." Ultimately, if the problem is ever to be solved, advertisers must stop "borrowing" ideas from each other and demand greater creativity from themselves.

Questions

1. Some art directors claim that "independent invention" explains why many ads look the same. Is that possible? If so, does it excuse running imitative advertising?

2. Should clients become more concerned about the ethics of copycat advertising? What if you were an art director and a client asked you to do an ad that copied the style of one that was already running?

Types of Television Commercials

The ads we have discussed have all been "presenter" commercials, where one person or character presents the product and carries the whole sales message. Sometimes, these presenters are celebrities, like Lynn Redgrave for Weight Watchers or Michael Jackson for Pepsi-Cola. Other times, they are corporate officers of the sponsor, like Frank Perdue for Perdue Chicken or Lee Iacocca, the chairman of Chrysler Corporation. In the Jarman commercial, a professional actor plays the role of a fictitious character acting as a spokesperson. Other sponsors, like Bank of America, may use a noncelebrity actor who simply delivers a straight pitch rather than playing a particular role.

The presenter format is only one type of commercial. In fact, there may be almost as many ways to classify television commercials as there are advertisers. The six basic categories, though, in addition to the presenter category, are the *straight announcement, demonstration, testimonial, slice of life, lifestyle,* and *animation.* We discuss each of these types briefly. These divisions often overlap, though, and should not be considered ironclad.

Straight Announcement

The **straight announcement** is the oldest and simplest type of television commercial. An announcer delivers a sales message directly into the camera or off-screen while a slide or film is shown on-screen. It is a safe method and can be effective if the script is well written and the announcer convincing. The appeal may be either "hard sell" or relaxed. The straight announcement is a relatively simple approach and needs no elaborate facilities, so the advertiser saves money. It may be combined with a demonstration.

By and large, the straight announcement has given way to more creative concepts. However, this type of commercial is still often used on late-night TV programs, as well as by local advertisers and political organizations.

Demonstration

Studies have shown that a **demonstration** convinces an audience better and faster than an oral message.[24] Memorable demonstrations have been used to show the product advantages of car tires, ballpoint pens, and paper towels, to mention just a few.

Products may be demonstrated in three ways—in use, in competition, or before and after. These techniques enable the viewer to project the product's performance if he or she owned it. Therefore, the theme of the demonstration should be as clear, simple, graphic, and relevant as possible. And it should be interesting—like the one in Exhibit 9-16, for example.

Testimonial

People are often persuaded by the opinions of individuals they respect, and this holds true whether the "product" is a political candidate or a bar of soap. The true **testimonial**—where a satisfied user tells how effective the product is—can make TV advertising highly effective.

Satisfied customers are the best sources for testimonials. While they may be camera shy, their natural sincerity is usually persuasive. Ogilvy suggests shooting candid testimonials when the subjects don't know they're being filmed.[25] But be sure to get their permission before use.

Using celebrities to endorse a product may gain attention, as we've discussed. But the celebrities must be believable and not distract attention from the product. Additionally, research has shown that presenters with moderate

EXHIBIT 9-16

The "big idea" demonstrated in this 30-second commercial is being able to catch fish where "you'd swear fish don't exist." Simple visuals and sound accentuate the message.

SFX: Footsteps

VO: This is the lure that won last year's National Walleye Championship. A lure so powerful . . .

SFX: Splash

VO: . . .it catches fish in places . . . you'd swear fish don't exist.

to high physical attractiveness score greater credibility due to perceived trust, perceived expertise, and audience liking.[26]

Actually, people from all walks of life endorse products—from known personalities to unknowns and nonprofessionals. Which person to use in a specific commercial depends on the product and the strategy.

Slice of Life (Problem/Solution)

The **slice-of-life** commercial is a little drama that portrays a real-life situation. It usually starts with just plain folks before they discover the solution to their problem. The situation is usually tense, full of stress—for example, the need to get a package delivered overnight for an important meeting. Often, the situation deals with something of a personal nature—bad breath, loose dentures, dandruff. A friend drops the hint, the product is tried, and the next scene shows a happier, cleaner person off with a new date, or someone finally able to bite into an apple. Such commercials are often irritating to viewers and hated by copywriters, but their messages still break through and sell.[27]

The key to effective slice-of-life commercials is simplicity. The ad should concentrate on one product benefit and make it memorable. Often, a **mnemonic device** can dramatize the product benefit and trigger instant recall. Users of Imperial margarine suddenly discover a crown on their head, for example; or the doorbell rings for the Avon representative.

Joe Sedelmaier, a Chicago television producer, has developed a unique style of humor out of the slice-of-life form.[28] He turns Everyman's trials of daily life into caricatures, builds sympathy for his beaten-down characters, and then offers the solution, as for Alaska Airlines in Exhibit 9-17 on p. 348.

Some variations on the slice-of-life technique make the believability almost painful to watch. Anacin, for example, combined the slice-of-life and testimonial forms by showing highly believable, depressing headache complaints from a sooty coal miner, a weather-beaten farmer, and a plain-looking housewife—all actors, of course. Such ads, which approach the cinema verité art form with their natural lighting, subdued colors, erratic motion, extreme close-ups, and grainy film quality, have been used by a variety of advertisers, including AT&T, Home Savings, and Hospital Corporation of America.[29]

Believability is difficult to achieve in slice-of-life commercials. People don't really talk about "ring around the collar," so the actors must be highly credible to put the fantasy across. That's why most local advertisers don't—and shouldn't—use the slice-of-life technique. Creating that believability takes professional talent and money, as we shall see in Chapter 11.

Lifestyle

When they want to present the user rather than the product, advertisers often use the lifestyle technique. For example, Levi's targets its 501 Jeans messages to young, contemporary men working, walking, and playing in a variety of different occupations and pastimes with a bluesy, modern musical theme. Likewise, beer and soft drink advertisers frequently target their message to active, outdoorsy, young people, focusing on who drinks the brand rather than on specific product advantages.

Animation

Cartoons, puppet characters, and animated demonstrations have traditionally been very effective in communicating difficult messages and in reaching specialized markets such as children. The way in which aspirin or other

EXHIBIT 9-17

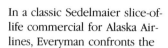

In a classic Sedelmaier slice-of-life commercial for Alaska Airlines, Everyman confronts the

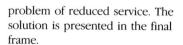

problem of reduced service. The solution is presented in the final frame.

ANNCR: Many airlines offer reduced rate fares. Unfortunately, that's not all they've reduced. It makes you wonder . . . what's next?

MAN (addressing other passengers): I'd appreciate it. Do you have four quarters for a dollar?

Anybody have two quarters for a dollar?

Yes, miss. Do you have two quarters for two dollars? Two quarters for five dollars, please?

Oh, boy, I'd appreciate it. Anybody have two quarters for five dollars?

ANNCR: On Alaska Airlines, we have low fares, too. But you'd never know it by the way we treat you.

medications affect the human system is difficult to explain. Animated pictures of headaches and stomachs, however, can simplify the subject and make a demonstration understandable.

Today, computer-generated graphics animate television commercials for everything from high-technology products to bathroom cleaner. This is discussed in Chapter 11, "Creative Production: Electronic Media." Its use, though, has required a great deal of faith on the part of advertisers, since most of this very expensive work is done right in the computer and there is nothing to see until the animation is well developed.[30]

The Role of Art Direction in Perspective

To conclude our discussion of creative art direction, it is important to understand that the many guidelines often offered as "rules" of good design—whether for television or for print—are merely expressions of accumulated thought and experience. They are merely *guidelines*. All the rules in the world will not make a great ad or design a great package. To do his or her job, the art director needs to push—to bend and sometimes break—rules while still maintaining standards of good taste. That's a ticklish task. But then, art direction is not science. And that's why they call it *art*.

Summary

Every advertisement uses art. In advertising, *art* refers to the whole visual presentation of the commercial or advertisement. This includes how the words in the ad are arranged, what size and style of type are used, whether photographs or illustrations are used, and how actors are placed in a television commercial.

The many types of artists involved in advertising include art directors, graphic designers, illustrators, and production artists, to name a few. Each has been trained to handle a particular specialty.

For print advertising, the first work from the art department is seen in the form of a layout, which is a design of the advertisement within specified dimensions. The layout has two purposes. One is a mechanical function to show where the parts of the ad are to be placed. The other is a psychological or symbolic function to demonstrate the visual image a business or product will present.

Several steps are used in laying out an ad: thumbnail sketch, rough layout, comprehensive layout, and mechanical. For brochures and other multipage materials, the layout is referred to as a *dummy*. For television, the layout is referred to as a *storyboard*.

A great deal of responsibility for the success of an advertisement is placed on the visual. The picture may be used to capture the attention of the reader, to identify the subject of the advertisement, to create a favorable impression, or for a host of other reasons.

The two basic devices for illustrating an advertisement are photography and drawings. Photography can make several important contributions to an advertisement, including realism; a feeling of immediacy; a feeling of live action; the special enhancement of mood, beauty, and sensitivity; and speed, flexibility, and economy.

Drawn illustrations can do many of these things, too, and may be used if the art director feels they can achieve greater impact than photographs.

The chief focus for visuals may be on the product in a variety of settings, or on a user benefit, a humorous situation, a testimonial, or even on some negative appeal.

More money is spent on packaging today than on advertising, primarily because of increased emphasis on self-service. This requires the package to play an important role in both advertising and selling.

Factors to consider in packaging design include how the package communicates verbally and nonverbally, the prestige desired, and the stand-out appeal required.

Package design is often changed because of a desire to align the package more closely with the product's marketing strategy, emphasize the product's benefits, emphasize the product's name, or take advantage of new materials.

In radio and television advertising, art also plays an important role and includes concept development, character definition, set and scene design, costuming, lighting, scripting, and camera angles—everything having to do with the visual value of the commercial.

The basic layout of a television commercial is called a *storyboard* and includes sketches of the scenes along with the script of the commercial. To supplement the storyboard and pretest a commercial, an animatic may be used.

There are numerous types of television commercials, including straight announcement, demonstration, testimonial, slice of life, lifestyle, and animation.

Questions for Review and Discussion

1. Choose any television commercial shown in this text. How would you describe the "art" in that commercial?

2. Select a print ad of your choice. What do you suppose the art director contributed to that advertisement?

3. What is a layout? What is its purpose?

4. What color stimulates sales best? Why?

5. What is a mechanical? How is it used?

6. What color is white space?

7. What is the purpose of a picture in an advertisement? When would you not use a visual?

8. What is a storyboard and how is it developed?

9. How is an art director important to the creation of a radio commercial?

10. What television spots can you think of that typify the six major types of television commercials?

CREATIVE PRODUCTION: PRINT MEDIA

Objective: To introduce the creative and technically complex field of print production. The computer has had such a dynamic effect on the production process that advertisers must be aware of some of the many alternatives available to them today—to save money, enhance their production quality, and accelerate the production phase of advertising. Yet, even with the computer, a basic knowledge of typology and printing is still very important to all advertisers.

After studying this chapter, you will be able to:

☐ Discuss the role of computers in the print production process.

☐ Explain the process advertisements and brochures go through from concept through final production.

☐ Describe the characteristics of the five major type groups.

☐ Understand how type is structured and measured.

☐ Discuss how print materials are prepared for the press.

☐ Define common printing terms like *sheetwise* and *work & turn.*

☐ Debate the advantages of the major printing methods used today.

They finally decided to let Raphaële do it—with Bob's help.

Steve Makransky, the art director at Young & Rubicam, had come up with a great idea for NYNEX's business-to-business campaign. The ads were supposed to run in special-interest sports publications like *Tennis* and *Golf Digest*—magazines read by top business executives and corporate CEOs who attend sporting events and belong to the country club set. The campaign was supposed to communicate the fact that NYNEX was more than the local telephone company for New York and New England. In fact, for corporations with sophisticated communications or computer networking problems, NYNEX was the one-stop supplier for the Fortune 500 companies.

Steve and his writing partner decided to tie into the sporting theme with a series of ads characterized by stunning visuals and teasing word-play headlines. One layout called for a city skyline under the header: "With us it's not a game." At first glance, the cityscape would look typical. But the second glance would let the eye spot something awry—chess pieces the size of skyscrapers? Nifty idea. But it presented a real problem—how to do it.

Illustration had come to mind first, but the client rejected the idea. It just wasn't realistic enough. Photography was the next logical choice. However, the subject of the photo was a *concept,* not a real object. Any photography here would need some heavy modification. They turned to a special-effects photographer. His suggestion: construct a model city. How long would this take? Too long. At what cost? Too much. They had to look elsewhere.

During the conceptual phase, the creative team had readily envisioned the cityscape in their minds, and Makransky had sketched out the idea easily enough. But to actually produce the image was another matter entirely—a common problem in advertising. The production process is where ingenious creative approaches—conceived in the mind—crash head-on into the physical realities of life.

A third approach was considered: Transfer images of buildings onto heat-sensitive materials that could then be shrink-wrapped onto the chess pieces. The chess pieces would be photographed and then photocomposited onto a stock photograph of the city. This was a step in the right direction, but as it turned out, still not good enough to work in real life. When wrapped around the chess pieces, the images warped to such an extent that they became totally unattractive and unbelievable.

Y&R's senior vice president and top art buyer, Alistair Gillett, remembered a Budweiser campaign with some striking images created by a retoucher using sophisticated computer imaging. Gillett fired off a call to Houston, Texas, and contacted Raphaële, a transplanted French woman who owned her own company, Raphaële Digital Transparencies, and a secret, multimillion-dollar mainframe computer system—named "Bob." When Alistair explained the job, Raphaële promised she and Bob could deliver the desired image. All she needed was the shot of the cityscape and the photographs of the chess pieces.

Makransky worked with photographer Bill White to shoot the chess pieces. They needed shots of each ivory chess piece, taken from eight different angles. For the cityscape, the agency reviewed a wide variety of **stock photos**—pictures already photographed for a different purpose and available for lease. The shot they selected was a beautiful business skyline of Dallas by photographer Marc Siegel.

With the photos in hand, Raphaële first used a scanner to digitize each image of the chess pieces and the cityscape into the computer. Then she edited out the buildings where the chess pieces were to fit, cloned a section of blue sky, and dropped that into the spaces where the buildings had been.

EXHIBIT 10-1

A specialized computer system was needed to produce this remarkably realistic image, so finding the right supplier was the key. Once discovered, the process still took five weeks to complete—and that's considered fast.

With us it's not a game.

Your company's information and communications strategy has to include a lot more than an opening gambit.

Which is one reason why over half of the Fortune 500 companies use NYNEX.®

From our broad range of telecommunications expertise, to the way we can optimize your network, our Companies can provide the communications and information systems that will work with your existing operations and expand along with your business.

NYNEX can move you to the latest software and computer systems. Customize a solution. Link all your systems, whether they're local, wide area or positively global. And, provide the training and maintenance to maximize your investment.

We invite you to call NYNEX at 1 800 535-1535.

We won't leave you in a stalemate.

Need to communicate? Need to compute? The answer is

NYNEX

Next, the textured facade images of the buildings had to be digitally mounted and wrapped around the images of the chess pieces. To do this, Raphaële created a three-dimensional computer model of each chess piece. Using specially designed software, the computer then wrapped the building textures around each model and even put reflections in the windows to appropriately match the new surrounding environment. To complete the effect, Raphaële overlaid shadows and light from the photos of the original chess pieces onto the buildings. To achieve perfection, the entire process—including minor adjustments requested by the agency—took about five weeks from beginning to end.

Finally, the completed image was output on an $11'' \times 14''$ transparency and shipped to the agency for the assembly of type and completion of the production process. The finished full-page ad shown in Exhibit 10-1 created such a stunning effect that it was later adapted to a full-page, black-and-white newspaper ad and run in *The Wall Street Journal* and *The New York Times*. But without the new, sophisticated production technologies available to advertisers today, it could never have been accomplished.

THE PRODUCTION PROCESS

The average reader of advertisements has no inkling of the intricate, detailed, technical stages printed advertisements and promotional materials go through from start to finish. But experienced advertising people do—especially art directors, designers, and print production managers. In fact, they pay very close attention to every detail. They know it's the details that give an advertisement added impact and completeness. And when an approved design goes into the production stage, they remain vigilant because the entire advertising effort can be radically affected by the outcome of the production process.

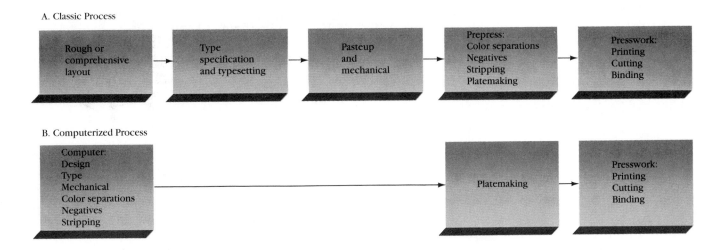

A. Classic Process

| Rough or comprehensive layout | → | Type specification and typesetting | → | Pasteup and mechanical | → | Prepress: Color separations Negatives Stripping Platemaking | → | Presswork: Printing Cutting Binding |

B. Computerized Process

| Computer: Design Type Mechanical Color separations Negatives Stripping | → | Platemaking | → | Presswork: Printing Cutting Binding |

EXHIBIT 10-2

A. Classic print production process.
B. Computerized print production process.

Role of the Production Manager

Every print ad presents numerous production complexities. These range from the reproduction of fine technical illustrations in full color, with precise specification and placement of type around the illustrations, to the need to have all printing materials checked, approved, duplicated, and shipped to the newspapers or magazines in time for a specific deadline. These tasks are the typical responsibilities faced by every production manager.

The term **print production** refers to the systematic process a layout for an ad or brochure goes through from concept to final printing. The primary role of the print production manager, therefore, is to see that the art director's or graphic designer's layout—which is often in color—is successfully converted into a final assembly of black-and-white artwork called a **mechanical** or **pasteup** (or set of mechanicals) that the printer can use to make printing plates. Exhibit 10-2A shows a model of the classic print production process. The reason for converting the artwork to black-and-white centers upon the modern printing process. Printers use high-contrast, black-and-white photographic film negatives to place an image on the printing plate; so artwork must be photographed in black-and-white only. To create full color, the printer must make four plates—one to print each of four colors: magenta (red), cyan (blue), yellow, and black. Each plate must be made from black-and-white artwork ready for the printer's camera to shoot. (This process will be discussed more thoroughly under the heading "Printing in Color.")

A powerful or beautiful ad can be destroyed when a production person fails to follow the designer's final layout correctly. For example, when type is spaced too widely, lines are drawn too thick, photographs go unretouched, or an inappropriate illustration technique is chosen, the look of the ad may be weakened or even destroyed. Failure to choose the proper printing process, papers, or inks can result in higher costs and may even lead to reprinting the entire job. For instance, if an advertiser makes the mistake of using oil-based inks to print promotional information on cereal boxes, rather than the lawfully required vegetable-based inks, the entire job will have to be scrapped and reprinted. Art directors and print production managers have occasionally lost tens of thousands of their client's or agency's dollars—and sometimes their jobs—by not paying attention to the details of print production.

Any person connected with advertising, therefore, needs a fundamental grasp of basic production procedures. This knowledge and understanding saves a lot of money and disappointment in the long run.

Impact of Computers on Print Production

In recent years, mechanical production procedures have become more complex. Enormous technological progress has taken place in the graphic arts field due in particular to the revolutionary application of computers and electronics. As the model in Exhibit 10-2B shows, much of the work previously performed by hand retouchers and pasteup artists, for example, can now be accomplished by artists and graphic designers using a variety of computer graphics or imaging programs on large ($100,000 range) or small, very affordable (less than $10,000) computers. The smaller IBM PC and Macintosh-based systems are commonly used for **desktop publishing**—the process that enables individuals, through the use of desktop computers, to personally prepare, and occasionally even print, relatively high-quality ads, documents, and publications. All these programs offer the artist the ability to treat printed pages—as well as photos and illustrations—as images that can be easily altered and corrected by the manipulation of the computer images on a monitor screen.

The larger, more costly minicomputer systems—such as the Hell ScriptMaster, Scitex, and Crosfield workstation—present other opportunities and benefits to major advertisers and agencies. Featuring a wide range of electronic options, these systems are considered the top guns for high-quality image enhancements and **prepress production**—the whole process of converting page art and visuals into materials (generally film negatives and color separations) needed for printing.[1] This process is rapidly replacing traditional hardcopy versions of artwork and photographs. Dealing with the images on a screen offers the artist great flexibility. Changes can be made immediately; high-quality proofs are immediately available; and sophisticated software tools allow the image to be flipped, twisted, rotated, or reversed—instantaneously. Finally, the output from these systems is of the highest quality, whether it is on paper for the printer to photograph or as a negative the printer can use outright. The chart in Exhibit 10-3 shows the various configurations of desktop publishing and related computerized equipment that might be used for producing different quality levels of prints or negatives. As we mentioned in Chapter 9, the desktop computer approach has not only proven very practical for print advertising, but is now also used to create storyboards for television commercials—video comps, if you will.[2]

Sophisticated software features previously only available on large computer systems have now made their way to the personal computer. Now desktop publishing software programs for page making (QuarkXpress® and Aldus PageMaker®), for painting and drawing (Aldus FreeHand®, Adobe Illustrator®), and for image manipulation (ColorStudio and Adobe Photoshop™) are available to the small business person as well as the agency creative department.[3] While these programs have only recently begun to offer the quality of big agency art, they are proven tools for the small business, offering both flexibility and savings in printing, typesetting, and advertising costs. A great feature of the personal computer graphics programs is that they allow users a wide choice of classic and designer type styles at low cost.

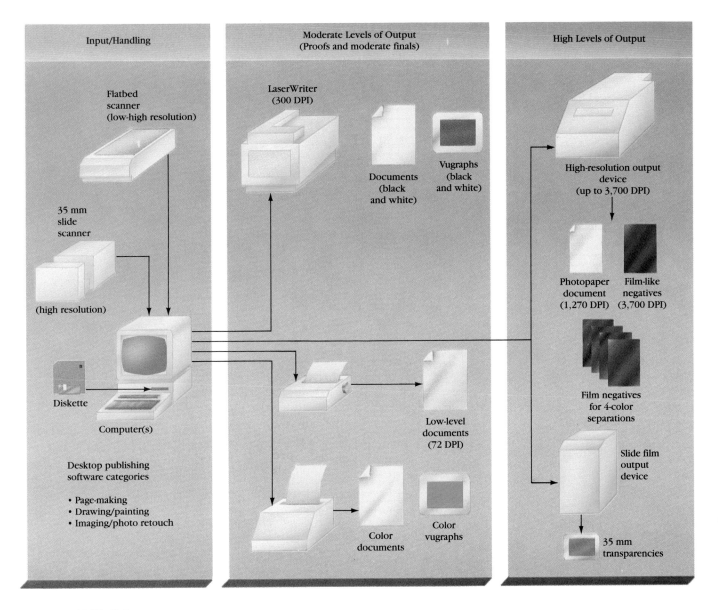

EXHIBIT 10-3

Typical desktop publishing configurations. Desktop and minicomputer systems can produce the artwork needed for printing. Images are electronically scanned into the computer or transferred from diskette. Specialized software is then used to manipulate the images, set type, and create a layout. Proofs, which show exactly what the finished ad will look like, can be printed out in color or black and white on moderately priced laser and dot-matrix printers. However, the negatives and transparencies needed for the actual printing process must be produced on a more expensive device that can create highly detailed, accurate images.

Today, small shops like Farago Advertising in New York—which produced the Barnes & Noble Bookstores advertisement in Exhibit 10-4—are producing camera-ready art on disk ready to be printed by a high-resolution phototypesetting machine as a paper mechanical or in the form of final negatives.[4]

Now nonartists have the tools to render simple to moderately difficult drawings, charts, and photo-retouch work as never before. These systems do not turn an unskilled artist into a skilled one, however. Notwithstanding the

This Barnes & Noble ad was produced on a desktop computer system. Notice the complexity of the layout, with varied column widths and type "wrapped" around images. Notice also the various type sizes and the distinctive graphics produced just for this ad.

influence of computers, the role of the traditional advertising artist and illustrator will likely remain extremely important to the company and the agency wishing to retain quality and individuality in their advertising. Despite the reputed speed of computers, many advertising creatives have found that the artistic detailing needed in using the computer actually takes *more* time in the design stage. This is more than compensated for in the production stage, though—since the essential production is handled electronically by the software at the time of design rather than later by a production artist working manually.[5]

As a result, today's first-rate graphic artist, illustrator, and retoucher must be computer literate and highly experienced in a number of art and page-making programs—in addition to having a thorough knowledge of aesthetics, rendering, and design.

PLANNING PRINT PRODUCTION

Once a print ad has been designed and the layout and copy have been approved, the ad falls under the supervision of the print production manager and a staff of production artists and assistants. In the smaller agencies and in-house art departments, the art director may also be responsible for overseeing print production.

The print production department specifies the style and size of the type-faces used in the ad. If the shop doesn't have its own typesetting machines or computer systems, it must order the type from a typesetting company. If it has its own computers, the production people can instantly select the size and style of type on the screen. The black-and-white type may be positioned electronically within the computer or output onto paper to be glued in place on an artboard (usually a thick posterboard with a smooth, glossy surface) within an area the size of the final printed image. If an additional color is to

EXHIBIT 10-5

A pasteup (or mechanical) combines the main image (or base art) with one or more plastic overlay sheets (sometimes called Rubylith or Amberlith). Each sheet shows the placement of a different color, and each may be photographed separately. In the printing process, the colors are printed one after the other to make up the total image.

be printed, another artboard marked to the same dimensions is used for the second image. Sometimes, the second image is glued onto a clear plastic **overlay** that lies on top of the first image (called the **base art**). The artists place crossmarks in the corners of the overlay and the base art to precisely register their position, as shown in Exhibit 10-5. When the printer goes to make the two plates, each pasteup (mechanical) has to be photographed separately. If an overlay is used, it is removed and photographed separately from the base art. Then each plate is printed one after the other in its own color, and the final printed piece comes together into a single page featuring both colors.

An ad that is to be placed in a publication is made **camera-ready** for the newspaper's or magazine's printer to make "negs" and plates. In most cases, the magazine provides a sheet of specific instructions and measurements for preparing camera-ready art for each of the ad sizes it offers.

When camera-ready art is prepared for a brochure, the print production manager may also be responsible for getting comparative prices from several printers and then ordering the printing. The manager must be sure the printer understands all the technical instructions.

The manager must make a crucial decision at the earliest possible time—which is most important for a particular project: speed, quality, or economy? The answer determines the nature of the production methods used and type of personnel employed. Typically, one criterion will be sacrificed in favor of the other two. If cost is more important than quality, a high-grade copy machine may be used to resize the artwork rather than a huge, wall-mounted production camera. If speed is most important, then costs for rush fees (which can easily triple costs) and overnight express deliveries will be justifiable.

Working backward from the **closing dates** (deadlines) of the publications, the production manager determines when each step of the work must be completed to meet the deadline. Deadlines can vary from months to hours. Generally, the manager tries to build extra time into each step. This is because every word, every art element, and most of the aesthetic choices are potential problems; and at the last minute, they may be changed to improve the ad.

The production manager informs the art director and copywriter of the opportunities and limitations of various production techniques and keeps them abreast of the progress of each job. In some cases, teams of art directors and writers are employed on just one account.

Finally, the production manager must check all proofs for errors and obtain approvals from agency and client executives before releasing the advertisements to the publications. This is generally a very time-consuming task because not everyone is available when the work is ready for approval.

For the production process to run smoothly, everybody concerned must understand the whole procedure. Consider the problem of correcting errors. Once the advertisement has been delivered to the typographer, photoplatemaker, printer, or publication, it costs substantially more to make any changes than it would before the actual production begins. For example, the cost of changing a single comma after the copy has been typeset may reach as much as $50. It becomes 10 times that once the negatives have been made by the printer, and it becomes 10 times more costly again if the job has already been printed.[6]

Thus, the production process requires good planning, and the people involved need to develop a recognition and understanding of art, graphics, and type. They must learn all they can about typography, platemaking, printing, and color, and they must be familiar with the technical jargon of printing.

TYPOGRAPHY

The art of selecting and setting type is known as **typography.** Because almost every advertisement has some reading matter, type has tremendous importance in advertising. The typeface chosen affects the advertisement's general appearance, design, and readability. Although good type selection cannot compensate for a weak headline, poorly written body copy, or a lack of appropriate illustrations, it can create interest and attract readers to the advertisement.

Successful print ads—as well as brochures and other promotional pieces—embody a particular personality, mood, or tone. One ad may feature a visual of a skier in action while another may picture a still shot of technical equipment. To complement the tone or mood of the visual, as in Exhibit 10-6, art directors carefully select type styles that will enhance the desired personality of the product or the ad.

In the end, it is hoped that the flavor imparted by the type helps to meet the objectives and strategy of the campaign by creating a link between the mood of the ad and the target audience's mental files and attitude. We discuss this subject more completely in the section titled "Type Selection."

Classes of Type

Type is divided into two classes: *display type* and *text type*. **Display type** is larger and heavier than text type. It is used in headlines, subheads, logos, and addresses, and for emphasis in an advertisement. Smaller **text type** is used for body copy in an advertisement.

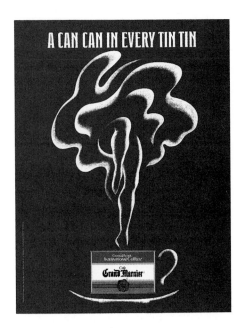

EXHIBIT 10-6

Each of the type styles used in this ad for International Coffees (from General Foods of Canada) sets a different mood. Notice the difference between the type styles used on the can and in the headline of the ad.

Type Groups

Thousands of typefaces are available, and type designers continually develop new ones. Typefaces are classified into various groups by their similarity in design. There is no reason to learn the names of all the faces, because each typesetting house or printer has only a limited number of typefaces, depending on requirements and the kind of equipment it uses. Except for people who wish to become art directors or type specialists, an understanding of the five major type groups shown in Exhibit 10-7 is sufficient.

Roman (Serif)

The most popular type group is called **roman type.** A good example of this is the type style you are reading right now. The two most distinguishing characteristics of roman type are the small lines or tails (called **serifs**), that finish the ends of the main strokes, and variations in the thickness of the strokes. These features tend to give the type a warm personality—more human and sensual. Roman offers the greatest number of designs, so contrast can be achieved without a basic design change. It is also considered the most readable. Roman type comes in a variety of sizes and has dozens of sub-classifications that differ in the thickness of the strokes, the way the letters are designed (letterforms), and the size and regularity of the serifs.

Gothic (Sans Serif)

The second most popular type group is **gothic** or **sans serif** (French for "without serif") **type.** Also referred to as *block* or *contemporary,* this large group of typefaces is characterized by the lack of serifs (hence the name *sans serif*) and the relatively uniform thickness of the strokes.

Sans serif text typefaces are usually not as readable as roman faces. But they are widely used—especially for highly technical product ads—because of their simple and clean lines, which give a slick, modern appearance.

EXHIBIT 10-7

The five major type groups include roman, gothic, square serif, cursive, and ornamental.

ROMAN TYPE	SQUARE SERIF TYPE
Typography	Typography
Typography	
Typography	SCRIPT TYPE
Typography	Typography
Typography	Typography
SANS SERIF TYPE	ORNAMENTAL TYPE
Typography	Typography
Typography	TYPOGRAPHY
TYPOGRAPHY	

Square Serif

Combining sans serif and roman typefaces produces **square serif type,** which has the same uniform thickness of strokes as sans serif type. Square serif is similar to roman typefaces in that it has serifs. However, the serifs have the same weight and thickness as the main strokes of the letters.

Cursive or Script

The **cursive** (or **script**) **typefaces** resemble handwriting—because they're based on handwriting. The letters are often connected, and they may convey a feeling of femininity, formality, classicism, or beauty. Since they are rather difficult to read, they are used primarily in headlines or formal announcements. Also, they are used in cosmetic and fashion advertising. The word *Advertising* on the cover of this text is in cursive calligraphy (done by hand) to help convey the concept of creativity in contemporary advertising.

Ornamental

The **ornamental typefaces** include designs that provide novelty and are highly embellished and decorative. They are used for special effects but are often difficult to read. The title pages of the section openers in this text contain some ornamental type—also done by hand.

Type Families

Each major type group includes type families. A **type family** is made up of related faces identified by such names as Cheltenham, Futura, Goudy, Souvenir, Bodoni, and Caslon. The roman typeface you are reading right now is called ITC Garamond Light. The basic design remains the same within a family but varies in the proportion, weight, and slant of the characters. Exhibit 10-8 shows the versions commonly available, including light, medium, bold, extra bold, condensed, extended, and italic. These variations enable the typographer to provide contrast and emphasis in an ad without changing type

EXHIBIT 10-8

Meet the Cheltenham family. Note the variety of looks that can be achieved without leaving the family. Art directors may use a boldface in the headline and lightface in the copy, as well as different sizes—or even italics for emphasis. Most art directors try to use only one type family in a single ad, and they rarely use more than two.

Cheltenham	**Cheltenham Bold**
Cheltenham Italic	***Cheltenham Bold Italic***
Cheltenham Bold	**Cheltenham Ultra**
Cheltenham Bold Italic	***Cheltenham Ultra Italic***
Cheltenham Bold Condensed	Cheltenham Light Condensed
Cheltenham Bold Condensed Italic	*Cheltenham Light Condensed Italic*
Cheltenham Bold Extra Condensed	Cheltenham Book Condensed
Cheltenham Nova	*Cheltenham Book Condensed Italic*
Cheltenham Bold Nova	**Cheltenham Bold Condensed**
Cheltenham Light	***Cheltenham Bold Condensed Italic***
Cheltenham Light Italic	**Cheltenham Ultra Condensed**
Cheltenham Book	***Cheltenham Ultra Condensed Italic***
Cheltenham Book Italic	

styles. A **font** consists of a complete assortment of capitals, small capitals, lowercase letters, numerals, and punctuation marks for a particular typeface and size of type.

To control the exclusivity of how their advertising looks, some advertisers commission the design of a unique type style. The Volvo ad in Exhibit 10-9, for example, shows a bold, sans serif headline set in Volvo's own type style designed by John Danza, a creative director at Volvo's former advertising agency.

Other advertisers might go in the opposite direction for uniformity. Some, for example, tailor their ads to blend well with the typography and design elements of the different magazines they are placed in. This gives the ads an editorial look and, the advertiser hopes, enhanced credibility (or at least interest).

Type Structure and Measurement

Graphic designers, production managers, and desktop publishers must have some understanding of how to measure type. *Points, picas, uppercase, lowercase,* and *commoncase* are terms used to describe the way type is structured and measured.

Points

The depth (or height) of type is measured in **points.** There are 72 points to the inch, so one point equals $\frac{1}{72}$ of an inch. The height of a line of type is measured from the bottom of the **descenders** (extensions downward from the body of the type—j, g, p) to the top of the **ascenders** (extensions upward from the body of the type—b, d, k).

The most common type sizes used in advertising have traditionally been 6, 8, 10, 11, 12, 13, 14, 18, 24, 36, 42, 60, 72, 84, 96, and 120 points. Some of these are shown in Exhibit 10-10. However, with computerized phototypesetting

EXHIBIT 10-10

The smaller type sizes are typically used for text, the larger
sizes for display (headlines).

text type		display type	
SIZE of type	6 POINT	SIZE of type	16 POINT
SIZE of type	8 POINT	SIZE of type	18 POINT
SIZE of type	9 POINT	SIZE of type	20 POINT
SIZE of type	10 POINT	SIZE of type	24 POINT
SIZE of type	12 POINT	SIZE of type	30 POINT
SIZE of type	14 POINT	SIZE of type	36 POINT

EXHIBIT 10-10

The smaller type sizes are typically used for text, the larger sizes for display (headlines).

equipment, any type size is possible. Most computer programs will print out type at any size, and, with recent improvements in graphics display technology, allow the designer to see an accurate on-screen representation of the final printed piece. The smaller sizes, 6 through 14 points, are used for text type, and the larger sizes are normally used for display (headline) type. This text, for example, is set in 10-point type.

Picas

The unit of measurement for the horizontal width of lines of type is the **pica.** There are exactly six picas to the inch and 12 points to the pica.

The width of a single letter of type depends on the style of the typeface and whether it is regular or bold, extended or condensed. The width also depends on the proportions of the letter. The averages for each type style and size are provided by the manufacturer of the type.

Uppercase, Lowercase, and Commoncase

Capital letters (caps) are called **uppercase,** and small letters are called **lowercase.** These terms came about when type was set by hand and compositors stacked the case containing the capital letters above the one with the small letters.

Note from the material you are now reading how easy it is to read a combination of uppercase and lowercase. However, type can also be set using all caps (uppercase) or **commoncase** (caps and small caps). Advertising copy set in caps and lowercase is more readable than copy set in all capitals, and that goes for headlines as well as body copy. Type set in solid capitals can be used for emphasis, but this should be done very sparingly. For more information on type structure and measurement, see Exhibit 10-11.

Type Selection

Knowledge of the effects and symbolism of typefaces requires expertise. This ability requires the experience and skill usually only acquired through study and trial and error. As a result, among local advertisers, type selection is often the most overlooked aspect of advertising creativity.

This illustrated guide to type shows how type is structured and measured.

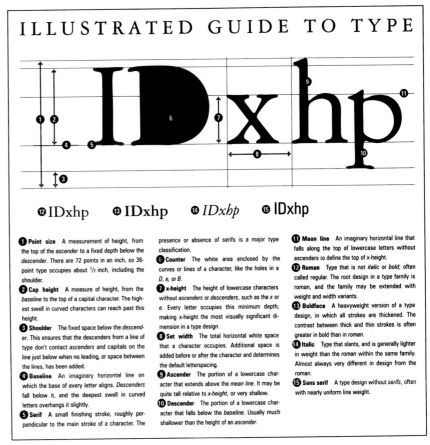

First published in Macworld, July 1991. Copyright © 1991 Macworld Communications, Inc.

Four important points should be considered in the selection of type: readability, appropriateness, harmony or appearance, and emphasis. We discuss each of these briefly.

Readability

The most important consideration in selecting a typeface is readability. As David Ogilvy says, good typography helps people read; bad typography prevents them from doing so.[7] General factors that contribute to readability include the style of type, boldness, size, length of the line, and spacing between the words, lines, and paragraphs. An advertisement is printed so that it can be read, and reduced readability kills interest. Difficult-to-read typefaces should be used infrequently and only to create special effects.

Large, bold, and simply designed typefaces are, of course, the easiest to read. However, advertisers are limited by the amount of space in the advertisement and the amount of copy that must be written. Readability is also affected by the length of the line the copy is set in. Newspaper columns are usually less than 2 inches wide; magazine columns, slightly wider. For advertisements, it is usually recommended that columns of copy be less than 3 inches (18 picas) wide.

The spacing between lines of type also influences the readability of an ad. A small amount of space between lines of type is always allowed for descenders (j, g, p) and ascenders (b, d, k). When this is the only space between lines, type is "set solid." Sometimes an art director decides to add extra space between the lines to give a more "airy" feeling. In this case, **leading** (pronounced *ledding*) between lines is called for. The term dates back to the time when thin lead strips were actually inserted between lines of metal type.

A line of type set in 10-point type with 2 points of space (leading) between lines is specified as "10 on 12," or "10/12," which is exactly what this text is set in. This same terminology is used today in computer typesetting.

Appropriateness

A typeface must be appropriate to the product being advertised. With many varieties of type available in terms of both style (typeface) and size, a host of moods and feelings can be conveyed quite apart from the meanings of the words themselves. Some typefaces suggest ruggedness and masculinity; others give a feeling of delicateness and femininity. One typeface can whisper "luxury", another can scream "bargain!" A typeface that conveys the feeling of something old-fashioned obviously would be inappropriate in an ad for a space-age electronic watch.

Harmony/Appearance

Advertising novices commonly make the mistake of mixing typefaces, which often results in disharmony and a feeling of clutter. Type should harmonize with the other elements of an advertisement—including the illustration and the layout. Therefore, typefaces that belong to the same family or are closely related should normally be chosen.

Emphasis

Emphasis with type selection can be achieved by using contrast. Contrast can be created by using more than a single type style or by using italic versus roman or upright type, lowercase versus uppercase, or small versus large type. Care must be taken, however—trying to emphasize *all* elements in an ad results only in emphasizing *none* of them. (For an interesting view on this, see Ad Lab 10-A, "Celestial Seasonings.")

Type Specification and Copy Casting

Type must fit into the space designated for it in the layout. Today, those who use the computer for type placement can simply change the size of the type instantly on the screen until it fits the area. But for those who don't use a computer, the number of characters in the copy has to be determined through a process called **copy casting** before the type can be selected. This is important so that type can be ordered from a typesetter and be delivered correctly sized to fit the space on the mechanical. Two ways are used to fit copy to a particular space: the *word-count method* and the *character-count method.*

With the **word-count method,** the words in the copy are counted and then divided by the number of words per square inch that can be set in a particular type style and size, as given in a standard table.

The **character-count method** gives greater accuracy. An actual count is made of the number of characters (letters, word spaces, and punctuation marks) in the copy. In a type specimen book or chart provided by the

AD LAB 10-A
Celestial Seasonings Uses Some Unforgettable Characters

Most ads use only one type family—or maybe two. Obviously, Celestial Seasonings decided to break this rule.

Laboratory Applications

1. How many different kinds of type have been used in this ad? Classify the base type by (*a*) type class and (*b*) type group.
2. Analyze the effect of the ad in terms of the type's readability, appropriateness, harmony, and emphasis.

typographer, the average number of characters per pica is given for each typeface and type point size. From this information, it is relatively simple to determine how much space a given piece of copy set in a particular typeface will use.

Copy sent to a typographer or publication should be marked with the type specifications written beside the copy. Usually, the copy is accompanied by a layout. When specifying type, the art director or type director should provide the typographer with at least the following information: the typeface by name, the type size and the leading desired, and the width of the line of type in picas.

The specification of type in advertising agencies is handled by art directors, type directors, or the print production staff. However, it is also important for copywriters and account executives to understand the basics of type specification and copy casting since copy must often be written to fit a particular space in an advertisement. Otherwise, the ad risks looking either overly crowded or too empty—thereby impairing its visual impact.

Typesetting Methods

In recent decades, technology has rapidly revolutionized the printing industry in general and typesetting methods in particular. The old methods of metal type composition (where letters were formed by pouring molten lead into brass molds) have become obsolete and virtually disappeared. The "hot-type" era included a variety of composition processes with such names as Linotype, Monotype, and Ludlow. But it has now yielded to the "cold-type" era in which letters can be easily imprinted directly onto photosensitized film or paper. This era, characterized by sophisticated, high-speed, electronic photocomposition equipment and operators schooled in computer technology, actually began in the 1950s and brought tremendous changes in the tools available to art directors, designers, and writers. Today's desktop publishing explosion is the heir of that technology. Surprisingly, desktop publishing is just newer, faster-running, smaller computers using the same high-resolution photo output devices of the 1970s and 80s.

Today's typesetting methods generally fall into two broad classifications: strike-on composition and photocomposition.

Strike-On Composition

Strike-on or **direct-impression composition** can be done on a regular typewriter or on intelligent electronic typewriters, and word processors that have microprocessors can perform basic text-editing functions automatically and may also include limited storage capabilities. Offering substantial savings over professional typesetting methods, this means of composition is used when economy is the overriding consideration.

This equipment is used primarily for typesetting direct-mail advertising, flyers, and house organs. But today, reasonably priced laser printers and desktop publishing software programs have all but replaced pure strike-on composition.

Photocomposition

Photocomposition—a combination of computer technology, electronics, and photography—is the most dominant method of producing advertising materials today. It offers an almost unlimited number of typefaces and sizes, faster reproduction at relatively low cost, and improved clarity and sharpness of image.

The basic function of all phototypesetting machines is to expose photosensitive paper or film to a projected image of the character being set. The most commonly used equipment today operates by cathode-ray tube (CRT) technology or by laser scanning.

CRT Typesetters The first digital, computerized typesetters used an electron beam to write digitized letterforms onto a cathode ray tube (CRT). The type image on the CRT is then projected onto photosensitive paper or film.[8] These machines can store hundreds of fonts and have extremely high-speed capabilities. Digital typesetters replaced the original photo-optic machines and have now themselves nearly been replaced by personal computers running desktop publishing programs.

Laser Typesetters With new computer-laser technology, type fonts and software programs can be stored digitally in a computer. As the computer turns the laser on and off, the laser beam "writes" onto the paper or film. High-end machines use photosensitive paper and films producing resolutions of from 1,270 dots per inch (dpi) on paper to 2,700+ dpi on films. Low-end laser printers attach to personal computers and work like plain-paper copiers, melting a black plastic dust to shape the letters. The resolution on these

The quality of print varies widely with the printer used to produce it. Notice the significant difference in sharpness between the low-resolution 300 dpi (dots per square inch) laser printer and the higher-resolution 2,400 dpi laser typesetter.

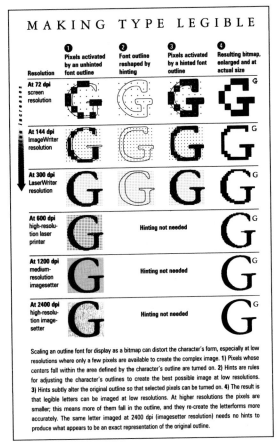

First published in Macworld, July 1991. Copyright © 1991 Macworld Communications, Inc.

printers is up to 300 dpi and, as Exhibit 10-12 shows, is quite suitable for low-level artwork like sales letters and coupon books. Laser printers offer high speeds and great reliability and versatility. In fact, laser printers can even output graphics and pictures as well as type.

THE PRINTING PROCESS

The objective of all printing methods is to transfer an image from one surface to another. Printed advertising materials are reproduced today by four major methods: letterpress, rotogravure, offset lithography, and screen printing.

We will discuss each of these methods shortly. But first, let's examine some basic principles of prepress and printing.

Preparing Materials for the Press (Prepress)

All of today's modern, high-speed presses, whether the method is letterpress, rotogravure, or offset lithography, require printing plates. A process called **photoplatemaking** is used to create the printing surface on the plates.

The photoplatemaking process can be compared to taking a picture with your own camera. When you snap a picture, you produce a negative. The picture is then made by shining a light through the negative onto sensitized paper in an enlarger. Photoplatemaking also begins with a negative. However, in this case, the negative is laid onto a photosensitive metal plate rather than

65-line screen.

100-line screen.

150-line screen.

EXHIBIT 10-13

A halftone screen is used to break a photographic image into dots. The coarser screen (65 lines) is used for rougher paper. Glossy, magazine-quality paper can be used to reproduce finer, sharper images.

on paper, and the image is exposed onto the plate with ultraviolet light. This plate is then used for printing.

Before this plate can be made, though, the artwork has to be prepared properly.

Line Films

Unlike a piece of *photographic paper,* which prints its image in continuous tones from black to white with any variety of shades of gray in between, *printed paper* has only areas of solid ink and areas of no ink. Printers use **orthographic film,** a high-contrast film yielding only black-and-white images, no gray tones. Thus, to be camera-ready, the artwork has to be made without color and in black-and-white. All's fine if the artwork is simply typeset copy, pen-and-ink drawings, or charcoal illustrations. In that event, the artwork is simply photographed to create what is called a **line film.** From that, a **line plate** is produced for printing.

However, a photograph or other illustration requiring graduations in tone cannot be reproduced on orthographic film or a plate without using an additional process—namely, a *halftone screen.*

Halftones

Where line plates print lines and solid areas (like type), halftone plates print dots. The key element in making such a plate is the **halftone screen** that breaks up continuous-tone artwork into dots. The screen itself is glass or plastic, crisscrossed with fine black lines at right angles like a window screen. This screen is placed in the camera between the lens and the negative. When the artwork is photographed, this screen breaks up the picture into a series of tiny black dots of varying shapes and sizes.

In the dark areas of the (halftone) photograph, the dots are many and large; in the gray areas, they are fewer and smaller; and in the white areas, they almost disappear completely. The combination of big and little dots with a little or a lot of white space between them produces the illusion of shading in the photograph. The human eye, seeing minute dots of ink, mixes them and perceives them as gradations of tone. But in reality, the screened illustration is still made up of only two tones, black and white.

The fineness of the halftone screen determines the quality of the illusion. A fine screen has more lines and thus more dots per square inch. Screens generally range from 50 to 150 lines to the inch each way, and the printed halftone may be described, for example, as a 50-line or a 150-line screen. Variation in the fineness of the screen is necessary because the paper the halftone is printed on may be coarse and ink-absorbent or smooth, glossy, and nonabsorbent. Halftones printed on newsprint must be screened coarsely, whereas fine-quality, glossy magazine paper can take fine-screen halftones. Note that with a coarse screen the dots can be seen quite easily with the naked eye, as shown in Exhibit 10-13.

When shooting halftones, printers often **flash** the film, a technique for lightening the darker areas of the halftone in order to keep them from plugging up with ink and looking blotchy.

Different types of screens may also be used for artistic effect. Exhibit 10-14 demonstrates the result of using various types of screens to reproduce the same photograph.

Two-color texture.

Random line.

Mezzo tint.

Wavy line (dry brush).

EXHIBIT 10-14

Many effects are possible through the use of special screens. Whether they use lines, scratches, or some other technique, they all work on the same principle as the dot screen. However, special screens require much more careful photo work.

Stripping

Typically a single negative must be made of all the line and halftone artwork for each plate. Negatives are always mounted onto orange paper or plastic sheets that serve as masks and extend beyond the size of the actual negative and hook up with registration pins at the edge of the light table. **Stripping** is the act of mounting negatives onto these sheets of masking material and registering the negative within the dimensions of the plate and with any "sister" negatives used to print other colors. Once this is done, the plate is **burned,** a term referring to the process of exposing the photosensitive plate to light. Of course, the light is being masked in some places by the negative.

Thinking like a Printer

Advertising designers face many complex challenges. Stripping is just one of them. Knowing the complex process a printer has to go through to prepare a job for the press can save time and money for both parties.

Likewise, when designing the art for some jobs, the art director or designer should determine early on what kind of press the job will be run on. Different presses accommodate different sheet sizes. A finished piece that is to be folded down to a 9″ × 12″ brochure would most likely be run on a press that prints a 25″ × 38″ sheet. But if a piece is designed to fold down to a 9½″ × 12½″ brochure, then a larger sheet of paper would have to be used, as well as a different press. In such a case, there would probably be a substantial waste of paper, and that could be costly.

Another example of thinking like a printer is to understand **imposition**— the positioning of the image on the sheet of paper. Paper and press operation are the two major expenses of any big printing job.

Because printing is a very competitive business, a printer must find ways to get as many images onto one sheet of paper as possible in order to give the best bids and get the work. So, imposition is extremely important. There are two kinds of imposition: *sheetwise* and *work & turn*.

Sheetwise Imposition

In **sheetwise imposition,** as Exhibit 10-15A shows, half the pages are printed on one side of the sheet and the other half on the reverse. This arrangement gives the designer two good options. First, a third color can be added to the job for very little money by simply printing the third color in place of the second color on one side. This will create the effect of a three-color piece. Second, the designer can position full-color pages so they only run on one side of the sheet. When the piece is folded down, full color will be distributed throughout the brochure even though only one side of the sheet was printed in full color.

Work & Turn Imposition

In **work & turn imposition,** both sides of the art are printed on one side of the sheet. After the first side has been run, the sheets are then turned over to the blank side, and the same plate is used to run the final side of the sheets. The images are registered so that the front and the back of the piece are printed on opposite sides of the paper and can be cut and folded down to make a complete set of pages in sequence (see Exhibit 10-15B). Work & turn

| 5 | 12 | 6 | 8 |
| 4 | 13 | 16 | 1 |

| 3 | 14 | 15 | 2 |
| 6 | 11 | 10 | 7 |

9	3	4	5
11	14	13	12
10	15	16	6
7	2	1	8

A. Sheetwise imposition is a pattern in which all the pages printed on one side of the sheet are different from the pages printed on the other side. This enables the use of a different second color, for example, on one side at very little extra cost.

B. Work & turn imposition, in contrast, is running the sheet through the press twice, using only one plate and one set of ink colors. When the paper is flipped over for the second run, page 7 ends up on the back of page 8, page 11 on the back of page 12, and so on.

imposition requires a sheet twice the size of the total image to be printed. But since it requires only one set of negatives and one plate, it is the least expensive way to run multiple colors on every page.

Methods of Printing

Few advertisers maintain all the necessary capital equipment and personnel required for producing printed materials. Instead, they usually hire outside print production companies who work at their direction. These suppliers may include a typesetting house, a color separator, a photoplatemaker, a printer, or a duplicating house for newspaper material. All these sources are particularly important when media schedules include publications that print by different methods or when it is desirable to convert material from one printing process to another to save time and money.

Now that we understand some of the basics of printing, let's discuss the major printing methods used today.

Letterpress

For many years, letterpress was the universal method of printing. It was used in the reproduction of newspapers and many magazines that needed reason-

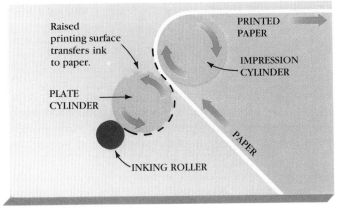

LETTERPRESS
Relief printing

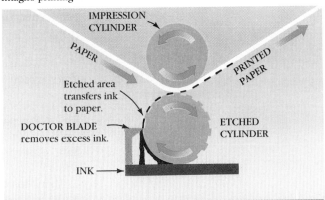

GRAVURE
Intaglio printing

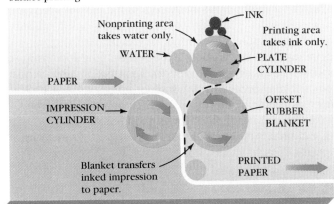

OFFSET
Surface printing

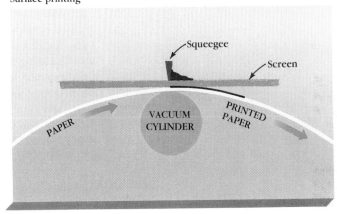

SILKSCREEN
Surface printing

EXHIBIT 10-16

The four major printing processes include letterpress, rotogravure, offset lithography, and screen printing.

able quality with sharp contrast. However, with the advent of newer, higher-quality methods, very little letterpress printing is done in the United States anymore. Still, it may be helpful to understand the basics of letterpress printing, not only for historical reasons but to have a well-rounded understanding of the printing process.

In **letterpress,** the printing is done from a metal or plastic printing plate on a large round drum or cylinder (see Exhibit 10-16). The process is similar to the way a rubber stamp works. Like a stamp, the image to be transferred is backward ("wrong reading") on the plate. The ink is applied to a raised (relief) surface on the plate and then transferred to the paper.

To produce the letterpress plate, the negative of the photographed image is laid on top of a sensitized plastic or copper plate and exposed to light. Since everything on a negative is in reverse, the image areas on the negative are transparent. This allows light to pass through the negative to the plate, which has been treated with a light-sensitive emulsion. The emulsion hardens in the areas exposed to the light, forming an acid-resistant protective covering over the image area of the plate. The plate is then placed in an acid bath that etches away the nonprinting areas—leaving the desired printing image raised on the surface of the plate.

The result is the line plate we discussed earlier. Sometimes a plastic plate may be used, in which case a photochemical process, called **photopolymerization,** followed by a simple washout is used to produce a relief plate.

Rotogravure

The process used in **rotogravure** differs from letterpress in several ways. First, two separate films are made—one for all type and line illustrations and the other for halftone illustrations. The negatives are combined into a single film "positive." In the gravure process, though, even type and line art are screened.

Then, instead of printing from a raised surface as in letterpress, the rotogravure process prints from a depressed surface. Like letterpress, the image to be transferred is backward ("wrong reading"). The design is etched or electromechanically engraved into a metal plate or cylinder, leaving depressions one- or two-thousandths of an inch deep. As the plate is inked and wiped clean with a metal blade, ink is left in the tiny depressions. It transfers this ink to the paper by pressure and suction (see Exhibit 10-16).

Preparing the printing plates or cylinders is time-consuming and costly, so rotogravure is practical and economical only for long press runs. Sunday newspaper supplements, mail-order catalogs, some major magazines, packaging, and other materials requiring a great number of photographs are well suited to this method. Rotogravure is noted for its good reproduction of color on both newsprint and quality paper stocks and for its ability to stand up to the rigors of long press runs.

Offset Lithography

Today, **offset lithography** is the most popular printing process used in North America. The printing plates cost less than for other printing methods, the printing can be done on almost any paper quality, and the preparation time is short. Because the process is photographic, it meshes well with the most popular form of typesetting, photocomposition. Advertisers simply have to provide pasted-up art for the printer's camera (*camera-ready materials*) or film for the platemaker.

Offset lithography employs the same line and halftone processes used to make letterpress plates. However, to the naked eye, the image on the lithographic printing plate appears to be flat instead of raised, as in letterpress, or depressed, as in rotogravure. Unlike letterpress and rotogravure, the image on the plate is "right reading."

The principle underlying lithography is that oil and water do not mix. To start, a photograph is made of the material to be printed. The negative from the photograph is laid on top of a zinc or aluminum printing plate and exposed to light. Chemicals are applied to the plate after the exposure, and the image takes the form of a greasy coating. The plate is then attached to a cylinder on a rotary printing press, and water is applied with a roller. The greasy image repels the water, but the blank portions of the plate retain it. As the plate is covered with an oily ink, the moist, blank portions of the plate repel the ink. The greasy-coated image retains the ink for transfer to an intermediate rubber surface called a **blanket,** which comes in contact with the paper and enables the image to be printed (see Exhibit 10-16).

EXHIBIT 10-17

The high-speed Heidelberg five-color offset press is used for printing magazines. The first four units are used for four-color process printing. The fifth may be used to varnish the printed page or to lay down a specific fifth color. Some art directors, for example, may want a "company blue," a specific color of ink rather than a combination of process colors.

Lithography is used extensively for inexpensive advertising materials prepared at "instant" printing shops. Most newspapers and magazines are now printed by this process on high-speed offset presses. Exhibit 10-17 shows a high-speed, five-color offset press widely used today. Likewise, most books (including this one), direct-mail materials, and catalogs are printed by offset. And because it is suitable for printing on metal, most packaging materials, including cans, are also printed by lithography.

Screen Printing (Serigraphy)

The signs and billboards planted along the highway often are examples of **screen printing.** Billboards use sheets of paper that have historically been too large for many printing presses. Also, the quantities required for many outdoor advertising campaigns, especially local ones, are so small that it is often uneconomical to use other printing processes, like offset, that might be used for national campaigns.

Screen printing, an old process based on the stencil principle, requires no plates. A special screen is stretched tightly on a frame. The frame is placed on the surface the message or image is to be printed on. A stencil, either hand cut from film or photographically prepared, is used to block out areas that are not to be printed. Ink is squeezed through the screen by a squeegee (rubber rollers) sliding across the surface, transferring the image onto the paper or other surface, as shown in Exhibit 10-16. For printing in color, a separate stencil is made for each color.

Printing stencils are made of nylon or stainless steel mesh. Originally, silk was used, hence the old term **silk screen.** Today, automatic presses for screen printing are also available, making the process economical for even longer runs.

Printing in Color

If an advertiser wants to print an ad or a brochure in blue, green, and black, then three different plates are required (one for each color), and the job is referred to as a *three-color job.* Typically, the advertiser specifies that the job be printed in black and two specific Pantone® colors—each of which is a solid color ink specifically created for blending Pantone Basic Color according to a specific formulation from the **PANTONE MATCHING SYSTEM® (PMS),** displayed in Exhibit 10-18.[9]

The method for printing full-color advertisements with tonal values, such as photographs and paintings, is called a **four-color process.** This is based on the principle that all colors can be printed by combining the three primary colors—**process red** (also called magenta), **process blue** (cyan), and **process yellow** (yellow)—plus black (which provides greater detail and density as well as shades of gray).

Each of the printing processes we have discussed can print color. However, a printing plate can print only one color at a time. Therefore, if a job is to be printed in full color, the printer must prepare four different printing plates—one for each color, including black.

The artwork to be reproduced is photographed through color filters that eliminate all the colors except one. For example, one filter eliminates all colors except red and extracts every light ray of red to be blended into the final reproduced picture. An electronic scanning device may be used to make these color separations. Thus, four separate, continuous-tone negatives are

produced to make a set of four-color plates: one for yellow, one for magenta, one for cyan, and one for black. The resulting negatives are in black and white and are called **color separation negatives.**

These color separations are photographed through a halftone screen to make a set of screened negatives from which the plates are made. In photographing the color separations, the halftone screen is rotated to a different angle for each separation. As a result, the dots do not completely overlap because the four plates superimpose the dots over one another during printing. On the printed page, tiny clusters of halftone dots of the four colors in various sizes and shapes give the eye the optical illusion of seeing the colors of the original photograph or painting. In printing, transparent inks are used, so people can see all colors through the four overlapping coatings of ink on the paper. For example, even though green ink is not used, green can be reproduced by the overlapping of yellow and cyan dots. Dark green would have larger blue halftone dots than yellow. (See Creative Department: From Concept through Production of a Magazine Advertisement, p. 376.)

Electronic scanners can perform four-color separations and screening in one process, along with enlargement or reduction. In a single operation, an operator can achieve highlight/shadow density changes, contrast modification, color change, or removal of an area or a whole piece. All this can be accomplished in several minutes instead of the hours or days that were previously needed for camera work and hand etching. Today, these scanners have evolved into complete computerized color prepress systems capable of positioning all illustrative and text elements as well as electronic retouching.[10]

Selecting Papers for Printing

When preparing materials for printing, it is important to know the kind of paper the advertisement will be printed on. Some advertisers are so concerned about the appearance of their ads they have them printed on a higher quality of paper stock than the regular pages of a newspaper or magazine. The advertisers then ship the printed material to the publication for insertion or binding.

Paper used in advertising can be broken down into three categories: writing, text, and cover stock.

Writing Paper

Writing paper is commonly used in letters and other direct-mail pieces. Bond writing paper is the most durable and also the most frequently used.

Text Paper

Many different types of text paper are available. Major classifications—news stock, antique finish, machine finish, English finish, and coated—range from less expensive, very porous, coarse papers (used for newspapers) to very smooth, expensive, heavier papers used for magazines, industrial brochures, and fine-quality annual reports.

(text continued on p. 381)

CREATIVE DEPARTMENT

FROM CONCEPT THROUGH PRODUCTION OF A MAGAZINE ADVERTISEMENT

Marketing Considerations

As a strategic defense against the recent introduction of a dry soup mix by Campbell Soup, the Thomas J. Lipton Company introduced a new product of its own, Lipton International Soup Classics. Designed to fit the contemporary consumer lifestyle, the product was a high-quality, single-serving convenience food. It could serve as an integral part of a light meal (e.g., salad, cheese, soup), as an appetizer for a formal dinner, or as a nutritious between-meal snack. Available in five creamy recipes, the product could satisfy a wide range of tastes. The Soup Classics were distinctively packaged in black cartons with dramatic product photos prominently positioned to display the soup's creamy texture and large, freeze-dried pieces of meat or vegetables. Distribution of the product was best developed in the East, followed by the central and western regions and, lastly, the South.

Creative Concepts

Lipton wanted to target upscale audiences in its primary market areas. Its advertising agency, Young & Rubicam, suggested showing both the distinctive packaging and the appetite appeal of the product in one shot. Since the package face displayed a picture of the product, the art director, Gary Goldstein, proposed a *trompe l'oeil* (optical illusion) layout where a beauty shot of a spoon in a steaming bowl of soup would replace the straight product shot. The idea even included having the spoon extend beyond the edge of the package—making the soup look ready-to-eat right off the front of the box (see A).

A. Rough layout.

Shooting the Ad

To achieve the desired look, the concept required at least four photographs: one main visual of the package itself, one for the soup, one for the steam, and one for the row of other flavors. Working with a tight layout and acetates, the photographer carefully positioned the package shot and the soup shot so that the perspective and lighting would match. The hot soup shot was slightly overexposed to capture the steam, which was an important element both for the *tromp l'oeil* and the appetite appeal.

Preparing for Production

The creative department reviewed the film (shot in an 8 × 10 format) based on the original layout. Four *chromes* were selected, each having the color density needed for high-quality, four-color reproduction. Then a composite print was created to show the client for approval. Subsequently, a mechanical retouching and stripping guide was developed from stats of the photos and type and shown to the agency art buyer and print producer for their input.

During a preproduction meeting, it was decided that it would be best to retouch this job on an electronic pagination system. Once client approval was obtained, the mechanical was given to the color separator, Potomac Color Industries, along with a timetable and the original transparencies. Reviewing the task with the separator, the following directions were developed:

1. Utilize the steam from chrome D (B.) and photocompose into main visual (C.). The steam should be transparent, allowing the background package to come through.
2. Photocompose the soup bowl (D.) into main visual. Create a shadow of the spoon in chrome A on the surface of the table.
3. Photocompose the package shots from chrome B (E.) into the main visual.
4. Color balance all packages and the background of the main visual.

A cost estimate was requested, and once approved, the job proceeded.

B. Chrome D, showing steam.

C. The main visual.

D. Chrome A, showing soup bowl.

E. Chrome B, showing package shots.

F. Marked copy for typesetter.

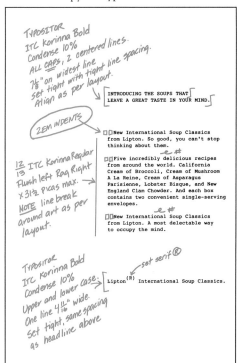

G. Photomechanical.

Production

First, each transparency was scanned into the electronic system, converting each of the images to digitized pixels. Next, at the computer workstation, the retoucher superimposed the bowl of soup on the main package shot and then added the steam to this composition. Behind the steam, the color had to be corrected very carefully to make the whole composition believable. Moreover, the steam itself was extended to break over the headline. A little soup was added to the spoon, and the drop shadow was created beneath the spoon.

From the computer's memory bank, the system was able to use a variety of selected applications as needed in the process, such as cloning, imaging, photocomposing, silhouetting, and vignetting.

When all adjustments had been made and the electronic retouching was finalized, Chromalins (slick, color reproductions) were sent to the agency for review and evaluation. After approval, the digitized film data with all corrections was stored in the computer for later disposition.

Typesetting

While this photo work was in process, type had to be set for the ad. The art director and the copywriter, Marvin Waldman, submitted the rough layout and the approved copy to the agency type director. Together they selected a suitable type style for the ad. The type director then determined the size of the headline and carefully marked up the copy for the style of typeface, spacing, and size (see F.).

The layout and copy were sent to the typographer, who set the headline and body copy with photodisplay equipment. From the film put out by this equipment, a photomechanical of the ad was created, according to the rough layout. The copywriter, art director, and type director then proofed the mechanical for errors and made whatever aesthetic or technical adjustments were required. The ad was then submitted to the client in this form for approval (see G.).

When all adjustments and corrections in copy and artwork had been determined, the mechanical was returned to the typographer. The corrections were made, and the new photomechanical was then used to make a negative line film for delivery to the photoplatemaker.

Photoplatemaking

Once the corrected film data of the main visual was retrieved from the computer, four-color screened film was manufactured. A line negative of the typographic elements was then incorporated with these screened separations. From the negative, four-color offset plates were made and placed on the press. A set of proofs and progressive proofs showing the single colors was pulled off the press and sent to the agency for approval (see H.). Minor

H. Progressive proofs (color separations).

Yellow

Magenta

Yellow and magenta

Cyan

Yellow, magenta, and cyan

Black

corrections were handled by sending the job back to the computer or by hand through a process called dot etching on the offset film masters.

After client and agency product group approval, the master films were duplicated by the platemaker, and the necessary quantity of films, proofs, and progressive proofs were sent to each of the publications involved. The proofs were then used by the publications as a guide for color at the press to be sure that a faithful reproduction would be achieved (see I.).

I. Completed ad.

Cover Paper

Because of its tough, durable quality, cover paper is used for softcover book covers and sometimes for direct-mail pieces. Advertisers can choose from many finishes and textures.

Preparing Materials for Print Media

Most local newspapers and magazines are willing and able to work with advertisers to help produce their advertisements. Frequently, this service is free. The local dress shop or furniture store works with the newspaper's ad salesperson and provides the copy and illustrations, and the newspaper's production department takes care of the rest.

At some point, however, advertisers may decide to exercise more control over the production process to ensure consistency and quality. Major agencies always like to maintain complete control over the preparation of materials used for reproduction rather than giving the media that responsibility.

Media schedules frequently contain numerous publications that will run the advertisement at about the same time, requiring the advertiser to provide duplicate materials to each publication.

Production specifications can be obtained directly from the publication. It is often more convenient, however, to use the Standard Rate and Data Service *Print Media Production Data* directory. This directory contains critical information, such as that shown in Exhibit 10-19, about the printing specifications

EXHIBIT 10-19

The advertising specifications and measurements used in the major print media are detailed in a directory published by the Standard Rate and Data Service.

OUTDOOR & TRAVEL PHOTOGRAPHY
A Harris Publications, Inc. Publication

Location ID: 18 PCLS 39   Mkd 050225-000
Published quarterly by Harris Publications, Inc., 1115 Broadway, New York, NY 10010. Phone 212-807-7100. FAX: 212-627-4678.

1. PERSONNEL
Assoc Pub—Elaine T. Sexton, 212-807-7100;
    FAX: 212-627-4678

2. GENERAL REQUIREMENTS
Printing Process: Offset Full Run
Trim Size: 8 x 10-7/8.
Binding Method: Saddle Stitched.
AD PAGE DIMENSIONS

1 pg	7 x	10	1/3 v 2-1/4 x	10
2/3 v 4-5/8 x	10		1/3 h 4-3/4 x 4-3/4	
1/2 v 4-3/4 x	7		1/4 v 3-3/8 x 4-3/4	
1/2 h	7 x 4-3/4		1/6 v 2-1/4 x 4-3/4	

3. BLEED
BLEED AD PAGE DIMENSIONS
1 pg .... 8-1/8 x 11-1/4
        LIVE MATTER 7 x 10

4. MATERIAL SPECIFICATIONS
SWOP Standards Apply.
Preferred Material: Positives, (Right Reading Emulsion side down).
Negatives, (Right Reading Emulsion side up).
PROOFING
Progressives 4 sets.
Rotation of colors: Black, cyan, magenta, yellow.
Inking TEXT: Type of ink 4A Standard Process; Paper weight 70 lb.; Paper stock type Machine Coated Stock. Ink proofing: R.O.P. Head to foot; Black & White Head to foot; Black/Color Head to foot; 4-color Head to foot; Cover Head to foot.

7. ISSUE AND CLOSING DATES
Published quarterly.

	—— Closing ——		
Issue:	On sale	(+)	(*)
Aug (Fall)	8/26	6/25	7/2
Oct (OTP buyers guide)	10/8	8/6	8/13
Nov (Winter)	11/26	9/24	10/1
Mar (Spring)	3/3	12/30	1/7
May (Summer)	5/26	3/24	3/31
Aug	8/25	6/23	6/30

(+) Space
(*) Material

and mechanical measurements (dimensions of advertising space acceptable) of every major publication.

For publications printed by rotogravure or offset lithography, duplicate materials consist of duplicate sets of color-separated film positives (for rotogravure) or photographic copies of the mechanical and screened art (for offset lithography). These photographic copies may be in the form of **photoprints** (a screened print or a Velox) or color-separated contact **film negatives,** depending on the requirements of the particular publication. Publications make their own printing plates from these materials.

We have barely scratched the surface in our discussion of the print production process. But we have shown that this field is very complex and, with expanding technology, becoming highly technical. That also means, though, that it offers many new and exciting challenges and opportunities for those interested in specializing in the printing side of the advertising business.

Summary

The production process in print advertising is so critical that if it is not handled correctly, an otherwise beautiful ad can be destroyed. With the advent of computerized prepress systems, the production process has been greatly facilitated on the one hand, but also made more complex. A fundamental understanding of production techniques, therefore, can save a lot of money and disappointment.

The print production manager's job is to ensure that the final advertisement reflects what the art director had in mind. That is often a nearly impossible task, as the print production manager must work within the limited, specified confines of time, quality, and acceptable budget constraints.

The typeface chosen for an advertisement affects its appearance, design, and legibility. Type can generally be divided into two broad classes: display type and text type. In addition, typefaces can be classified by their similarity of design. The major type groups are roman, sans serif, square serif, cursive or script, and ornamental. Within each group are many type families, such as Bodoni, Futura, Goudy, and Caslon. In a type family, the basic design remains the same, but variations of weight, slant, and size are available.

Type is measured in points and picas. Points measure the vertical size of type. There are 72 points to an inch. Picas measure the horizontal width of a single line of type. There are six picas to an inch. Type may further be referred to as *uppercase* (capital letters), *lowercase* (small letters), and *commoncase* (large and small capitals).

Four important points should be considered when selecting type: readability, appropriateness, harmony or appearance, and emphasis. The process of determining how much type will fit a specified area in an advertisement is called *copy casting*. There are several methods used to cast copy today.

There are also several methods used to set type. The most important of these are the various photocomposition techniques, including cathode-ray tube (CRT) techniques and laser exposure.

Printing processes have undergone great technological changes in recent decades. Today, the most common types of printing methods are offset lithography, rotogravure, and screen printing. Each method has its unique advantages and disadvantages.

Preparing plates for printing involves exposing an image to a sensitized metal plate. Two types of images are used for printing: line images and halftone images. Line images print only two tonal values—black and white. For gradations of tone, as in an illustration or photograph, halftone images are used. These print a series of black dots of various sizes, thus producing an optical illusion of tonal grades.

When full color is required, four halftone plates are used, one for each primary color and one for black. These print the colored dots in tiny clusters, creating the illusion of full color. For efficiency and economy, advertisers should understand impositioning—how printers fit several pages on a sheet of paper—especially in light of the high cost of paper today.

Questions for Review and Discussion

1. What effect has the introduction of the computer had on the print production process?

2. What is the primary role of the print production manager?

3. What are the characteristics of the five major type groups?

4. What does *copy casting* mean? Explain the ways in which it is done.

5. What is the importance of these terms: *readability, appropriateness, harmony/appearance, emphasis?*

6. What terms are used to describe how type is measured? What do the terms mean?

7. What are the major differences between rotogravure and offset lithography?

8. What is a halftone? Why is it important, and how is it produced?

9. How are color photographs printed? What are the potential problems with printing color?

10. What do the terms *sheetwise* and *work & turn* mean to a printer?

CREATIVE PRODUCTION: ELECTRONIC MEDIA

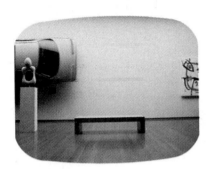

Objective: To present an overview of how radio and television advertisements are produced. As in print production, the computer has had a dynamic effect on the production of commercials for electronic media. However, the technology used is still subject to the creativity of those using it. Advertisers must be aware of some of the many alternatives available to them today—to save money, enhance their production quality, and facilitate the production process.

After studying this chapter, you will be able to:

☐ Discuss how the production of commercials for radio and television differs.

☐ Explain the process television and radio commercials go through from concept through final production.

☐ Describe the major types of radio and TV commercials.

☐ Understand how to save money in television production.

☐ Discuss the opportunities for special effects in television.

☐ Define common electronic production terms.

☐ Debate the advantages of using film or videotape to produce television commercials.

In 1985, the Dallas-based chain of economy motels lost $20 million. It had no marketing department, and it had never had an advertising campaign. Its occupancy rate was down to 59 percent and still sinking. Then it was sold in a leveraged buyout. The new owners—Kohlberg, Kravis, Roberts & Co.—brought in new management, a new advertising agency, and a folksy radio announcer named Tom Bodett from Homer, Alaska.

They added a few amenities, started building and acquiring more properties, and launched an aggressive nationwide advertising campaign—on radio. Within a year, things changed dramatically.

As Tom Bodett fessed up that "we don't put a chocolate on your pillow like those big, fancy chains," he convinced the American car-driving public to pull into a clean, friendly Motel 6.

"We'll only charge you about $20," he promised, "and we'll leave the light on for you."

By 1988, his laid-back, folksy humor and the endearing, award-winning ads written and placed by The Richards Group (see Exhibit 11-1 for an example) had contributed significantly to a 73 percent occupancy rate and a record 12.6 million rooms sold. Today, Motel 6 is the largest chain of budget motels in the United States and faring well—thanks to radio.[1]

EXHIBIT 11-1

A simple radio script featuring the low-key, folksy humor of Tom Bodett enabled Motel 6 to turn its financial fortunes around. In a nonvisual medium like radio, the goal is to draw listeners in and get them personally involved in the message. Today, Motel 6 is the largest economy motel chain in the United States.

ANNCR: Hi. Tom Bodett for Motel 6 with a few words about roughin' it. Well when you stay at Motel 6 you'll have to turn the bed down all by yourself, and go without that little piece of chocolate those fancy hotels leave on your pillow. Well I know it's a lot to ask, but for around 20 bucks, the lowest prices of any national chain, well you can't expect the moon now can you? After all, you do get a clean comfortable room, free TV, movies and local calls. And no service charge on long distance calls. No, we won't bring meals to your room on a silver cart, but that doesn't mean you can't get room service. Since local calls are free, just look up a pizza joint that delivers and give 'em a buzz. They'll bring that large pepperoni pineapple right to your door. So if you can tough it out all in the name of savin' a few bucks, well Motel 6 is where you oughta stay. We've got over 420 locations coast to coast. Just call 505-891-6161 for reservations. I'm Tom Bodett for Motel 6 and we'll leave the light on for you.

PRODUCING RADIO COMMERCIALS

The production of radio and television commercials is similar in several aspects. Radio uses the same basic types of commercials as television—namely, testimonials, slice of life, straight announcements, or music—and generally follows the same developmental patterns as television. But the details differ significantly.

Writing Radio Copy

Radio listeners usually decide within the first five to eight seconds whether they want to pay attention to a commercial. Research indicates that the primary determinant is the product category.[2] Therefore, to get and hold the attention of listeners not automatically attracted to a product category, radio copy must be intensive. To accomplish this, many techniques and devices can be used (see the Checklist for Creating Effective Radio Commercials). Creativity knows no limits.

The radio listener may be busy doing something else—driving, washing dishes, or reading the paper—so the message has to be catchy, interesting, and unforgettable. In the effort to gain attention, though, the advertiser must take care to avoid offending the listener. That can cause resentment. As in the case of Motel 6, a personal, relaxed, and cheerful style will usually be more effective.

Checklist for Creating Effective Radio Commercials

□ *Identify your sound effects.* A sound effect is only effective when the listener knows what it means.

□ *Don't be afraid to use music as a sound effect.* The commercial will work if the meaning of the music is clearly explained.

□ *If you use a sound effect, build your commercial around it.* It pays to make the message all about the relationship of the sound effect to your product.

□ *Give yourself time.* You need time in radio to set a scene and establish a premise. A 30-second commercial that nobody remembers has zero efficiency. Fight for 60-second commercials.

□ *Consider not using sound effects.* A distinctive voice or a powerful message straightforwardly spoken can be more effective than noises from the tape library.

□ *Beware of humor.* Professional comedians devote their lives to their art. It's rare for anyone else to sit down at a typewriter and match the skill of the best comedians.

□ *If you insist on being funny, begin with an outrageous*

premise. The best comic radio commercials begin with a totally ridiculous premise from which all subsequent developments logically follow.

□ *Keep it simple.* Radio is a good medium for building awareness of a brand. It's a rotten medium for registering long lists of copy points or making complex arguments.

□ *What one thing is most important about your product?* That is what your commercial should spend 60 seconds talking about.

□ *Tailor commercials to time, place, and specific audience.* Radio is a local medium. You can adjust your commercials to talk in the language of the people who will hear them and to the time of day in which they'll be broadcast.

□ *Presentation counts a whole lot.* Most radio scripts—even the greatest radio scripts—look boring on paper. Acting, timing, vocal quirks, and sound effects make them come alive.

Humor can be one of the best attention-getting devices and is being used with increasing success. But the advertiser must beware; humor is difficult to master. Poorly done humor is worse than none at all.

Other guidelines for writing radio copy include:

☐ If the commercial doesn't offer humor, then offer drama.

☐ Mention the advertiser's name early and mention it often—at least three times.

☐ Remember that radio has no visual enhancements like TV, so if the name is tricky, spell it—at least once.

☐ Be conversational. Use easy-to-pronounce words and short sentences. Avoid tongue twisters.

☐ Keep the message simple. Omit unneeded words.

☐ Concentrate on one main selling point. Make the *big idea* crystal clear.

☐ Paint pictures with the words. Use descriptive language. Familiar sounds, such as a fire engine siren or a car engine, can help create a visual image.

☐ Stress action words rather than passive words. Use verbs rather than adjectives.

☐ Emphasize the product benefits repeatedly—with variations.

☐ Make the script fit the available time.[3]

A good rule of thumb for the number of words in a commercial is as follows:

10 seconds: 20-25 words

20 seconds: 35-45 words.

30 seconds: 55-60 words.

60 seconds: 100-120 words.

And be sure to *ask for the order.* Try to get the listener to *do* something. The story is told that a radio disc jockey once made a bet. Figuring that many women drove from New Jersey to New York to shop, he bet he could persuade some of them by radio to turn around, go back through the tunnel, and buy their dresses from his New Jersey sponsor. He did, they did, and he won the bet.

Types of Radio Commercials

Although not all radio commercials can be rigidly cataloged, advertising writers have come up with myriad creative categories. Some of them are listed in Ad Lab 11-A. For our discussion here, we consider four common types of radio commercials: *straight announcement, musical, slice of life,* and *personality.*

Straight Announcement

The **straight announcement** commercial is probably the easiest to write. Delivered by one person—like Tom Bodett—it typically has no special sound effects. Music, if any, is played in the background. Straight announcements are adaptable to almost any product or situation and thus are used frequently. A straight announcement can also be designed as an **integrated commercial**—woven into a show or tailored to a given program. Getting

AD LAB 11-A
Creative Ways to Sell on Radio

Product demo The commercial tells how a product is used or the purposes it serves.

Voice power The power of the commercial is in the casting of a unique voice.

Electronic sound Synthetic sound-making machines create a memorable product-sound association.

Customer interview A product spokesperson and customer discuss the product advantages—often spontaneously.

Humorous fake interview The customer interview is done in a lighter vein.

Hyperbole or exaggerated statement Overstatement arouses interest in legitimate product claims that might otherwise pass unnoticed; often a spoof.

Fourth dimension Time and events are compressed into a brief spot involving the listener in future projections.

Hot property Commercial adapts a current sensation—a hit show, performer, or song.

Comedian power Established comedians do commercials in their own unique style, implying celebrity endorsement.

Historical fantasy Situation with revived historical characters is used to convey product message.

Sound picture Recognizable sounds are used to involve listener by stimulating imagination.

Demographics Music or references appeal to a particular segment of the population, such as an age or interest group.

Imagery transfer Musical logo or other sound reinforces the effects of a television campaign.

Celebrity interview Famous person endorses product in an informal manner.

Product song Music and words combine to create musical logo selling product in the style of popular music.

Editing genius Many different situations, voices, types of music, and sounds are combined in a series of quick cuts.

Improvisation Performers work out the dialogue extemporaneously for an assigned situation; may be postedited.

Laboratory Applications

1. Select three radio commercials with which you are familiar and discuss which creative techniques they use.
2. Select a radio commercial with which you are familiar and discuss how a different creative technique might increase its effectiveness.

and holding the listener's attention is its greatest problem; but once accomplished, the aural opportunity to educate the listener is almost unbeatable.

Musical

Jingles, or **musical commercials,** are among the best—and the worst—advertising messages produced. If done well, they can bring enormous success—well beyond that of the average nonmusical commercial. Done poorly, they can waste the advertising budget.

Musical commercials have several variations. The entire message may be sung, jingles may be interspersed throughout the copy, or orchestras may play symphonic or popular arrangements. Many producers use consistent musical themes for background color or to close the commercial. After numerous repetitions of the advertiser's theme, the listener begins to associate the music with the product being advertised. This is called a **musical logotype.**

Advertisers have three principal sources of music. They can buy the use of a tune from the copyright owner, which is usually expensive. They can use a melody in the public domain, which is free. Or they can hire a composer to write an original tune. Several of these original tunes, including Coke's song, "I'd Like to Teach the World to Sing," mentioned in Chapter 1, have later actually turned into hits.

Slice of Life (Problem Solution)

As in television, the **slice-of-life commercial** is a situation commercial in which professional actors discuss a problem and propose the product as its solution. Played with the proper drama, such commercials can get attention and create interest. "Slice" commercials can be produced with or without a humorous effect. In all cases, the story should be relevant to the product and simply told.

Radio Personality

It is sometimes desirable to have a **radio personality**—a disc jockey or talk show host—ad lib the advertising message live in his or her own style. When such a commercial is done well, it is often better than anything the advertiser could supply.

However, in doing this, the advertiser surrenders control of the commercial to the personality. The main risk, outside of occasional blunders, is that the personality may criticize the product. Even so, this sometimes lends realism that is hard to achieve otherwise.

If the advertiser decides to use this technique, the personality is given a highlight sheet listing the product's or the company's features, the main points to stress, and the phrases or company slogans to be repeated. But most of the specific wording and the mode of delivery are left to the discretion of the announcer.

THE RADIO PRODUCTION PROCESS

Radio commercials—frequently referred to as *spots*—are often among the quickest, simplest, and least expensive ads to produce. When local advertisers think of producing a radio spot, they typically just use the radio station—which often provides the production service at no charge.

Some commercials may simply be read live by the radio announcer, in which case the radio station is sent a copy of the script and any recorded music that is to be used. Care must be taken, though, to ensure that the material is accurately timed for length. A live commercial script should run about 100 to 120 words per minute, enabling the announcer to deliver the message at a normal, conversational pace.

The disadvantage of using live commercials is that announcers may not be consistent in their delivery. In addition, the use of sound effects is quite limited. If uniformity in the delivery of the commercial is critical, a recorded commercial must be used. The process of producing a recorded commercial is diagrammed in Exhibit 11-2, and includes *preproduction, production,* and *postproduction* or finishing phases.

Preproduction

In the **preproduction** phase, an agency may assign a radio producer from its staff or hire a free-lance producer to develop the commercial. The radio

Radio commercial

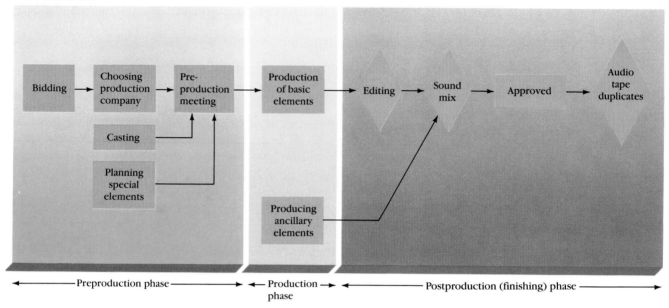

Preproduction phase | Production phase | Postproduction (finishing) phase

The process for producing a radio commercial has three phases. Notice how involved the preproduction and finishing phases are. Preplanning and then postproduction editing and mixing typically require far more time than the actual recording session does.

producer first estimates the costs and then presents a budget to the advertiser for approval. For recorded commercials, the producer selects a studio and a casting director.

Generally, most ad agencies go to independent recording studios to have greater control of the production process and to attain the highest quality of sound reproduction possible. The best studios offer highly experienced sound directors and capable technicians, have close ties to well-known talent, and feature the latest equipment.

The casting director casts professional actors for roles in a slice-of-life commercial or finds the right "voice" if there is only an announcer. If the script calls for music, the producer decides whether to use music already recorded or to hire a composer. The producer may also hire a music director, musicians, and singers. This is often done after listening to audition tapes of the recommended talent. Depending on the script, sound effects may be created or taken from prerecorded sources.

Next, a director supervises rehearsals until everything is ready for recording the commercial.

Production: Cutting the Spot

The recording and mixing of sound takes place at what's often called a **session.** Here, the voice and music talent perform in the studio into microphones set up by technicians. The sound engineer and director take command of an audio console in a control room, setting the recording levels and channeling sound data to the recording equipment—taking care to keep the levels of pitch and loudness within acceptable levels for broadcast.

At this point, we should briefly discuss the nature of sound and the use of microphones.

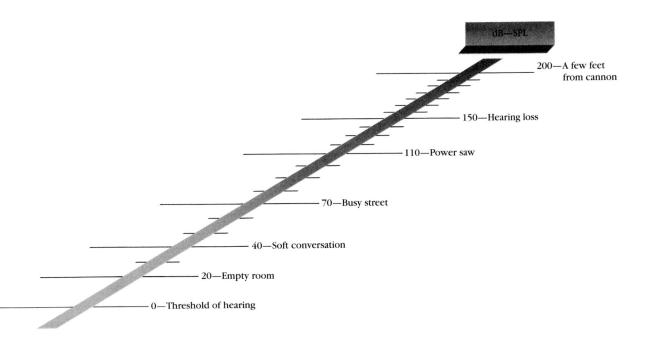

dB—SPL

200—A few feet
from cannon

150—Hearing loss

110—Power saw

70—Busy street

40—Soft conversation

20—Empty room

0—Threshold of hearing

EXHIBIT 11-3

The loudness of a sound is measured in decibels. The chart shows the range of human perception of sound.

The Nature of Sound

Sound is created when air molecules are vibrated to form alternating rings of compressed and rarefied (decompressed) air. One compressed section of air plus one decompressed section is considered a **cycle,** and is measured on the hertz scale. The greater the number of cycles hitting the eardrum per second, the higher the hertz, and the higher the sound's **pitch.** Most humans hear low pitches like rumbling sounds beginning at the 40-hertz (Hz) area and stop hearing high sounds like whistles at just above 15 kilohertz (1 kilohertz equals 1,000 cycles per second). The hertz cycles represent the number of high and low pressures passing by in a second, but they do not represent loudness.

Loudness is measured in **decibels**—the volume of air compressed in each cycle. Sounds become louder when air pressure is increased. As Exhibit 11-3 shows, an empty room has a general noise level of 20 decibels and a cannon blast has the highest pressure level of 200 decibels. Pressures greater than 150 decibels cause hearing loss.

The Use of Microphones

A wide range of **microphones** (or *mikes*) are used to capture sound for radio or television commercials. Although all are designed to convert sound energy into electrical impulses, each design does it in a slightly different way. The three basic types of structures used by professionals are: *moving coil, condenser,* and *ribbon.* The low-impedance moving-coil mike, diagrammed in Exhibit 11-4, is the most widely used in broadcasting today.[4] The flow of electrical impulses may be impeded (slowed) by the electronics and materials in any microphone. If the impedance is low, though, the pulses flow more quickly and are less likely to be affected by electrical noise such as "hums" and static.

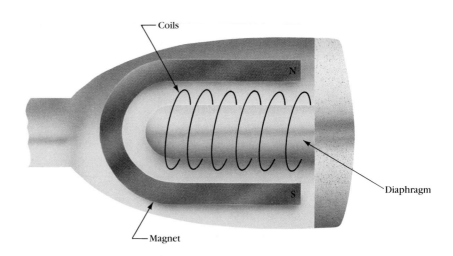

EXHIBIT 11-4

In a moving-coil microphone, sound vibrations cause the coil to move through a magnetic field, creating an electrical signal. The resulting electrical energy goes to an amplifier and then to an audio console for mixing and channeling to other equipment such as tape recorders or loudspeakers.

Another way professionals categorize microphones is by their *field of sensitivity,* a factor directly related to how the microphone is to be used in making the commercial. A mike that captures sound from all directions is referred as an **omnidirectional microphone.** Its key feature is a spherical screen that protrudes from the shaft of the mike. The **unidirectional microphone** captures sound from one direction only, and generally has a nonprotruding screen that is flat or recessed into the end of the microphone's shaft. A **bidirectional microphone** is designed to capture sounds from two opposing directions simultaneously. Its head is generally structured with a large, flat, two-sided screen protruding from the shaft. Here, back-to-back sound reception allows each of the two flat sides of the screen to capture sound.

Although all mikes will fit into one of the categories mentioned above, the function of the microphone can play an important role in its final design. The *shotgun* microphone and the *lavalier* microphone are two examples. The **shotgun microphone** is unidirectional and is engineered to capture sound from long distances. It is ideal for sporting events where the sound crew needs to capture the talk of players out on the field. The **lavalier microphone** is used on TV and radio talk shows because it's small and unobtrusive, and can hook onto a person's lapel, shirt, or tie.

Microphones are carefully selected, dispersed, and aimed to form the best combination needed to clearly capture the full spectrum of sounds. For radio commercials, mikes are usually placed on booms and held over the heads of the talent or placed on stands directly in front of the announcer. For television and film, mikes may also be *boomed* over the actors' heads out of the camera's view. The general rule in placement is to keep a distance between microphones of about three times the space between the voice talent and his or her microphone.

The Studio, the Sound Booth, and the Control Room

The **studio** is where the talent performs. It generally features sound-dampening wall surfaces, a carpeted floor, microphones, a window to the control room, and a variety of wall plugs for directly connecting equipment and instruments to the control room.

Standard items in the sound studio are the microphones, headphone sets, and speakers. An announcer wears headphones to keep verbal instructions

EXHIBIT 11-5

A sophisticated audio console (in the center) can manipulate electrical sound waves in many ways. It is used for both recording radio commercials and for mixing, editing, and enhancing the various tracks during the postproduction phase.

from the control room from entering and interrupting the sound environment of the studio. Also, singers wear headphones to monitor prerecorded, instrumental tracks as they sing, thereby keeping the music track from being recorded onto the voice track.

In addition to microphones and headphones, the studio may feature a **sound booth**—a small windowed room or practice area. Here, certain instruments such as drums or louder back-up talent may be totally or partially isolated, so the sound technicians can better balance the overall group of sounds.

The **control room** is where the producer, director, and sound engineer sit, monitoring and controlling all the sounds generated in the sound studio. Here, the **audio console,** also called the **board,** is used to channel sounds to the appropriate recording devices. The board is also a sound mixer, blending both live and prerecorded sounds for immediate or delayed broadcast. The board is generally wired to a range of recording and playback units, including multitracking, reel-to-reel or cartridge ("cart") tape recorders, and compact disc (CD) recorders. Although records are no longer manufactured, a turntable may be a part of the control room's equipment for the mixing of music and sound effects that are not available on more modern recording mediums.

The audio console shown in Exhibit 11-5 features a number of switching and volume controls. The **keys** are toggle switches that send the sounds either to the active program line or to an audition line (generally used for reviewing sounds for possible use on the program line). There is a set of **potentiometers** (also called *pots*)—relatively large dials or sliding linear buttons for controlling the volume of each device. The dial used to control the overall master volume is called the **gain.** To ensure that the total sound is not too weak or too loud (when overly loud, the sound becomes fuzzy), **volume unit meters** (better known as *VU meters*) are used. The VU meters have a needle that moves from left to right as the sound becomes louder.

The board plays a role in both recording and postproduction. Disc jockeys often run their live radio programs from a control room using a board and mixing sounds from carts and CDs into the program line along with their voices. Radio station producers use the same technique to record radio commercials. The distinct difference is that radio stations use tapes with 4 and 8 tracks on one side, while professional sound studios use special tape decks that record 16 to 32 tracks on one side. Here, the sound studio can blend many tracks together, perfectly synchronized to create a very powerful commercial. Professional studios use enormous audio consoles featuring keys, linear sliding pots, and VU meters for all 32 tracks. When using such equipment, it's not unusual for more than one sound engineer to monitor a board during a session.

Postproduction: Finishing the Spot

When the commercial has been recorded several times, the best *takes* are selected. Music, sound, and vocals are usually recorded separately and then mixed and *sweetened* during the **production,** or finishing, phase. Once completed, the final recording is referred to as the **master tape.**

From the master tape, duplicates of the commercials, called **dubs,** are recorded onto ¼-inch magnetic tape and sent to the selected radio stations for broadcast.

As the next section will demonstrate, this process of producing a radio spot is relatively simple compared to the enormous complexity of producing television commercials today.

PRODUCING TELEVISION COMMERCIALS

Imagine that you are the creative director of the agency we've just hired. You have received an assignment. We need a television commercial that will introduce our new line of beachwear, communicate the California surfer mystique, incorporate the bright colors and splash graphics of our well-recognized print ads, punch our company name and brand hard enough to get national awareness, stay true to the grass-roots surfers who have been our traditional customers while broadening our appeal to nonsurfing young people, and get our spot noticed in the fast-paced, highly graphic MTV visual environment. You have 30 seconds.

That was the very assignment given to graphic designer Mike Salisbury when he met with the people at Gotcha surfwear.[5] Fortunately for Salisbury, this assignment did not just come out of the blue. He had been designing the print ads for Gotcha since the company had been founded in a Laguna Beach garage back in 1978. So it was natural to turn to Salisbury first when Gotcha decided to move into TV—especially since the idea was to create a set of commercials that were consistent with the print campaign and would maintain the label's authenticity.

By 1990, the little surfwear company was doing over $100 million in annual sales. While it was certainly not underground anymore, the company was still not in a position to launch a nationwide network television campaign. But MTV was affordable. And the demographics of MTV were perfectly matched to their market—mostly young males in their teens. Further, the highly graphic visual environment of MTV seemed a good setting for the same graphic style Salisbury had set in the print ads. Exhibit 11-6 is an example of that style.

Translating this concept to television, though, was no simple task. The company wanted an approach that was graphically interesting, fast-paced, and

EXHIBIT 11-6

The complex, colorful images featured in Gotcha's print ads were replicated in its television commercials. Technically complex, they incorporated live-action film, animation, and special effects.

hard-hitting—and would not alienate the loyal grass-roots audience. The overriding visual concern was to capture the fashions in a thoroughly modern California lifestyle setting—to update the surfing film look of the 60s—and to capture the contemporary look of beach culture. Gotcha had produced its own surfing film two years earlier, so all this footage was a good beginning place for conceptualizing the ads. But as we shall see, Salisbury ended up using a lot more than live-action surfing shots. In fact, he used every major production technique available to television producers today.

Advertisers produce more than 50,000 television commercials every year in an effort to sell their goods and services. No one knows exactly how much is spent in the production of all these commercials, but most estimates are in the hundreds of millions of dollars.

Producing commercials for television has always been expensive, but in recent years these costs have soared.[6] For a local advertiser, a simple spot might cost anywhere from $1,000 to $20,000. For national quality spots, though, the costs are considerably higher. The lowest figure is probably around $30,000, with the average now well over $125,000.[7]

As the technology of electronic commercial production has increased, so have its costs and complexity, resulting in greater specialization in the production process. Major agencies, for example, used to maintain complete production facilities in-house. Not anymore. The trend for several decades now has been to use outside producers, directors, production companies, and other technical suppliers, and to seek more economical venues for both location and studio shooting. Many U.S. film and video producers, for example, now shoot in Canada for that very reason.[8]

As a result, the advertising agency producers must be generalists, able to bring a spot's creative essence to life. They must have a vast knowledge of the video and filmmaking craft—as well as the suppliers. And they must have the savvy to juggle the many dollars involved in commercial production. With technological development has come an increased need for knowledge of all related disciplines and the diplomacy and tact to deal with a wide variety of creative specialists. The agency producer profession has also experienced a gender change in recent years—women now often outnumber men.[9]

☑
Checklist for Creating Effective TV Commercials

☐ *Create a pertinent, relevant, unforced opening.* This permits a smooth transition to the rest of the commercial.

☐ *Use a situation that lends itself naturally to the sales story.* Avoid extraneous, distracting gimmicks.

☐ *Develop a plot that is high in human interest.*

☐ *Create a situation the viewer can easily identify with.*

☐ *Keep the number of elements in the commercial to a minimum.*

☐ *Present a simple sequence of ideas.*

☐ *Use short sentences with short, realistic, conversational words.* Be sure the script avoids "ad talk."

☐ *Let the words interpret the picture and prepare the viewer for the next scene.*

☐ *Write concise audio copy.* Fewer words are needed for

TV than for radio. Fewer than two words per second is effective for demonstrations. Sixty-second commercials with 101 to 110 words are most effective; those with more than 170 words are least effective.

☐ *Synchronize audio and video.*

☐ *Run scenes five or six seconds on average.* In general, no scene should run less than three seconds.

☐ *Avoid static scenes—use movement.*

☐ *Offer a variety of scenes without "jumping."*

☐ *Handle presenters properly.* See that they are identified, compatible, authoritative, pleasing, and nondistracting.

☐ *Ensure that the general video treatment is interesting and the commercial looks fresh and new.*

Today, virtually everybody involved in advertising must have a general understanding of basic television production concepts. This means recognizing the types of commercials most commonly used, which are most effective, the basic terms and techniques for producing a commercial, and how the production process is organized.

The student of advertising should have a knowledge of these concepts in order to understand how commercials are made, why commercial production is so expensive, and what methods can be used to cut costs without sacrificing quality or effectiveness. The Checklist for Creating Effective TV Commercials is a good place to start..

Television Production Techniques

Three major categories of production techniques are available to television advertisers today: *live action, animation,* and *special effects.* Mike Salisbury decided to use all of them for Gotcha..

Live Action

The **live-action** production technique portrays people and things in lifelike, everyday situations. The surfing film Gotcha had shot, for example, was live action; and the typical slice-of-life TV commercials we see regularly also use the live-action technique.

Salisbury's basic idea for Gotcha was to employ live-action shots to illustrate the California beach scene and bring it to life in a dynamic, realistic, and credible way. For example, to immediately grab the attention of the 15-year-old male audience, one commercial opened with a live shot of a bikini-clad

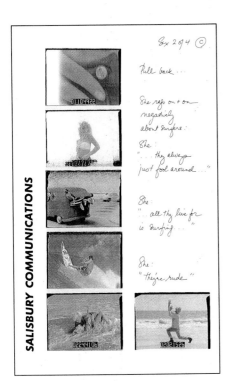

SALISBURY COMMUNICATIONS

Storyboards incorporating actual photographs of live-action beach and surfing scenes were used to show Gotcha executives how the finished commercials would look and feel.

model. Throughout the commercials, as shown in Exhibit 11-7, scenes of surfers, crashing waves, vans with surfboards, and couples on beach blankets were interspersed with other effects in rapid-fire order to create the motion and impact typical of the MTV environment.

Live action gives the greatest realism, but it lacks the unique distinctiveness of other production techniques—animated or special-effect commercials—so Salisbury decided to incorporate these methods, too.

Animation

Cartoons, dancing puppets, and demonstrations in which inanimate objects come to life on the screen are typical examples of **animation** and have traditionally been very effective for communicating difficult messages and for reaching specialized markets such as children. The way aspirin or other medications affect the human system, for example, is difficult to explain. Animated pictures of headaches and stomachs, however, can simplify the subject and make a demonstration understandable.

The traditional animation techniques involve the use of *cartoons, photo animation, stop-motion photography,* and *video animation.*

Cartoons Commercials featuring **cartoons** often have the highest viewer interest, the longest life, and therefore the lowest cost per showing. However, many viewers consider them childlike, and the initial production of film animation is very expensive. A fully animated commercial, for example, can easily run from $150,000 to $200,000.[10] The technique is achieved by drawing illustrations of each step in the action and photographing them one frame at a time. Then, when the film is projected at 24 frames per second, it gives the illusion of movement.

There are several animation styles, including Disney, contemporary, psychedelic, and others. Cartoons are sometimes supplemented by live action, especially when a serious purchase decision is to be made and the product benefits are described.

Photo Animation This technique uses still photography instead of illustrations or puppets. **Photo animation** is especially effective for making titles move. Making slight movements of the photos from one frame to the next creates the animated illusion. However, it is considered a very low-budget technique.

Stop-Motion Photography **Stop-motion photography** is an animation technique whereby objects and animals come to life—walk, run, dance, and do tricks. One of the best-known examples of this special effect is the charming "claymation" campaign created for the California Raisin Advisory Board, a segment of which is shown in Exhibit 11-8 (p. 398). The raisin characters, fashioned from plasticene clay, dance in a conga line and perform on a construction worker's sandwich. Created by Will Vinton Productions (Portland, Oregon), the raisins are flexible figures with movable joints. The arms and legs can be bent to simulate walking or dancing. Each frame of film is shot individually. An arm may be moved only 1/32 of an inch on each frame, but when the frames are assembled, the effect is smooth and natural, combining the whimsy of animation with the substance of live action. Since film is projected at 24 frames per second, this means 1,440 frames must be shot for each minute of raisin dancing.[11] Stop-motion is typically used with other famous puppet and doll characters like the well-known Pillsbury Doughboy and the Snuggles bear.

EXHIBIT 11-8

Through stop-motion animation techniques, the "claymation" California Raisins sang and danced their way to advertising fame.

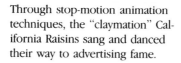

SFX: (LIQUID BEING POURED INTO A CONTAINER.)
(MUSIC IN.)

SFX: (LUNCH BOX TOP SLAMMING CLOSED.)
(MUSIC OUT.)

SFX: (SQUEAKY TOP OF LUNCH BOX OPENING.)
(MUSIC IN.)

LEAD RAISIN SINGER: Ooh, ooh, I heard it through the grapevine . . .

BACKUP RAISIN SINGERS: Ooh.

LEAD RAISIN SINGER: . . . raised in the California sun . . . shine.

BACKUP LEAD RAISIN (SPOKEN): California raisins . . . from the California vineyards.

LEAD RAISIN SINGER: Don'cha know that I . . .

BACKUP RAISIN SINGERS: . . . heard it through the . . .

BACKUP RAISIN SINGERS VO: . . . grapevine.

STEELWORKER: Sounds better'n what I got.

SFX: (AUTOMOBILE HORN.)

Video Animation Today, computer-generated graphics are used to animate television commercials for everything from high-technology products to bathroom cleaners. Using computer graphics, though, has required a great deal of faith on the part of advertisers, since most of this very expensive work is done right on the computer, and the client sees little or nothing until the animation is well developed.

For Gotcha, Salisbury's initial ideas for film animation were too expensive, so he decided to use computer-generated graphics. In one case, he wanted to frame a live shot in a border of wiggling leaves. To accomplish this effect, he created the collage of leaves shown in Exhibit 11-9 and shot it on videotape. Then he created a second collage, repositioning the leaves slightly, and shot that. The next step was simply two-frame animation—by toggling between the two tapes running simultaneously, the leaves seemed to wiggle. This was recorded onto another tape called a *B-roll.* Then, by running the B-roll at the same time as the live-action tape, the two were combined into a final shot.

Special Effects

Much video animation can be done with a computer joystick. Likewise, most of the **special effects** in video, such as moving titles and whirling logos, are handled this way. All major video production companies today use dedicated **digital video effects units (DVEs)** that can manipulate graphics on the screen in a variety of ways—fades, wipes, zooms, rotation, and so on.

Salisbury, for example, wanted the image of fish swimming across the screen. The fish graphic was simply shot to video and imported into the DVE. There it was altered digitally into two different shapes and then, with the

EXHIBIT 11-9

To create a border of wiggling leaves for a Gotcha commercial, two different collages of leaves were videotaped. Computerized editing equipment allowed rapid switching from one collage to the other, creating the illusion that the leaves were wiggling. The live-action tape was then super-imposed on this border.

EXHIBIT 11-10

Sophisticated video equipment enabled the creators of the Gotcha commercials to manipu-late graphics of fish and other animals to create the illusion that they were "swimming" through the basic scene. Such special ef-fects are entertaining and may be effective, but they can be expen-sive and are also appropriate only in certain circumstances—such as this.

joystick, moved across the screen, producing the swimming effect.[12] As shown in Exhibit 11-10, the fish were incorporated with other graphic elements to create a psychedelic effect on the screen reminiscent of some of the images used in the design of Gotcha's surfwear fashions.

Music and sound can also be manipulated digitally by computer. In fact, sound design has become its own specialty field in which technicians use computers to blend sound effects and music through the use of a program-mable synthesizer. This work is exemplified by the seductively intrusive sound in an AT&T spot in which fragments of a woman's day flit by as she is seen at work, at home, and commuting, while her voice-over complains about the hidden charges and restrictions of a competing long-distance service. The sound designer for this spot, Hein Hoven, used the sound of windshield wipers as the underlying rhythm combined with a synthesized ballad music underscore. There's also a discernible hiss of water, but the source is not revealed until the very end of the spot when we see the woman in her living room and rain streaming down her window.[13]

Special effects often entertain viewers and win advertising awards. But if the sales message is complex or based on logic, another technique might be more successful. The obvious precaution is not to let the technique so enthrall the viewers that they pay more attention to it than to the product.

Under normal circumstances, special effects should be limited to one fantasy or mnemonic device: the Energizer bunny, a jolly green giant, the Imperial crown, or the water skier crashing through the lifelike photo of the yacht in the Fuji film commercials. In these cases, the fantasy is directly related to the product's claims, and heavy repetition makes strong impressions on the viewer.[14]

The Television Production Process

Now that we have seen the various techniques producers use to create commercials, it's important to understand the process a commercial goes through from concept to completion. Regardless of which—or how many—production techniques are employed, the process of producing a commercial always involves three stages, as shown in Exhibit 11-11 (p. 402):

ETHICAL DILEMMA IN ADVERTISING
In Political Advertising, the Nays Have It

Since its earliest days, U.S. politics has often been a brutish affair with candidates leveling outrageous accusations against one another. Those early attacks seldom went beyond the "smoke-filled rooms," however. But today, contemporary electronic media have brought unprecedented immediacy to campaigning. Now, when politicians malign each other, radio and television flash the news from coast to coast. The electronic media also provide an arena for political advertising, much of which is decidedly negative.

Negative political advertising took center stage during the 1980s primarily because complex issues like drugs, crime, and the federal deficit are far more difficult to grasp than simplistic 30-second commercials focusing on other issues. Another reason for the increase in negative advertising is that it's intrusive enough to cut through the clutter of commercials that choke the electronic media. But the most important reason for the proliferation of these ads is the advertiser's belief that they almost always work.

Surprisingly, however, recent studies have suggested that negative advertising doesn't work and serves only to make people even more cynical about the political process. In 1989, a study reported by Professor Ronald Hill in the *Journal of Advertising* concluded that "voters' overall responses . . . are more positive for sponsor-positive advertisements than for sponsor-positive/opponent-negative or opponent-negative political advertisements." However,

the study also indicated that negative advertising is effective when an unknown challenger uses it against a well-known incumbent. As Larry Sabato, professor of government at the University of Virginia, says, "If you're the challenger and you have to make up 30 or 40 points in the polls, . . . anything's fair game."

Most political consultants believe negative advertising will be used even more in the future, simply because there are no restraints or regulations to prevent candidates from running even the most hostile attacks. Furthermore, the American Association of Political Consultants has yet to discipline a single member for violating its Code of Ethics. So candidates who believe they have an edge tend to use it quickly and decisively. As Democratic pollster Paul Maslin says: "The weapons [are] so powerful, that if you don't use them, you will lose them, because the other side will use them on you."

Michael Dukakis certainly learned that lesson during the 1988 presidential campaign. He tried to make George Bush's competence the central issue. Bush, on the other hand, portrayed Dukakis as soft on crime, and successfully exploited the pollution, tax, and patriotism issues. The "lowlight" was the infamous Willie Horton TV spot that implied Dukakis cared more about criminals than victims. Dukakis failed to return the volley immediately, and when he did counterattack, it was too little, too late. Bush won,

1. Preproduction—all the work prior to the actual day of filming.
2. Production—the actual day (or days) that the commercial is filmed or videotaped.
3. Postproduction (or finishing)—all the work done after the day of shooting to edit and finish the commercial.

Since all these steps have a dramatic impact on the cost and the eventual quality of the commercial, we shall discuss each briefly. For a look at how all three affect the end product, read Creative Department: From Concept through Production of a Television Commercial (pp. 414-18).

Preproduction

The greatest waste of money in commercial production inevitably occurs because of a lack of adequate preproduction planning. The converse is also true: The greatest savings can be effected by proper planning before the day of production.[15]

Casting, for example, is a crucial decision and must be completely settled before the day of shooting. Children and animals are unpredictable and often cause production delays. Rehearsals before production, therefore, are a must.

---

but only 26.77 percent of eligible voters cast their ballots for him. It seems that while negative political advertising can destroy opponents, it may also discourage voters from going to the polls.

Paradoxically, candidates who use negative advertising to prove they are worthy of governing us often end up proving they aren't. The 1988 presidential race spawned so many copycat campaigns over the next two years that Joseph Napolitan, a pioneer in the political use of television, observed, "Now the idea is to attack first, last, and always." Roger Ailes, considered the master of negativity, contends, "There's nothing wrong with negative advertising as long as it's accurate and fair. It's perfectly right to discuss an opponent." In 1988, Ailes handled Lynn Martin's campaign against Illinois Senator Paul Simon. The incumbent Simon easily defeated Martin despite her negative advertising. Afterward Simon called for a candidate code of conduct that would limit negative ads, but no action was taken.

The heart of the matter is that some politicians care more about winning than about ethics. As former Bush political adviser David Keene says, "If a poll shows that 70 percent of the voters won't vote for someone who smoked pot and your opponent is known to have smoked it, then the question you have to ask is, 'Why not run that kind of ad?' The answer is, you would." Of course you would, if you believe that the end justifies the means.

Recent polls indicate that negative advertising harms both candidates and destroys their credibility. It's one reason voters so often feel they're choosing between the lesser of two evils. Eventually, politicians and voters alike must realize that elections are too important to be decided by negative advertising. Politicians have the power to influence the course of the world's history. That's why they, and their advertising, should be held to the highest ethical standards.

Questions

1. Do you think it's unethical to use political advertising to reveal an opponent's personal problems?
2. Bob Garfield, an editorialist for *Advertising Age,* has proposed that all political advertising should carry the following standard disclaimer: "This has been a paid political announcement. The station is compelled by law to run it, but we have no right and no means to verify its accuracy or untruthfulness. We encourage you to seek other sources for more complete information. WARNING: POLITICAL ADVERTISING CAN LEGALLY DISTORT THE TRUTH." Do you agree with him? If so, why?

Film commercial

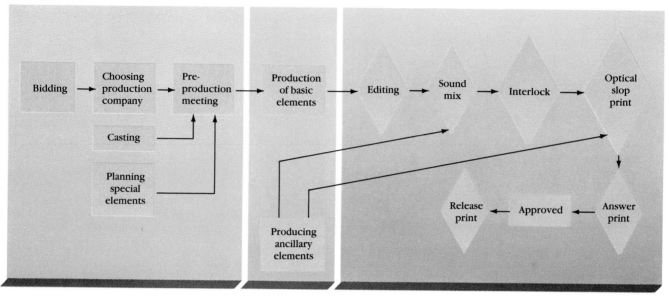

Videotape commercial

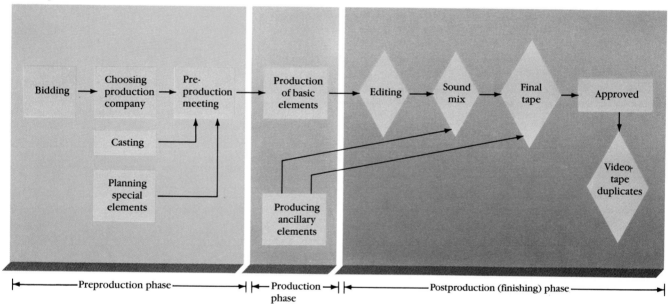

|←————Preproduction phase————→|←—Production—→|←——————————Postproduction (finishing) phase——————————→|
                                     phase

The production process for film and videotape commercials is quite similar to the process for producing radio commercials. They differ most in the finishing phase. Computerized video editing speeds up this phase considerably.

Once the advertiser approves a storyboard and budget, the production process begins. Because few people have the background to handle the entire production from start to finish, the commercial is a group effort. The team includes a writer, an art director, a producer, a director, and sometimes a musical composer and a choreographer. The person responsible for completion on schedule and within budget is the producer, who may be either in-house or free-lance.

The agency producer seeks competitive bids, usually sending copies of the storyboard to three studios. The bids include the services of a director, camera operators, electricians, and other technicians. The studio may do the film or tape editing, or it may be done elsewhere. A typical advertising agency contract, which puts the preproduction agreements in writing, is provided in Exhibit 11-12.

EXHIBIT 11–12

Commercial production contract form. A radio or television commercial involves many specialists. Because it is a business matter as well as a creative task, signed written contracts about who will do what—and for how much—are a necessity.

WARWICK BAKER & FIORE INC.

DATE: _____
JOB #: _____

ADVERTISING
100 AVENUE OF THE AMERICAS, NEW YORK, NY 10013
(212) 941-4200 FAX: (212) 941-4277
A PARTNER IN ALLIANCE INTERNATIONAL

This will confirm our understanding and serve as a complete agreement between you and us (sometimes herein referred to as "Agency"), for our client, _____, for the production and delivery of   commercial motion picture film(s) and/or tape(s) subject to our approval and acceptance and in accordance with scripts and/or storyboards supplied by us, and in compliance with the attached "Film/Tape Commercial Production Specifications and Quotations" for use under any circumstances, on the following terms and conditions:

1. (a) Code number(s), title(s), and product(s) to be inscribed on the negative leader of each film or at the beginning of each tape.

CODE #	TITLE	LENGTH	PRODUCT

    (b) Film(s)/tape(s) to be photographed in ☐ 35mm ☐ 16mm ☐ B/W ☐ Color suitable for television use.

2. Film(s)/tape(s) to be produced at mutually agreeable locations and studios.

3. You will be responsible for supplying every item and element for the above production as specified in the attached "Film/Tape Commercial Production Specifications and Quotations" sheet. You are hereby directed to use _____ as your subcontractor for the editing and completion of the commercials.

4. **Production Schedule:** It is agreed that the essential dates are as follows:

    Photography: _____   # of 35mm Film(s)/Master(s): _____

    Answer Print(s)/Master(s): _____   # of 3/4" Videocassettes: _____

5. **Delivery:** Upon completion of the commercial(s), you will deliver all material as indicated on the attached "Proof of Performance & Delivery" sheet.

6. **Price:**

    Shooting through dailies: $ _____
    Editing through completion: $ _____
    Duplicating master(s): $ _____
    TOTAL CONTRACT PRICE: $ _____

    Weather contingency: out-of-pocket costs up to $ _____ (any excess costs to be borne by you). The above prices do not include agency commission or sales tax. You will add total sales tax to your final invoice, if applicable. You agree to look solely to Agency for payment.

7. **Payment Schedule:**

    1/3 upon signing of this agreement
    1/3 upon completion of photography
    1/3 upon delivery of the film/tape materials and your final billing

8. Time of Production and Delivery are of the essence.

9. This agreement, with "Proof of Performance & Delivery" and "Film/Tape Commercial Production Specifications and Quotations" attached hereto constitutes the entire understanding between the parties and there are no other agreements or understandings, written or oral, in effect between the parties relating to the subject matter hereof. This agreement may not be modified or terminated orally.

10. Final 1/3 payment will not be made unless we have heard from the subcontracted editor that he has received payment.

11. All provisions and clauses on the reverse side hereof are part of this contract.

WARWICK BAKER & FIORE INC.

For and on behalf of: _____

By: _____

Agreed and Accepted:

_____
(Contractor)

By: _____

(Title) _____   (Date) _____

When the studio has been chosen, the cast is selected and an announcer, if needed, is chosen. Next, the set is built and the crew and cast rehearse under the director's supervision.

In the case of Gotcha, a very unusual event took place. Salisbury had a difficult time communicating his concept in the normal, sketched-out storyboard form (discussed in Chapter 9). His clients had never seen a storyboard, and they couldn't visualize what was intended. So Salisbury did something radical. He booked a production crew and spent a day at the beach shooting scenes in 16 mm film. From this, he pulled color still shots that he pasted down next to his storyboard sketches. The next time he showed the storyboard the clients got excited—they could see real pictures—and the concept was approved. Now Salisbury could book the studios and the specialists he needed to actually produce the commercial. He decided to shoot the live action in 16 mm film, which would then be converted to video for doing the editing and adding the special effects.

Shooting days are expensive. The cost of studios, casts, crews, and equipment are normally figured on a full-day basis. Therefore, any delays that could throw the production into an unexpected second shooting day must be avoided. This also suggests a problem for location shooting. Weather must be considered. Locations should be selected close to home whenever possible; extra days on location are extremely expensive. Fortunately, it is no longer necessary to travel to the major cities like New York and Los Angeles to find quality production houses.

All these factors should be taken into consideration during the preproduction phase, and every aspect of the commercial production should be discussed, decided, and approved by the client, agency, and production company prior to the shooting day.

During this preparatory period, preproduction meetings should be held with the producer, the agency account representatives, the writer, the art director, the studio director, possibly the advertiser, and anyone else deemed important to the production. Last-minute problems can be ironed out and final decisions made on the scenes, the actors, and the announcer at this time. Music, sets, action, lighting, and camera angles are all reviewed. The more details settled at this time, the better. A finished 60-second film commercial takes only 90 feet of film, but the shooting often requires several days and from 3,000 to 5,000 feet of film.

The soundtrack may be recorded before, during, or after the actual production of the film or videotape. Recording the sound in advance ensures that the commercial will be neither too long nor too short. This technique is used when the subject of the commercial has to move or dance to a specific rhythm. Sometimes, though, the music or voice-over is recorded after shooting.

Production: The Shoot

The actual shooting day (or days) of a commercial can be very long and tedious. Starting very early in the morning, the crew may take several hours just to light the set to the director's liking. The needs to control sound, lighting, and staging are basic demands that consistently challenge producers. Today, a great deal of technology exists to deal with these factors. Fortunately, a basic understanding of a few key fundamentals can provide the advertising student with a working perspective of the role of today's technology in the production of a television commercial.

Quiet on the Set: Sound As in radio, sound is extremely important to any television commercial. The ring of a high-pitched bell, properly timed, can make a smile seem brighter, add extra sparkle to a glass, or announce when a character experiences a smart idea. On the other hand, if the actor's lips move out of sync with his voice, the distraction will kill the effectiveness of a spot.

Today, the recording and control of sound is highly technical. But the overall procedure of recording and controlling music and sounds for commercials, films, or videos is relatively straightforward and similar to the process we discussed in radio production. Microphones capture sound; recorders are used to transfer sounds onto mediums like electronic tape that store the sounds; and with the use of a multichannel control board, stored sounds are manipulated for effect and then recorded onto film, video, or a playback system synchronized with film.

It is imperative to understand, though, that the original recording is the key to success—for two reasons. First, the original sound recording is synchronized with the original visual recording, both with the timing of the action and with the emotion expressed by the actors. A re-creation of those sounds and emotions will never quite match the timing nor have the feeling of the original.

EXHIBIT 11-13

A light meter like this can measure both incident and reflective light. It enables the cinematographer to determine how much additional light is necessary in a scene, where to aim the light sources, and how to set the camera's lens aperture.

Second, before it reaches its final form, the original recording will undergo rerecording many times—with some loss of fidelity each time. Therefore, the most reliable and highest-quality sound-recording equipment is mandatory for making a successful commercial. And any extraneous sounds must be absent from the recording. Hence the well-known order: "Quiet on the set!"

Lights In making a commercial, the director and the cinematographer must deal with a variety of light sources that affect the scene. For example, a scene with a person standing a few feet from a window may have daylight coming through a window, high-intensity studio lighting for brightening the subject and the inside of the room, and a regular table lamp on the table as a prop—all shedding different kinds of light that could adversely affect the scene. To control this effect, photographers need to first measure the light and then style it to suit the scene.

The accurate measurement of light is critical to the ability to create exciting images and capture moods. A major consideration is to ensure that the different types of light in the scene are balanced. All light sources must be coordinated to work properly with the designed receptivity of the film or videotape—in order to record the correct color and brightness.

An experienced **cinematographer**—a motion picture photographer—can generally guess the range and intensity of light by briefly studying the sources of light. However, he or she will depend on a reliable light meter as the primary instrument for determining how to set the lens **aperture** on the camera—the opening that controls the amount of light reaching the film or videotape. Too much light can overexpose film or cause *flares* and *burn-ins* on video equipment, while light that is too low fails to produce any image at all. Color shifts may occur as well.

Photographers measure light by its *intensity* (brightness) and by its *temperature* (color). Using an **incident light meter,** the intensity—or volume—of light directly emitted by a light source can be measured by pointing the meter at the source. The meter will display the amount of light measured and indicate the correct aperture setting for the type of film being used. Another way of measuring intensity is by using a **reflected light meter** that measures the volume of light reflected off the subject. A number of light meters, as shown in Exhibit 11-13, have features that allow measurement of both incidental and reflected light.

The second way to measure light is by its temperature or color range. Because light is electromagnetic energy—like heat—it can be measured by degrees on the *Kelvin scale.* This is done with a **color light meter.** In essence, this type of meter indicates the overall degrees on the Kelvin scale of

EXHIBIT 11-14	Temperature Kelvin (K) for Different Light Sources

Source	Color temperature
Candle flame	1,500°K
60-watt household bulb	2,800
Film-studio lights	3,200
Photoflood lights	3,400
Sunset in Los Angeles	3,000–4,500
Noon summer sunlight	5,400
Hydrargyrum medium arc-length iodide (HMI) lamp	5,600

the light reflecting from an area within the light meter's view. It can tell you if the scene is generally too blue, green, or red in relation to daylight or tungsten film. This is important, because various light sources can discolor an image, making it greener or redder than it appears to your eye. Daylight is considered *white light* and measures 5,400 degrees Kelvin. Red light ranges from 2,500 to 3,300 degrees; and light between 3,300 and 4,200 degrees Kelvin is in the bluish ranges.

Most manufactured light sources generate light that is not white. White light contains all the degrees Kelvin that we can see. We see individual colors when white light hits a material that absorbs all of the white light *except* for one color, which is reflected to our eye.

When a light source generates light in just one broad area of the color spectrum, it may not contain the range of temperatures needed to reflect all of the visible colors off the object. For example, while the eye sees fluorescent lighting as being white, it is actually generated in the green temperature range and appears green to video cameras and film. On the other hand, the incandescent light generated from a typical light bulb in your house emits light in the redder portion of the light spectrum.

Theater lamps, film lamps, and video production lamps are designed to create the higher intensities of manufactured light, but do so in differing Kelvin ranges, as shown in Exhibit 11-14. High-intensity lights may be quartz-halogen (about 3,200 degress Kelvin) or arc lamps (about 5,600 degrees Kelvin). The quartz-halogens emit a redder light while the arc lamps emit a wavelength that is most nearly equal to daylight.

It is extremely important for the cinematographer to be sure that the lighting on the set is consistent in temperature, or mixed only to create a desired effect. (And for any advertising people involved in producing commercials, it's similarly important to understand what the cinematographer is doing.) Balancing light for film may be done with filters that fit over lenses or light sources, as shown in Exhibit 11-15. For video, the camera operator simply aims the camera at a white card and adjusts the dials to shift the discolored image back to a true white—a process that takes only a few minutes.

There is more to lighting, though, than measuring it—it must also be styled. The arrangement of lights in the studio, on the studio lot, or on

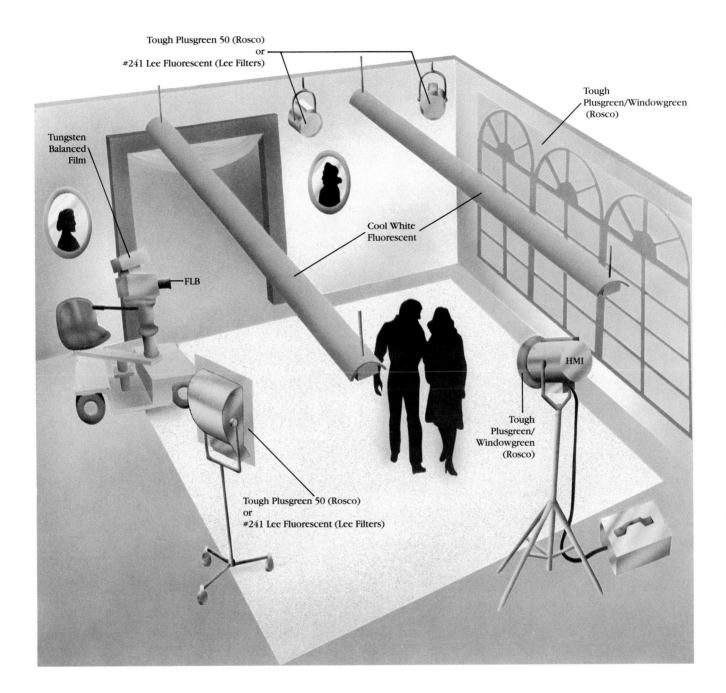

Tough Plusgreen 50 (Rosco)
or
#241 Lee Fluorescent (Lee Filters)

Tough
Plusgreen/Windowgreen
(Rosco)

Tungsten
Balanced
Film

Cool White
Fluorescent

FLB

HMI

Tough
Plusgreen/
Windowgreen
(Rosco)

Tough Plusgreen 50 (Rosco)
or
#241 Lee Fluorescent (Lee Filters)

EXHIBIT 11-15

For filming, an array of lens filters and light gels are used to
balance the overall color temperature of the scene with the
particular film being used. In
video, color balancing is achieved
electronically.

location must establish the proper visual mood. Intense light from a single
source gives a harsh appearance to the subject—which may be purposefully
used to create anxiety in the viewer. A reddish, more consistent, soft illumina-
tion can be established by using filters, lights in the warmer Kelvin range,
diffusion screens, and reflectors to set a more romantic mood for the scene.
Here, the director works with the art director and lighting engineer to choose
the types, intensities, and placement of the lights.

There are standard terms for different types of lighting, as shown in
Exhibit 11-16 (p. 408). The **keylight** is the primary light to fall upon the
subject. **Fill light** is much dimmer than a key light and is used to slightly
brighten up the shadow area to reveal details without losing the overall effect
of the shadow. **Backlight** is either directly behind or behind and above the

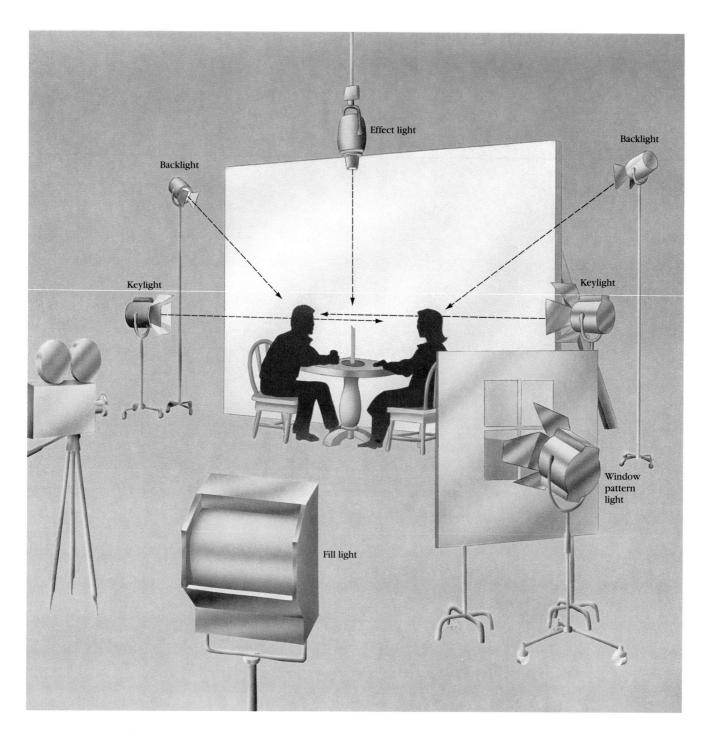

Effect light

Backlight

Backlight

Keylight

Keylight

Fill light

Window
pattern
light

EXHIBIT 11-16

Different types of lighting are used to style and enhance the scene and achieve special effects. For example, the light above the table produces the effect of a burning candle and helps develop the mood of the scene.

subject, aimed toward the camera to outline the subject and set the subject apart from the background. And **special-effects lighting** is used to create enhancements and distortions to add visual excitement to the scene.

Generally, a scene needs several types of lighting to give it life, but few scenes need all of these types at one time. It's the careful and skillful combination of lighting that adds the full measure of artistic and emotional appeal to the scene.

Camera Professional film cameras for shooting television commercials include models that shoot 16 mm, 35 mm, and 65 mm film—the diagonal measure-

EXHIBIT 11-17

This Panaflex studio film camera has an option for video assist so the director can see a video image while filming.

ment of a single film frame. Major brands such as Arriflex and Panaflex (shown in Exhibit 11-17) offer a variety of models for synchronized sound or high-speed shots. Many models can convert to a hand-held mode and may offer video assists for simultaneous video viewing during the shot.

Traditionally, local TV commercials were shot on the grainier but less expensive 16 mm film, while national spots were shot on 35 mm to gain the extra quality and precision offered by the larger format. While film is still widely used for national spots, most local spots are now shot on video.

Video cameras can be classified by their function. Studio video cameras are heavy-duty units that include a built-in stand with wheels. A number of accessories can be carried by the unit, the lens-mounted teleprompter being one of the most important. The **teleprompter** has a two-way mirror that allows the camera to see a spokesperson through the back of the mirror while he or she reads moving text that is reflected off the front side of the mirror. The video cameras used by professionals in the field feature shoulder mounts and a sound-recording unit, and are significantly larger than home units.

Unlike film cameras, studio video cameras are tied to a control room by large cables. Here, multiple video screens and sound channels are wired to a control panel. Specialized technicians keep the cameras and control rooms operating. Working at the control panel, the director switches from one camera to another and simultaneously sets the input and output levels of sound and visuals for both recording and editing on a number of recording systems. The control panels also feature special-effects devices for creating text or visual effects on the screen.

Action (Staging and Talent) The staging for a commercial may be done in the isolation of a studio, outside on a studio lot, or on location. The studio offers the greatest degree of control.

Most film and video studios are heavily soundproofed to eliminate outside sounds such as the sirens of emergency vehicles and the engine noise of low-flying aircraft. They feature corrugated wall surfaces to dampen echoes on the set. They are also lightproof and allow for complete lighting control. Special energy requirements and equipment are most easily used in the controlled environment offered by the studio. One drawback, however, is that studio lighting can give an artificial appearance to a scene.

For scenes requiring large amounts of space, historic or unique architecture, scenery, and the full effect of outdoor lighting, the studio lot offers the best control. The lot can be shielded from most stray, off-site sounds. Sets can be constructed conveniently close to the studio's carpentry shop and left standing until all shootings and retakes are completed. Usually, the lot is also conveniently situated near the studio's postproduction facility. Special energy needs and unique equipment can be better handled on the studio lot than on location. Unfortunately, though, natural events such as rain can create costly changes of schedule.

Shooting on location is generally a technical and logistical nightmare, but it may add great realism and authenticity to the scene. And because the building of sets is not required, on-site shooting is ideal for the lower-budget commercials.

Every location has natural and manufactured features that create obstacles. For example, natural lighting is strong, creating bright highlights contrasted with harsh shadows. Large, reflective screens and high-intensity lights, like those shown in Exhibit 11-18, are therefore required to brighten up the shadows for a more even-toned exposure. Likewise, energy sources for lighting and equipment may be insufficient on location, requiring long cabling and mobile generators. And again, natural events such as rain and fog can cause costly interruptions.

Shooting on location sets up special challenges for directors using video. A truck, van, motor home, or trailer is wired for video and sound control recording. Video screens and a multichannel control panel are mounted inside to control the recording of input from a number of cameras running simultaneously.

Whether at the studio or on location, when the scenes are being shot, it is usually necessary to try several "takes" for the **talent** (actors) to get them right. During this time, the lighting may be readjusted several times as

EXHIBIT 11-18

The existing light of a film location may be enhanced with reflector screens and high-intensity lights to create the desired effects.

unexpected shadows pop up. The director usually requires two or three good takes of every scene. In addition, each scene is probably shot from two or three different angles: one to establish the characters, one to show only the person speaking, and one to show the reaction of the person listening.

Scenes are not necessarily shot in order. For example, scenes with no synchronized sound are usually shot last, since they don't require the full crew to be present.

A long interval may be required between the shootings of each scene to move the camera, reset the lights, reposition the talent, and pick up the action, sound, and look to match the other scenes. This is extremely important, for each piece of action must match what comes before and after. Otherwise, the commercial will contain disconcerting jumps that can potentially destroy the credibility of the message.

Once all the scenes are "in the can," the commercial enters the postproduction phase, or finishing. Some reshooting may be necessary if the postproduction process is unable to make the commercial fit together smoothly or if the client dictates some changes at a later date.

Postproduction

In the **postproduction** phase, the commercial is actually put together. It is also the phase that usually determines how good a commercial is. At this point, the responsibilities of the film editor, the sound mixer, and the director are enormous.

Mike Salisbury, for instance, had to create the Gotcha commercials almost entirely in the postproduction stage. Everybody agreed on the need to establish the Gotcha name early and often, since the spots were intended to introduce the line of surfwear to a new audience. So each commercial started with an *academy leader*—as at the beginning of a reel of movie film—that spelled out the name G-O-T-C-H-A, one letter at a time. To accomplish this, the line art for each frame was created on a Macintosh computer using Adobe graphics software. This art was then colored and shot on video. Using the on-line edit bay at Master Communication in Los Angeles, Salisbury then married the academy leader graphics to some live-action footage to create a dynamic, attention-getting opening to the spots, such as the one for the "Danger" spot shown in Exhibit 11-19.

There were five tapes for the live action and several more tapes of the graphic footage during the edit session. The computers then selected either live or graphic elements to record to the master tape at the direction of Salisbury and the editor, Robert Master. Likewise, additional tapes of desired sound and music were created and then selected by the computer at their direction. As shown in Exhibit 11-20 (p. 412), the editor can switch from tape to tape and add any desired effects such as wipes and dissolves—all electronically. Salisbury's total editing session lasted 72 hours to create the four Gotcha commercials, considerably less than would have been required for film editing and lab work.

Many professionals, however, still prefer the film medium. When working with film, the visual portion of the commercial is first assembled on one piece of celluloid without the extra effects of dissolves, titles, or **supers** (words superimposed on the picture). The sound portion of the film is assembled on another piece of celluloid. This is called the **work print** (also called a **rough cut** or **interlock**). At this time, scenes may be substituted, music and sound effects added, or other last-minute changes made.

EXHIBIT 11-19

The academy leader mixed with live-action shots at the beginning of the Gotcha commercial was an attention getter designed to immediately communicate the sponsor's name. The "dial" on the left side of the image spells out both *Gotcha* (around the perimeter) and *Danger* (in the center letters).

EXHIBIT 11-20

In the postproduction phase for the Gotcha commercials, Mike Salisbury and Robert Master saved a lot of time and money by using computerized video and sound editing.

Next, the external sound is recorded. This includes the actors' voices, the announcer, the music track, the singers, and the sound effects. The announcer records the voice-over narrative. The music is recorded by musicians and singers, or prerecorded stock music may be bought and integrated into the commercial. Sound effects such as doorbells ringing or doors slamming are mixed.

The finished sound is put on one piece of celluloid that, combined with the almost-completed visual celluloid, is called the **mixed interlock.** When these two are joined, along with all the required optical effects and titles, a print called the **answer print** is made. This is the final commercial. If it receives all the necessary approvals, **dupes** (copies) are made and delivered to the networks or TV stations for airing.

The Film versus Tape Debate

Today, very few commercials are done live. Even those that look live are usually videotaped, and most national commercials are made on color film. Film projects a soft texture that live broadcasts and videotape do not have. Because film is the oldest method of showing moving pictures, there is a large pool of skilled talent in this field. Also, film is extremely flexible and versatile. It can be used for numerous optical effects, slow motion, distance shots, mood shots, fast action, and animation. Duplicate film prints are also cheaper than videotape dupes.

On the other hand, recording a commercial on 1- or ¾-inch magnetic videotape offers a more brilliant picture and better fidelity than film. It certainly looks more realistic and appears to have a "live" quality. Tape is also more consistent in quality than film stock. The chief advantage of tape, though, is that it can provide an immediate playback. This permits the work to be checked and redone while the props and actors are still assembled. Computerization has cut editing time up to 90 percent of the time involved in film. Videotape can be replayed almost forever, but a film commercial can be run only about 25 times.

Today, many directors shoot their commercials on film to gain the advantages of texture and sensitive mood lighting. But then, like Mike Salisbury, they dub the processed film onto videotape to do their editing. This is more costly, but it gives them the advantage of faster finishing and the opportunity to see the optical effects instantly as they are added. Some directors, however, still prefer to edit on film because of the wider range of effects possible, thereby achieving a higher level of "creative storytelling." (For an additional example of creative storytelling, see Creative Department: From Concept through Production of a Television Commercial.)

Costs

Many factors, some of which we've already mentioned in this chapter, contribute to the rising cost of commercial production. Some of these factors are listed below.[16]

☐ Inadequate planning and lack of preparation.
☐ Unnecessary production luxuries.
☐ Use of children and animals.
☐ Superstar talent and directors.
☐ Large casts.
☐ Night or weekend filming.
☐ Animation.
☐ Involved opticals, special effects, stop-motion photography.
☐ Location shooting.
☐ Both location and studio shooting for one commercial.
☐ Expensive set decoration or construction.
☐ Special photographic equipment.
☐ Additional shooting days.
☐ Major script changes during a shoot.
☐ Hierarchy of decision makers, approvers, and lawyers.

About the last factor, there's an old saw about too many cooks. In advertising, too many approvers may make an exceptionally expensive stew out of what was meant to be a reasonably economical commercial.

CREATIVE DEPARTMENT

FROM CONCEPT THROUGH
PRODUCTION OF A
TELEVISION COMMERCIAL

Marketing Background

Taster's Choice was introduced by Nestlé in 1967 as the first nationally distributed freeze-dried coffee. In advertising, it was positioned as the instant coffee that "tastes closest to fresh brewed, because freeze-drying locks in the coffee's flavor." This premium image allowed Nestlé to charge a premium price. As a result, dollar sales of Taster's Choice rapidly rose to the upper reaches of the market.

In the late 1980s, competitors were outspending Taster's Choice four to one in advertising and promotion. Rather than sit and watch the product's market share continue to erode, Nestlé decided in 1990 to jettison the advertising focus on the product and to develop a more emotionally driven campaign.

Creative Strategy

Nestlé's ad agency, McCann-Erickson, started by conducting an Emotional Bonding test among instant-coffee drinkers. This test, which the agency developed, helps identify the emotional components that "bond" consumers to brands, making them loyal to one or two products. The results of this test for Taster's Choice were consistent with the brand's premium image. Typical users were discriminating, self-assured, and sophisticated.

Nestlé was also interested in trying a totally new approach in its advertising campaign, something that its main competitors, Folgers and Maxwell House, had never tried. After reviewing the competition, the client and the agency agreed that romance was conspicuously absent in coffee advertising. Adding a touch of romance to the brand's sophisticated image would make Taster's Choice advertising distinctive.

Creative Concept

Meanwhile, Nestlé U.K. was promoting a premium instant coffee in London with a McCann-Erickson campaign. The unusual series of ads featured a couple whose relationship was developing in each episode of the series. This campaign technique was rare enough in Great Britain—and virtually unknown in the United States. But it was increasing sales by 20 to 30 percent.

The serial campaign technique seemed to fit perfectly with the creative strategy that Nestlé and McCann-Erickson had settled on for the U.S. campaign. So they decided to test it on American consumers. They simply used the first commercial in the British campaign and replaced the British announcer with an American one. The commercial tested surprisingly well when it was aired. Viewers recalled both the story and the product, and they believed that Taster's Choice would be appropriate for more discriminating, sophisticated coffee drinkers.

PRODUCT TASTERS CHOICE   LENGTH 1 x :45

TITLE "DINNER PARTY"

1. Tony entering hall of Sister's apartment.
TONY: "You're not going to believe what happened."

2. Sister passes Tony.
SISTER: "You're right... I'm not."
TONY: "You don't believe your own brother? Look - I'm sorry I'm late."

(They exit frame)

3. Sister enters kitchen followed by Tony.
SISTER: "Late!? We're having..."

4. BCU Taster's Choice jar F/G. Sister picks up cup in B/G.
SISTER: "...coffee!"

5. MCU Tony: Sister wipes through.
TONY: "Taster's Choice. Just in time."

6. Int. Dining room. The guests turn to see...

7. Sister & Tony entering.
SISTER: "...Well, I think you know..."

8. MCU Sharon.
SISTER: "(cont.) "... everyone except..."

9. As 7.
TONY: "We've already met'."

10. As 8.
SHARON: "We share the same taste in coffee."

11. ECU coffee poured.
MVO: "Savour the sophisticated taste..."

EXISTING FOOTAGE.....

12. ECU Taster's Choice jar.
MVO: "...of Taster's Choice..."

.... 5 SECONDS

13. Tony sits beside Sharon.
SHARON: "Are you always this late?"
TONY: I won't be tomorrow."

14. SHARON: "What's happening tomorrow?"

15. TONY: "I'm inviting you to dinner."

16. SHARON: "What makes you think I'll accept?"

17. TONY: "You can't resist my coffee."

Storyboard, Script, and Production Estimate

For efficiency's sake, Nestlé asked the agency to provide an estimate of the cost of producing the first two commercials in the series. The client was confident that the first spots would be successful. Nestlé also wanted a bid on commercials of two lengths: 45 seconds and 30 seconds.

The British originals had been 40 seconds long. Revising them to 45 seconds was easy; the extra 5 seconds was used to lengthen the dramatic pauses, increasing the romantic tension between the two characters (see the storyboards). Reducing the originals to 30 seconds was more difficult. Each line of dialogue was critical to the character and plot development. Finally, McCann-Erickson cut 10 seconds by using fewer words to convey the same thought and by eliminating a few scenes.

Bidding and preproducing the commercials were relatively easy. The client and the agency decided to use the same actor and actress, the same director, and the same production company as in the British campaign. They also decided to produce the commercials in London.

Preproduction

Because the critical casting decisions had already been made, preproduction focused on finding the "other women," who each have a line in the first two episodes. Finding two actresses in London who could speak English with an American accent was something of a challenge. "Americanizing" the set, props, wardrobe, and lead actor's accent was equally challenging. The client and the agency decided to leave the lead actress's accent British, however, to lend an air of sophistication to the commercials.

Shooting the Commercials

Many scenes were involved, and each had to be shot once from the actor's point of view and once from the actress's. The two leads had been hired for only three days. Thus, shooting had to proceed at a breakneck pace. Two days were spent filming them in scenes together, and one day was spent filming each of them in their scenes with the "other women."

Dailies to Distribution Prints

After each day of shooting, the director and McCann-Erickson representatives reviewed the "dailies" to ensure that the lighting, sound, and other creative aspects were correct. After the shoot was completed, the director cut together his recommended edits and sent them to the agency. Simultaneously, he shipped the original film to the United States. It took a week to clear customs.

TASTER'S CHOICE
DINNER PARTY :45

Tony: "You're not going to believe what happened."

Sister: "You're right . . . I'm not."

Tony: "You don't believe your own brother? Look, I'm sorry I'm late."

Sister: "Late!? We're having . . ."

Sister: ". . . coffee!"

Tony: "Taster's Choice. Just in time."

Sister: "Well, I think you know . . ."

Sister: ". . . everyone except . . ."

Tony: "We've already met."

Sharon: "We share the same taste . . ."

Sharon: ". . . in coffee."

Sharon: "Are you always this late?"

Tony: "I won't be tomorrow."

Sharon: "What's happening tomorrow?"

Tony: "I'm inviting you to dinner."

Sharon: "What makes you think I'll accept?"

Tony: "You can't resist my coffee."

After reviewing the director's cut, the agency's creative department edited their own version of the first two commercials. They then showed their rough cuts to the agency account group, who asked for minor revisions. Once these changes were made, the rough cuts were presented to the client. After the client's revisions were made, the rough cuts were finished. A voice-over was added, colors were adjusted, the cuts between scenes were made smoother, and finished music was added. The client approved these finished spots.

The final step was to transfer the commercials from film to videotape, to make duplicate tapes, and to ship them to the networks.

Campaign Results

After six months, the first two episodes had generated more positive consumer mail and phone calls than any other campaign in Nestlé's history. Television, print, and radio stories on the campaign and on its actor and actress have generated unprecedented levels of PR for Taster's Choice. And even though Folgers and Maxwell House have both reduced their price, Taster's Choice sales have gone up.

As for the romance that started in the first two episodes, it does continue. The third episode is shown here, and episodes four and five (following the British scenarios) will soon follow. Stay tuned!

Summary

Producing radio and television commercials is similar in several aspects. Both use the same basic types of commercials, and the production process follows the same general developmental pattern. Only the details and the cost differ.

Radio offers a wide range of creative possibilities—it is an excellent medium for humor and drama. Because the radio listener is often busy doing something else while the radio is on, the message should be catchy, memorable, simple, and intensive. Radio commercials should be written to create a visual image in the mind of the listener. Action words should be used rather than passive words. The copy should fit the available time. The four basic types of radio commercials are musical, slice of life, straight announcement, and personality.

Radio commercials may be produced at local radio stations or at independent production studios. At a recording session, the sounds of music, voices, and effects are picked up by microphones and recorded on audio tape. The pitch of sound is measured on the hertz scale, while loudness is measured in decibels. Many types of microphones are used today, but the most common one for broadcast commercials is the low-impedance moving-coil mike. In a recording session, the talent works from a sound booth, and the director and editor work at an audio console in a control room to record, mix, and fine-tune the spot. The final commercial is dubbed and distributed on ¼-inch tape.

Producing television commercials is expensive, and in recent years these costs have soared. People in advertising must be familiar with the production process, therefore, or risk wasting untold thousands of dollars.

Three major techniques used for producing television commercials are live action, animation, and special effects. Animation techniques include cartoons, photo animation, stop-motion photography, and video animation. The computer has dramatically affected the use of special effects in commercial production for everything from video and graphic manipulation to sound design and synthesized music.

Producing a television commercial involves three stages: preproduction, production, and postproduction or finishing. The preproduction stage includes all the work prior to the actual day of filming—casting, arranging for locations, estimating costs, finding props and costumes, and other work. During the production stage, the commercial is filmed or videotaped. Postproduction refers to the work done after the day of shooting. This includes editing, processing film, recording sound effects, mixing, and duplicating final films or tapes.

Most national commercials are still shot on film. Film is extremely flexible and versatile, it can be used for numerous optical effects, and film prints are cheaper than videotape dubs. In recent years, though, many more commercials—especially local ones—have been shot on tape. Videotape offers a more brilliant picture and better fidelity than film, it looks more realistic, and tape quality is more consistent than that of film stock. The chief advantage of tape, though, is that it can provide an immediate playback of the scene that was shot, and it greatly speeds up the editing process.

Questions for Review and Discussion

1. Why is an understanding of broadcast production techniques important for people involved in advertising today?

2. Why is radio often described as theater of the mind? Explain.

3. What do the terms *hertz* and *decibel* refer to?

4. If you wanted to record the action sounds of a football game for use in a commercial, what kind of microphone would you use?

5. What are the advantages and disadvantages of using animation in television advertising?

6. What leads to the greatest waste of money in broadcast commercial production? Explain.

7. At what stage of production do all the elements of a commercial come together?

8. When would it be better to use film in producing a television commercial?

9. What are the advantages of using videotape in television production?

10. How can an advertiser cut the cost of television production?

ADVERTISING MEDIA

Advertising media are the channels of communication through which advertising messages are conveyed. Choosing media for an advertising campaign is a critical task, requiring a sound knowledge of the benefits each channel provides for the products being advertised and the audiences being targeted.

Chapter 12, "Media Planning and Selection," introduces the media plan, including how target audiences are determined and objectives established for reaching those audiences. The chapter explains media strategy as well as how to select specific media vehicles and how to schedule their use.

Chapter 13, "Print Media," discusses the advantages and disadvantages of advertising in newspapers and magazines, and includes the consideration of factors such as flexibility, audience selectivity, reproduction quality, and circulation.

Chapter 14, "Electronic Media," presents the advantages and disadvantages of advertising on television and radio. The chapter discusses television's creativity and high cost, as well as radio's high reach and frequency at an efficient cost.

Chapter 15, "Direct Mail and Outdoor Media," offers the advantages and disadvantages of advertising by direct mail and through various channels that make up the outdoor media. The chapter discusses direct mail's effectiveness and expense, and it covers outdoor media's much less expensive channels such as poster panels, bulletins, and transit advertising.

Chapter 16, "Sales Promotion and Supplementary Media," discusses how sales promotion techniques supplement advertising by offering direct inducements. The chapter covers the push and pull strategies that are used to move products through distribution channels. Finally, the chapter discusses such supplementary media as specialty advertising, trade shows, and Yellow Pages directories.

Making Lasting Impressions

FOR THOSE WISHING TO BOOK THE SUN:
A RAY OF HOPE.

After gracing the Seven Seas during a much heralded 100-day inaugural cruise, The Royal Viking Sun returns to Europe and North America for the summer. There, she will begin passages of slightly shorter duration—two and three weeks—but of no less splendor. At last, *all* your clients can truly reach the sun. For reservations call (800) 422-8000, for sales assistance dial (800) 346-8000.

ROYAL VIKING LINE

Bahamian Registry.

© Royal Viking Line, 1989.

MEDIA PLANNING
AND SELECTION

Objective: To show how media planners accomplish marketing and advertising goals and strategies through the selection and scheduling of media. Even a breakthrough product with stunning advertising would languish if no one received the message it was available. Media planning involves a series of decisions that direct the advertising message to the right people at the right time in the right amount. To make sound decisions, the planner uses several analytical tools as well as experienced judgment.

After studying this chapter, you will be able to:

☐ Describe how a media plan accomplishes marketing and advertising objectives.

☐ Name some of the secondary research sources available to planners and describe how they are used.

☐ Define reach and frequency.

☐ Calculate gross rating points (GRPs) and cost per thousand (CPM).

☐ Explain why advertisers use a "media mix."

☐ Describe different types of advertising schedules and the purpose for each.

☐ Tell how reach, frequency, and continuity are related.

Have you ever wanted to make a big impression on somebody but were limited by your budget? That was the dilemma Del Monte Foods faced in 1988. The 100-year-old manufacturer of canned fruits, vegetables, and snacks had traditionally used network television for most of its advertising. But escalating costs, viewer fragmentation, and the clutter of countless other commercials made it more and more difficult for the brand to maintain a presence in the market. As Del Monte's media budget remained flat, the cost of TV advertising time rose until it looked as though the company could no longer afford to advertise regularly enough to reinforce its message.

It was time for a major overhaul of Del Monte's media plan. The company's media team and its agency, McCann-Erickson, wanted the brand to maintain a presence for more than just a few weeks in a quarter, which was all television allowed them to do at their spending level. So they decided to pull the plug on television and shift almost their entire budget into magazines.

It made sense financially. Magazine advertising rates were becoming more and more negotiable. And Del Monte's parent company could pass on corporate discounts and buying clout to Del Monte. All these factors added up to a more efficient use of the advertising budget—and allowed Del Monte to maintain a more regular and continuous presence than could be achieved through television.

Of course, cost efficiency of a media plan is not enough. The plan has to be effective, too. Del Monte believed that strong brand awareness in several product categories enabled it to forfeit some of the advantages that television provided, such as instant awareness and brand recognition. Magazines, with their color photography, allowed Del Monte to present food in an appealing way, giving readers a positive perception of taste. The ads, in *Good Housekeeping, Woman's Day,* and *People,* to name a few, featured new recipe ideas and serving suggestions. As Exhibit 12-1 illustrates, they carried the same graphic format so consumers would instantly recognize them as Del Monte ads as they turned the page. This graphic consistency along with the media plan was designed to build preference for the overall brand name while promoting individual products as different as green beans, Cajun stewed tomatoes, and vanilla pudding cups.

As Exhibit 12-2 (p. 424) shows, the shift from TV to magazines has been dramatic. In 1987, more than two-thirds of the $30.1 million media budget was spent primarily on network television. In 1988, the numbers flip-flopped, with more than two-thirds of the budget going to magazines. By 1989, that proportion increased to 90 percent; and for 1990, almost all the dollars spent went into magazines.

Best of all, this shift in media strategy has had a positive effect on sales. According to Nielsen Marketing Research, Del Monte's overall sales volume for the year May 1989 to April 1990 increased 10 percent in a category that grew only 5 percent during the same period. All four of the Del Monte advertised categories (vegetables, fruits, snack cups, and stewed tomatoes) increased their market share. And as you can see in Exhibit 12-2, this growth occurred in spite of fewer media dollars spent overall, which dropped from $30.1 million in 1987 to $22.4 million in 1990.

Del Monte plans to stick mainly to magazines that target women 25 to 54 years old and to use different categories of magazines for more specific product usage targeting, such as epicurean magazines to deliver recipe messages, and young family-oriented magazines for snack-food products. Will the company return to television? Only on a selective basis, such as new product launches and other strategic needs.[1]

EXHIBIT 12-1

Del Monte's shift from expensive TV advertising to more affordable magazine advertising allows the company to maintain a media presence that is more consistent and more regular. As a result of Del Monte's new media plan, brand-name preference has increased and so have sales.

EXHIBIT 12-2	Del Monte's Dramatic Shift from Television to Print Advertising (thousands of dollars)		
	Magazines	**Television**	**Total**
1987	$ 8,723.0	$20,504.5	$30,142.9
1988	14,206.5	8,094.1	26,627.3
1989	22,349.1	2,362.9	25,502.4
1990	21,962.7	479.9	22,442.6

In short, Del Monte was able to take a limited budget and spend it efficiently and effectively through sound media planning and selection.

MEDIA PLANNING: AN OVERVIEW

The decisions made by media planners frequently require as much creativity as the decisions made by senior art directors and copywriters. As we shall see in this chapter, media decisions, like good art and copy ideas, are made in the context of the larger marketing and advertising framework. They must be based on sound marketing principles and research as well as experience and intuition.

A product may be the greatest breakthrough of the century. Its advertising message may be intriguing and beguiling. But if that message is not delivered to the right people at the right time, the message will not be heard, the product will go unnoticed, and sales will be disappointing.

Media planning is the process that directs the advertising message to the right people at the right time. It involves many decisions, such as:

☐ In what areas of the country should we advertise?
☐ Which media should we use?
☐ When during the year should we concentrate our advertising?
☐ How often should we run the advertising?

The Players

You can find media people working in several kinds of department structures. These structures vary depending on the nature of the advertiser whose business they serve. Here are three of the most common places in which media people work:

1. *An advertising agency's media department.* Large, full-service advertising agencies have departments that perform all media functions for their clients. In many of these large agencies, the media *planning* function is separated from the media *buying* function. Traditionally, the media planner has a more strategic role, deciding where and how often the ads will run. The media buyer executes these plans, buying space in print media and time in broadcast media and negotiating price and

position of the ads. These traditional roles are becoming less pronounced, however. At some agencies, they have evolved into planner/buyer generalists who specialize in a single subject such as print, for example.

2. *In-house media departments.* Some advertisers have personnel on staff to handle their media services. These departments may do all the planning and buying for the company, or may leave some of it for an advertising agency or independent media buying service.

3. *Independent media buying services.* These companies buy advertising space and time in bulk, which they sell to advertisers or small ad agencies that don't have their own media departments.

The Challenge

The people involved in media planning seem to have a relatively low profile compared to their counterparts in the creative and account service departments. The glamour of the ad business portrayed in movies or on TV is usually reserved for those who create the ads and those who land new clients. But the importance of the media function should not be underestimated.

Consider that one media planner can be directly responsible for millions of dollars of a client's money. Joe De Deo, president of the New York-based agency Young & Rubicam, predicts that media work will become even more critical as the field becomes more complex. "Media will come into prominence, particularly on an international basis in the '90s," he says. "Clients are putting pressure on agencies to be more than efficient. They want creative buys."[2]

What makes media planning so much more complicated than it was even 5 or 10 years ago?

Increasing Media Options

For one thing, there are more media to choose from today, and each medium offers an increasing number of choices. "When I started 20 years ago, there were three networks, two independents, and eight big magazines," says Stacey Lippman, director of corporate media at Chiat/Day/Mojo. "It was an easy, easy job. It's not easy anymore. There's too much to keep track of and too many things to explore."[3]

Television, for example, has fragmented into network, syndicated, and local television, and network and local cable. Magazines are now aimed at every possible population segment. Even generalized national magazines produce editions for particular regions of the country or specific demographic groups, offering advertisers literally hundreds of insertion choices. In addition, nontraditional media, from videotape and theater-screen advertising to blimps, balloons, and shopping carts widen the scope of choices. Other nontraditional media available to advertisers are described in Ad Lab 12-A.

Increasing Fragmentation of the Audience

The increasing fragmentation of the audience, which is picking and choosing from an increasingly diverse array of media options, also complicates the media planner's job. Rather than reading a whole newspaper at one sitting or

AD LAB 12-A
Off-the-Wall Media that Pull Customers off the Fence

Advertising can be found everywhere these days, even places where we least expect it. Here are but a few of the unusual media being explored.

Videotapes

Advertisers are either sponsoring complete tapes, such as Mr. Boston's *Official Bartender's Guide* and Red Lobster Inns' *Eat to Win,* or are placing ads on the tapes for popular films, which helps keep the price of the tapes down.

Aerial Banners and Lights

Banners carrying ad messages can be pulled by low-flying planes. After dark, traveling aerial lights can display messages of up to 90 characters. Slow-flying helicopters can also carry 40-by-80 signs lit by thousands of bulbs.

Blimps

Besides the familiar Goodyear blimp, you can now see blimps bearing messages for Citibank, Coca-Cola, and Fuji Film, among others. Computer-run lighting systems allow the blimps to advertise at night.

In-Flight Ads

Many airlines offer in-flight audio and video entertainment that is available for advertising. The travel industry and advertisers wanting to reach business fliers are the main purchasers of this type of advertising.

Parking Meters

In Calgary, Alberta, or Baltimore, Maryland, you can't put money in a parking meter without seeing the signs on top advertising national products and local businesses. In development are solar-powered meters with liquid crystal displays for ad messages.

Electronic Billboards

Most modern sports stadiums and arenas have giant electronic displays on which ad space is sold.

Inflatables

Several companies are in the business of producing giant inflatable versions of beer cans, mascots, cereal boxes, and other items that can be used for advertising purposes.

Litter Receptacles

Some major cities offer ad space on concrete litter receptacles at major commercial intersections.

Taxicab Advertising

In addition to the familiar ads on the roofs and backs of taxis, some companies have taken to offering ad space inside, facing the riders. The most sophisticated system has an electronic message scrolling across a screen in the rider's view.

Milk Cartons

Government agencies and other noncommercial advertisers have used the sides of milk cartons to advertise issues deemed important to the public, such as missing children and immigration amnesty.

Laboratory Applications

1. What other off-the-wall media can you think of that are being used today?
2. How effective do you think off-the-wall media are for advertisers?

watching one network for a whole evening, people are essentially acting as their own programmers, very selectively choosing what to read, watch, and listen to as they go through the day. This makes it increasingly difficult to find the consumer in the marketplace.[4]

Increasing Costs

Another factor contributing to media-planning difficulties is the increasing cost of almost all media. From 1980 to 1990, the cost of exposing 1,000 people

EXHIBIT 12-3

To keep their production and broadcast costs as low as possible, West Coast Video had Comcast Cablevision in Willow Grove, Pennsylvania, produce this

slapstick spot for only $200. The video store also took advantage of this cable channel's moderate advertising rates.

Welcome, welcome, welcome to West Coast Video where the secret word is *movies*. Say the secret word, the West Coast Video duck will drop down with thousands of movies for you to choose from. Or adventures, comedies, dramas, horror films,

kids' films, and more copies of the hits. I could go on forever but I'm about to hit a wall. And of course every movie rents for just $1.98 overnight. Come to think of it, renting a movie anywhere but West

Coast Video is the most ridiculous thing I've ever heard!

West Coast Video–in the Leo Mall, Krewstown Shopping Center, and Welsh and the Boulevard.

You bet your life!

to each of the major media (called **cost per thousand** and abbreviated as CPM) rose faster than inflation. These rising costs make media planning more challenging than ever, especially for advertisers with relatively small budgets such as West Coast Video (see Exhibit 12-3). Advertisers are demanding more proof that their money is wisely spent, putting more pressure on the media planner to justify each decision.

Increasing Complexity in the Way Media Buys Are Made

Buying and selling media is not the straightforward process it once was. Many media companies, eager to bundle their various properties for advertisers, put together massive multimedia packages they sell as "value-added" programs designed to add value to traditional media placements. For example, media conglomerate Meredith Corp., which publishes magazines such as *Better Homes and Gardens* and *Ladies' Home Journal,* put together a program for advertiser Sherwin-Williams that combined products from Meredith's various divisions: magazine, special-interest publication, video, book, and real estate.[5]

Media planners face growing pressure to learn how to evaluate and execute these complex deals. Sometimes, the deals encompass marketing disciplines outside the traditional realm of media planning, such as public relations, promotion, and direct marketing. It is often difficult to evaluate these deals because the value of some of the nonmedia elements of these deals is hard to quantify.

When Perrier sponsored the 1989 U.S. Open tennis tournament, the media buy included everything from Perrier logos on packages of tennis balls to tickets to the event, to ads in *Tennis* magazine, to hospitality tents. But how do you assign a value to hospitality tents or logos on tennis balls? Some observers predict this trend toward integrating marketing communications will result in the evolution of a new breed of media planner—a "renaissance" planner schooled in many marketing disciplines beyond traditional media.[6]

In this chapter, we examine how media planners go about developing a basic plan, devising strategies to carry out the plan, and scheduling media buys. But first we need to see how media planning fits into the overall marketing plan.

THE ROLE OF MEDIA IN THE MARKETING FRAMEWORK

Let's step back for a moment and look at the big picture. By helping to ensure that the message goes to the right people at the right time, media planning is an important function in the advertising process. Similarly, advertising is an important function in the marketing process. So the relationship among media planning, advertising, and marketing is such that media planning is a component of advertising, which in turn is a component of marketing. Before media planning begins—indeed, before advertising is even considered—an overall marketing plan for the product, brand, or service is established, as we discussed in Chapter 7.

Marketing Objectives and Strategy

To briefly review our discussion in Chapter 7, the marketing plan contains both objectives or sales goals that the company wants to achieve with the brand and strategies that map out a plan of action for attaining those objectives. A look at Exhibit 12-4 shows that these objectives and strategies result from an analysis of the marketing situation. This analysis uncovers both problems and opportunities for the brand. Marketing objectives may focus on solving a problem, such as: "To regain sales volume lost to major competitive introductions over the past year." Or they may be designed to take advantage of an opportunity, such as: "To increase share in the growing male segment of the frozen food market."

Marketing strategies outline the steps to meet these objectives by using the four Ps of the marketing mix. Thus, if a company's marketing objective is to increase sales volume of a particular brand in a certain part of the country, the corresponding marketing strategies might include adapting the product to suit regional tastes (product), lowering the price to compete with local brands (price), gaining access to new retail outlets (place), and increasing awareness of the product with an advertising campaign (promotion). Advertising, then, is one of the strategic tools a company can use to achieve its marketing objectives.

Advertising Objectives and Strategy

As Exhibit 12-4 illustrates, the advertising plan extends from the marketing plan. Like the marketing plan, it too contains objectives and strategies. Advertising objectives differ from marketing objectives, though, in that they focus specifically on communication goals, such as:

☐ To increase awareness of the brand by 25 percent in southern states in the next 12 months.

☐ To increase intent to purchase the brand among men ages 18 to 24 by 20 percent within the next year.

☐ To increase recall of the advertising message among children 7 to 12 years old by 15 percent within the next six months.

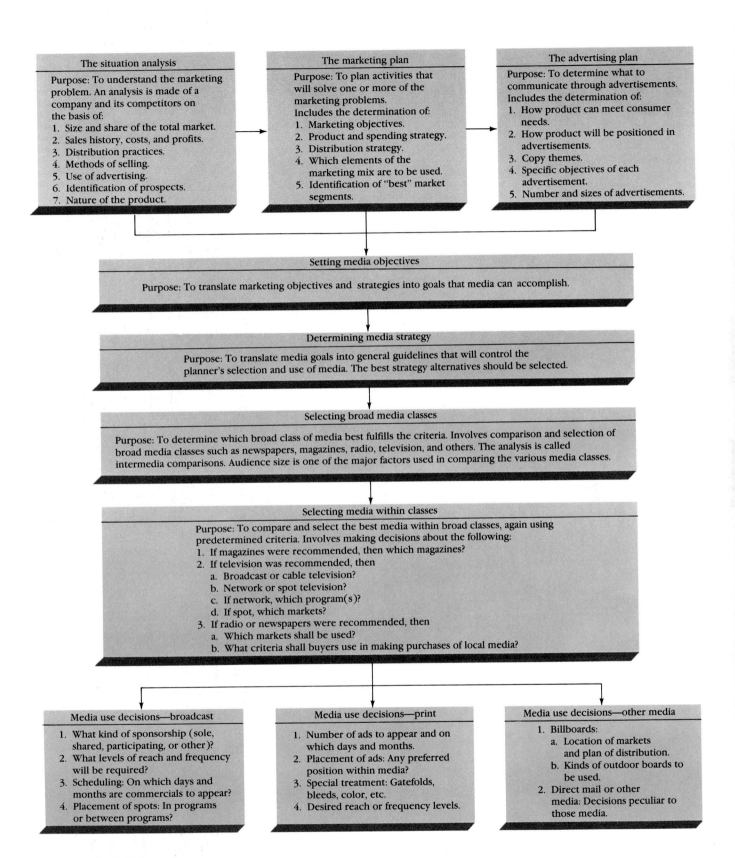

EXHIBIT 12-4

This diagram outlines the scope
of media planning activities.

Advertising strategies make up the action plan designed to accomplish objectives such as these. In an advertising agency, they involve an integrated effort from people in several departments. The account executives, with their marketing counterparts at the client company, have already established the marketing plan, which identified the target market and the target audience for advertising and the product concept. The research department may determine what the advertising message should focus on, based on consumers' attitudes toward the brand, its competitors, and the product category. Research would also track the progress toward the advertising goals by periodically testing advertising recall and effectiveness, and brand awareness.

The creative department develops a campaign that communicates the advertising message to the target audience. Creative is charged with not only sticking to that message strategy, but communicating it in a compelling, memorable, and effective manner. The media department makes sure the advertising message (developed by the creative department) gets to the correct target audience (established by the marketing managers and account executives) in an effective manner (as measured by the research department).

DEFINING MEDIA OBJECTIVES

The media plan, like a marketing and advertising plan, begins with a statement of objectives. These objectives, as outlined in Exhibit 12–4, flow directly from the marketing and advertising plans. They are designed to implement marketing or advertising objectives and strategies, but to do so specifically through the use of media.

Here is an example of some general media objectives for marketing and advertising a new food product:

1. To target large families, with special emphasis on the homemaker, who is usually the chief purchasing agent.
2. To concentrate the greatest weight of advertising in urban areas where prepared foods traditionally have greater sales and where new ideas normally gain quicker acceptance.
3. To provide advertising continuity and a fairly consistent level of impressions throughout the year except for extra weight during the announcement period.
4. To deliver advertising impressions over the entire country in direct relation to food-store sales.
5. To use media that will strengthen the copy strategy and put major emphasis on convenience, ease of preparation, taste, and economy.
6. To attain the greatest possible frequency of advertising impressions consistent with the need for broad coverage and the demands of the copy plan.[7]

Such objectives can be broken down into several component parts, but for convenience, we will focus on two main categories: audience objectives and message-distribution objectives.

Audience Objectives

Audience objectives define the specific types of people we want to communicate the advertising message to and are therefore essential in determining

EXHIBIT 12-5

TV ads for Apple's Macintosh are targeted at businesspeople who are enticed with the promise of "the power to be your best."

JOEY: Hey, Baldwin, how you doin'?

BALDWIN: Pretty good, Joey, how are you?

SAL: Ah, finished already.

WOMAN: Hey, I thought we were supposed to be doing this in-house.

BALDWIN: That's right. Pass the salt, would you?

SAL: Hey, your group did this?

BALDWIN: New computer. The salt?

SAL: Quintile analysis? Gimme a break.

BALDWIN: Well, Segall did that.

SAL: I thought he was in the L.A. office.

BALDWIN: So's Edwards—she did the graphics.

SAL: The market projections?

BALDWIN: Garnett. Chicago.

SAL: How'd you get everybody together in the same place?

BALDWIN: I told you. New computer.

SAL: What kind of system can do that?

BALDWIN: (UNINTELLIGABLY): Mcntsh.

SAL: What?

BALDWIN: Mcntsh.

SAL: Pardon me?

FADE TO BLACK.

SUPER: Macintosh. The power to be your best.

media objectives and strategy. The whole media effort will be wasted if the right people are not exposed to the ads in the campaign. In our sample objectives, the target audience is homemakers with large families who live in urban areas.

The target audience may consist of people in a specific income, educational, occupational, social, or ethnic group, as illustrated in the Apple Computer ad in Exhibit 12-5. And they may not necessarily be the actual consumers of the product. When Del Monte switched from television to print advertising, it had to sell the idea to the trade, the grocery retailers who carry Del Monte products. These people, whose jobs depend on moving the product off the shelves and into consumers' homes, may have felt that stopping TV advertising would be a loss of advertising support. If they believed the switch to print would decrease consumer demand for the brand, retailers could have been reluctant to give Del Monte products as much space on their grocery shelves.

So Del Monte created an advertising campaign targeted to the trade in which it emphasized the company's leadership in the product category. As

Exhibit 12-6 shows, the ads had the same bold graphic look used in consumer advertising, and they were designed to associate Del Monte brands with three of the magazines that would be used in its consumer magazine schedule. Says Del Monte vice president of corporate communications Dee Ann Campbell, "We basically said to them, 'You sell this magazine in your store, and you sell our products in your store, and the combination of the two is going to work all month long.'" Del Monte's media objectives for communicating to the trade were quite different than those targeting the consumer.

The target audience is often determined from the marketer's past research or through research studies conducted specifically to identify present and future users of the product. However, media planners sometimes rely on secondary research such as Simmons Market Research Bureau (SMRB) or Mediamark Research, Inc. (MRI) (see Exhibit 12-7). These syndicated reports give a demographic profile of the heavy and light users of various products and brands and enable the planner to define the target audience. The reports also specify which kinds of TV programs or magazines these heavy and light users have been exposed to, thus guiding the planner in selecting media that may have particularly large audiences of heavy users. As we will see in the section on media selection and scheduling, planners select media **vehicles,** particular magazines or broadcast programs, according to how well they "deliver" or expose the message to an audience that closely parallels the desired target audience.

Message-Distribution Objectives

Whereas audience objectives answer the question of to *whom* advertising will be aimed, distribution objectives answer the questions of where, when, and how often advertising should appear. Should advertising be more heavily concentrated in particular geographic areas? Our sample food-product objectives specify urban areas all over the country but in relation to food sales. Should the level of advertising be continuous, or should it be greater at certain times of the year? Our example specifies greater emphasis during the announcement period. How much of the target market should be exposed to the advertising, and how often? To answer these questions, a media planner

EXHIBIT 12-6

To ease retailers' worries about abandoning TV advertising, Del Monte designed a campaign just for people in the trade. Rather than setting media objectives such as brand recognition (as they would for consumers), Del Monte set media objectives for communicating to the trade that emphasized the company's leadership, consumer loyalty, and retailer support.

EXHIBIT 12-7   A Media Planner's Toolbox

These are just a few of the secondary sources of information to help media planners do their jobs:

☐ Simmons Market Research Bureau (SMRB) and Mediamark Research, Inc. (MRI): report data on product, brand, and media usage by both demographic and lifestyle characteristics.

☐ Broadcast Advertisers Reports (BAR), Leading National Advertisers (LNA), and Media Records: report advertisers' expenditures by brand, media type, market, and time period.

☐ Standard Rate & Data Service (SRDS): provides information on media rates, format, production requirements, and audience.

☐ Audit Bureau of Circulations (ABC): verifies circulation figures of publishers.

must fully understand such concepts as *reach, frequency,* and *gross rating points.*

Reach

The term **reach** refers to the total number of *different* people or households exposed to an advertising schedule during a given time, usually four weeks. For example, if 80 percent of a total of 10,000 people in the target market hear a program on radio station KKO at least once during a four-week period, the reach is 8,000 people. Reach, then, measures the unduplicated extent of audience exposure to a media vehicle and may be expressed either as a percentage of the total market (80 percent) or as a raw number (8,000).

This number, however, doesn't take into account the quality of that exposure. In other words, some people exposed to the message still may not be aware of it. Since one goal of advertising is to create awareness of a product or service, reach is not necessarily the best measure of advertising success. The term **effective reach** is often used to indicate quality of exposure. It measures the number or percentage of the audience who have been exposed to the message enough times to be aware of it.

Frequency

Frequency refers to the number of times the same person or household is exposed to a vehicle in a specified time span. Across a total audience, frequency is calculated as the average number of times individuals or homes are exposed to the vehicle. The figure is used to measure the *intensity* of a specific media schedule.

For example, suppose 4,000 people listened to a radio program three times during a four-week period and another 4,000 people listened to it five times. To determine the **average frequency,** the following formula would be used:

$$
\begin{aligned}
\text{Average frequency} \quad &= \text{Total exposures} \div \text{Audience reach} \\
&= (4{,}000 \times 3) + (4{,}000 \times 5) \div 8{,}000 \\
&= 32{,}000 \div 8{,}000 \\
&= 4
\end{aligned}
$$

Thus, for the 8,000 listeners reached, the average frequency or number of exposures was four. Frequency, then, is an important planning tool because it offers a measure of the repetition that can be achieved by a specific media schedule. Repetition is important, of course, because the more times people are exposed to a message, the more likely they are to remember it.

What is the correct frequency for a given message in a given medium? This can be expressed by the term **effective frequency.** Just as effective reach takes into account the advertising goal of awareness in the reach measurement, so too does effective frequency. It establishes the average number of times a person must see or hear a message before becoming aware of it. At the other end of the spectrum, it establishes the number of times beyond which further exposures would be a waste. So effective frequency falls somewhere between a minimum level that achieves awareness and a maximum level that starts to become overexposure. Overexposure is not only wasteful (as when an individual continues to be exposed to a message after a purchase decision has already been made) but can also lead to "wearout," which occurs when additional exposure to the commercial starts to irritate the consumer.

Conventional advertising wisdom holds that three to six contacts over a four-week period is the effective frequency for getting a message across, but there really is no magic number that works for every commercial and for every product. There are many factors to consider. Some are product-related. For example, researchers found that dishwashers, photographic film, and facial moisturizers were products the target consumers were extremely interested in. These consumers only needed to see an ad two times before they absorbed all the information. Product categories in which consumers were less interested, such as instant cereal, frozen pizza, and instant coffee, required more exposure to the advertising.[8]

Other factors that determine effective frequency relate to the advertising itself. For example, the complexity of the message, the size of the creative unit, the clutter of the media, and the entertainment value of the commercial should all be considered in establishing effective frequency levels.[9]

Message Weight

Sometimes media planners want to determine the size of the audience for several commercials or ads combined, or for an entire media plan. This is considered the **message weight** of the plan. It is calculated by simply adding up all the audience size numbers for each ad, disregarding any overlap or duplication that results. Message weight can be expressed in two ways: gross impressions and gross rating points.

Gross Impressions **Gross impressions** are the total of all the audiences delivered by a media plan. In the radio listener example, it would be the same as total exposures. It is calculated by multiplying the number of people who receive a message by the number of times they receive it—in this particular case, 32,000.

Gross Rating Points The gross impressions of a specific media schedule might run into the millions, so a more convenient and common method of expressing this information is in **gross rating points (GRPs).** A single rating point represents 1 percent of the audience.

GRPs can be computed in two ways. One way is to divide the total number of impressions by the size of the target population and multiply this number by 100. In our radio example, the total gross impressions delivered was 32,000 and the target audience was 10,000 people. So we can determine the gross rating points of this radio schedule using the formula:

$$(\text{Total gross impressions} \div \text{Target audience}) \times 100 = \text{Gross rating points}$$
$$(32,000 \div 10,000) \times 100 = 320 \text{ GRPs}$$

Another way to calculate GRPs is to multiply the reach, expressed as a percentage of the population, by the average frequency. In our example, 80 percent of the radio households heard a program an average of four times during the four-week period. We can determine the gross rating points of this radio schedule using the following formula:

$$\text{Reach} \times \text{Frequency} = \text{GRPs}$$
$$80 \times 4 = 320 \text{ GRPs}$$

It is important to understand that GRPs describe the total message weight of a media schedule, without regard to audience duplication, over a given period of time. For broadcast media, GRPs are often calculated for a week or a month. In print media, they are often calculated for the number of ad insertions in a campaign. And for outdoor advertising, they are calculated on the basis of daily exposure.

Once these media objectives have been determined—that is, the best mix of reach and frequency and the message weight—the media strategy can be developed.

DEVELOPING A MEDIA STRATEGY

The **media strategy** describes how the advertiser will achieve the stated media objectives. The strategy reflects the specific course of action to be taken with media: which media will be used, how often each will be used, how much of each, and when.

Generally, media-strategy decisions fall into one of two broad areas: selection of media and choice of vehicles within each medium. Should the advertiser, for example, use television, radio, magazines, outdoor, or some combination? When Del Monte felt it had maximized its print schedule, the company placed an aggressive outdoor schedule in about half the country during the summer of 1990. This was designed to be a "contraseasonal" strategy to its magazine effort. With the warm summer weather encouraging people to take to the road, Del Monte wanted to increase its brand visibility by taking advantage of the heavier traffic. Outdoor also brought Del Monte's advertising closer to the point of sale. By strategically placing the billboards, Del Monte could position its advertising to expose consumers to it on their way to the grocery store.[10]

Strategy decisions must take into account a wide variety of factors: geographic scope; the nature of the medium and the message; consumer purchase patterns; message size, length, and placement considerations; and competitive strategy and budget considerations.

Geographic Scope

A key strategic decision relates to the breadth of the media plan, which is determined by the location and makeup of the target audience.

Normally, advertising should be limited to areas where the product is available. A *local* plan may be used, for example, if the product is available in only one city or if that market has been chosen to introduce or test-market a new product.

A *regional* plan, on the other hand, may cover several adjoining metropolitan areas, an entire state, or several neighboring states. Regional media objectives can be achieved by using local media, regional editions of national magazines, or spot television and radio. Regional plans are also used to accommodate sectional differences in taste or preference that affect product sales. For example, more instant coffee is sold in the Midwest than in New England.

Advertisers who want to expose consumers to their advertising throughout the country generally use a *national* plan. The media used in such a plan usually include network TV and radio, full-circulation national magazines and newspapers, and nationally syndicated Sunday newspaper supplements. Exhibit 12-8 includes local and national expenditures and shows how much money is spent on each of the major media.

The scope of the media plan might also be based on other geographical considerations, such as the sales potential of each area. This factor is especially critical when determining how to allocate the advertising budget geographically. There are several ways planners can determine the sales potential of an area. Two that will be mentioned here are the **brand development index** and the **category development index.**

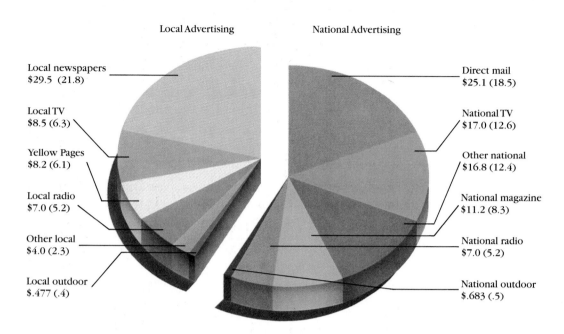

Local Advertising   National Advertising

Local newspapers
$29.5 (21.8)

Local TV
$8.5 (6.3)

Yellow Pages
$8.2 (6.1)

Local radio
$7.0 (5.2)

Other local
$4.0 (2.3)

Local outdoor
$.477 (.4)

Direct mail
$25.1 (18.5)

National TV
$17.0 (12.6)

Other national
$16.8 (12.4)

National magazine
$11.2 (8.3)

National radio
$7.0 (5.2)

National outdoor
$.683 (.5)

Dollars in billions (percent of total)

EXHIBIT 12-8

Expenditures for advertising
(1990), broken down by media,
are shown here.

The Brand Development Index

The **brand development index (BDI)** indicates the sales potential of a
particular brand in a specific market area. Essentially, it compares the percentage of the brand's total U.S. sales in that area to the percentage of the total
U.S. population in the area. The larger the brand's sales in the area relative to
the area's percentage of the U.S. population, the higher the BDI, and the
greater the sales potential for the brand. Here's how it is calculated:

$$BDI = [(\text{Percent of brand's total U.S. sales in the area}) \div$$
$$(\text{Percent of total U.S. population in the area})] \times 100$$

Let's say that sales of a brand in Los Angeles is 1.58 percent of the brand's
total U.S. sales. And suppose that the population of Los Angeles is 2 percent of
the total U.S. population. Then we can calculate the BDI for the brand in Los
Angeles:

$$BDI = [(\text{Percent of the brand's total U.S. sales in Los Angeles}) \div$$
$$(\text{Percent of total U.S. population in Los Angeles})] \times 100$$

$$\text{Los Angeles BDI} = [(1.58) \div (2)] \times 100 = 79$$

The Category Development Index

The **category development index (CDI)** is based on the same concept as
the BDI and is calculated in much the same way. The difference is that while
BDI considers brand sales, CDI is based on sales of the entire product
category, not any particular brand. Thus, we calculate CDI using the following
formula:

$$CDI = [(\text{Percent of the product category's total U.S. sales in the area}) \div$$
$$(\text{Percent of total U.S. population in the area})] \times 100$$

Let's say that we want to determine the CDI for Los Angeles. Category sales in Los Angeles are 4.92 percent of the total U.S. category sales. We already know that the population of Los Angeles is 2 percent of the total U.S. population. So the CDI in Los Angeles would be:

$$\text{Los Angeles CDI} = [(4.92) \div (2)] \times 100 = 246$$

The BDI and CDI, when considered together, can help the planner determine a media strategy for the market. In our example, the low BDI and high CDI in Los Angeles indicate that the product category has high potential, but the brand is not selling well. This could be a problem or an opportunity. If the brand has been in the market for some time, the low BDI raises a red flag: Some marketing problems are standing in the way of brand sales. But if the brand is relatively new in the market, the low BDI may not be alarming. Instead, the high CDI may point toward an opportunity for the brand to grow substantially, given more time and marketing support in the market.

Nature of the Medium and the Message

An important determinant in media strategy is the nature of the media themselves. Some media lend themselves better to certain types of messages or creative approaches than to others. For an introduction to the creative advantages and disadvantages of each of the major media, see Ad Lab 12-B, p. 438.

Often a combination of media will work together to get across the overall message. For example, television is quite effective in creating awareness of a product and getting people to understand its attributes. If they are done right and repeated often enough over time, TV ads can establish product value and a positive brand image in consumers' long-term memories. Once this foundation is set, it is often easier for other media such as radio, outdoor, newspaper, or direct mail to pull the consumers through to action. Thus, television can be used to create a mindset, while other media may be more effective at pull-through because they are closer to the point of action.[11]

Ben Givauden, president of the Givauden Agency in New York, appreciates the media "synergy" between newspapers and magazines. He notes, for example: "Newspapers can be used to detonate an idea, with magazines following up for the harder sell." He points out that newspapers offer in-depth circulation, whereas magazines offer retentive value.[12]

Media strategy is not only affected by the nature of the medium, it is also driven by the advertising message. Advertising messages differ in many ways. Some are simple, dogmatic messages: "AT&T: The right choice." Others are based on an emotional attitude, appealing to people's needs for safety, security, social approval, love, beauty, or fun: "You're in good hands with Allstate." Many advertisers use a reason-why approach to explain their product's advantages: "Twice the Room. Twice the Comfort. Twice the Value. Embassy Suites. Twice the Hotel."

Some messages are complex, requiring considerable space or time for explanation. Others announce a new product or product concept and are thus unfamiliar to the consuming public. Each of these circumstances considerably affects the media strategy.

A message that is either new or highly complex may require greater frequency and exposure to be understood and remembered (see the Conti-

AD LAB 12-B
Media Selection: As the Creative Person Sees It

	Creative disadvantages	Creative advantages
Newspapers	Loss of fidelity, especially in reproduction of halftone illustrations. Difficulty in controlling ad position on page.	Almost any ad size available. Impact of black against white (still one of the most powerful color combinations). Sense of immediacy. Quick response; easy accountability. Local emphasis. Changes possible at short notice.
Magazines	Size not as large as those of newspapers or posters. Long closing dates, limited flexibility. Lack of immediacy. Tendency to cluster ads. Possible difficulties in securing favorable position in an issue.	High-quality reproduction. Prestige factor. Accurate demographic information available. Graphic opportunities (use of white space, benday screen, reverse type). Color.
Television	No time to convey a lot of information. Air clutter (almost 25 percent of broadcasting is nonprogramming material). Intrusiveness (TV tops list of consumers' complaints in this respect). Capricious station censorship.	Combination of sight and sound. Movement. A single message at a time. Viewer's empathy. Opportunity to demonstrate the product. Believability: "What you see is what you get."
Radio	Lack of visual excitement. Wavering attention span (many listeners tune out commercials). Inadequate data on listening habits (when is the "listener" really listening?). Fleeting nature of message.	Opportunity to explore sound. Favorable to humor. Intimacy. Loyal following (the average person listens regularly to only about two stations). Ability to change message quickly.
Direct mail	Damper of state, federal, and postal regulations on creative experimentation. Censorship often unpredictable. Formula thinking encouraged by "proven" direct-mail track records.	Graphic and production flexibility, such as use of three-dimensional effect (folding, die-cuts, pop-ups). Measurable. As scientific as any other form of advertising. Highly personal.
Posters	Essentially a one-line medium with only a limited opportunity to expand on the advertising message. Inadequate audience research, especially in transit advertising.	Graphic opportunities. Color. Large size. High-fidelity reproduction. Simple, direct approach. Possibility of an entirely visual message.
Point of sale	Difficulty in pinpointing audience. Failure of retailers to make proper use of material submitted to them.	Opportunities for three-dimensional effects, movement, sound, and new production techniques.

Laboratory Application

What creative disadvantages and advantages can you add to the list?

nental Bank ad in Exhibit 12-9.) A dogmatic message, like "AT&T: The right choice," for example, may require a surge at the beginning of the campaign to communicate the idea. But then it is usually advantageous to maintain low frequency and strive for greater reach.

Reason-why messages may be complex to understand at first. But once the explanation is understood, a pulsing of advertising exposures at irregular intervals is often sufficient to remind customers of the explanation. On the other hand, emotionally oriented messages are usually more effective if spaced at regular intervals to create a continuing feeling about the product.[13]

The length and complexity of a message such as this one often require greater frequency to give readers a chance to absorb its meaning. The new information about Continental Bank, that it now specializes in serving businesses, also needs greater reinforcement in the initial stages of the campaign.

Message Size, Length, and Position Considerations

Considerations of *how* to use the selected media may greatly affect the overall media strategy. For example, greater attention can usually be gained from a full-color ad than from a black-and-white ad (see Exhibit 12-10A on p. 440). Likewise, a full-page ad attracts more attention than a quarter-page ad (see Exhibit 12-10B). With limited advertising budgets, though, larger units of space or time cost dearly in terms of such things as reach and frequency.

Is it better for a small advertiser to run a full-page ad once a month or a quarter-page ad once a week? Should TV advertisers use 60-second announcements or a lot of 15- and 30-second commercials? The answers to these questions are not simple. Some messages require more time and space to be explained. Competitive activity often dictates more message units. The nature of the product itself may demand the prestige of a full page or full color. On the other hand, the need for high frequency may demand smaller units. It is sometimes better to run several small ads consistently than to run one large ad occasionally.

Other considerations affecting media strategy include where to position the ad in various media. The preferred positions of magazine advertisements are on front and back covers. Perhaps the equivalent in television is the sponsorship of prime-time shows. Special positions, sponsorships, and other such opportunities are usually sold at a premium by the media. The media planner must, therefore, carefully weigh the benefits of these additional costs in terms of the potential sales impact against the loss of reach and frequency.

Competitive Strategy and Budget Considerations

Media strategy must consider what competitive advertisers are doing, particularly if their advertising budgets are larger. Media planners have access to several services that report competitive advertising expenditures in the different media. (Review Exhibit 12-7 for competitive spending sources available to planners.)

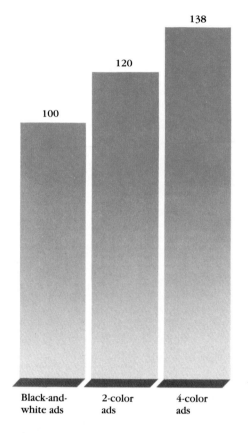

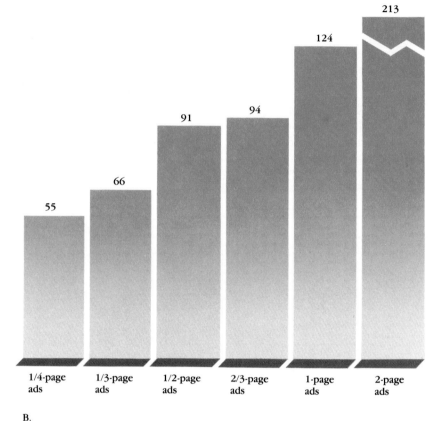

A.

B.

A. Readership scores for ads with various degrees of color.

B. Readership scores for ads of various sizes. Although readership is the greatest for four-color, two-page ads, the increased readership may not offset the additional cost in some publications.

This information can help the planner see what the brand's competitors are up to and can be used in several ways. It can tell you the size of competitors' budgets, what media they are using, and the regionality and seasonality of their sales. It can tip you off to new product tests and introductions. It can give you clues about competitors' strategies, such as their target audience and their goals in positioning the product. All this information is vital in planning a counterstrategy.[14]

After finding out how the competition is spending its budgets, how do you plan your brand's strategy? A lot depends on the size of the advertising budget. If it's much smaller than the competition's, your brand could get lost in the shuffle. One general rule is to bypass media that competitors dominate and to choose instead media that offer a strong or dominant position. When Stresstabs vitamins were introduced, for example, the campaign was entirely in print. According to the agency handling the campaign, "We wanted to avoid what was then a large arena of TV advertising, and our target audience was exposed to our message more efficiently and effectively in print."[15] On the other hand, it would make sense to use media similar to the competition if your target audiences are the same, or if competitors are not using their media effectively.

Stating the Media Strategy

A written statement of the media strategy is an integral part of any media plan. Without one, it is difficult for the client and agency management to analyze the logic and consistency of the recommended overall media schedule.

Generally, the strategy statement should indicate which media types will be used, how they will be used, and the rationale for these choices. It should start with a brief definition of the target audiences and the priorities for weighting them, and it should outline specific reach and frequency goals. The nature of the message should be explained. Then it should provide a breakdown of the various types of media to be used over the period of the campaign, the budget for each, and the cost of production and any collateral materials. Finally, the intended size of message units, along with any ad position or timing considerations, should be stated as well as the effect of budget restrictions.

MEDIA SELECTION AND SCHEDULING

Once the media strategy has been developed, the media planner is ready to select specific media vehicles and schedule their use. The planner usually bases each vehicle's value on a set of specific criteria. Some of these are quantitative, allowing the vehicles to be assigned numerical values. Others are qualitative and not so cut and dried. Both are important in the evaluation process.

Considerations in Selecting Individual Media

The media planner's job is to match the right media vehicles with the right audiences at the right time in the best environment in the most logical place—so that the advertising message will achieve the desired exposure, attract attention, and motivate customers to some action. And the planner must do this with cost efficiency in mind so that the reach and frequency goals can be met.

In evaluating specific media vehicles, the planner considers several factors: (1) overall campaign objectives and strategy; (2) size and characteristics of each medium's audience; (3) attention, exposure, and motivational value of the media being considered; and (4) cost efficiency. Several of these factors for major media are compared in Exhibit 12-11 (p. 442).

Overall Campaign Objectives and Strategy

When the selection process begins, the media planner's first job is to review the nature of the product or service, the intended objectives and strategies, and the primary and secondary target markets and audiences.

The nature of the product itself may suggest the type of media to be used. For example, when a product—such as a fine perfume—has a distinct personality or image, it might be advertised in media with personality traits that reinforce this image. The media planner would consider how various magazines and TV programs are regarded—such as feminine or masculine, highbrow or lowbrow, serious or frivolous—and determine their appropriateness for the brand.

The editorial content of the media vehicle and its compatibility with the product being advertised should also be considered. *Tennis* magazine may not be a good vehicle for cigarettes or an alcoholic beverage, even though the demographic profiles and image might match.

People use different media vehicles because they decide a specific reward can be gained from reading, listening to, or watching it. The rewards may include self-improvement, financial advice, career improvement, or entertainment. Advertising would be most effective if it positioned the product as

EXHIBIT 12-11   Comparative Evaluation of Advertising Media

	Spot television	Network television	Spot radio	Network radio	Consumer magazines	Business publications	Farm publications	Sunday supplements	Daily newspapers	Weekly newspapers	Direct mail	Outdoor	Transit	Point of purchase
Audience considerations														
Attentiveness of audience	M	M	M	M	M	M	M	M	M	M	M	W	W	W
Interest of audience	M	S	M	M	S	S	S	S	S	S	W	W	W	W
Avoids excess selection by audience	M	M	M	M	W	W	W	W	W	W	W	W	W	W
Offers selectivity to advertiser	W	W	M	M	S	S	S	W	W	W	S	W	W	W
Avoids waste	W	W	W	W	S	S	S	M	W	W	S	W	W	W
Offers involvement	M	S	M	M	M	S	S	M	M	M	W	W	W	W
Avoids distraction	M	S	M	M	S	S	S	M	M	M	S	W	W	W
Avoids resistance	N	N	N	N	N	N	N	N	N	N	N	N	N	N
Provides impact	V	V	V	V	V	V	V	V	V	V	V	V	V	V
Offers prestige	M	S	W	M	S	S	M	S	M	W	W	W	W	W
Good quality of audience data	M	M	M	M	S	S	M	M	M	W	M	W	W	W
Timing factors														
Offers repetition	S	S	S	S	M	M	M	W	M	W	V	S	S	M
Avoids irritation	W	W	W	M	M	M	M	M	M	M	M	M	M	M
Offers frequency	S	S	S	M	M	M	M	W	M	W	M	S	S	M
Offers frequency of issuance	S	S	S	S	V	V	W	W	M	W	V	N	N	N
Offers flexibility in scheduling	S	S	S	S	V	V	W	W	M	W	V	N	N	N
Long life	W	W	W	W	S	S	S	M	W	M	W	W	W	W
Low mortality rate	W	W	W	W	S	S	S	M	W	M	W	W	W	W
Avoids perishability	W	W	W	W	S	S	S	M	W	M	W	W	W	W
Allows long message	M	M	M	M	S	S	S	S	S	S	S	W	W	W
Provides product protection	V	M	V	M	M	M	M	M	V	V	S	W	W	M

Note: W = Weak; M = Medium; S = Strong; N = Not a factor for this medium; V = Varies from one vehicle to another within the medium.

part of the solution the consumer seeks. Otherwise it may be seen as an intrusion.[16]

If one objective of the marketing and advertising campaign is to gain greater product distribution, the selected media should influence both consumers and potential dealers. Suppose the goal is to stimulate sales of a nationally distributed product in certain isolated markets. Advertisements should then be concentrated in the local and regional media that penetrate those markets rather than in national media. On the other hand, if the goal is to elevate product image or company reputation, the advertiser may willingly

	Spot television	Network television	Spot radio	Network radio	Consumer magazines	Business publications	Farm publications	Sunday supplements	Daily newspapers	Weekly newspapers	Direct mail	Outdoor	Transit	Point of purchase
Geographic considerations														
Offers geographic selectivity	S	W	S	W	M	M	M	S	S	S	S	M	M	S
Offers proximity to point of sale	W	W	W	W	W	W	W	W	W	W	M	M	M	S
Provides for local dealer "tags"	M	W	M	W	M	M	M	M	S	S	S	M	M	S
Creative considerations														
Permits demonstration	S	S	W	W	M	M	M	M	M	M	S	W	W	S
Provides impact	S	S	M	M	M	M	M	M	M	M	S	W	W	M
Permits relation to editorial matter	M	M	W	M	S	S	S	M	M	M	S	N	N	N
Competitive factors														
Light use of medium by competitors	W	S	W	S	W	S	S	M	M	S	M	M	S	S
Low amount of total advertising	W	W	V	S	M	V	S	M	M	M	S	M	W	S
Control considerations														
Advertiser control of media content	W	M	W	M	W	W	W	W	W	W	S	N	N	N
Favorable environment	W	M	W	M	W	W	W	W	W	W	S	W	W	S
Advertiser control of location	N	S	N	S	M	M	M	W	W	W	S	W	W	M
Amount of government regulation	W	N	W	N	N	N	N	N	N	N	W	W	N	N
Number of other restrictions	W	W	W	W	V	V	V	V	V	V	W	W	W	W
Mechanical and production factors														
Ease of insertion	M	S	M	S	S	S	S	M	M	W	S	M	M	W
High reproduction quality	M	M	M	M	S	S	S	S	V	V	S	V	V	S
Flexibility of format	M	M	M	M	S	S	S	W	N	N	S	M	W	W
Avoids vandalism	N	N	N	N	N	N	N	N	N	N	N	W	W	W
Financial considerations														
Low total cost	M	W	M	W	W	W	W	M	S	S	W	M	M	M
High efficiency	M	S	S	M	M	M	M	M	M	W	S	S	S	W

sacrifice the sales potential of popular local programming in favor of the prestige of high-quality programs on network TV.

The price of the product and the pricing strategy may influence media choices, too. Pricing is often a key consideration in product positioning. For example, a premium-priced product may require the use of prestigious or "class" media to support its market image.

Reviewing the product's target market and the campaign's target audience is another vital step in media selection. The more the media planner knows about the market, the better the media selections are likely to be. Data gathered on the target market should include its size, location, and demographic profile, such as age, sex, education, occupation, income, and religion. Psychographic characteristics such as lifestyle, personality, and attitudinal traits, and behavioral characteristics such as purchase cycles, benefits sought, and product-use habits should be studied.

The task of the media planner is then (1) to select from these data the characteristics most relevant to the acceptance, purchase, and use of the product and (2) to match these data to the characteristics of the audiences of the specific media vehicles under consideration.

Characteristics of Media Audiences

When we speak of a medium's **audience,** we refer to the total number of people or households exposed to a medium. Importantly, exposure measurements indicate nothing about whether the audiences saw, heard, or read the advertisements or editorial contents of the medium. The media planner needs to know how many people are exposed to a message by a station or a publication to make a realistic judgment of that medium's potential effectiveness. Data on the size and characteristics of media audiences are readily available from a wide variety of media research organizations. Media vehicles often use these research findings about audience demographics to attract advertisers.

In addition, the planner will want to know the degree of interest in the publication or program and how closely the characteristics of the medium's audience match the profile of the target market.

Readership and audience studies conducted by various media have yielded data that enable the media planner to determine how closely the audience characteristics match the profile of the target market prospects. For example, if the product is intended for a Hispanic audience, it is essential that the medium selected be the one that exposes Hispanics to the message the most efficiently. Such information is available from various media research organizations and from the media, such as SpanAmerican and the National Hispanic Magazine Network. Earlier we mentioned Simmons Market Research Bureau. This company provides research data on age, income, occupational status, and other characteristics of a wide range of magazine readers. Simmons also publishes demographic and psychographic data on product usage among a varied group of consumers.

The *content* of a medium will also reflect the type of people in its audience. For instance, some radio stations emphasize in-depth news or sports; others, jazz or rock; and still others, symphonic music or operas. Each type of programming attracts a different audience, the character of which can be determined by analysis.

As we discussed in Chapter 7, some advertisers believe that, because people are more responsive when treated as individuals, there will be a movement away from mass marketing and toward commitments to smaller and smaller audience segments. The focus will be on building relationships through maximarketing techniques, rather than just trying to sell something and moving on. This requires the collection and management of a database of individual customers and prospects to enable advertisers to create special communications with each individual based on his or her needs, habits, and inclinations.

Some auto manufacturers integrate general advertising, telemarketing, and direct mail to build a relationship with customers and potential customers. For example, their ads may contain an 800 number for more information. The 800 calls are received by a telemarketing firm that collects key information about the callers for the company's database. The firm sends a targeted direct-mail package to the callers, referring them to the nearest dealer. These leads and all pertinent information are then sent to the dealer and the manufacturer. The telemarketing firm follows up with the prospects to see if they received the material and to find out whether they visited or were contacted by the dealer. These complex programs involving several communications techniques can lead toward a sale, provide support after the sale, or encourage repeat business.[17]

Exposure, Attention, and Motivational Value

As we have already pointed out, the goal of the media planner is to match the right media with the target audience so that the ads not only achieve the desired *exposure* but also attract *attention* and *motivate* prospective customers to act. This is no easy task, and it is made even more difficult because little reliable data have been developed to measure the relative strength of one medium over another in exposure, attention, or motivation values. However, experienced media planners still must consider these important issues daily.

Exposure To understand the concept of **exposure,** think in terms of how many people your ad "sees" rather than the other way around. If you place an ad in a magazine with 3 million readers, how many of those 3 million will your ad actually see? If a given TV program has an audience of 10 million viewers, how many people will your commercial actually see?

The numbers are usually considerably less than the total audience or readership. That's because even though a person may have read a particular magazine or watched a certain program, it doesn't mean he or she saw any of the ads. Some people read only one article in a magazine, set it aside, and never pick it up again. Others thumb through every page with as much interest in the ads as in the articles. Many people watch television until the commercial, then change the channel or leave the room to get a snack. Thus, comparing the exposure of one publication, radio station, or TV program with another is a very difficult task. And without statistics, it is up to the media planner to use his or her best judgment—based on experience.

The deputy director of media services at D'Arcy Massius Benton & Bowles has outlined five basic factors that can affect the probability of ad exposure:[18]

1. The senses required to perceive messages from the medium.
2. The amount and type of attention required by the medium.
3. Whether the medium is used as an information source or a diversion.
4. Whether the medium or program is aimed at a general audience or a targeted one.
5. The placement of the advertisement within the vehicle (within or between broadcast programs, adjacent to editorial material or other ads in print media).

Attention The degree of attention paid to ads by those exposed to them is another consideration. If you are not interested in motorcycles or cosmetics, you probably don't even notice ads for them when you do see them. On the other hand, if you are in the market for a new automobile, you probably notice every new-car ad you see.

Whereas exposure value relates only to the medium itself, **attention value** relates to the advertising message and copy just as much as to the medium. It is logical to assume that special-interest media, such as boating magazines, offer good attention value to a boating product. But what kind of attention value does the daily newspaper offer to a boating product? Will the boating enthusiast be thinking about a boat while reading the newspaper? These questions have no simple answers, and much research still needs to be done. But six factors have been found to positively affect the attention value of a medium:[19]

1. Audience involvement with editorial content or program material.
2. Specialization of audience interest or identification.
3. Number of competitive advertisers (the fewer, the better).
4. Audience familiarity with advertiser's campaign.
5. Quality of advertising reproduction.
6. Timeliness of advertising exposure.

Motivation These same factors affect a medium's **motivation value.** In some cases, though, they contribute more to motivation than to attention, and vice versa. For instance, familiarity with the advertiser's campaign may affect attention significantly but motivation very little. On the other hand, good-quality reproduction and timeliness can be very motivating to someone interested in a product such as flowers, as shown in an ad by the American Floral Marketing Council (see Exhibit 12-12). Therefore, attention value and motivation value should be considered separately when assessing alternative media.

EXHIBIT 12-12   The American Floral Association took advantage of the quality reproduction in this four-color print ad. The witty headline hits home with men who may have, on occasion, used flowers to get themselves out of trouble with a disgruntled female.

One way to boost motivation value is to determine why people read, watch, or listen to a particular media vehicle. Usually there is a need or motivation behind their choice, such as the pursuit of an emotional lift, humor, instruction, or escape. The advertised product should address these needs and participate in the solution offered by the vehicle when it is read, watched, or heard.[20]

One method media planners use to analyze these values is to assign a specific numerical value to their subjective assessment of a medium's various strengths and weaknesses. Then, using either a simple or complex weighting formula, they basically just add them up. Similar weighting methods are used for evaluating other considerations, such as the relative importance of age demographics against income characteristics.

Cost Efficiency

The final step in determining which media to select is to analyze the cost efficiency of each medium available. A common term used in media planning and buying is **CPM, or cost per thousand.** For example, if a daily newspaper has 300,000 subscribers and charges $5,000 for a full-page ad, then the cost per thousand is calculated as:

$$\text{CPM} = \$5{,}000 \div (300{,}000 \div 1{,}000) = \$16.67$$

A weekly newspaper with a circulation of 250,000 that charges $3,000 for a full page would promote itself as less expensive because its cost per thousand would be considerably less:

$$\text{CPM} = \$3{,}000 \div (250{,}000 \div 1{,}000) = \$12$$

However, media planners are normally more interested in the **cost efficiency** of exposing the target audience to the message, not the cost of exposing the medium's total circulation. Thus, if the target audience is males ages 18 to 49, and 40 percent (100,000) of the weekly newspaper's readers fit in this category, the CPM will actually be $30 [$3,000 ÷ (100,000 ÷ 1,000)] to reach this target audience. The daily newspaper might turn out to be more cost-efficient if 60 percent of its readers (180,000) belong to the target audience:

$$\$5{,}000 \div (180{,}000 \div 1{,}000) = \$27.78$$

Note that comparison of media based on CPM, while important, does not take into account other advantages and disadvantages of each medium. Thus, the media planner must evaluate all the criteria to determine (1) how much of each medium's audience matches the target audience, (2) how each medium satisfies the needs of the campaign's objectives and strategy, and (3) how well each medium measures up in attention, exposure, and motivation value. After such an evaluation, the planner can decide whether the daily or weekly newspaper is a better buy.

The Media Mix

Another media selection decision planners face is whether to use a single medium or several different kinds of media. A combination of media is called a **media mix.** The reasons for using a media mix include the following:

EXHIBIT 12-13

Nissan developed separate campaigns for print, broadcast, and direct mail, producing a synergistic media mix. This TV ad targeted business executives.

ANNCR VO: Nissan wants you to succeed in business, so lets define the following business terms: Conference room, executive decision making, client entertainment, risk management, hostile takeover.

ANNCR VO: This real world business course was brought to you. . . by Maxima,

SFX: CLUNK, CLUNK, CLUNK, CLUNK.

ANNCR VO: the four-door sports car.

1. To reach people not reached with only one medium.
2. To provide additional repeat exposure in a less expensive secondary medium after optimum reach is obtained in the first medium.
3. To utilize some of the intrinsic values of a medium to extend the creative effectiveness of the advertising campaign (such as music on radio or long copy in print media).
4. To deliver coupons in print media when the primary vehicle in the media plan is broadcast.
5. To produce **synergism,** an effect achieved when the sum of the parts is greater than that expected by adding the individual parts.[21] An example of a synergistic media mix is presented in Exhibit 12-13.

Nissan used an extensive media mix to communicate several messages about its 1989 Maxima to various segments in the target audience. The model was positioned as a four-door sedan with a difference—sports car performance. Nissan spent the bulk of its Maxima budget on the more visceral medium of TV because the message of sportiness was calculated to appeal to the emotions. The commercials ran during sporting events and prime-time shows such as "thirtysomething," "China Beach," "L.A. Law," "Wise Guy," "60 Minutes," and "20/20" to expose the message to the target audience of professionals and business executives with incomes of over $50,000, 25- to 34-year-olds for the Maxima SE and 35- to 49-year-olds for the GXE (see Exhibit 12-13).

Nissan also used print extensively. Clutter-busting multiple-page inserts in *Forbes, Fortune,* and *Business Week* communicated the car's suitability for bankers, doctors, and architects. When an automotive survey revealed that Nissan was the top-rated Asian automobile brand, followed by Honda, Toyota, and Acura, the company ran a campaign called "Re-Orient Your Thinking" each week in *The Wall Street Journal, USA Today, Time, Sports Illustrated, Newsweek,* and *U.S. News & World Report* to exploit the news value of the report. A print campaign also ran consistently in auto-enthusiast magazines throughout the year, to expose the message to the people who pick up those magazines only when in the market for a new car.

A direct-mail effort was aimed at Nissan's database of pre-1989 Maxima owners and invited them to test-drive the 1989 model. Print ads supporting the direct-mail campaign included an 800 number for a free preview kit that encouraged a test drive at a local dealership.

In short, each level of advertising drove home a different message about the Maxima. The national campaigns focused on its four doors, sports car performance, and trouble-free status. Regional ads underscored its price value, and dealer displays and direct-mail pieces touted its positive press reviews.[22]

Scheduling Criteria

After selecting the media vehicles, the media planner must decide how many of each vehicle's space or time units to buy and over what period of time they should be used.

Continuity, Flighting, and Pulsing

A major objective in the media plan is to schedule the advertising so that consumers are exposed to it at the point when they are ready to buy. Several terms describe how an advertising campaign is scheduled and sustained:

continuity, flighting, and *pulsing.* The differences between continuity, flighting, and pulsing are illustrated in Exhibit 12-14.

In **continuity,** advertising runs continuously and varies little over the campaign period. For example, a commercial might be scheduled on radio stations KKO and KXA for an initial four-week period. But then, to maintain continuity in the campaign, additional spots might be scheduled to run continuously every week throughout the year on station KXA. Products that are purchased on a regular basis with little fluctuation in demand usually follow this scheduling pattern.

Flighting is an intermittent scheduling pattern that alternates periods of advertising with periods of no advertising at all. The advertiser might decide to introduce the product with a four-week *flight* and then schedule three additional flights to run during seasonal periods later in the year. This pattern makes sense for products and services that experience large fluctuations in demand throughout the year, such as tax services, turkeys, and cold remedies.

Tyco Toys surprised its competitors by waiting until *after* Christmas to begin a $10 million advertising and promotional push for its Dino-Riders line of dinosaur action figures. Christmas gifts account for roughly 60 percent of all toy sales. Tyco reasoned that children would be on vacation and glued to their TV sets after Christmas and that relatively few toy commercials would compete with Dino-Rider ads for attention. The company counted on kids to spend their Christmas gift money or exchange presents for Dino-Riders.[23]

A third alternative, **pulsing,** mixes continuity and flighting strategies. Using this approach, the advertiser maintains a low level of advertising all year but uses periodic **pulses** to "heavy-up" during peak selling periods.

EXHIBIT 12-14

This is a comparison of three ways to schedule the same number of total GRPs: flighting, continous, and pulsing.

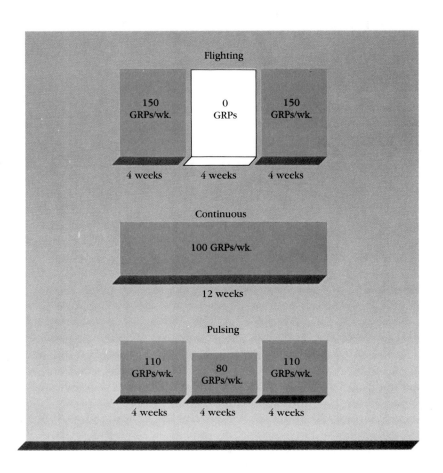

Michael Drexler, executive vice president of media at Bozell, Jacobs, Kenyon, & Eckhardt, compares pulsing to flicking a light switch on and off: "If I flip it on and off fast enough, you may never know the light is off."[24] This strategy would be appropriate for a product that is purchased throughout the year, but with moderate fluctuations in demand. Soft drinks, which are consumed at all times of the year, but more heavily in the summer, may benefit from a pulsing strategy.

Consumer Purchase Patterns

The degree to which a product is repurchased also affects media strategy. Some products with short purchase cycles, such as convenience foods and paper towels, may require somewhat more constant levels of advertising than products like refrigerators and furniture that are purchased infrequently. These short purchase cycles call for relatively high frequency and high continuity, depending on the length of time of the purchasing cycle. As the purchasing cycle gets longer, the pulsing of messages becomes more appropriate. For high-ticket items that require careful consideration, **bursting**— for instance, running the same commercial every half-hour on the same network in prime time—can be effective. A variation on this is **roadblocking,** or buying airtime on all three networks simultaneously. Chrysler used this technique to give viewers the impression that the advertiser was all over the place, even if the ad only showed for a few nights. Ramada Inns used **blinking** to stretch its slim ad budget, putting everything into Sunday to expose traveling salespeople to its advertising while they were still at home anticipating the forthcoming week.[25]

In some cases (such as the buying of camera film), the purchase cycle is erratic but susceptible to influence by advertising. In these situations, advertising exposures should be spaced, alternating periods of high frequency with periods of low exposure. The purpose is to try to reduce the length of time between purchases.

Products bought on impulse require steady, high-frequency advertising. Those bought after great deliberation may require pulsing with alternately high and low frequencies, depending on market conditions and competitive activity.

Products with a high degree of brand loyalty can usually be served with lower levels of frequency, allowing the advertiser to achieve greater reach and continuity.

EXHIBIT 12-15

Reach and frequency have an inverse relationship. For example, for the same budget it might be possible to reach 6,000 people 1 time, 3,000 people 5.5 times, or 1,000 people 9 times.

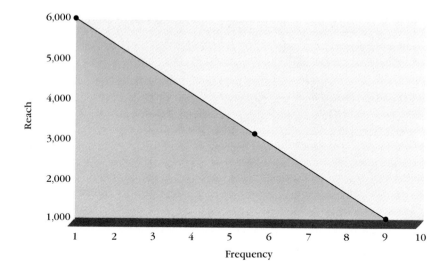

Determining the Reach, Frequency, and Continuity Combination

The continuity of a campaign affects how many people can be exposed to the message and how many times. It also affects how well the message is remembered over time. The ideal in most cases, of course, would be achieved if a company could simply advertise heavily all year long. However, the reach, frequency, and continuity of a media plan all depend on the advertiser's media budget. Because all budgets are limited, so are the attainable media objectives. In addition, these objectives have an inverse relationship to each other within the limits of the budget, as shown in Exhibit 12-15. To achieve greater reach, some frequency may have to be sacrificed. Likewise, to gain greater continuity, short-term reach or frequency must be sacrificed. See Exhibit 12-16 for a summary of guidelines for determining the

---

EXHIBIT 12-16   Guidelines for Determining the Reach, Frequency, Continuity, and Pulsing Combination

| | Objectives | | | |
Considerations	Reach	Frequency	Continuity	Pulsing
Needs				
New or highly complex message, strive for:		✔		
Dogmatic message, surge at beginning, then go for:	✔		✔	
Reason-why messages, high frequency at first, then use:				✔
With emotionally oriented messages, strive for:			✔	
When message is so creative or product so newsworthy that it forces attention, seek:	✔			
When message is dull or product indistinguishable, strive for:		✔		
Consumer purchase patterns				
To influence brand choice of regularly purchased products, use:		✔	✔	
As purchase cycle lengthens, use:		✔		✔
To influence erratic purchase cycles, strive for:				✔
To influence consumer attitudes toward impulse purchases, seek:		✔	✔	
For products requiring great deliberation, alternate between:	✔	✔		
To reinforce consumer loyalty, concentrate on:	✔		✔	
To influence seasonal purchases, anticipate peak periods with:	✔	✔		
Budget levels				
Low budget, use:				✔
Higher budgets, strive for:			✔	
Competitive activity				
Heavy competitive advertising, concentrate on:		✔		
When competitive budgets are larger, use:				✔
Marketing objectives				
For new product introductions to mass market, use:	✔			
To expand share of market with new uses for product, strive for:	✔			
To stimulate direct response from advertising, use:		✔		✔
To create awareness and recognition of corporate status, use:	✔		✔	

best reach, frequency, and continuity combination. The goal of the media planner is to optimize these objectives by getting enough reach, enough frequency, and the proper continuity to make the media plan work for the advertiser, keeping in mind these basic research findings:

1. Continuity is important because advertising is often quickly forgotten when consumers are not continually exposed to it. In most cases, it is a waste of money for advertisers to run an ad one week, wait six weeks, and then run another ad. Achieving continuity requires committing dollars over some continuous period of time.

2. Repeated exposures are needed to impress a message on the memories of a large proportion of consumers. The advertiser who runs only four or five radio spots per week gives up so much frequency (usually for the sake of continuity) it makes the schedule almost worthless.

3. As the number of exposures increases, both the number of persons who remember it and the length of time they remember it increase. This is why so many media planners believe frequency is the most important media objective; it's the key to remembering.

4. An intensive burst of advertising is more likely to cause a very large number of people to remember it (at least for a short time) than is spreading a schedule thinly over a 12-month period. This is the most common strategy for building frequency on a limited budget and is the rationale behind pulsing advertising schedules.

5. Fewer exposures per prospect in a comparatively large group promote greater memory of the advertising than do more exposures per prospect in a smaller group. In other words, there's a point at which reach becomes more important than frequency in promoting memory.

6. As additional exposures per prospect are purchased, the dollar efficiency of advertising decreases. At some point, therefore, it is again more important to seek reach rather than additional frequency.

The Use of Computers in Media Selection and Scheduling

Computers have been an important part of media planning since the early 1970s. They can eliminate much of the drudgery of planning by performing the tedious "number crunching" needed to arrive at GRPs, CPMs, reach, frequency, and so on. And they can save time and money, too. Ogilvy & Mather found that planning TV, radio, and print co-op budgets for each of client Ford's 1,000 dealers took only three people with a software system in place. The year before, it had taken 70 staffers working for a week and a half to get the plans out manually.[26]

Computers can be used to construct media schedules, to evaluate various media vehicles geared to the target market, to cross-tabulate demographic data (such as the age and income of light, medium, and heavy users of a product), and to assess the cost efficiency of alternative media plans. Does this mean, then, that human media planners will soon be replaced by computers? To answer that question, we need to know what computers can and can't do.

What they *can* do is manipulate numbers. Once a computer is given data on the audience demographics of radio stations in Pittsburgh, for example, it can rank the stations based on how closely their audience profile matches a product's target audience profile. Given information on the Pittsburgh stations' ad rates, ratings, and so on, the computer can produce several alternate radio advertising schedules that fit within the ad budget. As each radio buy is made, the computer can track how much of the budget has been spent, the percentage of the budget spent to expose the message to the primary demographic group, the cost per ratings point, and the CPM by **daypart** (a part of the broadcast day, such as morning, daytime, afternoon, or evening for radio, or early fringe, prime time, or late fringe for TV). All these activities certainly make the media planner's job easier. And that's not all computers are used for.

Three main types of computer programs have been developed for use in media planning. One of the oldest types is the **linear programming model,** designed to create a complete media schedule that maximizes exposure within a given budget. Although this type of program would indeed replace many traditional functions of the media planner, a fully practical linear model has not been developed because there are too many real-world variables that such a model has to take into account.[27]

A second type of program is the **simulation model,** used to estimate the ability of already-chosen media vehicles to expose target individuals within an audience to a message. Simulation programs do not plan media schedules but are useful in evaluating individual vehicles' target audience, cost efficiency, and so on. Specialized simulation models have also been developed for such purposes as calculating the optimum timing of an ad campaign.

Finally, **formula models** calculate reach, frequency, and other statistics for alternative media vehicles and can rank the vehicles according to selected parameters: the best reach, the best frequency, and so on. With any of these models, the computer instantly recalculates results whenever an assumption or factor is changed.

Since the advent of microcomputers in the early 1980s, software programs for media planning have proliferated, developed not only by software companies but also by ad agencies and by marketing or ad departments within companies. Some of these programs are highly customized, such as J. Walter Thompson U.S.A.'s special program to help 20th Century Fox plan newspaper buys as it introduces films in various markets. Others are for general use in the advertising industry, such as Media Management Plus, a set of programs for planning, buying, and managing all forms of advertising media (see Exhibit 12-17 on page 454).

Another major change that has occurred with the increasing use of microcomputers is the form in which media planners receive and keep data (audience demographics, broadcast ratings, readership statistics, and so forth). In the past, ad agencies used computer terminals plugged into huge mainframe computers to gain access to such data provided by various research services. Now microcomputer users have a choice of going on-line and paying for access to giant databases or of subscribing to services that provide data in the form of hard disks or floppy disks.

The problem for ad agencies is to make the best use of all this computerized data—which brings us to the issue of what computers *cannot* do. They cannot decide which medium or which environment is best for the message. They cannot evaluate the content of a magazine or the image of a TV program. Computers can manipulate numbers, but they cannot judge whether the numbers they are fed are valid or reliable, and they cannot interpret the meaning of the numbers. Thus, computers can aid in the planning process, but they cannot take the place of human planners, at least as long as subjective judgment is an important part of the process.

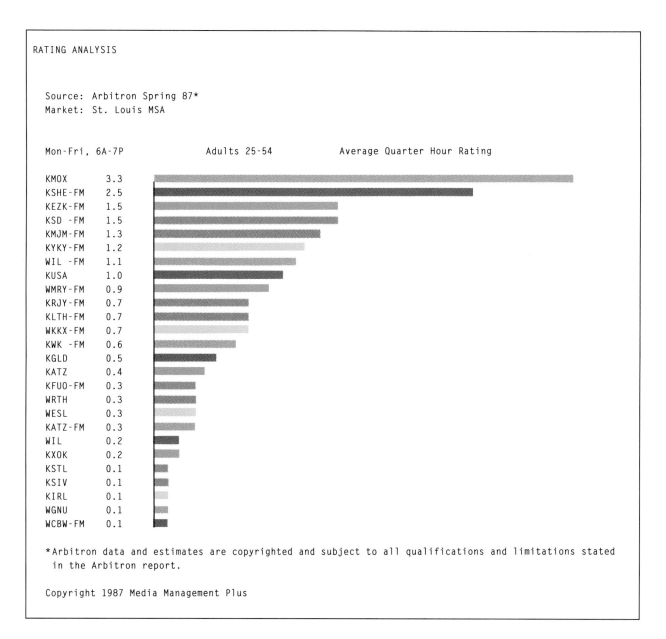

```
RATING ANALYSIS


Source: Arbitron Spring 87*
Market: St. Louis MSA


Mon-Fri, 6A-7P            Adults 25-54        Average Quarter Hour Rating

KMOX        3.3
KSHE-FM     2.5
KEZK-FM     1.5
KSD -FM     1.5
KMJM-FM     1.3
KYKY-FM     1.2
WIL -FM     1.1
KUSA        1.0
WMRY-FM     0.9
KRJY-FM     0.7
KLTH-FM     0.7
WKKX-FM     0.7
KWK -FM     0.6
KGLD        0.5
KATZ        0.4
KFUO-FM     0.3
WRTH        0.3
WESL        0.3
KATZ-FM     0.3
WIL         0.2
KXOK        0.2
KSTL        0.1
KSIV        0.1
KIRL        0.1
WGNU        0.1
WCBW-FM     0.1
```

*Arbitron data and estimates are copyrighted and subject to all qualifications and limitations stated
 in the Arbitron report.

Copyright 1987 Media Management Plus

EXHIBIT 12-17

This is an example of the type of
computer data (in this case, radio
ratings) supplied by the Media
Management Plus software system. This system can be used to
analyze various media vehicles
and then to plan media buys.

Summary

Media planning is the process that directs the advertising message to the right people at the right time. It involves many decisions, such as where to advertise geographically, which media to use, when during the year to concentrate the advertising, and how often to run the advertising, to name just a few. The decisions made by media planners frequently involve as much creativity as the decisions made by art directors and copywriters. And like good art and copy ideas, media decisions should be based on sound marketing principles and research, not just on experience and intuition.

The media function involves two basic processes: media planning and media selection. Media planning begins by defining the specific types of people to whom the advertising message will be directed and then setting goals or objectives for communicating with those audiences. This target audience is often determined from the marketer's past research, through special research studies conducted specifically to identify present and future users of the product, or through secondary research sources such as Simmons Market Research Bureau and Mediamark Research (MRI). Once the target audience is determined, the planner sets message distribution objectives that specify where, when, and how often the advertising should appear. These objectives may be expressed in terms of reach, frequency, impressions, gross rating points, and continuity.

In developing the appropriate media strategy, the planner must consider many variables: the geographic scope of the media plan, which is determined by the location and makeup of the target audience; the nature of the medium and the message, since some media lend themselves better to certain types of message or creative approaches than others; the size, length, and position of the message in the selected media, all of which affect not only the impact of the message but also the cost of placement; and the strategy of the brand's competitors, which will determine how the planner will counter competitive moves.

After the media strategy is developed, the task of selecting specific media vehicles begins. The planner usually bases each vehicle's value on a set of criteria and selects those vehicles that best meet these criteria. Some of the criteria are quantitative, and the vehicles can be assigned numerical values. Others are qualitative, less cut and dried, and require more subjective judgment. Both are important in the evaluation process. Some of the numerous factors that influence the selection process include campaign objectives and strategy; the size and characteristics of each medium's audience; geographic coverage; the attention, exposure, and motivation value of each medium; cost efficiency; and the media mix.

Once the particular media vehicles have been selected, the media planner must decide how to schedule their use—that is, how many of each medium's space or time units should be bought and over what period of time. There are many ways to schedule a media campaign, from steady, continuous advertising to erratic pulses of commercials. These decisions are affected by the seasonality of the product, the consumer purchase patterns, and the balance of reach, frequency, and continuity that can meet the planner's media objectives within the limits of the advertiser's budget.

The final plan must be the selecting and scheduling of media in a way that maximizes the effectiveness of the campaign as well as the efficiency of the dollars spent. Arriving at such a plan can be facilitated by computers but also requires subjective judgment.

Questions for Review and Discussion

1. What are the major factors contributing to the increased complexity of media planning?
2. What must the media planner take into consideration before planning can begin?
3. What are some of the secondary sources available to planners and how are they used?
4. What is the rule of thumb for determining the "right" frequency for a given message?
5. What is the difference between GRPs and CPMs? How is each calculated?
6. What major factors influence the choice of general advertising media?
7. What major factors influence the choice of individual media vehicles?
8. Why do advertisers use a media mix?
9. Why do advertisers use different scheduling approaches?
10. How are reach, frequency, and continuity related?

PRINT MEDIA

Objective: To explain how print advertising enhances the advertiser's media mix. Newspapers and magazines, with their unique communicative qualities, can complement broadcast, direct mail, and other media selections. By using print wisely, advertisers can greatly expand the impact of their campaigns without spending more than the media budget permits.

After studying this chapter, you will be able to:

☐ Explain the advantages and disadvantages of newspaper advertising.

☐ Describe how newspapers are categorized.

☐ Define the major types of newspaper advertising.

☐ Discuss how newspaper rates are determined.

☐ Explain the advantages and disadvantages of magazine advertising.

☐ Discuss several categories of magazines.

☐ Describe several sources of print media data.

I f records were kept for creating the most successful newspaper campaign in the least time and for the least money, a campaign for a Minneapolis haircutting salon, 7 South 8th for Hair, might well hold the world title.

"This was a very easy campaign to create, really painless," says Jarl Olsen, the copywriter at Fallon McElligott. "The whole thing took less than a day to plan."

The campaign ran in local newspapers because of their ability to reach a large audience quickly at reasonable cost. Newspapers were also best for getting across the simple, straightforward message planned for the campaign.

"We wanted to generate some talk value, so we used something everyone could laugh at." The instructions from the client were sparse; the only requirement was that the salon's name be on the ads. "We were all over the board," says Olsen, "and all of the ideas were weird."

Random scrawlings eventually led to the ad shown in Exhibit 13-1, featuring the snake-haired Medusa. "We sat around trying to think of bad haircuts," Olsen recalls with a laugh. "We thought of several, but we could only think of a few copy lines that made any sense." The rest of the campaign was the result of spin-offs of that original idea.

The ads consisted of stock photos of famous bad haircuts, a witty line of copy, and the salon's name and address. They appeared all over Minneapolis newspapers and later in local magazines and on posters. The campaign took the city by storm.

"These ads were everywhere," says Olsen, "and everyone was talking about them. Other shops were cutting the ads out and sticking their own logos on them. I called 7 South 8th to tell them about it. They laughed and said they knew. They thought it was funny."[1]

EXHIBIT 13-1

Newspaper ads for 7 South 8th for Hair, a Minneapolis hair salon, consisted of stock photos of "bad haircuts" with witty headlines. This inexpensive-to-produce campaign was highly successful.

A bad haircut is a real can of worms.

7 South 8th for Hair
804 LaSalle Avenue / Call 333-1376 for appointment

USING NEWSPAPERS IN THE CREATIVE MIX

Advertising people are constantly looking for *creative* solutions to their clients' marketing problems, as we pointed out in Chapter 7. However, many factors besides advertising creativity are involved in sales: the product, value offered, price, availability, competitive pressures, timing, and even the weather. Nevertheless, creative advertising can give the advertiser a chance to be heard, to present an offer. A fresh creative approach can do that superbly. The printed page in general and the newspaper in particular provide a unique, flexible medium for makers of advertising to express their creativity.

Thanks to a print advertising slump in the early 1990s, newspapers and magazines became more creative themselves in pursuing advertisers. They began to offer a number of new services, both in the production of quality ads and in the use of marketing techniques, to assure advertisers their ads would reach the targeted audience.

Advantages of Newspapers

Newspapers have inherent features that have traditionally set them apart from the other media that advertisers rely on.[2] For example:

☐ Newspapers are a *mass medium,* penetrating every segment of society. Almost everybody who can reasonably be thought of as a consumer reads them.

☐ Newspapers are a *local medium,* covering a specific geographic area that comprises both a market and a community of people sharing common concerns and interests.

☐ Newspapers are *comprehensive* in scope, covering an extraordinary variety of topics and interests.

☐ Newspapers are *read selectively* as readers search for what is personally interesting and useful.

☐ Newspapers are *timely* because they primarily cover the news.

☐ Newspaper readership is *concentrated* in time. Virtually all the reading of a particular day's paper happens that day.

☐ Newspapers represent a *permanent record* that people use actively. The advertiser's printed message stands still for rereading and reconsideration, for clipping, and for sharing.

Newspaper advertising also has credibility. Studies have found that newspaper ads rank highest in believability over other kinds of ads. In fact, one survey showed that 42 percent of respondents considered newspaper ads to be the most believable. TV commercials came in a distant second, with only 26 percent ranking them as most believable.[3]

These features give rise to several special attributes of newspapers that offer clues to the ad maker who is seeking what will work best creatively:

☐ Newspapers provide the opportunity for massive same-day exposure of an advertising message to a large cross section of any market. That gives the advertiser very broad *reach.*

☐ Newspapers combine broad reach with highly *selective attention* from the relatively small number of active prospects who, on any given day, are interested in what the advertiser is trying to tell them or sell them.

☐ Newspapers offer great *creative flexibility* to the advertiser. The ad's physical size and shape can be chosen and varied to give the degree of dominance or repetition that suits the advertiser's purpose. The San Diego Zoo, for example, has used full-page ads to attract the attention of newspaper readers

The San Diego Zoo has a lot of experience using its collection of varied and distinctive animals to get the public's attention. In this full-page newspaper ad, some of the zoo's less cuddly residents are pictured. The size and uniqueness of the drawings are eye-catching, cleverly reminding readers of what awaits them at the zoo.

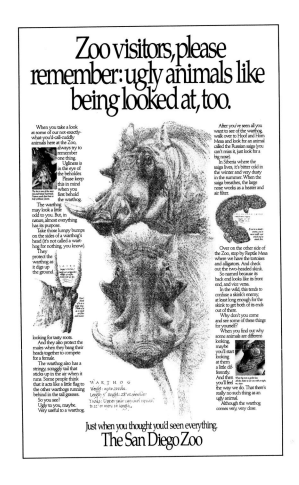

(see Exhibit 13-2). The advertiser can use black-and-white, color, Sunday magazines, or custom inserts. The newspaper, therefore, is almost a media mix by itself.

☐ With newspapers, the advertiser can go *where the customers are*. That may mean concentrating the messages in one market or spreading them out over a national schedule. It may mean running the ad in one part of the paper, in several sections, or just in certain demographic areas served by a single paper. The national advertiser can place ads on short notice, localize copy, and work with retailers by using co-op programs.

☐ The newspaper is an *active medium* rather than a passive one. Readers turn the pages, clip and save, write in the margins, and sort through the contents, screening out what they don't want from things they want to concentrate on. This reader-involving quality of newspapers offers unlimited creative opportunities to advertisers.

Some Drawbacks to Newspapers

Newspapers, like all media, also have their drawbacks. Newspapers enable advertisers to be geographically selective, but they *do not isolate and cover specific socioeconomic groups*. Instead, most newspapers reach broad, diverse groups of readers. The desires and needs of these broad groups may not match the marketing segmentation objectives of the advertiser. For example, a newspaper sports section may be a good place to advertise general sports products or services, such as surfboards or football tickets, but it would be a highly inefficient medium for advertising sports products to retail sporting goods dealers because of the tremendous waste of circulation.

A second disadvantage is the daily paper's *short life span*. Unless readers clip and save a newspaper ad or coupon, it may be lost forever.

In addition, advertisers must accept that newspapers often *lack production quality*. There is no time for high-quality reproduction techniques. The coarse paper newspapers use generally produces a far less impressive image than can be achieved with the slick, smooth paper stock of magazines. Moreover, many large metropolitan newspapers, including *The New York Times,* are not equipped for run-of-press color printing (color throughout the whole paper). Newspapers that do have color capabilities have yet to match the quality of color printing that readers are used to seeing in magazines.[4]

Another drawback is *clutter:* Because there is so much editorial content and advertising in the newspaper, each ad competes for notice with every other ad on the same page or spread. So many advertisements appear in a single issue of a newspaper (nearly 63 percent of the average daily paper), the potential for any one ad to capture major attention is minimized. A related problem is that, unless advertisers pay a premium rate for special placement, they have no control over where in the paper their ad will run.

Finally, many areas are served by newspapers that have *overlapping circulation;* that is, some residents read not one, but two or more different newspapers. Thus, advertisers may be paying for circulation that their ads have already reached in a different newspaper.

Newspapers are trying to overcome some of these shortcomings by providing special services to advertisers. For example, many papers offer "zoned" editions that go to specific neighborhoods or regions of the market area, and they are doing extensive marketing research to help link advertisers with their target audiences. Newspapers are also attempting to broaden their own audience appeal by including material of interest to certain demographic segments of their market area and by changing their focus to reflect changing lifestyles.

Who Uses Newspapers?

Newspapers are the dominant medium in terms of advertising volume, receiving more than 26 percent of the dollars spent by advertisers in the United States.[5]

Consider these important facts:

☐ Daily papers are read by more than 113 million U.S. adults each weekday. Nearly two out of three Americans read a paper every day.

☐ The typical daily newspaper reader spends an average of 45 minutes a day reading one or more newspapers and 62 minutes a week reading a Sunday paper.

☐ An average of 2.1 persons read each of the more than 62 million daily papers circulated in the United States each day.

☐ In 1989, there were 1,626 daily newspapers in the United States with a total circulation of 62.6 million. In 1990, the nation's 7,550 weekly newspapers had a combined circulation of more than 55 million.

☐ U.S. advertising volume in daily newspapers increased by 3.8 percent in 1989, with total sales of more than $32 billion—$5 billion more than its nearest competitor.[6]

EXHIBIT 13-3	Top 10 Newspaper Advertisers in the United States

Rank	Advertiser	Newspaper ad expenditures, 1990*
1	May Department Stores Co.	$218.2
2	R.H. Macy & Co.	160.1
3	Sears, Roebuck & Co.	136.8
4	Federated Department Stores	134.5
5	Dayton Hudson Corp.	106.2
6	Montgomery Ward & Co.	82.1
7	Kmart Corp.	80.1
8	Carter Hawley Hale Stores	72.8
9	J. C. Penney Co.	70.6
10	American Stores Co.	69.6

*Dollars are in millions.

Although the newspaper is the major community-serving medium for both news and advertising, the huge growth of radio and television over the past 25 years has caused more and more national advertising to be shifted to these electronic media. As a result, radio and TV today carry most of the national advertising in the United States, while 88 percent of newspaper advertising revenue comes from local advertising. As Exhibit 13-3 shows, retailers are the primary national newspaper advertisers, along with the airlines.

How Newspapers Are Categorized

Newspapers may be classified by their frequency of delivery, their physical size, or the type of audience they reach.

Frequency of Delivery

Advertisers have a choice of two basic types of newspapers: **dailies** and **weeklies.** Dailies are published at least five times a week, Monday through Friday.

Dailies are produced as either morning or evening editions. Of the 1,626 dailies in the United States, 1,125 are evening papers and 530 are morning papers. (The total exceeds 1,626 because 29 of the papers consider themselves morning *and* evening papers, or "all-day" newspapers.)[7] Morning editions tend to have a broader geographic circulation and a larger male readership; evening editions are read more by women. Despite these broad characteristics, each daily newspaper has its own circulation traits, determined chiefly by the geographic region it serves and the demographic makeup of its readers.

Weekly newspapers characteristically serve readers in small urban or suburban areas or farm communities. Recently, this has become the fastest-growing class of newspapers, due in part to its exclusive emphasis on local news and advertising. Weekly newspapers offer readers relief from unsettling national and international crises in the form of familiar names, news of local personalities, and hometown sports, entertainment, and social coverage.

The weekly newspaper usually offers advertisers a high degree of readership but at a cost per thousand (CPM) that is often higher than that of the daily paper. This higher rate may be justified, however, as the weekly has a longer life than the daily and is often exposed to more readers per copy. (Recall from Chapter 12 that CPM refers to how much it costs the advertiser to reach 1,000 members of the target audience.)

Physical Size

The two basic newspaper formats are **standard size** and **tabloid.** The *standard-size newspaper* is about 22 inches deep and 13 inches wide and is divided into six columns. The *tabloid newspaper* is generally about half the size of a standard-size newspaper, about 14 inches deep and 11 inches wide. Three national tabloid newspapers, all using sensational news stories to fight for single-copy sales through grocery supermarkets across the country, are the *National Enquirer, The Star,* and the *Globe.* In contrast, other national tabloids, such as the *New York Daily News,* emphasize "straight" news and features.

Prior to 1984, placing ads in papers across the country was a complex task because papers varied greatly in their dimensions, number of columns, and methods of calculating ad space. But the 1984 initiation of a new **standard advertising unit (SAU)** system changed all that. This system uses inches, or **column inches,** as the main unit of measure. The SAU system standardized the newspaper column width at 2¹⁄₁₆ inches; an SAU column inch is 2¹⁄₁₆ inches wide by 1 inch deep. Previously, "agate lines," or "lines," each a column wide and ¹⁄₁₄-inch deep, were the standard unit of measure. The SAU system also standardizes page and ad sizes, as shown in Exhibit 13-4. There are now 56 standard ad sizes for standard papers and 32 sizes for tabloids, each with a defined width and depth. Previously, newspapers used about 400 different ad sizes. Virtually all dailies have converted to the SAU system—some at great expense—but only about half the weekly papers have adopted the system.

Specialized Audience

Some dailies and weeklies are aimed at particular special-interest audiences, a fact not lost on advertisers. Their specialized news and features enable them to achieve high readership. They generally contain advertising oriented to their special audiences, and they may have unique advertising regulations.

Among these newspapers, for example, are those that specifically serve black readers. Today, more than 200 dailies and weeklies, such as the Ft. Worth, Texas, *Times* and the New York *Amsterdam News,* are black oriented. Other specialized papers serve foreign-language groups, such as Spanish, German, Polish, Chinese, or Armenian readers. The United States has newspapers published in 43 languages other than English.

Specialized newspapers are also produced for business and financial audiences. *The Wall Street Journal* is the leading national business and financial daily; its national edition enjoys circulation of nearly 2 million. Other papers are published for fraternal, labor union, or professional organizations, and some for religious groups or hobbyists. Some weekly newspapers are put out just for stamp and coin collectors, for example.

More than 1 million overseas armed services personnel read the daily and Sunday European and Pacific editions of the leading U.S. military newspaper, *Stars and Stripes.*

EXHIBIT 13-4

The SAU Grid shows the various standardized sizes for ads in tabloid-size and standard-size newspapers. As the grid indicates, each column is 2¹⁄₁₆ inches wide.

The Expanded SAU® Standard Advertising Unit System

Depth in Inches	1 COL. 2-1/16"	2 COL. 4-1/4"	3 COL. 6-7/16"	4 COL. 8-5/8"	5 COL. 10-13/16"	6 COL. 13"
FD*	1xFD*	2xFD*	3xFD*	4xFD*	5xFD*	6xFD*
18"	1x18	2x18	3x18	4x18	5x18	6x18
15.75"	1x15.75	2x15.75	3x15.75	4x15.75	5x15.75	
14"	1x14	2x14	3x14	4x14	N 5x14	6x14
13"	1x13	2x13	3x13	4x13	5x13	
10.5"	1x10.5	2x10.5	3x10.5	4x10.5	5x10.5	6x10.5
7"	1x7	2x7	3x7	4x7	5x7	6x7
5.25"	1x5.25	2x5.25	3x5.25	4x5.25		
3.5"	1x3.5	2x3.5				
3"	1x3	2x3				
2"	1x2	2x2				
1.5"	1x1.5					
1"	1x1					

1 Column 2-1/16"
2 Columns 4¹⁄₄"
3 Columns 6-7/16"
4 Columns 8⁵⁄₈"
5 Columns 10-13/16"
6 Columns 13"

Double Truck 26³⁄₄"
(There are four suggested double truck sizes:)
13xFD*   13x18
13x14   13x10.5

*FD (Full Depth) can be 21" or deeper. Depths for each broadsheet newspaper are indicated in the Standard Rate and Data Service. All broadsheet newspapers can accept 21" ads, and may float them if their depth is greater than 21".

Tabloids: Size 5 x 14 is a full page tabloid for long cut-off papers. Mid cut-off papers can handle this size with minimal reduction. The N size, measuring 9⁷⁄₈ x 14, represents the full page size for tabloids such as the New York Daily News and News-day and other short cut-off newspapers. The five 13 inch deep sizes are for tabloids printed on 55 inch wide presses such as the Philadelphia News. See individual SRDS listings for tabloid sections of broadsheet newspapers.

Printed in U.S.A. 11/83

Other Types of Newspapers

In the United States, there are 847 Sunday newspapers, mostly Sunday editions of daily papers, with a combined circulation of 62 million.[8] Sunday newspapers generally combine standard news coverage with their own special functions, such as

☐ Much greater classified advertising volume.

☐ Much greater advertising and news volume.

☐ In-depth coverage of developments in the arts, business, sports, housing, entertainment, and travel.

☐ Review and analysis of the past week's events.

Most Sunday newspapers also feature a newspaper-distributed magazine, or **Sunday supplement.** Some publish their own supplement, such as "Los Angeles Magazine" of the *Los Angeles Times.* The remaining newspapers

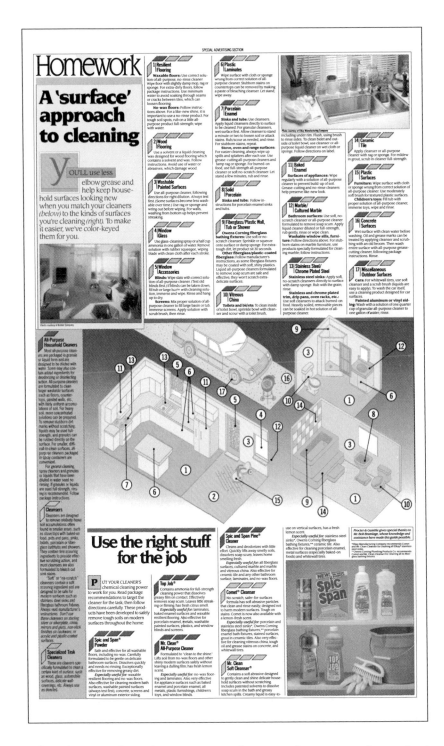

subscribe to syndicated magazine supplements, where a central organization compiles, edits, and prints the supplement and ships it to individual newspaper publishers for insertion in their Sunday editions.

Sunday supplements are distinct from other sections of the newspaper in that they are printed by rotogravure on smoother paper stock. This heavier, higher-quality paper is more conducive to quality color printing, making Sunday supplements attractive to national advertisers who want higher-quality reproduction.

Another type of newspaper, the **independent shopping guide** or free community newspaper, offers advertisers local saturation. Sometimes called *pennysavers* or *shoppers,* most newspapers of this type carry little news and practically no features. Instead, they are distributed free and are filled with advertising aimed at essentially the same audience as the weekly newspapers—urban and suburban community readers. Shoppers may be published weekly, biweekly, or monthly. Readership is generally high, and the publisher strives to achieve maximum saturation of the circulation area. A study of one chain of shoppers in the Long Island, New York, area found, for example, that 83 percent of those receiving the papers read them regularly, and 91 percent said these papers give them information they couldn't get from other newspapers.[9]

There are also several national newspapers in the United States, including *USA Today* and the *Christian Science Monitor.* Since its debut in 1982, *USA Today*'s national edition has achieved a circulation of almost 1.4 million, making it second only to *The Wall Street Journal* in national distribution and first among general-interest dailies, surpassing the *New York Daily News.* In mid-1986, *USA Today* became the number-one print vehicle for automotive ads.[10] The newspaper also has a distinctive look that savvy advertisers take advantage of, as in the Procter & Gamble insert in Exhibit 13-5.

Types of Newspaper Advertising

The major classifications of newspaper advertising are *display, classified, public notices*, and *preprinted inserts*. Advertisers use the different types of ads to achieve various advertising goals.

Display Advertising

Display advertising differs from **classified advertising** in that it includes not only copy, but illustrations or photographs, headlines, and other visual components. Classified ads usually include only copy. The newspaper ads for 7 South 8th for Hair, discussed at the beginning of this chapter, are examples of display advertising.

The size of display ads varies, and they are featured in all areas of the newspaper except on page one, the editorial page, the obituary page, the classified section, and the first page of major sections.

Display ads can be black-and-white or color, with or without pictures. Most local display advertising is either black-and-white or multicolored with a few basic colors. One common variation of the display ad, the **reading notice,** looks like editorial matter and sometimes costs more than normal display advertising. To prevent readers from mistaking it for editorial matter, the word *advertisement* appears at the top of the reading notice. Many, but not all, newspapers accept reading notices.

The two principal types of display advertising are *local* and *general (national).* As noted earlier, about 88 percent of all newspaper display advertising is local, and the largest source of newspaper display revenue is local retail merchants. See the Sangertown ad in Exhibit 13-6, for example. Retailers often run newspaper ads through **cooperative,** or co-op, **programs** sponsored by the manufacturers whose products they sell. The manufacturer pays fully or partially to create and run the ad, which features the local retailer's name and logo.

Most newspapers charge local and national advertisers different rates. The national rate averages 62 percent higher than the local rate, with some papers

Display ads give retailers the cost-effective exposure they need to remain top-of-mind with their customers. This sidewalk sale ad uses a tongue-in-cheek headline and humorous copy to put a new twist on an old idea.

MISPLACED OUR LEASE. EVERYTHING MUST GO.

It was in the top drawer yesterday. Today we can't seem to find it. In fact, we had to move all our merchandise out in the hall so we could look for it. Until we get our hands on it, practically all that merchandise will be on sale. (Our lease is bound to turn up any day now, so hurry.)
The "Misplaced Our Lease" Sidewalk Sale. July 13th Through 16th.

Shopping Hours 10-9:30 Monday-Saturday, 12-5 Sunday.
Located at the intersection of Routes 5 & 5A, New Hartford, New York 13413
Try our gift certificate program. Call 315-797-8520.

© The Pyramid Companies 1989

charging as much as 254 percent more for national ads.[11] Newspapers attribute these higher national rates to the added costs they incur in serving national advertisers. For instance, this advertising is usually placed by an advertising agency, which receives a 15 percent commission from the newspaper. Some newspapers serve these agencies through media representatives, who also receive a commission. If the advertising comes from another city or state, then additional costs, including long-distance telephone calls, are involved. Therefore, publishers feel the higher national rates are justified.

This dual rate system has been controversial among advertisers, however. In fact, many national advertisers rebel against the high rates and take their business elsewhere—only about 3 percent of national ad dollars now go to newspapers, and that proportion may shrink even further.[12] In response to declining national ads, newspapers began experimenting with national discount rates in 1987. At that time, a group of 258 papers joined forces to offer packaged goods advertisers an average 30 percent discount on orders of a quarter page or larger size that ran 13 times. This special rate was still 25 percent above local rates but lower than the usual 62 percent differential.[13] Smaller groups of papers have also joined forces to test other types of discount plans in an attempt to lure back national accounts.

Classified Advertising

Classified advertisements are a unique and important feature of newspapers. They provide a community marketplace for goods, services, and opportunities of every type, from real estate and new-car sales to employment opportunities and business proposals of major magnitude. They are also a significant source of ad revenues for papers. Such ads are usually arranged under subheads that describe the class of goods or the need the ads seek to satisfy. For example, you would look for a job under the classification "Help Wanted" and for an employee in the listings headed "Situations Wanted." Classified rates are typically based on the number of lines the ad occupies and may vary depending on whether the ad is for real estate, employment, or some other category. Most employment, housing, and automotive advertising takes the form of classified advertising.

Some newspapers also accept **classified display advertising.** Such ads run in the classified section of the newspaper and are generally characterized by larger-size type, photos, art borders, abundant white space, and sometimes even color.

Public Notices

For a nominal fee, newspapers will carry legal notices of changes in business and personal relationships, public governmental reports, notices by private citizens and organizations, and financial reports. These ads follow a preset format and thus require little creativity.

Preprinted Inserts

Preprinted inserts are inserted into the fold of the newspaper and sometimes look like a separate, smaller section of the paper. Printed by the advertiser, these inserts are delivered to the newspaper plant to be inserted into a specific edition either by machine or by the newsdealers. Insert sizes range from a typical newspaper page to a piece no larger than a double postcard; formats include catalogs, brochures, mail-back devices, and perforated coupons.

Some large metropolitan dailies allow advertisers to limit their inserts to specific circulation zones only. A retail advertiser that wants to reach shoppers in its immediate area only can place an insert in the local-zone editions. Retail stores, auto dealers, large national advertisers, and others have found it less costly to distribute their circulars in this manner than to mail them or deliver them door-to-door.

HOW TO BUY NEWSPAPER SPACE

To get the most from the advertising budget, it is important that the media buyer and advertiser know the characteristics of a newspaper's readership—the median age, sex, occupation, income, educational level, and buying habits of the typical reader.

Understanding Readership and Circulation

Readership information is available in standardized form from Simmons Market Research Bureau and Scarborough Research Corporation for 50 major United States markets, covering more than 150 dailies. In addition, most large papers can provide extensive readership data, including data on various geographic editions.

In single-newspaper cities, the demographic characteristics of readers are likely to reflect some cross section of the general population. In cities with two or more newspapers, however, these characteristics may vary widely. Los Angeles, for example, has the *Los Angeles Times,* directed to a broad cross section of the community, and *La Opinion*, directed specifically to the growing Hispanic population of the area. Each newspaper has a somewhat different readership, and that colors the overall attractiveness of the paper to different types of advertisers.

Readership is also determined by the time of day a newspaper is published. An advertiser, for example, may have to decide between advertising a bedding sale in a morning newspaper that has a 60 percent male readership or an evening newspaper with high female readership. Each alternative has its advantage. The morning paper can advertise the sale that day and attract immediate shoppers, but the evening paper can be read by husband and wife together and motivate them to come to the sale the following day. The advertiser must evaluate these and other factors to determine the optimum timing for the ad's placement.

In addition to understanding the newspaper's readership, the advertiser must know the facts of its circulation. The paper's total circulation includes subscribers; secondary readers, or people who read a copy of the paper that someone else subscribes to; and readers who buy the newspaper from a machine, newsstand, or retailer. Only by analyzing the paper's total readership can advertisers know how far their newspaper advertising dollars will go.

Rate Cards

Newspapers provide potential advertisers with a printed information form called a **rate card** that lists the advertising rates, mechanical and copy requirements, advertising deadlines, and other information the advertiser needs to know before placing an order. Because rates vary greatly from paper to paper, advertisers must be able to calculate which papers deliver the most readers for their money.

Flat Rates and Discount Rates

National advertisers, as noted earlier, usually pay a higher rate than local advertisers. Local advertisers sometimes earn even lower rates by buying large or repeated amounts of space at **volume discounts.** Not all newspapers offer such discounts, however. Many national papers charge **flat rates,**

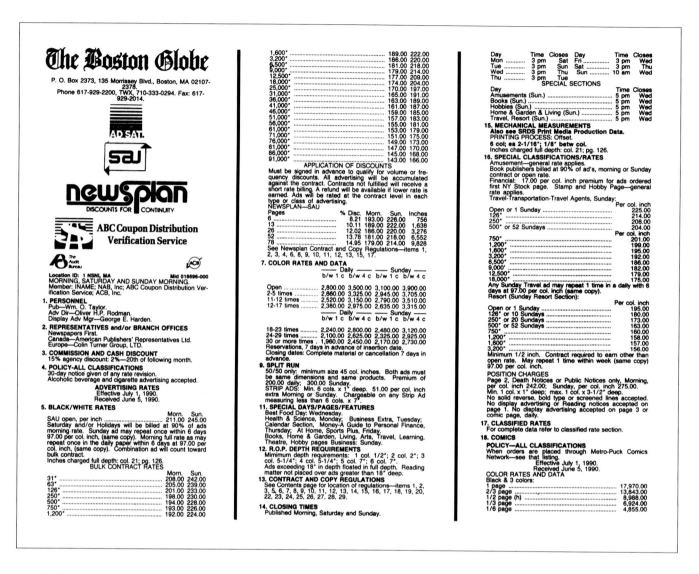

An example of newspaper advertising rates.

which means they allow no discounts for large or repeated space buys. A few newspapers offer a single flat rate to both national and local advertisers.

Newspapers that offer volume discounts have an **open rate**—their highest rate for one-time insertions—and **contract rates** or **earned rates,** whereby local advertisers can obtain discounts of up to 70 percent by signing a contract for frequent or bulk space purchases. Bulk discounts offer advertisers decreasing rates (calculated by multiplying the number of inches by the cost per inch) as the number of inches used increases. Advertisers earn *frequency discounts* by running a given ad repeatedly in a specific time period. More than 1,000 newspapers also participate in Newsplan, a Newspaper Advertising Bureau program that gives national and regional advertisers discounts for purchasing six or more pages per year. Exhibit 13-7 shows a rate card for *The Boston Globe,* listing various contract rates.

Short Rate

An advertiser who contracts to buy a specific amount of space during a one-year period at a discount rate and then fails to buy this amount of space is charged a **short rate.** This is computed by determining the difference between the earned rate for the inches run and the discount rate contracted.

Conversely, an advertiser who buys more inches than the number contracted may be entitled to a rebate or credit because of the additional advertising.

Combination Rates

Combination rates are offered for placing a given ad in (1) morning and evening editions of the same newspaper; (2) two or more newspapers owned by the same publisher; and (3) in some cases, two or more newspapers affiliated in a syndicate or newspaper group. Publishers sometimes offer advertisers combination rates for placing a given ad in consecutive Saturday and Sunday editions of the same newspaper. At one time, some newspapers required advertisers to buy combinations, but courts declared this practice illegal, and combinations are now optional.

Run of Paper (ROP)

ROP advertising rates entitle a newspaper to place a given ad on any newspaper page or in any position it desires—in other words, where space permits. Although the advertiser has no control over where the ad appears in the paper, most newspapers will try to place an ad in the position the advertiser requests. ROP rates are lower than those for preferred positions.

Preferred Position

An advertiser can ensure a choice position for an ad by paying a higher **preferred position** rate. For example, a dictating machine manufacturer must pay this rate if it wants to ensure placement of its ad on the business or financial page. And a tire manufacturer or retailer may do the same to ensure a position in the sports section.

There also are preferred positions on the newspaper page. The preferred position near the top of a page or on the top of a column next to reading matter is called **full position.** It's usually surrounded by reading matter and may cost the advertiser 25 to 50 percent more than ROP rates. Slightly less desirable, but also a preferred position, is placement *next to reading matter (NR),* which generally costs the advertiser 10 to 20 percent more than ROP rates.

Color Advertising

Color advertising such as the full-page newspaper ad for American International Rent A Car in Exhibit 13-8 is available in many newspapers on an ROP basis. As mentioned earlier, newspapers are not noted for their high-quality color printing because of high-speed presses and porous paper stock, so advertisers frequently preprint ads using processes known as HiFi color and Spectacolor. The advertisement is printed on a roll, and the roll is fed into the press by the newspaper, which prints its own material on the blank side. Some national advertisers preprint their color ads on magazine-supplement-type paper. The cost of a color ad is usually based on the black-and-white rate; the rate card simply lists an amount to add for each additional color the advertiser desires.

Split Runs

Many newspapers (and magazines) offer **split runs.** The advertiser runs two ads of identical size but different content for the same product in the same or

EXHIBIT 13-8

Because most newspaper ads are printed in black-and-white, this ROP American International Rent A Car ad gets lots of attention simply because it appears in four-color.

different press runs on the same day. This way, the advertiser tests the pulling power of one ad against the other. Newspapers set a minimum space requirement and charge extra for this service.

Co-op Insertions

As an aid to national advertisers wanting to place ads in several markets and several papers, the **Newspaper Advertising Bureau (NAB)** has instituted the **Newspaper Co-op Network** (NCN). With this system, advertisers can use salespeople from the respective newspapers to line up retailers for dealer-listing ads, for example. (Such ads are produced by the advertiser and include a blank space for insertion of the retailer's name.) The system also helps manufacturers control local advertising tie-ins to national campaigns and themes. Before the development of NCN, national advertisers placed ads individually and recruited local dealers individually—a process that could require hundreds of phone calls and a lot of paperwork. Now an insertion in up to 1,500 daily newspapers entails only a few phone calls.[14]

Another type of group insertion program, pioneered by *The New York Times,* places a particular ad in a comparable position in multiple major dailies on the same day. For example, the *Times* arranged for a Merrill Lynch ad to appear on the New York Stock Exchange quotes page in 26 major metropolitan newspapers every other Tuesday for a year.[15]

Insertion Orders and Tear Sheets

An advertiser who is ready to run an ad submits an **insertion order** to the newspaper. This form states the date(s) on which the ad is to run and its size, the desired position, and the rate. It also states the type of artwork—finished art, mechanicals, Velox prints (high-quality prints suitable for reproduction), or mats—that will be furnished with the ad.

When the newspaper creates advertising copy and art, it gives the advertiser a **proof copy** to check before running the ad. In contrast, most national advertising is submitted to newspapers with the art, copy, and layout in final form. It is important that the agency or advertiser receive verification that the ad has run. Therefore, the newspaper tears out the page on which the ad appeared and sends it to the agency or advertiser. Today most **tear sheets** for national advertisers are forwarded through a private central office, the Advertising Checking Bureau.

When a tear sheet arrives, the advertiser examines it to make sure the ad ran according to instructions—particularly with regard to the section of the paper in which it ran, its page position, and its reproduction. If the advertisement did *not* run as instructed, the agency or advertiser may be entitled to an adjustment. This may be a percentage discount or even a free rerun of the ad.

WE DELIVER TO EVERY CORNER OF THE EARTH. (INCLUDING THE CORNER OF 東 AND 西.)
Federal Express now serves more than 100 countries worldwide.

EXHIBIT 13-9

When an advertiser "absolutely, positively" has to make an outstanding impression, magazines are the media of choice. In this ad, Fallon McElligott pulls out the stops to colorfully illustrate the far-reaching growth of Federal Express's worldwide service.

USING MAGAZINES IN THE CREATIVE MIX

Like newspapers, magazines offer advertisers many advantages. For example, magazines give the advertiser flexible design options, lush color, and excellent reproduction quality. Magazines can also offer authority, prestige, permanence, excellent audience selectivity, and cost efficiency. Exhibit 13-9 illustrates several advantages of magazines as an element of the creative mix.

Advantages of Magazines

The advantages of magazines as an advertising medium differ from those of newspapers. For example:

☐ Magazines offer *flexibility* in both readership and advertising. They cover the full range of prospects—with a wide choice of both regional and national coverage. Each magazine lends itself to a variety of lengths, approaches, and editorial tones. The advertiser has many choices: long copy, black-and-white editorial ads; short copy, colorful poster ads; humorous cartoons; or any of an infinite variety of approaches. (See the Portfolio of Award-Winning Magazine Advertisements in this chapter.)

(continued on p. 477)

PORTFOLIO OF AWARD-WINNING MAGAZINE ADVERTISEMENTS

A. This striking spread employs a unique combination of spectacular photography and cryptic copy to help Nike stay a step ahead of the competition. It proves that effective ads don't always have to show the product— or even refer to it.

B. The sweeping grandeur of this ad makes the San Diego Wild Animal Park seem more like the plains of Africa than a big-city zoo. The magnificent panoramic photograph is complemented by an intriguing headline and captivating copy.

C. Sometimes you just gotta break the rules. And this bold headline does exactly that by mentioning the competition rather than the advertiser. It's a risky approach that assumes the audience already appreciates the ultimate reward of owning a Ferrari.

D. Creative advertising is sometimes as awe-inspiring as true art. This execution looks like an oil painting, but it leaves no doubt that Timberland clothes are for rugged individualists who battle the elements—and win.

E. Selling tires with minimal copy is an uncommon advertising approach, but the high-impact art makes this stunningly beautiful Pirelli ad stand apart from competitors.

F. There's an old saying in advertising: "If you want people to pay attention, put a baby or a dog in your ad." Hush Puppies tried to do both, and the sad-eyed pup in the white bonnet is simply irresistible.

G. The Art Director's Club of Los Angeles honored this ad for the innovative and engaging way it showed that Blue Diamond almonds go with everything, from uncommon delicacies to animal crackers.

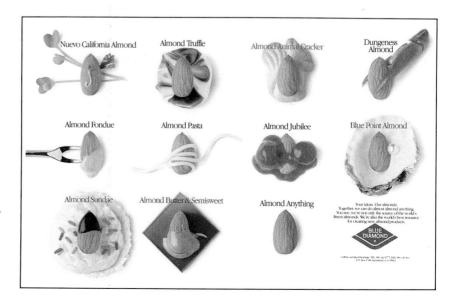

☐ Magazines are exciting. Their *color* spreads a spectrum of visual pleasure before the reader. And nowhere is color reproduction better than in slick magazines. Color in such publications as *National Geographic* enhances image and identifies the package. In short, it sells.

☐ Magazines endow the advertiser with an aura of *authority* and *believability* that enhances the commercial message. People believe what magazines say. Their influence affects people's ideas, opinions, and desires. Marketing expert Stephen Martin quotes John Naisbett as having said, "We are drowning in information but starving for knowledge and meaning." Martin points out that TV, radio, and newspapers offer lots of information but little knowledge or meaning, while "magazines are one place we can often find all three."[16]

☐ Magazines offer *permanence,* or long shelf life. For the advertiser who wants to communicate lasting information and enjoyment, magazines give the reader more opportunity to appraise ads in considerable detail. Magazine ads can deliver a more complete education/sales message and effectively communicate the total corporate personality. As Judith Ranzer, vice president for advertising and sales promotion at MCI, has emphasized, "It really does pay off to tell your story comprehensively. . . . The ad is not just a teaser to a product but a complete description of everything you need to know about it."[17] Magazines also enable advertisers to generate reprints and merchandising materials that help them get more mileage out of their advertising campaigns.

☐ Certain magazines, such as *Architectural Digest* and *Connoisseur,* also lend *prestige* to advertised products.

☐ Perhaps most important, magazines are the most *selective* of all media except for direct mail. The predictable editorial environment selects the audience and enables advertisers to pinpoint their sales campaigns. For example, the Pella window ad in Exhibit 13-10 (p. 478) runs in magazines read by architects and builders. Most magazines are written for special-interest groups. *Golf Digest* helps a golf club manufacturer reach golfers; *Business Week* reaches businesspeople; *Seventeen* reaches teenage girls; *Ebony* helps advertisers reach upscale members of the black community; *American Photographer* is aimed at professional and semiprofessional photographers; and *Modern Maturity,* the most widely circulated magazine, targets older readers. According to Steve Kurtzer, media supervisor at BBDO, the proliferation of specialized magazines has been a real boon to advertisers: "Such specialized vehicles enable marketers to target their messages to a well-defined segment of consumers in what can be a highly compatible editorial environment."[18]

☐ Finally, magazines can be very *cost-efficient.* By selecting the specific magazines and editions that reach prospects, the advertiser can minimize wasted circulation. The selling power of magazines has been proven and results are measurable, so they are the growing choice of many leading advertisers. Exhibit 13-11 (p. 479) is a list of the top 10 magazine advertisers in 1990. In addition, publishers are forming print networks in which advertisers receive reduced prices by advertising in two or more of the network's publications. Some networks include only one publisher's titles, while others include the magazines of two or three publishers. For example, in 1991, a network emerged encompassing *Newsweek;* Meredith Corp., which publishes *Ladies' Home Journal, Better Homes and Gardens,* and seven other women's magazines; and Times-Mirror, which publishes men's magazines such as *Outdoor Life* and *Field and Stream.*[19]

Why sit around and watch summer re-runs, when you can watch summer? Or see the kind of fall programming Mother Nature brings to trees?

A Pella® window brings new meaning to the expression

THE REASON SOME PEOPLE RUSH HOME FROM WORK ISN'T TO WATCH TV.

"a room with a view."

The fact is, Pella windows are preferred by more architects than any other window. And that's not just because they're well

 made. It's because they open up a wealth of new design

BUILT TO IMPOSSIBLY HIGH STANDARDS. OUR OWN.®

possibilities. Pella standard and custom windows not only make a house spectacular to look out of, but stunning to look at.

So if you're building or remodeling a home, come to the company that invented the idea of Windowscaping.℠

And discover how beautiful the world can be when it's not confined to a 21" screen.

If you'd like a little preview, call 1-800-524-3700 for a free Windowscaping Idea Book and the location of The Pella Window Store® nearest you.

Magazines also have some other advantages. They generate loyalty among readers that sometimes borders on fanaticism; they may reach prospects that salespeople can't because of geographic or other reasons; and they have extensive "pass-along" readership, meaning nonsubscribers read the magazine after the subscribers are finished with it. In addition, magazines readily communicate with hard-to-reach occupational groups, such as physicians and entertainment personalities.

Some Drawbacks to Magazines

Magazines offer excellent options for advertisers who understand how to use print media. (See the Checklist of What Works Best in Print, p. 480.) However, magazines also have some drawbacks. The immediacy of newspapers, for example, is lost in magazines. Likewise, magazines don't offer the depth of geographic coverage or the local reach of newspapers. Nor do they offer the national reach of the broadcast media. They're also unable to deliver high-frequency figures or mass audiences at a low price.

Another disadvantage is that advertising in magazines requires a long **lead time.** The advertiser or agency must buy the space and prepare the ad well in

EXHIBIT 13-11	Top 10 Magazine Advertisers in the United States	

Rank	Advertiser	Magazine ad expenditures, 1990*
1	Philip Morris Cos.	$260.0
2	General Motors Corp.	207.2
3	Ford Motor Co.	148.9
4	Procter & Gamble Co.	146.6
5	Chrysler Corp.	103.5
6	RJR Nabisco	78.8
7	Toyota Motor Corp.	77.9
8	Grand Metropolitan	76.7
9	Unilever NV	70.8
10	Nestlé SA	69.4

*Dollars are in millions.

advance of the date of publication—sometimes as long as three months. Weekly magazines, particularly those that run color ads, often require submission of advertising materials weeks in advance of the publication date. And once the closing date has been reached, no changes in copy or art can be allowed. Some magazines are trying to overcome this drawback by offering a "fast-close" service at no extra charge.

Magazines also have trouble offering *reach* and *frequency*. Unless it is a major marketing consideration, using selective magazines is very costly for reaching broad masses of people. The advertiser can actually build frequency faster than reach by adding numerous small-audience magazines to the schedule. However, most magazines are issued only monthly—or at best weekly—so building frequency in one publication is very difficult.

Popular magazines have the problem of heavy *advertising competition*. This can deter other advertisers. In the 50 or so magazines that account for the majority of total magazine circulation, the average relationship is 51.9 percent advertising to 48.1 percent editorial matter.[20]

In addition, the *cost* of advertising in magazines can be very high. National consumer magazines offer an average black-and-white cost per thousand that ranges from $5 to $12 or more; some trade publications with highly selective audiences have a CPM of more than $20 for a black-and-white page.

Magazines also must contend with the problem of *declining circulations*. In particular, single-copy sales dropped by almost 12 percent between 1980 and 1989.[21] The loss of newsstand sales stems from a number of things, including increased subscription sales, the ever-increasing number of magazines on the stands, changing consumer buying patterns, and competition from VCRs. Magazine publishers are quick to point out, however, that what they may be losing in reader quantity is made up for in reader quality. Using sophisticated research techniques, they can often back this claim with extensive demographic and psychographic data on their readers. Magazines also court advertisers by offering a number of creative methods for getting their ad messages across, as we will see in the next section and in Ad Lab 13-A (p. 481).

Checklist of What Works Best in Print

□ *Use simple layouts.* One big picture works better than several small pictures. Avoid cluttered pages. (Layouts that resemble the magazine's editorial format are well read.)

□ *Always put a caption under a photograph.* Readership of picture captions is generally twice as great as of body copy. The picture caption can be an advertisement by itself.

□ *Don't be afraid of long copy.* The people who read beyond the headline are *prospects for your product or your service.* If your product is expensive—like a car, a vacation, or an industrial product—prospects are hungry for the information long copy gives them. Consider long copy if you have a complex story to tell, any different product points to make, or an expensive product or service to sell.

□ *Avoid negative headlines.* People are literal minded and may remember only the negatives. Sell the positive benefits in your product—not that it won't harm or that some defect has been solved. Look for emotional words that attract and motivate, like *free* and *new* and *love.*

□ *Don't be afraid of long headlines.* Research shows that, on the average, long headlines sell more merchandise than short ones.

□ *Look for story appeal.* After the headline, a striking visual is the most effective way to get a reader's attention. Try for story appeal—the kind of visual that makes the reader ask: "What's going on here?"

□ *Photographs are better than drawings.* Research says that photography increases recall an average of 26 percent over artwork.

□ *Look at your advertisement in its editorial environment.* Ask to see your ad pasted into the magazine in which it will appear—or, for newspapers, photostated in the same tone as the newspaper page. Beautifully mounted layouts are deceptive. The reader will never see your advertisement printed on high-gloss paper, with a big white border, mounted on a board. It is *misleading* for you to look at it this way.

□ *Develop a single advertising format.* An overall format for all print advertising can double recognition. This rule holds special meaning for industrial advertisers. One format will help readers see your advertisements as coming from one large corporation, rather than several small companies.

□ *Before-and-after photographs make a point better than words.* If you can, show a visual contrast—a change in the consumer or a demonstration of product superiority.

□ *Do not print copy in reverse type.* It may look attractive, but it reduces readability. For the same reason, don't surprint copy on the illustration of your advertisement.

□ *Make each advertisement a complete sale.* Your message must be contained in the headline. React to the overall impression as the reader will. Only advertisers read all their advertisements. Any ad in a series must stand on its own. *Every one* must make a complete sale. Assume it will be the only advertisement for your product a reader will ever see.

Special Possibilities with Magazines

Magazines offer advertisers a wide variety of creative possibilities through various technical or mechanical elements. These include *bleed pages, cover positions, inserts* and *gatefolds,* and *special-size ads* such as *junior pages* and *island halfs.* We discuss these elements briefly below.

When the dark or colored background of the ad extends to the edge of the page, it is said to "bleed" off the page. The Nike Air ad featured in the Portfolio of Award-Winning Magazine Advertisements is an example of a bleed ad. Most magazines offer **bleed pages,** but advertisers usually have to pay a 10 to 15 percent premium for them. The advantages of bleeds include greater flexibility in expressing the advertising idea, a slightly larger printing area, and a more dramatic impact than might be achieved with a white border.

AD LAB 13-A
Innovations in Magazine Advertising

In the past few years, magazines have worked closely with advertisers to develop new technologies for creative presentations of ideas and products. From these efforts have come such innovations as fragrance strips, color strips, and pop-ups.

Since **fragrance strips** first came on the scene in the early 1980s, they have become a great favorite with perfume advertisers. Through a unique method called the *Scentstrip,* perfume samples can be tucked into magazines, yielding their scents to readers upon opening of a sealed insert. Despite some consumer complaints about allergies and not wanting to smell like perfume after reading a magazine, Scentstrips have become incredibly popular as they offer perfume makers a direct way to give consumers samples of their product. Odors have been used for other products as well—for example, a Rolls-Royce ad in *Architectural Digest* carried a Scentstrip bearing the essence of leather.

Following on the heels of fragrance samples has been the development of a method for including cosmetic samples with magazine ads. Now cosmetics manufacturers can insert **color strip** samples of eye shadow, blusher, lipstick, and makeup that readers can try immediately. Production of the color strips doesn't come cheap, but many advertisers think the expense is worth it.

Another costly production innovation that appeals to certain advertisers is the **pop-up ad.** Corporate advertisers such as Honeywell and TransAmerica were among the first to experiment with this eye-catching approach; and product ads, such as a pop-up Dodge Dakota, were not far behind.

Other intriguing approaches explored recently include **3-D ads** (complete with 3-D glasses), other forms of product samples (such as facial tissues and paper towels), and unusual shapes and sizes for inserts. An ad for Sarah Lee cheesecake, for example, took the form of a single heavy-

stock page with what appeared to be a bite taken out of the large-as-life cheesecake slice. A half-page insert for Gleem toothpaste featured a metallicized graphic of a mirror with the slogan "Check Your Mirror," asking readers to check whether their teeth were white enough.

Additional research is probing the possibilities of holographic ads and of ads that "talk" when a device is passed across the page. There are already ads that "sing"—liquor companies have included microchips that play Christmas carols in their December magazine ads, and Camel cigarette ads played "Happy Birthday" on the occasion of the brand's 75th anniversary in 1988.

All these innovative approaches are designed not only to attract the attention of readers but to *involve* them in the ad experience by appealing to more than just the visual sense.

Laboratory Application
What kinds of products besides perfumes and cars, could Scentstrips be used to advertise?

The front cover of U.S. magazines is commonly referred to as the *first cover.* Few publishers sell the first cover. They do sell the inside front, inside back, and outside back covers, typically at a premium. These are called the *second, third,* and *fourth covers,* respectively.

An insert consisting of a section of paper folded one or more times so that its folded size matches the other pages of the magazine is called a **gatefold.** The folded page swings out like a gate to present the advertisement. It may occupy the cover position or the centerfold. Gatefolds are useful in making spectacular and impressive announcements. Not all magazines provide gatefolds, and they are always sold at a premium.

An advertiser often has an ad printed on a special paper stock to add weight and drama to the message. This can then be inserted into the magazine at a special price. Another option is multiple-page inserts. Such inserts may be exclusively devoted to the product being advertised, or they may have editorial content and ads consistent with the magazine's focus. For example, Calvin Klein promoted its jeans in a 116-page insert—in *Vanity Fair*. Almost half as thick as the magazine itself, the insert was reported to cost more than $1 million. It contained 107 pictures portraying the hedonistic life of a rock band, had no copy, and showed models with few clothes. Widely written about in major newspapers and magazines, the publicity value of the campaign was enormous.[22]

Another way to make creative use of magazine ad space is to place the ad in very unusual places on the page or dramatically across spreads. For example, a **junior unit** is a large ad (60 percent of the page) placed in the middle of a page and surrounded with editorial material. Similar to junior units are **island halves,** except more editorial matter surrounds them. The island sometimes costs more than a regular half-page, but because it dominates the page, many advertisers consider the premium a small price to pay. Exhibit 13-12 shows other space combinations that can create a big impact.

How Magazines Are Categorized

Magazines may be classified in many ways. Commonly, advertisers categorize them by content, geography, and size.

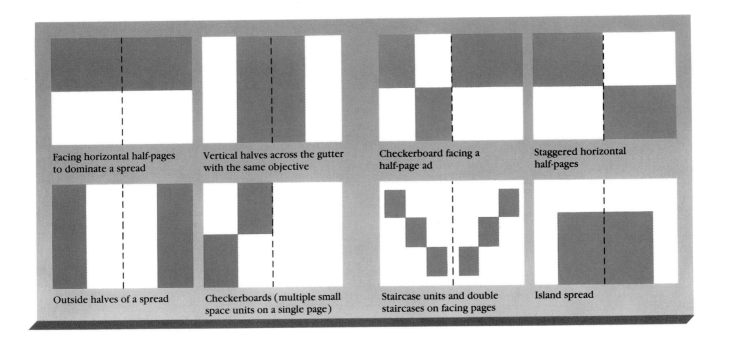

Facing horizontal half-pages to dominate a spread

Vertical halves across the gutter with the same objective

Checkerboard facing a half-page ad

Staggered horizontal half-pages

Outside halves of a spread

Checkerboards (multiple small space units on a single page)

Staircase units and double staircases on facing pages

Island spread

EXHIBIT 13-12

These magazine space combinations can create big impact.

Content

One of the most dramatic developments in publishing over the last three decades has been the emergence of magazines with specialized appeal and content. Although specialization has not guaranteed success in the field, it has given many publications good prospects for long-term growth.

The broadest classifications of content are *consumer magazines, farm magazines,* and *business magazines.* Each of these, though, may be broken down into hundreds of categories.

☐ **Consumer magazines** are purchased for entertainment, information, or both, and consumer magazine publishers edit them for people who buy products for their own consumption.

☐ **Farm publications** are magazines directed to farmers and their families or to companies that manufacture or sell agricultural equipment, supplies, and services. The most widely circulated farm publications are the *Farm Journal, Progressive Farmer, Prairie Farmer,* and *Successful Farming.*

☐ **Business magazines,** by far the largest category, target business readers. They include *trade publications,* which target retailers, wholesalers, and other distributors; *industrial magazines,* which target businesspeople involved in manufacturing; and *professional magazines,* which target lawyers, physicians, dentists, architects, teachers, and other groups of professional people. The ad in Exhibit 13-13, which promotes Lee Jeans to retailers and distributors, appeared in a trade magazine.

Magazines may also be classified as local, regional, or national. *Local magazines* have become popular, and now most major U.S. cities have magazines named after them: *San Diego Magazine, New York, Los Angeles, Chicago, Philadelphia, Palm Springs Life,* and *Crain's Chicago Business,* to name a few. Their readership is usually upscale, professional people interested in the arts, fashion, culture, and business.

Regional publications are targeted to a specific area of the country, such as the West or the South. Examples include *Sunset, Southern Living, Yankee,* and

EXHIBIT 13-13

When it comes to creativity in trade ads, the sky's the limit. This rather surreal execution promised retailers that Lee's Sky Wash jeans would really make sales take off.

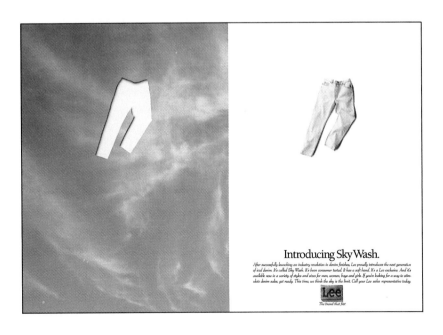

Introducing Sky Wash.

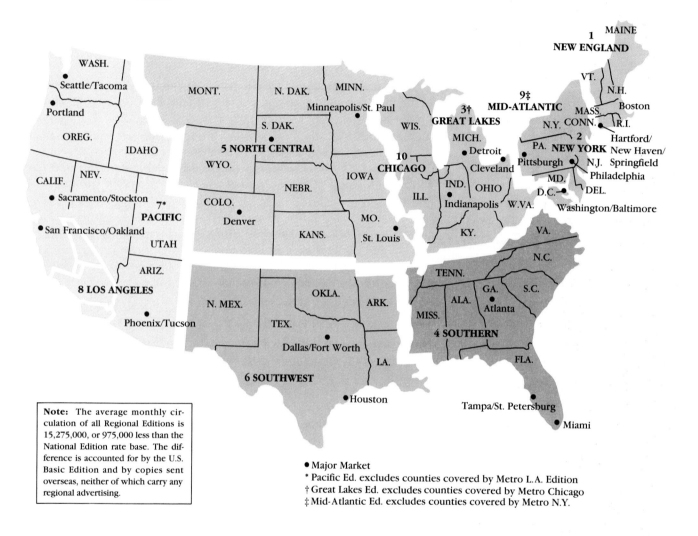

7 Hawaii   7 Alaska

Note: The average monthly circulation of all Regional Editions is 15,275,000, or 975,000 less than the National Edition rate base. The difference is accounted for by the U.S. Basic Edition and by copies sent overseas, neither of which carry any regional advertising.

● Major Market
* Pacific Ed. excludes counties covered by Metro L.A. Edition
† Great Lakes Ed. excludes counties covered by Metro Chicago
‡ Mid-Atlantic Ed. excludes counties covered by Metro N.Y.

EXHIBIT 13–14

The 10 major geographic editions of *Reader's Digest* are shown here.

Pacific Northwest. In addition, national magazines sometimes offer advertisers special market runs that allow the selection of specific geographic regions. *Time, U.S. News & World Report, Newsweek, Woman's Day,* and *Sports Illustrated* have developed their coverage to such an extent that an advertiser wishing to buy a single major market can easily do so. See, for example, Exhibit 13–14, which shows the 10 major geographic editions of *Reader's Digest.*

There are thousands of *national magazines* as well. They range from those with enormous circulations, such as *TV Guide,* which in 1990 had circulation of more than 15.8 million, and *Reader's Digest,* with a national circulation of 16.4 million, to lesser-known national magazines with circulations well under 100,000, such as *Modern Drummer* and *Volleyball Monthly.*[23]

Size

It doesn't take a genius to figure out that magazines come in different shapes and sizes, but sometimes it takes one to figure out how to get one ad to run in different-sized magazines and still look the same. Magazine sizes run the gamut from very large to very small, which makes production standardization an occasional nightmare. The most common magazine sizes might be grouped as follows:

Classification	Magazine	Approximate size of full-page ad
Large	*Life*	4 col. × 170 lines (9⅜ × 12⅛ inches)
Flat	*Time, Newsweek*	3 col. × 140 lines (7 × 10 inches)
Standard	*National Geographic*	2 col. × 119 lines (6 × 8½ inches)
Small or pocket	*Reader's Digest, TV Guide*	2 col. × 91 lines (4½ × 6½ inches)

HOW TO BUY MAGAZINE SPACE

The effective media buyer considers the selection of magazines on the basis of circulation, readership, cost and mechanical requirements, and ad closing dates. To serve the advertiser well, the buyer must understand the magazine's circulation statistics and rate card information.

Understanding Magazine Circulation

In addition to studying the rate card, advertisers must assess the magazine's audience. Data useful in this process include primary and secondary readership figures, the number of subscription and vendor sales, and the number of copies the publisher expects to sell versus those that are actually sold.

Primary and Secondary Readership

Data from the Audit Bureau of Circulations and other verified reports tell the media buyer what the magazine's total circulation is. This is **primary circulation,** and it represents the number of people who receive the publication. They may subscribe or buy it at the newsstand. **Secondary readership,** or **pass-along readership,** can be very important to some magazines—in some cases more than six different people read the same copy of a publication. Consider, for example, how many people read one copy of *Time* in a doctor's waiting room. Multiply that by a million subscribers, and the magazine can boast substantial readership beyond primary readers.

Vertical and Horizontal Publications

The two classifications of business publications are vertical and horizontal. A choice of one or the other depends on how deeply an advertiser wishes to

EXHIBIT 13-15

Apple Computer advertises in both horizontal and vertical magazines. This ad, which describes the benefits of Apple products in a general way, would be appropriate in magazines serving readers in a wide range of industries.

penetrate a particular industry or how widely the advertiser wishes to spread the message. Apple Computer advertises in both horizontal and vertical publications using ads such as that in Exhibit 13-15.

A **vertical publication** covers a specific industry in all its aspects. For example, Cahners Publishing Co. produces *Restaurants & Institutions* strictly for restauranteurs and food service operators. The magazine's editorial content includes everything from news of the restaurant industry to institutional-size recipes.

Horizontal publications, in contrast, deal with a particular job function that exists across a variety of industries. For example, *Packaging* magazine addresses only issues of concern to package engineers and designers, such as new materials that can be used to package various products. Likewise, readers of *Purchasing* work for companies in many different industries; their common link is purchasing management.

Subscription and Vendor Sales

Since World War II, the ratio of subscriptions to newsstand sales has increased. Today, subscriptions account for the majority of sales for most magazines. Newsstands (which also encompass magazine sales in bookstore chains) are still a major outlet for sales of single copies, but no newsstand can handle more than a fraction of the magazines available. Display space is limited, and vendors sometimes complain that distributors make them take publications they do not want in order to get other magazines they do.

From the advertiser's point of view, newsstand sales are impressive because they indicate that the purchaser really wants the magazine and is not merely taking a subscription out of habit. Revenues from single-copy sales account for 34 percent of total revenues for a representative sampling of leading magazines, according to the Magazine Publishers Association. Some publications are sold entirely through newsstand sales. Others, such as most trade publications, are sold entirely by subscription.

Paid and Controlled Circulation

Business publications are distributed on either a **paid circulation** or **controlled circulation** basis. If the publication is available on a paid basis, the recipient must pay the subscription price in order to receive it. *Business Week,* for example, is a paid circulation business magazine.

Circulation that is controlled (free) means the magazine is mailed to a selected list of individuals the publisher feels are in a unique position to influence the purchase of advertised products. *Corporate Video Decisions,* for example, is mailed without charge to managers of corporate video departments. To receive a controlled circulation publication, these people must indicate in writing a desire to receive it and must give their professional designation or occupation. Ordinarily, to qualify for the subscription list, they must also include information about their job title, function, and purchasing duties. In other cases, paying annual dues to an organization entitles the members to a free subscription. Members of the National Association for Female Executives, for example, receive free copies of *Executive Female.*

Advertising rates are based principally on circulation; advertisers don't want to pay to reach subscribers who have little or no interest in what they are selling. Publishers of paid circulation magazines say that subscribers who pay are more likely to read the publication than are those who receive free copies. On the other hand, controlled circulation magazines can characterize their readers as good prospects for the goods and services advertised in their pages. Publishers of controlled circulation publications say giving the publication away free is the only way to get good coverage of the market and that there is little or no effect on readership.

Guaranteed versus Delivered Circulation

A magazine's rate structure is based on its circulation. The *rate base* is the circulation figure upon which the publisher bases its rates, and the **guaranteed circulation** figure is the number of copies of the magazine the publisher expects to circulate. The latter is particularly meaningful for advertisers, because they buy space with the assurance of reaching a certain number of people. Because some copies counted as guaranteed circulation are usually sold on newsstands, it is possible that the publisher may not reach its guaranteed circulation figure. If this *delivered figure* is not reached, the publisher will have to provide a refund. For that reason, most guaranteed circulation figures are stated safely below the average actual delivered circulation.

Merchandising Services

Like newspapers, magazines often provide special services to advertisers. These include mailings prepared for the advertiser to notify dealers of the impending advertisement. Also, countertop cards for use in stores stating "As advertised in" are sometimes forwarded to retailers. Magazines also may provide

☐ Special promotions to stores.

☐ Marketing services that help readers find local outlets through a central phone number.

☐ Response cards that allow readers to send for brochures and catalogs from a variety of advertisers.

☐ Aid in handling sales force, broker, wholesaler, and retailer meetings.

☐ Advance editions for the trade.

☐ Research into brand preference, consumer attitudes, and market conditions.

All of these services are useful tools for the advertiser. Individually or in combination, they increase the effectiveness of magazine advertising.

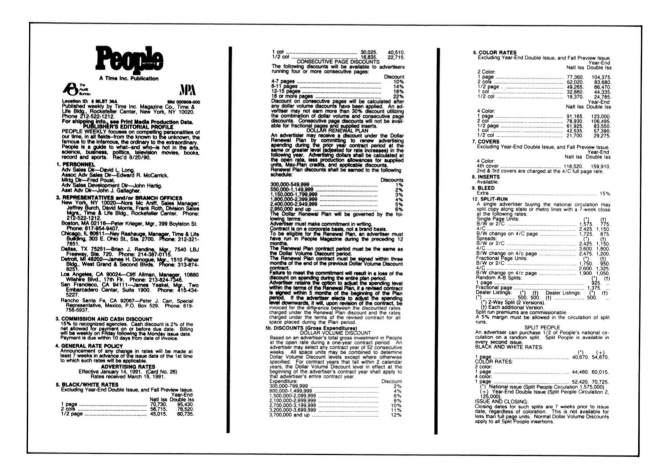

EXHIBIT 13-16

An example of magazine advertising rates.

Rate Cards

Magazine rate cards, like newspaper rate cards, follow a standard format like the rate card for *People* magazine shown in Exhibit 13-16. This helps advertisers readily determine advertising costs, discount opportunities, the magazine's mechanical requirements, the issue and closing dates, special editions, and additional costs for features like color, inserts, bleed pages, split runs, or preferred positions.

Rates

One way to compare magazines is to look at the one-time cost for a full-page, black-and-white ad, multiplied by 1,000, and divided by the publication's total circulation:

$$\frac{\text{Page rate} \times 1,000}{\text{Circulation}} = \text{Cost per page per thousand (CPM)}$$

For example, in 1990, the page rate for a one-time, black-and-white ad in *Flying* magazine was $12,560 on total paid circulation of 321,801. At the same time, *Plane & Pilot* magazine offered a full-page, black-and-white ad for $4,270 on total paid circulation of 103,670. Both aviation publications claimed substantial pass-along readership. Which was the better buy from the standpoint of cost per thousand?

EXHIBIT 13-17   Selected Consumer Magazines: Circulation, Readership, and Cost

Magazine	Total paid circulation	Readers per copy			Page cost for four-color ad
		Men	Women	Total	
Modern Maturity	21,033,000	.62	1.03	1.65	$218,215
Reader's Digest	16,602,000	1.27	1.72	2.99	124,730
TV Guide	16,334,000	1.29	1.59	2.88	112,900
National Geographic	8,571,000	1.93	1.76	3.69	139,280
Better Homes and Gardens	8,078,000	3.12	1.04	4.16	119,000
Family Circle	5,195,000	.67	3.82	4.49	82,165
Ladies' Home Journal	5,083,000	.49	3.31	3.80	78,200
Good Housekeeping	4,880,000	.96	5.08	6.04	103,190
Time	4,515,000	2.12	1.83	3.95	120,130
Woman's Day	4,358,000	.44	4.04	4.48	73,075
Redbook	3,846,000	.49	2.90	3.39	71,530
Sports Illustrated	3,739,000	4.64	1.43	6.07	113,220
National Enquirer	3,705,000	1.90	2.96	4.86	47,200
Playboy	3,347,000	3.02	.87	3.89	65,280
Star	3,206,000	1.02	1.99	3.01	37,300
People Weekly	3,203,000	4.28	6.99	11.28	91,165
Newsweek	3,173,000	3.94	2.89	6.83	100,980
Cosmopolitan	2,512,000	.89	4.26	5.15	58,435

Exhibit 13-17 lists the circulations, readership, and color page rates for 18 leading consumer magazines. Using these data, you can calculate which national buys offer the best CPMs.

As with newspapers, magazines give discounts based on frequency and volume. *Frequency discounts* are generally based on the number of insertions; *volume discounts* are offered on the total space used during a specific period. Almost all magazines offer *cash discounts* (usually 2 percent), and some offer discounts on the purchase of four or more consecutive pages in a single issue. Recent declines in the amount of magazine advertising have led many publications to offer other forms of discounts, as well. Recent evidence suggests that more than 50 percent of magazine publishers are willing to negotiate their rates, with discounts of up to half off formal rates. This rate-cutting trend is expected to continue.[24]

Color, if available, normally costs 25 to 60 percent more than black-and-white. Some publications, such as *Money,* even offer metallic and aluminum-based inks and special colors (beyond the four typically used in color printing) by special arrangement.

Bleed pages add as much as 20 percent to regular rates, although the typical increase is about 15 percent.

Second and third cover rates (the inside covers) are typically less than the rate for the fourth (back) cover. The cover rates usually include color, whether the ad is to be run in color or not. *Newsweek* charges $108,050 for second and third covers and $138,505 for the fourth cover, for example.

Magazines offer different rates for advertisements in issues that go to particular geographic or demographic markets. While geographic editions target geographic markets, demographic editions allow the advertiser to reach readers who share a demographic trait, such as age, income level, or professional status. For example, *Time* offers one-page four-color ads (one-time insertion) in Boston for $10,779 (166,000 circulation); in Texas for $12,698 (210,000 circulation); to college students for $21,100 (413,042 circulation); and to the 50 largest metropolitan markets for $107,200 (3,100,000 circulation). Thus, advertisers pay more for geographic or demographic editions with broader reach.

Issue and Closing Dates

Three dates significantly affect magazine advertising purchases:

☐ **Cover date**—the date appearing on the cover.

☐ **On-sale date**—the date the magazine is actually issued.

☐ **Closing date**—the date when all ad material must be in the hands of the publisher for inclusion in a specific issue. The closing date is sometimes the first thing the advertiser looks at. After determining whether the advertising materials can be ready by a certain date and which issue would be best, the advertiser or agency can buy space according to the factors we have discussed.

SOURCES OF PRINT MEDIA INFORMATION

To make informed media buying decisions, advertisers and their agencies require information about newspapers and magazines. There are many general sources of such information. The publication itself can provide more detailed information about its readership, circulation, rates, advertising policies, and editorial focus. Here are some principal sources of information that media planners commonly analyze.

☐ *Audit Bureau of Circulations (ABC).* The **Audit Bureau of Circulations** was formed in 1914 to verify circulation and other marketing data on magazines and newspapers. Each publication submits a semiannual statement, which specially trained ABC field auditors check. They examine all records necessary to verify the figures that the publisher reports.

The information the publisher supplies includes paid circulation (for a specified period) for its regional, metropolitan, and demographic editions, broken down by subscription, single-copy sales, and average paid circulation. The ABC also analyzes new and renewal subscriptions by price, duration, sales channel, and type of promotion.

☐ *Simmons Market Research Bureau.* SMRB is a well-respected syndicated research organization that publishes magazine readership studies. Its annual *Study of Media and Markets* report provides data on the purchase behavior and demographics of readers, based on personal interviews. In addition, SMRB publishes the *National College Study* and the *Simmons Teen-Age Research Study* twice a year.[25]

☐ *Mediamark Research Inc.* MRI also conducts personal interviews to determine readership patterns. In addition to reporting the audiences and readership demographics for leading consumer magazines and national newspapers, MRI publishes annual studies on the affluent market, business-purchase decision makers, and the top 10 local markets.[26]

☐ *Newspaper Advertising Bureau.* Several industry organizations and publications offer helpful aids for planning newspaper advertising. One of them is the **Newspaper Advertising Bureau** of the American Newspaper Publishers Association, the promotional arm of the nation's newspaper industry. The bureau provides its newspaper members with market information by conducting field research and collecting case histories. And, as mentioned earlier, it has created such programs as Newsplan and the Newspaper Co-Op Network to aid national advertisers in obtaining better rates and reaching multiple markets in a timely fashion.

☐ *Magazine Publishers Association (MPA).* The **Magazine Publishers Association** has a total membership of more than 230 publishers, representing 1,200 magazines. This trade group makes available the circulation figures of all ABC member magazines (general and farm) from 1914 to date, with annual figures related to population. It estimates the number of consumer magazine copies sold by year from 1943, and it lists the 100 leading ABC magazines according to circulation. MPA provides a sales, research, and promotion arm that attempts to stimulate greater and more effective use of magazine advertising.

☐ *Standard Rate and Data Service (SRDS).* **Standard Rate and Data Service** publishes *Newspaper Rates and Data, Consumer Magazine and Agri-Media Rates and Data,* and *Business Publication Rates and Data,* as well as other monthly directories that eliminate the necessity for advertisers and their agencies to obtain rate cards for every publication.

SUBSCRIBER DEMOGRAPHICS

Male/Female	73%/27%
Median Age	37.8 years
18-34	39%
18-49	88%
Median Household Income	$56,660
Average Household Income	$67,000
Professional/Managerial[1]	63.3%
Attended/Graduated College	86%

RUNNING

Average Weekly Miles Run	23.9 miles
Average Running Days/Week	4.2 days
Average Time Running	9.4 years
Competed in Running Event*	77%
Plan to Enter Competitive Running Event*	89%

FOOTWEAR

Average Number of Pairs of Running Shoes Owned	3.0 pairs
Purchased Running Shoes*	86%
Average Amount Spent**	$156
Total Pairs Purchased**	1,209,869
Total Amount Spent**	$60.5 million

Gave Advice:

% of Time Recommended Specific Brand/Company	93%
Number of People Advised*	1,476,601

(Based on circulation rate base of 425,000)

APPAREL
(Excluding Shoes)

Total Amount Spent*	$47.3 million
Purchased*	
Running Socks	65%
Running Shorts	64
Sunglasses	40
Sport-Tights	38
Bicycle Clothing	25
Sweat Suits	22

FITNESS ACTIVITY

Participate*

Bicycling	78%
Swimming	72
Weight Lifting	69
Health Clubs/ Gym Workout	55
Aerobic Exercise	53
Hiking/Backpacking	42
Golf	38
Skiing	36
Tennis	36
Overnight Camping	35

SPORTING EQUIPMENT

Own

Sports Watch/ Chronograph	71%
Weights	68
Bicycle	63
Tennis Racquet	47
Stationary Bicycle	36
Skis	35
Weight Workout Bench	33
Bike Helmet	31
Rowing Machine	18

☐ *Audience studies provided by publications.* Circulation figures are not enough. Newspapers and magazines also offer media planners many other types of statistical reports. The data in these reports detail reader income, demographic profiles, percentages of different kinds of advertising carried, and more. Exhibit 13-18 is an example of this type of audience information supplied by *Runner's World* magazine.

Summary

The printed page in general and the newspaper in particular provide a unique, flexible medium for advertising creativity. The newspaper is a mass medium that is read by almost everybody. It offers great flexibility, which assists creativity, and its printed message lasts. However, newspapers also have their disadvantages: lack of audience selectivity, short life span, poor production quality, heavy advertising competition, potentially poor ad placement, and overlapping circulation. Still, the newspaper is the major community-serving medium today for both news and advertising.

The newspaper's rates, mechanical requirements, and other pertinent information are printed on its rate card. The rates listed vary for local and national advertisers. Also listed are the newspaper's short-rate policy, combination rates, frequency discounts, run-of-paper rates, and other data.

Magazines offer different advantages. They are the most selective of all media and are flexible in both readership and advertising. They offer unsurpassed availability of color, excellent reproduction quality, authority and believability, long shelf life, and prestige at an efficient cost. However, they often require long lead times, have problems offering reach and frequency, and are subject to heavy advertising competition. And the cost of advertising in some magazines is very high.

In selecting magazines for advertising, the media buyer must consider a publication's circulation, its readership, and its cost and mechanical requirements. A magazine's rates may be determined by several factors: its primary and secondary readership, the number of subscription and vendor sales, and the number of copies guaranteed versus those actually delivered.

Magazine rate cards, like newspaper rate cards, follow a standard format so advertisers can readily determine advertising costs. They list black-and-white and color rates, discounts, issue and closing dates, and mechanical requirements.

Questions for Review and Discussion

1. Retailers are the leading local newspaper advertisers. Why do you think they rely so heavily on this medium?
2. In what ways can advertisers improve the selectivity of their newspaper ads?
3. What factors should advertisers consider in deciding which of several local papers (including dailies and weeklies) to use for advertising?
4. Do you agree with newspaper publishers that national advertisers should be charged a higher rate than local advertisers? Support your position.
5. How do advertisers benefit from split runs?
6. If you worked in the advertising department of a premium-priced furniture manufacturer, would you recommend magazine advertising? Why or why not?
7. If you were the advertising manager for a magazine aimed at senior citizens, what advantages would you cite to potential advertisers?
8. What is the advantage of magazine advertising to businesses that sell to other businesses?
9. If you were buying magazine space for a jeans manufacturer, what factors would you take into account in choosing the magazines?
10. What is the importance of the Audit Bureau of Circulations?

ELECTRONIC MEDIA

Objective: To describe the various factors advertisers must consider when using broadcast and cable television and radio in the creative mix. Each medium has its own unique characteristics, advantages, and drawbacks. Therefore, to achieve positive results, the advertiser must be able to judge the merits of each medium and know how to buy cost-effective advertising time.

After studying this chapter, you will be able to:

☐ Differentiate between the advantages and drawbacks of broadcast television as an advertising medium.

☐ Describe the types of broadcast advertising and the process of television audience measurement.

☐ Delineate the primary factors to consider when buying television time.

☐ Outline the advantages and drawbacks of cable television as an advertising medium.

☐ Compare the process of buying time on cable television with that of buying time on broadcast television.

☐ Analyze the advantages and drawbacks of using radio in the creative mix.

☐ Explain the major factors to consider when buying radio time.

Suppose you're marketing a product that's about as dull as they come. When consumers need one, they'll grab a package or two at the supermarket checkout stand without giving much thought to the benefits of one brand versus another. Although your product leads in overall market share, your chief competitor has taken the lead in one important segment of the $3 billion market. What do you do to get the consumer's attention on a grand scale and in a relatively short period of time?

In case you haven't guessed by now, the product is a common household battery—specifically, the Eveready Energizer. Its chief competitor is Duracell, which is number one in the fast-growing alkaline segment of the market. To keep Duracell from gaining even more ground, Eveready needed to come up with an advertising campaign that would put the spotlight on Energizer. Not only did it succeed in grabbing the spotlight, but Energizer made advertising history as well.

Fortunately, Energizer and its ad agency, Chiat/Day/Mojo Inc., chose the perfect advertising medium for their campaign. Where else but on television could a battery-powered pink bunny so delight viewers that it may well join the ranks of other commercial and cultural icons like Speedy Alka-Seltzer, the Pillsbury Doughboy, and the California Raisins?

What made ad history, however, was that the drum-beating Energizer Bunny (E.B.) tried something no other celebrity had dared to before. E.B. marched right out of its own ads and then seconds later interrupted pitches for other products. Viewers who might have tuned out during the commercial were jolted back to consciousness by something obviously out of the ordinary. Eventually they realized they'd been had—E.B. was not interrupting real ads but merely interrupting dead-on spoofs of typical TV commercials, as shown in Exhibit 14-1.

EXHIBIT 14-1

The Energizer bunny shocked television audiences into paying attention when it appeared to interrupt other, supposedly unrelated, commercials. Whether or not the bunny increased market share, it certainly achieved name recognition for Energizer while soaring to stardom and showing how effective television advertising can be.

ANNCR: Don't be fooled by commercials where one battery company's toy outlasts the other's. Energizer was never invited to their playoffs. Because nothing outlasts the Energizer.

SUPER: ENERGIZER

ANNCR: They keep going and going and going . . .

(MUSIC: PIANO)

WOMAN 1: I love the sound of the rain.

WOMAN 2: And I love the taste of your fresh-brewed coffee.

WOMAN 1: Thanks, but it's not fresh-brewed. It's new Tres Caf . . .

(SFX: DRUMS)

ANNCR: . . . still going. Nothing outlasts the Energizer.

SUPER: ENERGIZER

ANNCR: They keep going and going and going . . .

Ad critics hailed the campaign as one of the best. But the real evidence of E.B.'s impact was its instant assimilation into popular culture, thanks to the help of real live celebrities like David Letterman on "Late Night" and the comedy cast of "Saturday Night Live." Eveready even started getting calls from customers desperately seeking E.B. dolls for their kids. During one eight-week period, the company sold 20,000 E.B. look-alikes, which undoubtedly helped cover the $90,000 it cost to build the two robot rabbits used in the commercials.[1]

But how about selling batteries? Although Eveready is not yet boasting about impressive market share gains, neither is Duracell. More important for the long-term, the Energizer campaign succeeded in claiming a prominent position in the minds of consumers nationwide. In fact, Energizer made it onto *Advertising Age*'s list of top ten best-recalled ads for the first time in November 1990.[2]

The Energizer campaign is a stunning example of how advertisers can make effective use of broadcast television to quickly reach a large proportion of the population, get their attention, and establish product identity. This chapter explores other advantages of broadcast TV and its various drawbacks. The chapter also addresses the characteristics of other electronic media, including how cable television, videocassette rentals, and radio compete with broadcast television and how they are used as important parts of the creative mix.

OVERVIEW OF THE BROADCAST TELEVISION MEDIUM

There are approximately 1,100 commercial TV stations in the United States. Approximately half are VHF (very high frequency—channels 2 through 13) and the other half are UHF (ultrahigh frequency—channels 14 through 83). Any station not affiliated with one of the four national networks (ABC, NBC, CBS, Fox) operates as an independent station. Both network affiliates and independent stations may subscribe to nationally syndicated programs as well as originate their own programming. The increasing competition from **cable television** has caused the national networks to lose viewers during recent years. To compensate, some of the networks have invested in cable TV systems or started their own. NBC, for example, started CNBC, and ABC has an 80 percent interest in ESPN.[3]

Audience Trends

Middle-income, high school-educated individuals and their families are the heaviest viewers of **broadcast television.** Most television programming, therefore, is directed at this group. People with considerably higher income and education usually have a more diversified range of interests and entertainment options.

The average number of television viewing hours ranges from a low of 23 hours per week to a high of 36. Children under 12, for example, view an average of 23 hours per week; middle-aged men, 24 hours; teens, 26 hours; and middle-aged women, 28. Older women watch TV the most (36 hours a

EXHIBIT 14-2

Audience composition (shown here by selected program type) varies considerably.

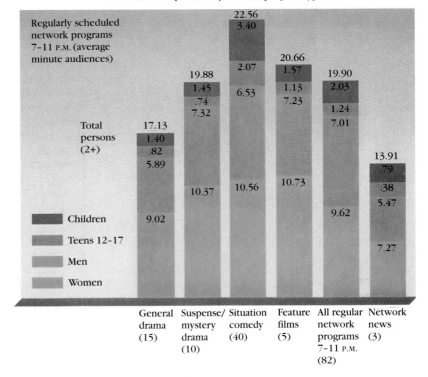

Audience composition by selected program type

( ) = Number of programs, November 1989

week). By age 18, the average child has watched more than 22,000 hours (two and one-half years) of TV.[4]

Individual program audiences vary a great deal. A sports event, for example, attracts proportionately more men in the 18 to 34 age category than any other group. Look at the audience composition statistics in Exhibit 14-2. How would you describe the primary viewers of network feature films?

The audience for broadcast TV may be changing as more households acquire cable and VCRs. Households with cable already watch less network TV than noncable households do, and predictions are that home video will have a 25 percent share of overall TV viewing by 1995.[5] As a result of such audience fragmentation, advertising on network TV will become less cost-effective. In fact, many advertisers are already shifting a portion of their advertising dollars to cable TV. Although advertising on home videos is still somewhat controversial, more advertisers are likely to consider it a worth-while option if the practice becomes more widely accepted.

Growth of Television Advertising

In 1950, only 3 percent of total U.S. advertising volume was placed on television. That amounted to $171 million. By 1990, however, that figure had grown to over $26 billion and accounted for more than 21 percent of all ad spending.[6] The major network television advertisers and their expenditures are listed in Exhibit 14-3.

EXHIBIT 14-3	Top 10 Network TV Advertisers in the United States	

Rank	Advertiser	TV ad expenditures, 1990*
1	General Motors Corp.	598.4
2	Procter & Gamble Co.	556.1
3	Philip Morris Cos.	402.2
4	Kellogg Co.	301.3
5	Sears Roebuck & Co.	253.8
6	AT&T Co.	244.9
7	McDonald's Corp.	231.0
8	Johnson & Johnson	211.4
9	Ford Motor Co.	196.9
10	PepsiCo	193.4

* Dollars are in millions.

Types of Broadcast Advertising

Advertisers can buy time on broadcast television several ways: they may sponsor an entire program, participate in a program, purchase spots from syndicators, or use spot announcements between programs.

Network Advertising

One way to advertise in the United States is to purchase airtime from one of the national **networks:** Columbia Broadcasting Company (CBS), National Broadcasting Company (NBC), American Broadcasting Company (ABC), or the Fox Broadcasting Company (FBC). Networks offer the large advertiser convenience and efficiency because the message can be broadcast simultaneously through network affiliates throughout the country.

When an advertiser presents a program alone, it is called a **sponsorship.** The advertiser is responsible for the program content and the cost of production as well as the advertising. This is so costly that single sponsorships are usually limited to specials.

Companies that sponsor programs (AT&T, Xerox, and Hallmark, for example) have two important advantages. First, the public more readily identifies with the product(s), and the company gains from the prestige attached to sponsoring first-rate entertainment. Second, the sponsor controls the placement and content of the commercials. The commercials can be fit to the program and run any length desired so long as they remain within network or station regulations.

The centralization offered by networks also simplifies bookkeeping, as the advertiser gets only one bill. The total cost per thousand is low—lower even than time purchased on a spot basis, which will be discussed later.

The high cost of sponsoring a program has encouraged many advertisers to **cosponsor** programs, permitting them to realize some of the advantages of sponsorship but at lower cost and risk. They often sponsor on alternate weeks or divide the program into segments. Most sports events, for instance, are sold as multiple sponsorships.

Most network TV advertising is sold on the **participation basis,** with several advertisers buying 30- or 60-second segments within the program. Advertisers can participate in a program once or several times on a regular or irregular basis. This allows the advertiser to spread out the budget and makes it easier to get in and out of a program without a long-term commitment. It also enables smaller advertisers to buy a limited amount of time and still have nationwide coverage.

Network advertising has its disadvantages, however. An advertiser who desires to buy fewer stations than the full network lineup often finds preference given to those willing to buy more. The advertiser who seeks to advertise to a limited market usually finds that the network lineup does not coincide with that need. Furthermore, placing network ads requires a long lead time, which reduces flexibility. Finally, all ads accepted by networks must go through their standards and practices departments and meet strict rules and guidelines.

Spot Announcements

National **spot announcements** offer the advertiser greater flexibility since commercials can be concentrated in the desired markets. In addition, spots are less expensive than participations because they run in clusters between programs. Spots may also be used to introduce a new product into one area at a time, which advertisers with limited distribution and budgets find advantageous.

Spots may be sold nationally or locally in segments of 10, 15, 30, or 60 seconds. Spot advertising is more difficult to purchase than network advertising because it involves contacting each station directly. However, the station rep system, in which individuals act as sales and service representatives for a number of stations, has helped reduce this problem.

The late 1980s saw a significant shift toward greater regional advertising through the use of national spots. Campbell Soup, for example, increased its local spot TV ad budget to address regional differences in eating habits. Other companies such as Procter & Gamble invested more heavily in spots to support new products in regional markets.

But spot advertising is available only at network station breaks and when network advertisers have purchased less than the full lineup. Thus, spot ads are likely to be lost in the clutter and tend to have lower viewership.

Syndication

An increasingly popular alternative to network advertising is advertising on syndicated programs. Television syndication comes in three forms: off-network, first-run, and barter. **Offnetwork syndication** includes programs that originally appeared on the networks and are now available to individual stations for rebroadcast. **First-run syndication** includes original shows produced specifically for the syndication market. Finally, **barter syndication** includes first-run programs that are offered free or for a reduced rate to stations but come with some of the ad space presold to national advertisers. The most popular barter syndication programs, including "Wheel of Fortune," "Entertainment Tonight," and "The Oprah Winfrey Show," can be found on stations in nearly every U.S. city. Barter syndication is one of the fastest-growing trends in television.[7] Exhibit 14-4 shows how barter syndication works.

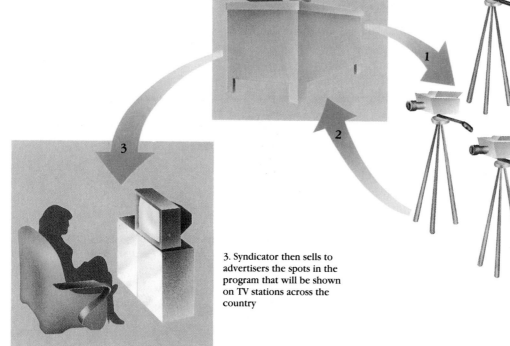

1. Barter syndicator provides a TV program either at reduced rates or for no cash

3. Syndicator then sells to advertisers the spots in the program that will be shown on TV stations across the country

2. TV stations: in return, the stations agree to give up some advertising spots in that program to the syndicator

EXHIBIT 14-4

This diagram illustrates how barter syndication works.

Local

Retailers, often in cooperation with nationally known manufacturers, may buy time from local stations. As a rule, local airtime is sold as spot announcements, but sometimes programs are developed and sponsored by local advertisers. Local firms may also buy the rights to a syndicated film series and sponsor it in their own market.

USING BROADCAST TELEVISION IN THE CREATIVE MIX

Although TV advertising seems to come under severe attack on a somewhat regular basis, no one ever denies its power and creative potential. Without television advertising, Federal Express, for example, may have never gotten off the ground. However, it is television's very potential for impact and creativity that has fueled so much criticism. As a means of reaching a mass audience, no other medium today has the unique creative abilities of television: the combination of sight, sound, and movement; the opportunity to demonstrate the product; the potential to use special effects; the empathy of the viewer; and the believability of seeing it happen right before your eyes. In fact, 57 percent of viewers surveyed said that television is the most authoritative advertising source, compared to only 20 percent for newspapers, 11 percent for magazines, and 9 percent for radio.[8]

Advantages of Broadcast Television

Broadcast television has grown faster than any other advertising medium in history. From its beginnings after World War II, TV has emerged as the medium that attracts the largest volume of national advertising—totaling more than $19 billion in 1990.[9] Why? Because contemporary television offers advertisers unique advantages over competing media.

Mass Coverage and Low Cost

A substantial portion of broadcast television's national advertising revenue comes from the packaged goods industry (foods and drugs). Procter & Gamble, for instance, is a leading spender in TV advertising. Its broadcast TV expenditures in 1990 were nearly $980 million, of which more than $556 million went to network advertising.[10] For Procter & Gamble's nationwide marketing of high-volume, low-profit packaged goods products, it uses television to reach a mass audience and presell its brand names at a very low cost per consumer.

A full 98 percent of all U.S. homes have a TV set, and most have more than one. Of the households that own TV sets, 90 percent view TV at least once during the average day and 98 percent tune in during an average week. Viewing time for the average household has increased over the past few decades, from five hours, six minutes per day in 1960 to more than seven hours per day in 1991.[11]

Typical network nighttime programs reach 15 percent of all television households. The more popular shows and special attractions reach 25 percent and more. For example, over 40 percent of TV households are usually reached by a Super Bowl game.

Broadcast television, therefore, has historically been a mass medium for mass-consumption products. Despite the often huge initial outlays for commercial production and advertising time, television's equally huge audiences bring the per exposure cost for each commercial down to a comparatively low level.

Selectivity

Television audiences are mass audiences, but they can vary a great deal depending on the time of day, the day of the week, and the nature of the programming. This permits the advertiser to present the message when the potential audience is best (as AT&T was able to do with its commercial, shown in Exhibit 14-5 on p. 502). Furthermore, advertisers can reach select geographic audiences by buying local and regional markets.

Impact

The ability to bring a moving picture with sound into the living rooms of a nation is tantamount to having an army of door-to-door sellers. Television offers an immediacy that other forms of advertising are unable to achieve, with the product being demonstrated in full color right before the customer's eyes. Seeing a hamburger cooked and eaten on the living room screen has stimulated many a viewer to go to a fast-food outlet for a similar meal.

EXHIBIT 14-5

Aired during network news shows when viewership by businesspeople is at its highest, this

corporate ad strives to do more than simply create a positive image for the company. It also

communicates a message about the company's products and services.

SINGERS: *We can help put people together . . . "*

AT&T can help your business grow . . .

VO: For us at American Express, building one worldwide nerve center was a dream come true.

Finding the communications and information systems that could grow with us might have been a nightmare.

We chose AT&T.

You don't trust your dream to just anyone.

ANNCR VO: Whether it's telephones, information systems, long distance services or computers . . .

SINGERS: *The Right Choice. AT&T.*

Creativity

Television's creative potential is limited only by the commercial creator's talents. The various facets of the TV commercial—sight, sound, motion, and color—permit infinite original and imaginative appeals. For some interesting facts on creating effective TV commercials, see the Checklist of What Works Best in Television.

Prestige

Hallmark, Xerox, Mobil, Exxon, and IBM have all experienced an increase in prestige and corporate awareness by sponsoring dramatic presentations and other cultural programs. Potential distributors, the company's sales force, and customers are impressed by a product's association with quality programming.

Social Dominance

Television has exhibited a power that goes beyond impact and prestige. The entire nation has been emotionally stirred by TV screenings of the Olympic Games, space travel, assassinations, wars, and political scandals. Most people in North America under age 35 don't know what life is like without television—they have grown up with TV as an important part of their environment.

Checklist of What Works Best in Television

□ *The picture must tell the story.* Forget every other rule in this chapter, and you will still be ahead of the game. Television is a *visual* medium. That's why the people in front of a set are called *viewers.* Try this trick for looking at a storyboard. *Cover the words.* What is the message of the commercial with the sound turned off? Is there a message at all?

□ *Look for a "key visual."* Here's another test to apply to the storyboard. Can you pick out *one* frame that visually sums up the whole message? Most good commercials can be reduced to this single key visual. A commercial with many different scenes may look interesting in storyboard form but can turn out to be an overcomplicated piece of film.

□ *Grab the viewer's attention.* The *first five seconds* of a commercial are crucial. Analysis of audience reaction shows either a sharp drop or a sharp rise in interest during this time. *Commercial attention does not build.* Your audience can only become less interested, never more. The level you reach in the first five seconds is the highest you will get, so don't save your punches. Offer the viewer something right off the bat. *News. A problem* to which you have the solution. A *conflict* that is involving.

□ *Be single-minded.* A good commercial is uncomplicated. Direct. It never makes the viewer do a lot of mental work. The basic commercial length in U.S. television is 30 seconds. The content possible in that time is outlined in the phrase: "name-claim-demonstration"—the name of your product, your consumer benefit, and the reason the consumer should believe it. Longer commercials *should not add copy points.* A 60-second commercial tells the same story as the 30-second one, with more leisure and detail. Or—best of all—*repetition.* The 60-second allows time for

a mood to be created; the 30-second generally does not. The 10-second and 15-second commercials are one-point messages. The 10-second registers the brand name and promise. The 15-second makes the promise more explicit.

□ *Register the name of your product.* Too often, a viewer will remember the commercial but not the name of your brand. This is a particularly troublesome problem with new products. Showing the package on screen and mouthing the name is not enough. Take extra pains to implant your product name in the viewer's mind.

□ *The tone of your advertising must reflect your product personality.* If you are fortunate enough to have a product with an established brand image, your advertising *must* reflect that image. It takes dedication on the part of advertiser and agency to build a brand personality. Discipline yourself to reject advertising that conflicts with it. (It helps to have a written "personality statement" of your product; if it were a person, what sort of person would it be?) When you launch a new product, the very *tone* of your announcement commercial tells viewers what to expect. From that moment on, it is hard to change their minds. Once you have decided on a personality for your product, sustain it in every commercial. Change campaigns when you must but retain the same tone of voice.

□ *Avoid "talky" commercials.* Look for the simplest, and most memorable, set of words to get across your consumer benefit. Every word must work hard. A 30-second commercial usually allows you *no more* than 65 words, a 60-second commercial twice that amount. Be specific. Pounce on clichés, flabbiness, and superlatives. Try this discipline: When you ask for 10 words to be added to a commercial, decide which 10 you would *delete* to make room for them.

The real relationship between the power of television and the sale of an advertiser's product is difficult to gauge. However, we can safely assume that the magnetic attraction of television events gives this medium a potential for advertising unlike any other.

Drawbacks of Broadcast Television

Although television's power as a creative tool may be unmatched, broadcast television still has many drawbacks that keep it from being used by most advertisers. In many instances, television just doesn't "fit" in the creative mix.

EXHIBIT 14-6   Network Television Advertising Rates

	Average rating		Cost of 30-second commercial	
	Low	High	Low	High
Daytime				
Early morning (7-9 A.M.)	1.3	4.4	$ 2,200	$ 19,000
Weekday (10 A.M.-4:30 P.M.)	2.2	8.1	4,600	30,000
Weekend (children)	1.3	6.7	3,000	23,400
Prime time	6.9	26.4	45,000	307,600
Late night	1.0	3.5	1,800	40,000

Advertising time on top-rated programs shown during the best viewing times carries a higher price tag because of the larger audience.

This may be because of cost, lack of audience selectivity, inherent brevity, or the clutter of competitive messages.

Cost

Broadcast television suffers its greatest handicap from the high cost of producing commercials and buying airtime. The production costs for a TV spot vary with the way the advertiser chooses to present the product. National advertisers, for example, film their most expensive commercials at a cost of $200,000 to more than $1 million each.[12] The second major area of expense is network time, as shown in Exhibit 14-6. A single 30-second commercial during prime time may cost as much as $300,000 for top-rated shows that claim the largest percentage of viewers. The average cost of a prime-time commercial is about $125,000. Special attractions can cost much more. A half-minute of commercial time during the 1991 Super Bowl cost about $800,000, for example.[13]

For the large advertiser, television can be relatively efficient, with the cost per thousand households running from $2 for advertising on shows rated at the lower end of the scale to $10 for top-rated shows. But the cost of large coverage, even at relatively low rates, usually prices the small and medium-sized advertisers out of the market.

Limits to Selectivity

Broadcast television is not cost-effective for advertisers seeking a very specific, small audience. Broadcast television is also losing some of its selectivity because of changing audience trends. For example, daytime network TV used to deliver a large female audience, but now fewer women tune in during the day. Women are working outside the home or are watching programs on cable or independent stations.[14] This frustrates advertisers who have traditionally promoted their products on soap operas to reach the target audience of women under age 50.

Brevity

An advertising message on broadcast television usually lasts only 30 seconds. The objective is to grab viewers' attention and leave them with a favorable attitude toward the product (or at least make them remember it). But in 30 seconds, that's a tall task.

Studies have shown that most TV viewers can't remember the product or company promoted in the most recent TV ad they watched—even if it was within the last five minutes.[15] Recall is improved with the length of the commercial—60-second spots are remembered better than 30-second spots.

In 1984, all three major networks began offering **split-30s,** which are 30-second spots in which the advertiser promotes two separate products with separate messages. Then, in the fall of 1985, CBS started accepting 15-second spots. A year later ABC and NBC followed suit. Now more than a third of commercials aired are :15s (15 seconds). Fifteen-second spots are popular with advertisers because they typically sell for half as much as :30s in network TV.[16] However, the percentage of :15s declined from a high of nearly 39 percent in 1989 to an estimated 35 percent in 1990. Buyers and sellers of network time offer various reasons for the decline, including creative considerations, bargain prices for network time, and increasing restrictions by the Big 3 networks.[17]

Clutter

One major drawback to television advertising is that a commercial is seldom seen in an isolated position. It is usually surrounded by station-break announcements, credits, public-service announcements, and "billboards" (just the name or slogan of a product), not to mention six or seven other commercials. With all these messages competing for attention, the viewer often comes away annoyed and confused and with a high rate of product misidentification.

Zipping and Zapping

With the advent of videocassette recorders (VCRs) and other home electronic gadgets, TV advertisers are faced with the additional challenges of zipping and zapping. **Zipping** refers to the ability of VCR users to skip through the commercials when replaying programs they have taped; **zapping** refers to the tendency of remote-control users to change channels at the beginning of a commercial break.

To counteract zipping, zapping, clutter, and brevity, the creators of TV commercials must concentrate on devising messages that immediately capture viewer attention, present a single message in an entertaining way, and avoid irritating or insulting the intelligence of their audience. But what is an advertiser to do when its brilliantly created, captivating message is sandwiched in with four or five other ads during a commercial break? The viewer may already be gone and the advertiser's dollars wasted.

TELEVISION AUDIENCE MEASUREMENT

Audience measurement is an important consideration for television advertisers. It helps ensure that a specific commercial is reaching the target market and that the price paid is in proportion to the number of viewers who will see the commercial.

Audience statistics, for example, helped TRW decide whether TV was the right medium for an advertising campaign. TRW needed to do something to spur investor interest in its securities—financial analysts were ignoring it, and shareholders were becoming dissatisfied with the stock's performance. The company decided to use television advertising to inform financial decision makers (analysts, pension fund managers, bank portfolio managers, investment bankers, stockbrokers, and corporate executives) about TRW, its activities, its growth, and its future.

But first TRW had to be sure it could reach its target audience efficiently through the medium of television. That meant studying the audiences of various programs and analyzing the programs' impact and cost-effectiveness against those of other media vehicles. It required an understanding of audience measurement techniques and the terminology used for television advertising.

ETHICAL DILEMMA IN ADVERTISING
Children's Television Advertising: The Medium and the Message

Kids have become a potent force in America's economy. They spend over $6.2 billion of their own money each year, and for the first time in history, they're also helping their parents make important purchasing decisions. In fact, according to James McNeal, a Texas A&M University marketing professor and author of *Children as Consumers,* kids influence their parents' buying decisions to the tune of $50 billion each year. It's no surprise then that the number of "adult" products being advertised to children has doubled over the last decade.

Advertisers love kids, because kids love to shop. That's why every day children are barraged by television advertising urging them to buy, buy, buy. Some say that's a good thing. Cy Schneider, author of *The Electronic Pied Piper: The Business and Art of Children's Television,* believes that "Enlightened ads that really understand what's going on in the home, in terms of buying, are creating dialogues between parents and children about products and the pluses and minuses of buying one brand instead of another."

Consumers Union disagrees. CU charges that children's advertising is anything but enlightened and that naive youngsters are sitting ducks for the sophisticated tactics of advertisers who see them only as a market. CU believes that advertisers must cultivate a sense of responsibility toward kids and accuses companies of "creating demand for products that are often unnecessary, shortlived, overpriced, or worthless."

Some experts say children are particularly vulnerable to television advertising because they're highly impressionable viewers who spend almost everything they earn, don't comparison shop, and don't make logical purchasing decisions. They're also anxious to keep up with the other kids on the block, which is why fad products come and go so quickly. In the make-believe world of television, the boundaries between fantasy and reality are often further blurred by programming that's been spawned by successful consumer products. Which came first: the Teenage Mutant Ninja Turtles or their Saturday morning cartoon show? Kids couldn't care less; they're just mesmerized by the images, and they buy the products associated with those images. Frank Orme, president of the National Association for Better Broadcasting, finds such programs "deceptive and cynical because kids can't tell when they are being pitched."

Or can they? Recent studies suggest that children are becoming increasingly savvy about messages from advertisers and that they display considerable skepticism about TV and commercials. Perhaps. But do they understand that Batman may fall out of favor tomorrow only to be replaced by a more popular character? Or that a cereal doesn't taste any better because it has Barbie on the box? TV advertising ignores these realities.

If children's advocates are concerned about television advertising in the home, they're absolutely livid about it in

Rating Services: "The Book"

A number of rating services measure the program audiences of TV and radio stations for advertisers and broadcasters. They pick a representative sample of the market and furnish data on the size and characteristics of the audiences that view or listen to the programs. Several research organizations gather the data at their own expense and publish it. Companies interested in their findings subscribe to the service and use it as a basis for making media advertising plans.

The most commonly used TV services are provided by A. C. Nielsen Company and Arbitron Ratings Company. For demographic studies of TV audiences, advertisers also commonly use the Simmons Market Research Bureau and Mediamark Research, Inc. These research companies publish their findings two or more times per year, depending on the size of the market, in a publication generally referred to as *The Book*. The Book reports a wide array of statistics on how many people, what age groups, and which sex watch TV at various times of the day within a specific market area. Ad Lab 14-A (p. 508) describes how methods such as the "people meter" are used to arrive at the TV ratings provided by Nielsen.

the classroom. Recently, financially strapped school districts have begun to invite advertisers into their classrooms in return for free teaching materials.

The most controversial of these programs is Whittle Communications' "Channel One." The 10-minute news broadcast for students carries an additional 2 minutes of commercials. Whittle has sold more that $200 million worth of advertising time to M&M/Mars, Burger King, and other companies that target children and expected to have 7,000 schools signed by early 1991. Schools that participate receive an average $50,000 worth of free television equipment in return for making the program required viewing for pupils. Child psychologist Lee Salk opposes "Channel One," stating that "kids are entitled to an education without having to be the object of commercial promotion." But he also concedes that "this is a free-enterprise system, and selling to kids comes with the territory."

And that territory seemingly knows no bounds. Today's children are subjected to movies that quietly showcase products, including cigarettes and alcohol, for a fee. Athletes and entertainers appear in commercials and ads hawking products to their young fans. And organizations like the Nickelodeon Club do little more than sell products and build brand loyalties among members.

It certainly seems clear that on children's television, the name of the game is selling, and the message is to buy brand names without regard to quality, price, or need. But

parents and schools can make a difference, if they teach their children well. The best defense against irresponsible advertisers is a child who grows up to be a smart, responsible consumer—one who knows how to spend money wisely.

Questions

1. Charlotte Baecher, director of educational services for Consumers Union, contends that "when a commercial message is delivered in school, it's an implicit endorsement." Do you agree? If so, should it ever be allowed? For what kinds of products and in what format?

2. "Advertisers have the responsibility to really get their messages across in a fair and reasonable way," says Nina Link, publisher of "Children's Television Workshop." What do you think Link means by "fair and reasonable"? What guidelines would you lay down to regulate or restrict the style and substance of children's advertising?

AD LAB 14-A
Where Do Those Infamous TV Ratings Come From?

For four decades, the life and death of network TV programs has been in the hands of the "Nielsen families"—the randomly chosen households **A. C. Nielsen** uses to measure audience viewing patterns. Originally there were two types of such families: those who kept diaries and those who simply had a "black box" attached to their TV sets. Someone in each of 2,400 diary homes kept a written record of which shows were watched by each member of the household during the week. Those in the 1,700 black-box households had an audimeter device attached to their TV sets that kept track of when the set was on and what channel it was tuned to. On the basis of data from these 4,100 households, Nielsen computed its Nielsen Television Index (NTI), the sole source of national TV ratings.

But that method of determining national ratings has been replaced by the **people meter,** an electronic device that automatically records a household's TV viewing. The people meter records the channels watched, the number of minutes of viewing, and who in the household is watching. This last data item requires that each person "punch in" and "punch out" on a keypad whenever beginning or ending a viewing session. The microwave-based people meter keeps track of second-by-second viewing choices of up to eight household members and relays the data to a central computer, which tabulates all the data overnight.

The original people meter was developed by AGB Research, a British company, and was first tested in the United States in 1984. It appeared to eliminate a lot of problems that had plagued the diary system. The diary approach had been criticized on several counts: The diarist would often record several days' viewing at one time, trying to recall what had been watched by the family in the previous week; one person usually kept track of the diary for the whole family; and the diarist often had difficulty tracking the burgeoning number of channels available for viewing and the time spent recording and playing back shows with a VCR. All these factors tended to bias the NTI toward major network shows, which were easier for diarists to remember. In addition, the black boxes were unreliable in that they could not indicate who was watching—only that the set was on.

AGB immediately found clients in ad agencies, cable networks, and syndicators—all of whom felt that broadcast network shows were overreported and other types of shows underreported. However, Nielsen had been developing its own people meter system and wasn't about to let AGB take over its market. AGB later abandoned the U.S. market after racking up losses of $67 million.

Unfortunately, the people meter has had its share of problems. At one point, Nielsen's numbers showed millions of people suddenly ceasing to watch TV. The networks hit the roof and insisted something had to be wrong, but Nielsen officials defended their system as proven and accurate. Still, when it came to guaranteeing ratings to advertisers, the networks decided to use eight-year trends instead of just the current year's ratings. Critics are convinced that the people meter numbers are flawed.

Now that Nielsen is looking less formidable, AGB has announced plans to reenter the U.S. market, saying it had been "invited" by the three networks. Meanwhile, even more sophisticated methods of audience measurement are in the works. Arbitron, which provides ratings of local TV programming, has developed a new service called ScanAmerica, which tracks both TV viewing and product purchases by the same sample of families.

However, advertisers who are fond of TV diaries may be happy to learn that this method of audience measurement has not been abandoned completely. Arbitron still uses the diary method during the four "sweeps" periods of each year. Both Arbitron and Nielsen conduct surveys of major market areas during these special ratings periods and publish "sweeps books" that provide the basis for local stations' ad rates.

Laboratory Applications

1. What are the advantages and disadvantages of the various television audience measurement methods?
2. Which audience rating method do you consider to be the best? Why?

Television Markets

Television rating services use a precise definition of their markets to minimize the problem of overlapping TV signals: *areas of dominant influence* and *designated market areas.*

Areas of Dominant Influence

Arbitron introduced the concept of calling TV markets **areas of dominant influence (ADI).** An *ADI* is defined as "an exclusive geographic area consisting of all counties in which the home market stations receive a preponderance of total viewing hours." Thus, the Charlotte ADI is all counties in which the Charlotte TV stations are the most watched.

Designated Market Areas

The Nielsen station index uses a similar method known as **designated market areas (DMA),** which also refers to geographical areas in which TV stations attract most of the viewing. When TRW decided to try TV advertising to spur investor interest, the company discovered that approximately half its shareholders were in the top 10 DMAs, which include the nation's largest cities from New York to Pittsburgh. Therefore, the company's first ads were scheduled in these top 10 markets with one exception: Houston was substituted for Pittsburgh because of the number of TRW customers in that area.

Dayparts

The next questions for TRW were when to air its commercials and on which programs. Unlike radio, there is little or no station loyalty in television. Viewer loyalty is to programs, and programs continue to run or are canceled depending on the size of their ratings (percentage of the population watching). Ratings also depend on the time of day a program runs.

Television time is divided into **dayparts** as follows:

	Daytime:	9 A.M.–4 P.M. (EST)
Combine as early fringe	Early fringe:	4–5:30 P.M. (EST)
	Early news:	5 or 5:30–7:30 P.M. (EST)
	Prime access:	7:30–8 P.M. (EST)
	Prime:	8–11 P.M. (EST)
Combine as late fringe	Late news:	11–11:30 P.M. (EST)
	Late fringe:	11:30 P.M.–1 A.M. (EST)

There are different levels of viewing during each daypart. The highest viewing level, of course, is in **prime time** (8 to 11 P.M.). Late fringe time also ranks fairly high in most markets among adults. Daytime and early fringe tend to be viewed most heavily by women.

To reach the greatest percentage of the advertiser's target audience with maximum frequency, all within budget, the media planner determines a **daypart mix** based on the TV usage levels reported by the rating services.

TRW's initial studies showed that its target audience watched TV for entertainment and information, principally during prime time and late evening news; they listened to the radio on the way to work; and they read trade publications related to their work. When TRW scheduled its first TV commercials, it bought enough time during late evening news from the two top-rated stations in each market to achieve a balance of good reach and frequency totaling a minimum of 50 gross rating points per week. Exhibit 14-7 shows an example of one of TRW's commercials. The company's TV schedule was supported with additional ads on morning radio and in major business publications.

Audience Measures

Rating services and media planners use numerous other terms to define a television station's audience, penetration, and efficiency. For example, **TV households (TVHH)** refers to the number of households that own television sets. By looking at the number of households that own TVs in a particular market, an advertiser can gain a sense of the size of that market. Likewise, by looking at the number of TVHH tuned in to a particular program, the advertiser can get a sense of the popularity of the program and how many people a commercial is likely to reach.

The percentage of homes in a given area that have one or more TV sets turned on at any particular time is expressed as **households using TV (HUT).** If there are 1,000 TV sets in the survey area and 500 are turned on, the HUT figure is 50 percent.

We're all familiar with TV shows that have been canceled because their ratings slipped. What does that really mean? The percentage of TV households in an area tuned in to a specific program is called the **program rating.**

$$\text{Rating} = \frac{\text{TVHH tuned to specific program}}{\text{Total TVHH in area}}$$

Networks are interested in high ratings because they are a measure of a show's popularity. If a show is not popular, advertisers will not want to advertise on it, and a network's revenue will fall. Similarly, local stations often change their programming to increase their popularity—and thereby their ratings.

The percentage of homes that have sets in use (HUT) tuned in to a specific program is called the program's **share of audience.** A program with only five viewers could have a 50 share if only 10 sets are turned on. For that reason, the program rating figures are important because they measure the audience as a percentage of all TVHH in the area, regardless of whether the TV sets are on or off.

The total number of homes reached by some portion of a program is referred to as **total audience.** This figure is normally broken down to determine **audience composition** (the distribution of audience into demographic categories).

Gross Rating Points

In television, **gross rating points (GRPs)** represent the total rating points achieved by a particular media schedule over a specific period, such as a week or a month. Thus, a weekly schedule of five commercials on programs with an average household rating of 20 would yield 100 GRPs.

TRW determined that a schedule of 50 GRPs per week would be sufficient at the beginning of its television campaign. TRW could have accomplished this by buying 10 spots with an average rating of 5 or only 2 spots with an

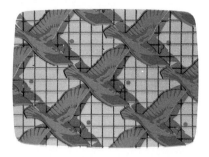

average rating of 25. The latter might have been feasible by using a highly rated prime-time program, but then the frequency would have been very low. So TRW opted to use the late evening newscasts, which had lower ratings against total TV households but higher shares of adults watching. It also afforded the company the ability to gain frequency.

The results of TRW's decision demonstrated the wisdom of its choice. Surveys taken in key markets where the commercials ran showed that the number of respondents who perceived TRW as an attractive investment alternative had increased 20 percent—to more than 60 percent total. In control markets where the TRW commercials did not air, the company's image remained virtually unchanged.

BUYING TELEVISION TIME

The process of buying TV time can be rather lengthy. Advertisers must determine which programs are available at what cost, analyze the various programs for efficiency, negotiate with stations or reps on price, determine what reach and frequency they are achieving, eventually sign the broadcast contracts, and finally review the affidavits of performance to be sure the commercials ran as agreed.

The buying procedures for television are so complex that most large advertisers seek the assistance of advertising agencies or media-buying services. Buying services are gaining in popularity because they charge less than ad agencies and can save advertisers money by negotiating for desirable time slots at reduced rates.[18] For the local advertiser, the assistance of station reps also proves invaluable in determining the best buys for the money.

Requesting Avails

Media buyers contact the sales reps for the stations they are considering to find out which programs are available. These reps may be local station salespeople, national media rep organizations that sell for one station in each market, or network reps. The media buyer gives the rep information about the advertiser's media objectives and target audiences and asks the rep to supply a list of **avails** (available time slots) along with their prices and estimated ratings.

The avails submitted by the rep should include all the data requested based on the most recent Nielsen or Arbitron book. Many media buyers ask for the information based on the last two or three books to see whether a show's ratings are consistent or have an upward or downward trend.

Selecting Programs for Buys

The media buyer must select the most efficient shows to buy in relation to the target audience. To do this, a simple computation is made of the **cost per rating point (CPP)** and the cost per thousand for each program, as follows:

$$\text{CPP} = \frac{\text{Cost}}{\text{Rating}} \qquad\qquad \text{CPM} = \frac{\text{Cost}}{\text{Thousands of people}}$$

For example, assume "People's Court" has a rating of 25, reaches 200,000 people in the primary target audience, and costs $140 for a 30-second spot with a fixed guarantee on station WALB-TV in Albany, Georgia. Then,

$$CPP = \frac{\$2,000}{25} = \$80 \qquad\qquad CPM = \frac{\$2,000}{200} = \$10$$

The lower the cost per thousand, the more efficient the show is against the target audience. The media buyer's task, therefore, is to compare the packages of each station, substituting stronger programs for less efficient ones.

Negotiating Prices and Contracts

While print media normally adhere to rate cards because of their guaranteed circulation, broadcast stations are willing to negotiate prices since their audiences are, at best, estimated (see Exhibit 14-8).

The purpose of price negotiation from the advertiser's standpoint is to get the best schedule possible within the budget. The media buyer contacts the rep and explains what efficiency the advertiser needs in terms of delivery and CPM to make the buy. The buyer may negotiate lower rates by working out a package deal; by accepting run-of-schedule positioning, which means the station chooses when to run the commercial; or by taking advantage of **preemption rates.** Preemption rates are lower rates that stations charge when the advertiser agrees to give the station the right to sell the spot to another advertiser who is willing to pay a higher rate. In a preemption situation, the advertiser saves money if demand is down, and the station minimizes the risk of unsold airtime.

Each station's advertising contract is a legal document. It is thus imperative that the media buyer catch any discrepancies before signing it. The contract indicates the dates, times, and programs on which the advertiser's commercials will run, the length of the spots, the rate per spot, and the total amount. The reverse side of the contract defines the various obligations and responsibilities of the advertiser, the agency, and the station and the terms of payment.

After the spots run, the station returns a signed and notarized **affidavit of performance** to the advertiser or agency, indicating when spots aired and what **makegoods** are available. (*Makegoods* refer to free time an advertiser receives to compensate for spots the station missed or ran incorrectly.) The affidavit of performance is the station's legal proof that the advertiser got what was paid for.

OVERVIEW OF THE CABLE MEDIUM

For over 30 years, broadcast TV, especially network TV, was the dominant entertainment medium in the lives of most Americans. But today, other electronic media are threatening to change that dominance forever. Chief among the challengers is cable television.

WBRZ
(Airdate April 4, 1955)
BATON ROUGE

BLAIR TELEVISION ⬛

ABC Television Network

N/AB
BROADCASTERS

TVB

Location ID: 6 TLST LA   Mid 007461-000
Louisiana Television Broadcasting Corp.
1650 Highland Rd., Baton Rouge, LA 70802. Phone 504-
   387-2222, Sales, 504-336-2226, Easylink, 62044844.
   FAX: 504-336-2246.
Mailing Address: Box: 2906, Baton Rouge, LA 70821.

1. PERSONNEL
Gen Mgr—Richard F. Manship.
Asst Gen Mgr—Patricia L. Cheramie.
Station Mgr—John M. Spain.
Dir of Sales—Jim Daboval III.

2. REPRESENTATIVES
Blair Television.

3. FACILITIES
Video 100,000 w., audio 15,000 w.: ch 2. Stereo.
Antenna ht.: 1,690 ft. above average terrain.
Operating schedule. 24 hours day. (except Sun sign off
   12:30 am, Mon sign on 5 am). CST.

4. AGENCY COMMISSION
15/0 to recognized agencies; 15 days.

5. GENERAL ADVERTISING REGULATIONS
General: 2a, 2b, 3a, 3b, 3c, 3d, 4a, 5, 6a, 7a, 8.
Rate Protection: 16b.
Contracts: 20c, 21, 22a, 25, 26, 28, 31b, 32a.
Basic Rates: 40b, 41b, 41c, 41d, 42, 43a, 45a, 47a, 47j,
   51, 52a.
Cancellation: 70b, 70f, 71, 72, 73a, 73b, 73d.
Prod. Services: 80, 83, 84, 85, 86.
Affiliated with ABC Television Network.

6. TIME RATES
No. 33 Effective January 1, 1990.
Rev. Received January 14, 1991.

7. SPOT ANNOUNCEMENTS

                                                          30 sec

7-10 pm Mon thru Sat; 6-10 pm Sun,
   Prime Time 900-400
6:30-7 pm Mon thru Sat; 10:30-11:40 Mon thru Fri; 10:30-
   11:30 pm Sat & Sun,
   Prime Access 500-150
5-5:30 pm Mon thru Fri; 5:30-6 Sun; 6-6:30 pm Mon thru
   Sat; 10-10:35 pm Mon thru Sun,
   Eyewitness News 600-150
5 am-3 pm Mon thru Fri,
   Weekday Daytime 250-30
3-5 pm Mon thru Fri,
   Weekday Early Fringe 300-80
11:40 pm-approx 1:30 am Mon thru Fri; 11:30 pm-approx
2 am Sat & Sun,
   Late Fringe 300-30
   Late Night 80-10
6 am-6 pm Sat & Sun,
   Family & Children's Programming 200-30
60 sec: double the 30 sec.
90 sec: 3 ti the 30 sec.
120 sec: 4 ti the 30 sec.
Spots ordered for all time periods & time blocks include
adjacencies & may run as much as 120 seconds prior to
the start of the segment due to station breaks preceding
the clock hour.
10 sec & 15 sec spots are priced by daypart & program, &
are subject to immediate preemptions by 30 or 60 sec
spots on breaks which do not accommodate natural 10
sec or 15 sec spots.

11. SPECIAL FEATURES
                             COLOR
Schedules network color, film, slides, tape and live.
Equipped with 1" reel.

13. CLOSING TIME
48 hours prior on all commercial copy; 72 hours if station
is to prepare video or audio tags.

EXHIBIT 14-8

The *Spot Television Rates and Data* listing for WBRZ-TV in Baton Rouge, Louisiana, shows the rates charged for various dayparts.

Cable TV has been around since the late 1940s. For most of its existence, its main purpose was to carry TV signals by wire to areas that had poor reception. But in the 1970s, the advent of satellite TV signals, cable's capacity to carry dozens of channels, and the introduction of uncut first-run movies in the home via pay-cable channels such as Home Box Office and Showtime suddenly made cable more attractive to viewers.

At first, many subscribers felt cable was worthwhile simply to receive a full array of regional channels and to have access to the premium services such as HBO. But once the novelty wore off, subscribers started to want more for their money. The need for more cable programming was soon filled by a variety of advertiser-supported cable networks, more-diversified pay services, and increased local cable programming, all of which drew more and more subscribers.

Cable's growth in the last decade has been extraordinary. In 1960, only 1 percent of TV households had cable. In 1975, that proportion had grown to 13 percent. Today, 54 percent of all households (59 million) are cable subscribers. By 1994, cable is expected to be in 65 percent of all households. Cable now reaches every county in the United States.[19]

Subscribers to cable TV pay a monthly fee to receive TV signals over wires that are laid into the home. The basic price covers as many as 50 advertiser-supported stations, including both the local network affiliates and independents and cable networks, superstations, and local cable system channels. Subscribers can also pay additional fees to receive premium services, such as HBO, the Disney Channel, and Cinemax, and to see special events such as first-run films, boxing matches, and baseball games (pay-per-view service).

There are now more than 25 national cable networks and a growing number of regional networks. Exhibit 14-9 (p. 514) provides a rundown of the most widely carried networks. There are also a handful of **superstations,** which are local television stations that broadcast to the rest of the country via satellite and carry national advertising. The best-known superstation is Ted Turner's WTBS–Atlanta, for which the term was coined.

Audience Trends

The presence of cable in U.S. and Canadian homes has significantly altered both TV viewing patterns and the use of other media. For example, households with cable spend less time watching *broadcast* TV than their counterparts who don't have cable. They also spend less time listening to the radio, reading, or going out for drives or to the movies. These statistics seem to indicate that, in many cases, cable is reaching an audience that is difficult to get to in any other way.

However, when it comes to overall TV viewing (both cable and broadcast TV), cable households watch more television than noncable TV households—56.4 hours per week for cable households versus 43.9 hours for noncable households. Market research also indicates that cable households seem to watch cable at all times of the day, although they tend to watch cable more often in the late fringe period and less often in the early fringe period. In all, they watch about 20.3 hours of cable per week.[20]

EXHIBIT 14-9   Major Cable Networks

Network	Estimated home coverage (millions)	Cost range*		Program type
CNN	57.9	$ 800-$	8,600†	News/information
ESPN	57.8	$ 750	8,500	Sports
Lifetime	55.0	400	10,000	News/information/women's interest
Nickelodeon	53.2	1,500	3,500	Youth interest
Nick at Night	53.2	1,500	2,600	Family/variety
MTV	52.9	2,500	7,500	Music (video)
The Discovery Channel	52.8	550	4,000	Family/health/news/information/technology/science
The Family Channel	51.7	500	4,000	Family/general/original
Arts & Entertainment	49.9	1,700	5,000	Family/variety
Headline News	46.3	800	8,600†	News/information
Financial News Network	35.1	400	2,500	News/information
Black Entertainment TV	29.0	350	1,000	Ethnic
FNN: Sports	26.2	400	2,500	Sports/news/information
CNBC	19.0	350	1,000	News/information
Entertainment Television	17.5	250	350	Entertainment/news/gossip
The Comedy Channel	11.0	225	400	Comedy
Ha!	10.0	300	600	Comedy

* Average prime time cost for 30-second spot.
† CNN and Headline News sold in combination.

Ratings

Integrated information on exactly who watches which cable programs has been hard to come by because traditional audience measurement techniques rely on too small a sample for findings on cable to be statistically significant. Therefore, each major cable programming service provides advertisers with reports of varying timeliness, daypart division, and reporting by show.[21]

Interpreting cable ratings is a confusing process because of the need to integrate the different sources of information. Therefore, cable advertisers are eagerly awaiting the upcoming increased sample size of people-meter surveys.

Who Uses Cable?

Cable advertising revenues have grown steadily since 1980, exceeding the $2 billion level in 1990, as shown in Exhibit 14-10. The lion's share of these revenues has gone to the cable networks.

National advertisers have been actively using cable since the late 1970s, and by the end of 1981, the top 50 nationally advertised brands could all be seen on cable. One company that has gone into cable advertising in a big way is Anheuser-Busch, which advertises regularly on several cable networks, with special emphasis on sports programming. As Charles B. Fruit, media director at Anheuser-Busch, explained, the broadcast networks can program only a limited amount of sports, and "we felt that the hard-core sports fan wanted more and would search it out. . . . Cable TV offered us another way to reach this important segment of our target audience. Cable TV also allowed

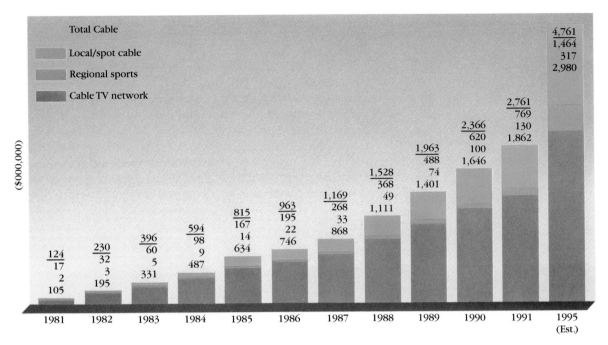

EXHIBIT 14-10

Cable ad revenues have grown dramatically.

us program and team associations prohibitively costly on network television."[22]

Local retailers also find cable a good place to advertise. Fisher Big Wheel, a discount department store in Midvale, Ohio, decided to run a series of special promotions only on cable after their first cable promotion brought an extra 15,000 customers into the store. Even tiny businesses have found cable advertising affordable and effective. For instance, a luncheonette on Main Street in Beacon, New York, placed a single spot on the local cable newscast and was deluged with hungry customers the next day.[23]

USING CABLE TELEVISION IN THE CREATIVE MIX

Most advertising on cable is done through the networks, but local and regional advertising is experiencing impressive growth. According to Paul Kagan Associates, a media consulting company, local cable ad revenues more than doubled between 1987 and 1990, and regional advertising tripled.[24] Although cable systems still derive their main income from subscribers and the premium and pay-per-view services, they need other forms of revenue as well and are starting to actively woo advertisers. We may also see advertising on the pay channels in the near future, most likely at intermissions between programs.

Advantages of Cable

The primary advantages of cable TV are its selectivity, low cost, and great flexibility.

Selectivity

According to cable's supporters, this medium reaches the kinds of households advertisers like best. Cable subscribers are younger, better educated, and more affluent, have higher-level jobs, and live in larger households than nonsubscribers. Those in cable households are also more likely to try new products and buy more high-ticket items, such as cars, appliances, and high-tech equipment.[25]

In addition to delivering this highly desirable audience, cable offers specialized programming aimed at particular types of viewers. Exhibit 14-11 shows how one cable network attracts boxing fans, for example. There are also cable networks devoted solely to sports, news, business, children's programming, and music. Furthermore, specific cable shows may deliver desirable demographics. Among the highest-rated shows on the Cable News Network (CNN) are the financial programs "Your Money" and "Inside Business," which appeal to an affluent audience. According to people-meter findings, the viewers of "Your Money" are 92 percent more likely to have a

EXHIBIT 14-11

Selectivity allows advertisers to target a small, well-defined audience the way that HBO targeted boxing fans with its Mike Tyson spot.

ANNOUNCER: Everyone has a talent.

Some people can paint.

Some people can sing.

Some people can write short stories.

Mike Tyson makes short stories out of some people.

HBO. The undisputed best time on TV.

household income over $40,000, while viewers of "Inside Business" are 85 percent more likely.[26] Such **narrowcasting** allows advertisers to choose programming with the viewer demographics that best match their target customers.

Low Cost

Cable advertising costs are much lower than those for broadcast television, and in many cases are comparable to radio ad costs. Thus, many small companies can benefit from TV's immediacy and impact without the enormous expenditures of broadcast TV. One award-winning spot for a video store cost only $200 to produce. In fact, cable costs are low enough for advertisers to run longer commercials and even to sponsor entire programs inexpensively. Many national advertisers are finding sponsorship particularly attractive, since an entire cable series can cost less to produce than a single broadcast TV commercial.[27]

Flexibility

One of the most appealing things about cable advertising is its great flexibility. Commercials can be of just about any length, they can be tailored to fit the programming environment, and they can be used for experimentation and test marketing.

Broadcast TV commercials need to be short because of the high costs of production and airtime, but cable ads can run up to two minutes and longer. Such long spots are desirable when a minute or less is just not enough to tell a product's story. One highly praised cable commercial was a two-minute ad for the State of Alaska Division of Tourism. This minitravelog revealing Alaska's wonders might have been much less effective at 30 seconds.

One long form of commercial popular on cable TV is the **infomercial.** The purpose of this longer format (usually three to eight minutes) is to give consumers detailed information about the product or service. It may demonstrate how to use the product, show how the product is made, or highlight the product's special features. Another type of longer commercial is the 90-second segment that devotes 60 seconds to a brief feature and 30 seconds to the actual product pitch.

Cable also allows advertisers to produce commercials to fit a specific programming environment. Thus, different ads for the same product could be developed to fit well on MTV, the Nashville Network, and the Arts & Entertainment Network.

Finally, cable is a good place to experiment, testing both new products and various advertising approaches. Major marketers such as Campbell soup, Bristol-Myers, Colgate-Palmolive, and Johnson & Johnson have used cable to experiment with such variables as ad frequency, copy impact, and media mix.[28] Many of the larger cable systems are working on technical innovations to help in test-marketing efforts, taking advantage of the fact that cable lines reach into individual households.

Drawbacks of Cable

While cable's greatest strength is selectivity, its main weakness is limited reach. Although all areas of the country now have access to cable, the proportion of cable homes is only about 60 percent, leaving 40 percent of the population without coverage. However, cable subscriptions are growing at a rate of over 300,000 households a month, so the percentage of TV homes without cable should continue to shrink with each passing year.

Another drawback is cable's audience fragmentation. With more than 50 channels at their disposal, cable viewers do not watch any one show in enormous numbers. Thus, reaching the majority of the cable audience in a particular market requires advertising on a great many stations.

Cable, particularly local cable, also has a bit of an image problem to overcome. Because of its sometimes poorer production quality and less desirable programming than broadcast TV, many advertisers consider cable less than glamorous. This image is improving, however, as cable network programming becomes stronger and as local cable systems become more sophisticated in their production techniques.

Cable TV is also subject to some of the same drawbacks as broadcast TV, including zipping and zapping. Well-produced longer-form commercials and infomercials that integrate programming with subtle promotion should help to combat these electronic enemies.

Buying Cable Time

Cable can be bought at the national, regional, and local levels. As with broadcast TV, national advertising is divided into network and local spots. Cable network advertising operates much like broadcast network advertising—the media buyer can sponsor network shows or purchase spot ads on network shows. Sponsorships are much more common on cable networks than on broadcast networks, however, because of the lower costs. See Exhibit 14-12 for a list of the top cable TV advertisers.

Purchasing national spot advertising on local cable systems has been time consuming for media buyers, who must deal with over 1,000 cable systems. However, the larger local systems are becoming more sophisticated in their ad sales and are receiving more assistance from the networks in filling local spots on network shows.

Regional cable advertising is facilitated by the use of **interconnects,** groups of cable systems joined together for advertising purposes. An advertiser can use an interconnect to buy the same ad time on all systems in a particular area. The largest interconnect, New York Interconnect, serves 3.1 million subscribers in the greater New York metropolitan area.

Ad spots and sponsorships on local cable stations are purchased in much the same way as ad time on local broadcast TV stations. Local advertisers are particularly attracted to community-oriented local programs, such as newscasts and sports events, that reach customers in their immediate area. However, local cable stations have not as yet provided the level of support that broadcast stations do to advertisers. For example, local cable advertisers need to invest more of their own time in quantifying the demographics and tracking their spots to ensure that they run as scheduled.

Other Forms of Television

Cable is not the only electronic challenger to traditional broadcast television. Cable has its own competitors, although they are all in minor usage at

EXHIBIT 14-12   Top 10 Cable TV Advertisers*

Rank	Advertiser	Cable TV network spending, 1990
1	Procter & Gamble Co.	$57.7
2	Time Warner	50.7
3	General Mills	27.4
4	Anheuser-Busch Cos.	26.8
5	Philip Morris Cos.	26.6
6	General Motors Corp.	26.0
7	RJR Nabisco	21.7
8	Sears, Roebuck & Co.	19.8
9	AT&T Co.	15.3
10	PepsiCo	13.1

Dollars are in millions.
* Includes CNN, MTV, USA, ESPN, WTBS, and Family Channel.

present. The various electronic systems go by the initials of DBS, MDS, STV, and SMATV.

- **DBS (direct broadcast satellite)** involves beaming programs from satellites to special satellite dishes mounted in the home or yard. Because DBS is expected to carry only four or five channels, it is not considered a major competitor to cable.
- **MDS (multipoint distribution system)** is a microwave delivery system that can carry up to a dozen channels. It is offered in some areas where cable is not available.
- **STV (subscription television)** is over-the-air pay TV. Subscribers pay for a descrambler that allows them to watch programs that are carried over a regular TV channel.
- **SMATV (satellite master antenna television)** uses a satellite dish to capture signals for TV sets in apartment buildings and other complexes, acting as a sort of minicable system.

So far, none of these systems has managed to capture the public's imagination the way cable has—and since most are more expensive and carry fewer channels, they have yet to pose much of a threat to either broadcast or cable television.

Advertising on Videocassette Rentals

Another challenger to both broadcast and cable TV is the rented videocassette. Ever since Pepsi sponsored the successful home-video release of *Top Gun* a few years ago, industry analysts have been expecting advertising on videocassette rentals to take off.[29] Although the video market hasn't been deluged with advertisers wanting to buy time, there has been increasing interest in the medium.

In 1989, Nielsen Media Research conducted a pilot study of video audiences using a meter-based prerecorded video tracking system it plans to syndicate.[30] The metering system tracks the videos by encoding each copy with an invisible marking that is "read" by a device installed in the Nielsen family homes. The tracking system allows Nielsen to follow how often a movie is viewed and exactly which scenes, if any, are watched more than once. Preliminary results of the study show that home-video renters are older than expected, with most renters falling between the ages of 25 and 49, and that 25 percent earn more than $50,000 a year.

Even more surprising was the fact that the majority of video renters watched the commercials appearing before the movie—sometimes even more than once. Nielsen found that the most popular commercial—a Schweppes ad starring comedian John Cleese preceding CBS/Fox's *A Fish Called Wanda*—was viewed by an astounding 95 percent of households renting the video.[31]

The study also showed that households watched the films they rented an average of 1.3 times during the typical two-day rental period. The most popular films were watched even more often. When metered data become regularly available, more advertisers are likely to give serious consideration to placing commercials on videos. So long as consumers don't rebel, it could become another important advertising vehicle.

OVERVIEW OF THE RADIO MEDIUM

Unlike watching TV or reading a newspaper, radio listening is usually done by one person alone. It is a personal, one-on-one medium. And it is mobile. Radio can entertain a person who is driving, walking, and at home or away from home. Radio is a particularly strong medium where commuting is done by automobile.

Radio is also adaptable to moods. In the morning, some people may want to hear the news, upbeat music, or interesting chatter from a disc jockey to help them wake up. In the afternoon, the same people may want to unwind with classical or easy-listening music. Thus, most people consistently listen to two or three different radio stations representing different types of programming, although they tend to be quite loyal to their chosen stations.

Who Uses Radio?

Increasing numbers of national advertisers are discovering the reach and frequency potential of radio. Schering Corporation, for example, decided to test radio's selling effectiveness on Tinactin, an antifungal product used primarily for athlete's foot. For two months in four western cities, Schering aired a Tinactin commercial featuring a lawyer, a math teacher, and an umpire. Tinactin's chief competitors, Desenex and Micatin, appeared regularly on TV during that same period. But with an 85 percent reach and a frequency of nine, Tinactin's market share jumped 12 points after the trial. Maria Boerlage, group brand director at Schering, said, "We do believe we have a good commercial, but we know the medium delivered those share points."[32]

Although many big-budget national companies, such as AT&T, Anheuser-Busch, PepsiCo, General Motors, and Chrysler, spend a lot of money on radio advertising, smaller national companies are also choosing radio to try to gain on the competition. Dial Corporation, which makes Purex laundry products and has nowhere near the ad budget of giants such as Procter & Gamble, calls radio its giant killer.

Local retailers also like the medium because they can tailor it to their immediate needs. It offers defined audiences, and retailers can create an identity for themselves by doing their own ads. In recent years, many types of local businesses have significantly increased their radio advertising expenditures. Grocery stores and supermarkets spent 335 percent more on radio advertising in 1990 than they did in 1980; and major spending increases have also been posted by automobile dealers, home improvement stores, banks and savings and loans, and the makers of drug products.[33]

Radio Programming and Audiences

Radio stations plan their programming carefully to reach specific markets and to capture as many listeners as possible. The larger its audience, the more a station can charge for commercial time. Therefore, extensive planning and research go into radio programming and program changes.

Stations have a number of options in program planning. They can use tried-and-true formats, subscribe to network or syndicated programming, or devise their own unique approaches. One successful station in Santa Fe, New Mexico, for example, plays sets of classical, jazz, and light rock music back-to-back. However, programming choices are greatly influenced by whether a station is on the AM or FM band.

For most of the history of radio, AM dominated the airwaves. But in the 1960s, with the advent of stereo and the growth of underground programming on FM, things began to change. Today, FM has more than 70 percent of the radio audience, and AM stations are scrambling for listeners.[34] It's not surprising that FM is so popular: It has much better sound fidelity (AM is more subject to interference), fewer commercial interruptions, and more varied programming. These features have attracted the younger listeners away from AM.

To counteract the inroads made by FM, many AM stations have switched to programs that do not rely heavily on sound quality, such as talk, news, and sports. Some AM stations are also experimenting with new formats, such as all-comedy, midday game shows with audience participation, children's programming, and formats geared to unique regions, such as KHJ's "car radio" in Los Angeles, which provides traffic reports every 10 minutes, tips on driving, and features on cars and travel.[35] AM stations are also trying to win back music listeners by improving their sound quality and by offering AM stereo broadcasting.

The great majority of stations, whether AM or FM, tend to adopt one of the dozen or so standard programming formats: contemporary hit radio (CHR), adult contemporary, country, album-oriented rock, easy listening, news/talk, black/urban, middle of the road (MOR), nostalgia (big band), classical, religious, and so on. Each of these formats tends to appeal to specific demographic groups, as shown in Exhibit 14-13. The most popular format, contemporary hit radio, appeals primarily to teenagers and to women under age 30. This format, always found on FM stations, emphasizes a constant flow of "Top 40" hits, usually with minimal intrusion by disc jockeys (although the talky, zany "zoo" approach to CHR has caught on in several markets). Another

EXHIBIT 14-13   Profile of Daily Adult Listeners of Radio Stations, by Format, in the United States

Format	Percent male	Percent female	Median age	Median household income	Percent with 1+ years college
Adult contemporary	46	54	39.1	$31,300	43
Album-oriented rock	62	38	30.8	33,600	45
All news	58	42	44.7	37,700	44
Black	55	45	36.0	21,000	8
Classic rock	62	38	31.8	35,500	51
Classical	54	46	40.0	38,800	59
CHR/rock	47	53	32.0	30,800	41
Country	51	49	41.5	28,400	32
Easy listening	46	54	48.2	30,100	43
Golden oldies	54	46	38.3	32,900	42
Lite/soft contemporary	43	57	36.2	36,500	50
MOR/nostalgia	50	50	53.0	27,900	33
News/talk	54	46	46.1	34,300	46
Religious	43	57	38.8	26,300	38
Urban contemporary	44	56	31.9	22,500	34
U.S. adult population	**48**	**52**	**39.2**	**31,100**	**37**

popular format, adult contemporary (or "easy oldies"), is often advertised as "light rock, less talk." This format aims at the desirable target group of working women aged 25 to 44.[36] The news/talk, easy-listening, and nostalgia formats all tend to have high listenership among men and women over age 50.

Advertisers can take advantage of listenership studies to determine which radio formats in a particular market deliver the greatest share of the target audience for a product. A company selling denture cream would want to place spots on a nostalgia or talk-oriented station, for example, while a manufacturer of acne cream would go for CHR stations.

A major trend in radio today has been a resurgence by the radio networks. Unlike TV networks, which supply affiliates with the bulk of their programming, radio networks offer services and programs that stations can subscribe to, in order to complement their local programming. Thus, a single station might subscribe to ABC's hourly newscasts, to CBS's weekly "Entertainment Coast-to-Coast," and to Mutual Broadcasting System's nightly "Larry King Show."

There are now some 18 national radio networks, including the multiple "mininetworks" of ABC, NBC, and CBS. In addition, numerous syndicators offer a variety of programs, from live rock concerts and sporting events to public-affairs programs and talk shows. To stand out in an increasingly competitive radio environment, more and more stations are opting for syndicated and network offerings.[37] And as more stations carry these programs and more listeners tune in, national advertisers are finding them increasingly attractive as a means for reaching target audiences.

USING RADIO IN THE CREATIVE MIX

How do you go about marketing a product when just saying its name causes people to laugh? That was the challenge for BBDO/Minneapolis when their client, George A. Hormel & Co., asked them to create a campaign for Spam canned luncheon meat that would draw a younger group of consumers to their product.

The ad agency decided to place the major thrust of its campaign in radio advertising. It chose radio for two main reasons: its frequency, offering a constant reminder of the product to listeners, and its reach to a younger audience. BBDO also felt that people are well enough aware of the appearance of Spam's familiar blue and yellow can that visuals were not necessary to their main message.

The main problem to overcome was Spam's image as a joke food—something that Johnny Carson and David Letterman love to make fun of and that Monty Python created a memorable sketch around. The agency chose to go with the humor and capitalize on it. The ads recorded conversations with consumers who had just sampled crepes, quiche, and other foods containing Spam. When they were told the main ingredient, their spontaneous laughter was infectious. The interviewer then unobtrusively cleared up some common misconceptions about the product, pointing out that it contains no fillers, just pork shoulder and ham. The radio script for the Spam radio campaign is shown in Exhibit 14-14.

As Jerry Figenskau, director of marketing and advertising for Hormel's grocery product division, explained, "By taking that kind of lighthearted look at the product, we can kind of contemporize it and put it in a position where we might be able to attract some of the new, young users."[38]

EXHIBIT 14-14

This script for BBDO's Spam radio campaign will give you some idea of the approach taken, but its appeal becomes more obvious when you can hear the voices and the infectious laughter.

SFX:	(PARTY CONVERSATION, LAUGHTER UNDER THROUGHOUT)
DICK:	We've just served up an elegant brunch with recipes made from SPAM luncheon meat, but our guests don't know it's SPAM.
	Hi. What have you tried so far?
JAY:	The crepe thing.
DICK:	What else?
JAY:	And, uh, it was like the crepe thing, only it was a different shaped thing.
DICK:	(LAUGHING) That's called quiche. Did you enjoy it?
JAY:	(LAUGHS) I went back twice.
DICK:	You enjoyed it. Is there anything you won't eat?
JAY:	Zucchini.
DICK:	All right. And how about you? Did you like it?
BARB:	I loved it.
DICK:	Do you pride yourself as a cook. I mean, do you know food?
BARB:	Well, I'm Italian. So food is my life.
DICK:	So you know food. What was the meat in the crepes and quiche and so on then?
BARB:	It tasted like ham to me.
DICK:	You're sure it's ham.
BARB:	I think I'm sure ... should I not be sure?
DICK:	No, no. What would you say if I told you it was SPAM!
MICHAEL:	SPAM?
THERESA:	(LAUGHS) It was very good!
BARB:	I'd be shocked. And it was delicious.
DICK:	O.K., What is SPAM? Do you know, Jay?
JAY:	Zucchini ...
DICK:	No, no. SPAM is pork shoulder and ham. No fillers. Just very good meat. So what do you think?
JAY:	Uh, it was good.
DICK:	And, would you have SPAM again?
JAY:	I certainly would, as long as I didn't have to make it with zucchini.
DICK:	O.K. Come on, America, discover the great taste of SPAM. It just might surprise you.
JAY:	Can I go back for thirds? (Laughter)

Hormel placed a high priority on the advertising of Spam, giving it a $1.6 million budget. Of that, $1.1 million was committed to radio, "for the acknowledged benefits of the medium."

Advantages of Radio

Radio is an integral part of our daily lives. We rely on clock radios to wake us in the morning. At breakfast, we tune in the morning news. Radio informs and entertains us while we drive to work or school or do household chores. And chances are good that if you work in an office or plant, you enjoy background music supplied by a local radio station. With its unique ability to relax, inform, and entertain, radio has become the daily companion of millions at work, at play, and on the highway.

EXHIBIT 14-15

Daily and weekly reach of radio exceeds other major media.

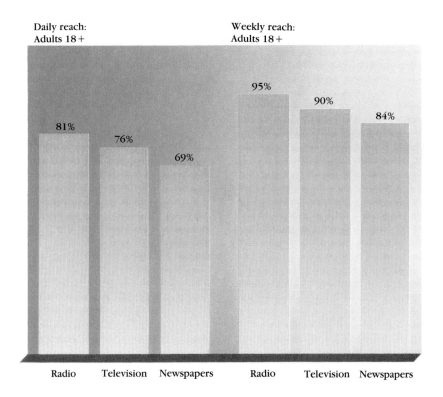

Daily reach:
Adults 18+

Weekly reach:
Adults 18+

95%

90%

84%

81%

76%

69%

Radio   Television   Newspapers   Radio   Television   Newspapers

In an average week, 96 percent of all the people in the United States listen to the radio—almost 80 percent on an average day. The average American spends almost three hours per day listening to the radio.[39] In fact, as Exhibit 14-15 shows, radio leads all other media in both daily and weekly reach. This has tremendous implications for advertisers; as a result, radio's advertising revenues have grown steadily.

The largest national radio advertisers are retail stores, automotive companies, beer and wine producers, telecommunications companies, and the U.S. government. Exhibit 14-16 lists the top 10 national radio advertisers.

But radio's biggest source of revenue is composed of the many thousands of local businesses that use the medium to reach out and talk to their local customers. Of the $8.8 billion spent in radio in 1990, over $6.6 billion came from local advertisers.[40] Among the features of radio that both national advertisers like Hormel and local advertisers like banks and car dealers find appealing are its reach and frequency, its selectivity, and its cost-efficiency.

Reach and Frequency

Radio offers an excellent combination of reach and frequency. With the average adult listening more than three hours a day, radio builds a large audience quickly, and a normal advertising schedule easily allows repeated impact on the listener. This ability to quickly expose people a sufficient number of times to motivate them to buy makes radio particularly attractive to local merchants.

Selectivity

The wide variety of specialized radio formats available, with their prescribed audiences and coverage areas, enables advertisers to select just the market

---

EXHIBIT 14-16   Top 10 National Radio Advertisers

Rank	Advertiser	Ad expenditures, 1989*
1	Sears, Roebuck & Co.	$107.1
2	General Motors Corp.	74.8
3	Chrysler Corp.	53.6
4	Philip Morris Cos.	51.5
5	Anheuser-Busch Cos.	49.8
6	Procter & Gamble Co.	38.5
7	AT&T Co.	26.0
8	Ford Motor Co.	24.6
9	Kmart	24.4
10	U.S. government	24.3

* Dollars are in millions.

---

they want to reach. Commercials can be aimed at listeners of a specific sex, age group, ethnic or religious background, income group, employment category, educational level, or special interest. General Electric, for example, has been working to increase its product recognition among Hispanics and blacks by placing commercials on stations aimed at those groups.

Cost-Efficiency

Radio's strong appeal to advertisers is largely its economy. Radio has the ability to offer its reach, frequency, and selectivity at one of the lowest costs per thousand. Thus, the budget for an effective radio schedule is often less than that needed for newspapers, magazines, or television.

Radio production is also relatively inexpensive. National spots can usually be produced for one-tenth the cost of a TV commercial. And in some cases, there are no production costs at all because local radio stations frequently produce commercials free for their local advertisers.

Radio has a number of other advantages as well. It has a timeliness and immediacy that few other media can match—see, for example, the copy for a *Crain's New York Business* commercial in Exhibit 14-17. The low cost adds to

EXHIBIT 14-17

Radio advertisers can often take advantage of timely topics in a way that television advertisers cannot.

"Soviets"

Anncr: Recently, senior Soviet officials appearing on American television indicated that in their effort to restructure their ailing economy, they hope to receive American aid. Not financial aid, mind you. But informational aid. Suddenly, they want to learn about competition. About corporate deal making. About how big business profits fuel big-city economies. However, it doesn't take an expert in geo-political economies to figure out what the Soviets are really after: A complimentary subscription to *Crain's New York Business*. To which we'd like to respond: No deal. They're going to have to pay for a subscription just like everybody else.

radio's creative flexibility (the commercial message can be changed for each market segment, for instance), and its local flavor helps build an identity for the advertiser in the community.

Drawbacks to Radio

In spite of its great advantages, radio has traditionally suffered from certain limitations: it is only an aural medium; its audience is highly segmented; the advertiser's commercials are short-lived, and often they are only half heard; and each ad must compete with the clutter of other ads.

Limitations of Sound

Radio is heard but not seen. This fact can limit the effectiveness of commercials for products that need to be seen to be understood. Advertising agencies often prefer the freedom of creating with sight, sound, color, and motion, as in television. Some agencies see radio as restricting their creative options.

Nevertheless, many brilliant creative efforts have been achieved with radio through the use of "theater-of-the-mind" techniques. Pittsburgh Paints, for example, used a campaign that actually capitalized on radio's aural limitation. "Imagine yellow . . ." the announcer said, and soft music swelled in the background. The campaign, which used the same concept to describe other colors with music, proved to be highly effective. (See the Checklist of What Works Best in Radio.)

Checklist of What Works Best in Radio

□ *Stretch the listener's imagination.* Voices and sounds can evoke pictures.

□ *Listen for a memorable sound.* What will make your commercial stand out from the clutter? Offer a distinctive voice, a memorable jingle, a solution to the listener's problem.

□ *Present one idea.* It is difficult to communicate more than one idea in a television commercial. In radio, which is subject to more distractions, it is nearly impossible. Be direct and clear.

□ *Select your audience quickly.* It pays to flag your segment of the audience at the beginning of the commercial—before they can switch to another station.

□ *Mention your brand name and your promise early.* Commercials that do so get higher awareness. It heightens awareness if you mention the brand name and promise *more than once.*

□ *Capitalize on events.* Exploit the flexibility of radio to tie in with fads, fashions, news events, or the weather.

□ *Use radio to reach teenagers.* Teenagers don't watch much television. They do listen to a lot of radio. Media experts say it's the best way to reach teens. Some say it's the *only* way.

□ *Music can help.* It is particularly effective in reaching teenagers who prefer the "now sounds" offered by music stations. You can give your campaign infinite variety with the same lyrics arranged in different ways and sung by different people.

□ *Ask listeners to take action.* People respond to radio requests for action. They call the station to exchange views with the disc jockey or ask for certain music. Don't be afraid to ask listeners to call now, or write in, or send money.

□ *Make use of radio's merchandising services.* Associate your business with a popular on-air personality; sponsor promotions such as contests and give-aways.

Segmented Audiences

Radio's ability to deliver highly selective audiences can also be a handicap to some advertisers. The large number of radio stations competing for the same audience may make the purchase of effective airtime difficult for the advertiser. For example, while one city may have only three TV stations, it may have 20 radio stations competing for a market of, say, 1.5 million people. Clearly, the advertiser who seeks to blanket this market will have to buy multiple stations, which may not be cost-effective.

Short-Lived and Half-Heard Commercials

A radio commercial is brief and fleeting. You can't keep it like a newspaper or a magazine ad. It lasts only moments, and then it's gone.

For many listeners, radio provides only a pleasant background sound while they are driving to work, reading, studying, or entertaining. Thus, radio must compete with other activities for their attention, and it does not always succeed.

Clutter

The more successful a radio station is, the more commercials it carries. Therefore, stations that have the greatest appeal for advertisers also offer the most competition from other commercials. The challenge is to produce a commercial that stands out from the rest.

BUYING RADIO TIME

As with television, advertisers need a basic knowledge of the medium to buy radio time effectively. First, it's important to be aware of the types of radio advertising available for commercial use. Second, a basic understanding of radio terminology is necessary. And, finally, the advertiser needs to know the steps in preparing a radio schedule.

Types of Radio Advertising

An advertiser may purchase network, spot, or local radio time. Local purchases account for 75 percent of all radio time sold; spot radio, another 20 percent; and networks, 5 percent.

Networks

Advertisers may use one of the national radio networks (ABC, CBS, NBC, Mutual, United Stations) to carry their messages to the entire national market simultaneously via the networks' affiliated stations. In addition, more than 100 regional radio networks in the United States operate as news, sports, and farm networks with information oriented toward specific geographic markets.

The use of networks provides national and regional advertisers with simple administration and low effective net cost per station. The amount of paperwork and clerical time is greatly reduced, and the cost per station is usually lower than if comparable times were bought on individual stations. Typical costs of advertising on various national radio networks are listed in Exhibit 14-18. However, the disadvantages lie in the lack of flexibility in

EXHIBIT 14-18	Network Radio Advertising Rates (cost of :30 commercial) by Dayparts and Demographic Segments			
	Monday-Sunday 6 A.M.-midnight	Monday-Friday 6-10 A.M.	Monday-Friday 3-7 P.M.	Saturday/Sunday 6 A.M.-midnight
Adults 18+	$4,045	$4,359	$4,965	$4,027
Men 18+	3,981	4,588	5,133	3,940
Men 18-34	3,468	3,171	3,427	4,209
Men 25-54	4,195	4,255	4,703	4,150
Women 18+	3,727	4,043	4,541	3,693
Women 18-34	3,632	4,286	4,533	3,616
Women 25-54	4,196	4,243	4,943	4,474
Teens 12-17	2,552	2,747	2,161	2,456

choosing the affiliated stations, the limitation of the number of stations on the network's roster, and the long lead time required to book time.

Spot Radio

Buying **spot radio** affords national advertisers great flexibility in their choice of markets, stations, airtime, and copy. The advertiser can choose as long or as short a flight as desired. In addition, spot advertising enables the message to be presented to listeners at the most favorable times.

By purchasing radio spots, advertisers can tailor commercials to the local market. The commercials can be put on the air quickly—some stations are willing to run a commercial with as little as 20 minutes' lead time.

Spot advertising also enables advertisers to build local listener acceptance of their product or service by using local personalities or by purchasing airtime on locally produced programs.

Local Radio

Local time denotes radio spots purchased by a local advertiser. It involves the same procedure as national spots; the sole difference is the location of the advertiser.

Radio advertising can also be classified live, taped, or transcribed (a form of record). In recent years, the trend has been toward recorded shows with live news in between. Nearly all radio commercials today are recorded to reduce costs and maintain broadcast quality.

Radio Terminology

Buying radio time requires a basic understanding of radio terminology. Much of the language used for radio advertising is the same as that used for other media. But radio also has many terms that are either peculiar to it or have a special meaning when applied to radio advertising. The most common of these are the concepts of *dayparts, average quarter-hour audiences,* and *cumes* (cumulative audiences).

Dayparts

The radio day is divided into five basic dayparts:

6 A.M.–10 A.M.	Morning drive
10 A.M.–3 P.M.	Daytime
3 P.M.–7 P.M.	Afternoon (or evening) drive
7 P.M.–12 A.M.	Nighttime
12 A.M.–6 A.M.	All night

The rating services measure the audiences for only the first four of these dayparts, because all-night listening is very limited and not highly competitive. Ad Lab 14-B describes the three major audience rating services offered to radio broadcasters and advertisers. The heaviest radio use occurs during drive times (6–10 A.M. and 3–7 P.M.) during the week (Monday–Friday).

This information is important to advertisers because usage and consumption vary for different products. For example, radio's morning drive time

---

AD LAB 14-B
The Reports that Make or Break Radio Stations

Three major audience rating services are offered to radio broadcasters and advertisers. Media buyers use the data obtained from these services to determine which programs and stations will deliver the greatest number of target listeners.

Arbitron

The **Arbitron** rating service chooses a group of representative listeners in each of 257 cities and gives them a diary for keeping track of all the time they spend listening to radio. Listeners return the diaries to Arbitron at the end of each week for tabulation, and Arbitron compiles the results into a quarterly report.

The Arbitron "book" reports not only the number of listeners to particular stations and shows but also their age, sex, and preferred listening times. The service is available to clients on a subscription basis. The major clients are radio stations, but some ad agencies and radio sales representatives also subscribe.

Birch Research

Birch Research uses telephone surveys rather than diaries to obtain listener data. Interviewers talk to representative listeners in 130 major radio markets. Results are published on a monthly basis, with quarterly summaries. Birch also offers **Birchscan,** a monthly computerized report.

RADAR

Ratings of network radio programs are determined by **RADAR** (Radio's All-Dimension Audience Research). RADAR audience estimates are based on telephone interviews with listeners. Each listener is called daily for a week and asked about listening habits from the day before until that moment. The research is conducted year-round and is published annually in *Radio Usage* and *Network Radio Audiences.* A number of specialized reports are also available.

Laboratory Applications

1. What do you think might be the advantages and disadvantages of these radio audience measurement methods?

2. Which audience measurement method, diary or phone interview, would you consider better? Why?

EXHIBIT 14-19

The *Spot Radio Rates and Data* listing for KWOD–FM radio in Sacramento, California, shows that spot announcement rates vary from a high of $260 to a low of $112 per minute, depending on the number bought and the dayparts selected.

coincides perfectly with most people's desire for a steaming, fresh cup of coffee, so it is a great time for advertising coffee brands. Late evening, on the other hand, is a poor time to advertise coffee.

Radio stations base their rates on the time of day the advertiser wants commercials aired, but the rates are highly negotiable according to supply and demand at any given time. Exhibit 14-19 shows standard rates for airtime on KWOD-FM in Sacramento, California, for instance. To achieve the lowest rate, an advertiser can order spots on a **run-of-station (ROS)** basis, similar to ROP in newspaper advertising. However, this leaves total control of spot placement up to the station. Most stations, therefore, offer a **total audience plan (TAP)** package rate, which guarantees a certain percentage of spots in the better dayparts if the advertiser buys the total package of time.

Average Quarter-Hour Persons

The term **average quarter-hour persons** is used to identify the average number of persons who are listening to a specific station for at least 5 minutes during a 15-minute period of any given daypart. For example, station KKDA in Dallas/Ft. Worth, Texas, in Exhibit 14-20 has an average quarter-hour listenership of 33,800, meaning that any day, during any 15-minute period between 3 P.M. and 7 P.M., it is probable that 33,800 persons over age 12 are tuned in to the station.

This same idea can be expressed in terms of "share" if the station's audience is shown as a percentage of the total listening audience in the area. For example, in our illustration, the total average quarter-hour listening audience for all stations is 676,000. Therefore, the average quarter-hour audience of radio station KKDA could be expressed as an average quarter-hour share of .05:

$$\frac{33,800}{676,000} = .05 \text{ or } 5 \text{ percent}$$

Average Quarter-Hour Rating Points

By extending our computations a little further, this same audience (Exhibit 14-20) could be expressed in terms of rating points if we show it as a percentage of the population. For example, with radio station KKDA located in an area of 3,072,727 people, its average quarter-hour persons could be expressed as an **average quarter-hour rating** of 1.1:

$$\frac{33,800}{3,072,727} = .011 \text{ or } 1.1 \text{ percent}$$

Determining the gross rating points of a radio schedule simply requires multiplying the average quarter-hour rating by the number of spots. For example,

$$\text{Rating points} \times \text{Number of spots} = \text{GRPs}$$
$$1.1 \times 24 = 26.4$$

The GRPs could also be determined by multiplying the average quarter-hour persons by the number of spots and dividing by the population. For example,

$$\text{Average quarter-hour audience} \times \text{Number of spots} = \text{Gross impressions}$$
$$33,800 \qquad \times \qquad 24 \qquad = \qquad 811,200$$

Therefore,

$$\frac{811,200}{3,072,727} = .264 \text{ or } 26.4 \text{ GRPs}$$

Cume Estimates

The **cume persons** is the total number of *different* persons who listened to a radio station for a minimum of five minutes in a quarter-hour within a reported daypart.

Specific Audience
MONDAY–FRIDAY   3PM–7PM

KKDA-FM		Persons 12+	Persons 18+	Men 18+	Men 18-24	Men 25-34	Men 35-44	Men 45-54	Men 55-64	Women 18+	Women 18-24	Women 25-34	Women 35-44	Women 45-54	Women 55-64	Teens 12-17
MET AQH	PER (00)	338	260	107	20	54	15	8	9	153	52	42	31	1	4	78
MET AQH	RATING	1.1	.9	.8	1.0	1.4	.4	.4	.7	1.0	2.5	1.1	.9		.3	2.5
MET AQH	SHARE	5.0	4.2	3.6	4.0	6.3	2.1	1.7	3.2	4.8	9.4	4.9	4.1	.2	1.5	14.9
MET CUME	PER(00)	1678	1282	626	93	314	117	45	35	656	224	202	141	8	17	396
MET CUME	RATING	5.2	4.4	4.5	4.6	8.2	3.5	2.2	2.7	4.4	11.0	5.3	4.3	.4	1.2	12.7
TSA AQH	PER(00)	368	283	123	29	58	15	8	12	160	53	45	31	3	4	85
TSA CUME	PER(00)	2021	1547	800	208	328	117	45	69	747	246	227	141	39	17	474

EXHIBIT 14–20

The Arbitron *Radio Market Report* includes both average quarter-hour and cume audience data. The survey data shown here are for station KKDA-FM in Dallas/Fort Worth.

MET AQH PER (00) (Metropolitan Average Quarter Hour Persons) = The estimated number of persons who listened to a station for a minimum of five minutes within a quarter-hour. The estimate is the average of the reported listening in the total number of quarter-hours the station was on the air during a reported daypart. AQH Persons estimates are expressed in hun-

dreds (00). This estimate is also shown for the TSA (Total Survey Area), which may include counties surrounding the MET (metropolitan area).

MET AQH RATING (Rating Point) = The Metropolitan Average Quarter Hour Persons estimate expressed as a percentage of the appropriate estimated population.

MET AQH SHARE = The Metropolitan Average Quarter Hour Persons estimate for a given station expressed as a percentage of the total MET AQH estimate within a reported daypart.

MET CUME PER = The esti-

mated number of *different* persons who listened to a station for a minimum of five minutes in a quarter-hour within a reported daypart. (Cume estimates may also be referred to as *cumulative* or *unduplicated* estimates.) Cume Persons estimates are expressed in hundreds (00) in this report. This estimate is also shown for the TSA.

MET CUME RATING = The estimated number of Cume Persons expressed as a percentage of the appropriate estimated Metropolitan population.

In our example, we generated 811,200 gross impressions with our schedule on station KKDA. But that does *not* mean that 811,200 *different* people heard our commercials. Many people might have heard our commercials three, four, or five times.

By measuring the cumulative number of different persons who listened to KKDA, the rating services give us an idea of the reach *potential* of our radio schedule, which in this case is 167,800.

The **cume rating** is the estimated number of cume persons expressed as a percentage of the estimated population. For example,

$$\frac{167,800}{3,072,727} = .052 \text{ or } 5.2\%$$

Preparing a Radio Schedule

The procedure advertisers use to prepare their radio schedules is similar to that used to prepare their TV schedules. The steps are as follows:

1. Identify stations with the greatest concentration (cume) of the advertiser's target audience by demographics (e.g., men aged 25 to 34).

2. Identify stations whose format typically offers the highest concentration of potential buyers. The advertiser may know, for instance, that while many men and women between the ages of 35 and 49 listen to beautiful music stations, the best format for potential tire purchasers in that age group is an all-news or sports format.

3. Determine which time periods (dayparts) on those stations offer the greatest number (average quarter-hour) of potential buyers. Here again, it is more likely that prospective tire buyers will be concentrated in drive time rather than midday.

4. Using the stations' rate cards for guidance, construct a schedule with a strong mix of these best time periods. An average weekly spot load per station may be anywhere from 12 to 30 announcements, depending on the advertiser's budget. At this point, it is often wise to contact the station reps, give them a breakdown of the advertiser's media objectives, suggest a possible budget for their station, and ask what they can provide for that budget. This gives the media buyer a starting point for analyzing costs and negotiating the buy.

5. Determine the cost for each 1,000 target people each station delivers. The operational word here is *target*. The media buyer is not interested in the station's total audience.

6. Negotiate and place the buy.

7. Assess the buy (with the help of the agency's or radio station's computer) in terms of reach and frequency.

These steps are far from all-inclusive, but they demonstrate some of the complexity media planners and buyers deal with daily in their efforts to match an advertiser's message with a target audience on radio.

Summary

As a means of reaching the masses, no other medium today has the unique creative ability of television. Broadcast television has grown faster than any other advertising medium in history because of the unique advantages it offers advertisers: mass coverage at low cost, audience selectivity, impact, prestige, and social dominance.

Television's power as a creative tool may be unmatched, but the medium still has many drawbacks. These include high cost, limited selectivity, brevity, clutter, and susceptibility to zipping and zapping.

The four forms of television advertising are network, spot, syndication, and local. Within these classifications are many commercial opportunities for advertisers.

To determine which shows to buy, the media buyer must select the most efficient ones against the target audience. The task, therefore, is to compare the packages of each station, substituting stronger programs for the less efficient ones, and negotiating prices to get the best buy.

Broadcast television's dominance is being challenged by new electronic media, particularly cable. Cable offers the visual and aural appeal of television at a much lower cost and with greater flexibility. The cable audience is highly fragmented, which helps advertisers target specific markets but is a drawback for those wanting to reach the mass audience. Cable advertising can be done at the national, regional, or local level and can take the form of program sponsorships, segment sponsorships, and spots of varying lengths, including the longer infomercials.

Like television, radio is recognized as a highly creative medium. However, its greatest attribute is probably its ability to offer excellent reach and frequency to selective audiences at a very efficient price. Its drawbacks relate to the limitations of sound, the fact that radio audiences are very segmented, and the nature of short-lived and half-heard commercials.

Radio stations are normally classified by the programming they offer and the audiences they serve. Radio stations may be AM or FM, may make use of network or syndicated programs, and may follow one of a dozen or more popular formats.

Advertisers may purchase radio time in one of three forms: local, spot, or network.

Buying radio time requires a basic understanding of radio terminology. The most common terms are *dayparts, average quarter-hour,* and *cumulative audiences.*

Questions for Review and Discussion

1. What are the advantages of broadcast television advertising for a product such as Energizer batteries?
2. What are the advantages of 15-second commercials? What are the drawbacks?
3. How can advertisers overcome the problems of zipping and zapping?
4. Why has advertising on network TV come to be seen as less desirable in recent years?
5. What would you do to purchase time from a local television station? Outline the procedure you would follow.
6. In what ways is cable TV's selectivity a strength? In what ways is it a drawback?
7. Why do you suppose some advertisers don't believe in the effectiveness of radio advertising?
8. What is the format of the radio station you listen to most? How would you describe the demographics of its target audience?
9. What is the difference between average quarter-hour and cume audiences? Which is the better measure for media planners?
10. What is the importance of dayparts to advertisers?

DIRECT MAIL AND OUTDOOR MEDIA

Objective: To present the media that advertisers commonly use to complement print and broadcast in the media mix, or use in place of those mass media; to evaluate the advantages and disadvantages of the direct-mail, outdoor, and transit media; and to explain the basics of buying direct-mail and outdoor advertising.

After studying this chapter, you will be able to:

☐ Differentiate between direct marketing and direct mail.

☐ Identify the three distinct forms of mail-order advertising.

☐ Cite the advantages and disadvantages of direct-mail advertising.

☐ Discuss database marketing.

☐ Explain how outdoor advertisers measure exposure.

☐ Describe the types of outdoor advertising structures.

☐ Identify the variables that influence the cost of transit advertising.

W hen Champion International wanted to create enthusiasm for a new paper stock among industrial purchasing decision makers, its target audience consisted of only 315 publishing executives.

Because the audience was so small, the Stamford, Connecticut-based paper company decided to pour several hundred thousand dollars into an extremely targeted direct-mail campaign. Working with an agency that develops dimensional mailings, Champion created a nine-part mailing with a billiards theme. (Dimensional mailings, as the name suggests, rely on three-dimensional items instead of, or in addition to, flat enclosures.)

Each of the nine mailings tied the pool theme together with a point about Champion or its new high-gloss paper product, named "Influence." The first mailing was a miniature pool table. Supporting copy explained that the company is "in position to pool our resources. . . . and being in position is everything in our industry." A later mailing included seven striped pool balls in a box headlined, "We've earned our stripes." Additional copy explained how Champion had worked to become an industry leader. Yet another mailing held a cue ball printed with the "Influence" name; copy described product benefits, as shown in Exhibit 15-1.

Other mailings included items such as a full-size cue stick, chalk, a pool bridge, and a ball rack. The mailings were "a succinct way to get a key point

EXHIBIT 15-1

Champion's "Influence" direct-mail campaign consisted of a series of nine packages. Each contained a billiards-related item and copy associating the item to Champion or its products.

across to our customers about our product and Champion," says John H. Hildenbiddle, the company's vice president of creative services. Champion fielded the dimensional campaign a few months before the product was commercially available, to prime the market.

The mailings, designed to pique the recipients' curiosity about the product and pave the way for sales calls by Champion sales representatives, were a great success. Reps were able to make personal sales presentations to 95 percent of the executives who received the mailings. "All of the people have said, 'if [Influence is] as good as you say it is, we'll try it,'" Hildenbiddle reports.[1]

DIRECT-MAIL ADVERTISING

Direct-mail advertising is the term given to all forms of advertising that are sent directly to prospects through the U.S. Postal Service or through private delivery services. In dollars spent, direct mail is the third-ranked advertising medium today, surpassed only by newspapers and TV.

No matter how large or small a company may be, it nearly always uses direct mail in its advertising program. When a firm starts in business, its first medium of advertising is generally direct mail, and as it grows, it usually continues to use direct mail. The reason is clear: The shortest distance between two points is a straight line. And of all the media, direct mail offers the "straightest" line to reach the desired prospective customer.

Direct Mail versus Direct Marketing

Several other terms are frequently confused with direct mail. These include *direct advertising, direct marketing,* and *direct-response* and *mail-order advertising.* How are these concepts similar, and how do they differ?

Direct Advertising

Direct advertising is any form of advertising issued directly to the prospect through the use of the mails, fax machines, on-line computer services, interactive electronic kiosks, salespeople, dealers, or other means rather than through the traditional mass media. Such advertising may take the form of door-to-door circulars, telephone solicitations, handbills, computer diskettes, videocassettes, or direct mail.

Direct Mail

Direct mail is any form of direct advertising that is sent through the mail. It is perhaps the most popular form of direct advertising today. A brochure sent to a prospect by mail is *direct-mail advertising.* But if the same brochure is distributed door-to-door, it is not direct mail. (It is still direct advertising.) The difference, then, is in the distribution method.

Direct Marketing

With **direct marketing,** advertising media are used to build a *database* of customer information. The choice of media includes direct mail, newspapers, magazines, radio, or television used alone or in combination. The goal of direct marketing is to get inquiries, to sell merchandise or services direct, to provide support to salespeople and distributors, to encourage feedback, to get contributions, or to get people to visit stores.[2]

Underlying all direct-marketing success is the ability to trigger a direct, measurable action that is cost-effective. This can be achieved by using any of these selling methods: (*a*) buyer seeks out seller through a retailer or exhibit, (*b*) seller seeks out buyer through personal selling, or (*c*) buyer seeks out seller by mail or phone to obtain a mail order.[3]

Direct Response

Direct-response advertising is a message that asks the reader, listener, or viewer for an immediate response. A newspaper or magazine ad, for example, may ask the reader to fill in and mail a featured coupon to obtain information or to actually order the advertised product, as shown in Exhibit 15-2. Direct-response advertising can take the form of mailings (direct mail), or it can use a wide range of other media, including matchbook covers, magazines, radio, TV, or even outdoor posters (billboards). With the advent of toll-free phone numbers, television ads that urge viewers to "Call now! Operators are standing by!" have become much more common. Exhibit 15-3 (p. 538) is an example of such advertising. Advertisers of both consumer goods and industrial products use direct-response advertising to stimulate

EXHIBIT 15-2

This direct-response ad for Perform dog food lists a toll-free telephone number to make ordering easy.

EXHIBIT 15-3

Direct-response TV ads, which ask viewers to use an 800 number to order, are now used for everything from kitchen appliances to telephone systems.

(MUSIC UNDER)

ANNCR: (VO) The owner of this small business has found a way to do more in a day than he ever thought possible. Now he has the power to stay next to his phone without being tied to his chair. This . . . is his competitive edge. He's discovered the first cordless phone specifically designed for business: the revolutionary new AT&T MERLIN Cordless. Now he's free to make, take, hold, or transfer calls from up to five people—all while he's on the move. And since it works with his AT&T Small Business Phone System, he doesn't have to give up AT&T quality. He isn't just working harder, he's working smarter. To find out more about the new MERLIN CORDLESS, call 1 800 367-6784. You'll wonder how you ever competed without it. 1 800 367-6784.

(MUSIC OUT)

sales. For business-to-business marketers, print and direct mail are the primary direct-response media. The usual objective of direct-response advertising for high-ticket industrial products is to generate sales leads for follow-up by a sales representative.

Another burgeoning area of direct-response advertising is **telemarketing,** in which prospective customers are called directly on the phone and given an oral sales presentation. One poll indicated that about 1 in 10 adults who had made a direct-marketing purchase within the prior two weeks had done so because of a promotional phone call.[4] However, consumers particularly dislike this form of advertising—the poll also discovered that nearly 90 percent of respondents were annoyed to some extent when salespeople called them at home.[5] Advertisers of many consumer goods and services now use telemarketing, and as the cost of direct sales calls has risen in the past 10 years, business-to-business advertisers have also begun to rely on this medium. In the industrial arena, telemarketing is particularly efficient for selling low-priced products, such as replacement parts and office supplies.

Mail Order

Mail-order advertising is both a form of direct-response advertising and a method of selling in which the product or service is promoted through advertising and the prospect orders it *through the mail.* It involves no intermediate salespeople. As it is practiced today, mail-order advertising may be received in any of three distinct forms: mail-order catalogs (like Lands' End or Spiegel), advertisements in a wide variety of print and electronic media, and direct-mail advertising.

EXHIBIT 15-4	Top 10 Mail-Order Product Categories	
Rank	Category	Sales ($ billions)
1	Insurance/financial	$13.3
2	Department stores	11.7
3	General merchandise	9.5
4	Apparel	8.6
5	Magazines	5.7
6	Sporting goods	3.6
7	Electronic goods	2.7
8	Collectibles	2.1
9	Books	2.0
10	Crafts	1.2

Growth of Direct Mail

Direct marketing, direct mail, and telemarketing in particular, have grown astronomically in the past 10 years. Just the number of catalogs mailed grew from 5.8 billion in 1980 to 13.6 billion in 1990. Between 1983 and 1990, the number of adult Americans shopping by mail and phone increased from 36 percent to 55 percent. By 1989, U.S. mail-order sales had reached $183.3 million, of which about $87 million were consumer purchases. Direct mail represents 19 percent of all advertising spending.[6]

Direct mail is successful because it uniquely meets the needs of today's changing lifestyles. With more and more women in the work force, families find they have more discretionary income but less time to shop. Shopping at home, by mail, is much easier than going to stores, and consumers can often get more detailed information about products from catalogs and sales brochures than they can get from harried or unknowledgeable retail salespeople.

Direct-mail advertising also has boomed as a result of the consumer credit-card explosion. Credit-based mass marketers have expanded their profits by stuffing monthly customer statements with tempting mail-order product offers for everything from small personal items to major appliances. And the increased availability of credit has enabled them to sell high-priced items to consumers. Products that are innovative, can be shipped fairly easily, and are not readily available through other distribution channels are the best candidates for direct-mail sales. Leading consumer mail-order products include books, housewares, clothing, electronic gadgets, and the other products and services listed in Exhibit 15-4.

With more and more major companies entering the field, the direct-mail image is improving daily. Consumers seem more comfortable ordering by mail, knowing that when they deal with reputable companies, they can get quality merchandise, often at a reduced price. Many mail-order companies have highly sophisticated systems for ordering, fulfillment, and after-sale follow-up designed to make shopping easy and satisfying.

Among the biggest users of direct-mail advertising are insurance companies, financial institutions, and marketers of other types of financial services. American Express, for example, is one of the strongest believers in direct mail. And Charles Schwab & Company, one of the country's leading discount brokerage houses, originally achieved its status through the exclusive use of direct marketing, primarily direct-mail advertising.[7]

USING DIRECT MAIL IN THE CREATIVE MIX

Direct mail is an efficient, effective, and economical medium for sales and business promotion. Thus, it is used by a wide variety of retail, commercial, and industrial companies; charity and service organizations; and individuals. Direct mail can also increase the effectiveness of advertising in other media if carefully coordinated. Publishers Clearinghouse, for example, uses TV spots in conjunction with its direct-mail campaigns. These commercials alert viewers to the impending arrival of direct-mail sweepstakes promotions.

Types of Direct Mail

Direct-mail advertising has many forms. These include sales letters, brochures, and even handwritten postcards. The message can be as short as one sentence or as long as dozens of pages. And within each format—from tiny coupon to thick catalog—an almost infinite variety is possible.

Sales letters are the most common form of direct mail. They can be typewritten, typeset and printed, printed with a computer insert (such as your name), or fully computer-typed. They are often mailed with brochures, price lists, or reply cards and envelopes.

Postcards are generally used to announce sales, offer discounts, or otherwise generate customer traffic. Postcards may travel by first- or third-class mail. The first-class postcard may feature a handwritten message, but third-class postcards must be printed and may not contain handwriting.

Some advertisers use a double postcard, enabling them to send both an advertising message and a perforated reply card. A recipient who wants the advertised product or service simply tears off the reply card and mails it back to the advertiser. To encourage response, some advertisers use a postpaid reply card. This requires having a first-class postal permit, which is available for a nominal fee from the local postmaster.

Leaflets or **flyers** are generally single, standard-size ($8\frac{1}{2}$-by-11-inch) pages printed on one or both sides and folded one or more times. They usually accompany a sales letter and are used to supplement or expand the information it contains.

Folders, larger than leaflets in most cases, are printed on heavier paper stock. Their weight and size enable them to "take" a printed visual image well. They are often designed with photos or other illustrations, usually in full color. Folders can accommodate a longer, more detailed sales message than most leaflets. Often they are folded and sent as self-mailers, without envelopes, for increased economy.

Broadsides are larger than folders. Though sometimes used as window displays or wall posters in stores, they can be folded to a compact size that will fit into a mailbag.

Self-mailers are any form of direct mail (postcards, leaflets, folders, broadsides, brochures, catalogs, house organs, magazines) that can travel by

EXHIBIT 15-5

Parker Pen used striking photography in its catalog to convey the quality of its writing instruments and to gain reader attention.

mail without an envelope. Such mailers are often folded and secured by a staple or seal. They have a special blank space on which the prospect's name and address can be written, stenciled, or labeled.

Reprints are direct-mail enclosures frequently sent by public relations agencies or departments. They are duplications of publication articles that show the company or its products in a favorable light.

Statement stuffers are advertisements enclosed in the monthly customer statements mailed by department stores, banks, or oil companies. Many different types of products—from camping equipment to stereo systems—are sold this way. To order, the customer simply writes the credit card number on the reply card.

House organs are publications produced by business organizations. They take many forms, including stockholder reports, newsletters, consumer magazines, and dealer publications. Most are produced by the company's advertising or public relations department or by its agency. Today, an estimated 10,000 different house organ publications are mailed in the United States each year and read by more than 3.5 million people.

Catalogs are reference books that list, describe, and often picture the products sold by a manufacturer, wholesaler, jobber, or retailer. Nearly everyone is familiar with the Sears Roebuck and J. C. Penney catalogs, but similar catalogs are mailed by the millions each year by industrial, mail-order, and retail firms. The catalog in Exhibit 15-5 was distributed by Parker Pen. With more people shopping at home, specialized catalogs have become big business in recent years. In 1990, there were more than 7,000 mail-order catalogs of all types. Sears, logging catalog sales of more than $3.9 billion a year, now has 30 different "Focus" catalogs that feature specific types of merchandise, such as children's clothing, farm and ranch products, and items for mobile home owners.[8] Other mail-order companies that have prospered with specialized approaches offer outdoor clothing and equipment (L. L. Bean, Campmor), electronic gadgets (Sharper Image), gourmet foods (Balducci's), and children's items (Childcraft, Just for Kids).[9]

The downside of the catalog boom is that with so many choices available, consumer response per catalog is down, while the costs of preparing and mailing catalogs are increasing. As a result, some companies, including Montgomery Ward, have gone out of the mail-order business, and many firms that were exclusively mail order have begun to open retail stores. Royal Silk, for example, started out selling clothing solely through the mail but opened several stores after consumers displayed an interest in buying at retail.[10] And Sharper Image, which originally sold only through its catalogs, now makes 80 percent of all sales through its retail stores.[11]

Buying Direct-Mail Advertising

Direct-mail advertising entails three basic costs: list rental or purchase; conception, production, and handling of the direct mailer; and distribution.

ETHICAL DILEMMA IN ADVERTISING
The Direct-Mail Privacy Crisis

Direct-mail advertisers succeed by aiming their pitches at very specific targets, so the single most important element—the very foundation—of any given campaign is the mailing list. Countless companies provide lists to help direct mailers sell billions of dollars in products each year. The quality of information the lists provide is crucial; the better the list, the better the response and the bigger the profits.

To maximize profits, direct mailers seek out highly personalized profiles of potential customers, including intimate information about their purchasing habits and lifestyles. The most effective lists categorize people in such detail that it sometimes seems like an invasion of privacy. A business called Jewish Introductions International offers a list of 16,000 Jewish singles with incomes of $50,000-plus, and a prominent chain of ice-cream parlors sells its birthday club list to the Selective Service System. Today, nobody's safe from the long arm of list compilers.

Although most direct mailers contend they follow sound ethical principles, some obviously don't. The sleaziest have made a science of targeting special groups like impulse buyers or elderly consumers who scare easily and are more vulnerable to certain sales pitches. And, of course, a small minority are frauds who tout investment deals that are outright scams.

According to the U.S. Office of Consumer Affairs, the most common consumer complaint about mailing lists is that information collected for one purpose (such as credit applications) is often sold to direct mailers. When Consumer Affairs Director Bonnie Guiton testified before Congress, she voiced the concern that once individuals provide information in good faith, they lose all control over its use. And that, Guiton believes, constitutes a threat to personal privacy.

With consumer discontent growing, the direct-marketing industry is on the defensive. Direct Marketing Association president Jonah Gitlitz maintains, "I think people don't mind disclosing information about themselves to get a more specific sales offer." But he acknowledges that "information collected for one purpose should not be used for another." Gitlitz also points out that consumers can register with the DMA to have their names removed from mailing lists. According to DMA director of ethics and consumer affairs Lorna Christie, over a million people have filed such requests since 1985. DMA members must also subscribe to the association's standard of ethics, and the organization does follow up on mail-order complaints. Gitlitz says, "When we receive no cooperation on vio-

Direct-Mail Lists

Bob Stone, author of *Successful Direct Marketing Methods,* calls mailing lists the "heart" of every direct-mail operation. Each list, he points out, actually defines a market segment. The lists may be grouped as house lists, mail-response lists, and compiled lists.[12]

☐ **House lists.** A company's customers are its most important asset. It stands to reason, therefore, that its list of customer and prospect names compiled over a long time is also the company's most important and valuable direct-mail asset. This list may contain current, recent, and long-past customers or future prospects. The general manager of Ogilvy & Mather Direct has suggested six ways a store can build its own house list: (1) offer a credit plan; (2) offer to send useful booklets or other service information; (3) exchange names with other retailers with similar customer profiles; (4) capture the names of customers who ask for home delivery; (5) offer warranties or service plans; and (6) ask current customers to provide names of friends and neighbors.[13]

One way GE Consumer Electronics Products gathers customer data for mailings is by enclosing an owner registration form with appliances such as

lations, we have a process through our ethics committee in which we present their files to the Federal Trade Commission for possible action." Sounds good—but only about half the nation's direct marketers belong to the DMA.

Though the direct-mail industry professes concern about mailing list abuse, it often seems content with winning narrow legal victories and lobbying against its opponents rather than imposing strict ethical standards on its members. But if self-regulation fails, the time bomb of consumer privacy will explode. Roy Schwedelson, CEO of WMI/Worldata, a list management and brokerage firm, says, "Direct marketers in all industries have to realize that they are playing with fire. They are bringing on regulations that no one wants."

With the threat of strict regulation right around the corner, some advertisers have begun to build their own lists. Quaker Oats compiled an inventory of 30 million households, then sent out a questionnaire that was apparently designed to profile select consumers in microscopic detail. Privacy watchdog groups called the survey an intolerable invasion of privacy because it asked questions about household income, credit card usage, and the consumer feelings about mandatory drug testing, the right to own guns, and school prayer. Nobody was forced to reply, but

Robert Smith, publisher of the *Privacy Journal,* says, "Consumers' participation is by rote," so it's almost automatic. Smith also argues that most consumers are ignorant of how their answers might be used.

In the final analysis, following self-imposed ethical standards should be a matter of simple common sense for direct mailers. As copywriter Milt Pierce says, "We in direct marketing live or die by the trust of people who never see our store, never see our product, and often become our customers by . . . mere faith. Such faith demands a higher standard of ethics."

Questions

1. You and a friend work at the same list brokerage firm. You accidentally learn that your friend is helping an important client fraudulently misuse the information on a mailing list. Would you blow the whistle on your friend? Would you testify against your friend if the case went to court?

2. In the Quaker Oats example given above, do you think the company should be compelled to tell consumers exactly how it proposes to use the information obtained?

Doubleday Book Club

Doubleday List Marketing

Location ID: 10 DCLS 564   Mid 019694-000
Member: D.M.A.
Participant D.M.A. Mail Preference Service.
Doubleday Mailing Lists.
501 Franklin Ave., Garden City, NY 11530. Phone 516-873-4477. Fax: 516-873-4774.
Specific list selections are located in each appropriate classification in their normal alphabetical sequence.

1. **PERSONNEL**
Manager, List Marketing—Diane Silverman.
Assistant Manager, List Mktg.—Liz Maletta.
List Mktg. Coordinator—Linda Jackson.
Broker and/or Authorized Agent
All recognized brokers.

2. **DESCRIPTION**
Doubleday Book Club members.
ZIP Coded in numerical sequence 100%.

3. **LIST SOURCE**
Direct mail and space ads.

4. **QUANTITY AND RENTAL RATES**
Rec'd Mar. 8, 1990.

	Total Number	Price per/M
Members	900,000	75.00
Hotline	479,000	80.00
Completers (1989-90)	433,000	40.00
Age-coded names	2,130,000	80.00

Selections: enrollment date, 5.00/M extra; dollar select, 6.00/M extra; Mr./Mrs./Miss/Ms., sex, 3.00/M extra; state, SCF, ZIP tape, 4.00/M extra.

5. **COMMISSION, CREDIT POLICY**
20% commission to all recognized brokers. Payments due 30 days after billing.

6. **METHOD OF ADDRESSING**
4/5-up Cheshire labels. 4-up pressure sensitive labels, 5.00/M extra. Magnetic tape (9T 1600/6250 BPI).

7. **DELIVERY SCHEDULE**
Ten working days.

8. **RESTRICTIONS**
Sample mailing piece required for approval.

9. **TEST ARRANGEMENT**
Minimum 10,000.

11. **MAINTENANCE**
Cleaned and updated quarterly.

EXHIBIT 15-6

This is a typical listing from *Direct Mail List Rates and Data (Consumer Lists),* published by Standard Rate and Data Service.

radios and stereos. The company also sells the information to other direct-mail advertisers. On the mail-in form, purchasers reveal their name, address, telephone number, birth date, occupation, income range, credit card preferences, home ownership status, and number of children. They also indicate their hobbies and interests, such as golf, foreign travel, photography, and bowling. After reporting an interest in wine tasting and real estate investment on the owner registration form, the consumer can expect to start receiving mailings from advertisers selling those products and services.

☐ **Mail-response lists.** Next to customers, the advertiser's second most important prospects are those who have responded to the direct-mail solicitations of other companies, especially firms whose efforts are complementary to the advertiser's. For example, if you plan to advertise wool scarves and sports-car caps, you might find the most attractive response list to be held by a company that markets driving gloves. Thousands of such response lists are available from an array of firms. They are simply the house lists of other direct-mail advertisers, and they are usually available for rental with a wide variety of demographic breakdowns.

☐ **Compiled lists.** The third kind of list is the most readily available in volume but offers the lowest response expectation. It is simply a list compiled for one reason or another by a source. These may include lists of automobile owners, new-house purchasers, city business owners, Chamber of Commerce presidents, union members, and so on. Compiled lists are often computer merged with mail-response and house lists. This **merge and purge** process involves merging all names and purging all duplicates so that no more than one piece of a mailing is sent to one name.

Direct-mail lists can be purchased or rented. Advertisers who buy the list may use it unlimitedly; those who rent are usually granted the right to use it for only a single mailing. One way list owners discover whether renters use the list more than once is to plant decoy names in the list.[14] Most list owners, to make sure the advertiser does not mail anything that reflects poorly on them or competes with their own products or services, require the prospective renter to submit sample mailers.

Many lists are handled by **list brokers.** A list owner who does not want to bother with the details of renting the list can retain a broker to handle it. The list owner pays the broker a commission (usually 20 percent) for this service. The advertiser in turn benefits from the broker's direct-mail knowledge and expertise without paying more than the rental cost of the list.

Lists can be brokered or exchanged with list houses or other noncompetitive companies. The variety of lists available today is virtually unlimited. Advertisers can rent lists of endocrinologists, farm equipment dealers, North American sports enthusiasts, and would-be entrepreneurs, for example. Lists may be tailored to reflect customer location (ZIP code); demographics such as age, income, and credit card ownership; or psychographic characteristics, such as personality and lifestyle. The SRDS *Direct Mail List Rates and Data* comes in two volumes: Volume I, *Consumer Lists,* and Volume II, *Business Lists.* These resources contain more than 50,000 list selections in hundreds of different classifications. Exhibit 15-6 shows an SRDS listing.

The quality of mailing lists varies enormously. One owner of a wine store in San Francisco found this out firsthand when he purchased a mailing list that turned out to include hundreds of out-of-date addresses and names of people who lived too far away to patronize his store, who were not wine drinkers, or who could not afford his fine, expensive wines. The wine retailer learned from his experience, hired a mailing list broker, and purchased a second list that produced much better results. The second list included the names of people who lived near his wine shop, subscribed to an expensive wine journal, and owned moderately expensive homes.[15]

The prices of mailing lists vary according to their quality. Rental rates average about $30 per thousand names, but lists can be secured for as little as $15 per thousand or as much as $400 per thousand. The more stringent the advertiser's selection criteria, the more expensive the list. As the San Francisco wine store owner discovered, spending an extra $10 per thousand is often well worth the savings in wasted mailers and postage that result from using an imprecise list.

The average mailing list changes more than 40 percent a year. One reason for this is that some 20 percent of the nation's population relocates to a new address each year. Large numbers of people also make job changes, get married, or die. Therefore, mailing lists must be continually updated. This *cleaning,* as it is called, ensures that the list is current and correct.

Computers can also be used to enhance mailing lists, turning them into valuable databases. The process of **overlaying,** for example, combines information from several different sources to produce an in-depth profile of each customer or company on the list. The profile may include the customer's purchasing history as well as demographic information. Such detailed databases pave the way for the *maximarketing* techniques discussed in Chapter 7, in which advertisers pinpoint customers and narrowly target mailings to those who are most likely to be interested in the product or service. Some experts believe direct mail will eventually be so specific that "junk mail" will disappear—all mailers will be meaningful to the recipients.[16]

With the computer, an advertiser can also test the validity and accuracy of a given list. This is done by renting or buying every *n*th name and sending a mailer to that person. If the results are favorable, additional names can be purchased, usually in lots of 1,000.

Production and Handling

The advertiser can create a direct-mail package or retain the services of an advertising agency or free-lance designer and writer. Some agencies specialize in direct mail.

Once the mailing package is conceived and designed, it is ready for printing. The size and shape of the mailing pieces as well as the specified type, illustrations, and colors all influence printing costs. Special features such as simulated blue-ink signatures, cardboard pop-ups, and die cutting (the cutting of paper stock into an unusual shape) add to the cost. But the larger the printing volume, or "run," the lower the printing cost per unit.

The remaining production tasks can be handled by a local **letter shop** unless the advertiser prefers to do them internally. On a cost-per-thousand basis, letter shops stuff and seal envelopes, affix labels, calculate postage, and sort, tie, and stack the mailers. Some shops also offer creative services. If the advertiser plans to use third-class bulk mail, the mailers must be separated by ZIP code and tied into bundles to qualify for low bulk rates. When these tasks are finished, the letter shop delivers the mailers to the post office.

Distribution

Distribution costs are chiefly based on the weight of the mailer and the delivery method. Advertisers have a choice of several such methods, including the U.S. Postal Service, United Parcel Service, air freight, and private delivery services.

Direct mail has been found to be most effective when it arrives on Tuesdays, Wednesdays, and Thursdays. This may be because some people are affected by Monday back-to-work blues and Friday can't-wait-for-the-weekend elation, or because the growing acceptance of the four-day workweek and expanded weekends means fewer people are "in town" from Friday through Monday.

The most common means of delivery is the U.S. Postal Service. It offers the advertiser a choice of several types of mail delivery.

☐ *First-class mail.* Contrary to popular belief, a large amount of direct-mail advertising is sent first class. **First-class mail** ensures fast delivery, returns any mail that is undeliverable, and forwards mail (without additional charge) if the addressee has moved and filed a forwarding address.

☐ *Business reply mail.* **Business reply mail** enables the recipient to respond without paying postage. The advertiser must first obtain a special permit number, which is available from the local postmaster. This number must be printed on the face of the return card or envelope. On receiving a response, the advertiser must pay postage plus a few cents handling fee. This "postage-free" incentive tends to increase the rate of response.

☐ *Third-class mail.* The four types of **third-class mail** are single piece, bulk, bound books or catalogs, and nonprofit organization mail. Most direct-mail advertising travels by third-class mail, which offers a significant savings over first-class rates.

☐ ***Fourth-class mail.*** This class applies only to mail that weighs over 16 ounces, typically merchandise, books, printed matter, and all mailable matter not in first, second, or third class.

Advantages of Direct Mail

Next to the personal sales call, direct mail is the most effective medium an advertiser can use to put a message in front of a prospect. As Ad Lab 15-A shows, advertisers of many kinds can benefit from direct mail. However, the medium is also the most expensive on a cost-per-exposure basis.

As a medium competing for advertisers' dollars, direct mail traditionally offers several key advantages over its competition..

Selectivity

Direct mail enables advertisers to select the desired prospects. By mailing only to these prime prospects—the ones most likely to buy the product or service—the advertiser can reduce sales costs and increase profits.

For example, if you wanted to advertise a 10-gallon paint compressor to professional painters, you wouldn't want to use TV. The medium's reach is too broad, and you would have to pay for the total audience. But by acquiring a list of professional painters and mailing your message directly to them, you could reach your desired audience more efficiently, at a lower cost, and with greater results. Today, computerized mailing lists enable advertisers to obtain names of people in a variety of occupational groups, in specific regions or

AD LAB 15-A
College Grad Gets Job through Mail

A 21-year-old college graduate of Glassboro State College (B.A. in communications/liberal arts) skillfully used his education in direct-response marketing to get a job.

He decided to test a direct-mail package and personal sales presentation in the Philadelphia area before going to New York to meet industry leaders, to secure at least 10 interviews at direct-response marketing agencies in New York City, and to obtain two job offers.

His marketing plan included a direct-mail package, a mailing envelope, a letter to spark interest, a folder to explain the product, and a reply card to make responding easier.

Chief executive officers or the presidents of direct-response marketing agencies or of direct-response divisions of advertising agencies were contacted. The test market comprised medium-sized to large advertising agencies in the Philadelphia area that listed direct-mail or direct-response advertising as part of their media breakdown. The Philadelphia list was compiled from an area business publication, *Focus Magazine,* which annually devotes one issue to Philadelphia's advertising agencies.

The initial mailing consisted of 43 pieces to Philadelphia (mailed the first week of June) and later, 24 pieces to New York (mailed the first week of July). Two weeks following the mail drop, he initiated a telephone call to each nonrespondent. The purpose was to confirm receipt of the direct-mail package and to ask for a personal interview. The total allocated budget for this program was $723.

As a result of this campaign, the graduate secured nine interviews in New York City and received two job offers there.

Attention Advertising Executives! When You're Ready To Make A Sound Investment . . .
Here Are Five Profitable Reasons Why You Should Hire This Adman

Laboratory Application

If you were to prepare a job-hunting direct-mail advertising campaign for yourself, what reader benefits would you include? (See Chapter 8 on copywriting.)

states, in given age groups, in particular income categories, and in other demographic classifications.

Baby food, diaper, and toy manufacturers wanting to advertise their products to new parents can, for example, obtain mailing lists compiled by *American Baby* magazine or by companies that buy names from diaper services, maternity shops, or childbirth training instructors. In fact, each year millions of parents with new babies receive numerous direct-mail pitches targeted specifically at them.[17]

The gradual fragmentation of the mass consumer market, combined with the availability of low-cost, high-powered computer hardware and software, has made **database marketing** increasingly common among direct-mail advertisers. Unlike traditional direct mail, in which the marketer targets groups of customers, database marketers try to pinpoint the needs of specific consumers. The advertiser creates and updates a customer database that includes information on purchasing habits and lifestyles. The customers provide this information through marketing surveys, product registration cards, mail-in rebate coupons, "frequent flier" club applications, and other response vehicles. By tracking and analyzing the purchasing patterns of specific customers in the database, the advertiser can achieve rifle-shot accuracy with their mailings.[18]

The advertiser may manage the customer database in-house or rely on an outside supplier. When the Quaker Oats Company launched its Quaker Direct marketing program nationally in 1990, it used consumer profiles from a database managed by Computerized Marketing Technologies. That supplier uses consumer surveys to gather information on buying preferences and habits. Quaker mailed its promotional package, a set of coupons, to 18 million households. The coupons in each direct-mail package were chosen specifically for the household that received the mailing. Households without dogs did not receive dog food coupons, for example, and consumers who buy Cap'n Crunch cereal received coupons for that product.[19]

Intensive Coverage and Extensive Reach

Most of the mass media are limited in the number of readers, viewers, or listeners they can reach. Not all viewers, for example, have their TV sets tuned to the same channel at the same time to see a given commercial. Not everyone in a community subscribes to and reads the local newspaper on the day a given ad runs. But virtually everyone has a mailbox, and by using direct mail, an advertiser can reach 100 percent of the homes in a given area. Direct mail literally reaches out and touches everyone the advertiser selects.

Flexibility

Few limitations exist on direct-mail format, style, or capacity. In addition, the wide variety of materials and processes available enable direct-mail advertising to be uniquely creative and novel, limited only by the ingenuity of the advertiser, the size of the advertising budget, and the regulations of the U.S. Postal Service.

The direct-mail piece may be a simple postcard or letter, or it may be a large folded broadside, a multipage brochure, or even a box containing

EXHIBIT 15-7

Direct mail sometimes plays on the curiosity of the recipient, as this Continental mailer suggests.

Recipients opened the main package, just to find another, and another, and another.

several elements. The direct-mail piece in Exhibit 15-7, from Continental Bank, shows how multiple enclosures can help communicate an advertising point. With direct mail, the advertiser can tell the prospect a little bit or include all the details necessary to understand a complex product. Moreover, the advertiser can usually produce a direct-mail piece and distribute it in considerably less time than it would take with most mass media. When speed is important, direct mail is usually considered.

Control

Advertisers have more control over direct-mail circulation and the quality of the message than with the print or broadcast media. Advertisers can choose the exact audience they want, the number of recipients and their locations, ages, gender, and other factors.

Preprinted direct-mail pieces enable a large advertiser, such as a department store chain, to control the quality of advertising reproduction for all its outlets. In contrast, a retail organization conducting a chainwide advertising campaign in 16 different newspapers is likely to encounter significant differences in the quality of printing, page placement, position, and reader response.

Personal Impact

Advertisers can personalize direct mail to the needs, wants, and whims of specific audiences. The privacy of the medium also allows the advertiser to make special offers to a specific group without offending other prospects or customers. A customer acquired by mail typically remains a mail-oriented customer and can be sold repeatedly, often through highly targeted direct-mail promotions instead of expensive sales calls. As Exhibit 15-8 (p. 550) shows, advertisers also may use targeted direct-mail campaigns to build awareness.

These factors, however, can also cause occasional problems for unwary advertisers. One major airline invited company executives to bring their wives along on their next flight and then sent a cordial thank you note to each wife. Unfortunately, some of the wives who received these notes hadn't gone on the flights. The airline's gracious effort not only unsettled a number of households but also lost at least a few executive customers—perhaps permanently. The personal nature of direct mail requires more advertiser caution—and discretion—than most other media. (See the Checklist of What Works Best in Direct Mail, p. 551.)

Exclusivity

When the prospect opens the mailbox and takes out a piece of direct-mail advertising, competitive distractions are at a minimum. In contrast, a magazine contains many eye-catching ads as well as articles, stories, and illustrations. These distractions reduce the attention the reader is likely to give a single ad.

Response

Direct mail normally achieves a higher percentage of responses per thousand people reached than any other advertising medium. And with direct mail, it's easy to measure the results. In addition, direct mail has a unique ability to

Talk about personalized target marketing! This bold self-promotion piece was aimed at an ad agency that had a specific job opening. The fact that it worked proves that one way to win a creative job is to do something creative.

measure the performance of a campaign strategy. As a rule of thumb, the direct-mail advertiser receives about 15 percent of the responses within the first week of a mailing and therefore knows almost immediately whether the campaign is going to be successful.

This relatively short-term measurement affords the advertiser still another advantage. The early stages of a campaign can test prospect reactions to product acceptability, pricing, audiences, offers, copy approaches, sales literature, and so on. Direct-mail advertisers often test two or more different approaches to a campaign before choosing the final format and contents. In fact, each element of the mailing can be tested individually, including the offer, the mailing list, and the writing and graphics of the package itself.[20]

Drawbacks to Direct Mail

Although direct mail has many unique advantages, it also has some disadvantages compared with other media.

High Cost per Exposure

Direct mail has the highest cost per exposure of any of the major media—about 14 times as much as most magazine and newspaper advertising. Why? Postal rates have soared in recent years and continue to climb. Paper costs also have risen sharply. Production and printing costs, particularly for full-color mailers, are at an all-time high. Even a one-page sales letter cannot be produced and printed and prepared for mailing for much less than $100 per thousand—and that doesn't include postage, which has also gone up. Advertisers typically use computer software to estimate costs and profits for a direct-mail campaign.

Checklist of What Works Best in Direct Mail

☐ *Make sure your offer is right.* More than any other element, what you offer the consumer—in product, price, or premium—will make the difference. Consider combinations instead of single units, optional extras, different opening offers, and commitment periods. *Free* is the most powerful offer you can make, but beware of its attracting lookers instead of buyers.

☐ *Demonstrate your product.* Offer a free sample, or enclose a sample if you can. Sampling is the most expensive promotion in absolute cost but is often so effective the investment is quickly paid back with a larger business base. If you measure response on a profit per piece mailed, it sometimes pays to spend a few more cents.

☐ *Use the envelope to telegraph your message.* Direct mail must work fast. Your envelope has only seconds to interest the prospect—or go unopened into the wastebasket.

☐ *Have a copy strategy.* Like any other advertising medium, direct mail will be more productive if you decide *in advance* the important issues of target audience, consumer benefit, and support, tone, and personality. While your promise should relate specifically to your product, experts say the most potent appeals in direct mail are how to make money, save money, save time, or avoid effort.

☐ *Grab the reader's attention.* Every beginning copywriter in direct mail learns the AIDA formula. The letters stand for the ideal structure of a sales letter: Attention, Interest,

Desire, Action. Look for a dramatic opening that speaks to the reader in a very *personal* way.

☐ *Don't be afraid of long copy.* The more you tell, the more you sell—particularly if you're asking the reader to spend a great deal of money or invest time. A Mercedes-Benz letter was five pages long. A Cunard Line letter for ocean cruises was eight pages. The key to long copy is *facts.* Be specific, not general. Make the letter visually appealing. Break up the copy into smaller paragraphs and emphasize important points with underlines or handwritten notes. Including several pieces in a direct-mail package often improves response.

☐ *Don't let the reader off the hook.* Leave your readers with something to do, so they won't procrastinate. It's too easy to put off a decision. Use action devices like a yes/no token to be stuck on a reply card. *Involvement* is important. Prod them to act *now.* Set a fixed period of time, like 10 days. Or make only a limited supply available. Make it extremely easy for the reader to respond to your offer. But always ask for the order.

☐ *Pretest your promises and headlines.* Don't guess at what will appeal to the reader. There are many ways to sell your product benefits and as many inexpensive testing methods. Avoid humor, tricks, or gimmicks. It pays to be serious and helpful.

Delivery Problems

A newspaper offers subscribers precise delivery times. The Sunday morning paper, for example, is home-delivered on Sunday mornings. Radio and TV shows are nearly always aired at the exact time scheduled. However, the U.S. Postal Service makes no delivery commitments on third-class mail. This may pose problems, particularly for "dated" mailers. Large retail stores generally allow 48 to 72 hours for the mail delivery of sale announcements. In some cases, however, sale mailers have arrived four to six days after a sale ended. Other times, the mailer never reaches its destination at all because of mistakes in the recipient's name or address. Depending on the advertiser's direct-mail list, up to 10 percent of the mailings may be undeliverable.[21]

Lack of Content Support

Magazine advertising usually owes its readership to the articles, stories, and illustrations that surround it. Direct mail, on the other hand, must stand alone; it must capture and hold the reader's attention without assistance. It must also stand out in some way from the handful of other direct-mail appeals that may arrive the same day. Thus, direct-mail advertising must combine

EXHIBIT 15-9

Direct mail is just too expensive to waste on people who don't want it. For those who want to reduce the amount of direct mail they receive, the Direct Marketing Association offers a unique service: removal of their names from many national lists. The DMA also offers consumers a chance to receive *more* direct mail if they want.

strong verbal and nonverbal appeals in an attractively laid out and well-produced format, and it must be conceived, written, and produced very carefully. The Musical Heritage Society, a direct-mail record club, learned this lesson the hard way when several recipients of a club mailing called in to complain about misspelled words and incorrect grammar in German copy in the mailer.[22]

Selectivity Problems

If the advertiser incorrectly identifies the prime audience for the mailing or does not obtain a good list of prospects, the mailing may fail.

Some groups of prospects have been so saturated by volumes of mail they have become less responsive to direct-mail advertising. Physicians, for example, are targeted by many financial, real estate, and insurance advertisers because of their favorable income image. The result is that the physician response rate is lower than that of most other professionals.

To avoid sending mail to people who do not want it, advertisers can use the name-removal service offered by the Direct Marketing Association. This unique service is described in Exhibit 15-9.

Negative Attitudes

Many consumers have negative attitudes toward what they perceive as "junk mail" and automatically throw it away—or are at least suspicious of mail solicitations. Consumers may not respond to direct-response offers because they distrust the advertiser or believe it's too difficult to return merchandise. Advertisers must respond to such attitudes to win consumers with direct mail.

Environmental Concerns

Consumers are also concerned about the problem of overflowing landfills and may perceive direct mail as just more landfill fodder. The use of non-biodegradable or environment-unfriendly mailing materials such as plastic catalog wrappers and the expanded polystyrene "peanuts" used to pack mail-order items also fuels consumer distaste for direct mail.

Recognizing that consumer concerns with environmental issues are not going to fade, direct-mail advertisers are taking steps to be more environmentally responsible. In 1989, the Direct Marketing Association established a Task Force on the Environment to identify ways direct marketers could become more environment-friendly. The Task Force is investigating the environmental merits of using recycled and recyclable paper and packaging, purging duplicates from mailing lists, establishing in-house recycling programs, and more.

Direct marketers such as Eddie Bauer and L. L. Bean print parts of their catalogs on paper with recycled content. Meanwhile, Esprit de Corp., Mac-Connection, Patagonia, and Seventh Generation are printing their entire catalogs on paper with recycled content. Patagonia is also reducing its annual catalog mailings from four to two, at least partly for environmental reasons. As dozens of paper de-inking facilities for coated paper stocks become operational in the mid-1990s, catalog recycling will become possible.[23] Ironically, several proenvironment groups rely heavily on direct-mail campaigns to solicit contributions.

OUTDOOR ADVERTISING

Anderson Travel, based in Winston-Salem, North Carolina, was leery of using outdoor advertising at first. Although the travel agency had used broadcast and print, "It was a strain to get Anderson in outdoor," recalls Julie Budd, of Morphis & Friends, the agency that created Anderson's first outdoor ads in 1988. "In the beginning, our client was a bit cautious, because he wasn't sure outdoor could say what he wanted to say in so few words," she explains. To reassure Anderson, Morphis created a campaign in which each outdoor ad featured high-quality graphics and memorable wordplay: "Sea It Our Way," "Try Our Lei Away Plan," "Waterwaytogo," and "Don't Miss Our Sail." Between the time the campaign broke in 1988 and the first quarter of 1990, Anderson's cruise bookings rose 200 percent. Today, the travel agency places all its ads on billboards.[24]

Standardization of the Outdoor Advertising Business

Media like outdoor advertising and transit advertising that reach prospects outside their homes are referred to as **out-of-home media.** Most advertising that appears out of doors consists of on-premise signs that identify a place of business. This type of sign, though certainly helpful to a business, does not provide market coverage. Conversely, **standardized outdoor advertising** locates its structures scientifically to deliver an advertiser's message to an entire market. Standardized outdoor advertising is a highly organized medium available to advertisers in more than 15,000 communities across the country. The structures on which the advertising appears are owned and maintained by individual outdoor advertising companies known as *plants.* The structures are built on private land the outdoor plant operators own or lease and are concentrated in commercial and business areas where they conform to all local building code requirements.

The industry consists of about 600 local and regional plant operators. They find suitable locations, lease or buy the property, erect the outdoor structures, contract with advertisers for poster rentals, and post the panels or paint the bulletins. Exhibit 15-10 (p. 554) shows how an outdoor ad is assembled. Plant operators also maintain the outdoor structures so lights are working and torn sheets are replaced, and they keep the areas surrounding the structures clean and attractive.

Usually, the smaller the market, the larger the percentage of local advertisers. The outdoor firm may employ an art staff to perform creative services for local advertisers, but the creative work for national advertisers is usually handled by advertising agencies. By far the biggest outdoor advertisers are retailers and makers of tobacco products, which together accounted for about 24 percent of all outdoor expenditures in 1990.[25]

Buying Outdoor Advertising

To buy outdoor advertising, the media planner must understand the different types of outdoor structures. The standardized structures have three basic forms: the poster panel, the bulletin, and the spectacular.

Poster Panels

Poster panels ("billboards") are the basic form of outdoor advertising and the least costly per unit. A poster is a structure consisting of blank panels with

EXHIBIT 15-10

A. Printed poster sheets are collated, prepasted, and vacuum-sealed in plastic bags. The glued sheets will remain moist for weeks. Erecting the poster begins with pasting on "blanking paper" to form a border. Next, beginning at the bottom, the prepasted sheets are applied to the first section of the panel.

B. By starting at the bottom and working upward, each sheet can overlap the previous section. This forms a "rain-lap" and helps prevent flagging or tearing of the poster. Because the sheets have been prepasted, a dry brush can be used to make the paper adhere to the panel. Prepasting also eliminates glue streaks from dark backgrounds.

C. Sheet by sheet, the giant paper mosaic is assembled to build the advertiser's message into a clean, colorful 12' by 25' display. Since a poster is a series of sheets, some sections of the poster can be varied for specific locations. Thus, some posters may have a different dealer's name.

a standardized size and border. It is usually anchored in the ground, but it may be affixed to a wall or roof. Its advertising message is first printed at a lithography or silk screen plant on large sheets of paper. These are then mounted by hand on the panel.

Poster sizes are referred to in terms of sheets. At one time, covering a structure 12' by 25' required 24 of the largest sheets a printing press could hold. The designation "24-sheet" is still used even though press sizes have changed and most poster sizes are larger. The poster is still mounted on a board with a total surface of 12' by 25', but today there are two basic sizes of posters:

☐ 30-sheet poster—with a 9'7" by 21'7" printed area surrounded by a margin of blank paper. The 30-sheet provides 25 percent more copy area than the old 24-sheet size of 8'8" by 19'6".

☐ Bleed poster—with a 10'5" by 22'8" printed area extending all the way to the frame. The bleed poster is about 40 percent larger than the old 24-sheet poster.

One way some local advertisers get high-quality outdoor advertising at lower than usual cost is to use ready-made 30-sheet posters. These stock posters are available in any quantity, and they often feature the work of first-class artists and lithographers. Local advertisers simply order as many as they need and have their name placed in the appropriate spot. These ready-made posters are particularly suitable for such local firms as florists, dairies, banks, and bakeries.

Advertisers of grocery products and many local advertisers like to use smaller poster sizes, such as "junior panels." These are also referred to as

EXHIBIT 15-11

As this custom-made board points out, some things are worth waiting for. After all, there's only one aquarium in town that has turtles that stand head and shell above the rest.

8-sheet posters and offer a 5′ by 11′ printing area on a panel surface 6′ wide by 12′ deep.

Painted Bulletins

Painted bulletins or **displays** are meant for long- term use and are usually placed in only the best locations where traffic is heavy and visibility is good. Painted bulletins are usually painted in sections in the plant's shop and then brought to the site, where they are assembled and hung on the billboard structure.

Although usually standardized in width and height, actual sizes depend on the available location, the advertiser's budget, and the character of the message. Bulletins are more often custom-made than posters, are generally larger, and are usually longer. Typical bulletins are 14′ by 48′; however, some even extend to 18′ by 62′10″.

Painted displays are normally illuminated and are repainted several times each year to keep them looking fresh. Some are three-dimensional or embellished by cutouts that extend beyond the frames, as shown in Exhibit 15-11. Variations include the use of cutout letters, plastic facing, backlighting, moving messages, clocks, thermometers, electric time and temperature units called jump clocks, and novel treatment of light and color. Ad Lab 15-B (p. 556) explains how advertisers can use color to best effect in outdoor advertising.

Some advertisers overcome the higher expense of painted bulletins by using a **rotary plan.** The bulletins are rotated to different choice locations in the market every 30, 60, or 90 days, giving the impression of wide coverage over time.

Spectaculars

Spectaculars are giant electronic signs that usually incorporate movement, color, and flashy graphics to grab the attention of viewers in high-traffic areas. Spectaculars are very expensive to produce and are found primarily in the largest cities, such as the Times Square area of New York City. Exhibit 15-12 (p. 557) shows the visual impact of spectaculars.

AD LAB 15-B
How to Use Color in Outdoor Advertising

Color Contrast and Value

The availability of a full range of colors, vividly and faithfully reproduced, is an outstanding advantage of outdoor advertising. A huge poster or bulletin alive with brilliant reds and greens and yellows and blues can produce an effect approached by no other medium.

In choosing colors for outdoor, the designer should seek high contrast in both hue (the identity of the color, such as red, green, yellow) and value (the measure of the color's lightness or darkness). Contrasting colors work well at outdoor-viewing distances, but colors lacking contrast blend together and obscure the message.

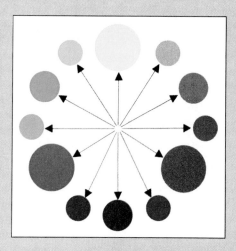

The color wheel illustrates the need for contrast in both hue and value. For example, green and red are opposite each other on the wheel and are therefore complementary colors. They represent a good contrast in *hues,* but are very similar *values*. As a result, they set up an annoying vibration. The same is true of blue and orange.

Blue and green and orange and red are especially poor combinations because they are similar in both hue *and* value.

On the other hand, yellow and purple—*dis*similar in both hue and value—provide a strong and effective con-

trast for outdoor. White goes well with any dark-value color, while black is good with colors of light value.

Color Impact

Among the color combinations shown, legibility ranges from best in combination 1 (upper left) to poorest in combination 18 (lower right).

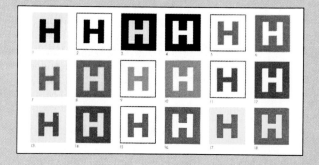

Color Combinations

Color combinations illustrate need for contrast in hue and value. Blue and green do *not* work well together; yellow and purple *do*.

Laboratory Applications

1. Which outdoor advertisements in this chapter use color the most effectively?
2. What examples of outdoor advertising have you seen that use color effectively?

Advantages of Outdoor Advertising

Outdoor advertising offers numerous and distinct advantages. They relate to the medium's reach, frequency, flexibility, impact, and cost.

EXHIBIT 15-12

Spectaculars are expensive, elaborate animated signs found primarily in the heart of large cities such as New York and Tokyo.

Reach

Often an advertiser requires saturation of a market to accomplish objectives such as the introduction of a new product or feature or a change in package design. Outdoor advertising is a mass medium that makes broad coverage possible overnight.

The term describing the basic unit of sale for billboards, or posters, is *100 gross rating points daily* or a 100 **showing.** One rating point is equal to 1 percent of a particular market's population. Buying 100 gross rating points does not mean, however, that the message will appear on 100 posters within a market. It means the message will appear on as many panels as needed to provide a daily exposure theoretically equal to 100 percent of the market's population. In actuality, however, an advertiser who buys a showing of 100 gross rating points will reach about 88.1 percent of adults in a market per day over the 30-day period during which the posters are "bought."[26]

An advertiser desiring less saturation can decrease the number of posters, and the units of sale would be expressed as fractions of the basic unit, such as 75, 50, or 25 gross rating points (GRPs). An advertiser desiring more saturation can increase the number of posters to reach as high as 200 or 300 GRPs per day. The map in Exhibit 15-13 shows the locations of billboards in Los Angeles and Orange Counties that provide 100 or more GRPs per day.

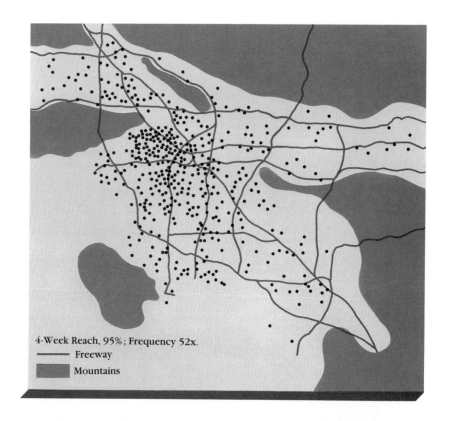

EXHIBIT 15-13

This map shows billboard locations throughout Los Angeles and Orange counties that would achieve at least 100 GRPs each day for four weeks. The cost of such a showing would be about $400,000.

EXHIBIT 15-14

An important advantage of billboards is that they can be targeted to a desired audience by careful placement. This billboard for UTA French Airlines was placed in rotating locations in Los Angeles and San Francisco targeted to high-income households. Studies have shown that outdoor advertising delivers a more affluent audience than television because younger, wealthier consumers tend to be on the go—eating out, attending the theater and concerts—rather than staying home watching TV.

Even more important to most advertisers is the audience reached by outdoor advertising. For the most part, its audience is a young, educated, affluent, and mobile population, and one very attractive to most national advertisers. That audience makes outdoor a particularly suitable medium for advertising luxury automobiles and travel, as shown in Exhibit 15-14.

EXHIBIT 15-15

The in-house agency for Robinson's Department Stores has produced an award-winning series of outdoor boards featuring products that expand beyond the confines of the traditional billboard. Most of these are co-op ads depicting products not normally seen in the outdoor medium.

Frequency

Outdoor offers *frequency of impressions*. According to the Institute for Outdoor Advertising, the 9 out of 10 people reached with a 100 GRP showing receive an average of 29 impressions each over a 30-day period. This frequency increases for groups that are better educated and have higher incomes—again, very attractive.

Data on frequency and reach for more than 8,000 markets are available from Audience Market by Market for Outdoor (AMMO), one of the services of the Institute for Outdoor Advertising.

Flexibility

In addition, outdoor offers advertisers great flexibility. They can place their advertising geographically where they want it—in any of 9,000 markets across the country—nationally, regionally, or locally. An outdoor advertiser can buy just one city or even a small section of that city. For a local advertiser such as Robinson's Department Stores, whose billboard ad is shown in Exhibit 15-15, the ability to deliver an advertising message with geographic selectivity is quite attractive.

The flexibility can be demographic. Messages can be concentrated in areas frequented or traversed by young people, upper-income people, or people of specific ethnic backgrounds. One outdoor company, Winston Network, has even developed a computerized method for characterizing outdoor audiences by age, sex, income, and lifestyle down to the block level.[27]

Outdoor can even target consumers by activity, reaching shoppers on their way to the store, businesspeople on their way to and from work, or travelers on their way to the airport, for example.

Cost

Outdoor advertising offers the lowest cost per message delivered of any major advertising medium. Rates vary depending on the size of the particular market and the intensity desired.

If a showing provides 750,000 total impression opportunities daily in a market with a population of 1 million, it is said to deliver 75 GRPs daily. Over

EXHIBIT 15-16	Monthly Rates for Standard Posters (12' by 25') in Selected Metropolitan Markets						

Market	25 daily GRPs		50 daily GRPs		100 daily GRPs		Average/ poster for 100 daily GRPs
	Number	Cost	Number	Cost	Number	Cost	
Atlanta	30	$13,800	60	$ 27,000	120	$ 51,600	$430
Denver	21	11,100	39	20,000	78	39,500	506
Detroit	45	29,700	90	59,400	180	118,800	660
Las Vegas	9	4,150	16	7,190	31	13,415	101
Los Angeles	120	78,000	240	154,800	480	306,000	638
Minneapolis/St. Paul	45	21,825	90	43,650	180	87,300	485
New Orleans	20	9,500	40	19,000	80	38,000	475
Phoenix	22	13,500	44	26,000	88	52,000	591
Seattle	29	15,573	58	31,146	116	62,292	537
St. Louis	32	17,757	64	35,514	128	71,030	555

Note: Costs are for space only; they do not include production. Discounts are available.

a period of 30 days, this showing would earn 2,250 GRPs (30 × 75). The GRP system makes cost comparison possible from market to market.

Local and national advertisers are charged the same rates. These are quoted on a monthly basis for various GRP levels and vary considerably from market to market. Differences are due to variations in property rentals, labor costs, and market size. Higher rates are found in larger markets where traffic volume is high. Exhibit 15-16 lists the space rates for standard posters in Los Angeles and several other cities.

The *Buyers Guide to Outdoor Advertising,* published twice a year by the Institute of Outdoor Advertising, contains detailed rate information.

Impact

All this adds up to economical intensity of impressions for the advertiser. With relatively low cost, the advertiser can build up GRPs very fast by hitting a large percentage of the market many times over a short period. This, of course, is ideal for advertisers who have a short, simple, dogmatic message. (See Portfolio of Outdoor Advertising: A 20th-Century Art Form, pp. 563-65.)

The inherent features of outdoor add impact and unique creative possibilities to the advertiser's message. Outdoor offers the largest display of any medium, and advertisers can use the size of the outdoor ad to dramatize their marketing messages. Outdoor advertising also offers the spectacular features of lights, animation, and brilliant color. Outdoor technologies, such as fiber optics and backlit displays for billboards, offer even more creative options to outdoor advertisers. Observers predict that billboards incorporating giant video screens could even become a reality.[28]

Finally, whereas other media carry the message to the prospect, outdoor sells continuously day and night, catching people on their way to shop, work, or play. Thus, posters like the popcorn ad in Exhibit 15-17 can influence

This eye-catching billboard from Smartfood makes it appear as though someone literally accepted the invitation posed in the headline.

grocery shoppers immediately before they make a purchase decision. Outdoor's ability to catch consumers en route gives it additional impact for impulse products as well as for hotels, motels, restaurants, tourist attractions, and auto-related services.

Drawbacks to Outdoor Advertising

Just as outdoor has numerous advantages, it also has numerous disadvantages. For example, customers pass posters very quickly, so outdoor advertising must intrude to be effective. The design and copy must tell a story briefly and crisply, and they must sell. Further, outdoor messages are influenced by their environment. Placement in a run-down area detracts from the outdoor medium's ability to lend prestige to the advertised product. Other limitations relate to audience measurement, costs, planning, and the visual impact of outdoor advertising on the environment. (See the Checklist of What Works Best in Outdoor on p. 562.)

Audience Measurement

Although outdoor advertising is fine for reaching a wide audience, it has limitations for reaching a narrow demographic group. Furthermore, the demographics of outdoor audiences are difficult to measure. Realizing that not every passing vehicle and pedestrian will see or read the outdoor ad, some outdoor buyers distrust the space seller's estimates of reach.

Checklist of What Works Best in Outdoor

□ *Look for a big idea.* This is no place for subtleties. Outdoor is a bold medium. You need a poster that registers the idea quickly and memorably—"visual scandal" that shocks the viewer into awareness.

□ *Keep it simple.* Cut out all extraneous words and pictures and concentrate on the essentials. Outdoor is the art of brevity. Use only one picture and no more than seven words of copy—preferably less.

□ *Personalize when you can.* Personalized posters are practical, even for short runs. Mention a specific geographic area ("New in Chicago") or the name of a local dealer.

□ *Look for human, emotional content for memorability.* It can be an entertainment medium for travelers who are hungry or bored.

□ *Use color for readability.* The most readable combination is black on yellow. Other combinations may gain more attention, but stay with primary colors—and *stay away from reverse* (white letters against a dark background).

□ *Use the location to your advantage.* Many new housing developments capitalize on their convenient locations with a poster saying: "If you lived here, you'd be home now." Use outdoor to tell drivers that your restaurant is down the road, your department store is across the street. Don't ignore the ability of outdoor to reach ethnic neighborhoods. Tailor the language and the models to your consumer.

Another disadvantage is the difficulty of physically inspecting each outdoor poster panel (as opposed to checking tear sheets of space advertising or monitoring commercials). This makes it difficult to measure the results of outdoor advertising.

Planning and Costs

Because printing and posting outdoor messages are very time-consuming, outdoor campaigns must be planned far in advance. Usually a six- to eight-week lead time is required.

The high initial preparation cost may discourage local use. For national advertisers, buying outdoor can be a major headache; sales are highly fragmented among different outdoor companies serving different markets. In a single market, as many as 30 companies may be selling ad space.

Visual Impact

Outdoor advertising is also hampered by its past history. Countrysides dotted with advertising messages gave rise to complaints about billboards despoiling the landscape and "polluting" the scenery. Governments responded with laws banning outdoor advertising in certain areas and limiting it in others. The Highway Beautification Act of 1965 was enacted to control outdoor advertising on the U.S. interstates and other federally subsidized highways. The Federal Highway Administration reports that 709,760 billboards have been removed so far under the Highway Beautification Act. At the state level, outdoor advertising is prohibited in Maine, Vermont, Hawaii, and Alaska. Ironically, some of these states use outdoor advertising in *other*

(continued on p. 566)

PORTFOLIO OF OUTDOOR ADVERTISING: A 20TH-CENTURY ART FORM

A. The best billboards are often those specifically targeted at the people most likely to see them—motorists. No one expects drivers to read all these signs, but they should still get the message that taking the bus could reduce some of the stresses they are no doubt currently experiencing.

B. Motorists in California and Florida were treated to this high-impact painted bulletin. The cleaning woman is a 500-pound sculpture.

Celebrate the San Diego Zoo's 70th birthday.

C. Motorists in San Diego were grabbed by this series of striking billboards along one of the city's major freeways.

D. Outdoor advertising offers many creative possibilities, as this seemingly folded poster illustrates.

E. If this startling outdoor ad doesn't catch your attention, nothing will. It demonstrates that the medium has no limits for those who approach it imaginatively.

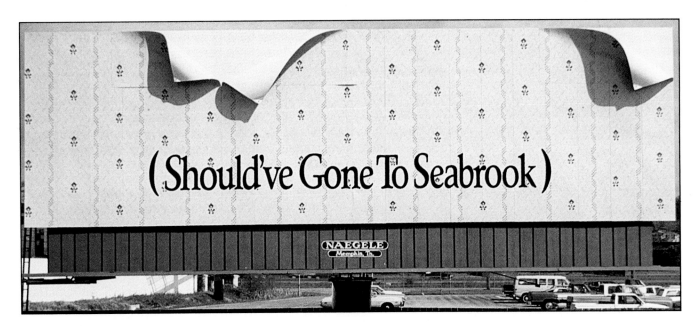

F. Seabrook Wallcoverings used unusual effects on this billboard to help cut through the visual clutter of the outdoors and grab the attention—albeit briefly—of motorists and pedestrians.

states. Maine's tourism advertising runs on billboards in Massachusetts, for example.[29]

The reputation of outdoor advertising has improved in recent years, with governmental control of the medium and more innovative and entertaining uses of this "art form." In fact, outdoor has become such a popular medium among advertisers that demand for outdoor ad space has overwhelmed the supply.

TRANSIT ADVERTISING

In 1910, Wrigley's Gum decided to undertake a new test campaign in Buffalo, New York, because gum had been so difficult to sell there. Wrigley's contacted the Collier Service Company in New York City, which had been established to provide copy and illustration service as well as to sell transit (bus) advertising. At the time, Collier employed some of the best writers in America, including F. Scott Fitzgerald and Ogden Nash. Collier's organization developed the famed "spear man" for Wrigley.

Wrigley's spear man logo was then printed on cards and carried on buses throughout Buffalo. The Buffalo program was so successful that Wrigley's repeated it in city after city across the nation.

It was around the same time that the Campbell Soup Company began to think of using advertising to sell its products. Spending its first $5,000 on car card advertising, Campbell contracted to place its ads on one-third of the buses in New York City for one year. After only six months, the campaign was so obviously successful the contract was enlarged to include all the other surface vehicles in New York City. This produced a 100 percent increase in business, and for 12 years transit advertising was Campbell's only medium.

As the transit advertising industry has progressed, it has developed more efficient standardization, better research, additional statistical data, and measured circulation. All this has made transit advertising more attractive to national advertisers. In recent years, national marketers of products such as tobacco, petroleum products, financial services, proprietary medicines, and foods and beverages have used transit advertising. Warner Lambert, for example, advertises its candy products with transit ads like the one in Exhibit 15-18. The medium is especially suitable for reaching middle- to lower-income urban consumers, providing supplemental coverage to these groups.

Transit advertising is equally popular with local advertisers. Such advertisers as theaters, restaurants, and retailers find it a productive medium for reminders and special announcements.

Types of Transit Advertising

Transit advertising depends on the millions of people who use commercial transportation (buses, subways, elevated trains, commuter trains, trolleys, and airlines) plus pedestrians and auto passengers.

Transit advertising includes several media forms: inside cards; outside posters; and station, platform, and terminal posters.

Inside Cards

The standard size of the **inside card,** placed in a wall rack above the windows, is 11″ by 28″. Four other widths are available (11″ by 21″, 11″ by 42″,

EXHIBIT 15-18

J. Walter Thompson (Toronto) created an amusing series of transit ads for Warner Lambert's Junior Caramels.

11″ by 56″, and 11″ by 84″). Cost-conscious advertisers print both sides of the card so it can simply be reversed to change the message, thus saving on paper and shipping charges.

Inside car-end posters (in "bulkhead" positions) are usually larger, and sizes vary. A common size is 22″ by 21″. Some top-end or over-door cards are 16″ by 39″ or 16″ by 44″. The end and side positions carry premium rates. Exhibit 15-19 (p. 568) shows common sizes for both inside cards and outside posters.

Outside Posters

Printed on high-grade cardboard and often varnished to make them weather resistant, the most widely used **outside posters** are (1) side of bus—king size (30″ by 144″), queen size (30″ by 88″), and traveling display (21″ by 44″); (2) rear of bus—taillight spectacular (21″ by 72″); and (3) front of bus—headlight (17″ by 21″ and 21″ by 44″).

Terminal Posters

In many bus, subway, and commuter train stations, space is sold for one-sheet, two-sheet, and three-sheet **terminal posters.** Also, major train and airline terminals offer a variety of special advertising forms that might be compared to outdoor spectaculars. These are usually custom designed and include such attention getters as floor displays, island showcases, illuminated signs, dioramas (three-dimensional scenes), and clocks with special lighting and moving messages. In cities with major mass-transit systems, advertisers can also buy space on bus shelters and on the backs of bus-stop seats. Exhibit 15-20 (p. 569) is a bus-shelter ad placed by the Minnesota Department of Health.

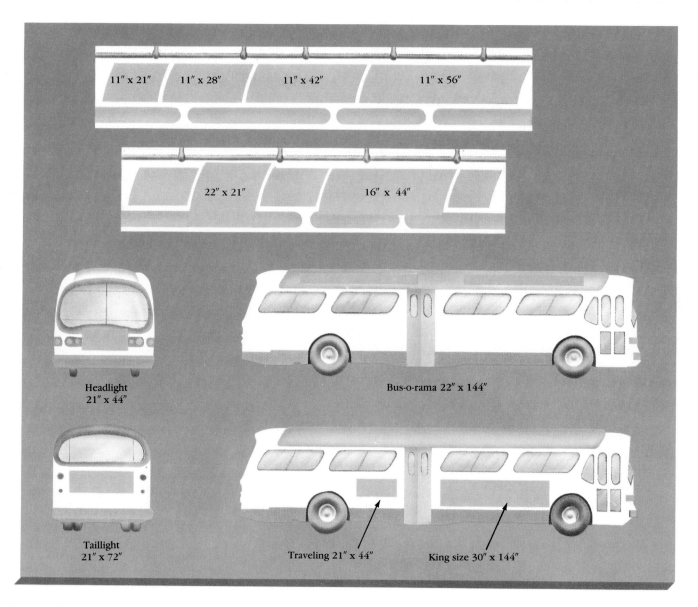

11″ x 21″ 11″ x 28″ 11″ x 42″ 11″ x 56″

22″ x 21″ 16″ x 44″

Headlight
21″ x 44″

Bus-o-rama 22″ x 144″

Taillight
21″ x 72″

Traveling 21″ x 44″

King size 30″ x 144″

EXHIBIT 15-19

The common sizes for inside cards and outside posters available in transit advertising.

Taxi Exteriors

Advertisers may also buy space on taxi-cab roofs, generally for periods of 30 days. In large markets, these internally illuminated, two-sided posters measure 14″ by 48″. Sizes vary in smaller markets.[30]

Buying Transit Advertising

One of the most cited advantages of transit advertising is the cost per exposure. Just a few cents will buy 1,000 exposures.

The unit of purchase is a showing, also known as a run or service. In transit advertising, a full showing (or No. 100 showing) means that one card will appear in each vehicle in the system. Space may also be purchased as a one-half (or No. 50) showing or a one-quarter (or No. 25) showing. Exterior

EXHIBIT 15-20

The Minnesota Department of Health placed ads on bus shelters to communicate the evils of smoking.

EXHIBIT 15-21

Basically, transit advertising is a billboard on wheels, so it's perfect for covering a big market. The City of Minneapolis used this example to suggest that trashy newspapers could be reincarnated as useful ones, if only people would remember to recycle.

displays like the one shown in Exhibit 15-21 are purchased on a showing basis.

Rates are usually quoted for 30-day showings—with discounts for 3-, 6-, 9-, and 12-month contracts. The advertisers must supply the cards at their own expense.

Cost depends on the length of the showing, the saturation of the showing, and the size of the space. Rates vary extensively, depending primarily on the size of the transit system.

Rates for specific markets may be obtained from the local transit company and from the Transit Advertising Association's *TAA Rate Directory of Transit Advertising,* the industry's rate book.

Special Inside Buys

In some cities, advertisers may buy all the inside space on a group of buses, thereby gaining complete domination. This buy is called the **basic bus.** In addition, pads of business reply cards or coupons (called **take ones**) may be affixed to interior advertisements for an extra charge. This allows passengers to request more detailed information, send in application blanks, or receive some other advertised product benefit.

Special Outside Buys

Some transit companies offer **bus-o-rama signs.** This is a jumbo roof sign, which is actually a full-color transparency backlighted by fluorescent tubes, running the length of the bus. Two bus-o-rama positions are on each side of the bus. A single advertiser may also buy a **total bus**—all the exterior space on a bus including the front, rear, sides, and top. This gives the product message powerful exclusivity.

Some transit companies offer other unique capabilities. With the introduction of new advance-design buses, for instance, the Winston Network (WN) transit advertising company offers advertisers up to 20 feet of sign space along the street side of the bus. WN applies pressure-sensitive vinyl to the smooth outer surface of the futuristic buses. Available in several reflective colors and textures, the 30″ by 240″ vinyl signs offer a versatile alternative to advertisers. In addition, they can be die cut to any shape within the sign area, so anything from soft-drink bottles to carpenter's pencils can travel the streets daily.

The industry has two organizations to keep advertisers informed of opportunities in transit advertising: the Transit Advertising Association (TAA) and the American Public Transit Association. The TAA is the main source of information, performing research and supplying industry data on the number of vehicles, trends, and rider demographics. The TAA is the national trade organization and promotion arm of the industry. Its members represent 80 percent of the transit advertising volume in the United States and Canada.

One variation on out-of-home advertising being experimented with is the "mobile billboard," which is something of a cross between traditional billboards and transit advertising. Exhibit 15-22 shows a mobile billboard used by *Woman's Day.* The mobile billboards were first conceived of as ads on the sides of tractor-trailer trucks. After seeing an American Trucking Association's survey showing that 10.1 million people see the average tractor-trailer in a year and that 91 percent notice trucks displaying words and pictures, the president of a ready-made salad company came up with the idea. He had his fleet of 50 trucks outfitted with 9′ high by 48′ long billboards touting his "Salad Singles." The company, Orval Kent Food Company, also leases space to other advertisers on its 250 other trucks.[31]

Although the idea of advertising on trucks has yet to catch on, a variation of this theme has appeared in some large cities, where specially designed flatbed trucks carry 10′ high by 22′ long billboards up and down busy thoroughfares. Unlike the tractor-trailers, which display their advertising on

Mobile billboards—ads on the sides of tractor-trailers or on specially designed flatbed trucks— are starting to appear in some areas of the country, to mixed reaction.

long hauls, the flatbeds can be limited to a specific local area, reaching a particular target audience. Local routes for mobile ads are also available on delivery trucks in San Francisco, Los Angeles, and Seattle. *Entrepreneur* magazine predicts that rolling advertising will become a common sight on our streets and freeways.[32]

Advantages of Transit Advertising

The many advantages of transit advertising include high reach, frequency, exposure, and attention values at very low cost. Transit fares cover the medium's capital costs, and federal subsidies have created larger and better transit systems and even some new ones. This medium reaches mass audiences and offers the geographic flexibility to reach ethnic or neighborhood groups. New York Subway Advertising claims that 89 percent of all blacks and 90 percent of Hispanic adults in New York can be reached through the subways.[33] Transit advertising's further advantages include:

☐ Long exposure to ads, because the average ride is 25 minutes.

☐ Repetitive value; many people take the same routes day after day.

☐ Eagerly read messages by bored riders. Readership of ads in the New York subway trains is high, and ad recall averages 55 percent.[34]

☐ Low cost, in fact generally lower than for any other medium.

☐ Special constructions and color effects at relatively low cost.

☐ It can target the needs of riders—with ads for cool drinks in summer, for example. Food ads also do well, as evening riders contemplate dinner.

☐ It is well positioned environmentally, as social pressure to use public transportation instead of private cars increases.

Drawbacks to Transit Advertising

Among the weaknesses of transit advertising, especially inside cards, is its general lack of coverage of some segments of society, such as suburbanites who drive their own cars, rural dwellers, and business and professional people who seldom use mass transportation. Other disadvantages include:

☐ Transit lacks the status of an important advertising medium.

☐ Rush-hour crowds limit the opportunity and ease of reading.

☐ Transit reaches a nonselective audience, which may not meet the needs of some advertisers.

☐ Cards are so numerous and look so similar they may be confusing.

☐ The transit vehicle environment, which may be crowded and dirty, may not lend prestige to the product.

☐ The trend to outlying shopping centers means fewer shoppers make trips downtown.

☐ Although transit cards may carry longer messages than billboards, copy is still somewhat limited.

Summary

Direct-mail advertising includes all forms of advertising sent directly to prospects through the mail. As an advertising medium, it ranks third in dollars spent, surpassed only by newspapers and television.

Next to the personal sales call, direct mail is the most effective way an advertiser can put a message in front of a prospect. It is also the most expensive on a cost-per-exposure basis. As an advertising medium, it offers several advantages. These include selectivity, intensive coverage, flexibility, control, personal impact, exclusivity, and response performance.

The drawbacks to direct mail include the high cost per exposure, the delays often experienced in delivery, the lack of other content support for the advertising message, certain problems with selectivity, and negative attitudes toward the medium.

Direct-mail advertising comes in many forms. Sales letters, brochures, and even handwritten postcards all qualify as direct-mail advertising. The message can be as short as one sentence or as long as dozens of pages.

The direct-mail list is the heart of the medium because each list actually defines a market segment. The three types of direct-mail lists include house lists, mail-response lists, and compiled lists. Their prices vary according to their quality.

Of the major advertising media, outdoor advertising offers the lowest cost per message delivered. In addition, the medium offers other attractive features. These include instant broad coverage (reach), very high frequency, great flexibility, and high impact. Drawbacks include the necessity for brief messages, the limitations for reaching narrow demographic groups, the lead time required, and the medium's past reputation. In addition, the high initial preparation costs and difficulty of physically inspecting each billboard discourage some advertisers.

The standardized outdoor advertising industry consists of about 600 local and regional plant operators. National advertising makes up the bulk of outdoor business.

The two most common forms of standard outdoor advertising structures are the poster panel and the painted bulletin. The poster panel is the basic form, is the least costly per unit, and is available in a variety of sizes. Painted bulletins are meant for long use and are usually placed in the best locations where traffic is heavy and visibility is good. Some advertisers overcome the relatively higher expense of painted bulletins by using a rotary plan. An additional form of outdoor available in some cities is the spectacular, an expensive electronic display.

Transit advertising offers the features of high reach, frequency, exposure, and attention values at very low cost. Furthermore, it gives long exposure to the advertiser's message and offers repetitive value and good geographic flexibility. In addition, advertisers have a wide choice in the size of space used.

The disadvantages of transit advertising are also numerous. It does not cover some segments of society, it reaches a nonselective audience, it lacks prestige, and copy is still somewhat limited.

Questions for Review and Discussion

1. What advantage did direct mail offer Champion International that the mass media could not?
2. What is the difference between direct-mail and direct-response advertising?
3. Although direct mail offers the advantage of selectivity, what are the associated problems?
4. What are the three types of mailing lists? Which is the best? Why?
5. What costs are advertisers likely to incur in a direct-mail campaign?
6. Which advertising objectives are the outdoor media mostly suitable for?
7. Do you feel outdoor is an effective advertising medium for a politician? Why?
8. What is the difference between a poster panel and a painted bulletin?
9. Why is transit advertising considered three separate media forms?
10. Which characteristics of transit advertising benefit advertisers the most?

CHAPTER

16

SALES PROMOTION AND SUPPLEMENTARY MEDIA

Objective: To define sales promotion, explain its changing role in the marketing mix, and describe the most commonly used types of sales promotions. Since dealers and customers are attracted to different types of promotion techniques, advertisers need to understand how to effectively apply both push strategies and pull strategies to promotional programs. Advertisers must also be aware of the growing number of supplementary media that can offer cost-effective alternatives for advertising and promoting their products.

After studying this chapter, you will be able to:

☐ Define *sales promotion* and explain its changing role in the marketing mix.

☐ Identify the benefits and drawbacks of sales promotion.

☐ Describe the various push strategy techniques used in trade promotions.

☐ Outline the pull strategy techniques used in consumer promotions.

☐ Discuss the primary issues in specialty advertising programs.

☐ List the factors to consider in planning exhibits or trade-show booths.

☐ Describe the role of Yellow Pages advertising and the factors to bear in mind when placing ads in the Yellow Pages.

uess who owns the kids' market when it comes to fast food? None other than McDonald's, of course. But maybe not forever. The number-two contender, Burger King, recently developed a sales promotion program that looks like a winner, and it might even turn Ronald McDonald into a middle-aged has-been.

Ronald's new competition is the Burger King Kids Club (see Exhibit 16-1). The club's centerpiece is "Kid Vid." His backups include other characters representing contemporary interests such as video and computer games, photography, sports, and even brainy pursuits. But this is no ordinary club, mind you. The Burger King Kids Club is a multifaceted promotional effort brought to life by some of the best in the business, including the Promotion Group of Irvine, California; London-based Passion Pictures, the creative forces behind *Roger Rabbit;* LucasFilms; and Saatchi & Saatchi Advertising.

Kids who sign up as members of the Kids Club receive a "Super Official Totally Secret Membership Kit" that includes a personalized membership card and letter (which guarantees them free meals on their birthdays), stickers featuring Kids Club characters and logos, an autographed poster, and the Club's official iron-on transfer. Then there are the special Kids Club meals that come in kids meal bags (made with recycled newspapers) that carry the promoted menu items and display the premium character being offered through a transparent window. Premiums include food-action figures called *Lickety Splits,* Teenage Mutant Ninja Turtles "rad" badges, figurines, free-wheeling kid transporters, and high-performance race cars. Special "Burger-N-Books" bookmarks are mailed to Kids Club members. Kids are asked to read four books and write the names of the books on the bookmarks. Free meals are given to kids who redeem the completed bookmark lists. If that isn't enough, kids receive a full-color magazine called *Funstuff,* which includes games, puzzles, coupons, and special promotions, to lure them back to Burger King. In addition, they can buy an official Kids Club clubhouse at any Burger King restaurant. And to top it all off, members get a "Birthday Party Pack" so they can throw a "Burger King Birthday Party" at home.

So how do today's kids respond to something akin to the Mickey Mouse Club of the 50s and 60s? Within just two months, Burger King attained its membership goal for the entire first year—nearly 1 million kids. Membership

now exceeds 2.7 million children. The company is also gaining a valuable database on which to base future promotions. And last but not least, franchise owners reported an increase in sales of kids' meals by as much as 200 to 300 percent.[1]

ROLE OF SALES PROMOTION

What would have happened to the sales of Burger King kids' meals without the promotion—if Burger King had simply placed all its efforts into advertising? The answer to this question is the key to understanding what sales promotion is and how it works.

The purpose of all marketing tools such as advertising, public relations, and sales promotion is to help the company achieve its marketing objectives (discussed in Chapters 4 and 7). Types of marketing objectives may include the following:

☐ To introduce new products.
☐ To induce present customers to buy more.
☐ To attract new customers.
☐ To combat competition.
☐ To maintain sales during off-seasons.
☐ To increase retail inventories so more goods may be sold.
☐ To obtain shelf space.

As we know, the marketing strategy the company uses to achieve these objectives may include a high degree of personal selling. It may also include activities such as advertising the company's products in the national media or in trade journals read by its dealers. It may include public relations activities such as feature stories and magazine interviews. Or it may include a major sales promotion campaign like Burger King's.

By definition, **sales promotion** is a direct inducement offering extra incentives all along the marketing route—from manufacturers through distribution channels to customers—to enhance the movement of the product from the producer to the consumer. Therefore, three important things should be remembered about sales promotion:

1. It is an acceleration tool designed to speed up the selling process.
2. It normally involves a direct inducement (such as money, prizes, extra products, gifts, or specialized information) that provides extra incentives to buy, visit the store, request literature, or take some other action.
3. It may be used *anywhere along the marketing route:* from manufacturer to dealer, from dealer to customer, or from manufacturer to customer.

Sales promotion is sometimes considered *supplementary* to advertising and personal selling because it binds the two together, making both more effective by increasing sales. In reality, however, sales promotion is far more than supplementary. In the mid-1970s, marketers began to shift marketing dollars from advertising to the promotion side of the mix. By the end of the 1980s, sales promotion had averaged a 13 percent annual growth rate, while advertising averaged a 10 percent growth rate.[2] Promotion spending now represents 66 percent of the typical marketing budget versus 34 percent for advertising.

Benefits of Sales Promotion

The ultimate benefit of effective sales promotion is that it *maximizes* sales volume. Ideally, sales promotion generates sales that would not otherwise be achieved. However, for products already on a strongly rising sales trend, a promotion can often put sales a notch higher than they were at the beginning of the promotion.[3]

In some cases, a promotion is more effective than advertising in motivating customers to select a particular brand when they consider all brands about equal. In other cases, a promotion generates additional sales by motivating customers who have been unmoved by any other advertising efforts. Another benefit of certain types of sales promotion is that they tend to generate a more immediate and easy-to-measure payoff than traditional advertising campaigns.

Drawbacks of Sales Promotion

Although sales promotion plays an important role in the marketing mix, it also has its drawbacks. A primary drawback of many sales promotions is that they rarely stimulate repeat purchases once the promotion ends. In fact, some customers are so conditioned to respond to promotions they simply won't buy unless the product is promoted. As the participant of a focus group once said, "What's the point of buying cereal without a coupon?"[4]

A second drawback of promotion is the cost. An analysis of promotions directed toward retailers for 65 different product categories revealed that only 16 percent of the promotions were profitable. In other words, for the majority of manufacturers, the promotion cost to generate an extra $1 of sales was greater than $1.[5]

A third drawback of promotion is its tendency to draw the competition into a promotion war. When competitors constantly try to outdo each other's promotions, the result can be reduced sales increases for everyone and the elimination of profits altogether.

To get the most out of promotion dollars, a company should invest sufficient resources to develop and test creative, hard-to-imitate promotions. At the same time, advertisers should not go overboard with unprofitable promotions that go way beyond what is necessary to counter the competition and to maintain competitive levels of display. In most cases, it's better to achieve a lower level of profitable sales than a higher level of unprofitable sales.

SALES PROMOTION TECHNIQUES

Any manufacturer who markets through normal channels must secure the cooperation of retailers by using **push strategies,** or **trade promotions.** Trade promotions are primarily defensive tactics, designed to protect shelf space against competitors. **Pull strategies,** or **consumer promotions,** on the other hand, are offensive tactics designed to attract customers. Although

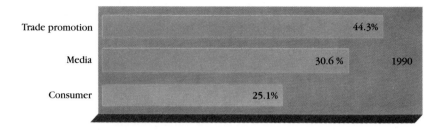

EXHIBIT 16-2

Trade promotion dollars continue to dominate the marketing mix.

push and pull strategies are both important and can work successfully together, advertisers spend significantly more of their promotion dollars on trade promotions versus consumer promotions, as shown in Exhibit 16-2.

Push Strategy Techniques

In today's crowded supermarkets, shelf space and floor space are hard to come by. To maintain their own images, department stores have been forced to set standards for manufacturers' displays. This means that retailers often cannot use the special racks, sales aids, and promotional literature supplied by the manufacturers. Many retailers are also pressed for time and lack the personnel to effectively use the flood of manufacturers' sales promotion materials. So packages of promotion literature remain unopened, and displays remain unassembled in a stock room.

Despite these problems, many manufacturers do an excellent job of implementing push strategy in sales promotion with a wide range of trade promotions closely keyed to retailer needs. Taos Furniture, for example, provides retailers with the materials shown in Exhibit 16-3.

One example of a far-sighted trade promotion was that of an appliance manufacturer. Dealers and distributors complained to the manufacturer about a constant barrage of separate and unrelated bulletins and letters from different factory departments concerning new products, display material, promotion booklets, service problems, policy, ad mats, and countless other topics. The manufacturer responded by incorporating all necessary information into one compact monthly newsletter, a newsy publication that the dealers and distributors actually looked forward to receiving.

Manufacturers use many sales promotion techniques to offer dealers extra incentives to purchase, stock, and display their products. Among the more common trade promotions are *trade deals, slotting allowances, display allowances, buy-back allowances, advertising allowances, cooperative advertising and advertising materials, dealer premiums and contests, push money, collateral materials,* and *company conventions* and *dealer meetings.*

Trade Deals

Trade deals offer short-term discounts on the cost of the product or other dollar inducements to sell the product. Trade deals must comply with the Robinson-Patman Act by being offered on an equal basis to all dealers. Dealers pass the savings on to customers through short-term sales on the products.

Overreliance on trade deals to boost short-term sales has become a controversial issue in marketing. As summarized in *Advertising Age,* "The

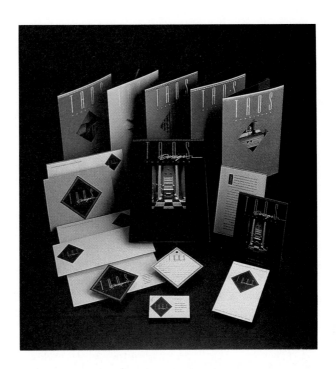

EXHIBIT 16-3

Taos Furniture provides retailers with a variety of promotional materials.

main bone of contention for marketers is whether trade promotions bring about incremental profits through increased use of products, or whether the products eventually would have been sold anyway, regardless of promotions."[6]

Trade deals are also seen as a threat to brand loyalty, for they encourage customers to buy whatever brand happens to be "on special" this week. Furthermore, marketers who use trade discounts extensively find themselves in a trap—if they cut back on the promotions, they face the prospect of losing market share.

The issue is further complicated by the fact that many retailers abuse trade discounts by engaging in forward buying and diverting. With **forward buying,** a retailer stocks up on a product when it is on discount and buys smaller amounts when it is at list price. **Diverting** is purchasing large quantities of an item at a regional promotion discount and shipping portions of the buy to areas of the country where the discount is not offered. The result is not only large fluctuations in a manufacturer's sales coinciding with promotions but also fluctuations in work-force and other production needs in response to sales.[7]

Slotting Allowances

Slotting allowances are fees (typically ranging from $15,000 to $40,000) that manufacturers often pay to retailers for the privilege of obtaining shelf or floor space for a new product. The practice is controversial because manufacturers feel they are being forced to subsidize the retailer's cost of doing business, and the Federal Trade Commission is looking into the legality of requiring such allowances. Retailers say the allowances are justified because of the proliferation of new products. Indeed, new-item proliferation in the supermarket arena has increased 61 percent each year, from 7,000 in 1984 to 12,000 in 1989.[8] That means dealers must spend more time redesigning shelves, finding warehouse space, entering information into computer systems, and relaying new product information to employees.

Campbell soup, however, found a way to get around the slotting allowance. It rewarded stores that agreed to stock its new Swanson Great Starts frozen breakfasts with free television commercial time.[9] The only catch was that the supermarket ads, which aired immediately after a Great Starts commercial, had to mention the Swanson product at least once.

Display Allowances

Display allowances are similar to slotting allowances, but they pertain to the product display materials rather than the actual shelf space required to stock the product. More and more stores charge display-hungry manufacturers a fee to make room for and to set up the display as specified. Such in-store displays include counter stands, floor stands, and special racks that give the retailer ready-made, professionally designed vehicles for selling more of the featured products. In some cases, a well-designed dealer display is enough to induce dealers to stock more of the product than they normally would.

Surprisingly, the display allowance is the least important factor when it comes to retailers accepting display materials. More important factors (in order of importance) are: increased profitability, display quality, service, graphics, ease of set-up, and size.[10]

Buy-Back Allowances

Manufacturers introducing a new product will sometimes offer retailers a **buy-back allowance** that essentially pays for the old product that hasn't sold, or that will be taken off the shelf to make room for the new product. Some manufacturers convince retailers to take on their product line in place of an existing vendor's merchandise by including a buy-back allowance for the competitor's leftover stock. In fact, this practice (which is legal) is becoming so common with certain types of merchandise that many retailers *expect* prospective vendors to offer a buy-back allowance.

Small companies as well as industry giants incorporate buy-back allowances into their trade promotions. For example, a little-known wholesaler of plumbing hardware with annual revenues under $1 million included a $15,000 buy-back allowance in its proposal to a regional chain of home improvement stores in order to improve its chances of replacing the existing vendor. The chain store accepted the proposal and took a portion of the buy-back allowance each month in the form of a 10 percent discount on the previous month's purchases.

Advertising Allowances

Advertising allowances are either a percentage of gross purchases or a flat fee paid to the retailer for advertising the manufacturer's product. Although advertising allowances are offered primarily by large companies, small companies may offer them to high-volume customers. For example, the small plumbing hardware wholesaler mentioned above offered one retailer an advertising allowance of 3 percent of gross purchases (in addition to the buy-back allowance). Advertising allowances are more common for consumer products than for industrial products.

Cooperative Advertising and Advertising Materials

National manufacturers often reimburse local retailers for advertising the manufacturer's products in the local media. This practice is referred to as **cooperative (co-op) advertising.** The manufacturer may repay 50 to 100 percent of the dealer's advertising costs or some other amount based on sales. Sometimes, special co-op arrangements are made to introduce new lines, advertise certain products, or combat competitive activity.

Unlike advertising allowances, which may not require a specific accounting of how the allowance was spent, co-op advertising programs typically require the retailer to submit proof of advertsing. To receive their advertising reimbursement, retailers must submit tear sheets for newspaper ads or an affidavit of performance for radio and television commercials.

Many manufacturers provide extensive prepared **advertising materials:** ads, glossy photos, sample radio commercials, preprinted inserts, and other advertising components. Most appliance manufacturers, for instance, supply the material and insist that it be used in order for their dealers to qualify for co-op advertising money.

Dealer Premiums and Contests

Prizes and gifts are often used to get retail dealers and salespeople to reach specific sales goals or to stock or display a certain product. Hanes Hosiery, for example, encouraged salesclerks to become more knowledgeable about the Hanes line by offering them free pairs of panty hose and the chance to win larger prizes such as a hot tub. In another type of promotion, KLM Dutch Airlines ran a **sweepstakes** for travel agency employees to help increase U.S. air travel to Amsterdam. Two grand prizes of dinner/dance parties were awarded in each of five U.S. regions. Exhibit 16–4 shows the KLM sweepstakes materials.

EXHIBIT 16-4

To increase awareness of KLM Royal Dutch Airlines among travel agency employees, the airline staged a sweepstakes: "It All Begins in Amsterdam." Two grand prizes were awarded in each of five regions of the United States. The prize was a dinner and dance party at a hotel in the winner's hometown, with all the winner's co-workers invited.

Concerns are often raised about the ethics of awarding prizes and gifts to dealers and salespeople. Travel-related contests in particular have received increased scrutiny in recent years. Critics are concerned that agents are not looking out for the best interests of the traveler. To win a fur coat, jewelry, trips, or commissions, for example, agents may be inclined to push products they know are inappropriate for certain customers. In response to such concerns, Voit Gilmore, president of the American Society of Travel Agents, said, "Every professional travel agent knows he proceeds at his own peril if he lets some gimmick or temptation influence his professional judgment."[11]

Push Money

Retail salespeople are encouraged in many ways to push the sale of particular products. One of these inducements is **push money (PM),** also called **spiffs.** For example, when you buy a pair of shoes, frequently the salesperson pushes special cushioned insoles or shoe polish or some other high-profit "extra." For each item sold, the salesperson may receive a 25- to 50-cent spiff, depending on the product.

Collateral Sales Material

In industrial sales and high-ticket consumer product sales, it is usually difficult to get a purchase decision from the buyer without giving considerable data on every aspect of the product. For this reason, dealers request catalogs, manuals, technical specification sheets, brochures, presentation charts, films, audiovisual materials, or other sales aids available from the manufacturer. As a category, these are all referred to as **collateral sales material.**

Company Conventions and Dealer Meetings

Most major manufacturers hold **company conventions and dealer meetings** to introduce new products, sales promotion programs, or advertising campaigns. These are also opportune times to conduct sales and service training sessions. Meetings are frequently promoted as opportunities to learn and also to share experiences with other company salespeople and executives. As such, they can be a dynamic sales promotion tool for the manufacturer.

Much of the advertising created and placed by companies today is invisible to the customer because it appears only in trade journals read by particular businesspeople. Also usually invisible are the push techniques of sales promotion used to help accelerate sales by offering inducements to dealers, retailers, and salespeople. If the inducements are successful, the product will be given more shelf space, special display, or extra interest and enthusiasm by salespeople. The difference between no interest and extra interest can spell the difference between product failure and success in today's competitive marketplace.

Pull Strategy Techniques

The list of consumer promotions used to accelerate the sales of products is long; and it is constantly growing as new techniques are devised. One reason for the increased focus on consumer promotions may be the proliferation of

EXHIBIT 16-5   Consumer Promotion Scorecard

Types of promotion	Percent of respondents using	
	Larger firms*	Smaller firms†
Couponing consumer direct	93%	97%
Couponing in retailer's ad	71	46
Cents-off promotions	82	92
Money-back offers/ cash refunds	75	71
Premium offers	79	49
Sampling new products	82	70
Sampling established products	68	57
Sweepstakes	75	62
Contests	43	22

* Annual sales = $1 billion or more.
† Annual sales = Less than $1 billion.

To Get Eggs Any Fresher,
You'd Have to Ruffle a Few Feathers

FREE EGGS

EXHIBIT 16-6

Coupons are distributed in a multitude of ways, from newspaper ads to direct mail to in-store handouts. Advantage stores made use of magazine ads to distribute coupons for fresh eggs.

cable TV channels and the use of VCRs, which have altered TV viewing habits and reduced the proportion of the audience seeing any one program. With media audiences becoming increasingly fragmented, major manufacturers are turning to methods that will reach mass numbers of consumers, such as coupons, sweepstakes, and in-store displays.

Some of the most common and successful consumer promotions include coupons, cents-off promotions, refunds/rebates, premiums, sampling, combination offers, sweepstakes and contests, and point-of-purchase advertising. Exhibit 16-5 shows the percentages of large and small firms that use various consumer promotions. A successful promotional campaign, such as Burger King's Kids Club, uses a combination of these techniques to achieve its objectives. Basic "commandments" for consumer promotion campaigns are outlined in Ad Lab 16-A (p. 584).

Coupons

A **coupon** is a certificate with a stated value that is presented to the retail store for a price reduction on a specified item (see Exhibit 16-6). A record 306.8 billion coupons were distributed in 1990; however, only a small percentage were actually presented at the checkout counter.[12] Of all the coupons redeemed in 1990, the largest percentage were for health and beauty aids (38.9 percent), followed by prepared foods (20.7 percent), frozen foods (19.6 percent), household products (19 percent), and cereals (15.4 percent).[13]

Coupons may be distributed in newspapers or magazines, door-to-door, on packages, in stores, and by direct mail. By far, the greatest number of coupons are distributed through **free-standing inserts (FSIs)** in newspapers—a full 68 percent reach consumers by this means.[14] One reason for

AD LAB 16-A
The 10 Commandments of Creative Promotion

Creativity is not limited to the advertising sphere—sales promotion calls for some creative effort as well. You should find these 10 commandments handy for both developing and reviewing promotions.

1. *Thou shalt set specific objectives.* Undisciplined or undirected creative work is a frivolous waste. The first step in developing a promotion is to exercise your creativity by setting meaningful goals. Lack of creativity at this stage results in vague and useless directions—and wasted time. You need to determine at this point whether your goal is to increase brand awareness, build up trade inventories, bring in triers, or whatever.

2. *Thou shalt know how basic promotion techniques work.* Knowing what a promotion technique can and cannot do is an important part of the creative challenge. A sweepstakes shouldn't be used to encourage multiple purchases nor a refund used to get new customers. A price-off deal cannot reverse a brand's downward sales trend.

3. *Thou shalt have simple, attention-getting copy.* Although there are times when promotional concepts become so complex that it seems impossible to write a simple or even understandable headline, most promotions are built around a simple idea such as "save 75 cents." The trick is to emphasize this idea and not get bogged down trying to be cute.

4. *Thou shalt lay out contemporary, easy-to-track graphics.* This task usually falls to the art director, but design considerations must be taken into account when developing a promotion. For example, a designer shouldn't be expected to fit 500 words of text and illustrations of 20 items into a quarter-page, free-standing insert.

5. *Thou shalt clearly communicate your concept.* Words and graphics must work together to get the message across.

6. *Thou shalt reinforce your brand's advertising message.* When a brand has a big-budget, long-term ad campaign, promotions should be tied to it. It takes an extra shot of creativity on everyone's part to tie in a prize or premium with advertising, but it does make the marketing effort easier in the long run.

7. *Thou shalt support the brand's positioning and image.* What would you think if Kraft offered a recipe book of potent drink recipes? Especially for image-sensitive brands and categories—like family-oriented Kraft—it is important to be creative about supporting positioning and image.

8. *Thou shalt coordinate your promotional efforts with other marketing plans.* In other words, let the right hand know what the left hand is doing when it comes to scheduling and planning. A promotion that requires a lengthy sales pitch to the trade should not be scheduled when salespeople are slated to go to a national sales convention for a week. Creative scheduling would time a consumer promotion to break simultaneously with a big trade promotion or set up a free sample promotion in conjunction with the introduction of a new line.

9. *Thou shalt know the media you work through.* This means determining which media will work best for achieving a particular promotion's goals. If you plan to distribute samples, would it be best to use in-store, door-to-door, or direct-mail distribution? Should you provide newspaper or magazine support? These creative decisions require expert knowledge of the media.

10. *Thou shalt know when to break the other nine commandments.* This is the ultimate creative exercise. It takes a confidently creative person to know when breaking any of these rules is really the smartest way to go.

Laboratory Application

Choose a currently running promotion for a product and determine whether the creators of the campaign have followed these commandments.

---

the growing reliance on FSIs is that they have a higher redemption rate than regular newspaper and magazine coupons—4.2 percent as compared to about 2.3 percent. Coupons in or on the package have the highest redemption levels (15.4 and 12.2 percent, respectively).[15]

After consumers redeem coupons, the retailer sorts the coupons, submits them to the manufacturer or a coupon clearinghouse, and is then reimbursed for the coupons' face value plus a handling charge.

Fraudulent submission of coupons costs the industry some $250 million annually. Coupon fraud comes in a variety of forms, including counterfeiting and submitting coupons for products that were never purchased. Quaker Oats has been in the forefront of manufacturers battling coupon fraud, or "misredemption." Unlike other companies, which generally randomly check 5 percent of coupons, Quaker employees examine 100 percent of submitted coupons and enter pertinent data about each into their computerized system. With this system, Quaker can spot fraud and also gather useful data about how the coupons have been used for particular products in various areas of the country. According to Quaker officials, the computerized process has allowed the company to cut costs and increase efficiency as well as gather marketing data.[16]

Cents-Off Promotions and Refunds/Rebates

Cents-off promotions are short-term reductions in the price of a product. They take various forms, including basic cents-off packages, one-cent sales, free offers, and box-top refunds. One common method is for a package to bear a special sticker indicating "25 cents off on this package" or something similar. The sticker is removed by the clerk at the check-out counter.

Another common approach is to offer a refund in the form of cash or coupons that can be applied to future purchases of the product. To obtain the refund, the consumer must supply proof of purchase of the product, such as three box tops. The coupon method is gaining in popularity among manufacturers, since it has been found that 9 out of 10 coupons sent to consumers as refunds are redeemed. With cash refunds, manufacturers have no way of knowing whether any of the money is actually spent to buy more of their product. Rebates are generally larger cash refunds on items such as cars or household appliances. A $700 rebate on the purchase of a car, for example, is handled by the seller—the consumer doesn't send in a rebate coupon. For an electric mixer or coffee maker, however, the consumer must send in a coupon to receive a $5 or $10 rebate.

Cents-off and refund promotions are often combined with other promotional techniques, such as sweepstakes and contests. Peter Paul, for example, sponsored an "Exotic Island Game" in which purchasers of Almond Joy and Mounds candy bars could be instant winners of various prizes and could also collect inner wrappers that in the right combination would win them a $6,000 island vacation. Accompanying the contest was an offer of a $1 refund for six Peter Paul wrappers. Not only did sales of the candy bars increase 50 percent over the period of the promotion, but more than 400,000 consumers sent in the proofs of purchase for the $1 refund.[17]

Premiums

A **premium** is an item offered free or at a bargain price to encourage the consumer to buy an advertised product. A recent survey shows that premiums have the same effect as rebates on purchase behavior, but tend to be more effective in getting consumers to buy a product they didn't really need.[18] Exhibit 16-7 shows some of the survey results. Premiums are intended to improve the product's image, gain goodwill (provided the product and premium don't disappoint the consumer), broaden the customer base, and produce quick sales. Procter & Gamble accomplished all these objectives with a campaign for Spic and Span in which a gem (garnet, emerald, sapphire,

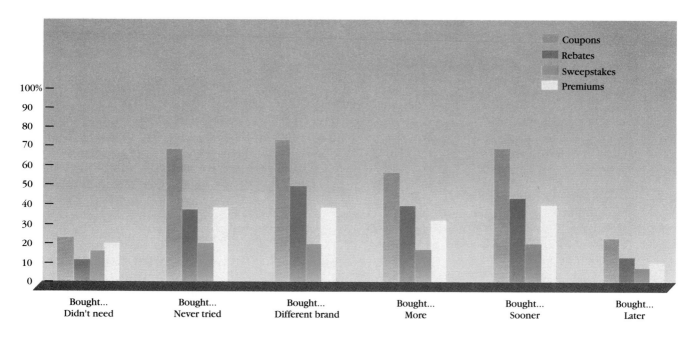

EXHIBIT 16-7

Next to coupons, premiums are one of the most effective promotion techniques for changing consumer behavior.

or diamond) was inserted in each package. Lots of new customers bought the product, and P&G gained a higher-quality image through its association with the precious stones.[19]

A good premium should have strong appeal and value and should be useful or unusual. It could be included in the product's package, or mailed free or for a certain amount of money, on receipt of proof of purchase (box top or label). Or the premium may be given with the product at the time of purchase. Cosmetics companies, for example, often have department-store promotions in which scarves, purses, and cosmetics samplers are given free with a purchase or may be purchased (for a low price) with a cosmetics purchase. A growing trend in recent years has been for companies to jointly sponsor premium offers. Coca-Cola and Sony, for example, teamed up to sponsor a multimillion dollar campaign during which Coke gave away 5.6 million miniature compact discs featuring pop stars on Sony's Epic label.[20]

The purchased cosmetics sampler is an example of a **self-liquidating premium**—the consumer pays the cost of the premium. The seller does not attempt to make a profit on such a premium but only tries to break even. A variation of the self-liquidating premium is the continuity premium. This type of premium is given weekly to customers who return to the store to complete their sets of dinnerware or encyclopedias, for example. To be eligible, however, the customer must buy a minimum dollar amount of other items.

In-pack premiums, such as the Spic and Span diamonds or the prizes in Cracker Jack, are particularly popular in the food field, especially with cereals. **On-pack premiums** (those attached to the outside of the package) have good impulse value, but they may encourage pilferage. Another drawback to on-pack premiums is that they sometimes are difficult for the retailer to stack on the shelves. As a result, the product causes problems for the retailer.

Coupon premiums, which require customers to save and collect in-pack coupons for later redemption of valuable premiums, can create great consumer loyalty. General Mills, for example, includes coupons on its breakfast cereal boxes that can be collected and redeemed for savings on hundreds of kitchen, home, gift, and children's items.

Related to coupon premiums are **trading stamps.** This promotion device was introduced by the Sperry & Hutchinson Company in 1896. For years, the popularity of S&H Green Stamps in department stores, supermarkets, and service stations fluctuated. Finally, as discount stores and suburban shopping centers grew and the energy crisis affected service stations, interest in trading stamps began to wane. Today, trading stamps in general have largely given way to other forms of retail promotion such as games.

Sampling

Sampling is the most costly of all sales promotions. However, it is one of the most effective promotions for new products because it offers consumers a free trial in hopes of converting them to habitual use. To be successful, sampling must deal with a product that is available in small sizes and purchased frequently. The success of a sampling campaign depends heavily on the merits of the product. Also, the sampling effort should be supported by advertising.

Samples may be distributed by mail, door-to-door, in stores, or via coupon advertising. They may be given free or for a small charge. Among products that have lent themselves to direct-mail sampling are cold remedies, candy, teabags, shampoos, disposable shavers, and laundry products. Sometimes, samples are distributed with related items, but this limits their distribution to those who buy the other product.

In-store sampling has experienced a recent surge in popularity, with demonstrators on hand to dispense samples of foods, beverages, and other products to passing shoppers. Campbell Soup, for example, had men in tuxedos dishing out samples of its new entrees in Washington, D.C., supermarkets. Most sampling programs hinge on the products being appealing enough for samplers to want to buy more, and are usually tied to a coupon campaign: "If you liked that taste of the new Cherry 7UP, here's a coupon to get 50 cents off the purchase of a six-pack." Among sampling flops have been samples of instant baby food, a line of microwave pasta that shoppers said tasted overcooked, and a gourmet mustard dip that the Price Choppers supermarket chain mistakenly served with hot dogs.[21]

Many times samples are distributed to target markets, such as cosmetics to college women (pull strategy), new drugs to physicians (push strategy), or shampoo to beauticians (push strategy). Several firms provide specialized sample distribution services, such as Welcome Wagon and Gift Pax.

Combination Offers

Food and drug marketers have successfully used **combination offers,** such as a razor and a package of blades or a toothbrush with a tube of toothpaste, at a reduced price for the two. For best results, the items should be related. Sometimes a combination offer may be used to introduce a new product by tying its purchase to an established product at a special price.

Contests and Sweepstakes

A **contest** offers prizes based on the skill of the entrants. A **sweepstakes** offers prizes based on a chance drawing of entrants' names (see Exhibit

EXHIBIT 16-8

One of the best-known national contests is for Publishers Clearing House. In addition to direct mail (shown here), the contests are promoted through TV ads.

16-8). A **game** has the chance element of a sweepstakes but is conducted over a longer time. Games include local bingo-type games designed to build store traffic. Their big marketing advantage is that customers must make repeat visits to the dealer to continue playing.

Both contests and sweepstakes have the common purpose of encouraging consumption of the product by creating consumer involvement. These devices are highly popular and pull millions of entries. Usually, contest entrants are required to send in some proof of purchase, such as a box top or label. For more expensive products, the contestant may only have to visit the dealer to pick up an entry blank.

Contests range from puzzle solving (such as Cap'n Crunch's "Where's the Cap'n?"), to cooking competitions (Pepto-Bismol's chili cook-offs; Pillsbury's bake-offs), to photo contests (Johnson & Johnson's annual "Adorable Babies Photo Contest;" Mazda's family photo contest).

In recent years, sweepstakes and games have become more popular than contests. They are much easier to enter and take less time than contests and, therefore, have greater appeal for many consumers. Exhibit 16-9 shows participation in sweepstakes by age, income, and education level. Sweepstakes require careful planning. No purchase can be required as a condition for entry, or the sweepstakes becomes a lottery and therefore illegal. All postal laws must be obeyed in planning contests and sweepstakes.

To encourage a large number of entries, sponsors try to keep their contests as simple as possible. The prize structure must be clearly stated and rules clearly defined. National contests and sweepstakes are handled and judged by independent, professional contest firms.

Contests and sweepstakes must be promoted and advertised to be successful. This can be expensive. An important element of this promotion is dealer support, and to ensure dealer cooperation, many contests and sweepstakes require the entrant to give the name of the particular product's local dealer. In these cases, prizes may also be awarded to the dealer who made the sale.

Point-of-Purchase Advertising

As a push technique, good dealer displays may induce a retailer to carry a certain line or promote a new product. However, **point-of-purchase (P-O-P) advertising** is primarily a pull technique consisting of advertising or display materials at the retail location to build traffic, advertise the product,

EXHIBIT 16-9

Sweepstakes participation by classification group is shown here. The more affluent, better-educated, and older consumer is more likely to participate in a sweepstakes.

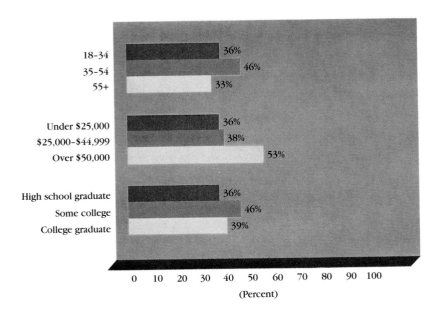

and promote impulse buying. Ad Lab 16-B discusses the use of artificial aromas in point-of-purchase advertising.

Point-of-purchase programs have become increasingly important in light of the fact that more than 80 percent of purchase decisions are not made until the customer is in the store. Spurred by this startling finding (reported by the Point of Purchase Advertising Institute), manufacturers have greatly increased their P-O-P budgets.[22]

AD LAB 16-B
Smell: Powerful Armament in the Retailer's Arsenal

You are strolling past the bakery in your local shopping mall. Isn't that the irresistible aroma of fresh-baked chocolate chip cookies wafting your way?

Maybe not.

International Flavors & Fragrances, Inc., has succeeded in synthesizing the mouth-watering aroma of not only chocolate chip cookies but also hot apple pie, fresh pizza, baking ham, and even nongreasy french fries.

IF&F packages the artificial odors in aerosol cans and markets them along with time-released devices that periodically fire a burst of scent into the shopping mall to tempt customers. The sprays are reportedly selling briskly and cost retailers just pennies a day.

Ledan, Inc., a New York promotion firm, is developing scented materials that stick to in-store displays. The com-

pany is already marketing chocolate scents for candy racks and piña colada aromas for the liquor department, and it hopes to have the smell of bacon available before long.

The purpose of these smells is, of course, to make people feel hungry or thirsty. What has some people concerned, however, is the possibility of a store full of competing odors. With that kind of result, the idea of using smells as a promotional gimmick could turn out to be a real stinker.

Laboratory Application

Do you think that using artificial odors is a legitimate sales promotion technique?

P-O-P materials may include window displays, counter displays, floor and wall racks to hold the merchandise, streamers, and posters. Often, the product's shipping cartons are designed to double as display units. At times, a complete "information center" provides literature, samples, and product photos. Exhibit 16-10 shows an example of effective P-O-P advertising for a car rental company.

In-store materials have increased in importance with the trend toward self-service retailing. With fewer and less knowledgeable salespeople available to help them, customers are on their own to make purchasing decisions. Eye-catching and informative displays can give them the push they need to make a choice. Even in well-staffed stores, display material can offer extra selling information and make the product stand out from the competition.

The proliferation of P-O-P displays has led many retailers to be more discriminating in what they actually use. Most are beginning to insist on well-designed, attractive materials that will blend harmoniously with their store atmosphere. Some retailers actively work with manufacturers to develop appropriate P-O-P displays; a few even design their own P-O-P materials to create an in-store identity.

The emphasis on P-O-P has led to the development of a variety of new approaches, including ads on shopping carts, "talking" antacid boxes, beverage jingles activated by opening in-store refrigerator doors, and interactive computer systems for selecting everything from shoe styles to floor coverings. One technique gaining attention is the **product information center (PIC).** A video-display terminal located primarily in supermarkets, the PIC carries a series of 15-second "commercials" in a five-minute rotation, interspersed with community-interest items. Some PIC spots are used in conjunction with overall promotional campaigns. Johnson & Johnson found that a promotion for Band-Aid Medicated 20's resulted in sales increases of 24 to 38 percent in cities without PIC supplementation but saw a 75 percent sales increase in Ft. Worth, Texas, where the PIC spots were used.[23]

On an expense report it looks like any other car.

≋*National* Car Rental. *Florida Funwheels.*

SUPPLEMENTARY MEDIA

Many miscellaneous promotional media are difficult to classify because they are tailored to individual needs and do not necessarily fall into any major category. They include *specialty advertising, trade shows* and *exhibits, directories* and *Yellow Pages,* and a variety of emerging alternative media.

Specialty Advertising

The Specialty Advertising Association International (SAAI) defines **specialty advertising** as an advertising, sales promotion, and motivational communication medium that employs useful articles of merchandise imprinted with an advertiser's name, message, or logo.[24] Today, nearly every business uses advertising specialties to some degree, including everything from matchbooks and staplers, to sports bags and Pierre Cardin leather goods (see Exhibit 16-11). There are said to be as many as 15,000 different specialty items sold, representing an annual volume of more than $3 billion.

An advertising specialty is different than a premium. For one thing, premiums can run the gamut from inexpensive trinkets to automobiles worth several thousand dollars. Because premiums can be fairly expensive items, they often bear no advertising message. However, the recipient of a premium must give some consideration to the advertiser—buy a product, send in a coupon, witness a demonstration, or perform some other action of advantage to the advertiser. An advertising specialty, on the other hand, typically carries the advertiser's name on it and is given free as a goodwill item with no strings attached. Some specialty items, particularly if they are useful, may be kept for years and thereby serve as continuous, friendly reminders of the advertiser's business.

Companies often spend substantial sums for these goodwill items; they must also exercise care. It is the one business in the advertising field where industry practice dictates that the advertiser pay for any production overage incurred, up to an agreed-on limit. Since specialty items are often produced according to each advertiser's unique specifications (such as imprinting the advertiser's name or making a replica of the product), the overage is difficult if not impossible for the manufacturer to adapt and resell to another advertiser.

EXHIBIT 16-11

Among the many items used for specialty advertising are office supplies such as staplers. Office and business items are popular because they serve as a daily reminder of the advertiser's name in the place where the customers do their ordering.

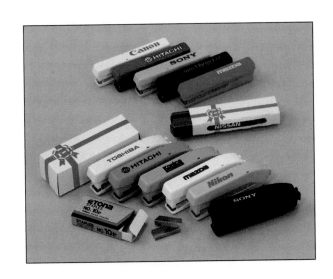

Consumer Specialties

Because consumers tend to associate the quality of a specialty item with the quality of the company providing it, there has been a definite trend toward more expensive gifts for consumers as well as for business customers. According to SAAI, items costing $3 to $5 are becoming the norm, as opposed to cheap key rings and pencils, for example.[25]

Specialties designed for consumers are particularly advantageous to small-business owners with a limited audience because they enable the company to reach a targeted market economically. For example, Jim Graven of Louisville, Kentucky, used a unique specialty item to reach consumers being lured away by the competition. What prompted the move was the loss of $30,000 in sales of Graven's regulation-size pool tables when a competitor started advertising undersized pool tables at a discount price. Instead of spending $1,500 on a one-time newspaper ad, or $1,000 on a local 30-second TV commercial, Graven spent $100 for 500 measuring sticks with the exact width of his regulation-size pool tables. It took only 10 days to get the custom-made sticks imprinted with regulation pool-table dimensions, the company logo, and comparative-shopping suggestions. Graven then handed them out to comparison shoppers, encouraging them to measure the competitor's table. The result: Graven's sales increased 28 percent over the next two years.[26]

Business-to-Business Specialties

The business-to-business arena has seen a trend toward structured promotions, in which target customers receive a series of specialties. Beckman Instruments, for example, wanted to increase its number of clients in a four-state area before assigning sales personnel to that region. To gain the attention of clinical lab supervisors and purchasing agents in 250 hospitals and clinics, Beckman sent them a series of specialty gifts, including coffee mugs, calendars, paper-clip dispensers, and a jigsaw puzzle, over a 12-month period.[27]

Does a specialty's dollar value play a significant role in influencing business buying or referral decisions? One test conducted with a mortgage company and realtors produced some interesting results. In the test, one group of realtors received a $1.49 ball point pen imprinted with the mortgage company's name, a second group received a $10 sports bag also imprinted, and a third group received nothing. In a follow-up questionnaire that asked if the realtors would recommend a specific banking product to their clients, the realtors who received no gift were least inclined to recommend the product. Although the "sports bag" group was most inclined to recommend the product, the "ball point" group responded almost as positively. The conclusion was that the gift recipients felt obliged to *reciprocate* in a favorable way, but the value of the gift was not a crucial issue. Therefore, the $1.49 pen was a much better investment than the $10 bag because it produced nearly the same results.[28]

Inappropriate specialty items can backfire no matter what the cost, however. For example, the recipient may perceive an overly expensive gift as a form of bribery. A cheap-looking trinket, on the other hand, could make a quality-conscious business look chintzy in the eyes of prospective customers. The objective of any specialty program, therefore, should be to give a gift "small enough to activate reciprocal relations but not large enough to backfire."[29]

Trade Shows and Exhibitions

Every major industry sponsors annual **trade shows** and exhibitions where manufacturers, dealers, and buyers of the industry's products can get together for demonstrations and discussion. Exhibitors have the opportunity to expose their new products, literature, and samples to new customers as well as old. At the same time, they can meet potential new dealers for their products. Exhibit 16-12 shows an example of a well-designed exhibit.

More than 9,000 industrial, scientific, and medical shows are held in the United States each year, and many companies exhibit at more than one show. As a result, the construction of booths and exhibits has become a major factor in sales promotion plans for many manufacturers. To stop traffic, booths must be simple in design and attractive, with good lighting. The exhibit should also provide a comfortable atmosphere to promote conversation between salespeople and prospects.

Many regular trade-show exhibitors use state-of-the-art technology, such as holograms, fiber optics, and interactive computer systems, to communicate product features quickly and dramatically. Pratt & Whitney, for example, uses holograms to present quarter-scale cutaway images of its aircraft engines. The company has found that holograms are easier to transport, less expensive to make, and more dramatic than traditional engine models.[30]

In planning exhibits or trade-show booths, advertisers need to consider the following factors:

☐ Size and location of space.
☐ Desired image or impression of the exhibit.
☐ Complexities of shipping, installation, and dismantling.
☐ The number of products to be displayed.
☐ The need for storage and distribution of literature.
☐ The use of preshow advertising and promotion.
☐ The cost of all these factors.

Companies that promote their products at trade shows must carefully plan their booths, sales materials, and special trade-show promotions.

Trade-show costs have increased substantially in the last decade. In fact, it's not uncommon for a large company to spend $1 million on its booth at one trade show. Between 1987 and 1989, the average cost per visitor reached was approximately $89. When advertisers factor in personnel, travel, living and salary expenses, and preshow promotion, the cost per visitor reached rises to more than $141.[31] Despite the high costs involved, many companies find exhibiting at trade shows to be a cost-effective means of reaching sales prospects in person.

Directories and Yellow Pages

Thousands of directories are published each year not only by phone companies but by trade associations, industrial groups, and others. While serving mainly as locators, buying guides, and mailing lists, they may also carry advertising aimed at specialized fields. When Yellow Pages advertising is combined with other media, the reach increases significantly, as illustrated in Exhibit 16-13. Numerous factors affect the overall success of Yellow Pages advertising, but studies indicate that ad content (not size) is most important.[32] In general, the ad content should tell people *how to make the purchase*, not try to convince them to make a purchase.

In the United States, there are approximately 6,000 local telephone directories with a combined circulation of 286 million. Since deregulation of the

EXHIBIT 16-13

Overall advertising reach from media combinations. When Yellow Pages advertising is used in conjunction with other media, the advertising reach increases significantly.

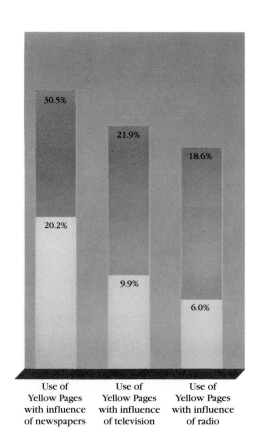

| Use of Yellow Pages with influence of newspapers | Use of Yellow Pages with influence of television | Use of Yellow Pages with influence of radio |

30.5% / 20.2%   21.9% / 9.9%   18.6% / 6.0%

phone industry and the 1984 breakup of AT&T, the Yellow Pages business has been booming, with advertising revenues reaching more than $8.5 billion in 1990.[33] Nine big operators—the seven regional Bell companies, Reuben H. Donnelley, and GTE Directories—account for more than 90 percent of the industry's advertising revenues.[34] In addition, 200 other publishers produce their own brands of Yellow Pages and compete for advertising dollars. Since neither the name *Yellow Pages* nor the walking-fingers logo is a protected trademark, anyone can use them.

Because of stiff competition, phone and directory companies have been coming up with ways to make their particular Yellow Pages more distinctive. Some are beefing up the contents, offering emergency medical guides, color street maps, and other useful information. Others contain discount coupons. Also, highly specialized directories are aimed at particular audiences, such as the Chinese-language Yellow Pages in San Francisco, a directory for students at the University of Massachusetts, and a business directory so technical that the Ohio edition lists 22 different entries for ball bearings. Exhibit 16-14 shows an ad for a Nynex business-to-business directory.

Yellow Pages are often the sole advertising medium for local businesses. In fact, nearly 90 percent of Yellow Pages revenue is derived from local advertisers.[35] However, Yellow Pages directories can be an important advertising medium for national advertisers, too. U-Haul, for example, spends more than $10 million a year on Yellow Pages ads.

To attract more national advertisers, Pacific Bell Directory has been testing a phone-book version of national brand advertising.[36] Category headings for specific products don't exist, and the brand ads are placed in related categories. For example, a Teledyne Water Pik ad appears in the section for dentists as well as in the section for pharmacies. It features an 800 number and "Call for the dealer nearest you" in the copy. Although the test ads were free, a similar half-page ad in the Pacific Bell directory would cost about $12,000 in the Los Angeles market.

For national advertisers with a smaller budget, a company called Yellow Spots sells filler space—a by-product of every directory's layout.[37] National advertisers who choose filler space are given the option of having their logo/image ads appear every 5, 10, or 15 pages.

The main complaint from Yellow Pages advertisers is the difficulty in verifying the amount of business their advertisements attract. However, two directory companies (Nynex and Donnelley) are testing special metered telephone lines that track customer responses.

Emerging Media

As the traditional advertising media become more expensive, and as audiences become more fragmented, many advertisers are being forced to seek new ways of reaching their customers. As a result, several types of alternative media are emerging as potentially viable options.

Movie Theaters

Advertising in movie theaters is a growing but controversial practice. Some theater audiences boo and hiss during commercials, while others seem indifferent. Yet studies have shown that 87 percent of viewers can recall

EXHIBIT 16-14

A national trend in highly populated areas is the publication of phone directories in two versions: one for consumers, and another for businesses, such as the business-to-business directory by Nynex, shown in this ad. In order to get complete coverage in an area, many businesses feel it's necessary to advertise in both versions, which has substantially increased phone company advertising revenue.

theater ads the following day, in comparison to a 20 percent recall rate for television ads.[38] Not all movie theater chains permit filmed advertising, for fear of offending their audience. Others, such as Cineplex Odeon, welcome commercials. The cost of placing a commercial in about 5,700 of the nation's first-run theaters can run as high as $650,000.[39] Unfortunately for advertisers, Walt Disney Company recently announced that it will no longer allow U.S. theaters to run commercials before any of its movies.

An alternative way to reach movie audiences is to pay a fee to have the product written into the movie itself. This practice (called **product placement**) is becoming more common, but is also controversial.

Videotapes

With over 65 million videos going out to 22 million homes a week, video movies cannot be overlooked as an advertising medium.[40] However, placing commercials on movie videos is as controversial as theater advertising. Advertisers such as Chrysler, PepsiCo, and Nestlé spend hundreds of thousands of dollars a year on video advertising, hoping they will positively influence viewers rather than offend them. A less intrusive type of video advertising involves placing ads on the videocassette boxes. A third type of video advertising is the video brochure, such as "FreeVee," which is distributed to 1,000 video stores by Video Information Network.[41] The advertisers make their own video and then pay Video Information to distribute the tapes to video stores, which in turn make them available to customers.

Parking Meters and Public Telephones

Thanks to a couple of enterprising companies that saw a new opportunity to sell advertising space, marketers can now advertise on parking meters and on public telephones. The two primary companies that place such advertising are American Parking Meter Advertising and American Telephone Advertising (ATA). For advertisers who want to reach a specific market, ATA offers 20 market segments, such as hotels and restaurants, airports, college campuses, and convenience stores.[42]

Computer Software

More and more companies are using **computer software** as an advertising medium for reaching both consumers and business buyers. Software ads include disks distributed by individual manufacturers and ad spots on computer information services such as Prodigy. Most disk ads feature games, animation, slick graphics, and other interactive features. MCI Communications, for example, uses software with sound effects and sophisticated graphics to sell its phone services to business managers. Advertisers spend about $10 million a year on software ads, but some companies actually get customers to pay for their advertising. For example, more than 100,000 computer enthusiasts paid $6.95 each to view Ford's Simulator disk.[43]

Interactive Television

Although it is still in the developmental stage, it's not too early for advertisers to think about the potential of **interactive television.** In fact, some advertisers are helping to fund its development. Once in place, the technology will allow viewers who sign up for the service to use a hand-held device to change camera angles or zero in on a particular scene, for example.[44] More important to advertisers will be the viewer's ability to respond to questions during a commercial, which will enable advertisers to develop a wealth of demographic information for future promotions.

Electronic Couponing

A growing number of supermarkets and retail chains are introducing electronic couponing into their marketing mix. **Electronic couponing** refers to frequent-shopper cards or **"smart" cards** that automatically credit cardholders with coupon discounts when they check out. One such smart card is the Vision card, developed by Advanced Promotion Technologies of Deerfield Beach, Florida. When combined with a touch-sensitive video screen, computer graphics, printer, and laser videodisc player, Vision cardholders can take advantage of a variety of retailer and manufacturer promotions by simply touching the video screen.[45] Exhibit 16-15 shows a customer taking advantage of a state-of-the-art electronic couponing system.

Grocery Cart Videos

Not to be outdone by smart cards, shopping carts are getting smarter, too. Information Resources Inc. (IRI), Chicago, introduced the VideOcart, which comes equipped with a video screen that shows spots from national advertisers as well as store specials. During a nine-week test of the VideOcart, participating advertisers saw an average sales gain of 33 percent.[46] Grocers also saw their sales increase. VideOcart advertisers are guaranteed category exclusivity and first right of refusal in every store for their category. After national expansion, IRI expects its ad rates to be $4 per 1,000 households delivered per week.

EXHIBIT 16–15

Electronic couponing eliminates the time-consuming chore of clipping and sorting printed coupons.

Electronic Signs

Electronic signs are similar to the VideOcart concept, but they display text and graphic messages much like the big screens in sports stadiums. In Store Advertising, headquartered in New York, offers one of the more innovative electronic message board systems. Advertisers pay In Store Advertising to program and transmit weekly commercial messages to hundreds of chain stores where shoppers will see them on the electronic signs. The retail stores pay nothing for the signs, and they receive 25 percent of the weekly gross revenues that In Store Advertising gets from its various advertisers.[47] For 50 minutes each hour, the signs display the advertisers' commercials. The other 10 minutes are turned over to the individual stores for their own promotions.

Summary

Sales promotion supplements advertising and personal selling for the purpose of stimulating or accelerating sales. However, since the mid-1970s, marketers have increasingly shifted marketing dollars from advertising to the promotion side of the mix. Sales promotion includes a wide variety of promotional activities with unlimited applications aimed at salespeople, distributors, retailers, consumers, and industrial buyers. By offering direct inducements, such as money, prizes, gifts, or other opportunities, sales promotion provides extra incentives to buy a product, to visit a store, to request literature, or to take some other action.

Sales promotion techniques are used in the trade to *push* products through the distribution channels or, with the ultimate consumer, to *pull* them through the channel.

Manufacturers use a variety of sales promotion techniques to offer dealers extra incentives to purchase, stock, and display their products. These include trade deals, slotting allowances, buy-back allowances, display allowances, advertising allowances, co-operative advertising and advertising materials, dealer premiums and contests, push money, collateral material, and company conventions and dealer meetings.

The most visible forms of sales promotion are those aimed at the ultimate purchaser of the product. They include coupons, cents-off promotions and refunds/rebates, premiums, sampling, combination offers, contests and sweepstakes, and point-of-purchase advertising.

Supplementary media are quite diverse. They include specialty advertising, trade shows and exhibits, and Yellow Pages directories, to mention just a few. Emerging media that advertisers are beginning to experiment with and use include: movie theaters, videotapes, public telephones, parking meters, computer software, interactive television, electronic couponing, grocery cart videos, and electronic signs.

Questions for Review and Discussion

1. How does the definition of *sales promotion* differ from the definition of *advertising?*
2. What are the main purposes of sales promotion?
3. Why have trade deals become controversial?
4. What are the most commonly used push strategies? Which would you use if you were a major cosmetics manufacturer?
5. What are the most common pull strategies? Which would you use if you wanted to launch a new soft drink?
6. Why is there a trend away from push strategies and toward pull strategies?
7. Why are FSIs the most popular means for distributing coupons?
8. What is the difference between an advertising specialty and a premium?
9. What is the importance of trade shows to marketers?
10. Should advertisers be interested in using directories and the Yellow Pages? Why?

P A R T

V

SPECIAL TYPES
OF ADVERTISING

Advertising can be used for a variety of special purposes. Local businesses advertise within a particular geographic area rather than nationwide, corporations sometimes advertise to enhance their reputations rather than to sell products, and international businesses advertise around the world. Part V presents thorough coverage of these special types of advertising.

Chapter 17, "Local Advertising," discusses the advertising done by businesses trying to reach customers within their immediate geographic area. Chapter topics include establishing local objectives, analyzing local markets, determining local strategies, establishing realistic budgets, and planning local media strategies. Other topics include analyzing seasonal patterns and determining creative direction.

Chapter 18, "Public Relations, Corporate Advertising, and Noncommercial Advertising," discusses managing a corporation's relationships through public relations, including openly sponsored media communications and corporate advertising. The chapter discusses public relations activities (publicity, lobbying, special-events management, and fund raising) and tools (media kits, feature articles, and audiovisual materials). Finally, the chapter covers noncommercial advertising as used by schools, charitable organizations, and labor groups.

Chapter 19, "International Advertising," discusses advertising's worldwide growth since World War II and its varying status from country to country. It covers foreign advertising activities and distinguishes between international, multinational, and global advertising. Also discussed are differences in international advertising's creative strategies, media, advertising messages, and governmental and cultural restrictions.

From Local to Global

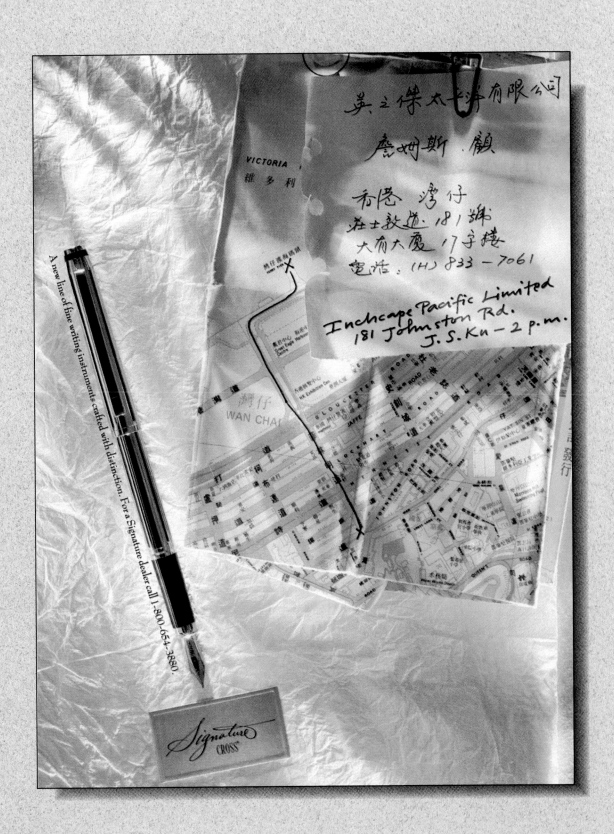

CHAPTER 17

LOCAL ADVERTISING

Easter's Coming, And Pier 1's Hopping.

Objective: To define *local advertising* and describe how basic advertising principles are applied locally. The advertising person who works at the local level faces unique circumstances and special problems that stem from the practical realities of marketing in the local community. A general understanding of the nature of local advertising will help the advertising person use available media, community resources, and advertising dollars to the best advantage.

After studying this chapter, you will be able to:

☐ Define *local advertising* and describe the most common types of advertising used by local advertisers.

☐ Differentiate between the typical objectives of local advertisers and national advertisers.

☐ List the steps involved in planning the local advertising effort.

☐ Outline the types of market research local advertisers should conduct.

☐ Delineate the primary factors that can affect the local advertiser's budget.

☐ Describe the advantages and disadvantages of the various media available to local advertisers.

☐ Identify the common sources of creative assistance available to local advertisers.

When Ralph Rubio opened his own Mexican restaurant in 1983, he specialized in fish tacos—lightly battered and fried whitefish served in soft-shelled corn tortillas with white sauce, salsa, cabbage, and a wedge of lime. But at the time, few of the other local Mexican eateries even offered fish tacos on their menus, and none featured them. Even using a secret batter recipe (given to him by a street vendor from San Felipe, Mexico), Rubio found fish tacos hard to sell.

Rubio had worked his way through college as a waiter and managed several restaurants after graduating from San Diego State University. He saw a need in San Diego for better Mexican food, and he geared his restaurant's offerings to his own taste. After all, if he liked the more sophisticated and highly seasoned food, others probably would, too. At least, that was the theory. But the first month's daily sales at the restaurant averaged only $163. Would advertising help?

Rubio began with print advertising, placing coupons in many of his newspaper ads (see Exhibit 17-1). He later expanded his advertising to radio and TV, targeting his market further by advertising on Hispanic stations. In addition, he reached customers aged 18 to 34 by advertising on cinema slides at the local movie theaters. Business began to pick up; Rubio soon opened another restaurant . . . and another.

With each new opening, Rubio distributed direct-mail flyers throughout the surrounding area, and the restaurant gave out free samples to employees in nearby stores. Also, Rubio worked with an artist to create a fish taco cartoon character called Pesky Pescado. He also purchased a 15-foot inflatable Pesky to appear at his restaurants. Employee uniforms were T-shirts sporting Pesky's picture, and Rubio sold Pesky T-shirts and sweatshirts to enthusiastic patrons at slightly above his cost. He also ordered bumper stickers and antenna balls to promote his growing restaurant chain. Finally, to gain even more visibility, Rubio took an active part in community affairs, including tie-ins with a blood bank, a literacy program, and fund-raising activities for both a Tijuana medical clinic and a local university's athletic program.

EXHIBIT 17-1

Rubio's made fish tacos world famous with the help of local advertising and a character named Pesky Pescado.

The growing popularity of the fish taco enabled Rubio's to double revenues every year for the first five years. After eight years, Rubio's had expanded to 10 restaurants serving over 16,000 fish tacos per day. Rubio trademarked the phrase "Rubio's. Home of the fish taco." And a local restaurant critic called the fish taco "the food San Diegans would miss the most." Rubio plans to expand his restaurants throughout Southern California and eventually statewide. He believes fish tacos are a food that will be around for a long time.[1]

LOCAL ADVERTISING: WHERE THE ACTION IS

Local advertising, as opposed to regional or national advertising, refers to advertising by businesses within a particular city or county to customers within the same geographic area. In 1990, approximately 44 percent of all dollars spent on advertising were for local advertising.

Quite often, local advertising is referred to as **retail advertising** because it is commonly performed by retail stores. However, retail advertising is not necessarily local—it can be regional or national as well, as witnessed by the volume of commercials run by national retail firms such as Sears and J. C. Penney. Moreover, many businesses not usually thought of as retail stores use local advertising—real estate brokers, banks, movie theaters, auto mechanics, plumbers, radio and TV stations, restaurants, museums, and even funeral homes. Local businesses of all types often use public service or issue advertising.

Local advertisers fit into three categories:

☐ Dealerships or local franchises of regional or national companies that specialize in one main product or product line (such as Toyota, McDonald's, or H&R Block).

☐ Stores that sell a variety of branded merchandise, usually on a non-exclusive basis (such as department stores).

☐ Specialty businesses and services (such as music stores, shoe repair shops, florists, hair salons, travel agencies).

Businesses in each of these categories have different advertising goals and approaches.

Local advertising is very important because most sales are made or lost locally. A national auto manufacturer may spend millions advertising new cars, but its nationwide network of local auto dealers spend just as much or more on a combined basis to bring customers into their showrooms to buy the cars. In fact, if the dealers don't make a strong effort on the local level, the efforts of the national advertisers may be wasted. So when it comes to consummating the sale, local advertising is where the action is.

The basic principles used by national advertisers are also applicable to local advertising, but local advertisers have special problems that stem from the simple, practical realities of marketing in a local area. Local and national advertisers differ in basic objectives and strategies, perceived needs of the marketplace, amount of money available to spend on advertising, greater emphasis by local advertisers on newspaper advertising, use of price as a buying inducement, and the use of specialized help in preparing advertisements.

Drive Drunk And We'll See You Real Soon.

If you saw drinking and driving from our point of view,
you wouldn't drink and drive.

Goodwine
Funeral Homes

Caring For Families The Way Only A Family Can.

Flat Rock 584-3200
Palestine 586-2067
Robinson 544-2131

Types of Local Advertising

The two major types of local advertising are product and institutional. As its name implies, **product advertising** is designed to sell a specific product or service and to get immediate action, as shown in Exhibit 17-2. **Institutional advertising,** on the other hand, attempts to obtain favorable attention for the business as a whole, not for a specific product or service the store or business sells. The effects of institutional advertising are intended to be long term rather than short range.

Product Advertising

Local advertisers usually expend most of their advertising efforts on three major types of product advertising.

Regular Price-Line Advertising This type of advertising informs consumers about the services available or the wide selection and quality of merchandise offered at regular prices. An accounting firm, for example, may advertise its accounting and tax services for small businesses. A jewelry store may advertise a specific category of jewelry that has widespread appeal. Exhibit 17-3 (p. 606), for example, shows an effective ad for pierced earrings.

Sale Advertising To stimulate the movement of particular merchandise or generally increase store traffic, local merchants advertise items on sale, emphasizing specially reduced prices. Service businesses may also do sale advertising. A travel agency, for instance, may advertise a special sale on cruises, or a hair salon may advertise perms at a reduced price.

If you love this ad, you must have holes in your head.

Zell Bros has hundreds of ways to fill those tiny holes. At hundreds of different prices, from $20 to $25,000. Now, if you don't happen to have holes in your head, don't despair. We also have a rather impressive collection of clasp-type earrings.

Open Sunday. Downtown Store 12-5 pm / 227-8471, Clackamas Town Center 10am-9pm / 654-6504, Washington Square 10am-10pm / 620-3610. Items enlarged individually to show detail. Subject to prior sale.

EXHIBIT 17-3

Zell Bros. jewelers found a unique way to advertise its wide selection of pierced earrings at regular prices.

Clearance Advertising Local advertisers may do clearance advertising to make room for new product lines or new models or to rid themselves of slow-moving product lines, floor samples, broken or distressed merchandise, or items that are no longer in season. For example, Sew Pro's, a sewing and vacuum center, ran ads in a local newspaper for a spring clearance sale in order to sell its demo models and make room for newer models.[2]

Institutional Advertising

Institutional advertising sells an *idea* about the company. It is usually designed to make the public aware of the company and to build a solid reputation or image. An institutional ad might stress longer hours of operation, a new credit policy, store expansion, or company philosophy, or it might simply be educational. This type of advertising is expected to reap long-term rather than short-term benefits. Many types of businesses, including stores, restaurants, banks, professional firms, and hospitals, use institutional advertising from time to time. In fact, today more and more hospitals rely on

Institutional advertising, such as this handsome newspaper ad, helps create an image for the advertiser and builds public awareness.

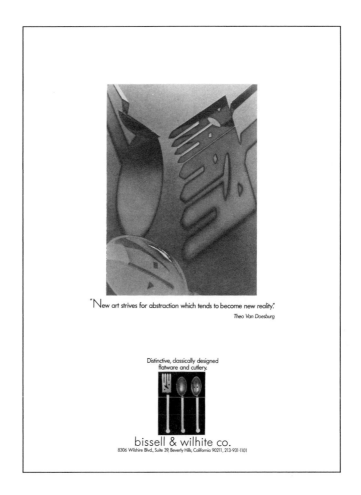

"New art strives for abstraction which tends to become new reality."
Theo Van Doesburg

Distinctive, classically designed flatware and cutlery.

bissell & wilhite co.
8306 Wilshire Blvd., Suite 39, Beverly Hills, California 90211, 213-931-1101

institutional advertising to increase their visibility. For example, Children's Hospital and Health Center in San Diego ran an ad thanking its nurses for the care they provide to their patients.[3]

Readership of institutional advertising may sometimes be lower than that of product advertising. But if done effectively, institutional ads can be very helpful in building a favorable image and identity for the business, attracting new patronage, and developing loyalty from existing customers. Exhibit 17-4 is an institutional ad run by Bissell & Wilhite, a business that specializes in flatware and cutlery.

Objectives of Local Advertising

The objectives of local advertising differ from the objectives of national advertising in both emphasis and time. National manufacturers tend to emphasize long-term objectives of awareness, image, and credibility. On the local, retail level, the advertiser's needs tend to be more immediate, as shown in the Checklist of Local Advertising Objectives on p. 608. The emphasis is on keeping the cash register ringing—increasing traffic, turning over inventory, and bringing in new customers among other things. As a result, on the local level, there are constant promotions, sales, and clearances, all designed to create immediate activity. The trade-off, of course, is that the day after the

Checklist of Local Advertising Objectives

☐ *To introduce new customers.* Every year, many old customers are lost due to relocation, death, inconvenience, or dissatisfaction. To thrive, a business must continually seek new customers, primarily through advertising.

☐ *To build awareness and image.* Because many local businesses provide essentially the same services, stores can use advertising techniques to distinguish themselves from each other.

☐ *To help retain old customers and increase their frequency of visits.* More customers are lost because of inattention than any other single reason. In addition, a barrage of advertising from competitors may lure customers away. A steady, consistent program of advertising can keep present customers informed and reinforce their desire to remain customers and visit your business more often.

☐ *To reduce sales expense.* By preselling many customers, advertising lightens the load on sales personnel. By increasing traffic, it allows salespeople to make more sales in a shorter time. Both contribute to reducing the cost of sales.

☐ *To curtail seasonal peaks.* Each year there are dips and swings in the business cycle. One way to level off the peaks and valleys is to advertise consistently.

☐ *To accelerate inventory turnover.* Some businesses sell all the merchandise in a store four or five times a year. Others turn over the inventory 15 to 20 times. The more times inventory is turned, the more profit can be made. Rapid inventory turnover also keeps prices down. In this way, advertising contributes to lower customer prices.

promotion or sale the traffic may drop. So to increase traffic again, the merchant may plan another sale or another promotion. Then another and another. This can result in a cycle of sporadic bursts of activity followed by inactivity, sharp peaks and valleys in sales, and the image of a business that should be visited only during a sale.

Long-term and short-term objectives work against each other when one is sought at the expense of the other. Successful local advertisers must therefore think of long-term objectives first and then develop short-term goals to help achieve their long-term objectives. This usually increases the emphasis on institutional and regular price-line advertising, improves customer service, and reduces the reliance on sales and clearances for creating traffic.

PLANNING THE ADVERTISING EFFORT

The key to success in any advertising program, local or national, is adequate planning. Planning is not a one-time occurrence, however, but a continuous process of research, evaluation, decision, execution, and review. On the local level, more advertising dollars are wasted because of inadequate planning than for any other reason. The success of Rubio's was due to the fact that Ralph Rubio made planning a continuous, flexible process that allowed for change, improvement, new facts, and new ideas. Several steps are involved in planning the local advertising effort: analyzing the local market and the competition, conducting adequate research, determining objectives and strategy, establishing a realistic budget, and planning media strategy. However, as we mentioned in Chapter 7, the small advertiser will often profit from a bottom-up planning approach. Rubio's success, for example, can be attributed to his starting with a tactic—the fish taco—and then building a complete strategy around it, from the bottom up.

Analyzing the Local Market and Competition

Careful research must be used to identify the type of local market in which the business is located. Whenever possible, local advertising should reflect the needs of the immediate area. Items to consider, therefore, are whether the area is rural or urban, conservative or progressive, high- or low-income, white-collar or blue-collar. A thorough knowledge of the local market and potential customers influences the goods and services the business offers, the prices established, and the design and style of advertising. Accurate analysis at this point prevents advertising misfires later on.

Similarly, a careful study should be made of all competitors in the local area. What merchandise and services do they offer? What is their pricing strategy? Where are they located? How large are they? What is their advertising strategy? What media do they use? How much do they spend on advertising? Do their places of business invite customers to shop there or do they repel customers?

Constant competitive research alerts the advertiser to new ideas, comparative advantages and disadvantages, new merchandising techniques, and new material for advertising campaigns.

Conducting Adequate Research

The local advertiser usually cannot afford to hire a specialized firm to conduct formal market research programs. However, because of its proximity to the marketplace, a local store or business should be well attuned to the attitudes of customers and should be able to conduct informal research to measure customer reaction to merchandise and advertising campaigns. A good local advertising agency might assist in this regard.

Chapter 6 thoroughly discussed the field of advertising and marketing research. This chapter examines only aspects of research unique to the local advertiser. As discussed in Chapter 6, there are two types of research: primary research, which is data collected firsthand, and secondary research, which is data accumulated by others that can be adapted to the needs of the advertiser.

Primary Research

To be successful, a local advertiser must have the answers to many important questions. Who are our present customers? Who are our potential customers? How many are there? Where are they located? How can our company best appeal to them? Where do they now buy the merchandise or services we want to sell to them? Can we offer customers anything they are not getting at the present time? If so, what? How can we convince them to do business with us? To answer these questions, local advertisers should conduct primary research in the following areas.

Customer and Sales Analysis It is important to keep track of customers—both charge and cash customers—to correlate their addresses to census tract information. Census information includes such data as average income, family size, education, vehicle and home ownership, and age.

In retail stores, sales should be tabulated by merchandise classification. Careful analysis of this information helps identify changes in consumer buying patterns—which in turn affect the merchandise or services that will be bought and advertised in the future.

A comparison should be made of a company's sales by merchandise lines in relation to those of other companies in the area. (Information about other companies' market share can be obtained from several sources mentioned later in this section.)

Customer Attitudes and Satisfaction Feedback from sales personnel can provide valuable information about customers. In addition, having salespeople solicit information about customers can forestall problems by pinpointing areas of customer satisfaction and dissatisfaction at an early stage. Customers will also feel that the store cares if it actively seeks such information from them. One way to solicit information is to provide response forms that allow customers to offer comments about the business's products and services and to make suggestions for improvement, such as carrying certain merchandise not currently stocked. Response forms are particularly common in restaurants, where customers have time before and after meals to fill them out.

Advertising Testing Because of the vast number of ads prepared by most local advertisers, it's unusual to test advertisements in advance of their placement. However, posttesting would determine the advertising campaign's effect on sales, if any. One method for posttesting is to provide a discount coupon with an ad and to tabulate the number of customers who take advantage of the coupon offer. A similar way to test the effectiveness of broadcast ads is to give customers a special discount or premium if they mention some slogan or line from the commercial. Some businesses also make a point of having employees ask customers where they heard about the business or the particular promotion being staged.

Secondary Research

Local advertisers should be aware of the many secondary sources of information that are available and can be adapted to their particular needs. These sources include manufacturers and suppliers, trade publications and associations, local advertising media, and various government organizations.

Manufacturers and Suppliers Manufacturers and suppliers want their dealers to succeed. Their dealer-aid programs usually include valuable research on the retail market for their products. Many manufacturers conduct dealer seminars to explain these research results.

Retail Trade Publications and Associations Trade publications are excellent sources of information for a local advertiser's business. They contain news of important trends, new technology, and research studies relating to the businesses the publication is directed toward. Just a few of the hundreds of such publications are *Stores, The Merchandiser, Progressive Grocer, Automotive News, Farm Supplier, Hotel & Motel Management, Modern Jeweler,* and *Shopping Center World.* A complete list of publications is available in *The Standard Periodical Directory* or *Ulrich's International Periodicals Directory.*

Advertising is a common topic in other publications as well. A glance under "Advertising" in the *Business Periodicals Index* will give local business owners an idea of some of the publications that cover aspects of advertising they may be concerned with.

The National Retail Federation (NRF) (100 W. 31st Street, New York, NY 10001) publishes an extensive list of materials on research topics of interest to retailers. Another source of information is the Mass Retailing Institute's study of shoppers' behavior, available at reasonable cost (579 7th Avenue, New York, NY 10018).

Typical of the many associations that are good sources of research information are the National Office Products Association, National Association of Drug Stores, Menswear Retailers of America, United States Savings and Loan League, National Sporting Goods Association, and American Society of Travel Agents. The *Encyclopedia of Associations,* available at most libraries, indicates the associations pertinent to a particular area of interest. A short letter will bring the desired research data.

Advertising Media and Media Associations The amount of research data that will be provided by local media depends on the size of the community. In large cities, the major newspapers and broadcast stations provide in-depth market data about the communities they serve.

Even if a local advertiser lives in a community too small for the media to provide their own research data, the newspaper and broadcasters probably belong to national associations that conduct extensive research that can be passed along to advertisers. Organizations of particular interest are the Direct-Mail Advertising Association, Newspaper Advertising Bureau, Radio Advertising Bureau, Magazine Publishers Association, Television Bureau of Advertising, and Institute of Outdoor Advertising.

Government Organizations Various government bureaus can provide information to the local advertiser, including data on population projections, birth and death information, marriage license statistics, and so on. In every state government, departments in charge of commerce, taxation, labor, highways, and justice provide reports and data. These materials can be useful in measuring local markets and making projections. Of particular interest to most local advertisers is the Small Business Administration (SBA). It publishes a wealth of information on a wide variety of topics, most of it free or available for only a nominal charge.

The U.S. Department of Commerce also offers pertinent materials, including *Retail Data Sources for Market Analysis, Business Service Checklist* (a weekly guide to Department of Commerce reports, books, and news releases); *Bureau of Census Catalog, Census Tract Studies;* the annual edition of the *U.S. Industrial Outlook; Current Retail Trade; Survey of Current Business; Monthly Department Store Sales; County Business Patterns;* the annual edition of the *Statistical Abstract of the United States;* and the *County and City Data Book.*

Determining Objectives and Strategy

The stated objectives of any marketing and advertising program determine the particular marketing mix or strategy to be used. A local advertiser has the same general options as a national advertiser when it comes to developing its local marketing strategy: product, price, place, and promotion.

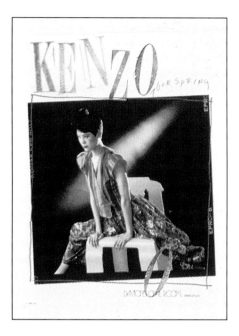

EXHIBIT 17-5

This award-winning ad for the Oval Room, a boutique in Dayton's department store, ran in Minneapolis/St. Paul-area magazines. The high production values of the magazines allowed the art director to use unconventional design elements, such as hand-drawn rules and hand-stamped type.

Product

What merchandise should be sold? What services should be offered? Should some lines be expanded or dropped? How wide a selection should be offered? If a store intends to be a discount house, it may want to carry a broad line. If it wants to be a specialty shop, it may opt to carry only selected lines. In short, what is the business's product/service concept? Exhibit 17-5 shows how one advertiser differentiates itself by focusing on high-quality clothing products. For the existing business, these questions are answered by experience and research. For the new or expanding business, research is a must in order to avoid the substantial losses that can result from carrying the wrong lines of merchandise or providing the wrong service.

Price

What will the local market support? Should prices be high, low, or moderate? What should be included in the price? What about terms and warranties? What about the use of charge cards? What policy should be established on refunds? Are all these policies in keeping with the desired image of the business? Local advertisers have the tendency to cut prices first rather than seek other ways to compete. That strategy is often self-defeating in the long run.

Place

Where should the business be located? What is the trading area? For a bank, how many branches can be established? What kinds of areas should be served? What is the cost of doing business in different areas? How large should the facilities be? Additional branches or locations can create great economies in advertising costs, but these economies may be offset by greater problems and costs in the management and administration of the business.

Promotion

Should the business be highly promotional, semipromotional, or nonpromotional? A business that has few regular customers and must rely on discount prices, sales, and other promotions to bring customers in (such as an auto dealer) will have to do a great deal of advertising (**highly promotional strategy**). A business that has regular customers but uses periodic sales and promotions to increase store traffic (such as a men's clothing store) will need a **semipromotional strategy.** Finally, a business that relies on a clientele that returns regularly to the business (a hair salon, for example) may have less need for advertising and related types of promotion—**nonpromotional strategy**—and may use greater amounts of institutional advertising.

Other promotional questions local advertisers will need to answer include: Should advertising concentrate on the regular price line, special sales, or clearances? What percentage of advertising should be institutional? How do advertising activities affect this type of business? How much advertising should be done, and in what media?

Determining the objectives and strategies of any business—local, regional, or national—is the most important policy decision management ever makes. The chosen objectives and strategies determine the whole complexion of the business in the years that follow. They give direction to the enterprise, continuity to its promotional efforts, and an understanding of the company in the marketplace. The objectives and strategies should be highly specific. They should be written down, reviewed frequently, and updated or revised on a regular basis as the business situation warrants.

Perhaps the biggest mistake a local advertiser can make is to put too little thought or effort into integrating its advertising with its overall business objectives. This lack of integration can lead to a number of advertising difficulties, as discussed in Ad Lab 17-A.

AD LAB 17-A
Mistakes Commonly Made by Local Advertisers

Even the best-laid plans for local advertisers may go awry. However, chances of success are much greater if certain potential pitfalls are avoided.

Inattention to the Advertising Effort Advertising is sometimes not given the attention it deserves, whether because of distractions, lack of time on the part of the local advertiser, or lack of skill or interest in this aspect of the business.

Ego Involvement Local advertisers sometimes succumb to the temptation to become celebrities by appearing in their own television commercials or placing photographs of themselves (or their family) in ads. This practice is dangerous. Most local advertisers are not effective spokespeople.

Inadequate Supply of Merchandise If the business has an insufficient supply of merchandise to meet the demand generated by the advertising, the advertiser loses more than the potential sales revenue—the money spent on the advertising is wasted, and harm is done to customer goodwill.

Unqualified Individuals Handling the Advertising Successful advertising requires competent individuals to plan, produce, and implement it. The smaller the establishment, the greater the chance that the person who handles the advertising will be unqualified to do so. Large stores have the advantage of being able to afford an advertising manager.

Compensating for Mistakes by Advertising Even the best advertising efforts cannot compensate for a bad location, poor selection of merchandise, untrained personnel, unreasonably high prices, or a host of other difficulties. A good advertising campaign only speeds up the failure of a poorly run business.

Lack of Knowledge about What to Advertise One of the most important decisions involves what to advertise. If an adver-

tisement is to be successful, it must contain merchandise or services in which people have some interest. A good rule of thumb is to advertise items that are selling well already. Promote items that build traffic and feature items in advertisements that are nationally advertised brands. These get attention because of the identifiable name, they take less explanation because of national promotion by manufacturers, and they help the local advertiser build a good reputation by association with a well-known brand.

Overspending on Noncommercial Advertising A host of charitable causes and nonprofit organizations are always waiting for contributors. Particularly difficult to turn down are requests for advertising in high school yearbooks, church bulletins, athletic programs, and publications of fraternal organizations. Rarely do these ads prove cost-effective, however. If contributions are made by placing advertisements, the expense should be charged to "contributions to charitable organizations" rather than calling it an advertising expense.

Lack of Coordination Advertising must be coordinated with buying of merchandise. Employees should be informed about the advertising so they can answer customers' questions. Merchandise must be properly priced and marked. Displays need to be in position. And local advertising should be coordinated with national advertising by manufacturers so that the advertising efforts reinforce each other.

Laboratory Applications

1. As an observer of local advertisers, identify and describe mistakes you feel they make in addition to those given above.

2. What should they do to correct their mistakes?

Establishing the Budget

How much should a local business invest in advertising? New businesses usually require greater advertising expenditures than established ones. Once the public becomes familiar with a company's goods or services, advertising costs should settle at a natural, profitable level. But an advertising budget must be precisely designed for a particular business.

Exhibit 17-6 lists the average percentage of sales invested in advertising by different types of establishments. These figures are national averages and do not reflect the tremendous variety of factors that can affect the budget. The most important variable is the promotion policy established when the company's objectives and strategies are determined. Other influences include:

☐ Location of the business. A business that depends on walk-in traffic will probably need to do more advertising if it is located in an isolated, hard-to-find area rather than a shopping center.

☐ Age and character of the firm. New businesses typically need to advertise more than well-established businesses.

☐ Size of the business. A small business cannot afford to spend as much on advertising as a large business.

☐ Type of product or service offered. A restaurant that serves outstanding food, for example, may only need a minimal ad budget because of word-of-

EXHIBIT 17-6   Average Advertising Investments of Retail Businesses

Commodity or class of business	Average percent of sales	Commodity or class of business	Average percent of sales
Appliance, radio, TV dealers	2.3%	Insurance agents, brokers	1.8%
Auto accessory and parts stores	0.9	Jewelry stores	4.4
Auto dealers	0.8	Laundromats (under $35,000 in sales)	1.3
Bakeries	0.7	Liquor stores (under $50,000 in sales)	0.7
Banks	1.3	Lumber and building materials dealers	0.5
Beauty shops	2.0	Meat markets	0.6
Book stores	1.7	Men's wear stores (under $300,000)	2.4
Camera stores (under $100,000 in sales)	0.8	Motels	3.7
Children's and infants' wear stores	1.4	Motion picture theaters	5.5
Cocktail lounges	0.9	Music stores ($25,000 to $50,000)	1.8
Credit agencies (personal)	2.4	Office supplies dealers (under	
Department stores ($1 million–$2 million)	2.5	$100,000)	1.0
Discount stores	2.4	Paint, glass, and wallpaper stores	1.3
Drugstores (independent, under $70,000 in sales)	1.1	Photographic studios and supply shops	2.4
		Real estate (except lessors of buildings)	0.6
Dry cleaning shops (under $50,000 in sales)	1.7	Restaurants (under $50,000)	0.6
		Savings and loan associations	1.5
Florists	2.1	Shoe stores	1.9
Food chains	1.1	Specialty stores ($1 million and over)	3.0
Furniture stores	5.0	Sporting goods stores	3.5
Gift and novelty stores	1.4	Taverns (under $50,000)	0.7
Hardware stores	1.6	Tire dealers	2.2
Home centers	1.3	Travel agents	5.0
Hotels (under 300 rooms)	6.7	Variety stores	1.5

mouth advertising. A travel agent, on the other hand, continually needs to entice people to travel with ads for special fares and exotic cruises.

☐ Size of the trading area. A large advertising budget may not be justified if the trading area is relatively small.

☐ Amount and kind of advertising done by competitors. If competitors do minimal advertising, a small advertising budget may go a long way. On the other hand, if competitors advertise heavily, a comparable advertising budget may need to be established.

☐ Media available for advertising, their coverage of the trading area of the business, and their costs. If the primary local newspaper, for example, has 100,000 subscribers, the advertising rates will be higher than if it had only 5,000 subscribers. Likewise, television advertising rates in large cities will usually be higher than in smaller communities.

☐ Results obtained from previous advertising. Positive results from previous advertising almost always justifies a similar or larger budget. If results were disappointing, the budget is likely to be reduced.

The goal of the local advertiser is to set a budget in which the optimum amount of advertising money will be spent. If more money is spent on advertising than necessary, the advertiser wastes the excess money. On the other hand, if the advertiser doesn't spend enough to generate the necessary sales, the entire advertising expenditure may be a waste.

Budgeting Strategy

Advertising programs should be continuous; one-shot ads are almost always ineffective. Also, advertising money should be spent when prospects are most receptive to buying a local advertiser's goods or services. In practice, this requires that advertising dollars be allocated in relation to sales volume. A company that sells swimming pools and spas, for example, will allocate more advertising dollars during the spring and summer months than during the winter months.

Local advertisers can choose several strategies or methods to budget their advertising expenditures. (Some of these were discussed in Chapter 7.) However, most advertisers still use the percent-of-sales method, since it is the simplest to calculate and the easiest to defend with company bookkeepers and accountants.

To achieve the objective of selling more merchandise at lower unit cost, well-timed advertising should be run to create month-by-month sales and advertising patterns like those illustrated in Exhibits 17-7 and 17-8 on the following pages.

Advertising has become such a large and complicated activity for many companies that marketers use computers to determine the advertising budget. A computer can analyze the previous year's sales along with various influencing factors to determine a budget based on anticipated sales for the current year. The result is an advertising expenditure curve that, month by month, slightly precedes the sales curve, as illustrated by the dashed line in Exhibit 17-8.

Developing the Annual Sales and Advertising Plan

Not all local advertisers have a computer to forecast sales for the coming year. However, by doing some research, an advertiser can make a fairly accurate sales forecast. Basic questions a local merchant might ask include: What is the anticipated increase in population for the local area during the next year?

EATING AND DRINKING PLACES
($47,514,000,000)

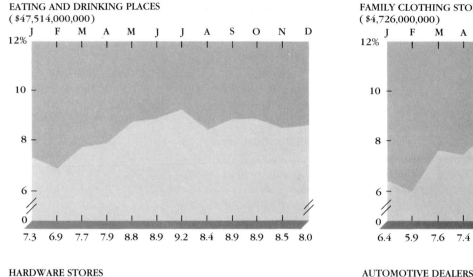

7.3   6.9   7.7   7.9   8.8   8.9   9.2   8.4   8.9   8.9   8.5   8.0

FAMILY CLOTHING STORES
($4,726,000,000)

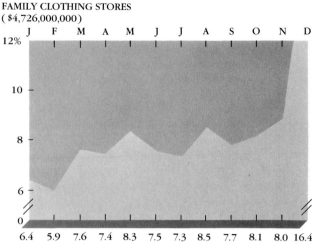

6.4   5.9   7.6   7.4   8.3   7.5   7.3   8.5   7.7   8.1   8.0   16.4

HARDWARE STORES
($5,772,000,000)

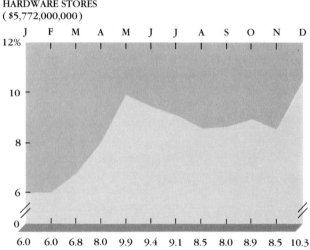

6.0   6.0   6.8   8.0   9.9   9.4   9.1   8.5   8.0   8.9   8.5   10.3

AUTOMOTIVE DEALERS
($93,046,000,000)

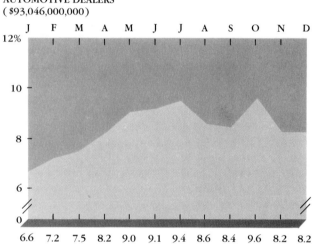

6.6   7.2   7.5   8.2   9.0   9.1   9.4   8.6   8.4   9.6   8.2   8.2

EXHIBIT 17-7

Total retail sales by types of stores.
Percentage of the year's total
sales is indicated for each month.
Note how important each month
is to the sale of certain types of
products and services: Clothing
sales are highest in December;
hardware sales are highest in May
and December. Advertising budgets should be geared to these
fluctuations.

What is the anticipated increase or decrease in overall retail sales? What is the
outlook for local employment? How are similar businesses doing?

Local accountants, bankers, trade associations, Chambers of Commerce,
and media representatives can help answer these questions. After all the
factors that affect finance, production, and marketing have been considered, a
realistic sales plan for the year, month by month, and even week by week,
should be developed. From that sales plan, an advertising expense plan can
be formulated. (See the Checklist for Setting Local Advertising Budgets, on
p. 618.)

Advertising should precede sales promotions. The most advertising dollars
should be spent just before customers are most likely to respond, such as
when a new store is opening, a new product is introduced, or prices are

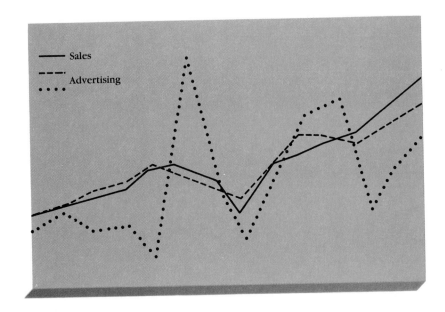

EXHIBIT 17-8

If you want well-timed advertising to sell more merchandise at lower unit costs, you want a sales advertising pattern that month by month looks like this---- not this·····

reduced. To determine the appropriate ad expenditures, a retailer first computes the percentage of yearly sales anticipated for each month (or, better yet, each week) of the year and plots this information on a graph. Next, the retailer plots an advertising curve that slightly precedes the sales curve, as shown with the dashed lines in Exhibit 17-8. (Note that advertising peaks are slightly lower than sales peaks, but the valleys are slightly higher, indicating that the unit cost of advertising is typically a little higher when sales are low.) The advertising curve indicates what percentage of the annual advertising expenditure should be spent each month.

Plotting anticipated sales patterns enables business owners to allot a percentage of the total yearly advertising to each month. By plotting actual sales as the year progresses, the advertiser can compare weekly and monthly expenses to weekly and monthly sales goals.

A simple device commonly used by local advertisers is a **monthly promotional calendar.** The calendar should be large enough to accommodate information about media schedules, costs, in-house promotions, sales, and special events. The advertiser should enter all the holidays as well as traditional community events like "Washington's Birthday Specials." The local media, trade associations, and trade publications can be especially helpful in supplying this information. The calendar then enables the advertiser to tell at a glance the shape and direction of the advertising program.

Planning Media Strategy

Choosing the right local advertising media is important for two reasons. First, most local advertisers' budgets are too limited to use all media that might be appropriate. Ralph Rubio, for example, started out with newspaper ads for his Deli-Mex restaurant, then expanded to radio and TV commercials when his business started growing. Second, certain media are more effective than others if the business is restricted geographically, by type of customer, or by some other factor. For instance, an exclusive art gallery may achieve better results by advertising in an upscale magazine than in the daily newspaper.

Checklist for Setting Local Advertising Budgets

Set a Sales Goal

☐ Write down the sales figures for each month last year—for the whole store and for each department. Then, in view of this performance and your own knowledge and judgment of this year's picture, rough in sales goals for next year. Use the following profit pointers as a reminder of the factors to be considered in making your sales goal realistic but challenging:

Your sales last year.

Population, income, employment levels.

New and expanded departments.

Tie-ins with merchandising events.

What competitors are doing, getting.

More aggressive selling and advertising.

Decide How Much Advertising

☐ Write down how much advertising you used each month last year. Then, considering your planned sales goal and what your competition is likely to do, write in your planned advertising budget for the coming year. Your budget as a percent of sales can be checked against the expenditure of other stores in your classification. The following profit pointers can be used to double-check your own thinking on the advertising budget you can afford and need to do the job:

Stores in less favorable locations advertise more.

So do those that are new and expanding.

Strong competition raises the size of the budget needed.

Stores stressing price appeal usually promote more.

Special dates and events offer additional sales opportunities.

Added sales produced by increased expenditure are more profitable—more money can be spent to get them.

Taking advantage of co-op support can stretch ad dollars and increase ad frequency.

Decide What to Promote

☐ Let your business experience guide you in weighting the advertising you will invest in each of your departments each month. For instance, if the sales goal of Department A is 9 percent of the total store sales objective this month, then earmark for it something like 9 percent of the month's planned advertising space. Your list shouldn't be a straightjacket, but a basic outline.

Check the month's heavy traffic pullers.

Look for departments whose seasonal curve drops next month and should be cleared now.

Dig for "sleepers," currently hot, but that don't show up in last year's figures.

Promote newly expanded departments harder.

Calculate co-op support available for each line of merchandise.

Make a Schedule

☐ For each month, fill in a day-by-day schedule to take full advantage of:

Payroll days of important firms.

Days of the week traffic is heaviest.

National and local merchandising events offering tie-in possibilities.

New or expanded departments.

Current prices and your stock on hand—jot down items, prices, and ad sizes for each day.

Newspapers

Local advertisers give newspapers the greatest emphasis—for a number of reasons. The local newspaper is the shopper's most trusted source of local information. Recognizing this fact, retailers look to the medium for informing the community about their stores, merchandise, and services.[4] Exhibit 17-9 shows how one local advertiser used newspaper advertising to get the attention of prospective customers. Newspapers offer other advantages as well:

Bullock's uses a consistent format and placement for its *Los Angeles Times* ads to build identity and continuity.

- Most newspapers are oriented to the local community. This makes it possible for the local advertiser to reach the desired audience with a minimum of wasted circulation.
- The cost is typically low, considering the large number of prospects reached—so low, in fact, that it is affordable for most businesses. Also, most newspapers have a special rate for local advertisers that is considerably lower than their national rates.
- Advertising can be placed in the newspaper on very short notice.

☐ Some selectivity is possible by advertising in special-interest sections of the newspaper, such as sports or business news.

☐ Consumers read newspapers at their leisure, and when they see ads of interest, they may clip and save them for future reference.

Drawbacks to newspapers include their limited selectivity, their sometimes poor reproduction, and potential ad clutter. Nevertheless, newspapers remain by far the number-one medium for local advertising. More than 50 percent of local advertising expenditures go to newspapers, with television and radio far behind at 13 and 11 percent, respectively. The rest of the local advertising pie goes to direct mail, outdoor advertising, magazines, and miscellaneous forms of advertising.

To compete with such increasingly popular ad media as free papers, direct mail, and "shoppers" (to be discussed shortly), most daily newspapers have also instituted a service called **total market coverage (TMC).** A TMC is a free advertising vehicle sent out weekly to 100 percent of the residents in the newspaper's market area. It may be in tabloid or similar format and may contain varying amounts of editorial matter as well as ads. However, the primary function of the TMC is advertising. Some newspapers prefer to call the TMC "alternative distribution," particularly since the publication may be either sent through the mail or hand delivered by newspaper employees.[5] Since the ads in TMCs are the same as those run in the paper, no ad production costs are incurred, which makes it handy for the local advertiser who wants to reach everyone in the local market area. The biggest drawback to TMCs is uncertainty of readership. Just because people receive something doesn't mean they'll read it. So readership must always be analyzed carefully.

Newspapers have both display and classified advertising departments. These departments are usually equipped to help advertisers prepare the complete advertisement, including copy, art, typesetting, and layout/design. Often, the service is given without charge. For example, advertising professionals at the *San Diego Business Journal* created an entire identity (complete with name, logo, and artwork) for a group of independent management consultants who pooled their resources to purchase advertising space in the paper. Large papers even have personnel who will visit an advertiser's place of business to do artwork for ads.

For more details on newspaper advertising, review Chapter 13. .

Shoppers and Free Papers

A growing number of cities have all-ad publications, called **shoppers,** that are published as a forum for local advertisers. Some shoppers distribute their publications through the mail and offer total circulation in a given area. This can be ideal for a local advertiser seeking distribution to the immediate trading area. For advertisers who want to run ads only in areas of the city their businesses serve, shoppers offer an advantage over newspaper TMCs because they often print separate editions for various ZIP code groupings.

Some shopper publications respond to competition from TMCs by adding editorial content. On Long Island in New York, for example, the *Center Island Pennysavers* used to be 100 percent ads. But with competition from *Newsday Extra,* a weekly TMC of the giant daily paper, the shopper switched to a format with 70 percent ads and 30 percent local news. The shopper's publisher explained the decision to add editorial content: "We went to local news because our advertisers wanted it and because *Newsday* couldn't really cover the local news."[6]

In addition to shoppers, many cities have free newspapers, usually geared toward entertainment information. These papers are usually distributed in establishments that advertise in them and at other key locations throughout the city. The advantage of free papers is that people tend to like them and read them, often because the papers provide information they can't get elsewhere. The disadvantage is that distribution can be erratic.

Magazines

The growth of local, slick, special-interest magazines has given local advertisers the opportunity to communicate with upper-income prospects through a prestigious medium. Exhibit 17-10 shows a magazine ad for an upscale inn. Publications such as *Palm Springs Life, Dallas Home and Garden,* and *Los Angeles Magazine* offer excellent photographic reproduction as well. Local

WHALES LEAP, CLIFFS RISE, SEA GULLS SOAR BUT, ON WEEKDAYS, ROOM RATES PLUMMET.

On Monday, our coastline is just as spectacular as it is on Saturday. Our Spa tubs as soothing. Our

$190.⁰⁰ WEEKNIGHTS

cuisine as divine. But our prices, like Carmel's weekend crowds, abruptly subside. So come bask in our finest spa suites Sunday through

HIGHLANDS INN
A Member of Small Luxury Hotels and Resorts.

Thursday. When paradise belongs to the whales, the sea gulls, and the fiscally wise.

Four Miles South of Carmel on Hwy One. (408) 624-3801 (800) 682-4811 (CA)

EXHIBIT 17-10

Highlands Inn, near Carmel, California, chose an upscale magazine for this ad directed at prospective guests who are affluent, but "fiscally wise."

advertisers who seek even greater prestige and selectivity can also use special city or regional editions of major national publications such as *Time, Newsweek,* and *Sports Illustrated.* The attractiveness of using magazine advertising may be limited because of cost or because a store's trading area may be much smaller than the market reached by the magazine. In addition, magazines require that advertising be submitted long before the publication date.

Review Chapter 13 for further information about magazine advertising.

Electronic Media

Local advertisers find buying time on area radio and TV stations attractive because it usually reaches a strictly local audience, offers high impact, and has a relatively low cost per thousand. Exhibit 17-11 is an example of a low-cost local TV commercial. Because effective electronic media advertising requires multiple exposures, however, some advertisers might consider the total cost too high.

Radio and TV commercial time is highly selective since time slots can be purchased next to the most suitable programs for the product or service being offered. This is especially true with local cable TV stations. Likewise, Top-40 radio stations are ideal advertising media for record dealers.

Immediacy and believability are additional benefits of electronic media, since local personalities, or the advertisers themselves, can present the commercial message personally. In Chicago, for example, one men's clothing store used well-known baseball and football players and a college president,

EXHIBIT 17-11

Local television advertising doesn't need to cost an arm and a leg. This witty TV commercial for radio station AM 1000 was done on a very low budget.

GARRY: VO: AM 1000, AM 1000, AM 1000.

STEVE: So, Garry . . .

GARRY: Yep.

STEVE: How does it feel to have your own radio station? AM 1000, the Loop.

GARRY: The Loop.

STEVE: 'Scuse me?

GARRY: What?

STEVE: I'm not done with my part of the commercial yet.

(SFX: Static under)

GARRY: Forget about that. The new Loop AM 1000.

STEVE: VO: Yeah, the Loop AM 1000 . . .

(SFX: "El" train under)

STEVE: VO: And we have control of it. Hey, it's a big mistake, let's be honest. But it's too late.

GARRY: Listen.

STEVE: So deal with it.

among others, in a popular radio campaign. In a typical commercial, a man reminisces about a key life event that at some point involved wearing a suit from Bigsby & Kruthers men's clothiers. A narrator then humorously identifies the speaker and his suit size, such as "Chicago Cub Rick Sutcliffe wears the Cy Young Award from the National Baseball League and a 46 extra-long from Bigsby & Kruthers. They both fit." Interestingly enough, none of the spokesmen is paid to do the ads—they are all volunteers who happen to like the store.[7]

Local advertisers are also finding that certain Hollywood celebrities are even willing to pitch their products for an affordable fee. Former sitcom stars often work for scale—$366 a day for TV ads, less for radio commercials.[8] Tom Poston ("Newhart") pitched a sale at J. H. Biggar furniture stores, and Adrienne Barbeau ("Maude") did ads for the Campbell Automotive Group, a cluster of car dealerships.

Most radio and TV stations gladly offer assistance in the writing and production of commercials for local advertisers. Normally, this assistance is provided at a nominal charge for studio time plus additional fees for talent, special set designs, and tape dubbing.

For additional information on electronic media advertising, review Chapters 11 and 14.

Signs

The most direct method for businesses to invite customers into their stores or to use their services is through the use of signs. Three types of signs are used by local advertisers: in-store signs, outdoor advertising, and transit advertising. Exhibit 17-12 is an example of attention-grabbing outdoor advertising. Signs offer mass exposure with color, potentially large size, and very low cost per viewer. When signs are used to promote specific products, it is usually for items that have continuous appeal, such as automobiles or fast-food restaurant items.

One disadvantage of signs is the advertiser's inability to make frequent changes. This limits the use of signs for promotion of many types of merchandise. Another consideration is that most local governments have strict sign ordinances that merchants must comply with. In Beverly Hills, for example, an upscale supermarket named Mrs. Gooch's was allowed only one sign—the name of the store, minus the logo.[9]

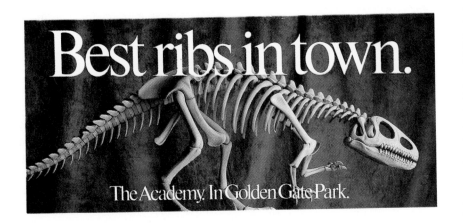

EXHIBIT 17-12

This eye-catching billboard turned out to be an effective means of advertising for the California Academy of Sciences.

Sign companies offer copy and art services, frequently without charge. However, producing signs is usually quite expensive and should be investigated thoroughly.

Chapter 15 gives more complete information on the use of outdoor and transit advertising.

Classified Directories

Yellow Pages directories published by both telephone companies and private companies are a vital advertising medium for most local businesses because the Yellow Pages are kept in the home or office as a ready source of information. In fact, the Yellow Pages are the sole means of advertising for some businesses. Every business that has a telephone qualifies for a one-line listing without charge. Additional advertising in the directories must be paid for, however.

Local communities in large urban areas and military bases usually have privately published classified telephone directories, which are less expensive than the large telephone company directories. These private directories cater to the special interests of the immediate locale and therefore offer excellent support to the small retail merchant or local professional service.

The main problem faced by small businesses now is that the proliferation of directories makes it difficult to decide which ones to choose. If advertisers appear in every available directory, their ad budget will be shot; but staying out of key directories might be a mistake as well. Adding to the problem is the skyrocketing costs of directory ads. A quarter-page ad in Bell Atlantic's 1990 Baltimore directory, for example, is over $5,000.[10]

Chapter 16 provides additional information on the use of Yellow Pages advertising.

Handbills

Handbills may be single sheets **(flyers)** or multiple-page ads **(circulars)** and can be distributed on the street, in parking lots, or door-to-door. The main advantages of handbills are low cost, high speed of production, flexibility, and direct distribution to the target audience. Disadvantages include a high level of throwaways, usually poor production quality, and clutter.[11] Handbills are especially useful for making grand opening announcements, for advertising sales, and for periodically reminding people of the merchandise or service offered. Handbills should be carefully planned to create a good appearance, and attention should also be given to the message so that effective appeals are built into the headline and body copy. A good printer can provide sound advice about the quality of paper to use, colors, size, cost, and general appearance. The copy itself is the advertiser's responsibility, however.

Direct Mail

Although it can also be used to reach mass markets, the superior advantage of direct-mail advertising is its ability to reach specific market segments. Perhaps the greatest use of direct mail is envelope stuffers that accompany monthly bills mailed to charge-account customers. Direct mail may also take the form of catalogs, flyers, postcards, letters, or coupon packets.

One popular type of direct mail is **shared mail,** in which ads of two or more advertisers are included in a single mail package targeted by ZIP code. Introduced by Advo-Systems of Windsor, Connecticut, in 1980, this method accounted for more than 18 billion ad pieces mailed in 1990 for that company alone.[12] Two-thirds of Advo-Systems' client list of more than 25,000 advertisers consists of small, local businesses. The majority fall into four distinct groups: retail stores, food stores, do-it-yourself stores, and chain drugstores. A major appeal of shared mail is that a particular piece can be sent to selected ZIP codes to reach only those households in the advertiser's targeted area.

Whatever the vehicle for delivery, direct mail is likely to get the reader's undivided attention because it has no competition from other advertisers at the same time. Local advertisers with limited budgets can use direct mail to great advantage—the number of pieces mailed and the printing costs are simply adjusted to the budget, and unlimited graphic possibilities can be used to meet the requirements for most any product or service. Most local direct-mail houses can offer copy, art, and printing as well as mailing services.

For more on direct-mail advertising, review Chapter 15.

Sales Promotion

Many sales promotion methods discussed in Chapter 16—including coupons, sampling, specialty advertising, and contests and special events—can be uniquely effective for local advertisers.

Coupons Coupons provide a special inducement to the customer to make a purchase. Usually, the customer receives a price reduction upon presenting the coupon, which has been clipped from a newspaper ad or handbill or received in the mail. Coupons can be used to build store traffic, to encourage the use of a product for the first time, and to test the effectiveness of a particular ad. Exhibit 17-13 is an example of a coupon that customers can clip from a newspaper ad.

Sampling Mrs. Fields Cookies has discovered that giving the customer a small sample of the product is highly effective. Other businesses that lend themselves to sampling are ice-cream stores, delicatessens, bakeries, and fabric stores.

Specialty Advertising Specialty items, including calendars, rulers, shoehorns, and pens, are inexpensive for the retailer but can be valuable to the customer. These items generally contain the store name, address, and telephone number, and often a brief sales message.

Contests and Special Events Local advertisers often schedule a variety of contests and special events, ranging from grand opening contests to product demonstrations to lectures and films, to get customers in the door. For example, the First Wisconsin Bank of Appleton designed several grand opening contests as part of a promotional extravaganza that cost about $100,000 and brought in a remarkable $8 million in deposits within three months.[13]

Many retailers develop their own demonstrations tailored to their product line and market. Bridal shops give sessions on how to plan for a wedding, and sporting goods stores hire a golf pro to give lessons. Other retailers rely on manufacturers to present demonstrations. Thus, a camera store might have a

You can always count on an Amoco station to give you good directions.

1. Cut out this coupon.
2. Bring it to Amoco Quick Lube.
3. Get $2 off on your oil change.

At Amoco Quick Lube, our service technicians will give you a complete oil and lube job in twenty minutes or less. No appointment necessary.

Expiration date: _____ Not good in conjunction with other Amoco coupon offers.

EXHIBIT 17-13

Fallon McElligott came up with a different twist on using coupons in this ad for Amoco.

demonstration of video cameras conducted by a representative from a video equipment company. Other types of special events might include a travel film sponsored by a travel agency or a talk on vitamins presented by a health food store.

Another type of special event a business can sponsor is a show. Probably the most common type of local show is the fashion show given by a clothing retailer. Others include building and home shows staged by hardware stores and new-car shows staged by local car dealers.

Free Publicity

The media are always on the lookout for unusual items that may be of interest to their readers or listeners. Stores that hold major grand openings, have important personnel changes, or have new and unusual lines of merchandise are often newsworthy and might be covered by the local media. Moreover, publicity is often more cost-effective than advertising and offers greater credibility. However, the advertiser must take the initiative to call the media or send a well-written press release—and then hope the media will follow through with the desired publicity.

Examples of newsworthy events might include an autograph signing by a celebrity, an unusual display (such as a runner jogging on a treadmill for hours at a time to demonstrate a sport shoe), or a tie-in with a local sports event (say, giving away free baseball caps to everyone who attends a particular major league baseball game).

Aaron Hull, founder of Office Furniture Warehouse, a 10-store chain in Chicago, is a master of free publicity. For example, when construction work was being done outside one of his stores, Hull decided to have a "sidewalk sale"—and donned a hard hat and jackhammer and distributed chopped-up slabs of cement sidewalk as souvenirs of Chicago. On another occasion, Hull acquired a batch of canvas bags bearing a logo for the "Six Million Dollar Man" TV series. He advertised them as "bionic bags" carrying a list price of $6 million but on sale for 99.5 percent off list price: $3. These and similar promotions received plenty of attention from the local media. Hull believes that once people stop laughing at his outrageous promotions, "they discover that our company offers the best savings on office furniture and supplies."[14]

Community Involvement

Making contributions to the community can effectively enhance a business's image. It can involve sponsoring a local activity such as a baseball team, a summer camp for needy youngsters, or a scholarship. Another way to become involved with the community is to allow store facilities to be used by social or civic organizations for fund-raisers or meetings. Many businesses such as banks and savings associations have rooms specifically designed for community use.

The Media Mix

As with a national advertising plan, the local plan involves a mixture of kinds of advertising. Take the example of Younkers department stores in Des Moines, Iowa. Although the primary advertising effort is made in the Des Moines *Register,* the store also uses smaller newspapers, radio, TV, telemarketing, and direct mail to reach customers.

In the *Register,* Younkers runs "hard-sell ads" every Thursday, Friday, and Saturday and then runs an "idea ad" on Sundays, focusing on prestige goods that promote the store's image. Radio stations are carefully selected for specific commercials: country and western for jeans, rock for teenage outerwear, easy listening for women's fashions. TV commercials are used only for major promotions, such as spring and fall sales. Finally, major emphasis is placed on telemarketing and direct mail. Even though direct mail is the most expensive advertising medium for Younkers, management considers it the most dollar-effective. The store mails primarily to its own list of charge customers, but the direct-mail program has been so successful that many dormant and random-purchase customers have become steady buyers.[15]

The great majority of Younkers' direct-mail pieces take the form of tabloids or catalogs. Customers can order through the mail or by phone in addition to purchasing the items in the store. Younkers makes double use of the direct-mail pieces by transforming them into inserts for the *Register* and other papers. Although this leads to a lot of duplication with charge customers, management believes the results justify the practice.

This media mix works well for a department store in the Midwest. The particular mix that is best for any one type of business in a specific location will vary depending upon a number of factors. As Chapter 12 pointed out, choosing an appropriate media mix for a business can be an art in itself.

CREATING THE LOCAL ADVERTISEMENT

One of the most competitive businesses in any local market is the grocery business. Characterized by high overhead, low profit margins, heavy discounting, constant promotion, and massive doses of advertising, food retailing is a difficult and highly competitive business at best.

The Tom Thumb Page grocery stores in Dallas had an additional problem. They had elected to avoid price competition whenever possible and to compete instead on the basis of quality and service. This policy made it potentially difficult to attract new customers and create store traffic, because grocery customers tend to be very price-oriented.

The Tom Thumb chain had been doing "maintenance advertising" in routine food-day newspaper sections for about four years. When they hired a new advertising agency, KCBN, Inc., chain owners Bob and Charles Cullum explained their situation and their objectives. They asked the agency to develop a campaign that would show that Tom Thumb was, in fact, very competitive in giving top value even though the prices might be slightly higher.

Barbara Harwell and Chuck Bua, the agency's creative directors, responded by developing a local institutional campaign that made grocery advertising history. They suggested opening the campaign with a television promotion for Thanksgiving turkeys. They convinced the Cullums and Tom Hairston, the chain's president, that to present a truly quality image they would have to create an absolutely outstanding commercial in terms of production quality. Furthermore, to communicate that Tom Thumb's policies truly warranted higher prices, they persuaded the clients to make a bold, risky statement that would impress the viewing public. Hairston and the Cullums agreed. Two weeks before Thanksgiving, the campaign began.

The commercial opened with a tight close-up of a live turkey. As the off-camera announcer spoke, the camera pulled slowly back, and the turkey reacted to the copy with an occasional "gobble."

The announcer said:

At Tom Thumb we stand behind everything we sell . . . and that's a promise. It's always been that way. Even when we started, Mr. Cullum said, "We want our customers to be happy with everything they buy in this store. If a woman buys a turkey from us and comes back the day after Thanksgiving with a bag of bones and says she didn't like it, we'll give her her money back . . . or give her another turkey."

The moment he said that, the turkey reacted with a big "gobble" and ran off-camera. The commercial closed on the company logo with the announcer saying, "That's the way we do business at Tom Thumb . . . we stand behind everything we sell, and that's a promise" (see Exhibit 17-14).

The company merchandised the campaign by printing the slogan "We stand behind everything we sell . . . and that's a promise" on grocery sacks, on red lapel buttons for employees, and on outdoor billboards. The audio portions of the commercials were aired as radio spots. Most important, employee-orientation meetings were held to explain the concepts to the company's personnel and to make absolutely sure that any customers returning merchandise received a friendly, cordial smile from the employee handling the transaction.

The reaction to the campaign was astounding. First, it became the topic of local conversation. Then people began to wonder how many turkeys might be returned for the money. Local TV newspeople began to talk about the campaign and showed the commercial in their newscasts. Finally, the top disc jockey in Dallas sponsored a contest inviting listeners to guess how many turkeys would be returned to Tom Thumb. The day after Thanksgiving, the local TV film crews waited at the stores to count and interview people carrying in bags of bones.

One customer said she returned a turkey and got her money back with no questions asked. Another said she was given her money immediately but that she then gave the money back. She had just wanted to test them to see whether they were telling the truth.

The final score was 30,000 turkeys sold and only 18 returned—a fantastic marketing, advertising, and publicity success. Since then, the story has been reported in numerous grocery and advertising trade journals, and Tom Thumb Page successfully continued the "We stand behind everything we sell" advertising campaign theme.

This "talking turkey" example shows that creativity in developing an ad campaign is just as important at the local level as it is on the national level. Local advertisers often fail to realize that their print and broadcast messages compete for attention with national messages in the same media. And with the budgetary constraints of local businesses, creativity becomes even more important in grabbing the consumer's attention. The final section of this chapter addresses elements that go into creating local ads, and the kinds of creative assistance available to local advertisers.

Creating the Message

It was 1951 when Cal Worthington first started appearing on Los Angeles television stations to pitch his car dealership. Sponsoring third-rate movies on late-night and Saturday afternoon TV, Worthington appeared in a western outfit and cowboy hat and introduced a variety of hillbilly singers who were on hand all weekend to entertain the customers who were looking at cars.

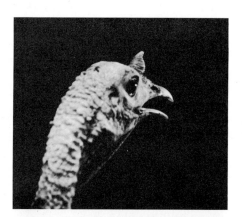

EXHIBIT 17-14

Tom Thumb stores talked turkey with customers by promising to stand behind everything they sell.

It's A Stretch. But You Can Afford It.

Renting a limousine for the evening isnt as expensive as you might think. Call Premier **Premier Limousine**
Limousine at 722-4467 for our rates and package information. And go out on the town without going into the red.

EXHIBIT 17-15

The advertiser's service inspired the clever pun used in this ad for Premier Limousine.

Thirty-eight years later, Worthington was still at it, but the zaniness had increased. He is noted for appearing in his TV ads with any of a variety of domesticated wild animals (all introduced as "my dog Spot") and crooning a tune promising to "stand upon my head" to make a deal on a new or used car.

Worthington has achieved far more than just sales success. He has been ribbed by talk show host Johnny Carson, and people stop him in airports to get his autograph. Thus, Worthington's fame has spread well beyond the local market he serves. The same thing has happened to local advertisers in St. Louis, New York, Des Moines, and around the country. Some of these low-budget, do-it-yourself advertisers have been so successful they have engendered a near-cult following of viewers and imitators.

On the other hand, others who have tried the same approach of producing an assortment of low-budget, in-house commercials for viewing on late-night TV have failed miserably and eventually quit trying to use such commercials.

In print advertising, many local advertisers have achieved remarkable success using what some professional advertising agency artists might refer to as a "schlock" approach. Heavy bold type, items crowded into advertising space, loud headlines, and unsophisticated graphic design contribute to the "schlock" look.

So long as the creative message is honest, consistent, and effective, many people say that's all that matters. Invariably, the question comes down to whether the objectives of the company are being met. To direct and control the creative aspects of advertisements and commercials, local advertisers should develop a checklist of creative do's and don'ts for their particular businesses and follow it. This will at least ensure consistency. (See the Checklist for Creating Local Advertising on p. 630.)

Coming up with ideas for local ad campaigns can be extremely difficult. When the editors of *Ad/Pro* magazine asked various sales promotion and advertising executives, "Where do your ideas come from?" the answers were wide ranging. Some looked to the merchandise for ideas; others looked to the customer. Magazines, scrapbooks, photography exhibits, and recent movies were also mentioned as idea sources.[16] Exhibit 17-15 shows an ad idea that was inspired by an important aspect of the advertiser's service.

Checklist for Creating Local Advertising

☐ *Make your ads easily recognizable.* Studies have shown that advertisements that are distinctive in their use of art, layout techniques, and typefaces usually enjoy a higher readership than run-of-the-mill advertising. Try to make your ads distinctively different in appearance from the advertising of your competitors—and then keep your ads' appearance consistent. This way, readers will recognize your ads even before they read them.

☐ *Use a simple layout.* Ads should not be crossword puzzles. The layout should carry the reader's eye through the message easily and in proper sequence from headline to illustration to explanatory copy to price to your store's name. Avoid the use of too many different typefaces, overly decorative borders, and reverses (black on white).

☐ *Use a dominant element—a large picture or headline—to ensure quick visibility.* Photographs and realistic drawings have about equal attention-getting value, but photographs of real people and action pictures win more readership. Photographs of local people or places also have high attention value. Color increases the number of readers.

☐ *Use a prominent benefit headline.* The first question a reader asks of an ad is: "What's in it for me?" Select the main benefit that your merchandise offers and feature it in a compelling headline. Amplify this message in subheads. Avoid generalized quality claims. Your headline will be easier to read if it is black on white and is not surprinted on part of the illustration.

☐ *Let your white space work for you.* Don't overcrowd your ad. White space is an important layout element in newspaper advertising because the average page is so heavy with small type. White space focuses the reader's attention on your ad and will make your headline and illustration stand out. When a "crowded" ad is necessary, such as for a sale, departmentalize your items so that the reader can find his or her way through them easily.

☐ *Make your copy complete.* Know all there is to know about the merchandise you sell and select the benefits most appealing to your customers. These benefits might have to do with fashion, design, performance, or the construction of your merchandise. Sizes and colors available are important, pertinent information.

☐ *State price or range of prices.* Dollar figures have good attention value. Don't be afraid to quote your price, even if it's high. Readers often will overestimate omitted prices. If the advertised price is high, explain why the item represents a good value—perhaps because of superior materials or workmanship or extra luxury features. Point out the

actual saving to the reader and spell out your credit and layaway plans.

☐ *Specify branded merchandise.* If the item is a known brand, say so in your advertising. Manufacturers spend large sums to sell their goods, and you can capitalize on their advertising while enhancing the reputation of your store by featuring branded items.

☐ *Include related items.* Make two sales instead of one by offering related items along with a featured one. For instance, when a dishwasher is advertised, also show a garbage disposal.

☐ *Urge your readers to buy now.* Ask for the sale. You can stimulate prompt action by using such phrases as "limited supply" or "this week only." If mail-order coupons are included in your ads, provide spaces large enough for customers to fill them in easily.

☐ *Don't forget your store name and address.* Check every ad to be certain you have included your store name, correct address, telephone number, and store hours. Even if yours is a long-established store, this is important. Don't overemphasize your signature, but make it plain. In a large ad, mention the store name several times in the copy.

☐ *Don't be too clever.* Many people distrust cleverness in advertising, just as they distrust salespeople who are too glib. Headlines and copy generally are far more effective when they are straightforward than when they are tricky. Clever or tricky headlines and copy often are misunderstood.

☐ *Don't use unusual or difficult words.* Many of your customers may not understand words familiar to you. Words like *couturier, gourmet, coiffure,* as well as trade and technical terms, may be confusing and misunderstood. Everyone understands simple language. Nobody resents it. Use it.

☐ *Don't generalize.* Be specific at all times. Shoppers want all the facts before they buy. Facts sell more.

☐ *Don't make excessive claims.* The surest way to lose customers is to make claims in your advertising that you can't back up in your store. Go easy with superlatives and unbelievable values. Remember: If you claim your prices are unbelievable your readers are likely to agree.

☐ *Plan ad size carefully.* Ad attention increases with the size of the ad.

☐ *Consider your target customers.* People note more ads directed at their own sex.

☐ *Use tie-ins with local or special news events.* These have proven effective in attracting readers.

This Kasle Recycling ad shows how a small local company can use creativity to achieve greater impact in advertising.

An important goal of local advertisers is to achieve a consistent, distinctive look that makes the ads both appealing and immediately identifiable. Bullock's department store in Los Angeles provides a good example. Since 1985, readers of the *Los Angeles Times* have been accustomed to seeing a Bullock's ad on the back page of every Sunday edition. The ad is always in the same place on the same day, and the layout is always the same: a dramatic four-color photograph (usually a fashion shot), a script letter *B* at the top, and the Bullock's logo at the bottom. In speaking of the award-winning newspaper campaign, Judy Farris, vice president for sales and promotion, noted, "The ad's position is important. It is a consistent statement. Repetition in advertising is important. You can establish an image over time. It has a cumulative effect."[17]

Of course, not all local businesses are as large as Bullock's with a separate advertising department that can devise such a major campaign. Fortunately, smaller businesses with smaller budgets also have a number of creative options to choose from. Exhibit 17-16 illustrates that even a local recycling company can be creative.

Seeking Creative Assistance

Local businesses have a number of sources they can turn to for creative help, including advertising agencies, the local media, free-lancers and consultants, creative boutiques, syndicated art services, and wholesalers, manufacturers, and trade associations.

Advertising Agencies

Because they are not usually equipped to do their own advertising work, local advertisers increasingly turn to agencies for help. One misconception is that all agencies are large and handle only sizable accounts. Many communities have small agencies that assist local advertisers. Local advertisers find they need help in locating markets, determining media mixes, developing better ads, and following up their advertising with effective evaluation. The quality

THERE IS A SPELLING MISTAKE IN THIS ADVERTISEMENT. THE FIRST PERSON TO SPOT IT WILL RECIEVE $500.

No, it's not in this line.

Or, you'll have guessed, in this line, either.

You're going to have to read this entire page, with the eyes of a school examiner, to spot it.

Which, when you think, makes it rather a good advertisement, doesn't it? Since ads, like the editorial they sidle up to, are written to be read.

How many of the other ads in this week's 'Media' are going to get this amount of attention?

One, maybe? Two?

It's more than likely that you haven't read *any* of them. Be honest, now:

You've given them the same treatment you give those suspiciously friendly encyclopaedia salesmen, who knock on your door and ask for five minutes of your time.

No, thank you: Slam the door. (Or in this case, turn the page.)

No sale. And we don't blame you. You saw the sell coming. Why waste your time?

The majority of ads are like that, too. Predictable, dull, and not very well presented.

They resolutely ignore the fact that the average consumer sees one thousand, six hundred advertising messages every day, and would be perfectly content not to see any at all.

You see, with the possible exception of seven year old brats with a passion for Teenage Mutant Ninja Turtles, PEOPLE DON'T LIKE ADS. There, we've said it. In a publication dedicated to the creed that advertising is a profession comparable only in its saintliness and altruism with being one of Mother Teresa's little helpers, we've spilt the beans:

We are not universally popular: If spacemen came down and took every person connected with advertising away for dissection, it would be a long time before we were missed. And even then, it would be because people discovered that their newspapers had become more interesting, and their TV programmes more enjoyable, for our absence.

(See? Heresy spoken out loud. And still we write. No thunderbolts from on high. God doesn't like ads, either.)

And yet...

And yet, in the face of reams of irrefutable evidence to the contrary, the majority of advertising agencies (and let's spread the blame a bit, their clients, too), persist in the belief that this just ain't so.

They sincerely believe that buying a space also guarantees readership of whatever they fill it with.

Sadder still, the higher the cost of the space, the more tense and creatively constipated they become, and the more safe and generic is their message: It's a new rule; the bigger the budget, the blander the ads.

Even the relatively enlightened feel that if they find, and mention, some semblance of a benefit in that space, they've *really* done a good job.

That by some miracle, the consumer is going to home in on their ad, shrieking "Just what I've always wanted!"

Sure. If your benefit is "Free Beer".

OK; *definitely*, if your benefit is "Free Beer". But if it's not, you're in big trouble.

You're going to be thrown in there with washing powders that get clothes whiter, toothpastes that taste nicer, tires that grip better ...

In other words, you're going to be ignored.

Don't misunderstand us, please. If your product has a substantial benefit over its competitors, you'd be mad not to tell everyone. The point is, it'd be mad to think that's *all* you had to do.

The public, as we've said, has become immune to everyday advertising.

For an ad to succeed these days, it has to work on many levels. It has to be relevant to the reader: It has to speak to him in language he can relate to: If there *is* a benefit to crow about, it has to be a benefit that's important to the *consumer*, not just to the manufacturer: To revert to the door-to-door salesman analogy, it has to look good ...the sort of person you'd invite into your home; the sort of advertisement you'd welcome into your mind...

But most of all, it has to be 'different'.

It has to jump from the page, or leap off the screen, screaming "Read me! Watch me!"

And it has to do so with a degree of seduction in its voice, rather than the foot-in-the-door brazen insistence, that leads only to the zap, the flip, and the broken toe.

Now. Doubtless there are sceptics out there who may say that this particular advertisement meets none of the criteria that it has been at such pains to expound.

That it is visually dull, dull, dull.

That it's criminally overwritten: That it's also a stupid concept, and that the one and only reason that they're reading it is to find the spelling mistake and qualify for $500 in the currency of their choice.

They may, of course, be right. (Found it yet, by the way? Keep going; concentrate.)

But at the Ball Partnership we'll do anything to get people to read ads.

Ours. Or yours.

This advertisement has cost us $22,336 to run. As you can imagine we're more than happy to give away $500 to make sure that everybody reads it. If you've found the spelling mistake (and if you haven't by now, you've missed it), call The Ball Partnership in Hong Kong, Malaysia, Singapore, Taiwan or Thailand and ask to speak to the Managing Partner. Of course, you're almost certainly too late to get the five hundred bucks, but call anyway. We like to chat about ads.

of agencies varies tremendously, and only a competent agency can be a real aid to an advertiser. Exhibit 17-17 is an example of an effective ad that an agency developed to promote itself. Specifically, an agency can help a local advertiser in the following ways:

☐ Analyze the local advertiser's business, and the product or service being sold; evaluate the markets for the business, including channels of distribution.

☐ Evaluate the advertiser's competitive position in the marketplace.

☐ Determine the best advertising media and provide advice on the costs and effectiveness of each.

☐ Devise an advertising plan and, once approved, implement it by preparing and placing the ads.

☐ Simplify the advertiser's administrative work load by taking over media interviewing, analysis, checking, and bookkeeping.

The Best Way To Judge A Photographer's Work Is By His Self-Promotion Piece.

Obviously, I Need Some Work.

My name's Kerry Wetzel. I've assisted some of the best photographers in Portland and L.A. On shoots for Nike, Burgerville and PGE.

Don't get me wrong. Working with Pete Stone, Steve Bonini and C.B. Harding taught me a lot about lighting, composition and big ideas.

Even if they did get to walk off with all the awards. While I got stuck with all the heavy lifting.

So why should you give me a shot instead of one of those other guys? For starters, I'm fast. I'm easy to work with. And I'll give you my firstborn child for $700 a day.

If you have a job sitting around that needs a photograph instead of a big name photographer, call 233-3947 and take a look at my portfolio. Plus:

And I promise you'll never have to look at another self-promotion piece like this one again.

Kerry Wetzel. Photographer.

EXHIBIT 17-18

Free-lance advertising suppliers often use bold and innovative ads for their own services to attract local clients.

☐ Assist in other aspects of the advertising and promotion effort by helping with sales contests, publicity, grand openings, and other activities.

Advertising agencies tend to be used less extensively by local advertisers than by national advertisers. A major reason is that most media, including newspapers, have two sets of advertising rates—one for national advertisers and another for retail or local advertisers. The local rate is lower and is not commissionable. Because the vast majority of local advertising is placed directly by the local advertiser rather than through an advertising agency, the advantage is a lower cost to the retailer for advertising media. Frequency and quantity discounts also give additional savings to the local advertiser.

Many advertisers simply don't spend enough money on advertising to warrant the hiring of an advertising agency. And many advertising agencies do not accept local advertisers as clients because of low budgets.

For a complete discussion of advertising agencies, review Chapter 3.

Local Media

The advertising media, in addition to selling space or time, offer a multitude of advertising services to local advertisers. These services range from planning advertising campaigns to actually preparing the advertisement.

Free-Lancers and Consultants

Because some advertising people like to be their own bosses, they act as free agents who often work out of their homes preparing copy, art and layout, photography, or other services. Exhibit 17-18 is an example of a clever ad for a free-lancer's own services. Free-lancers often specialize not only in the type of service they perform but also in the type of advertisers they serve, such as car dealerships, clothing stores, or travel agencies.

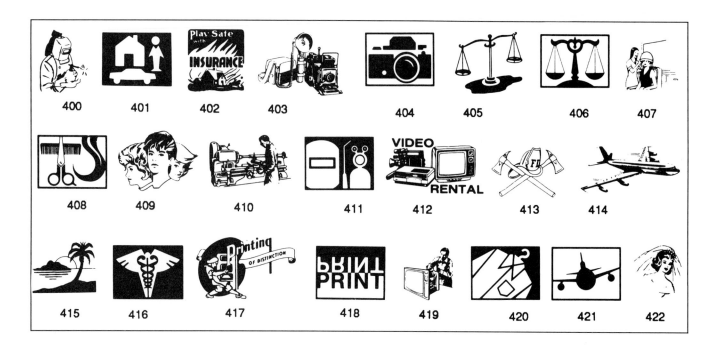

EXHIBIT 17-19

EXHIBIT 17-19

Using clip art is a convenient and relatively inexpensive way to illustrate advertisements.

Creative Boutiques

A boutique performs only the creative work. Employees of such shops specialize as copywriters, graphic designers, and illustrators. They charge a negotiated fee or a percentage of the media expenditure. Local advertisers who want the best creative work but are not interested in any other services provided by a full-service agency frequently turn to this source for help.

Syndicated Art Services

Syndicated art services can be useful to local advertisers by offering them a large book of artwork, called **clip art,** ready to be clipped and used in an advertisement. Clip art is available for various types of businesses and is often tied in to seasons, holidays, and other promotional angles. Clip art is available by direct subscription or through the advertising department of a local newspaper. Exhibit 17-19 shows examples from a clip art book.

Wholesalers, Manufacturers, and Trade Associations

As a service to their distributors and dealers, wholesalers and manufacturers as well as some trade associations often provide ready-made advertising.

The most common type of help local advertisers receive from manufacturers is called **vertical cooperative advertising.** The manufacturer normally provides the ad and a percentage of the cost of the advertising time or space. For some local businesses, the amount of co-op money provided by manufacturers is quite substantial, as shown in Exhibit 17-20. The local advertiser only has to have the local newspaper drop in the name and address of the business or have the radio and TV station add a tag line with the name, address, and telephone number of the firm. Co-op advertising has both advantages and disadvantages—see Ad Lab 17-B, p. 636.

EXHIBIT 17-20	The Importance of Co-Op Advertising Dollars

Store	Co-op dollars as a percentage of total ad budget
Appliance dealers	80%
Clothing stores	35
Department stores	50
Discount stores	20
Drugstores	70
Food stores	75
Furniture stores	30
Household goods	30
Jewelers	30
Shoe stores	50

EXHIBIT 17-21

Members of the Tri-State Cadillac Dealers Association pooled their advertising dollars to develop and air a television commercial beneficial to all Cadillac dealers in the area.

COMMUTER: Don't need a lift, Jack . . . there's my wife in our Lincoln Continental. Ahhh! You're

not Doris. And this isn't my car—it's a Taurus. I'm sorry!

VO: It's funny, how much *alike* Ford cars can look these days.

Horizontal cooperative advertising is a joint effort by real estate agents, insurance agents, pharmacies, car dealers, or travel agents, for example, to pay for an ad to create traffic for their *type* of business rather than for one particular business. Auto dealers in a central area of town often attempt to build traffic for all their businesses by pooling their advertising dollars and advertising the central area as the place to shop for cars. See Exhibit 17-21 for an example of this.

AD LAB 17-B
The Co-Op Battleground

On the surface, co-op advertising seems like a great arrangement for retailers. A manufacturer will supply advertising materials (saving the retailer production costs) and will also pay a percentage of the cost of running the ad. All the retailer needs to do is drop in the store's logo, arrange for the ad to run, and collect the co-op dollars from the manufacturer.

By using co-op advertising, the retailer not only is able to stretch an always too-small ad budget but is able to associate his or her business with a nationally advertised product. Furthermore, the retailer can be proud of professionally prepared ads and acquires greater leverage with the local media that carry the co-op ads.

There are, however, a few significant drawbacks to the co-op system. For one thing, a retailer has to sell a lot of merchandise to qualify for significant co-op funds. And some retailers who do qualify for co-op funds do not take advantage of them because they feel the supplied ads will not fit with their store's image. However, the major problem is that the retailer and manufacturer often have different advertising objectives and, thus, different ideas of how the ads should actually be executed.

Often, the manufacturer wants to exert total control, specifying when, where, and in what form the ad will run. As a national advertiser, the manufacturer expects co-op ads to tie in with national advertising promotions. It wants the right product to be advertised at the right time. Retailers, on the other hand, have their own ideas of which products they want to advertise at a particular time. They are more concerned with daily volume and with projecting an image of value and variety. Thus, an appliance store might prefer to advertise the most inexpensive models of a refrigerator line, even though the appliance manufacturer wants to emphasize the top-of-the-line models.

Manufacturers also worry that retailers will place a picture of their product in the midst of a cluttered, ugly ad, that their up-scale product will be featured next to inferior products, that the ad will run in inappropriate publications, and that it will not come out at optimal times. Retailers counter with the argument that they know the local market better than the manufacturer does and should be trusted to advertise appropriately. In short, manufacturers feel they do not have enough control over co-op ads, while retailers think the manufacturers have too much control.

A retailer who is contemplating using co-op funds should consider the following questions:

What advertising qualifies, in terms of products and special requirements?

What percentage is paid by each party?

When can advertisements be run?

What media can be used?

Are there special provisions regarding message content?

What documentation is required for reimbursement?

How does each party benefit?

Do cooperative advertisements obscure the image of the individual retailer?

Laboratory Application

Look through today's edition of a daily paper in your city. Try to determine which ads qualify as co-op. Do the ads fit the particular store's image? What effect do the ads have on the images of the national products being featured?

Shopping centers often do the same thing. Even a group of four psychotherapists in Verona, New Jersey, found cooperative advertising effective. They budgeted $15,000 for their joint campaign, which included newspaper and Yellow Pages ads, a mailing to potential clients, and free workshops. Aharon Ungar, a New York consultant who works extensively with psychologists, helped the group come up with a descriptive name, Comprehensive Psychological Services, and designed an ad that emphasized one specialty for each member.[18]

Summary

Local advertising is placed by businesses within a particular city or county and aimed at customers in the same geographic area. Local advertising is important because it is in the local arena that most sales are made or lost. While the basic principles used by national advertisers are applicable to local advertisers, local advertisers have special problems they must address. Local advertising appears as either product advertising or institutional advertising. Product advertising can be further subdivided into regular price-line advertising, sale advertising, and clearance advertising.

The objectives of local advertising differ from those of national advertising in emphasis and time frame. The needs of local advertisers tend to be more immediate. Therefore, advertising is usually intended to increase traffic, turn over inventory, or bring in new customers right away.

Successful local advertisers realize the importance of marketing and advertising planning. This includes analyzing the local market, analyzing the competition, conducting adequate research, determining objectives and strategy, establishing a realistic budget, and planning media strategy.

Local businesses are often highly seasonal. By plotting anticipated sales patterns throughout the year, business owners can allot a percentage of their total yearly advertising to each month. In general, the most advertising dollars should be spent just before the time when customers are most likely to respond.

There are many media normally available to local advertisers. These include newspapers, individual shopping guides, local magazines, local radio and television, and outdoor advertising. In addition, many local advertisers use direct mail, classified directories, sales promotion, and free publicity.

Perhaps the biggest problem for local advertisers is determining creative direction. Fortunately, there are a number of sources they can turn to for help. These sources include local advertising agencies, the local media, free-lancers and consultants, creative boutiques, syndicated art services, and wholesalers, manufacturers, and trade associations.

Questions for Review and Discussion

1. What are the objectives of the various types of local advertising?

2. What does a local advertiser expect to learn by analyzing the local market?

3. How can analyzing the competition give local advertisers the competitive edge?

4. What kind of primary research could you conduct to find out what customers think of your retail business?

5. What sources of secondary research data could inform local advertisers about future retail trends?

6. What are the most important factors influencing the advertising budget of a shopping-mall tenant?

7. What basic questions would a local merchant need to answer to formulate an annual advertising plan?

8. Which media usually receive the most emphasis by local advertisers? Explain why.

9. Which sales promotional tools would be uniquely useful for local advertisers? Why?

10. If you were a local advertiser, which sources would you turn to for creative assistance? Why?

PUBLIC RELATIONS, CORPORATE ADVERTISING, AND NONCOMMERCIAL ADVERTISING

Objective: To explain the role of public relations and corporate advertising in the marketing mix. PR activities and institutional advertising can improve the effectiveness of product ads by enhancing the image of the advertiser. A separate section on noncommercial advertising illustrates how advertising can be used to sell ideas and behaviors rather than products.

After studying this chapter, you will be able to:

☐ Distinguish between advertising and public relations.

☐ Discuss some key elements of crisis communications.

☐ Describe the difference between press agentry and publicity.

☐ Identify several public relations tools.

☐ Define advocacy advertising.

☐ Explain the role of corporate identity advertising.

☐ Discuss the purpose of public service announcements.

The name *Exxon Valdez* conjures up a variety of images: oil-soaked sea birds and otters, a four-mile-long slick oozing over the formerly pristine Alaskan waters, and workers struggling to clean the birds, mop up the oil, and restore the violated shoreline. But another image, one troubling in its own way, lingers in the minds of advertising and marketing professionals. That's the televised picture of Lawrence G. Rawl, chairman of Exxon Corp., tersely fielding reporters' questions about the disaster his company had caused.

When the tanker *Valdez* ran aground on the Bligh Reef of Prince William Sound on March 24, 1989, it precipitated the worst oil spill the United States had ever experienced. (Exhibit 18-1 is a reminder of the accident's impact.) For Exxon, it also signaled an unprecedented public relations challenge, one the petroleum giant fumbled on a scale the size of the spill. The company broke every rule of crisis communications in its tardy, defensive media response.

The company was unprepared for a crisis of this magnitude, or perhaps for any crisis, and that became clear as the disaster unfolded. Exxon made a major public relations error by disseminating false information about the disaster, perhaps unintentionally. For example, while the tanker was still leaking, an Exxon spokesperson estimated minimal environmental damage. Even after tens of thousands of dead animals had been counted and the public had been inundated with televised images of the damage, Exxon stuck to its count of 300 dead birds and 70 dead otters.

Exxon also erred in failing to produce Chairman Rawl immediately for media interrogation. When Rawl did comment, he and his company came across badly as he tried to shift the blame for cleanup delays to Alaska officials and the U.S. Coast Guard. Another mistake was to set up media headquarters in Valdez, Alaska, the site of the accident, rather than in a metropolitan area such as New York, where it would have been easier to handle the deluge of press inquiries.

Thanks to the multilevel PR fumble, Exxon rapidly lost credibility with the public. A month after the spill, an NBC News/Wall Street Journal poll showed that 77 percent of those surveyed thought the company "could have done

EXHIBIT 18-1

When the *Valdez* dumped 11 million gallons of crude oil off the coast of Alaska, Exxon representatives mishandled public relations, making it extremely difficult to salvage the company's image.

more" to clean up the spill. In addition, 41 percent said they would seriously consider boycotting Exxon. In a separate poll, conducted two months after the spill, 11 percent of adult respondents said they refused to buy Exxon gasoline.[1]

THE ROLE OF PUBLIC RELATIONS

Public relations (PR) is a term that is widely misunderstood and misused to describe anything from selling to hosting, when in fact it is a very specific communications process. Every company, organization, association, and government body deals with groups of people affected by what that organization does or says. They might be employees, customers, stockholders, competitors, suppliers, or just the general population of consumers. Each of these groups may be referred to as one of the organization's publics. The process of public relations manages the organization's relationships with these publics.

As soon as word of the *Valdez* spill got out, the PR staff at Exxon assumed responsibility for handling the barrage of phone calls from the press and the public and for managing all company communications with the media. Simultaneously, other company departments had to deal with numerous local, state, and federal government agencies and with the community at large—not just in Valdez, Alaska, but anywhere in the world where someone was touched by the disaster. In addition, myriad other publics suddenly popped into the spotlight demanding special attention and care: Alaskan fishermen, both houses of Congress, local politicians, the financial community, stockholders, employees, the local press, national networks, Exxon dealers, and environmental groups, for starters.

Companies and organizations know they must consider the public impact of their actions and decisions because of the powerful effect of public opinion. This is especially true in times of crisis, emergency, or disaster. But it is just as true for major policy decisions concerning changes in business management, pricing policies, labor negotiations, introduction of new products, or changes in distribution methods. Each of these decisions affects different groups in different ways. Conversely, effective administrators can use the power of these groups' opinions to bring about positive changes.

In short, the purpose of everything labeled *public relations* is to influence public opinion toward building goodwill and a positive reputation for the organization. In one instance, the PR effort might be to rally public support; in another, to obtain public understanding or neutrality; or in still another, simply to respond to inquiries. Well-executed public relations is a long-term activity that molds good relationships between an organization and its publics.

Put yourself in the position of Exxon's top public relations manager at the time of the *Valdez* accident. What do you suppose was the major thrust of the PR staff's efforts in the days immediately following the discovery of the oil spill? What might they have been called on to do?

We will discuss these and other questions in this chapter. But first it is important to understand the relationship between public relations and advertising—they are so closely related but so often misunderstood.

Advertising versus Public Relations

Advertising is generally described as openly sponsored and paid for media communications between sellers and buyers. Certainly, like public relations, the purpose of advertising is to affect public opinion. However, this is normally accomplished through the open attempt to sell the company's products or services. Although corporate advertising, discussed later in this chapter, is used for image enhancement and other nonselling purposes, it is still advertising, and as such it is bought and paid for.

Public relations activities, like product advertising, may involve media communications, but these communications are not normally openly sponsored or paid for. Usually they take the form of news articles, editorial interviews, or feature stories. One means of relaying a public relations message, though, is through corporate advertising.

As public relations expert Amelia Lobsenz has pointed out, public relations is less precise than advertising. Advertising can be strictly controlled so that its reach and impact can be charted in advance, but public relations communications are not so easily quantifiable: "PR's results depend more on the experience, ingenuity, and tenacity of the people engaged in its day-to-day execution."[2] Although PR communications may be less controlled than advertising, such communications often have greater credibility.

Advertising versus Public Relations Practitioners

Another interesting difference between public relations and advertising is the orientation or perspective of professional practitioners in the fields. Advertising professionals tend to be sales- or marketing-oriented (the perspective of this text, for example). They view marketing as the umbrella process companies use to determine what products the market needs and what means will be required to distribute and sell the products to the market. To advertising professionals, advertising and public relations are primarily marketing tools used to promote sales of the company's products and services. As a rule, therefore, they tend to use advertising and public relations as "good news" vehicles for the company and its products.

Public relations professionals, on the other hand, consider public relations as the umbrella process companies should use to manage their continuing relationships with various publics. From the PR perspective, marketing and advertising are simply public relations tools that should be used in the company's sales relationship with customers and prospects.

Very few companies are structured with a public relations orientation, but the "news" perspective and open information orientation of the professional public relations person are important and interesting to understand. In times of crisis or emergency, PR is normally considered the better perspective to adopt.

To achieve the greatest effectiveness, advertising and public relations efforts should be closely coordinated. In fact, many advertising agencies have public relations departments or perform public relations services. Many company advertising departments also supervise company PR activities.

PUBLIC RELATIONS ACTIVITIES AND TOOLS

As the *Exxon Valdez* episode illustrates, one of the most important public relations tasks for any corporation is **crisis communications.** Even companies that have earned the public's trust and goodwill over years or decades can lose their status as responsible corporate citizens if they mismanage their response to an accident or other crisis.

Crisis Communications

Johnson & Johnson's response to the Tylenol poisonings of 1982 provides an example of exemplary crisis communications. The company manufactures and markets the pain reliever Tylenol, several bottles of which were laced with cyanide by a madman in October 1982. The tampering, which took place at the retail level, led to several deaths.[3] Although J&J had no ongoing public relations program for Tylenol and no emergency public information plan at the time of the tampering, it quickly prepared a course of action. Management strategists at Johnson & Johnson and McNeil Products Company (the J&J subsidiary that markets Tylenol) worked together to formulate three stages of action:

1. Identify the problem and take immediate corrective action. This meant getting information from the press, police, FDA, and FBI; identifying the geographic dimensions of the problem; correcting rumors; and immediately withdrawing all affected products from the marketplace.

2. Cooperate with the authorities in the investigation to find the killer. Rather than simply reacting to situations as they developed, Johnson & Johnson got actively involved by helping the FBI and other law enforcement agencies in their efforts to generate leads and investigate security at the McNeil plants. The firm offered a $100,000 reward for information leading to the arrest and conviction of the murderer.

3. Rebuild the Tylenol name and capsule line, including the Regular Strength capsules, which had been recalled along with the Extra-Strength brand. (The specific product that had been tampered with was Tylenol Extra-Strength.)

The first job was to ensure that the tampering had not occurred at McNeil. The company's two capsule production lines were shut down and dog teams were brought in to search for evidence of cyanide. Everyone believed the problem was probably confined to the retail end of the chain, but they needed to be sure.

Simultaneously, the insatiable appetite of the news media for background information and updates on the crisis, plus a flood of inquiries from anxious consumers, put J&J's PR people under enormous pressure. Faced with a crisis of such magnitude, a firm has little choice but to handle inquiries openly. All communications between the media and the company had to be channeled through the corporate communications department, however. In addition, all customer, trade, and government communications had to be coordinated within the company. Only in this way could open, clear, consistent, *legal,* and credible communications be maintained. And only in this way could the potentially disastrous effects of rumormongering, political backbiting, and corporate defensiveness be minimized.

In the first 48 hours after the Cook County, Illinois, coroner confirmed in a press conference that cyanide-laced Tylenol had killed several people, phone calls to Johnson & Johnson and McNeil were incessant. The moment one caller hung up, the telephone rang again. In the basement at McNeil, a bank of phones usually used for sales was pressed into service and staffed by employees. But employees had to know what to say, what not to say, and where unanswerable questions should be referred. That, of course, depended on who was calling and what they were asking.

At the same time, management and employees had to be notified, various authorities had to be contacted, and many others who were involved had to be reached. All this had to be planned, coordinated, and supervised efficiently. And that was suddenly the job of the J&J and McNeil public relations managers and staff.

As infrequent as disasters might be, dealing with them is the most important activity of PR professionals and public information officers in highly sensitive organizations such as airlines, law enforcement agencies, military organizations, chemical and oil companies, and public utilities. These industries are characterized by a high demand for news and information. And their press relations activities are often performed in a variety of pressure-cooker situations.

Since the Tylenol incident, many other companies in normally nonsensitive areas have directed their public relations departments to develop crisis-management plans. As noted by PR expert Art Stevens, "How a corporation handles news during crises determines in large measure the impact that news has on the public. When corporations have no plans for coping with crisis news, the resulting press coverage can be disastrous."[4] The crisis may range from a small noninjury fire in an office to a run on a bank to criminal behavior on the part of an employee. The main advice all experts on crisis management give is to follow J&J's example by being open and candid. Says Stevens, "Withholding information or evading questions is almost certain to backfire."[5] Exhibit 18-2 (p. 644) is a classic example of an advertiser coming clean. The crisis in this case occurred during the Cold War when Toshiba breached U.S. security by selling submarine technology to the Soviet Union.

Public Relations Activities

Fortunately, most public relations professionals do not spend most of their time handling crisis communications. Rather, they are employed to *generate* news from basically low-news-demand organizations—and their activities reflect that fact. These activities range from publicity and press agentry to special-events management and speech writing.

One of the most important functions of a PR practitioner is to plan and execute the overall public relations program. To do so, the practitioner has to analyze the relationships between the organization and its publics; evaluate public attitudes and opinions toward the organization; assess the organization's policies and actions as they relate to the organization's publics; and finally, plan and execute the various PR activities.

Publicity and Press Agentry

Publicity and public relations are often thought of as the same thing, when in fact publicity is a subset of public relations. Publicity refers to the generation of news about a person, product, or service that appears in broadcast or print media.[6]

Publicity is usually thought of as being "free" because the media do not bill anyone for the publicity they run, and the media cannot normally be "bought" to run the publicity. The organization seeking the publicity may go to considerable expense in an effort to get it, but there's no bill for the space or time received and no guarantee, in fact, of receiving any publicity at all. Typically, the return on investment in publicity positions it favorably vis-à-vis other communications strategies. In contrast to running a large advertising campaign, which might require an investment of 5 to 20 percent of sales, a major publicity program would typically only require an investment of 1 to 2 percent of gross sales.[7]

TOSHIBA CORPORATION EXTENDS ITS DEEPEST REGRETS TO THE AMERICAN PEOPLE.

Toshiba Corporation shares the shock and anger of the American people, the Administration and Congress at the recent conduct of one of our 50 major subsidiaries, Toshiba Machine Company. We are equally concerned about the serious impact of TMC's diversion on the security of the United States, Japan, and other countries of the Free World.

Toshiba Corporation had no knowledge of this unauthorized action by TMC. And the United States and Japanese Governments have not claimed that Toshiba Corporation itself had any knowledge or involvement.

Nevertheless, Toshiba Corporation, as a majority shareholder of TMC, profoundly apologizes for these past actions by a subsidiary of Toshiba.
- As a measure of *personal* recognition of the grievous nature of TMC's action, both the Chairman and the President of Toshiba Corporation have resigned. *For the Japanese business world, this is the highest form of apology.*
- In TMC, the subsidiary where the diversion occurred, wrongdoers are now being prosecuted.

For the future, Toshiba Corporation takes full responsibility to insure that never again will such activity take place within the Toshiba Group of companies.
- We are working with the Governments of the United States and Japan in this endeavor.

The relationship of Toshiba Corporation, its subsidiaries and their American employees with the American people, one marked by mutual trust and cooperation, has developed over many years of doing business together. We pledge to do whatever it takes to repair, preserve, and enhance this relationship.

Toshiba Corporation already has begun to take corrective measures throughout its hundreds of subsidiaries and affiliate companies:
- We immediately directed all our companies to institute stringent measures guarding more securely against this kind of misconduct.
- We obtained the resignation of the President of TMC and the three other Board members who had corporate responsibility for the conduct of those TMC employees actually involved.

- We also obtained TMC's commitment to stop exports to the Soviet Bloc countries for an unlimited time.
- We have authorized an extensive investigation to find all the facts concerning TMC's actions and to design safeguards to prevent repetition of such conduct. This investigation is being directed by American counsel, assisted by a major independent accounting firm.
- We will discharge all officers and employees found to have knowingly participated in this wrongful export sale.
- We have appointed the former senior auditing official of Toshiba Corporation to TMC's Board with direct responsibility for Toshiba's policy of full observance of the law and of Japan's security arrangements with its allies.
- We are going to develop a rigid compliance program in cooperation with the Governments of Japan and the United States.
- We intend to establish Toshiba's new compliance program as a model for all future export controls throughout Japanese industry.

In its 22 years of doing business with the United States, Toshiba Corporation has been a leader in introducing American products to the Japanese market, and also has significantly shifted the manufacture of Toshiba products to the United States. At a time when many of the U.S.-based corporations competing with Toshiba are moving production facilities and jobs abroad, Toshiba's American companies are steadily expanding the extent to which their products are manufactured in the United States. Today, Toshiba employs thousands of Americans in 21 states from New York to Texas to California. It is these Americans who have played a large and crucial part in earning Toshiba its reputation for producing top quality products, reliable service, and ongoing innovation that millions of American consumers and industrial customers know they can trust.

These bonds of cooperation are signs of our commitment to America. We earnestly wish to continue our efforts to develop our relationship with America.

We ask our American friends to work with us and help us to do so.

Joichi Aoi

Joichi Aoi
President/CEO
Toshiba Corporation

EXHIBIT 18–2

This apology by the president of Toshiba Corporation ran in 60 American publications following the revelation that one of Toshiba's subsidiaries had sold submarine technology to the Soviets. This public apology was made on the assumption that the American people hate coverups and are more forgiving if parties admit guilt and offer reparation.

Publicity must be newsworthy to be effective. Opportunities for publicity include the introduction of a new product, awards, company sales and earnings, mergers, retirements, parades, and speeches by company executives. Sometimes publicity will accrue without the advertiser intending it. Exxon, for example, received a lot of publicity when the *Valdez* accident occurred. As that example suggests, publicity may be good or bad for the company. And because publicity can originate from any source, it can sometimes be difficult—or impossible—to control.

Press agentry refers to the activity of planning and staging events to attract attention and generate publicity that will be of interest to the media. Although celebrities, circuses, sports events, politicians, motion pictures, and rock stars come to mind as requiring press agentry, many PR people also use it to bring attention to new products or services or to put their company or organization in a favorable light. For example, if a company makes a major donation to a charitable cause or alters its product formulation to be environment-friendly, press agentry can be used to bring the donation or the new product formula to the attention of the public.

For print media, the publicity person deals with editors and feature writers. For broadcast media, he or she deals with a program director, assignment editor, or news editor. One of the most important functions of public relations is to develop and maintain ties with such editorial contacts.

Public Affairs and Lobbying

Frequently, companies and organizations need to deal with public officials, regulatory and legislative bodies, and various community groups. This is the task of **public affairs** people. Sometimes this work is handled by the public relations office; other times, by specialists in public affairs. Although public affairs and public relations have at times been viewed as separate disciplines, there is growing sentiment that they should be integrated. Says Robert Keith Gray, chairman of public relations powerhouse Hill and Knowlton USA, "We in public affairs and public relations too long have labored under our own Berlin Wall, our belief that public affairs and public relations are disciplines as separate as East and West. . . . To succeed with [today's] issues, we must put together the public affairs skills that include policy expertise on a wide range of issues—analysis, monitoring, and lobbying—and combine those skills and information with the nuts and bolts of public relations such as media relations, community outreach, and grassroots efforts."[8]

Lobbying, meanwhile, refers to informing and persuading government officials to promote or thwart administrative action or legislation in the interests of the client. Because every organization is affected by the government, lobbying has become big business at both the federal and state levels.

Community Involvement

The goal of community involvement is "to have the company officers, management, and employees contribute to the community's social and economic development."[9] Such contributions may take the form of providing leadership for civic and youth groups, participating in fund-raising drives for local charities, sponsoring medical programs, providing educational programs for schools, and sponsoring cultural or recreational activities. One role of the company public relations department is to help set up such programs and to publicize their existence to the community.

Promotion and Special-Events Management

In profit-making organizations, **promotion** means using advertising and public relations techniques to sell a product or service and to enhance the reputation of the organization. Promotion can be achieved through press parties, open houses, celebrations, sponsoring of contests, or a variety of other activities.

There are two kinds of public relations events: those designed to create publicity and those designed to improve public relations through personal contact. Often these two purposes overlap. For example, Macy's Thanksgiving Day parade in New York generates tremendous publicity as well as a great deal of community goodwill because of personal contact. Also, an event designed to improve public relations among members of an association—such as the annual convention of the American Bar Association—can generate vast amounts of publicity.

An increasingly popular event used as a public relations tool is the company-sponsored cultural or sports event. One such event is the America's Marathon that Beatrice sponsors, shown in Exhibit 18-3. Corporate sponsorship of events has grown rapidly in the past decade. In 1984, 1,200 companies spent a total of $340 million to sponsor events. By 1991, 1,800 companies spent a total of $2.94 billion on event sponsorship.[10]

Some corporations spend hundreds of millions of dollars per year solely on sports marketing. Such sums are necessary to cover the fees and other costs of sponsoring large-scale or international events. For example, 3M Company paid about $12 million to become an official sponsor of the 1988 Olympic Games.[11] The company was sufficiently impressed with the return on that investment to become one of several corporate sponsors of the 1992 Games. Firms with more modest event-marketing budgets have a variety of options, ranging from local golf tournaments and dance concerts to surfing contests.

EXHIBIT 18-3

Among companies that have used sports event sponsorship as a means of promotion is Beatrice, which sponsors the America's Marathon in Chicago.

Some companies associate their names with existing events. For example, Mercedes-Benz, Perrier, and Seiko have been among the sponsors of the New York Marathon; NutraSweet sponsored the Soviet Union's first professional skating competition; and Visa sponsored Paul McCartney's 1990 concert tour.[12]

Other companies devise their own events to sponsor: Compaq Computer Corporation sponsors its own tennis tournaments, Kentucky Fried Chicken sponsors gospel music concerts, McDonald's has its All-American High School Band and its All-American High School Basketball Game, and Fujitsu has sponsored its own annual jazz festival for more than 20 years.

Sponsorship of charity events is another tried-and-true public relations activity. A number of large corporations, including Chevrolet, AT&T, American Airlines, PepsiCo, and Eastman Kodak, enhanced their identities by cosponsoring the Live Aid concert in 1985. "Helping the less fortunate is good business," says one of the organizers of Live Aid.[13]

Publications

Public relations persons are often responsible for company publications; news releases and media kits; booklets, leaflets, pamphlets, brochures, manuals, and books; letters, inserts, and enclosures; annual reports; posters, bulletin boards, and exhibits; audiovisual materials; and speeches and position papers. We discuss these communication tools in more detail later in this chapter.

Research

Because the purpose of all public relations activities is to influence public opinion, the PR person must be concerned with measuring and analyzing changes in public attitude and sentiment. For example, Perrier used research to monitor its standing with the public after benzene, a carcinogen, was found in bottles of Perrier water in 1990. Perrier conducted several surveys through an independent research organization and found that 82 percent of its customers had heard about the benzene contamination. But the research results also indicated that 80 percent of the customers planned to buy the water when it became available again, after the product recall.[14]

A common form of public relations research is **opinion sampling.** Standard techniques for such research include interviewing consumers in shopping malls or by telephone. Or, the advertiser may set up communications channels for consumer feedback, such as toll-free phone lines. Other research techniques include focus groups, analysis of incoming mail, field reports, and panel studies.

Fund Raising and Membership Drives

A public relations person may be responsible for soliciting money for a nonprofit organization or for a cause the company deems worthwhile, such as the United Way or a political action committee (PAC).

Charitable organizations, labor unions, professional societies, trade associations, and other groups rely on membership fees or contributions as a primary means of support. The public relations specialist, often considered the chief communicator of an organization, must communicate to potential contributors or members the purposes and goals of the organization.

Public Speaking

Because public relations practitioners frequently represent their employers at special events, it's essential that they be able to speak well in public. They also prepare speeches for company officials to present at stockholder meetings, conferences or conventions, and other such functions. They arrange for speaking opportunities and develop answers for the most common questions a representative from the company might be asked. Similar preparations must be made for press conferences and interviews.

Public Relations Tools

The communication tools at the PR person's disposal vary widely—from news releases and photographs to audiovisual materials and even advertising.

News Releases and Media Kits

A **news release,** or **press release,** is one or more typewritten sheets of information (usually 8½ by 11 inches) issued to generate publicity or shed light on a subject of interest. Topics may include the announcement of a new product, promotion of an executive, an unusual contest, landing of a major contract, or establishment of a scholarship fund, to name a few. Exhibit 18-4 shows the standard press release format. For pointers in preparing releases, see the Checklist for Writing News Releases.

A **media kit,** or **press kit,** is used to gain publicity at staged events such as press conferences or open houses. Such a kit includes a basic fact sheet detailing the event, a program or schedule of the activities, and a list of the participants and their biographical data. In addition, the kit contains bro-

Checklist for Writing News Releases

For a news release to be effective, it must be read and accepted by a busy editor who may have only a moment or two to glance at it. Here are some guidelines for producing successful press releases.

☐ *Identify yourself.* Include not only the name and address of the company (preferably on a letterhead) but also the name and number of whom to contact for further information.

☐ *Provide a release date.* Even if the item is marked "for immediate release," it is helpful to the editor to know when the item was sent.

☐ *Use wide margins.* Copy should be double-spaced for print media and triple-spaced for broadcast media.

☐ *Keep it short.* One page is the preferred length. If the release needs to be longer, don't break in the middle of a paragraph.

☐ *Proof your copy.* Typos, grammatical errors, and other mistakes will detract from your message.

☐ *Update your mailing list.* Editors change, offices move. Make sure you have the most recent information on the media you are informing.

☐ *Don't call to see whether the editor has received your release.* Editors don't like to be pressured into using PR materials; calling won't help your case.

☐ *Don't ask for tear sheets.* If the item gets published, don't expect the editor to take time out to send you a copy.

☐ *Don't promise you'll advertise if the item is published.* You will only offend the editor, who usually has nothing to do with the advertising department of the publication.

☐ *Send a thank you.* If an article is run, send the editor a note saying you appreciated the write-up.

EXHIBIT 18-4

Note in this example of a news release that the style follows that of a regular news story, complete with headline. Note also that information is provided on whom to contact at Johnson Wax for additional information.

Glade
Litter
fresh

FOR IMMEDIATE RELEASE   CONTACT: Jamie Diamond
                                          -or-
                                          Julie O'Rourke
                                          Golin/Harris Communications
                                          312/836-7279

NEW BROCHURE IS THE CAT'S MEOW

Pet lovers can now get firsthand information on living compatibly with their pets in a free booklet from Glade® LitterFresh. "Coexisting With Your Two-Footed Friend," a brochure written from a cat's perspective, is full of tongue-in-cheek tips on "domesticating humans" and includes helpful hints for cat owners as well.

This delightful brochure gives "hints for humans" on topics such as preventing household "cat-astrophe," plants that may be poisonous to cats, and keeping the litter box smelling fresh. The "author" describes his first experience at the veterinarian, his favorite pastimes and the important bonds that are formed between pet and owner.

To obtain a free copy of "Coexisting With Your Two-Footed Friend," send a self-addressed, stamped business-size envelope to: Glade Litter Fresh, P.O. Box 11172, Chicago, IL 60610.

                                # # #

Johnson 1525 Howe Street • Racine, WI 53403
Wax

chures prepared for the event, appropriate photos, a news story for the broadcast media, and news and feature stories for use by the print media.

Photography

Photographs of events, products in use, new equipment, or newly promoted executives can lend credence or interest to an otherwise dull news story. Photos may even persuade an art-poor editor to accept an article for publication. Photos must be of good quality, however, and are most effective if they need little or no explanation. Typed captions describing the subject of the photo and accurately identifying the people in it should be taped to the back of each photo.

Feature Articles

Many publications, particularly trade publications, will run feature articles about companies, products, or services. Such articles may be written by

EXHIBIT 18-5

Rather than being dry summaries of financial data, many annual reports, such as this one from McDonnell Douglas, are elaborate, full-color booklets with photos, illustrations, and sophisticated designs.

someone on the public relations staff or at the publication, or by a third party (such as a free-lance business writer). Feature articles can be invaluable, because they give the company or product credibility.

Features may include case histories, illustrated how-to's (such as how to use the company's product), problem-solving scenarios (how the company's product was used by a customer to increase production, for example), and state-of-the-art updates. Other formats include roundups of what's happening in a specific industry and editorials (such as a speech or essay by a company executive on a current issue).[15]

Printed Materials

Printed materials are used extensively in public relations. They may take the form of brochures or pamphlets about the company, letters to customers, inserts or enclosures that accompany monthly statements, the **annual report** to stockholders, other reports, or house organs. Exhibit 18-5, an annual report from McDonnell Douglas, demonstrates the creative potential of such publications.

A **house organ** (or **house publication**) is a company publication. Internal house publications are for employees only. External house publications may go to company-connected persons (customers, stockholders, suppliers, and dealers) or to the public. They may take the form of a newsletter, a tabloid newspaper, or a magazine. The house organ shown in Exhibit 18-6 is a quarterly newsletter. The purpose of house organs is to promote goodwill, increase sales, or mold public opinion. A well-produced house organ can do

EXHIBIT 18-6

House organs circulated outside the company can be an important public relations tool, worth the extra expense for strong editorial content, glitzy design, and high production values.

a great deal to get employees or customers to feel they know the people who make up a company. However, writing, printing, and distributing a house organ can be expensive.

Posters, Exhibits, and Bulletin Boards

Posters used internally can stress safety, security, reduction of waste, and courtesy. Externally, they can impart production information or other news of interest to the consumer.

Exhibits can give a history of the organization, present new products, show how products are made, or tell about future plans of the organization. Exhibits are often prepared for local fairs, colleges and universities, and trade shows.

Bulletin boards can be used to announce new equipment, meetings, promotions, new products, construction plans, and recreation news.

Audiovisual Materials

Audiovisual materials can take many forms, including slides, films, filmstrips, and videocassettes used for training, sales, or public relations. Considered a form of corporate advertising, "nontheatrical" or "sponsored" films (developed for public relations reasons) are furnished without charge to movie theaters, organizations, and special groups, particularly schools and colleges. Classic examples of these films include *Why Man Creates,* produced for Kaiser Aluminum, and Mobil Oil Corporation's *A Fable,* starring the famous French mime Marcel Marceau.

Many public relations departments provide **video press releases**—news or feature stories prepared by a company and offered free to TV stations. The TV stations may use the whole video story or just segments of it. Video press releases are somewhat controversial, for critics see them as subtle commercials or even propaganda. The critics take particular issue with stations running the stories without disclosing that they came from a public relations firm and were not developed by the station's news staff.[16]

CORPORATE ADVERTISING

As mentioned earlier, corporate advertising is a basic tool of public relations. It includes public relations advertising, institutional advertising, corporate identity advertising, and recruitment advertising. Their use depends on the particular situation, the audience or public being addressed, and the message the firm needs to communicate. (For examples, see the Portfolio of Corporate Advertising on pages 654–57.)

Public Relations Advertising

Public relations advertising is often used when a company wishes to communicate directly with one of its important publics to express its feelings or enhance its point of view to that particular audience. The Claris ad in Exhibit 18-7, for example, targets customers, investors, and stock analysts. Public relations ads are typically used to improve the company's relations with labor, government, customers, or suppliers.

When companies sponsor art events, programs on public television, or charitable activities, they frequently place public relations ads in other media to promote the programs and their sponsorship. These ads are designed to enhance the company's general community citizenship and to create public goodwill. The ad in Exhibit 18-8 promotes an art exhibit and Southwestern Bell's sponsorship role.

Corporate/Institutional Advertising

In recent years, the term **corporate advertising** has come to denote that broad area of nonproduct advertising used specifically to enhance a company's image and increase lagging awareness. The traditional term for this is **institutional advertising.**

Institutional or corporate ad campaigns may serve a variety of purposes—to report the company's accomplishments, to position the company competitively in the market, to reflect a change in corporate personality, to shore up stock prices, to improve employee morale, or to avoid a communications problem with agents, dealers, suppliers, or customers.

(*continued on p. 658*)

EXHIBIT 18-7

This PR ad addresses the ex-president of software publisher Claris, but it speaks to publics concerned about the company's future without him: customers, investors, and stock analysts. Claris is a subsidiary of Apple Computer, which has used PR advertising many times to communicate with key publics.

So long, Coach.

Claris has just lost one of our hardest-working employees.

Bill Campbell is on his way to lead another bunch of impossible dreamers over at GO Corporation, those guys with the pen-based notebook computing system.

And the bunch he left behind would like to publicly tender him the biggest compliment we can conjure:

Bill, we'll miss your leadership, your vision, your wisdom, your friendship and your spirit.

But—thanks to all of the above—we're going to be fine without you.

In 1987, when Apple decided to get out of the software business, you volunteered to start a spin-off company.

You began with a handful of nearly-free Apple software products, a few rebels, a name, "Claris," and built us into the world's leading Mac software company.

We just finished our best quarter ever in sales, profits, market share and growth.

You taught us how to stand on our own.

You built us to last.

And even though you're no longer coaching our team, we're going to do our best to keep making you proud.

CLARIS

EXHIBIT 18-8

Many corporations provide funding for cultural events and activities, and it's good public relations to advertise such corporate sponsorship.

*"Still–in a way–nobody sees a flower–really–
it is so small–we haven't time–
and to see takes time, like to have a friend takes time."*
—*Georgia O'Keeffe*

Red Poppy, 1927   Oil on canvas 7" x 9", Private collection, Geneva   Photography by Malcolm Varon

GEORGIA O'KEEFFE 1887-1986

National Gallery of Art, Washington · November 1, 1987-February 21, 1988
The Art Institute of Chicago · March 12-June 26, 1988
Dallas Museum of Art · July 31-October 16, 1988
The Metropolitan Museum of Art, New York · November 19, 1988-February 5, 1989

Southwestern Bell Corporation

An exhibition organized by the National Gallery of Art and made possible by a grant from Southwestern Bell Foundation.

PORTFOLIO OF CORPORATE ADVERTISING

A. Corporate advertising often spotlights the company's history. This ad for Dreyfus stresses its historical involvement in mutual funds.

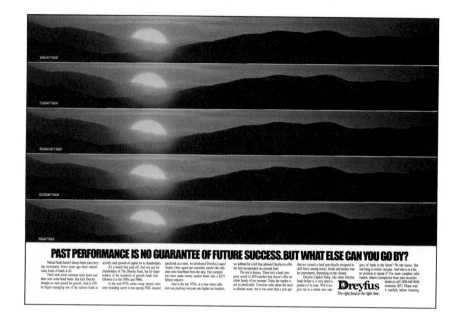

B. Alluring photographs by award-winning photographer Jay Maisel set this and other ads in a series for United Technologies one cut above the others.

C. Looking almost like a magazine editorial spread, this ad for 3M emphasizes a lesser-known aspect of the company—its health technology expertise.

D. Long, interesting copy and a zingy layout make this corporate ad for Denny's Restaurants inviting and different.

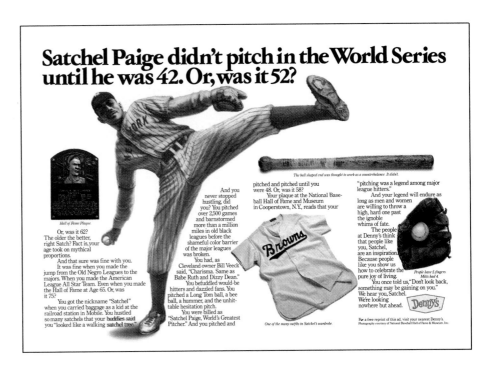

E. The high-tech look and sophistication of this ad contribute to the image Rockwell International wants to establish.

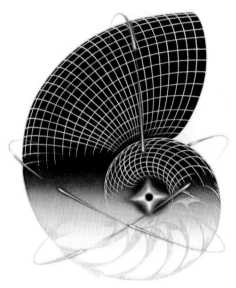

'ek·sə·ləns

Excellence
• *Distinguished by superiority; e.g., 123,000 committed, dedicated employees—highly skilled in complementary technologies.*
• *A standard, like the quality of products being developed in our five core business areas.*
• *A surpassing achievement, such as '85 sales exceeding $11 billion.*

$$F = FR_1 / \frac{d}{da} \left[\log \left(T - T_{pv} - T_{oe} \right) \right]$$

The Nautilus Configuration: It is nature's inspiration for excellence in science and engineering. It is also a symbol of the commitment of Rockwell employees.

The quest for excellence by our 25,000 engineers, scientists and supporting technical personnel shapes the work of Rockwell's 123,000 employees worldwide. And results in the elegant solutions to customer needs that make Rockwell a leader in five diverse areas of commercial and government business.

Excellence is also a major reason for the ongoing record of financial growth that brought us more than $11 billion in sales and record earnings in 1985.

To learn more about us, write: Rockwell International, Department 815B-3, 600 Grant Street, Pittsburgh, PA 15219.

Rockwell International

...where science gets down to business

Aerospace / Electronics / Automotive
General Industries / A-B Industrial Automation

F. The Japanese electronics firm Mitsubishi uses handsome ads such as this to tell Americans that it is a good corporate neighbor.

G. John Hancock's "Real life, real answers" campaign revolution-ized TV advertising for financial services and helped blur the line between product and corporate advertising.

BRO: Ah gee, I don't know. You remember . . . Maggie . . . I certainly remember. When he could pick up the both of us in one hand. One hand.

SIS: I know. I remember.

BRO: Oh man. Now . . . it's like it's our turn. You know what I mean?

SIS: I know. I know.

BRO: He can't drive at night any-more. Did you know that? Mom told me that.

SIS: I know. I know.

BRO: But that's really nothing. I mean 5 years or 7 years from now, what happens then? He won't ask us. Even if he needs our help he won't ask us. The thing is . . . we've got to do something. We're the ones . . . you know. Michael isn't even working.

Companies and even professional advertising people have historically questioned, or simply misunderstood, the effectiveness of corporate advertising. Retailers, in particular, have clung to the idea that institutional advertising may be pretty or nice but that it "doesn't make the cash register ring." However, a series of marketing research studies sponsored by *Time* magazine and conducted by the Yankelovich, Skelly & White research firm offered dramatic evidence to the contrary.

In the first of these studies, 700 middle- and upper-management executives were interviewed in the top 25 U.S. markets. The researchers evaluated five companies that were currently doing corporate advertising and five that were not. They found that the companies using corporate advertising registered significantly better awareness, familiarity, and overall impression than companies using only product advertising. In fact, the five corporate advertisers in the study drew higher ratings in every one of 16 characteristics measured, including being known for quality products, having competent management, and paying higher dividends.[17] Perhaps the most interesting aspect of the research was the fact that the five companies with no corporate advertising spent far more for total advertising than did the firms engaged in corporate advertising.

David Ogilvy, the founder and creative head of Ogilvy & Mather, has been an outspoken advocate of corporate advertising. However, he has been

ETHICAL DILEMMA IN ADVERTISING
When Is Advertising Not Really Advertising?

The **advertorial** is a strange creature. It's half advertising, half editorial, and totally controversial. Advertorials are the primary form of advocacy advertising, and their aim is to sway public opinion rather than to sell products. Although advertorials account for only 5 percent of all corporate advertising, they can sometimes move mountains.

Take the case of AT&T, for instance. In 1908, the company used advertorials to extol the virtues of private monopoly and lay the foundation for its telecommunications empire. Strategically, the AT&T campaign was the classic prototype for much advocacy advertising. It defined the issue, presented facts selectively, and argued for the conclusion that best served its interests.

Since AT&T's pioneering effort, a few corporations like Mobil Oil have developed reputations as outspoken companies by routinely using advertorials as an integral part of their corporate advertising effort. In general, though, most companies have avoided addressing controversial issues for fear of making unnecessary enemies. According to Tom Garbett, a corporate ad consultant, "Advocacy advertising never happened as big as anybody thought . . . at no time could you count more than a dozen active corporations doing [it]."

But in the 1970s, activist groups began to use the media to demand greater social responsibility from corporations, and embattled companies and business associations rose to defend their industries. Many used advertorials to educate people about what they believed to be the proper role and responsibilities of business in an open, free, capitalistic society.

As the political climate changed in the 1980s, advocacy advertising decreased significantly. During the Reagan years, there was little need for it, because as Barry Biederman, chairman of Biederman & Co., said, "I think a lot of groups that used advocacy advertising prior to the Reagan administration felt they had a warmer friend in Washington. They've used lobbying activities rather than the advocacy advertising they would have used [before]."

Advertorials will probably always be with us because, when done well, they can be quite effective in influencing public opinion. A classic study done by Harold Mendelsohn in 1973 revealed that advocacy advertising was most successful when it presented facts that helped convince people they weren't really as well-informed as they had believed. Another study in 1985 revealed that advocacy advertising often succeeds because it "may be perceived as more interesting and more informative, and hence, be more persuasive than a message presented in a news appalled by most corporate advertising, characterizing it as filled with "pomposity," "vague generalizations," and "fatuous platitudes." (For more on Ogilvy's views, see Ad Lab 18-A.) Corporate advertising has also been criticized for being beautiful but bland, self-serving, and oblivious to the needs of the audience.

Responding to such criticisms and to other forces in the marketplace, corporations have made major changes in their corporate advertising policies and campaigns. Expenditures for this type of advertising have increased dramatically over the last decade.[18] The primary medium used for corporate advertising is consumer (primarily business) magazines, followed by network television.[19]

A change in message strategy has also accompanied this increase in corporate ad spending. In the past, most corporate ads were designed primarily to create goodwill for the company. Today, with many corporations diversifying and competition from foreign advertisers increasing, these same firms find their corporate ads must do much more. Their ads must accomplish specific objectives—develop awareness of the company and its activities, attract investors, improve a tarnished image, attract quality employees, tie a diverse product line together, and take a stand on important public issues.

Another category of corporate advertising is called **advocacy advertising.** Corporations use it to communicate their views on issues that affect their

format." That leads to a key distinction that corporations and the FTC can't seem to agree on: Is an advertorial actually news in an advertising format or vice versa?

It's a crucial issue. If advertorials are treated like all other advertising, the FTC can review their content for truth and accuracy. Corporations contend that advertorials are editorial rather than commercial in nature and shouldn't fall under the purview of the FTC. For example, R. J. Reynolds Tobacco ran a series of ads questioning the validity of scientific studies that proved smoking is harmful. The FTC maintained that the ads distorted the facts and would mislead unsuspecting consumers. Reynolds countered that the ads were actually editorials, so it could advance any opinion it pleased. The company never addressed the question of whether the ads were ethical or not.

Television has balked at running advocacy advertising. George Schweitzer, VP-communications of CBS-TV news, says, "We haven't accepted advocacy advertising for the simple reason that we feel it would allow those with the biggest wallets to have the loudest voices." Deep pockets certainly do help shape public opinion. In May 1987, Drexel Burnham Lambert spent $600,000 running 11 ads that sold the idea that high-yield junk bonds were important to the economy. The ads were persuasive, but

Drexel—and some of its customers—eventually went broke.

Corporations undeniably have the same right as anyone else to express their views on *any* subject. Furthermore, the government should not be allowed to cripple corporate advertisers with strict regulations while allowing their adversaries to have unfettered First Amendment freedoms. Perhaps, then, the guiding principle should be this: If it looks like an ad and talks like an ad, then it is an ad, and as such, ethics demand that it be closely scrutinized by the FTC and the public, just as any other form of advertising would be.

Questions

1. Do you think it's unethical for corporations to use persuasive advertising techniques to influence specific target groups of key decision makers?

2. How can you determine if an advocacy ad is deceptive? If deception is established, what do you think the penalty should be?

AD LAB 18-A
David Ogilvy Talks about Corporate Advertising

I have had some experience with corporate advertising—for Shell, Sears, IBM, International Paper, Merrill Lynch, General Dynamics, Standard Oil of New Jersey, and other great corporations.

Big corporations are increasingly under attack—from consumer groups, from environmentalists, from governments, from antitrust prosecutors who try their cases in the newspapers. If a big corporation does not take the initiative in cultivating its reputation, its case goes by default.

If it were possible, it would be better for corporations to rely on public relations (i.e., favorable news stories and editorials) rather than paid advertising. But the media are too niggardly about disseminating favorable information about corporations. That is why an increasing number of public relations directors have come to use paid advertising as their main channel of communication. It is the only one they can control with respect to *content,* with respect to *timing,* and with respect to *noise level.* And it is the only one which enables them to *select their own battleground.*

So I guess that corporate advertising is here to stay. Why is most of it a *flop?*

First, because corporations fail to define the *purpose* of their corporate campaigns.

Second, because they don't *measure the results.* In a recent survey conducted by *The Gallagher Report,* only one in four of U.S. corporate advertisers said that it measured changes in attitude brought about by its corporate campaigns. The majority fly blind.

Third, because so little is known about what works and what doesn't work in corporate advertising. The marketing departments and their agencies know a good deal about what works in *brand* advertising, but when it comes to *corporate* advertising they are amateurs. It isn't their bag.

Fourth, very few advertising agencies know much about corporate advertising. It is only a marginal part of their business. Their creative people know how to talk to housewives about toilet paper, and how to write chewing-gum jingles for kids, and how to sell beer to blue-collar workers. But corporate advertising requries copywriters who are at home in the world of big business. There aren't many of them.

I am appalled by the *humbug* in corporate advertising. The *pomposity.* The *vague generalities* and the *fatuous platitudes.*

Corporate advertising should not insult the intelligence of the public.

Unlike product advertising, a corporate campaign is the voice of the chief executive and his board of directors. It should not be delegated.

What can good corporate advertising hope to achieve? In my experience, one or more of four objectives:

1. It can build *awareness* of the company. Opinion Research Corporation states, "The invisibility and remoteness of most companies is the main handicap. People who feel they know a company well are five times more likely to have a highly favorable opinion of the company than those who have little familiarity."
2. Corporate advertising can make a good impression on the financial community, thus enabling you to raise capital at lower cost—and make more acquisitions.
3. It can motivate your present employees and attract better recruits. Good public relations begins at home. If your employees understand your policies and feel proud of your company, they will be your best ambassadors.
4. Corporate advertising can influence public opinion on specific issues.

Abraham Lincoln said, "With public opinion against it, nothing can succeed. With public opinion on its side, nothing can fail."

Stop and Go—that is the typical pattern of corporate advertising. What a waste of money. It takes time, it takes *years,* for corporate advertising to do a job. It doesn't work overnight—even if you use television.

A few companies—a *very* few—have kept it going long enough to achieve measurable results.

Laboratory Application

Discuss a corporate advertisement with which you are familiar that demonstrates what David Ogilvy refers to as the humbug in corporate advertising, the pomposity, the vague generalities, and the fatuous platitudes.

business. Whatever the issue, the company tailors its stand to protect its position in the marketplace.[20]

Corporate advertising is also increasingly being used to set the company up for future sales. Although this is traditionally the realm of product advertising, many advertisers have instituted "umbrella" campaigns that simultaneously communicate messages about the products and the company. This has been termed **market prep corporate advertising.** A GTE umbrella campaign, for example, emphasized the company's products and services in a way that pointed up its overall technological sophistication.[21]

Of course, no amount of image advertising can accomplish desired goals if the image does not match the corporation. As noted image consultant Clive Chajet put it, "You can't get away with a dissonance between the image and the reality—at least not for long."[22] If, for example, a sophisticated high-tech corporation like IBM tried to project a homey, small-town family image, it would lose credibility very quickly.

Corporate Identity Advertising

Companies take pride in their logos and corporate signatures. In fact, the graphic designs that identify corporate names and products are considered valuable assets of the company, and great effort is expended to protect their individuality and ownership. The corporate logo may even dominate advertisements, as shown in Exhibit 18-9. What does a company do, though, when

The legendary twin-supercharged, twin-engine, twin-driveshaft 1935 Alfa Romeo Bimotore Monoposto.

Coming soon: A legend for the new age. The incredible Pininfarina-designed Alfa Romeo 164 high-performance luxury sedan. With an Alfa Romeo Assurance Program so comprehensive, it even pays for tune-ups. See your dealer for details. For more information, call 1-800-245-ALFA.

© 1990 Alfa Romeo Distributors of North America.

Alfa Romeo. The legendary marque of high performance.

EXHIBIT 18-9   A unique, distinctive logo is like a corporation's fingerprint. Alfa Romeo calls its logo "the legendary marque of high performance," and the company has used it as the focal point for a teaser campaign touting a newly designed luxury sedan.

it decides to change its name, logos, trademarks, or corporate signatures, as when it merges with another company? How does it communicate that change to the market it serves and to other influential publics? This is the job of **corporate identity advertising.**

When software publisher Productivity Products International changed its name to Stepstone Inc., it faced an interesting dilemma. It needed to advertise the change. But in Europe, a key market for the firm, a corporate name change implies that the business has gone bankrupt and is starting over with a new identity. So, rather than announcing its new name in the print media, Stepstone used a direct-mail campaign. It mailed an announcement of its name change to customers, prospects, investors, and the press. The campaign was a success: Within days of the mailing, almost 70 customers and prospects called Stepstone to find out more about the company and its products.[23]

More familiar corporate name changes from the recent past include the switch from American Harvester to Navistar International; the renaming of Western Bankcorporation to First Interstate Bankcorp; the change of Consolidated Foods to Sara Lee Corporation; and the creation of Unisys to replace the premerger identities of Burroughs and Sperry.

Recruitment Advertising

When the prime objective of corporate advertising is to attract employment applications, companies use **recruitment advertising** such as the Chiat/Day ad in Exhibit 18-10. Recruitment advertising is most frequently found in the classified sections of daily newspapers and is typically the responsibility of the personnel department rather than the advertising department. Recruitment advertising has become such a large field, though, that many advertising agencies now have recruitment specialists on their staffs. In fact, some agencies specialize completely in recruitment advertising, and their clients are corporate personnel managers rather than advertising department managers. These agencies create, write, and place classified advertisements in newspapers around the country and prepare recruitment display ads for specialized trade publications.

NONCOMMERCIAL ADVERTISING

So far in this chapter, we have discussed only the advertising of commercial organizations. But nonprofit organizations also advertise. The government, charities, trade associations, and religious groups, for example, use the same kinds of creative and media strategies as their counterparts in the for-profit sector to convey messages to the public. But unlike commercial advertisers, whose goal is to create awareness, image, or brand loyalty on the part of consumers, noncommercial organizations use advertising to affect consumer opinions, perceptions, or behavior—with no profit motive. While commercial advertising is used to stimulate sales, **noncommercial advertising** is used to stimulate donations, to persuade people to vote one way or another, or to bring attention to social causes.

If a specific commercial objective for a new shampoo is to change people's *buying* habits, the analogous noncommercial objective for an energy conservation program might be to change people's *activity* habits, such as turning off the lights. The latter is an example of *demarketing,* which means the advertiser is actually trying to get consumers to buy less of a product or service. Exhibit 18-11 compares objectives of commercial and noncommercial advertisers.

EXHIBIT 18-10

Although most corporate recruitment advertising is found in the
classified sections of newspapers
and business publications, some
national corporate magazine ads
are used for recruitment purposes.

THIS SHOULD HAVE RUN LAST WEEK.

We're looking for a media buyer with at least
1½ years experience in television and print buying.
If you're interested in placing ads
rather than reading them,
call David Cairns at 585-9992.

CHIAT/DAY

EXHIBIT 18-10

Although most corporate recruitment advertising is found in the classified sections of newspapers and business publications, some national corporate magazine ads are used for recruitment purposes.

EXHIBIT 18-11   Comparison of Advertising Objectives

Product advertising	Noncommercial advertising
Create store traffic.	Stimulate inquiries for information.
Stimulate brand loyalty.	Popularize social cause.
Change buying habits.	Change activity habits.
Increase product use.	Decrease waste of resources.
Communicate product features.	Communicate political viewpoint.
Improve product image.	Improve public attitude.
Inform public of new product.	Inform public of new cure.
Remind people to buy again.	Remind people to give again.

Examples of Noncommercial Advertising

One example of noncommercial advertising conducted on a large scale is the antidrug campaign created by the Partnership for a Drug-Free America. In 1987, this coalition of more than 200 ad agencies, the media, and many other companies in the communications business launched an all-out attack on drug abuse. The coalition set its goal as the "fundamental reshaping of social attitudes about illegal drug usage." The $1.5 billion program entails the efforts of ad agencies across the country, each developing components of the campaign at their own cost.

The antidrug program includes hundreds of newspaper and magazine ads as well as 200 different commercials and print ads. The space and time allotted for the ads, all donated by the media, are worth an estimated $310 million per year.[24] Similarly, most of the creative and production suppliers have donated their services.

EXHIBIT 18-12

Many of the print ads produced
by the Partnership for a Drug-
Free America have focused on
the drugs that adults are most
likely to abuse, especially cocaine
and crack. This is one in a series
of magazine ads created by DDB
Needham Worldwide.

The wide variety of ads have been created to reach specific target groups. Some are aimed at cocaine users, some at marijuana smokers; some are aimed at parents, some at children. Most ads present hard-hitting messages about the dangers of drug abuse, depicting drug use as a sure route to the hospital or the cemetery. In a TV commercial targeted at teenaged marijuana smokers, for example, the Ayer agency suggests that pot smokers are subjecting themselves to the risk of physical and mental health problems. Other commercials compare the brain on drugs to an egg in a frying pan or show dead rats that have succumbed to cocaine abuse. Print ads have also emphasized the dangers of cocaine abuse, including a series of ads developed by DDB Needham Worldwide that enumerate cocaine's effects. Exhibit 18-12 is from that series of ads. In addition, some ads speak to parents who use drugs ("If parents stop, kids won't start"), to women tempted to use cocaine ("What to do if he hands you a line"), and to parents who have put off talking to their children about drugs ("If everybody says it can't happen to their kids, then whose kids is it happening to?").

The effort is being billed as the "largest and most ambitious private-sector, voluntary peacetime effort ever undertaken." Believing that the United States cannot succeed as a drug culture and that advertising can "demoralize" drug use, the organization wants nothing less than a drug-free America.

Not all public service advertising is done on such a massive scale. We see advertisements daily for intangible humanitarian social causes (Red Cross), political ideas or issues (political candidates), philosophical or religious positions (Church of Latter Day Saints), or particular attitudes and viewpoints (labor unions). In most cases, these advertisements are created and placed by nonprofit organizations, and the product they advertise is their particular mission in life, be it politics, welfare, religion, conservation, health, art, happiness, or love.

Research conducted by the Partnership for a Drug-Free America proves that noncommercial advertising does change consumer attitudes. Specifically, the coalition's ads have changed attitudes about drug use. Thus, by providing information to the public on issues such as health, safety, education, and the environment, noncommercial advertising helps build a better society. Public service announcements emphasizing the dangers of unsafe sex and drunk driving and those stressing the virtues of recycling and continuing education demonstrate that noncommercial advertising can help to enhance the quality of life.

Types of Noncommercial Advertising

One way to categorize the various types of noncommercial advertising is by the organizations that use them. For instance, advertising is used by churches, schools, universities, charitable organizations, and many other **nonbusiness institutions.** We also see advertising by *associations*, such as labor groups, professional organizations, and trade and civic associations. In addition, we witness millions of dollars' worth of advertising placed by *government organizations:* the U.S. Army, Navy, Marine, Corps, and Postal Service; the Social Security Administration; the Internal Revenue Service; and various state chambers of commerce. In addition, in election years we are bombarded with all sorts of political advertising that qualifies as noncommercial.

Among organizations that use public service advertising are those wanting to prevent child abuse, diseases such as AIDS, drunk driving, and unwanted teenage pregnancy.

Advertising by Nonbusiness Institutions

"It's a matter of life and breath" is a familiar line to anyone who watches television. Every year the American Lung Association places an estimated $10 million worth of advertising on television and radio, in newspapers and magazines, and on outdoor and transit media. All this space and time are donated as a public service by the media involved. Such donated ads are termed *public service announcements (PSAs)*. In its effort to educate the public about the damaging effects of smoking or the early warning signs of emphysema, lung cancer, and tuberculosis, the Lung Association joins a long list of nonbusiness institutions that use noncommercial advertising to achieve their objectives. The Children's Defense Fund uses PSAs like the one shown in Exhibit 18-13.

The objectives of nonbusiness institution advertising are varied. The Foster Parents Plan uses massive doses of advertising to ask readers to adopt children from the country of their choice by spending $22 per month for their care and support. The Church of the Nazarene advertises "Our church can be your home" to build an image of a church in which members can be personally involved. The National Council on Alcoholism wants children and teenagers to say *no* to drinking "And say yes to life."

Not all nonbusiness institution advertising is donated. If you live in a large metropolitan area and want to place a newspaper ad for your favorite charitable organization, you will probably be charged a special nonprofit institution rate by your local city newspaper. Newspaper, radio, and TV advertising departments are besieged by requests from local churches, charity groups, hospital guilds, and other social organizations to donate advertising space and time to these "favorite causes." In self-defense, the media are forced to charge for most local nonbusiness institution advertising, such as that in Exhibit 18-14.

Many nonprofit organizations and religious groups are turning to paid advertising to get their message to the public.

PRESTO CHANGO: I know I should drink milk 'cause it will help me grow up big and strong. Milk's got stuff that's good for my bones and stuff that's good for my muscles. And I guess that's okay, but I'm more interested in having fun! That's what makes milk so neat; you can drink a lot of it and it tastes cool. Milk can be a real pick-me-up! Milk, it does a body good.

On the national level, a sizable number of organizations seek to place free public service ads on the three major U.S. networks. ABC, NBC, and CBS each received ads from about 300 organizations and ran about 8,000 spots in 1990.[25] In light of this tough competition, sponsors of PSAs are forced to create more sophisticated campaigns, supplying ads that are more likely to be aired.

Advertising by Nonprofit Business Associations

Business, professional, trade, labor, farm, and civic associations all use advertising to achieve their individual objectives. Frequently, nonprofit business associations advertise simply to create goodwill and a positive impression of the association's members by spotlighting the good works of individuals within the organization. Labor unions, for example, use advertising to inform the public how important union workers are to the nation's economy. By stimulating goodwill in this way, they are potentially able to enlist more public support during labor disputes.

Other business association ads promote the product that members produce: dairy products, California raisins, Florida grapefruit, and so on. See, for example, the National Dairy Board spot in Exhibit 18-15. And the Beef Industry Council has run TV commercials featuring James Garner and Cybill Shepherd talking about how they like "real food for real people." The objective of these associations' advertising is sometimes indirectly—and often directly—commercial.

Finally, some business association ads are devoted to specific causes that are in some way linked to their business. Thus, the Magazine Publishers' Association has sponsored a $26 million campaign against adult illiteracy.

Advertising by Government Organizations

Government bureaus and departments have been highly effective advertising and propaganda practitioners for years. In its effort to communicate with the voters, the government employs advertising agencies and public relations firms and maintains well-staffed in-house graphics, communications, and press-relations departments.

Much government advertising announces the availability of government services such as consumer assistance, welfare aid, or career guidance. Similarly, great effort is given to instructing people how to use government services correctly. The U.S. Postal Service, for example, has maintained a strong campaign for years to persuade and remind citizens to use ZIP codes and also to mail early for Christmas.

The 1970s also saw the Army, Navy, Air Force, and Marine Corps enter the paid advertising arena. With the end of the Selective Service draft came the need to recruit for the all-volunteer force, so the military waged aggressive advertising campaigns to draw young men and women to its ranks. The Army, which has had the biggest advertising budget, has relied heavily on paid television commercials. The Navy, with its "Live the Adventure" and, more recently, "You are tomorrow, You are the Navy" campaign themes, has also used paid spots when its budget has permitted. Advertising by the individual armed services is supplemented by the Defense Department's joint military ad program.[26]

Beyond the national level, many state governments use advertising to attract new businesses, tourists, or workers to aid their economy. Exhibit 18-16 is from a TV commercial that Illinois uses to draw tourists. Ohio

EXHIBIT 18-16

To draw tourists, the Illinois Bureau of Tourism ran this television ad, offering the beauty and tranquillity of nature as an escape from fax machines, car phones, and even TV commercials.

(SFX: Frogs croaking)
SUPER: No fax machines
(SFX: Owl hooting)
SUPER: No heavy metal
(SFX: Geese honking)
SUPER: No car phones

(SFX: Crickets chirping)
SUPER: The parks and forests of Illinois' 635,357 acres of nothing but nature.
(SFX: Loon calling)
SUPER: No TV commercials

SUPER: Illinois, the American Renaissance, 1-800-223-0121, Illinois Bureau of Tourism, Department of Commerce and Community Affairs.

advertises the availability of skilled workers and placement services for industrial concerns; North Carolina beckons with a rural, homey image; and California offers a wide variety of attractions.

Political Advertising

Federal, state, and local politicians also use advertising to influence voters. Making registered voters aware of the candidate's legislative record, stand on issues, and political vision can be achieved through the same advertising media that for-profit organizations use, namely print, broadcast, direct mail, and outdoor. Political candidates also use advertising to discredit their opposition.

Presidential candidates and other politicians with millions of dollars to spend on advertising typically use television commercials to sway large blocks of voters. They also may enlist top talent from the world of commercial advertising to create their advertising campaigns. The candidate may run some ads with a positive message early on, to build credibility with voters, then follow up with ads that sling mud at opposing candidates.[27]

Political advertising has grown significantly with the expansion of broadcast media in the past two decades. One study revealed that television advertising by gubernatorial and congressional candidates in the six nonpresidential election years between 1970 and 1990 ballooned from $12 million to $230.5 million.[28]

The Advertising Council

Most of the national PSAs you see on television have been placed there by the **Advertising Council,** a private, nonprofit organization that links noncom-

EXHIBIT 18-17

The Ad Council has produced many memorable campaigns, including this announcement about the dangers of fatty foods.

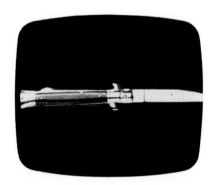

ANNCR (VO): The stiletto. Outlawed in most major cities.

The trench knife—it boasts a seven-inch, solid steel blade.

The survival knife. Designed to cut through virtually anything.

Yet the most dangerous knife of all may be the one we use to eat too much high-fat food: the ordinary table knife.

For a free booklet on how to help reduce your risk of cancer and heart disease through low-fat eating, call 1-800-EAT-LEAN.

mercial campaign sponsors with ad agencies. The sponsors pay for production costs, while the ad agencies donate their creative services.

The Ad Council's policy today is basically the same as when it began during World War II: "Accept no subsidy from government and remain independent of it. Conduct campaigns of service to the nation at large, avoiding regional, sectarian, or special-interest drives of all kinds. Remain nonpartisan and nonpolitical. Conduct the Council on a voluntary basis. Accept no project that does not lend itself to the advertising method. Accept no campaign with a commercial interest unless the public interest is obviously overriding."

Among familiar campaigns created by the Ad Council are those for the United Negro College Fund ("A mind is a terrible thing to waste"); child abuse prevention ("Help destroy a family tradition"); the United Way ("It works for all of us"); crime prevention ("Take a bite out of crime"); and the U.S. Department of Transportation ("Drinking and driving can kill a friendship"). Exhibit 18-17 shows frames from an Ad Council commercial that advocates a healthy diet. The Ad Council's two longest-running campaigns are those for the American Red Cross and forest fire prevention. According to the Ad Council's research, the number of forest fires has been cut in half over the life of the Smokey Bear campaign.[29] The council is currently playing a role in overseeing the Partnership for a Drug-Free America effort.

Summary

Public relations is a process used to manage an organization's relationships with its various publics. These publics include the organization's employees, customers, stockholders, and competitors as well as the general populace. Many public relations activities involve media communications. However, unlike product advertising, these communications are not normally openly sponsored or paid for.

Public relations activities include publicity and press agentry, public affairs and lobbying, promotion and special-events management, publication preparation, research, fund-raising and membership drives, and public speaking.

The tools used in public relations are many and varied. They include news releases and media kits, photography, feature articles, all sorts of printed materials, posters and exhibits, and audiovisual materials.

To help create a favorable reputation in the marketplace, companies use various types of corporate advertising, including public relations advertising, corporate (or institutional) advertising, corporate identity advertising, and recruitment advertising.

Noncommercial advertising includes advertising by non-business institutions (churches, schools, charitable organizations), associations (labor groups, business and professional organizations), political candidates, and governments.

To assist with important causes, members of the advertising profession formed the Advertising Council during World War II. During its more than four decades of operation, the Ad Council has conducted memorable campaigns for such projects as child abuse prevention and the United Way.

Questions for Review and Discussion

1. How does the definition of *public relations* differ from the definition of *advertising*?

2. How is the perspective of advertising practitioners different from that of PR professionals?

3. What is the importance of establishing a crisis-management plan? What types of companies are most likely to need such a plan?

4. If you handled the public relations for a utility company, what activities do you think would be the most useful?

5. What do you think are the most important public relations tools for a major corporation? Why?

6. What are the various types of corporate advertising? Describe them.

7. In what ways is the line between product and corporate advertising beginning to blur?

8. What is the purpose of recruitment advertising? Why is it under the domain of corporate advertising and public relations?

9. What is the difference between commercial and noncommercial advertising?

10. What are the major types of noncommercial advertising? Which are more likely to receive free media space?

CHAPTER

19

INTERNATIONAL ADVERTISING

Objective: To convey how advertisers plan, create, and organize for worldwide advertising. To succeed in the global marketplace, advertisers must know how to select and work with an ad agency on international campaigns. They must also understand the environments their ads will appear in, with attention to market, media, and message considerations.

After studying this chapter, you will be able to:

☐ Describe worldwide marketing structures.

☐ Explain the difference between an international ad agency and an export agency.

☐ Define the environments that influence international advertising.

☐ Explain the importance of marketing research in international advertising.

☐ Describe the types of international media available to advertisers.

☐ Explain why campaign transferability can be difficult in international advertising.

☐ Describe some legal constraints international advertisers face.

Gillette Company believes that people are similar the world over. Backing up its conviction, the firm more than once has used a single campaign to advertise a shaving product worldwide. For example, to launch the twin-bladed Sensor razor in 1990, the company spent $110 million on television and print advertising in North America and Europe. The theme throughout the international campaign was "The best a man can get," as shown in Exhibit 19-1.

Gillette introduced the Sensor product to U.S. men with sporty commercials during the Super Bowl. The next month, the company started running nearly identical commercials in 18 other countries. All the commercials used diagrams of the Sensor blades efficiently cutting whiskers and featured manly, if not macho, spokesmen. The only elements of the campaign that changed from country to country were language and specific sports images. Gillette translated the commercial into 26 languages, taking into consideration linguistic subtleties that could undermine the effectiveness of the campaign's theme in various parts of North America and Europe. The French theme line, for example, became "La perfection au masculin," or "Perfection, male style." That translation overcame the problem of "Perfection" as a feminine noun in French. As for sports imagery, the European commercials replaced U.S. football scenes with shots of soccer action.

Gillette chose the pan-Atlantic approach for the Sensor razor partly because of its previous success with a similar ad campaign for the Contour Plus razor in Europe (called Atra Plus in the United States). In 1986, Gillette launched the Contour Plus in 15 European countries using the same commercials throughout. By using a single ad campaign, the company reportedly

EXHIBIT 19-1

To promote its razors, Gillette uses international advertising without varying much of the content. Because consumers tend to react the same to this product, Gillette doesn't have to worry about differing consumer habits or cultural attitudes. Some small adjustments are made, however, such as changing the sports imagery (from football to soccer) or the precise wording of the slogan (from "The best a man can get" to "Perfection, male style").

VO: Gillette announces a razor so revolutionary it can sense the individual needs of your face. Introducing the extraordinary Gillette Sensor Shaving System.

SONG: Gillette. The Best a Man Can Get.

VO: Sensor twin blades are indi-

vidually mounted on remarkably responsive springs. They continuously sense and automatically adjust to the individual curves and contours of your face.

SONG: And we know how to make the most of who you are.

VO: The extraordinary Gillette

Sensor. Closer, smoother, safer than ever before. To give you the best shave a man can get.

SONG: Where the race is run, you're the champion. Gillette. The Best a Man Can Get.

VO: New Gillette Sensor. The Best a Man Can Get.

saved millions of dollars on advertising and other marketing expenses while racking up significant sales at retail.

Some advertisers oppose the use of international advertising that doesn't vary significantly from country to country. They believe consumer habits, customs, and attitudes differ too much between countries for a one-note campaign to work. And that's true for some products, but not so applicable for products that most consumers tend to react similarly to—like razors. "We are blessed with a product category [shaving systems] where we're able to market across multinational boundaries as if they were one country," one of Gillette's marketing vice presidents explained. Another of the company's executives added, "If you accentuate the similarities of human beings, it's amazing what you can do."[1]

GROWTH AND STATUS OF INTERNATIONAL ADVERTISING

In this text, we have discussed marketing and advertising planning, advertising creativity, and the advertising media. We have also offered overall advertising perspectives and focused on some special types of advertising. However, most of this discussion has centered on advertising as practiced in the United States and Canada. The question arises, therefore, as to how well such practice applies to advertising in the rest of the world. Companies advertising abroad face a variety of difficulties and opportunities, as we will see in this chapter.

A bit of history will help put the current explosion of international advertising into perspective. As U.S. companies entered world markets after World War II, consumption of U.S. products grew tremendously. By 1990, U.S. advertising expenditures accounted for $130 billion, or 47 percent of the world total.[2] However, in the last 15 years, expenditures by foreign advertisers increased even more rapidly than U.S. expenditures, thanks to improved economic conditions and a desire for expansion. As national economies have expanded and personal incomes have increased, the use of advertising has also increased.

Organizations in every country of the world practice advertising in one form or another. Actual figures are not available, but recent estimates of worldwide advertising expenditures outside the United States exceed $145.6 billion per year, or 53 percent of the worldwide total.[3] The emphasis on advertising in individual countries, though, depends on the country's level of development and its national attitude toward promotion. Generally, advertising expenditures are higher in countries with higher personal income.

Today, advertising is used worldwide to sell ideas, policies, and attitudes as well as products. From Procter & Gamble in Cincinnati to Fiat in Turin, Italy, major marketers believe in international advertising, and they back their convictions with sizable advertising budgets. As Exhibit 19–2 shows, the top 10 worldwide advertisers are based in many different countries.

Communist countries, including China, once condemned advertising as an evil of capitalism. But now, with the Soviet Union's economy broadening to include private enterprise, even the Soviets are starting to admit the benefits of advertising. Although decades of propaganda have conditioned Soviet consumers to distrust or ignore advertising, some Western advertisers are successfully gaining the attention of Soviet citizens by featuring instructional or entertaining fare in ads.[4] Ad Lab 19-A (p. 674) discusses how Pepsi has successfully used advertising techniques within the Soviet market.

EXHIBIT 19-2   Top 10 International Advertisers

Rank	Advertiser	Headquarters	Primary business	Countries in which spending was reported
1	Unilever NV	Rotterdam/London	Soaps	Argentina, Australia, Austria, Brazil, Britain, Canada, Denmark, France, Germany, Greece, India, Italy, Japan, Malaysia, Mexico, Netherlands, Pan Arabia, Portugal, Puerto Rico, South Africa, Spain, Switzerland, Taiwan, Thailand, Turkey
2	Procter & Gamble Co.	Cincinnati	Soaps	Australia, Austria, Britain, Canada, France, Germany, Greece, India, Italy, Japan, Malaysia, Mexico, Netherlands, Pan Arabia, Puerto Rico, Taiwan, Thailand, Turkey
3	Nestlé SA	Vevey, Switzerland	Food	Argentina, Australia, Austria, Brazil, Britain, France, Germany, India, Japan, Malaysia, Mexico, Netherlands, Pan Arabia, Portugal, Puerto Rico, Spain, Switzerland, Taiwan, Thailand
4	Renault SA	Paris, France	Automotive	Argentina, Austria, Britain, France, Germany, Italy, Netherlands, Pan Arabia, Portugal, Spain, Switzerland, Thailand
5	Philip Morris Cos.	New York	Food	Argentina, Australia, Austria, Brazil, Britain, Canada, Denmark, France, Germany, Hong Kong, Japan, Malaysia, Mexico, Netherlands, Pan Arabia, Spain, Taiwan, Thailand
6	Fiat SpA	Turin, Italy	Automotive	Brazil, Britain, Denmark, France, Germany, Italy, Netherlands, Portugal, Spain, Switzerland
7	Matsushita Electric Industrial Co.	Osaka, Japan	Electronics	Brazil, Britain, Hong Kong, Japan, Malaysia, Pan Arabia, Taiwan, Thailand
8	PSA Peugeot-Citroen SA	Paris, France	Automotive	Argentina, Austria, Britain, Denmark, France, Germany, Netherlands, Pan Arabia, Portugal, Spain, Switzerland, Thailand
9	Nissan Motor Co.	Tokyo, Japan	Automotive	Australia, Britain, Germany, Japan, Mexico, Pan Arabia, Switzerland, Thailand
10	Volkswagen AG	Wolfsburg, Germany	Automotive	Brazil, Britain, France, Germany, Mexico, South Africa, Spain, Sweden, Switzerland, Thailand

Certainly, as a communication form, international advertising contributes to the unification of the world. And one benefit is enhanced international understanding as advertisers introduce foreign products, values, and ideas into new markets. As technology and ideologies evolve, international advertising will continue to flourish. As a creative director for Ogilvy & Mather in Paris has said, "Nous n'avons pas mal de budgets," which can be loosely translated as, "We're not hurting for business."

AD LAB 19-A
Advertising in the Soviet Union

The idea of Michael Jackson selling soft drinks on Soviet television was, until fairly recently, inconceivable. According to traditional Marxist-Leninist doctrine, advertising is a tool of capitalistic exploitation. It siphons off the surplus value belonging to underpaid workers and puts it in the hands of overpaid white-collar workers who are nonproductively employed in such tasks as writing jingles.

However, thanks to *glasnost* and *perestroika*, advertising is gradually infiltrating the Soviet Union. In 1988, Pepsi-Cola International, Visa International, and Sony became the first non-Soviet companies to buy television advertising time in that country. Two of Pepsi's first commercials featured Michael Jackson—a distinct change from the days when Soviets were adamantly against celebrity endorsements.

"The Pepsi commercials were some of the best I have seen," said Vladimir Posner, who hosted the program during which the ads ran. "Many people who watched them were amazed by the creativity and artistry involved. We do not have much of a history of advertising or of marketing in the Western sense. Our ads generally say: 'Here's a product, here's what it does, and here's where you can buy it if you want.' As our economy goes through a process of reform, and state enterprises and cooperatives begin to compete among themselves, advertising will become much more important." He added that the Pepsi ads signified "a breakthrough of sorts."

Pepsi, which has marketed its products in the Soviet Union since 1974, learned to be creative with Soviet media before they were permitted to use paid television advertising. The company sponsored sports events, bought space on bus placards, purchased newspaper ads, and sometimes used billboards.

Laboratory Application

Why did the Pepsi commercials represent a "breakthrough" in Soviet advertising?

MANAGING INTERNATIONAL ADVERTISING

Imagine you are the advertising manager of a U.S. company planning to market its products abroad. You are aware that you may need to use a different creative strategy in the foreign market. You will be speaking to a new audience with a different value system, a different environment, and probably a different language. Your foreign customers will probably have different purchasing abilities, habits, and motivations than the average North American. The media that U.S. and Canadian advertisers generally use may be unavailable or ineffective in foreign markets. And the advertisements may need to be different, too.

You also face another problem. How will you manage and produce the advertising? Will your in-house advertising department do it? Will your domestic advertising agency do it? Or will you have to set up a foreign advertising department or hire a foreign advertising agency?

To answer these questions, we need to ask two more: How does your company structure its worldwide marketing operations? Within that structure, what are the most economical and effective means to conduct advertising activities?

Worldwide Marketing Structures

Just as in domestic situations, managing advertising in foreign markets depends to a great extent on the company's foreign marketing structure. Does the advertiser intend to market its products internationally, multinationally, or globally? What's the difference?

Advertisers frequently use the terms *international, multinational,* and *global* interchangeably. The differences in these terms relate to the degree of involvement in foreign markets.

International Structure

Many advertisers break into **international marketing** simply by exporting the products they already produce. But as companies get more involved, they may contract for manufacture, form joint ventures, or invest in foreign sales offices, warehouses, plants, manufacturing subsidiaries, or other facilities. The advertiser's headquarters office typically operates and views all these operations as "foreign marketing divisions."

At first, the home office controls the foreign marketing and advertising. But as the complexities of foreign operations expand, pressure to decentralize grows. For years, the 3M Company has operated internationally with autonomous units in various countries. Similarly, many large retailers structure their foreign operations internationally, with local management responsible for its own product lines, marketing operations, and its own profit and losses.

Multinational Structure

As companies grow and prosper, they may become true **multinational** corporations with direct investment in several countries and make business decisions based on choices available anywhere in the world.[5] They strive for full and integrated participation in world markets. Foreign sales, a large part of the multinational's activities, usually grow faster than domestic sales. Well-known U.S. multinationals today range from Exxon and IBM, which earn about 50 percent of their sales abroad, to firms such as Kodak and Xerox, which earn about 25 percent of their total sales abroad. The top 25 U.S. multinational corporations derive 42 percent of their revenues and 69 percent of their profits from overseas.[6] Exhibit 19-3 shows the type of advertising Xerox uses in Japan.

A multinational typically exerts strong centralized control and coordination over all marketing activities, including advertising. Companies like Coca-Cola are called multinational organizations because they sell in many countries, have strong direction and coordination from one central headquarters, and have a standardized product line and a uniform marketing structure. The chairman of Coca-Cola called this strategy, "One site, one sound, one sell."

EXHIBIT 19-3

Compare Dentsu's creative director Yasuhiro Ohnishi's approach to advertising Xerox color photocopiers in Japan (carp swimming on paper) with ads you may have seen for Xerox color copiers in the United States.

VO: Apply colors with an electronic palette. Increase the number. Change the size. Documents can have new colors. Just a little fantastic. XEROX's color copier Palette. Now on sale.

EXHIBIT 19-4

Coca-Cola's trademark varies from country to country, but the overall look is retained through use of similar letterforms and style, even with different alphabets.

Exhibit 19-4 shows how Coca-Cola retains its famous logo even in foreign markets.

Global Structure

As the multinational company develops a worldwide marketing and advertising strategy, it faces the choice that confronted Gillette in the European Community: whether to use the same ads in all countries or to create unique campaigns for each. Harvard marketing professor Theodore Levitt would encourage the multinational to use the same advertising and marketing in all countries and thereby create a *global brand*. Gillette, with its one-theme worldwide campaigns, is a good example of a **global** advertiser.

Grey Advertising suggests three questions companies should ask before attempting a global strategy:

☐ Has the market developed in the same way from country to country? (The continued popularity of clotheslines in Europe has discouraged demand for fabric softening products used in dryers.)

☐ Are the consumer targets similar in different nations? (Canon found that while Japanese consumers like sophisticated, high-tech products, many U.S. consumers fear technologically complex products.)

☐ Do consumers share the same wants and needs around the world? (Tang was successfully positioned as an orange juice substitute in the United States. But in France, where people don't drink orange juice at breakfast, Tang had to be repositioned as a daytime refreshment, as shown in Exhibit 19-5.)

Grey suggests that, if the answer to any of these questions is *no*, a global marketing attempt will probably fail.[7]

Levitt envisions total worldwide product, marketing, and advertising standardization. In his 1983 book, *The Marketing Imagination,* Levitt theorizes that companies that do not use true **global marketing** with global brands

GOÛT FRAMBOISE SUR FRÉQUENCE TANG.

TANG TOUT PRÊT.
TOUT NOUVEAU. TOUT BON.

EXHIBIT 19-5

This French ad for Tang positions it as a refreshing beverage rather than a breakfast drink. The youngster is floating along listening to his Tang "radio," which plays "raspberry taste on the Tang frequency." The copy below says Tang is "All ready. All new. All good."

will surely perish on the rough seas of what he calls the *new global realities*. An excellent example of a global product—one standardized worldwide—is Coca-Cola.

Levitt argues that, thanks to cheap air travel and new telecommunications technology, the world is becoming a common marketplace in which people have the same tastes and desires and want the same products and lifestyles no matter where they live. This, he believes, allows for world-standardized products at low prices sold the same way around the world.[8]

Levitt's admittedly exaggerated theory stirred up a lot of dust on Madison Avenue. In fact, several large multinationals dumped their multiple agency relationships in favor of one worldwide agency. Meanwhile, the large international agencies raced to prove they were each best equipped to handle global brands.

Nevertheless, many advertisers believe Levitt's approach is incorrect. Some say global advertising presupposes a global consumer—who doesn't exist. Others say advertising should communicate the gestures, nuances, and idiosyncrasies of a country and its culture, which global ads cannot. In fact, even Coca-Cola is advertised differently in different countries. Its "General Assembly" commercial, which features a thousand children from around the world singing a song of hope at St. George's Hall in Liverpool, is available in 21 languages. For each of the 16 countries in which the ad runs, the company has edited the commercial to focus on children from that country (see Exhibit 19-6).

As the global marketing debate has evolved, a third view—one that accepts Levitt's argument, but only to a point—has emerged. International ad agencies such as Backer Spielvogel Bates Worldwide and D'Arcy Masius Benton & Bowles have developed research tools to identify the "global consumer." Through surveys, the agencies have found that consumers worldwide do share some similarities, but those prospective customers also maintain distinct differences.

EXHIBIT 19-6

Coca-Cola's commercial "General Assembly" shows 1,000 teenagers from around the world joining together in a song of hope for tomorrow. There are actually 16 different versions, each beginning with a teen from the target country singing in his or her own language, "I am the future of the world. I am the hope of my nation . . ." Coke's ad agency in each country has the freedom to edit the commercial for its market so that more can be shown of the teens from that country.

GIRL SOLO: I am the future of the world.

I am the hope of my nation.

I am tomorrow's people.

I am the new inspiration and we've got a song to sing to you.

GROUP: (Under solo) Ooh.

GIRL SOLO: We've got a message to bring to you.

Please let there be for you and for me a tomorrow . . .

ALL TOGETHER: Tomorrow.

If we all can agree, there'll be sweet harmony tomorrow, tomorrow . . .

GROUP: (Under solo) Aah.

GIRL SOLO: And we all will be there, Coca-Cola to share . . .

GROUP: Coca-Cola to share . . .

GIRL SOLO: Feelings so real and so true.

GROUP: Feelings so real and so . . .

ALL TOGETHER: True.

GIRL SOLO: Promise us tomorrow and we'll build a better world for you.

GROUP: Build a better world for you.

Young & Rubicam's research, conducted in six countries, identified product benefits shared by consumers in different cultures. However, Margaret Mark, director of consumer insights with Young & Rubicam, advises advertisers not to "develop one strategy and one commercial and force-feed it to different cultures. As you get closer to execution, you need to be acutely sensitive to cultural differences. But at the origin, it's one enormous benefit to be able to think about people who share common benefits across cultures."[9]

Ultimately, the advertising direction a company takes depends on many variables, including breadth of product line, availability of qualified management, ability to use similar marketing techniques across countries, and the costs of particular marketing strategies. Nonetheless, advertisers cannot discount the importance of their choice to operate internationally, multinationally, or globally.

Agency Selection

All advertisers have a wide choice of agencies when conducting advertising activities outside their own countries. They may choose an international or global agency, a local foreign agency, an export agency, their normal domestic agency, or their house agency. The best choice depends on the advertiser's foreign marketing structure and business needs.

EXHIBIT 19-7   Top 10 Agencies by Worldwide Billings

Agency	1990*
WPP Group	$2,712
Saatchi & Saatchi Co.	1,729
Interpublic Group of Cos.	1,649
Omnicom Group	1,335
Dentsu Inc.	1,254
Young & Rubicam	1,073
Eurocom Group	748
Hakuhodo Inc.	586
Grey Advertising	583
Foote, Cone & Belding Communications	536

*Dollars are in millions.

International and Global Agencies

Many multinational advertisers find that only a large agency with widespread offices or affiliates can do an adequate job. Thus, some large U.S. general agencies have established themselves in major foreign markets and shifted their focus from domestic advertising to international and even global marketing. Thanks to a 1980s wave of merger-mania that reduced the number of advertising agencies, several mega-agencies now wield significant clout in international media buying and worldwide advertising coordination. Exhibit 19-7 lists the 10 largest ad agencies worldwide.

Advertisers planning large multinational campaigns often deal with a large international agency. The agency's overseas offices usually employ multilingual, multinational creative specialists and administrators who can create distinct campaigns for different markets or coordinate and control one central campaign for a series of countries. An alternative is to hire various international agencies for different regions. For example, Rolex uses J. Walter Thompson in 25 countries, Pimo in the Middle East, Ogilvy & Mather for Southeast Asia, and Intercom in South Africa.

Because of differences in attitudes, buying habits, business systems, and laws, it's seldom practical to simply translate U.S. advertising into other languages. A foreign-based staff of advertising specialists can transform and adapt basic concepts and strategies and add verbal and visual elements with local appeal.

Local Foreign Agencies

An advertiser may select a local foreign agency to coordinate activities in a particular market. The foreign agency, of course, understands local attitudes and customers as well as the local media. General Motors worked with a foreign agency, DPZ-Propaganda, to create the ad in Exhibit 19-8.

If the advertiser plans to promote the product differently to various markets, it may appoint several local agencies that understand the needs of those particular markets. A problem with that approach, for the multinational advertiser, lies in coordinating the various agencies.

EXHIBIT 19-8

Multinational advertisers like General Motors often employ local ad agencies in foreign markets. This ad, done by DPZ-Propaganda in Italy, uses a whimsical visual to address a most serious subject: the potentially deadly dangers of mixing drinking and driving.

Export Agencies

Some agencies specialize in creating ads for exporters. These **export agencies** may work with domestic agencies on particular accounts or perform their specialty for clients of their own.

Export agencies typically prepare ads for particular language groups or geographic areas. They employ writers and specialists familiar with the market and its media.

Domestic and House Agencies

Small companies exporting their products abroad may simply ask their domestic agency to prepare their first international ads, which many agencies can do quite adequately. Some domestic agencies are affiliated with foreign shops that provide media counsel, translation services, or production assistance. Other domestic agencies join international **agency networks** to receive similar services and other specialized services such as arranging local press conferences or trade fairs. One problem with using a domestic agency, however, is that it may not have experience in the pitfalls of international advertising.

Some companies, especially industrial firms, use their company advertising departments or house agencies for foreign advertising. While they may lack the creativity and objectivity of outside agencies, in-house services must please only one master and can immerse themselves in the advertiser's projects. Moreover, house agencies may know more about product intricacies and subtleties and offer economies over outside agencies. Again, though, in-house help may lack expertise in foreign advertising, and that can prove far more costly in the long run.

CREATIVE STRATEGIES IN INTERNATIONAL ADVERTISING

As we have discussed throughout this text, advertisers set a creative strategy based on the mix of product concept, target audience, communications media, and advertising message. The same holds true in international advertising, except that advertisers often use different creative strategies in foreign markets than they would in the United States and Canada. There are several reasons for this:

☐ Influenced by their own particular environment, foreign markets reflect their local economy, social system, political structure, and degree of technological advancement. Therefore, the advertiser's *target audiences* may be different, too.

☐ The media the advertiser uses in domestic markets may not be available, or as effective and economical, in foreign markets. Therefore, the company may need to alter its *media strategy*.

☐ Foreign consumers may not want to buy, or be able to buy, the same products (or product concepts). They may have different motivations and buying habits. Therefore, the advertiser may need to alter the *advertising message* and possibly even the *product concept*.

In this section, we discuss these three Ms of advertising strategy—markets (audiences), media, and messages—and their relationship to international advertising and the products marketed abroad.

Market Considerations

What is the difference between the foreign market for a product and the U.S. market for the same product? The answer is simply *environment*. The environment in France is different from that in Japan. The environment in Brazil is different from that in Saudi Arabia. And, sometimes—as in the case of Switzerland—environments even vary widely within a single country.

Many countries have more than one official language. Canada and Norway have two; Belgium, three; and Switzerland, four. Canadians may be used to this situation, as shown by the ads in Exhibit 19-9 (p. 684), but it presents an immediate problem to the U.S. advertiser.

As in domestic markets, the advertiser who wants to communicate with foreign consumers must consider the environments that influence people's attitudes, tastes, and the way in which they think, speak, and feel. These are the social environments (including language) and the economic, technological, and political environments. We consider each of these briefly.

Social Environments

In the United States and Canada, our social environment is based on our family background; our language, education, and religion; the friends we associate with; and our lifestyle. Similarly, the social environments in Italy, Indonesia, and Upper Volta are based on language, culture, literacy rate, religion, and lifestyle.

In North America, advertising encourages and coaxes us to keep our mouth clean, our breath fresh, and our teeth scrubbed. On the other hand, in some southern European countries, it is considered vain and improper to

(continued on p. 684)

PORTFOLIO OF INTERNATIONAL ADVERTISING

A. This ad was part of an unusual campaign that used the names of well-known Austrians to help promote greater tolerance toward foreigners. The headline asks: "Where would we be without Busek?" Erhard Busek is the Austrian Minister of Science; Branca Busek is the nurse holding the babies. The tag line proclaims: "Vienna is home. For all of us."

B. Leo Burnett, Bangkok, created this fanciful motor oil ad that proves that it really pays to understand local idioms. The headline reads: "One of 108 ways to use dead motorbikes." "108 ways" is a Thai expression meaning "many ways."

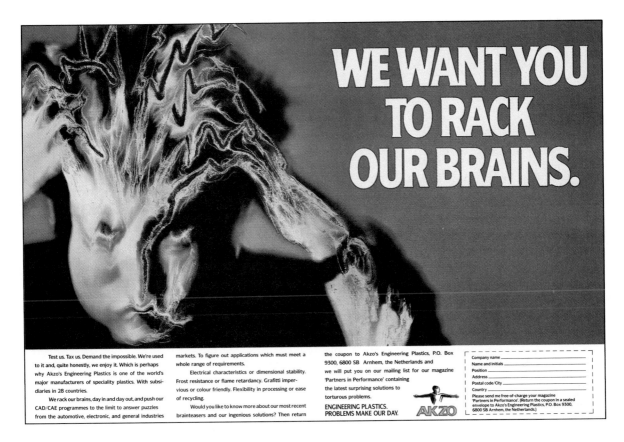

WE WANT YOU TO RACK OUR BRAINS.

Test us. Tax us. Demand the impossible. We're used to it and, quite honestly, we enjoy it. Which is perhaps why Akzo's Engineering Plastics is one of the world's major manufacturers of speciality plastics. With subsidiaries in 28 countries.

We rack our brains, day in and day out, and push our CAD/CAE programmes to the limit to answer puzzles from the automotive, electronic, and general industries markets. To figure out applications which must meet a whole range of requirements.

Electrical characteristics or dimensional stability. Frost resistance or flame retardancy. Grafitti impervious or colour friendly. Flexibility in processing or ease of recycling.

Would you like to know more about our most recent brainteasers and our ingenious solutions? Then return the coupon to Akzo's Engineering Plastics, P.O. Box 9300, 6800 SB Arnhem, the Netherlands and we will put you on our mailing list for our magazine 'Partners in Performance' containing the latest surprising solutions to torturous problems.

**ENGINEERING PLASTICS.
PROBLEMS MAKE OUR DAY.**   AKZO

Company name _____
Name and initials _____
Position _____
Address _____
Postal code/City _____
Country _____
Please send me free-of-charge your magazine 'Partners in Performance'. (Return the coupon in a sealed envelope to Akzo's Engineering Plastics, P.O. Box 9300, 6800 SB Arnhem, the Netherlands.)

C. No, this isn't a Post-Impressionist painting; it's a trade ad for a specialty plastics manufacturer in the Netherlands. The photographer, Ralph Steadman, is also an artist known for his unique illustrations. Here, his photographic technique gives the headline a novel interpretation.

D. This ad's artful layout creates a setting of simple elegance and good taste. And the copy—a mix of French and German—impeccably complements the imagery by being short, sweet, and direct: "Beautiful moments" [from] "Rosalp. The cream of butter."

de bons moments

Rosalp

Rosalp

Die Butter aus feinstem Süssrahm

No matter what the job is, we always work from the same blueprint.

The document pictured here is the starting point for every job we undertake.

And what it says, in a nutshell, is that your home renovation will be carried out to your satisfaction or Sears will fix it. Simple as that. No qualifiers. No escape clauses.

If you're not happy, we fix it. You've got it in writing.

You've got it in writing for roofing, siding, central heating and air conditioning – in short, for any installed home improvement that Sears offers.

So give us a call. We'll come to your home and provide a free, written estimate, and if you like, we can arrange financing with no down payment on approved credit.

So whether you're considering the services mentioned above, or things like kitchen remodelling or replacement windows and entry doors, there's no safer way to do it than with Sears Guaranteed Home Improvements.

Because starting a job is always the first step in finishing it right.

Sears Guaranteed Home Improvements
Someone you know

Quel que soit le projet de rénovation, nous partons toujours des mêmes plans.

Le document représenté ici est le fondement de tous les travaux que nous entreprenons.

Il explique que vous serez entièrement satisfait de vos rénovations ou Sears corrigera le problème. Rien de plus simple. Pas de déterminatifs, ni d'échappatoire.

Si vous êtes mécontent de quelque chose, nous rectifions la situation.

C'est écrit noir sur blanc.

Cette promesse s'applique aux toitures, aux revêtements extérieurs, aux systèmes de chauffage central et aux appareils de climatisation – en somme à tous les travaux de rénovation domiciliaire offerts par Sears.

N'hésitez pas à nous appeler. Nous irons chez-vous gratuitement pour préparer un devis et vous le remettre par écrit. Nous pourrons aussi arranger le financement des travaux sans aucun acompte de votre part, sous réserve d'une approbation de crédit.

Que vous considériez les services mentionnés ci-dessus ou des projets comme la modernisation d'une cuisine ou le remplacement de portes et fenêtres, les produits de rénovation garantis par Sears sont le moyen le plus sûr de les réaliser.

En effet, quand on part du bon pied avec un projet, il a de meilleures chances de bien finir.

Produits de rénovation garantis par Sears
Où l'on se sent en confiance

EXHIBIT 19-9

These two Canadian ads for Sears home improvements use the same creative concept and say approximately the same thing.

overindulge in the use of toiletries. Consumers in the Netherlands and United Kingdom use three times as much toothpaste as those in Spain and Greece. To communicate effectively with Spanish consumers, who view toothpaste as a cosmetic product, advertisers use chic creative executions rather than dry, therapeutic pitches.[10]

Economic Environments

The economic environment comprises several things: the country's standard of living, wealth and its distribution, the amount of business transacted, principal occupations, and people's material possessions. In countries where people earn less money, the demand for expensive products is low. In relatively poor countries, the creative strategy for automobile advertisers might be to target the small group of wealthy, upper-class consumers. In a country with a large middle class, the advertiser would be better off mass marketing the car and positioning it as a middle-class product.

Technological Environments

The degree to which a country has developed its technology affects its economic and social conditions. It also affects the prospects for advertisers of certain goods and services. For example, countries that don't manufacture computers might not be good markets for components such as disk drives and microprocessors. On the other hand, advertisers of low-priced, imported computers might do very well there.

Political Environments

Some foreign governments exert far greater control over their citizens and businesses than the U.S. government does. For example, until fairly recently, there was virtually no market for American-made products in many Eastern bloc countries or in China. They simply weren't allowed. Political control often extends to which products companies may advertise and sell, which media they may use, and what they may say in commercials.

The political environment affects media availability, as well. For example, the fall of communism in the Eastern bloc spurred the introduction of a Hungarian edition of *Playboy;* distribution of *The Wall Street Journal/Europe* in Hungary, Poland, and Yugoslavia; and sales of *USA Today International* in Hungary and in Poland.[12] Eastern Europeans, hungry for news from the West, provide a motivated market for these types of publications, examples of which are shown in Exhibit 19-10.

Meanwhile, in the European Community (EC), the so-called 1992 initiative has fostered a unified system of pan-European trade, finance, labor, and regulatory codes. Barriers to the flow of people, goods, and money within the EC have gradually fallen, making it easier than ever for advertisers to coordinate pan-European ad campaigns. U.S. advertisers are well aware of the opportunity the initiative represents: A barrier-free EC means a $4 trillion market comprising 320 million consumers.

To better reach the changing European market, IBM started pan-European image advertising in the 1980s and followed up with its first pan-European product ad campaign in 1991. "The more Europe becomes integrated, the more important it is to have really consistent brands and advertising throughout the European Community," says Felix Bjorklund, IBM's European communications vice president. The pan-European approach has also saved IBM money. By eliminating duplicate creative and production costs—only the language of the voice-overs in the pan-European product ads varied—the company saved $2 million.[12]

EXHIBIT 19-10

The Wall Street Journal/Europe and *USA Today International* give advertisers new opportunities for reaching the European market. These newspapers also publish Asian editions.

The Importance of Marketing Research

As in the domestic market, companies conduct marketing research in international markets to understand the advertising environment and make better advertising decisions. Unfortunately, the research skills available in some developing countries don't compare with those found in industrialized countries such as the United States, Canada, and Japan. Some secondary research statistics may be available, but they may also be out-of-date or invalid. When evaluating secondary data developed outside their firm, advertising managers should ask the following questions:

☐ Who collected these data and why?
☐ What research techniques did they use?
☐ Would the data source have any reason to bias the data?
☐ When were the data collected?

It may be difficult to answer these questions, but with or without the answers, the international advertising manager should exercise caution when presented with "facts" about foreign markets.

Primary research conducted overseas is often more expensive than domestic research. But the advertiser planning a worldwide or even a regional foreign campaign must know if the message will be viable in the individual markets. Companies that ignore a society's particular "design for living" risk the failure of their entire international marketing effort.[13]

Examples of mistakes made because of inadequate (or no) research abound. Pepsodent failed in Southeast Asia because it promised white teeth to people who considered black or yellow teeth symbols of prestige. Maxwell House advertised its product as the "great American coffee" in Germany until General Foods discovered that Germans have little respect for U.S. coffee. Germans were also unresponsive to ads for Imperial margarine in which crowns miraculously appeared on consumers' heads, because Germans pride themselves on their democracy and are offended by references to monarchy.

Advertisers need more than just factual information about a particular country's culture. They need to understand and appreciate the special nuances of cultural traits and habits—difficult to do without living in a country and speaking its language. Thus, the international advertiser consults with experienced, bilingual nationals with marketing backgrounds—and conducts primary research when necessary.

Mattel Toys International learned the value of primary research the hard way. For years, Mattel tried unsuccessfully to market the Barbie Doll in Japan. The company finally granted the manufacturing license to a Japanese company, Takara. Takara did its own research and found that most Japanese girls and their parents thought Barbie's breasts were too big and her legs too long. Takara modified the doll accordingly, changed the blue eyes to brown, and sold 2 million dolls in two years.

Conducting original research, though, can be fraught with problems. First, the researcher must operate in the language of the country under study. But translating questionnaires can be very tricky. Second, reliable customer information depends on people's willingness and ability to give researchers accurate information about their lives, opinions, and attitudes. In many cultures, however, people view strangers suspiciously and wish to keep their personal lives private. For example, U.S. companies have learned that mail surveys and telephone interviews simply don't work in Japan the way they do in the United States, and that in many cases the personal interview (an expensive and time-consuming technique) is the most fruitful research method.[14] But even with the interview method, Japanese respondents invariably answer all yes or no questions with *hai* (meaning yes). They mean, "Yes, I heard the question." When asked to amplify, the person may go on to give a negative answer to the question.

Local conditions may further interfere with data collection. Many Latin American countries tolerate tax evasion, for example, and interviewers aren't likely to get accurate information about income or even major appliance ownership from research respondents in those countries. In fact, some respondents in the region have mistaken interviewers for tax collectors and treated them accordingly.[15]

Despite these problems, advertisers should realize the importance of continuous research. Competent research personnel are available in all the developed countries, and in most developing nations research assistance is available through local offices of major international research firms.

Media Considerations

U.S. advertisers often adapt quickly to foreign styles of advertising, but they don't take so readily to foreign media. In the United States, if you want to

Countries vary in the types of advertising media available. A familiar sight in Paris, for example, is the advertising kiosk.

promote a popular soft drink as a youthful, fun refresher, you use television. In several European countries and many countries of Asia, South America, and Africa, you cannot. Governments around the world own and control most broadcast media, and many do not permit commercials. Others may limit advertising to a certain number of minutes per hour or per day.

In countries that do allow television advertising, advertisers may have another problem. How many people own television sets, and who are they? In Europe, the vast majority of the population now owns TVs. But in less-developed nations, only upper-income consumers have them—and thus a different media mix is called for.

One way to develop an international media plan is to formulate individual national plans first, based on market research about the reach and targeting that various media in the country provide. By fitting together the multiple national plans, the advertising manager can coordinate an international media plan. That's tougher than it sounds, though, because reliable information about media is not so available overseas as in the United States and Canada. Circulation figures are not necessarily audited, audience demographics may be sketchy, and in countries where rate negotiation prevails, even ad rates may not be what they seem.[16]

Because of the media variations in each country, even global advertisers may entrust national media plans to in-country media specialists rather than run the risk of faulty, centralized media planning.

Types of Media Available

Virtually every country has radio, television, newspapers, magazines, outdoor, and direct mail. The cinema is a very popular medium in many countries, as are other specialty media that do not exist in the United States or are not widely used, such as the advertising kiosk shown in Exhibit 19-11. Generally, the foreign advertiser's media choices are either international or local, depending on the medium's audience.

International/Global Media Several large U.S. publishers, including Time, McGraw-Hill, and Scientific American, circulate international editions of their magazines abroad. Likewise, the *International Herald Tribune, The Wall Street Journal,* and London's *Financial Times* are widely read in Europe, the Middle East, and Asia. Because well-educated, upper-income consumers tend to read these publications, which are typically printed in English, they are the closest things to global media for reaching this audience. The *Reader's Digest,* no doubt the oldest global mass-audience medium, is distributed in 170 foreign countries. However, because the Reader's Digest Association prints the magazine in local languages and tailors it to each country, advertisers sometimes view it more as a local medium.

Recently, the number of international business, trade, or specialty publications has grown. For example, *European Business* is published in Switzerland in English but is distributed throughout Europe. *Electronic Product News,* published in Belgium, is likewise printed in English and distributed throughout Europe.

Political changes in the Soviet Union and the Eastern bloc have spurred many new trade publications within those countries. The magazines are often produced locally in conjunction with foreign publishers. For example, in 1990, McGraw-Hill, which has long published an international edition of *Business Week,* launched Russian-language editions of *Aviation Week & Space*

Technology and *Business Week* plus a Hungarian-language edition of the latter. Also in 1990, International Data Group launched several trade publications in the Soviet Union and Eastern bloc countries; titles include *PC World USSR* and *Computerworld Poland.*[17]

In the past, international media consisted mainly of newspapers and magazines. However, in recent years, the Superchannel and Sky Channel pan-European satellite-to-cable broadcast options have emerged to supplement print media. And for decades, the Voice of America (VOA) and Radio Luxembourg have served as examples of international broadcast media. To help correct the U.S. trade deficit, the VOA now carries spots for U.S. products.

Local Media Because effective international media are scarce, international advertisers often must use local media in the countries where they do business. Foreign media cater to their own local national audience. This, of course, requires the advertiser to produce ads in the language(s) of each country. In countries with more than one official language, some magazines produce two separate editions.

Spillover Media Local media that a substantial number of consumers in a neighboring country inadvertently receive are called **spillover media.** For example, French media may spill over into Belgium and Switzerland. Media also tend to spill over into countries lacking indigenous-language publications, particularly specialty publications. English and German media enjoy a large circulation in Scandinavian countries. French and English media are popular in Spain, Italy, North Africa, and various Middle Eastern countries. And a wide variety of foreign language media spill into the Eastern bloc countries.

According to a study by the Foote, Cone & Belding advertising agency, spillover media pose a threat for the multinational advertiser because they expose readers to multiple ad campaigns. If the advertiser runs both international and local campaigns for the same products, discrepancies in product positioning, pricing, or advertising messages could confuse potential buyers. With spillover media becoming more common, the advertiser's local subsidiaries or distributors need to coordinate local and international ad campaigns to preclude such confusion. On the positive side, spillover media offer potential cost savings through regional campaigns.

Within the broad categories of international, foreign, and spillover media are the media we recognize from the United States—radio, magazines, television, newspapers, and so on. The difference lies not so much in the media's availability as in their coverage and economics.

Media Coverage

U.S. and foreign advertisers may reach the broad U.S. middle class using any number of media, but this is not necessarily true in many foreign markets. For one thing, lower literacy rates and education levels in some countries restrict the coverage of mass press media. Where income levels are low, television ownership is similarly low. These factors lead to a natural segmentation of the market by the selective coverage of the various media.

In countries dominated by national newspapers, circulation may be primarily limited to upper-class, well-educated people. On the other hand, both Pepsi and Coke have reached lower-income markets successfully through radio, which enjoys almost universal ownership. Moreover, in some developing countries, many stores and bars blare their radios into the street for passersby to hear. Auto manufacturers successfully use television and magazine advertising to reach the upper class. And cinema advertising can reach whole urban populations where TV ownership is low, because motion picture attendance in such countries is still very high. The advertiser may exercise some selectivity with cinema advertising by restricting the commercials to upper-income areas or to lower-class theaters, depending on the target market. The Checklist for International Media Planning outlines some basic considerations for media buyers entering the international arena.

Economics of Foreign Media

As we pointed out in Chapter 1, a major purpose of advertising is to communicate with customers less expensively than through the use of personal selling. In some underdeveloped countries, however, it may actually be cheaper to send people around with baskets of samples periodically. For mass marketers selling in the United States, this kind of personal contact is impossible.

In North America, legislation and labor costs have inhibited the growth of outdoor advertising. In most foreign markets, though, outdoor enjoys far greater coverage, because it costs less to have people paint the signs, and there is often less government restriction about billboard placement. In Mexico, for example, almost every street seems to have a "Disfrute Coca-Cola" sign. In Nigeria, billboards with the slogan "Guiness gives you power" next to the bulging biceps of an African arm kept Guiness stout ale the best seller for many years—despite an 80 percent illiteracy rate. Exhibit 19-12 shows an outdoor ad for the Wiener Festwochen, an annual Viennese arts festival.

In addition to availability, another factor that inhibits the growth of TV is its cost. The cost factor, however, causes some countries to consider opening TV to commercial use to help pay for it. Advertisers may expect, therefore, that as more countries allow commercial broadcasts, and as international satellite channels gain a bigger foothold, TV advertising will proliferate. On the other hand, as labor rates increase, advertisers may see fewer print and outdoor media options in foreign markets. Likewise, the use of personal selling and sales promotion could decrease as those costs rise.

Message Considerations

Developing the message strategy for foreign markets involves many considerations. Consider, for example, the efforts of Galeries Lafayette to market fake furs in the United States. The company took out a two-page ad in *Elle* magazine and pitched the product as it would have in France: as an upmarket, haute couture garment. But U.S. consumers don't think of fake furs in those terms, and the company did not sell much in the United States.[18]

As this example suggests, advertisers must base their appeals on the foreign consumer's purchasing abilities, habits, and motivations. Language is another important factor to consider, as are national advertising regulations. We consider these factors next.

Checklist for International Media Planning

Basic Considerations (Who Does What?)

□ *What is the client's policy regarding supervision and placement of advertising?* Make sure you know when, where, and to what degree client and/or client branch offices abroad want to get involved.

□ *Which client office is in charge of the campaign?* North American headquarters or local office or both? Who else has to be consulted? In what areas (creative or media selection and so forth)?

□ *Is there a predetermined media mix to be used?* Are there any "must" media? Can international as well as foreign media be used?

□ *Who arranges for translation of copy if foreign media are to be used?*

 □ Client headquarters in North America.

 □ Client office in foreign country.

 □ Agency headquarters in North America.

 □ Foreign media rep in North America.

 □ Other.

□ *Who approves translated copy?*

□ *Who checks on acceptability of ad copy in foreign country?* Certain ads, especially those of financial character, sometimes need special approval by foreign government authorities.

□ *What is the advertising placement procedure?*

 □ From agency branch office in foreign country, after consultation with agency headquarters, directly to foreign media.

 □ From North American agency to American-based foreign media rep to foreign media.

 □ From North American agency to American-based international media.

 □ From North American agency to affiliated agency abroad to foreign media.

 □ Other.

□ *What are the pros and cons of each of these approaches?* Is a commission split with foreign agency branch or affiliate office necessary or can campaign be equally well placed directly from North America? Does the client save money by placing from North America to save certain ad taxes (in Belgium and the Netherlands, for instance)? Some publications quote local rates and higher U.S. dollar rates. In those instances, local ad placement results in a lower rate. Therefore, in what currency does client want to pay?

□ *Who receives checking copies?*

□ *Will advance payment be made to avoid currency fluctuation possibilities?* What will the finance folks in the back room have to say about your choice?

□ *Who bills whom?* What currency is used? Who approves payment?

Budget Considerations

□ *Is budget predetermined by client?*

□ *Is budget based on local branch or distributor recommendation?*

□ *Is budget based on recommended media schedule of agency?*

□ *Is budget based on relationship to sales in the foreign markets?*

□ *What is the budget period?*

In almost every foreign country, outdoor advertising continues to grow in popularity. This poster, done for an annual arts festival in Vienna, boasts a visual that's distinctive enough to have stopping power and a headline that communicates clearly and instantly.

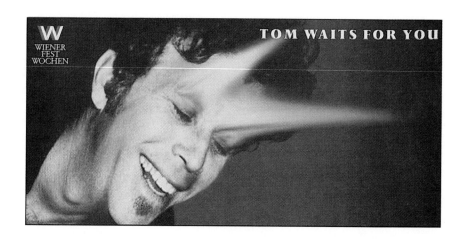

□ *What is the budget breakdown for media,* including ad taxes, sales promotion, translation, production and research costs?

□ *What are the tie-ins with local distributors, if any?*

Market Considerations

□ *What is your geographical target area?*
  □ Africa and Middle East.
  □ Asia, including Australasia.
  □ Europe, including U.S.S.R.
  □ Latin America.
  □ North America.
□ *What are the major market factors in these areas?*
  □ Local competition.
  □ GNP growth over past four years and expected future growth.
  □ Relationship of country's imports to total GNP in percent.
  □ Membership of country in a common market or free trade association.
  □ Literacy rate.
  □ Attitude toward North American products or services.
  □ Social and religious customs.
□ *What is your basic target audience?*
  □ Management executives across the board in business and industry.
  □ Managers and buyers in certain businesses.
  □ Military and government officials.
  □ Consumers; potential buyers of foreign market goods.

Media Considerations

□ *Availability of media to cover market:* Are the desired media available in the particular area (e.g., business magazines, news magazines, trade and professional magazines, women's magazines, business and financial newspapers, TV, radio)?

□ *Foreign media and/or international media:* Should the campaign be in the press and language of a particular country, or should it be a combination of the two types?

□ *What media does the competition use?*

□ *Does medium fit?*
  □ Optimum audience quality and quantity.
  □ Desired image, editorial content, and design.
  □ Suitable paper and color availability.
  □ Justifiable rates and CPM (do not forget taxes on advertising, which can vary by medium).
  □ Discount availability.
  □ Type of circulation audit.
  □ Availability of special issues or editorial tie-ins.

□ *What are the closing dates at North American rep and at the publication headquarters abroad?*

□ *What is the agency commission* (when placed locally abroad at the agency, commission is sometimes less than when placed in North America)?

□ *For how long are contracted rates protected?*

□ *Does the publication have a North American representative* to help with media evaluation and actual advertising placement?

Purchasing Characteristics in Foreign Markets

Advertising messages—foreign or domestic—must address the market that can afford to buy the product. In low-income countries where only the wealthy can afford to buy homes, housing ads that stress luxury qualities should draw an interested audience. But in a market with many financially pressed middle-class consumers, messages stressing the housing's functional or economical aspects would probably be more effective.

How and *when* consumers normally make purchases are also important considerations. Most important, though, is *who* makes the buying decision. In North America and Europe, for instance, spouses usually exercise about the same control over purchasing decisions. In Latin American countries, though, the husband often controls major decisions. In the United States, even children may have a strong influence (especially in the choice of breakfast cereals, snacks, toothpastes, and fast-food chains), but this is much less common in foreign markets.

These differences vary from country to country and product to product, and advertisers must consider the issues carefully before creating ads or buying media. One company introduced a new detergent in Holland by advertising solely in one magazine for children under 10. The company offered a miniature sports car as an in-pack premium. The introduction's success showed, in this case at least, that children did strongly influence the buying decision.

Consumer Motives and Appeals

Advertisers also need to understand the personal motivations in each market. Selling deodorant in Japan is difficult because most Japanese don't think they have body odor—and they don't, thanks to their low-protein diet. A commercial for Feel Free deodorant, therefore, positioned the product as youthful, chic, and convenient rather than as an odor fighter. The advertiser accomplished this by showing a young girl, on her way out for a date, suddenly remembering her deodorant and using it quickly before leaving.

National pride is another important consideration for foreign advertisers. Some lower-income, less-developed nations respect and desire U.S. products while fearing and resenting U.S. influence and power. U.S. advertisers should toe a careful line to avoid aggravating this national sensitivity in certain foreign markets.

Another important consideration is social roles. In Saudi Arabia, for example, husbands traditionally make the purchasing decision for durable goods such as cameras and cars (women don't drive), and women decide which food, toiletries, clothing, and household furnishings to buy. Shopping is a social affair, and Saudi Arabians almost always shop in groups. Thus, an ad campaign that stresses peer approval might be more appropriate than one emphasizing individual growth or self-indulgence.[19]

Differences in taste and attitude may not be so apparent or important in business-to-business advertising as in consumer advertising. Businesspeople's problems are fairly universal, as are the advertising appeals to solve them. The difference in approach comes down to the region's economics. The ad in Exhibit 19-13, created by the London office of BBDO, illustrates the universality of industrial advertising messages.

The Question of Language and Campaign Transfer

In Western Europe, people speak at least 15 different languages and more than twice as many dialects. This presents a problem of potentially enormous magnitude to North American advertisers entering Europe. A similar problem exists in Asia, to a lesser extent in South America, and to an even greater extent in Africa.

As we noted earlier in this chapter, international advertisers have debated the transferability of campaigns for years. One side believes it's too expensive to create a unique campaign for each national group. They feel it is acceptable to simply translate one campaign into the necessary languages, as shown in Exhibit 19-14. Other advertisers believe that this approach never works well and that the only way to ensure success is to create a special campaign for each market. Still others feel both solutions are uneconomical and unnecessary. They simply run their ads in English worldwide.

EXHIBIT 19-13

Industrial advertising generally addresses the same problems worldwide, but attention must still be paid to subtle differences in the local economy. For instance, this British ad emphasizes the durability of slate roofing because the English value longevity over initial cost.

EXHIBIT 19-14

In global advertising, a single basic ad is used and is translated into the languages of the various countries where it will be run. This global campaign for Visa ran simultaneously in dozens of countries.

None of these solutions is always correct. Advertisers probably need not create different campaigns for every country. Moreover, the hard fact of life is that advertisers must weigh the economics of various promotional strategies against anticipated promotional objectives. The advertiser must look at each situation individually. Identifying the target audience and knowing the market's cultural preferences are basic, and so is the issue of translation.

Classic examples of mistranslations and faulty word choices abound in international advertising. Braniff once advertised the comfortable leather seats on its jets in Spanish terms that readers understood as an invitation to sit naked. And a faulty Spanish translation for an ad for Frank Perdue chicken read, "It takes a sexually excited man to make a chick affectionate."[20]

EXHIBIT 19-15   Advertising Regulations in Selected Countries of Western Europe

| Country | General regulations | | Limitations on |
	Comparative advertising	Advertising to children	Alcoholic beverages
Austria	Banned if denigrating.	Direct appeal forbidden.	None.
Belgium	Banned if denigrating.	Banned by law in all media.	Ads for absinthe drinks banned.
Denmark	Minor restrictions.	None.	None.
Finland	None.	None.	Banned on TV.
France	Banned.	Prebroadcast screening of commercials.	Hard liquor banned on all media, others on radio and TV.
Germany	Banned.	Voluntary for TV and radio.	Voluntary limits by industry.
Italy	Direct comparisons banned; indirect OK if substantiated.	Cannot show children eating.	Some restrictions on TV ads.
Netherlands	OK if comparison is fair, detailed.	Voluntary restraints.	Voluntary restraints on TV and radio.
Sweden	Banned if denigrating.	Ban on showing children in danger.	Voluntary control on ads for wine and hard liquor.
Switzerland	None.	None.	Banned on all media.
United Kingdom	Banned if denigrating.	Voluntary rules designed to protect children.	No commercials before 9 P.M.

In other cases, a poorly chosen or badly translated product name has undercut advertising credibility in foreign markets. Ford, for example, had to change the name of a product after initially introducing it in Brazil under its U.S. name, Pinto. In Portuguese, Pinto means "small male appendage." Even Coke has endured linguistic problems. Its product name was once widely translated into Chinese characters that sounded like "Coca-Cola" but meant "bite the wax tadpole."[21]

People in the United States, Canada, England, Australia, and South Africa all speak English, but with wide variations in vocabulary, word usage, and syntax. Similarly, the French spoken in France, Canada, Vietnam, and Belgium may be as different as the English spoken by a British aristocrat and a Tennessee mountaineer. Language variations exist even within single countries. For example, the Japanese use five lingual "gears," ranging from haughty to servile, depending on the speaker's and the listener's respective stations in life. Japanese translators must know when to change gears.

Advertisers in general must follow some basic rules in using translators.

☐ The translator must be an effective copywriter. Just because the translator speaks a foreign language doesn't mean he or she can write advertising

specific products		Media regulations	
Tobacco	Drugs and medicine	Restricted or banned media	Limitations on commercials
Voluntary ban on TV ads.	Ads need approval of government.	None.	Maximum length of 30 seconds.
Cigarette ads banned in cinema, TV, and radio.	Banned by law in all general media.	No commercial TV or radio.	Not applicable.
Voluntary control over cigarette ads.	Banned in all general media.	No commercial TV or radio.	Not applicable.
Banned on TV and media directed at youth.	Voluntary control over copy.	No domestic radio.	No television commercials on certain days.
Cigarettes banned on TV and radio.	Copy clearance needed.	Total receipts from one advertiser limited to 8 percent of total TV.	Blocks, or groups, of commercials only (no spots).
Banned on TV and radio.	Banned in all media.	None.	TV commercials between 6 and 8 P.M., none on Sunday.
All tobacco banned in all media.	Copy clearance needed.	None.	Sold in broadcast packages.
Voluntary restraints on TV and radio.	None.	None.	No more than two TV commercials per week per product.
Banned in all media.	Prescription drug ads banned.	No commercial TV or radio.	Not applicable.
Banned in all media.	Banned in all media.	No commercial radio.	No more than two TV commercials per week per product.
Cigarette ads banned on TV and radio.	Voluntary control.	None on major media.	None.

copy. The logic of this should be clear: All of us can speak English, yet relatively few of us are good writers, and even fewer are good copywriters. Still, advertisers too often fall into the trap of simply having a translation service rewrite their ads in the foreign language. That's rarely a good solution.

☐ The translator must understand the product, its features, and its market. It is always better to use a translator who is a product or market specialist rather than a generalist.

☐ Translators should translate into their native tongue, and they should live in the country where the ad will appear. Only in this way can the advertiser be sure the translator has a current understanding of the country's social attitudes, culture, and idiomatic use of the language.

☐ The advertiser should give the translator easily translatable English copy. Double meanings and idiomatic expressions, which make English such an interesting language for advertising, usually don't translate well. They only make the translator's job more difficult.

Finally, remember the Italian proverb, *Tradutori, traditori* ("Translators are traitors"). There is perhaps no greater insult to a national market than to misuse its language. The translation must be accurate, and it must also be good copy.

English is rapidly becoming the universal language for corporate advertising campaigns directed to international businesspeople. However, some industrial firms, completely baffled by the translation problem, have printed their technical literature and brochures in English. This is a poor solution that may incite nationalistic feelings against the company. Worse yet, this approach automatically limits a product's use to people who read and understand technical English. It also greatly increases the probability of misunderstanding and, thus, additional ill will toward the company.

Legal Restraints on International Advertisers

International advertisers' creative messages, including what the ads say, show, or do, are at the mercy of foreign governments and cultures. Many countries strongly regulate advertising claims and prohibit superlatives. In Germany, for example, advertisers may use only scientifically provable superlatives. McCann-Erickson once tried to translate the old Coca-Cola slogan, "Refreshes you best," into foreign languages. Realizing the slogan couldn't be used in Germany, the agency substituted "Das erfrischt richtig," or "Refreshes you right," in that market.

Many European countries also bar two-for-one offers, coupons, premiums, one-cent sales, box-top gimmicks, free tie-in offers, and the like. And in Europe, companies may only advertise price cuts during "official sales periods" or risk extremely high fines. Further, advertisers typically need government approval before publishing a sale ad in Europe. Exhibit 19-15 lists the regulations some Western European countries impose on advertising.

Meanwhile, in Saudi Arabia, companies may not advertise alcohol or pork, or even images of pigs, such as stuffed toys and piggy banks. Saudi Arabia also bans pictures of anything sacred. Ads in this country may show only people with Arabic appearance, and no women's faces. Furthermore, the government bans all TV and radio advertising.[23] The only solution to these and the myriad legal problems of international advertising is to retain a good local lawyer who knows advertising law.

Summary

Since the end of World War II, advertising has grown worldwide. As economic conditions and the standard of living have improved in foreign lands, the use of advertising has also increased. However, the status of advertising varies from country to country depending on local attitudes toward promotional activities in general.

The way a company manages its advertising activities in foreign markets depends on its marketing structure and strategy and on the availability of qualified talent. Some companies are organized to market internationally; others. multinationally; and some, globally. Depending on the needs of their international advertising program, these companies may choose to use large U.S. or foreign-based international agencies, local foreign agencies, export agencies, their normal domestic agencies, or even an in-house agency.

In overseas markets, companies often find it necessary to use different creative strategies than they use in their domestic campaigns. For one thing, foreign markets are characterized by different social, economic, technological, and political environments. And in some developing countries, market research may not be so reliable as in North America, which makes it more difficult to understand local customs, culture, and attitudes.

Second, the media in foreign markets are different. Some media may not be available, others may not be as effective, and still others may not be economical.

Third, advertising messages often must be different. They must reflect the purchasing ability, habits, and motivations of the consumer in that foreign market. And usually they must be in the consumer's language.

Finally, advertisers must be ever mindful of foreign cultural and governmental restrictions on what they may or may not say, show, or do in ads. Some restrictions are legal; others are moral and ethical and define the boundaries of good taste.

Questions for Review and Discussion

1. Since the European Community became one united market as of January 1, 1992, why don't all marketers use pan-European ad campaigns?

2. What is the difference between an international firm, a multinational firm, and a global firm? How do these differences affect the way they manage their advertising?

3. What are the pros and cons of the global advertising debate? How would you evaluate each side's position?

4. What kinds of products lend themselves best to global advertising? What kinds are more likely to require individual variations?

5. What factors differentiate U.S. markets from foreign markets?

6. How could a country's political environment affect media planning?

7. What do you suppose is the primary advertising medium in most foreign countries? Why?

8. What major factors influence the creation of advertising messages in foreign markets?

9. What are "official sales periods," and why are they important?

10. Overall, what is the basic difference between advertising in the United States or Canada and advertising in overseas markets?

MARKETING PLAN OUTLINE

DATE:

COMPANY NAME:

TITLE OR PRODUCT:

Encapsulation, for executive review, of entire marketing plan in no more than two or three pages.

I. Executive Summary

    A. Summary of situation analysis
    B. Summary of marketing objectives
    C. Summary of marketing strategies
    D. Budget summary

Complete statement of where the organization is today and how it got there.

What business the organization is in and characteristics of the industry as a whole. Information available from industry trade publications, trade association newsletters, consumer business press, Department of Commerce publications.

II. Situation Analysis

    A. The industry
       1. Definition of industry and company business
       2. History of industry
         a. Technological advances
         b. Trends
       3. Growth patterns within industry
         a. Demand curve
         b. Per capita consumption
         c. Growth potential
       4. Characteristics of industry
         a. Distribution patterns and traditional channels
         b. Regulation and control within industry
         c. Typical promotional activity
         d. Geographical characteristics
         e. Profit patterns

All relevant information on the company and its capabilities, opportunities, and/or problems. Information may be found in annual reports, sales records, warranty card records, customer correspondence, sales staff reports.

    B. The company
       1. Brief history
       2. Scope of business
       3. Current size, growth, profitability
       4. Reputation
       5. Competence in various areas
         a. Strengths
         b. Weaknesses

Complete description and all relevant information on the product/service mix, sales, and the strengths and weaknesses therein. See sales literature, sales reports, dealer correspondence, and so on.

C. The product/service
  1. The product story
    a. Development and history
    b. Stage of product life cycle
      (1) Introduction
      (2) Growth
      (3) Maturity
      (4) Decline
    c. Quality factors
    d. Design considerations
    e. Goods classification
      (1) Consumer or industrial good
      (2) Durable or nondurable good or service
      (3) Convenience, shopping, or specialty good
      (4) Package good, hard good, soft good, service
    f. Packaging
    g. Price structure
    h. Uses
      (1) Primary
      (2) Secondary
      (3) Potential
    i. Image and reputation
    j. Product/service strengths
    k. Product/service weaknesses
  2. Product sales features
    a. Differentiating factors
      (1) Perceptible, imperceptible, or induced
      (2) Exclusive or nonexclusive
    b. Position in mind of customer
    c. Advantages and disadvantages (customer perception)
  3. Product research and development
    a. Technological breakthroughs
    b. Improvements planned
    c. Technical or service problems
  4. Sales history
    a. Sales and cost of sales
      (1) By product/service
      (2) By model
      (3) By territory
      (4) By market
    b. Profit history for same factors
  5. Share of market
    a. Industry sales by market
    b. Market share in dollars and units
    c. Market potential and trends

All relevant information about the people or organizations that comprise the current and prospective market for the firm's offerings. See market research reports, consumer/business press, trade publications, Census of Manufacturers, trade association reports.

D. The market
  1. Definition and location of market
    a. Identified market segments
      (1) Past
      (2) Potential
    b. Market needs, desires
    c. Characteristics of market
      (1) Geographic
      (2) Demographic

                (3) Psychographic

                (4) Behavioral

           d. Typical buying patterns

                (1) Purchase patterns

                (2) Heavy users/light users

                (3) Frequency of purchase

           e. Buying influences on market

      2. Definition of our customers

           a. Present, past, and future

           b. Characteristics

                (1) Shared characteristics with rest of market

                (2) Characteristics unique to our customers

           c. What they like about us or our product

           d. What they don't like

      3. Consumer appeals

           a. Past advertising appeals

                (1) What has worked

                (2) What has not worked and why

           b. Possible future appeals

      4. Results of research studies about market and customers

E. The competition

      1. Identification of competitors

           a. Primary competitors

           b. Secondary competitors

           c. Product/service descriptions

           d. Growth and size of competitors

           e. Share of market held by competitors

      2. Strengths of competition

           a. Product quality

           b. Sales features

           c. Price, distribution, promotion

      3. Weaknesses of competition

           a. Product features

           b. Consumer attitude

           c. Price, distribution, promotion

      4. Marketing activities of competition

           a. Product positioning

           b. Pricing strategies

           c. Distribution

           d. Sales force

           e. Advertising, publicity

           f. Estimated budgets

F. Distribution strategies

      1. Type of distribution network used

           a. History of development

           b. Trends

      2. Evaluation of how distribution is accomplished

      3. Description and evaluation with channel members

      4. Promotional relationship with channel members

           a. Trade advertising and allowances

           b. Co-op advertising

           c. Use of promotion by dealer or middlemen

           d. Point-of-purchase displays, literature

           e. Dealer incentive programs

Complete information about the competition, the competitive environment, and the opportunities or challenges presented by current or prospective competitors. See SEC Form 10-Ks, consumer/business press articles, *Moody's Industrial Manual,* Standard & Poor's reports, Dun & Bradstreet report, *Thomas Register of American Corporations.*

Complete discussion of how the firm's products/services are distributed and sold, what channels are available, and characteristics of channel members. See dealer and distributor correspondence, sales staff reports, advertising reports, trade publication articles.

Background and rationale for firm's pricing policies and strategies, discussion of alternative options. Study sales reports, channel-member correspondence, customer correspondence, competitive information.

All relevant data concerning the firm's personal sales efforts and effectiveness as well as complete discussion of the firm's use of advertising, public relations, and sales promotion programs. Examine sales reports, advertising reports, articles in *Advertising Age, Marketing Communications,* and so on, in-house data on advertising, sales, and training.

Enumeration of those environmental factors that may be beyond the firm's immediate control but affect the firm's business efforts. See government reports and announcements, consumer/business press, trade association articles.

Recitation of relevant attitudes and directives of management as they pertain to the firm's marketing and advertising efforts. Information available from corporate business plan, management interviews, internal memos and directives.

Enumeration or summary of those problems considered most serious to the firm's marketing success.

Summary of those opportunities which offer the greatest potential for the firm's success.

G. Pricing policies
  1. Price history
    a. Trends
    b. Affordability
    c. Competition
  2. Price objectives and strategies in past
    a. Management attitudes
    b. Buyer attitudes
    c. Channel attitudes
H. Promotion strategies
  1. Past promotion policy
    a. Personal versus nonpersonal selling
      (1) Use of sales force
      (2) Use of advertising, public relations, sales promotion
    b. Successes and failure of past policy
  2. Sales Force
    a. Size
    b. Scope
    c. Ability/training
    d. Cost per sale
  3. Advertising programs
    a. Successes and failures
    b. Strategies, themes, campaigns
    c. Appeals, positionings, and so on
    d. Expenditures
      (1) Past budgets
      (2) Method of allocation
      (3) Competitor budgets
      (4) Trend
I. Environmental factors
  1. Economy
    a. Current economic status
    b. Business outlook and economic forecasts
  2. Political situation
  3. Societal concerns
  4. Technological influences
J. Corporate objectives and strategies
  1. Profitability
    a. Sales revenue
    b. Cost reductions
  2. Return on investment
  3. Stock price
  4. Shareholder equity
  5. Community image
  6. New product development
  7. Technological leadership
  8. Mergers and/or acquisitions
K. Potential marketing problems

L. Potential marketing opportunities

What general and specific needs the firm seeks to satisfy. Determine through study of situation analysis factors and management discussions and interviews.

Organization sales goals defined for whole company or for individual products by target market, by geographic territory, by department, or by some other category. Must be specific and realistic based on study of company capabilities, funding, and objectives.

The method(s) by which the organization plans to achieve the objectives enumerated above.

A general description of the type of marketing strategy the organization intends to employ.

A detailed description of the marketing mix(es) the firm intends to use to achieve its objectives.

The detailed tactical plans for implementing each of the elements of the firm's marketing mix.

III. Marketing Objectives

    A. Market need objectives
        1. Market need-satisfying objectives
        2. Community need-satisfying objectives
        3. Corporate need-satisfying objectives
    B. Sales target objectives
        1. Sales volume
            a. Dollars
            b. Units
            c. Territories
            d. Markets
        2. Share of market
        3. Distribution expansion
        4. Other

IV. Marketing Strategy

    A. General marketing strategy
        1. Positioning strategy
        2. Product differentiation strategy
        3. Price/quality differentiation strategy
    B. Specific market strategies
        1. Target market A
            a. Product
            b. Price
            c. Place
            d. Promotion
                (1) Personal selling
                (2) Advertising
                (3) Sales promotion
                (4) Public relations
        2. Target market B
            a. Product
            b. Price
            c. Place
            d. Promotion
                (1) Personal selling
                (2) Advertising
                (3) Sales promotion
                (4) Public relations

V. Action Programs (Tactics)

    A. Product plans
    B. Pricing plans
    C. Distribution plans
    D. Promotional plans
        1. Sales plan
        2. Advertising plan
        3. Sales promotion plan
        4. Public relations plan

Description of the methods the firm will use to review, evaluate, and control its progress toward the achievement of its marketing objectives.

Determination of the amount of money needed to conduct the marketing effort, the rationale for that budget, and the allocation to various functions.

Details of information, secondary data, or research conducted to develop information discussed in the marketing plan.

VI. Measurement, Review, and Control

    A. Organizational structure
    B. Methodology for review and evaluation

VII. Marketing Budget

    A. Method of allocation
    B. Enumeration of marketing costs by division
      1. New product research
      2. Marketing research
      3. Sales expenses
      4. Advertising, sales promotion, public relations

VIII. Appendixes

    A. Sales reports
    B. Reports of market research studies
    C. Reprints of journal or magazine articles
    D. Other supporting documents

ADVERTISING PLAN OUTLINE

Brief encapsulation, for executive review, of entire advertising plan in no more than two or three pages.

Condensed review of pertinent elements presented in the marketing plan.

DATE:

COMPANY (PRODUCT) NAME:

I. Executive Summary

    A. Premises—summary of information presented in marketing plan
    B. Summary of advertising objectives
    C. Summary of advertising strategy
    D. Budget summary

II. Situation Analysis

    A. Company's (or product's) current marketing situation
        1. Business or industry information
        2. Description of company, product, or service
            a. Stage of product life cycle
            b. Goods classification
            c. Competitive or market positioning
        3. General description of market(s) served
        4. Sales history and share of market
        5. Description of consumer purchase process
        6. Methods of distribution
        7. Pricing strategies employed
        8. Implications of any marketing research
        9. Promotional history
    B. Target market description
        1. Market segments identified
        2. Primary market
        3. Secondary markets
        4. Market characteristics
            a. Geographic
            b. Demographic
            c. Psychographic
            d. Behavioral
    C. Marketing objectives
        1. Generic market objectives
        2. Long- and short-term sales target objectives
    D. Marketing mix for each target market—summarized from marketing plan
        1. Product
        2. Price

3. Place
4. Promotion
E. Intended role of advertising in the promotional mix
F. Miscellaneous information not included above

Analysis and statement of what the advertising is expected to accomplish—see Checklist for Developing Advertising Objectives (Chapter 7).

III. Advertising Objectives

A. Primary or selective demand
B. Direct action or indirect action
C. Objectives stated in terms of advertising pyramid
  1. Awareness
  2. Comprehension
  3. Conviction
  4. Desire
  5. Action
  6. Repurchase reinforcement
D. Quantified expression of objectives
  1. Specific quantities or percentages
  2. Length of time for achievement of objectives
  3. Other possible measurements
    a. Inquiries
    b. Increased order size
    c. Morale building
    d. Other

Intended blend of the creative mix for the company as a whole, for each product, or for each target market.

IV. Advertising (Creative) Strategy

A. Product concept—how the advertising will present the product in terms of:
  1. Product or market positioning
  2. Product differentiation
  3. Life cycle
  4. Classification, packaging, branding
  5. FCB Grid purchase-decision position
    a. High/low involvement
    b. Rational/emotional involvement
B. Target audience—the specific people the advertising will address
  1. Detailed description of target audiences
    a. Relationship of target audience to target market
    b. Prospective buying influences
    c. Benefits sought/advertising appeals
    d. Demographics
    e. Psychographics
    f. Behavioristics
  2. Prioritization of target audiences
    a. Primary
    b. Secondary
    c. Supplementary

The strategy for selecting the various media vehicles that will communicate the advertising message to the target audience—see Chapters 12-16.

C. Communications media
  1. Definition of media objectives
    a. Reach
    b. Frequency
    c. Gross rating points
    d. Continuity/flighting/pulsing
  2. Determination of which media reach the target audience best

What the company wants to say and how it wants to say it, verbally and nonverbally—see Chapters 8-11.

        a. Traditional mass media
          (1) Radio
          (2) Television
          (3) Newspapers
          (4) Magazines
          (5) Outdoor
        b. Other media
          (1) Direct mail
          (2) Publicity
        c. Supplemental media
          (1) Trade shows
          (2) Sales promotion devices
          (3) Off-the-wall media
    3. Availability of media relative to purchase patterns
    4. Potential for communication effectiveness
    5. Cost considerations
        a. Size/mechanical considerations of message units
        b. Cost efficiency of media plan against target audiences
        c. Production costs
    6. Relevance to other elements of creative mix
    7. Scope of media plan
    8. Exposure/attention/motivation values of intended media vehicles
D. Advertising message
    1. Copy elements
        a. Advertising appeals
        b. Copy platform
        c. Key consumer benefits
        d. Benefit supports or reinforcements
        e. Product personality or image
    2. Art elements
        a. Visual appeals
          (1) In ads and commercials
          (2) In packaging
          (3) In point-of-purchase and sales materials
         b. Art platform
          (1) Layout
          (2) Design
          (3) Illustration style
    3. Production elements
        a. Mechanical considerations in producing ads
          (1) Color
          (2) Size
          (3) Style
        b. Production values sought
          (1) Typography
          (2) Printing
          (3) Color reproduction
          (4) Photography/illustration
          (5) Paper
          (6) Electronic effects
          (7) Animation
          (8) Film or videotape
          (9) Sound effects
          (10) Music

The amount of money to be allocated to advertising and the intended method of allocation.

V. The Advertising Budget

A. Impact of marketing situation on method of allocation
  1. New or old product
  2. Primary demand curve for product class
  3. Competitive situation
  4. Marketing objectives and strategy
  5. Profit or growth considerations
  6. Relationship of advertising to sales and profits
  7. Empirical experience
B. Method of allocation
  1. Percentage of sales or profit
  2. Share of market
  3. Task method
  4. Unit of sale
  5. Competitive parity

The research techniques that will be used to create the advertising and evaluate its effectiveness—see Chapter 6.

VI. Testing and Evaluation

A. Advertising research conducted
  1. Strategy determination
  2. Concept development
B. Pretesting and posttesting
  1. Elements tested
    a. Markets
    b. Motives
    c. Messages
    d. Media
    e. Budgeting
    f. Scheduling
  2. Methodology
    a. Central location tests
    b. Sales experiments
    c. Physiological testing
    d. Aided recall tests
    e. Unaided recall tests
    f. Attitude tests
    g. Inquiry tests
    h. Sales tests
    i. Other
  3. Cost of testing

CAREER PLANNING IN ADVERTISING

The cliché is old but true: The process of looking for a job is a full-time job in itself. It should not be approached haphazardly. With careful research and planning (and lots of patience), an individual aspiring to work in advertising can obtain not only a job but one that fits with his or her abilities, interests, and career goals.

The job-hunting process, in advertising or any other field, can be broken down into five main steps:

1. Self-assessment and goal setting.
2. Conducting the job search.
3. Preparing a résumé, cover letter, and portfolio.
4. Interviewing.
5. Following up.

Self-Assessment and Goal Setting

The first (and some would argue the most important) step in the job search process is to determine exactly what you have to offer potential employers and what you really want out of a career. You have a variety of ways to go about assessing your interests, marketable skills, strengths and weaknesses, and other characteristics that will influence the kind of job you will do best in and enjoy the most. There are many books on career planning that provide inventories and questionnaires to help you in such a self-assessment.

Through self-evaluation, you can determine not only your interests and job qualifications but also your career goals and objectives. What type of work would you like to do? What do you expect to get out of your work—Money? Power? Fame? Personal fulfillment? What kind of work environment do you prefer? You should be able to make a list of musts and preferences regarding size of company, location, salary, benefits, training programs, and other employer characteristics. Again, career planning books provide guidelines that can help you set goals and objectives.

After completing your self-assessment, you may find you are simply unprepared to enter the career of your choice. At this point, you have the opportunity to undertake any additional schooling you might need, to get some job experience (even if summer or part-time) in a related field, or to serve as an intern (unpaid worker) at an advertising agency, in a company advertising department, with the media, or with a supplier. Your object should be to improve your marketability so you can get the job you really want.

Conducting the Job Search

Before looking into specific jobs that might be available, you will need to investigate the advertising field to determine what types of jobs will fit your career goals. Advertising jobs can be broken down into six main areas: creative (art direction, copywriting), account services, media (planning, scheduling, buying), production (print, broadcast), research, and public relations. (See Exhibit C-1 for specific jobs and their salaries.) Most advertising jobs are found in agencies, but they are also available in the advertising departments of large and small companies, in media, and in allied services (such as media-planning agencies or production companies). To find out about jobs in the advertising field, you can read books on the topic, write to organizations that have career information, and keep up with the most popular trade periodicals, especially *Advertising Age* and *Adweek.* See the listings at the end of this appendix.

In addition to exploring the types of jobs available in advertising, you will want to find out more about what the industry is really like and what is actually involved in doing the work. One way is to obtain interviews with people in the business. Find out the names of people who are highly regarded in their advertising jobs in your community and ask for a few moments of their time for an informative interview. Many will be flattered to be sought out as experts in their field. Be sure to be prepared with specific questions, not take up too much of the person's time, and thank him or her in person and in a follow-up note.

When the time comes to begin conducting your actual job search, you can draw on a number of sources. The most obvious source is want ads in your local paper or in the city where you would like to work. However, it has been estimated that some 80 percent of jobs are filled without an ad ever appearing. How do you hear about these job openings? Cracking this hidden job market will require a great deal of time and effort on your part because you will need to create a network of people who can help you get a job. That will entail telling everyone you know that you are looking for a job and asking everyone you encounter whether he or she knows of any job openings in your field or of anyone who works in that field. You can begin with relatives, friends, and teachers. You should follow up on every lead they give you and ask each new person for additional leads. Networking should eventually land you some interviews for the kind of job you want.

While you are setting up your network, you should also be preparing a list of target employers. These are the companies you most want to work for. That will entail doing some research, such as checking the *Standard Directory of Advertisers* and *Standard Directory of Advertising Agencies.* Also helpful are publications such as the *Advertising Career Directory.* (See the listings at the end of this appendix.) You should make a file card for each company, including information on who is in charge of the specific department where you would like to work.

Other leads for potential employers include college placement offices, employment sections of industry trade papers, and employment agencies (some specialize in jobs in the advertising field).

Preparing a Résumé, a Cover Letter, and a Portfolio

Armed with your list of potential employers, including those obtained through networking and your own research, you are ready to begin contacting them to apply for a job. In most cases, your initial contact will be through

EXHIBIT C-1	Careers in Advertising			

Job title	Job description	Requirements	Salary range	Entry level
Art director	Responsible for visual elements in print and broadcast ads; supervises or creates layouts, hires photographers, illustrators.	B.A. desirable but not required; art school degree helpful; portfolio a must.	$27,600–$70,150 (senior art director)	Assistant art director ($20,700)
Copywriter	Writes copy for print and broadcast advertisements; works with art director to develop ad concept; can work for ad agency or advertiser.	B.A. with courses in advertising, marketing, liberal arts, social sciences; portfolio a must.	$28,750–$70,150 (senior copywriter)	Junior copywriter ($20,700)
Account executive	Serves as link between client and ad agency; acts as business manager for account; does market planning; coordinates advertising planning process.	B.A. in business; M.B.A. often preferred; marketing background desirable.	$39,100–$94,300	Junior account executive (B.A.: $20,700–$26,450; M.B.A.: $29,900–$39,100)
Media planner	Decides media to advertise in and plans media mix; chooses media vehicles; conducts media tests.	B.A. with emphasis in marketing, merchandising, or psychology.	$29,900–$172,500 (media director)	Trainee ($13,500–$16,100)
Media buyer	Buys space in print media and time in electronic media; negotiates price and position of ads; may work for ad agency or media-buying firm.	B.A. with emphasis in marketing, economics, mathematics, or statistics; M.B.A. preferred.	$29,900–$172,500 (media director)	Trainee ($13,000–$16,100)
Traffic manager	Schedules, supervises, and controls an ad agency's work flow.	B.A. not required but highly desirable; good general education helpful.	$23,000–$43,700	Traffic assistant ($15,525)
Print production manager	Prepares ads for printing; works with typesetters, color separators, printers, and other suppliers.	B.A. helpful but not essential; background in graphic arts, printing useful.	$25,300–$64,400	Production assistant ($14,950–$17,250)
Broadcast producer	Supervises all aspects of production for radio and TV commercials, including hiring the director and production company and controlling budget.	B.A. preferred; background in some area of broadcasting helpful.	$31,500–$102,350	Production assistant ($14,950–$17,250)

Job title	Job description	Requirements	Salary range	Entry level
Market researcher	Conducts studies of consumers and their buying habits; conducts tests of consumer reactions to products and ads; may work in ad agency or with research firm.	Degree a must; M.B.A. or Ph.D. desirable; background in statistics useful; computer literacy an advantage.	$42,550–$105,800 (market research manager)	Trainee ($15,525)
Public relations manager	Obtains publicity for clients; serves as intermediary between client and public; handles contacts with press; may work for ad agency, client company, or public relations firm.	College degree with emphasis on liberal arts; journalism or marketing background helpful.	$29,900–$96,600	PR assistant or trainee ($17,250–$19,550)
Advertising director/ manager	Runs advertising department at company, managing all advertising and coordinating with any outside agencies used.	B.A. in marketing or M.B.A.	$36,800–$52,900	Advertising assistant ($19,550–$23,000)
Brand/product manager	Is responsible for the marketing of a specific product or brand at a company, including sales and advertising.	B.A. in marketing or M.B.A.	$40,250–$52,900	Advertising assistant ($19,550–$23,000)
Copywriter for retail ad department	Writes copy for newspaper ads, catalogs, direct-mail pieces for retail business.	B.A. preferred, with courses in advertising, English, sociology, psychology; portfolio helpful.	$31,050–$36,800	($17,250–$25,300)
Artist for retail ad department	Illustrates print ads, catalogs, and direct-mail pieces for retail business.	B.A. desirable; commercial art courses useful; portfolio a must.	$32,200–$36,800	($22,500–$26,450)
Photographer	Photographs products, other setup shots for ad agency or in-house ad department.	B.A. from professional art school; portfolio a must.	$25,300–$37,950	Usually free-lance
Sales representative	Handles advertising sales for a particular newspaper, magazine, radio or TV station, or other medium.	B.A. preferred, with emphasis on business courses; sales experience valuable.	Commission	—
Jingle creator	Writes the music and lyrics for jingles used in radio and TV commercials, usually on a contract or free-lance basis.	B.A. preferred (but not required), with emphasis on music and business.	$40,250–$690,000	$28,750

a résumé and cover letter. Because these items are tools for marketing your product—you—they must be carefully prepared to create a good first impression.

Your résumé should be attractive, well written, and professional. There's no need to do anything fancy—colored paper, professional typesetting, slick design—as most employers will ignore the trappings (unless they're particularly sloppy or amateurish) and focus on the content. For an impressive-looking résumé, stick with clean black type on white bond paper. Leave generous margins to enhance readability. And keep it short—two pages at the most. Always proofread your résumé (even better—have someone else proof it for you) to make sure there are no errors in grammar, punctuation, and spelling.

An example of a résumé is shown in Exhibit C-2. Following are specific tips for preparing your résumé.

Heading

The heading should include a title (such as "Résumé") and basic information about you (name, address, phone number). It should also include your career objective. The objective should be stated as specifically as possible

EXHIBIT C-2

An example of a résumé.

SHARON LEE ANDERSON

4150 Prairie Avenue   Elgin, Illinois 60120   Phone (708) 888-7043

Career Objective: Copywriter in a medium-sized Chicago agency. Advancement to creative supervisor within five years.

Education for Advertising

Bachelor of Arts (1989), University of Illinois, Chicago, Illinois. Major: Advertising and Journalism. Minor: Marketing.

Honors: Dean's list, six semesters. Graduated in upper 10 percent of class.

Advertising Experience

Junior Copywriter (part-time)
Goldblatt's Department Store
Skokie, Illinois
(May 1989-September 1990)

Advertising Salesperson
Campus newspaper
University of Illinois
(October 1988-March 1989)

Responsible for creative copy
for direct-mail brochures

Serviced existing accounts and
contracted with 22 new accounts

Awards, Activities, Affiliations

First-place winner. Copywriting category. National Student Advertising Campaign Competition, 1991. Sponsored by the Federation of Advertising Agencies.

Program Chairman, 1990-91. University of Illinois Advertising Club.

Recipient. Summer 1990 scholarship from Advertising Institute.

Other Relevant Information

Write and speak Spanish. Type 70 wpm. Proficient with WordPerfect and Microsoft Word programs for IBM PC and PageMaker for Macintosh.

Personal Data

Hobbies include reading (science fiction, history, behavioral sciences), flute playing, dancing, racquetball.

References

Dr. Harold G. Simpson, Professor of Advertising, School of Journalism, University of Illinois, Chicago, Illinois 60680

Dr. Barbara Wasserman, Professor of Marketing, School of Business, University of Illinois, Chicago, Illinois 60680

Linda Dolan, Director of Advertising, Goldblatt's Department Store, Skokie, Illinois 60076 (e.g., "an entry-level position in the media department of a large ad agency with a long-term goal of media planning for major accounts"), as opposed to something vague ("a challenging position in the advertising industry" or "a job where I can put my enthusiasm and interpersonal skills to good use").

Education

Include any degrees you have already earned and any outstanding honors or scholarships. If you have little work experience, this section should emphasize courses you have taken that might prepare you for your chosen career.

Work Experience

Emphasize jobs that are relevant to your target field. Include any part-time or volunteer work that shows an interest in the type of job you are seeking. For all relevant work experience, be sure to include a brief description of your duties and any worthy accomplishments. Briefly list other jobs held to show that you have the ability to get and hold a job and have at least contributed to your support.

Activities and Achievements

This section is a good spot to include any other information that might be of interest to an employer, such as language skills, relevant hobbies, and community activities.

References

If you wish to include names of past employers who can be contacted about your skills and experience, be sure to get their permission first before listing them. If you have good references, it's best to list them. It's acceptable to state "References available upon request."

Accompanying the résumé should be a cover letter that catches the reader's attention, provides evidence of your qualifications, and requests an interview (see Exhibit C-3). Like the résumé, the letter should be professionally presented (not handwritten, for instance) and businesslike. It should answer the employer's question, "What's in it for me?" A number of books provide help with writing good résumés and cover letters. Several are listed at the end of this appendix.

If you are looking for a job as an art director or a copywriter, you will also need to prepare a portfolio, or "book," to show potential employers. This portfolio can include published pieces, pieces done for school courses, or self-projects. What it should *not* include is bad work. The fact that something you did was published does not automatically qualify it for your portfolio, especially if it is not among your best work. A portfolio should be carefully thought out and prepared, as it may be the sole basis on which some employers do their hiring. It should contain a small number of items that represent the kinds and quality of work you can do.

Interviewing

The purpose of the résumé and cover letter is to land you a job interview. It is usually on the basis of the interview (and your portfolio, if you have one) that employers will make their decision. You should therefore work on develop-

EXHIBIT C-3

An example of a letter of application.

4150 Prairie Avenue
Elgin, IL 60120
June 10, 1991

Mr. Harold Lessler
Henley, Schmidt and Kaiser Advertising
5948 Lakeshore Drive
Chicago, IL 60034

Dear Mr. Lessler:

If a woman were seeking a copywriting position in your agency, would you be interested if you discovered she'd had experience as a department store copywriter? Would you become even more interested to find she'd had practical selling experience with a campus newspaper and had graduated in the top 10 percent of her class from a major university? I'm just such a woman, Mr. Lessler.

Writing brochure copy aimed at women with young children and at working women age 25-40 taught me the importance of adapting advertising to a specific target audience. My year and a half of experience at Goldblatt's Department Store in Skokie, Illinois, gave me training in copywriting that can be put to work for your agency.

As helpful as this experience was, a fledgling copywriter also needs to know what real selling is all about. That is why I believe you'll find my newspaper ad-selling experience valuable. It helped me immeasurably in learning to turn out copy that sells.

I majored in advertising at the University of Illinois. To make sure I understood the world in which advertising works, I minored in marketing. My courses paid off: I was the first-place winner, copywriting category, in the 1989 National Student Advertising Campaign Competition. I like to win awards. And I'd try to win many for your agency!

My research shows that you have several accounts needing copywriting in Spanish. I speak and write Spanish fluently. In addition, my 70 wpm typing ability, my proficiency in using word processing programs, and my ability to work constructively with others (as evidenced by my tour of duty as Program Chairman of the campus Advertising Club) make up a background that will enable me to serve your agency well.

After you've had an opportunity to review the enclosed resume, please call me at (312) 698-5894. I'd be grateful for an interview to discuss my qualifications with you.

Cordially yours,

Sharon Lee Anderson
Sharon Lee Anderson

Enclosure

ing your interviewing skills. Learn the most commonly asked interview questions and rehearse your answers. Read about preparing for interviews and follow suggestions for scheduling, attire, and appropriate interview behavior.

Before an interview, you should find out about the company. If it is an advertising agency, how big is it? How is it structured? What are its major accounts? Who are the major figures? Who will you be talking to, and what is the correct pronunciation of his or her name?

At the close of the interview, be sure to thank the interviewer and to politely inquire about what will happen next. Should you expect additional interviews? Will someone from the company be in touch? Show that you are interested—but not desperate.

Following Up

Record-keeping is a must when you are conducting a job search. You should have files or cards for recording letters and résumés sent, dates of interviews, and so forth. If, within a reasonable time, you have not had responses to your letters to certain target employers, write follow-up letters. After an interview, it is always a good idea to write a brief thank-you note, reiterating your interest in the job. Such notes should always be typed.

Eventually, as the result of your employment-seeking efforts, you will receive one or more job offers. Accept the job that best fits your objectives, and you will at last be on your way to a career in advertising.

CAREER PLANNING PUBLICATIONS

Books

Advertising Career Directory. 2nd ed. Hawthorne, N.J.: The Career Press, Inc., 1987.

Bolles, Richard N. *What Color Is Your Parachute? A Practical Manual for Job Hunters and Career Changes.* Berkeley, Calif.: Ten Speed Press, 1992.

Chorba, Thomas, and Alex York. *Winning Moves: Career Strategies for the Eighties.* New York: Anchor Books, 1986.

College Placement Manual. Bethlehem, Penn.: College Placement Council, Inc., 1985.

Corwen, Leonard. *There's a Job for You in Advertising, Commercial Art, Fashion, Films, Public Relations and Publicity, Publishing, Television and Radio, Travel and Tourism.* New York: New Century, 1983.

Craig, James. *Graphic Design Career Guide.* New York: Watson-Guptill Publications, 1983.

Deckinger, E. L., and Jules B. Singer. *Exploring Careers in Advertising.* New York: Rosen Publishing Group, 1985.

Greenberg, Jan. *How Advertising Works and the People Who Make It Happen.* New York: Henry Holt and Company, 1987.

Haas, Ken. *How to Get a Job in Advertising.* New York: Art Direction Book Company, 1979.

Holtz, Herman. *Beyond the Résumé.* New York: McGraw-Hill, 1984.

Katz, Judith A. *The Ad Game.* New York: Harper & Row, 1984.

Lareau, William. *The Inside Track: A Successful Job Search Method.* New York: New Century Publishers, 1986.

Laskin, David. *Getting into Advertising: A Career Guide.* New York: Ballantine Books, 1986.

Mogel, Leonard. *Making It in the Media Professions: A Realistic Guide to Career Opportunities in Newspapers, Magazines, Books, Television, Radio, the Movies, and Advertising.* Chester, Conn.: Globe Pequot, 1987.

Paetro, Maxine. *How to Put Your Book Together and Get a Job in Advertising.* New York: Executive Communications, 1980.

Public Relations Career Directory. 2nd ed. Hawthorne, N.J.: The Career Press, 1987.

Schmidt, Peggy J. *Making It on Your First Job: When You're Young, Inexperienced, and Ambitious.* New York: Avon Books, 1981.

Shelling, Robert O. *Jobs: What They Are . . . Where They Are . . .* New York: Simon & Schuster, 1986.

Wasserman, Dick. *How to Get Your First Copywriting Job.* New York: Center for Advancement of Advertising, 1985.

West, Jonathan P. *Career Planning Development and Management: An Annotated Bibliography.* New York: Garland Publishing, 1983.

Wilson, Robert F., and Adele Lewis. *Better Résumés for Executives and Professionals.* Woodbury, N.Y.: Barron's Educational Series, 1983.

Periodicals

Business Week's Guide to Careers, 1221 Avenue of the Americas, New York, NY 10010.

Career Opportunity News, Garrett Park Press, Garrett Park, MD 20896.

Journal of Career Planning and Employment, College Placement Council, 62 Highland Avenue, Bethlehem, PA 18017.

Occupational Outlook Quarterly, Superintendent of Documents, U.S. Government Printing Office, Washington, DC 20402.

Pamphlets

Advertising: A Guide to Careers in Advertising, American Association of Advertising Agencies, 200 Park Avenue, New York, NY 10017.

Where Shall I Go to Study Advertising, Advertising Education Publications, 3429 Fifty-Fifth Street, Lubbock, TX 79413.

SELECTED PERIODICALS

Advertising Age, 740 North Rush Street, Chicago, IL 60611.

Advertising Techniques, 10 East 39th Street, New York, NY 10016.

Adweek, 49 East 21st Street, New York, NY 10010.

Adweek's Marketing Week, 49 East 21st Street, New York, NY 10010.

Applied Arts Quarterly, 20 Holy Street, Suite 208, Toronto, Ontario, Canada M4S 3B1

Archive, P.O. Box 6338, Syracuse, NY 13217.

Art Direction, 10 East 39th Street, New York, NY 10016.

Broadcasting, 1735 DeSales Street N.W., Washington, DC 20036.

Business Marketing, 740 Rush Street, Chicago, IL 60611.

Canadian Business, 70 The Esplanade, 2nd Floor, Toronto, Canada M5E 1R2

Canadian Journal of Communication, St. Thomas More College, 1437 College Drive, Saskatoon, Saskatchewan, Canada S7N 0W6.

Communication Arts, P.O. Box 10300, Palo Alto, CA 94303.

Direct Marketing, 224 Seventh Street, Garden City, NY 11530.

Editor & Publisher, 575 Lexington Avenue, New York, NY 10022.

Incentive Marketing, 633 Third Avenue, New York, NY 10017.

Info-Presse Communications, 4316 Rue St-Laurent, Suite 400, Montreal, Quebec, Canada H2W 1Z3

Journal of Advertising, American Academy of Advertising, c/o Ron Lane, School of Journalism, The University of Georgia, Athens, GA 30602.

Journal of Advertising Research, Advertising Research Foundation, 3 East 54th Street, New York, NY 10022.

Journal of Broadcasting, Broadcast Education Association, 1771 N Street N.W., Washington, DC 20036.

Journal of Marketing, American Marketing Association, 250 South Wacker Drive, Suite 200, Chicago, IL 60606.

Marketing, Maclean-Hunter Ltd., 777 Bay Street, Toronto, Ontario, Canada, M5W 1A7.

Marketing News, American Marketing Association, 250 South Wacker Drive, Suite 200, Chicago, IL 60606.

Mediaweek, 1515 Broadway, New York, NY 10036.

MIN/Media Industry Newsletter, 145 East 49th Street, New York, NY 10017.

Modern Packaging, 205 East 42nd Street, New York, NY 10017.

Print, 355 Lexington Avenue, New York, NY 10017.

Public Relations Journal, 845 Third Avenue, New York, NY 10020.

Sales and Marketing Management, 633 Third Avenue, New York, NY 10164.

Sales and Marketing Management in Canada, 1077 St. James Street, Winnipeg, Manitoba, Canada R3C 3B1

Stores, National Retail Merchants Association, 100 West 31st Street, New York, NY 10001.

Television/Radio Age, 1270 Avenue of the Americas, New York, NY 10020.

Zip, 401 North Broad Street, Philadelphia, PA 19108.

REFERENCE BOOKS AND DIRECTORIES

Standard Directory of Advertisers. Wilmette, Ill.: National Register Publishing Company, 1989.

Standard Directory of Advertising Agencies. Wilmette, Ill.: National Register Publishing Company, 1989.

RESEARCH AND INFORMATION SERVICES

A. C. Nielsen Company, Nielsen Plaza, Northbrook, IL 60062.

Advertising Checking Bureau, 165 North Canal Street, Chicago, IL 60606.

Audit Bureau of Circulations, 900 North Meacham Road, Schaumburg, IL 60195.

Broadcast Advertisers Report (BAR), 500 Fifth Avenue, New York, NY 10036.

Gallup & Robinson, Research Park, Princeton, NJ 08540.

Leading National Advertisers (LNA), 515 Madison Avenue, New York, NY 10022.

Mediamark Research, 341 Madison Avenue, New York, NY 10017.

Simmons Marketing Research Bureau, 219 East 42nd Street, New York, NY 10017.

Starch INRA Hooper, 566 East Boston Post Road, Mamaroneck, NY 10543.

The Arbitron Company, 1350 Avenue of the Americas, New York, NY 10019.

PROFESSIONAL AND TRADE ASSOCIATIONS

The Advertising Council, 825 Third Avenue, New York, NY 10022.

Advertising Research Foundation (ARF), 3 East 54th Street, New York, NY 10022.

American Advertising Federation, 1400 K Street N.W., Suite 1000, Washington, DC 20005.

American Association of Advertising Agencies, 666 Third Avenue, 13th Floor, New York, NY 10017.

American Business Press, 205 East 42nd Street, New York, NY 10017.

American Marketing Association, 250 South Wacker Drive, Chicago, IL 60606.

Association of National Advertisers, 155 East 44th Street, New York, NY 10017.

Business/Professional Advertising Association, 205 East 42nd Street, New York, NY 10017.

Council of Better Business Bureaus, 1515 Wilson Boulevard, Arlington, VA 22209.

Direct Marketing Association, 6 East 43rd Street, New York, NY 10017.

International Advertising Association, 475 Fifth Avenue, New York, NY 10017.

Magazine Publishers Association, 575 Lexington Avenue, New York, NY 10022.

Marketing Communications Executives International, 2602 McKinney Avenue, Dallas, TX 75204.

Marketing Research Association, 111 East Wacker Drive, Suite 600, Chicago, IL 60601.

National Advertising Review Board (NARB), 845 Third Avenue, New York, NY 10022.

National Association of Broadcasters, 1771 N Street N.W., Washington, DC 20036.

National Council of Affiliated Advertising Agencies, 6 East 45th Street, New York, NY 10017.

National Retail Merchants Association, 100 West 31st Street, New York, NY 10001.

National Yellow Pages Service, 999 West Big Beaver Road, Troy, MI 48084.

Newspaper Advertising Bureau, 1180 Avenue of the Americas, New York, NY 10036.

Outdoor Advertising Association of America, 1899 L Street N.W., Suite 403, Washington, DC 20036.

Point-of-Purchase Advertising Institute, 2 Executive Drive, Ft. Lee, NJ 07024.

Public Relations Society of America, 845 Third Avenue, New York, NY 10022.

Radio Advertising Bureau, 304 Park Avenue South, New York, NY 10010.

Sales and Marketing Executives International, 6151 Wilson Mills Road, Suite 200, Cleveland, OH 44143.

Specialty Advertising Association International, 1404 Walnut Hill Lane, Irving, TX 75062.

Television Bureau of Advertising, 477 Madison Avenue, New York, NY 10022.

Transit Advertising Association, 1025 Thomas Jefferson Avenue, Suite 502E, Washington, DC 20007.

ENDNOTES

Chapter 1

1. "A New Look for Coca-Cola: A Synopsis of the 70s," Coca-Cola Company, 1970.

2. Stan Rapp and Tom Collins, *MaxiMarketing: The New Direction in Advertising, Promotion and Marketing Strategy* (New York: McGraw-Hill, 1987), pp. 17-30.

3. Marshall McLuhan, *Understanding Media: The Extensions of Man* (New York: McGraw-Hill, 1965), pp. 45-58; Desmond Smith, "Tomorrow's Media Are in Place Today," *Advertising Age,* December 19, 1983, pp. M-14, M-16; Walter A. Kleinschrod, "The Management Message in Electronic Messaging Media," *Administrative Management,* October 1987, p. 13; H. T. Eckhardt, "Electronics and Print Co-Exist in the Wired City," *American Printer,* July 1988, pp. 94, 96; Deborah Pfeiffer and Czatdana Inan, "The Times They Are a Changin'," *Telephony,* January 7, 1991, pp. 22-30.

4. James Burke, *The Day the Universe Changed* (Boston: Little, Brown, 1985), pp. 91-92.

5. Al Ries and Jack Trout, *Positioning: The Battle for Your Mind,* rev. ed. (New York: McGraw-Hill, 1986), pp. 23-27, 39, 101.

6. Daniel Thomas Seymour, "Demarketing: New Segmenting Tool," *United States Banker,* August 1983, pp. 71-72, 74; Lawrence R. Lepisto, "Demarketing Strategies: Assessment and Implementation," *Mid-Atlantic Journal of Business,* Winter 1983-1984, pp. 31-41; Linda Hersch, "The Demarketing Zone," *ZIP/Target Marketing,* October 1984, pp. TM38-TM39; Kathleen A. Krentler, "Maintaining Quality Control during the 'Crunch' in Service Firms," *Journal of Services Marketing,* Winter 1988, pp. 71-74; Allan C. Reddy, "Reducing Health Care Cost by Demarketing Benefits," *Health Marketing Quarterly,* 1989, pp. 137-45.

7. Al Ries and Jack Trout, *Marketing Warfare* (New York: McGraw-Hill, 1986), pp. 49-54.

8. Raymond Serafin and Cleveland Horton, "Chrysler Rides Pro-U.S. Tide," *Advertising Age,* March 5, 1990, pp. 1, 42, 2.

9. Debra Goldman, "Study: Advertisers Aren't Talking to Consumers," *Adweek,* August 27, 1990, p. 25.

10. Mark Evans, "Tom McElligott's a Man on a Mission in New York," *Adweek,* August 27, 1990, p. 25.

11. John McManus, "Cable Proves It's Media's Live Wire," *Advertising Age,* November 26, 1990, p. S6; see also, "Media & Measurement Technologies (Part 1)," *Direct Marketing,* March 1991, pp. 25-27, 79.

12. McGraw-Hill Laboratory/Laboratory of Advertising Performance, 1985 study.

13. George Garneau, "Slight Ad Growth Expected for Newspapers," *Editor & Publisher,* January 5, 1991, pp. 14, 73; R. Craig Endicott, "P&G Spends $2.28 Billion, Surges to Head of Top 100," *Advertising Age,* September 25, 1991, pp. 1, 67, 72.

14. Ernest Dichter, *Handbook of Consumer Motivations* (New York: McGraw-Hill, 1964), pp. 6, 422-31.

15. Richard E. Kihlstrom and Michael H. Riordan, "Advertising as a Signal," *Journal of Political Economy,* June 1984, pp. 427-50.

16. John Kenneth Galbraith, "Economics and Advertising: Exercise in Denial," *Advertising Age,* November 9, 1988, pp. 80-84.

17. Rebecca Colwell Quarles, "Marketing Research Turns Recession into a Business Opportunity," *Marketing News,* January 7, 1991, pp. 27, 29.

Chapter 2

1. John O'Toole, "Afterword," *Madison Avenue,* May 1980, p. 98.

2. Abraham Maslow, *Motivation and Personality,* 2nd ed. (New York: Harper & Row, 1970), pp. 39-51.

3. Jack Haberstroh, "Can't Ignore Subliminal Ad Charges," *Advertising Age,* September 17, 1984, p. 42.

4. Michael Shudson, *Advertising, the Uneasy Persuasion* (New York: Basic Books, 1985), p. 24.

5. "Importance of Image," *The Wall Street Journal,* August 12, 1985, p. 19.

6. Robert J. Samuelson, "The Sovereign Consumer," *Newsweek,* July 29, 1985, p. 54.

7. "Ads That Shatter an Old Taboo," *Time,* February 2, 1987, p. 63.

8. Jeffrey A. Trachtenberg, "It's Become Part of Our Culture," *Forbes,* May 5, 1986, p. 134.

9. Lucy A. McCauley, "The Face of Advertising," *Harvard Business Review,"* November-December 1989, pp. 155-59; "TV Ads Show Struggle to Replace Bygone Images of Today's Mothers," *The Wall Street Journal,* October 5, 1984, p. 29.

10. Trachtenberg, "It's Become Part of Our Culture," p. 135.

11. Laurie P. Cohen, "Sex in Ads Becomes Less Explicit, as Firms Turn to Romantic Images, *The Wall Street Journal,* February 2, 1988, sec. 2, p. 25.

12. Neal Templin, "The Latest Model at the Auto Show Wears Pin Stripes," *The Wall Street Journal,* January 8, 1991, p. A1.

13. Federal Trade Commission, 1991.

14. James Bredin, "Out of Control?" *Industry Week,* April 17, 1989, p. 38.

15. Bill Shaw, "Foreign Corrupt Practices Act: A Legal and Ethical Analysis," *Journal of Business Ethics,* October 1988, pp. 789-95.

16. Joanne Lipman, "Brand-Name Products Are Popping Up in TV Shows," *The Wall Street Journal,* February 19, 1991, p. B1.

17. Ibid.

18. "Volvo Admits That Its 'Car-Crusher' Ads Were Fakes," *The San Diego Union,* November 6, 1990, p. A-9.

19. Arthur S. Hayes, "Judicial Campaign Comes In for Scrutiny," *The Wall Street Journal,* October 26, 1990, p. B1.

20. Janice Castro, "Volunteer Vice Squad," *Time,* April 23, 1990, p. 60.

21. Joanne Lipman, "Ad Industry Debates about Line between Patriotism, Opportunism," *The Wall Street Journal,* January 30, 1991, p. B6.

22. Brian Bremner, "A New Sales Pitch: The Environment," *Business Week,* July 24, 1989, p. 50.

23. Judith D. Schwartz, "Wal-Mart's 'Green' Campaign to Emphasize Recycling Next," *Adweek's Marketing Week,* February 12, 1990, p. 61.

24. Jane Bryant Quinn, "New Handcuffs on the Cops," *Newsweek,* September 3, 1984, p. 62.

25. Richard W. Anderson, "Wanna Watch Miami Vice or a Half-Hour Ad?" *Business Week,* November 28, 1988, p. 114.

26. David Riggle, "Say What You Mean, Mean What You Say," *In Business,* May-June 1990, pp. 50-51.

27. Dean Keith Fueroghne, *"But the People in Legal Said . . .,"* (Homewood, Ill.: Dow Jones-Irwin, 1989), p. 14.

28. Robert J. Watkins, "Government Controls of Advertising," in *Legal and Business Aspects of the Advertising Industry,* ed. Felix H. Kent and Elhanan C. Stone (New York: Practising Law Institute, 1986), p. 83.

29. Robert Garfield, "Advertisers: All's Fair in Commercials," *USA Today,* April 19, 1985, p. 83.

30. Watkins, "Government Controls," p. 88.

31. Steven A. Meyerowitz, "Endorsements: What You Can and Cannot Do," *Business Marketing,* March 1986, p. 8.

32. "The Growing Brouhaha over Drug Advertisements," *New York Times,* May 14, 1989, p. F-8.

33. Ibid.

34. William Mueller, "Who Reads the Label?" *American Demographics,* January 1991, pp. 36, 39.

35. Thomas R. King, "For Perrier, New Woes Spring Up," *The Wall Street Journal,* April 26, 1990, p. B1.

36. Douglas T. Brownlie, "Protecting Marketing Intelligence: The Role of Trademarks," *Marketing Intelligence and Planning* 6, no. 4 (1988), pp. 21-26; Steven A. Meyerowitz, "Don't 'Xerox' This Article! How to Defend Your Trademarks," *Business Marketing,* December 1984, p. 64.

37. Wayne E. Green, "Lawyers Give Deceptive-Trade Statutes New Day in Court, Wider Interpretations," *The Wall Street Journal,* January 24, 1990, p. B1.

38. Steven A. Meyerowitz, "The Marketing Downside to States' Rights," *Business Marketing,* November 1986, p. 64.

39. "Volvo Admits That Its 'Car-Crusher' Ads Were Fakes," p. A-1.

40. Robert Johnson and John Koten, "Sears Has Everything, Including Messy Fight over Ads in New York," *The Wall Street Journal,* June 28, 1988, p. A1.

41. Steven A. Meyerowitz, "The New Threat to Advertising Freedom," *Business Marketing,* October 1986, p. 20.

42. Ellen Joan Pollock, " 'I Love My Lawyer' Ads May Spread to More States," *The Wall Street Journal,* December 7, 1990, p. B1.

43. Ibid.

44. Steven Meyerowitz, "When Privacy Goes Public in Advertising," *Business Marketing,* March 1987, p. 104.

45. Michele Galen, "A Comeback May Be Ahead for Brand X," *Business Week,* December 4, 1989, p. 35.

46. Ibid.

47. Bruce Buchanan and Doron Goldman, "Us vs. Them: The Minefield of Comparative Ads," *Harvard Business Review,* May-June 1989, p. 38.

48. Steven A. Meyerowitz, "The Developing Law of Comparative Advertising," *Business Marketing,* August 1985, p. 81.

49. Felix H. Kent, "Control of Ads by Private Sector," *New York Law Journal,* December 27, 1985; reprinted in Kent and Stone, eds., *Legal and Business Aspects of the Advertising Industry,* 1986, pp. 207-9.

50. *"Dear***, Your Advertising Has Recently Come to the Attention of the National Advertising Division . . ."* (New York: Council of Better Business Bureaus, 1983), p. 1.

51. *NAD Case Report,* National Advertising Division, Council of Better Business Bureaus, 20, no. 10 (January 21, 1991).

52. Paul Farhi, "Agencies, Networks Battle over Censors' Role," *Adweek,* November 14, 1983, p. 50.

53. Thomas R. King, "In More TV Ads, the Fine Print Gets Evil Eye," *The Wall Street Journal,* July 12, 1990, p. B1.

54. Public Relations Department, KLBJ, Austin, Texas, 1991.

55. Public Relations Department, KDWB, Minneapolis-St. Paul, Minnesota, 1991.

56. Public Relations Department, KSDO, San Diego, California, 1991.

57. David Shaw, "Newspapers Draw Foggy Lines on Ads," *Los Angeles Times,* February 15, 1987, p. 1.

58. Ibid.

Chapter 3

1. "Is Frank Perdue Chicken?" *Forbes,* November 5, 1984, pp. 223-24; Nancy Giges, "Holly Farms, Perdue Face Off in Chickie Run," *Advertising Age,* September 16, 1985, p. 4.

2. Private correspondence, Perdue Farms, April 1991.

3. Christian McAdams, "Frank Perdue Is Chicken!" *Esquire,* April 1973, pp. 113-17. Copyright 1973 by Esquire Publishing, Inc.; and "Frank Perdue," *Inc.,* February 1984, pp. 21-23; private correspondence, Perdue Farms, April 1991.

4. Frederick R. Gamble, *What Advertising Agencies Are—What They Do and How They Do It,* 7th ed. (New York: American Association of Advertising Agencies, 1970), p. 4; Ralph S. Blois, "Do You Really Need an Agency," *Sales & Marketing Management,* October 1988, pp. 120-23.

5. John K. Smalley, "Creative Ad Ventures/Automatic Returns/Great Moments in Advertising/Zapping Viewer Apathy," *World,* January-February 1986, pp. 8-20.

6. "The Mice That Roar," *Venture,* June 1985, pp. 110-14.

7. Dianne Lynne Kastiel, "Are You Using Your Agency Enough?" *Business Marketing,* January 1987, pp. 85-89.

8. John H. Taylor, "Western International Media: Running Scared," *Forbes,* May 28, 1990, pp. 146-48.

9. *Inside the AAAA,* American Association of Advertising Agencies, Copyright 1990, p. 5.

10. Ibid., pp. 40-41.

11. Blois, "Do You Really Need an Agency."

12. George A. Hathaway III, "Account Execs—Choosing the Right Path," *Advertising Age,* September 2, 1985, p. 30.

13. "15% System: Fair or Faulty," *Advertising Age,* May 1, 1989, pp. 20, 76.

14. Jon Lafayette and Cleveland Horton, "Shops to Clients: Pay Up—4A's Members Call for an End to Free Services," *Advertising Age,* March 19, 1990, pp. 1, 66.

15. Edward Tashjian, "Marketing Services Has Big Role in Biz-to-Biz Advertising and PR," *Marketing News,* March 4, 1991, pp. 11, 30.

16. John Micklethwait, "Cut the Ribbon," *The Economist,* June 9, 1990, pp. S16-S17; Tom Eisenhart, "'Guaranteed Results' Plan May Suit Business Marketers," *Business Marketing,* July 1990, p. 32.

17. Franchellie Cadwell and Herman Davis, "Why Is It That Advertising Agencies Don't Advertise?" *Advertising Age,* November 19, 1979, p. 51; Rena Sonnenrich, "At Agencies, Small Is Beautiful, Not Easy (Part 2)," *Advertising Age,* October 7, 1985, p. 40; Carys Bowen-Jones, "Knowingly Undersold," *Marketing* (UK), August 6, 1987, pp. 22-23.

18. Bowen-Jones, "Knowingly Undersold,"; Nancy Zeldis, "A Bit of Sweden in Connecticut," *Management Review,* October 1987, pp. 12-14.

19. Stephanie Overman, "A Company of Champions," *HR Magazine,* October 1990, pp. 58-60; R. Craig Endicott, "P&G Spends $2.28 Billion, Surges to Head of Top 100," *Advertising Age,* September 25, 1991, pp. 1, 33, 72.

20. R. Craig Endicott, "Where Those Ad Dollars Go," *Advertising Age,* August 20, 1987, pp. 134-36, 210-12; *D&B—Dun's Market Identifiers,* April 1991.

21. Laurie Freeman, "The House that Ivory Built," *Advertising Age,* August 20, 1987, pp. 4-14, 162-200; R. Craig Endicott, "P&G Spends $2.28 Billion," p. 1.

22. Joseph M. Winski, "One Brand, One Manager," *Advertising Age,* August 20, 1987, pp. 86-90, 204-5.

23. Jolie Solomon and Carol Hymowitz, "Team Strategy: P&G Makes Changes in the Way It Develops Its Products," *The Wall Street Journal,* August 11, 1987, pp. 1, 10.

24. Ibid.; see also Lenore Skenzay, "Brand Managers Shelved? Professors Offer Alternative for Changing Market," *Advertising Age,* July 13, 1987, p. 81.

25. Robert Selwitz, "Media Buying Moves In-House," *Marketing Communications,* September 1986, pp. 19-23, 79, 86.

26. Ibid.

27. M. E. Ziegenhagen, "Advertising: Which Is Best . . . In-House or Outside Agency?" *Sales & Marketing Management in Canada,* August 1986, pp. 10-11; Blois, "Do You Really Need an Agency"; Micklethwait, "Cut the Ribbon."

28. Sam Sparrow, "Design: In-House or Agency?" *Industrial Marketing Digest* (U.K.), 2nd Quarter 1987, pp. 35-39.

29. Pradeep K. Korgaonkar and Danny N. Bellenger, "Correlates of Successful Advertising Campaigns: The Manager's Perspective," *Journal of Advertising Research,* December 1986-January 1987, pp. 29-41. See Also Pradeep K. Korgaonkar, Danny N. Bellenger, and Allen E. Smith, "Successful Industrial Advertising Campaigns," *Industrial Marketing Management,* May 1986, pp. 123-38.

30. Daniel B. Wackman, Charles T. Salmon, Caryn C. Salmon, "Developing an Advertising Agency-Client Relationship," *Journal of Advertising Research,* December 1986-January 1987, pp. 21-28.

31. Jennifer Pendleton, "Matches Made in Heaven: Some Agencies, Clients Stay Wed for Decades," *Advertising Age,* March 14, 1988, pp. 3, 74.

32. "Sure You've Been a Great Agency for 16 Years, But Here's the Door," *The San Diego Union,* July 7, 1991, pp. 11, 6.

33. Paul C. Katz, "Getting the Most of Your Advertising Dollars: How to Select and Evaluate an Ad Agency," *Bottomline,* March 1987, pp. 35-38.

34. Christy Marshall, "In Spite of Image, Agency-Client Links Do Often Endure," *Advertising Age,* July 1982, pp. 33-34, 41; Mat Toor, "Fear and Favour in Adland," *Marketing* (UK), November 15, 1990, pp. 30-32.

35. Paul C. N. Mitchell, "Auditing of Agency-Client Relations," *Journal of Advertising Research,* December 1986-January 1987, pp. 29-41.

36. Steven A. Meyerowitz, "Ad Agency Conflicts: The Law and Common Sense," *Business Marketing,* June 1987, p. 16.

37. Joanne Lipman, "Colgate Drops Ted Bates as Its Agency; Move Seen as Blow to Ad-Firm Mergers," *The Wall Street Journal,* June 2, 1986; see also Andy Zipser, "Advertising: Mad as in Madison Avenue," *Barron's,* December 3, 1990, pp. 12-13, 32-39.

Chapter 4

1. Gary Kurzbard and Gary F. Soldow, "Towards a Parametric Definition of Marketing," *European Journal of Marketing* (UK) 21, no. 1 (1987), pp. 37-47; and O. C. Farrell and George H. Lucas, Jr., "An Evaluation of Progress in the Development of a Definition of Marketing," *Journal of the Academy of Marketing Science* 15, no. 3 (Fall 1987), pp. 12-23.

2. Adapted from AMA definition of marketing; see "AMA Board Approves New Marketing Definition," *The Marketing News,* March 1, 1985, p. 1.

3. Louis E. Boone and David L. Kurtz, *Contemporary Marketing* (Hinsdale, Ill.: Dryden Press, 1986), p. 6.

4. The classic studies on this subject were performed by Edwin A. Locke, "Toward a Theory of Task Motivation and Incentives," *Organizational Behavior and Human Performance,* May 1968, p. 161; and Richard M. Steers and Lyman W. Porter, "The Role of Task-Goal Attributes in Employee Performance," *Psychological Bulletin,* July 1974, p. 446; also, for a discscussion of goal hierarchies, see J. Paul Peter and Jerry C. Olson, *Consumer Behavior and Marketing Strategy,* 2nd ed. (Homewood, Ill.: Richard D. Irwin, 1990), pp. 186-88.

5. William F. Allman, "Science 1, Advertisers 0: New Research Is Undermining Conventional Ideas on What Sells." *U.S. News & World Report,* May 1, 1989, pp. 60-61.

6. Courtland L. Bovée and John V. Thill, *Business Communication Today* (New York: McGraw-Hill, 1989), pp. 38-40.

7. Del I. Hawkins, Roger J. Best, and Kenneth A. Coney, *Consumer Behavior: Implications for Marketing Strategy,* 4th ed. (Homewood, Ill.: Richard D. Irwin, 1989), pp. 66-67.

8. The classic quote: "The medium is the message," came from Marshall McLuhan, *Understanding Media: The Extensions of Man* (New York: McGraw-Hill, 1965), pp. 45-58; see also Desmond Smith, "Tomorrow's Media Are in Place Today," *Advertising Age,* December 19, 1983, pp. M-14, M-16; Paul Levinson, "Marshall McLuhan and Computer Conferencing," *IEEE Transactions on Professional Communication,* March 1986, pp. 9-11; Walter A. Kleinschrod, "The Management Message in Electronic Messaging Media," *Administrative Management,* October 1987, p. 13.

9. David Cravens, Gerald E. Hills, and Robert B. Woodruff, *Marketing Management* (Homewood, Ill.: Richard D. Irwin, 1987), p. 124.

10. Michael J. McCarthy, "Mind Probe—What Makes an Ad Memorable? Recent Brain Research Yields Surprising Answers," *The Wall Street Journal,* March 22, 1991, p. B3.

11. Robert B. Settle and Pamela L. Alreck, *Why They Buy* (New York: John Wiley & Sons, 1986), pp. 71-73.

12. Boone and Kurtz, *Contemporary Marketing,* p. 164.

13. "Maidenform Tries New Approach in Latest Lingerie Ad Campaign," *The Wall Street Journal,* April 23, 1987.

14. E. Jerome McCarthy and William D. Perreault, Jr., *Basic Marketing,* 10th ed. (Homewood, Ill.: Richard D. Irwin, 1990), p. 175.

15. McCarthy, "Mind Probe."

16. Al Ries and Jack Trout, *Positioning: The Battle for Your Mind,* rev. ed. (New York, McGraw-Hill, 1986), pp. 30-32.

17. Ibid., p. 29.

18. Adapted from Hawkins, Best, and Coney, *Consumer Behavior,* pp. 320-29.

19. John O'Toole, *The Trouble with Advertising,* 2nd ed. (New York: Random House, 1985), p. 21.

20. Larry Gaudet, "Les Annonces de Provigo," *Applied Arts Quarterly,* Spring 1990, pp. 25-28.

21. J. Paul Peter and Jerry C. Olson, *Consumer Behavior and Marketing Strategy,* p. 434.

22. Don E. Schultz, "Add Value to the Product and the Brand," *Marketing News,* October 23, 1989, p. 13.

23. Ken Dychtwald and Greg Gable, "Portrait of a Changing Consumer," *Business Horizons,* January-February 1990, pp. 62-74.

24. McCarthy and Perreault, *Basic Marketing, p. 172.*

25. B. Rice, "The Selling of Life-Styles: Are You What You Buy? Madison Avenue Wants to Know," *Psychology Today,* March 1988, pp. 46-51.

26. George P. Moschis, "The Role of Family Communication in Consumer Socialization of Children and Adolescents," *Journal of Consumer Research,* March 1985, pp. 898-913.

27. Jeffrey Zaslow, "Children's Search for Values Leading to Shopping Malls," *The Wall Street Journal,* March 13, 1987.

28. John Koten, "The Shattered Middle Class," *The Wall Street Journal,* March 9, 1987, p. 19.

29. John Wall, "Minorities Slice the Advertising Pie," *Insight,* March 9, 1987, pp. 46-47; U.S. Census Bureau, 1991.

30. Ibid.

31. Boone and Kurtz, *Contemporary Marketing,* p. 174.

32. The classic studies on cognitive dissonance were initiated by Leon Festinger, *A Theory of Cognitive Dissonance* (Evanston, Ill.: Row, Peterson, 1957), p. 83; for more recent views, see also Hugh Murray, "Advertising's Effect on Sales—Proven or Just Assumed?" *International Journal of Advertising* (UK) 5, no. 1 (1986), pp. 15-36; Hawkins, Best, and Coney, *Consumer Behavior,* pp. 663-65; and Ronald E. Milliman and Phillip J. Decker, "The Use of Post-Purchase Communication to Reduce Dissonance and Improve Direct Marketing Effectiveness," *Journal of Business Communication,* Spring 1990, pp. 159-70.

33. Allman, "Science 1, Advertisers 0," pp. 60-62.

Chapter 5

1. Ken Dychtwald and Greg Gable, "Portrait of a Changing Consumer," *Business Horizons,* January-February 1990, p. 62. Copyright 1990 Indiana University School of Business.

2. "Forecasters Can Tell Weather to Advertise," *Advertising Age,* January 31, 1985, p. 38.

3. Values and Lifestyles Program, Descriptive Materials for the VALS2 Segmentation System (Menlo Park, Calif.: SRI International, 1989).

4. William F. Allman, "Science 1, Advertisers 0: New Research Is Undermining Conventional Ideas on What Sells," *U.S. News & World Report,* May 1, 1989, p. 60.

5. B. Rice, "The Selling of Lifestyles: Are You What You Buy? Madison Avenue Wants to Know," *Psychology Today,* March 1988, p. 46.

6. Rebecca Piirto, "Measuring Minds in the 1990s," *American Demographics,* December 1990, p. 33.

7. Ibid., p. 32.

8. Ibid., pp. 46-51; and B. Rice, "The Selling of Lifestyles."

9. Values and Lifestyles Program.

10. Michael Hedges, "Radio's Lifestyles," *American Demographics,* February 1986, pp. 32-35.

11. Values and Lifestyles Program.

12. Frank P. McDonald, "Whither the New Segmentation Systems," *Marketing & Media Decisions,* May 1985, pp. 94, 96.

13. Ed Zotti, "Thinking Psychographically," *Public Relations Journal,* May 1985, pp. 26-30.

14. John H. Mather, "No Reason to Fear Frightening Reality of VALS," *Marketing News,* September 13, 1985, p. 15.

15. E. Jerome McCarthy and William D. Perreault, Jr., *Basic Marketing,* 10th ed. (Homewood, Ill.: Richard D. Irwin, 1990), pp. 195-208.

16. David Cravens, Gerald E. Hills, and Robert B. Woodruff, *Marketing Management* (Homewood, Ill.: Richard D. Irwin, 1987), pp. 156-78.

17. Ibid.

18. McCarthy and Perreault, *Basic Marketing,* pp. 62-89.

19. The now widely popularized conceptual model of the 4 Ps was originally developed by E. J. McCarthy, *Basic Marketing* (Homewood, Ill.: Richard D. Irwin, 1960); and the usage of the *marketing mix* derived from Neil H. Borden, "The Concept of the Marketing Mix," *Journal of Advertising Research,* June 1964, pp. 2-7.

20. McCarthy and Perreault, *Basic Marketing,* pp. 250-61; Harper W. Boyd, Jr., and Orville C. Walker, Jr., *Marketing Management: A Strategic Approach* (Homewood, Ill.: Richard D. Irwin, 1990), pp. 250-53.

21. Meg Cos, "More Work Leaves Less Time for Arts, Harris Survey Says," *The Wall Street Journal,* March 16, 1988; also Greg Clarkin, "The Marketing Successes of 1989—Entertainment: Fast Forward," *Marketing & Media Decisions,* March 1990, pp. 57-59.

22. Boyd and Walker, *Marketing Management,* pp. 252-53.

23. Adapted from Louis E. Boone and David L. Kurtz, *Contemporary Marketing,* 5th ed. (Hinsdale, Ill.: Dryden Press, 1986), p. 228.

24. Allan J. McGrath, "Segmentation and Differentiation Positioning Strategies Are Timeless," *Marketing News,* October 24, 1988, p. 18.

25. Cass Bettinger, "Developing Marketing Strategy," *Banker's Magazine,* January-February 1987, pp. 64-71.

26. Tom Eisenhart, "Breaking Away from the Faceless Pack," *Business Marketing,* June 1988, pp. 74-78.

27. Ann Keely, "From Experience—Maxi-Niching the Way to a Strong Brand: Positioning According to Systemic Dynamics," *Journal of Product Innovation Management,* September 1989, pp. 202-6.

28. Kay Satow, "The Changing State of Research in the United States," *Journal of the Market Research Society* (UK), October 1989, pp. 521-25.

29. Cyndee Miller, "Jeans Maker Has No Excuses for Its Unusual Ads," *Marketing News,* November 20, 1989, p. 9.

30. Adapted from McCarthy and Perreault, *Basic Marketing,* pp. 236-37.

31. Margaret Henderson Blair, Allan R. Kuse, David H. Furse, and David W. Stewart, "Advertising in a New Competitive Environment: Persuading Customers to Buy," *Business Horizons,* November-December 1987, pp. 20-26; also James C. Schroer, "Ad Spending: Growing Market Share," *Harvard Business Review,* January-February 1990, pp. 44-48.

32. John S. Blyth, "Packaging for Competitive Advantage," *Management Review,* May 1990, p. 64.

33. Ibid.

34. Dick Berry, "Marketing Mix for the '90s Adds an S and 2 Cs to 4Ps," *Marketing News,* December 24, 1990, p. 10.

35. Shlomo Kalish, "A New Product Adoption Model with Price, Advertising, and Uncertainty," *Management Science,* December 1985, pp. 1569-85.

36. Jack Cohen, "Planning an Effective Pricing Strategy," *Supermarket Business,* January 1991, pp. 27-35, 66, 74.

37. Tom Nash, "The Price of Success," *Chief Executive* (UK), July-August 1987, pp. 14-16.

38. Murray Roman, "What Telemarketing Can Do," *Banker's Magazine,* March-April 1984, pp. 55-58; see also, Stan Rapp and Tom Collins, *MaxiMarketing: The New Direction in Advertising, Promotion, and Marketing Strategy* (New York: McGraw-Hill, 1987), pp. 77-82.

39. McCarthy and Perreault, *Basic Marketing,* p. 15.

40. Boone and Kurtz, *Contemporary Marketing,* pp. 289-92.

41. U.S. Department of Commerce.

42. Terry Paul and John Wong, "The Retailing of Health Care," *Journal of Health Care Marketing,* Fall 1987, pp. 23-34.

43. Michael Etgar, "Effects of Adminstrative Control on Efficiency of Vertical Marketing Systems," *Journal of Marketing Research,* February 4, 1976, pp. 12-24; also Leon Richardson, "Miracles of Modern Business Method," *Asian Business* (Hong Kong), June 1990, pp. 104-5.

44. Mollie Neal, "Coupon Clutter: A 'Unique' Alternative," *Direct Marketing,* November 1989, pp. 23-24, 32, 99; Associated Press, "306.8 Billion Grocery-Store Coupons Were Issued in 1990," *The San Diego Union,* April 6, 1991, p. C1.

Chapter 6

1. Richard Gibson, "Marketers' Mantra: Reap More with Less," *The Wall Street Journal,* March 22, 1991, p. B1.

2. E. Jerome McCarthy and William D. Perreault, *Basic Marketing,* 10th ed. (Homewood, Ill.: Richard D. Irwin, 1990), p. 124.

3. Ibid., p. 127.

4. Jack J. Honomichl, "Marketing/Advertising Research: Top Worldwide Research Companies," *Advertising Age,* December 5, 1988, pp. S1, S11-S18.

5. Louis E. Boone and David L. Kurtz, *Contemporary Marketing,* 5th ed. (Hinsdale, Ill.: Dryden Press, 1986), p. 110.

6. "Researcher Says Test First, Then Advertise," *Bank Advertising News* 11, no. 17 (April 20, 1987), p. 7.

7. Gerald J. Eskin, "Applications of Electronic Single-Source Measurement Systems," *European Research* 15, no. 1 (1987), pp. 12-20.

8. Dan Fost, "Business Software: Keep It Simple, Make It Fun," *American Demographics,* December 1990, p. 19.

9. Gibson, "Marketers' Mantra."

10. Leo Bogart, "What the Scanners Show," *Advertising Age,* June 8, 1987, pp. 18, 20.

11. McCarthy and Perreault, *Basic Marketing,* p. 135.

12. William F. Allman, "Science 1, Advertisers 0: New Research Is Undermining Conventional Ideas on What Sells," *U.S. News & World Report,* May 1, 1989, p. 60.

13. McCarthy and Perreault, *Basic Marketing,* p. 135.

14. "Heartbeat," *Advertising Age,* January 12, 1987, pp. 3, 44.

15. Pamela L. Alreck and Robert B. Settle, *The Survey Research Handbook* (Homewood, Ill.: Richard D. Irwin, 1985), pp. 64-66.

16. David W. Cravens, Gerald E. Hills, and Robert B. Woodruff, *Marketing Management* (Homewood, Ill.: Richard D. Irwin, 1987), p. 639.

17. Ibid.

18. Alreck and Settle, *The Survey Research Handbook,* p. 98.

19. Ibid., p. 665.

20. R. B. Gill, "The Promise: 'Fashion comes to life' Delivers a Pledge to Consumers," *JC Penney Today* 55, no. 11 (1990), p. 6.

21. Ibid.

22. R. Craig Endicott, "P&G Spends $2.28 Billion, Surges to Head of Top 100," *Advertising Age,* September 25, 1991, pp. 1, 72.

23. Van Wallach, "Pretesting—A Necessary Evil or a Creative Tool," *Advertising Age,* February 13, 1986, pp. 18-19.

24. William R. Dillon, Teresa Domzal, and Thomas J. Madden, "Evaluating Alternative Product Positioning Strategies," *Journal of Advertising Research,* August-September 1986, pp. 18-19.

25. Mary McCabe English, "Test Marketing: Higher Costs Boost Test Commercials," *Advertising Age,* February 13, 1986, pp. 14-15.

26. R. B. Gill, "The Promise," p. 7.

27. Michael J. McCarthy, "Mind Probe: What Makes an Ad Memorable? Recent Brain Research Yields Surprising Answers," *The Wall Street Journal,* March 22, 1991, p. B3.

28. Shona McKay, "Advertising Signs Up for Analysis," *Applied Arts Quarterly,* Spring 1987, pp. 30-32.

29. Gibson, "Marketers' Mantra."

30. Robert Judson, "Marketing Mature Brands Requires Ad Analysis," *Marketing News,* January 2, 1987, pp. 20-21.

Chapter 7

1. "Ten Best Sellers," *Car and Driver,* March 1989, p. 31.

2. Lloyd Garrison, "The Honda Way," *Time,* September 8, 1986, pp. 50-56; Stewart Toy, "The Americanization of Honda," *Business Week,* April 25, 1988, pp. 90-96; Jack R. Nerad, "The Acura Integra LS," *Motor Trend,* July 1988; "The Acura Concept (1986-1988)," Report presented at the Acura dealer meeting, 1989.

3. William Giles, "Marketing Planning and Customer Policy," *Management Decision* (UK) 24, no. 3 (1986), pp. 19-27.

4. Margaret L. Friedman, "How to Write a Marketing Plan for Your Service Organization," *Agency Sales Magazine,* February 1987, pp. 42-46.

5. G. A. Marken, "Success Is No Accident; You Need a Plan," *Marketing News,* May 23, 1986, p. 28; Ralph S. Blois, "Do You Really Need an Agency," *Sales & Marketing Management,* October 1988, pp. 120-22.

6. David W. Nylen, "Making Your Business Plan and Action Plan," *Business,* October-November-December 1985, pp. 12-16; "Preparing a Marketing Plan," *International Journal of Bank Marketing* (UK), 1989, pp. vii-viii; Thomas McCaghren, "Putting Ill-Conceived Marketing Plans on Track," *National Underwriter,* June 5, 1989, pp. 41, 44-45.

7. David W. Cravens, Gerald E. Hills, and Robert B. Woodruff, *Marketing Management* (Homewood, Ill.: Richard D. Irwin, 1987), pp. 245-46; McCaghren, "Putting Ill-Conceived Marketing Plans on Track."

8. Kenichi Ohmae, "Getting Back to Strategy," *Harvard Business Review*, November-December 1988, p. 149.

9. "Preparing a Marketing Plan," pp. vii-viii; E. Jerome McCarthy and William D. Perreault, Jr., *Basic Marketing*, 10th ed. (Homewood, Ill.: Richard D. Irwin, 1990), p. 95.

10. Ohmae, "Getting Back to Strategy."

11. Donald P. Robin and R. Eric Reidenbach, "Social Responsibility, Ethics, and Marketing Strategy: Closing the Gap between Concept and Application," *Journal of Marketing*, January 1987, pp. 44-58; P. Rajan Varadarajan and Anil Menon, "Cause-Related Marketing: A Coalignment of Marketing Strategy and Corporate Philanthropy," *Journal of Marketing*, July 1988, pp. 58-74; Mark Evans, "Education Marketing Basics: Advertising in the Classroom," *Advertising Age*, October 10, 1988, p. 18.

12. Fred Posner, "Smart Strategy + Superb Execution = Great Advertising," Speech before the American Marketing Association, Marketing Management Conference, New York, March 31, 1982.

13. David Ogilvy, *Ogilvy on Advertising* (New York: Random House, 1985), p. 12.

14. Pat Sloan, "Olay Bath Bar Takes Aim at Dove," *Advertising Age*, February 4, 1991, p. 9.

15. "Barricades to Strategic Marketing Thinking," *Planning Review*, February 1987, pp. 8-15.

16. Richard L. Erickson, "Marketing Planning: There Is No Magic," *Journal of Business & Industrial Marketing*, Fall 1986, pp. 61-67; Sharon Wolf, "Focused Strategy Can Assist the Communications Process," *Marketing News*, December 4, 1987, p. 20.

17. Louis E. Boone and David L. Kurtz, *Contemporary Marketing* 5th ed. (Hinsdale, Ill.: Dryden Press, 1986), pp. 66-68.

18. Robert M. Cohen, "Advertising Effectiveness: First Know Your Objectives," *Sales & Marketing Management in Canada*, October 1989, pp. 10-12.

19. John O'Toole, *The Trouble with Advertising*, 2nd ed. (New York: Random House, 1985), p. 103.

20. The classic treatise on measurable advertising objectives was written by Russell H. Colley, *Defining Advertising Goals for Measured Advertising Results* (New York: Association of National Advertisers, 1961), p. 1; see also, Russell Abratt, "Advertising Objectives of Industrial Marketers," *International Journal of Advertising* (UK) 6, no. 2 (1987), pp. 121-31; Steven W. Hartley and Charles H. Patti, "Evaluating Business-to-Business Advertising: A Comparison of Objectives and Results," *Journal of Advertising Research*, April-May 1988, pp. 21-27; Cohen, "Advertising Effectiveness"; Raymond R. Burke, Arvind Rangaswamy, Jerry Wind, and Jehoshua Eliashberg, "A Knowledge-Based System for Advertising Design," *Marketing Science*, Summer 1990, pp. 212-29.

21. Calvin L. Hodock, "Strategies behind the Winners and Losers," *The Journal of Business Strategy*, September-October 1990, p. 7.

22. O'Toole, *The Trouble with Advertising*, pp. 128-30; David Clark Scott, "Finding Out What Makes Us Tick," *Christian Science Monitor*, January 27, 1987, pp. 1, 16; Beate von Keitz, "Consumer Involvement—Does It Affect Advertising Testing?" *Marketing & Research Today* (Netherlands), February 1990, pp. 37-45.

23. Adapted from Al Ries and Jack Trout, *Bottom-Up Marketing* (New York: McGraw-Hill, 1989), p. 8.

24. Robert D. Buzzell and Frederick D. Wiersema, "Successful Share-Building Strategies," *Harvard Business Review*, January-February 1981, p. 135; Siva K. Balasubramanian and V. Kumar, "Analyzing Variations in Advertising and Promotional Expenditures: Key Correlates in Consumer, Industrial, and Service Markets," *Journal of Marketing*, April 1990, pp. 57-68.

25. Lacy Glenn Thomas, "Advertising in Consumer Goods Industries: Durability, Economies of Scale, Heterogeneity," *Journal of Law & Economics*, April 1989, pp. 163-193; James C. Schroer, "Ad Spending: Growing Market Share," *Harvard Business Review*, January-February 1990, pp. 44-48.

26. William Band, "Quality Is King for Marketers," *Sales & Marketing Management in Canada* (Canada), March 1989, pp. 6-8.

27. Bernard Ryan, Jr., *Advertising in a Recession: The Best Defense Is a Good Offense* (New York: American Association of Advertising Agencies, 1991), pp. 13-29; Priscilla C. Brown, "Surviving with a Splash," *Business Marketing*, January 1991, p. 14; Edmund O. Lawler, "A Window of Opportunity," *Business Marketing*, January 1991, p. 16; Rebecca Colwell Quarles, "Marketing Research Turns Recession into Business Opportunity," *Marketing News*, January 7, 1991, pp. 27, 29.

28. Leo Bogart, *Strategy in Advertising*, 2nd ed. (Chicago: Crain Books, 1984), pp. 45-47.

29. Schroer, "Ad Spending"; John Philip Jones, "Ad Spending: Maintaining Market Share," *Harvard Business Review*, January-February 1990, pp. 38-42.

30. James M. Oliver and Paul W. Farris, "Push and Pull: A One-Two Punch for Packaged Products," *Sloan Management Review*, Fall 1989, pp. 53-61.

31. Marsha Lindsay, "Establish Brand Equity through Advertising," *Marketing News*, January 22, 1990, p. 16; Robert D. Buzzell, John A. Quelch, and Walter J. Salmon, "The Costly Bargain of Trade Promotion," *Harvard Business Review*, March-April 1990, p. 142.

32. Kent M. Lancaster and Judith A. Stern, "Computer-Based Advertising Budgeting Practices of Leading Consumer Advertisers," *Journal of Advertising* 12, no. 4 (1983), pp. 4-9; James E. Lynch and Graham J. Hooley, "Advertising Budgeting Practices of Industrial Advertisers," *Industrial Marketing Management*, February 1987, pp. 63-69; Pierre Filiatrault and Jean-Charles Chebat, "How Service Firms Set Their Marketing Budgets," *Industrial Marketing Management*, February 1990, pp. 63-67.

33. Jan Calloway, "Cashing In on Your Advertising," *Cellular Business*, February 1987, pp. 20-21; Peter Barrow, "How Much Is It Going to Cost Me?" *Canadian Manager* (Canada), December 1989, pp. 14-15.

34. Gordon Willis, Sherril H. Kennedy, John Cheese, and Angela Rushton, "Maximizing Market Effectiveness: Promotion Decisions," *Management Decision* (UK) 28, no. 2 (1990), pp. 103-27.

35. Richard Vaughn, "How Advertising Works: A Planning Model Revisited," *Journal of Advertising Research*, February-March 1986, pp. 57-66.

36. Amiya K. Basu and Rajeev Batra, "ADSPLIT: A Multi-Brand Advertising Budget Allocation Model," *Journal of Advertising* 17, no. 2 (1988), pp. 44-51; Peter Doyle and John Saunders, "Multiproduct Advertising Budgeting," *Marketing Science*, Spring 1990, pp. 97-113; Glen L. Urban, John R. Hauser, and John H. Roberts, "Prelaunch Forecasting of New Automobiles," *Marketing Science*, April 1990, pp. 401-21; Bay Arinze, "Market Planning with Computer Models: A Case Study in the Software Industry," *Industrial Marketing Management*, May 1990, pp. 117-29.

37. Ahmet Aykac, Marcel Corstjens, David Gautschi, and Ira Horowitz, "Estimation Uncertainty and Optimal Advertising Decisions," *Management Science*, January 1989, pp. 42-50.

Chapter 8

1. Peter C. Yesawich, "The Final Steps in Market Development: Execution and Measurement of Programs," *Cornell Hotel & Restaurant Administration Quarterly,* February 1989, pp. 82-91.

2. Marvin Schoenwald, "Marketing a Political Candidate," *Journal of Consumer Marketing,* Spring 1987, pp. 57-63.

3. John O'Toole, *The Trouble with Advertising,* 2nd ed. (New York: Random House, 1985), p. 131.

4. Ibid., p. 132; Fred Danzig, "The Big Idea," *Advertising Age,* November 9, 1988, pp. 16, 138-40.

5. O'Toole, *The Trouble with Advertising,* pp. 132-33.

6. John Caples, "A Dozen Ways to Develop Advertising Ideas," *Advertising Age,* November 14, 1983, pp. M4-M5, M46; "Can Creativity Be Systematized?" *Advertising Age,* November 18, 1985, pp. 46, 48; Luther Brock and Milton Pierce, "Check Your Swipe File for Direct Mail Ideas/A Good Swipe File Is Better than a College Education," *Direct Marketing,* December 1986, pp. 111, 116-17; Murray Raphel, "How to Get A-Head in Direct Mail," *Direct Marketing,* January 1990, pp. 30-32, 52.

7. "Copy Chasers: When the Client Must Take Charge," *Business Marketing,* July 1989, pp. 70-73; Julie Liesse, "Finding the Perfect Print Ad," *Advertising Age,* August 13, 1990, p. 52.

8. David Ogilvy, *Ogilvy on Advertising* (New York: Random House, 1985), pp. 17-18.

9. Milton Pierce, "How to Write a Powerful Headline," *Direct Marketing,* September 1988, pp. 90, 95.

10. Herbert L. Kahn, "Your Own Brand of Advertising for Non-Consumer Products," *Harvard Business Review,* January-February 1986.

11. E. Jerome McCarthy and William D. Perreault, Jr., *Basic Marketing,* 10th ed. (Homewood, Ill.: Richard D. Irwin, 1990), p. 175; Michael J. McCarthy, "Mind Probe—What Makes an Ad Memorable? Recent Brain Research Yields Surprising Answers," *The Wall Street Journal,* March 22, 1991, p. B3.

12. Raphel, "How to Get A-Head in Direct Mail."

13. Liesse, "Finding the Perfect Print Ad."

14. Ogilvy, *Ogilvy on Advertising,* p. 71; Murray Raphel, "Ad Techniques—Off with the Head!" *Bank Marketing,* February 1988, pp. 54-55.

15. Ogilvy, *Ogilvy on Advertising,* pp. 10-11.

16. Ivan Levison, "Six Battle-Tested Tips for Success in Print Ads," *High-Tech Marketing,* February 1987, pp. 62-63.

17. Andrew J. Byrne, "The Most Important Part of an Advertisement," *National Underwriter,* November 7, 1986, pp. 48-49; Levison, "Six Battle-Tested Tips."

18. Marie Spadoni, "Fallon McElligott Rolls Stone into the 80s: Trade Advertising," *Advertising Age,* August 18, 1986, pp. S3, S9-S10.

19. Pierce, "How to Write a Powerful Headline," pp. 90, 95.

20. Harold M. Spielman, "In Copy Research, Practice Makes Almost Perfect," *Advertising Age,* November 1, 1984, pp. 16-22; "Eleven Ways to Write Copy That Gets Results," *National Public Accountant,* July 1985, pp. 31-32; "Copy Chaser Criteria," *Business Marketing,* January 1991, p. 33.

21. Ogilvy, *Ogilvy on Advertising,* p. 119.

22. Spielman, "In Copy Research."

23. O'Toole, *The Trouble with Advertising,* p. 149.

24. Ibid., p. 148.

25. Ogilvy, *Ogilvy on Advertising,* pp. 118-20.

26. Kahn, "Your Own Brand of Advertising," p. 24.

Chapter 9

1. Adapted from Sharon Edelson, "Elemental Considerations: Making Idyllic Images under Less than Ideal Circumstances," *American Photographer,* November 1989, pp. 18, 19, 22.

2. Murray Raphel, "Ad Techniques—Off with the Head," *Bank Marketing,* February 1988, pp. 54-55.

3. Glenn Mohrman and Jeffrey E. Scott, "Truth(s) in Advertising? Part II," *Medical Marketing & Media,* October 1, 1988, pp. 28-32.

4. J. Douglas Johnson, *Advertising Today* (Chicago: Science Research Associates, 1978), pp. 91-92; Julie Liesse, "Finding the Perfect Print Ad," *Advertising Age,* August 13, 1990, p. 52.

5. John O'Toole, *The Trouble with Advertising,* 2nd ed. (New York: Random House, 1985), p. 149.

6. David Ogilvy, *Ogilvy on Advertising* (New York: Random House, 1985), pp. 88-89.

7. Ibid.

8. Ibid.

9. Richard H. Stansfield, *Advertising Manager's Handbook* (Chicago: Dartnell Corporation, 1969), pp. 640-41; Julia M. Collins, "Image and Advertising," *Harvard Business Review,* January-February 1989, pp. 93-97.

10. Mark Spaulding, "Packaging's 100 Giants," *Packaging,* July 1990, pp. 36-54.

11. Hester Thomas, "Design Packs a Punch," *Marketing* (UK), November 20, 1986, pp. 47-50; Francis Lancaster, "Body Language in Packages," *Marketing* (UK), September 29, 1988, pp. 27, 30.

12. Walter P. Margulies, *Packaging Power* (New York: World Publishing, 1970), p. 62; Lancaster, "Body Language in Packages"; Karen Hogan, "Brand Strategy: Mint Conditions," *Marketing* (UK), February 9, 1989, pp. 27-28; Wright Ferguson, "Health & Beauty Aids," *Supermarket Business,* September 1989, pp. 194-95, 222, 230.

13. Michael Gershman, "Packaging's Role in Remarketing," *Management Review,* May 1987, pp. 41-45.

14. Sheila Clark, "Packaging—Not Just a Pretty Design," *Chief Executive* (UK), November 1986, pp. 80-81.

15. Teresa Reese, *Print Casebooks 7, 1987/1988: The Best in Packaging* (Bethesda, Md.: R.C. Publications, 1986), pp. 46-49, 88-90; Ellen Opat Inkeles, *Print Casebooks 8, 1989/1990: The Best in Packaging* (Bethesda, Md.: R.C. Publications, 1989), pp. 85, 99.

16. Karen Hogan, "Packaging/Design/Point-of-Sale: Metal Works," *Marketing* (UK), October 4, 1990, pp. 33-36.

17. Phyllis Furman, "Grocery Marketing: Redesign Puts Old Packages in New Light," *Advertising Age,* May 4, 1987, pp. S20-S21; "Marketing Guide: 14—3-D Packaging Design," *Marketing* (UK), March 29, 1990, pp. 21-24.

18. Ogilvy, *Ogilvy on Advertising,* p. 109.

19. Hooper White, "TV Commercial Production: Creatives Redirect a Complex Scene," *Advertising Age,* March 31, 1986, pp. S1-S2.

20. Mary McCabe English, "Test Marketing: Higher Costs Boost Test Commercials," *Advertising Age,* February 13, 1986, pp. 14-15.

21. Betsy Sharkey, "Software Lets Thrifty Clients 'CLIP' and Save," *Adweek,* November 7, 1988.

22. Terry Kattelman, "Future Shop," *Advertising Age,* January 7, 1991, p. S18.

23. Ogilvy, *Ogilvy on Advertising,* pp. 103-13.

24. Ibid., pp. 107-8.

25. Ibid., p. 105.

26. Gordon L. Patzer, "Source Credibility as a Function of

Communicator Physical Attractiveness," *Journal of Business Research,* June 1983, pp. 229-41.

27. Ogilvy, *Ogilvy on Advertising,* p. 105.

28. Dylan Landis, "Sedelmaier Spots Have Alaska Airlines Roaring," *Adweek,* July 29, 1985, p. 10.

29. "Forget Jingles and Jokes in These Cinema Verité Ads," *The Wall Street Journal,* April 16, 1987.

30. Judith Reitman, "Cutting the Clutter with Computer Graphics," *Marketing & Media Decisions,* May 1985, pp. 52-58, 168.

Chapter 10

1. Gordon Graham, "Computer Wizardry: The Wild, Wild West of Desktop Color," *Applied Arts Quarterly* (Canada), Fall 1990, pp. 13, 16, 18, 20.

2. Winnie O'Kelley, "Computers Create Graphic Palette," *Advertising Age,* April 28, 1986, p. 54; Cathy Madison, "Desktop Video Editing Has Ad Makers Clicking," *Adweek,* March 11, 1991, pp. 46-47.

3. "70 Case Studies of Computers in Business," *Technology Solutions,* supplement to *Publish,* Summer 1991, pp. 100-102.

4. Terry Kattelman, "Desktop Creativity: Future Shop, At Tiny High-Tech Farago Advertising in New York, Small Is Potentially Beautiful," *Advertising Age,* January 7, 1991, p. S18.

5. "70 Case Studies of Computers in Business," pp. 61-63.

6. Kathleen Loomis, "Printing: Teach Your Boss a Lesson," *In House Graphics,* February 1990, pp. 8-9.

7. David Ogilvy, *Ogilvy on Advertising* (New York: Random House, 1985), pp. 96-97.

8. Alex Brown, "Type Renaissance," *Macworld,* July 1991, pp. 204-5.

9. PANTONE® is a registered trademark of Pantone, Inc.

10. Stephanie Cook, "The Electronic Palette Has Retouchers on the Run," *Business Week,* Industrial/Technology edition, January 12, 1987, pp. 122H-122I; Graham, "Computer Wizardry," pp. 13, 16, 18, 20; Suzanne Weber, "Commercializing on the Power of the Mac," *Technology Solutions,* Summer 1991, pp. 61-63.

Chapter 11

1. Stewart Toy and Amy Dunkin, "Cheap Dreams: The Budget Inn Boom," *Business Week,* July 14, 1986, pp. 76-77; Beverly Narum, "Regional Profiles: Dallas," *Advertising Age,* November 9, 1988, pp. 24, 141-42; Marcia Parker, "Room at the Inn: Motel 6 Sites Finance Expansion," *Pensions & Investment Age,* December 12, 1988, pp. 27-28; Carol Hall, "Travel: Motel 6—King of the Road," *Marketing & Media Decisions,* March 1989, pp. 80-86; Skip Hollandsworth, "Ad Men at War," *Best of Business,* Summer 1991, p. 60, reprinted from *Texas Monthly,* November 1990.

2. Murphy A. Sewall and Can Sarel, "Characteristics of Radio Commercials and Their Recall Effectiveness, *Journal of Marketing,* January 1986, pp. 52-60.

3. David Ogilvy, *Ogilvy on Advertising* (New York: Random House, 1985) pp. 113-16; Bob Weinstein, "Radio Is a Riot," *Madison Avenue,* June 1985, pp. 70-74; Rachel Simpson, "Radio Advertising: Creativity's Short Wave," *Marketing* (UK), December 15, 1988, p. 31.

4. Michael C. Keith, *Radio Production, Art and Science* (Stoneham, Mass.: Butterworth-Heinemann, 1990), p. 91.

5. Gotcha story and information adapted from Greg Hofman, "Splash Graphics That Say 'Gotcha,'" *Step-by-Step Graphics,* May-June, 1991, p. 40.

6. Miner Raymond, "How to Cut Commercial Production Costs without Anyone Knowing You've Done It," *Sales & Marketing Management in Canada* (Canada), December 1987, pp. 20-22; Janet Myers and Laurie Freeman, "Marketers Police TV Commercial Costs," *Advertising Age,* April 3, 1989, p. 51; "Marketing Guide 19: Advertising Production," *Marketing* (UK), February 7, 1991.

7. "Cost of TV Spot Production Escalates to Nearly $125,000," *Marketing News,* September 26, 1986, p. 6; Alex Ben Block, "Where the Money Goes," *Forbes,* September 21, 1987.

8. Cam Sylvester, "Mavericks: North Star," *Canadian Business* (Canada), August 1989, pp. 25-26.

9. Andrew Olds, "Creativity-Production: The Generalists," *Advertising Age,* January 1, 1990, pp. S26-S29, S31.

10. Hofman, "Splash Graphics," p. 44.

11. Joan Hamilton, "You've Come a Long Way, Gumby: Claymation Is the Hottest Thing in Commercials, and Will Vinton's Ad for California Raisins Is the Reason," *Business Week,* December 8, 1986; p. 74; Albert R. Karr, "Lively Raisins on TV Are Grapes of Wrath to One Distributor," *The Wall Street Journal,* January 21, 1987.

12. Hofman, "Splash Graphics," p. 48.

13. Terry Kattleman, "Creativity: Sound Design—Roll Over Hein Hoven," *Advertising Age,* March 5, 1990, pp. SS20-SS22.

14. Ogilvy, *Ogilvy on Advertising,* pp. 113-16.

15. Miner Raymond, "How to Cut Commercial Production Costs," pp. 20-22.

16. Kenneth Roman and Jane Maas, *How to Advertise* (New York: St. Martin's Press, 1976), pp. 79-81; Miner Raymond, "How to Cut Commercial Production Costs," pp. 20-22; "Marketing Guide 19: Advertising Production," pp. 21-24.

Chapter 12

1. Joe Mandese, "Del Monte's Can-Do," *Marketing & Media Decisions,* November 1990, pp. 47-49.

2. Jon Lafayette, "Agency Media Staffs Gain Clout," *Advertising Age,* March 4, 1991, p. 12.

3. Ibid.

4. Page Thompson, "The Big Picture," *Inside Print,* 1989 Media Planner's Guide, pp. 31-33.

5. Scott Donaton, "Roles Expand in Value-Added Era," *Advertising Age,* April 9, 1990, pp. S-26, S-28.

6. Joe Mandese, "Decoding the Deal," *Marketing & Media Decisions,* September 1989, pp. 33-39.

7. Jack Z. Sissors and Lincoln Bumba, *Advertising Media Planning,* 3rd ed. (Lincolnwood, Ill.: NTC Business Books, 1989), pp. 235-36.

8. "Studying the Academic Studies," *Adweek Special Report,* December 7, 1987, p. 31.

9. David C. Lehmkuhl, "Mediology," *Marketing & Media Decisions,* May 1989, p. 79.

10. Mandese, "Del Monte's Can-Do," pp. 47-49.

11. Stephen H. Martin, "Mediology," *Marketing & Media Decisions,* November 1990, pp. 57, 60.

12. "Effective Use of Print: The Current Thinking," *Inside Print,* January 1987, p. 119.

13. Kenneth Longman, *Advertising* (New York: Harcourt Brace Jovanovich, 1971), pp. 211-12.

14. Sissors and Bumba, *Advertising Media Planning,* p. 126.

15. "Effective Use of Print," p. 119.

16. Neil Kelliher, "Magazine Media Planning for 'Effectiveness': Getting the People Back into the Process," *The Journal of Consumer Marketing,* Summer 1990, pp. 47-55.

17. Joe Coogle, "Research: Data-Base Marketing," *Marketing & Media Decisions,* January 1990, pp. 75-76.

18. Stephen P. Phelps, "Media Planning: The Measurement Gap," *Marketing & Media Decisions,* July 1986, p. 151.

19. Longman, *Advertising,* p. 351.

20. Kelliher, "Magazine Media Planning for 'Effectiveness,'" pp. 47-55.

21. Jim Surmanek, *Media Planning* (Lincolnwood, Ill.: NTC Business Books, 1985), p. 24.

22. Michael Garry, "To the Max," *Marketing & Media Decisions,* March 1990, pp. 39-42.

23. "Tyco Toys Will Avoid Christmas Rush," *The Wall Street Journal,* November 5, 1987, p. 39.

24. Andrea Rothman, "Timing Techniques Can Make Small Ad Budgets Seem Bigger," *The Wall Street Journal,* February 3, 1989, p. B4.

25. Ibid.

26. Joe Mandese, "The Merge/Purge Program," *Marketing & Media Decisions,* October 1989, pp. 48-58.

27. Sissors and Bumba, *Advertising Media Planning,* p. 358.

Chapter 13

1. Tom Goss, *The Best in Advertising,* Print Casebooks, Vol. 6, 1984-85 edition (Washington, D.C.: R. C. Publications, 1984), pp. 25-26.

2. Leo Bogart, "Newspapers Fight Off Broadcast Challenge, Survive, and Prosper," *Advertising Age,* April 30, 1980, p. 176.

3. Michael J. Robinson and Andrew Kohut, "Believability and the Press," *Public Opinion Quarterly,* Summer 1988, pp. 174-89; Opinion Research Corporation Study, reported in *Key Facts about Newspapers and Advertising* (New York: Newspaper Advertising Bureau, 1982), p. 1.

4. Russell Shaw, "Papers Losing Ground in National Advertising," *Advertising Age,* July 25, 1985, p. 52.

5. *'90 Facts about Newspapers* (Washington, D.C.: American Newspaper Publishers Association, 1990), p. 10.

6. Ibid., p. 2.

7. Ibid.

8. Ibid., p. 3.

9. Eileen Norris, "Ad Vehicles Bombard Consumers," *Advertising Age,* November 7, 1985, p. 16.

10. Margaret Rosser, "*USA Today,* Yesterday and Tomorrow," *Marketing & Media Decisions,* December 1986, p. 108; *'90 Facts about Newspapers.*

11. *Newspaper Rate Differentials* (New York: American Association of Advertising Agencies, 1990).

12. *'90 Facts about Newspapers,* p. 10.

13. William F. Gloede, "Newspapers Cut National Ad Rate," *Advertising Age,* June 8, 1987, p. 1.

14. "A Network of Co-op Power," *Marketing Communication,* June 1986, p. 80.

15. "Effective Uses of Print: The Current Thinking," *Inside Print,* January 1987, p. 119.

16. Stephen H. Martin, "Magazines: A Medium to Watch," *Marketing & Media Decisions,* August 1985, p. 79.

17. "Reader's Choice: Ads with Impact," *Inside Print,* January 1987, p. 35.

18. Steve Kurtzer, "Magazines: The Next Decade," *Marketing & Media Decisions,* June 1985, p. 142.

19. Joanne Lipman, "Time, Newsweek Concoct Package Deals," *The Wall Street Journal,* March 8, 1991, sec. b, p. 4.

20. Hall's Magazine Reports, Magazine Publishers of America, January 1990.

21. Magazine Publishers of America, April 1990.

22. Scott LaFee, "It's Chic, and Quite the Thing," *The San Diego Union,* September 16, 1991, p. C1.

23. Pat Guy, "Circulations Drop; Shakeout Possible," *USA Today,* August 28, 1990, sec. b, p. 4.

24. John Potenzano, "The Added Value of Added-Value," *Marketing & Media Decisions,* June 1990, pp. 58-59.

25. *Guide to Consumer Magazines* (New York: American Association of Advertising Agencies, 1988), p. 10.

26. Ibid.

Chapter 14

1. Stuart Elliott, "Energizer's E. B. Parades into Ad History," *USA Today,* January 26, 1990, p. 1B.

2. Kate Fitzgerald, "Energizer Hops onto Top 10," *Advertising Age,* January 7, 1991, p. 39.

3. John Motavalli, "Cable TV," *Media in the 90s,* September 11, 1989, p. 160.

4. *Nielsen Television Index,* Nielsen Media Research, 1990, pp. 2-3.

5. Joe Mandese, "Is Home Video the Real Fourth Network?" *Adweek,* March 18, 1986, p. 4.

6. *TV Basics 1990-91* (New York: Television Bureau of Advertising), p. 6.

7. Frank Sommerfield, "Anything but Money," *Marketing & Media Decisions,* December 1989, p. 28; Richard W. Stevenson, "Bartering for TV Ad Time," *The New York Times,* August 3, 1985, p. 19.

8. *TV Basics 1990-91,* p. 3.

9. "Tracking Ad Dollars," *The Wall Street Journal,* March 22, 1990, p. B4.

10. R. Craig Endicott, "P&G Spends $2.28 Billion, Surges to Head of Top 100," *Advertising Age,* September 25, 1991, pp. 1, 58, 72.

11. *TV Basics 1990-91,* p. 5.

12. David Kalish, "Putting the Touch on Media," *Marketing & Media Decisions,* July 1989, pp. 14-15.

13. *Adweek's Marketer's Guide to Media* 14, no. 1, January 1991.

14. Ronald Alsop, "Advertisers Go Beyond Soaps to Reach Daytime Audience," *The Wall Street Journal,* September 19, 1985, p. 33.

15. "Terminal Television," *American Demographics,* January 1987, p. 15.

16. Wayne Walley, "Popularity of :15s Falls," *Advertising Age,* January 14, 1991, p. 3.

17. Ibid.

18. Aimee Stern, "New Power in Buying TV Time," *Dun's Business Month,* June 1985, p. 59.

19. "1991 Advertisers Guide to Cable," *Advertising Age,* February 11, 1991, p. 22.

20. Rajeev Batra and Rashi Glazer, *Cable TV Advertising* (New York: Quorum Books, 1989), p. 21.

21. *Cable TV Facts 90,* pp. 6-7.

22. David Samuel Barr, *Advertising on Cable: A Practical Guide for Users* (Englewood Cliffs, N.J.: Prentice Hall, 1985), p. 34.

23. Ibid., p. 43.

24. *Cable TV Facts 90,* p. 5.

25. "1991 Advertisers Guide to Cable," p. 21.

26. Len Strazewski, "Advertisers Wired about Cable's Reach," *Advertising Age,* October 19, 1987.

27. Barr, *Advertising on Cable,* p. 71.

28. Judan Dagnoli, "Cable Test Hot-Wired to Consumer Preferences," *Advertising Age,* December 1, 1986, p. S-10.

29. Hanna Rubin, "Home Video," *Media in the 90s,* September 11, 1989, p. 168.

30. Ibid.

31. Joanne Lipman, "Video Renters Watch the Ads, Zapping Conventional Wisdom," *The Wall Street Journal,* April 28, 1989, p. B1.

32. "Radio Ads for Athlete's Foot Medicine Outdo TV Spots," Radio Advertising Bureau.

33. *Radio Facts for Advertisers 1990* (New York: Radio Advertising Bureau, Inc., 1990), pp. 34-37.

34. Helen Rogan, "AM Radio Fights to Win Listeners with Stereo and Format Changes," *The Wall Street Journal,* October 21, 1985, p. 25.

35. Janice Steinberg, "New Formats Gain Frequency on AM Band," *Advertising Age,* August 19, 1985, p. 18.

36. Michael Hedges, "Radio's Life Styles," *American Demographics,* February 1986, p. 3.

37. Julie Liesse Erickson, "Networks Sharing Airwaves with Syndicators," *Advertising Age,* August 29, 1985, p. 28.

38. Marianne Miller, "SPAM's Media Plan: It Might Surprise You," *Marketing & Media Decisions,* October 1985, p. 69.

39. *Radio Facts for Advertisers 1990.*

40. "Tracking Ad Dollars," p. B4.

Chapter 15

1. Tom Eisenhart, "Breakthrough Direct Marketing," *Business Marketing,* August 1990, pp. 20-28.

2. Carol Nelson, "If It Isn't Direct, It Doesn't Follow," *Direct Marketing,* March 1990, pp. 66-67; "Direct Marketing: A Useful Advertising Medium and a Valuable Sales Tool," *Small Business Report,* September 1985, p. 71.

3. "Direct Marketing: What Is It?" *Direct Marketing,* September 1983, p. 20.

4. "Ringing Up Annoyance," *Target Marketing,* February 1987, p. 30.

5. Ibid.

6. Christine Adamec, "Niche Marketing by Mail," *In Business,* November-December 1986, p. 32; Jean Li Rogers, "Consumer Response to Advertising Mail," *Journal of Advertising Research,* December 1989-January 1990, pp. 18-23; "Mail Order Top 250+," *Direct Marketing,* October 1990, pp. 27-46; "USA Snapshots: Home Becomes the Mail," *USA Today,* December 19, 1990, sec. d, p. 1; "USA Snapshots: More Catalogs in the Mail," *USA Today,* December 19, 1990, sec. b, p. 1; "Tracking Ad Dollars," *The Wall Street Journal,* March 22, 1991, sec. b, p. 4.

7. Albert Haas, Jr., "How to Sell Almost Anything by Direct Mail," *Across the Board,* November 1986, p. 49.

8. Penny Gill, "Targeting Direct Mail," *Stores,* July 1990, pp. 42-47; Pat Sloan, "Avon Is Calling on New Tactics," *Advertising Age,* January 7, 1991, pp. 3, 41.

9. Louise Tutelian, "Catalogs Turn a Page in Marketing," *USA Today,* October 17, 1986, sec. b, p. 1.

10. John Schneider, "Direct to the Consumer," *Nation's Business,* June 1985, pp. 29, 32; Edmund L. Andrews, "A Catalog of Woes," *Venture,* May 1986, p. 54.

11. John B. Hinge, "Catalog Houses that Once Boomed Find the Checks Are No Longer in the Mail," *The Wall Street Journal,* April 4, 1991, sec. b, pp. 1, 8.

12. Bob Stone, *Successful Direct Marketing Methods* (Chicago: Crain Books, 1987), p. 101.

13. William R. Morrisey, "Gain Competitive Edge with Data-Based Direct Marketing," *Marketing News,* March 15, 1985, p. 22.

14. Allen Miller, "Workshop: How to Develop a Direct-Mail Mailing List," *Public Relations Journal,* April 1988, pp. 31-32.

15. Diane C. Donovan, "Marketing," *Nation's Business,* July 1986, p. 35.

16. Peter Finch, "The Direct Marketing Data Base Revolution," *Business Marketing,* August 1985, p. 46.

17. Bob Davis, "Baby Goods Firms See Direct Mail as the Perfect Pitch for New Moms," *The Wall Street Journal,* January 29, 1986, p. 33.

18. David Shepard Associates, Inc., *The New Direct Marketing* (Homewood, Ill.: Business One Irwin, 1990), pp. 6, 21, 254.

19. Mollie Neal, "Quaker's Direct Hit," *Direct Marketing,* January 1991, pp. 52-53, 70; Laurie Petersen, "Quaker Bets Direct Promotion Is the Right Thing to Do," *Adweek's Marketing Week,* January 8, 1990, pp. 4-5.

20. Haas, "How to Sell Almost Anything," p. 50.

21. Karen Hochman, "15 Direct Mail Tips from the Pros: 8 Ways to Get Better Results," *Bank Marketing,* November 1988, pp. 28-30.

22. William Matheson, "Sprechen Sie Deutsch? Yeah—Well, Sort Of," *The Wall Street Journal,* February 5, 1988, sec. 1, p. 25.

23. Hinge, "Catalog Houses that Once Boomed."

24. "Sea It Anderson's Way," *Institute Insights,* First Quarter 1990.

25. *Billboard Basics* (Washington, D.C.: Outdoor Advertising Association of America, 1991), pp. 6, 11.

26. Press release, Institute of Outdoor Advertising, 1991.

27. Robert Levy, "Breakout in Billboards," *Dun's Business Month,* May 1985, p. 44.

28. *Guide to Out-of-Home* (New York: American Association of Advertising Agencies, 1988), p. 18.

29. *Billboard Basics,* pp. 2, 10, 14, 19.

30. *Guide to Out-of-Home,* p. 12.

31. Nancy L. Croft, "Spiels on Wheels," *Nation's Business,* February 1987, p. 14.

32. Murray Raphel, "Miniature Billboards," *Direct Marketing,* December 1989, pp. 30, 32; Grandesigns Turns Truck Space into Sales," *Entrepreneur,* October 1985, p. 9.

33. Ruth Hamel, Tim Schreiner, and Brad Edmondson, "Billboards Want Respect: Cracking the Code," *Direct Marketing,* July 1988, pp. 45-49; Barbara Walton, "How to Reach a Very Specific Market Target Rather Efficiently," *Madison Avenue,* November 1985, p. 98.

34. Ibid.

Chapter 16

1. Bruce Horovitz, "The Pratfalls in Promotions," *Los Angeles Times,* April 28, 1991, pp. D1, D8; "Burger King Sees Kids as Future," *Adweek's Marketing Week,* January 8, 1990, p. 5; Laurie Peterson, "BK's Kids Club Takes on Ronald," *Adweek,* January 1, 1990, p. 3; Laurie Petersen, "Promote's 1990 All-Stars: Sharon Fogg," *Promote,* March 5, 1990, p. 13.

2. Russ Bowman, "Sales Promotion," *Marketing & Media Decisions,* July 1989, p. 124.

3. John Philip Jones, "The Double Jeopardy of Sales Promotions," *Harvard Business Review,* September-October 1990, p. 149.

4. Laurie Petersen, "The Pavlovian Syndrome," *Adweek's Marketing Week "Promote,"* supplement, April 9, 1990, p. 7. 1990, p. 51.

5. Magid M. Abraham and Leonard M. Lodish, "Getting the Most Out of Advertising and Promotion," *Harvard Business Review,* May-June 1990, p. 51.

6. Richard Edel, "Trade Wars Threaten Future Peace of Marketers," *Advertising Age,* August 15, 1985, p. 18.

7. Ronald Alsop, "Retailers Buying Far in Advance to Exploit Trade Promotions," *The Wall Street Journal,* October 9, 1986, p. 35.

8. Earl Lifshey, "Do Retailers Ask Too Much of Vendors?" *Scan,* March-April 1991, p. 18.

9. David Kalish, "Creative Concepts: Space Invaders," *Marketing & Media Decisions,* November 1988, p. 31.

10. Amy E. Gross, "Promote: What Retailers Want," *Adweek's Marketing Week,* October 29, 1990, p. 42.

11. Robert L. Rose, "Travel Agents' Games Raise Ethics Issue," *The Wall Street Journal,* November 23, 1988, p. B1.

12. "306.8 Billion Grocery-Store Coupons Were Issued in 1990," *The San Diego Union,* April 6, 1991, p. C-1.

13. Suzy Parker, "USA Snapshots: A Look at Statistics that Shape Our Lives," *USA Today,* March 13, 1987, p. 1D.

14. "Consumers' Use of Coupons Rose in 1991," Manufacturers Coupon Control Center, special release, 1991.

15. *Thirteenth Annual Survey of Promotional Practices* (Stamford, Conn.: Donnelly Marketing, 1991), p. 24.

16. "Computers Help Foil Coupon Fraud," *Marketing News,* August 15, 1986, p. 1.

17. William A. Robinson, *Best Sales Promotions,* 6th ed. (Lincolnwood, Ill.: NTC Business Books, 1987), p. 261.

18. "Study: Some Promotions Change Consumer Behavior," *Marketing News,* October 15, 1990, 12.

19. Edward D. Meyer, "Promotion Magic," *Boardroom Reports,* January 1, 1987, p. 6.

20. "Coke Disc-o," *The San Diego Union,* March 6, 1991, p. E-2.

21. Alix M. Freedman, "Use of Free Product Samples Wins New Favor as Sales Tool," *The Wall Street Journal,* August 28, 1986, p. 19.

22. Point of Purchase Advertising Institute, New York, 1987.

23. Mark Paul, "The Electronic Salesman," *Marketing Communications,* December 1986, p. 32.

24. Specialty Advertising Association International.

25. Kevin T. Higgins, "Specialty Advertising Thrives," *Marketing News,* October 11, 1985, p. 20.

26. Nancy L. Croft, "Smart Selling: Take a Cue, and Dive In," *Nation's Business,* Deccember 1987, p. 54R.

27. Richard G. Edel, "Specialties: Gifts of Motivation," *Marketing Communications,* April 1986, p. 106.

28. Avraham Shama and Jack K. Thompson, "Promotion Gifts: Help or Hindrance?" *Mortgage Banking,* February 1989, pp. 49-51.

29. Ibid., p. 52.

30. Kate Bertrand, "Attention-Grabbing Trade Show Gadgetry," *Business Marketing,* November 1986, p. 106.

31. Frank Sommerfield, "The Other Show Business," *Marketing & Media Decisions,* August 1990, p. 16.

32. Doug R. Berdie and Elaine M. Hauff, "Surprises Are Found in Consumer Reactions to Ads in Yellow Pages," *Marketing News,* September 11, 1987, p. 8.

33. Edmund L. Andrews, "Changing Shopping Habits Keep Those Fingers Walking," *The New York Times,* July 1, 1990, p. 4-F.

34. Janice Castro, "Invasion of the Yellow Pages," *Time,* October 5, 1987, p. 52.

35. Carol Hall, "Branding the Yellow Pages," *Marketing & Media Decisions,* April 1989, p. 59.

36. Ibid., p. 60.

37. Ibid., p. 62.

38. Betsy Bauer, "New Quick Flicks: Ads at the Movies," *USA Today,* March 13, 1986, p. D1.

39. Joanne Lipman and Kathleen A. Hughes, "Disney Prohibits Ads in Theaters Showing Its Movies," *The Wall Street Journal,* February 9, 1990, p. B1.

40. "For These Video Ads, You Don't Need a VCR," *The Wall Street Journal,* May 9, 1988, p. 25.

41. Joanne Lipman, "Need a Commercial Break? Viewers Take Ads Home to Play on VCRs," *The Wall Street Journal,* June 5, 1987, p. 21.

42. "ATA Reaches Your Markets" (Great Falls, Mon.: American Telephone Advertising, February 1987), pp. 2-4.

43. Annetta Miller and Judy Howard, "Turning PCs into Salesmen," *Newsweek,* March 12, 1990, p. 69.

44. Maureen O'Donnell, "New Media," *Adweek's Marketing Week,* September 11, 1989, p. 202.

45. Lynn Coleman, " 'Smart Card,' Coupon Eater Targeted to Grocery Retailers," *Marketing News,* June 6, 1988, p. 1.

46. Cyndee Miller, "VideOcart Spruces Up for New Tests," *Marketing News,* February 19, 1990, p. 19.

47. "Electronic Promo: The Subject Was Roses," *Chain Store Age Executive,* September 1988, pp. 64-70.

Chapter 17

1. Personal interview, Ralph Rubio, January 22, 1990.

2. Advertisement by Sew Pro in *The San Diego Union,* May 5, 1991, p. D10.

3. Advertisement by Children's Hospital and Health Center in *The San Diego Union,* May 5, 1991, p. D3.

4. Irving Burstiner, *Basic Retailing* (Homewood, Ill.: Richard D. Irwin, 1986), p. 577.

5. Mary McCabe English, "Total Market Coverage: Shared Mail Digging In," *Advertising Age,* June 14, 1984, p. 17.

6. Eileen Norris, "Total Market Coverage: Ad Vehicles Bombard Consumers," *Advertising Age,* November 7, 1985, p. 16.

7. "Bigsby & Kruthers Puts 'Suitbook' on Radio," *Ad/Pro,* March 1987, p. 5.

8. Thomas R. King, "In Hollywood Stars Come Out in Local Ads," *The Wall Street Journal,* July 25, 1990, p. B1.

9. Bob Hughes, "Mrs. Gooch's Makes a Fashion Statement with Its Beverly Hills Shop," *Supermarket Business,* May 1988, p. 72.

10. Bell Atlantic, 1991.

11. Barry Berman and Joel R. Evans, *Retail Management: A Strategic Approach* (New York: Macmillan, 1986), p. 401.

12. Advo-Systems, Inc., annual report, 1990, p. 1.

13. James Rubenstein, "A G-R-A-N-D Opening," *Bank Marketing,* January 1989, p. 28.

14. Susan Sachs, "The P. T. Barnum of the Office Furniture Trade," *Entrepreneur,* December 1985, p. 74.

15. "Younkers' Carl Zitz, Marketing VP, Tells How Store Is Changing," *Ad/Pro,* October 1986, p. 4.

16. "Creativity in Ads: How Ideas Flow," *Ad/Pro,* February 1987, p. 1.

17. "At Bullock's: Always on Sunday, in Four Color," *Ad/Pro,* March 1987, p. 1.

18. Rifka Rosenwein, "Psychotherapists Begin to Lose Reluctance to Self-Promotion," *The Wall Street Journal,* August 27, 1987, p. 25.

Chapter 18

1. Ben Yagoda, "Cleaning Up a Dirty Image," *Business Month,* April 1990, pp. 48-52; E. Bruce Harrison with Tom Prugh, "Assessing the Damage," *Public Relations Journal,* October 1989, pp. 40-45.
2. Amelia Lobsenz, "How to Blend PR into Your Marketing Mix," *Marketing News,* March 15, 1985, p. 37.
3. "Product Survival: Lessons of the Tylenol Terrorism" (Washington, D.C.: Washington Business Information, 1982), pp. 11-17.
4. Art Stevens, "How to Handle Bad News," *Industry Week,* October 14, 1985, p. 63.
5. Ibid., p. 64.
6. Doug Newsom, Alan Scott, and Judy Vanslyke Turk, *This Is PR: The Realities of Public Relations* (Belmont, Calif.: Wadsworth Publishing Company, 1989), p. 203.
7. "Public Relations: Creating a Company Image," *Small Business Report,* February 1987, pp. 49-54.
8. Lloyd B. Dennis, "Public Affairs: Deja Vu All Over Again," *Public Relations Journal,* April 1990, pp. 14-17.
9. "Public Relations: Creating a Company Image," p. 49.
10. Steven Morris, "Corporate Sponsorship Becomes Life of the Party," *Chicago Tribune,* March 27, 1988, sec. 7, p. 1; statistical data supplied by International Events Group, May 1991.
11. Pat McGeehan, "Signing 3M an Olympian Effort," *Advertising Age,* November 9, 1987.
12. Data supplied by International Events Group.
13. A. Craig Copetas, "Make Profits, Not War," *Inc.,* January 1986, p. 21.
14. Jane Weaver, "Perrier: Fighting Crisis with Laughter," *Adweek,* March 19, 1990, p. 12.
15. John A. Platta, "Energizing Sales with Public Relations," *Business Marketing,* June 1986, p. 133.
16. Jeanne Saddler, "Public Relations Firms Offer 'News' to TV," *The Wall Street Journal,* April 2, 1985, p. 6.
17. *Corporate Advertising/Phase II,* an Expanded Study of Corporate Advertising Effectiveness, conducted for *Time* magazine by Yankelovich, Skelly & White, Inc. Undated.
18. Meryl Davids, "16th Annual Review of Corporate Advertising Expenditures," *Public Relations Journal,* September 1987, p. 29.
19. Ibid.
20. Newsom et al., *This Is PR,* p. 193.
21. Maureen F. Hartigan and Peter Finch, "The New Emphasis on Strategy in Corporate Advertising," *Business Marketing,* February 1986, p. 48.
22. Anne B. Fisher, "Spiffing Up the Corporate Image," *Fortune,* July 21, 1986, p. 72.
23. Tom Eisenhart, "What's in a Name? Plenty," *Business Marketing,* October 1988, pp. 88-94.
24. *What We've Learned about Advertising* (New York: American Association of Advertising Agencies, 1990), p. 3.
25. Data supplied by ABC, NBC, and CBS.
26. John Moes, "Military Asks What It Can Do for Recruits," *Advertising Age,* July 19, 1984, p. 36.

27. Patricia Sellers, "The Selling of the President in '88," *Fortune,* December 21, 1987, pp. 131, 132, 136; Walecia Konrad, "The Selling of the President, 1988" *Business Week,* September 12, 1988, p. 37; Gerry Braun, "Will High Road Lead to Victory?" *The San Diego Union,* May 27, 1990, sec. a, p. 1.
28. "Political Ads on TV Rise," *USA Today,* September 26, 1990, sec. b, p. 1.
29. Annetta Miller, "Peddling a Social Cause," *Newsweek,* September 1, 1986, pp. 58-59.

Chapter 19

1. Joshua Levine, "Global Lather," *Forbes,* February 5, 1990, pp. 146, 148; Alison Fahey, "International Ad Effort to Back Gillette Sensor," *Advertising Age,* October 16, 1989, p. 34.
2. Gary Levin and Jon Lafayette, "Ad Spending Hikes May Lag Inflation," *Advertising Age,* December 17, 1990, pp. 3, 34.
3. Ibid.
4. David Lanchner, "The Rush to Russia," *Adweek's Marketing Week,* February 20, 1989, pp. 24-32.
5. E. Jerome McCarthy and William D. Perreault, *Basic Marketing,* 10th ed. (Homewood, Ill.: Richard D. Irwin, 1990), p. 577.
6. "U.S. Firms with the Biggest Foreign Revenues," *Forbes,* July 23, 1990, pp. 362.
7. "Efficacy of Global Ad Projects Is Questioned in Firm's Survey," *The Wall Street Journal,* September 13, 1984, p. 29.
8. "The Ad Biz Gloms onto 'Global,'" *Fortune,* November 12, 1984, p. 77.
9. Rebecca Piirto, "Global Psychographics," *American Demographics,* December 1990, p. 8.
10. Laurel Wentz, "1992: A False Sense of 'Europhoria'?" *Advertising Age,* October 10, 1988, pp. 2, 74.
11. "Eastern Europe Beckons," *Advertising Age,* November 20, 1989, pp. 1, 45.
12. Richard L. Hudson, "IBM Strives for a Single Image in Europe," *The Wall Street Journal,* April 16, 1991, sec. b, p. 6.
13. Philip R. Cateora, *International Marketing* (Homewood, Ill.: Richard D. Irwin, 1990), pp. 85-87.
14. Michael Brizz, "How to Learn What Japanese Buyers Really Want," *Business Marketing,* January 1987, p. 72.
15. John Fayerweather, *International Marketing* (Englewood Cliffs, N.J.: Prentice Hall, 1970), pp. 92-93.
16. Erdener Kaynak, *The Management of International Advertising* (Westport, Conn.: Quorum Books, 1989), pp. 70, 148.
17. Tom Eisenhart, "Opportunities Ripening for U.S. Business Publishers in Eastern Europe," *Business Marketing,* October 1990, p. 42.
18. Steven Weed, "Expanding the Marketplace," *Direct Marketing,* November 1989, pp. 42-45.
19. Maria Katz, "No Women, No Alcohol; Learn Saudis Taboos before Placing Ads," *International Advertiser,* February 1986, p. 11.
20. Richard N. Weltz, "How Do You Say, 'Oops!'" *Business Marketing,* October 1990, pp. 52-53.
21. Lennie Copeland, "Foreign Markets: Not for the Amateur," *Business Marketing,* July 1984, pp. 112-18.
22. Katz, "No Women, No Alcohol."

CREDITS AND ACKNOWLEDGMENTS

PART I The power of imagination ad   Courtesy Pratt & Whitney/Canada; Agency, BCP Strategy/Creativity.

CHAPTER 1

Coke ad   Coke and Coca-Cola are registered trademarks of The Coca-Cola Company; permission for use of this ad granted by The Coca-Cola Company.

Exhibit 1-1   Jacobs' Pharmacy: Courtesy of the Archives, The Coca-Cola Company.

Exhibit 1-3   Canadian Macintosh ad: Courtesy Baker Lovick Advertising.

Exhibit 1-4   Westvaco Sterling Litho Gloss: © 1988 Westvaco Corporation; photographer, Jim Huibregtse.

Exhibit 1-5   Pierre Cardin ad: Courtesy BBDO International, Inc.

Exhibit 1-6   Adler Planetarium ad: Courtesy Adler Planetarium, Chicago.

Exhibit 1-7   Kaiser Permanente ad: Creative director, Jon Hyde; art director, Andy Vucinich; copywriter, Paul Cuneo; producer, Ann Johnston; agency, J. Walter Thompson/San Francisco; client, Kaiser Permanente.

Exhibit 1-8   Pearle Vision ad: © 1991 Pearle, Inc.

Exhibit 1-9   Tailor's shop sign: Colonial Williamsburg Foundation.

Exhibit 1-10   Health jolting chair ad: Dick Supten, *The Mad Old Ads* (New York: McGraw-Hill, 1966).

Exhibit 1-11   Palmolive ad: Reprinted with permission from April 30, 1980, issue of *Advertising Age.* Copyright 1980 by Crain Communications, Inc.

Ethical Dilemma   Adapted from Howard Schlossberg, "The Simple Truth: Ads Will Have to Be Truthful," *Marketing News,* December 24, 1990, p. 6; Ed Fitch, "Truth Be Told, Deception Is 'In,'" *Advertising Age,* April 20, 1987, p. 56; Robert Pitofsky, "Should Puffery Be Outlawed—Former FTC Man Says No," *Advertising Age,* April 7, 1975, p. 15; Steven Mitchell Sack, "Legal Puffery—Truth or Consequences," *Sales & Marketing Management,* October 1986, pp. 59–60; Herbert J. Rotfeld and Kim B. Torzoll, "Is Advertising Puffery Believed?" *Journal of Advertising* 3 (1980), pp. 16–20, 45; Richard Kurnit, "Truth in Advertising—The Latest Word," *Advertising Age,* July 21, 1986, p. 55; James E. Lukaszewski, "Three Grand Delusions and Five False Assumptions," *Across the Board,* November 1990, pp. 55–57; Jennifer Lawrence, "How Volvo's Ad Collided with the Truth," *Advertising Age,* November 12, 1990, p. 76; Jon Lafayette, "Scandal Puts Focus on Ad Visuals," *Advertising Age,* November 26, 1990, p. 62; Ralph Nader, "Rise of the Consumerists," *Advertising Age,* June 18, 1990, pp. 68, 72; Krystal Miller and Jacqueline Mitchell, "Car Marketers Test Gray Area of Truth in Advertising," *The Wall Street Journal,* November 19, 1990, pp. B1, B6; Paul Hawken, "Truth or Consequences," *Inc.,* August 1978, pp. 48–50, 52; Michael A. Kamins and Lawrence J. Marks, "Advertising Puffery: The Impact of Using Two-Sided Claims on Product Attitude and Purchase Intention," *Journal of Advertising* 4 (1987), pp. 6–15.

Exhibit 1-12   Hathaway shirt ad: Courtesy Ogilvy & Mather.

Exhibit 1-13   VW think small ad: this ad has been copyrighted by and is reproduced with the permission of Volkswagen of America, Inc.

Exhibit 1-14   Minnesota Dept. of Health animals smoking storyboard: Courtesy Martin Williams Advertising Incorporated.

Exhibit 1-15   John Pemberton: Courtesy The Coca-Cola Company.

Exhibit 1-17   Old Coke coupons: Courtesy The Coca-Cola Company.

Exhibit 1-18   Old Coke bottles: Courtesy The Coca-Cola Company.

Portfolio   Coke and Coca-Cola are registered trademarks of the Coca-Cola Company and permission for use granted by The Company. Permission for use of ads granted by The Coca-Cola Company. **Max Headroom photo**   Courtesy of McCann-Erickson/New York.

Exhibit 1-19   Save the Battlefield Coalition ad: Courtesy The Martin Agency/Richmond, VA.

Exhibit 1-21   Aspirin: Michael J. Hruby.

Exhibit 1-22   Lotus 1-2-3 3.1 ad: Lotus Development Corp.; Agency: Hill, Holiday, Connors, Cosmopoulos.

Exhibit 1-23   Union Oil logos: Courtesy Union Oil of California.

Exhibit 1-24   Cereals: Concialdi Design.

Exhibit 1-25   Studebaker ad: Historical Pictures Service, Chicago.

CHAPTER 2

Sierra Club ad   ADs/CDs, Ken Neiheisel, Greg Conyers; design studio, Marsh; illustrator, Mark Fox; client, The Sierra Club/San Diego Chapter.

Exhibit 2-1   Dexter shoe ad: Art Director/creative director, Woody Kay; copywriter, Steve Bautista; photographer, Aaron Jones; agency, Pagano Schenck & Kay; client, Dexter Shoe Company.

Exhibit 2-2   Pounce see no weevil ad: Courtesy Harry Kerker-HCM.

Exhibit 2-3   American Lung Association truth in advertising ad: © 1990, Christopher Conerly/American Lung Association.

Exhibit 2-4   Baylor College of Medicine second chance brochure: Writer, Baylor College of Medicine/Office of Public Affairs/Health Promotion, Houston, TX; developed through a grant from the National Heart, Lung, and Blood Institute, National Institutes of Health; designer, Uri Kelman; illustrator, Lee Lee Brazeal; agency/studio, Kelman Design Studio; production company, AW Printing.

Exhibit 2-5   Northwestern Bell storyboard: Courtesy Northwestern Bell.

Exhibit 2-6   Volvo photo: Cindy Lewis.

Exhibit 2-7   Amoco recycling: Courtesy Amoco Corporation/Amoco Chemical Company.

Exhibit 2-9   Technics Johnny Cash ad: Courtesy Matsushita Electric Corporation of America, Technics Division.

Exhibit 2-10   Flowchart of the FTC complaint procedure: Gary Armstron and Julie Ozanne, "An Evaluation of NAD/NARB Purpose and Performance," *Journal of Advertising* 12, no. 3 (1983), p. 24. Reprinted with permission.

Exhibit 2-11   California Milk Advisory Board butter ad: Courtesy Foote, Cone & Belding.

Exhibit 2-12   Trademark terminology: logos courtesy of The Coca-Cola Company; GM trademark is used with permission of General Motors Corporation; Nabisco Brands, Inc.; The Prudential Insurance Company of America; The Pillsbury Company; The Du Pont Company; Federal Deposit Insurance Corporation.

Exhibit 2-13   Once a Xerox ad: Courtesy Xerox Corporation.

Exhibit 2-14   Hyatt Legal Services storyboard: Courtesy Hyatt Legal Services.

Exhibit 2-15   Rhode Island Hospital mammogram ad: Courtesy Pagano Schenck & Kay.

Exhibit 2-16   Visa ad: Courtesy VISA U.S.A., San Francisco.

Ad Lab 2-B   Advertising to Children: Daniel M. Gold, "The Backlash over Clutter in Kidland," *Adweek's Marketing Week,* October 8, 1990, p. 4. Storyboard Courtesy The Procter & Gamble Company.

Exhibit 2-17   NAD misleading ads can run ad: Courtesy Bozell Inc./Council of Better Business Bureaus, Inc. *Note:* any future form of this ad will include the word *commercial* immediately prior to the last word (*advertising*) in the first paragraph.

Ad Lab 2-C   Issue ad: storyboard Courtesy W. R. Grace & Co.

CHAPTER 3

Coffee with a twist ad Courtesy Kraft General Foods Canada Inc.

Exhibit 3-1 Perdue takes a tough man ad: Courtesy Scali, McCabe, Sloves, Inc.

Ad Lab 3-A Reprinted with permission from the March 25, 1991, issue of *Advertising Age*. Copyright 1991 by Crain Communications, Inc.

Exhibit 3-4 Sledgehammer ad: Agency, Franklin Dallas Kundinger; writer, Peter Holmes; art director, Peter Holmes; photography, Shin Sugino.

Exhibit 3-5 Resist the usual ad: Courtesy Young & Rubicam Ltd./Toronto.

Exhibit 3-6 Hyatt ad: Reproduced with permission from Hyatt Hotels Corporation.

Exhibit 3-7 *Crain's New York Business* "stock photo" ad: Courtesy Goldsmith/Jeffrey; *Crain's New York Business*.

Exhibit 3-8 Perdue chicken oven stuffer ad: Courtesy Scali, McCabe, Sloves, Inc.

Exhibit 3-9 Gigante Vaz ad: Courtesy Gigante Vaz and Partners Advertising Inc.

Exhibit 3-10 Slimebucket account ad: Courtesy Young & Rubicam Inc.

Exhibit 3-14 Minneapolis for the winter ad: Courtesy Martin-Williams.

Exhibit 3-15 New York Lung Association ad: Courtesy New York Lung Association, New York City, New York.

Exhibit 3-17 Crest yum yum ad: Courtesy Benton & Bowles, Inc. and The Procter & Gamble Company.

Exhibit 3-19 Benetton ad: Courtesy United Colors of Benetton, Benetton Cosmetics Corp.

Exhibit 3-21 Apple ad: Courtesy Chiat/Day.

Ethical Dilemma Adapted from Steven A. Meyerowitz, "Ad Agency Client Conflicts: The Law and Common Sense," *Business Marketing*, June 1987, p. 16; "Saatchi and Saatchi Co. Is Brought to Court Over a Client Conflict," *The Wall Street Journal*, April 17, 1987, p. 18; Lauren Ames, "The Great Conflict Conflict," *Madison Avenue*, June 1985, pp. 66–69; Herbert Zeltner, "Conflict Issue Still a Problem," *Advertising Age*, June 16, 1986, pp. 3, 24, 28, 30–32; Marianne Paskowski, "Client Conflict Woes—As Told from the Agency Side," *Marketing & Media Decisions*, October 1984, pp. 70, 73–74, 96; Marianne Paskowski, "Conflict Woes as Told from the Client Side," *Marketing & Media Decisions*, November 1984, pp. 61–62, 176.

PART II BYU Chart a good course poster: Courtesy Brigham Young University.

CHAPTER 4

Obsession perfume ad Courtesy Calvin Klein, Inc.

Exhibit 4-1 Edsel ad: Henry Ford Museum/Edison Institute.

Ad Lab 4-A Needs and utility: E. Jerome McCarthy and William D. Perreault, Jr., *Basic Marketing*, 10th ed. (Homewood, Ill.: Richard D. Irwin, 1990), pp. 5–6.

Exhibit 4-2 Ford Explorer curiosity runs ad: Courtesy Ford Division Advertising Department.

Exhibit 4-3 Iacocca storyboard: Courtesy Kenyon & Eckhardt, Inc.

Exhibit 4-5 AT&T fence-sitter ad: Courtesy American Telephone and Telegraph Company.

Exhibit 4-7 Wrangler jeans comfortable suit ad: Courtesy The Martin Agency/Richmond, VA.

Exhibit 4-10 Colombian Coffee ad: Courtesy The National Federation of Coffee Growers of Colombia.

Exhibit 4-11 Alpine CD ad: Courtesy Franklin Dallas Kundinger Advertising.

Exhibit 4-12 Maidenform pushed around ad: Copywriter, Rochelle Klein; art director, Michael Vitiello; photographer, Mark Coppos; agency, Levine, Huntlye, Vick and Beaver; client, Maidenform.

Exhibit 4-13 Dos Locos restaurant ad: Copy, James Hauptman; Art, Dan Ventura; Type, Teenage Mutant Typography.

Exhibit 4-14 *Rolling Stone* mouse ad: Courtesy Fallon McElligott.

Exhibit 4-16 French billboards Les histoires de Mario; Le poisson de Provigo; La Bagnole de Marcel; Le citron de Provigo: Client, Provigo; creative directors, Jean-Jacques Stréliski and Paul Lavoie; art director, Lili Côte; photographer, Michel Pilon.

Ad Lab 4-C Adapted from Harold W. Berkman and Christopher C. Gilson, *Consumer Behavior: Concepts and Strategies*, 2nd ed. (Boston: Kent Publishing Co., 1981), p. 249. Reprinted by permission of Kent Publishing, a Division of Wadsworth Inc.; and Jack Haberstroh, "Can't Ignore Subliminal Ad Charges," *Advertising Age*, pp. 3, 42, 44.

Exhibit 4-17 Harley Davidson ad: Courtesy Carmichael Lynch, Inc.

Exhibit 4-18 Contemporary social classes: Equifax National Decision Systems.

Exhibit 4-19 Chicago Cutlery ad: Courtesy Martin/Williams Advertising/Minneapolis.

Exhibit 4-20 Look ski binding ad: Copyright 1990 Look Performance Sports, Inc.; agency, Jim Mitchell Advertising, Longmont, Colorado.

Exhibit 4-21 State Farm ad: Courtesy State Farm Insurance Companies.

Ad Lab 4-D Jonathan's Uptown ad: Art directors, Kathy Izard, Jim Mountjoy; writers, Steve Lasch, Julie Dalton; agency, Loeffler, Ketchum & Mountjoy; client, Jonathan's Uptown.

CHAPTER 5

State of Texas ad Courtesy GSD&M; art director, Larry Martin; creative director and writer, Guy Bommarito.

Exhibit 5-1 Clearwater Federal ad: Courtesy Clearwater Federal.

Exhibit 5-4 Heavy usage patterns: Adapted from David L. Kurtz and Louis E. Boone, *Marketing* (New York: Dryden Press, 1981), p. 146.

Ethical Dilemma Adapted from Michael Specter, "Reynolds Cancels Plan to Market New Cigarette," *Washington Post*, January 20, 1990, p. A3; James R. Schiffman, "After Uptown, Are Some Niches Out?" *The Wall Street Journal*, January 22, 1990, pp. B1, B6; Anthony Lewis, "Merchants of Death," *New York Times*, May 19, 1988, p. A31; Marlene Cimons, "Tobacco Firms' Sports Ties Assailed," *Los Angeles Times*, February 24, 1990, p. A23; Bryant Robey, "The 'Uptown' Fiasco Highlights U.S. Inequality," *Adweek's Marketing Week*, March 12, 1990, p. 58; Judann Dagnoli, "Uptown Downfall Scares Industry," *Advertising Age*, January 29, 1990, p. 57; Editorial, "The Downing of Uptown," *Advertising Age*, January 29, 1990, p. 32; Bruce Horovitz, "Cigarette Ads: A Matter of Conscience," *Los Angeles Times*, May 2, 1989, sec. IV, pp. 1, 6; Editorial, "When Ads Leave a Bad Aftertaste," *Los Angeles Times*, January 23, 1990, p. B6; Howard Schlossberg, "Segmenting Becomes Constitutional Issue," *Marketing News*, April 16, 1990, pp. 1–2; Michael Specter, "Sullivan Denounces Reynolds Tobacco," *Washington Post*, January 19, 1990, pp. A1, A8; Alix M. Freedman and Michael J. McCarthy, "New Smoke from RJR under Fire," *The Wall Street Journal*, February 20, 1990, pp. B1, B8; Djata, "The Marketing of Vices to Black Consumers," *Business & Society Review*, Summer 1987, pp. 47–49.

Exhibit 5-5 Porsche resale ad: Courtesy Fallon McElligott.

Exhibit 5-6 Usage rates: Adapted from Dik Warren Twedt, "How Important to Marketing Strategy Is the 'Heavy User'?" *Journal of Marketing*, January 1964, p. 72.

Exhibit 5-7 Segmenting toothpaste market: Adapted from Russell I. Haley, "Benefit Segmentation: A Decision-Oriented Research Tool," *Journal of Marketing* 32 (July 1968), p. 33.

Exhibit 5-8 Used with permission © American Demographics, July, 1989.

Exhibit 5-9 SIC codes: Adapted from E. Jerome McCarthy and William D. Perreault, Jr., *Essentials of Marketing*, 5th ed. (Homewood, Ill.: Richard D. Irwin, 1991), p. 156.

Exhibit 5-10 U.S. proportional map: Adapted from U.S. Department of Commerce, Bureau of the Census, Census of Manufactures, Area Statistics (Washington, D.C.: U.S. Government Printing Office, 1977), p. 749.

Ad Lab 5-A Reebok photo: Reprinted by permission of Reebok International Ltd.

Exhibit 5-11 map: Courtesy Equifax National Decision Systems.

Exhibit 5-12 Product life cycle: Adapted from Ben M. Ennis, *Marketing Principles* (Santa Monica, CA: Goodyear Publishing, 1980), p. 351.

Exhibit 5-13 Intel 486 PC ad: Reprinted with the permission of Intel Corporation, 1991.

Exhibit 5-14 Crest ad: Courtesy Benton & Bowles, Inc. and The Procter & Gamble Company.

Exhibit 5-16 Amtrak Empire Builder ad: Creative director, Alan Fraser; art director, Jay Morales; copywriter, Marcia Lusk; producer, Joe Scibetta; director, John St. Clair; agency, DDB Needham Worldwide; client, Amtrak.

Exhibit 5-17 Xerox ad: Courtesy Young & Rubicam/Xerox Corporation.

Exhibit 5-18 Sunkist orange ad: Courtesy Sunkist Growers, Inc.

Exhibit 5-19 Omni Hotels items: Courtesy Omni Hotels.

Exhibit 5-20 Speedo: Courtesy Maddocks & Company, Los Angeles.

Exhibit 5-21 Music Construction set ad: Designed by Jamie Davison.

Exhibit 5-22 Certifiably Nuts ad: Courtesy Thomas Binnion/Jon Reeder Design Firm.

Exhibit 5-23 Demand, supply vs. price: Adapted from Elwood S. Buffa and Barbara A. Pletcher, *Understanding Business Today* (Homewood, Ill.: Richard D. Irwin, 1980), p. 37.

Exhibit 5-24 Cornes Motors ad: Courtesy USP Automotive Advertising/ Cornes Motors.

Exhibit 5-25 Birks pens ad: Courtesy Birks.

Exhibit 5-26 PIP Printing ad: This advertisement was used with the permission of PIP Printing, The Best Business Printer in the Business.

CHAPTER 6

J. C. Penney ad   Courtesy J. C. Penney Company, Inc.

Exhibit 6-1   J. C. Penney store: Courtesy N. W. Ayer Incorporated.

Exhibit 6-3   CACI ad: Appears courtesy CACI Marketing Systems, Fairfax, VA.

Exhibit 6-5   Comparison data methods: Pamela L. Alreck and Robert B. Settle, *The Survey Research Handbook* (Homewood, Ill.: Richard D. Irwin, 1985), p. 41.

Exhibit 6-6   Campbell's billboard: Courtesy Ogilvy & Mather/Toronto.

Exhibit 6-7   Focus group: Burgess Blevins.

Exhibit 6-8   Reliability diagram: Pamela L. Alreck and Robert B. Settle, *The Survey Research Handbook* (Homewood, Ill.: Richard D. Irwin, 1985), p. 65.

Ad Lab 6-B photos   Adapted from *Everything You've Always Wanted to Know about TV Ratings*, A. C. Nielsen Company, 1978.

Exhibit 6-9   Penney questionnaire: Courtesy Ayer Incorporated.

Exhibit 6-11   Research costs: The Professional Research Group.

Exhibit 6-12   Penney's Arizona jeans: Courtesy J. C. Penney Company, Inc.

Exhibit 6-13   Research categories: Adapted from Edmund W. J. Faison, *Advertising: A Behavioral Approach for Managers* (New York: John Wiley & Sons, 1980), p. 664.

Exhibit 6-14   Penney's Hunt Club: Courtesy J. C. Penney Company, Inc.

Exhibits 6-15, 6-16   Penney ads: Courtesy Ayer Incorporated.

Exhibit 6-17   Researcher: Burgess Blevins.

Exhibit 6-18   *Parade* magazine ad: Created by Baker & Fiore Inc. for PARADE Magazine. Reprinted with permission of Parade Publications, Inc.

Exhibit 6-19   Penney storyboard: Courtesy Ayer Incorporated.

Exhibit 6-20   Penney clothes you can live in ad: Courtesy J. C. Penney Company, Inc.

Exhibit 6-21   Direct-mail questionnaire: Courtesy Bruzzone Research Company.

Exhibit 6-22   Burger King ad: Courtesy J. Walter Thompson USA and Starch INRA Hooper.

CHAPTER 7

Claris Corporation Cheops ad   Agency, BBDO/Los Angeles; client, Claris Corporation.

Exhibit 7-1   Acura badges and labels ad: ®1988 Acura Division of American Honda Motor Co., Inc. Acura, Legend, and Integra are trademarks of Honda Motor Co., Ltd.

Ad Lab 7-A   Jack Trout and Al Ries, "Marketing Warfare," *Southern Advertising*, July 1978; photos by Michael J. Hruby.

Exhibit 7-2   Acura look what happens ad: ®1989 Acura Division of American Honda Motor Co., Inc. Acura, Legend, and Integra are trademarks of Honda Motor Co., Ltd.

Exhibit 7-4   Army Nurse Corps ad: Army photographs courtesy U.S. Government, as represented by the Secretary of the Army.

Exhibit 7-5   Mirolin Microcast Whirlpool ad: Courtesy Franklin Dallas Kundinger Inc. Advertising.

Exhibit 7-6   Acura you've arrived ad: ®1989 Acura Division of American Honda Motor Co., Inc. Acura, Legend, and Integra are trademarks of Honda Motor Co., Ltd.

Exhibit 7-7   Acura Integra antilock brakes storyboard: Client, Acura Division of American Honda Motor Co., Inc.; agency, Ketchum Advertising.

Exhibit 7-8   L'Oreal ad: Courtesy of the L'Oreal Hair Care Division.

Exhibit 7-9   Acura most expensive part ad: Courtesy Mendelsohn Zien Advertising, Inc.

Exhibit 7-10   American Express pediatrician ad: Courtesy Marketplace Advertising and Promotion.

Exhibit 7-13   Cereal ads: Total courtesy General Mills, Inc.; Frosted Flakes courtesy *Kellogg's Frosted Flakes*®.

Exhibit 7-14   FCB grid: David Clark Scott, "Modern Advertising, 'The Subtle Persuasion,'" *The Christian Science Monitor*, January 27, 1987.

Exhibit 7-15   Acura forget everything ad: ®1990 Acura Division of American Honda Motor Co., Inc. Acura, Legend, and Integra are trademarks of Honda Motor Co., Ltd.

Ad Lab 7-C   *Sweet 'N Low*: Courtesy Pedone & Partners Advertising, Inc. *BMW before/after ad*: Client, Kasle Recycling; agency, Meyer & Wallis; creative director/writer, Tim A. Wallis; art director, Jim Brooks; photographer, Dan Wilson. *Snyder hairspray storyboard*: Courtesy Martin/Williams Advertising/Minneapolis. *Sail magazine ad*: Courtesy Mullen Advertising, Inc. *Nissan Pathfinder ad*: Courtesy Chiat/Day/Mojo Inc. Advertising/San Francisco. *K2 Corp snowboard ad*: Agency, Cole & Weber; copywriter, Hugh Saffel; art director, Fred Hammerquist.

Exhibit 7-16   Domino Pizza ad: © 1991 Domino's Pizza Inc.

Exhibit 7-17   AAAA recession ad: Courtesy American Association of Advertising Agencies.

Exhibit 7-18   Bermuda less green ad: Courtesy FCB/Ronalds-Reynolds, Ltd./Toronto.

Exhibit 7-19   Advertising expenditures: *Advertising Age,* September 25, 1991.

PART III   Adobe Systems ad: © 1987 Adobe Systems Incorporated; POSTSCRIPT is a registered trademark of Adobe Systems Incorporated. Glypha, Helvetica and Optima are registered trademarks of Linotype Company. ITC Franklin Gothic, ITC Avant Garde, ITC Cheltenham, ITC Garamond, ITC Bookman, ITC Souvenir, ITC Galliard, ITC Lubalin Graph and ITC New Baskerville are registered trademarks of International Typeface Corporation.

CHAPTER 8

Dog-Frisbee Championship ad   Courtesy Earle Palmer Brown/Bethesda, MD.

Exhibit 8-1   Ford Model T ad: Courtesy Henry Ford Museum/Edison Institute.

Exhibit 8-4   Honda more of a good thing ad: Courtesy Rubin Postaer & Associates; photographer, Jim Hall/Lamb & Hall.

Exhibit 8-5   Air Canada Cargo flamingo ad: Courtesy Air Canada.

Exhibit 8-7   Luis Gomez Dog Trainer ad: Art director, James Offenhartz; writers, Marian Allen Godwin and Todd Matthew Godwin; agency, Levine, Huntley, Schmidt and Beaver; client, Luis Gomez.

Ethical Dilemma   Adapted from Darrel Muehling, Donald Stem, Jr., and Peter Raven, "Comparative Advertising: Views from Advertisers, Agencies, Media and Policy Makers," *Journal of Advertising Research,* October-November 1989, pp. 38-48; Meryl Freeman, "Comparative Cautions," *Marketing & Media Decisions,* September 1987, pp. 78, 82, 84-85; Jeffrey Trachtenberg, "New Law Adds Risk to Comparative Ads," *The Wall Street Journal,* June 1, 1989, p. B6; Liza Frenette, "Trademark Proposals Could Threaten Free Speech," *Folio: The Magazine for Magazine Management,* April 1989, p. 23; Joe Flint, "Network Handling of Comparative Ads Causing Concerns," *Broadcasting,* October 29, 1990, pp. 53, 55; Thomas King, "Comparative TV Ad Reviews Criticized," *The Wall Street Journal,* October 23, 1990, p. B8; Steven Meyerowitz, "Brand X Strikes Back: The Developing Law of Comparative Advertising," *Business Marketing,* August 1985, pp. 81-84, 86; Slade Metcalf, "The Limits of Comparative Advertising," *Folio: The Magazine for Magazine Management,* August 1989, pp. 135-37; Cornelia Pechmann and David Stewart, "The Effect of Comparative Advertising on Attention, Memory, and Purchase Intentions," *Journal of Consumer Research,* September 1990, pp. 180-91; Caryn Beck-Dudley and Terrell G. Williams, "Legal and Public Policy Implications for the Future of Comparative Advertising: A Look at *U-Haul v. Jartran,*" *Journal of Public Policy & Marketing* 8 (1989), pp. 124-42.

Exhibit 8-8   United Way ad: Courtesy Earle Palmer Brown/Lawler Ballard Advertising.

Ad Lab 8-A   Stanley ad: Provided by Lawner Reingold Britton & Partners/Boston, MA.

Exhibit 8-9   Barry Wilson's Auto Repair ad: Copywriter, Dirk Mitchell; art director, James Howe; designers, James Howe, Dirk Mitchell; client, Barry Wilson's Auto Repair; agency, Mitchell & Howe.

Exhibit 8-10   *San Francisco Examiner* ad: Creative director, Rich Silverstein; art director, Steve Stone; copywriter, David Fowler; photographer, Dan Escobar; account director, Rene Cournoyer; production supervisor, Max Fallon; agency, Goodby, Berlin & Silverstein; client, *San Francisco Examiner.*

Exhibit 8-11   *Rolling Stone* van/sedan ad: Courtesy Fallon McElligott.

Exhibit 8-12   Prudential Bache ad: Courtesy Prudential Securities, Inc.

Exhibit 8-13   Microsoft ad: Courtesy Ogilvy & Mather/Los Angeles.

Exhibit 8-14   GTE Telephone radio script: Courtesy DDB Needham Worldwide, Inc.

Ad Lab 8-B   Reprinted with permission from *Advertising Age,* March 14, 1983. Copyright Crain Communications, Inc.

Exhibit 8-15   U S West Communications radio script: Courtesy the Martin Agency/Richmond, VA.

Exhibit 8-16   Life preserver storyboard: Courtesy U.S. Coast Guard and National Safe Boating Council.

Portfolio   *Tourisme Quebec ad*: Agency, BCP Strategy/Creativity; creative directors, Jean Gamache and Caroline Jarvis; art director, Caroline Jarvis; copywriters, Penny Cadrain and Cheryl Rae. *Certs ad*: Used with the permission of Warner-Lambert Company. Certs is a registered trademark of Warner-Lambert Company. © 1989 Warner-Lambert Company. *U.C. Berkeley ad*: Courtesy Goldberg, Moser O'Neill. *Spalding ad*: Courtesy Leonard, Monahan, Lubars & Kelly/Spalding. *Minnesota Orchestra ad*: Courtesy McCool & Co./Minnesota Orchestra.

Exhibit 8-17 First Interstate Corvette loan ad: Art director, Clifford Goodenough; copywriter, Norah Delaney; creative director, Roger Livingston; photographer, Larry Gilpin; agency, Livingston & Company (Seattle); client, First Interstate Bank of New Mexico.

Exhibit 8-18 Alaska Airlines little things work storyboard: Courtesy Sedelmaier Films/Alaska Airlines.

CHAPTER 9

School of Visual Arts ad Provided by the School of Visual Arts, New York City; creative director, Silas H. Rhodes; designer, Tony Palladino; copywriter, Dee Ito.

Exhibit 9-1 Timberland elements of design ad: Courtesy Mullen Advertising, Inc.

Exhibit 9-2 Timberland because the earth ad: Courtesy Mullen Advertising, Inc.

Exhibit 9-3 Chicago cutlery layout and finished ad: Courtesy Martin/Williams Advertising, Inc./Minneapolis.

Ad Lab 9-B Adapted from Mike Turner, "What Makes a Good Account Executive?" *Viewpoint* I (1980), pp. 27-28.

Exhibit 9-4 Dental-Eye Camera montage: Courtesy Kyocera America, Inc., Bioceram Division, and Tom Michael and Bob Hines, Market Design, Inc.

Exhibit 9-5 3M wrong clinical code ad: Courtesy Martin/Williams Advertising, Inc./Minneapolis.

Exhibit 9-6 Godiva Chocolates ad: Courtesy Margeotes Fertitta & Weiss, Inc.

Exhibit 9-7 Vepco ad: Courtesy The Martin Agency.

Exhibit 9-8 Talon zipper banana ad: Courtesy Talon.

Ad Lab 9-D Adapted from Walter Margulies, "What Colors Should You Use?" *Media Decisions* (New York: Decision Publications).

Portfolio *Garuda ancestors ad:* Courtesy Garuda, Indonesia/FCB. *TCF ad:* Courtesy Chuck Ruhr Advertising/Minneapolis. *Nature Company:* Courtesy The Nature Company; agency, Goodby, Berlin & Silverstein. *Mona Lisa/McDonald's:* Courtesy Cossette Communications-Marketing. *Nissan brochure:* Courtesy Chiat/Day/Mojo/Los Angeles.

Exhibit 9-9 Hombre beer: Design firm, Hermsen Design Associates, Inc.; client, Rubinoff Importing Company, Inc.; illustrator, Bart Forbes.

Exhibit 9-10 Gold Seal salmon ad: Courtesy Sam Payne & Associates/Specialty Seafoods.

Exhibit 9-11 Bill Demby storyboard: Courtesy BBDO/New York.

Exhibit 9-12 Bill Demby sketches: Courtesy BBDO/New York.

Ethical Dilemma Adapted from Jon Berry, "Creative Inspiration or Blatant Rip-Off," *Adweek Eastern Edition*, January 29, 1990, pp. 34-35; Bruce Horovitz, "Imitation Not Always Flattering in Advertising," *Los Angeles Times*, March 28, 1989, part IV, p. 6; David Kalish, "Copy-Cat Advertising," *Marketing & Media Decisions*, March 1987, pp. 22-23; Seymour Luft, "Imitation: The Highest Form of Blather-y," *Advertising Age*, November 15, 1982, p. M-30; Dale Arden, "Something Borrowed: When Is It Plagiarism?" *Back Stage/Shoot*, July 27, 1990, pp. 102-3.

Exhibit 9-13 AT&T script: Courtesy of Ayer, Inc. Reprinted with permission of AT&T; copyright 1990, AT&T; all rights reserved.

Exhibit 9-15 Jarman shoes manhole storyboard: Courtesy Genesco Inc.

Exhibit 9-16 Champion Tournament Lures ad: Director/Cameraman, Michael Caporale; production company, Caporale Studios.

Exhibit 9-17 Alaska Airlines reduced fares storyboard: Courtesy Sedelmaier Films/Alaska Airlines.

CHAPTER 10

Amity Leather ad Courtesy Frankenberry, Laughlin & Constable, Inc.

Exhibit 10-1 NYNEX ad: Courtesy of NYNEX Corporation; photo by Marc Segal/PSI.

Exhibit 10-4 Barnes & Noble ad: Courtesy Farago & Associates.

Exhibit 10-5 Designer working with mechanical: Michael J. Hruby.

Exhibit 10-6 General Foods Grand Marnier coffee ad: Courtesy Kraft General Foods Canada Inc.

Exhibit 10-9 Design every Volvo ad: © 1989 Volvo North America Corporation.

Exhibit 10-11 Illustrated Guide to Type: First published in *Macworld*, July 1991. Copyright © 1991 Macworld Communications, Inc.

Ad Lab 10-A Celestial Seasonings ad: © 1990 Celestial Seasonings, Inc., 4600 Sleepytime Drive, Boulder, Colorado, 80301.

Exhibit 10-12 Making type legible: First published in *Macworld*, July 1991. Copyright © 1991 Macworld Communications, Inc.

Exhibit 10-13 Forest preserve shelter: John Patsch/Journalism Services.

Exhibit 10-17 Heidelberg press: Courtesy Heidelberg Eastern, Inc.

Exhibit 10-18 Pantone ad: PANTONE is a registered trademark of Pantone, Inc.

Creative Department Courtesy Young & Rubicam, Inc.

Exhibit 10-19 Printing requirements: *Print Media Production Data* August 1991 issue, published by Standard Rate & Data Service, a Maxwell Macmillan Company.

CHAPTER 11

Honda Accord storyboard Courtesy Rubin Postaer & Associates.

Exhibit 11-1 Motel 6 radio script: Courtesy The Richards Group.

Ad Lab 11-A Adapted from Wallace A. Ross and Bob Landers, "Commercial Categories," in *Radio Plays the Plaza* (New York: Radio Advertising Bureau, 1989).

Exhibit 11-2 Adapted with permission of Macmillan Publishing Co., Inc., from *Advertising*, by William M. Weilbacher, p. 273. Copyright 1962 by The Free Press.

Exhibit 11-3 Sound pressure chart: Michael C. Keith, *Radio Production: Art and Science* (Stoneham, MA: Betterworth-Heinemann, 1990), p. 90.

Exhibit 11-4 Moving coil microphone: Michael C. Keith, *Radio Production: Art and Science* (Stoneham, MA: Betterworth-Heinemann, 1990), p. 90.

Exhibit 11-5 Audio console: Scott Wanner/Journalism Services.

Exhibit 11-6 Gotcha ad: Courtesy Salisbury Communications.

Exhibit 11-7 Beach scenes storyboard: Courtesy Salisbury Communications.

Exhibit 11-8 California raisins storyboard: Courtesy Foote, Cone & Belding.

Exhibit 11-9 Wiggling leaves creation: Courtesy Salisbury Communications.

Exhibit 11-10 Fish photo/storyboard frame: Courtesy Salisbury Communications.

Ethical Dilemma Adapted from James Perry and David Shribman, "The Negative Campaign Ad Comes of Age in Eastern Races, Stealing the Limelight," *The Wall Street Journal*, November 2, 1989, p. A22; Ronald Paul Hill, "An Exploration of Voter Responses to Political Advertisements," *Journal of Advertising* 18, no. 4 (1989), pp. 14-22; Steven W. Colford, "Political Advisers Veer from Smear, *Advertising Age*, November 23, 1987, p. 53; George Will, "The Other Guy Started It," *Advertising Age*, January 18, 1988, pp. 66-67; Bob Garfield, "Let Voters Take Warning: Political Advertising in This Country Is a Travesty," *Advertising Age*, November 5, 1990, pp. 28-29; Gary Levin, "Negative Ads Win on Election Day '90," *Advertising Age*, November 12, 1990, p. 3; "One Vote for Negative Ads," *Advertising Age*, November 7, 1988, p. 16; Jack Honomichl, Rance Crain, Richard Gordon, and Steven Colford, "Negative Spots Likely to Return in Election '88," *Advertising Age*, September 14, 1987, pp. 3, 70, 72, 74, 76, 78.

Exhibit 11-17 Panavision camera: Courtesy Panavision.

Exhibit 11-18 Shooting Pepsi commercial: Diana Lyn/Shooting Star.

Exhibit 11-19 Gotcha animation: Courtesy Salisbury Communications.

Exhibit 11-20 Edit bay photo: Courtesy Salisbury Communications.

Creative Department (Taster's Choice): Courtesy McCann-Erickson.

PART IV Royal Viking Line.

CHAPTER 12

Celestial Seasonings Lemon Zinger ad © 1990 Celestial Seasonings, Inc., 4600 Sleepytime Drive, Boulder, Colorado 80301.

Exhibit 12-1 Del Monte consumer ad: Reprinted with permission of Del Monte Corporation.

Exhibit 12-2 Del Monte print/TV advertising: Joe Mandese, "Del Monte's Can-Do," reprinted with permission of *Adweek's Marketing and Media Decisions*, November 1990, pp. 47-49.

Exhibit 12-3 West Coast Video: Courtesy Comcast Cablevision.

Exhibit 12-4 Media planning activities: Adapted from Jack Z. Sissors and E. Reynold Petray, *Advertising Media Planning* (Chicago: Crain Books, 1976).

Exhibit 12-5 Apple power lunch storyboard: Courtesy BBDO/Los Angeles.

Exhibit 12-6 Del Monte trade ad: Reprinted with permission of Del Monte Corp.

Exhibit 12-8 Ad expenditures by media: data from *The Wall Street Journal*, March 22, 1991, p. B4.

Exhibit 12-9 Continental Bank ad: Courtesy Fallon McElligott.

Exhibit 12-10 Ad readership scores: Adapted from *Cahners Advertising Research Report*.

Exhibit 12-11 Evaluation of advertising media: From Donald W. Jugenheimer and Peter B. Turk, *Advertising Media* (Columbus, Ohio: Grid Publishing, 1980), p. 90.

Exhibit 12-12 American Floral Marketing Council ad: Courtesy Earle Palmer Brown, Bethesda, Maryland.

Exhibit 12-13 Maxima TV campaign: Courtesy of Chiat/Day/Mojo Inc. Advertising.

Exhibit 12-14 Scheduling GRPs: Adapted from Jim Surmanek, *Media Planning* (Lincolnwood, IL: NTC Books, 1988), p. 125.

Exhibit 12-17 Rating analysis chart: Copyright 1987 Media Management Plus and The Arbitron Company.

CHAPTER 13

Hershey's chocolate milk ad Courtesy of Hershey Foods Corporation. HERSHEY'S is a trademark of Hershey Foods Corporation.

Exhibit 13-1 Hair salon ad: Courtesy Fallon McElligott.

Exhibit 13-2 San Diego Zoo ad: Courtesy Franklin & Associates.

Exhibit 13-3 Top newspaper advertisers: Reprinted with permission from *Advertising Age*, September 25, 1991. Copyright Crain Communications, Inc.

Exhibit 13-4 Standard advertising units grid: Courtesy Standard Rate & Data Service.

Exhibit 13-5 P&G newspaper insert: Courtesy of The Procter & Gamble Company.

Exhibit 13-6 Sangertown Square misplaced lease ad: Courtesy Sangertown Square; Pyramid Management Group, Inc.

Exhibit 13-7 *Boston Globe* newspaper rate card: Reprinted from May 12, 1991, *Newspaper Rates and Data*, published by Standard Rate & Data Service, a Maxwell Macmillan Company.

Exhibit 13-8 American International Rent A Car: Courtesy American International Rent A Car Corporation.

Exhibit 13-9 Federal Express Chinese ad: Courtesy Fallon McElligott.

Portfolio *San Diego Wild Animal Park:* Courtesy Franklin & Associates. *Nike:* Courtesy Wieden & Kennedy. *Cornes Motors:* Courtesy USP Automotive Advertising/Cornes Motors. *Timberland:* Courtesy Mullen Advertising, Inc. *Hush Puppies:* Courtesy Fallon McElligott. *Blue Diamond Growers:* Courtesy Saatchi & Saatchi DFS/Pacific. *Pirelli Tires:* Courtesy Pirelli Armstrong Tire Corporation.

Exhibit 13-10 Pella Windows ad: Courtesy Scali, McCabe, Sloves, Inc.

Exhibit 13-11 Top magazine advertisers: Reprinted with permission from *Advertising Age*, September 25, 1991, p. 72. Copyright Crain Communications, Inc.

Exhibit 13-12 Adapted from "Magazine Newsletter of Research," Magazine Publishers Association, vol. 8, no. 1.

Ad Lab 13-A Innovations in magazine advertising: ad Courtesy Delta Airlines.

Exhibit 13-13 Lee's skywash jeans ad: Courtesy Fallon McElligott.

Exhibit 13-14 *Reader's Digest* map: Courtesy The Reader's Digest Association.

Exhibit 13-15 Apple Desktop Media ad: Used with permission, Apple Computer, Inc.

Exhibit 13-16 *People* magazine advertising rates: Reprinted from April 27, 1991, *Consumer Magazine* and *Agri-Media Rates and Data*, published by Standard Rate & Data Service, a Maxwell Macmillan Company.

Exhibit 13-17 Magazine circulation: *Consumer Magazine* and *Agri-Media Rates and Data* (Standard Rate & Data Service), and *1990 Media Modules*, Grey Advertising, pp. 77–90.

Exhibit 13-18 *Runner's World* ad: Courtesy *Runner's World*.

CHAPTER 14

Snyder hairspray ad Courtesy Martin/Williams Advertising/Minneapolis.

Exhibit 14-1 Eveready Energizer Bunny: Courtesy Chiat/Day/Mojo/Los Angeles.

Exhibit 14-2 Audience composition chart: *Nielsen Report on Television*, 1990.

Exhibit 14-3 Top TV advertisers: *Advertising Age*, September 25, 1991, p. 38.

Exhibit 14-4 Barter syndication, "Business Day," *The New York Times*, August 3, 1985, p. 19. Copyright © 1985 by The New York Times Company. Reprinted with permission.

Exhibit 14-5 AT&T storyboard: Courtesy AT&T.

Exhibit 14-6 Network TV rates: reprinted with permission of *Adweek's Marketer's Guide to Media*, January–March 1991, p. 19.

Ethical Dilemma Adapted from Kim Foltz, "Kids as Consumers: Teaching Our Children Well," *Adweek*, November 30, 1987, p. 40; Noreen O'Leary, "Study Portrays Children as Complex, Savvy Media Mavens," *Adweek*, November 30, 1987, p. 42; Susan Dillingham, "Food Makers Hunger for Younger Market," *Insight*, June 18, 1990, p. 43; Patricia Sellers, "The ABC'S of Marketing to Kids," *Fortune*, May 8, 1989, pp. 114–20; Ellen Graham, "Children's Hour: As Kids Gain Power of Purse,

Marketing Takes Aim at Them," *The Wall Street Journal*, January 19, 1988, pp. 1, 15; "Selling to Children," *Consumer Reports*, August 1990, pp. 503, 518–21; Susan Dillingham, "The Classroom as a Marketing Tool," *Insight*, September 24, 1990, pp. 40–41; Michael J. McCarthy, "Tobacco Critics See a Subtle Sell to Kids," *The Wall Street Journal*, May 3, 1990, pp. B1, B6; John Wilke, Lois Therrien, Amy Dunkin, and Mark Vamos, "Are the Programs Your Kids Watch Simply Commercials?" *Business Week*, March 25, 1985, pp. 53–54.

Exhibit 14-7 TRW storyboard: Courtesy Wyse Advertising.

Exhibit 14-8 Blair TV spot rates: *Spot Television Rates and Data*, August 15, 1991, issue; published by Standard Rate & Data Service, a Maxwell Macmillan Company.

Exhibit 14-9 Major cable networks: Reprinted with permission of *Adweek's Marketer's Guide to Media*, January–March, 1991, p. 41, Major Cable Networks.

Exhibit 14-10 Cable ad revenues: Data, Paul Kagan Associates, Inc., chart, *Cable TV Facts 1990*, p. 5.

Exhibit 14-11 HBO Mike Tyson storyboard: Courtesy R/Greenburg Associates; Paul Fuentes, director.

Exhibit 14-12 Top cable TV advertisers: *Advertising Age*, September 25, 1991, p. 50.

Exhibit 14-13 Adult radio listeners: Printed with permission of *Adweek's Marketer's Guide to Media*, January–March 1991, p. 80.

Exhibit 14-14 Spam radio script: Courtesy George A. Hormel & Co.

Exhibit 14-15 Daily/weekly radio reach: Adapted from Radio Advertising Bureau data.

Exhibit 14-16 Top radio advertisers: *Advertising Age*, September 26, 1990, pp. 61, 64.

Exhibit 14-17 *Crain's New York Business* "Soviets" radio script: Courtesy Goldsmith/Jeffrey.

Exhibit 14-18 Radio advertising rates: Reprinted with permission of *Adweek's Marketer's Guide to Media*, January–March 1991, p. 75, Network Radio Advertising.

Exhibit 14-19 KWOD-FM radio spot rates: *Spot Radio Rates and Data*, September 1, 1991, issue; published by Standard Rate & Data Service, a Maxwell Macmillan Company.

Exhibit 14-20 Listening rates: Courtesy The Arbitron Company.

CHAPTER 15

Heinz Pet Products direct-mail package Courtesy Heinz Pet Products and Leo Burnett USA.

Exhibit 15-1 Direct-mail ad: Courtesy Champion International Corporation.

Exhibit 15-2 Perform Premium Dog Food direct-response print ad: Courtesy Ogilvy & Mather Direct.

Exhibit 15-3 AT&T competitive edge direct-response storyboard: Courtesy Ogilvy & Mather Direct.

Exhibit 15-4 Top 10 mail-order product categories: *The United States Mail Order Industry*, Maxwell Sroge Publishing, Inc., Chicago, Ill.

Exhibit 15-5 Parker Pen ad: Courtesy Samata Associates, Design Consultants.

Ethical Dilemma Adapted from Laura Bird, "Marketing in Big Brother's Shadow," *Adweek's Marketing Week*, December 10, 1990, pp. 26–27, 30; John Osborn, "Abuses Draw Congress' Fire," *Advertising Age*, September 25, 1989, pp. S8–S9; Marvin Schwartz, "List Usage Ethics and Marketing Opportunities in Merge/Purge," *Direct Marketing*, May 1987, pp. 40, 44, 46, 48, 156–57; Rose Harper, "List Security: A Matter of Ethics," *Folio: The Magazine for Magazine Management*, December 1988, pp. 193–94; Stephen Toman, "Consumer Confidence: A Top Priority," *Direct Marketing*, April 1988, p. 96; Robert J. Posch, "Nuisance/Privacy Infractions—Part Two," *Direct Marketing*, January 1988, p. 103; Terrence Witkowski, "Self-Regulation Will Suppress Direct Marketing's Dark Side," *Marketing News*, April 24, 1989, p. 4; Milton Pierce, "The Morality of Direct Marketing," *Direct Marketing*, October 1987, pp. 118, 120, 122.

Exhibit 15-6 Doubleday Buyers list: *Direct Mail List Rates and Data (Consumer Lists)*, August 1991 issue; published by Standard Rate & Data Service, a Maxwell Macmillan Company.

Exhibit 15-7 Continental Bank boxes: Courtesy Fallon McElligott.

Exhibit 15-8 Martin Agency hiring ad: Courtesy The Martin Agency/Richmond, VA.

Exhibit 15-9 Mailer Preference Service: Courtesy Direct Marketing Association, Inc.

Exhibit 15-10 Pasting up poster sheets: Courtesy Patrick Media Group, Inc.

Exhibit 15-11 New England Aquarium ad: Courtesy Arnold Advertising/Boston.

Exhibit 15-12 Night scene: Noel A. Silverston/Stock Imagery.

Exhibit 15-13 Billboard location map: Courtesy Pacific Outdoor Advertising Co.

Exhibit 15-14 UTA French Airlines ad: Courtesy Vogel Communications Group.

Exhibit 15-15 Robinson's Department stores ad: Courtesy Robinson's.

Exhibit 15-16 Monthly rates for posters: Gannett's Outdoor Network USA, *1991 Ratebook & Almanac.*

Exhibit 15-17 Smartfood billboard: Courtesy Mullen Advertising.

Portfolio *Traffic signs billboard:* Courtesy Cole & Weber. *Kodak billboard:* Reprinted courtesy of Eastman Kodak Company. *San Diego Zoo:* Courtesy San Diego Zoo/Phillips-Ramsey. *Museum of Flight:* Art director, Matt Myers; copywriter, Rick Rosenberg; creative director, Jim Copacino; illustrator, Matt Myers; agency, Livingston & Company (Seattle); client, Museum of Flight. *Seabrook Decorating Centers ad:* Billboard created by Thompson & Company/Memphis TN for Seabrook Decorating Centers; Trace Hallowell, art director; Mickey Hodges, copywriter; Michael H. Thompson, creative director.

Exhibit 15-18 Junior Caramels transit ad: Courtesy J. Walter Thompson Co. Ltd./Toronto.

Exhibit 15-19 Sizes for transit cards: Courtesy The Transit Advertising Association, Inc.

Exhibit 15-20 Minnesota Dept. of Health antismoking mouthwash outdoor poster: Courtesy Martin Williams Advertising Incorporated/Minnesota Department of Health.

Exhibit 15-21 Recycle, Minnesota transit ad: Agency, Clarity Coverdale Rueff/Minneapolis; art director, David Fox; copywriter, Joe Alexander; creative director, Jac Coverdale; photographer, Mark Lavor; client, City of Minneapolis Recycling.

Exhibit 15-22 *Woman's Day* mobile billboard: Courtesy *Woman's Day.*

CHAPTER 16

Jell-O-jigglers ad © 1990 Kraft General Foods, Inc.

Exhibit 16-1 Burger King Kids Club: Rob Crandall/Picture Group.

Exhibit 16-2 Share of promotional dollars: *Thirteenth Annual Survey of Promotional Practices,* p. 7, 1991. Courtesy of Donnelley Marketing, Inc.

Exhibit 16-3 Taos Furniture ad: Courtesy Vaughan/Weeden Creative, Inc.

Exhibit 16-4 KLM sweepstakes: Courtesy W. L. Harvey Communications, Inc.

Exhibit 16-5 Consumer promotion scorecard: *Thirteenth Annual Survey of Promotional Practices,* p. 27, 1991. Courtesy of Donnelley Marketing, Inc.

Exhibit 16-6 Lucky Supermarket ad: Courtesy Grey Advertising.

Ad Lab 16-A Reprinted by permission from March 16, 1981, issue of *Advertising Age.* Copyright 1981 by Crain Communications, Inc.

Exhibit 16-7 chart: "Study: Some Promotions Change Consumer Behavior," *Marketing News,* October 15, 1990, p. 12.

Exhibit 16-8 Sweepstakes ad: Courtesy of Publishers Clearing House.

Exhibit 16-9 Sweepstakes participation: Reprinted with permission of *Adweek's Marketing Week,* April 9, 1990, pp. 6, 7, Sweepstakes Participation.

Ad Lab 16-B Adapted from Bernard Wysocki, Jr., "Sight, Smell, Sound: They're All Arms in Retailer's Arsenal," *The Wall Street Journal,* April 17, 1979.

Exhibit 16-10 National Car Rental ad: Courtesy Chiat/Day/Mojo/New York.

Exhibit 16-11 Specialty staplers: Courtesy The Advertising Specialty Institute.

Exhibit 16-12 Trade show: Cathy Melloan: TSW Click/Chicago.

Exhibit 16-13 Yellow Pages chart: reprinted with permission of Yellow Pages Publishers Association (YPPA).

Exhibit 16-14 NYNEX business-to-business Yellow Pages ad: Courtesy Goldsmith/Jeffrey, Inc.

Exhibit 16-15 Electronic couponing photo: Barth Falkenberg.

PART V   Signature Cross Pen ad Courtesy of Hill, Holliday, Connors, Cosmopoulos, Inc., Boston; art director, Nancy Wovers.

CHAPTER 17

Pier 1 Imports ad Courtesy Pier 1 Imports.

Exhibit 17-1 Rubio's Fish Tacos: John Brice & Associates/Bill Pike, illustrator.

Exhibit 17-2 Goodwine Funeral Homes ad: Art director, David Straka; creative director, Pat Fagan; copywriter, Pat Fagan; agency, Keller-Crescent Co.; client, Goodwine Funeral Homes.

Exhibit 17-3 Zell Bros. ad: Courtesy Borders, Perrin & Norrander, Inc.

Exhibit 17-4 Bissell & Wilhite silverware ad: Creative art director/art director/copywriter, Gary D. Johns; photographer, Marc Coppos; agency, Gary D. Johns, Inc.; client, Bissell & Wilhite Co.

Exhibit 17-5 Kenzo ad: Courtesy Dayton Hudson Department Store.

Exhibit 17-6 Average advertising investment: Data from Newspaper Advertising Bureau, Inc.

Exhibit 17-7 Retail sales by types of stores: Data from Newspaper Advertising Bureau, Inc.

Exhibit 17-8 Advertising expenditure curves: Data from Newspaper Advertising Bureau, Inc.

Exhibit 17-9 Bullock's ad: Courtesy Bullock's.

Exhibit 17-10 Highlands Inn ad: Courtesy Zechman & Associates.

Exhibit 17-11 Loop AM 1000: Courtesy Loop AM 1000; agency, Eisaman, Johns and Laws Advertising, Inc.

Exhibit 17-12 Golden Gate Park best ribs in town: Art director, Matt Myers; copywriter, Jim Copacino; creative director, Jim Copacino; photographer, Stewart Tilger; model maker, Mike Dillion; agency, Livingston & Company (Seattle); client, California Academy of Sciences.

Exhibit 17-13 Amoco Quick Lube ad: Courtesy Fallon McElligott.

Exhibit 17-14 Tom Thumb turkey ad: Courtesy KCBN, Inc.

Exhibit 17-15 Premier Limousine ad: Courtesy Premier Limousine Co.

Checklist for Creating Local Advertising Data from Newspaper Advertising Bureau, Inc.

Exhibit 17-16 Kasle Recycling Cadillac ad: Client, Kasle Recycling; agency, Meyer & Wallis; creative director/writer, Tim A. Wallis; art director, Jim Brooks; photographer, Dan Wilson.

Exhibit 17-17 Ball Partnership ad: Writers, Neil French/Ben Hunt; art director, Neil French; agency, The Ball Partnership.

Exhibit 17-18 Kerry Wetzel ad: Art director, Joe Shands; writer, Ron Saltmarsh, client, Kerry Wetzel Photographer; agency, Cole & Weber/Portland.

Exhibit 17-21 Tri-State Cadillac Dealers storyboard: Courtesy Biederman, Kelly & Shaffer.

CHAPTER 18

Ad Council drink/drive ad Courtesy The Advertising Council Inc.

Exhibit 18-1 Exxon oil spill photo: Paul Fusco/Magnum Photos, Inc.

Exhibit 18-2 Toshiba ad: Courtesy Calet, Hirsch & Spector, Inc.

Exhibit 18-3 Beatrice marathon: William Meyer: Click/Chicago.

Exhibit 18-4 Glade Litter Fresh: Courtesy Golia/Harris Communications, Inc.

Exhibit 18-5 Annual report: Courtesy McDonnell Douglas.

Exhibit 18-6 Innova house organ: Courtesy Creel Morrell, Inc.-Atlanta, Newport Beach, Washington, D.C.; design principle, Eric G. Morrell; executive vice president/design, Cinda K. Debbink; project description: a quarterly publication produced for an international audience and sponsored by Innova.

Exhibit 18-7 Claris Corporation so long Coach ad: Courtesy Claris Corporation.

Exhibit 18-8 Georgia O'Keefe poster: Courtesy Southwestern Bell Corporation.

Portfolio *Dreyfus ad:* Courtesy Levine, Huntley, Vick & Beaver. *Carrier Transcold Refrigeration ad:* Courtesy United Technologies. *3M ad:* Courtesy 3M. *Denny's ad:* Courtesy Denny's. *Rockwell International ad:* reprinted with permission of copyright holder, Rockwell International Corporation, All Rights Reserved. *Mitsubishi Electric ad:* Courtesy David Nathanson. *John Hancock ad:* Courtesy John Hancock Mutual Life Insurance Company.

Ethical Dilemma Adapted from Richard Nelson, "Bias versus Fairness: The Social Utility of Issues Management," *Public Relations Review,* Spring 1990, pp. 25-32; Bob Cutler and Darrel Muehling, "Advocacy Advertising and the Boundaries of Commercial Speech," *Journal of Advertising* 18, no. 3 (1989), pp. 40-50; Thomas Garbett, "Look What We're Doing for Humanity," *Across the Board,* May 1989, pp. 45-52; Janice Steinberg, "Advocacy Approach Past Its Prime," *Advertising Age,* October 5, 1987, pp. S8-S9; Robert Heath and William Douglas, "Issues Advertising and Its Effect on Public Opinion Recall," *Public Relations Review,* Summer 1986, pp. 47-56; Robert Heath and Richard Nelson, "Image and Issue Advertising: A Corporate and Public Policy Perspective," *Journal of Marketing,* Spring 1985, pp. 58-68; Peter Chippindale and Chris Horrie, "It All Ads Up. Democracy Is Being Replaced by 'Advertocracy' When It Comes to Shaping Public Opinion," *New Statesman and Society,* October 7, 1988, pp. 10-11; Herbert Waltzer, "Corporate Advocacy Advertising and Political Influence," *Public Relations Review,* Spring 1988, pp. 41-55; Phyllis Furman, "Farley Industries' Image Goes Public," *Advertising Age,* October 5, 1987, pp. S-12; Roland Marchand, "The Fitful Career of Advocacy Advertising: Political Protection, Client Cultivation, and Corporate Morale," *California Management Review,* Winter 1987, pp. 128-56.

Ad Lab 18-A David Ogilvy photo: Courtesy Ogilvy & Mather/New York.

Exhibit 18-9 Alfa Romeo ad: © 1990, Alfa Romeo Distributors of North America. Used with permission.

Exhibit 18-10 Chiat/Day/Mojo ad: Art director, Karen Prince; copywriter, Isidoro Debellis; agency/client, Chiat/Day/Mojo/Toronto.

Exhibit 18-12 Partnership for a Drug-Free America anti-cocaine ad: creative director, Tom Yobbagy; art director, Tom Schwartz; copywriter, Dean Hacohen; photography, Larry Sillen; agency, DDB Needham Worldwide; client, Partnership for a Drug-Free America.

Exhibit 18-13 Children's Defense Fund hot date ad: Reproduced with permission of the Children's Defense Fund.

Exhibit 18-14 Episcopal Church ad: Courtesy Fallon McElligott.

Exhibit 18-15 National Dairy Board presto chango storyboard: Courtesy America's Dairy Farmers/National Dairy Board.

Exhibit 18-16 Illinois Department of Tourism storyboard: Courtesy Illinois Bureau of Tourism, Department of Commerce and Community Affairs. "No Commercials" :30 TV; agency, McConnaughy Stein Schmidt.

Exhibit 18-17 Ad Council Eat Lean TV storyboard: courtesy of the Advertising Council.

CHAPTER 19

All Nippon Airways ad agency, FCB Paris, in partnership with Dentsu Tokyo; creatives, A. D. Oliver Vouktchevitch; copy, Bertand Suchet; account personnel (FCB) Tony Crowther, (Dentsu) Takashi Ichikura; client, Mr. Yasuda, ANA Tokyo and Mr. Takei, ANA Paris.

Exhibit 19-1 Gillette Sensor storyboard: Courtesy The Gillette Company.

Exhibit 19-2 Top 10 international advertisers: *Advertising Age,* November 19, 1990, p. S-4.

Exhibit 19-3 Fuji Xerox storyboard: Client, Fuji Xerox Co., Ltd.; agency/creative, Dentsu Inc., Tokyo; production, Spoon Inc.

Exhibit 19-4 Coke logos: Coke and Coca-Cola are registered trademarks of the Coca-Cola Company and permission for use granted by The Company.

Ad Lab 19-A Michael Jackson photo: Sam Emerson/Shooting Star.

Exhibit 19-5 French Tang ad: Courtesy GreyCom, Inc.

Exhibit 19-6 Coke's general assembly storyboard: Coke and Coca-Cola are registered trademarks of The Coca-Cola Company and permission for use granted by The Company.

Exhibit 19-7 Top 10 agencies: *Advertising Age,* March 26, 1991.

Exhibit 19-8 GM cat ad: Courtesy DPZ/Propaganda/Sao Paulo.

Exhibit 19-9 French/English Sears ads: Courtesy Franklin Dallas Kundinger Inc. Advertising.

Exhibit 19-10 International *USA Today/Wall Street Journal:* photo by Michael J. Hruby.

Portfolio *Busek Ad:* Courtesy CAA, Vienna. *Mobil Oil ad:* Leo Burnett (Thailand). *AZKO Engineering:* Courtesy PMSvW/Y&R; art director, Jan Pastoor; copywriter, Hans Born/Joris Gergsma; photographer/illustrator, Ralph Steadman. *Rosalp butter ad:* Werbeagentur BSW, Atelier Jaquet AG, Bern.

Exhibit 19-11 Parisian advertising kiosk: Stephen Dunn.

Exhibit 19-12 Weiner Fest Wochen ad: Courtesy Demner & Merlicek/Vienna.

Checklist for International Media Planning Courtesy Directories International, Inc.

Exhibit 19-13 Richmond Slate ad: Courtesy First City/BBDO Ltd., London.

Exhibit 19-14 Visa ads: Courtesy of Visa International.

Exhibit 19-15 Advertising regulations in Western Europe: Adapted from *Advertising Age: Its Role in Modern Marketing,* 5th ed, by S. Watson Dunn and Arnold M. Barban. Copyright 1982 by The Dryden Press, a division of Holt, Rinehart and Winston, Publishers. Reprinted by permission of Holt, Rinehart and Winston.

GLOSSARY*

AAAA (2) See *American Association of Advertising Agencies*.

AAF (2) See *American Advertising Federation*.

ABC (13) See *Audit Bureau of Circulations*.

abundance principle (1) The idea that in an economy that produces more goods and services than can be consumed, advertising serves two purposes: keeping consumers informed of selection alternatives and allowing companies to compete more effectively for consumer dollars.

account executive (3) The liaison between the agency and the client. The account executive is responsible both for mustering all the agency's services for the benefit of the client and for representing the agency's point of view to the client.

A. C. Nielsen (13) An organization which provides a wide variety of audience and market data to the advertising industry; produces the *Nielsen Station Index*, which provides a wide array of statistics on how many people, in what age groups, and of what sex are watching TV at various times of the day within a specific market area.

action advertising (1)(7) Advertising intended to bring about immediate action on the part of the reader or viewer.

action block (7) The top step in the advertising pyramid, in which people actually go out and test the product or even purchase it.

action programs (7) See *tactics*.

ADI (14) See *area of dominant influence*.

administered system (5) A type of vertical marketing system in which a dominant channel member has strong retailer support.

advertisers (3) See *clients*.

advertising (1) The nonpersonal communication of information, usually paid for and usually persuasive in nature, about products (goods and services) or ideas by identified sponsors through various media.

advertising agency (3) An independent organization of creative people and businesspeople who specialize in developing and preparing advertising plans, advertisements, and other promotional tools for advertisers. The agency also arranges for or contracts for the purchase of space and time in various media.

advertising allowance (16) Either a percentage of gross purchases or a flat fee paid to the retailer for advertising the manufacturer's product.

Advertising Council (18) A nonpartisan, nonpolitical volunteer organization supported by the American Association of Advertising Agencies. It conducts public service ad campaigns to the nation at large, avoiding regional, sectarian, or special-interest drives of all kinds.

advertising manager (3) The advertiser's person who is in charge of planning, coordinating, budgeting, and directing the company's advertising program.

advertising materials (16) Ads, photos, sample radio commercials, preprinted inserts, and related items that manufacturers supply to dealers.

advertising medium (1) See *media*.

advertising message (7) An element of the creative mix comprising what the company plans to say in its advertisements and how it plans to say it—verbally and nonverbally.

advertising objectives (7) What the advertiser hopes to achieve through advertising, usually with respect to customer awareness, attitude, and preference.

advertising plan (7) The plan that directs the company's advertising effort. A natural outgrowth of the marketing plan, it analyzes the situation, sets advertising objectives, and lays out a specific strategy from which ads and campaigns are created.

advertising pyramid (7) A simple five-step model for understanding some of the tasks advertising can perform and for setting advertising objectives. The five steps include awareness, comprehension, conviction, desire, and action.

advertising research (6) The systematic gathering and analysis of information specifically to facilitate the development or evaluation of advertising strategies, ads and commercials, and media campaigns.

* Numbers in parentheses after term indicate chapter(s) where term is discussed.

advertising strategy (7) The methodology advertisers use to achieve their advertising objectives. The strategy is determined by the particular creative mix of advertising elements the advertiser selects, namely: target audience; product concept; communications media; and advertising message. (Also called the *creative mix.*)

advertorial (18) An advertisement with the aim of swaying public opinion rather than selling a product; a form of advocacy advertising.

advocacy advertising (18) Advertising used to communicate a company's views on issues that affect business.

affidavit of performance (14) A signed and notarized form sent by a television station to an advertiser or agency indicating what spots ran and when. It is the station's legal proof that the advertiser got what was paid for.

agency commission (3) Compensation paid by a medium to recognized advertising agencies, usually 15 percent (16⅔ percent for outdoor), for advertising placed with it.

agency network (19) An international affiliation of advertising agencies organized to give and receive media counsel, translation services, production assistance, or other specialized services in unfamiliar markets.

agricultural advertising (1) See *farm advertising.*

American Advertising Federation (AAF)(2) A nationwide association of advertising people. The AAF helped to establish the Federal Trade Commission, and its early "vigilance" committees were the forerunners of the Better Business Bureaus.

American Association of Advertising Agencies (AAAA)(2) The national organization of the advertising business. It has members throughout the United States and controls agency practices by denying membership to any agency judged unethical.

ANA (2) See *Association of National Advertisers.*

animatic (9) A rough television commercial produced by photographing storyboard sketches on a film strip or video with the audio portion synchronized on tape. It is used primarily for testing purposes.

animation (9)(11) The use of cartoons, puppet characters, or demonstrations of inanimate characters come to life in television commercials; often used for communicating difficult messages or for reaching specialized markets, such as children.

annual report (18) A formal document issued yearly by a corporation to its stockholders to reflect the corporation's condition at the close of the business year.

answer print (11) The final print of a filmed commercial, along with all the required optical effects and titles, used for review and approval before duplicating.

aperture (11) The opening in a camera that determines the amount of light that reaches the film or videotape.

appeal (8) The specific approach advertisers use to communicate how their products will satisfy customer needs. There are two broad types of appeals advertisers use: rational and emotional appeals.

Arbitron (14) A commonly used rating service that regularly publishes statistics on how many people, in what age groups, and of what sex are watching TV or listening to radio at various times of the day within a specific market area.

area of dominant influence (ADI)(14) Arbitron's term for a television market—defined as "an exclusive geographic area consisting of all counties in which the home market stations receive a preponderance of total viewing hours."

art (9) The whole visual presentation of a commercial or advertisement. Art also refers to the style of photography or illustration employed, the way color is used, and the arrangement of elements in an ad so that they relate to one another in size and proportion.

art direction (8) The act or process of managing the visual presentation of an ad or commercial.

ascender (10) In typography, any letter that rises above the x-height; for example, d, t, l.

Association of National Advertisers (ANA)(2) An organization composed of 400 major manufacturing and service companies that are clients of member agencies of the AAAA. These companies, which are pledged to uphold the ANA code of advertising ethics, work with the ANA through a joint Committee for Improvement of Advertising Content.

attention value (12) A consideration in selecting media based on the degree of attention paid to ads in a particular medium by those exposed to them. Attention value relates to the advertising message and copy just as much as to the medium.

attitude (4) The acquired mental position—positive or negative—that we hold in regard to some idea or object.

attitude test (6) A type of posttest that usually seeks to measure the effectiveness of an advertising campaign in creating a favorable image for a company, its brand, or its products.

audience (12) The total number of households exposed to a particular medium.

audience composition (14) The distribution of an audience into demographic categories.

audio (8)(9) The sound portion of a commercial. Also, the right side of a script for a television commercial, indicating spoken copy, sound effects, and music.

audio console (11) In a sound studio control room, the board that channels sounds to the appropriate recording devices and that blends both live and prerecorded sounds for immediate or delayed broadcast.

Audit Bureau of Circulations (ABC)(13) An organization supported by advertising agencies, advertisers, and publishers that verifies circulation and other marketing data on newspapers and magazines for the benefit of its members.

avails (14) An abbreviated term referring to the TV time slots that are *available* to an advertiser.

average frequency (12) Total exposures divided by audience reach.

average quarter-hour persons (14) A radio term referring to the average number of people who are listening to a specific station for at least 5 minutes during a 15-minutes period of any given daypart.

average quarter-hour rating (14) The average quarter-hour persons estimate expressed as a percentage of the estimated population.

awareness advertising (1) Advertising that attempts to build the image of a product or familiarity with the name and package.

awareness block (7) The foundation block of the advertising pyramid, in which people are acquainted with the company, good, service, or brand.

backlight (11) A light that is either directly behind or behind and above a subject, aimed toward the camera to outline the subject and set the subject apart from the background.

barter syndication (14) Marketing of first-run television programs to local stations free or for a reduced rate because some of the ad space has been presold to national advertisers.

base art (10) The first image on an artboard on which an overlay may be placed.

basic bus (15) In transit advertising, all the inside space on a group of buses, which thereby gives the advertiser complete domination.

behavioral sciences (4) The social sciences: anthropology, sociology, psychology, and so on.

behavioristic segmentation (5) Method of determining market segments by aggregating consumers into product-related groups based on their knowledge, attitude, use, or response to actual products or product attributes.

benefit headline (8) Type of headline that makes a direct promise to the reader.

benefits (5) The particular product attributes offered to customers, such as high quality, low price, status, speed, sex appeal, good taste, etc.

benefit segmentation (5) Method of segmenting markets by determining the major benefits consumers seek in a product (high quality, low price, status, speed, sex appeal, good taste, etc.).

Better Business Bureau (BBB) (2) A business-monitoring organization funded by dues from over 100,000 member companies. It operates primarily at the local level to protect consumers against fraudulent and deceptive advertising.

bidirectional microphone (11) A microphone designed to capture sounds from two opposing directions simultaneously.

big idea (8) The flash of creative insight—the bold advertising initiative—that captures the essence of the strategy in an imaginative, involving way and brings the subject to life to make the reader stop, look, and listen.

billboards (15) See *poster panel*.

Birch Research (14) A radio research service that relies on telephone surveys to obtain listener data.

Birchscan (14) A monthly computerized report of radio data, published by Birch Research.

blanket (10) In offset printing, the intermediate rubber surface that comes in contact with the paper.

bleed pages (13) Magazine advertisements in which the dark or colored background of the ad extends to the edge of the page. Most magazines offer bleed pages, but they normally charge advertisers a 10 to 15 percent premium for them.

blinking (12) A type of media schedule in which ads are run only on specific days when the target audience is most likely to be reading or watching.

board (11) See *audio console*.

body copy (8) The text of an advertisement that tells the complete story and attempts to close the sale. It is a logical continuation of the headline and subheads and is usually set in a smaller type size than headlines or subheads.

boldface (8) Heavier type.

bottom-up marketing (7) The opposite of standard, top-down marketing planning, bottom-up marketing focuses on one specific tactic and develops it into an overall strategy.

boxes and panels (8) A *box* is copy around which a line has been drawn, while a *panel* is an elongated box that usually runs the whole length or width of an ad. Boxes and panels are generally used in advertisements to set apart coupons, special offers, contest rules, and order blanks.

brand (4) The combination of name, word, symbols, or design that identifies one particular product and differentiates it from competing products.

brand development index (BDI) (12) The percentage of a brand's total sales in an area divided by the total population in the area; it indicates the sales potential of the particular brand in the specific market area.

brand equity (5) The totality of what consumers, distributors, dealers, and competitors feel and think about a brand over an extended period of time; in short, it is the value of the brand's capital.

brand insistence (5) The consumer's refusal to accept substitutes for a particular brand.

brand loyalty (4) The consumer's conscious or unconscious decision—expressed through intention or behavior—to repurchase a brand continually. This occurs because the consumer perceives that the brand has the right product features, image, quality, or relationship at the right price.

brand manager (3) The individual within the advertiser's company who is assigned the authority and responsibility for the successful marketing of a particular brand.

brand nonrecognition (5) The consumer's lack of awareness of a brand.

brand preference (5) The consumer's tendency to choose a particular brand over its competitors.

brand recognition (5) The consumer's awareness and recognition of a brand.

brand rejection (5) The consumer's refusal to buy a brand again unless it changes its quality or image.

broadcast television (14) Television sent over airwaves as opposed to over cables.

broadside (15) A form of direct-mail advertisement, larger than a folder and sometimes used as a window display or wall poster in stores. It can be folded to a compact size and fitted into a mailer.

budget buildup method (7) See *objective/task method.*

bulletin boards (18) An internal public relations means for announcing new equipment, meetings, promotions, new products, construction plans, and recreation news.

burn (10) The process of exposing a photosensitive plate to light.

bursting (12) A media scheduling method for promoting high-ticket items that require careful consideration, such as running the same commercial every half-hour on the same network in prime time.

business advertising (1) Advertising directed at people who buy or specify goods and services for business use.

business magazines (13) Periodicals that target business readers; they may be trade, industrial, or professional magazines.

business markets (4) Organizations that buy natural resources, component products, and services that they either resell or use in making another product or running their business.

business reply mail (15) A type of mail that enables the recipient of direct-mail advertising to respond without paying postage.

bus-o-rama (15) In transit advertising, a jumbo roof sign, which is actually a full-color transparency backlighted by fluorescent tubes, running the length of the bus.

buy-back allowance (16) A manufacturer's offer to pay for an old product so that it will be taken off the shelf to make room for a new product.

cable television (14) Television signals carried to households by cable and paid for by subscription.

camera-ready (10) A finished ad that is ready for the printer's camera to shoot—to make negatives or plates—according to the publication's specifications.

cartoon (11) Animation technique achieved by drawing loose, childlike illustrations of each step in the action and photographing them one frame at a time such that when the film is projected, it gives the illusion of movement.

catalogs (15) Reference books mailed to prospective customers that list, describe, and often picture the products sold by a manufacturer, wholesaler, jobber, or retailer.

category development index (CDI) (12) The percent of a product category's total U.S. sales in an area divided by the percent of total U.S. population in the area.

centers of influence (4) Customers, prospective customers, or opinion leaders whose actions are respected and may be emulated by others.

centralized organization (3) A staff of employees, usually located at corporate headquarters, responsible for all the organization's advertising. The department is often structured by product, advertising subfunction, end user, media, or geography.

central location test (6) A type of pretest in which videotapes of test commercials are shown to respondents on a one-to-one basis, usually in shopping center locations.

cents-off promotion (16) A short-term reduction in the price of a product designed to induce trial and usage. Cents-off promotions take various forms, including basic cents-off packages, one-cent sales, free offers, and box-top refunds.

channels of distribution (5) See *distribution channel.*

character-count method (10) A method of copy casting in which an actual count is made of the number of characters in the copy.

cinematographer (11) A motion picture photographer.

circulars (17) Multipage handbills.

classified advertising (13) Newspaper and magazine advertisements usually arranged under subheads that describe the class of goods or the need the ads seek to satisfy. Rates are based on the number of lines the ad occupies. Most employment, housing, and automotive advertising is in the form of classified advertising.

classified display advertising (13) Ads that run in the classified section of the newspaper but have larger-size type, photos, art borders, abundant white space, and sometimes color.

clearance advertising (17) A type of local advertising designed to make room for new product lines or new models or to get rid of slow-moving product lines, floor samples, broken or distressed merchandise, or items that are no longer in season.

clients (3) The various businesses that advertise themselves or their products and for whom advertising agencies work in an effort to find customers for their goods and services.

close (8) That part of an advertisement that asks customers to do something and tells them how to do it—the action step in the ad's copy.

closing date (10) The final deadline for supplying printing material for an advertisement to a publication.

clutter tests (6) Method of pretesting in which commercials are grouped with noncompetitive control commercials and shown to prospective customers to measure their effectiveness in gaining attention, increasing brand awareness and comprehension, and causing attitude shifts.

cognition (4) The point of awareness and comprehension of a stimulus.

cognitivie dissonance (4) See *theory of cognitive dissonance.*

cognitive theory (4) An approach that views learning as a mental process of memory, thinking, and the rational application of knowledge to practical problem solving.

collateral sales material (5) (16) All the accessory nonmedia advertising materials prepared by manufacturers to help dealers sell a product—booklets, catalogs, brochures, films, trade-show exhibits, sales kits, etc.

color light meter (11) A type of light meter that indicates the overall degrees on the Kelvin scale for the light reflecting from an area within the light meter's view. Thus, it indicates whether a scene is generally too blue, green, or red in relation to daylight or tungsten film.

color separation negatives (10) Four separate continuous-tone negatives produced by photographing artwork through color filters that eliminate all the colors but one. The negatives are used to make four printing plates—one each for yellow, magenta, cyan, and black—for reproducing the color artwork.

color strip (13) A sample of eye shadow, blusher, lipstick, or makeup provided in a magazine advertisement.

column inch (13) In newspaper advertising, a measurement of depth one inch deep by one column wide. Most newspapers now sell advertising space by the column inch.

combination offers (16) A sales promotion device in which two related products are packaged together at a special price, such as a razor and a package of blades. Sometimes a combination offer may be used to introduce a new product by tying its purchase to an established product at a special price.

combination rates (13) Special newspaper advertising rates offered for placing a given ad in (1) morning and evening editions of the same newspaper; (2) two or more newspapers owned by the same publisher; or (3) two or more newspapers affiliated in a syndicate or newspaper group.

command headline (8) A type of headline that orders the reader to do something.

commercial advertising (1) Advertising that promotes goods, services, or ideas for a business with the expectation of making a profit.

commoncase (10) Typeset material that appears in capital letters and small caps.

communicating arts (4) Writing and printing, drama and theatrical production, graphic design, photography, and so on.

communications media (7) An element of the creative mix, comprising the various methods or vehicles that will be used to transmit the advertiser's message.

commission (3) See *agency commission.*

company conventions and dealer meetings (16) Events held by manufacturers to introduce new products, sales promotion programs, or advertising campaigns.

comparative advertising (2) Advertising that claims superiority to competitors in some aspect.

compiled list (15) A type of direct-mail list that has been compiled by another source, such as lists of automobile owners, new-house purchasers, business owners, union members, and so forth. It is the most readily available in volume but offers the lowest response expectation.

comprehension block (7) In the advertising pyramid, the stage at which target consumers are not only aware of the product but also recognize its purpose and perhaps some of its features.

comprehensive layout (9) A facsimile of a finished ad with copy set in type and pasted into position along with proposed illustrations. The "comp" is prepared so the advertiser can gauge the effect of the final ad.

computer software (1) Used as an advertising medium, disks distributed by individual manufacturers and ad spots on computer information services.

conceptualization (8) See *visualization.*

conditioning theory (4) Also called stimulus-response theory, the idea that learning is a trial-and-error process.

consumer advertising (1) Advertising directed at the ultimate consumer of the product or at the person who will buy the product for someone else's personal use.

consumer behavior (4) The activities, actions, and influencers of people who purchase and use goods and services to satisfy their personal or household needs and wants.

consumer decision-making process (4) The series of steps a consumer goes through in deciding to make a purchase.

consumerism (2) Social action designed to dramatize the rights of the buying public.

consumer magazines (13) Information- or entertainment-oriented periodicals directed toward people who buy products for the own consumption.

consumer promotions (16) Marketing, advertising, and sales promotion activities aimed at inducing trial, purchase, and re-purchase by the consumer. (Also called *pull strategy.*)

consumers, consumer market (1) (4) People who buy products and services for their own, or someone else's, personal use.

contest (16) A sales promotion device for creating consumer involvement in which prizes are offered based on the skill of the entrants.

continuity (12) The length of an advertising campaign and the manner in which it is scheduled and sustained over an extended period of time.

contract rate (13) A special rate for newspaper advertising usually offered to local advertisers who sign an annual contract for frequent or bulk space purchases. As the number of inches contracted for increases, the rate decreases.

contractual systems (5) Vertical marketing systems consisting of voluntary contractual arrangements among independent members; examples include retail co-ops and franchises.

controlled circulation (13) A free publication mailed to a select list of individuals the publisher feels are in a unique position to influence the purchase of advertised products.

control room (11) In a recording studio, the place where the producer, director, and sound engineer sit, monitoring and controlling all the sounds generated in the sound studio.

conviction block (7) In the advertising pyramid, the stage at which a certain number of people believe in the value of the product.

cooperative advertising (5)(13)(16) The sharing of advertising costs by the manufacturer and the distributor or retailer. The manufacturer may repay 50 or 100 percent of the dealer's advertising costs or some other amount based on sales. See also *horizontal cooperative advertising; vertical cooperative advertising.*

copy (3)(8) The words that make up the headline and message of an advertisement or commercial.

copy casting (10) The process of determining how much type will fit into an advertisement. The two methods of copy casting include the word-count and the character-count methods.

copy platform (8) A document that serves as a guide for writing an ad. It describes the most important issues that should be considered in writing the copy, including a definition and description of the target audience; the rational and emotional appeals to be used; the product features that will satisfy the customer's needs; the style, approach, or tone that will be used in the copy; and, generally, what the copy will say.

copy points (5) Copywriting themes.

copyright (2) An exclusive right granted by the Copyright Act to authors and artists to protect their original work from being plagiarized, sold, or used by another without their express consent.

copywriters (3) People who create the words and concepts for ads and commercials.

copywriter's pyramid (8) A simple, five-step model for setting copy objectives in writing ads and commercials.

copywriting (8) Creating the verbal element of the advertising message.

corporate advertising (1)(18) The broad area of nonproduct advertising aimed specifically at enhancing a company's image and increasing lagging awareness.

corporate marketing system (5) A type of vertical marketing system that occurs when a single corporation owns the manufacturers, distributors, and dealers of many of the products it sells.

corporate objectives (7) Goals of the company stated in terms of profit or return on investment. Goals may also be stated in terms of net worth, earnings ratios, growth, or corporate reputation.

cosponsor (14) One of multiple sponsors of a television program or series.

cost efficiency (12) The cost of reaching the target audience through a particular medium as opposed to the cost of reaching the medium's total circulation.

cost per rating point (CPP)(14) A simple computation used by media buyers to determine which broadcast programs are the most efficient in relation to the target audience. The CPP is determined by dividing the cost of the show by the show's expected rating against the target audience.

cost per thousand (CPM)(12) A common term describing the cost of reaching 1,000 people in a medium's audience. It is used by media planners to compare the cost of various media vehicles.

coupon (16) A certificate with a stated value that is presented to retail stores for a price reduction on a specified item.

coupon premiums (16) Premiums for which consumers must collect in-pack coupons.

CPM (12) See *cost per thousand.*

creative boutique (3) An organization of creative specialists (such as art directors, designers, and copywriters) who work for advertisers and occasionally advertising agencies to develop creative concepts, advertising messages, and specialized art. A boutique performs only the creative work.

creative department (3) That department in an advertising agency responsible for conceiving, writing, laying out, and producing ads and commercials.

creative mix (7) Those advertising elements the company controls to achieve its advertising objectives, including the target audience, the product concept, the communications media, and the advertising message. (See also *advertising strategy.*)

crisis management (18) A company's plan for handling news and public relations during crises.

cue (5) The stimulus that triggers a consumer's need or want, which in turn creates a drive to respond. An advertisement might be a cue.

cume persons (14) The total number of *different* people listening to a radio station for at least one 15-minute segment over the course of a given week, day, or daypart.

cume rating (14) The estimated number of cume persons expressed as a percentage of the estimated population.

current customers (4) People who have already purchased something from a business and who may purchase on a regular basis.

cursive type (10) A type style that resembles handwriting. Also called *script.*

customers (4) The people or organizations who consume goods and services. See also *centers of influence, current customers,* and *prospective customers.*

cycle (11) One compressed section of air plus one decompressed section which, in concert with other cycles, produces sound. Cycles are measured on the hertz scale, and the more cycles per second, the higher the sound's pitch.

dailies (13) Newspapers published at least five times a week, in either morning or evening editions.

database marketing (15) Tracking and analyzing the purchasing patterns of specific customers in a database and then targeting direct-mail advertising to their needs.

daypart (12) A part of the broadcast day. See also *radio dayparts; television dayparts.*

daypart mix (14) A media scheduling strategy based on the TV usage levels reported by the rating services.

decentralized organization (3)   The establishment of advertising departments by products or brands or in various divisions, subsidiaries, countries, regions, or whatever other categories must suit the firm's needs.

deceptive advertising (2)   According to the FTC, any ad in which "there is a misrepresentation, omission, or other practice that is likely to mislead the consumer acting reasonably in the circumstances, to the consumer's detriment."

decibel (11)   Unit of measure for the loudness of sound determined by measuring the *volume* of air compressed in each cycle.

decline stage (5)   The last phase of the product life cycle when the product has become obsolete due to changing consumer taste or new technology.

decoding (4)   The interpretation of a message by the receiver.

defamation (8)   Making a false statement or allegation about a person or holding a person up to contempt.

defensive strategy (1)   In marketing warfare, the strategy used by the dominant company in a given market, which must defend itself against the onslaught of competitors.

demarketing (1)   The marketing and advertising techniques used by some companies and organizations to discourage the purchase or use of certain products.

demographics (5)   The study of the numerical characteristics of the population.

demonstration (9)   A type of TV commercial in which the product is shown in use.

departmental system (3)   The organization of an ad agency into departments based on function: account services, creative services, marketing services, and administration.

descender (10)   In typography, a letter that drops below the base line; for example, p, g, y.

designated market areas (DMA) (14)   The geographical areas in which TV stations attract most of their viewers, according to the Nielsen station index.

desire block (7)   In the advertising pyramid, the group of people who actually desire the product.

desktop publishing (10)   The process that enables individuals, through the use of desktop computers, to personally prepare, and occasionally even print, relatively high-quality ads, documents, and publications.

development stage (3)   In the agency-client relationship, the honeymoon period when both agency and client are at the peak of their optimism and are most anxious to quickly develop a mutually profitable mechanism for working together.

device copy (8)   Advertising copy that relies on wordplay, humor, poetry, rhymes, great exaggeration, gags, and other tricks or gimmicks.

dialog/monolog copy (8)   A type of body copy in which the characters illustrated in the advertisement do the selling in their own words either through a quasi-testimonial technique or through a comic strip panel.

digital video effects (DVE) unit (11)   In video, special-effects equipment for manipulating graphics on the screen to produce fades, wipes, zooms, rotations, and so on.

direct advertising (15)   Any form of advertising issued directly to the prospect through the use of mails, fax machines, on-line computer services, interactive electronic kiosks, salespeople, dealers, or other means rather than through the traditional mass media.

direct broadcast satellite (DBS) (14)   A television delivery system that involves beaming programs from satellites to special satellite dishes mounted in the home or yard.

direct-impression composition (10)   See *strike-on composition*.

direct-mail advertising (15)   All forms of advertising sent directly to prospects through U.S. or private postal services.

direct marketing (15)   A marketing system in which the seller does not rely on the traditional channels of distribution but rather builds and maintains its own database of customers and uses a variety of media to communicate directly with those customers.

direct questioning (6)   A method of pretesting designed to elicit a full range of responses to the advertising. Direct questioning is especially effective for testing alternative advertisements in the early stages of development.

direct-response advertising (15)   An advertising message that asks the reader, listener, or viewer for an immediate response. Direct-response advertising can take the form of direct mail or it can use a wide range of other media, from matchbook covers or magazines to radio, TV, or billboards.

display advertising (13)   Newspaper and magazine ads that normally use not only copy but also illustrations or photos, headlines, and other visual components.

display allowances (16)   Fees paid to retailers to make room for and set up manufacturers' displays.

display type (10)   Large, bold type, heavier than text type, used in headlines, subheads, logos, addresses, or wherever there is a need for emphasis in an advertisement.

distribution channel (5)   The network of all the firms and individuals that take title, or assist in taking title, to the product as it moves from the producer to the consumer.

diverting (16)   Purchasing large quantities of an item at a regional promotional discount and shipping portions to areas of the country where the discount isn't being offered.

DMA (14)   See *designated market areas*.

dubs (11)   Duplicates of radio commercials made from the master tape and sent to stations for broadcast.

dummy (9)   A layout of a brochure or other multipage advertising piece. It is put together, page for page, just like the finished product will eventually appear.

dupes (11)   Copies of a finished television commercial that are delivered to the networks or TV stations for airing.

dutch doors (13) See *gatefold.*

earned rate (13) See *contract rate.*

effective frequency (12) The range of exposures between the minimum number of times a person must see or hear a message before becoming aware of it and the maximum level that starts to become overexposure.

effective reach (12) The number or percentage of the audience who have been exposed to a message enough times to be aware of it.

electronic couponing (16) In supermarkets, the use of frequent-shopper cards that automatically credit cardholders with coupon discounts when they check out.

electronic signs (16) Signs in supermarkets that electronically display text and graphic messages, including advertisements.

emotional appeal (8) Advertising appeal that relates to the consumer's psychological, social, or symbolic needs or wants.

empirical research method (7) A method of allocating funds for advertising that uses experimentation to determine the best level of advertising expenditure. By running a series of tests in different markets with different budgets, companies determine the most efficient level of expenditure.

encoding (4) Translating an idea or message into words, symbols, and illustrations.

entrepreneurial agency (3) Any of the thousands of small advertising agencies that inhabit every major city in the country.

equipment-based service (5) A service business that relies mainly on the use of equipment.

ethical dilemma (2) A situation in which there are two conflicting but valid sides to an issue.

ethical lapse (2) A situation in which an advertiser makes a clearly unethical and sometimes illegal decision.

euphemism (8) The substitution of an inoffensive, mild word for a word that is offensive, harsh, or blunt.

evaluation of selection alternatives (4) Choosing among brands, sizes, styles, and colors.

evaluative criteria (4) The standards a consumer uses for judging the features and benefits of alternative products.

evoked set (4) The particular group of alternative goods or services a consumer considers when making a buying decision.

exchange (4) The trading of one thing of value for another thing of value.

exclusive distribution (5) The strategy of limiting the number of wholesalers or retailers who can sell a product in order to gain a prestige image, maintain premium prices, or protect other dealers in a geographic region.

exhibits (18) A public relations approach that involves preparing displays that tell about an organization or its products; exhibits may be shown at fairs, colleges and universities, or trade shows.

experimental method (6) A method of scientific investigation in which a researcher alters the stimulus received by a test group or groups and compares the results with that of a control group that did not receive the altered stimulus.

exploratory research (6) See *informal research.*

export agency (19) An agency that specializes in creating ads for American companies engaged in international advertising.

exposure (12) A consideration in selecting media based on the number of people who actually see an advertisement in a given medium as opposed to the total audience of that medium. (Or, from another perspective, how many people an ad sees in a given medium.)

family brand (5) The marketing of various products under the same umbrella name.

farm advertising (1) Advertising directed to farmers as businesspeople and to others in the agricultural business.

farm publications (13) Magazines directed to farmers and their families or to companies that manufacture or sell agricultural equipment, supplies, and services.

FCB grid (7) A conceptual model developed by Foote, Cone & Belding advertising to illustrate the nature of product purchases from the consumer's point of view. The grid has two dimensions: one to illustrate the degree of personal involvement (high or low) required to make a purchase, and the other to demonstrate the kind (think or feel) of involvement required.

FCC (2) See *Federal Communications Commission.*

FDA (2) See *Food and Drug Administration.*

Federal Communications Commission (FCC) (2) Federal regulatory body with jurisdiction over radio, television, telephone, and telegraph industries. Through its licensing authority, the FCC has indirect control over broadcast advertising.

Federal Trade Commission (FTC) (2) The major federal regulator of advertising used to promote products sold in interstate commerce.

fee-commission method (3) Compensation method whereby an ad agency establishes a fixed monthly fee for all its services to the client and retains any commissions earned for space or time purchased on behalf of the client.

feedback (4) A message that acknowledges or responds to an intitial message indicating that the first message was received.

fill light (11) A light used to slightly brighten up a shadow area to reveal details without losing the overall effect of the shadow.

film negatives (10) Photographic negatives of camera-ready ads, from which printing plates are made.

first-class mail (15) A U.S. Postal Service classification of mail delivery used by direct-mail advertisers to ensure fast delivery, mail forwarding (at no additional charge), and return of undeliverable mail.

first-run syndication (14) Programs produced specifically for the syndication market.

flanking strategy (1) (7)   In marketing warfare, the strategy adopted by middle companies in the hierarchy, who must point out the qualities that make them different from the top three companies.

flash (10)   A technique for lightening the dark areas of a halftone in order to keep them from plugging up with ink and looking blotchy.

flat rate (13)   A standard newspaper advertising rate with no discount allowance for large or repeated space buys.

flighting (12)   An intermittent media scheduling pattern in which periods of advertising are alternated with periods of no advertising at all.

flyer (15) (17)   A form of direct-mail advertising that is usually a single, standard-size (8½ by 11 inches) page printed on one or both sides and folded one or more times. It often accompanies a sales letter to supplement or expand on the information it contains.

focus-group method (6)   A qualitative method of research in which 8 to 10 people, "typical" of the target market, are invited to a group session to discuss the product, the service, or the marketing situation for an hour or more.

folders (15)   Large, heavy-stock flyers, often folded and sent out as self-mailers.

font (10)   For a particular typeface and size of type, the complete assortment of capitals, small caps, lowercase letters, numerals, and punctuation marks.

Food and Drug Administration (FDA) (2)   Federal agency that has authority over the labeling, packaging, and branding of packaged foods and therapeutic devices.

formal research (6)   Collecting primary data directly from the marketplace using qualitative or quantitative methods.

formula model (12)   A type of computer program used to calculate the reach, frequency, and other statistics for various media vehicles and to rank the vehicles according to selected parameters.

forward buying (16)   A retailer's stocking up on a product when it is discounted and buying smaller amounts when it is at list price.

four-color process (10)   The method for printing color advertisements with tonal values, such as photographs and paintings. This process is based on the principle that all colors can be printed by combining the three primary colors—yellow, magenta (red), and cyan (blue)—plus black (which provides greater detail and density as well as shades of gray.

four Ps (5)   See *marketing mix*.

fourth-class mail (15)   A class of mail designed for merchandise, books, printed matter, and all other mailable matter not in first, second, or third class.

fragrance strips (13)   Perfume samples included in sealed inserts in magazines.

franchising (5)   A type of vertical marketing system in which dealers pay a fee to operate under the guidelines and direction of the manufacturer.

free-standing inserts (FSIs) (16)   Coupons distributed through inserts in newspapers.

frequency (12)   The number of times the same person or household is exposed to a vehicle in a specified time span. Across a total audience, frequency is calculated as the average number of times individuals or homes are exposed to the vehicle.

FTC (2)   See *Federal Trade Commission*.

full position (13)   In newspaper advertising, the preferred position near the top of a page or on the top of a column next to reading matter. It is usually surrounded by editorial text and may cost the advertiser 25 to 50 percent more than ROP rates.

full-service advertising agency (3)   An agency equipped to serve its clients in all areas of communication and promotion. Its advertising services include planning, creating, and producing advertisements as well as performing research and media selection services. Nonadvertising functions include producing sales promotion materials, publicity articles, annual reports, trade show exhibits, and sales training materials.

gain (11)   On an audio console, the dial used to control the overall master volume.

game (16)   A sales promotion activity in which prizes are offered based on chance. The big marketing advantage of games is that customers must make repeat visits to the dealer to continue playing.

gatefold (13)   A magazine cover or page extended and folded over to fit into the magazine. The gatefold may be a fraction of a page or two or more pages, and it is always sold at a premium.

general agency (3)   An agency that is willing to represent the widest variety of accounts but that concentrates on companies that make goods purchased chiefly by consumers.

geographic segmentation (5)   A method of segmenting markets by geographic regions based on the shared characteristics, needs, or wants of people within the region.

global advertising (19)   Using the identical ad, with translation, in all international markets.

global brand (19)   A brand for which the same marketing and advertising is used throughout the world.

global marketing (19)   The theory that, thanks to cheap air travel and modern telecommunications technology, the world is becoming a common marketplace in which people have the same tastes and desires and want the same products and lifestyles no matter where they live—thus allowing for world-standardized products at low prices sold the same way around the world.

goods (1)   Tangible products such as suits, soap, and soft drinks.

gothic type (10)   See *sans serif type*.

government markets (4)   Governmental bodies that buy products for the successful coordination of municipal, state, federal, or other government activities.

gross impressions (12) The total of all audiences delivered by a media plan.

gross rating points (GRPs) (12) (14) (15) The total audience delivery or weight of a specific media schedule. It is computed by dividing the total number of impressions by the size of the target population and multiplying by 100, or by multiplying the reach, expressed as a percentage of the population, by the average frequency. In television, gross rating points are the total rating points achieved by a particular media schedule over a specific period. For example, a weekly schedule of five commercials with an average household rating of 20 would yield 100 GRPs. In outdoor advertising, a 100 gross rating point showing (also called a number 100 showing) covers a market fully by reaching 9 out of 10 adults daily over a 30-day period.

group system (3) System in which an ad agency is divided into a number of little agencies or groups, each composed of an account supervisor, account executives, copywriters, art directors, a media director, and any other specialists required to meet the needs of the particular clients being served by the group.

growth stage (5) The period in a product life cycle that is marked by market expansion as more and more customers make their first purchases while others are already making their second and third purchases.

GRPs (12) (14) (15) See *gross rating points.*

guaranteed circulation (13) The number of copies of a magazine that the publisher expects to sell. If this figure is not reached, the publisher must give a refund to advertisers.

guerrilla strategy (1) (7) In marketing warfare, carving out a small niche that one can defend successfully in the larger marketplace.

habit (4) An acquired or developed behavior pattern that has become nearly or completely involuntary.

halftone screen (10) A glass or plastic screen, crisscrossed with fine black lines at right angles like a window screen, which breaks continuous-tone artwork into dots so that it can be reproduced.

halo effect (6) In ad pretesting, the fact that consumers are likely to rate the one or two ads that make the best first impression as the highest in all categories.

handbills (17) Low-cost flyers or other simple brochures distributed by hand on the street, in parking lots, or door-to-door.

headline (8) The words in the leading position of an advertisement—the words that will be read first or that are positioned to draw the most attention.

hidden differences (5) Imperceptible but existing differences that may greatly affect the desirability of a product.

hierarchy of needs (4) Maslow's theory that the lower biologic or survival needs are dominant in human behavior and must be satisfied before higher, socially acquired needs become meaningful.

highly promotional strategy (17) In retailing, doing a great deal of advertising in order to keep bringing customers in.

horizontal cooperative advertising (17) Joint advertising effort of related businesses (car dealers, realtors, etc.) to create traffic for their type of business.

horizontal publications (13) Business publications targeted at people with particular job functions that can cut across industry lines, such as *Purchasing* magazine.

households using TV (HUT) (14) The percentage of homes in a given area that have one or more TV sets turned on at any particular time. If 1,000 TV sets are in the survey area and 500 are turned on, the HUT figure is 50 percent.

house list (15) A company's most important and valuable direct-mail list, which may contain current, recent, and long-past customers or future prospects.

house organs (15) (18) Internal and external publications produced by business organizations, including stockholder reports, newsletters, consumer magazines, and dealer publications. Most are produced by a company's advertising or public relations department or by its agency.

house publications (15) (18) See *house organs.*

ideas (1) Economic, political, religious, or social viewpoints that advertising may attempt to sell.

illustrators (9) The artists who paint, sketch, or draw the pictures we see in advertising.

imperceptible differences (4) Distinguishing characteristics of products that are not readily apparent without close inspection or use.

imposition (10) The positioning of images on a sheet of paper for the purpose of printing.

incentive system (3) A form of compensation in which the agency shares in the client's success when a campaign attains specific, agreed-upon goals.

incident light meter (11) A light meter that indicates the intensity, or volume, of a light source. The meter displays the amount of light measured and indicates the correct aperture setting for the type of film being used.

independent shopping guide (17) Weekly local ad vehicles that may or may not contain editorial matter. They can be segmented into highly select market areas.

in-depth interview (6) An intensive interview technique that uses carefully planned but loosely structured questions to probe respondents' deeper feelings.

individual brand (5) Assigning a unique name to each product a manufacturer produces.

induced differences (5) Distinguishing characteristics of products effected through unique branding, packaging, distribution, merchandising, and advertising.

industrial advertising (1) (3) Advertising aimed at individuals in business who buy or influence the purchase of industrial products.

industrial agency (3) An advertising agency representing client companies that sell products to other businesses.

industrial buyers (4) The people who purchase industrial goods and services for use in their business.

industrial markets (4) Individuals or companies that buy products needed for the production of other goods or services such as plant equipment and telephone systems.

industrial products (1) Goods and services that are used in the manufacture of other goods or that become a physical part of another product. Industrial goods also include products that are used to conduct business and that do not become part of another product such as capital goods (office machines, desks, operating supplies) and business services for which the user contracts.

informercial (14) A long (three to eight minutes) TV commercial that gives consumers detailed information about a product or service.

informal research (6) The second step in the research process, designed to explore a problem by reviewing secondary data and interviewing a few key people with the most information to share. Also called *exploratory research*.

in-house advertising agency (3) Agency wholly owned by an advertiser and set up and staffed to do all the work of an independent full-service agency.

in-pack premiums (16) Sales promotion device, popular in the food field, in which inexpensive gifts are placed inside the package for the buyer.

inquiry test (6) A form of test in which consumer responses to an ad for information or free samples are tabulated.

insertion order (13) A form submitted to a newspaper or magazine when an advertiser wants to run an advertisement. This form states the date(s) on which the ad is to run, its size, the requested position, and the rate.

inside card (15) A transit advertisement, normally 11 by 28 inches, placed in a wall rack above the windows.

institutional advertising (1) (17) (18) A type of advertising that attempts to obtain favorable attention for the business as a whole, not for a specific product or service the store or business sells. The effects of institutional advertising are intended to be long term rather than short range.

institutional copy (8) A type of body copy in which the advertiser tries to sell an idea or the merits of the organization or service rather than the sales features of a particular product.

in-store sampling (16) The handing out of free product samples to passing shoppers.

integrated commercial (11) A straight radio announcement, usually delivered by one person, woven into a show or tailored to a given program to avoid any perceptible interruption.

intensive distribution (5) A distribution strategy based on making the product available to consumers at every possible location so that consumers can buy with a minimum of effort.

intensive techniques (6) Qualitative research aimed at probing the deepest feelings, attitudes, and beliefs of respondents through direct questioning. Typical methods include in-depth interviews and focus groups.

interactive television (16) Television in which the viewer is able to alter the images on the screen, respond to questions, and so on.

interconnects (14) Groups of cable systems joined together for advertising purposes.

interlock (11) See *work print*.

internal data (6) Company records, such as product shipment figures, billings to customers, advertising expenditures, etc.

international advertising (1) Advertising directed at foreign markets.

international marketing structure (19) Organization of companies with foreign divisions, typically decentralized with autonomous units in various foreign countries.

international markets (4) Consumer, business, or government markets located in foreign countries.

interpersonal influences (4) Social influences on the consumer decision-making process, including family, society, and cultural environment.

interview (6) See *in-depth interview*.

introductory phase (5) The initial phase of the product life cycle (also called the *pioneering phase*) when a new product is introduced, costs are highest, and profits the lowest.

inverted pyramid (7) A simple model shaped like an upside-down pyramid, which represents the growing number of people who have joined the action block of the advertising pyramid and developed the repurchasing habit.

island half (13) A half-page of magazine space that is surrounded on two or more sides by editorial matter. This type of ad is designed to dominate a page and is therefore sold at a premium price.

issue advertising (18) A type of corporate advertising that advocates a particular point of view on a public issue.

jingle (11) A musical commercial, usually sung with the sales message in the verse.

junior unit (13) A large magazine advertisement (60 percent of the page) placed in the middle of a page and surrounded by editorial matter.

key light (11) The primary light to fall upon a subject.

keys (11) On an audio console, the toggle switches that send sounds either to the active program line or to an audition line.

kicker (8) A subhead that appears above the headline.

lavaliere microphone (11) A small, unobtrusive microphone that can hook onto a person's lapel, shirt, or tie.

layout (3) (9) An orderly formation of all the parts of an advertisement. In print, it refers to the arrangement of the headline, subheads, visuals, copy, picture captions, trademarks, slogans, and signature. In television, it refers to the placement of characters, props, scenery, and product elements, the location and angle of the camera, and the use of lighting.

leading (10) Pronounced *ledding*, the space between lines of type. Art directors may vary this space to give a slightly more airy or condensed feeling.

lead-in paragraph (8) In print ads, a bridge between the headlines, the subheads, and the sales ideas presented in the text. It transfers reader interest to product interest.

lead time (13) The length of time between the closing date for the purchase of advertising space or time and the publication or broadcast of the ad. Advertising in magazines requires a long lead time—sometimes as long as three months. And once the closing date has been reached, no changes in copy or art can be allowed.

leaflet (15) See *flyer*.

learning (4) A relatively permanent change in thought processes or behavior that occurs as a result of reinforced experience.

letterpress (10) The forerunner of today's printing processes, but now rarely used. In letterpress, the process is similar to the way a rubber stamp works. Like a stamp, the image to be transferred is backward ("wrong reading") on the plate. The ink is applied to a raised (relief) surface on the plate and then transferred to the paper.

letter shop (15) A firm that stuffs envelopes, affixes labels, calculates postage, sorts pieces into stacks or bundles, and otherwise prepares items for mailing.

libel (8) Defaming a person in print.

Library of Congress (2) The federal body that registers and protects all copyrighted material, including advertising.

licensed brands (5) Brand names that other companies can buy the right to use.

lifestyle (9) Type of commercial in which the user is presented rather than the product. Typically used by clothing and soft drink advertisers to affiliate their brands with the trendy lifestyles of their consumers.

linear programming model (12) A type of computer program designed to create a complete media schedule that maximizes exposure within a given budget.

line film (10) Film made from typeset copy and solid black and white (no tonal values) illustrations. From the line film, a line plate is produced for printing.

line plates (10) The plates used to print solid black-and-white images (not tonal values) such as typeset copy, pen-and-ink drawings, or charcoal illustrations.

lines (13) A unit for measuring space in newspapers and magazines: 14 lines to a column inch.

list broker (15) an intermediary who handles rental of mailing lists for list owners on a commission basis.

live action (11) The basic production technique in television that portrays people and things in lifelike, everyday situations.

local advertising (1) (17) Advertising by businesses within a city or county directed toward customers within the same geographical area.

local time (14) Radio spots purchased by a local advertiser.

logotype (8) Special design of the advertiser's name (or product name) that appears in all advertisements. Also called a *signature cut,* it is like a trademark because it gives the advertiser individuality and provides quick recognition at the point of purchase.

lowercase (10) Small letters, as opposed to capital letters.

Magazine Publishers Association (MPA) (13) A trade group made up of more than 230 publishers who represent 1,200 magazines. It compiles circulation figures on ABC member magazines and promotes greater and more effective use of magazine advertising.

mail-order advertising (15) A form of direct-response advertising and a method of selling in which the product or service is promoted through advertising and the prospect orders it. Mail-order advertising is usually received in three distinct forms: catalogs, advertisements in magazines and newspapers, and direct-mail advertising.

mail-response list (15) A type of direct-mail list, composed of people who have responded to the direct-mail solicitations of other companies, especially those whose efforts are complementary to the advertiser's.

maintenance stage (3) In the client-agency relationship, the day-to-day interaction that, when successful, may go on for years.

majority fallacy (5) A common marketing misconception that, to be successful, a product or service must appeal to the majority of people.

makegoods (14) TV spots that are aired to compensate for spots that were missed or run incorrectly.

management supervisors (3) Managers who supervise account executives and who report to the agency's director of account services.

market (4) A group of potential customers who share a common interest, need, or desire, who can use the offered good or service to some advantage, and who can afford or are willing to pay the purchase price.

marketer (4) Any person or organization that has a good, service, or idea to sell.

marketing (4) The process of planning and executing the conception, pricing, promotion, and distribution of ideas, goods, and services to create exchanges that satisfy the perceived needs, wants, and objectives of individuals and organizations.

marketing exchange cycle (4) A cycle that consists of (1) discovering, locating, and measuring the needs, attitudes, and desires of prospective customers; (2) interpreting this information for management so that goods and services may be improved and new ones developed; and (3) devising and implementing a system to make the good or service available, to inform prospective customers about the product's need-satisfying capabilities, and to execute the exchange.

marketing information system (6) A set of procedures and methods for generating an orderly flow of pertinent information for use in making marketing decisions.

marketing mix (5)(7) Four elements, called the four Ps (product, price, place, and promotion), that every company has the option of adding, subtracting, or modifying in order to create a desired marketing strategy.

marketing objectives (7) Goals of the marketing effort that may be expressed in terms of the needs of specific target markets and specific sales objectives.

marketing-oriented period (4) The modern marketing era in which companies determine in advance what customers want and then develop goods and services that will satisfy those needs or desires.

marketing plan (7) The plan that directs the company's marketing effort. First, it assembles all the pertinent facts about the organization, the markets it serves, and its products, services, customers, and competition. Second, it forces the functional managers within the company to work together—product development, production, selling, advertising, credit, transportation—to focus efficiently on the customer. Third, it sets goals and objectives to be attained within specified periods of time and lays out the precise strategies that will be used to achieve them.

marketing research (6) The systematic gathering, recording, and analysis of information to help managers make marketing decisions.

marketing strategy (7) The statement of how the company is going to accomplish its marketing objectives. The strategy is the total directional thrust of the company, that is, the "how-to" of the marketing plan and is determined by the particular blend of the marketing mix elements (the four Ps) which the company can control.

market-need objectives (7) Marketing objectives that orient the company as a satisfier of target market needs rather than as a producer of goods or services.

market prep corporate advertising (18) Corporate advertising that is used to set the company up for future sales; it simultaneously communicates messages about the products and the company.

market research (4)(6) The systematic gathering of information about a specific market or market segment, including its size, composition, structure, and so forth.

market segmentation (5) The strategic process of (1) identifying groups of people with certain shared characteristics within the broader product market and (2) aggregating these groups into larger market segments according to their mutual interest in the product's utility.

master tape (11) The final recording of a radio or TV commercial, with all the music, sound, and vocals mixed, from which dubs (duplicates) are recorded and sent to radio or TV stations for broadcast.

maturity stage (5) That point in the product life cycle when the market has become saturated with products, the number of new customers has dwindled, and competition is most intense.

mechanical (9)(10) The set type and illustrations or photographs pasted into the exact position in which they will appear in the final ad. Also called a *pasteup,* this is then used as the basis for the next step in the reproduction process.

media (1)(3)(4) Plural of *medium,* referring to communications vehicles paid to present an advertisement to its target audience.

media-buying service (3) An organization that specializes in purchasing and packaging radio and television time.

media classes (6) The broad media categories: print, electronic, outdoor, and direct mail.

media commission (3) See *agency commission.*

media kit (18) A package of materials used to gain publicity at staged events such as press conferences or open houses.

media mix (12) Combining several kinds of media in an advertising program.

media planning (12) The process that directs the advertising message to the right people at the right time.

media research (6) The systematic gathering and analysis of information on the reach and effectiveness of media vehicles.

media strategy (12) A description of how the advertiser will achieve stated media objectives: which media will be used, how often, and when.

media subclasses (6) Smaller divisions of media classes, such as radio, TV, magazines, newspapers, and so on.

media units (6) Specific units of advertising in each type of medium, such as half-page magazine ads, 30-second spots, etc.

media vehicles (6) See *vehicles.*

medium (1)(4) See *media.*

mental files (4) Stored memories in the consumer's mind.

merge and purge (15) In compiling mailing lists, the process of merging mail response and house lists and purging all duplicates.

message strategy (8) The specific determination of what an ad or campaign will say and how it will say it. The elements of the message strategy include the copy platform, art direction, and production values.

message weight (12) The size of the audience for several commercials or ads combined or for an entire media plan.

microphone (11) An instrument used to capture sound for radio or television commercials.

middleman (5) A business firm that operates between the producer and the consumer or industrial purchaser—someone who deals in trade rather than in production.

mixed interlock (11) The edited version of a filmed television commercial mixed with the finished sound track. Used for initial review and approval prior to being duplicated for airing.

mnemonic device (9) A gimmick used to dramatize the product benefit and make it memorable, such as the Imperial margarine crown or the Avon doorbell.

monthly promotional calendar (17) A local advertiser's

monthly schedule of sales, special events, in-house promotions, ad placements, and so on.

motivation (4) The underlying drives that stem from the conscious or unconscious needs of the consumer and contribute to the individual consumer's purchasing actions.

motivation research (6) Qualitative research used to give advertisers a general impression of the market, the consumer, or the product.

motivation value (12) A consideration in selecting media based on the characteristics of a particular medium that might enhance that medium's ability to motivate its audience to action; for example, good quality reproduction or timeliness.

MPA (13) See *Magazine Publishers Association.*

multinational marketing structure (19) An approach to international marketing in which a corporation has full and integrated participation in world markets and a view toward business based on choices available anywhere in the world. The multinational's marketing activities are typically characterized by strong centralized control and coordination. See also *international marketing structure.*

multipoint distribution systems (MDS) (14) A microwave TV delivery system that can carry up to a dozen channels.

musical commercial (11) See *jingle.*

musical logotype (11) A jingle that becomes associated with a product or company.

NAB (13) See *Newspaper Advertising Bureau.*

NAD (2) See *National Advertising Division.*

NARB (2) See *National Advertising Review Board.*

NARC (2) See *National Advertising Review Council.*

narrative copy (8) A type of body copy that tells a story. It sets up a problem and then creates a solution using the particular sales features of the product or service as the key to the solution.

narrowcasting (14) The ability of cable networks to offer specialized programming aimed at particular types of viewers.

national advertisers (1) Companies that place advertising in more than one region of the country.

national advertising (1) Advertising aimed at customers in several regions of the country.

National Advertising Division (NAD) (2) The National Advertising Division of the Council of Better Business Bureaus. It investigates and monitors advertising industry practices.

National Advertising Review Board (NARB) (2) A five-member panel, composed of three advertisers, one agency representative, and one layperson, selected to review decisions of the NAD.

National Advertising Review Council (NARC) (2) An organization founded by the Council of Better Business Bureaus and various advertising industry groups to promote and enforce standards of truth, taste, morality, and social responsibility in advertising.

national brands (5) Product brands that are marketed in several regions of the country.

NCN (13) See *National Co-op Network.*

needs (4) The basic, often instinctive, human forces that motivate a person to do something.

networks (14) Any of the national television or radio broadcasting chains or companies such as Columbia Broadcasting System (CBS), National Broadcasting Company (NBC), or American Broadcasting Company (ABC). Networks offer the larger advertiser convenience and efficiency because the message can be broadcast simultaneously throughout the country.

news/information headline (8) A type of headline that includes many of the "how-to" headlines as well as headlines that seek to gain identification for their sponsors by announcing some news or providing some promise of information.

Newspaper Advertising Bureau (NAB) (13) A bureau of the American Newspaper Publishers Association. It provides newspapers with market information by conducting field research and offers national advertisers help with obtaining better newspaper ad rates and with timely placement of ads in multiple markets.

Newspaper Co-op Network (NCN) (13) The NAB's system by which advertisers are able to line up local dealers for ads through a central clearinghouse.

news release (18) A typewritten sheet of information (usually 8½ by 11 inches) issued to print and broadcast outlets to generate publicity or shed light on a subject of interest.

Nielsen Station Index (14) See *A. C. Nielsen.*

nonbusiness institutions (18) Nonprofit organizations whose primary objective is noncommercial: churches, schools, universities, charitable organizations, and so forth.

noncommercial advertising (1)(18) Advertising sponsored by or for a charitable institution, civic group, religious order, political organization, or some other nonprofit group to stimulate donations, persuade people to vote one way or another, or bring attention to social causes.

nonpersonal influences (4) Factors influencing the consumer decision-making process that are often out of the consumer's control, such as time, place, and environment.

nonpersonal selling (5) All selling activities that use some medium as an intermediary for communication, including advertising, public relations, sales promotion, and collateral materials.

nonprobability samples (6) Research samples that do not provide every unit in the population with an equal chance of being included. As a result, there is no guarantee that the sample will be representative.

nonproduct advertising (1) Advertising designed to sell ideas or a philosophy rather than products or services.

nonpromotional strategy (17) For local businesses, reliance on word-of-mouth and return customers as opposed to advertising and related types of promotion.

objectives (7) See *marketing objectives.*

objective/task method (7) A method of determining advertising allocations, also referred to as the *budget-buildup method,* that defines objectives and how advertising is to be used to accomplish them. It has three steps: defining the objectives, determining strategy, and estimating the cost.

observation method (6) A method of research used when researchers actually monitor the overt actions of the person being studied.

offensive strategy (1) In marketing warfare, the strategy used by the second- and third-place companies to capture portions of the number-one company's market.

Office of Consumer Affairs (2) The chief consumer protection agency of the federal government.

off-network syndication (14) The availability of programs that originally appeared on networks to individual stations for re-broadcast.

offset lithography (10) The most popular printing process in the United States and Canada today. Unlike letterpress and rotogravure, the image on the offset plate is right reading. As the plate is covered with an oily ink, the moist, blank portions of the plate repel the ink. The greasy-coated image retains the ink for transfer to an intermediate rubber surface called a blanket, which comes in contact with the paper and enables the image to be printed.

omni-directional microphone (11) A microphone that captures sound from all directions.

on-camera (8) Actually seen by the camera, as an announcer, a spokesperson, or actors playing out a scene.

on-pack premium (16) A premium designed to have a good impulse value attached to the outside of a package.

open rate (13) The highest newspaper advertising rate for one-time insertions.

opinion leader (4) Someone whose beliefs or attitudes are respected by people who share an interest in some specific activity.

opinion sampling (18) A form of public relations research in which consumers provide feedback via interviews, toll-free phone lines, focus groups, and similar methods.

ornamental type (10) A group of typefaces comprising designs that provide novelty and are decorative or highly embellished.

orthographic film (10) A high-contrast photographic film yielding only black-and-white images, no gray tones.

out-of-home media (15) Media such as outdoor advertising (billboards) and transit advertising (bus and car cards) that reach prospects outside their homes.

outside posters (15) The variety of transit advertisements appearing on the outside of buses, including king size, queen size, traveling display, rear of bus, and front of bus.

overlay (10) A piece of clear plastic containing a second image from which a second printing plate can be made for color printing.

overlaying (15) In developing mailing lists, the process of combining information from several sources to produce an in-depth profile of each customer or company.

packaging (4) (9) The container for a product—encompassing the physical appearance of the container and including the design, color, shape, labeling, and materials used.

paid circulation (13) The total number of copies of the average issue of a newspaper or magazine that are distributed through subscriptions and newsstand sales.

painted bulletins (15) Large outdoor painted displays and walls, normally 14′ by 48′ or larger, meant for long use and usually placed in only the best locations where traffic is heavy and visibility is good.

panels (8) See *boxes and panels.*

Pantone Matching System (PMS) (10) A set of solid colors for printing created by blending inks according to formulations specified by the Pantone company.

participation basis (14) The basis on which most network television advertising is sold. Advertisers can participate in a program once or several times on a regular or irregular basis by buying 30- or 60-second segments within the program. This allows the advertiser to spread out the budget and makes it easier to get in and out of a program without a long-term commitment.

pass-along readership (13) Readers of a publication in addition to the purchaser or subscriber.

pasteup (9) See *mechanical.*

people-based service (5) A service that relies on the talents and skills of individuals rather than on highly technical or specialized equipment.

people meter (14) An electronic device that automatically records a household's TV viewing, including channels watched, number of minutes of viewing, and who is watching.

perceived value (5) The value of a product in the customer's eyes, which may be created through actual differentiation or through unique branding, distribution, dealer service, and advertising.

percentage-of-sales method (7) A method of advertising budget allocation based on a percentage of the previous year's sales, the anticipated sales for the next year, or a combination of the two.

perceptible differences (5) Differences between products that are visibly apparent to the consumer.

perception (4) Our personalized way of sensing and comprehending the stimuli to which we are exposed.

perceptual screens (4) The physiological or psychological perceptual filters that messages must pass through.

personal processes (4) The three internal, human operations—perception, learning, and motivation—which govern the way consumers discern raw data (stimuli) and translate them into feelings, thoughts, beliefs, and actions.

personal selling (5) A sales method based on person-to-person contact, such as by a salesperson at a retail establishment or by a telephone solicitor.

photo animation (11) An animation technique that uses still photography instead of illustrations or puppets. By making slight movements of the photos from one frame to the next, the animated illusion is created.

photocomposition (10) A method of typesetting that combines computer technology, electronics, and photography. It offers an almost unlimited number of typefaces and sizes, fast reproduction at relatively low cost, and clear, sharp images.

photographers (9) The artists who use cameras to create visuals for advertisements.

photoplatemaking (10) A process for making printing plates, similar to taking a picture, in which an image is photographed and the negative is printed in reverse on a sensitized metal plate rather than on paper. This plate is then used for printing.

photopolymerization (10) A photochemical process used in the manufacture of plastic printing plates.

photoprints (10) Screened prints or Veloxes, which publications can use for making their own printing plates.

physiological screens (4) The perceptual screens that use the five senses—sight, hearing, touch, taste, and smell—to detect incoming data and measure the dimension and intensity of the physical stimulus.

pica (10) The unit of measurement for the horizontal width of lines of type. There are six picas to the inch and 12 points to the pica.

picture-caption copy (8) A type of body copy in which the story is told through a series of illustrations and captions rather than through the use of a copy block alone.

pitch (11) The perception of the highness or lowness of a sound depending on the number of cycles per second of sound waves hitting the eardrum—as measured on the hertz scale.

place element (5) In the marketing mix, how and where customers purchase a good or service; distribution.

PMS (10) See *Pantone Matching System*.

point (10) The unit of measurement for the depth (or height) of type. There are 72 points to the inch, so 1 point equals 1/72 of an inch.

point-of-purchase (P-O-P) advertising (16) Materials set up at a retail location to build traffic, advertise the product, and promote impulse buying. Materials may include window displays, counter displays, floor and wall displays, streamers, and posters.

pop-up ad (13) A three-dimensional magazine ad.

positioning (4)(5) The way in which a product is ranked in the consumer's mind by the benefits it offers, by the way it is classified or differentiated from the competition, or by its relationship to certain target markets.

positioning era (1) The 1970s, when marketers focused on how their product ranked against the competition in the consumer's mind.

postcards (15) Cards sent by advertisers to announce sales, offer discounts, or otherwise generate consumer traffic.

poster panel (15) The basic form of outdoor advertising and the least costly per unit. It is a structure of blank panel with a standardized size and border, usually anchored in the ground, with its advertising message printed by lithography or silkscreen and mounted by hand on the panel.

posters (18) For public relations purposes, signs that impart product information or other news of interest to consumers or that are aimed at employee behavior, such as safety, courtesy, or waste reduction.

postproduction (11) The finishing phase in commercial production—the period after recording and shooting when a radio or TV commercial is edited and sweetened with music and sound effects.

postpurchase dissonance (4) See *theory of cognitive dissonance*.

postpurchase evaluation (4) Determining whether a purchase has been a satisfactory or unsatisfactory one.

posttesting (6) The fourth stage of advertising research, designed to determine the effectiveness of an advertisement or campaign *after* it runs.

potentiometer (11) On an audio console, the dial or sliding linear button for controlling volume; also called a *pot*.

preemption rates (14) Lower TV advertising rates that stations charge when the advertiser agrees to give the station the right to sell to another advertiser willing to pay a higher rate.

preferred position (13) A choice position for a newspaper or magazine ad for which a higher rate is charged.

premium (16) An item offered free or at a bargain price to encourage the consumer to buy an advertised product.

prepress production (10) The process of converting page art and visuals into materials (generally film negatives and color separations) needed for printing.

preprinted inserts (13) Newspaper advertisements printed in advance by the advertiser and then delivered to the newspaper plant to be inserted into a specific edition. Preprints are inserted into the fold of the newspaper and look like a separate, smaller section of the paper.

preproduction (11) The period of time before the actual recording or shooting of a commercial—the planning phase in commercial production.

prerelationship stage (3) All the time before an agency and client officially get together to do business.

press agentry (18) The planning of activities and the staging of events to attract attention to new products or services and to generate publicity about the company or organization that will be of interest to the media.

press kit (18) See *media kit*.

press release (18) See *news release*.

pretesting (6) The third stage of advertising research, used to increase the likelihood of preparing the most effective advertising messages.

price element (5) In the marketing mix, the amount charged for the good or service—including deals, discounts, terms, warranties, and so on. The factors affecting price are market demand, cost of production and distribution, competition, and corporate objectives.

primary circulation (13) The number of people who receive a publication, whether through direct purchase or subscription.

primary data (6) Research information gained directly from the marketplace.

primary demand (5) Consumer demand for a whole product category.

primary demand trend (5) The projection of future consumer demand for a whole product category based on past demand and other market influences.

prime time (14) The highest TV viewing time of the day, namely 8 to 11 P.M.

print production (10) The systematic process a layout for an ad or a brochure goes through from concept to final printing.

private brands (5) Personalized brands applied by distributors or dealers to products supplied by manufacturers. Private brands are typically sold at lower prices in large retail chain stores.

process (4) A series of actions or methods that take place sequentially.

process blue, red, and yellow (10) The three primary colors (plus black) that are combined in four-color printing.

product (1)(6)(7) The particular good or service a company sells. See also *product concept*.

product advertising (1)(17) Advertising intended to promote goods and services; also a functional classification of advertising.

product concept (5)(7) The consumer's perception of a product as a "bundle" of utilitarian and symbolic values that satisfy functional, social psychological, economic, and other wants and needs. Also, as an element of the creative mix used by advertisers to develop advertising strategy, it is the bundle of product values the advertiser presents to the consumer.

product differentiation (5) The competitive strategy of creating a difference in a product to appeal to the preferences of a distinct market segment.

product element (5) The most important element of the marketing mix: the good or service being offered and the values associated with it—including the way the product is designed and classified, positioned, branded, and packaged.

product information center (16) A video-display terminal in stores such as supermarkets that carries a series of 15-second "commercials" in a five-minute rotation, interspersed with community-interest items.

production (10)(11) The whole physical process of producing ads and commercials; also the particular phase in the process when the recording and shooting of commercials is done.

production-oriented period (4) An era when there were few products and many consumers, and companies only had to worry about creating and producing enough products to satisfy the huge demand.

production values (8) One of the elements of message strategy. Production values determine what is to be created mechanically and how it is to be created.

product life cycle (5) Progressive stages in the life of a product—including introduction, growth, maturity, and decline—that affect the way a product is marketed and advertised.

product marketing process (5) The sequence of activities marketers perform to select markets and develop marketing mixes that eventually lead to exchanges.

product placement (16) Paying a fee to have a product included in a movie.

product shaping (4) Designing and building products to solve the customer's problems.

professional advertising (1) Advertising directed at individuals who are normally licensed to operate under a code of ethics or set of professional standards.

program rating (14) The percentage of TV households in an area that are tuned in to a specific program.

projective techniques (6) In marketing research, asking indirect questions or otherwise involving consumers in a situation where they can express feelings about the problem or product. The purpose is to get an understanding of people's underlying or subconscious feelings, attitudes, opinions, needs, and motives.

promotion (5)(7)(18) The marketing-related communication between the seller and the buyer. For profit-making organizations, promotion means using advertising and public relations techniques to sell a good or service and to enhance the reputation of an organization. See also *promotion element*.

promotional mix (7) The combination of personal selling, advertising, public relations, sales promotion, and collateral materials that an advertiser uses to develop a promotional strategy. See also *promotion element*.

promotion element (5)(7) The aspect of the marketing mix that consists of marketing-related communications between seller and buyer.

proof copy (13) A copy of a newspaper-created ad provided to the advertiser for checking purposes before the ad runs.

prospective customers (4) People who are about to make an exchange, are considering it, or may consider it.

provocative headline (8) A type of headline written to provoke the reader's curiosity so that, to learn more, the reader will read the body copy.

psychographics (5) The grouping of consumers into market segments on the basis of psychological makeup—values, attitudes, personality, and lifestyle.

psychological screens (4) The perceptual screens consumers use to evaluate, filter, and personalize information according to subjective standards, primarily emotions and personality.

public affairs (18) All activities related to the community citizenship of an organization, including dealing with community officials and working with regulatory bodies and legislative groups.

publicity (18) The generation of news about a person, product, or service that appears in broadcast or print media.

public relations (5) (18) Communications activities, usually not overtly sponsored, that act as supplements to advertising to inform various publics about the company and its products and to help build corporate credibility and image.

pull strategy (5) (16) Marketing, advertising, and sales promotion activities aimed at inducing trial, purchase, and repurchase by consumers.

pulse (12) An increased schedule of advertising above normal levels, usually during peak selling periods.

pulsing (12) Mixing continuity and flighting strategies in media scheduling.

purchase occasion (5) A method of segmenting markets on the basis of *when* consumers buy and use a good or service.

push money (16) A monetary inducement for retail salespeople to push the sale of particular products. Also called *spiffs.*

push strategy (5) (16) Marketing, advertising, and sales promotion activities aimed at getting products into the dealer pipeline and accelerating sales by offering inducements to dealers, retailers, and salespeople. Inducements might include introductory price allowances, distribution allowances, and advertising dollar allowances to stock the product and set up displays.

qualitative research (6) The use of in-depth, open-ended questions to get people to share their thoughts and feelings on a subject in order to gain impressions rather than definitions.

quantitative mathematical models (7) Specialized computer-based techniques for budgeting and allocating advertising dollars.

quantitative research (6) A data collection method used by market researchers to develop hard numbers so they can completely and accurately measure a particular market situation.

question headline (8) A type of headline that asks the reader a question.

RADAR Report (14) Radio's All-Dimension Audience Research audience estimates (ratings), based on daily telephone interviews that cover seven days of radio listening behavior.

radio dayparts (14) The five basic parts into which the radio day is divided: morning drive, daytime, afternoon drive, nighttime, all night. The rating services measure the audiences for only the first four of these dayparts, as all-night listening is very limited and not highly competitive.

radio personality (11) A disc jockey or talk show host.

random probability samples (6) A sampling method in which every unit in the population universe is given an equal chance of being selected for the research.

rate card (13) A printed information form listing a publication's advertising rates, mechanical and copy requirements, advertising deadlines, and other information the advertiser needs to know before placing an order.

ratings (14) See *program rating.*

rational appeal (8) Advertising appeal based on the consumer's practical, functional need for the product or service.

reach (12) The total number of *different* people or households exposed to an advertising schedule during a given time, usually four weeks. Reach measures the *unduplicated* extent of audience exposure to a media vehicle and may be expressed either as a percentage of the total market or as a raw number.

reading notice (13) A variation of a display ad designed to look like editorial matter. It is sometimes charged at a higher space rate than normal display advertising, and the law requires that the word *advertisement* appear at the top.

recall tests (6) Posttesting methods used to determine the extent to which an advertisement and its message have been noticed, read, or watched.

recruitment advertising (18) A special type of advertising, most frequently found in the classified sections of daily newspapers and typically the responsibility of a personnel department, aimed at attracting employment applications.

reference groups (4) People we try to emulate or whose approval concerns us.

reflected light meter (11) Light meter that measures the volume of light reflected off a subject.

regional advertising (1) Advertising for products sold in only one area or region of the country. The region might cover several states but not the entire nation.

regular price-line advertising (17) A type of retail advertising designed to inform consumers about the services available or the wide selection and quality of merchandise offered at regular prices.

reinforcement advertising (7) Advertising designed to remind people of their successful experience with a product and to suggest using it again.

reliability (6) An important characteristic of research test results. For a test to be reliable, it must be repeatable, producing the same result each time it is administered.

reprints (15) Duplications of published articles that show the company or its products in a favorable light, used as direct-mail enclosures and frequently sent by public relations agencies or departments.

reseller markets (4) Individuals or companies that buy products for the purpose of reselling them.

retail advertising (1) (17) Advertising by retail stores, primarily at the local level (although it can also be regional or national).

retainer (3) See *straight-fee method.*

roadblocking (12) Buying simultaneous airtime on all three television networks.

roman type (10) The most popular type group, considered to be the most readable and offering the greatest number of designs. It is characterized by the serifs (or tails) that cross the ends of the main strokes and by variations in the thickness of the strokes.

ROP (13) Run of paper. A term referring to a newspaper's normal discretionary right to place a given ad on any page or in any position it desires—in other words, where space permits. Most newspapers make an effort to place an ad in the position requested by the advertiser.

rotary plan (15) In outdoor advertising, the rotation of painted bulletins to different choice locations in the market every 30, 60, or 90 days, giving the impression of wide coverage over time.

rotogravure (10) A printing process that works in the reverse of letterpress. Instead of the printing design being raised above the printing plate as in letterpress, the rotogravure process prints from a depressed surface. Ink in the tiny depressions is transferred to the paper by pressure and suction.

rough cut (11) See *work print*.

run of paper (13) See *ROP*.

run of station (ROS) (14) Leaving placement of radio spots up to the station in order to achieve a lower ad rate.

sale advertising (17) A type of retail advertising designed to stimulate the movement of particular merchandise or generally increase store traffic by placing the emphasis on special reduced prices.

sales letters (15) The most common form of direct mail. Sales letters may be typewritten, typeset and printed, printed with a computer insert (such as your name), or fully computer typed.

sales-oriented period (4) An era when the marketplace was glutted with products and the selling function was characterized by business's use of extravagant advertising claims and an attitude of *caveat emptor* (let the buyer beware).

sales promotion (5) (16) A direct inducement offering extra incentives all along the marketing route—from manufacturers through distribution channels to customers—to accelerate the movement of the product from the producer to the consumer.

sales-target objectives (7) Marketing objectives that relate to a company's sales. They should be specific as to product and market, quantified as to time and amount, and realistic. They may be expressed in terms of total sales volume; sales by product, market segment, or customer type; market share; growth rate of sales volume; or gross profit.

sales tests (6) Methods used to obtain information on the sales-producing value of specific ads or whole campaigns.

sample (6) A portion of the population selected by market researchers to represent the appropriate targeted population.

sample unit (6) The actual individuals chosen to be surveyed or studied.

sampling (16) Offering consumers a free trial of the product, hoping to convert them to habitual use.

sans serif type (10) A large group of typefaces characterized by the lack of serifs (thus the name, sans serif) and by a relatively uniform thickness of the strokes. Also referred to as *block, contemporary,* or *gothic.*

satellite master antenna television (SMATV) (14) A method for TV signal delivery that makes use of a satellite dish to capture signals for TV sets in apartment buildings and other complexes.

SAU systems (13) See *standard advertising unit system.*

screen printing (10) An old printing process that requires no plates and is based on the stencil principle. As ink is squeezed through a special stencil screen stretched tightly on a frame, the desired image is reproduced. For printing in color, a separate stencil is made for each color.

script (10) See *cursive type.*

seal (8) A type of certification mark offered by such organizations as the Good Housekeeping Institute and Underwriters' Laboratories when a product meets standards established by these institutions. Seals provide an independent, valued endorsement for the advertised product.

secondary data (6) Information that has previously been collected or published.

secondary readership (13) The number of people who read a publication in addition to the primary purchasers.

selective demand (5) Consumer demand for the particular advantages of one brand over another.

selective distribution (7) Strategy of limiting the distribution of a product to select outlets in order to reduce distribution and promotion costs.

selective perception (4) The ability of humans to select from the many sensations bombarding their central processing unit those sensations that fit well with their current or previous experiences, needs, desires, attitudes, and beliefs, focusing attention on some things and ignoring others.

self-concept (4) The images we carry in our mind of the type of person we are and who we desire to be.

self-liquidating premium (16) A special offer in which the consumer pays the cost of the premium. The seller does not attempt to make a profit on such a premium but only tries to break even.

self-mailer (15) Any type of direct-mail piece that can travel by mail without an envelope. Usually folded and secured by a staple or a seal, self-mailers have a special blank space for the prospect's name and address.

semipromotional strategy (17) An approach to local advertising that entails using periodic sales and promotions to increase store traffic for a business that otherwise has regular customers.

serifs (10) Delicate curved tails that cross the end of each letter stroke of roman type.

service (1) (5) A bundle of benefits that may or may not be physical, that are temporary in nature, and that come from the completion of a task.

session (11) The time when the recording and mixing of a radio commercial takes place.

shared mail (17) A direct-mail vehicle in which ads from two or more advertisers are included in a single mail package targeted by ZIP code.

share of audience (14) The percentage of homes that have sets in use (HUT) tuned in to a specific program. A program with only five viewers could have a 50 share if only 10 sets are turned on.

share-of-market/share-of-voice method (7) A method of allocating advertising funds based on determining the firm's goals for a certain share of the market and then applying a slightly higher percentage of industry advertising dollars to the firm's budget.

sheetwise imposition (10) An arrangement for printing in which half the pages are printed on one side of the sheet and the other half on the reverse.

shoppers (17) Weekly local ad vehicles that may or may not contain editorial matter. They can be segmented into highly selected market areas.

short rate (13) The rate charged to advertisers who, during the year, fail to fulfill the amount of space for which they have contracted. This is computed by determining the difference between the standard rate for the lines run and the discount rate contracted.

shotgun microphone (11) A unidirectional microphone engineered to capture sounds from long distances.

showing (15) A traditional term referring to the relative number of outdoor posters used during a contract period, indicating the intensity of market coverage. For example, a 100 showing provides an even and thorough coverage of the entire market.

SIC codes (5) See *Standard Industrial Classification codes.*

signature cuts (8) See *logotype.*

silk screen (10) See *screen printing.*

simulation model (12) A type of computer program used to estimate the ability of specific media vehicles to reach target individuals.

situation analysis (7) A statement in the marketing plan telling where the organization is and how it got there. It includes relevant facts about the company's history, growth, goods and services, sales volume, share of market, competitive status, markets served, distribution system, past advertising programs, results of market research studies, company capabilities, and strengths and weaknesses.

slander (8) Defamation of a person in broadcast advertising or verbal statements.

slice-of-life commercial (9)(11) A type of commercial consisting of a short play that portrays a real-life situation in which the product is tried and becomes the solution to a problem.

slogan (8) A standard company statement (also called a *tag line* or a *theme line*) for advertisements, salespeople, and company employees. Slogans have two basic purposes: to provide continuity for a campaign and to reduce a key theme or idea to a brief, memorable positioning statement.

slotting allowances (16) Fees that manufacturers pay to retailers for the privilege of obtaining shelf or floor space for a new product.

smart cards (16) Frequent-shopper cards, issued by supermarkets and retail chains, that are used for electronic couponing and other purposes.

social sciences (4) see *behavioral sciences.*

sound booth (11) A small windowed room or practice area in a sound studio.

special effects (11) Unusual visual effects created for commercials.

special-effects lighting (11) Lighting used to create enhancements or distortions to add visual excitement to a scene.

specialty advertising (16) An advertising, sales promotion, and motivational communication medium that employs useful articles of merchandise imprinted with the advertiser's name, message, or logo.

spectaculars (15) Giant electronic signs that usually incorporate movement, color, and flashy graphics to grab the attention of viewers in high-traffic areas.

speculative presentation (3) An agency's presentation of the advertisement it proposes using in the event it is hired. It is usually made at the request of a prospective client and is often not paid for by the client.

spiff (16) See *push money.*

spillover media (19) Foreign media aimed at a national population that is inadvertently received by a substantial number of the consumers in a neighboring country.

split run (13) A feature of many newspapers (as well as magazines) that allows advertisers to test the comparative effectiveness of two different advertising approaches by running two different ads of identical size, but different content, in the same or different press runs on the same day.

split-30s (14) Thirty-second TV spots in which the advertiser promotes two separate products with separate messages.

sponsorship (14) The presentation of a radio or TV program by a sole advertiser. The advertiser is responsible for the program content and the cost of production as well as the advertising. This is generally so costly that single sponsorships are usually limited to specials.

spot announcement (14) An individual commercial message run between programs but having no relationship to either. Spots may be sold nationally or locally. They must be purchased by contacting individual stations directly.

spot radio (14) National advertisers' purchase of airtime on individual stations. Buying spot radio affords advertisers great flexibility in their choice of markets, stations, airtime, and copy.

In addition, spot advertising enables the message to be tailored to the local market and presented to listeners at the most favorable times.

square serif type (10) A kind of typeface that combines sans serif and roman. The serifs have the same weight and thickness as the main strokes of the letters.

SRDS (13) See *Standard Rate and Data Service.*

standard advertising unit (SAU) system (13) A system of standardized newspaper advertisement sizes that can be accepted by all standard-sized newspapers without consideration of their precise format or page size. This system allows advertisers to prepare one advertisement in a particular size or SAU and place it in various newspapers regardless of the format.

Standard Industrial Classification (SIC) codes (5) Method used by the U.S. Department of Commerce to classify all businesses. The SIC codes are based on broad industry groups, which are then subdivided into major groups, subgroups, and detailed groups of firms in similar lines of business.

standardized outdoor advertising (15) Specialized structures located scientifically to deliver an advertiser's message to an entire market.

Standard Rate and Data Service (SRDS) (13) A publisher of media information directories that eliminate the necessity for advertisers and their agencies to obtain rate cards for every publication.

standard size (13) A newspaper size generally 22 inches deep and 13 inches wide, divided into six columns.

statement stuffers (15) Advertisements enclosed in the monthly customer statements mailed by department stores, banks, or oil companies.

stimulus (4) Physical data that can be sensed.

stock photos (10) Existing photos that can be purchased for advertising purposes, usually from stock photo agencies.

stop-motion photography (11) An animation technique whereby objects and animals come to life—walk, run, dance, and do tricks. Each frame of film is shot individually. An arm may be moved only $\frac{1}{32}$ of an inch on each frame, but when the frames are assembled, the effect is smooth and natural.

storyboard (3)(9) Drawings of a series of sequential frames to indicate the conception of a television commercial.

straight announcement (9)(11) The oldest type of radio or television commercial, in which an announcer delivers a sales message directly into the microphone or on-camera or does so off-screen while a slide or film is shown on-screen.

straight-fee method (3) A method of compensation for ad agency services in which a straight fee, or *retainer,* is based on a cost-plus-fixed-fees formula. Under this system, the agency estimates the amount of personnel time required by the client, determines the cost of that personnel, and multiplies by some factor.

straight-sell copy (8) A type of body copy in which the text immediately explains or develops the headline and visual in a straightforward attempt to sell the product.

strategy (7) The methodology a company uses to achieve its objectives—the "how to" of a plan. See *marketing strategy.*

strike-on composition (10) A simple method of setting type, also called *direct-impression composition,* which can be done on a regular typewriter, an electronic typewriter, or a word processor.

stripping (10) Assembling line and halftone negatives into one single negative, which is then used to produce a combination plate.

studio (11) The place where commercials are recorded.

subheads (8) Secondary headlines in advertisements that may appear above or below the headline or in the text of the ad. Subheads are usually set in a type size smaller than the headline but larger than the body copy or text type size. They may also appear in boldface type or in a different ink color.

subscription television (STV) (14) Over-the-air pay TV. Subscribers pay for a descrambler that allows them to watch programs carried over a regular television channel.

Sunday supplement (13) A newspaper-distributed Sunday magazine. Sunday supplements are distinct from other sections of the newspaper since they are printed by rotogravure on smoother paper stock.

supers (11) Words superimposed on the picture in a television commercial.

superstations (14) Local TV stations that broadcast to the rest of the country via satellite and carry national advertising. The best-known superstation is Ted Turner's WTBS out of Atlanta, for which the term was coined.

suppliers (3) People and organizations that assist both advertisers and agencies in the preparation of advertising materials, such as photography, illustration, printing, and production.

survey method (6) The most common way to gather primary research data. By asking questions of current or prospective customers, the researcher hopes to obtain information on attitudes, opinions, or motivations.

sweepstakes (16) A sales promotion activity in which prizes are offered based on a chance drawing of entrants' names. The purpose is to encourage consumption of the product by creating consumer involvement.

syndicated research services (6) Companies that continuously monitor and publish information on subjects of interest to marketers, such as the reach and effectiveness of media vehicles.

syndication (14) See *barter syndication, first-run syndication, off-network syndication.*

synergism (12) An effect achieved when the sum of the parts is greater than that expected from simply adding together the individual components.

tabloid (13) A newspaper size generally about half as deep as a standard-sized newspaper; it is usually about 14 inches deep and 11 inches wide.

tactics (7) The precise details of a company's marketing strategy that spell out the specific details of the methods that will be used to achieve its marketing objectives.

tag line (8)   See *slogan.*

take ones (15)   In transit advertising, pads of business reply cards or coupons, affixed to interior advertisements for an extra charge, that allow passengers to request more detailed information, send in application blanks, or receive some other product benefit.

talent (11)   The actors in commercials.

target audience (1) (7)   The specific group of individuals to whom the advertising message is directed.

target market (5) (6) (7)   The group of market segments toward which all marketing activities will be directed.

telemarketing (5) (15)   Selling products and services by using the telephone to contact prospective customers.

teleprompter (11)   A two-way mirror mounted on the front of a studio video camera that reflects moving text to be read by the speaker being taped.

television dayparts (14)   The various parts of the day into which TV programming and viewing is divided. These include daytime, early fringe, early news, prime access, prime time, late news, and late fringe.

terminal posters (15)   One-sheet, two-sheet, and three-sheet posters in many bus, subway, and commuter train stations as well as in major train and airline terminals. They are usually custom designed and include such attention getters as floor displays, island showcases, illuminated signs, dioramas (three-dimensional scenes), and clocks with special lighting and moving messages.

termination stage (3)   The ending of a client-agency relationship.

testimonial (9)   The use of satisfied customers and celebrities to endorse a product in advertising.

testing (6)   See *posttesting; pretesting.*

text (8)   See *body copy.*

text type (10)   The smaller type used in the body copy of an advertisement.

theme line (8)   See *slogan.*

theory of cognitive dissonance (4)   The theory that people try to justify their behavior by reducing the degree to which their impressions or beliefs are inconsistent with reality.

third-class mail (15)   The inexpensive type of U.S. mail delivery usually used for direct-mail advertising. The four types of third-class mail are single piece, bulk, bound books or catalogs, and nonprofit organization mail.

3-D ads (13)   Magazine ads requiring the use of 3-D glasses.

thumbnail sketch (9)   A rough, rapidly produced pencil sketch, approximately one-fourth to one-eighth the size of the finished ad, that is used for trying out ideas.

top-down planning (7)   The planning process of analyzing a situation, establishing objectives, setting strategy, and determining tactics, in that order.

total audience (14)   The total number of homes reached by some portion of a TV program. This figure is normally broken down to determine the distribution of audience into demographic categories.

total audience plan (TAP) (14)   A radio advertising package rate that guarantees a certain percentage of spots in the better dayparts.

total bus (15)   In transit advertising, all the exterior space on a bus, including the front, rear, sides, and top, giving the product message powerful exclusivity.

Total market coverage (TMC) (17)   A free advertising vehicle delivered weekly to 100 percent of residents in a newspaper's market area.

trade advertising (1)   The advertising of goods and services to middlemen to stimulate wholesalers and retailers to buy goods for resale to their customers or for use in their own businesses.

trade deals (16)   Short-term dealer discounts on the cost of a product or other dollar inducements to sell a product.

trademark (2)   Any word, name, symbol, device, or any combination thereof adopted and used by manufacturers or merchants to identify their goods and distinguish them from those manufactured or sold by others.

trade promotions (16)   See *push strategy.*

trade shows (16)   Exhibitions where manufacturers, dealers, and buyers of an industry's products can get together for demonstrations and discussion; expose new products, literature, and samples to customers; and meet potential new dealers for their products.

trading stamps (16)   A once-popular sales promotion device for department stores, supermarkets, and service stations in which customers making purchases received stamps that could be redeemed for valuable products.

transit advertising (15)   An out-of-home medium that actually includes three separate media forms: inside cards; outside posters; and station, platform, and terminal posters.

trial close (8)   In ad copy, requests for the order that are made before the close in the ad.

TVHH (TV households) (14)   The number of households in a market area that own television sets.

type families (10)   Related typefaces in which the basic design remains the same but in which variations occur in the proportion, weight, and slant of the characters. Variations commonly include light, medium, bold, extra bold, condensed, extended, and italic.

typography (10)   The art of selecting and setting type.

unfair advertising (2)   According to the FTC, advertising that causes a consumer to be "unjustifiably injured" or that violates public policy.

unidirectional microphone (11)   A microphone that captures sound from one direction only.

Universal Product Code (6)   A series of linear bars and a 10-digit number that identify a product and its price.

universe (6)   The entire target population of a research study.

uppercase (10)   Capital letters.

usage rates (5)   The extent to which consumers use a product: light, medium, or heavy.

user-status (5)   A method of segmenting markets by types of product users, such as nonusers, ex-users, potential users, new users, and regular users.

USP (1)   The *unique selling proposition,* or the differentiating features, of every product advertised; a concept developed by Rosser Reeves of the Ted Bates advertising agency.

utility (4)   A product's ability to provide both symbolic or psychological want satisfaction and functional satisfaction. A product's problem-solving potential may include form, time, place, or possession utility.

validity (6)   An important characteristic of a research test. For a test to be valid, it must reflect the true status of the market.

values and lifestyles (VALS) (5)   A psychographic typology for segmenting U.S. consumers and predicting their purchase behavior.

vehicles (6) (12)   Particular media programs or publications.

vertical cooperative advertising (17)   Co-op advertising in which the manufacturer provides the ad and pays a percentage of the cost of placement.

vertical marketing system (5)   A centrally programmed and managed system that supplies or otherwise serves a group of stores or other businesses.

vertical publications (13)   Business publications aimed at people within a specific industry; for example, *Restaurants & Institutions.*

video (9)   The visual part of a television commercial. Also, the left side of a television script, indicating camera action, scenes, and stage directions.

video press release (18)   A news or feature story prepared in video form and offered free to TV stations.

visual (9)   The picture or illustration in an advertisement.

visualization (8)   The creative point in advertising where the search for the "big idea" takes place. It includes the task of analyzing the problem, assembling any and all pertinent information, and developing some verbal or visual concept of how to communicate what needs to be said.

voice-over (8)   In television advertising, the spoken copy or dialog delivered by an announcer who is not seen but whose voice is heard.

volume discounts (13)   Reduced newspaper ad rates earned by purchasing large or repeated amounts of space.

volume segmentation (5)   Defining consumers as light, medium, or heavy users of products.

volume unit (VU) meter (11)   On an audio console, a needle indicating the loudness of sounds.

wants (4)   Needs learned during a person's lifetime.

weeklies (13)   Newspapers that are published once a week and characteristically serve readers in small urban or suburban areas, or farm communities, with exclusive emphasis on local news and advertising.

word-count method (10)   A method of copy casting in which all the words in the copy are counted and then divided by the number of words per square inch that can be set in a particular type style and size, as given in a standard table.

work & turn imposition (10)   A method of printing in which both sides of the art are printed on one side of the sheet. After the first side has been run, the sheets are then turned over to the blank side, and the same plate is used to run the second side. The images are registered so that the front and the back of the piece are printed on opposite sides of the paper and can be cut and folded down to make a complete set of pages in sequence.

work print (11)   The first visual portion of a filmed commercial, assembled without the extra effects or dissolves, titles, or supers. At this time, scenes may be substituted, music and sound effects added, or other changes made.

zapping (14)   The tendency of remote-control users to change TV channels during commercials.

zipping (14)   The ability of VCR users to skip through commercials when replaying taped programs.

NAME AND COMPANY INDEX

ABC, 496, 505, 522, 665-66
Abdul, Paula, 195
Abraham, Magid M., E-10
Abratt, Russell, E-6
Abraxas, 212
Acura automobiles, 237, 240, **241**
  advertising plan for, 255, 259-60, 261, 262, **262, 263**
  marketing plan for, 242, 244, 247, 249, **249**, 250, **250, 251**
Adidas, 172, 193
Adler Planetarium (Chicago), **13**, 14
Adobe Systems Incorporated, **277**
Advanced Promotion Technologies, 597
Advantage, **583**
Advertiming, 160
Advertising Checking Bureau, 473
Advertising Council, **638**, 667-68
ADVO-System, 625
AGB Research, 508
Ailes, Roger, 401
Air Canada, 286, **286**, 331
AIWA, 89
Akzo's Engineering Plastics, **683**
Alaska Airlines, 311, **311, 348**
Alaska Division of Tourism, 517
Alcohol and Tobacco Tax Division, 56
Alfa Romeo, **662**
Alka-Seltzer, 495
Allman, William F., E-3, E-4, E-5
Allstate, 437
Alpine car CD player, **135**
Alpo Petfoods, 67
Alreck, Pamela L., E-4, E-5
Alsop, Ronald, E-9, E-11
Altman, William F., E-4
American Advertising Federation, 68, 76
American Airlines, 296
American Association of Advertising Agencies (AAAA), E-2, 68, 76, 89, 266, **267**
American Association of Political Consultants, 400
American Bar Association, 65, 646
American Broadcasting Corp., 496, 505, 522, 655-66
American Dental Association, 239
American Express, 73, **253**, 539
American Floral Marketing Council, **446**
American Harvester, 662
American Home Products, 272
American International Rent-A-Car, **472**
American Lung Association, **47**, 665
American Motors, 238
American Newspaper Publishers Association, 491
American Public Transit Association, 570
American Red Cross, 664, 668
American Society of Travel Agents, 582, 611
American Stores Co., 461
American Trucking Association, 570
Amity Leather, **350**
Amoco, **55, 625**
Amore, **534**
Amtrak, **178**
ANA Airways, **670**
Anderson, Richard W., E-2
Anderson Travel, 553
Andrews, Edmund L., E-11
Anheuser-Busch, 138, 272, 512, 520, 525
A-1 steak sauce, 312
Aponte, Angelo J., 64
Apple Computer, **10**, 11, **108**, 240, **431, 486**

Arbitron, 165, 202, 507, 508, 529, **531**
Arco, 88
Arinze, Bay, E6
Armco vacuum cleaner, 310
Arpege, 297
Arriflex, 408
Arrow shirts, 312
Arts & Entertainment Network, 514, 517
Ashland Chemical, 87
Ashley Whippet Dog Frisbee Championships, 278
Association of National Advertisers, 68, 76, 161
AT&T, 344, 347, 498, 595, 647
  advertorials, 658
  Ayer and, 108, 200
  calling card ad, **342**
  commercials, 24
  disclaimers by, 71
  expenditures by, 272, 525
  industrial market ad, **128**
  program sponsorship by, 498
  radio ads by, 520
  slogan of, 200, 308, 437, 438
  television commercial, 399, **502, 538**
Audi, 237
Audit Bureau of Circulations, 432, 485, 491
Audubon Society, 149
Avis, 23
Avon, 347
Ayer, 18, 25, 86, 108, 109, 344, 664
  J. C. Penney and, 199, 200, 201, 212, 224, 225, 229, 231, 232
Aykac, Ahmet, E6

Backer Spielvogel Bates Worldwide, 85, **108**, 677
Baecher, Charlotte, 507
Baker Lovick/BBDO, 10
Balasubramanian, Siva K., E-6
Balducci's, 541
Ball Partnership, **632**
Band, William, E-6
Band-Aid bandages, 63, 590
Bangkok, **682**
Bank of America, 346
Barbeau, Adrienne, 623
Barnes & Noble Bookstores, **356**
Barr, David Samuel, E-9
Barrow, Peter, E-6
Bartles & Jaymes, 312, 341, 344
Basu, Amiya K., E-6
Ted Bates Worldwide, 113, 114
Batra, Rajeev, E-6, E-9
Eddie Bauer, 552
Bauer, Betsy, E-11
BBDO Worldwide, 85, 113, 163, 339, 522, 692
BCP, 86
L. L. Bean, 541, 552
Beatrice, 646
Beckman Instruments, 592
Beef Industry Council, 64, 666
Bellenger, Danny N., E-3
Benetton, **105**
Benson & Hedges, 109
Berdie, Doug R., E-11
Berman, Barry, E-11
Bermuda Department of Tourism, **270**
Bermudez Associates, 87
Berry, Dick, E-5
Bertrand, Kate, E-11

Best, Roger J., E-3, E-4
Better Business Bureau, 66-67
Bettinger, Cass, E-4
Betty Crocker, 101, 312
Bic pens, 192
Biederman, Barry, 658
J. H. Biggar furniture stores, 623
Bigsby & Kruthers, 623
Birch Research, 529
Birks, **192**
Bissell & Wilhite Co., **607**
Bjorklund, Felix, 685
Black Entertainment TV, 514
Blair, Margaret Henderson, E-5
Block, Alex Ben, E-8
Blois, Ralph S., E-2, E-3, E-5
Bloom, Robert, 113
Bloom Agency, 343
Blue Diamond almonds, **476**
Blyth, John S., E-5
BMW, 237
Bodett, Tom, 344, 385
Boerlage, Maria, 520
Bogart, Leo, E-5, E-6, E-9
Bolles, Richard N., 715
Boone, Louis E., E-3, E-4, E-5, E-6
Borden, Neil H., E-4
Boston Globe, The, **470**
Bovée, Courtland L., E-3
Bowen-Jones, Carys, E-3
Bowman, Russ, E-10
Boyd, Harper W., Jr., E-4
Bozell, Jacobs, Kenyon, Eckherdt, 113, 449
Braniff, 695
Braun, Gerry, E-12
Bredin, James, E-1
Bremner, Brian, E-2
Bristol-Myers, 104, 239, 272, 517
British Knights, 193
Brizz, Michael, E-12
Broadcast Advertisers Reports, 432
Brock, Luther, E-7
Brown, Alex, E-8
Brown, Priscilla B., E-6
Brownlee, Douglas T., E-2
R. H. Bruskin Associates, 215
Bruzzone Research Co., **233**
Bryers ice cream, 111
Bua, Chuck, 627
Buchanan, Bruce, E-2
Budd, Julie, 553
Bufferin, 33-34, **34**
Bullock's, **619**, 631
Bumba, Lincoln, E-8, E-9
Burger King, **234**, 507, **575**, 575-76, 583
Burke, James, E-1
Burke, Raymond R., E-6
Leo Burnett, 344, **682**
Burrell Advertising, 87
Burroughs, 662
Burstiner, Irving, E-11
Busek, Erhard and Brance, **682**
Bush, George, 61, 400
Buzzell, Robert D., E-6
Byrne, Andrew J., E-7

Cable News Network, 514, 516
CACI Marketing Systems, 205, **208**

NOTE: Page numbers for advertising appear in **boldface** type.

Cadillac, **635**
Cadwell, Franchellie, E-3
Cahners Publishing Co., 486
California Academy of Sciences, **623**
California Milk Advisory Board, **61**
California Raisin Advisory Board, 397, **398**
Calloway, Jan, E-6
Calvin Klein, 50, 482
Camel cigarettes, 481
Campbell, Dee Ann, 432
Campbell Automotive Group, 623
Campbell Soup, 211, **212**, 376, 461, 499, 517, 560, 580, 587
Campmor, 541
Candler, Asa G., 26
Canon, 676
Caples, John, E-7
Carney, Art, 30
Carpenter, Scott, 344
Carson, Johnny, 522, 629
Carter Hawley Hale Stores, 461
Cash, Johnny, 58
Castor Spanish International, 87
Castro, Janice, E-2, E-11
Cateora, Philip R., E-12
CBS, 496, 505, 519, 522, 665-66
Celestial Seasonings, **365, 442**
Certifiably Nuts, **185**
Certs, **304**
Chajet, Clive, 661
Champion International, **535**, 535-36, **537**
Charmin, 297
Chart a Good Course, **117**
Chebat, Jean-Charles, E-6
Cheese, John, E-6
Chesebrough-Pond's, 67
Chevrolet, 213, 289, 647
Chevron, 54
Chiat/Day/Mojo, **109**, 495, **663**, 696
Chicago Cutlery, **146, 323**
Childcraft, 541
Children's Defense Fund, **665**
Children's Hospital and Health Center (San Diego), 607
Chorba, Thomas, 715
Christie, Lorna, 542
Chrysler Corp., 180, 192, 346
    competition for, 238
    disclaimers by, 73
    Dodge, 51
    expenditures by, 272, 479, 525
    Lee Iacocca commercials, 24-25, 124, **125**
    radio ads by, 520
    roadblocking by, 450
    video ads by, 596
Church of Latter Day Saints, 664
Church of the Nazarene, 665
Cinemax, 513
Cineplex Odeon, 596
Citgo, 14
Citibank, 89
Civil Aeronautics Board, 57
Clairol, 296
Clancy Shulman, 113
Claris-Cheops, **236, 278, 653**
Clark, Agi, 199, 200, 202, 224, 225, 229
Clark, Eric, 51
Clark, Sheila, E-7
Clarkin, Greg, E-4
Clausewitz, Carl von, 238, 239-40
Clearwater Federal, 155, **155**, 156, 157, 168-70, 170-71, 177, 178-79
Cleese, John, 519
CNBC, 496, 514
CNN, 514, 516
Coca-Cola, **4**, 138, 183
    advertising economics for, 38
    Bill Cosby and, 90-91, 341
    as brand, 181
    comparison advertising and, 288, 289

Coca-Cola—*Cont.*
    history of, **5**, 5-7, 26-27, **26-31**
    international advertising, 675, **676**, 677, **678**, 689, 692, 695
    Pepsi versus, 24, 141, 288
    premiums from, 586
    subliminal perception and, 144
    in trade advertising, 11-12
Cohen, Jack, E-5
Cohen, Laurie P., E-1
Cohen, Robert H., E-6
Coke. *See* Coca-Cola
Coleman, Lynn, E-11
Coleman, Ronald, 110
Colgate-Palmolive, 110, 113, 114, 239, **239**, 517
Colley, Russell H., 255, E-6
Collier Service Co., 566
Collins, Julia M., E-7
Collins, Tom, E-1, E-5, 257
Columbia Broadcasting System, 496, 505, 519, 522, 665-66
Colombian coffee, **134**
Comedy Channel, 514
Compaq Computer Corp., 647
Comprehensive Psychological Services, 636
Compton Advertising, 113
CompuServe, 205
Computerized Marketing Technologies, 547
Coney, Kenneth A., E-3, E-4
Confucius, 299
Consolidated Foods, 662
Consumer Federation of America, 75
Consumer-Product Safety Commission, 57
Consumers' Research, 75
Consumers Union, 75, 506, 507
Continental Bank, **439, 548,** 549
Converse, 172, 193
Coogle, Joe, E-9
Cook, Stephanie, E-8
Copeland, Lennie, E-12
Copetas, A. Craig, E-12
Cornes Motors, **190, 475**
Corstjens, Marcel, E-6
Corwen, Leonard, 715
Cos, Meg, E-4
Cosby, Bill, 290-91, 341
Cossette Communications-Marketing, 86, 139, 140, 286
Council of Better Business Bureaus, 68
Craig, James, 715
Crain's New York Business, **88, 525**
Cravens, David W., E-4, E-5, E-6
Creative Media, 88-89
Crest, **69**
Croft, Nancy L., E-10, E-11
Cross pen, **601**
Cullum, Bob and Charles, 627, 628

Dagnoli, Judan, E-10
Dancer Fitzgerald Sample, 113
Danzig, Fred, E-7
D'Arcy Massius Benton & Bowles, 445, 677
Davids, Meryl, E-12
Davis, Bob, E-10
Davis, Herman, E-3
Dayton Hudson Corp., 461
Dayton's department store, **612**
DDB Needham Worldwide, 85, 98, **134**, 664
DeBeers, 200, 308
Decker, Phillip J., E-4
Deckinger, E. L., 715
De Deo, Joe, 425
Della Femina, Jerry, 20
Della Femina McNamee, 109
Del Monte Foods, **423**, 423-24, 431-32, **432**, 435
Del Taco, 136, 312
Deluxe software, **185**
Demby, Bill, 339-40, 341
Dennis, Lloyd B., E-12

Denny's Restaurants, 143, **655**
Dentsu Inc., **675**, 679
Detroit Auto Works, 312
Deutsch, Donnie, 21
Dexter USA, **44**
Dial Corp., 520
Diamond Star Motors, 180
Dichter, Ernest, E-1, 33
Dictaphone, 89
Diddley, Bo, 657
Dillon, William R., E-5
Direct-Mail Advertising Association, 611
Direct Marketing Association, 542-43, 552, **552**
Discovery Channel, 514
Walt Disney, 88, 397, 596
Disney Channel, 513
Dr Pepper, 165
Dodge Dakota, 481
Dole fruit cocktail, 134
Domino's pizza, **266**
Domzal, Teresa, E-5
Donaton, Scott, E-8
Reuben H. Donnelley, 595
Donovan, Diane C., E-10
Dos Locos, **136**
Dove soap, 287
Doye, John, 317-18, 320
Doyle, Peter, E-6
Doyle Dane Bernbach, 113
DPZ-Propaganda, 680
Drexel Burnham Lambert, 659
Drexler, Michael, 449
Dreyfuss, **654**
Dukakis, Michael, 400
Dun & Bradstreet, 201
Dunkin, Amy, E-8
Du Pont, 339-40, **340, 341**
Duracell, 495, 496
Dychtwald, Ken, E-4

Eastman, George, 312
Eastman Kodak, 110, 165, 272, 312, **562**, 647, 675
Eckhardt, H. T., E-1
Edel, Richard G., E-11
Edelson, Sharon, E-7
Edmondson, Brad, E-10
Eisenhart, Tom, E-4, E-10, E-12
Eliashberg, Jehoshua, E-6
Elliott, Stuart, E-9
Embassy Suites, 437
Endicott, R. Craig, E-1, E-3, E-5, E-9
Energizer Bunny, 400, **495**, 495-96
English, Mary McCabe, E-5, E-7, E-11
English Leather, 303
Entertainment Television, 514
Environmental Protection Agency (EPA), 58, 59
Episcopal Church, **666**
Epstein, Michael, 288
Equifax, 145
Erickson, Julie Liesse, E-7, E-10
Erickson, Richard L., E-6
Escada perfume, **118**
Eskin, Gerald J., E-5
ESPN, 496, 514
Esprit de Corp., 552
Etgar, Michael, E-5
Evans, Joel R., E-11
Evans, Mark, E-1, E-6
Eveready Bunny, 400, **495**, 495-96
Exxon, 502, 639-40, 641, 645, 675

Fahey, Alison, E-12
Fallon McElligott, 457, 473, 625
Falstaff Brewing Company, 75
Family Channel, 514
Farago, Peter, 341
Farago Advertising, 355
Farhi, Paul, E-2

Farrell, O. C., E-3
Farris, Judy, 631
Farris, Paul W., E-6
Fayerweather, John, E-12
FCB/Leber Rate Partners-New York, 664
Federal Communications Commission, 56, 61
Federal Express, **473**, 500
Federal Highway Administration, 562
Federal Trade Commission, 55-59, **60**, 311, 543, 579
    advertising review by, 53
    advertorials and, 659
    comparative advertising and, 290
    pricing and, 34
    truth in advertising and, 20, 21
Federated Department Stores, 461
Ferguson, Wright, E-7
Festinger, Leon, E-4
Fiat SpA, 673
Fidelity Federal, 298
Figenskau, Jerry, 522
Filiatrault, Pierre, E-6
Financial News Network, 514
Finch, Peter, E-10, E-12
Fireman, Paul, 172
First Interstate Bank, 308, **309**, 662
First Wisconsin Bank (Appleton), 625
Fisher, Anne B., E-12
Fisher Big Wheel, 514
Fitzgerald, Kate, E-9
Fitzgerald Sample, 113
Fitzpatrick, Sean, 21
Fizdale, Rick, 344
FNN: Sports, 514
Fogg, Sharon, E-10
Folgers, 414, 418
Food and Drug Administration, 56, 59, 61
Foote, Cone & Belding, 43, 86, 108, 261, 274, 679, 689
Ford, Henry, 279-80
Ford Motor Co., 312
    Bill Cosby and, 341
    Chevrolet versus, 289
    competition for, 238
    copywriting for, 279, **279**, 280
    Edsel and, 22, **119**, 119-20, 123, 201
    expenditures by, 272, 479, 498, 525
    Explorer ad, 122-23, **123**
    international ads, 695
    Simulator disk, 596
    stereotypes and, 51
Fost, Dan, E-5
Foster Parents Plan, 665
Joseph W. Foster & Sons Athletic Shoes, 172
4-Day Tire Stores, 135-36
Fox (network), 496, 519
Franklin Dallas Kundinger Advertising, **86**
Freeberg, Stan, 294
Freedman, Alix M., E-11
Freeman, Laurie, E-3, E-8
Friedman, Margaret L., E-5
Fruit, Charles B., 514
FTC. *See* Federal Trade Commission
Fueroghne, Dean Keith, E-2
Fujitsu, 400, 647
Fulgoni, Gian, 210
Furman, Phyllis, E-7
Furse, David H., E-5

Gable, Greg, E-4
Galbraith, John Kenneth, 37, E-1
Galen, Michele, E-2
Galeries Lafayette, 689
Gallup, George, 20
Gamble, Frederick R., E-2
Garbett, Tom, 658
Garfield, Robert, E-2, 401
Garneau, George, E-1
Garner, James, 666
Garrison, Lloyd, E-5

Garry, Michael, E-9
Garuda Airlines, **333**
Gaudet, Larry, E-4
Gautschi, David, E-6
Gayner, Joel, 345
GE, 143, 163, 525, 543
General Dynamics, 660
General Electric. *See* GE
General Foods, 104, 111, 184, **359**, 686
General Mills, 100-102, **260**, 272, 586-87
General Motors, 233
    competition for, 238
    expenditures by, 272, 478, 499, 525
    international ads, **680**
    radio ads, 520
Gerber, 312
Gershman, Michael, E-7
Gibson, Richard, E-5
Gift Pax, 587
Gigante Vaz & Partners, **90**
Giges, Nancy, E-2
Giles, William, E-5
Gill, Penny, E-10
Gill, R. B., E-5
Gillers, Stephen, 53
Gillett, Alistair, 351
Gillette Co., 233, **671,** 671-72, 676
Gilmore, Voit, 582
Gitlitz, Jonah, 542
Givaudan, Ben, 437
Glazer, Rashi, E-9
Gleem toothpaste, 481
Gloede, William F., E-9
Godiva chocolates, **329**
Golden, Jim, 345
Goldman, Debra, E-1
Goldman, Doron, E-2
Gold Seal salmon, **338**
Goldsmith/Jeffrey, 88
Goldstein, Gary, 376
Gomez, Luis, **289**
Good Housekeeping Institute, 308
Lyle Goodis and Associates, 86
Goodwine Funeral Homes, **605**
Goss, Tom, E-9
Gotcha surfwear
    advertisements, **395, 397, 399, 411, 412**
    commercial goals, 394-95
    commercial postproduction, 411
    commercial shooting, 396-97, 398, 399, 403
W. R. Grace, 72, **72**
Graham, Gordon, E-8
Grand Metropolitan PLC, 272, 479
Graven, Jim, 592
Gray, Robert Keith, 645
Great Cuts, 89
Green, Wayne E., E-2
Greenberg, Jan, 715
Grey Advertising, 85, 676, 679
Gross, Amy E., E-11
GTE, **302,** 595, 661
Guiness, 689
Guiton, Bonnie, 542
Gulf, 312
Gutenberg, Johannes, 17
Guy, Pat, E-9
Gyrostar II Snowboard, **265**

Ha!, 514
Haas, Albert, Jr., E-10
Haas, Ken, 715
Haberstroh, Jack, E-1, 144
Hairston, Tom, 627
Hakuhodo, Inc., 679
Hall, Carol, E-8, E-11
Hallmark, 308, 498, 502
Hamel, Ruth, E-10
Hamilton, Alexander, 79
Hamilton, Joan, E-8

Hanes Hosiery, 581
Harley-Davidson, **142**
Hartigan, Maureen F., E-12
Hartley, Steven W., E-6
Harwell, Barbara, 627
Hathaway, George A., III, E-3
Hathaway shirts, **22, 324**
Hauff, Elaine M., E-11
Hauser, John R., E-6
Hawkins, Del I., E-3, E-4
Hayes, Arthur S., E-2
HBO, 513, **516**
HCM/New York, 87
Headline News, 514
Hedges, Michael, E-4, E-10
Heinz, 180, 183
Helm, Jelly, **550**
Hersch, Linda, E-1
Hershey's Chocolate Milk Mix, **456**
Hertz, 138
Higgins, Kevin T., E-11
Highlands Inn, **621**
Hildenbiddle, John H., 536
Hill, Ronald, 400
Hill and Knowlton USA, 645
Hills, Gerald E., E-4, E-5, E-6
Hinge, John B., E-10
Hochman, Karen, E-10
Hodock, Calvin L., E-6
Hofman, Greg, E-8
Hogan, Karen, E-7
Holiday Inns, 233
Hollandsworth, Skip, E-8
Holtz, Herman, 715
Hombre beer, **337**
Home Box Office, 513, **516**
Home Savings, 347
Honda Motor Co., 21, 237, 246, 284, **286,** 344, **384.**
    See also Acura automobiles
Honeywell, 481
Honomichi, Jack J., E-5
Hooley, Graham J., E-6
Hoover, William, 53
George A. Hormel & Co., 522-23, **523**
Horovitz, Bruce, E-10
Horowitz, Ira, E-6
Horton, Cleveland, E-1, E-3
Horton, Willie, 400
Hospital Corporation of America, 347
Hoult, Peter, 160
Hoven, Hein, 399
Howard, Judy, E-11
Howell, William, 202
H&R Block, 604
Hudson, Richard L., E-12
Hughes, Bob, E-11
Hughes, Kathleen A., E-11
Hull, Aaron, 626
Hume, Peter, 211, 212
Hyatt, Joel, 65
Hyatt Hotels & Resorts, **87**
Hyatt Legal Services, **65**
Hymowitz, Carol, E-3

Iacocca, Lee, 24-25, **125,** 346
IBM, 87, 138, 240, 312, 502, 675, 685
IGA Food Stores, 193
Illinois Bureau of Tourism, **667**
Imperial Margarine, 347, 400, 686
Inan, Czatdana, E-1
Information Resources, 209-10, 597
Inkeles, Ellen Opat, E-7
Institute for Outdoor Advertising, 559, 611
In Store Advertising, 598
Intel, **175**
Intercom, 679
Internal Revenue Service, 268
International Coffees, **78**
International Data Group, 688

International Flavors & Fragrances, Inc., 589
International Harvester, 57
International Paper, 660
Interpublic Group of Cos., 679
Isuzu, 109
Isuzu, Joe, 20
Ivory soap, 287
Izard, Kathy, 151

Jackson, Bo, 657
Jackson, Michael, 346, 674
Jackson, Ron, 21
Jacob's Pharmacy, **5**
Jarman shoes, 343–44, **345,** 346
Jartran, 66
Jell-O, 63, 111, 291, 341, **574**
Jewish Introductions International, 542
Jig-a-Whopper, **347**
John Hancock Financial Services, **657**
Johnson, J. Douglas, E-7
Johnson, Robert, E-2
Johnson & Johnson, 239, 272, 498, 517, 588, 590, 642–43
Johnson Wax, **649**
Jonathan's Uptown restaurant, 151, **151**
Jones, John Philip, E-6, E-10
Jordan, Michael, 31
Joseph, Charles, E-12
Judson, Robert, E-5
Just for Kids, 541

Paul Kagan Associates, 515
Kahn, Herbert L., E-7
Kaiser Aluminum, 652
Henry J. Kaiser Family Foundation, **668**
Kaiser Permanente, 14, **14**
KAKZ (Wichita), 530, 531–32
Kalish, David, E-9, E-11
Kalish, Shlomo, E-5
Karr, Albert R., E-8
Kasle Recycling, **264, 631**
Kastiel, Dianne Lynne, E-2
Kattelman, Terry, E-7, E-8
Katz, Maria, E-12
Katz, Paul C., E-3
Kaynak, Erdener, E-12
KCBN, 627
KDWB (Minneapolis-St. Paul), 73
Keely, Ann, E-4
Keene, David, 401
Keith, Michael C., E-8
Kelliher, Neil, E-8, E-9
Kellogg's, 260, **260,** 272, 498
Kennedy, Sherreil H., E-6
Kent, Felix H., E-2
Kenyon & Eckhardt, 113
Kerlick, Switzer & Johnson Advertising, **92**
Ketchum Advertising, 262, 263, 344
Keys, Wilson Bryan, 144
KHJ (Los Angeles), 521
Kihstrom, Richard E., E-1
King, Thomas R., E-2, E-11
KKDA-FM (Dallas), **531**
KLBJ (Austin), 73
Kleenex, 34, 63, 186, 312
Kleinschrod, Walter A., E-1, E-3
KLM Royal Dutch Airlines, **581**
Kmart, 14, 223, 272, 525
Kodak. *See* Eastman Kodak
Kohlberg, Kravis, Roberts & Co., 385
Kohut, Andrew, E-9
Konrad, Walecia, E-12
Korgaonkar, Pradeep K., E-3
Kornhauser, Henry, 111
Koten, John, E-2, E-4
Kraft, 98, 111, 184, 302
Krentler, Kathleen A., E-1
KSDO (San Diego), 73
K-Swiss, 193

Kumar, V., E-6
Kurnit, Rick, 20
Kurtz, David L., E-3, E-4, E-5, E-6
Kurtzer, Steve, E-9, 477
Kuse, Allan R., E-5
KWOD-FM (Sacramento, Ca.), **530**
Kyocera's Yashica Dental-Eye camera, **326**

L. A. Gear, 173, 193
Lafayette, Jon, E-3, E-8, E-12
LaFee, Scott, E-9
Lancaster, Francis, E-7
Lancaster, Kent M., E-6
Lanchner, David, E-12
Landis, Dylan, E-8
Lareau, William, 715
La Scala, 312
Lasker, Albert, 6
Laskin, David, 715
L'Auberge, 312
Lawler, Edmund O., E-6
Leading National Advertisers, 432
Ledan, 589
Lee denims, **483**
Lehmkuhl, David C., E-8
Lepisto, Lawrence R., E-1
Letterman, David, 496, 522
Lever Brothers. *See* Unilever
Levin, Gary, E-12
Levine, Huntley, Schmidt & Beaver, 161
Levine, Joshua, E-12
Levinson, Paul, E-3
Levi's, 12, 347
Levison, Ivan, E-7
Levitt, Theodore, 676–77
Levy, Robert, E-10
Lewis, Adele, 715
Library of Congress, 56, 63
Liesse, Julie, E-7, E-10
Lifetime, 514
Lifshey, Earl, E-11
Lincoln, Abraham, 660
Linde, 180
Lindsay, Marsha, E-6
Link, Nina, 507
Lipman, Joanne, E-2, E-3, E-9, E-10, E-11
Lippman, Stacey, 425
Lipson, David, 161
Thomas J. Lipton Co., 376, **376–81**
Listerine, 59, 239, **239**
Lobsenz, Amelia, E-12, 641
Locke, Edwin A., E-3
Lodish, Leonard M., E-10
Loeffler Ketchum Mountjoy, 151
Londre, Larry, 295
Longman, Kenneth, E-8, E-9
Look ski bindings, **147**
Loomis, Kathleen, E-8
Lopez, Ernie, 148
L'Oreal, 23–24, 187, 250, **251**
Lorillard, 54
Los Angeles City Fire Department, 295
Lotus 1-2-3, **35**
Lucas, George H., Jr., E-3
Lucky Supermarket, 141
Lynch, James E., E-6

Maas, Jane, E-8
Mac-Connection, 552
Maclaren/Lintas, 87
Macy's, 134, 461, 646
Madden, Thomas J., E-5
Madison, Cathy, E-8
Magazine Publishers Association, 487, 491, 611, 666
Magnavox, 193
Maidenform, 135, **135**
Makransky, Steve, 351
Mandese, Joe, E-8, E-9
Marceau, Marcel, 652

Margulies, Walter P., E-7
Mark, Margaret, 678
Mark, Reuben, 113
Marken, G. A., E-5
Market Design, 326
Mars, 507
Marshall, Christy, E-3
Martin, Lynn, 401
Martin, Stephen H., 477, E-8, E-9
Martin Agency, 86, **550**
Martin/Williams, **98,** 99
Maslin, Paul, 400
Maslow, Abraham, E-1, 141–42
Mass Retailing Institute, 611
Master, Robert, 411
Mather, John H., E-4
Matheson, William, E-10
Matsushita Electric Industrial Co., 673
Mattel Toys International, 686
Maxell recording tape, 90
May Department Stores Co., 461
Mazda, 588
McAdams, Christian, E-2
McCabe, Ed, 79, 91
McCaghren, Thomas, E-5, E-6
McCann-Erickson, 6, 85, 414, 416, 423, 667, 692
McCarthy, E. Jerome, E-4, E-5, E-6, E-7, E-12
McCarthy, Michael J., E-4, E-5, E-7
McCartney, Paul, 647
McCauley, Lucy A., E-1
McDonald, Frank P., E-4
McDonald's, 12, 604
  agencies and, 110
  Bill Cosby and, 341
  expenditures by, 272, 498
  kids targeted by, 260, 575
  Quebec ad, **334**
  sponsorship by, 647
McDonnell Douglas, **650**
McElligott, Fallon, 295
McElligott, Tom, 25
McEnroe, John, 657
McGeehan, Pat, E-12
McGrath, Allan J., E-4
McGraw-Hill, 27, 687, 688
MCI Communications, 596
McKay, Shona, E-5
McLuhan, Marshall, 16, 130, E-3
McNamara, Robert S., 123
McManus, John, E-1
McNeal, James, 506
McNeil Products Co., 642–43
Media-Advertising Partnership for a Drug-Free America, 663–64, **664,** 665
Mediamark Research, 432, 491, 507
Media Records, 432
Meding, Chuck, 200
Mendel, Cathy, 339
Mendelsohn, Harold, 658
Menon, Anil, E-6
Menswear Retailers of America, 611
Meola, Eric, 317
Mercedes-Benz, 192, 237, 240, 248, 647
Mercury Capri, 165
Meredith Corp., 427, 477
Merrill Lynch, 165, 473, 660
Merryman, Walker, 161
Meyer, Edward D., E-11
Meyerowitz, Steven A., E-2, E-3
Michael, Tom, 326
Michelob, 138
Micklethwait, John, E-3
Microlab, **593**
Microsoft, 298
Miller, Allen, E-10
Miller, Annetta, E-11, E-12
Miller, Cyndee, E-4, E-11
Miller, James C., III, 56
Miller, Marianne, E-10
Miller Myers Bruce DellaCosta, 232
Milliman, Ronald E., E-4

Minneapolis (City of), **569**
Minneapolis Planetarium, 302
Minneapolis Star, **564**
Minnesota Department of Health, **24**
Minnesota Department of Public Health, **569**
Minnesota Orchestra, **306**
Mirolin, **247**
Mitchell, Arnold, 164
Mitchell, Kent, 110
Mitchell, Paul C. N., E-3
Mitsubishi, 180, **657**
M&M/Mars, 507
Mobil, 502, 652, 658
Moes, John, E-12
Mogel, Leonard, 715
Mohrman, Glenn, E-7
Monaghan, Tom, 263
Montgomery Ward, 461, 541-42
Morphis & Friends, 553
Morris, Steven, E-12
Morrisey, William R., E-10
Morton Salt, 308
Moschis, George P., E-4
Motavalli, John, E-9
Motel 6, 344, 385, **385**, 386
MRCA, 205
Mrs. Fields Cookies, 625
Mrs. Gooch's, 623
MTV, 514, 517
Mueller, William, E-2
Mullen Advertising, 317
Murray, Hugh, E-4
Museum of Flight, **563**
Musical Heritage Society, 552
Myers, Jane, E-8
Myers, Marty, 231-32

Nabisco. *See* RJR Nabisco
Naisbett, John, 477
Napolitan, Joseph, 401
Narum, Beverly, E-8
Nash, Tom, E-5
Nashville Network, 517
National Broadcasting Corp., 496, 505, 522, 665-66
National Advertising Division (NAD), 68, **70**
National Advertising Review Board (NARB), 68, 70, 71
National Advertising Review Council, 67, 68-70
National Association for Better Broadcasting, 506
National Association for Female Executives, 487
National Association of Drug Stores, 611
National Car Rental, **590**
National Cash Register, 138
National Consumer League, 74
National Council of Senior Citizens, 75
National Council on Alcoholism, 665
National Dairy Board, **667**
National Decision Systems, 169
National Hispanic Magazine Network, 444
National Office Products Association, 611
National Retail Federation, 611
National Rifle Association (NRA), 149
National Sporting Goods Association, 611
Nature Company, The, **334**
Navistar International, 662
NBC, 496, 505, 522, 665-66
NCR, 138
Neal, Mollie, E-5, E-10
Needham Harper Worldwide, 113
Nelson, Carol, E-10
Nerad, Jack R., E-5
Nestlé, 272, 414, **415**, 416, **417**, 418, 479, 596, 673
Networks, radio, 71, 73
New England Aquarium, **555**
Newport cigarettes, 312
Newsom, Doug, E-12
Newspaper Advertising Bureau, 470, 472, 491, 611
New York City Department of Consumer Affairs, 64
New York Interconnect, 518
New York Lung Association, **99**
New York Subway Advertising, 571

Nick at Night, 514
Nickelodeon, 507, 514
Nielsen, A. C., 20, 202, 205, 507, 508, 509
Nielsen Marketing Research, 423
Nielsen Media Research, 519
Nike, 172, 173, 181, 193, 294, **479**, 480
Nikon, 89
Nissan, 233, 236, **265**, **335**, **448**, 448, 673
Norris, Eileen, E-9, E-11
Northwestern Bell, 50
Nurse Corps, **245**
Nutech Spectra-flanstran, 310
NutraSweet, 647
Nylen, David W., E-5
NYNEX, 351, **352**, 595, **595**

Obsession perfume, **118**
O'Donnell, Maureen, E-11
Office Furniture Warehouse, 626
Office of Consumer Affairs, 56
Ogilvy, David, 22, 250, 287, 294, 301, 308, 327, 341, 342, 346, 363
    bibliography, E-6, E-7, E-8
    on corporate advertising, 658-59, 660
Ogilvy & Mather, 85, 86, 113, 250, 324, 453, 542, 673, 679
Ohmae, Kenichi, E-6
Ohnishi, Yasuhisro, 675
O'Kelley, Winnie, E-8
Olds, Andrew, E-8
Oldsmobile, 344
Oliver, James M., E-6
Olsen, Jarl, 457
Olson, Jerry C., E-3, E-4
Olson, Millie, 344
Omnicom Group, 679
Omni Hotels, **182**
Opinion Research Corp., 660
Original Arizona Jean Co., 221
Orme, Frank, 506
Orval Kent Food Co., 570
O'Sullivan, Maureen, 5, 29
O'Toole, John, 43, 139, 303, E-1, E-4, E-6, E-7
Overman, Stephanie, E-3

Pacific Bell Directory, 595
Packard, Vance, 144
Paetro, Maxine, 715
Palmer, Volney B., 18
Palmolive shampoo, **19**
Panaflex, **409**
Pantone, 374
Parade magazine, **228**
Parents Institute, 308-9
Parker, Marcia, E-8
Parker, Suzy, E-11
Parker pen, **541**
Parks, Michael, E-12
Partnership for a Drug-Free America, 663-64, **664**
Patagonia, 552
Patent and Trademark Office, 56
Patti, Charles H., E-6
Patzer, Gordon L., E-7
Paul, Mark, E-11
Paul, Terry, E-5
Pesale Vision, **15**
Peckham, J. O., 273
Pella windows. 90
Pemberton, John S., 5, 26
Pendleton, Jennifer, E-3
J. C. Penney, 109, 244, 604
    campaign theme, 229, **229**
    catalog, 541
    concept testing by, 224-25, **225**, **226**
    image of, **198**, **199**, 199-200
    information system of, 204
    marketing research by, 201, 202-3, 210-11, 213, 214-15
    marketing strategy of, 220-21

J. C. Penney—*Cont.*
    newspaper advertising by, 461
    Original Arizona Jean Company brand, **221**
    posttesting for, 232-33
    print ads for, 229, 231
    problem and research objectives of, 208-9
    product concept definition by, 222-23, **223**
    questionnaire of, **217**
    target market selection by, 223-24
    TV commercials for, **229**
Pepsi-Cola, 346
    Coke versus, 24, 141, 290
    expenditures by, 272, 498
    international advertising, 12, 689
    radio ads by, 520
    Soviet Union ads, 674, **674**
    video ads, 25, 596
    videocassette ads, 519
Pepsodent, 686
Pepto-Bismol, 588
Perdue, Frank, 79, 80, 89, 92, 346
Perdue Farms/Chickens, **79**, 79-80, **89**, 90, 91, 287, 347, 695
Perform dog food, **537**
Perreault, William D., Jr., E-4, E-5, E-6, E-7, E-12
Perrier, 61, 427, 647
Pesky, Alan, 91
Peter, J. Paul, E-3, E-4
Peter Paul, 585
Petersen, Laurie, E-10
Pfeiffer, Deborah, E-1
Phelps, Stephen P., E-9
Philip Morris, 272, 345, 479, 498, 525, 673
Piedmont Grocery, 540
Pierce, Milton, 543, E-7
Pier I, **602**
Pierre Cardin, 12, **13**, 591
Piirto, Rebecca, E-4, E-12
Pillsbury, 397, 495
PIP Printing, 193, **194**
Pirelli, **476**
Pittsburgh Paints, 526
Plake, Glen, 147
Platta, John A., E-12
Plymouth Laser, 180
Poe, Edgar Allan, 18
Point of Purchase Advertising Institute, 589
Polaroid, 233, 312
Pollock, Ellen Joan, E-2
Porsche, 181, 302, **558**
Porter, Lyman W., E-3
Posner, Fred, E-6, 25, 248
Posner, Vladimir, 674
Postaer, Larry, 344
Poston, Tom, 623
Potenzano, John, E-9
Pounce, **45**
J. D. Power & Associates, **241**
Powers, John, 110
Pratt & Whitney, **3**, 593
Premier Limousine, **629**
Price Choppers, 587
Prime Cuts haircutting salon, 295
Procter & Gamble, 520
    agencies and, **102**, 102-4, 110, 113, 114
    comparative advertising by, 67
    Crest, 176, **176**, 191, 239, **239**
    expenditures by, 272, 479, 498, 525, 673
    newspaper insert, 466
    premiums from, 585-86
    spot announcements by, 499
    TV use by, 501
Productivity Products International, 662
Profile bread, 59
Provigo grocery stores, 139, **140**
Prudential-Bache Securities, 296, **297**
PSA Peugeot-Citroen SA, 673
Publishers Clearing House, 540
Puma, 193
Python, Monty, 522

Quaker Oats, 543, 547, 548, 585
Quarles, Rebecca Colwell, E-1, E-6
Quebec Tourism, 301, **304**
Quelch, John A., E-6
Quinn, Jane Bryant, E-2

RADAR, 529
Radio Advertising Bureau, 611
Radio Luxembourg, 688
Ralston Purina, 66, 272
Ramada Inns, 450
Rangaswamy, Arvind, E-6
Ranzer, Judith, 477
Raphael, Murray, E-7, E-10
Raphaële Digital Transparencies, 351
Rapp, Stan, 257, E-1, E-5
Rawl, Lawrence G., 639
Raymond, Miner, E-8
RCA, 23, 312
Reader's Digest, **484,** 484-85
Reader's Digest Association, 685
Red Cross, 664, 668
Reddy, Allan C., E-1
Redenbacher, Orville, 240
Redgrave, Lynn, 346
Redland Roof Tiles, **690**
Reebok, 156, 172-73, **173,** 191, 193, 195
Reese, Teresa, E-7
Reeves, Rosser, 22
Reidenbach, R. Eric, E-6
Reinhard, Keith, 110-11
Reitman, Judith, E-8
Renault SA, 673
Revson, Charles, 246
R.J. Reynolds. *See* RJR Nabisco
Rhode Island Hospital, **66**
Rice, B., E-4
Richards Group, 385
Richardson, Leon, E-5
Richmond Slate, **690**
Ries, A1, 22-23, 24, 138, 160, 222, 238, 240, 263, 299
   bibliography, E-1, E-4, E-6
Riggle, David, E-2
Riney, Hal, 20
Riordan, Michael H., E-1
Ritz crackers, 144
RJR Nabisco, 54, 160-61, 272, 478, 659
Roberts, John H., E-6
Robin, Donald B., E-6
Robinson, Frank M., 26
Robinson, Michael J., E-9
Robinson, William A., E-11
J. W. Robinson's Department Store, **559**
Rockwell, Norman, 322
Rockwell International, **656**
Rogan, Helen, E-10
Rogers, Buck, 302
Rolex, 679
Rolling Stone, **137,** 295, **296**
Rolls-Royce, 22, 294, 481
Roman, Kenneth, E-8
Roman, Murray, E-5
Rosalp, **683**
Rose, Robert L., E-11
Rosenwein, Rifka, E-11
Rosser, Margaret, E-9
Rothman, Andrea, E-9
Royal Silk, 542
Royal Viking Lines, **421**
Rubenstein, James, E-11
Rubin, Hanna, E-10
Rubin Postaer & Associates, 86, 344
Rubio, Ralph, 603-4, 608, 617
Rubio's Deli-Mex, **603,** 603-4, 608
Ruhaak, John, 289
Ruhr/Paragon, 86
Runner's World, **492**
Rushton, Angela, E-6
Ryan, Bernard, Jr., E-6

Saatchi, Charles, 113
Saatchi, Maurice, 113
Saatchi & Saatchi, 85, 86, 113, 114, 679
Sabato, Larry, 400
Sachs, Susan, E-11
Saddler, Jeanne, E-12
Sail magazine, **265**
St. Joseph aspirin, 143
Saks Fifth Avenue, 150
Salisbury, Mike, 394, 395, 396, 398, 403, 411
Salk, Lee, 507
Salmon, Caryn C., E-3
Salmon, Charles T., E-3
Salmon, Walter J., E-6
Samuelson, Robert J., 48, E-1
San Diego Zoo, **459, 474, 563**
San Francisco Examiner, **295**
Sangertown Square, **467**
Sara Lee, 481, 662
Sarel, Can, E-8
Satow, Kay, 28
Saunders, John, E-6
Save the Battlefield Coalition, **32**
Savin, 138
Scali, McCabe, Sloves, 79, **89,** 89-90, 93
Scali, Sam, 91
Scarborough Research Corp., 469
Schering Corp., 520
Schernecker, Jim, 65
Schmidt, Peggy J., 715
Schmidt, Robert, 161
Schneider, Cy, 506
Schneider, John, E-10
Schoenwald, Marvin, E-7
School of Visual Art, **316**
Schreiner, Tim, E-10
Schroer, James C., E-5, E-6
Schultz, Don E., E-4
Charles Schwab & Co., 539
Schwartz, Judith D., E-2
Schwedelson, Roy, 543
Schweitzer, George, 659
Schweppes, 519
Scientific American, 687
Scope mouthwash, 239, **239**
Scotch tape, 63
Scott, Alan, E-12
Scott, David Clark, E-6
Scott, Jeffrey E., E-7
Seabrook, **564**
Sears Roebuck & Co., 14, 193, 461, 498, 604, 660
   Canadian ads, **682**
   catalog, 541
   expenditures by, 272, 461, 525
   New York City suit, 64
   J. C. Penney and, 223
Sea World, 295
Second Chance, **49**
Securities and Exchange Commission, 57
Sedelmaier, Joe, 347
Seiko, 647
Sellers, Patricia, E-12
Selwitz, Robert, E-3
Serafin, Raymond, E-1
Settle, Robert B., E-4, E-5
7 South 8th for Hair, 457, **457,** 466
Seventh Generation, 552
7UP, 23
Sewall, Murphy A., E-8
Sew Pro's, 606
Seymour, Daniel Thomas, E-1
Shalek, Nancy, 344
Shama, Avraham, E-11
Sharkey, Betsy, E-7
Sharper Image, 542
Shaw, Bill, E-2
Shaw, David, E-2
Shell, 312, 660
Shelling, Robert O., 715
David Shepard Associates, E10

Shepherd, Cybill, 666
Sherwin-Williams, 427
Showtime, 513
Shudson, Michael, E-1, 47
Siegel, Marc, 351
Sierra Club, **42**
Simmons Market Research Bureau, 202, 432, 444, 469, 491, 507
Simon, Paul (senator), 401
Simpson, Rachel, E-8
Singer, Jules B., 715
Sissors, Jack Z., E-8, E-9
Skenzay, Lenore, E-3
Sloan, Pat, E-6
Small Business Administration, 611
Smalley, John K., E-2
Smartfood popcorn, **561**
Smith, Allen E., E-3
Smith, Desmond, E-1, E-3
Smith, Robert, 543
Smith Corona typewriters, 294
Smucker's, 288, 289
Snow board, **265**
Snuggles, 397
Snyder hairspray, **264, 494**
Soldow, Gary F., E-3
Solomon, Jolie, E-3
Sommerfield, Frank, E-9, E-11
Sonnenrich, Rena, E-3
Sony, 586, 674
Sorrell Ridge, 288, 289
Sosa & Associates, 87
Southwestern Bell, **653**
Spadoni, Marie, E-7
Spalding, 146, **307**
SpanAmerican, 444
Sparrow, Sam, E-3
Spaulding, Mark, E-7
Specialty Advertising Association International, 591, 592
Speedo, **183**
Sperry, 662
Sperry & Hutchinson, 587
Spielman, Harold M., E-7
Sport Chalet, 134
SRI International, 163, 164
Standard Oil of New Jersey, 660
Standard Rate & Data Service, 73, 202, 205, **381,** 432, 491, **544**
Stansfield, Richard H., E-7
Starch, Daniel, 20
Starch INRA Hooper, **234**
State Farm, **148**
Steadman, Ralph, 683
Steers, Richard M., E-3
Stein, Sid, 202-3
Steinberg, Janice, E-10
Steinem, Gloria, 50
Stepstone, Inc., 662
Stern, Aimee, E-9
Stern, Judith A., E-6
Stevens, Art, E-12, 643
Stevenson, Richard W., E-9
Stewart, David W., E-5
Stone, Bob, 542, E-10
Stone, Elhanan C., E-2
Strazewski, Len, E-9
Stresstabs, 440
Studebaker, **39**
Sullivan, Louis, 160, 161
Sunkist, 108, 180, **181,** 196, 285, 312
Supreme Court, 65
Surmanek, Jim, E-9
Suzuki, **554**
Sweet 'N Low, **264**
Sylvania, 329
Sylvester, Cam, E-8

Takara, 686

Talon, Inc., **332**
Tang, 676, **677**
Taos Furniture, **579**
Tappan, James, 113
Tashjian, Edward, E-3
Taylor, John H., E-2
TCF, **333**
Technics electronic piano, **59**
Teledyne, 595
Television Bureau of Advertising, 611
Templin, Neal, E-1
Texaco, 312
Texas Dept. of Tourism, **154**
Thill, John V., E-3
Thomas, Hester, E-7
Thomas, Lacy Glenn, E-6
Thompson, Jack K., E-11
Thompson, Page, E-8
J. Walter Thompson Co., 85, 108, 113, 453, **567,** 679
Thrasher, Hugh, 344
3M Company, 297, **327,** 646, **655,** 675
Tide detergent, 312
Timberland Company, **475**
    ad design development for, 317-18, **318**
    ad layout for, 319, **320,** 321, 323, 324
    visuals for, 328, 329
Timberline boots, **305**
Time, 687
Times-Mirror, 88, 477
Time Warner, 272, 685
Timex watches, 192
Tom Thumb Page stores, 627-28, **628**
Toor, Mat, E-3
Toshiba Corp., 643, **644**
Toy, Stewart, E-5, E-8
Toyota, 237, 272, 479, 604
Toys "Я" Us, 266
Trachtenberg, Jeffrey A., E-1
TransAmerica, 481
Transit Advertising Association, 570
Trident, 180
Tri-State Cadillac Dealers Association, **635**
Trout, Jack, 22-23, 24, 138, 222, 238, 240, 263, 299
    bibliography, E-1, E-4, E-6
TRW, 506, **510,** 511
Tully, John P., 53
Turk, Judy Vanslyke, E-12
Turner, Mike, 324
Tutelian, Louise, E-10
20th Century Fox, 453
Tyco Toys, 449
Tyson, Mike, 516

U-Haul, 66, 595
Underwriters Laboratories, 75, 308
Ungar, Aharon, 635
Unilever, 108, 180, 250, 272, 479, 673
Union Oil, **36**
Unisys, 662

United Negro College Fund, 668
U.S. Army, 145, **245,** 246, 287, 666
U.S. Coast Guard, **303,** 305, 308
U.S. Department of Agriculture, 56-57
U.S. Department of Commerce, 166, 204
U.S. Department of Justice, 57
U.S. Department of Transportation, 668
U.S. Food and Drug Administration, 56, 59, 61
U.S. Navy, 666
U.S. Office of Consumer Affairs, 542
U.S. Postal Service, 56, 545, 546, 551, 666
United States government, 524
United States Savings and Loan League, 611
United Technologies, 87, **654**
United Way, **292,** 647, 668
Upjohn, 61
Urban, Glen L., E-6
USAir, 88
USA Today International, **685**
USWest, **303**
UTA French Airlines, **558**

Varadarajan, P. Rajan, E-6
Vaughn, Richard, E-6
Vepco, **330**
Vicks, 263
Video Information Network, 596
Vienna, **682**
Will Vinton Productions, 397
VISA, **66,** 89, 647, 674, **691**
Voice of America, 688
Volkswagen, 23, **23**
Volvo, 20, 53, **54,** 239, 361, **361**
von Keitz, Beate, E-6
Von's, 141

Wackman, Daniel B., E-3
Waldman, Marvin, 378
Walker, Orville C., Jr., E-4
Wall, John, E-4
Wallach, Van, E-5
Walley, Wayne, E-9
Wall Street Journal/Europe, **685**
Wal-Mart, 54
Walton, Barbara, E-10
Warner Lambert, 272, **567**
Warwick, John, 111
Wasserman, Dick, 715
Watkins, Robert J., E-2
WBRZ (Baton Rouge, La.), **573**
Weaver, Jane, E-12
Weber, Suzanne, E-8
Weed, Steven, E-12
Weight Watchers, 346
Weinstein, Bob, E-8
Weismuller, Johnny, 29
Welcome Wagon, 587
Wells Rich Green, 109

Weltz, Richard N., E-12
Wendy's, 193
Wentz, Laurel, E-12
West, Jonathan P., 715
West Coast Video, **427**
Western Bankcorporation, 662
Western International Media, 88
Westvaco paper, **11,** 12
Wetzel, Kerry, **633**
Whirlpool appliances, 312
White, Bill, 351
White, Hooper, E-7
Whittle Communications, 507
Wiener Festwochen, **690**
Willis, Gordon, E-6
Wilson, Robert F., 715
Barry Wilson's Auto Repair, **294**
Wind, Jerry, E-6
Winski, Joseph M., E-3
Winston Network, 559, 570
Wolf, Bob, 288
Wolf, Sharon, E-6
Woman's Day, **571**
Wong, John, E-5
Woodruff, Robert B., E-4, E-5, E-6
Worthington, Cal, 628-29
WPP Group, 113, 679
Wrangell, George, 22
Wrangler jeans, **130**
Wrigley's Gum, 566

Xerox, 312
    international sales, 675
    Palette ad, **675**
    positioning by, 178, **179**
    program sponsorship by, 498, 502
    Savin versus, 183
    trademark, **62,** 63

Yagoda, Ben, E-12
Yamaha, 246
Yankelovich, Skelly and White, 113, 163, 658
Yesawich, Peter C., E-7
York, Alex, 715
Young & Rubicam, 85, 86, **87,** 111, 113, 165, 351, 376, 678, 679
Younkers department stores, 626-27

Zaslow, Jeffrey, E-4
Zell Bros., **606**
Zenith, 308
Ziegenhagen, M. E., E-3
Zipser, Andy, E-3
Zotti, Ed, E-4
Zurzhard, Gary, E-3

SUBJECT INDEX

AAAA Standards of Practice, 76
Abundance principle, 38-39
Academy leader, 411
Account executives, 90
Account management, by agencies, 90
Action, ad copy and, 291, 292, 293
Action advertising, 253
Action programs, in marketing plan, 250, 252
Acura automobiles, 66, 237, 240-41
    advertising plan for, 255, 259-60, 261, 262, 263
    Integra, 247, 250
    Legend, 247, 262
    marketing plan for, 242, 244, 247, 249, 250, 251
Ad/Pro, 629
Advertisements
    from concept through production, 376-82
    creation of, 84
    posttesting, 232-34
    pretesting, 228-31
    readership studies of, 327
Advertisers, 84
    agency relationship with, 107-14
    checklist for, 114
    communication by, 128-31
    expenditures by, 272
    large, 100-106
    self-regulation by, 76
    small, 106-7
Advertising
    action, 15, 16
    awareness, 15
    business components of, 80-82
    career planning, 708-18
    codes, 75
    commercial, 15
    comparative (*see* Comparative advertising)
    cooperative, 192, 581, 634-36
    corporate (*see* Corporate advertising)
    corrective, 59
    definition of, 6-8
    early broadcast, 21
    early regulation of, 18, 20
    economic impact of, 32-40
    English language and, 43, 45-46
    ethics (*see* Ethical dilemmas; Ethics)
    evolution, 16-21
    functions and effects, 26-27, 32
    government, 666-67
    institutional, 14, 606-7, 653 (*see also* Corporate advertising)
    international (*see* International advertising)
    job titles, 710-11
    local (*see* Local advertising)
    manager, 106
    noncommercial (*see* Noncommercial advertising)
    nonproduct, 14
    objectives (*see* Objectives)
    persuasiveness of, 8
    place and, 189, 191-94
    price and, 186-89, 190
    product and, 172-86
    proliferation of, 48
    promotion and, 194-96
    public relations versus, 640-41
    regulation (*see* Regulation)
    reinforcement, 256
    sales and, 268-69, 274
    social impact of, 43-54
    sponsors, 8
    subliminal, 144
    unfair and deceptive, 52
Advertising, the Uneasy Persuasion, 47

Advertising Age, 120, 201, 205, 226, 401, 496, 578, 709
Advertising agencies. *See* Agencies
Advertising allowances, 580
Advertising associations, self-regulation by, 75, 76
Advertising budgets, 270-74. *See also* Budgets/budgeting
Advertising Career Directory, 709
Advertising classifications, 8, 9
    geographic area, 12-14
    medium, 14
    purpose, 14-16
    target audience, 8-12
Advertising departments
    organization of, 100-106
    people in, 80-82
    tasks of, 82-84
Advertising development, research categories, 222
Advertising expenditure curves, 617
Advertising materials, 581
Advertising plan, 252
    creative mix, 258-63, 264-65
    fund allocation, 266-74
    for local advertisers, 615-16
    objectives, 252-59
    outline, 704-7
"Advertising Principles of American Business," 76
Advertising production. *See* Production
Advertising pyramid, 254-56
Advertising research, 199-200
    cost of, 220
    creative-concept testing, 224-26
    definition of, 202
    interpreting and reporting findings, 219
    local, 609-11
    need for, 200-201, 202
    posttesting, 226, 232-34
    pretesting, 226-32
    strategy determination, 221-24
    surveys, 227
    types of, 221, 222
Advertising strategy
    copywriting and, 280-87
    creative mix and, 258-63, 264-65
    research, 221-24
Advertorials, 658-59
Advocacy advertising, 659, 661
Adweek, 709
Aerial banners and lights, 426
Affidavit of performance, 512
Africa, 686, 694
Age groups, merchandise purchased by, 159
Agencies. *See also* Advertising departments
    administration of, 93
    à la carte services, 88-89
    checklist review of, 108
    client relationship with, 107-14
    client sources of, 98-100
    commission for, 86
    definition of, 80, 84
    financial data on, 85
    income sources of, 96-98
    in-house, 104-6
    international, 678-80
    largest, 85
    for local advertisers, 631-33
    mergers of, 113
    role of, 84, 86
    self-regulation by, 75-76
    structure of, 94-96
    tasks of, 89-93
    types of, 86-89
Agency networks, 680

Agricultural advertising, 12
Aided recall, 232
AIDS, 48, 54
Aim toothpaste, 180
Airbrush, 332
Alaska, 562, 639-40
Alcohol advertising, 143, 692
Almond Joy, 585
Alpine car CD player, 135
AMC Jeep, 238
American Airlines, 647
American Baby, 547
American Demographics, 205
American Photographer, 477
American Vegetable Grower, 12
America's Marathon, 646
AM radio, 520-21
Amsterdam News, 462
Anacin, 347
Animatic, 341
Animation, 348, 397
Annual reports, 650
Answer print, 412
A-1 steak sauce, 312
Appeals, 282-83, 689-90
Applied Arts Quarterly, 716
Architectural Digest, 477, 481
Archives of Ophthalmology, 12
Area probability sampling, 216
Areas of dominant influence, 509
Arkansas, 64
Armco vacuum cleaner, 310
Arpege, 297
Arriflex camera, 408
Arrow shirts, 312
Art
    definition of, 318-19
    layout, 319, 321, 323-28
    in package design, 336-39
    in print ads, 319, 321, 323-32
    in radio and TV ads, 339-48
Art direction, 284, 317-18
Art director, 322, 334-37
Artist, role of, 322
Artistic principles, 320-21
Art services, for local advertising, 634
Ascenders, 361
Atlanta, 5, 26, 560
Atra Plus razor, 671
AT&T calling card, 344
Attention, 288, 289, 293, 445-46
Attitude(s), 141, 610
Attitude tests, 232, 234
Audience composition, 510
Audience Market by Market for Outdoor, 559
Audience objectives, 430-32
Auding, 299
Audio, for script, 341
Audio console, 393
Audiovisual materials, for public relations, 652
Audis, 250
Austin, Texas, 73
Australia, 695
Austria, 694-95
Automotive advertising, expenditures on, 272
Automotive News, 610
Avails, 511
Average quarter-hour, 530
Aviation Week & Space Technology, 688
Awareness, of product, 123
Awareness advertising, 15

Bait-and-switch, 52
Balance, in art, 320
Baltimore, 14
Band-Aid bandages, 63, 590
Barbie Doll, 686
Barter syndication, 499, 500
Base art, 357
Basic bus, 570
Baton Rouge, La., 513
Bayer aspirin, 33-34
Beacon, New York, 515
Behavior, consumer. *See* Consumer behavior
Behavioristic segmentation, 159-63
Belgium, 681, 687, 688, 694-95
Benefits
    of advertising, 51-52
    in headlines, 295
    in visuals, 329-30
Benefit segmentation, 160
Bermuda, 270
Better Homes and Gardens, 427, 477, 489
Betty Crocker, 312
Beverly Hills, 623
Biarritz, 312
Bic pens, 192
Big idea, 284, 286-87
Billboard ads, 553-55
    advantages and disadvantages, 438
    locations map, 558
    for Provigo, 139, 140
    rates, 560
    for Wrangler, 130
Billboards
    electronic, 426
    mobile, 571
Billiard ball principle, 33
Birchscan, 529
Black, in art design, 333
Blacks, advertising to, 160-61, 571
Blanket, 373
Bleed pages, 480
Blimps, 426
Blinking, 450
Blue, in art design, 333
BMW, 250
Body copy, 298, 300-305, 308
Book, The, 507
Boston, 490
Boston Globe, The, 74, 470
Boston Newsletter, 17
Bottom-Up Marketing, 240
Bottom-up marketing, 262-63, 266-67
Boxes, for copy, 308
Brain-pattern analysis, 230
Brand development index, 436
Branding, 180-82
Brand loyalty, 140-41
Brand managers, 103
Brazil, 681, 695
Broadcast advertising. *See also* Radio; Television
    pretesting, 228-29, 230
    rise of, 21
    types, 498-500
Broadcast commercials, 339-45. *See also* Radio commercials; Television commercials
Broadcast media, for local advertising, 622-23
Broadcast production, 92
Broadsides, 540
Brown, in art design, 333
Budgets/budgeting, 82, 83
    buildup method, 273-74
    for international advertising, 690-91
    for local advertising, 614-17, 618
    pretesting, 227-28
Bulletin boards, for public relations, 651
Bureau of Census Catalog, 611
Burger King Kids Club, 575-76, 583
Bursting, 450
Business advertising, 9-12, 690
Business cycles, advertising effect on, 37-38

Business environment, fund allocation and, 269-70
Business magazines, 483
Business markets, 127, 165-67
Business Periodicals Index, 204, 610
Business Publication Rates and Data, 491
Business purchasing procedures, 166
Business reply mail, 546
Business Service Checklist, 611
Business Week, 11, 205, 448, 477, 487, 688
Bus-o-rama signs, 570
Buy-back allowances, 580
Buyers Guide to Outdoor Advertising, 560

Cable television, 25
    advantages, 515-17
    audience trends, 513
    buying time on, 518
    competition for, 518-19
    cost of, 517
    in creative mix, 515-19
    disadvantages, 517-18
    history, 512-13
    major networks, 514
    ratings, 513-14
    revenues, 515
    viewers of, 514-15
Cadillac, 22, 240
California, 166, 667
California raisins, 397, 398, 495
Camel cigarettes, 481
Camera-ready art, 357
Cameras, for TV commercials, 408-9
Campbell soups, 211, 212, 499
Canada, 181, 212, 273, 687. *See also specific locations*
    advertising agencies in, 85, 86, 87
    Air Canada ad, 286
    Bermuda Department of Tourism ad, 270
    cable TV in, 513
    film and video production in, 395
    General Foods ad, 359
    languages in, 681, 682, 695
    market segmentation for, 157
    Mirocast Whirlpool ad, 247
    social environment of, 681
    subculture in, 147
    target marketing in, 158
    transit ads in, 570
Canadian Advertising Rates & Data, 205
Canadian Business, 205, 716
Canadian Consumer, 205
Cap'n Crunch cereal, 548, 588
Careers, in advertising, 708-18
Carmel, California, 621
Cartoons, 397
Case, of type, 362
Catalogs, 541
Category development index, 436-37
Cease-and-desist order, 59
Celebrity endorsements, 52, 58, 65, 330, 346-47
Census Tract Studies, 611
Center Island Pennysavers, 620
Central location tests, 229, 230, 231
Cents-off promotions, 585
Cereals, 38, 162
Certifiably Nuts, 186
Certs, 304
"Channel One," 507
Character-count method, 364-65
Charlotte, North Carolina, 151, 509
Charmin bathroom tissue, 297
Chattanooga, Tennessee, 26
Cheltenham type family, 360
Cherry 7UP, 587
Chevrolet trucks, 291
Chicago, 13, 85, 622-23, 626
Chicago magazine, 483
Chicago Tribune, 74
Children, advertising to, 68, 506-7, 692
Children as Consumers, 506

Children Protection Act of 1966, 57
"Children's Television Workshop," 507
China, 685, 695
Choice, advertising effect on, 37
Christian Science Monitor, 466
Cigarette advertising, 47, 54, 160-61
Cincinnati, 311
Cinematographer, 405
Circulars, for local advertising, 624
Circulation, magazine, 485-88
Circulation information, 469
Clairol, 296
Clarity, in art, 321
Classes, social, 144-45
Classified advertising, 468
Classified directories, 624
Clearance advertising, 606
Clearwater, Florida, 169
Clients. *See* Advertisers
Clip art, 634
Close-up toothpaste, 180
Closing dates, 357-58
Clutter tests, 229
Coca-Cola
    bottle design, 27
    Chinese ad, 691
    clothing, 181
    history of, 5-7, 26-31
    Pepsi versus, 288
    in trade advertising, 11-12
Cognition, in consumer behavior, 136
Cognitive dissonance, 152
Cognitive theory, 139
Coke. *See* Coca-Cola
Colgate toothpaste, 239
Collateral sales material, 582
Colombian coffee, 134
Color, 19, 20, 336, 556
Color advertising, in newspapers, 471
Color separation negatives, 375
Color strips, in magazines, 481
Combination offers, 587
Command headlines, 297
Commercial artist, role of, 322
Commercials, 339-45. *See also* Radio commercials; Television commercials
Commission, for agencies, 86, 96
Communication(s), 18, 61, 129-31
Communications Act of 1934, 56, 61, 72
Communications media, in creative mix, 262
Community involvement, 99, 626, 645
Company conventions, 582
Comparative advertising, 24
    court rulings on, 66-67
    ethics of, 290-91
    false and misleading, 52
    international regulations, 692
Comparative pricing, 188
Competition
    abundance principle and, 39
    advertising effect on, 36-37
    in local advertising, 609
    in magazines, 479
    price and, 187-88
Compiled lists, 544
Comprehension, in consumer behavior, 136
Comprehensive layout, 325
Computer-generated drawings, 332
Computer Marketing, 205
Computers, 10-11, 354-56, 452-54
Computer software, 596
Computer technology, 25
Computerworld Poland, 688
Concept testing, 224-26
Conceptualization, in copywriting, 284
Conditioning theory, 139
Condoms, 48-49
Connoisseur, 477
Consent decree, 58
Consultants, local advertising and, 633

Consumer advertising, 9
Consumer agencies, 86-87
Consumer behavior
  from advertising perspective, 131-32
  cultural influence on, 147-48
  decision making, 132, 150
  definition of, 131
  environment influence on, 149
  familial influence on, 143
  learning, 137, 139-41
  motivation, 141-43
  perception, 133-37
  personal processes in, 132, 133
  place influence on, 149
  positioning and, 138
  societal influence on, 143-47
  time influence on, 149
Consumer groups, regulation by, 74-75
Consumerism, 74
Consumer Magazine and Argi-Media Rates and
  Data, 491
Consumer magazines, 483
Consumer markets, 128
Consumer movement, 19, 20, 23
Consumer promotions, 577. See also Pull strategies
Consumers
  choice by, 37
  demand by, 37
  international, 689-90
  knowledge of, 131
Contests, 581-82, 587-88, 625
Continuity, 449, 451-52
  in art, 321
Contour Plus razor, 671
Contrast, in art, 321
Controlled circulation, 487
Control room, 393
Conventions, 582
Cooperative advertising, 192, 581, 634-36
Copy
  approval process, 313
  definition of, 91
  radio, 386-87
Copy blocks, effective size of, 327-28
Copy casting, 364-65
Copy platform, 281-82, 284, 285
Copy points, 183
Copyright, 63
Copywriters, 91, 286-87, 301
Copywriter's pyramid, 287-91, 293
Copywriting
  advertising strategy and, 280-87
  appeals in, 282-83
  big idea in, 284, 286-87
  copy approval, 313
  creating product names, 312
  by Henry Ford, 279-80
  message strategy, 280-84
  pitfalls, 309-11, 313
  process of, 313-14
  product marketing facts for, 282-83
  seeing vs. hearing, 299-300
  setting objectives, 287-91
  subheads, 297-98
  Sunkist copy platform, 285
  writing checklist, 301
Copywriting terminology, 291-92
  body copy, 298, 300-303, 308
  boxes and panels, 308
  headlines, 292, 294-97
  seals, logotypes, signatures, 308-9
  slogans, 308
Cordova, 312
Corporate advertising, 652, 658-59, 661-62. See also
  Institutional advertising
  definition of, 14, 652
  identity advertising, 661-62
  portfolio, 654-57
  recruitment advertising, 661-62
Corporate Canada Online, 205
Corporate Video Decisions, 487

Corrective advertising, 59
Cosmetics ads, in 1980s, 23-24
Cosmopolitan, 489
Cost efficiency, of media, 447
Cost per rating point, 511-12
Cost per thousand, 447, 450, 462, 489-90
County and City Data Book, 611
County Business Patterns, 611
Couponing, electronic, 597
Coupons, 583-87, 625
Court rulings, recent, 64-67
CoverStory, 209
CPM, 447, 453, 462, 489-90
CPP, 511-12
Cracker Jack, 586
Craftsman, 181
Cragmont, 181
Crain's Chicago Business, 483
Crain's New York Business, 87, 88, 525
Creative boutiques, 88, 634
Creative Code, 76
Creative concepts, in agencies, 91
Creative-concept testing, 224-26
Creative mix, 227, 258-63, 264-65
Credibility, of ad copy, 290-91, 293
Crest toothpaste, 12, 68, 176, 191, 239
Crisis communications, 642-43
Criticisms, social, 44-52
Crosfield workstation, 354
CRT typesetters, 366
Culture, consumer behavior and, 147-48
Cume audience, 531-32
Current Retail Trade, 611
Cursive type, 360
Customer analysis, for local advertising, 609-10
Customers, definition of, 126

Dakota cigarettes, 54
Dallas, 627-28
Dallas Home and Garden, 621
Data, research, 204, 211, 213, 214
Database marketing, 547
Datril, 239
Dayparts, 453, 509-10, 529-30
DBS, 519
Deadlines, 357-58
Dealer meetings, 582
Decadence fragrance, 312
Deceptive advertising, 50, 52, 56-57. See also Unfair
  advertising
Decision making, consumer, 132, 150
Decoding, in communication, 130
Defamation, in copy, 311, 313
Delaware, 64
Deluxe software, 185
Demand
  advertising effect on, 37
  price and, 186-87
  primary, 174
  selective, 175
Demarketing, 24, 663
Demographic segmentation, 157-59
Demonstration commercial, 346
Denmark, 694-95
Dentists, advertising by, 65
Denver, 560
Descenders, 361
Desenex, 520
Designated market areas, 509
Desire, ad copy and, 290-91, 293
Desktop publishing, 354-56
Des Moines Register, 626-27
Detroit, 560
Detroit Free Press, 73
Device copy, 301-2
Dialogue copy, 301
DIALOG Information Service, 205
Diet Coke, 290
Diet Pepsi, 290
Digital video effects units, 398

Dino-Riders, 449
Direct advertising, 536
Direct broadcast satellite, 519
Direct-impression composition, 366
Direct mail
  advantages, 438, 547-50
  buying, 542-46
  in creative mix, 540-52
  definition of, 536
  direct marketing versus, 536-38
  disadvantages, 438, 550-52
  distribution, 545-46
  growth of, 538-39
  guidelines, 551
  lists, 542-45
  for local advertising, 624-25
  privacy issue, 542-43
  production and handling, 545
  top product categories, 539
  types, 540-41
Direct mail, tests, 230
Direct Mail List Rates and Data, 544
Direct marketing, direct mail versus, 537-37
Directories, 594-95, 624
Directory of Associations in Canada, 204
Directory of National Trade Associations, 204
Direct questioning, 230, 231
Direct-response advertising, 253, 537-38
Disclaimers, 70-71
Disclosures, 52, 58
Disney animation style, 397
Display advertising, 466
Display allowances, 580
Displays, 555
Display type, 358
Distribution, 187, 189, 191-94
Diverting, 579
Dodge automobiles, 50, 294, 481
Domino's pizza, 266
Donnelley Directory, 595
Dove soap, 250, 287
Dow Jones News Retrieval Service, 205
Drug advertising, 59, 60-61, 693
Dubs, 394
Dummy, 321, 324-25
Dupes, 412
Dutch doors, 481

Ebony, 234, 477
Economics, 32-40, 268-69
Edsel, 22, 119-20, 123, 201
Electronic billboards, 426
Electronic couponing, 597
Electronic Pied Piper, The: The Business and Art of
  Children's Television, 506
Electronic Product News, 687
Electronics, 11
Electronic signs, 598
Elle, 150, 152, 689
Emotional appeals, 282
Empirical research method, for funds allocation, 274
Encoding, in communication, 129
Encyclopedia of Associations, 611
Endorsements, 52, 58, 65, 330, 346-47
Energizer Bunny, 400, 495-96
English language, advertising effect on, 43, 45-46
English Leather, 303
"Entertainment Coast-to-Coast," 522
"Entertainment Tonight," 499
Environment, 149, 552, 565, 681-85
Escada, 150, 152
Esquire, 79
Ethical dilemmas, 53
  advertorials, 658-59
  childrens' TV ads, 506-7
  cigarettes targeted to blacks, 160-61
  client-agency conflicts, 110-11
  comparative advertising, 288-89
  direct-mail privacy, 542-43

Ethical dilemmas—*Cont.*
  imitation vs. plagiarism, 344-45
  political advertising, 400-401
Ethics
  advertiser's responsibility, 52-54
  lapses, 53-54
  laws and, 53
  subliminal manipulation, 144
  truth in advertising, 20-21, 50, 52
Ethnic groups, advertising portrayal of, 49-50
Ethnic specialty ads, 87
Euphemisms, in copy, 311
Europe
  advertising regulations in, 694-95
  athletic shoes in, 193
  automobiles from, 240
  economic community 685
  languages in, 693-94
  purchasing decision in, 691-92
  TV sets in, 686-87
European Business, 687
Evaluation and testing, 226-34
Evaluations, 132, 152
Eveready Energizer battery, 495-96
Exchanges, marketing and, 124, 125, 126
Executive Female, 487
Exhibits, for public relations, 651
Expenditures, 267-74, 617
Experimental method, in research, 210
Explorer, 122-23
Export agencies, 680
Exposure, 445
Exxon Valdez, 639-40, 641, 643
Eye-movement camera, 230
Fable, A, 652
Fairness Doctrine, 72
Family, consumer behavior and, 143
Family Circle, 489
Farm Journal, 483
Farm publications, 483
Farm Supplier, 610
FCB grid, 261
Feature articles, in public relations, 649-50
Federal Hazardous Substances Act of 1960, 57
Federal regulation. *See* Regulation, federal
Feedback, in communication, 130-31
Field and Stream, 477
Film, tape versus, 412-13
Film negatives, 382
Financial Times (London), 687
Finland, 694-95
First amendment rights, 65-66, 72
First-class mail, 546
First-run syndication, 499
Fish Called Wanda, A, 519
Flammable Fabrics Act of 1954, 57
Flighting, 449
Flights, ads during, 426
Flyers, 540, 624
Flying, 489
FM radio, 520-21
Focus groups, 212-13, 230
Focus Magazine, 546
Folders, 540
Font, 361
Food advertising, 59, 61, 272
Forbes, 205, 448
Ford automobiles, 294, 312
Ford Model T, 279, 280
Ford Mustang, 295, 296
Formula models, in media planning, 453
Form utility, 122
For Oily Hair Only, 160
Ft. Worth, Texas, 462, 590
Fortune, 113, 205, 448
Forward buying, 579
Four-color process, 374
Fragrance strips, in magazines, 481
France, 676, 677, 681, 689, 694-95
Franchises, 193
Free-lancers, local advertising and, 633

Free-standing inserts, 583-84
French language, 695
Frequency, 433, 450, 451-52
Fuji film, 400
Fuji film, 400
Full-service agencies, 86-87
Fund raising, public relations and, 647
Funds allocation, 270-74
Funstuff, 575

Gallagher Report, The, 660
Galvanometer, 230
Games (promotion), 588
Gasoline prices, 36
Gatefolds, 481
Geographic segmentation, 157
Gerber baby foods, 312
Germany, 686, 694-95
Gleem toothpaste, 481
Global structure, 676-78
Globe, 462
Godiva chocolates, 329
Gold Seal salmon, 338
Golf Digest, 477
Good Housekeeping, 73, 423, 489
Goodwill, 14
Gotcha surfwear, 394-95, 396-97, 398, 399, 403, 411
Gothic type, 359-60
Government
  advertising, 666-67
  local advertising and, 611
  markets, 128
  regulation, 20
Graphic designers, 322
Great Britain, 414, 416, 681, 693, 694-95
Greece, 681
Green, in art design, 333
Grocery cart videos, 597
Gross impressions, 434
Gross rating points (GRPs), 434-35, 510-11, 557-58, 559-60
GTE Directories, 595
Guaranteed circulation, 487
Guiness stout ale, 689

Habits, 140-41
Halftone screen, 368, 375
Hallmark cards, 308
Halo effect, 231
Handbills, 624
Hanes hosiery, 581
Harley-Davidson motorcycles, 142
Hathaway shirts, 22, 322
Hawaii, 562
Headlines
  definition of, 292
  effective use of, 327
  illustrated, 327, 334
  role of, 292, 294
  types of, 294-97
Health gimmicks, 18-20
Hearing, seeing versus, 299-300
Heidelberg five-color offset press, 373
Hidden Persuaders, The, 144
Highway Beautification Act, 562
Hispanics, 148, 158, 444, 525, 571, 603
Holland, 681, 694-95
Hombre beer, 337
Honda Accord, 237, 284, 286
Honda automobiles, 21, 294, 342
Honda Civic, 237
Honda station wagon, 284, 286
Horizontal cooperative advertising, 634-35
Horizontal publications, 486
Hotel & Hotel Management, 610
Households using TV, 510
House lists, 542-43
House organs, 540, 650-51
Houston, 509
Humor, 330, 387

Hungary, 685
Hunt Club label, 223

IBM-compatible microcomputers, 298
IBM computers, 53, 312
IBM PC, 354
Idea, strategy versus, 284
Illinois, 668
Illustration, benefits of, 331-32
Illustrators, 322, 328
Imitation, plagiarism, versus, 343-43
Imperial margarine, 347, 400, 683
Imposition, 369-70
Industrial advertising, 10-11, 692
Industrial agencies, 87
Industrial buyers, 131
Industrial magazines, 483
Industrial markets, 128, 165-67
Industrial Revolution, 17-18
Industry Guides, 59
Inflatables, 426
In-flight ads, 426
Infomercial, 517
Information age, 25
Information headlines, 295
Information services, for advertising careers, 717
Information system, marketing, 203
Info-Presse Communications, 716
In-pack premiums, 586
Inquiry tests, 232, 234
Insertion order, 473
"Inside Business," 516-17
Inside card, 566-67, 568
Institutional advertising, 14, 606-7, 653. *See also* Corporate advertising
Institutional copy, 300-301
In-store sampling, 587
Integrated commercial, 387
Intel 486 microprocessor, 175
Interactive television, 596-97
Interconnects, 518
Interest, in ad copy, 290, 293
Interlock, 411-12
International advertising, 12, 13
  agency selection, 678-80
  budget, 690-91
  creative strategies, 681
  growth and status, 672-73
  largest advertisers, 673
  legal restraints, 692
  managing, 674-80
  market considerations, 681-86
  media considerations, 686-89
  message considerations, 689-96
  portfolio, 682-83
  worldwide marketing structures, 675-78
International Coffees, 359
International Herald Tribune, 687
International markets, 128
Interviews
  for advertising jobs, 713-14
  in-depth, 212, 227
IQuest, 205
Iron Age, 11
Island halves, 482
Issue advertising, 72
Italy, 680, 688, 694-95
Ivory soap, 287

Janitor in a Drum, 184
Japan, 675, 681, 685, 686, 692
Japanese automobiles, 237
Japanese language, 695
Jarman shoes, 343-44, 345
Jell-O, 63, 574
Jig-a-Whopper, 347
Jingles, 388-89
Jolly green giant, 400
Journal of Advertising, 400

Junior Caramels, 567
Junior Mints, 54
Junior unit, 482

Kansas City Star and Times, 73
Kenmore, 181
Kentucky Fried Chicken (KFC), 647
Kicker, 297
Kleenex, 34, 63, 186, 312
Kraft cheese, 184
Kraft marshmallows, 302

"L.A. Law," 53
Ladies' Home Journal, 48, 427, 477, 489
Language
    advertising effect on, 43, 45-46
    campaign transfer and, 693-96
    in Canada, 681, 682
    hearing vs. reading, 299-300
Lanham Trade-Mark Act of 1947, 56, 61, 67
"Larry King Show," 522
Laser typesetters, 36-37
Las Vegas, 560
"Late Night," 496
Latin America, 686, 691
Law. *See* Regulation
Lawyers, advertising by, 65
Layout
    definition of, 321, 323
    effective, 327-28
    purposes of, 323-24
    steps in, 325-27
    of Timberland ad, 319
Leading, 364
Leaflets, 540
Learning, consumer, 137, 139-41
Lee denims, 483
Letterpress, 371-72
Letter shop, 545
Levi's jeans, 12, 347
Libel, in copy, 311
Life, 485
Life Savers, 23
Lifestyle commercial, 347
Lifestyles and values, 164-65
Lighting, for TV commercials, 405-7, 408, 410
Light meters, 405-6
Lincoln automobiles, 240
Linear programming, in media planning, 453
Line drawings, 331
Line films, 368
Line plate, 368
Lipton International Soup Classics, 376-870
List brokers, 544
Listerine, 59, 239
Litter receptacles, 426
Live-action production, 396
Live Aid, 647
Lobbying, 645
Local advertising, 13, 14, 604-5
    budget, 614-17, 618
    creating, 627-36
    expenditures, 614
    guidelines, 630
    market and competition analysis, 609
    media strategy, 617-27
    mistakes, 613
    objectives, 607-8, 611-13
    planning, 608
    research for, 609-11
    retail advertising versus, 604
    strategy, 611-13
    types, 605-7
Local magazines, 483
Local (radio) time, 528
Local regulation, 63-64
Local stations, 500
Logos, 309, 328, 335
London, 414, 416, 679

Look ski bindings, 147
L'Oreal cosmetics, 23-24
L'Oreal hair coloring products, 251
Los Angeles
    advertising agencies in, 85
    billboard locations in, 558
    poster rates in, 560
    sales potential in, 436-37
    transit ads in, 571
Los Angeles Magazine, 483, 621
Los Angeles Times, 73, 74, 464, 469, 619, 630
Loss-leader pricing, 189
Lotus software, 34, 35
Loyalty, brand, 140-41

Macintosh computers, 10, 11, 431
    working with, 341, 354
Magazine, circulation, 485-89
Magazine advertisement, from concept through production, 376-82
Magazines
    ad portfolio, 474-76
    advantages, 438, 473, 477, 479
    buying space in, 485-90
    classifications, 483-85
    cost, 480
    Del Monte ads in, 423-24
    disadvantages, 438, 478-79
    largest advertisers, 479
    for local advertising, 621-22
    rates of, 488-90
    regulation by, 73
    services provided by, 487-88
    special possibilities, 480-82
Maidenform bras, 135
Mail delivery, 545-46
Mailing lists, 541-45
Mail-order advertising, 538
Mail-order product categories, 539
Maine, 562, 566
Majority fallacy, 155-56
Makegoods, 512
Management supervisors, 90
Manipulation, 46-48, 144
Market concentration, 166-67
Market demand, price and, 186-87
Marketers, 128
Marketing
    bottom-up, 262-63, 266-67
    definition of, 121
    direct vs. indirect, 190
    exchanges and, 124
    importance of, 120-21
    needs and, 122-23
    participants in, 125-28
    perception and, 123-24
    as process, 121
    satisfaction and, 125
    target, 170-72
    utility and, 122
    warfare strategies, 24
Marketing (Canada), 205
Marketing communication, 129-31
Marketing exchange cycle, 126
Marketing Imagination, The, 676
Marketing information system, 203
Marketing mix, 171-72, 249-50
Marketing objectives, 246-48, 428
Marketing plan
    action programs, 250, 252
    advertising and, 242-44
    definition of, 242
    elements of, 244
    fund allocation, 267-74
    objectives, 244, 246-48
    outline, 698-703
    situation analysis, 244, 245
    strategy, 248-50, 251
Marketing research
    costs, 220

Marketing research—*Cont.*
    definition of, 201
    formal, 209-19
    informal (exploratory), 203-4
    for international advertising, 683-84
    interpreting and reporting findings, 219
    need for, 201
    objectives, 208-9
    process, 202-20
    qualitative, 209-11
    quantitative, 211-13
    questionnaire design, 215, 217-18, 219
    sampling theories, 214-15
    secondary data in, 204-5, 208
    strategy and, 220-21
Marketing segments, business, identifying, 165-67
Marketing strategy, 220-21
    case illustration, 237, 240-42
Marketing structures, worldwide, 675-78
Marketing systems, vertical, 193-94
Marketing theory, evolution of, 125
Marketing Warfare, 24, 238
Marketing warfare, 238-40
Market-need objectives, 246, 247
Market prep corporate advertising, 661
Markets
    definition of, 127
    for international advertising, 681-86, 691
    pretesting, 227
    types, 127-28
Market segmentation
    by age groups, 159
    behavioristic, 158, 159-63
    cigarette for blacks, 160-61
    demographic, 157-59
    geographic, 157, 158
    methods, 158
    process, 156-57
    psychographic, 158, 163-65
    for toothpaste, 163
Market segments, 157, 168-70
Marlboro, 344
Massachusetts, 566
Master tape, 394
Materialism, advertising and, 46
Maxi/marketing, 256, 257
Maxwell House coffee, 414, 418, 685
Mazda automobiles, 294
MDS, 519
Mechanical, 325, 353, 357
"Me" decade, 23-24
Media
    agency use of, 92
    buying services, 88-89
    classes/subclasses, 227
    comparative evaluation, 442-43
    in creative mix, 262
    definition of, 8, 80
    expenditures, 436
    fragmented audience for, 425-26
    increasing complexity of, 427-28
    increasing costs of, 426-27
    increasing options in, 425
    for international advertising, 685-89, 690-91
    international regulations, 692
    for local advertising, 611, 617-27
    in marketing framework, 428-30
    objectives, 429, 430-35
    pretesting, 227
    print (*see* Print media)
    regulation by, 70-74
    supplementary, 591-98
    unusual, 426
Media associations, for local advertisers, 611
Media audience, 444-45
Media commissions, for agencies, 96
Media kit, 648-49
Media Management Plus, 453, 454
Media mix, 447-48, 626-27
Media placement, by small advertisers, 106
Media planners, information sources for, 432

Media planning, 424-29
Media research, 202
Media scheduling, computers for, 452-54
Media scheduling criteria, 448-52
Media selection
  advantages and disadvantages, 438
  attention and, 445-46
  audience characteristics and, 444-45
  campaign objectives and, 441-44
  computers for, 452-54
  considerations, 441
  cost efficiency, 447
  exposure and, 445
  motivation and, 446-47
Media Sexploitation, 144
Media strategy, 435
  competition and budget, 439-40
  geographic scope, 435-37
  message size, length, and position, 439
  nature of medium and message, 437-39
  stating, 440-41
Media units, 227
Media vehicle, 227
Medicines, patent, 18, 20
Medium, in communication, 129-30
Memory, in consumer behavior, 136-37
Mental files, 136-37
Mercedes, 250
Merchandiser, The, 610
Mergers, of agencies, 113
Message
  in creative mix, 262-63
  in international advertising, 687-93
  in local advertising, 628-29, 631
  pretesting, 227
  size, length, and position, 439
Message-distribution objectives, 432-35
Message strategy, 280, 281-84
Message weight, 434
Mexico, 687
Micatin, 520
Mickey Mouse watches, 181
Microphones, 391-92
Microsoft software, 298
Middleman, definition of, 191
Midvale, Ohio, 515
Milk cartons, 426
Minneapolis-St. Paul, 73, 98, 457, 560, 569, 612
Minorities, advertising portrayal of, 49-50
Mint Condition, 344
Mirocast Whirlpool, 247
Mississippi, 64
Mitsubishi Eclipse, 180
Mixed interlock, 412
Mnemonic device, 347
Mobile billboards, 571
Mock magazines, 230
Modern Drummer, 485
Modern Jeweler, 610
Modern Maturity, 477, 489
Money, 490
Monitor, 163
Monolog copy, 301
Monthly Department Store Sales, 611
Monthly promotional calendar, 617
Montreal, advertising agencies in, 85, 86
Morton salt, 308
Motel 6, 342, 385, 386
Motivation/motives, 446-47
  consumer, 141-43
  in international advertising, 689-90
  pretesting, 227
  research, 211
Mounds, 585
Movement, in art, 320
Movie theaters, 595-96
Ms. magazine, 50
Multipoint distribution system, 519
Musical commercials, 388-89
Musical logotype, 388
Music Education Journal, 12

Narrative copy, 301
Narrowcasting, 517
National advertising, 12
National Association of Broadcasters Television Code, 73
National College Study, 491
National Enquirer, 462, 489
National Geographic, 477, 485, 489
National magazines, 484-85
NBC News, 639
Needs, 47-48, 122-23, 141-42
Negative appeal, in visuals, 330
Netherlands, 681, 692-93, 695
Network advertising, 498-99
Network Radio Audiences, 529
Networks
  radio, 71, 73
  television, 70
New Mexico, 64
New Orleans, 560
Newport cigarettes, 312
Newsday Extra, 620
News headlines, 295
Newspaper Co-op Network, 472-73, 491
Newspaper Rates and Data, 74, 491
Newspapers
  advantages, 438, 458-59
  advertisement types in, 466-68
  buying space in, 469-73
  delivery frequency, 461-62
  disadvantages, 438, 459-60
  largest advertisers, 461
  for local advertising, 618-21
  national, 466
  rates of, 466-68, 469-71
  readership, 460-61
  regulation by, 73-74
  shopping guides, 466
  sizes, 462
  specialized audiences, 462
  Sunday, 463-65
NEWSPLAN, 470, 491
News releases, 648, 649
Newsweek, 48, 73, 448, 477, 484, 485, 489, 490, 622
New York City
  agencies, 85, 679
  cable TV, 518
  Department of Consumer Affairs, 64
  spectaculars, 555, 557
  transit ads, 566, 571-72
New York Daily News, 462, 466
New Yorker, The, 73
New York magazine, 483
New York Marathon, 647
New York Times, The, 49, 352, 460, 473
New York Times Index, 204
Nielson Television Index, 508
Nigeria, 689
Nike air, 480
Nissan automobiles, 294, 337
Nissan GXE, 448
Nissan Infiniti, 250
Nissan Maxima, 448
Nissan Pathfinder, 265
No Excuses clothing, 182
Noncommercial advertising, 15, 662-66
North Carolina, 667
Norway, 681
Nudity, 49
Nutech Spectra-flanstran, 310
Nutritional Labeling and Education Act of 1990, 61
Nyquil, 263

Objectives
  in advertising plan, 252-59
  for copywriting, 287-91
  corporate, 188, 246
  in marketing plan, 244, 246-48
  media and, 428, 430
  of product vs. noncommercial advertising, 663
  strategy versus, 248

Objective task method, for funds allocation, 273-74
Observation method, in research, 209
Obsession perfume, 50, 312
Offensiveness, advertising and, 48-49
Off-network syndication, 499
Offset lithography, 372-73
Ohio, 667
Oil companies, 36
Oldsmobile, 324
Olympic Games, 346
On-pack premiums, 586
On War, 238
La Opinion, 469
Opinion leaders, 146-47
Opinion sampling, 647
"Oprah Winfrey Show, The," 499
Orange, in art design, 333
Order-of-merit tests, 230
Orlando Sentinel, 74
Ornamental type, 360
Orthographic film, 368
Outdoor advertising
  advantages, 556-61
  buying, 553-55
  color in, 556
  disadvantages, 561-62, 564-65
  guidelines, 562
  portfolio, 562-64
  standardization, 553
Outdoor Life, 477
Out-of-home media, 553
Outside posters, 567, 568
Overlay, 357

Pacific Northwest, 483
Package design, art in, 336-39
Packages/packaging, 38, 183-86, 329, 339
Packaging, 486
Packaging forms and materials, 337-38
Packaging specialists, 338-39
Paid circulation, 487
Painted bulletins, 555
Paired comparison methods, 230
Palette copier, 675
Palmolive shampoo, 19
Palm Springs Life, 483, 621
Panaflex camera, 409
Panels, for copy, 308
Pantone Matching System Colors, 374
Papers, for printing, 375
Parade, 228
Parents Magazine, 73
Paris, 679, 687
Parking meters, 426, 596
Participation basis, 499
Party Pride, 181
Pass-along readership, 485
Pasteup, 325, 353, 357
Pasteup artists, functions of, 322
Patent and Trademark Office, 61-63
PC World USSR, 688
Penetration pricing, 189
People, 423
People meter, 508
People Weekly, 489
Pepsi-Cola, 24, 25, 290, 647
Pepsodent, 180, 685
Pepto-Bismol, 588
Percentage-of-sales method, for funds allocation, 271-72
Perception, 123-24, 133-37, 138, 144
Perceptual meaning studies, 230
Perceptual screens, 134, 138
Perdue chickens, 287, 691
Periodicals, for advertising careers, 716-17
Persuasion, 8
Pesky Pescadao, 603
Pharmaceuticals, 59, 272
Philadelphia, 18, 289, 311, 546
Philadelphia magazine, 483

Phoenix, 560
Photo animation, 397
Photocomposition, 366-67
Photographers, 328
Photography
  benefits of, 331
  impact of, 18
  in public relations, 649
  stop-motion, 397
  television, 405, 407-9
Photoplatemaking, 367-68
Photopolymerization, 372
Photoprints, 382
Physicians, advertising by, 65
Physiological screens, in consumer behavior, 134
Picas, 362
Picnic, 144
Picture-caption copy, 301
Pierre Cardin products, 12, 113
Pillsbury Doughboy, 397, 495
Pittsburgh, 509
Place
  consumer behavior and, 149
  in local advertising strategy, 612
  in marketing, 189, 191-94
  utility, 122
Plagiarism, imitation versus, 342-43
Plane & Pilot, 489
Playboy, 294, 489, 685
Plymouth Laser, 180
Point-of-purchase advertising, 588-90
Point of sale, advantages and disadvantages, 438
Points (type), 361
Poison fragrance, 312
Poland, 685
Polaroid, 312
Political advertising, 400-401, 667
P-O-P advertising, 588-90
Pop-up advertisements, in magazines, 481
Porsche, 302
Porsche sunglasses, 181
Portfolio tests, 230
Positioning, of products, 178-79
Positioning: the Battle for Your Mind, 138
Positioning strategies, 138, 250
Positions, in newspapers, 471
Possession utility, 122
Postcards, 540
Poster panels. See Billboard ads
Posters, for public relations, 651
Postpurchase evaluation, 152
Posttesting, 226, 232-34
Pounce, 45
Prairie Farmer, 483
Preemption rates, 512
Premiums, 581-82, 585-86
Prepress production, 354
Preprinted inserts, 468
Presentations, by agencies, 100
Press agentry, 645
Press kit, 648-49
Press releases, 648-49
Prestige pricing, 189
Pretesting, 226-32
Price
  advertising effect on, 34-35
  in local advertising strategy, 612
  in marketing, 186-89, 190
  Pricing strategies, 188-89
  Primary demand, 168, 174
Print advertisements, pretesting, 229, 230, 231
Print advertising, copywriter's pyramid and, 293
Printer, thinking like, 369
Printer's Ink, 63
Printing
  advertisement, 11, 12
  color, 373, 374-75
  impact of, 17
  methods, 370-74
  papers, 375
  process, 367-72

Print media, 457, 480, 490-92. See also Magazines;
  Newspapers
Print Media Production Data, 381
Print production, 91-92
  classic vs. computerized, 353
  computers and, 353-56
  definition of, 353
  planning, 356-58
Privacy Journal, 543
Privacy rights, 66
Prodigy, 596
Product advertising, 14, 605-6
Product concept, 171, 222-23, 260-61
Product engineers/designers, 81
Product information center, 590
Production
  developing values, 284
  print and broadcast, 91-92
  process, 352-56
  by small advertisers, 106
  traffic, 93
Production artists, functions of, 322
Production costs, price and, 187
Production manager, role of, 353
Product life cycle, 173-76
Product marketing process, 156
Products
  advertising value and, 33-34
  branding, 180-82
  claims, 74
  classifications, 176-77
  comparisons, in visuals, 329
  differentiation, 179-80
  disclaims, 70-71
  FDA and, 59, 61
  in local advertising strategy, 612
  in marketing, 172-86
  names, 312
  packaging, 183-86
  placement, 596
  positioning, 178-79
  samples, in magazines, 481
  shaping, 124
  utility, 122
Professional advertising, 12
Professional associations, for advertising careers,
  717-18
Professional magazines, 483
Profile bread, 59
Profits, advertising and, 268-69
Program rating, 510
Progressive Farmer, 483
Progressive Grocer, 610
Promises, false, 52
Promotion. See also Sales promotion
  in local advertising strategy, 612-13
  in marketing, 194-96
  public relations and, 646
Promotional mix, 258
Promotional pricing, 189
Proof copy, 473
Proportion, in art, 320
Provocative headlines, 295-96
Psychographic segmentation, 163-64
Psychological screens, in consumer behavior, 135
Public affairs, 645
Publications
  for advertising careers, 715-17
  for local advertisers, 610-11
  in public relations, 647
Public Information Service Bulletin, 204
Publicity, 626, 643, 645
Public notices, 468
Public relations, 196
  activities, 643-48
  advertising versus, 640-41
  corporate advertising, 652-62
  crisis communications, 642-43
  role of, 640-41
  tools, 648-52
Public service announcements, 665

Public speaking, in public relations, 648
Puerto Rico, 65
Pull strategies, 582-90
Pulsing/pulses, 449-50, 451
Pupilometric devices, 230
Purchase decision, postpurchase evaluation and,
  149-52
Purchase occasion, 159
Purchasing, 486
Purex, 520
Push money, 582
Push strategies, 578-82

Quaker Oats Squares, 53
Quantitative mathematical models, for funds alloca-
  tion, 274
Quebec, 139, 286, 301, 304, 335
Question headlines, 296
Questioning, direct, 230, 231
Questionnaire design, 215, 217-18, 219

Radio. See also Broadcast advertising
  advantages, 438, 523-26
  advertisers, 520
  AM vs. FM, 520-21
  audience profile, 521
  buying time on, 527-28
  cost of, 525-26, 527
  disadvantages, 438, 526-27
  largest advertisers, 525
  overview, 520
  programming and audiences, 520-22
  ratings services, 529
  reach of, 525
  regulation by, 71, 73
  terminology, 528-32
Radio advertising, types, 527-28
Radio commercials, 386-89, 526. See also Broadcast
  commercials
Radio copy, writing, 386-87
Radio Market Report, 531
Radio personality, 389
Radio production, 389-94
Radio schedule, preparing, 532
Radio Usage, 529
Random probability samples, 215
Rate cards
  for magazines, 489-90
  for newspapers, 469
Rational appeals, 282
RCA computers, 23
RCA televisions, 312
Reach, 433, 450, 451-52, 458
Readability, of type, 363
Reader's Digest, 73, 196, 484-85, 489, 687
Reader's Guide to Periodical Literature, 204
Readership information, 327, 440, 469
Reading notice, 466
Rebates, 585
Recall tests, 232, 233-34
Recruitment advertising, 662
Red, in art design, 333
Redbook, 489
"Red Book," 85
Reebok athletic shoes, 172-73, 190, 193, 195
Reference groups, 146
Refunds, 585
Regional advertising, 12, 14. See also Local
  advertising
Regional publications, 483-84
Regular price-line advertising, 605, 606
Regulation, 20
  federal, 55-63
  for international advertising, 693
  by media, 70-74
  nongovernment, 66-76
  recent court rulings, 63-67
  state and local, 63-64
Reinforcement advertising, 256

Reliability, of data, 213, 214
Repetition, for learning, 139
Reprints, 540
Research. *See also* Advertising research; Marketing research for public relations, 647
Research data, 204, 211, 213, 214
Research services, for advertising careers, 717
Reseller markets, 127
Responsibility, of advertisers, 54-55
Restaurant advertising, expenditures on, 272
Restaurants & Institutions, 486
Résumé, for advertising career, 712-13
Retail advertising, 272, 604
Retail businesses, advertising investments of, 614
Retail Data Sources for Market Analysis, 611
Retail sales, by types of stores, 616
Ritz crackers, 144
Roadblocking, 450
Robinson-Patman Act, 578
Rolling Stone magazine, 295, 296
Rolls-Royce, 22, 294, 481
Roman type, 359
ROP rates, 471
"Roseanne," 53
Rotary plan, 555
Rotogravure, 372
Rough cut, 411-12
Rough layout, 325, 326
Runner's World, 492
Run of paper rates, 471
Run-of-station, 530

Sacramento, Ca., 530
Sail magazine, 265
St. Louis, 560
Sale advertising, 605-6
Sales, advertising and, 268-69, 274
Sales analysis, for local advertising, 609-10
Sales and Marketing Management in Canada, 717
Sales experiments, 230
Sales letters, 540
Sales plan, for local advertisers, 615-16
Sales promotion, 195, 576-77
   advantages, 577
   disadvantages, 577
   expenditures, 578
   guidelines, 584
   for local advertising, 625-26
   pull strategies, 582-90
   push strategies, 578-82
   response by type, 583
Sales-target objectives, 247
Sales tests, 232, 234
Sampling (promotion), 587, 625
Sampling (research), 214-15, 216
San Diego, 73, 603-4
San Diego Business Journal, 620
San Diego Magazine, 483
San Francisco, 571
San Francisco Examiner, 295
Sanka, 184
Sans serif type, 359-60
Santa Fe, New Mexico, 520
Sara Lee cheesecake, 481
Satellite master antenna television, 519
Satisfaction, marketing and, 124
Saturday Evening Post, 279, 280, 322
"Saturday Night Live," 496
Saudi Arabia, 681, 692, 693
SAU system, 462, 463-65
ScanAmerica, 508
Scandinavia, 688, 694-95
Scents, in sales promotion, 589
Scentstrip, 481
Scheduling, pretesting of, 228
Scitex, 354
Scope mouthwash, 239
Scotch brand tape, 63
Scratchboard, 332
Screen printing, 373-74

Screens, 368, 369, 375
Script development, 341
Script type, 360
Seals, 308-9
Seattle, 560, 571
Seattle Foot, 339-40
Seeing, hearing versus, 299-300
Segmentation. *See* Market segmentation
Selection evaluation, 132
Selective demand, 175
Selective perception, 135
Self-concept, 135
Self-liquidating premiums, 586
Self-mailers, 540
Selling, personal vs. nonpersonal, 195
Sensationalism, 49
Sensor razor, 671
Sensory bombardment, 137
Serifs, 359
Serigraphy, 373-74
Service, definition of, 177
Service Standards, 89
Session, 390
Sets, for TV commercials, 410
Seventeen, 477
7UP, Cherry, 587
Sex, 50, 144
Sexual ads, subliminal perception in, 144
Shared mail, 625
Share of audience, 510
Share-of-market/share-of-voice method, 273
Sheetwise imposition, 369, 370
Shell, 312
Sherman Antitrust Act, 70
S&H Green Stamps, 587
Shoes, athletic, 172, 190, 193, 195
Shoppers, 620
Shopping Center World, 610
Shopping guides, 466
Showing, 557
SIC codes, 166, 167
Signatures, 309, 328, 335
Signs, 598, 623-24
Silk screen, 374
Simmons Teen-Age Research Study, 491
Simplicity, in art, 321
Simulation, in media planning, 453
Simulator disk, 596
Situation analysis, in marketing plan, 244, 245
Skimming, 189
Sky Channel, 688
Slander, in copy, 311
Slice of life commercial, 347, 389
Slogans, 308
Slotting allowances, 579-80
Small-print qualifications, 52
"Smart" cards, 597
SMATV, 519
Smell, in sales promotion, 589
Smith Corona typewriters, 294
Smucker's preserves, 290
Snoopy toothbrushes, 312
Snow board, 265
Snuggles bear, 397
Snyder hairspray, 264
Soaps and cleansers, advertising expenditure, 272
Social factors, 43-55, 144-45
Soft drinks, 5-7
Sorrell's preserves, 290
Sound
   for radio commercials, 391, 526
   in TV commercials, 404, 411-12
   visuals versus, 299-300
Sound booth, 393
South America, 687, 694
Southeast Asia, 686
Southern Living, 483
Southern Messenger, 18
Soviet Union, 672, 674, 687
Spain, 681, 685, 688
Spalding golf clubs, 307

Spalding tennis rackets, 146
Spam, 522-23
Special effects, 398
Specialty advertising, 591-92, 625
Spectaculars, 555
Speedy Alka-Seltzer, 495
Spic and Span, 585-86
Spiffs, 582
Spillover media, 688
Split runs, 471-72
Split-30s, 505
Sports Illustrated, 134, 448, 484, 489, 622
Spot announcements, 499
Spot radio, 528
Spot Radio Rates and Data, 530
Spot Television Rates and Data, 513
Square serif type, 360
Staging, for TV commercials, 409-10
Standard advertising unit, 462, 463-65
Standard Directory of Advertisers, 85, 709
Standard Directory of Advertising Agencies, 85, 709
Standard for the Flammability of Children's Sleep-wear of 1972, 57
Standard Industrial Classification (SIC) codes, 166, 167
Standardized outdoor advertising, 553
Standard Periodical Directory, The, 610
Standard Rate and Data Service, 73, 202, 205, 381, 432, 491
Star, The, 462, 489
Stars and Stripes, 462
Statement stuffers, 541
State regulation, 63-64
Statistical Abstract of the United States, 204, 611
Stereotypes, advertising and, 49-50
Sterling Litho Gloss paper, 11, 12
Stimulus, in consumer behavior, 133-34
Stimulus-response theory, 139
Stock photos, 351
Stop-motion photography, 397
Stores, 610
Storyboards, 91, 321, 325, 341, 397
Straight announcement, 346, 387
Straight-sell copy, 300
Strategy. *See also* Advertising strategy; Marketing strategy; Media strategy
   idea versus, 284
   in marketing plan, 248-50, 251
   objectives versus, 248
Stresstabs vitamins, 4400
Strike-on composition, 366
Stripping, 369
Studebaker automobiles, 39
Studio, 392-93
Study of Media and Markets, 491
STV, 519
Subculture, consumer behavior and, 147-48
Subheads, 297-98
Subliminal manipulation, 144
Subliminal Seduction, 144
Subscription television, 519
Substantiation, 58
Successful Direct Marketing Methods, 542
Successful Farming, 483
Sunday supplement, 464-65
Sunkist copy platform, 285
Sunkist oranges, 180
Sunkist vitamins, 180, 312
Sunset, 483
Superchannel, 688
Supers, 411
Superstations, 513
Suppliers, 79
Supreme Court, 72
Survey of Current Business, 611
Surveys, 210
Swanson Great Starts, 580
Sweden, 694-95
Sweepstakes, 581, 587-88, 589
Sweet 'N Low, 264
Switzerland, 681, 687, 688, 694-95

Syndication, 499, 500

TAA Rate Directory of Transit Advertising, 570
Tabloid newspaper, 462
Tacos, 136
Tag lines, 308
Take ones, 570
Talent, for TV commercials, 410-11
Talon zippers, 332
Tang, 676, 677
Tape, film versus, 412-13
Target audience, in creative mix, 259-60
Target marketing, 170-72, 223-24, 248-49
Taster's Choice, 414-18
Taxicab advertising, 426, 568
Tear sheets, 473
Teenage Mutant Ninja Turtles, 506, 575
Telecast tests, live, 230
Teledyne Water Pik, 595
Telemarketing, 190, 538
Telephones, public, 596
Teleprompter, 409
Television. *See also* Broadcast advertising
    advantages, 438, 501-3
    advertising growth in, 498
    audience measurement, 506, 510
    audience trends, 496-97
    buying time on, 511-12
    cable (*see* Cable television)
    in creative mix, 500
    disadvantages, 438, 505
    gross rating points, 510-11
    interactive, 596-97
    largest advertisers, 498
    markets, 508-9
    network vs. cable, 497
    rates, 504, 512
    rating services, 507
    ratings sources, 508
    regulation, 70-71
    stations, 496
Television commercials. *See also* Broadcast commercials
    art in, 339-48
    from concept through production, 414-18
    costs, 413
    films vs. tape, 412-13
    guidelines, 396, 503
    producing, 394-413
    types of, 346-48
Television production, 400-401
    postproduction, 411-12
    preproduction, 401-4
    shooting, 404-11
Television scripts, common abbreviations in, 343
Temperature, for light sources, 406
Tennis, 427, 441
Tennis and Golf Digest, 351
Terminal posters, 567
Testimonials, 52, 58, 65, 330, 346-47
Testing, 226-34, 610
Texaco, 312
Texas, 154, 490
Text type, 358
Thailand, 682
Theaters, movie, 595-96
Theater tests, 230
Theme lines, 308
Third-class mail, 547
"Thirtysomething," 53
3-D advertisements, in magazines, 481
Thumbnail sketches, 325, 326
Tide detergent, 312
Timberline boots, 305
Time, 14, 29, 73, 448, 484, 485, 489, 490, 622, 658
Time utility, 122
Timex watches, 192
Tinactin, 520

Tobacco advertising, 693
Toiletries ads, in 1980s, 23-24
Tokyo, 85
Toothpaste market, segmentation of, 163
Top Gun, 519
Toronto
    advertising agencies in, 25, 85, 86, 87, 211, 232, 696
    Birks ad, 192
    Warner Lambert ad, 567
Total audience, 510, 530
Total bus, 570
Total cereal, 260
Total market coverage, 620
Toyota Lexus, 250
Trade advertising, 11-12
Trade associations, for advertising careers, 717-18
Trade deals, 578-79
Trade-Mark Act of 1947, 56, 61, 67
Trademark Law Revision Act of 1988, 67, 288
Trademarks, 61-63
Trade promotions, 577. *See also* Push strategies
Trade publications, 483
Trade Regulation Rules, 59
Trade shows, 593-94
Trading stamps, 587
Trailer tests, 230
Transit advertising, 566
    advantages, 571-72
    buying, 568-71
    disadvantages, 572
    types, 566-68
Trident sugarless gum, 180
Truth in advertising, 20-21, 50, 52
TV Guide, 484, 485, 489
TV households, 510
Tylenol, 239, 642-43
Type
    classes, 358
    families, 360-61
    groups, 359-60
    illustrated guide, 363
    selection, 362-64
    sizes, 362
    specification, 364-365
    structure and measurement, 361-62
Typesetting methods, 365-67
Typography, 358

Ulrich's International Periodicals Directory, 610
Unaided recall, 232
Unfair advertising, 52, 57. *See also* Deceptive advertising
Unique selling proposition, 22
United Kingdom, 414, 416, 681, 694-95
United States
    advertising agencies in, 85
    market concentration in, 168
    subculture in, 147
Unity, in art, 321
Universal Product Code, 209-10
Uptown cigarettes, 54, 160-61
U.S. Industrial Outlook, 611
U.S. News & World Report, 448, 484
Usage rates, 162
USA Today, 49, 448, 466
USA Today International, 685
USP, 22

Valdez, Alaska, 639-40
Validity, of data, 213, 214
VALS 2, 163, 164
Values and lifestyles, 164-65
Vanity Fair, 482
VCRs, 25, 174-76, 505
Vermont, 565
Verona, New Jersey, 635

Vertical cooperative advertising, 634
Vertical marketing systems, 193-94
Vertical publications, 486
Video, for script, 341
Video animation, 398
VideOcart, 597
Videocassette recorders, 25, 174-76, 505
    life cycle of, 174-76
Videocassettes, advertising on, 519
Video effects, 398-400
Videography, 405, 407-9
Video Information Network, 596
Video press releases, 642
Videos, grocery cart, 597
Videotapes, 426, 596
Vienna, 689, 690
Vision card, 597
Visualization, in copywriting, 284
Visuals
    chief focus, 328-30
    choice, 330, 331
    definition of, 318
    distortions, 52
    purposes, 329
    sound versus, 299-300
    techniques for creating, 331-32
Vitamin market, 205-7
Voice-pitch analysis, 230
Vol de Nuit, 312
Volkswagen bus, 295, 296
Volleyball Monthly, 484
Volume segmentation, 162
Volvos, 250

Wall Street Journal, The, 12, 14, 296, 352, 448, 462, 466, 639, 687
Wall Street Journal/Europe, The, 685
Want Makers, The: Lifting the Lid Off the World Advertising Industry; How They Make You Buy, 51
Wants, needs and, 141-42
Wash drawings, 332
Washington, D.C., 587
WD-40, 302
Wheeler-Lea Amendment, 56-57
"Wheel of Fortune," 499
Whirlpool appliances, 312
White space, in art, 321
Why Man Creates, 652
Williamsburg, Virginia, 16
Woman's Day, 423, 484, 489, 571
Women, advertising portrayal of, 50
Word-count method, 364
Word of mouth advertising, 139
Words, printed vs. spoken, 299-300
Work print, 411-12
Work & turn imposition, 369-70
World Almanac and Book of Facts, 204
Wrangler jeans, 130
Wrigley's gum, 566
Wyndham collection, 229

Xerox Palette, 312

Yankee, 483
Yashica Dental-Eye camera, 326
Yellow, in art design, 333
Yellow Pages, 594-95, 624
"Your Money," 516-17
Yugoslavia, 685

Zapping, 505
ZIP codes, 625
Zipping, 505